NINTH EDITION

Advertising, Promotion, and other aspects of
Integrated Marketing Communications

Terence A. Shimp
University of South Carolina

J. Craig Andrews
Marquette University

SOUTH-WESTERN
CENGAGE Learning·

Australia • Brazil • Japan • Korea • Mexico • Singapore • Spain • United Kingdom • United States

SOUTH-WESTERN
CENGAGE Learning®

Advertising, Promotion, and Other Aspects of Integrated Marketing Communications, Ninth Edition
Terence A. Shimp and J. Craig Andrews

Senior Vice President, LRS/Acquisitions & Solutions Planning: Jack W. Calhoun

Editorial Director, LRS/Acquisitions & Planning: Erin Joyner

Executive Editor: Mike Roche

Developmental Editor: Sarah Blasco

Editorial Assistant: Megan Fischer

Market Development Manager: Gretchen Swann

Media Editor: John Rich

Senior Rights Acquisitions Specialist: Deanna Ettinger

Manufacturing Planner: Ron Montgomery

Senior Marketing Communications Manager: Jim Overly

Design Direction, Production Service, and Composition: PreMediaGlobal

Senior Art Director: Stacy Shirley

Cover Designer: Beckmeyer Design

Cover Images:
 © iStock Photo/stevecoleimages
 © iStock Photo/trekandshoot
 © iStock Photo/Neustockimages
 © iStock Photo/RapidEye
 © iStock Photo/Franckreporter
 © Shutterstock/Luba V Nel

For product information and technology assistance, contact us at
Cengage Learning Customer & Sales Support, 1-800-354-9706

For permission to use material from this text or product,
submit all requests online at **www.cengage.com/permissions**
Further permissions questions can be emailed to
permissionrequest@cengage.com

Library of Congress Control Number: 2012945620
ISBN-13: 978-1-111-58021-6
ISBN-10: 1-111-58021-9

South-Western
5191 Natorp Boulevard
Mason, OH 45040
USA

Cengage Learning is a leading provider of customized learning solutions with office locations around the globe, including Singapore, the United Kingdom, Australia, Mexico, Brazil, and Japan. Locate your local office at:
www.cengage.com/global

Cengage Learning products are represented in Canada by Nelson Education, Ltd.

For your course and learning solutions, visit **www.cengage.com**

Purchase any of our products at your local college store or at our preferred online store **www.cengagebrain.com**

Printed in the United States of America
2 3 4 5 6 7 16 15 14

Dedication

I dedicate this 9th edition of Advertising, Promotion, and Other Aspects of Integrated Marketing Communications *to my wife, Judy, who is my life partner and best friend. She endured long periods of absence while I was involved in an active career as a teacher, researcher, and author. Fortunately, the burden of effort for this ninth edition has been undertaken by my greatly respected friend and colleague, Craig Andrews. I owe him an immeasurable debt and wish him great success in the future as the sole author of subsequent editions. Finally, I dedicate this edition to the many professors around the world who have given me the greatest compliment possible when choosing to adopt various editions of my text. I dearly hope that I have not disappointed you. (TAS)*

This 9th edition of Advertising, Promotion, and Other Aspects of Integrated Marketing Communications *is dedicated to my wife Maura, and children Colleen, Patrick, and Brendan, as well as to my mother and father, and brothers and sister. I also appreciate the keen insights, never-ending inspiration, and creative ideas on IMC issues from my many colleagues and Marquette students over the years. I wish to offer a sincere "thank you" to my long-time friend and mentor, Terry Shimp, for giving me this wonderful opportunity to become involved with the text. (JCA)*

Brief Contents

iv

Contents

Responding to a Dynamic World

The field of marketing communications is rapidly changing. Brand managers continually attempt to gain advantage over competitors and endeavor to achieve larger market shares and profits for the brands they manage. Marketing communications, or *marcom* for short, is just one element of the marketing mix, but advertising, sales promotions, public relations, direct marketing, personal selling, and social media/online marketing tools are performing increasingly important roles in firms' attempts to achieve financial and nonfinancial goals. Marcom practitioners are confronted with the rising costs and challenges of placing ads in traditional advertising media (television, magazines, etc.) and the ever-changing opportunities found in social media and online/mobile advertising. It is for these reasons that advertising and promotion budgets are shifting away from traditional media as a means of both accessing difficult-to-reach groups (e.g., college-age consumers) and providing an economically viable option for conveying advertising messages and promotional offers.

Marketing communicators realize now more than ever that they must be held financially accountable for their advertising, promotion, and other marcom investments. As companies seek ways of communicating more effectively and efficiently with their targeted audiences, marketing communicators are continually challenged. They must use communication methods that will break through the clutter, reach audiences with interesting and persuasive messages that enhance brand equity and drive sales, and assure firms that marcom investments yield an adequate return on investment. In meeting these challenges, companies increasingly embrace a strategy of integrated marketing communications whereby all marcom elements must be held accountable and "speak with one voice" in delivering consistent messages and influencing action.

Focus of the Text

Whether students are taking this course to learn more about the dynamic nature of this field or as part of planning a career in advertising, sales promotion, or other aspects of marketing, *Advertising, Promotion, and Other Aspects of Integrated Marketing Communications* will provide them with a contemporary view of the role and importance of marketing communications. The text emphasizes the importance of integrated marketing communications (IMC) in enhancing the equity of brands, and provides thorough coverage of all aspects of an IMC program: advertising, sales promotion, packaging and branding strategies, social media, online and mobile advertising, direct marketing, point-of-purchase communications, public relations, word-of-mouth buzz creation, event- and cause-oriented sponsorships, and personal selling. These topics are made even more accessible in this edition through expanded use of examples and applications. And, of course, the text covers appropriate academic theories and concepts to provide formal structure to the illustrations and examples.

Advertising, Promotion, and Other Aspects of Integrated Marketing Communications is intended for use in undergraduate or graduate courses in marketing communications, advertising, promotion strategy, promotion management, or other courses with similar concentrations. Professors and students alike should find this book substantive but highly readable, eminently current but also appreciative of the evolution of the field. Above all, this ninth edition blends marketing communications practice in its varied forms with the rigors of research and theory. Throughout its previous eight editions, the attempt has been made to balance coverage in examining marketing communications both from the consumer's and the marketer's vantage points. This edition focuses more than ever not only on managerial and business-to-business aspects of marketing communications, but also on the latest developments in online/mobile advertising and social media.

Changes and Improvements in the Ninth Edition

The ninth edition of *Advertising, Promotion, and Other Aspects of Integrated Marketing Communications* reflects many changes beyond those just described. The textbook has been thoroughly updated to reflect the following:

- State-of-the-art coverage of major academic literature and practitioner writings on all aspects of marketing communications. These writings are presented at an accessible level to students and illustrated with examples and special inserts—*Marcom Insight* features, *IMC Focus* boxes, and *Global Focus* inserts.
  - *Marcom Insight*—Each chapter opens with a *Marcom Insight* that corresponds to the thematic coverage of the chapter, piques students' interest, and illustrates the content to follow. Most of these are new to this edition.
  - *IMC Focus*—Each chapter includes features that illustrate key IMC concepts by using real-company situations that showcase how various aspects of marketing communications are put into practice.
  - *Global Focus*—These features enhance the text's global perspective and spotlight international applications of marcom principles.
- This edition has expanded from 21 to 23 chapters. Most of the chapters have been substantially rewritten or rearranged to reflect a more logical progression of material coverage. The following updates and improvements are reflected in this new edition:
  - Chapter 1 updates its coverage of IMC examples and fundamentals and continues to provide a model of the marcom process that structures the text as well as provides a useful framework for comprehending the strategic and tactical aspects of marketing communications.
  - Marcom's role in enhancing brand equity and influencing behavior receives updated treatment in Chapter 2. The chapter emphasizes the importance of achieving marcom accountability and includes discussion of return on marketing investment and efforts to measure marcom effectiveness.

- Chapter 3 focuses on marcom's role in facilitating the success of new brands. Specifically, the chapter devotes substantial coverage to the role of brand naming, brand equity, and—new to this chapter—intellectual property issues covering patents, copyrights, and trademarks. In addition to these changes, Chapter 3 removes coverage of packaging and shifts that material to Chapter 22 which examines packaging with point-of-purchase communications and signage.

- Chapter 4, which is an update of Chapter 21 in the eighth edition, provides in-depth coverage of environmental marketing, marcom-related regulatory issues, and ethical issues in marketing communications. Expanded coverage is devoted to sustainability, recent regulatory cases, and public health initiatives involving IMC, as well as privacy issues affecting marketing communications.

- Chapters 5 through 8 focus on the fundamental marcom decisions that are based on the marcom-process model introduced in Chapter 1. These chapters include detailed coverage of marcom segmentation, targeting, and positioning (Chapter 5), the communications process and consumer behavior (Chapter 6), the role of persuasion in IMC (Chapter 7), and objective setting and budgeting (Chapter 8). Chapter 5 includes a thorough update of demographic facts and figures, Chapter 6 integrates the coverage of meaning creation with fundamentals of consumer behavior, Chapter 7—a new chapter—examines major routes to persuasion from IMC, and Chapter 8 examines challenging decisions in objective setting and marcom budgeting.

- Chapter 9, in its overview of advertising management, examines the role of messages, media, and measurement. The chapter devotes major coverage to the advertising management process and also presents a perspective on the case for investing or disinvesting in advertising.

- Chapter 10 describes the fundamentals and importance of advertising creativity.

- Chapter 11 examines: (1) endorser ("source") factors that influence the persuasiveness of messages and (2) specific forms of creative messages (e.g., appeals to fear and guilt, humor, sex) and what determines their effectiveness.

- Chapter 12 analyzes traditional ad media (newspapers, magazines, radio, and TV) and updates this coverage.

- Chapter 13 covers online and mobile advertising—a major overhaul of the previous chapter on Internet advertising. This chapter now displays the online advertising process and online advertising formats, including search engine advertising, banner ads, rich media, sponsored and corporate websites, blogs and podcasts, a major section on mobile advertising, and privacy. The chapter concludes with measurement of online advertising efforts.

- Chapter 14 represents a brand new and important addition to this edition—i.e., the role of social media in IMC programs. This chapter includes an analysis of social media's "landscape" (e.g., major players, advantages and disadvantages, categories, rankings), the role of Facebook and Twitter in IMC, examples of successful social media campaigns, how to advertise in social media, and measuring the effectiveness of social media efforts.

- Chapter 15 investigates direct marketing and other ad media, including direct response advertising, direct mail and database marketing, video-game advertising (adver-gaming), brand placements in movies and TV programs, cinema advertising, and a collection of alternative ad media.

- Chapter 16 treats media planning and analysis in detail and provides a common set of concepts, terms, and metrics for describing the specific media that are covered in Chapters 12 through 15.

- Chapter 17 is now placed after all media choice and planning discussion and provides an updated, expanded, and improved coverage of measures of advertising effectiveness.
- Chapter 18 introduces sales promotions and explores in detail trade-oriented promotions. The chapter also presents a series of generalizations regarding trade-promotion effectiveness.
- Chapters 19 and 20 explore consumer-oriented forms of sales promotions and provide a framework to categorize such promotions. Chapter 19 covers sampling and couponing. Chapter 20 examines all remaining forms of consumer promotions—premiums, price-offs, bonus packs, games, rebates and refunds, sweepstakes and contests, continuity promotions, overlay and tie-in promotions, and retailer promotions.
- Chapter 21 examines public relations (especially marketing-oriented PR), word-of-mouth influence, and sponsorships. The material on sponsorships was moved from Chapter 19 in the previous edition to this chapter and examines event sponsorships and cause-related marketing.
- Chapter 22 is a unique chapter that explores topics often neglected or receiving minimal coverage in most advertising and marcom texts: packaging, point-of-purchase communications, on-premise business signage, and out-of-home (off-premise) advertising.
- Chapter 23 returns the topic of personal selling to the text after several editions. The chapter discusses personal selling's role as an important part of the promotional mix and IMC, different types of personal selling jobs and activities, current technological aids for those in personal selling, the basic steps in personal selling as applied to a case, and factors accounting for salesperson performance and effectiveness.

A Premier Instructional Resource Package

The resource package provided with *Advertising, Promotion, and Other Aspects of Integrated Marketing Communications*, ninth edition, is specifically designed to meet the needs of instructors facing a variety of teaching conditions and to enhance students' experience with the subject. We have addressed both the traditional and the innovative classroom environments by providing an array of high quality and technologically advanced items to bring a contemporary, real-world feel to the study of advertising, promotion, and integrated marketing communications.

- Instructor's Manual. This comprehensive and valuable teaching aid includes the Resource Integration Guide, a list of chapter objectives, chapter summaries, detailed chapter outlines, teaching tips, and answers to discussion questions. The Instructor's Manual for this edition is revised by Tracy Tuten of East Carolina University.
- ExamView® Test Bank. The Test Bank, also revised by Tracy Tuten, provides testing items for instructors' reference and use. The Test Bank contains over 2,500 true/false, multiple-choice, and essay questions in varying levels of difficulty. ExamView® software makes test preparation, scoring, and grading easy. Featuring automatic grading, ExamView® allows you to create, deliver, and customize tests and study guides (both print and online) in minutes.
- PowerPoint® Presentations. The PowerPoint® package, revised by Craig Andrews and Jacob Bagha of Marquette University, covers all of the material found in the textbook in addition to outside supplemental examples and materials, including embedded commercials.
- Bring the experience of advertising to your classroom with *Ad Age on Campus*. Student access to *Ad Age on Campus* can be packaged with new

copies of this book free of charge which will provide students with access to the following:

- *Ad Age* weekly edition online
- *Ad Age* data center
- Creativity-online.com

Ad Age has been the leading source of news, analysis, research, and data on the advertising, marketing, and media industry for 80 years. With its daily news feed, columns from the brightest thinkers in the industry, exclusive industry statistics in the datacenter, and breakthrough work selected by the editors of Creativity, *Ad Age on Campus* offers students a way to enhance their classroom experience with real-world knowledge.

Acknowledgments

We sincerely appreciate the thoughtful comments from the colleagues who recommended changes and improvements for this edition. Previous editions also have benefited from the many useful comments from the following reviewers, friends, and acquaintances, whose affiliations may have changed:

Charles S. Areni, *Texas Tech University*

Guy R. Banville, *Creighton University*

Ronald Bauerly, *Western Illinois University*

M. Elizabeth Blair, *Ohio University*

Barbara M. Brown, *San José State University*

Gordon C. Bruner II, *Southern Illinois University*

Chris Cakebread, *Boston University*

Newell Chiesl, *Indiana State University*

Bob D. Cutler, *Cleveland State University*

Robert Dyer, *George Washington University*

Denise Essman, *Drake University*

P. Everett Fergenson, *Iona College*

James Finch, *University of Wisconsin, LaCrosse*

George R. Franke, *University of Alabama*

Linda L. Golden, *University of Texas, Austin*

Stephen Grove, *Clemson University*

Ronald Hill, *Villanova University*

Clayton Hillyer, *American International College*

Robert Harmon, *Portland State University*

Stewart W. Husted, *Lynchburg College*

Patricia Kennedy, *University of Nebraska, Lincoln*

Susan Kleine, *Bowling Green State University*

Russell Laczniak, *Iowa State University*

Geoffrey Lantos, *Bentley College*

Monle Lee, *Indiana University, South Bend*

William C. Lesch, *University of North Dakota*

J. Danile Lindley, *Bentley College*

Wendy Macias, *University of Georgia*

Therese A. Maskulka, *Lehigh University*

John McDonald, *Market Opinion Research*

Gordon G. Mosley, *Troy State University*

John Mowen, *Oklahoma State University*

Darrel Muehling, *Washington State University*

Kent Nakamoto, *Virginia Tech University*

D. Nasalroad, *Central State University*

Nusser Raajpoot, *Central Connecticut State University*

Cindy Raines, *University of Tennessee*

Jayanthi Rajan, *University of Connecticut*

Edward Riordan, *Wayne State University*

Alan Sawyer, *University of Florida*

Stanley Scott, *Boise State University*

Douglas Stayman, *Cornell University*

Jeff Stoltman, *Wayne State University*

Linda Swayne, *University of North Carolina, Charlotte*

John A. Taylor, *Brigham Young University*

Kate Ternus, *Century College*

Carolyn Tripp, *Western Illinois University*

Karen Faulkner Walia, *Long Beach City College*

Josh Wiener, *Oklahoma State University*

Liz Yokubison, *College of DuPage*

Our appreciation extends to a number of former Ph.D. students and colleagues—our friends, who have shared their experiences in using the textbook and have provided valuable suggestions for change: Avery Abernethy, Auburn University; Mike Barone, University of Louisville; Paula Bone, West Virginia University; Tracy Dunn, Benedict College; Satish Jayachandran, University of South Carolina; Jack Lindgren, University of Virginia; Ken Manning, Colorado State University; David Sprott, Washington State University; Elnora Stuart, University of South Carolina Upstate; and Scott Swain, Northeastern University.

Finally, we very much appreciate the excellent work of the Cengage team for their outstanding efforts in bringing to fruition this ninth edition. We especially appreciate the support, patience, insight, copyediting, and guidance of Sarah Blasco, Developmental Editor, Cengage; the extensive production management by Dewanshu Ranjan, Senior Project Manager, PreMediaGlobal; the encouragement and creative ideas of Mike Roche, Executive Editor, Cengage; research conducted by Marquette University graduate assistants, Jacob Bagha and Kelsey Otero; the contributions of the many hands that touched the book; and finally, we appreciate the help of the technology group in preparing the website and its contents.

Terence A. Shimp
Distinguished Professor Emeritus
University of South Carolina
November 2012

J. Craig Andrews
Professor and Kellstadt Chair in Marketing
Marquette University
November 2012

About the Authors

TERENCE A. SHIMP

Terence A. Shimp received his doctorate from the University of Maryland and taught for four years at Kent State University before moving to the University of South Carolina, where he was a faculty member for 29 years. While at the University of South Carolina, Shimp was the W. W. Johnson Distinguished Foundation Fellow and for 12 years was the chair of the Marketing Department in the Moore School of Business. He now is Distinguished Professor Emeritus.

Shimp earned a number of teaching awards during his career, including the Amoco Foundation Award that named him the outstanding teacher at the University of South Carolina in 1990. He has published widely in the areas of marketing, consumer behavior, and advertising. His work has appeared in outlets such as the *Journal of Consumer Research, Journal of Marketing Research, Journal of Marketing, Journal of Advertising, Journal of Advertising Research, Journal of Consumer Psychology*, and the *Journal of Public Policy and Marketing*. Shimp was the 2001 recipient of the American Academy of Advertising's lifetime award for outstanding contributions to research in advertising. He was elected Fellow of the Society for Consumer Psychology in 2003. For his dedication and years of service to the *Journal of Consumer Research*, Shimp received that journal's Distinguished Service Award in 2012.

Shimp is past president of the Association for Consumer Research and past president of the *Journal of Consumer Research* policy board. For many years, he served on the editorial policy boards of premier journals such as the *Journal of Consumer Research, Journal of Consumer Psychology, Journal of Marketing, Marketing Letters, Journal of Public Policy & Marketing*, and the *Journal of Advertising*. He has represented the Federal Trade Commission and various state agencies as an expert witness in issues concerning advertising deception and unfairness.

J. CRAIG ANDREWS

J. Craig Andrews is Professor and Charles H. Kellstadt Chair in Marketing, Marquette University, Milwaukee, Wisconsin. He received his Ph.D. in marketing from the University of South Carolina and has been a faculty member at Marquette University for 28 years. He has taught the Integrated Marketing Communications (IMC) course yearly since 1986. Andrews currently serves on the U.S. Food & Drug Administration's Risk Communication Advisory Committee in Washington, DC. He recently was responsible for ad copy testing on the Behavior Change Expert Panel for the National Youth Anti-Drug Media Campaign (working with Ogilvy & Mather) in New York. He also has been editor of the *Journal of Public Policy & Marketing*, for which he twice earned honors as Reviewer of the Year. Andrews also served as a Consumer Research Specialist in the Division of Advertising Practices with the Federal Trade Commission in Washington, DC, earning the FTC's Award for Meritorious Service. He has held visiting professor positions with Coca-Cola Foods in Houston and with the Fitzgerald & Co. advertising agency in Atlanta as part of the Advertising Education Foundation's Visiting Professor Program. Professor Andrews earned the first Marquette University, College of Business Administration "Researcher of the Year" Award in 2011.

Andrews currently serves on four editorial boards: *Journal of Public Policy & Marketing*, *Journal of Advertising*, *Journal of Current Issues & Research in Advertising*, and *Journal of Marketing Communications*. His work has appeared in the leading journals in marketing, international business, and public health, including *Journal of Marketing*, *Journal of Consumer Research*, *Journal of Public Policy & Marketing*, *Journal of Advertising*, *Journal of Current Issues & Research in Advertising*, *Journal of Retailing*, *European Journal of Marketing*, *Journal of International Business Studies*, and the *American Journal of Public Health*, among others. His recent research with colleagues includes work on warnings and disclosures (including graphic visual tobacco warnings), front-of-package nutrition symbols, corrective advertising, methodological issues in conducting social impact research and ad copy testing, nutrition advertising claims, covert marketing practices, and evaluating pharmacy leaflet prototypes.

Recently, Andrews and colleagues were awarded the 2012 *Thomas C. Kinnear/Journal of Public Policy & Marketing Award*, which honors the article published in *JPPM* between 2008 and 2010 that has made the most significant contribution to the understanding of marketing and public policy issues. The award was for the article, "Understanding How Graphic Pictorial Warnings Work on Cigarette Packaging," which he co-authored with Jeremy Kees, Scot Burton, and John Kozup. The authors' findings have been featured on the *CBS Early Show*, *NPR*, *Bloomberg Businessweek*, *USA Today*, *Forbes*, and *U.S. News & World Report*, among others. Currently, they are extending their research to both adolescent smokers and young adult smokers in the United States and throughout the European Union.

Advertising, Promotion,
and other aspects of
Integrated Marketing
Communications

© Jorg Hackemann/Shutterstock.co

PART

1

CHAPTERS

The Practice and Environment of Integrated Marketing Communications (IMC)

Part 1 introduces the fundamentals of integrated marketing communications (IMC). *Chapter 1* overviews IMC, what is meant by "marketing," and discusses the importance of marketing communications (marcom). Specifically, IMC emphasizes the need for integrating the promotional mix elements (advertising, sales promotions, personal selling, public relations, direct marketing, and online marketing/social media) with each other and with the brand's marketing mix such that all speak with one voice. The chapter describes five key IMC features and presents a model of the marcom decision-making process.

Chapter 2 explains how IMC enhances brand equity, influences behavior, and achieves accountability. Brand equity is then defined and the Brand Asset Valuator (with differentiation, relevance, esteem, and knowledge elements) is discussed in providing a measure of brand equity. The chapter also presents the relationships among brand concept (and how it is developed), brand equity, and brand loyalty.

Chapter 3 examines marcom's role in achieving acceptance for new products and how marketing communicators facilitate product adoption and diffusion. Chapter 3 also provides detailed descriptions of the brand development process, including the requirements for a good brand name, the steps involved in arriving at a good name, and the role of logos. Important aspects of intellectual property (patents, copyrights, and trademarks) affecting brands and marketing communications are then discussed.

Chapter 4 presents the related topics of environmental marketing and regulation, marcom regulation and self-regulation, and ethical issues in marcom. Environmental marcom practices and state and national environmental marketing regulation are first examined. Then, governmental regulations (especially for deception and unfair practices under the Federal Trade Commission) and industry self-regulation of marcom practices are described. Finally, ethical issues involving targeting vulnerable groups and specific unethical marcom practices conclude the chapter.

CHAPTER 1

An Overview of Integrated Marketing Communications

Let's Check In! Place-Based Apps, Mobile Scanning Devices, and Checking-In with Your "Friends"

Facebook has launched a placed-based "app" (application) to compete with foursquare that allows mobile device users with a Facebook account to share their exact location and find the whereabouts of their friends. Although the name may be evolving from Facebook "Places" to Facebook "Nearby Friends," the social media network is committed to location-based services. It joins other such services used by smartphone users, such as foursquare, Gowalla, Google Latitude, Loopt, Yelp, etc. to shop, communicate, socialize, and play games. Also, business owners, such as restaurant and retail managers, can search for, claim, and verify their locations on the Facebook sites, and then advertise a Facebook listing. Facebook Deals allows those with Facebook accounts to connect to special deals and specials by simply touching "Places" and then "Check In" on their mobile phones. Nearby Places with deals appear with a yellow icon that can be viewed to find out more on the deal and to claim it. Recent examples of Places deals from retailers include American Eagle Outfitters (20 percent off), Chipotle (two for one entrees), Golden State Warriors (exclusive event with

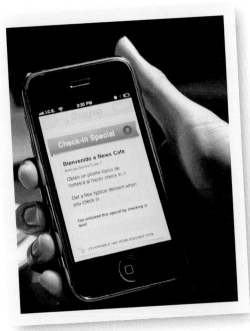

an NBA player), McDonald's ($1 per customer to Ronald McDonald House), North Face ($1 per customer to National Parks Foundation), and UC-Berkeley (those who check in can help form the human tunnel that football players run through). Facebook "Nearby Friends" locates all of your Facebook friends (who are checked in) on Google Maps interface with their check-in history displayed with lines traversing the map. This may incorporate companies in the future in the way that Places and Deals do currently.

So, what do consumers really want from using their mobile phones for placed-based check-ins? At this point, research suggests that deals and sharing information with friends are the key activities. As far as which app marketers should work with, Facebook appears to have an edge with more than 150 million of their 500 million users accessing their social network from their mobile devices. Such location-based (proximity) services are expected to soar in the United States from $200 million currently to $5.8 billion in 2015. This may bode well for Facebook given that their sheer size may overwhelm competitors. Yet, other apps, such as

© Mayela_Lopez/La Nacion de Costa Rica/Newscom

1 Appreciate the practice of marketing communications and recognize the marcom tools used by practitioners.

2 Differentiate among the following terms: the *marketing mix*, *marketing*, *communications*, *marketing communications*, the *promotional mix*, and *integrated marketing communications*.

3 Describe the philosophy and practice of integrated marketing communications (IMC) and the five key features of IMC.

4 Recognize the activities involved in developing an integrated communications program.

5 Identify obstacles to implementing an IMC program.

6 Understand and appreciate the components contained in an integrative model of the marcom decision-making process.

Foodspotting (tailored to foodies looking or new dishes), Re-drover (parents scheduling activities for kids), Shopkick (for retail shopping), and Checkpoints (for grocery stores) are more narrowly tailored.

Beyond personal mobile phones, placed-based scanning has revolutionized grocery shopping. For example, with Scan It!, shoppers at 250 Giant and Stop and Shop stores in the Northeast can use a scanning device to keep a running tally of items and prices, and to obtain strategically timed coupons as they move through the store. For example, after scanning coffee in the store, shoppers may see a coupon for coffee creamer. It is estimated that consumers who use Scan It! spend about 10 percent more than the average customer, but many appreciate the saved time and efficiency that comes with the device.

Stop and Shop (a subsidiary of Ahold) is testing is a way for shoppers to download Scan It! software directly onto their smartphones. Some retail experts predict that the new scanning software may spell the end for traditional cash registers in stores. New chips embedded into smartphones will enable customers to pay for many items with a quick wave of the phone over an electronic scanner. For example, a bar-code app for Starbucks already allows consumers to buy coffee in some of their 6,800 stores.

Google Checkout continues to partner with many payment processors to handle purchases, many made with smartphones. Google is trying to broaden these efforts to move consumers and merchants into a world in which the smartphone completely replaces the wallet for credit cards, coupons, and receipts. In a trial of Google Wallet, all consumers have to do is to touch their phone screen to select a card, then tap the phone to a credit card reader in the store or restaurant. The idea for Google is to make money by offering coupons and ads that come along with the experience. This service will be known as "Google Offers," and like Groupon,

Google will collect a fee from participating retailers each time a consumer redeems a coupon.

Yet, one major concern with the new technology may be privacy and security. Eavesdropping devices conceivably could steal all the money out of your phone, although apps are moving to encrypting data transmissions. In the past, privacy advocates have raised alarm over Facebook Places allowing friends apps to access information about your most recent check-in by default (or to check you in) as soon as you start using the app. Also, "geo-fencing" technology allows retailers to send text-message discounts or coupons when they are in the proximity of a store. Although assurances of privacy are important to many, company providers point out that those 13- to 30-years-old tend not to see sharing location and information as a major problem as long as they receive a compelling reward in exchange.

Sources: Aamoth, Doug, "Pay Phone. A New Chip Embedded in Smart Phones Could Let U.S. Consumers Leave their Wallets at Home," *Time*, February 21, 2011, p. 58; Patel, Kunur, "What Is a 'Check-in,' Anyway?" *Advertising Age*, February 28, 2011, 40; Bernard, Tara Siegel, "Google Unveils App for Paying with Phone," *New York Times* (online edition), March 26, 2011, http://www.nytimes.com/2011/05/27/technology/27google.html?_r=1&ref=business; Patel, Kunur and Natalie Zmuda, "Expecting Something in Return for your Check-In Efforts? Say No More," *Advertising Age*, August 23, 2000, 6; Rosman, Katherine, "A World in Which You Can be Mayor," *Wall Street Journal*, November 3, 2010, D1, D2; Svensson, Peter, "Smartphone Turned Wallet," *Milwaukee Journal-Sentinel*, May 27, 2011, 3D; Wortham, Jenna, "New Facebook Location Feature Sparks Privacy Concerns," NYTimes.com, August 18, 2010, http://bits.blogs.nytimes.com/2010/08/18/new-facebook-location-feature-sparks-privacy-concerns; Zimmerman, Ann, "Check Out the Future of Shopping," *Wall Street Journal*, May 18, 2011, D1, D2; Sarah Perez, "Nearby Friends: New Cyber-Stalking App for Tracing Facebook Places Check-Ins," *ReadWriteWeb*, August 30, 2010, http://www.readwriteweb.com/archives/nearby_friends_new_cyber-stalking_app_for_tracking_facebook_places_checkins.php; and M.G. Siegler, "One Year Later, Facebook Killing Off Places ... To Put Location Everywhere," *Tech Crunch*, August 23, 2011, http://techcrunch.com/2011/08/23/facebook-location-tagging.

Introduction

All firms employ marketing communications (marcom) to one degree or another, and it doesn't matter whether their efforts are directed at consumers—i.e., people like you and me in our day-to-day consumption activities—or focused on customers of other businesses. Consider the following examples of integrated marketing communications (IMC) programs. The first example is in a business-to-consumer (B2C) context, the second is in a business-to-business (B2B) environment, and the third represents a marcom program initiated through a partnership among a government agency, non-profit groups, and ad agency for consumers.

© Maria R. T. Deseo/PhotoEdit Inc.

"Eat. Drink. Loot!" is the slogan for the Pepsi Loot app for the iPhone, a location-based service (LBS) mobile phone initiative—and the first in geo-targeting—that allows consumers to find nearby restaurants that serve Pepsi products, including Taco Bell, Pizza Hut, Arby's, and Panda Express. Customers that check into restaurants offering Pepsi can then earn loyalty "loot" points that can be used to obtain downloadable songs from popular artists from the Pepsi Loot website (www.pepsilootstore.com). It also gives participating restaurants the opportunity to provide exclusive Pepsi Loot offers to their customers, such as a free drink with an entrée purchase. This innovative B2C marcom program has been expanded to include a partnership with location-based mobile network, foursquare, and features integration with Facebook and Twitter.

In another important campaign, PepsiCo used mobile advertising and content distributed to apps with 2D barcodes (also known as quick response [QR] codes) to engage a key target audience of 18- to 24-year-olds with the promotion of its Pepsi Max Brand. In the United Kingdom, Pepsi spread its "Pepsi Max Kicks" campaign virally, by offering mobile content that can be shared with friends, including a picture of British TV personality and model Kelly Brook delivered to phones via QR codes. The QR codes appeared on 400 million cans and bottles of Pepsi across Britain, and the media campaign also integrated mobile and Web-based advertising.[1]

A recent program by General Electric (GE) illustrates a successful B2B application of integrated marketing communications. With an objective of increasing awareness among business customers that GE is a company that does more than manufacture light bulbs and appliances, GE's advertising agency initiated an integrated campaign titled "Imagination at Work" to establish that GE also is successful in producing wind power, security systems, and jet engines, among other products. The intensive ad campaign involved a combination of TV, print (ads in business publications such as *Bloomberg Businessweek*, *Forbes*, and *Fortune*), and online advertising. For example, a clever TV advertisement dramatically illustrated that GE produces jet engines by showing a vintage Wright Brothers–era airplane equipped with a modern GE jet engine. This integrated campaign, which was conducted in Europe as well as in the United States, was quite successful in changing business customers' misperceptions of GE. Post-campaign research revealed that perceptions of GE as an innovative company increased by 35 percent, opinions of GE as offering high-tech solutions increased by 40 percent, and perceptions of it as being dynamic increased by 50 percent.[2]

Marcom campaigns also can help address problems in society through partnerships among governmental agencies, non-profits, and marcom agencies. Due to increases in adolescent drug use in the 1990s, the White House's Office of National Drug Control Policy (ONDCP) enacted the largest public health advertising campaign in U.S. history. The first phase of the campaign began in 1999, used the brand My Anti-Drug, and partnered with Ogilvy & Mather ad agency, the Partnership for a Drug-Free America, the Advertising Council, and Fleishman-Hilliard Communications. Although the bulk of the $180 million spent each year was on national TV ads (with themes of resistance skills, peer intervention, negative consequences, and modeling positive behavior), important public relations and online ad efforts were made for youth 11- to 13-years-old and parents (www.whatsyourantidrug.com). The second (and ongoing) phase began in 2005 with the development of the brand, Above the Influence (www.abovetheinfluence.org), which targeted adolescents aged 12- to 17-years-old. Rigorous copy testing of TV ads only allowed those spots that significantly increased anti-drug beliefs and/or reduced intentions to use drugs versus controls to appear in the televised media. Although there has been criticism of the campaign in not including an initial baseline measure, recent research has shown that greater exposure to the anti-drug ads resulted in lower rates of (marijuana) use for eighth-grade girls in one study, and for all adolescents in another study, which combined the ad campaign with an in-school, community intervention.[3]

Marketing Communcations Objectives and Terminology

As the preceding examples illustrate, marketing communications is a critical aspect of companies' overall marketing missions and a major determinant of success or failure. All organizations—whether firms involved in B2B exchanges, companies engaged in B2C marketing, or organizations delivering not-for-profit services (museums, symphony orchestras, anti-drug campaigns, etc.)—use various marketing communications to promote their offerings and achieve financial and nonfinancial goals. Companies have a variety of general objectives for their marcom programs: (1) *informing* customers about their products, services, and terms of sale; (2) *persuading* customers to choose certain products and brands, shop in particular stores, go to certain websites, attend events, and other specific behaviors; and (3) *inducing action* (e.g., purchase behavior) from customers that is more immediate than delayed in nature. These objectives usually are accomplished sequentially, although are pitted against one another at times (e.g., a government agency whose mission is to "just give the folks the facts" versus another with a mission affecting public health). These and other objectives can be achieved by using a variety of marcom tools, including mobile and TV advertising, salespeople, social media (Facebook, Twitter, and YouTube), point-of-purchase displays, interactive packages, direct mail literature, group online coupons (Groupon), free samples, publicity releases, and other communication and promotional devices.

We now present several marketing and marcom terms that will be useful in providing a foundation for future concepts and chapters in this text. As you may recall from your introductory marketing course, the marketing mix consists of the specific collection of certain levels of a brand's "4Ps"—product, price, place (distribution), and promotion—all usually aimed at a specific target market. As an example, Mountain Dew "Code Red" might be aimed at males 14 to 21, primarily using marcom tools of bright red labeling, flavored soda ingredients, a $1.50 price in a vending machine, online advertising, and snowboarding/skateboarding celebrities to generate interest.

Other important marcom terminology includes communications, the process whereby commonness of thought is established and meaning is shared between individuals or between organizations and individuals. This idea is illustrated in the Social Media Venn Diagram found in Figure 1.1. Although there have been numerous definitions of marketing over the years,[4] one that is concise and focuses directly on (customer) needs and wants is as follows: Marketing is human activity directed at satisfying (customer) needs and wants through exchange processes.[5] Taken together, marketing communications represents the collection of all elements in an organization's marketing mix that facilitate exchange by establishing shared meaning with its customers. Central to the definition of marketing communications is the notion that *all marketing mix variables*, and not just promotion alone, can communicate with customers. The definition permits the possibility that marketing communications can be both intentional (e.g., as with advertising and sales promotion) and unintentional (e.g., a product feature, package cue, store location, or price).

FIGURE 1.1 Social Media Venn Diagram

Promotional Mix Elements

Promotion management employs a variety of methods to meet customer needs and move them toward action. The blend of these primary promotional elements has evolved over time and is known as the promotional mix. Currently, the promotional mix elements include advertising, public relations, sales promotion, personal selling, direct marketing, and online marketing/social media.

Advertising is any paid form of non-personal communication of ideas, goods, or services by an identified sponsor.[6] This includes traditional mass media outlets such as television, magazines, newspapers, out-of-home (billboards), etc. The advertiser is an identified sponsor and it is nonpersonal because the sponsoring form is simultaneously communicating with multiple receivers (perhaps millions) rather than with a specific person or small group.

Public relations or PR is an organizational activity involved with fostering goodwill between a company and its various publics (e.g., employees, suppliers, consumers, government agencies, stockholders, etc.). The primary focus of public relations in IMC is with the marketing-oriented aspects of communications with publics (e.g., publicity, product releases, handling rumors, tampering, etc.). For example, publicity, like advertising, is non-personal communication to a mass audience. Yet, unlike advertising, it is not paid for by the company and usually comes in the form of news items or editorial comments about a company's products or services.

Sales promotion consists of all promotional activities that attempt to stimulate short-term buyer behavior (i.e., attempt to promote immediate sales). In comparison, advertising and public relations/publicity usually are designed also to accomplish other objectives, such as developing brand awareness or influencing consumer attitudes. Sales promotions are directed at the trade (wholesalers/distributors and retailers), consumers, and at times toward the company's own sales force. *Trade sales promotion* includes using display allowances, quantity

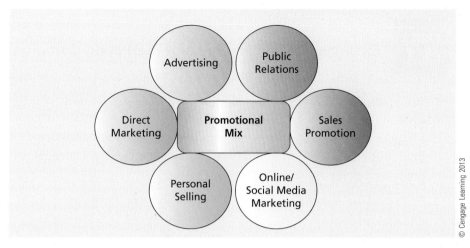

FIGURE **1.2**   The Promotional Mix

discounts, and merchandise assistance to activate wholesale and retailer responses. *Consumer sales promotion* includes the use of coupons, premiums, free samples, contests/sweepstakes, and rebates.

Personal selling is paid, person-to-person communication in which a seller determines needs and wants of prospective buyers and attempts to persuade these buyers to purchase the company's products or services. Depending on the situation, personal selling outreach efforts can range from face-to-face communication to telephone sales to online contacts.

Direct marketing represents an interactive system of marketing which uses one or more advertising media to effect a measurable response and/or transaction at any location. Primary methods of direct marketing include direct response advertising, direct selling, telemarketing, and the use of database marketing techniques. *Direct-response advertising*, a major form of direct marketing, involves the use of any of several media to transmit messages that encourage buyers to purchase directly from the advertiser. Such media might involve TV, direct mail, print, and online efforts. You may be familiar with some of the brands that have spent the most on direct response TV advertising recently in a tight economic climate: Proactiv, Rosetta Stone, Nutrisystem, Snuggie, Time Life, Cash4Gold, ShamWow, and PedEgg, among others.[7]

Online marketing is the promotion of product and services over the Internet (e.g., search engine marketing, banner ads, mobile advertising, and location-based apps), whereas social media marketing represents forms of electronic communication through which user-generated content (information, ideas, and videos) can be shared within the user's social network.[8] The use of IMC through social media networks (e.g., Facebook, Twitter, and YouTube) has literally exploded and has changed the entire IMC industry. At this point, we expand our discussion to the consideration of all primary marketing communication tools, focusing on, but not limited to, the promotional mix elements (see Figure 1.2).

The Primary Tools of Marketing Communications

The primary forms of marketing communications include many specific examples of promotional mix and other communication elements, including traditional mass media advertising (TV, magazines, etc.); online advertising (websites, opt-in e-mail messages, text messaging, etc.); sales promotions (samples, coupons, rebates, premium items, etc.); store signage, package labeling, and point-of-purchase communications; direct-mail literature; public relations and publicity releases; sponsorships of events and causes; presentations by salespeople; social media and online marketing; and various collateral forms of communication devices. Table 1.1 provides a listing of possible marketing communication elements.

TABLE 1.1	Examples of Primary Tools of Marketing Communications

1. Media Advertising
   - TV
   - Radio
   - Magazines
   - Newspapers
2. Direct Response Advertising
   - Direct mail
   - Telephone solicitation
   - Online advertising
3. Place Advertising
   - Billboards and bulletins
   - Posters
   - Transit ads
   - Cinema ads
4. Store Signage and Point-of-Purchase Advertising
   - External store signs
   - In-store shelf signs
   - Shopping cart ads
   - In-store radio and TV

5. Trade- and Consumer-Oriented Promotions
   - Trade deals and buying allowances
   - Display and advertising allowances
   - Trade shows
   - Cooperative advertising
   - Samples
   - Coupons
   - Premiums
   - Refunds/rebates
   - Contests/sweepstakes
   - Promotional games
   - Bonus packs
   - Price-off deals

6. Event Marketing and Sponsorships
   - Sponsorship of sporting events
   - Sponsorship of arts, fairs, and festivals
   - Sponsorship of causes
7. Marketing-Oriented Public Relations and Publicity
8. Personal Selling
9. Social Media
   - Facebook
   - Twitter
   - LinkedIn
   - YouTube
10. Online Marketing
    - Mobile advertising
    - Placed-based applications
    - Search engine marketing

Source: Adapted from Figure 1.1 in Kevin Lane Keller, "Mastering the Marketing Communications Mix: Micro and Macro Perspectives on Integrated Marketing Communication Programs," *Journal of Marketing Management* 17 (August, 2001), 823–51.

The Integration of Marketing Communications

Mountain Dew is a well-known brand that is consumed by predominately young, active, outdoor-oriented consumers and is the fourth-highest selling soft-drink brand in the United States. On the market for more than 50 years, Mountain Dew is positioned as a brand that stands for fun, exhilaration, and energy—FEE for short. Brand managers have been consistent over time and across communication media in maintaining the FEE theme that represents the brand's core meaning—its positioning. Various advertising media, event sponsorships, and consumer promotions have been employed over the years to trumpet the brand's core meaning. The brand managers of Mountain Dew use network TV commercials, as well as local TV and radio spots, online marketing, and social media to appeal to the brand's target audience.

Event sponsorships provide another major communication medium for Mountain Dew, which has sponsored leading alternative sports competitions such as the Dew Action Sports Tour (extreme sports tournament), the Summer and Winter X Games, and the Mountain Dew Vertical Challenge (a series of ski and snowboard races). Appealing giveaway items (T-shirts, videos, branded snowboards and mountain bikes, etc.) are distributed at these events to generate excitement and foster positive connections between the Mountain Dew brand and its loyal consumers.

Much of Mountain Dew's continued success is attributable to its brand managers' dedication to presenting *consistent* messages about the brand, both over time and across communication media. By contrast, many companies treat the various promotional mix elements—advertising, sales promotions, online marketing, social media, public relations, and so on—as virtually separate activities rather than as integrated tools that work together to achieve a common goal. Personnel responsible for advertising sometimes fail to coordinate adequately their efforts with individuals in charge of sales promotions or publicity. A better idea is to try to address the customer problems first, and then apply the most appropriate integrated solution, rather than forcing the promotional element (e.g., social media) up front.[9]

Why Integrate?

The logic underlying integration seems so clear and compelling that the student may be wondering: What's the big deal? Why haven't firms practiced IMC all along? Why is there reluctance to integrate? Good questions, all, but what sounds reasonable in theory is not always easy to put into practice.[10] Organizations traditionally have handled advertising, sales promotions, mobile advertising, social media, and other communication tools as virtually separate practices because different units within organizations have specialized in separate aspects of marketing communications—advertising *or* social media, etc.—rather than having generalized knowledge and experience with all communication tools. Furthermore, outside suppliers (such as advertising agencies, public relations agencies, social media firms, and sales promotion agencies) also have tended to specialize in single facets of marketing communications rather than to possess expertise across the board. There has been a reluctance to change from this single-function, specialist model due to managerial parochialism (e.g., a famous misguided quote is "TV is the answer, now what was the question?") and for fear that change might lead to budget cutbacks in their areas of control and reductions in their authority, perceived expertise, and power.

IMC Practices and Synergy

Although there is movement toward increased implementation of IMC, not all brand managers or their firms are equally likely to adopt IMC. In fact, experienced managers are more likely than novice managers to practice IMC. Firms involved in marketing services (rather than products) and B2C (versus B2B) companies are more likely to practice IMC. More sophisticated companies also are likely adherents to IMC.[11]

IMC is a goal worth pursuing because using multiple communication tools in conjunction with one another can produce greater results than tools used individually and in an uncoordinated fashion. There is a *synergistic effect* of using multiple well-coordinated marcom tools. A study of Levi Strauss' Dockers khaki pants illustrated this value of synergy.[12] Using regression modeling and sales trajectories, researchers determined that the use of both TV and print advertisements produced a synergistic effect on sales of pants that significantly added to the individual effects of each advertising medium. Another study demonstrated that TV and online advertising used in conjunction produced positive synergistic effects that were additional to each medium's individual effects. TV and online advertising used together produced more attention, more positive thoughts, and higher message credibility than did the sum of the two media when used individually.[13]

Definition of IMC

Proponents of IMC have provided slightly different perspectives on this management practice, and not all educators or practitioners agree on the precise meaning of IMC.[14] This text uses the following definition, which focuses on the origin and essence of IMC and provides a succinct view of the concept.

> IMC *is the coordination of the promotional mix elements (advertising, public relations, sales promotion, personal selling, direct marketing, and online marketing/social media) with each other and with the other elements of the brands' marketing mix (product, place, price) such that all elements speak with one voice.*[15]

Key IMC Features

Inherent in the definition of integrated marketing communications are several critical features, which are interdependent and listed in no particular order of importance in Table 1.2. Yet all five features are critical to both understanding the philosophy of IMC and appreciating what must be accomplished to implement this philosophy into practice.

Key Feature #1: IMC Should Begin with the Customer or Prospect

This feature emphasizes that the marcom process must *start with the customer or prospect* and then work backward to the brand communicator in determining the most appropriate messages and media to employ for the brand. The IMC approach starts with the customer ("outside-in") to determine which communication methods that will best serve their needs and motivate them to purchase the brand. It avoids an "inside-out" approach (from company to customer) in identifying communication vehicles.

Consumers in Control

It is widely acknowledged that marketing communications are governed by a key reality: The consumer increasingly wants to be in control! In today's marketplace, consumer-generated content has placed consumers clearly in control. Online marketing via location-based services (e.g., foursquare), social media (Twitter, Facebook, and YouTube), smartphone scanning, blogging, texting, etc. has enabled consumers to have communications and entertainment when and wherever they want. (See the *Global Focus* insert for a marcom program in China that puts consumers in control.)

Reduced Dependence on the Mass Media

Many marketing communicators now realize that communication outlets other than the mass media often better serve the needs of their brands. The objective is to contact customers and prospects effectively using touch points that reach them where, when, and how they wish to be contacted. Traditional mass media advertising (via TV, magazines, radio, and newspapers) is not always the most effective or cost-efficient avenue for accomplishing this objective. For example, Nike—in a

TABLE 1.2	Five Key Features of IMC

1. Start with the customer or prospect.
2. Use any form of relevant contact or touch point.
3. Speak with a single voice.
4. Build relationships.
5. Affect behavior.

GLOBAL FOCUS

Creating a Pepsi Commercial in China

In an effort to reach out to China's Internet-savvy youth and to engage their interest in Pepsi, the marketers of this soft drink brand created the Pepsi Creative Challenge contest. Consumers were invited to develop a TV spot that would star Jay Chow (also spelled Chou), who is a superstar in the entertainment business throughout Asia. Contest entrants were instructed to submit scripts for a commercial with a maximum of 200 words. Other consumers who logged on to a website then read and scored the submitted scripts. A panel consisting of Pepsi executives and Mr. Chow then selected the best five ideas from among the 100 highest-scoring entries during each two-week period. At the end of six weeks, 15 finalists were identified. The 15 scripts were posted on the website, and interested consumers then voted for the best script. The winner received $12,500 and an opportunity to participate in the production of the commercial. The remaining 14 finalists earned $1,250 cash prizes for their efforts and were invited to attend the party launching the new commercial.

As indicated by a Pepsi executive, the response was extremely positive with more than 27,000 commercial scripts submitted. A marketing researcher stated that "The reason why digital interactive marketing campaigns like the Pepsi Creative Challenge work is that they add value by creating a mechanism for consumers to get involved." Of course, "getting involved" is simply another way of saying that consumers' control over advertising content is increasing—in China as elsewhere around the globe.

Sources: Adapted from Normandy Madden, "Consumers to Create Pepsi Spot in China," *Advertising Age*, June 5, 2006, 15; and "Wharton's Take on the Internet in China," April 17, 2007, http://www.edelmanapac.com/edelman/blog/2007/04/17/Whartons-Take-on-the-Internet-in-China.html.

move that shocked the advertising community—dropped its ad agency of 25 years because it was dissatisfied with the agency's lack of digital expertise.[16] In actuality, many advertising agencies have been slow to adapt to advertisers' increasing use of the Internet and are understaffed with employees who possess digital expertise and experience.[17]

Although advertising in the digital media is increasing rapidly, this does not mean that mass media advertising is unimportant or in threat of extinction. The point instead is that other communication methods must receive careful consideration *before* mass media advertising is automatically assumed to be *the* solution. Many brand managers and their agencies have reduced the role of TV in their marcom budgeting because TV advertising may not be as effective or cost-efficient as it once was. TV audiences are more fragmented than in prior years and relatively fewer consumers can be reached by the advertising placed on any particular program. Moreover, other advertising and nonadvertising tools may be superior to TV in achieving brand managers' objectives. For example, Unilever's brand of Wisk detergent was historically advertised heavily on TV. Wisk's brand managers devised a media plan that minimized TV in the ad budget in lieu of using online media to reach people where "their passions get them dirty." Specifically, banner ads were placed on targeted websites where consumers were learning more about their passions (i.e., Foodies on Foodnetwork.com, do-it-yourselfers on DIY.com, etc.) and other touch points directed consumers to a Wisk website where further information was provided. Tag line: Wisk. Your passions get your dirty. Our power gets you clean.[18]

In the spirit of reducing dependence on TV advertising, McCann Worldgroup, a highly respected advertising agency, has developed the concept of a *media-neutral approach* when counseling its clients in selecting appropriate marcom tools. This approach requires that the brand marketer first identify the goal(s) a marcom program is designed to accomplish (building brand awareness, creating buzz, influencing behavior, etc.) and then determine the best way to allocate the marketer's budget.[19] This media-neutral or "agnostic" approach[20] is perfectly in accord with our earlier discussion about selecting the most appropriate communication tool given the task at hand.

Key Feature #2: Use Any Form of Relevant Contact

As carpenters, plumbers, and auto mechanics know, some tools are more appropriate for a given task at hand. Similarly, a truly professional marketing communicator selects the best tools (advertising, social media, publicity, etc.) for the job.

Touch Points and 360-Degree Branding

Now, as applied to marketing communications, IMC practitioners need to be receptive to using all forms of *touch points*, or *contacts*, as potential message delivery channels. Touch point and contact are used here as interchangeable terms to mean *any* message medium capable of reaching target customers and presenting the brand in a favorable light.

In many respects, this amounts to surrounding present or prospective customers with the brand message at every possible opportunity and allowing them to use whatever information about the brand they deem most useful.[21] Thus, the phrase, *360-degree branding*, suggests that a brand's touch points should surround the target audience. A marketing manager for Ford trucks put it this way: "We want to be everywhere that makes sense for our customer. We go to the places they are."[22]

Toyota Motor Sales U.S.A. and its advertising agency Saatchi & Saatchi illustrate the use of a multiple-touch point strategy during their introduction of the Yaris subcompact automobile.[23] In an effort to reach a market of 18- to 34-year-olds, Toyota's ad agency promoted the Yaris in branded entertainment venues that reached Yaris's youthful age-group target. The multiple-touch point strategy included the following elements: (1) A series of 26 mobile-phone episodes that were spun off the TV program *Prison Break*; each two-minute "mobisode" was preceded by a 10-second advertisement for the Yaris. (2) An Internet contest had consumers create their own three-minute TV commercials for the Yaris under the theme "What would you do with your Yaris?" (3) Yaris was the title sponsor in specially designed video games. (4) Yaris was featured in various sponsored events such as the South by Southwest Music festival held in Austin, Texas. (5) Finally, the subcompact Yaris was integrated into the TV comedy show, *Mad TV*, through a series of sketches that were built around the car.

Other brand touch-point examples include:

- MasterCard provided complimentary snacks, games, puzzles, and movie headphones on select American Airlines flights during the busy Christmas holiday season.
- Brand managers at Procter & Gamble placed the Tide detergent logo on napkin dispensers in pizza shops and cheesesteak shops in Boston and Philadelphia. These napkin dispensers held napkins imprinted with the Tide logo and the message "Because napkins are never in the right place at the right time."
- JELL-O pudding was promoted by affixing stickers with the JELL-O name to bananas—one product (bananas) was used as a contact channel for reaching consumers about another (JELL-O).
- In New York City, ads are placed on large vinyl sheets that cover scaffolding at construction sites. These ads sometimes extend for an entire city block and serve to convey the advertiser's message in prominent and dramatic fashion.
- Germany's Puma brand of athletic footwear promoted itself during soccer's World Cup hosted in Japan by spotlighting its new brand of Shudoh soccer cleats at sushi restaurants in major cities around Asia and Europe. The shoes were encased in stylish displays made of bamboo and glass and placed on tables.

© Richard Levine/Alamy

- Hershey Foods Corporation, makers of Hershey's Kisses among many other items, designed a huge display rising 15 stories high in New York City's Times Square district.
- BriteVision designed a unique touch point in the form of advertisements on coffee sleeve insulators that protect coffee drinkers from burning their hands.
- By partnering with the owner of 125 shopping malls, 20th Century Fox devised a creative solution to movie marketing. Under an exclusive deal, new movies from 20th Century Fox were advertised on huge banners in mall garages, on tray liners in restaurants, and elsewhere in malls.
- An outdoor media company in Denmark devised a creative way to reach consumers with advertising messages. The company gave parents free use of high-quality baby carriages (i.e., buggies or strollers) that carried the names of corporate sponsors on the sides.
- Another creative touch point is described in the *IMC Focus* insert.

Overall, the IMC objective is to reach the target audience efficiently and effectively using touch points that are appropriate. Also, marketing

IMC FOCUS

The Laundry Hanger as an Advertising Touch Point

Reaching large numbers of men with advertising messages is often difficult because most ad media are fragmented; that is, they appeal to relatively small groups of people who share common interests but fail to reach large numbers whose interests are highly diverse and thus do not watch the same TV programs, read the same magazines, listen to the same radio programs, and so on. It is for this reason that advertisers and their agencies are continuously seeking media alternatives that can make contact with difficult-to-reach consumers. Enter the mundane laundry hanger as a novel point of contact.

A small New York company, Hanger Network, is generating interest from some major advertisers who are constantly searching for unique ways to reach consumers economically. Hanger Network's advertising proposition is straightforward: It arranges with laundry-supply firms to make and distribute laundry hangers carrying advertising messages for distribution in dry cleaners throughout the United States. For example, the marketers of Mitchum deodorant used hangers as part of a multimedia campaign for its new brand of men's deodorant named Smart Solid. Smart Solid is positioned as a brand that won't leave a white residue on clothing as do other antiperspirants. Hanger ads for this brand

carried a variety of taglines such as "You won't find white residue on a Mitchum Man's shirt," "Chilidog stains are another story," and "A Mitchum Man doesn't wear his emotions on his sleeve, or his deodorant." Prior to fully committing to hanger advertising, Mitchum pretested hanger ads in two cities and experienced double-digit growth in consumer brand awareness and purchase intentions by the completion of the pretest. The decision to expand the campaign in other markets was a no-brainer based on these impressive results.

Hanger Network's ads have been used in approximately 40 percent of the 25,000 dry cleaning outlets in the United States. There have been some problems that need to be worked out, but it is likely that hanger advertising has a future. But, although it has the potential to achieve advertisers' needs, it isn't an inexpensive form of advertising. In fact, the price is around $45 for every thousand hangers that carry an ad, which on a cost-per-thousand basis is more expensive even than advertising during some high-profile sporting events on television!

Source: Adapted from Suzanne Vranica, "Marketers Try Hanging Out at Dry Cleaners," *Wall Street Journal Online*, March 12, 2007, http://online.wsj.com (accessed March 12, 2007).

© Jim Barber/Shutterstock.com

communicators have learned that the identical message has differential impact depending on the medium that carries the message. As the chair and chief executive officer of the Young & Rubicam ad agency succinctly stated, "At the end of the day, [marcom agencies] don't deliver ads, or direct mail pieces, or PR and corporate identity programs. We deliver results."[24]

Key Feature #3: Speak with a Single Voice

Since the early origins of IMC, it was clear that marketing communications must *speak with a single voice*. Coordination of messages and media is absolutely critical to achieving a strong and unified brand image and moving consumers to action. Failure to closely coordinate all communication elements can result in duplicated efforts or, worse, contradictory brand messages.

A vice president of marketing at Nabisco fully recognized the value of speaking with a single voice when describing her intention to integrate all the marketing communication contacts for Nabisco's Oreo brand of cookies. This executive captured the essential quality of "single voicing" when stating that, under her leadership, "whenever consumers see Oreo, they'll be seeing the same message."[25]

A general manager at Mars, Inc., maker of candy products, expressed a similar sentiment when stating, "We used to look at advertising, PR, promotion plans, each piece as separate. Now every piece of communication from package to Internet has to reflect the same message."[26]

In general, the single-voice principle involves selecting a specific positioning statement for a brand. A positioning statement is the key idea that encapsulates what a brand is intended to stand for in its target market's mind and then consistently delivers the same idea across all media channels. For example, at one of the authors' universities (Marquette University, www.marquette.edu) all communication is now branded with the theme encouraging students to "Be the Difference" and promoting the university's attributes of "Excellence, Faith, Leadership, and Service."

Key Feature #4: Build Relationships Rather Than Engage in Flings

Successful marketing communication requires building relationships between brands and their consumers/customers. A relationship is an enduring link between a brand and its customers. Successful relationships between customers and brands lead to repeat purchasing and, ideally, loyalty toward a brand.

The value of customer retention has been compared to a "leaky bucket," the logic of which is nicely captured in the following quote:

> *As a company loses customers out of the leak in the bottom of the bucket, they have to continue to add new customers to the top of the bucket. If the company can even partially plug the leak, the bucket stays fuller. It then takes fewer new customers added to the top of the bucket to achieve the same level of profitability. It's less expensive and more profitable to keep those customers already in the bucket. Smart business people realize that it costs five to 10 times more to land a new customer than to keep a customer they already have. They also recognize that increasing the number of customers they keep by a small percentage can double profits.*[27]

Loyalty Programs

One well-known method for building customer relations is the use of *loyalty programs* dedicated to creating customers who are

committed to a brand and encouraging them to satisfy most of their product or service needs from offering organizations.[28] Airlines, credit card companies, hotels, supermarkets, and many other businesses provide customers with bonus points—or some other form of accumulated reward—for their continued patronage.

For example, to encourage use of its debit/gift card and to retain loyal purchasers, the Caribou Coffee chain developed an incentive whereby consumers who used the Caribou Card and spent at least $1.50 per visit over 10 visits would receive a $4 credit on their Caribou Card.[29] Pizza Hut encouraged repeat purchasing from its customers by promoting a fee-based program in which customers paid an annual fee of $14.99; in return, they received an initial free large pizza and an additional free pizza every month if they placed two orders per month. This program enabled Pizza Hut to retain its best customers and keep them from switching their loyalties to other pizza makers.[30]

In step with the consumer-centric movement discussed in the context of IMC key feature #1, loyalty programs are increasingly being designed so that consumers are in control of how their reward points are used rather than restricting them to using the points only in a manner directed by the brand manager. As a case in point, Canada's Air Miles Reward Program enables its frequent fliers to use their reward miles for shopping at over 100 sponsors and allows them to acquire movie tickets, electronic merchandise, Walt Disney World tickets, gift cards, and literally hundreds of other product options of their choosing.[31]

Experiential Marketing Programs

Another way relationships between brands and customers are nurtured is by creating brand experiences that make positive and lasting impressions. This is done by creating special events or developing exciting venues that attempt to build the sensation that a sponsoring brand is relevant to the consumer's life and lifestyle. For example, Harley-Davidson (www.harley-davidson.com) has accomplished this for years through their Harley Owner's Group (HOG). HOG helped sponsor Harley's 100th celebration in Milwaukee with over one million riders returning to the home of Harley, and the four day 105th celebration with 70,000 enjoying Bruce Springsteen and the E-Street Band on Milwaukee's Lakefront. As another example, Toronto-based Molson beer conducted the Molson Outpost campaign that took 400 sweepstakes winners on a weekend escapade of outdoor camping and extreme activities such as mountain climbing. Lincoln automobiles, a sponsor of the U.S. Open tennis tournament, converted an unused building at the USTA National Tennis Center into a complex that immersed visitors in the history of tennis. The building featured soundstages, faux docks with real water, and images of the evolution of tennis around the world. Some 30,000 leads were obtained from people interested in Lincoln automobiles, prompting

© AP Images/Morry Gash

Lincoln's marketing communications coordinator to comment that "experiential marketing is permeating our entire marketing mix."[32]

Key Element #5: Don't Lose Focus of the Ultimate Objective: Affect Behavior

A final IMC feature is the goal of *affecting the behavior* of the target audience. This means that marketing communications ultimately must do more than just influence brand awareness or enhance consumer attitudes toward the brand. Instead, successful IMC requires that communication efforts be directed at encouraging some form of behavioral response. The objective, in other words, is to *move people to action*. For example, an

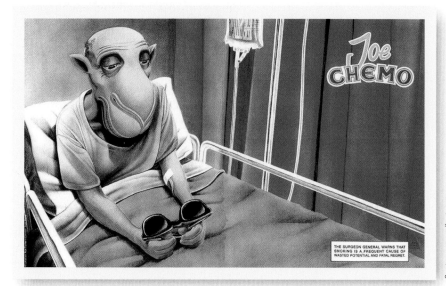

advertising campaign that reminds people of one of the recent tragedies (e.g., Hurricane Katrina, the earthquakes in Haiti and Japan, tornadoes in the Midwest) may be ineffective if it merely gets people to feel sorry for the plight of residents; rather, effectiveness is demonstrated by people contributing money to relief funds for these tragedies.

A similar challenge confronts antismoking proponents. Although most people understand intellectually that smoking causes cancer, emphysema, and other ailments, these same people often think that cancer and other problems will happen to smokers other than themselves. Hence, antismoking ads may serve to make people aware of the problems associated with smoking, but such campaigns may be ineffective if people continue to smoke. The IMC goal in such a case is to develop more compelling advertisements that influence smokers to discontinue this practice. For instance, creative appeals to normative influences (e.g., social disapproval) have been found to significantly reduce adolescent non-smoking intentions versus controls.[33] Similarly, adolescent aspirations and autonomy are found to aid anti-drug ad and school/community-based campaigns in reducing drug use.

One caution in all of this is that it would be simplistic and unrealistic to expect an action to result from every communication effort. Prior to purchasing a new brand, consumers generally must be made aware of the brand and its benefits and be influenced to have a favorable attitude toward it. Communication efforts directed at accomplishing these intermediate, or pre-behavioral, goals are fully justified. Yet eventually—and preferably sooner than later—a successful marcom program must ultimately affect behavior.

Obstacles to Implementing the Key IMC Features

Brand managers typically use outside suppliers, or specialized services, to assist them in managing various aspects of marketing communications. These include advertising agencies, public relations firms, sales promotion agencies, direct-advertising firms, social media firms, and special-event marketers. Herein is a major reason why marketing communication efforts often do not meet the ideals previously described. Integration requires tight coordination among all elements of a marcom program. However, this becomes complicated when different specialized services operate independently of one another.

Perhaps the greatest obstacle to integration is that few providers of marketing communication services have the far-ranging skills to plan and execute programs that cut across all major forms of marketing communications.

Advertising agencies, which traditionally have offered a greater breadth of services than do other specialists, are well qualified to develop mass media advertising campaigns; most, however, do not also have the ability nor scale to conduct direct-to-customer advertising, and even fewer have departments for sales promotions, special events, and publicity campaigns. In the final analysis, although most marketers consider themselves proponents of IMC, a major challenge facing brand marketers and their agencies is assuring that all marcom tools used in a particular marketing execution are consistently executed.[34]

The Marketing Communications Decision-Making Process

Figure 1.3 is a framework conceptualizing the various types of practical brand-level marcom decisions and the outcomes desired from those decisions. The model consists of a set of fundamental decisions, a set of implementation decisions, and program evaluation. The model in Figure 1.3 shows that *fundamental decisions* (targeting, positioning, setting objectives, and budgeting) influence *implementation decisions* regarding the mixture of communications elements and the determination of messages, media, and momentum. The expected *outcomes* from these decisions are enhancing brand equity and affecting behavior. Subsequent to the implementation of the marcom decisions, *program evaluation*—in the form of measuring the results from marcom efforts, providing feedback (see dashed arrow in Figure 1.3), and taking corrective action—is essential to determining whether outcomes match objectives. Corrective action is required when performance falls below expectations.

The objective of marketing communications is to enhance *brand equity*, the goodwill that an established brand has built up over its existence. In turn, improved brand equity is a means of moving customers to *favorable action toward the brand*—i.e., trying it, repeat purchasing it, and, ideally, becoming loyal

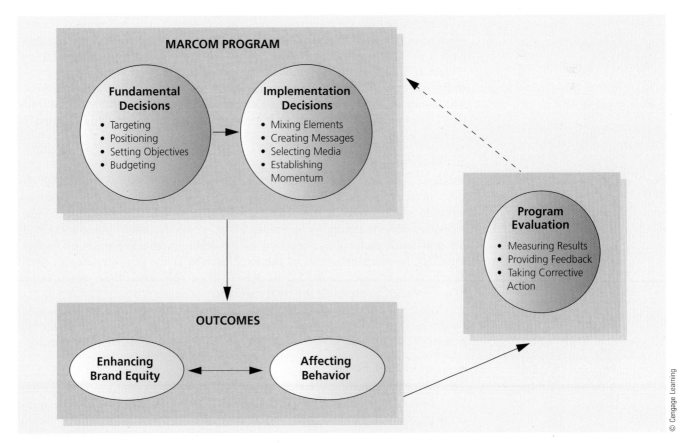

© Cengage Learning

FIGURE **1.3** Making Brand-Level Marcom Decisions and Achieving Desired Outcomes toward the brand. Enhancing equity and affecting behavior depend, of course, on the suitability of all marketing-mix elements—e.g., product quality and price level—and not just marcom per se. Marcom efforts nonetheless play a pivotal role by informing customers about new brands and their relative advantages and by elevating brand images.

Fundamental Marcom Decisions

Targeting

Targeting lets marketing communicators deliver messages more precisely and prevent wasted coverage to people falling outside the intended audience. Hence, selection of target segments is a critical step toward effective and efficient marketing communications for both B2B and B2C companies. Companies identify potential target markets in terms of demographics, lifestyles, product usage patterns, and geographic considerations. Targeting is covered in detail in Chapter 5.

Positioning

A brand's position represents the key feature, benefit, or image that it stands for in the consumer's or the target audience's collective mind. Brand communicators and the marketing team in general must decide on a *brand positioning statement*, which is the central idea that encapsulates a brand's meaning and distinctiveness vis-a-vis competitive brands in the product category. It should be obvious that positioning and targeting decisions go hand in hand: positioning decisions are made with respect to intended targets, and targeting decisions are based on a clear idea of how brands are to be positioned and distinguished from competitive offerings. Chapter 5 covers the topic of positioning in considerable detail.

Setting Objectives

Marketing communicators' decisions are grounded in the underlying objectives to be accomplished for a brand. For example, whereas mass media advertising is ideally suited for creating consumer awareness of a new or improved brand, point-of-purchase communications are perfect for influencing in-store brand selection, and personal selling is unparalleled when it comes to informing B2B customers and retailers about product improvements. The most important question to pose is this: "What is the communications supposed to do or accomplish?"[35] The choice of appropriate marketing communications tools and media naturally flows from the answer to this key question. Objective setting is covered in Chapter 8.

Budgeting

Financial resources are budgeted to specific marcom elements to accomplish desired objectives. Companies use different budgeting procedures in allocating funds to marketing communications managers and other organizational units. At one extreme is *top-down budgeting (TD)*, in which senior management decides how much each subunit receives. At the other extreme is *bottom-up budgeting (BU)*, in which managers of subunits (such as at the product category level) determine how much is needed to achieve their objectives; these amounts are then combined to establish the total marketing budget.

Most budgeting practices involve a combination of top-down and bottom-up budgeting (e.g., a *bottom-up/top-down process [BUTD]* or a *top-down/bottom-up process [TDBU]*).[36] Budgeting is covered in Chapter 8 along with objective setting.

A Concluding Point

The following statement serves as an important point to capture the preceding discussion of fundamental marcom decisions. You regularly should pose questions to yourself—and to your colleagues—such as these: Is our brand clearly positioned in the minds of consumers? What is the single most important aspect that they associate with our brand? Is our communication directed to a specific target? What specific objective is our advertising (or sales promotion, or event, etc.) attempting to accomplish? Is our proposed strategy within the budget available, or do we need to request more budget?

> *A Concluding Point: All marketing communications should be: (1) directed to a particular target market, (2) clearly positioned, (3) created to achieve a specific objective, and (4) undertaken to accomplish the objective within budget constraint.*

Marcom Implementation Decisions

The fundamental decisions just described are conceptual and strategic. Comparatively, the implementation decisions are practical and tactical. Here is where the proverbial rubber hits the road. Marcom managers must make various implementation decisions in the pursuit of accomplishing brand-level objectives and achieving the brand's positioning and targeting requirements. Initially they must choose how best to integrate, or mix, the various communications elements to achieve objectives toward the target market and within budget constraint. Then they must decide what types of messages will accomplish the desired positioning, which media are appropriate for delivering messages, and what degree of momentum is needed to support the media effort. Please refer again to Figure 1.3 to obtain a view of the "forest" prior to examining specific "trees."

Mixing Elements

A fundamental issue confronting all companies is deciding exactly how to allocate resources among the various marketing communications tools. For B2B companies, the mixture typically emphasizes, in the following order of budgeting importance, direct mail, online marketing, trade shows, brand advertising, and telemarketing.[37] For consumer goods marketers, mixture decisions are, in many respects, more complicated because greater options are available. The issue boils down in large part to a decision of how much to allocate to advertising and to sales promotions. (Note: In keeping with practitioner convention, the word *promotion* hereafter will be used interchangeably with *sales promotion*.) The trend during the past two decades has been toward greater expenditures on promotions and fewer on advertising.

Is there an *optimum mixture* of expenditures between advertising and promotion? There is not, unfortunately, because the marketing communications-mix decision constitutes an *ill-structured problem*.[38] This means that for a given level of expenditure, there is no way of determining the mathematical optimum allocation between advertising and promotion that will maximize revenue or profit. There are two reasons for this. First, advertising and promotions are somewhat interchangeable—both tools can accomplish some of the same objectives. Therefore, it is impossible to know exactly which tool or combination of tools is better in every situation. Second, advertising and promotions produce a synergistic effect—their combined results are greater than what they would achieve individually. This makes it difficult to determine the exact effects that different combinations of advertising and sales promotion might generate.

However, a satisfactory mixture can be formulated by considering the differing purposes of each of these marcom tools. A key strategic consideration is whether short- or long-term schemes are more important given a brand's life-cycle stage and in view of competitive realities. For example, new brands require larger investment in promotions such as couponing and sampling to generate trial purchases, whereas mature brands might need proportionately greater advertising investment to maintain or enhance a brand's image.

Brand equity considerations also play a role in evaluating a satisfactory combination of advertising and promotions. Poorly planned or excessive promotions can damage a brand's equity by cheapening its image. If a brand is frequently placed on sale or if some form of deal (price-offs, discounts, etc.) is regularly offered, consumers will delay purchasing the brand until its price is reduced. This can cause the brand to be purchased more for its price discount than for its nonprice attributes and benefits (see Figure 1.4).

FIGURE **1.4** A Buy-One-Get-One Free Promotion

A word of caution is in order in properly mixing advertising and sales promotion. A "short-term solution" in spending excessive amounts on promotion to create quick sales while failing to invest sufficiently in advertising to build a brand's long-term equity can spell trouble for a brand's future. An appropriate mixture involves spending enough on promotions to ensure sufficient sales volume in the short term while simultaneously spending enough on advertising to ensure the growth or preservation of a brand's equity position.

Creating Messages

A second implementation decision is the creation of messages in the form of advertisements, publicity releases, promotions, package designs, social media, and any other form of marcom message. Subsequent chapters will address specific message issues relating to each marcom tool. Suffice it to say at this point that systematic (versus ad hoc) decision making requires that message content be dictated by the brand's positioning strategy and aligned with the communications objective for the designated target audience.

Selecting Media

All marketing communications messages require an instrument, or medium, for transmission. Although the term *media* is typically applied to advertising (television, magazines, radio, mobile, Internet, etc.), the concept of *media* is relevant to all marcom tools. For example, personal sales messages can be delivered via face-to-face communications or by telemarketing; these media alternatives have different costs and effectiveness. Point-of-purchase materials are delivered via in-store signs, electronically, musically, and otherwise. Each represents a different medium. Detailed discussions of media (especially advertising) are reserved for specific chapters later in the text.

Establishing Momentum

The word *momentum* refers to an object's force or speed of movement—its impetus. A train has momentum as it races down the tracks, a spacecraft has momentum as it is launched into orbit, a hockey player has momentum when skating past the defensive opposition, a student has momentum when making good progress on a term paper or when finished studying for an exam. Marketing communications programs also have, or lack, momentum. Simply developing an advertising message, creating a buzz-generating viral campaign, or releasing publicity is insufficient. The effectiveness of each of these message forms requires both a sufficient amount of effort and continuity of that effort.

Toyota Motor Corporation had available in stock on one occasion only a 16-day supply of the fast-selling Camry. Yet it launched a major advertising campaign aggressively encouraging consumers to purchase Camrys. Critics declared that it was unwise for Toyota to advertise when insufficient product was available to fulfill orders. In response, the vice president of Toyota Motor Sales, U.S.A., asserted that even when demand is strong, it is important "to keep your momentum in the marketplace going."[39] This executive obviously appreciates the value of achieving and maintaining a brand's momentum. Unfortunately, this is not the case in every organization. For example, advertising is one of the first items cut during economic downturns, even when, by continuing to advertise, the advertised brand could gain market share over brands that have suspended or severely slashed their ad budgets.

Marcom Outcomes

Based on our conceptual framework, the outcomes for a marcom program are twofold: (1) enhancing brand equity and (2) affecting behavior. Figure 1.3 displays a double-headed arrow between these outcomes, which signifies that each outcome can influence the other. For example, an ad campaign can result in enhanced brand equity leading to trial behavior. Conversely, trial, via a free sample, may lead to more positive brand perceptions and equity.

As established previously, a fundamental IMC principle is that marcom efforts must ultimately be gauged by whether they *affect behavior*. Sales promotion is the marcom tool most capable of directly affecting consumer behavior. However, *excessive* reliance on promotions can injure a brand's reputation by creating a low-price and perhaps low-quality image. It is for this reason that marketing communicators often seek first to enhance a brand's equity as a foundation to influencing behavior. We will examine this topic in detail in Chapter 2.

Program Evaluation

The final step in the process is that a program evaluation must take place, accomplished by measuring the results of marcom efforts against the objectives that were established at the outset. For a local advertiser—say, a sporting goods store that is running an advertised special on athletic shoes for a two-day period in May—the results are the number of Nike, Reebok, Adidas, and other brands sold versus a comparable time period (e.g., the last month, the previous May). For a national manufacturer of a branded product, results typically are not so quick to occur. Rather, a company invests in point-of-purchase communications, promotions, and advertising and then waits, often for weeks, to see whether these programs deliver the desired sales volume in a specific time period.

Regardless of the situation, it is critical to evaluate the results of marcom efforts. Throughout the business world there is increasing demand for *accountability*, which requires that research be performed and data acquired to determine whether implemented marcom decisions have accomplished the objectives they were expected to achieve. Results can be measured in terms of behavioral impact (such as increased sales) or based on communication outcomes versus comparable time periods or control groups.

Measures of *communication outcomes* include brand awareness, message comprehension, attitude toward the brand, and purchase intentions. All of these are communication (rather than behavioral) objectives in the sense that an advertiser has attempted to communicate a certain message argument or create an overall impression. Thus, the goal for an advertiser of a relatively unknown brand may be to increase brand awareness in the target market by 30 percent within six months of starting a new advertising campaign. This objective (a 30 percent increase in awareness) would be based on knowledge of the baseline awareness level prior to the campaign's debut. Post-campaign measurement would then reveal whether the target level was achieved.

Failure to achieve targeted results may prompt corrective action (see the dashed arrow in Figure 1.3). For instance, corrective action might call for greater investment, a different combination of communications elements, revised creative strategy, different media allocations, or a host of other possibilities. Only by systematically setting objectives and measuring results is it possible to know whether marcom programs are working as well as they should and how future efforts can improve on the past.[40]

Summary

This opening chapter has overviewed the fundamentals of IMC and provided a framework for thinking about all aspects of marcom decision making. IMC is the coordination of the promotional mix elements with each other and with the other elements of the brand's marketing mix such that all elements speak with a one voice. One of several key features of IMC is the use of all sources of brand or company contacts as potential message delivery channels. Another key feature is that the IMC process starts with the customer or prospect rather than the brand communicator to determine the most appropriate and effective methods for developing persuasive communications programs. Consumers are increasingly in control of marketing communications both in their active choice of which media outlets to attend and by generating their own brand-related communications—via podcasting, blogging, and creating messages on social media sites such as Facebook, Twitter, and YouTube.

This chapter has provided a model of the marcom process to serve as a useful integrative device for better structuring and understanding the topics covered throughout the remainder of the text. The model (see Figure 1.3) includes three components: a marcom program consisting of fundamental and implementation decisions, outcomes (enhancing brand equity and affecting behavior), and program evaluation. Fundamental decisions include choosing target markets, establishing a brand positioning, setting objectives, and determining a marcom budget. Implementation decisions involve determining a mixture of marketing communications tools (advertising, promotions, social media, etc.) and establishing message, media, and momentum plans. These decisions are evaluated by comparing measured results against brand-level communications objectives.

It is our sincere hope that this introductory chapter has piqued your interest and provided you with a basic understanding of the many topics you will be studying while reading this text and participating in classroom lectures and discussions. Marketing communications truly is a fascinating and dynamic subject. It combines art, science, and technology and allows the practitioner considerable latitude in developing effective ways to skin the proverbial cat. It will serve you well throughout your studies and into your marketing career to remain ever mindful of the key elements of IMC described in this chapter. Organizations that truly succeed in their marcom pursuits must accept and practice these key elements.

Because the field of marketing communications involves many forms of practice, a number of specialty trade associations have evolved over time. The following appendix overviews, in alphabetical order, some of the more influential associations in the United States. Internet sites are provided to facilitate your search for additional information about these organizations. (Many countries other than the United States have similar associations. Interested students might want to conduct an Internet search to identify similar associations in a country of interest.)

Appendix

Some Important U.S. Trade Associations in the Marcom Field:

Advertising Research Foundation (ARF, www.thearf.org)—ARF is a nonprofit association dedicated to increasing advertising effectiveness by conducting objective and impartial research. ARF's members consist of advertisers, advertising agencies, research firms, and media companies.

American Association of Advertising Agencies (AAAA, www.aaaa.org)—The Four *As*, as it is referred to conversationally, has the mission of improving the advertising agency business in the United States by fostering professional development, encouraging high creative and business standards, and attracting first-rate employees to the advertising business.

Association of Coupon Professionals (ACP, www.couponpros.org)—This coupon redemption trade association strives to ensure coupons as a viable promotional tool and to improve coupon industry business conditions.

Association of National Advertisers (ANA, www.ana.net)—Whereas the AAAA serves primarily the interests of advertising agencies, ANA represents the interests of business organizations that advertise regionally and nationally. ANA's members collectively represent over 80 percent of all advertising expenditures in the United States.

Direct Marketing Association (DMA, www.the-dma.org)—DMA is dedicated to encouraging and advancing the effective and ethical use of direct marketing. The association represents the interests of direct marketers to the government, media, and general public.

Incentive Manufacturers and Representatives Alliance (IMRA, www.imraorg.net)—Members of IMRA are suppliers of premium merchandise. This association serves these members by promoting high professional standards in the pursuit of excellence in the incentive industry.

International Social Marketing Association (iSMA, www.isocialmarketing.org)—The iSMA's mission is to support the advancement of social marketing practice, research, and teaching, as one of the world's leading sources of authoritative information on social marketing. They are committed to improving people's lives through the transformative power of marketing.

Internet Advertising Bureau (IAB, www.iab.net)—IAB's mission is to help online, interactive broadcasting, e-mail, wireless, and interactive television media companies increase their revenues.

Mobile Marketing Association (MMA, www.mmaglobal.com)—The Mobile Marketing Association (MMA) is a global association dedicated to stimulating the growth of mobile marketing and its associated technologies.

Point-of-Purchase Advertising International (POPAI, http://popai.com)—This trade association serves the interests of advertisers, retailers, and producers/suppliers of point-of-purchase products and services.

Promotional Products Association International (PPAI, www.ppai.org)—PPAI serves the interests of producers, suppliers, and users of promotional products. The businesses PPAI represents used to be referred to as the specialty advertising industry, but promotional products is the term of current preference.

Promotion Marketing Association (PMA, www.pmalink.org)—PMA's mission is to foster the advancement of promotion marketing and facilitate better understanding of promotion's role and importance in the overall marketing process.

Discussion Questions

1. Explain how your college or university uses marketing communications to recruit students.
2. The combined use of different marcom tools—such as advertising a brand on TV along with sponsoring an event—can produce a synergistic effect for a brand. What does the concept of synergy mean in this context? Provide a practical illustration of how two or more marcom tools when used in combination are capable of producing results greater than the sum of their individual contributions.
3. Explain what it means to say that the consumers are in control of marketing communications. Provide an example from your own experience that supports the contention that marcom is becoming increasingly consumer-centric.
4. What steps can marketing communicators take to allow consumers to exercise their control of when, where, and how they receive brand messages? Provide specific examples to support your answer.

5. Based on your experiences and those of close friends with whom you discuss such matters, what might be the future role of social networking outlets (e.g., Twitter, MySpace, Facebook, foursquare, and You-Tube) in disseminating brand information? On the basis of your experience, is most brand-related information that appears on these sites positive or negative?

6. Explain the meaning of *360-degree branding*. What are the advantages and potential disadvantages of such a practice?

7. The following quote from an advertising executive appeared in the chapter in the section under IMC key feature #2: "At the end of the day, [marcom agencies] don't deliver ads, or direct mail pieces, or PR and corporate identity programs. We deliver results." Explain what you think this executive meant in making this statement.

8. One key feature of IMC is the emphasis on affecting behavior and not just its antecedents (such as brand awareness or favorable attitudes). For each of the following situations, indicate the specific behavior(s) that marketing communications might attempt to affect: (a) your university's advertising efforts, (b) a professional baseball team's promotion for a particular game, (c) a government agency's efforts to improve food safety, and (d) Gatorade's sponsorship of a volleyball tournament.

9. Assume you are in charge of advertising a product that is marketed specifically to college students. Identify seven contact methods (include no more than two forms of mass media advertising) you might use to reach this audience.

10. Objectives and budgets are necessarily interdependent. Explain this interdependency and construct an illustration to support your point.

11. Brand positioning and targeting also are necessarily interdependent. Explain this interdependency and provide an example to support your point.

12. What is the distinction between top-down (TD) and bottom-up (BU) budgeting? Why is BUTD used in companies that are more marketing oriented, whereas TDBU is found more frequently in finance-driven companies?

13. Why do you think that the trend in marcom budgeting is toward increased expenditures on promotions and reduced advertising spending?

14. Explain the concept of *momentum* and offer an account as to why momentum is important for a specific brand of your choosing.

15. Assume you are in charge of fundraising for an organization on your campus—a student club, a social fraternity or sorority, a business fraternity, a non-profit group, or any other such organization. It is your job to identify a suitable project and to manage the project's marketing communications. For the purpose of this exercise, identify a fundraising project idea and apply the subset of the model involving fundamental decisions. In other words, explain how you would position your fundraising project, whom you would target, what objective(s) you would set, and how much (ballpark figure) you would budget for marcom efforts.

End Notes

1. This description is adapted from Ron Callari, "Pepsi Loot & Shopkick, Social Media's First Location-based Loyalty Programs," *Investorspot.com*, March 9, 2010, http://inventorspot.com/articles/pepsi_loot_shopkick_social_medias_first_locationbased_loyalty_pr_41165; Clifford, Stephanie, "Linking Customer Loyalty With Social Networking," *New York Times* (online), April 28, 2010, http://www.nytimes.com/2010/04/29/business/media/29adco.html; and Dan Butcher, "Pepsi-Co Exec Reveals Top Mobile, Social Trends for 2011," *Mobile Marketer*, December 22, 2010, http://www.mobilemarketer.com/cms/sectors/food-beverage/8564.html.

2. Kate Maddox, "Special Report: Integrated Marketing Success Stories," BtoBonline.com, June 7, 2004, http://www.btobonline.com.

3. Robert Denniston, "Planning, Implementing, and Managing an Unprecedented Government-Funded Prevention Communications Initiative," *Social Marketing Quarterly*, 10 (2), Summer 2004, 7–12; Robert C. Hornik, "Evaluation Design for Public Health Communications Programs," in *Public Health Communication: Evidence for Behavior Change*, R.C. Hornik, ed, Mahwah, NJ. Lawrence Erlbaum, 2002, 385–405, Cornelia Pechmann and Craig Andrews, "Copy Test Methods to Pretest Advertisements," in *Wiley International Encyclopedia of Marketing*, v. 4, Jagdish Sheth and Naresh K. Maholtra, Editors-in-Chief, West Sussex, UK: John Wiley & Sons, Ltd., 2011, 54–62; Christopher S. Carpenter and Cornelia Pechmann, "Exposure to the Above the Influence Antidrug Advertisements and Adolescent Marijuana Use in the United States, 2006–2008," *American Journal of Public Health*, 101 (5), May 2011, 948–54; and Michael D. Slater, Kathleen J. Kelly, Frank R. Lawrence, Linda R. Stanley, and Maria Leonora G. Comello, "Assessing Media Campaigns Linking Marijuana Non-Use with Autonomy and Aspirations: "Be Under Your Own Influence" and ONDCP's "Above the Influence," *Prevention Science*, v. 12 (online), 2011, 12–22.

4. For an excellent historical review of more than 60 different definitions of marketing since 1920, see Debra Jones Ringold and Barton Weitz, "The American Marketing Association Definition of Marketing: Moving from Lagging to Leading Indicator,"

Journal of Public Policy & Marketing, 26 (2) (fall 2007), 251–60.

5. Philip Kotler, *Principles of Marketing*, Englewood Cliffs, NJ: Prentice-Hall, 1980, 10.

6. Adapted from E. Jerome McCarty and Willam D. Perreault, Jr., *Basic Marketing*, Homewood, IL: Irwin, 1987, 368.

7. Jack Neff, "Amid Cutbacks, ShamWow Marches On," *Advertising Age*, March 23, 2009, 1, 14.

8. Based on the Merriam-Webster Online Dictionary, http://www.merriam-webster.com/dictionary/social+ media, and Wikipedia, http://en.wikipedia.org/wiki/ Social_media (both accessed May 28, 2011).

9. Jonah Bloom, "Dedicated Social-Media Silos? That's the Last Thing We Need," *Advertising Age*, June 8, 2009, 11.

10. Bob Hartley and Dave Pickton, "Integrated Marketing Communications Requires a New Way of Thinking," *Journal of Marketing Communications* 5 (June 1999), 97–106; and Philip J. Kitchen, Joanne Brignell, Tao Li, and Graham Spickett Jones, "The Emergence of IMC: A Theoretical Perspective," *Journal of Advertising Research* 44 (March 2004), 19–30.

11. These findings are based on research by George S. Low, "Correlates of Integrated Marketing Communications," *Journal of Advertising Research* 40 (May/June 2000), 27–39.

12. Prasad A. Naik and Kalyan Raman, "Understanding the Impact of Synergy in Multimedia Communications," *Journal of Marketing Research* 40 (November 2003), 375–88.

13. Yuhmiin Chang and Esther Thorson, "Television and Web Advertising Synergies," *Journal of Advertising* 33 (Summer 2004), 75–84.

14. Philip J. Kitchen and Inga Burgmann, "Integrated Marketing Communication," in *Wiley International Encyclopedia of Marketing*, v. 4, Jagdish Sheth and Naresh K. Maholtra, Editors-in-Chief, West Sussex, UK: John Wiley & Sons, Ltd., 2011, 105–27.

15. Adapted from the 3rd edition (1993) and Adrienne Ward Fawcett, "Integrated Marketing—Marketers Convinced: Its Time Has Arrived," *Advertising Age*, November 6, 1993, S1–S2.

16. Suzanne Vranica, "On Madison Avenue, a Digital Wake-up Call," *Wall Street Journal Online*, March 26, 2007, http://online.wsj.com.

17. Brian Steinberg, "Ogilvy's New Digital Chief Discusses Challenges," *Wall Street Journal Online*, April 4, 2007, http://online.wsj.com.

18. Weber Shandwick, 919 Third Avenue, New York, NY, 10022.

19. Lisa Sanders, "'Demand Chain' Rules at McCann," *Advertising Age*, June 14, 2004, 6.

20. Jonah Bloom, "Want to Restore Marketers' Faith? Embrace Agnosticism," *Advertising Age*, September 24, 2007, 16.

21. David Sable, "We're Surrounded," *Agency* (spring 2000), 50–51.

22. Amy Johannes, "A Cool Moves Front," *Promo*, August 2006, 21.

23. Mare Graser, "Toyota Hits Touch Points as It Hawks Yaris to Youth," *Advertising Age*, May 1, 2006, 28.

24. Peter A. Georgescu, "Looking at the Future of Marketing," *Advertising Age*, April 14, 1997, 30.

25. Judann Pollack, "Nabisco's Marketing VP Expects 'Great Things,'" *Advertising Age*, December 2, 1996, 40.

26. Stephanie Thompson, "Busy Lifestyles Force Change," *Advertising Age*, October 9, 2000, s8.

27. This quote is from author Vicki Lenz as cited in Matthew Grimm, "Getting to Know You," *Brandweek*, January 4, 1999, 18.

28. The importance of creating committed customers is verified empirically in Peter C. Verhoef, "Understanding the Effect of Customer Relationship Management Efforts on Customer Retention and Customer Share Development," *Journal of Marketing* 27 (October 2003), 30–45.

29. Amy Johannes, "Coffee Perks," *Promo*, September 2006, 41.

30. Samar Farah, "Loyalty Delivers," *Deliver*, September 2006, 10–15.

31. Amy Johannes, "Top of Wallet," *Promo*, July 2007, 20–22.

32. Dan Hanover, "Are You Experienced?" *Promo*, February 2001, 48.

33. Cornelia Pechmann, Guangzhi Zhao, Marvin E. Goldberg, and Ellen Thomas Reibling, "What to Convey in Antismoking Advertisements for Adolescents: The Use of Protection Motivation Theory to Identify Effective Message Themes," *Journal of Marketing* 67 (April 2003), 1–18.

34. A survey of over 200 marketing professionals found that both brand marketers and agencies consider consistency of execution the major challenge to integrating marcom strategies. See Claire Atkinson, "Integration Still a Pipe Dream for Many," *Advertising Age*, March 10, 2003, 1, 47.

35. Don E. Schultz, "Relax Old Marcom Notions, Consider Audiences," *Marketing News*, October 27, 2003, 8.

36. Nigel F. Piercy, "The Marketing Budgeting Process: Marketing Management Implications," *Journal of Marketing* 51 (October 1987), 45–59.

37. Carol Krol, "DMA: Direct Response Gets Largest Share of B-to-B Marketing," *BtoB*, May 7, 2007, 3.

38. Thomas A. Petit and Martha R. McEnally, "Putting Strategy into Promotion Mix Decisions," *The Journal of Consumer Marketing* 2 (winter 1985), 41–47.

39. Quoted in Sally Goll Beatty, "Auto Makers Bet Campaigns Will Deliver Even If They Can't," *Wall Street Journal Online*, October 13, 1997, http:// online.wsj.com.

40. Tim Ambler, *Marketing and the Bottom Line: The New Metrics of Corporate Wealth* (London: Pearson Education Limited, 2000), especially Appendix A.

CHAPTER 2

Enhancing Brand Equity and Accountability

Are There Too Many Social Media Brands?

For many online "market mavens," it is really difficult to stay on top of all the new social media options, run the latest apps, and have all the "need to know" content and information on a 24/7 basis. Beyond the obvious (Facebook, YouTube, Twitter, Google$^+$, etc.), there are so many competing niche brands out there to consider! As to the social media content, just a few hours off (for some that could be not checking overnight), might mean missing that important blog, Facebook post, or breaking news Tweet.

Yet, trying to keep up with the latest social media brands and content, such as work connections (LinkedIn), location-based check-ins (foursquare, Facebook Places, and Facebook Nearby Friends),

© iStockphoto.com/Ismail Akin Bostanci

lifefstyle blogging (Word Press), etc., can easily create overflowing inboxes and information overload, even for the most tech-savvy consumer. Currently, many social media brands are vying to be the "owners" of different social media spaces. For example, recent social graph application programming interfaces (APIs) allow software programs to connect documents and people together across many different social media networks. So, if Joe or Sally starts a Twitter account with no followers or friends, social graph APIs can search their other public social networks (Facebook, LinkedIn, etc.) to help establish new connections. Yet, Google's Friend Connect, Facebook's Connect service, and MySpace's Data Availability all started social graph APIs within

1. Explain the concept of *brand equity* from both the company's and the customer's perspectives.

2. What are some of the positive outcomes that result from enhancing brand equity?

3. Describe the different models of brand equity from the customer's perspective.

4. Understand how marcom efforts must influence behavior and achieve financial accountability.

days of each other, providing a crowded brand space for this service.

As another example of social media brand crowding, lifestreaming is an e-collection (i.e., diary) of your electronic life. The tail of your steam contains documents from birth all the way to the most recent version. With the right filters, it can serve a purpose for sharing information with others. Lifestream brand battles are now taking place among MyBlog Log, FriendFeed, Lifestream. fm, Facebook, WordPress, Posterous, Tumblr, etc. The mobile social network brand space is even more crowded, with the following brands battling it out: BrightKite, MocoSpace, Friendstribe, Hobnoster, Dodgeball, Zyb, mig33, Mobiluck, MeetMoi, JuiceCaster, Loopnote, Rabble, Wadja, Treemo, groovr, flagr, LimeJuice, Loopt, and Next2Friends, among others. Other social media services, such as Twitter feed organizers, filtering RSS (real simple syndication) feeds, social news, and social media monitoring tools all are experiencing brand crowding. Although there are tools (e.g., Gizapage, Power.com) to help aggregate all of your social media feeds into one site, you are still left with all of that information.

The harsh reality is that many studies, across a broad range of product categories (e.g., gourmet jams, chocolates, retirement funds, and toothpaste), have shown that although consumers show an interest in larger brand assortments, they are 10 times as likely to make a purchase, say, among 6 brands than from 24 to 30. In this chapter, brand building is shown to be a challenging and never-ending process, with efforts directed at enhancing brand equity (e.g., via brand differentiation, relevance, esteem, and knowledge), and hopefully, leading to long-term brand loyalty. Those few social media brands that are adept (and fortunate) at enhancing brand equity and loyalty are likely to survive this "wild west" of social media brand battles.

Sources: Bamieh, M. "Too Many Social Networks … Too Little Time," *Thoughtpick Blog*, February 4, 2010, http://blog.thoughtpick. com/2010/02/too-many-social-networks-too-little-time.html; DeAngelis, Tori, "Too Many Choices?" *Monitor on Psychology*, June 2004, 35 (6), 56, http://www.apa.org/monitor/jun04/toomany.aspx; Hartzer, Bill, "Best Social Media Monitoring Tools," BillHartzer.com, March 26, 2010, http://www.billhartzer.com/pages/11-best-social-media-monitoring-tools; Iyengar, Sheena S. and Mark R. Leeper, "When Choice is Demotivating: Can One Desire Too Much of a Good Thing?" *Journal of Personality and Social Psychology*, 79 (6), 995–1006; Perez, Sarah, "Too Many Choices, Too Much Content," *ReadWriteWeb*, May 14, 2008, http://www.readwriteweb.com/archives/too_many_choices_ too_much_content.php; and Varanica, Suzanne, "Social Media Draws A Crowd," *Wall Street Journal*, July 19, 2010, B7.

Introduction

The previous chapter introduced the philosophy and practice of integrated marketing communications (IMC) and then presented a framework for thinking about all aspects of the marcom process. You will recall that this framework included four components: (1) a set of fundamental decisions (targeting, positioning, etc.), (2) a group of implementation decisions (mixing elements, creating messages, etc.), (3) two types of outcomes resulting from these decisions (enhancing brand equity and affecting behavior), and (4) a regimen for evaluating marcom results and taking corrective action. This chapter focuses on the third component in this framework, namely, the desired outcomes of marcom efforts for brands.

The basic issues addressed are these: What can marketing communicators do to enhance brand equity and, beyond this, affect the behavior of their present and prospective customers? Also, how can marketing communicators justify their investments in advertising, sales promotions, social media, and other marcom elements and demonstrate financial accountability? The chapter first discusses the concept of brand equity and explores this topic from both company and customer perspectives. A following section then addresses the importance of affecting behavior, including a discussion of accountability.

Brand Equity

Before we discuss the important concept of brand equity, we should be clear about the meaning of the term *brand*. The American Marketing Association defines a brand as a "name, term, sign, symbol, design, or a combination of them intended to identify the goods or services of one seller or group of sellers and to differentiate them from those of competition."[1] Thus, *identification* and *differentiation* are important aspects of a brand. Also, a brand includes what is known as trade dress, which refers to the appearance and image of the product, including its packaging, labeling, shape, color, sounds, design, lettering, and style. Examples of trade dress include the MGM Lion's roar, Kodak's gold-colored film box, the distinctive red and white lettering on Coca-Cola packages, the blue Twitter bird symbol, or red TV tube with the YouTube brand name. As with instances of the duplication of a regular brand trademark, copying a company's trade dress is actionable under the 1946 Lanham Act.[2]

© Susan Van Etten

Yet, a brand is more than *just* a name, term, symbol, and so on. A brand is everything that one company's particular offering stands for in comparison to other brands in a product category. A brand represents a set of values that its marketers, senior company officials, and other employees consistently embrace and communicate for an extended period.[3] That is, in consumers' minds, what does your brand stand for? For example, over time, Volvo has become virtually synonymous with safety; Crayola crayons stand for fun; Absolut vodka encapsulates hipness; Harley-Davidson embodies freedom and rugged individualism (see *IMC Focus*); Sony represents high quality and dependability; Chanel No. 5 means eloquence; Toyota's Prius personifies environmental consciousness; and Rolex watches represent master craftsmanship and sophistication. Each of these brands has embraced and communicated a particular set of values. All of these brands possess high equity because consumers believe these brands have the ability and willingness to deliver on their brand promises.[4]

IMC FOCUS

Harley-Davidson—An Iron Horse for Rugged Individualists, Including American Women

Brand managers at Harley-Davidson Motor Co. ran a magazine ad several years ago that captured the essence of this company's famous motorcycles. The ad depicted a driverless Harley-Davidson motorcycle on an open road in the American West in a fashion reminiscent of a wild mustang in a similar scène. The ad's headline declared, "Even Cows Kick Down the Fence Once in a While," and was supported with copy stating:

It's right there in front of you, Road, wind, country. A Harley-Davidson motorcycle. In other words, freedom. A chance to live on your own terms for a while ... Anyone who's been there knows: Life is better on the outside.

This advertising message was subtle but clear: if you cherish freedom, independence, and perhaps a sense of being a kindred spirit with others of like mind, then Harley-Davidson is the motorcycle for you. The cowboy spirit was encapsulated in this positioning, which tacitly equated Harley motorcycles with horses. (Harley-Davidson equals "iron horse.") Potential purchasers of Harley motorcycles probably as youngsters envisioned themselves riding horses in America's Old West.

What makes Harley-Davidson motorcycles such a unique and strong brand, indeed a brand of virtual iconic status? Informed observers and students of brand marketing would suggest that Harley, more so than most brands, has a deep emotional connection with present and prospective owners. As captured in the previous description of a Harley advertisement, the brand has been marketed as and has virtually become synonymous with American culture and values of personal freedom, rebelliousness, and

rugged individualism. Harley also has created a sense of brand community among owners of its brand, who share strong comradeship. In fact, when Harley celebrated its 100th anniversary, over 250,000 riders from around the world came to Milwaukee to participate in the big party. Needless to say, few brands anywhere in the world have such loyal and devoted followers.

An especially interesting aspect of Harley's consumer community is that it has become increasingly female—American women are a fast-growing segment of the motorcycle business, with annual purchases exceeding 100,000 cycles! Nearly one in eight sales of Harley motorcycles is to women, which is attributable in large part to Harley's concerted effort to appeal to the female segment. For example, its dealers hold "garage parties," organized gatherings at which dealer representatives inform women about Harley-Davidson motorcycles, appeal to their dreams of owning a motorcycle, and attempt to reduce their fears.

Sources: For a fascinating ethnographic analysis of Harley-Davidson owners and more detail on the Harley-as-horse metaphor, see John W. Schouten and James H. McAlexander, "Subcultures of Consumption: An Ethnography of the New Bikers," *Journal of Consumer Research* 22 (June 1995), 43–61; Some of the following comments are adapted from James D. Speros, chief marketing officer at Ernst & Young and chair of the Association of National Advertisers, in "Why the Harley Brand's So Hot," *Advertising Age*, March 15, 2004, 26; For an interesting treatment of rugged individualism in a marketing/advertising context, see Elizabeth C. Hirschman, "Men, Dogs, Guns, and Cars," *Journal of Advertising* 32 (spring 2003), 9–22; For further reading on brand communities, see Albert M. Muniz Jr. and Thomas C. O'Guinn, "Brand Community," *Journal of Consumer Research* 27 (March 2000), 412–32; and Clifford Krauss, "Harley Woos Female Bikers," *New York Times Online*, July 25, 2007, http://www.nytimes.com.

© Jim Barber/Shutterstock.com

So, what exactly is brand equity? For the purpose of our discussion, we define brand equity as the goodwill (i.e., equity) that an established brand has built up over its existence. As such, the concept of *brand equity* can be considered both from the perspective of the organization that owns a brand and from the vantage point of the customer.

A Firm-Based Perspective on Brand Equity

The firm-based viewpoint of brand equity focuses on outcomes extending from efforts to enhance a brand's *value* to its various stakeholders (e.g., final consumers, retailers, wholesalers, suppliers, and employees). As the value, or equity, of a brand increases, various positive outcomes result. These include (1) achieving a higher market share, (2) increasing brand loyalty, (3) being able to charge premium prices, and (4) earning a revenue premium.[5] Being able to charge premium prices means that a brand's elasticity of demand becomes less elastic as its equity increases; that is, brands with more equity can charge higher prices than brands with less equity. Consider household brands of paint, such as the Sears brand versus the Martha Stewart or Ralph Lauren brands. The quality differential between the Sears brand and the designer brands likely is considerably less than is the premium-price differential that the designer brands command due to their brand equity.

A revenue premium is defined as the revenue differential between a branded item and a corresponding private-labeled (store brand) item. With revenue equaling the product of a brand's net price × volume, a branded good enjoys a revenue premium over a corresponding private-label item to the degree it can charge a higher price and/or generate greater sales volume. In equation form, the revenue premium for brand b compared to a corresponding private-label item, pi, is as follows:

$$\text{Revenue premium}_b = (\text{volume}_b)(\text{price}_b) - (\text{volume}_{pl})(\text{price}_{pl}) \qquad (2.1)$$

It has been demonstrated that grocery brands possessing higher equity generate higher revenue premiums. In turn, there is a strong positive correlation between the revenue premiums brands enjoy and the market shares they realize.[6] The ability to charge higher prices and generate greater sales volume is due in large part to marcom efforts that build favorable images for well-known brands and, in turn, less perceived risk and greater shopper efficiency.

Finally, another form of firm-based brand equity is somewhat akin to the notion of revenue premium just described. We might label this unique form "taste-premium" brand equity. The fast-food chain McDonald's was the focus of a study involving the taste perceptions of a sample of 3- to 5-year-old preschool children from low-income backgrounds.[7] The study design had the children taste two versions each of five products (hamburger, chicken nuggets, french fries, milk/apple juice, and carrots). In one version, each product was presented to the preschool children in a package with McDonald's packaging graphics. In the second version, the same products were presented in plain-white packages absent McDonald's identification. (Note that this plain-white version might be roughly equated with the private-label brands in the case of the revenue premium form of brand equity.) With the exception of carrots, which are not sold at McDonald's restaurants, all other items were actual McDonald's products, regardless of whether they were presented to the children in McDonald's packages or in the plain-white packages. After tasting both versions of each product, the preschoolers were instructed to indicate whether they (1) liked the taste of the McDonald's version, (2) liked the taste of the plain-white version, or (3) whether they tasted the same. It is important to note that research assistants didn't actually ask children whether they preferred the McDonald's version or the plain-white version, but rather simply had them identify which item tasted the best, the food/drink located on the left or right side of the tray on which the two versions were placed.

Table 2.1 presents study results in terms of three percentages for each of the five products: (1) the percentage of children who considered the food/drink item with the McDonald's packaging to taste the best, (2) the percentage who thought the two versions tasted the same or gave no answer when asked "Tell me if they taste the same, or point to the food (drink) that tastes the best to you," and (3) the percentage who considered the food/drink item in the plain-white packaging to taste the best.

The percentages in Table 2.1 make it clear that the participating preschoolers preferred the taste of all five food and drink items when they had McDonald's packaging over the identical food/drink items with plain-white packaging.

TABLE 2.1	Children's Taste Preferences (in percents)			
Food or Drink Item	Preferred Taste of McDonald's Version	Thought the Two Versions Tasted the Same or Gave No Answer	Preferred Taste of Plain-White Version	P-value*
Hamburger	48.3	15.0	36.7	0.33
Chicken nugget	59.0	23.0	18.0	<0.001
French fries	76.7	10.0	13.3	<0.001
Milk or apple juice	61.3	17.7	21.0	<0.001
Carrot	54.1	23.0	23.0	0.006

*The probability level based on a test of significant difference among the percentages. P-values of 0.05 or less are conventionally considered statistically significant.

The percentage of children preferring McDonald's french fries was a whopping 76.7 percent. Even for carrots, *which is not a McDonald's menu item*, 54.1 percent considered the sampled carrot better tasting when it was served in a McDonald's package versus the 23.0 percent who preferred the carrot when served in a plain-white package.

These results convincingly indicate brand equity in action. Simply placing products in well-identified McDonald's packaging led children to regard these items to be superior tasting in comparison to identical items in plain-white packages. These preferences were especially strong among those children who lived in homes with more television sets and who more frequently ate food from McDonald's. As will be indicated in the following section on consumer-based brand equity, these results demonstrate the role that the speak-for-itself and message-driven approaches play in enhancing a brand's equity.

Brand Equity Models

Although there is considerable agreement on basic brand principles, several models of brand equity present slightly different perspectives on the concept. These include the Brand Asset Valuator,[8] Dimensions of Brand Knowledge,[9] the Brand Awareness Pyramid,[10] the Customer-Based Brand Equity Model,[11] and the Brand Dynamics Pyramid.[12] This chapter focuses on the first three of these brand equity models.

Brand Asset Valuator

The Chicago-based advertising agency, Young & Rubicam (Y&R), developed a model of brand equity entitled the BrandAsset® Valuator (BAV). The BAV is based on research with over 700,000 consumers in 50 countries, for over 45,000 brands, and provides a comparative measure of brand equity elements across many different categories. The BAV is composed of the following four key components or pillars of brand equity:

- *Differentiation* (or sometimes referred to as energized differentiation): the degree to which the brand is seen as unique or different from others.
- *Relevance*: the degree to which the consumer identifies with the brand or is involved in the brand in their everyday lives (e.g., "What's in it for me?").
- *Esteem*: the degree to which the brand is held in high regard and well respected.
- *Knowledge*: the degree to which consumers are familiar with and aware of the brand.

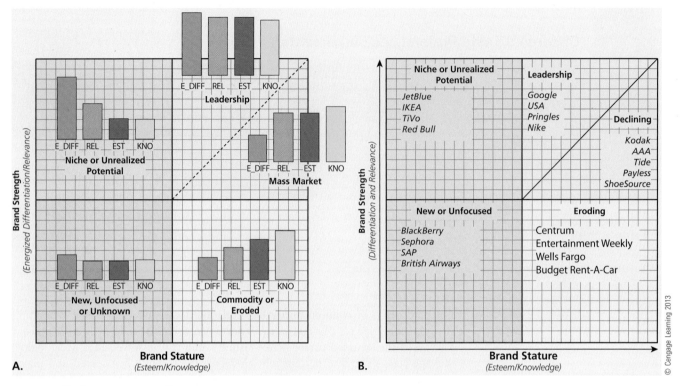

FIGURE **2.1** BrandAsset® Valuator's Power Grid

The relationships among these brand components or pillars can provide insight into the brand's current and future status. For example, as depicted in Figure 2.1, the BAV's Power Grid is based on the brand's strength (differentiation, relevance) and the brand's stature (esteem, knowledge), depicting successive stages of brand development from differentiation to relevance to esteem to knowledge. Figure 2.1 suggests that brands can cycle through stages of being new to a niche player to leadership and to eventual erosion. The second panel shows a representative placement of brands on the Power Grid.

Dimensions of Brand Knowledge

From the perspective of the customer, a brand can be said to possess equity to the extent that people are familiar with the brand and have stored in memory favorable, strong, and unique brand associations.[13] Such associations are the particular thoughts and feelings that consumers have linked in memory with a particular brand. For example, what thoughts/feelings come immediately to mind when you think of McDonald's, Facebook, or Apple? Thus, as suggested by Keller's "Dimensions of Brand Knowledge," another way of thinking about brand equity is that it consists of two forms of brand-related knowledge: *brand awareness* and *brand image*, as shown in Figure 2.2.

Brand awareness is an issue of whether a brand name comes to mind when consumers think about a particular product category and the ease with which the name is evoked. For example, regarding toothpaste brands in the United States, Crest and Colgate probably came to mind immediately, because these brands are the market share leaders. Yet, perhaps you also thought of Aquafresh, Mentadent, and Arm & Hammer insofar as these brands also obtain a large share of toothpaste purchases. But did you consider Close-Up, Pepsodent, or Aim? Maybe so, yet probably not, due to low awareness levels. As with the

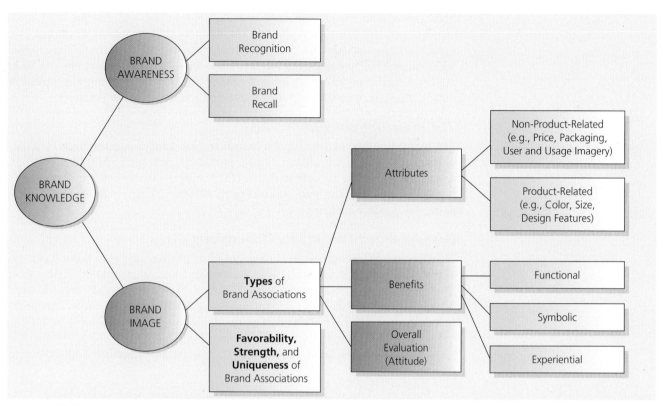

FIGURE **2.2** A Customer-Based Brand Equity Framework

Source: Adapted from Kevin Lane Keller, "Conceptualizing, Measuring, and Managing Customer-Based Brand Equity," *Journal of Marketing* 57 (January 1993), 7.

BAV's measure of knowledge, brand awareness and brand image (as depicted in Figure 2.2) can be important dimensions of brand equity.

Figure 2.2 shows two levels of awareness: brand recognition and recall. *Brand recognition* reflects a relatively superficial level of awareness, whereas *brand recall* indicates a deeper form. Consumers may be able to identify a brand if it is presented to them on a list or if hints/cues are provided. However, fewer consumers are able to retrieve a brand name from memory without any reminders.

The second dimension of consumer-based brand knowledge is a brand's image. Brand image represents the associations that are activated in memory when people think about a particular brand. As shown in Figure 2.2, these associations can be conceptualized in terms of *type, favorability, strength*, and *uniqueness*. For example, the *types* of associations in one consumer's memory about McDonald's might include childhood recollections of trips to McDonald's, the positive smell of cheeseburgers and fries, memories of Ronald McDonald in advertising, yet occasional retail service issues. All of these associations, with the exception of occasional service problems, represent *favorable* links with McDonald's as far as a consumer is concerned. These associations might be held *strongly* in the consumer's memory and some of the associations might be *unique* in comparison to other fast-food chains. For example, only McDonald's has golden arches and Ronald McDonald. No other fast-food chain has, in this consumer's mind, cheeseburgers and fries that taste nearly as good as McDonald's.

From this illustration and in the context of the specific elements portrayed in Figure 2.2, we can see that this consumer associates

McDonald's with various *attributes* (e.g., golden arches) and *benefits* (e.g., great tasting fries), and that they possess an overall favorable evaluation, or *attitude*, toward this brand. These associations are held strongly and are favorable and somewhat unique. McDonald's would love to have millions of consumers like this in its market, which it undoubtedly does. To the extent that this consumer is typical of other consumers, it can be said that McDonald's has high brand equity.

The Brand-Awareness Pyramid

The marcom imperative is to move brands from a state of unawareness, to recognition, on to recall, and ultimately to top-of-mind awareness (TOMA). This pinnacle of brand-name awareness (i.e., TOMA status) exists when your company's brand is the first brand that consumers recall when thinking about brands in a particular product category.

Brand-Related Personality Dimensions

Brands—just like people—can be thought of as having their own unique personalities. Research has identified five personality dimensions that describe most brands: sincerity, excitement, competence, sophistication, and ruggedness.[14] That is, brands can be described as possessing some degree of each of these dimensions, ranging from "the dimension doesn't describe the brand at all" to "the dimension captures the brand's essence."

The five brand-related personality dimensions are described and illustrated as follows.

1. *Sincerity*—This dimension includes brands that are perceived as being down-to-earth, honest, wholesome, and cheerful. Sincerity is precisely the personality that Disney has imbued in its brand.
2. *Excitement*—Brands scoring high on the excitement dimension are perceived as daring, spirited, imaginative, and up to date. The Apple iPhone perhaps epitomized this personality dimension when it originally was introduced in 2007 amid much fanfare and even consumer frenzy, as purchasers sought to be among the first to own this unique cell phone. This is still true for the Apple iPhone 4S in 2011 and its popular app, "Siri," the personal office assistant.

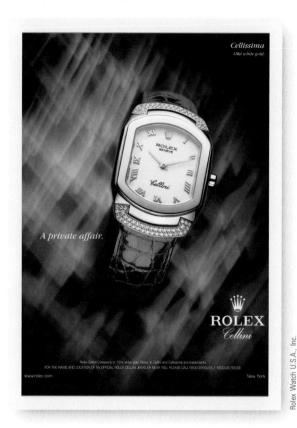

Cellissima
18kt white gold.

A private affair.

ROLEX
Cellini

www.rolex.com   New York

Rolex Watch U.S.A., Inc.

3. *Competence*—Brands scoring high on this personality dimension are considered reliable, intelligent, and successful. In the automobile category, with the exception of an accelerator recall in 2009, Toyota has done well on this dimension over the years. Toyotas are not particularly exciting or rugged, and have had some recent recalls on sticking accelerators, but consumers generally regard them as reliable and competent. J.D. Power, an organization that surveys automobile owners to assess levels of satisfaction, annually reports that Toyota is at or near the top of satisfaction ratings. This, of course, is due to the brand's overall success and reliability.

4. *Sophistication*—Brands that are considered upper class and charming score high on the sophistication dimension. Luxury automobiles, jewelry items, expensive perfume, and high-end kitchen appliances are just some of the many product categories that include brands that score high on the sophistication scale. In the jewelry category, for example, Rolex and Cartier are well-known sophisticated brands.

5. *Ruggedness*—Rugged brands are thought of as tough and outdoorsy. L.L. Bean, REI, North Face, and Patagonia typify retailers that offer brands regarded as rugged and outdoorsy. In the automobile category, the Honda Element, with its appeal to young, outdoor-oriented consumers, is another example of a brand that would score high on the ruggedness dimension.

Relationships among Brand Concepts, Brand Equity, and Brand Loyalty

In order to build brand equity, as measured by the BAV's pillars or the dimensions of brand knowledge, brand managers often focus first on the development of the brand concept. The brand concept is the specific meaning that brand managers create and communicate to their target market. (This often follows extensive research on their target market's interests and media habits.)

In turn, brand concept management (e.g., for McDonald's, Facebook, Burton, Netflix, and Harley-Davidson) represents the analysis, planning, implementation, and control of a brand concept throughout the life of the brand. This development can be achieved with appeals to consumers' functional, symbolic, and/or experiential needs.[15] Although we elaborate more on these appeals in Chapter 5's material on positioning, we briefly describe these now as they relate to brand concept building. An appeal to *functional needs* attempts to fulfill the consumer's consumption-related problems. For instance, a Rockport shoe commercial depicted two girls who needed the comfort of Rockport shoes in walking dogs around the hills of San Francisco. Next, an appeal to *symbolic needs* focuses on associating the brand with symbolic objects. For example, the Nike swoosh symbol has long been associated with their athletic shoes and celebrity endorsers. Often, symbolic appeals are directed at consumers' desires for self-enhancement, role position, group membership, and belongingness. Finally, appeals to *experiential needs* focus on messages that provide sensory pleasure, variety, and/or cognitive stimulation. An example of this is a commercial for Pictionary showing a house "exploding" in laughter from people playing this fun board game.

These appeal types all can help to develop a brand's concept, hopefully, leading to enhanced brand equity and long-term brand loyalty. Thus, the

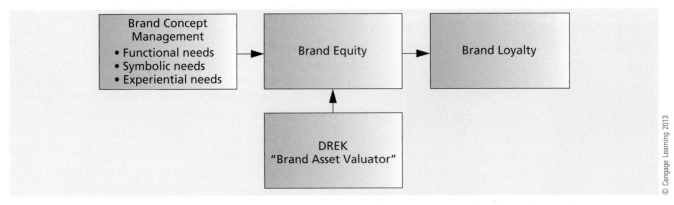

© Cengage Learning 2013

FIGURE **2.3**   Brands and Their Management

ultimate objective is to achieve brand loyalty, a consumer's commitment to continue using or advocating a brand, as demonstrated not only by repeat purchases, but also by other positive brand behaviors (e.g., word-of-mouth advocacy, brand identification).[16] Relationships among appeals used to develop brand concepts, brand equity, and brand loyalty are depicted in Figure 2.3.

A favorable brand image, brand equity, and strong loyalty does not happen automatically. Sustained marketing communications are generally required to create favorable, strong, and perhaps unique associations about the brand. For example, it could be claimed that one of the world's greatest brands, Coca-Cola, is little more than colored sugar water. In the United States alone, the Coca-Cola Company in a recent year commanded 43 percent of the carbonated soft-drink market, which totals over $50 billion in revenue. Coke Classic (Coke) held an individual brand share of nearly 18 percent, whereas its nearest competitor, Pepsi, had about an 11 percent share.[17] It is effective advertising, exciting sales promotions, creative sponsorships, social media, and other forms of marketing communications that are responsible for Coca-Cola's positive image and massive market share. Coca-Cola outperforms Pepsi not because Coke is necessarily a better tasting product, but because it has developed a more positive image with greater numbers of consumers. For a fascinating review of evidence supporting this contention, read the *IMC Focus* insert and its discussion of neuroscience and its application in commerce, known as *neuromarketing*.

Strategies to Enhance Brand Equity

What strategies can be taken to enhance a brand's equity? The following discussion identifies three ways by which brand equity may be enhanced and labels these the (1) speak-for-itself approach, (2) message-driven approach, and (3) leveraging approach.[18]

Enhancing Equity by Having a Brand Speak for Itself

As consumers, we often try brands without having much, if any, advance knowledge about them. Consumers form favorable (or perhaps unfavorable) brand-related associations merely by consuming a brand absent any significant brand knowledge prior to the usage experience. In effect, the brand "speaks for itself" in informing consumers of its quality, desirability, and suitability for satisfying their consumption-related goals.

Enhancing Equity by Creating Appealing Messages

Marcom practitioners can build positive brand-related associations via the power of repeated claims about the features a brand possesses and the benefits it delivers.

IMC FOCUS

Neuromarketing and the Case of Why Coca-Cola Outsells Pepsi

Coca-Cola (Coke) and Pepsi are two well-known carbonated beverages that have been marketed for over 100 years. These brands have been locked in fierce battles for decades, described sometimes as "the cola wars." One sensational battle began in 1975 when Pepsi sponsored a national taste test to determine which brand, Coke or Pepsi, was regarded as better tasting. Following this testing, Pepsi undertook an advertising campaign (called the "Pepsi Challenge") that directly compared Pepsi with Coke and claimed the research evidence (i.e., so-called "blind" taste tests) revealed that consumers prefer Pepsi over Coke. If in fact Pepsi is a better tasting beverage than Coke, why is Coca-Cola the higher selling and more popular beverage? For an answer, let's enter the world of neuromarketing and the technology of brain imaging.

Neuromarketing is a specific application of the field of brain research called *neuroscience*. Neuroscientists study activation of the brain to outside stimuli with the use of brain scanning machines that take functional magnetic resonance images (fMRIs) when individuals visually or otherwise employ their senses upon exposure to stimuli. Brain scans with fMRI machines reveal which areas of the brain are most activated in response to external stimuli. With this brief description in mind, we can describe research conducted by a neuroscientist at the Baylor College of Medicine in Texas, research that might be described as the "21st Century Pepsi Challenge."

The scientist, Read Montague, performed the Pepsi Challenge by scanning the brains of 40 study participants after they tasted intermittent squirts of Pepsi and Coke. When "blind" as to which brand they were tasting, Pepsi came out the clear winner. That is, the reward center of the brain, the ventral putamen, revealed a much stronger preference for Pepsi versus Coke when study participants were unaware of which brand they had tasted. However, this result flip-flopped when Montague altered the testing procedure by telling participants the name of the brand they were about to taste. Now a different region of the brain was more activated and Coca-Cola was the winner in this nonblind taste test. In particular, activation in the medial prefrontal cortex—an area of the brain associated with cognitive functions such as thinking, judging, preference, and self-image—revealed that participants now preferred Coke. In short, with blind taste tests, Pepsi was the winner. With nonblind tests, Coke prevailed. What happened?

The apparent answer is a difference in brand images, with Coke possessing the more attractive image earned through years of effective marketing and advertising effort. Past ad campaigns such as "It's the Real Thing," "I'd Like to Buy the World a Coke," and "Have a Coke and a Smile" have possibly resonated more positively with consumers than has Pepsi's marketing, which has concentrated more on aligning that brand with, as it turned out, ill-advised celebrities such as Michael Jackson and Britney Spears. In sum, this "21st century Pepsi Challenge" further demonstrates the importance of effective marcom efforts and the role that a positive brand image plays in determining brand equity and influencing consumer choices.

Sources: Edwin Colyer, "The Science of Branding," *Brandchannel*, March 15, 2004, http://brandchannel.com (accessed March 22, 2004); Clive Thompson, "There's a Sucker Born in Every Medial Prefrontal Cortex," *The New York Times*, October 26, 2003, http://rickross.com (accessed July 20, 2004); David Wahlberg, "Advertisers Probe Brains, Raise Fears," *The Atlanta Journal-Constitution*, February 1, 2004, http://cognitiveliberty.org (accessed July 20, 2004); Melani Wells, "In Search of the Buy Button," *Forbes.com*, September 1, 2003, http://forbes.com (accessed July 20, 2004); "The Cola Wars: Over a Century of Cola Slogans, Commercials, Blunders, and Coups," http://geocities.com/colacentury (accessed July 21, 2004).

This type of brand-equity-building can be thought of as the "message-driven approach." Such an approach is effective if marcom messages are creative, attention getting, believable, and memorable. Yet, we should note that the speak-for-itself and message-driven approaches are not necessarily independent; that is, consumers' associations about the brand can result from both first-hand experiences and message communications.

Timberland Earthkeepers.
Lightweight. Organic. Recycled.
Worship the ground you walk on.

The new lightweight Timberland® Earthkeepers boot. Made from 100% organic cotton canvas, a water repellent waxed upper and a 30% recycled rubber outsole. Gentle on you, gentle on the earth beneath your feet.

Timberland Make it better.
www.timberlandonline.co.uk

Timberland, ® the tree design and Earthkeepers are trademarks of The Timberland Company ©2008 The Timberland Company. All rights reserved.

FIGURE 2.4 An Appeal to Environmental Awareness

Enhancing Equity via Leveraging

A third equity-building strategy that increasingly is being used is "leveraging." Brand associations can be shaped and equity enhanced by having a brand tie into, or leverage, positive associations that already exist through socialization in culture and society. For example, the Lincoln Memorial and Ellis Island are signs of freedom to Americans. To Germans and many other people throughout the world, the now-crumbled Berlin Wall signified oppression and hopelessness. Comparatively, yellow ribbons signify crises and hopes for hostage release and the safe return of military personnel. Pink ribbons signal support for breast cancer victims. Red ribbons have grown into an international symbol of solidarity on AIDS. The Black Liberation flag with its red, black, and green stripes—representing blood, achievement, and the fertility of Africa—symbolizes civil rights. Recycled material in Timberland Earthkeepers boots represents an appeal to environmental awareness (see Figure 2.4).

Similarly, marketing communicators can *leverage* meaning and create associations for their brands by connecting them with other objects that already possess well-known meaning. Figure 2.5 portrays how brands leverage associations by forming connections with (1) other brands, (2) places, (3) things, and (4) people. There are numerous ways for leveraging favorable brand associations, and Figure 2.5 is a good starting point for appreciating these options.

Leveraging Associations from Other Brands Among other forms of leveraging, Figure 2.5 shows how a brand can leverage associations from *other brands*. In recent years, two brands often enter into an alliance or a co-branding relationship that potentially serves to enhance both brands' equity and profitability. You need only look at your bank card (e.g., Visa) to see that it likely carries the name of an organization such as your college or university. The common theme of many co-branding alliances is that their images are similar, that they appeal to the same market segment, and that the co-branding initiative is mutually beneficial. Thus, the brands should possess a *common fit* and that the combined marcom efforts maximize the advantages of the individual brands while minimizing the disadvantages.[19] This collaboration can happen by studying how consumers *naturally* use a particular brand (e.g., Post Grape Nuts cereal) with another brand (e.g., General Mills Yoplait yogurt).

Ingredient branding is a special type of alliance between branding partners. For example, Lycra, a brand of spandex from DuPont, initiated a multimillion-dollar global advertising effort to increase consumer ownership of jeans made with Lycra. Along the lines of the "Intel Inside" campaign, Lycra's advertising featured Lycra jeans by Levi Strauss, Diesel, DKNY, and other jean manufacturers. DuPont began this campaign in an effort to differentiate itself from cheaper unbranded spandex from Asia.[20] Other well-known instances of ingredient branding include various skiwear brands that prominently identify the Gore-Tex fabric from which they are made and cookware makers that tout

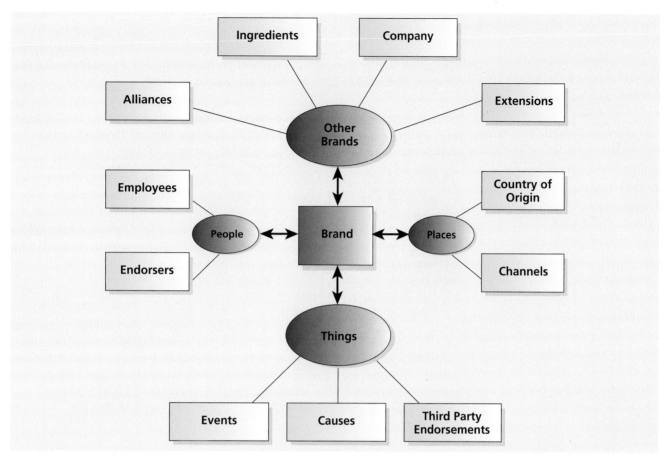

FIGURE 2.5 Leveraging Brand Meaning from Various Sources

Source: Kevin Lane Keller, "Brand Synthesis: The Multidimensionality of Brand Knowledge," *Journal of Consumer Research* 29:4 (March 2003), 598. Reprinted by permission of the University of Chicago Press.

the fact that their skillets and other cookware items are made with DuPont's Teflon nonstick coating. Although ingredient branding is in many instances beneficial for both the ingredient and "host" brands, a potential downside for the host brand is that the equity of the ingredient brand might be so great that it overshadows the host brand. This situation would arise, for example, if skiers knew that their ski jacket was made of Gore-Tex fabric but they had no awareness of the company that actually manufactured the jacket.

Leveraging Associations from People Beyond leveraging a brand's image by associating itself with another brand, Figure 2.5 points out that a brand can leverage its equity by aligning itself with *people*, such as its own employees or endorsers. A later chapter discusses the role of endorsers in detail, so nothing more will be said at this time other than to note that brand associations with endorsers can be fabulously successful (think Michael Jordan and Gatorade) or potentially disastrous (e.g., Tiger Woods and his public acknowledgement of affairs and the brands that quickly dropped their relationships with him—Accenture, AT&T, Gatorade, and Gillette).

Leveraging Associations from Things   Other forms of leveraging include associating a brand with *things* such as events (e.g., sponsorship of the World Cup soccer championship) and causes (e.g., sponsorship of a save-Darfur rally). Again, no further discussion is devoted to these topics at this point given that Chapter 21 describes these forms of association in depth.

Leveraging Associations from Places   Finally, a brand's equity can be leveraged by being associated with *places* such as the channel in which a brand is distributed or a country image (labeled country of origin in Figure 2.5). Imagine, for example, if a brand were carried in a mass merchandise store (e.g., Walmart) compared to being distributed in a high-end department store. If quality and price were held constant, in which store would the brand be regarded more positively?

Leveraging a brand by emphasizing its *country of origin* is a potentially effective way to enhance the brand's equity.[21] For example, brands with German and Swiss heritage often are perceived around the globe as being high in craftsmanship. Japanese electronic products are regarded as unparalleled in innovativeness, quality, and dependability. Also interestingly, older consumers, for example, are generally more concerned with where a brand comes from than are their more youthful counterparts, who are more comfortable living in a global world and buying products based on considerations other than where they are made.[22] In fact, research has shown that American college students are not as knowledgeable as to where the brands they consume originate.[23] For example, just 4.4 percent of 1,000 students knew that Nokia cell phones are made in Finland (53 percent thought Nokia to be Japanese), and just 8.9 percent knew LG cell phones are from Korea. Nearly 50 percent thought that Adidas clothing is from the United States rather than its true home country, Germany. Motorola, a long-established American brand, was misperceived to be Japanese by more than 40 percent of respondents.

When a brand leverages its country of origin, the potential exists for the brand to benefit from this association or possibly to suffer if the country is perceived in a less than positive light. It obviously is in brand marketers' best interest that their countries of origin are perceived favorably. The *Global Focus* insert provides a look at how the world perceives the United States.

What Benefits Result from Enhancing Brand Equity?

As previously noted, one major by-product of efforts to increase a brand's equity is that consumer *brand loyalty* might also increase.[24] Indeed, long-term growth and profitability are largely dependent on creating and reinforcing brand loyalty. The following quote from two respected marketing practitioners sums up the nature and importance of brand loyalty:

> *While marketers have long viewed brands as assets, the real asset is brand loyalty. A brand is not an asset. Brand loyalty is the asset. Without the loyalty of its customers, a brand is merely a trademark, an ownable, identifiable symbol with little value. With the loyalty of its customers, a brand is more than a trademark. A trademark identifies a product, a service, a Corporation. A brand identifies a promise. A strong brand is a trustworthy, relevant, distinctive promise. It is more than a trademark. It is a trustmark of enormous value. Creating and increasing brand loyalty results in a corresponding increase in the value of the trustmark.[26]*

Research has shown that when firms communicate unique and positive messages via advertising, personal selling, promotions, events, and other means,

The World's Perception of America

Strange as it may seem, nations themselves can be thought of as brands, meaning people form mental associations of nations that are equivalent to "brand" images. Firms marketing their products under the banner—the country of origin—of a particular nation are thus affected by how positive or negative that country's image is. Many countries actively market themselves with the goal of forging favorable and strong associations in the minds of people around the world. Regardless of whether a country actively markets itself, however, people nevertheless form associations based on that county's business climate, its international relations, its attractiveness as a tourist location, and so on.

A British market research firm has developed a Nations Brand Index (NBI) as a barometer of global opinion toward a large number of countries around the globe.[25] Each business quarter the NBI researchers poll over 25,000 people around the world on their perceptions of over 35 countries. Survey respondents are asked questions about each country in six areas:

1. *Exports*—their level of satisfaction with products and services produced in that country.
2. *People*—their thoughts and feelings about the people in the country based on questions such as "How much would you like to have a close friend from [name of country]?"
3. *Governance*—their perceptions of whether the country can be trusted to make responsible decisions and to uphold international peace and security.
4. *Tourism*—their perceptions of a country's natural beauty and historical heritage and the likelihood of visiting the country if money were no obstacle.
5. *Culture and Heritage*—their perceptions of a country's cultural heritage and feelings about its contemporary culture, such as its music, art and literature, sporting excellence, and film quality.
6. *Immigration and Investment*—their willingness to live and work in a country for an extended period and their perceptions of whether the country would be a good place to pursue further education.

A nation's "brand" image is the sum of its scores on these six dimensions. The most recent NBI results ranks the top 40 countries.

In this version of the NBI, the United States is ranked seventh among the 40 countries evaluated. Although the United States performs very well in four (exports, cultural heritage, tourism, and investment and immigration) of the six dimensions, it suffers in the two remaining areas (people and governance). Outside the United States, the poor performance on the governance and people dimensions may be due to given the widespread opposition to the wars in Iraq and Afghanistan, the U.S. government's record on treatment of enemy combatants (e.g., Abu Ghraib and Guantanamo Bay), its saber-rattling posture toward Iran and North Korea, and so on.

A country's image, like any brand image, is not immutable but can be changed by the actions of its leaders and its people. As noted previously, it is important as a matter of international relations and economics that a country have a positive image. Each of us has a role to play in this regard by the people we choose to lead us and by the behavior we display when traveling abroad.

they are able to differentiate their brands effectively from competitive offerings and insulate themselves from future price competition.[27]

Marketing communications plays an essential role in creating positive brand equity and building strong brand loyalty. However, this is not always accomplished with traditional advertising or other conventional forms of marketing communications. For example, Starbucks, the virtual icon for upscale coffee, does very little advertising, yet this brand has a near cult-like following. Nevertheless, Starbucks' chairman voiced concern that efforts to grow sales and profits—e.g., introducing breakfast items in some stores and replacing conventional espresso makers with automatic machines—may have damaged Starbucks' reputation for providing a unique consumption experience.[28]

An ex-CEO and chairman of PepsiCo provides us with a fitting section conclusion in the following implicit description of the importance of that company's efforts to build the equity of its brands:

> *In my mind the best thing a person can say about a brand is that it's their favorite. That implies something more than simply they like the package, or the taste. It means they like the whole thing—the company, the image, the value, the quality, and on and on. So as we think about the measurements of our business, if we're only looking at this year's bottom line and profits, we're missing the picture. We should be looking at market share, but also at where we stand vis-a-vis our competitors in terms of consumer awareness and regard for our brands. You always know where you stand in the [profit and loss statement] because you see it every month. But what you need to know, with almost the same sense of immediacy, is where you stand with consumers and your customers.*[29]

Characteristics of World-Class Brands

Some brands have such exceptional brand equity that they deserve the label "world class." The well-known EquiTrend survey by the market research firm Harris Interactive is conducted biannually and includes responses from more than 25,000 consumers who collectively, not individually, rate over 1,000 brands across 39 categories. Each respondent evaluates each of 80 brands in terms of (1) whether he or she is *familiar* with the brand, (2) how good the brand's *quality* is, and (3) whether he or she would *consider purchasing* the brand. These three scores then are combined to form a *brand equity* score for each brand, with a theoretical range from zero to 100.[30]

The EquiTrend survey in Table 2.2 reveals the 10 brands with the overall highest equity. Many of these brands regularly appear in EquiTrend's top-10 rankings. These brands possess high brand equity because they are well known and possess strong and favorable associations in consumers' memories.

Another brand-ranking analysis is undertaken annually by Interbrand, which ranks the 100 top global brands.[31] Its brand-ranking method is based on calculating (1) the percentage of a company's revenue that can be credited to a brand, (2) the strength of a brand in terms of influencing customer demand at the point of purchase, and (3) the ability of the brand to secure continued

| **TABLE 2.2** | **Top Ten World-Class Brands Overall (Among more than 1,000 total brands included in EquiTrend's Spring 2009 survey)** | |

Brand	Rank	Equity Score
M&M's Plain Chocolate Candy	1	79.5
Hershey's Kisses Chocolate Candy	2	79.5
Arm & Hammer Baking Soda	3	78.3
Reese's Peanut Butter Cups Chocolate Candy	4	78.1
Hershey's Milk Chocolate Bars	5	78.1
Kleenex Facial Tissues	6	77.5
Campbell's Soups	7	77.4
Google	8	76.7
M&M's Peanut Chocolate Candy	9	76.6
Crayola Crayons	10	76.6

Source: Spring 2009 EquiTrend brand study by Harris Interactive, http://www.harrisinteractive.com/news/pubs/Harris_Interactive_News_2009_06_08.pdf (accessed June 9, 2011).

TABLE 2.3	Interbrand's Top 20 Global Brands, 2010		
Rank	Brand	Country of Origin	Brand Value ($mil)
1	Coca-Cola	U.S.	70,452
2	IBM	U.S.	64,727
3	Microsoft	U.S.	60,895
4	Google	U.S.	43,557
5	GE	U.S.	42,808
6	McDonald's	U.S.	33,578
7	Intel	U.S.	32,015
8	Nokia	Finland	29,495
9	Disney	U.S.	28,731
10	Hewlett-Packard	U.S.	26,897
11	Toyota	Japan	26,192
12	Mercedes	Germany	25,179
13	Gillette	U.S.	23,298
14	Cisco	U.S.	23,219
15	BMW	Germany	22,322
16	Louis Vuitton	France	21,860
17	Apple	U.S.	21,143
18	Marlboro	U.S.	19,961
19	Samsung	South Korea	19,491
20	Honda	Japan	18,506

Source: Interbrand Report, "Best Global Brands 2010," http://www.interbrand.com/en/knowledge/best-global-brands/best-global-brands-2008/best-global-brands-2010.aspx. Used with permission.

customer demand as a result of brand loyalty and repurchase likelihood. Only those brands that provide public financial data (thus excluding private companies) and that secure at least one-third of their revenues from international operations are potential candidates for inclusion in Interbrand's rankings of "best global brands." This latter factor accounts for why some of the brands included in Table 2.2, which consists entirely of American brands, are not also included in Interbrand's top-20 list. Table 2.3 lists the top 20 "best brands" based on Interbrand's analysis in one recent year.

Affecting Behavior and Achieving Marcom Accountability

In Chapter 1, one major point was that marcom efforts should be directed, ultimately, at affecting behavior rather than merely enhancing equity. Creating brand awareness and boosting brand image may serve little positive effect unless individuals ultimately make purchases or engage in some other form of desired behavior. By "behavior" we mean that the customer takes some *action* such as contributing to a charitable organization, discontinuing smoking, voting for a political candidate, staying on a diet plan, attending a concert, and so on. All of these behaviors, or acts, contrast with pre-behavioral cognitions or emotions whereby one merely thinks that doing something is a good idea or feels good about the prospect of doing something. Ultimately, the proof of the behavioral pudding is in the *action*.

The effect of marcom, or of its specific elements such as advertising, can thus be gauged in terms of whether it generates a reasonable revenue return (i.e., volume × net price) on the marcom investment. This idea of return on investment (ROI) is referred to in marketing circles as return on marketing investment (ROMI). In a world of increased accountability, it is important that marketing people in all capacities, including marcom practitioners, demonstrate that additional investments in, say, advertising yield returns that meet or exceed alternative applications of corporate funds. The vast majority of chief executive officers (CEOs), as well as chief marketing officers (CMOs) and chief financial officers (CFOs), are increasingly asking, "What's my ROMI?"[32] Two primary motivations underlie this increased focus on measuring marketing performance, as explained in the following quote:

> *First, greater demands for accountability on the marketing function from the CEO, the Board, and other executives mandate a greater focus on measurement. For a CMO to truly command an equal seat at the executive table, a CMO must define and deliver quantitative measurements for the Corporation. And these metrics must be clearly and convincingly communicated to the appropriate audiences. A second, perhaps equally important driver is the imperative for a CMO to get better at what they do. As the budget battles become more frequent and uncomfortable, a CMO can make marketing a more effective organization only by measuring and understanding what is working and what isn't.[33]*

Difficulty of Measuring Marcom Effectiveness

Though most marketing executives agree that measuring marketing performance is critically important, a problem resides with the difficulty of measuring marcom effectiveness. Several reasons account for this complexity: (1) obstacles in identifying an appropriate measure, or metric, of effectiveness; (2) complications with getting people throughout the organization to agree that a particular measure is the most appropriate; (3) snags with gathering accurate data to assess effectiveness; and (4) problems with determining the exact effect that specific marcom elements have on the measure that has been selected to indicate effectiveness.

Choosing a Metric

An initial problem is one of determining which specific measures (also called *metrics*) should be used to judge marcom effectiveness. Although a variety of metrics are available, not all may be equally appropriate for judging how well a company's marcom efforts have performed. Consider, for example, the case of an automobile company that has increased its annual marcom budget for a particular model by 25 percent over the previous year's budget. The company will advertise this particular model using a combination of TV, magazine, and online advertising. It also will sponsor a professional golf tournament and have a presence at several other sporting and entertainment events. Moreover, it will use an attractive rebate program to encourage consumers to buy sooner rather than postpone purchases. What metric(s) should the company use to gauge the effectiveness of its marcom efforts? Possible options include changes in *brand awareness* before and after the aggressive marcom program is undertaken, improved *attitudes* toward the automobile model, increased *purchase intentions*, and larger *sales volume* compared to last year's performance. None of these options is without problems. For example, awareness is a good measure of marcom effectiveness only if increases in awareness ultimately translate in some known proportion to sales increases; likewise, improved attitudes and purchase intentions are suitable measures only if they predictably turn into increased sales in the current or subsequent periods. And sales itself is an imperfect measure, because marcom efforts in the current accounting period may not improve sales volume measurably until a later period. Moreover, other "3P" efforts (product, price, and place/distribution) may influence sales as well. In short, there typically is no perfect metric by which marcom effectiveness can be judged. All measures/metrics can be flawed in some way, though some may be more preferable given the right match between the marcom objective and the target market in question.

The difficulty of determining how best to measure marketing's return on investment is illustrated by a recent study that the Association of National Advertisers (ANA) conducted on its membership.[34] In response to a key question asking respondents to identify which metric is closest to their company's definition of marketing ROI, more than 15 versions of ROMI were revealed. Yet the five metrics in most frequent usage are these: (1) incremental sales revenue generated by marketing activities (66 percent of respondents identified this metric), (2) changes in brand awareness (57 percent), (3) total sales revenue generated by marketing activities (55 percent), (4) changes in purchase intention (55 percent), and (5) changes in attitudes toward the brand (51 percent).[35] (The percentages sum to greater than 100 because some companies use multiple metrics.) It also is noteworthy that three of the leading metrics (i.e., changes in brand awareness, attitudes, and purchase intentions) do not even involve sales revenue but instead are based on pre-sales diagnostics.

Gaining Agreement

As is generally the case when intelligent people are asked to select a particular solution to a problem, consensus may be lacking. This is primarily due to the fact that individuals from different backgrounds and with varied organizational interests often see their "world" differently or operate with varying ideas of what best indicates suitable performance. For example, those in finance may be inclined to view things in terms of *discounted cash flows* and *net present values* of investment decisions, whereas marketing executives have historically tended to use measures of brand awareness, image, and equity to indicate success.[36] Hence, arriving at a suitable system for measuring marcom performance requires gaining agreement from different company officials, who likely have different views regarding how performance should be assessed.

Collecting Accurate Data

Whatever the measure chosen, any effort to meaningfully assess marcom performance necessitates having data that are reliable and valid. Returning to the automobile illustration, suppose that sales volume is used to judge the effectiveness of this year's marcom efforts. It would seem a simple matter to measure how many units of the automobile model have been sold during the present fiscal period. However, some of the units sold this year are residual orders from last. Also, a number of the units sold are fleet sales to companies that are entirely independent of the marcom efforts directed to consumers. How sales should be calculated can also be problematic, given the difference between units sold to dealers and units moved through to end-user consumers. All in all, collecting accurate data is no slam dunk.

Calibrating Specific Effects

Our hypothetical automobile company will employ several marcom tools (e.g., advertising media, several events, and periodic rebates) to persuade consumers to buy their cars. Ultimately, brand managers and other marketing executives are interested in knowing more than just the overall effectiveness of the marcom program. They also need to identify the relative effectiveness of individual program elements in order to make better decisions in the future about how best to allocate resources. This is, perhaps, the most complicated problem of all. How much relative effect does each program element have on, say, sales volume compared to the effects of other elements? A technique called *marketing mix modeling* is increasingly being used for this purpose.

Assessing Effects with Marketing Mix Modeling

To understand and appreciate the nature and role of marketing mix modeling, let us return to our example of the automobile marketer that increased its marcom budget for a particular model by 25 percent over the previous year's budget. To advertise and promote the brand, the following marcom tools were used: (1) advertising via TV, magazine, and online media; (2) sponsorship of a professional golf tournament along with several other sporting and entertainment events; and (3) use of an attractive rebate program to encourage consumers to buy now rather than later.[37]

Each of these activities can be thought of as individual *elements* constituting the brand's marcom mix. The issue that marketing mix modeling addresses is this: what effect did each of these elements have in affecting this automobile model's sales volume in a prior period? Marketing mix modeling employs well-known econometric statistical techniques (e.g., multivariate regression analysis) to estimate the effects that the various advertising, promotion, and other marcom elements have in driving sales volume. Though it is beyond the scope of this text to offer a technical explanation of regression analysis or of other more sophisticated analytic techniques used in marketing mix modeling, the conceptual underpinnings are straightforward. Let us demonstrate this approach using the following multivariate regression equation:

$$Y_i = \beta_0 + \beta_1 X_{1i} + \beta_2 X_{2i} + \beta_3 X_{3i} + \beta_4 X_{4i} + \beta_5 X_{5i} + \beta_6 X_{6i} \qquad (2.2)$$

where:

Y_i = The number of automobiles sold during the period of analysis, designated as period i

X_{1i} = TV advertising expenditures (designated as element 1) during the ith period

X_{2i} = Magazine advertising expenditures (element 2) in the ith period

X_{3i} = Online advertising expenditures (element 3) in the ith period

X_{4i} = Amount spent sponsoring the golf tourney (element 4) in the ith period

X_{5i} = Amount spent sponsoring other, minor events (element 5) in the ith period

X_{6i} = Amount spent on rebates (element 6) during the ith period

β_0 = Baseline sales without any advertising or promotions

$\beta_1, \beta_2, \beta_3, \beta_4, \beta_5, \beta_6$ = Estimates of the individual effects the various advertising and promotion elements had on sales.

In order to employ marketing mix modeling, a relatively long series of longitudinal data is required. The data for each period would include the level of sales during that period (Y_i) along with corresponding advertising, promotion, and sponsorship expenditures for each program element (X_{1i} through X_{6i}). Imagine, for example, that our hypothetical automobile company records weekly sales and has meticulous records of precisely how much is spent weekly on each advertising and promotion element for a period of two full years. Records of this sort would produce a set of 104 observations (52 weeks × 2 years), which would provide a sufficient number of observations to produce reliable parameter estimates for the various program elements.

The analytic aspect of marketing mix modeling yields statistical evidence regarding the relative effects that each program element has had in influencing sales of this particular automobile model. Managers learn from such analysis which elements are outperforming others and can use this statistical information to shift budgets from program element to element. Obviously, more effective elements would in the future receive relatively greater budgets vis-a-vis the less effective elements.

Marketing mix modeling has been used off and on for nearly a quarter century, but current use is at a high point with leading marketers such as Procter & Gamble (P&G) and the Clorox Company benefiting greatly from the use of this analytic approach. In one recent year, for example, P&G's application of marketing mix modeling resulted in that firm's changing how it spent more than \$400 million of its advertising and promotion budget.[38] Based on its modeling, P&G substantially increased its advertising budget. Comparatively, Clorox's use of marketing mix modeling led it to shift some money away from advertising into promotions. The important point is that each application of marketing mix modeling is based on a unique set of marketing circumstances. One solution does not, in other words, fit all.

Any company (e.g., non-profits, B2B) can employ the techniques of marketing mix modeling provided it maintains (or can purchase from syndicated sources) sales data on a period-by-period basis as well as meticulous records of its expenditures on a period-by-period basis for all of its advertising, promotion, and other marcom elements. The example we've been working with for the automobile model could be more complicated in that a full marketing mix analysis could consider not just expenditures on, say, a particular advertising medium such as television, but would disaggregate the data for specific types of TV expenditures (e.g., network TV versus cable) and even different day parts (daytime, prime time, etc.). The finer, or more disaggregated, the data, the better analysts can determine which specific marketing mix elements are most and least effective in driving sales.

Summary

This chapter discussed the nature and importance of brand equity. Brand equity is defined as the goodwill (i.e., equity) that an established brand has built up over its existence. This value can be measured by the degree to which a brand is different, relevant, held in high esteem, and has developed consumer knowledge. High brand-name awareness and strong, favorable, and perhaps unique associations that consumers have in memory about a particular brand help in this regard. Enhanced equity, in turn, helps to bolster consumer brand loyalty, may increase market share, differentiates a brand from competitive offerings, and may permit charging relatively higher prices—depending on the target market.

The chapter also discussed the importance of not restricting the assessment of marcom performance to brand equity measures only, but of also considering whether marcom efforts have influenced behavior. By examining the effect that marcom has on behavior, it is possible to gauge financial accountability and thus better equip marketing communicators when they request increased budgets from CFOs. The technique of marketing mix modeling provides an analytic method for assessing the effectiveness of individual marcom elements and for determining how budgets should be shifted among program elements.

Discussion Questions

1. With reference to the *Marcom Insight* segment that opened the chapter and in view of the detailed section on brand equity later in the chapter, explain why brand awareness is a necessary, but insufficient indicator of brand equity.

2. Using the framework in Figure 2.2, describe all personal associations that the following brands hold for you: (a) Harley-Davidson motorcycles, (b) Groupon couponing service, (c) Burton snowboards, (d) *The Onion* newspaper, (e) basketball player LeBron James, and (f) the MINI Cooper automobile.

3. An ex-CEO of PepsiCo was quoted in the text as saying, "In my mind, the best thing a person can say about a brand is that it's their favorite." Identify two brands that you regard as your favorites. Describe the specific associations that each of these brands hold for you and thus why they are two of your favorites.

4. Provide examples of brands that in your opinion are positioned in such a way as to reflect the five

personality dimensions: sincerity, excitement, competence, sophistication, and ruggedness.

5. Provide several examples of co-branding or ingredient branding other than those presented in the chapter.

6. When discussing brand equity from the firm's perspective, it was explained that as the equity of a brand increases, various positive outcomes result: (1) a higher market share, (2) increased brand loyalty, (3) ability to charge premium prices, and (4) capacity to earn a revenue premium. Select a brand you are particularly fond of and explain how its relatively greater equity compared to a lesser brand in the same product category is manifest in terms of each of these four outcomes.

7. Compare and contrast the speak-for-itself and message-driven approaches to enhancing brand equity.

8. Select a brand of vehicle (automobile, truck, motorcycle, SUV, etc.) and with this brand describe

the type, favorability, strength, and uniqueness of brand associations that you hold in memory for this brand. Do the same for the brand's differentiation, relevance, esteem, and knowledge that it holds for you.

9. What are your reactions to the application of neuroscience to marketing (neuromarketing) that was described in the *IMC Focus*? Do you consider this technique ethical? Do you fear that with the knowledge obtained from its application marketers will be able to manipulate consumers?

10. Describe the leveraging strategy for enhancing brand equity. Take a brand of your choice and, referring to Figure 2.5, explain how that brand could build positive associations, thereby enhancing its equity, by linking itself to (a) places, (b) things, (c) people, and (d) other brands. Be specific.

11. What does it mean to say that marketing communications should be directed, ultimately, at affecting behavior rather than merely enhancing equity? Provide an example to support your answer.

12. Why is demonstrating accountability important for marcom practitioners?

13. Assume that your college or university has had difficulty getting nonstudent residents in the local community to attend basketball games. Your school's athletic director requests that an organization you belong to (say, a local chapter of the American Marketing Association) develop an advertising program that is to be targeted to local residents to encourage them to attend basketball games. What measures/metrics could you use to assess whether the advertising program you developed has been effective? How might you assess the ad campaign's ROMI?

End Notes

1. Cited in Kevin Lane Keller, *Strategic Brand Management: Building, Measuring, and Managing Brand Equity*, 2nd ed., Upper Saddle River, NJ: Prentice-Hall, 2003, p. 3.

2. Dorothy Cohen, *Legal Issues in Marketing Decision Making*, Cincinnati, OH: South-Western, 1995.

3. Jacques Chevron, "Unholy Grail: Quest for the Best Strategy," *Brandweek*, August 11, 2003, 20.

4. Brand credibility includes dimensions of expertise, or ability, and trustworthiness, or willingness to consistently deliver on brand promises. See Tülin Erdem and Joffre Swait, "Brand Credibility, Brand Consideration, and Choice," *Journal of Consumer Research* 31 (June 2004), 191–98.

5. Arjun Chaudhuri and Morris B. Holbrook, "The Chain of Effects from Brand Trust and Brand Affect to Brand Performance: The Role of Brand Loyalty," *Journal of Marketing* 65 (April 2001), 90; and Peter Doyle, *Value-Based Marketing: Marketing Strategies for Corporate Growth and Shareholder Value*, Chichester, England: John Wiley & Sons, 2000, 300.

6. Kusum L. Ailawadi, Donald R. Lehmann, and Scott A. Neslin, "Revenue Premium as an Outcome Measure of Brand Equity," *Journal of Marketing* 67 (October 2003), 1–17.

7. Thomas N. Robinson, Dina L. G. Borzekowski, Donna M. Matheson, and Helena C. Kraemer, "Effects of Fast Food Branding on Young Children's Taste Preferences," *Archives of Pediatric & Adolescent Medicine* 161 (2007), 792–97.

8. Brand Asset Valuator, Brand Asset Consulting, Young & Rubicam, http://www.brandassetconsulting.com (accessed June 11, 2011).

9. Kevin Lane Keller, "Conceptualizing, Measuring, and Managing Customer-Based Brand Equity," *Journal of Marketing* 57 (January 1993), 7.

10. David A. Aaker, *Managing Brand Equity*, New York: Free Press, 1991, 62.

11. Kevin Lane Keller, "Building Customer-Based Brand Equity," *Marketing Management*, July–August, 2001, 17.

12. Brand Dynamics Pyramid, "Brand Dynamics™—A Stronger Brand Starts Here," Milward Brown marketing research, http://www.millwardbrown.com/Solutions/ProprietaryTools/BrandDynamics/BrandDynamicsSlick/BrandDynamicsSlick-Page1.aspx (accessed June 18, 2011).

13. Kevin Lane Keller, "Conceptualizing, Measuring, and Managing Customer-Based Brand Equity," *Journal of Marketing* 57 (January 1993), 7.

14. Jennifer L. Aaker, "Dimensions of Brand Personality," *Journal of Marketing Research* 34 (August 1997), 347–56. See also, Jennifer Aaker, Susan Fournier, and S. Adam Brasel, "When Good Brands Do Bad," *Journal of Consumer Research* 31 (June 2004), 1–16.

15. C. Whan Park, Bernard J. Jaworski, and Deborah J. MacInnis, "Strategic Brand Concept-Image Management," *Journal of Marketing* 50 (October 1986), 136. The discussion of functional, symbolic, and experiential needs/benefits adheres to Park et al., conceptualizations.

16. Adapted from Alan S. Dick and Kanul Basu, "Customer Loyalty: Toward an Integrated Conceptual Framework, *Journal of the Academy of Marketing Science*, 22 (2), 1994, 99–113.

17. "Special Issue: All-Channel Carbonated Soft Drink Performance in 2005," *Beverage Digest* 48 (March 8, 2006).

18. This and subsequent comments in this section are adapted from Kevin Lane Keller, "Brand Synthesis: The Multidimensionality of Brand Knowledge,"

Journal of Consumer Research 29 (March 2003), 595–600.

19. Cited in Kevin Lane Keller, *Strategic Brand Management: Building, Measuring, and Managing Brand Equity*, Upper Saddle River, NJ: Prentice Hall, 1998, 285. For excellent theoretical treatments of this issue, see C. Whan Park, Sung Youl Jun, and Allan D. Shocker, "Composite Branding Alliances: An Investigation of Extension and Feedback Effects," *Journal of Marketing Research* 33 (November 1996), 453–66; and Bernard L. Simonin and Julie A. Ruth, "Is a Company Known by the Company It Keeps? Assessing the Spillover Effects of Brand Alliances on Consumer Brand Attitudes," *Journal of Marketing Research* 35 (February 1998), 30–42.

20. Sandra Dolbow, "DuPont Lycra Stretches Out Into Jeans," *Brandweek*, July 2, 2001, 8.

21. For further reading, see Terence A. Shimp, Saeed Samiee, and Thomas J. Madden, "Countries and Their Products: A Cognitive Structure Perspective," *Journal of the Academy of Marketing Science* 21 (1993), 323–30.

22. See, for example, Saeed Samiee, Terence A. Shimp, and Subhash Sharma. "Brand Origin Recognition Accuracy: Its Antecedents and Consumers' Cognitive Limitations" *Journal of International Business Studies* 36 (2005), 379–97.

23. "New National Research Study: It's from Where? College Students Clueless on Where Favorite Brands Come From," *Anderson Analytics*, May 24, 2007, http://www.andersonanalytics.com; and Beth Snyder Bulik, "Ditch the Flags; Kids Don't Care Where You Come From," *Advertising Age*, June 4, 2007, 1, 59.

24. Simon Anholt, "Anholt Nation Brands Index: How Does the World See America," *Journal of Advertising Research* 45 (September 2005), 296–304; Simon Anholt, "2008 Anholt-Gfk Nation Brands Index Ranking," http://nation-branding.info/2008/10/01/anholts-nation-brand-index-2008-released (accessed June 22, 2011); and "Nation Brands Index," http://en.wikipedia.org/wiki/Nation_branding#Nation_Brands_Index (accessed June 22, 2011).

25. For sophisticated discussions of the relationship between brand equity and brand loyalty, consult the following sources: Tülin Erdem and Joffre Swait, "Brand Equity as a Signaling Phenomenon," *Journal of Consumer Psychology* 7, 2 (1998), 131–58; Chaudhuri and Holbrook, "The Chain of Effects from Brand Trust and Brand Affect to Brand Performance: The Role of Brand Loyalty."

26. Larry Light and Richard Morgan, *The Fourth Wave: Brand Loyalty Marketing*, New York: Coalition for Brand Equity, 1994, 11.

27. William Boulding, Eunkyu Lee, and Richard Staelin, "Mastering the Mix: Do Advertising, Promotion, and Sales Force Activities Lead to Differentiation?" *Journal of Marketing Research* 31 (May 1994), 159–72.

28. Janet Adamy, "Starbucks Chairman Says Trouble May Be Brewing," *Wall Street Journal Online*, February 23, 2007, http://online.wsj.com.

29. "The PepsiCo Empire Strikes Back," *Brandweek*, October 7, 1996, 60.

30. Press release from Harris Interactive, June 8, 2009, http://www.harrisinteractive.com.

31. Interbrand Report, "Best Global Brands 2010," http://www.interbrand.com/en/knowledge/best-global-brands/best-global-brands-2008/best-global-brands-2010.aspx (accessed June 22, 2011).

32. For example, see Sunil Gupta, Donald R. Lehmann, and Jennifer Ames Stuart, "Valuing Customers," *Journal of Marketing Research* 41 (February 2004), 7–18; Roland T. Rust, Katherine N. Lemon, and Valarie A. Zeithaml, "Return on Marketing: Using Customer Equity to Focus Marketing Strategy," *Journal of Marketing* 68 (January 2004), 109–27; and "Measures and Metrics: The Marketing Performance Measurement Audit," The CMO Council, June 9, 2004.

33. The CMO Council, "Measures and Metrics: The Marketing Performance Measurement Audit," June 9, 2004, 3.

34. Hillary Chura, "Advertising ROI Still Elusive Metric," *Advertising Age*, July 26, 2004, 8.

35. Ibid.

36. The *net present value (NPV)* of an investment represents the present, or discounted, value of future cash inflows minus the present value of the investment. The related concept of *discounted cash flow* expresses the value of future cash flows in present dollars. For example, if a firm's cost of borrowing money is 10 percent, then $100 that will not be received for three years is worth in current value only about $75. That is, if you invested $75 today and received 10 percent interest on this investment, in three years it would grow in value to $100. The concept of discounted cash flow simply reverses this logic and examines what a future flow of cash is worth in today's dollars. If this remains unclear, please go online and identify a source that discusses the concept of *time value of money*.

37. The example given here focuses only on marketing communication elements. In actuality, a full-blown marketing mix modeling would include all elements of a brand's marketing mix (e.g., product, price, distribution channels/place) and not just marcom elements.

38. Jack Neff, "P&G, Clorox Rediscover Modeling," *Advertising Age*, March 29, 2004, 10.

CHAPTER 3

Brand Adoption, Brand Naming, and Intellectual Property Issues

MARCOM INSIGHT   Back to the Future! The Vibram FiveFingers Running Shoe

Each year, *Advertising Age* announces "America's Hottest Brands" and one of the recent surprise winners was the Vibram FiveFingers shoe brand. Vibram (pronounced "vee-bram," short for founder Vitale Bramani) is a 75-year-old Italian company that began as a maker of climbing shoe soles. As noted in *Advertising Age*'s feature on the award-winning brands, "It isn't easy to reinvent a 75-year old company, especially with a product that people have deemed 'ugly' and 'disgusting,' but that's exactly what Vibram has done...."

So, exactly how did the Vibram FiveFingers shoe become one of "America's Hottest

© Handout/MCT/Newscom

Brands"? The story begins with Vibram USA President-CEO Tony Post, a runner who injured his knee training for a marathon in 2005 and, subsequently, was forced to have surgery. When doctors recommended that he stop running, Mr. Post tried a prototype "barefoot" shoe developed by Robert Fliri and Marco Bramani (the founder's grandson). Although the prototype wasn't created for running, Mr. Post was able to run long distances in them without pain, and thus, a new brand was born.

In January 2006, FiveFingers began its public relations campaign (without advertising) and had a strong consumer advocate in "Barefoot" Ted McDonald, who ran the Boston Marathon in

1 Appreciate marcom's role in facilitating the introduction of new brands.

2 Explain the innovation-related characteristics that influence adoption of new brands.

3 Understand the role performed by brand names in enhancing the success of new brands.

4 Explain the activities involved in the brand-naming process.

5 Appreciate the role of logos.

6 Describe following intellectual property rights associated with brands: patents, copyrights, and trademarks.

FiveFingers shoes in April. By June, Vibram sold out of the brand and was named one of the best innovations of the year by *Time*. This positive feedback continued over time, with featured articles four years later in *Runner's World* citing the FiveFingers' long-term success, due in part to Christopher McDougall's *NY Times* Bestseller, *Born to Run*. In it, McDougall reports on the success of barefoot runners (e.g., Indians of Northern Mexico) who frequently race ultralong distances in their rubber sandals.

All this advocacy certainly helped the FiveFingers cause. Based on Herbert Kelman's famous 1961 article, "Processes of Opinion Change," the trustworthiness and expertise of such relevant sources can enhance internalization of beliefs about a brand and subsequent positive attitude change. Moreover, the appearance of the ultralight, chic shoes on the Emmy Awards, talk shows, and on the feet of celebrities Matthew McConaughey and former NFL star Eddie George certainly serve to aid the brand's *observability*, a key factor in brand adoption rates.

Sources: Adapted from Anna Baskin, "America's Hottest Brands: Vibram," *Advertising Age*, November 15, 2010, http://adage.com/ article/print-edition/vibram-fivefinger-shoes-america-s-hottest-brands-2010/147037; Vibram, Wikipedia, http://en.wikipedia.org/wiki/Vibram (accessed June 23, 2011); Bob Parks, "Is Less More?" *Runner's World*, November 2010, http://www.runnersworld.com/article/printer/1,7124,s6-240-400–13691-0,00.html; and Herbert C. Kelman, "Processes of Opinion Change," *Public Opinion Quarterly*, 25 (Spring), 1961, 57–78.

Introduction

Introducing new brands is critical for achieving continued growth and long-term success, and this chapter examines general factors that influence the acceptance of new brands and their likelihood of success. Also examined are considerations involved in developing brand names, which play a key role in influencing the initial success of new brands and the sustained success of mature brands. Finally, we examine the dimensions of intellectual property rights affecting brands, including patents, copyrights, and trademarks.

Introducing a stream of new brands is absolutely essential to most companies' long-term growth. Yet, despite the huge investments and concerted efforts in introducing new brands, many are never successful. Although it is impossible to pinpoint the exact percentage of unsuccessful new brands, once introduced, failure rates typically range between 35 and 45 percent, and the rate may be increasing.[1] Thus, facilitating the successful introduction of new brands is critical to the success of a company.

Marcom and Brand Adoption

The acceptance of new ideas, including new brands, has traditionally been referred to as *product adoption*, although the emphasis here will be with respect to specific brands rather than entire product categories. This process of brand adoption occurs when consumers and B2B customers become aware of new brands, undertake trial purchases of these brands, and possibly become repeat purchasers.[2] The notions of trial and repeat purchase are particularly apt for inexpensive consumer packaged goods, and low involvement situations,[3] but even expensive durable goods like automobiles are tried via test-drives and repeat purchased at longer inter-purchase rates than characterize consumer goods.

The model in Figure 3.1, termed the *Brand Adoption Process*, indicates—with circles—the three main stages through which an individual becomes an adopter of a new brand. These stages are the awareness, trier, and repeater classes, with the term *class* referring to a group, or category, of consumers who

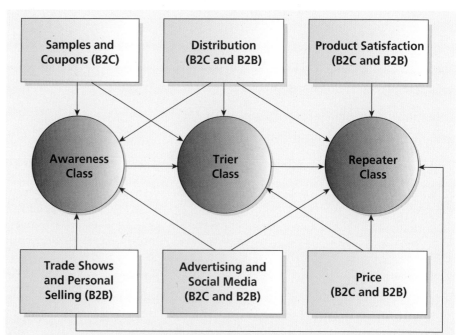

FIGURE 3.1 Model for the Brand Adoption Process

© Cengage Learning

FIGURE 3.2 Advertisement Illustrating the Brand Adoption Process

occupy the same stage. The blocks surrounding the circles are mostly marcom tools that play a role in moving consumers from initial awareness, through trial, and ultimately to becoming repeat purchasers.

The Fruit$_2$O advertisement in Figure 3.2, a brand from Kraft Foods, is used to demonstrate the Brand Adoption Process. The original Fruit$_2$0 brand was a fruit-flavored water beverage that came in eight flavors (raspberry, grape, lemon, etc.). Kraft Foods subsequently extended the product line with four versions of vitamin-enhanced fruit-flavored water beverages, named Immunity, Energy, Hydration, and Relaxation—each containing different vitamin enhancements. For example, Fruit$_2$O Immunity (see Figure 3.2) contains antioxidants and vitamin A; Fruit$_2$O Energy has caffeine and B vitamins.

The first step in facilitating adoption is to make consumers aware of a product's existence. Figure 3.1 illustrates four determinants of the awareness class: free samples and coupons, trade shows and personal selling, advertising and social media, and distribution. The first three of these are distinctly marcom activities; the fourth, distribution, is closely allied in that point-of-purchase materials and shelf placement are aspects of a brand's distribution. Successful introduction of new brands typically requires an effective advertising and social media campaign, widespread distribution backed up with point-of-purchase materials, and, in the case of inexpensive packaged goods, extensive sampling and couponing. Fruit$_2$O, for example, was sampled extensively when introduced, and coupons were available that reduced the expense for price-conscious consumers. In B2B marketing, trade shows and personal sales efforts are invaluable means of making prospective customers aware of new offerings. Although not shown in the Brand Adoption Process Model, word-of-mouth communication, a form of free advertising, also plays a significant role in facilitating brand awareness. (A later chapter will describe in detail efforts by marketing communicators to build buzz surrounding the introduction of brands.)

Once customers and consumers become aware of a new product or brand, there is an increased probability they will actually try the new offering.[4] Coupons, distribution, and price are the factors that affect the trier class (see Figure 3.1). That is, the availability of cents-off coupons, wide product distribution on retailer shelves and displays, and lower prices (such as introductory, low-price offers) all facilitate trial of new brands. For durable goods, trial may involve test-driving a new automobile or visiting an electronics store to acquire hands-on experience with a new digital camera, smartphone, or laptop computer. In the case of inexpensive packaged goods, trial more likely involves purchasing a new brand to test its performance characteristics—its taste, cleaning ability, or whatever attributes and benefits are pertinent to the product category.

Repeat purchasing, demonstrated by the repeater class, is a function of five primary forces: personal selling, advertising and social media, price, distribution, and product satisfaction. That is, customers and consumers are more likely to continue to purchase a particular brand if personal sales efforts, advertising, and social media continue to remind them about the brand, if the price is considered reasonable, if the product or service is easily accessed, and if product quality is deemed satisfactory. On this last point, it is undeniable that marcom efforts are critical to boosting repeat purchasing, but they cannot make up for poor product performance. Consumer satisfaction with a brand is the major determinant of repeat purchasing. Consumers typically will not stick with brands that fail to live up to expectations.

Brand Characteristics That Facilitate Adoption

Five brand-related characteristics influence consumers' attitudes toward *new* brands and their likelihood of adopting them. These are a brand's: (1) relative advantage(s), (2) compatibility, (3) complexity, (4) trialability, and (5) observability.[5]

Relative Advantage

Relative advantage represents the degree to which consumers perceive a new brand as being better than existing alternatives with respect to specific attributes or benefits. This is a function of consumer perception and is not a matter of whether a new brand in a new product category is actually better by objective standards.

Relative advantage is positively correlated with an innovation's adoption rate. That is, the greater an innovation's relative advantage(s) compared to existing offerings, the more rapid the rate of adoption, all other considerations held constant. (Conversely, a new brand's relative disadvantage(s)—high price, difficulty of learning how to use a new product, and so on—will retard the rate of adoption.) In general, a relative advantage exists to the extent that a new brand offers (1) better performance compared to other options, (2) savings in time and effort, or (3) immediacy of reward.

Consider the following illustrations of relative advantages (also see the *Global Focus* insert for another illustration of relative advantages for washing machines in developing countries):

- The cashless economy is becoming a reality due to new technology. Google Wallet is an app (application) that turns a user's smartphone into a payment device.[6]
- The sweetener brand Splenda affords consumers the distinct relative advantage of tasting like sugar but being calorie free.
- Hybrid automobiles (such as the Toyota Prius and Chevy Volt) offer meaningful relative advantages in the form of being more fuel efficient

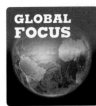

GLOBAL FOCUS

Washing Machines for the Masses in Brazil, China, and India

Millions of people throughout the developing world wash clothes the old-fashioned way: either with washboards and soap or with machines that are not fully automatic. (Most readers of this text may have never seen such a machine, but the authors and their friends remember seeing their parents wash the laundry in electric-powered machines that required individual items be manually "fed" through rollers to remove excess water prior to hanging the items on lines for drying.) This still is how it is done in much of the world. But Whirlpool Corp. has designs on changing the model of how people do their laundry. The secret to success is designing fully automatic washing machines that are functional and aesthetically appealing, yet affordable for the masses to purchase them. These relative advantages over traditional (non-automatic washer) solutions to doing the laundry will likely yield huge profits for Whirlpool in its global undertaking to alter laundry-washing behavior.

Whirlpool has designed a machine named Ideale for distribution in Brazil, China, India, and other developing countries. The retail price is in the range of $150 to $200, compared with the average automatic washer in the United States, priced at nearly $500. About one-quarter of Brazilian households have automatic washing machines, whereas the penetration levels in China and India are less than 10 percent. Importantly, Whirlpool has designed its washing machines to fit uniquely the consumption habits and preferences in each country. For example, in Brazil consumers are in the habit of washing floors beneath furniture and appliances; accordingly, the Ideale for Brazil was made to stand high on four legs. Also, because Brazilian homemakers want to see the machine operate, Whirlpool equipped the Ideale with a transparent, acrylic lid. In China, families often have shelves above their washers, so the tops of Whirlpool machines for that country were designed to be foldable. Moreover, because space constraints in China mean that many families locate their appliances in the living room, it was important that the washing machine for consumers in that country be aesthetically appealing. In India, washers often are placed in a position of pride in the home, but are moved around the house. Thus, washing machines for that market have caster wheels for easy mobility. Color preferences also vary from country to country. In Brazil, the Ideale comes only in white because Brazilians associate white with cleanliness. But Chinese dislike white appliances because they show dirt and grime, so Whirlpool produces light blue and gray machines for consumers in that country. Consumers in India can choose from white, blue, or green machines.

Source: Adapted from Miriam Jordan and Jonathan Karp, "Machines for the Masses," *Wall Street Journal Online*, December 9, 2003, http://online.wsj.com.

and environmentally friendly than conventional, fully gasoline-fueled automobiles.

- Flat-screen, plasma TVs take up less space, weigh less, and provide better resolution than conventional televisions. This technology was expensive for most consumers, which explained the initial slow rate of adoption in households. However, bars, hotels, and restaurants shifted in droves from conventional to flat-screen TVs, and households are now doing the same as prices come down.

- Brands in the so-called quick clean category have exploded in recent years. This includes items such as Procter & Gamble's Swiffer, which is a home mopping system that allows the consumer to mop hard surfaces easily by placing dirt-grabbing electrostatic sheets on pads that are attached to mop handles. Procter & Gamble's Mr. Clean Magic Eraser illustrates another quick-clean brand that offers distinct relative advantages over more traditional cleaning products.

- Unilever introduced a product long desired by parents: less drippy popsicles. Named Slowmelt Pops, these specially formulated popsicles reduce melting and dripping and stay on the stick longer.
- PepsiCo. recently introduced a "Social Vending Machine," giving consumers the option to gift a beverage to a friend, which they can redeem at participating machines with a SMS (text) code.[7]

Compatibility

The degree to which an innovation is perceived to fit into a person's way of doing things is termed compatibility. In general, a new brand is more compatible to the extent that it matches consumers' needs, personal values, beliefs, and past consumption practices. Incompatible brands are those that are perceived as incongruent with how people have learned to satisfy their consumption needs. For example, although horse meat is an alternative to beef in European countries such as Belgium, France, Italy, and Spain, it is hard to imagine North American consumers converting from their deeply ingrained preference for beef to this lean, sweet-tasting alternative.

Consider also the traditional manner by which wine bottles have been "corked." For hundreds of years, real cork—which is the outer bark of oak trees—has provided the stopper material for wine bottles. Alternatives to real cork are beginning to serve as substitutes, including plastic stoppers and even twist-off metal caps. Although these newer types of stoppers are as effective as cork (and may even be superior because they cannot contaminate wine with the sometimes musty smell of cork), many traditionalists consider non-cork stoppers unacceptable and not compatible with wine enthusiasts. For example, a survey of members of the U.S. wine trade (restaurateurs, hotel wine buyers, etc.) revealed that these experts believe their customers think that non-cork enclosures cheapen a bottle of wine, and that the reason consumers prefer cork enclosures is simply a matter of tradition rather than performance.[8]

In general, adoption rapidity is increased with greater compatibility. Innovations that are compatible with consumers' existing situations are less risky, more meaningful, and require less effort to incorporate into one's consumption lifestyle. Hybrid automobiles probably will experience a relatively slow rate of adoption because the idea of a combined gasoline and electric, or hybrid, automobile is somewhat incompatible with consumers' concept of how an automobile should be energized. However, with the rapid rise of gasoline prices, consumers have become more accepting of hybrid automobiles because of their lower operating cost.

Sometimes the only way to overcome perceptions of incompatibility is through heavy advertising to convince consumers that a new way of doing things truly is superior to an existing solution. For example, even though *Time* recognized the Apple iPad as one of the 50 best inventions of the year,[9] this line of tablet computers received mixed reviews when launched in 2010. As an example, some felt that the many details communicated on aspects of its hardware were less important than software and user interface issues. Yet, Apple went on to sell 15 million iPads, expecting to take 83 percent of the tablet computing market in the United States. A similar story occurred for Apple's promotion of the MacBook Air—"The World's Thinnest Notebook." Although criticized as omitting certain features, it is thin, lightweight, and stylish attributes caught on quickly with consumers.[10]

Complexity

Complexity refers to an innovation's degree of perceived difficulty. The more difficult an innovation is to understand or use, the slower the rate of adoption. As unlikely as it may seem in the twenty-first century, personal computers when first available were adopted slowly because many home-owners perceived them as too difficult to understand and use. The adoption of programmable TVs with hard drives (e.g., TiVo) also has been slower than expected, likely because many consumers fear they will be unable to use the technology successfully.

The success of Apple's iMac in the late 1990s attests to the value of making product use simple. The iMac was virtually an instant success, selling about one-quarter of a million units in the first six weeks after launch and becoming one of the hottest products on the market during the holiday season. Although a very good personal computer, the iMac's retail price of $1,299 at the time was, if anything, at a premium level compared to functionally competitive PCs. Indeed, in terms of specifications, the original iMac was nothing exceptional, with only 32 MB of RAM, a 4-GB hard drive, and a 233-MHz processing chip. However, the iMac's design was special. With a choice of five novel colors, translucent case, one-piece unit, rounded (versus angular) shape, and pre-installed software, the iMac was unlike any other personal computer. Beyond its unique design, the iMac was perhaps the most user-friendly computer to ever hit the market. Essentially, the user simply had to plug it in and turn it on—no setup, no hassle. This perhaps explains why nearly one-third of the iMac buyers were first-time computer owners who apparently believed that the iMac did not exceed their threshold for complexity.

Trialability

The extent to which an innovation can be used on a limited basis prior to making a full-blown commitment is referred to as trialability. In general, new brands that lend themselves to trialability are adopted at a more rapid rate. Trialability is tied closely to the concept of perceived risk. Test-driving new automobiles, eating free food products at local supermarkets, using a trial-sized version of a new shampoo, and trying out a new golf driver before purchasing it illustrate trial behaviors. The trial experience (e.g., through sampling) serves to reduce the consumer's risk of being dissatisfied with a product after having permanently committed to it through an outright purchase.

Facilitating trial is typically more difficult with durable products than with inexpensive packaged goods. Automobile companies allow consumers to take test-drives, but what do you do if you are, say, a computer manufacturer or a lawn mower maker? If you are creative, you do what companies like Apple Computer and John Deere did in novel efforts to give people the opportunity to try their products. Apple developed a "Test Drive a Macintosh" promotion that gave interested consumers the opportunity to try the computer in the comfort of their own homes for 24 hours at no cost. John Deere offered a 30-day free test period during which prospective mower purchasers could try the mower and then return it, no questions asked, if not fully satisfied. British-based Land Rover initiated a unique money-back offer to encourage purchases of Land Rover's Discovery Series II SUV model. Prospective buyers could drive the new SUV for 30 days or 1,500 miles and then return it for a full refund if they were dissatisfied with its performance.

© Getty Images for John Deere

Observability

Observability is the degree to which the user of a new brand or other people can observe the positive effects of new-product usage. The more a consumption behavior can be sensed (seen, smelled, heard, etc.), the more observable, or visible, it is. Thus,

FIGURE 3.3 Advertisement Illustrating Observability

wearing a new perfume with a subtle fragrance is less "visible" than adopting an avant-garde hairstyle. Driving an automobile with a new type of engine is less visible than driving one with a unique body design such as a BMW MINI Cooper, Zipcar, or a Hummer. In general, innovations that are high in observability lend themselves to rapid adoption if they also possess relative advantages, are compatible with consumption lifestyles, and so on. Products whose benefits lack observability are generally slower in adoptability.[11]

The important role of product observability is illustrated by Nike's long-standing use of showing the technology in its athletic shoes such as its Shox brand. Highly visible inserts in the heels of shoes convey the benefits of stability, cushioning, and increased lift through tiny shock absorbers that provide spring. Nike could have designed its shoes so that the shock absorbers are concealed from observation. Instead, the company made the feature conspicuous by "exposing the technology" and making the point that Nike shoes enable greater leaping ability than do competitive brands.

The importance of observability perhaps explains why Dell introduced its Inspiron notebook computers in eight colors not normally associated with this product category (e.g., pink, yellow, green, and red; see Figure 3.3). With languishing sales and slow growth, Dell created a new organizational unit that brought together personnel from industrial design, engineering, and marketing with the purpose of enabling Dell to respond to consumer trends quickly and to introduce a continuous stream of exciting new products.[12]

Because status from brand ownership is one form of consumption advantage, an advantage high in symbolism rather than functionality, it perhaps is not surprising that many well-known clothing brands plaster their apparel items with prominent brand names and logos that are observable to the world. Consumers have become walking billboards for designer brands, a case of observability incarnate.

Quantifying the Adoption-Influencing Characteristics

At this point, it would be useful to go beyond mere description and have a procedure whereby the five characteristics could be quantified to determine whether a proposed product concept stands a good chance of being successful. Table 3.1 illustrates a procedure for accomplishing this goal. Each of the five characteristics is rated in terms of its *importance* (from "1" to "5") in determining the success of a proposed new product and then multiplied by its *evaluation* (scored from "−5" to "+5"), i.e., with respect to how well the new brand performs on each characteristic. These scores are then summed into a total score, ranging from "−25" to "+25."

For illustration purposes, consider the issue of hair removal. Many women (and some men) go to doctors and salons to have unwanted hair removed by a laser procedure. It is estimated that professional hair removal in the United States commands annual revenues in excess of $2.5 billion.[13] Hair removal via the laser procedure stunts the growth of hair follicles by using light at a frequency and wavelength that is absorbed by the follicles but not by the surrounding skin tissue. Imagine how popular such a procedure would be if a product were available for *in-home use*. Or would it? Well, Gillette, a company famous for its razors and blades is betting that such a product will be highly demanded. Gillette had teamed up with a small company, Palomar Medical Technologies Inc., to develop an in-home laser-based hair-removal product. Palomar pioneered the field of laser hair removal and was the first company to obtain approval from the U.S. Food and Drug Administration for removing hair by such a procedure.[14] Gillette and Palomar kept adding tests and studies for the product, so at the time of this text's press date, it had yet to be launched.[15] Yet, for the purpose of its application to Table 3.1, we will assume it will be in order to quantify the success potential of the product.

TABLE 3.1	Hypothetical Illustration of Quantifying the Adoption-Influencing Characteristic

Characteristic	Importance (I)*	Evaluation (E)†	I × E
Relative advantage(s)	5	5	25
Compatibility	3	3	9
Complexity	4	−2	−8
Trialability	5	−1	−5
Observabiltiy	1	0	0
Total Score	NA	NA	21

© Cengage Learning 2013

*Importance is rated on a scale with values ranging from zero to five. A rating of zero would indicate that a specific characteristic has no importance in this particular case. High positive values indicate progressively increasing levels of importance.
†Evaluation is rated on a scale with values ranging from minus five to five. A rating of zero, the midpoint of the scale, would indicate that the proposed new product performs neither favorably or unfavorably on the characteristic at hand; negative values indicate poor performance, with minus five representing the worst possible performance; positive values indicate favorable performance, with five representing the best possible performance.

As shown in Table 3.1, relative advantage and trialability are judged to be the most important considerations in determining the success of this new laser product, both with importance ratings of five. This in-home hair-removal product must compete against conventional hair-removal procedures (e.g., shaving legs with blades or applying a chemical substance) in terms of ease of hair removal, length of effectiveness, and amount of effort and pain involved. The new brand (let's call it LaserGillette, for convenience) must possess these *relative advantages* vis-a-vis existing hair-removal products if it stands any chance of succeeding. Likewise, it is maximally important that potential purchasers be able to try the product in advance of actually purchasing it, so *trialability* also receives an importance score of five. *Compatibility*, however, is considered to be of only moderate importance (a score of three) insofar as potential users of LaserGillette may be willing to adopt a somewhat radical new method of removing hair if the procedure has distinct relative advantages that justify what will be a more expensive option compared to conventional methods. *Complexity of use*, with an importance score of four, is considered a very important determinant of product adoption as many potential users may be reluctant to switch from their present hair-removal procedure, say shaving, if the laser procedure is perceived as being difficult to use. Finally, *observability* receives an importance score of only one in that product adoption usually does not involve others seeing how well the product works because this is mostly a process done in private.

With importance ratings determined, we can turn to the evaluation of LaserGillette on each of the five adoption-influencing characteristics. On relative advantages, this new brand is assessed to have the highest possible score, a five. The importance rating multiplied by its evaluation score results in LaserGillette receiving a combined relative advantage score (I × E) of 25 points on this single dimension. Because the product is not drastically different than other hair-removal procedures (all involve moving an object, such as a razor, over the skin), its compatibility evaluation score is a three, which thus produces a combined I × E score of 9 points. It can be seen in Table 3.1, however, that Laser-Gillette scores on the negative side with respect to both complexity and trialability. The product is perceived as being somewhat difficult to learn to use, and cannot be tried prior to purchase other than by viewing a product-in-use video that is available at the point of purchase. Because observability is not really at issue, LaserGillette's I × E score on this dimension is 0. The total score, as shown in Table 3.1, is a 21. Based on its past new-product introduction efforts, let us assume that Gillette has learned that all brands with scores of 18 or higher typically are successful when introduced to the market. Hence, with a total score of 21, it is likely that LaserGillette will be a success.

Yet, brand managers can build spreadsheets based on the results, and ascertain what changes may be needed in order to increase the odds that a new product will succeed. For example, because Laser-Gillette is not evaluated favorably in terms of its trialability, the brand management team may seriously consider devising an in-store procedure that allows prospective users to try the product in a safe and hygienic manner.

Brand Naming

Choosing an appropriate brand name is a crucial decision, largely because that choice can influence early trial of a new brand and affect future sales volume. Indeed, brand names have been described as the "cerebral switches" that activate images in target audiences' collective minds.[16] Research has shown that even children (as young as 3 or 4) are aware of brand names and that by the age of 10 or so the brand name takes on conceptual significance whereby children think about brand names as more than simply another product feature. In other words, the name takes on a "life of its own," and children judge brands on the basis of their acquired reputations and evaluate people in terms of what brands they own.[17] A good brand name can evoke feelings of trust, confidence, security, strength, durability, speed, status, and many other desirable associations. A product's brand name plays a major role in determining its immediate success upon introduction and its sustained prosperity as it matures.

The name chosen for a brand: (1) affects the speed with which consumers become aware of the brand, (2) influences the brand's image, and (3) thus plays a major role in brand equity formation. Achieving consumer awareness of a brand name is the critical initial aspect of brand equity enhancement. Brand-name awareness has been characterized as the gateway to consumers' more complicated learning and retention of associations that constitute a brand's image.[18] Through brand names, a company can create excitement, elegance, exclusiveness, and influence consumers' perceptions and attitudes.[19]

What Constitutes a Good Brand Name?

This is a difficult question that is often left up to brand-naming professionals, such as Berkeley, California's Master-McNeil, one of the first firms formed exclusively for brand naming and research.[20] Even over 15 years ago, they were able to charge between $20,000 to $250,000 for brand-naming services, depending on the research involved and the product's global reach. Master-McNeil is responsible for such successful brand names as PayPal, Chevy Traverse, Buick LaCrosse, and the WE (women's entertainment) TV network. While at San Francisco–based Landor Associates before Master-McNeil, founder S.B. Master was responsible for naming Walt Disney's Touchstone Pictures and Westin Hotels. A focus on brand-naming objectives and criteria, conceptual support (e.g., metaphors), name availability and linguistic services, customer relations, and global contacts are all important in the brand-naming process.

Yet, it can be a real challenge in developing the right brand identification and differentiation needed for a successful brand name. For example, consider the following Internet-based company brands developed in part due to URL (uniform resource locator, i.e., web address) availability: Blish, Colib, Diigo, Eskobo, Gliffy, Gootodo, Gooay, Meebo, Noodly, Otavo, Oyogi, Qoop, Renkoo, Skobee, Tioti, Trumba, Woomp, Wrickr, Zlango, and Zoozio. (Readers will note that many of these contain double vowels, similar to Google and Yahoo!.) As noted by another leading brand-naming expert, "How …. are you supposed to remember, or even care in the first place, what Eskobo does, what makes Renkoo special, and what differentiates Otavo from Oyogi from Qoop?"[21]

At this point, and given these challenges, let's consider an actual brand name and the logic that went into choosing that name. In 2006, Microsoft introduced a music and video player to compete against brands such as Apple's iPod and named the brand Zune. Actually, Zune became the brand name for the media player itself. For Microsoft's hardware and Internet media store, it was named the Zune Marketplace, which enables customers to acquire songs, movies, TV programs, and software. Why the name Zune? As noted above, when picking a name for a new brand, companies such as Microsoft tend to select firms that specialize in brand naming—e.g., Lexicon Branding Inc. in this case. Lexicon's chief executive justified the choice of the Zune name when offering the following comments to a *Wall Street Journal* reporter:[22]

- The letter "Z" connotes an aura of strength and reliability and, in the English language, is among the most alive and energetic sounds.
- The branding objective was to find a short word, because short words are easier for people to pronounce and remember, and a short word would reflect the small size of Microsoft's media player.
- In choosing the Zune name, Lexicon Branding considered upward of 4,500 candidate names. Over the course of three months, Zune ultimately won out as the "best" name.
- In addition to suggesting strength, reliability, and energy, the name Zune was selected due to its ring of familiarity, as, for example, the easy leap one makes in moving from the word "tune" to Zune.
- Finally, a top marketing executive at Microsoft indicated that they wanted a brand name that would sound active and could be used both as a verb and a noun, as, for example, does the name Google.

Beyond this single name choice, marketing practitioners and researchers have attempted to specify factors that determine brand-name quality. There is general agreement that brand names should satisfy several fundamental requirements. First, a good brand name should distinguish the brand from competitive offerings. Second, it should facilitate consumer learning of desirable brand associations by describing or suggesting brand attributes or benefits. Third, it is important that the name achieve compatibility with the brand's desired image and with its product design and packaging. Fourth, it is useful for the name to be memorable and easy to pronounce and spell.[23] Finally, although not discussed subsequently as a fifth requirement, another important consideration is the suitability of the brand name for marketing a brand in multiple countries. Ideally, a brand name would satisfy requirements one through four equally well in all countries in which the brand is marketed. Needless to say, most brand names fail to satisfy this ideal. For example, it has been suggested that the Zune name is reminiscent of a profane word in Hebrew. Although that prospect has been contested, the possibility that the name may evoke such a word may diminish the Zune's success potential in Israel and other markets that use the Hebrew language.

Requirement 1: Distinguish the Brand from Competitive Offerings

It is desirable for a brand to have a unique identity, something that clearly differentiates it from competitive brands. Failure to distinguish a brand from competitive offerings creates confusion and increases the chances that consumers will not remember the name or mistakenly select another brand. Clinique selected the name Happy to

© Philip Lange/Shutterstock.com

suggest precisely that feeling for its perfume brand, a name choice that is striking in its differentiation from the usually sexually suggestive names chosen for perfumes such as Passion, Allure, and Obsession.

In the low-fare airline category, brand marketers have come up with unique names such as Ted Airlines (2004–2009; now part of United), Song (2003–2006; now part of Delta), Ryan Air (Europe), Spirit Airlines, and JetBlue Airways—unique names that provide each airline with a distinct identity. Compare these names with the stodgy monikers that historically dominated the U.S. airline industry, names such as United, Continental, TWA, Delta, American, Northwest, Eastern, Southwest, and so on. The new airline names seem intent on conveying brand personalities that suggest these airlines deliver something more than mere functionality. Moreover, all are memorable and easy to pronounce (see requirement #4).

Rather than using brand names to differentiate themselves from competitors, some marketers attempt to hitchhike on the success of other brands by using names similar to better-known and more respected brands. However, the Federal Trademark Dilution Act of 1995 protects owners of brand names and logos from other companies using the identical or similar names. (In legal terms, brand names and logos are referred to as *trademarks*.) The objective of this legislation is to protect trademarks from losing their distinctiveness.[24] Trademark infringement cases occur with some regularity in the United States, and stealing well-known brand names is widely practiced in some newly emerging market economies such as China.

Requirement 2: Facilitate Consumer Learning of Brand Associations

As described in Chapter 2, when discussing customer-based brand equity, a brand's image represents the *associations* that are activated in memory when people think about a particular brand. It is desirable that marcom efforts create associations that are favorable, strong, and perhaps unique. Brand names serve as *memory cues* that facilitate recall of product attributes and benefits and also predict product performance.[25]

Post-it (notepads), I Can't Believe It's Not Butter (margarine), I Can't Believe It's Not Chicken (a faux-chicken soy-based product), Healthy Choice (low-fat foods), Huggies (diapers), and Crocs (rubber shoes) illustrate brand names that do

© Ian Dagnall/Alamy

outstanding jobs in describing (or suggesting; see later discussion) their respective products' attributes or benefits. Consider also the name Liquid-Plumr, which is the brand name for a liquid product that is poured into sinks to open clogged drainage pipes. The name implies that the product is virtually like having your own plumber, without, of course, incurring the expense and inconvenience of hiring an actual plumber. The *IMC Focus* insert describes a very interesting product that has a brand name, Tooth Tunes, that clearly describes that brand's key product attribute/benefit. Finally, compare some of the many tech-sounding names for cell phones (e.g., Samsung's M300, Sony Ericsson's W300, and LG's VX series [VX5300, VX8300, VX8550, and VX9900]) with cell phone names that describe or suggest specific brand features or benefits (e.g., Samsung Hue and Sync, Motorola RAZR, Apple's iPhone, and LG's Chocolate and Revolution).

IMC FOCUS

A Musical Toothbrush That Encourages Children to Brush Longer

Moms and dads routinely have to remind their children to brush their teeth. With sufficient encouragement (coercion?), kids comply. But because most children consider brushing an undesirable task, the tendency is to spend too little time brushing and not doing a thorough job. Enter Tooth Tunes, the descriptive brand name of a product from Hasbro that encourages children to spend more time brushing, in fact, up to the dentist-recommended two full minutes. Tooth Tunes is a power toothbrush that plays pop songs lasting two minutes using a technology called dentamandibular sound transduction. The music cannot be heard outside the head, either by users or nonusers, and, to encourage good brushing technique, the songs sound best when kids use an up-and-down brushing stroke. Children push a button on the toothbrush; a minicomputer starts playing the song; and sound waves are transported from the front teeth, to the jawbone, and then to the inner ear.

Each Tooth Tunes brush comes loaded with a single song, with over 20 songs available from leading artists that appeal to children's musical tastes, such as Hillary Duff's *Wake Up*, the Black Eyed Peas' *Let's Get It Started*, Destiny Child's *Survivor*, and *Get 'cha Head in the Game* from the *High School Musical* movie. Tooth Tunes brushes are not inexpensive, with each being priced around $10. Hasbro hopes that kids will want to rotate the songs they listen to and thus encourage (pester?) their parents to purchase multiple brushes.

Sources: Adapted from Jack Neff, "Now There's Music for Molars," *Advertising Age*, October 23, 2006, 12; and http://www.hasbro.com/toothtunes (accessed August 21, 2007).

Brand-Name Suggestiveness Transmeta Corp., a manufacturer of computer chips that competes against the much larger Intel and its Pentium class of products, introduced a super-efficient chip designed for laptop computers. This new chip promised to extend laptop usage without battery recharge for many hours beyond the standard two or three hours enabled by conventional chips. Transmeta named the new chip Crusoe after the famous fictional character Robinson Crusoe, suggesting that a "stranded" user to continue working for many hours without access to an electrical outlet.

Researchers have carefully examined the issue of brand-name suggestiveness. *Suggestive* brand names are those that imply particular attributes or benefits in the context of a product category. Crusoe is a suggestive brand name. So is Healthy Choice for food products, intimating that this brand is low in fat content and calories. The name Outback for Subaru's SUV suggests a product that is durable and rugged—capable of taking on the challenge of the famous Australian outback. Ford Explorer is a name that suggests adventure for prospective purchasers of pickup trucks seeking the thrill of off-road driving. The name Crocs (rubber shoes) suggests that this brand is appropriate for wear in or around water as well as on land and is as tough as a crocodile's skin.

Suggestive brand names facilitate consumer recall of advertised benefit claims that are consistent in meaning with the brand names.[26] Suggestive names reinforce in consumers' memories the association between the name and the semantically related benefit information about the brand.[27] Conversely, these same suggestive names may reduce the recallability of benefit claims after a brand has been repositioned to stand for something different than its original meaning.[28]

Made-up Brand Names To convey key brand attributes/benefits, brand-name developers sometimes create names rather than select names from actual words found in dictionaries. Microsoft's Zune, as noted previously, is a made-up name. Many automobile brand names currently in use or used in the past are made-up names, including Acura, Altima, Geo, Lexus, Lumina, and Sentra.

© Jim Barber/Shutterstock.com

These names were created from *morphemes*, which are the semantic kernels of words. For example, Compaq, which now has merged with Hewlett-Packard, combined two morphemes (com and paq) and in so doing suggested the product benefit of a compact computer. The automobile name Acura is a derivative of "accurate" and suggests precision in product design and engineering. The name Lexus, by comparison, appears to be an entirely made-up name that does not suggest any particular product feature or benefit. The same is true for Exxon, as this computer-generated name had no prior meanings or connotations globally and was distinct from their prior name (Esso) and its tiger mascot that had carried with it varied interpretations throughout the world.

Sound Symbolism and Brand Naming   Research is increasingly showing that sound symbolism plays a major role in determining how consumers react to brand names and form judgments about brands.[29] Individual sounds, called *phonemes*, are the basis for brand names. Not only do phonemes serve to form syllables and words but also they provide meaning about a brand through a process of *sound symbolism*.[30] Consider, for example, the use of "front" vowels in brand names (i.e., vowels such as e as in "bee" and *a* as in "ate") compared to "back" vowels (vowels such as *ü* as in "food" and *o* as in "home"). Research has demonstrated that brand names that include front vowels (versus back vowels) convey attribute qualities such as smallness, lightness, mildness, thinness, femininity, weakness, and prettiness.[31]

A study using ice cream as the target product created the names Frosh and Frish for an allegedly new brand. These names differ only with respect to their phonetic sounds, with Frosh and Frish based on *o* (a back vowel) and *i* (a front vowel) sounds, respectively. The study determined that the name Frosh conveyed more positive brand attribute associations and more favorable brand evaluations than did Frish. The study further revealed that the effect of brand name sound symbolism occurred in an effortless, automatic fashion without cognitive involvement. It was this sound symbolism that led research participants to evaluate more favorably Frosh versus Frish ice cream.

Requirement 3: Achieve Compatibility with a Brand's Desired Image and with Its Product Design or Packaging

It is essential that the name chosen for a brand be compatible with a brand's desired image and also with its design or packaging. Suppose, for example, that you wanted to name a brand of all-natural foods that have no artificial colors, flavorings, or preservatives along with a line of organic produce that has been grown with no synthetic fertilizers or pesticides. What would you name that brand? The Florida-based supermarket chain, Publix, chose the name Green-Wise for its private-label collection of earth-friendly food items—a name compatible with the image desired. Many grocers have health food sections with their own brands (see Figure 3.4). Healthy Choice is an ideal name for a category of fat-free and low-fat food items targeted toward weight- and health-conscious consumers. The name suggests the consumer has a choice and that Healthy Choice is the right one.

Another name that fits well with a desired brand image is Swerve, which was Coca-Cola's now discontinued milk-based drink aimed at children and teens. The dictionary meaning of the word *swerve* is to make an abrupt turn in movement or direction. Prospective users of Swerve were thus promised a drink that was out of the ordinary and that would make them part of a "movement"—perhaps away from ordinary soft drinks. In a sense, this name suggested that drinking milk is a "cool" thing. Swerve's packaging graphics reinforced the name by displaying a grinning cow in dark glasses, suggesting a smart brand for young people who desire their own identity and perhaps march to their own drummer. However, even a good brand name cannot save a product that eventually fails to appeal to its intended target audience, as Coca-Cola discontinued the Swerve brand after only about three years on the market.

FIGURE **3.4** Health Food Sections of Grocery Stores Contain Many Image-Compatible Brands

Requirement 4: Be Memorable and Easy to Pronounce

Finally, a good brand name is easy to remember and pronounce. Although shortness is not an essential ingredient for a good name, many brand names are short, one-word names that facilitate ease of memory and pronunciation (Tide, Bold, Shout, Edge, Bounce, Cheer, Swatch, Smart, Zune, Crocs, etc.). Probably few words are as memorable as those learned in early childhood, and among the first words learned are animal names. This likely explains auto marketers' penchant for using animals as brand names (e.g., Mustang, Thunderbird, Bronco, Cougar, Lynx, Skyhawk, Skylark, Firebird, Jaguar, and Ram). In addition to their memorability, animal names conjure up vivid images. This is very important to the marketing communicator because concrete and vivid images facilitate consumer information processing. Dove soap, for example, suggests softness, grace, gentleness, and purity. Ram (for Dodge trucks) intimates strength, durability, and toughness.

In coming up with memorable names, companies often take liberties with standard dictionary spellings. For example, research shows that names with unusual spellings enhance consumer recall and recognition, perhaps explaining the naming decisions for Campbell's Invigor8 drink and Motorola's RAZR phone.[32]

Some Exceptions to the "Rules"

The previous discussion has identified four guidelines for brand naming (and also mentioned a fifth, although it—compatibility across cultures—was not discussed in detail). Yet, some successful brand names seem entirely at odds with the "rules" and become successful in spite of their names. The first brand in a new product category can achieve tremendous success regardless of its name if the brand offers customers distinct advantages over alternatives. Second, in all aspects of life there are exceptions to the rules, even in brand naming. For example, some successful brand names may not be short, but are memorable due to distinctive advertising, packaging, product features, or word-of-mouth campaigns (e.g., Haagen-Dazs ice cream, Leinenkugel beer, etc.).

A third major exception to the "rules" is that brand managers and their brand-name consultants sometimes intentionally select names that, at inception, are virtually meaningless (e.g., Exxon). As another example, the word *lucent* in Lucent Technologies was selected because for most people this word has relatively little meaning and few associations—the *empty-vessel philosophy* of brand naming. The empty-vessel expression can be useful in that subsequent marketing communications are able to create the exact meaning desired without contending with past associations already accumulated in people's memories.

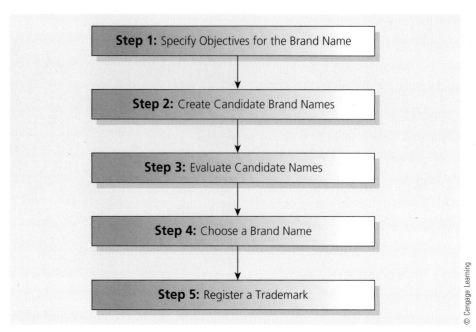

Step 1: Specify Objectives for the Brand Name

Step 2: Create Candidate Brand Names

Step 3: Evaluate Candidate Names

Step 4: Choose a Brand Name

Step 5: Register a Trademark

© Cengage Learning

FIGURE **3.5** The Brand-Naming Process

The Brand-Naming Process

Brand naming involves a rather straightforward process, as determined by a survey of over 100 product and brand managers who represent both B2C and B2B products. Figure 3.5 lists the steps, and the following discussion describes each.

Step 1: Specify Objectives for the Brand Name

As with all managerial decisions, the initial step is to identify the objectives to be accomplished. Most managers are concerned with selecting a name that will successfully position the brand in the minds of the target audience, provide an appropriate image for the brand, and distinguish it from competitive brands.[33] As previously described, the name Zune for Microsoft's media player was selected to be a short name that connoted energy, strength, and reliability.

Step 2: Create Candidate Brand Names

Brand-name candidates often are selected using creative-thinking exercises and brainstorming sessions. Companies frequently use the services of naming consultants to generate candidate names, as was the case in the selection of JetBlue, Verizon, Accenture, and Lucent. The survey of product and brand managers noted previously determined that nearly 50 candidate names were created for each brand-naming assignment.[34]

Step 3: Evaluate Candidate Names

The many names generated are evaluated using criteria such as relevance to the product category, favorability of associations conjured up by the name, and overall appeal. Product and brand managers consider it critical that names be easily recognized and recalled.

Step 4: Choose a Brand Name

Managers use the criteria noted in steps 1 and 3 to select a final name from the candidate field. In many firms, this choice is a matter of subjective judgment rather than the product of rigorous marketing research. For example, the airline name JetBlue was chosen subjectively based on hunch and insight.[35] JetBlue's chief executive and his associates were uncertain what they wanted in a name for their new airline, but they were absolutely certain what they did not want—namely, they didn't want

© Parypa/Shutterstock.com

(1) a geographic destination such as Southwest or Northeast; or (2) a made-up word such as brand names popular in automobile marketing (e.g., Lexus and Acura).

The marketing team at "New Air," which was the operating name for the airline while awaiting the selection of a permanent name, considered numerous name possibilities, including New York Air, Gotham, Taxi, the Big Apple, Imagine Air, Yes!, and Fresh Air. Taxi was the name that had the greatest appeal to a top marketing executive, who thought that the name had "a New York feel" and would enable a unique plane design with yellow and black checkering on the tails of planes (reminiscent of the look of New York City's Checker Cabs). The name *taxi* eventually was rejected, however, because in its verb usage, taxi describes what planes do on runways, and the Federal Aviation Administration rejected this usage for a brand name. Also, some feared that New York City taxi cabs may have had negative image associations for some riders.

"New Air's" marketing executives then considered other name possibilities, such as Blue, It, and even Egg. All three names were rejected, and as a last resort the company employed the services of Landor Associates, a firm that specializes in brand naming. Landor eventually came up with six candidate names: Air Avenues (too suggestive of New York's swank Park Avenue, which is an inappropriate association for a budget airline); Hiway Air (a made-up name, and rather silly at that); Air Hop (another silly name); Lift Airways (ultimately rejected for being suggestive of the emergency situation embodied in the similar sounding "airlift"); Scout Air (rejected because it implied an adventure destination and suggested the name of scouting organizations such as the Girl Scouts); and True Blue.

True Blue was the name initially selected. A key member of the marketing team shared these views: "The blue has a good visual aspect to it. It's the sky, it's friendship, it's loyalty." A long and arduous process was finally completed, and the new airline was prepared to trumpet its engaging name, True Blue. But just two weeks before launching public relations and advertising campaigns, the company learned that the True Blue name was already owned by Thrifty-Rent-A-Car, which had copyrighted the name for use in a customer service program. (As an aside, the fact that the name was already owned had escaped Landor's legal analysis, much to the dismay of this respected brand-naming company.) Just one week before announcing the new airline, a member of the marketing team recommended the name JetBlue. Everyone agreed that the name would work, and New Air became JetBlue Airways— a fledgling airline that may become a mainstay of American airline service.

Step 5: Register a Trademark

Most companies apply for trademark registration. Some companies submit only a single name for registration, whereas others submit multiple names (on average, five names). One survey found that three names are rejected for every registered name.[36] Trademarks and other intellectual properties are further discussed in a later section of this chapter.

The Role of Logos

As part of a brand's "trade dress" (name, design, shape, colors, sounds, etc.) associated with a brand, is a graphic design element called a *brand logo*. These design elements, or logos, can be thought of as a shorthand way of identifying a brand. For identifying their brands, companies use logos with or without brand names.[37] Not all brand names possess a distinct logo, but many do. Figure 3.6 presents a collection of six famous logos, ones that are readily recognizable to millions of

FIGURE **3.6** Famous Logos

Sources: © A3386 Uli Deck Deutsche Presse-Agentur/Newscom; © AP Images/PRNewsFoto/TASSIMO; © PORTAFOLIO - Casa Editorial El Tiempo/El Tiempo de Colombia/Newscom; © AP Images/ PRNewsFoto/Nike; © AP Images/ PRNewsFoto/Shell Oil Company; © HO/AFP/Getty Images/Newscom

people around the globe. For example, the Nike swoosh is virtually as famous as the company name, as are the logos for Shell Oil, Coca-Cola, and the other brands shown in Figure 3.6. Consumers learn these logos and easily recognize the brands on which the logos are emblazoned. (To test this, take a moment and visualize the logos for each of the following well-known brands: Pepsi, Ralph Lauren's Polo, Tommy Hilfiger clothing, Starbucks coffee, Mercedes-Benz automobiles, New York Yankees, Arm & Hammer baking soda, and Cracker Jack popcorn.)

Logo designs are incredibly diverse, ranging from highly abstract designs to those that depict nature scenes and from very simple to complex depictions. Generally, good logos (1) are recognized readily, (2) convey essentially the same meaning to all target members, and (3) evoke positive feelings.[38] Research has determined that the best strategy for enhancing the likeability of a logo is to choose a design that is moderately elaborate rather than one that is too simple or too complex. Also, natural designs (as opposed to abstract illustrations) were found to produce more favorable consumer responses (see Figure 3.7).[39]

Updating Logos

Because logos become dated over time, companies occasionally update logos to be more attuned with the times. For example, the logo representing General Mills' Betty Crocker brand is a created person named Betty Crocker. Betty Crocker has represented this brand for more than 85 years, and during this time has undergone a variety of changes. Figure 3.8 displays the four most recent incarnations of Betty Crocker. The current version, which was introduced in 1996 in celebration of Betty Crocker's 75th birthday, is a digitally morphed amalgam of the photos of 75 women.

Many other brands routinely update their logos. The URL presented in the following footnote provides a useful source for reviewing logo changes for a number of well-known brands such as Adidas, BP, Google, IBM, John Deere, Nike, Sony, and Yamaha.[40] Recently, Starbucks removed its angular text to leave a rounded logo. In fact, many logos have moved from an angular look to a more rounded appearance; however, recent research has shown that such a change is evaluated more negatively from consumers strongly

© iStockphoto.com/tbradford

FIGURE **3.7** A Natural Design Logo

FIGURE **3.8** The Changing Faces of Betty Crocker

committed to the brand.[41] Also, with relatively well-known brands (e.g., Gap), negative social media (e.g., via Twitter accounts) can hurt with major logo changes. However, angular to rounded logo changes are found to be more receptive in countries, such as India and China, that have cultures that are more interdependent and collectivist in nature.[42]

Intellectual Property

Intellectual property refers to a number of different author or company creations (e.g., a new brand name and/or logo) for which a set of exclusive rights are recognized under law.[43] Common types of intellectual property associated with product and brand protection include patents, copyrights, and trademarks.[44]

Patents

In the United States, federal patent protection is the exclusive method for retaining rights to publically disclosed inventions, according to Article I, sec. 8 of the U.S. Constitution. Under Congressional amendments, a patent permits an author or a firm to secure a monopoly or exclusive rights to the use of an invention for a period of 20 years, which is generally not renewable.[45] (This also is consistent with the World Trade Organization's [WTO] agreement on Trade-Related Aspects of Intellectual Property Rights.)

In the United States, there are three types of patents: utility, design, and plant.[46] The term *utility* patent is the most frequent type, and in the United States, is used to distinguish itself from the other two types. The utility category includes patents for inventions such as biological, business method, chemical, and software patents. In contrast, *design* patents protect the appearance or shape, rather than the utilitarian function found with utility patents. This could include the design of a soft drink bottle or other innovative consumer packaging. Finally, *plant* patents offer protection for discovery of certain naturally occurring and previously uncultivated plants or for the breeding of novel plants.[47]

U.S. patent applications are filed with the Patent & Trademark Office (www. uspto.gov); yet to obtain rights, certain criteria must be met. For example, the patent filer must demonstrate that they have a novel, useful, and nonobvious process or product. Legally, a patent provides the right to *exclude others* from making, using, selling, offering for sale, or importing the invention for the term of the patent (usually 20 years).[48] If another party infringes on an owner's patent, the owner must file suit (in federal court) to seek an injunction and recover damages. For example, in 1990, patent holder Robert Kearns was awarded a $10 million judgment from Ford Motor Company for their violation of Kearns' intermittent windshield wipers.[49]

Copyrights

A copyright is a set of exclusive rights, not for an actual idea or invention, but for the *form* in which it is expressed, and it should be in a tangible medium.[50] For example, one may play a captivating song on a guitar, but the musical work needs to be scored (e.g., sheet music) to receive copyright protection. The focus of copyright protection is on the originality of the expression by the owner. Initially, copyright law addressed the copying of books, but has expanded over many years to include maps, sheet music, dramatic works, paintings, photographs, architectural drawings, sound recordings, motion pictures, computer programs, etc.

Although registration is not a requirement for copyright protection in the United States, the work should be registered with the Copyright Office of the Library of Congress (www.copyright.gov) to receive these rights. A U.S. copyright is usually granted for the life of the author plus 70 years, or if "work for hire" (e.g., with an ad agency), 90 years from the date of publication or 120 years from its creation, whichever happens first. The registration application includes two copies of the work, a small filing fee, and the application form. Copyright laws are standardized via international agreements (e.g., Berne Convention, Trade-Related Aspects of Intellectual Property Rights [TRIPS], etc.).

Copyright protection has certain limits. For example, the *fair use* doctrine (sec. 107 of 1976 Copyright Act) states that use of the copyrighted work for the purpose of criticism, comment, news reporting, teaching, scholarship, or research is not an infringement of a copyright.[51] Another important defense is the *lack of use for commercial purposes*. Yet, the recent Digital Millennium Copyright Act prohibits the manufacture, importation, or distribution of devices whose intended use, or only significant commercial use, is to bypass an access or copy control put in place by a copyright owner.[52] Fair use is not a defense to such distribution, as found in the music recording industry.

Trademarks

A trademark is a distinctive sign, or indicator used by an individual, business organization, or other legal entity to *identify* the goods or services to consumers with which the trademark appears; and to *distinguish* its goods and services from competition. A trademark typically is a (brand) name, word, phrase, logo, symbol, design, image, or combination of these elements.[53] Trade dress may encompass these as well as unconventional categories, such as associations of the brand with color, smell, sounds, etc.

In the United States, the 1946 Lanham Act supplemented common law by offering federal protection through federal registration (via the Patent & Trademark Office: www.uspto.gov). Although registration is not mandatory, it is encouraged to provide trademark owners with benefits.[54] For example, registration offers nationwide protection that would only cover local areas under normal use. Interestingly, unlike the United States and most countries, registration trumps use in China.[55] Moreover, it is suggested that you register your mark in one or several Chinese languages (e.g., Mandarin). For instance, Starbucks used Xian Bake, as "Xian" translates to "star" in Chinese and "Bake" is pronounced like "bucks" in Chinese.[56] In addition to registration in other countries, experts suggest registration with your country's customs service (e.g., U.S. Customs Service for U.S. firms) that can seize infringing items imported into your country.

In many parts of the world—e.g., Africa—stopping *trademark counterfeiting* can be quite challenging. Fake Kiwi shoe polish, knockoff Rolexes, counterfeit Louis Vuitton handbags, and fake Viagra are commonplace.[57] As it turns out, the protection of intellectual property rights in many developing countries is a new concept. This means that many brand owners are at the mercy of (Chinese) counterfeiters in places like Uganda and Kenya.[58]

In addition to trademark counterfeiting, *trademark dilution* or *disparagement* cases have occurred (e.g., abuse of trademarked Disney characters online). In addition, a company could lose their trademark if the mark becomes a "common descriptive work" (i.e., becoming a generic term or referred to as the process of *genericness*). For example, through the generic usage of the brand, Kellogg lost the exclusive rights to their cereal *Shredded Wheat*. To avoid genericness, firms are told to use the word *brand* with their name (e.g., Xerox brand; JELL-O Brand) and to avoid using the name as a general product category term in their marketing communications.

Summary

The continual introduction of new brands is critical to the success of most business organizations. Marketing communications can facilitate the brand-adoption process by communicating a new brand's relative advantages, showing how it is compatible with consumers' existing purchase preferences and values, reducing real or perceived complexity, enhancing the brand's communicability, and making it easy to try.

The brand name is the single most important element for a product and plays an influential role in determining whether new brands succeed. The brand name works with advertising and other product features to communicate and position the brand's image. The brand name identifies the product and differentiates it from others on the market. A good brand name can evoke feelings of trust, confidence, security, strength, durability, speed, status, and many other desirable associations. A brand name should satisfy several fundamental requirements: it should describe the product's benefits, be compatible with the product's image, and be memorable and easy to pronounce. A major section in this chapter was devoted to a five-step process for selecting a brand name. Another section discussed the nature and role of brand logos.

The chapter concluded with a discussion of intellectual property rights associated with products and brands, including patents, copyrights, and trademarks. This discussion includes what each right entails, their application process, legal rights, and coverage limits.

Discussion Questions

1. Sugar-substitute products have been available for years. The two historically leading brands in this category are Equal (blue package) and Sweet'N Low (pink package). A yellow-packaged product named Splenda was the latest artificial sweetener introduced and is now the market-share leader. The company that markets this brand claims that it is "made from sugar, so it tastes like sugar." Using Splenda for illustration, explain the process by which marketing variables can influence consumers to become part of the awareness, trier, and repeater classes for this brand (refer to Figure 3.1).

2. What determines whether a new product or service has relative advantages over competitive offerings? Identify the relative advantages of each of the following: disposable cameras, hybrid automobiles, computer tablets, 3D TVs. Given that each of these products also has relative disadvantages compared to competitive products, present a general statement (i.e., a statement with universal applicability) that would explain why consumers are willing to adopt new products even though they almost invariably have relative disadvantages.

3. Pick a new brand of your choice and describe in detail how that brand satisfies, or fails to satisfy, the following success requirements: relative advantages, compatibility, complexity, trialability, and observability. Note: For the purposes of this assignment, it is better to select a brand that represents an innovative product category rather than a simple extension of an established category.

4. Assume you work for a company that is in the business of creating brand names for clients. One of your clients is a major automobile company. This company is in the process of introducing a new electric automobile to compete against Nissan's all-electric Leaf and Chevy's combination electric/gas Volt. Your task is to develop a name for this new automobile, either a real dictionary-word name or a made-up name along the lines of Lexus or Acura. Present and justify your choice of brand name.

5. Perform the same exercise as in question 4, but now develop a brand name for a new brand of soy milk. Perhaps the best-known brand in this category is Silk, which obviously is a conjunction of soy and milk.

6. Select a product category of personal interest and analyze the brand names for three competitive brands in that category. Analyze each brand name in terms of the fundamental requirements that were described in the chapter. Order the three brands according to which has the best, next best, and worst brand name. Support your ranking with specific reasons.

7. Based on your personal experience in using smartphones, propose a design for a new smartphone that, in your view, would make it a success among consumers in your age group. Based on the new attributes/benefits that your proposed smartphone would possess, provide a brand name for the phone and justify your rationale for this name.

8. A Boston diamond wholesaler developed a special way to cut diamonds that gives diamonds perfect symmetry and extra sparkle. The wholesaler developed a viewing device (called the proportion scope) that allows consumers to see a diamond with eight perfect hearts and eight arrows when they peer through the scope. The inventor of this specially cut diamond gave his gems the brand name Hearts on Fire. Evaluate this name by applying concepts from the chapter. Propose an alternative name.

9. SUVs have names such as the Ford Explorer, Chevy Tahoe, Nissan Armada, Mercury Mountaineer, Lincoln Navigator, Infinity QX-4, Jeep Wrangler, Toyota Highlander, Cadillac Escalade, and so on. Suppose you worked for an automobile company and that your company developed an SUV that was marketed as safer and more fuel efficient than other SUVs. What would you name this new vehicle? What is your rationale for this name?

10. Identify several brand logos other than those illustrated in this chapter and indicate why, in your view, these are effective logos.

11. Search online for recent cases involving the following trademark infringements and lost trademark rights: trademark counterfeiting, trademark disparagement and/or dilution, and genericness (common descriptive work). What might have the trademark owners done differently to protect their rights in each case?

End Notes

1. William Boulding, Ruskin Morgan, and Richard Staelin, "Pulling the Plug to Stop the New Product Drain," *Journal of Marketing Research* 34 (February 1997), 164.

2. The following discussion is adapted from Chakravarthi Narasimhan and Subrata K. Sen, "New Product Models for Test Market Data," *Journal of Marketing* 47 (winter 1983), 13–14.

3. Robert E. Smith and William R. Swinyard, "Information Response Models: An Integrated Approach," *Journal of Marketing*, 46 (winter 1982), 81–93.

4. A sophisticated and thorough empirical analysis of factors influencing the probability the people will undertake trial purchases of consumer packaged goods is provided by Jan-Benedict E. M. Steenkamp and Katrijn Gielens, "Consumer and Market Drivers of the Trial Probability of New Consumer Packaged Goods," *Journal of Consumer Research* 30 (December 2003), 368–84.

5. Everett M. Rogers, *Diffusion of Innovations*, 5th ed., New York: Free Press, 2003.

6. "Innovation Extravaganza," *Trend Briefing Blog*, http://trendwatching.com/briefing, June 2011.

7. Ibid.

8. Becky Ebenkamp, "Survey Says: Put a Cork in It!" *Brandweek*, March 6, 2006, 18.

9. Henry McCracken, "The 50 Best Innovations of 2010: iPad," *Time*, November 11, 2010, http://www.time.com/time/specials/packages/article/0,28804,2029497_2030652,00.html.

10. "MacBook Air," Wikipedia, http://en.wikipedia.org/wiki/MacBook_Air (accessed June 28, 2011).

11. For further discussion of the role of observability, see Robert J. Fisher and Linda L. Price, "An Investigation into the Social Context of Early Adoption Behavior," *Journal of Consumer Research* 19 (December 1992), 477–86.

12. Christopher Lawton, "Dell's Colorful Designs for Customers," *Wall Street Journal Online*, June 26, 2007, http://online.wsj.com.

13. Shari Roan, "Laser Hair Removal Is Coming to the Home," *The Courier-Journal*, August 2, 2007, http://www.courier-journal.com.

14. "Palomar Medical and Gillette Sign Agreement to Develop a Home-Use, Light-Based Hair Removal Device for Women," *PR Newswire*, February 19, 2007, http://www.prnewswire.com.

15. Alice Howe, "Gillette Laser Hair Removal," eHow Blog, http://www.ehow.com/way_5530928_gillette-laser-hair-removal.html (accessed June 30, 2011).

16. Rob Osler, "The Name Game: Tips on How to Get It Right," *Marketing News*, September 14, 1998, 50.

17. Gwen Bachmann Achenreiner and Deborah Roedder John, "The Meaning of Brand Names to Children: A Developmental Investigation," *Journal of Consumer Psychology* 13, no. 3 (2003), 205–19; See also Paul M. Fischer, Meyer P. Schwartz, John W. Richards, Jr., Adam O. Goldstein, and Tina H. Rojas, "Brand Logo Recognition by Children Aged 3 to 6 Years: Mickey Mouse and Old Joe the Camel," *Journal of the American Medical Association*, 266 (22), December 11, 1991, 3145–148.

18. Joseph W. Alba, J. Wesley Hutchinson, and John G. Lynch, "Memory and Decision Making," in *Handbook of Consumer Behavior*, ed. Thomas S. Robertson and Harold H. Kassarjian, Englewood Cliffs, NJ: Prentice Hall, 1991, 1–49.

19. France Leclerc, Bernd H. Schmitt, and Laurette Dubé, "Foreign Branding and Its Effects on Product Perceptions and Attitudes," *Journal of Marketing Research* 31 (March 1994), 263–70.

20. Dana S. Calvo, "It May Be the Name Game, but They're All Business," *New York Times*, September 4, 1994, F4.

21. Pam Baker, "Playing the Name Game: Sometimes, It's a Losing Effort," *E-Commerce Times*, September 24, 2001, http://naming.com/assets/news/newspage.php?news=2007_ecommerce.

22. Mark Boslet, "It's Alive! It's Also Small, Simple: The Ideas behind the Name 'Zune,'" *Wall Street Journal Online*, November 16, 2006, http://online.wsj.com.

23. These requirements represent a summary of views from a variety of sources, including Kevin Lane Keller, *Strategic Brand Management: Building, Measuring, and Managing Brand Equity*, Upper Saddle River, NJ: Prentice Hall, 1998, 136–40; Allen P. Adamson, *Brand Simple* (New York: Palgrave MacMillan, 2006), chapter 7; Daniel L. Doden, "Selecting a Brand Name That Aids Marketing Objectives," *Advertising Age*, November 5, 1990, 34; and Walter P. Margulies, "Animal Names on Products May Be Corny, but Boost Consumer Appeal," *Advertising Age*, October 23, 1972, 77.

24. For excellent coverage of trademark infringement, review the following sources: Jeffrey M. Samuels and Linda B. Samuels, "Famous Marks Now Federally Protected Against Dilution," *Journal of Public Policy & Marketing* 15 (fall 1996), 307–10; Daniel J. Howard, Roger A. Kerin, and Charles Gengler, "The Effects of Brand Name Similarity on Brand Source Confusion:

Implications for Trademark Infringement," *Journal of Public Policy & Marketing* 19 (fall 2000), 250–64; and Dorothy Cohen, *Legal Issues in Marketing Decision Making*, Cincinnati, OH: South-Western, 1995.

25. Chris Janiszewski and Stijn M. J. Van Osselaer, "A Connectionist Model of Brand-Quality Associations," *Journal of Marketing Research* 37 (August 2000), 331–50.

26. Kevin Lane Keller, Susan E. Heckler, and Michael J. Houston, "The Effects of Brand Name Suggestiveness on Advertising Recall," *Journal of Marketing* 62 (January 1998), 48–57. See also J. Colleen McCracken and M. Carole Macklin, "The Role of Brand Names and Visual Clues in Enhancing Memory for Consumer Packaged Goods," *Marketing Letters* 9 (April 1998), 209–26; and Richard R. Klink, "Creating Brand Names with Meaning: The Use of Sound Symbolism," *Marketing Letters* 11, no. 1 (2000), 5–20.

27. Sankar Sen, "The Effects of Brand Name Suggestiveness and Decision Goal on the Development of Brand Knowledge," *Journal of Consumer Psychology* 8, no. 4 (1999), 431–54.

28. Keller et al., "The Effects of Brand Name Suggestiveness on Advertising Recall." However, for an alternative perspective, see Sen "The Effects of Brand Name Suggestiveness and Decision Goal."

29. For example, Richard R. Klink, "Creating Brand Names with Meaning: The Use of Sound Symbolism," *Marketing Letters* 11 (February 2000), 5–20; and Eric Yorkston and Geeta Menon, "A Sound Idea: Phonetic Effects of Brand Names on Consumer Judgments," *Journal of Consumer Research* 31 (June 2004), 43–51.

30. Yorkston and Menon, "A Sound Idea," 43.

31. Klink, "Creating Brand Names with Meaning."

32. Tina M. Lowrey, L. J. Shrum, and Tony M. Dubitsky, "The Relation between Brand-Name Linguistic Characteristics and Brand-Name Memory," *Journal of Advertising* 32 (fall 2003), 7–18. See also Dawn Lerman and Ellen Garbarino, "Recall and Recognition of Brand Names: A Comparison of Word and Nonword Name Types," *Psychology & Marketing* 19 (July/August 2002), 621–39. This latter article provides preliminary evidence that created brand names (i.e., nonword names) generate higher recognition scores than do brand names that are based on actual words.

33. Chiranjeev Kohli and Douglas W. LaBahn, "Observations: Creating Effective Brand Names: A Study of the Naming Process," *Journal of Advertising Research* 37 (January/February 1997), 67–75.

34. Ibid., 69.

35. This description is adapted from Rebecca Johnson, "Name That Airline," *Travel & Leisure*, October 1999, 159–64; Bonnie Tsui, "JetBlue Soars in First Months," *Advertising Age*, September 11, 2000, 26; and "JetBlue Airways Open for Business" Company Press Release, January 11, 2000, http://jetblue.com/about/pressroom/pressreleases/pr.asp?year=2000&news=01112000_launch.

36. Kohli and LaBahn, 73.

37. When brand names are used, logos are set in any of a multitude of typefaces. Typeface design can have a substantial impact on the impressions formed when viewing a logo. Fascinating research on this issue is provided by Pamela W. Henderson, Joan L. Giese, and Joseph A. Cote, "Impression Management Using Typeface Design," *Journal of Marketing* 68 (October 2004), 60–72.

38. Pamela W. Henderson and Joseph A. Cote, "Guidelines for Selecting or Modifying Logos," *Journal of Marketing* 62 (April 1998), 14–30. This article is must reading for anyone interested in learning more about logos.

39. Henderson and Cote, "Guidelines for Selecting or Modifying Logos."

40. Adobe Systems Logo History, http://worldsbestlogos.blogspot.com/2007/08/adobe-systems-logo-history.html.

41. Michael F. Walsh, Karen Page Winterich, and Vikas Mittal, "Do Logo Redesigns Help or Hurt Your Brand? The Role of Brand Commitment," *Journal of Product & Brand Management*, 19 (2), 2010, 76–84; see also Gap's negative social media experience with their logo change in Rob Walker, "Good News, Bad News," *New York Times*, October 29, 2010, http://www.nytimes.com/2010/10/31/magazine/31fob-consumed-t.html.

42. Josh Sanburn, "Circles and Swooshes: What's Behind the Trend Toward Kindler, Gentler Logos?" *Time*, March 14, 2011, 62–63.

43. Richard Raysman, Edward A. Pisacreta, and Kenneth A. Adler, "Intellectual Property Licensing: Forms and Analysis," *Law Journal Press*, 1998–2008, ISBN 973-58852-086-9.

44. Dorothy Cohen, *Legal Issues in Marketing Decision Making*, Cincinnati, OH: South-Western, 1995.

45. Ibid, 84.

46. Ibid, 85.

47. Ibid, 85.

48. Ibid, 87; *Herman v. Youngstown Car Mfg. Co.*, 191 F. 579, 584–585, 1911.

49. Cohen, 88.

50. Adapted from Cohen, 94; "Copyright," Wikipedia, http://en.wikipedia.org/wiki/Copyright (accessed June 26, 2011).

51. Cohen, 96–97.

52. "Copyright," Wikipedia.

53. Adapted from *Restatement (Third) of Unfair Competition* at 9 (1995).

54. Cohen, 113.

55. Bart A. Lazar, "Protect Trademarks When Marketing in China," *Marketing News*, June 15, 2006, 7.

56. Ibid, 7.

57. David Rocks and Alex Halperin, "Stalking the Wild Copycats," *Businessweek*, August 18, 2008, 62–63.

58. Ibid, 63.

CHAPTER 4

Environmental, Regulatory, and Ethical Issues

Will Graphic Visual Tobacco Warnings in the United States Be Effective?

As a matter of U.S. public health and regulatory policy, the United States was the first nation in the world in 1966 to require a health warning on cigarette packages. This text warning read, "Caution: Cigarette Smoking May Be Hazardous to Your Health," and was updated in 1985 to include five rotating, specific text health warnings. However, although the United States began the trend of labeling cigarette packages with health warnings, it currently has one of the smallest and least prominent warnings in the world on packages. The "bottom line" is that the U.S. warnings have not changed in 25 years, often go unnoticed (due to familiarity and habituation), and fail to really convey relevant information to smokers in order to quit. Currently, more than 37 other countries already have adopted graphic visual tobacco warnings on packages.

At present, the health statistics for smokers in the United States are not encouraging, as some 440,000 Americans still die each year from smoking, approximately 6,000 people aged 12 and older become smokers daily, and overall adult smoking rates (21.6 percent) have remained virtually unchanged over the recent five-year reporting period.

Although there have been First Amendment challenges from the industry, and a temporary injunction by a federal judge, a major provision of the Family Smoking Prevention and Tobacco Control Act of 2009 will require color graphics with supplemental text that depict the negative consequences and to cover 50 percent of the front and back of each pack. On June 21, 2011, the U.S. Food & Drug Administration selected nine new graphic visual health warnings to

1 Appreciate the role of marketing communications in environmental (green) marketing.

2 Recognize the principles that apply to all green marcom efforts.

3 Explain the role and importance of governmental efforts to regulate marketing communications.

4 Be familiar with deceptive advertising and the elements that guide the determination of whether a particular advertisement is deceptive.

5 Be acquainted with the regulation of unfair business practices and the major areas where the unfairness doctrine is applied.

6 Know the process of advertising self-regulation.

7 Appreciate the ethical issues associated with advertising, sales promotions, and other marcom practices.

8 Understand why the targeting of marketing communications toward vulnerable groups is a heatedly debated practice.

include on cigarette packaging and advertising by October 2012.

The ultimate question, of course, is whether or not these regulatory and public health communication efforts will be effective. A recent review of 94 graphic visual tobacco health warning studies (with 72 quantitative ones) indicated that they indeed can be effective, as larger warnings with pictures are significantly more persuasive than smaller, text-only versions. More specifically, experimental research (with cause-and-effect inferences and control groups) has shown that adding a visual warning to the textual warning currently used in the United States can decrease the perceived attractiveness of the cigarette package and increase smokers' intentions to quit. In an extension of this research, it was reported that highly graphic visuals (versus a no-visual control, low graphic visual, or a moderately graphic visual) significantly increased evoked fear and smoker intentions to quit. Interestingly, it was evoked fear—and not warning message recall—that fully mediated the effect of the graphic visuals on smoker intentions to quit. (Interested readers are encouraged to review other experimental studies evaluating the graphic visuals.)

In the case of the nine, initial graphic warnings mandated for U.S. cigarette packages by October 2012, it likely that a longitudinal, pre-post tracking of a variety of key outcome measures (e.g., adult smoker quitting intentions and cessation behavior; adolescent intentions not to start and subsequent behavior) will help serve as the ultimate test of their effectiveness in the United States.

Sources: Duff Wilson, "U.S. Releases Graphic Images to Deter Smokers," *New York Times,* June 21, 2011, http://www.nytimes.com/2011/06/22/health/policy/22smoke.html?_r=1&hp; "Required Warnings for Cigarette Packages and Advertisements," *Federal Register,* U.S. Food & Drug Administration, 76 (120), June 22, 2011, 36628–36777; see also Bethany K. Dumas, "An Analysis of the Adequacy of Federally Mandated Cigarette Package Warnings," (Chapter 11) in *Language in the Judicial Press,* eds., J.N. Levi and A. G. Walker, New York: Plenum Press Corp., 1990, 309–52; *Federal Register,* 36629, 36631; Duff Wilson, "Court Blocks Graphic Labels on Cigarette Packs," *New York Times,* November 7, 2011, http://www.nytimes.com/2011/11/08/health/policy/court-blocks-graphic-labels-on-cigarette-packs.html; David Hammond, "Health Warning Messages on Tobacco Products: A Review," *Tobacco Control,* 2011, doi:10.1136/tc.2010.037630; Jeremy Kees, Scot Burton, J. Craig Andrews, and John Kozup, "Tests of Graphic Visuals and Cigarette Package Warning Combinations: Implications for the Framework Convention on Tobacco Control," *Journal of Public Policy & Marketing,* 25 (Fall 2006), 212–23; Jeremy Kees, Scot Burton, J. Craig Andrews, and John Kozup, "Understanding How Graphic Pictorial Warnings Work on Cigarette Packaging," *Journal of Public Policy & Marketing,* 29 (Fall 2010), 265–76; see other work by Michelle O'Hegarty, Linda L. Peterson, David E. Nelson, et al., "Reactions of Young Adult Smokers to Warning Labels on Cigarette Packages," *Journal of Preventive Medicine,* 30 (2006), 467–73; Ellen Peters, Daniel Romer, Paul Slovic, Kathleen Hall Jamieson, Leesha Wharfield, C.K. Mertz, and Stephanie M. Carpenter, "The Impact and Acceptability of Canadian-style Cigarette Warning Labels Among U.S. Smokers and Nonsmokers" *Nicotine & Tobacco Research,* 9 (April 2007), 473–81; C.I. Vardavas, G. Connolly, K. Karamanolis, et al., "Adolescent Perceived Effectiveness of the Proposed European Graphic Tobacco Warning Labels," *European Journal of Public Health,* 19 (2009), 212–17; L.I. Sabbane, F. Bellevance, J.C. Chebat, et al., "Recency Versus Repetition Priming Effects of Cigarette Warnings on Nonsmoking Teenagers: The Moderating Effects of Cigarette Brand Familiarity," *Journal of Applied Social Psychology,* 39 (2009), 656–82; and G.T. Fong, D. Hammond, J. Yuan, et al., "Perceptions of Tobacco Health Warnings in China Compared to Picture and Text-Only Health Warnings From Other Countries," *Tobacco Control,* 19 (2010) (Suppl. 2), i69–i77.

Introduction

This chapter examines three major topics: (1) *environmental issues in marketing communications*, (2) the *regulation* of marcom practices, and (3) *ethical issues* in marketing communications and their implications. All three topics are interrelated: Ethical issues confronting contemporary marketing communicators sometimes occur over environmental marketing efforts, and regulation (from federal and state governments and by industry self-regulators) is needed due in large part to some unethical marketing communications practices.[1] The discussion of graphic visual warnings on tobacco packages in the opening *Marcom Insight* represents a situation where issues of advertising regulation, ethics, and public health are involved.

Environmental Marketing Communications

People around the world are concerned with the depletion of natural resources and the degradation of the physical environment. The world's carbon footprint has grown larger with the rapid economic development of China and India, added to huge petroleum consumption by highly industrialized countries such as the United States and Canada. Although skeptics remain, the scientific community generally agrees that global warming is largely a man-made reality and that corrective measures are required. (See the *Global Focus* insert for discussion of environmentally sustainable consumption in 17 countries.)

Many companies are responding to environmental concerns by introducing environmentally-oriented products and undertaking marcom programs to promote them. These actions are referred to as green marketing.[2] Legitimate green marketing efforts must minimally accomplish two objectives: improve environmental quality and satisfy customers.[3] Anything short of meeting these objectives amounts to bogus environmental marketing, or what has been referred to as *greenwashing*. Yet, compared to the 1990s, the current climate for environmental claims is one of accountability and scrutiny.[4] For example, when Levi's launched its new line of "eco" organic cotton jeans, it still did not promote them as it still took one-third of a pound of chemicals to grow one pound of cotton.[5] So, companies that may be *relatively* better, may not be in an *absolute* sense—an ongoing challenge in marketing communications. The following section discusses illustrative marcom efforts that fall under the banner of credible green marketing.

Green Marketing Initiatives

Motivated for reasons such as achieving regulatory compliance, gaining competitive advantage, being socially responsible, and following the commitment of top management, some companies have made legitimate responses to environmental problems.[6] These responses mostly have been in the form of *new* or *revised products*. Perhaps the major environmentally responsive product initiative has been the introduction of electric-gas

© Boykov/Shutterstock.com

GLOBAL FOCUS

The Greendex: Environmentally Sustainable Consumption in 17 Countries

National Geographic magazine together with a global research firm measured consumer progress in 17 countries toward sustainable environmental consumption. The study included 17,000 consumers who were asked about their energy-use behavior, transportation choices, food usage, use of green versus traditional products, attitudes toward the environment, and knowledge of environmental issues. Answers to these questions led to the construction of a green consumer behavior index, or *Greendex*, for each of the 17 countries: Argentina, Australia, Brazil, Canada, China, France, Germany, Great Britain, Hungary, India, Japan, Mexico, Russia, South Korea, Spain, Sweden, and the United States. The higher a country's average score on the Greendex, the more environmentally friendly, or sustainable, consumer behavior is in that country.

Results from the survey revealed that consumers in India had the highest Greendex score at 62.6 points, followed by Brazil (58). Consumers from China (57.3), Mexico (54.5), Argentina (54.2), Russia (54.2), and Hungary (54.1) followed as the next highest-scoring countries on the Greendex. Considering consumers from wealthier countries, those in South Korea (52.8), Sweden (50.7), Spain (50.4), Australia (50.3), Germany (50), Japan (49.7), and Great Britain (49.6) followed closely on the Greendex. The lowest-scoring consumers were from France (48.9), Canada (47.9), and—in last place—consumers from the United States (45).

You can calculate your personal Greendex score by going to http://environment.nationalgeographic.com/environment/greendex/calculator. Perusal of this site will enable you to see why each of the 17 countries scored high or low on the Greendex. For example, Brazil, the highest scoring country along with India, received its high score because

Brazilian consumers (1) live in small residences, (2) rarely use home heating, (3) wash their clothes in cold water, (4) are far below average (compared to other countries) in ownership of vehicles, (5) use public transportation, and (6) are concerned more than consumers in other countries about environmental problems.

Comparatively, consumers in the United States scored the lowest on the Greendex because (1) heating and air-conditioning are commonplace and residences tend to be large, (2) a low percentage of American consumers use public transportation, (3) a small percentage of Americans walk or bike daily, (4) food consumption in the United States is the least environmentally sustainable of all countries (e.g., Americans are the least likely of all consumers in the 17 countries to consume locally grown foods, and over one-third of Americans drink bottled water daily), and (5) American consumers (along with Australian and European consumers) are much less concerned about environmental problems than those in emerging economies.

Fortunately or unfortunately, depending on perspective, those of us who live in wealthy countries and participate in the riches our countries offer will always generate more carbon and other greenhouse gases than will less economically fortunate consumers living elsewhere around the globe. Nonetheless, we all can do a better job in reducing our impact on the environment by altering consumption habits and making choices that may cost a little more in the short run but in the long run will benefit the environment and society at large.

Source: Adapted from "Consumer Choice and the Environment—A Worldwide Tracking Survey," http://environment.national geographic.com/environment/greendex (accessed July 9, 2011).

hybrid vehicles such as the Toyota Prius and Chevy Volt, and true electric vehicles, such as the Nissan Leaf.

Compact fluorescent lightbulbs (CFL) are increasingly prevalent because they are longer lasting and more energy efficient than traditional incandescent bulbs. In fact, the traditional incandescent bulb is targeted for an eventual phaseout in countries throughout the world.[7] In the United States, California's target date for the phaseout is 2018. Even Nike has gone green with its introduction of Air Jordan XX3 sneakers that have an outsole made of recycled material and almost no chemical-based glues.[8]

THANKS TO HIS STUBBORNNESS, THE WASTE ON THIS TRUCK CAN BE USED TO FUEL IT.

Patrick Foody Sr. is a determined man. Some 30 years ago, he had a visionary idea. He would produce ethanol, a vital ingredient in transportation fuels, from agricultural wastes like cereal straws and cornstalks. Contemporaries doubted him. Initial attempts were costly. Still, Pat and his colleagues at Iogen Corporation pressed on. After much dogged persistence, and with help from

Shell, they found ways to make large-scale production a commercial reality. It may be a while yet before alternatives such as EcoEthanol™ can become a major source of energy. But by seeking out partners like Pat, we're hoping to bring that day a step closer. For more information, visit www.shell.com.

Courtesy, Shell International

FIGURE 4.1 Green Advertising Addressing the Biophysical Environment

Green Advertising

Environmental appeals in advertising were commonplace in American advertising for a short period in the early to mid-1990s, but the initial fervor toward the deteriorating physical environment waned. In fact, for 10 years following this period it was difficult to find examples of environmentally oriented advertising. Now, however, with a rising tide of interest in green marketing and green consumption, environmental appeals have reemerged. Green advertising represents a wise marcom strategy, but only if brand marketers have something meaningful to say about the ecological efficacy of their brands vis-a-vis competitive brands. (As previously noted, this is due to greater scrutiny and accountability.) More advertisers would undoubtedly jump on the green bandwagon if their brands had environmentally based relative advantages.

There are three types of green advertising appeals: (1) ads that address a relationship between a product/service and the biophysical environment (e.g., the ad for Shell in Figure 4.1); (2) those that promote a green lifestyle without highlighting a product or service (see Figure 4.2); and (3) ads that present a corporate image of environmental responsibility (see Figure 4.3).[9]

Reduced Packaging Responses

Various efforts have been initiated to improve the environmental effectiveness of packaging materials. Early efforts included packaging soft drinks and many other products in recyclable plastic bottles, switching from polystyrene clamshell containers to paperboard packages for burgers and other sandwiches, and introducing concentrated laundry detergents to shrink packages and thus produce less waste disposal to be placed in already crowded landfills. More recently, we have seen efforts on the part of companies such as PepsiCo to reduce the amount of plastic used in bottles for some of its noncola beverages (e.g., Lipton iced tea and Tropicana juice drinks).[10] PepsiCo's Pepsi and Diet Pepsi cans are now made with 40 percent recycled aluminum,[11] and Coca-Cola has financially supported the world's largest bottle-to-bottle recycling plant and has promised to recycle 100 percent of its aluminum cans sold in the United States.[12]

In one of the major initiatives toward more ecologically friendly packaging, Walmart introduced a package-reduction program that requires its 60,000 worldwide suppliers to rate themselves in terms of various packaging-related factors (e.g., product-to-package ratio, percent of recycled content, and packing tightness of shipping pallets). Suppliers report their scores to Walmart and track the progress of their packaging-reduction efforts. Walmart uses this information as input into its selection of suppliers in competitive product categories. Walmart's objective is by 2013 to cut by 5 percent the amount of packaging on products carried in its stores. Packaging reduction of this magnitude would equate to savings of millions of trees and millions of barrels of oil that go into producing packaging materials.[13]

As counter to these positive packaging developments, there is evidence that package materials often are wasted due to a practice called *short filling*. For example, over 40 percent of juice containers, milk cartons, and other dairy products contain a smaller amount of product—from 1 to 6 percent less—than the package labels promise.[14] This short-filling problem is partially due to profit skimming and also results, more innocently, from poorly calibrated packing

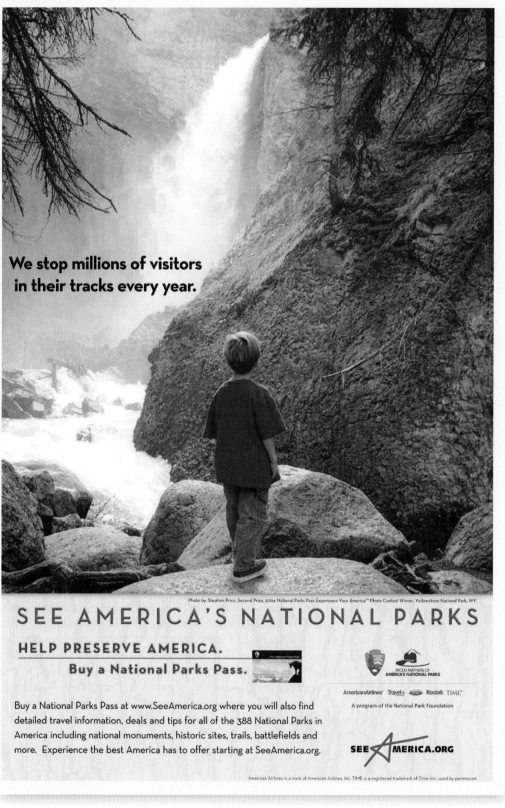

FIGURE 4.2 Green Advertising Promoting a Green Lifestyle

Image courtesy of The Advertising Archives

FIGURE 4.3 Green Advertising Presenting an Image of Environmental Responsibility

machines. Whatever the reason, the fact remains that short filling results annually in thousands of tons of wasted packaging materials.

Seal-of-Approval Programs

Organizations around the world have designed programs to assist consumers in identifying environmentally friendly products and brands. In Germany, for example, the Blue Angel seal represents a promise to consumers that a product carrying an environmental claim is legitimate. At present, there are 11,500 brands and services in 90 product categories that carry the Blue Angel eco-label.[15] For example, three printer products from Samsung recently received Blue Angel certification. Green Seal, a Washington, D.C. nonprofit organization, has developed standards and awarded seals to companies that meet environmental standards—which fewer than 20 percent of all products in the category are able to satisfy. General Electric, for example, received a seal for developing compact fluorescent lightbulbs. In addition to Green Seal, there are various product-category-specific seal programs. For example, the 100% Recycled Paperboard Alliance—a group of North American recycled paperboard manufacturers—allows participating members to identify their products with a logo that consists of a semi-circle of small arrows pointing to the words *100% Recycled Paperboard*. More than 80 companies have received certification from the 100% Recycled Paperboard Alliance.[16]

Sponsorship Programs: Cause-Related and Event Marketing

In general, sponsorship marketing is when companies sponsor or support worthy environmental or social programs in order to generate goodwill about the company or its brands (see Chapter 21). As an example of cause-related marketing (in which a contribution is linked to customer activity), Bank of America introduced an eco-friendly credit card and promised to contribute $1 to an environmental organization for every dollar consumers using the card spent.[17] Absolut vodka encouraged consumers to visit its website and select one of three environmental charities (the Ocean Foundation, the Fruit Tree Planting Foundation, and the Environmental Media Association) that the company would contribute $1 to up to a total of $500,000 to each charity.[18] Cause-related marketing programs can be effective if they are not overused and if consumers perceive a company's involvement in an environmental cause is sincere and not just raw commercialism.

Companies also are employing event sponsorships (with no strings attached) related to the environment. For example, Ben & Jerry's sponsored a "Campus Consciousness Tour" by combining a rock show (with rock band Guster) and an ecology-oriented fair to further students' understanding of global warming issues. Interested students were provided with postcards to send to Congress encouraging emission-reduction efforts for vehicles, and Ben & Jerry's website (www.lickglobalwarming.com) featured a videogame requiring users to make sound environmental decisions toward receiving backstage passes to a Guster concert.[19]

Point-of-Purchase Programs

Billions of dollars are invested in plastic, wood, metal, paper, and other display materials. Many of the displays manufacturers send to retailers are never used and simply end up in landfills. Closer consultations with retailers regarding their point-of-purchase needs would lead to fewer unused and discarded displays.

Also, increased use of permanent displays (those engineered to last at least six months) would substantially reduce the number of temporary displays that are quickly discarded, as well as the use of digital displays.

Direct Marketing Efforts

Direct marketing materials such as brochures, pamphlets, and especially catalogs are voluminous, requiring, of course, major consumption of trees and use of huge amounts of natural gas in their production. Unfortunately, research revealed that only 28 percent of the surveyed direct marketers said that the environment is a frequent factor in their decision making.[20] Companies that use direct marketing in their marcom programs can improve their stewardship of the environment by doing a better job in targeting customers and thereby cutting out waste circulation, by removing unlikely purchasers from their mailing lists, and by reducing the frequency of mailing catalogs and other solicitations to prospective customers.

Outdoor Advertising Responses

The highways and streets of America are inundated with tens of thousands of outdoor signs. With the exception of digital signs (see Chapter 21), nearly all of the billboards are covered either with banners made from polyvinyl chloride (PVC), a toxic petroleum-based product, or with thick paper that is impractical to reuse or recycle. Removal of these materials from billboards leads to massive waste that enters into landfills. CBS Outdoor, the second-largest billboard company in the United States, intends to discontinue using PVC vinyl sheets and replace them with a plastic that is reusable. Lamar Advertising, the third-largest outdoor ad firm, is in the process of replacing thick paper panels with a thinner and lighter-weight material. Finally, the leader in outdoor advertising in the United States, Clear Channel Outdoor, is reducing energy usage in its hundreds of thousands of displays by using more energy-efficient lights.[21] All in all, the outdoor advertising industry is making important strides toward "going green."

Social Media Campaigns

The beer brand Corona recently launched an environmental campaign on Facebook (www.facebook.com/savethebeach) and Twitter (e.g., for Spain: http://twitter.com/#!/savethebeach_es) that seeks to preserve beaches throughout Europe. It allows visitors (via a contest) to submit photos, videos, etc. to lobby for "save the beach" funds to save their own European beach. So far, the funds have resurrected Capocotta Beach, Italy, and Portman Bay, Cartagena, Spain.

Guidelines for Green Marketing

© Umberto Shtanzman/Shutterstock.com

The significance of the environmental problem demands that marketing communicators do everything possible to ensure that green claims are credible, realistic, and believable. To assist companies in knowing what environmental claims can and cannot be communicated in advertisements, on packages, and elsewhere, the FTC promulgated guides for environmental marketing claims, commonly referred to as the Green Guides.[22] These guides outline four general principles that apply to all environmental marketing claims: (1) qualifications and disclosures should be sufficiently clear and prominent to prevent deception; (2) claims should make clear whether they apply to the product, the package, or a component of either; (3) claims should not overstate an environmental attribute or benefit, either expressly or by implication; and (4) comparative claims should be presented in a manner that makes the basis for the comparison sufficiently clear to avoid consumer deception. The

Green Guides also discuss specific application areas and provides hypothetical examples for illustration to help avoid deceptive practices. These specific areas include the following: general benefit claims ("environmentally friendly"); degradability, biodegradable, and photodegradable claims; compostable claims; recyclable and recycled content claims; source reduction and refillable statements; and ozone-safe and ozone-friendly claims.

The Green Guides were last revised in 1996 and 1998 to update definitions of recyclable, recycled content, and seal of approval claims. Yet, in late 2010, the Federal Trade Commission (FTC) planned proposed revisions of the Green Guides to help avoid possible deception with new environmental issues and claims. This included marketers' use of unqualified product certification and seals of approval claims, and "renewable energy" claims.[23] At the time of this writing, the FTC is still involved in this Green Guide revision.

In addition to these general guidelines, marcom practitioners are offered four general recommendations for making appropriate environmental claims: (1) make the claims specific, (2) use claims that reflect current disposal options, (3) make the claims substantive, and (4) only use supportable claims.[24]

1. *Make Specific Claims.* This guideline is intended to prevent marketing communicators from using meaningless claims such as "environmentally friendly" or "safe for the environment." The use of specific environmental claims enables consumers to make informed choices, reduces the likelihood that claims will be misinterpreted, and minimizes the chances that consumers will think that a product is more environmentally friendly than it actually is. For example, a claim that a brand of washing detergent is "fully biodegradable" is more precise than an expression that this brand is "good for the environment."

2. *Reflect Current Disposal Options.* This recommendation is directed at preventing environmental claims that are technically accurate but practically unrealizable due to local trash-disposal practices. For example, many communities dispose of trash by burying it in public landfills. Because paper and plastic products do not degrade when buried, it is misleading for businesses to make environmental claims that their products are degradable, biodegradable, or photodegradable.

3. *Make Substantive Claims.* Some marketing communicators may use trivial and irrelevant environmental claims to convey the impression that a promoted brand is environmentally sound. For example, a claim that a package is "100% more recyclable than before," when it has gone from only 1 to 2 percent recycled material is trivial and is likely to be deceptive.

4. *Make Supportable Claims.* This recommendation is straightforward: Environmental claims should be supported by competent and reliable scientific evidence. The purpose of this recommendation is to encourage businesses to make only those environmental claims that can be backed by facts. The injunction to businesses is clear: Do not claim it unless you can support it.

Regulation of Marketing Communications

Advertisers, sales promotion managers, and other marcom practitioners are faced with a variety of regulations and restrictions that influence their decision-making latitude. The past century has shown that regulation is necessary to protect consumers and competitors from unethical, fraudulent, deceptive, and unfair practices that some businesses choose to perpetrate. Regarding unfair competition, monopoly power, and anti-trust issues (including pricing and distribution practices that may substantially lessen competition), interested readers may wish to visit the U.S. Department of Justice website (www.justice.gov/atr) or the Federal Trade Commission's Bureau of Competition (www.ftc.gov/bc), who share jurisdiction in this area. In market economies, there is an inevitable tension between the interests of business organizations and the rights of consumers. Regulators attempt to balance the interests of both parties while ensuring that an adequate level of competition is maintained.

When Is Regulation Justified?

Strict adherents to the ideals of free enterprise would argue that government should rarely if ever intervene in the activities of business. However, most observers believe that regulation is justified in certain circumstances, especially when consumer decisions are based *on false or limited information*.[25] Under such circumstances, consumers are likely to make decisions they would not otherwise make and, as a result, incur economic, physical, or psychological injury. Competitors also are harmed because they lose business they might have otherwise enjoyed when companies against whom they compete present false or misleading information. In theory, regulation is justified if the *benefits realized exceed the costs*. What are the benefits and costs of regulation?[26]

Benefits

Regulation offers three major benefits. First, *consumer choice* among alternatives is improved when consumers are better informed in the marketplace. For example, consider the Alcoholic Beverage Labeling Act, which requires manufacturers to place the following warning on all containers of alcoholic beverages:

> GOVERNMENT WARNING: (1) According to the Surgeon General, women should not drink alcoholic beverages during pregnancy, due to the risk of birth defects. (2) Consumption of alcoholic beverages impairs your ability to drive a car or operate machinery, and may cause health problems.[27]

This regulation informs consumers that drinking has negative consequences; yet the effects of such warnings can wear out or dissipate over time.[28] Pregnant women can help themselves and especially their unborn children by heeding this warning to refrain from drinking alcoholic beverages, although it is likely that additional prevention and communications efforts are needed in combination with warning labels to have a major impact in curbing drinking among pregnant women.[29] It should be noted that federal trade regulations with expenditures in excess of $100 million in any year are subject to a mandatory cost-benefit analysis.[30] For instance, in the case of the graphic visual tobacco warnings to be placed on all cigarette packages by October 2012 (due to the 2009 Family Smoking Prevention and Tobacco Control Act), the overall benefits are estimated by the Food & Drug Administration (FDA) to be $601 million on an annual basis and $9.4 billion overall.[31] These benefits include smoker lives saved, health status improvement, medical and other financial expenditures saved, and fire losses averted.[32]

A second benefit of regulation is that when consumers become better informed, *product quality tends to improve* in response to consumers' changing needs and preferences. For example, when American consumers began learning about the dangers of fat and cholesterol during the 1990s, and with the addition of the Nutrition Facts Panels mandated by Congress and implemented by the FDA, manufacturers started marketing healthier food products that now are widely available in grocery stores. The same can be expected to occur in restaurants with legislation in some states that requires restaurants to make available nutritional information for the levels of calories, fat, and sodium contained in menu items.

Consumers of packaged goods products in the United States recently have faced an onslaught of front-of-package

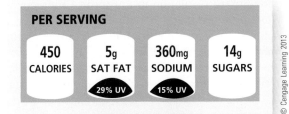

PER SERVING

| 450 CALORIES | 5g SAT FAT | 360mg SODIUM | 14g SUGARS |
| 29% UV | 15% UV |

© Cengage Learning 2013

(FOP) nutrition symbols and icons, including the controversial "Smart Choices" single summary indicator. Other front-of-package icons are proposed for the near future, including a simple FOP symbol from Walmart and the "Nutrition Keys" from the Grocery Manufacturers Association and the Food Marketing Institute. In general, the intent of the FOP symbols and icons is to help consumers make better choices in constructing a balanced diet due to their simplicity and suggested ease of use.

A third regulatory benefit is *reduced prices* resulting from a reduction in a seller's "informational market power." For example, prices of used cars undoubtedly would fall if dealers were required to inform prospective purchasers about a car's defects, because consumers would not be willing to pay as much for automobiles with known problems.

Costs

Regulation is not costless. Companies often incur the *cost of complying* with a regulatory remedy. For example, although there is a temporary injunction, U.S. cigarette manufacturers as of October 2012 are required to rotate one of nine different graphic visual warnings (with text) at a cost of $29.1 million annually ($434 million total). This obviously will be somewhat more costly than the currently required four rotating small text warning messages, yet is outweighed by the estimated $9.4 billion saved in total, primarily in medical costs.[33] *Enforcement costs* regulatory agencies incur and taxpayers pay represent a second cost category. For example, the FTC's Enforcement Division is necessary in tracking and enforcing the objectives and outcomes of deception and unfairness case orders.

The *unintended side effects* that might result from regulations represent a third cost to both buyers and sellers. A variety of potential side effects are unforeseen at the time legislation is written. For example, a regulation may unintentionally harm sellers if buyers switch to other products or reduce their level of consumption after regulation is imposed. The cost to buyers may increase if sellers pass along, in the form of higher prices, the costs of complying with a regulation. Both of these prospects are possible when food makers either choose to switch from hydrogenated oil or continue to make their products with hydrogenated oil, with the requirement that they must reveal the high levels of trans fat in their labeling. In sum, major trade regulation is theoretically justified only if the benefits exceed the costs.

When regulation is justified, federal and state agencies, along with the industry, work to oversee the integrity of marketing communications. The following sections examine the two forms of regulation that affect many aspects of marketing communications: governmental regulation and industry self-regulation.

Regulation by Federal Agencies

Governmental regulation takes place at both the federal and state levels. All facets of marketing communications are subject to regulation, but advertising is the one area in which regulators have been most active. This is because advertising is the most conspicuous aspect of marketing communications. The discussion that follows examines federal governmental regulation of advertising in the United States as performed by two agencies: the FTC and the FDA. Readers who wish to know more about advertising regulation in European Union countries are directed to the source cited in this endnote.[34]

The FTC is the U.S. government agency with primary responsibility for regulating advertising and promotion at the federal level. The FTC's regulatory authority cuts across three broad areas that directly affect marketing communicators: deceptive advertising, unfair practices, and information regulation.

Deceptive Advertising

Although the FTC makes most deception rulings on a case-by-case basis, there are guidelines in deciding whether deceptive advertising has occurred. Under current deception policy, the FTC will find a business practice deceptive if "… there is a representation, omission, or practice that is likely to mislead the consumer acting reasonably in the circumstances, to the consumer's detriment" (i.e., it is material representation, omission, or practice).[35] Thus, there are three elements that provide the essence of the FTC's deception policy: misleading, reasonable consumer, and material.[36]

(1) Misleading There must be a representation, omission, or a practice that is likely to mislead the consumer. The FTC defines a *misrepresentation* as an express or implied statement contrary to fact. For example, if a pharmaceutical company claimed that one of its over-the-counter (OTC) drugs did not contain a substance that it actually did, this would be considered a misrepresentation. A *misleading omission* is said to occur when qualifying information necessary to prevent a practice, claim, representation, or reasonable expectation or belief from being misleading is *not* disclosed. A misleading omission would exist, for example, if the same pharmaceutical company failed to disclose an important side effect of using its OTC drug.

(2) Reasonable Consumer The act or practice must be considered from the perspective of the "reasonable consumer." The FTC's test of reasonableness is based on the consumer's interpretation or reaction to an advertisement—that is, the Commission determines the effect of the advertising practice on reasonable members of the group to which the advertising is targeted. (This information normally is accessed in the "discovery process," in which the FTC has legal authority to all documents and material on a case, including target market details in marketing plans.) Although not required in FTC cases, ad copy tests are often conducted to determine the overall (net) impression of the ad claim(s) on consumers in the target market.[37] The following quote indicates that the FTC evaluates advertising claims case by case in view of the target audience's unique position—e.g., its education level, intellectual capacity, mental frame, and so on.

> *For instance, if a company markets a cure to the terminally ill, the practice will be evaluated from the perspective of how it affects the ordinary member of that group. Thus, terminally ill consumers might be particularly susceptible to exaggerated cure claims. By the same token, a practice or representation directed to a well-educated group, such as a prescription drug advertisement to doctors, would be judged in light of the knowledge and sophistication of that group.*[38]

(3) Material To be considered deceptive, the representation, omission, or practice must be "material." A *material representation* involves information that is important to consumers and that is *likely* to influence their *choice* or *conduct* regarding a product. In general, the FTC considers information to be material when it pertains to the central characteristics of a product or service (including performance features, size, and price). Hence, if an athletic-shoe company falsely claimed that its brand possesses the best shock absorption feature on the market, this would be a material misrepresentation to the many runners who make purchase choices based on this factor. In contrast, if this same company were to claim falsely that it has been in business for 28 years—when in fact it has been in business for only 25 years—this would not be regarded as material because most consumers would not be swayed much differently whether the company had been in business 25 or 28 years.

© mtkang/Alamy

An important case involving the issue of materiality was brought by the FTC against Kraft Foods and its advertising of Kraft Single American cheese slices. The FTC challenged Kraft on grounds that advertisements for Kraft Singles falsely claimed that each slice contains the same amount of calcium as *five* ounces of milk. In fact, each slice of Kraft Singles begins with five ounces of whole milk, but during processing 30 percent, or 1.5 ounces of milk, is lost. In other words, each slice contains only 70 percent of the amount of calcium claimed in Kraft's advertisements.[39] Kraft responded that its $11 million advertising campaign did not influence consumer purchases. Kraft's legal counsel argued that the advertisements (1) did not convey the misleading representation the FTC claimed, but (2) even if this representation had been conveyed, it would not have mattered because calcium is a relatively unimportant factor in consumers' decision to purchase Kraft Singles. (Out of nine factors consumers rated in a Kraft copy test, calcium was rated no higher than eighth—yet produced over 50 percent agreement.)

Whereas the FTC's position was that Kraft's advertising *was* likely to mislead consumers (i.e., 40 to 50 percent in the target market took the deceptive claims over control groups), Kraft's defense was that its calcium claim, whether false or not, is non-deceptive because they felt the difference between 5 ounces of milk and 3.5 ounces is an immaterial difference to consumers.

After hearing detailed testimony on the matter and following an appeal process, the FTC Commissioners determined that Kraft's advertising claim was indeed material.[40] The reasoning was that the 1.5-ounce reduction represented two-thirds of the daily calcium deficiency of young girls, a major end market for the cheese slices. According the FTC Deception Policy Statement, there are several factors for which *materiality is presumed*. In this case, the calcium deficiency represented an important health issue that is presumed to be important to consumers. In addition, Kraft did not show an actual ad in their copy test—an important criterion in bringing forth copy test evidence in such cases.

Following appeals all the way to the U.S. Supreme Court, the final FTC order had Kraft cease and desist (literally, "stop and go no more," or discontinue) further misrepresentations of Kraft Singles' calcium content. The Kraft case generated much discussion and controversy. The articles cited in the following end note are worth reading for this particular case, as well as for their broader significance to advertising practice and public policy involving deceptive advertising.[41]

Covert Marketing Practices and Deception A particularly cunning form of advertising deception occurs when consumers are exposed to covert forms of marcom messages, or what also is referred to as "masked marketing." These are messages that appear *not* to be marketing communications but that actually are.[42] The slyness of masked messages makes them especially potent and potentially deceptive because unsuspecting consumers are inclined to accept messages that appear to be from a nonmarketing source, whereas if they knew these claims were from a marketer they would be somewhat skeptical and more inclined to reject their validity.[43]

There are various forms of masked marketing communications, but just two forms are described.[44] First, buzz-building or viral campaigns (see Chapter 21) are sometimes conducted in person-to-person settings (e.g., in bars) where people are hired to say positive things about a new brand. Unsuspecting recipients of such messages presume that the favorable word of mouth is from an actual consumer who really likes the brand, when in fact the "buzzer" has been hired to deliver a disguised sales message. Not all viral campaigns are deceptive, but some are.

Infomercials are a second form of masked message. These messages often come across to viewers as TV programs when in actuality they are nothing more than "long advertisements" that mask their real intent by including testimonials from presumed experts and actors posing as real product users. Of course, not all infomercials are phony, but some are.

False infomercials, misleading viral campaigns, and other forms of masked messages are deceptive when they satisfy the three precepts of the FTC's deception policy, namely, (1) when they are delivered to reasonable consumers, (2) when they are misleading, and (3) when the content of the messages is material.

Unfair Practices

The FTC has legal authority to regulate unfair as well as deceptive acts or practices in commerce. The *old* ("Cigarette Rule") criteria used to evaluate whether a business act was unfair involved such considerations as whether the act (1) offends public policy as it has been established by statutes; (2) is immoral, unethical, oppressive, or unscrupulous; and (3) causes substantial injury to consumers, competitors, or other businesses.[45] However, this unfairness definition was a matter of considerable dispute for years because the precise interpretation of "unfairness" on these criteria was felt by some to be ambiguous. The dispute ended in 1994 when Congress devised a three-part definition of unfairness that was satisfactory to all parties. Currently, unfair advertising is defined as "acts or practices that cause or are likely to cause (1) *substantial injury to consumers* (e.g., health/safety, monetary), which is (2) *not reasonably avoidable* by consumers themselves, and (3) *not outweighed by countervailing benefits to consumers or competition*" (emphasis added).[46]

One example of an FTC unfairness case is that for AMF, Inc., which ran ads for their bicycles showing children riding in an unsafe manner (e.g., in and out of traffic).[47] Although there was nothing deceptive per se in the commercial, if children imitated the unsafe advertised riding practices, it is likely that substantial injury might result, which may not be reasonably avoidable due to limited reasoning ability of children. As part of the FTC order, the company agreed to prepare and distribute public service announcements (PSAs) on bicycle safety for use on children's TV programs.

The FTC has applied the unfairness doctrine in three major areas: (1) advertising substantiation, (2) promotional practices directed at children and other vulnerable populations, and (3) trade regulation rules.

1. *Advertising substantiation.* The ad-substantiation program is not a direct application, but is grounded in principle or theory. It is based on a simple premise: It is unfair for advertisers to make claims about their products without having a *reasonable basis* for those claims. The ad-substantiation program requires advertisers to have documentation (e.g., test results or other data) indicating that they have a reasonable basis for making a claim prior to the dissemination of the advertisements.[48]

   The following two FTC deceptive ad cases illustrate the ad substantiation program. The Dannon Co., Inc. (www.dannon.com), agreed to stop exaggerating the health benefits of its Activia yogurt and DanActive dairy drink due to a lack of scientific support for their claims involving beneficial bacteria, known as probiotics.[49] Specifically, Dannon agreed to stop claiming that one daily serving of Activia relieves irregularity, and that DanActive

© iStockphoto.com/Debbi Smirnoff

helps people avoid catching colds or the flu. Similarly, KFC (www. kfc.com) agreed to stop making unsubstantiated claims about the relative nutrition of its fried chicken and that its fried chicken was compatible with popular weight-loss programs.[50]

2. *Unfairness involving children and other vulnerable populations.* Because children are more credulous and less well equipped than adults to protect themselves, public policy officials are especially concerned with their protection. When applied to cases involving children (and other vulnerable populations), the unfairness doctrine is especially useful because many ad claims may not be deceptive per se, but are nonetheless unfair because children (and others who are vulnerable) may not have the cognitive capabilities to fully understand the risks associated with product claims (i.e., "not reasonably avoidable"). For example, the FTC considered one companies' use of Spider Man vitamins advertising to be unfair because such advertising was judged to be capable of inducing children to take excessive and dangerous amounts of vitamins.[51]

3. *Trade regulation rules.* Whereas most FTC actions are taken on a case-by-case basis, the use of its trade regulation rules (TRRs) enables the FTC to issue a regulation that restricts *an entire industry* for prevalent unfair and objectionable practices. For example, after website operators were found collecting personally identifiable information from children under 13, Congress passed the Children's Online Privacy Protection Act in 1998 and placed the FTC in charge of its implementation, as part of the Children's Online Privacy Protection Rule (COPPR).[52] COPPR affects all website operators collecting information from children under the age of 13, and sets provisions for privacy notice, parental consent (for collection), access to information collected, security, etc.

In recent years, the FTC has most actively applied the unfairness doctrine to numerous instances of telemarketing scams and Internet fraud.[53] Both technologies are ripe for fraudulent behavior by unscrupulous marketers, and such behavior can readily injure consumers (as well as competitors) because the tricks and scams cannot reasonably be avoided by consumers themselves. E-mail fraud is the most widely practiced abuse, and the FTC has brought over 200 enforcement actions under its unfairness power against such fraudulent behavior.[54]

Information Regulation

Although the primary purpose of advertising regulation is the prohibition of deceptive and unfair practices, regulation also is needed at times to provide consumers with information they might not otherwise receive. Usually, the FTC has some options regarding remedies for the order provisions in each case: cease and desist, mandated or triggered disclosures, corrective advertising, consumer redress (back payment), or even asset seizure (in federal court). However, even though it has been used sparingly, the corrective advertising program is arguably the most important of the FTC's information provision programs.[55]

Corrective advertising is based on the premise that a firm that misleads consumers should have to use future advertisements to rectify the deceptive impressions it has created in consumers' minds. Corrective advertising is designed to prevent a firm from continuing to deceive consumers rather than to punish the firm.

Consider the corrective advertising order the FTC issued against the Novartis Corporation and its Doan's Pills (an over-the-counter medicine for minor backache pain). Doan's advertisements referred to the brand's special or unique ingredients, called itself the "back pain specialist," and depicted the brand against packages of competitors Advil, Bayer, and Tylenol. The FTC concluded that the advertising campaign created the false impression that Doan's was more effective than other OTC drugs for combating back pain. The FTC ordered Novartis to undertake an $8 million advertising campaign to correct the misimpression that Doan's Pills outperform other OTC analgesics in treating back pain. This order required Doan's packaging and advertising to carry the message, "Although Doan's is an effective pain reliever, there is no evidence that Doan's is more effective than other pain relievers for back pain." Novartis' legal counsel claimed the order was excessive, whereas others have appraised the order as an inadequate remedy in the face of compelling evidence that Doan's advertising was deceptive.[56]

The FTC walks a fine line when issuing a corrective advertising order and specifying the remedial action a deceptive advertiser must take. The objective is to restore the marketplace to its original position prior to the deceptive advertising so that a firm does not continue to reap the rewards from its past deception. However, there is always the possibility that the corrective advertising effort may go too far and severely damage the firm and perhaps, unintentionally, hurt other companies in the industry.[57]

Product Labeling

The FDA is the federal body responsible for regulating information on the packages of food, tobacco, and drug products. The FDA has been active in regulating the type of nutritional information that must appear on food labels (e.g., Nutrition Facts Panels), nutrition content claims, and health claims (i.e., claims linking a disease with a nutrient). For example, the requirement that labels must include the amount of trans fats contained in a single serving was an important addition to the Nutrition Facts Panel. Future food labeling issues for the FDA include front-of-package symbols,[58] which are common (on a voluntary basis) in U.K. grocery stores.

Prescription Drug Advertising

Whereas the FTC is responsible for regulating deceptive and unfair advertising for all products (including OTC drugs), the FDA is charged with regulating advertisements for *prescription drugs*. This has been a major challenge in recent years with direct-to-consumer (DTC) advertising. As the name suggests, this form of advertising involves messages for prescription drugs that are directed toward consumers. Pharmaceutical companies expect DTC ads to motivate consumers to urge their physicians to prescribe advertised drug brands. The FDA's role is, in this regard, to police the truthfulness of DTC ads and to ensure that any claims made are supported by scientific evidence.

The FDA requires prescription drug advertisers to present a *balanced perspective* when advertising drugs. That is, in addition to touting product benefits, they must also identify the side effects and risks of using particular drugs. You may have noticed that TV commercials for DTC drugs show how wonderful a drug is in treating arthritis, cholesterol levels, weight problems, or other health issues. It is only at the end of the commercial that consumers are informed that in using the drug one may experience nausea, diarrhea, reduced sexual functioning, or any of a number of other undesirable consequences. Drug companies in some instances may wish not to mention these side effects, but doing so is required by the FDA—for the protection of consumers in the best spirit of regulation.

In serious cases, the FDA's Division of Drug Marketing, Advertising, and Communications (DDMAC) can issue warning letters to offending firms. For example, a recent warning letter to Bayer Healthcare stated that commercials for the birth control pill Yaz overstated the drug's efficacy (e.g., intended just for premenstrual dysphoric disorder [PMDD] and *not* PMS; and "moderate acne," not *all* acne) and minimized serious side effects (e.g., "heart and other health problems").[59]

In magazine ads, pharmaceutical companies provide detailed information about their products' undesirable side effects, but this information typically is placed on the back pages of ads and in very small print. Critics have questioned the value of such information on grounds that it is too technical, too detailed, and difficult to read because it typically is printed in very small print. Accordingly, the FDA proposed that drug makers present less detailed information about side effects in print ads, but that they explain the most serious problems in language accessible to typical consumers. Similarly, efforts are underway to make the prescription drug, pharmacy leaflet information more comprehensible.

False Advertising and Lanham Act Cases in Federal Court

Although there is not a private right to sue for false advertising under the Federal Trade Commission Act, these rights do exist and are available under Section 43 (a) of the federal Lanham Act of 1946.[60] Under the Lanham Act, in addition to fast injunctive relief from false advertising, monetary damages and attorney fees can be available to victorious plaintiffs. Yet, unlike FTC cases, plaintiffs *must* present extrinsic evidence (e.g., ad copy tests) as support for their complaint when *implied* ad claims are involved. (This does not apply to expressly false claims, e.g., "Our car gets 500 miles per gallon.")

One such famous Lanham Act false advertising case occurred over Papa John's implied claim of "Better Pizza. Better Ingredients" in comparison to Pizza Hut.[61] The ad claims in question implied that Papa John's "won big time" in taste tests over Pizza Hut and that Papa John's sauce and dough were better than Pizza Hut's due to fresh ingredients and filtered water.[62] The 5th Circuit Court of Appeals eventually ruled in favor of Papa John's, as it was argued that Pizza Hut failed to present evidence establishing that the implied "better" claims were material to consumers (i.e., likely to influence their purchase decisions regarding choice of pizza).[63] In general, there have been a considerable number of Lanham Act false advertising cases in industries for which comparative advertising is prevalent.

Regulation by State Agencies

Individual states have their own statutes and regulatory agencies to police the marketplace from fraudulent business practices. There is every indication that states will remain active in their efforts to regulate advertising deception and other business practices, which poses a potentially significant problem for many national advertisers who might find themselves subject to multiple, and perhaps inconsistent, state regulations.[64] It is somewhat ironic that many national companies would prefer to see a stronger FTC because these companies are better off with a single regulatory agency that institutes uniform national guidelines and keeps the marketplace as free as possible from the fly-by-night operators that tarnish the image of all businesses.

Advertising Self-Regulation

Self-regulation, as the name suggests, is undertaken by the advertising community itself (i.e., advertisers, industry trade associations, and ad media) rather than by governmental bodies. Self-regulation is a form of *private government* whereby peers establish and enforce voluntary rules of behavior.[65] Advertising self-regulation has flourished in countries such as Canada, France, the United Kingdom, and the United States.[66]

Media Self-Regulation

The *advertising clearance process* is a form of self-regulation ad media undertake that happens behind the scenes before a commercial or other advertisement reaches consumers. A magazine advertisement or television commercial undergoes a variety of clearance steps prior to its actual printing or airing, including (1) advertising agency clearance, (2) approval from the advertiser's legal department and perhaps also from an independent law firm, and (3) media approval (such as television networks' guidelines regarding standards of taste).[67] A finished ad that makes it through the clearance process and appears in advertising media is then subject to the possibility of post hoc regulation from federal (e.g., the FTC), state attorneys general, and self-regulators (e.g., the National Advertising Review Council).

Source: Courtesy of the Advertising Self-Regulatory Council

The Advertising Self-Regulatory Council (ASRC)

Self-regulation by the Advertising Self-Regulatory Council (ASRC) has been the most publicized and perhaps most effective form of self-regulation.[68] ASRC (founded as the National Advertising Review Council in 1971) is an organization formed via a partnership among the Association of National Advertisers, the American Association of Advertising Agencies, the American Advertising Federation, Council of Better Business Bureaus, Electronic Retailing Association, Direct Marketing Association, and the Interactive Advertising Bureau.

Advertising self-regulation under the ASRC has four investigative or compliance units and an appeals unit: the Children's Advertising Review Unit (CARU), the Electronic Retailing Self-Regulation Program (ERSP), the Online Interest-Based Accountability Program (Accountability Program), the National Advertising Division (NAD), and the National Advertising Review Board (NARB). CARU reviews advertising directed to children under the age of 12 (and websites directed at children under age 13) to assure that they adhere to CARU's guidelines and federal laws. ERSP examines direct-response advertising, including home shopping channels and infomercials. The Accountability Program, the most recent self-regulatory mechanism, was put into place to assure that advertisers comply with industry-backed principles for transparency and choice in online interest-based advertising. The NAD evaluates, investigates, and holds initial negotiations with an advertiser on complaints involving truth or accuracy of national advertising. Thus, the NAD only reviews advertisements that are national in scope rather than local. Finally, the NARB is an appeals court consisting of 70 representatives who are formed into five-member panels to hear appeals of NAD and CARU cases when an involved party is dissatisfied with the initial verdict.

The number of cases investigated and resolved varies, but the NAD often becomes involved in as many as 150 cases a year. Cases are brought to the NAD by competitors, initiated by the NAD staff itself, or originate from local Better Business Bureaus, consumer groups, and individual consumers. Under self-regulation, however, the ultimate resolution is based on the voluntary cooperation of the advertiser.

As an example of CARU in action, Campbell Taggart, the maker of Iron Kids Bread (a fortified white bread), was asked to modify their advertising produced by Publicis in which a boy makes fun of a girl eating wheat bread. Although the advertiser disagreed, it went against CARU principles to imply that the use of a product will lead to less acceptance by his/her peers, and the advertiser eventually modified their commercials.[69]

Another CARU case challenged a Tyson Chicken Nuggets commercial showing children *not* eating any portions of meals consisting of healthy ingredients; worse yet, they were shown giving them to pets, other kids, or hiding them in toys. Although Tyson strongly disagreed, they were found to violate CARU guidelines that advertising of food products should not discourage or disparage healthy lifestyle choices and that food products should be shown as part of a nutritionally-balanced meal.[70] Tyson had voluntarily discontinued the campaign prior to the CARU findings.

Finally, the NAD challenged a "Free Glasses" Facebook promotion by Coastal Contacts, Inc. that made express online ad claims such as "Like This Page! So You Too Can Get Your Free Pair of Glasses!" and "Save 70% and Get Fast, Free Shipping!" The NAD determined that the promotion failed to clearly and adequately disclose important information, such as limitations on the total number of glasses to be given away and the qualification of associated costs (i.e., they were not really free). The NAD also requested that Coastal Contacts, Inc. disclose that the total number of fans ("likes") displayed on the page was actually based on *all* of its many Facebook pages *globally*.[71]

In conclusion, advertising self-regulation reduces the need for government regulation and maintains the general integrity of advertising and, in so doing, protects both consumers and competitors. A president of ASRC has succinctly captured self-regulation's value:

> *Self-regulation is smart business. It provides a level playing field. Continuing NAD improvements provide the quickest, least expensive and most effective way for advertisers to challenge one another's claims. A court case can take over a year (vs. NAD's 60 business days) and cost 10 times as much as a NAD case.*[72]

Ethical Issues in Marketing Communications

Marketing communicators in their various capacities—as advertisers, sales promoters, package designers, public relations representatives, bloggers, point-of-purchase designers, and so on—regularly make decisions that have ethical ramifications. Ethical lapses and moral indiscretions sometimes occur under pressures of trying to meet business goals and attempting to satisfy the demands of the financial community.

With an understanding of how marketing communications is ripe for assertions of unethical actions—because marcom practitioners sometimes *do* engage in unacceptable behaviors—you will be better prepared by taking a moral check and resisting the temptation to do something that may be expedient but costly in the long run. A respected educator has framed the importance of examining ethical issues in the following terms:

> *I think most people—and [college] students are no different—know right from wrong. I believe they care about doing right. But even those of us with a rudimentary moral sensibility aren't always able to evoke those basic principles when dealing with fairly routine business decisions. For instance, we may do an enthusiastic sales pitch and promise things our company isn't quite ready to deliver, or we might highlight the positive aspects of our products and downplay the negative ones. We might formulate financial projections to favor the outcome we advocate. We might overstep the boundaries when advertising to children or go overboard when we use personal data to target customers.... Ethical dilemmas do not arrive bathed in red lights. There is no sign that says, "You're about to enter an ethical zone." Therefore, ethics education is not about defining for students what is right and what is wrong. Ethics education should aim to raise our students' antennae for recognizing ethical implications, conflicts of interest, and exercises of asymmetric power when such dilemmas pop up without warning.*[73]

Ethics in our context involves matters of right and wrong, or *moral*, conduct pertaining to any aspect of marketing communications. For our purposes, the terms ethics and morality will be used interchangeably and considered synonymous with societal notions of *honesty, honor, virtue*, and *integrity*. Although it is relatively easy to define ethics, the field of marketing—as well as elsewhere in society—lacks consensus about what ethical conduct actually entails.[74] We nonetheless can identify the following marketing communications practices that are especially susceptible to ethical challenges: (1) targeting marketing communications, (2) advertising, (3) public relations, (4) packaging communications, (5) sales promotions, and (6) online and social media marketing.

The Ethics of Targeting

Based on principles of marketing strategy, we know that firms should direct their offerings at specific segments of customers rather than use a scatter or shotgun approach. Nevertheless, ethical dilemmas are sometimes involved when special products and corresponding marketing communications efforts are directed at segments that may be vulnerable. For example, especially open to ethical debate is the practice of targeting products and communications efforts to segments that, for various psychosocial and economic reasons, are vulnerable to marketing communications—such as children, teens, and economically disadvantaged groups.[75]

Targeting Children and Teens

In-school marketing programs, advertisements in traditional media, and messages on the Internet continually urge children to desire various products and brands. In fact, one study has estimated that U.S. businesses spent $15 billion in one year advertising and marketing their brands to children ages 12 and under.[76] Critics contend that many of the products targeted to children are unnecessary and that the communications are exploitative. Because it would involve debating personal values to discuss what children do or do not need, the following examples present the critics' position and allow you to draw your own conclusions.[77]

Targeting Food and Beverage Products Consider a past advertising campaign that targeted Gatorade to children. Advertisements claimed that bottled Gatorade is the "healthy alternative for thirsty kids." Nutritionists and other critics charged that Gatorade is unnecessary for children and no better than water—no

harm or benefit arises from its consumption.[78] If indeed Gatorade does not benefit kids, is it ethical to urge them to encourage a parent to purchase this product?

Childhood obesity and the marketing of food products to children are especially hotly debated topics. According to the Centers for Disease Control and Prevention, nearly 1 in 6 children (17 percent or 12.5 million) are considered obese, a rate that compares to 1 in 16 cases of childhood obesity only about 25 years ago.[79] Many critics consider it unethical to market food products to children, perhaps especially through cartoon characters touting sugared cereals and unhealthy snacks.[80]

Consider targeting efforts by the famous food company, Campbell Soup. Campbell historically marketed its soup and pasta brands primarily to mothers with the expectation that they would make appropriate choices for their children. But the company's market research revealed that direct appeals to children would increase sales volume. Accordingly, Campbell at one time used rapper Bow Wow and soccer player Freddy Adu as spokespeople to reach older children. To appeal to younger children, Campbell advertised its products during TV programs such as *Dora the Explorer* and *Jimmy Neutron*.[81] Although sodium levels of soup and pasta sauce can be high at times, is targeting these products to children unethical?

Consider also an advertising effort by the Subway sandwich chain, which, as you may recall, achieved much success using spokesman Jared Fogle, a once morbidly obese man who supposedly lost nearly 250 pounds by dieting on Subway sandwiches and exercise. Subway extended the campaign several years ago in an effort directed at children. In one commercial, a preteen boy was overheard in the background saying, "When my brother had friends over, I would, like, stay up in my room because I was afraid they'd call me fat, or something. Now I'm not afraid of that at all. I started running and eating better stuff. I'm Cody. I'm twelve years old." After the child bared his soul, Jared Fogle came before the camera and declared, "More than anything, we [Subway] want your children to lead long and healthy lives." By implication, eating at Subway rather than at nutritionally challenged fast-food outlets is one means for children to reduce weight and to increase the quality of their lives. Critics asserted that this campaign was exploitive.[82] Defenders of Subway's advertising countered by claiming that this type of advertising serves to raise children's awareness of the importance of eating more nutritious foods and undertaking exercise regimens. Did Subway cross the exploitation line with this advertising?

Due to a combination of pressure from critics, fear of more regulations from the FTC, and perhaps their own high moral standards, 11 of the largest food and beverage companies in the United States (e.g., Campbell Soup, General Mills, Kellogg, and PepsiCo) adopted self-imposed rules that limit advertising to children under 12. Among other rules, the companies pledged to discontinue use of licensed characters in ads (i.e., characters from popular TV shows and movies) unless they are used for promoting healthier products—such as General Mills' use of SpongeBob SquarePants on packages to promote its frozen vegetable mixes. Additionally, the companies agreed to stop advertising in elementary schools.[83]

Targeting Tobacco and Alcohol Products Marketers have been criticized for targeting adult products to teens and college students. The Miller Brewing Company, for example, was criticized for running a television commercial for its Molson Ice brand that focused on a label displaying 5.6 percent alcoholic content while an off-camera announcer uttered that Molson Ice is a "bolder" drink. A spokesperson for the Center for Science in the Public Interest asserted that the Molson Ice commercial appealed to children because they "drink to get drunk" and higher alcohol content is "what they want in a beer."[84] The beer industry itself would be expected to oppose such advertising because one of the brewing industry's advertising guidelines explicitly states that beer advertisements "should neither state nor carry any implication of alcohol strength."[85]

In general, there is considerable concern regarding the marketing of beer and other alcoholic beverages to teens and young adults. A study by a watchdog group at Georgetown University reported that one-quarter of alcohol advertising was more likely seen by youths than adults.[86] Research undertaken by the Centers for Disease Control and Prevention monitored over 67,000 radio spots in 104 markets in the United States and concluded that 49 percent of those ads were aired on programs that are youth oriented. The study concluded that beer and liquor companies are not abiding by a self-imposed ban on advertising to teens.[87]

Lawsuits have been filed against major brewers and other companies that market alcohol products on the basis that their advertising and marketing practices increase underage drinking.[88] A consumer advocacy group, the Center for Science in the Public Interest, initiated an effort to reduce the amount of alcohol advertising on televised sports. Coaching legends Dean Smith (ex-basketball coach at the University of North Carolina) and Tom Osborne (ex-football coach, now athletic director, at the University of Nebraska) participated in the program, and The Ohio State University (OSU) became the first major school to get involved when it blocked its local media partners from airing any alcohol ads during the broadcast of OSU sporting events.[89]

By far the greatest recent controversy involved claims of unfair targeting of cigarettes to teens via advertisements and product placements in movies. This issue concerns many parents, consumer advocates, and academic researchers who have suggested that exposure to cigarette advertising leads youth to view cigarettes as a positive consumption symbol and to be more likely to smoke.[90] A group of 41 members of the U.S. Congress sent a letter to 11 women's magazines (e.g., *Cosmopolitan*, *Glamour*, and *Vogue*) urging the magazines to stop accepting tobacco ads because, according to these Congressional members, young women represent a large proportion of these magazines' readership and that their health is being threatened.[91] (Although the 2009 Family Smoking Prevention and Tobacco Control Act will now give the FDA oversight over tobacco advertising and marketing, specific provisions on product placements in movies and print ads for youth audiences were not included.[92]) Investigators also have found that antismoking campaigns using teen actors and tailored anti-tobacco themes for adolescents (e.g., FACT: Fighting Against Corporate Tobacco) are effective in lowering teenagers' attitudes toward smoking and their likelihood of beginning to smoke or discontinuing once the habit is started.[93] These effects held even when accounting for the prior influence of peer and family smokers and previous experimentation with smoking.

Source: FACT is a program of the Wisconsin Tobacco Prevention and Control Program, Wisconsin Department of Health Services

Targeting Miscellaneous Products Another criticized aspect of children-directed marketing communications is the practice of targeting posters, book covers, free magazines, and other so-called learning tools to children. Disguised as educational materials, these communications often are little more than attempts to persuade schoolchildren to want the promoted products and brands. Critics contend these methods are unethical because they use children's trust in educational materials to hawk merchandise.

There also has been criticism of the marketing of adult-oriented entertainment products to children and teens. The FTC has issued a regular series of reports, titled *Marketing Violent Entertainment to Children*, that admonishes the entertainment industry for targeting children with advertisements for violent films, video games, and music. However, the FTC has called on the entertainment industry to self-regulate and rigorously apply its own codes of conduct, although there are serious concerns that the industry is not as motivated or even capable of cleaning its own house.[94] An editor of *Advertising Age*, a publication widely read by advertising practitioners and a voice of reason in the ad industry, offers the following appropriate conclusion to this discussion:

> *This publication's editors ... almost always side with the advertising industry in preferring self-regulation to government intervention. But self-regulation is a privilege earned with responsible behavior and voluntary restraint. In the marketing of entertainment products to children, marketers have shown little restraint. If they continue to act irresponsibly, they will have invited the regulation they so desperately want to avoid.*[95]

Targeting Economically Disadvantaged Consumers

Makers of alcohol and tobacco products frequently employ billboards and other advertising media in targeting brands to economically disadvantaged consumers. Although billboard advertising of tobacco products is restricted under the Master Settlement Agreement between the federal government and firms in the tobacco industry, and under the Family Smoking Prevention and Tobacco Control Act, in the past billboards advertising tobacco and alcohol were disproportionately more likely to appear in inner-city areas.[96]

Three previous celebrated cases illustrate the concerns.[97] A national uproar ensued when R.J. Reynolds Tobacco Company (RJRT) was preparing to introduce Uptown, a brand of menthol cigarette aimed at African-Americans and planned for test marketing in Philadelphia, where African-Americans make up 40 percent of the population. Because African-Americans have more than a 50 percent higher rate of lung cancer than whites, the product launch incensed many critics, including the U.S. government's Secretary for Health and Human Services. In response to the public outcry, RJRT canceled test marketing, and the brand died.[98]

Following the wake of Uptown's demise, critics challenged another firm, the Heileman Brewing Company, for introducing its PowerMaster brand of high-alcohol malt liquor targeted to inner-city residents—a brand containing 5.9 percent alcohol compared with the 4.5 percent content of other malt liquors.[99] Brewing-industry supporters claimed that rather than being exploitive, PowerMaster and other malt liquors merely meet the demand among African-Americans and Hispanics, who buy the vast majority of malt liquor.[100] Nonetheless, the U.S. Treasury Department's Bureau of Alcohol, Tobacco, and Firearms (ATF), which regulates the brewing and liquor industries, would not permit the Heileman Brewing Company to market malt liquor under the name PowerMaster. The ATF considered the name PowerMaster as promoting the brand's alcoholic content, which violated federal regulations.

The R.J. Reynolds Tobacco Company was again widely criticized when preparing to introduce its Dakota brand of cigarettes to young, economically downscale women. RJRT's plans to test-market Dakota in Houston were squashed when critics created an outcry in response to what was considered to be exploitive marketing.[101]

In summary, the issue is more than "is targeting good or bad." The important ethical issues are concerned not about fulfilling needs and wants, but about when consumer vulnerabilities are exploited.

Ethical Issues in Advertising

The role of advertising in society has been debated for centuries. Advertising ethics is a topic that has commanded the attention of philosophers, practitioners, scholars, and theologians.[102] Even advertising practitioners are mixed in terms of their awareness of and concern for ethical issues in the day-to-day conduct of advertising.[103] The following is a succinct yet eloquent account of why advertising is so fiercely criticized:

> *As the voice of technology, [advertising] is associated with many dissatisfactions of the industrial state. As the voice of mass culture it invites intellectuals' attack. And as the most visible form of capitalism it has served as nothing less than a lightning-rod for social criticism.*[104]

A variety of ethical criticisms have been leveled against advertising. Because the issues are complex, it is impossible to treat each criticism in great detail. Also, it is important to note that there is a difference between one's attitude toward advertising in general and toward specific ads. Thus, the following discussion introduces some illustrative issues with the expectation that each will prompt more in-depth thought and perhaps class discussion.[105]

Advertising Is Untruthful and Deceptive

Roughly two-thirds of Americans think that advertising (in general) is often untruthful.[106] As was discussed previously, deception occurs when an ad claim misleads reasonable consumers and the claim is important enough to likely to affect the consumer's conduct (i.e., it is "material"). By this definition, it is undeniable that some advertising is deceptive—the existence of governmental regulation and industry self-regulation attests to this fact. It would be naïve, however, to assume that *most* advertising is deceptive.

Nonetheless, when advertising is deceptive, consumers may eventually be harmed and even competitors of deception perpetrators may be negatively affected because consumers become increasingly skeptical and develop diminished trust in the accuracy of subsequent advertising claims.[107] Advertisers of direct-to-consumer (DTC) pharmaceutical products have been scrutinized in recent years due to the magnitude of such advertising and the questionable honesty of some of the claims made for these products. For example, the cholesterol drug Vytorin—well known for its graphic advertising executions that characterized cholesterol as resulting from two sources, food and heredity, and portrayed images of older relatives dressed in apparel reminiscent of high-cholesterol food items—continued to advertise that it is an effective agent for reducing cholesterol even after a large scientific study revealed that Vytorin was ineffective for reducing plaque buildup in the arteries.[108]

Advertising Is Manipulative

The criticism of manipulation asserts that advertising can influence people to do things they would not otherwise do were it not for exposure to advertising. Taken to the extreme, this suggests that advertising is capable of moving people against their free wills. But people, when *consciously aware* that attempts are being made to persuade or influence them, have the cognitive capacity and defenses to resist efforts to motivate them in a direction they wish not to be moved.[109]

However (and it is a big however), there is growing evidence that much human behavior is *not under conscious control*. (This issue is discussed in Chapter 11 in the context of subliminal advertising.) Many of our actions occur virtually automatically (without cognitive intervention), as if we were on autopilot, especially if the action is compatible with our current need state.[110] There also is a limitation on the length of influence, for example, as found with point-of-purchase displays. In sum, advertising practitioners (along with communicators in other aspects of life) may be able to influence or "prime" consumers in very subtle ways.

Advertising Is Offensive and in Bad Taste

Advertising critics contend that advertisements are sometimes insulting to human intelligence, vulgar, and generally offensive to the tastes of many consumers. The critics have in mind such practices as sexual explicitness or innuendo, outlandish humor, and excessive repetition of the same advertisements. Many consumers consider ads for erectile dysfunction drugs (brands such as Cialis and Viagra) as especially offensive, particularly when they appear on programs children view. The American Pediatrics Association has encouraged marketers to restrict such ads to after 10 p.m. so that children do not learn to view sex as a "recreational sport."[111] Undeniably, some advertising might be viewed as disgusting and offensive.[112] Yet, the same might be said for all forms of mass-media presentations (e.g., some network reality programs, political pundits, YouTube clips, etc.).

Advertising Creates and Perpetuates Stereotypes

At the root of this criticism is the contention that advertising tends to portray certain groups in a very narrow and predictable fashion. For example, minorities may have been portrayed disproportionately in working-class roles rather than in the full range of positions they actually occupy; women may have been stereotyped as sex objects; and senior citizens sometimes are characterized as feeble and forgetful. Certainly, at times, advertising *has* been guilty of perpetuating stereotypes, and as noted above, this has occurred at times in network programming and in other form of media as well.

Advertising Persuades People to Buy Things They Do Not Really Need

A frequently cited criticism suggests that advertising causes people to buy items or services they do not need. Yet, this criticism might be viewed as a value-laden judgment. Do you need another pair of shoes? Do you need a college education? Who is to say what you or anyone else needs? Advertising most assuredly influences consumer tastes and encourages people to undertake purchases they may not otherwise make, but is this unethical (e.g., misleading, deceiving, taking advantage of vulnerable consumers)?

Advertising Plays on People's Fears and Insecurities

Some advertisements appeal to the negative consequences of not buying and using certain products—rejection by others, failure to have provided for the family if one should die without proper insurance coverage, not sending a contribution to save starving children in developing countries, and so on. Some advertisers are guilty of influencing consumer behavior by appealing to negative emotions such as fear, guilt, and humiliation. There certainly are self-regulatory protections on these actions for children, via the CARU. Yet, such appeals are quite common in society at large. For example, theologians sometimes threaten that non-believers will go to hell; politicians assert that our fate will be even worse if we vote for their opponent; teachers warn that our futures are in jeopardy if we do not get term papers in on time; and parents intimidate their children on a routine basis using a variety of "fear appeals." Looked at this way, it might be deduced that advertisers are rather innocent by comparison.

A Trade Association's Code of Ethical Standards

In sum, the institution of advertising is certainly not free of criticism, but advertising also reflects society.[113] Yet, responsible advertising practitioners, knowing their practice is particularly susceptible to criticism, have a vested interest in producing legitimate advertising. Accordingly, advertising practitioners typically operate under ethical codes of conduct, such as the American Association of Advertising Agencies' (AAAA) code of ethical standards.

The AAAA is the national trade association that represents advertising agencies in the United States. Its members are responsible for creating approximately three-quarters of the total advertising volume placed nationwide by ad agencies. AAAA's mission is to improve and strengthen the ad agency business, to advocate advertising, to influence public policy, to resist advertising-related legislation that it regards as unwise or unfair, and to work with government regulators to achieve desirable social and civic goals. The AAAA promulgated a code of high ethical standards in 1924 and updated the code in 1990. It is presented here verbatim because it represents, on the one hand, a set of lofty goals for the advertising industry and, on the other, a framework for evaluating whether advertisements these agencies produce meet these high standards.

We, the members of the American Association of Advertising Agencies, in addition to supporting and obeying the laws and legal regulations pertaining to advertising, undertake to extend and broaden the application of high ethical standards. Specifically, we will not knowingly create advertising that contains:

    a. False, or misleading statements or exaggerations, visual or verbal

    b. Testimonials that do not reflect the real opinion of the individual(s) involved

    c. Price claims that are misleading

    d. Claims insufficiently supported or that distort the true meaning or practicable application of statements made by professional or scientific authority

    e. Statements, suggestions, or pictures offensive to public decency or minority segments of the population.

We recognize that there are areas that are subject to honestly different interpretations and judgment. Nevertheless, we agree not to recommend to an advertiser, and to discourage the use of, advertising that is in poor or questionable taste or that is deliberately irritating through aural or visual content or presentation.

Comparative advertising shall be governed by the same standards of truthfulness, claim substantiation, tastefulness, etc., as apply to other types of advertising.

These Standards of Practice of the American Association of Advertising Agencies come from the belief that sound and ethical practice is good business. Confidence and respect are indispensable to success in a business embracing the many intangibles of agency service and involving relationships so dependent upon good faith.

Clear and willful violations of these Standards of Practice may be referred to the Board of Directors of the American Association of Advertising Agencies for appropriate action, including possible annulment of membership as provided by Article IV, Section 5, of the Constitution and By-Laws.[114]

Ethical Issues in Public Relations

Publicity, the aspect of public relations that establishes contacts with the news media, involves disseminating positive information about a company and its products and handling negative publicity when things go wrong. Because publicity is like advertising in that both are forms of mass communications, many of the same ethical issues apply and need not be repeated. The one distinct aspect worthy of separate discussion is the matter of *negative publicity*.

A number of illustrious cases have surfaced in recent years in which companies have been widely criticized for marketing unsafe products. For example, as discussed in Chapter 21, Merck & Co. came under attack after a scientific study revealed that patients taking Vioxx—the arthritis and acute pain medication—for 18 months or longer had double the risk of suffering heart attacks or strokes compared to a control group taking a placebo. The way firms confront negative publicity has important strategic and ethical ramifications. The primary ethical issue concerns whether firms confess to product shortcomings and acknowledge problems or, instead, attempt to cover up the issues.

Ethical Issues in Packaging and Branding

Four aspects of packaging involve ethical issues: (1) label information, (2) packaging graphics, (3) packaging safety, and (4) environmental implications of packaging.[115] *Label information* on packages can mislead consumers by providing exaggerated information or by unethically suggesting that a product contains more of desired attributes (for instance, nutrition) or less of undesired attributes (such as trans fat) than is actually the case. For example, there may be instances in which reduced nutrition ad claims ("lower sodium") may still be considered to be at high absolute levels of the nutrient, yet are taken as absolutely low by consumers without necessary nutrition knowledge.[116]

Packaging graphics may be unethical when the picture on a package is not a true representation of product contents (e.g., as when a children's toy is made to appear much bigger on the package than it actually is). Another case of potentially unethical packaging is when a store brand is packaged so that it looks virtually identical to a well-known national brand. *Unsafe packaging* problems are particularly acute when packaging is not tamperproof and contains dangerous products that are unsafe for children. Packaging information may be misleading and unethical when it suggests environmental benefits that cannot be delivered.[117]

Related to packaging ethics is *brand naming*. A marketer's choice of brand name engages ethical considerations when the chosen name suggests the brand possesses product features that it does not, or will deliver benefits that it cannot. Consider, for example, a hypothetical children's toy carrying the name "PowerGlider." Because this name suggests that the toy (a plastic airplane) has an actual power source such as an engine, consumers would be deceived when purchasing the brand if in fact the only source of power is the person who has to throw it.

Another ethical violation may occur when a company borrows (or steals) a brand name from a better known and established brand. In effect, by using another company's well-known brand for its own product, the violator is capitalizing on the power of *leveraging* as described in Chapter 2. Stealing another company's established brand name is not only unethical but can be illegal according to trademark law. A global form of brand-naming piracy occurs when marketers in one country use brand names for their products that are virtually the same as the names of established brands from another country.

Ethical Issues in Sales Promotions

Ethical considerations are involved with all facets of sales promotions, including manufacturer promotions directed at wholesalers and retailers and to consumers. As is discussed in Chapter 18, retailers have gained considerable bargaining power vis-a-vis manufacturers. One outcome of this power shift has been retailers' increased demands for deals, such as *slotting allowances*, that illustrate the power shift. This practice (thoroughly discussed in Chapter 18) requires manufacturers to pay retailers a per-store fee for their willingness to handle a new stock unit from the manufacturer. Critics of slotting allowances contend this practice represents a form of bribery and is therefore unethical.

Consumer-oriented sales promotions (including practices such as coupons, premium offers, rebates, sweepstakes, and contests) are unethical when the sales promoter offers consumers a reward for their behavior that is never delivered—for example, failing to mail a free premium object or to provide a rebate check. Sweepstakes and contests are potentially unethical when consumers think their odds of winning are much greater than they actually are.[118]

Ethical Issues in Online and Social Media Marketing

Ethical issues abound in the use of online marketing and social media as marcom choices, many of which overlap with the prior, general discussions involving the ethics of advertising and promotions. Aside from the general ethical issues already discussed, invasion of individuals' *privacy* is notable. Because online marketers can collect voluminous information about people's personal characteristics, online shopping behavior, and use of information, it is easy to invade individuals' privacy rights by selling information to other sources and divulging confidential information. It would take us too far afield to get into a detailed discussion of all the issues surrounding privacy invasion, but interested readers are encouraged to examine the articles listed in the following end note.[119] Recently, the FTC charged Google with deceptive privacy practices with their rollout of their social network, Google Buzz. The FTC had received thousands of complaints of public disclosure of e-mail contacts due to a failure of Google to fully allow users to opt-out of this disclosure.[120] Google agreed to implement a comprehensive privacy program as an agreement to the order provisions.

Another ethical violation in online marketing relates to the use of blogs and tweets. For example, companies are unethical when their blogs and tweets include positive testimonials from falsified consumers. Unethical blogging practices also are evidenced when companies pay individuals to write blogs that provide positive evaluations of a company's products. Needless to say, there is great potential for information on blogs to be exaggerated if not outright erroneous.

Fostering Ethical Marketing Communications

Primary responsibility for ethical behavior resides within each of us when we are placed in any of the various marketing communicator roles. In large part, it is a matter of our own personal integrity. Although difficult to define precisely, *integrity* generally means being honest and not acting in a deceptive or purely expedient manner.[121] As a case application of this point, see the *IMC Focus* dealing with a rigged promotion for Frozen Coke.

Businesses can foster ethical or unethical cultures by establishing *ethical core values* to guide marketing communications behavior. Two core values that would go a long way toward enhancing ethical behavior are (1) treating customers with respect, concern, and honesty—the way you would want to be treated or the way you would want your family treated—and (2) acting toward the environment as though it were your own property.[122]

Firms can foster ethical marcom behavior by encouraging their employees to apply each of the following tests when faced with an ethical predicament:[123]

1. Act in a way that you would want others to act toward you (the *Golden Rule test*).
2. Take only actions that an objective panel of your professional colleagues would view as proper (the *professional ethics test*).
3. Always ask, "Would I feel comfortable explaining this action on television to the general public?" (the *TV test*).
4. Consider "What if everyone acted in this manner?" (the *categorical imperative*).

During your business career (and otherwise in life), you undoubtedly will be confronted with times of moral/ethical predicament calling for one decision versus another. Thoughts such as these will enter your mind: "My supervisor wants me to do such and such (fill in the blank), but I am not sure it is the right thing to do." "I could increase my brand's sales and profits if I were to (fill in the blank), but although doing that would be expedient, I am concerned that it is not the right thing to do." When confronted with such dilemmas, stop before you act. Apply the four tests. For example, imagine yourself standing before a television camera and justifying your behavior or considering what if everyone acted in this way. Ask if this is how you would want someone to treat you. Ponder whether other professionals would endorse your behavior. In short, think before you act. Business can be tough.

A Rigged Promotion for Frozen Coke

Imagine that you are a mid-level marketing executive and that you are trying to increase your business with a major customer. You specifically are attempting to convince the customer that it should run a nationwide promotional contest featuring one of your products. This contest, if successful, will increase sales of your product and boost your customer's profits. However, the customer is not convinced the promotion will be effective and wants to conduct a trial run prior to undertaking the promotion nationally. The test will be conducted by comparing sales in a city where the promotion is run (the "test" city) against sales in another city that is not offering the promotion (the "control" city). Initial test results reveal your customer's business does not increase much in the test versus control city. The nationwide promotion is in jeopardy. Your job status is threatened. What should you do?

This hypothetical situation actually occurred several years ago. The protagonists were Coke and its customer, Burger King. Mid-level executives at Coca-Cola Co. pitched the idea to Burger King to run a promotion offering a free Frozen Coke (a product consisting of crushed ice blended with Coke) when customers bought a "value meal" at a Burger King outlet. The argument presented to Burger King was that by offering free Frozen Cokes it could significantly increase customer traffic and thus the sales of value meals.

Burger King's executives were unwilling to commit to an expensive, nationwide promotion until they had some evidence that it would significantly increase sales. They decided to run a test in Richmond, VA (the test city), where free Frozen Cokes would be offered when a value meal was purchased, and compare the number of value meal purchases in Richmond during the test period against value meal volume in Tampa, FL (the control city), where free Frozen Cokes would *not* be provided when consumers purchased value meals. This test involved, in other words, a simple field experiment where the presence (Richmond) or absence (Tampa) of free Frozen Cokes was the experimental treatment.

Unfortunately, initial sales results at the start of the Richmond promotion were disappointing, as value meal volume in Richmond was not much different than in Tampa. Under pressure that Burger King might reject the concept of a nationwide promotion, which would have adverse effects for sales of Frozen Coke, a couple of mid-level Coca-Cola executives created a scheme to boost sales of

value meals in Richmond during the remainder of the test. They hired a freelance consultant and gave him $9,000 to distribute to Boys & Girls Clubs in the Richmond area. The freelancer distributed cash to leaders of these clubs, who were instructed to treat children to value meals at Burger King.

Although this $9,000 in cash contributed less than 1 percent of the total number of value meals purchased in Richmond during the test period, it played a role in demonstrating that sales of value meals in Richmond increased by 6 percent during the test period in comparison to a Tampa sales increase of only 2 percent. On the basis of this differential, Burger King decided to take the promotion nationwide.

Needless to say, the rigged promotion eventually came to Burger King's attention, but only after the fast-food chain had invested in the nationwide Frozen Coke promotion. Coca-Cola's corporate office acknowledged that its employees improperly influenced the test results in Richmond, but the company denied any corporate wrongdoing and laid the blame on the mid-level employees who devised the rigged sales results. Coca-Cola agreed to pay Burger King up to $10 million to compensate it and its franchises for any financial losses.

In explaining his behavior to a supervisor, one of the mid-level executives rationalized that the monetary giveaway was necessary in Richmond to "deseasonalize the data in order to have an accurate measure [of sales response]." His justification, in other words, was that the weather was warmer in Tampa compared to Richmond at the time of the test, which would, according to his logic, have biased business in favor of greater value meal sales in Tampa than Richmond. In short, this executive rationalized what appears to be unethical behavior, but his argument appears to be somewhat self-serving and disingenuous. If he truly thought that seasonal differences would have biased test results, then he should have convinced Burger King's executives to pick a control city where the weather would have been comparable to Richmond's rather than selecting Tampa.

Sources: Christina Cheddar Berk, "Executive at Coke Gives Up His Post in Scandal's Wake," *Wall Street Journal Online*, August 26, 2003, http://online.wsj.com; Chad Terhune and Richard Gibson, "Coke Agrees to Pay Burger King $10 Million to Resolve Dispute," *Wall Street Journal Online*, August 4, 2003, http://online.wsj.com; and Chad Terhune, "How Coke Officials Beefed Up Results of a Marketing Test," *Wall Street Journal Online*, August 20, 2004, http://online.wsj.com.

Living with your own bad decisions (those reflecting anything other than high integrity) can be miserable. Moreover, in subfields of marketing, we often work in smaller circles than one would think, in which "everyone knows everyone."

We conclude this section by presenting the thoughts of a marketing practitioner who has urged his fellow practitioners to conduct their marcom activities in a manner that lifts the human spirit rather than appeals to human nature's most base instincts. He urges marcom practitioners to contemplate four questions before creating and transmitting messages.[124] These questions deserve our careful consideration.

- What lasting impact will this message have on our brand if we continue to communicate it over the long run?
- What lasting impact, if any, will my message have on society at large?
- Does my message appeal to the best in people and attempt to lift the human spirit?
- What response am I trying to elicit and what macro message does that send about our society?

Summary

This chapter examined a variety of issues related to green marketing initiatives, the regulation of marketing communications, and ethical marcom behavior. In the first section, environmental, or *green*, marketing was described, and implications for marketing communications were elaborated. Marketing communicators have responded to society's environmental interests by developing more environmentally friendly packaging and undertaking other communications initiatives. Recommendations provided to marketing communicators for making appropriate environmental claims are to (1) make the claims specific, (2) have claims reflect current disposal options, (3) make the claims substantive, and (4) make supportable claims.

The second section examined the regulation of marcom activities. The regulatory environment was described

with respect to both government regulation and industry self-regulation. The FTC's role was explained in terms of its regulation of deception and unfair practices. False advertising under the Lanham Act, as well as self-regulation by the Council of Better Business Bureaus' National Advertising Division (NAD) and National Advertising Review Board (NARB) were discussed.

The last major section examines implications of ethical (and unethical) marketing communications. The ethics of each of the following marcom activities were discussed: the targeting of marketing communications efforts, advertising, public relations, packaging communications, sales promotions, and online marketing and social media communications. A concluding discussion examined how firms can foster ethical behavior.

Discussion Questions

1. Some consumers are more concerned about the physical environment than others. Provide a specific profile of what in your opinion would be the socioeconomic and psychographic (i.e., lifestyle) characteristics of the "environmentally concerned" consumer.
2. The text mentioned—in the context of discussing packaging ethics—that an ethical infraction may occur when marketers package store brands so that they look virtually identical to well-known national brands. What are your thoughts on this?
3. From your experience, are most green marketing claims legitimate or do they represent green-wash? Support your answer with examples.
4. Are the profit motive and green marketing inherently in conflict?
5. Did Subway cross the exploitation line when it targeted its food products to obese children?
6. What is your opinion regarding the ethics of product placements (e.g., cigarettes, alcohol) in movies targeted to children? Identify the arguments on both sides of the issue, and then present your personal position.
7. Is targeting unethical or just good marketing? Identify the arguments on both sides of the issue, and then present your personal position.
8. What is your view regarding Anheuser-Busch's use in the early-to-mid 1990s of humorous TV commercials that portrayed animated characters Frank and Louie, and an accompanying cast of lizard and frog characters? Is this form of advertising simply a marvelous creative execution, or is it insidious in its potential to encourage children to like the concept of drinking beer, and perhaps Budweiser in particular? (Note: If you do not recall these commercials, ask your professor to provide a description.)

9. Are you in favor of the FDA requiring nutritional labeling, or do you consider such requirements an unnecessary intrusion into the free marketplace? Justify your position on this matter.

10. What is the distinction between a deceptive and an unfair business practice?

11. Give examples of advertising claims that, if found false, probably would be considered material and those that probably would be evaluated as immaterial.

12. What is your opinion of the defense Kraft used in claiming that calcium is an immaterial product attribute?

13. When discussing the criticism that advertising is manipulative, a distinction was made between persuasion efforts of which consumers are cognitively aware and those that fall below their conscious radar screens. First, explain in your own words the distinction between the potential for advertisers to "manipulate" consumers cognitively and unconsciously. Second, express your thoughts about the ethical ramifications of, say, retailers' potential use of in-store advertising to air subliminal messages.

14. What is your view of proposals that would ban all advertising and marketing in elementary schools? Require calorie and nutrition menu boards in fast food restaurants? Tax nutritionally inferior food that only provide added calories?

15. In theory, corrective advertising represents a potentially valuable device for regulating deceptive advertising. In practice, however, corrective advertising must perform a very delicate balancing act by being strong enough without being too forceful. Explain the nature of this dilemma.

16. In the late 1990s, the Distilled Spirits Council of the United States voted to lift its voluntary ban on advertising "hard" liquor on television and radio, a self-imposed ban that had been in effect for nearly a half-century. In your opinion, what are the arguments on both sides of the issue regarding the removal of this ban? If you were an executive the Distilled Spirits Council employed, would you have urged a return to the airways? Is this return to advertising distilled spirits via electronic media unethical or, alternatively, is it a matter of a gutsy business decision by the Distilled Spirits Council that was long overdue?

End Notes

1. For an interesting discussion of the interrelation between ethical issues and regulation, see George M. Zinkhan, "Advertising Ethics: Emerging Methods and Trends," *Journal of Advertising* 23 (September 1994), 1–4.

2. The concept of green marketing has various dimensions beyond this general explanation. For a review of the nuances, see William E. Kilbourne, "Green Advertising: Salvation or Oxymoron?" *Journal of Advertising* 24 (summer 1995), 7–20.

3. Jacquelyn A. Ottman, Edwin R. Stafford, and Cathy L. Hartman, "Avoiding Green Marketing Myopia," *Environment* 48 (no. 5, 2006), 23–36.

4. Mya Frazier, "Going Green? Plant Deep Roots," *Advertising Age*, April 30, 2007, 1, 54–55.

5. Ibid, 54.

6. Subhabrata Bobby Banerjee, Easwar S. Iyer, and Rajiv K. Kashyap, "Corporate Environmentalism: Antecedents and Influence of Industry Type," *Journal of Marketing* 67 (April 2003), 106–22; and Pratima Bansal and Kendall Roth, "Why Companies Go Green: A Model of Ecological Responsiveness," *Academy of Management Journal*, 43 no. 4 (2000), 717–36.

7. "Phase-out of Incandescent Light Bulbs," Wikipedia, http://en.wikipedia.org/wiki/Phase-out_of_incandescent_light_bulbs (accessed July 19, 2011).

8. Nicholas Casey, "New Nike Sneaker Targets Jocks, Greens, Wall Street," *Wall Street Journal*, February 15, 2008, B1.

9. This classification is based on Subhabrata Banerjee, Charles S. Gulas, and Easwar Iyer, "Shades of Green: A Multidimensional Analysis of Environmental Advertising," *Journal of Advertising* 24 (summer 1995), 21–32. For additional discussion of the types of environmental advertising claims and their frequency of use, see Les Carlson, Stephen J. Grove, and Norman Kangun, "A Content Analysis of Environmental Advertising Claims: A Matrix Method Approach," *Journal of Advertising* 22 (September 1993), 27–39.

10. Betsy McKay, "Pepsi to Cut Plastic Used in Bottles," *Wall Street Journal*, May 6, 2008, B2.

11. "Coming around Again," *Marketing News*, May 15, 2008, 4.

12. Michael Bush, "Sustainability and a Smile," *Advertising Age*, February 25, 2008, 1, 25.

13. Betsy Spethmann, "How Would You Do?" *Promo*, February 2007, 18.

14. For review of a report on the short-filling problem, see FTC, "Federal/State Report, "Milk: Does it Measure up?" Finds Widespread "Short-Filling" of Milk and other Products," July 17, 1997, http://www.ftc.gov/opa/1997/07/milk.shtm.

15. "The Blue Angel Eco-label with Brand Character," http://blauer-engel.de/en/blauer_engel/index.php (accessed July 19, 2011).

16. For list, see http://www.rpa100.com/recycled/look-whos-using-the-rpa-100-symbol (accessed June 1, 2008).

17. Based on a Bank of America press release, http://newsroom.bankofamerica.com/index.php?s=press_releases&item=7697 (accessed June 1, 2008).

18. Brian Quinton, "Absolut Zero," *Promo*, April 2008, 10.

19. Stephanie Thompson, "Ben & Jerry's: A Green Pioneer," *Advertising Age*, June 11, 2007, S-8.

20. Carol Krol, "Direct Marketers Not Feeling 'Green,'" *BtoB*, May 5, 2008, 14.

21. Information in this section is adapted from Shira Ovide, "Can Billboard Trade Go Green?" *Wall Street Journal*, September 19, 2007, B2.

22. Published in the *Federal Register* on August 13, 1992 [57 FR 36,363 (1992)]. These guides also available are online at http://www.ftc.gov/bcp/grnrule/green02.htm. See also, Jason W. Gray-Lee, Debra L. Scammon, and Robert N. Mayer, "Review of Legal Standards for Environmental Marketing Claims," *Journal of Public Policy & Marketing* 13 (spring 1994), 155–59.

23. "Federal Trade Commission Proposes Revised 'Green Guides'," *FTC News*, http://www.ftc.gov/opa/2010/10/greenguide.shtm (accessed May 25, 2011).

24. Julie Vergeront (principal author), *The Green Report: Findings and Preliminary Recommendations for Responsible Environmental Advertising* (St. Paul: Minnesota Attorney General's Office, November 1990). The following discussion is a summary of the recommendations in *The Green Report*. The Federal Trade Commission's guidelines are similar in stating that environmental claims should (1) be substantiated; (2) be clear as to whether any assumed environmental advantage applies to the product, the package, or both; (3) avoid being trivial; and (4) if comparisons are made, make clear the basis for the comparisons.

25. Michael B. Mazis, Richard Staelin, Howard Beales, and Steven Salop, "A Framework for Evaluating Consumer Information Regulation," *Journal of Marketing* 45 (winter 1981), 11–21.

26. The following discussion is adapted from Mazis, et al. Note, readers should not be confused with mandatory cost-benefit analyses that occur with major federal regulations, FTC unfairness cases, and FTC trade regulation rules.

27. Alcohol Beverage Labeling Act of 1988, S.R. 2047.

28. For reviews of the warnings and disclosures literature, see J. Craig Andrews, "Warnings and Disclosures" (Chapter 15), in *Evidence-Based Communications of Risks and Benefits: A Users Guide*, Baruch Fischhoff, Noel Brewer, and Julie Downs, eds., Silver Spring, MD: U.S. Food & Drug Administration, August 2011, 149–161; and David W. Stewart and Ingrid M. Martin, "Intended and Unintended Consequences of Warning Messages: A Review and Synthesis of Empirical Research," *Journal of Public Policy & Marketing* 13 (spring 1994), 1–19.

29. Janet R. Hankin, James J. Sloan, and Robert J. Sokol, "The Modest Impact of the Alcohol Beverage Warning Label on Drinking Pregnancy among a Sample of African-American Women," *Journal of Public Policy & Marketing* 17 (spring 1998), 61–69.

30. "Required Warnings for Cigarette Packages and Advertisements," *Federal Register*, June 22, 2011, 36705.

31. Ibid, 36705, 36708.

32. Ibid, 36708.

33. Ibid, 36705.

34. Ross D. Petty, "Advertising Law in the United States and European Union," *Journal of Public Policy & Marketing* 16 (spring 1997), 2–13.

35. "FTC Deception Policy Statement," Letter from James C. Miller III (former) Chairman, Federal Trade Commission to the Honorable John D. Dingle, Chairman, Committee on Energy and Commerce, U.S. House of Representatives, October 14, 1983, 4; also appended to *Cliffdale Associates, Inc., FTC Decisions*, 103 (1984), 110–202.

36. "FTC Deception Policy Statement," 1–19. For a thorough discussion of these elements and other matters surrounding FTC deception policy, see Gary T. Ford and John E. Calfee, "Recent Developments in FTC Policy on Deception," *Journal of Marketing* 50 (July 1986), 82–103.

37. For discussion regarding ad copy test guidelines for FTC deception cases, see Thomas J. Maronick, "Copy Tests in FTC Deception Cases: Guidelines for Researchers," *Journal of Advertising Research*, 31 (December 1991), 9–17; and J. Craig Andrews and Thomas J. Maronick, "Advertising Research Issues from *FTC Versus Stouffer Foods Corporation*," *Journal of Public Policy & Marketing*, 14 (fall 1995), 301–309.

38. Public copy of a letter dated October 14, 1983, from FTC Chairman James C. Miller III to Senator Bob Packwood, Chairman of Senate Committee on Commerce, Science, and Transportation.

39. This information is based on Jacob Jacoby and George J. Szybillo, "Consumer Research in FTC Versus Kraft (1991): A Case of Heads We Win, Tails You Lose?" *Journal of Public Policy & Marketing* 14 (spring 1995), 2.

40. Ruling of the Federal Trade Commission, Docket No. 9208, January 30, 1991.

41. Jef I. Richards and Ivan L. Preston, "Proving and Disproving Materiality of Deceptive Advertising Claims," *Journal of Public Policy & Marketing* 11 (fall 1992), 45–56; Jacoby and Szybillo, "Consumer Research in FTC Versus Kraft," 1–14; David W. Stewart, "Deception, Materiality, and Survey Research: Some Lessons from Kraft,"

Journal of Public Policy & Marketing 14 (spring 1995), 15–28; and Seymour Sudman "When Experts Disagree: Comments on the Articles by Jacoby and Szybillo and Stewart," *Journal of Public Policy & Marketing* 14 (spring 1995), 29–34.

42. Ross D. Petty and J. Craig Andrews, "Covert Marketing Unmasked: A Legal and Regulatory Guide for Practices That Mask Marketing Messages," *Journal of Public Policy & Marketing* 27 (spring 2008), 7–18.

43. Ibid.

44. See ibid., p. 8, for a typology of six forms of masked marcom messages.

45. Dorothy Cohen, "Unfairness in Advertising Revisited," *Journal of Marketing* 46 (winter 2008), 8.

46. Christy Fisher, "How Congress Broke Unfair Ad Impasse," *Advertising Age*, August 22, 1994, 34.

47. *AMF, Inc.*, FTC file no. 782-3025, (consent agreement), July 9, 1979.

48. For further discussion see Dorothy Cohen, "The FTC's Advertising Substantiation Program," *Journal of Marketing*, 44 (winter 1980), 26–35; and Debra L. Scammon and Richard J. Semenik, "The FTC's 'Reasonable Basis' for Substantiation of Advertising: Expanded Standards and Implications," *Journal of Advertising*, 12 (1) (1983), 4–11.

49. "FTC Approves Final Order Settling Charges that Dannon Made Deceptive Claims for Activia Yogurt and DanActive Dairy Drink," *FTC News*, February 4, 2011, http://www.ftc.gov/opa/2011/02/dannon.shtm.

50. "KFC's Claims That Fried Chicken Is a Way to 'Eat Better' Don't Fly," *FTC News*, June 2004, http://www.ftc.gov/opa/2004/06/kfccorp.shtm.

51. Cohen, "Unfairness in Advertising Revisited," 74.

52. "Children's Online Privacy," Bureau of Consumer Protection Business Center, Federal Trade Commission, http://business.ftc.gov/privacy-and-security/children's-online-privacy (accessed July 19, 2011).

53. J. Howard Beales III, "The FTC's Use of Unfairness Authority: It's Rise, Fall, and Resurrection," *Journal of Public Policy and Marketing* 22 (fall 2003), 192–200.

54. Ibid.

55. The following is based on the excellent review article by William L. Wilkie, Dennis L. McNeill, and Michael B. Mazis, "Marketing's 'Scarlet Letter': The Theory and Practice of Corrective Advertising," *Journal of Marketing* 48 (spring 1984), 11. See also Gardner and Leonard, "Research in Deceptive and Corrective Advertising."

56. See Michael B. Mazis, "FTC v. Novartis: The Return of Corrective Advertising?" *Journal of Public Policy & Marketing* 20 (spring 2001), 114–22; and Bruce Ingersoll, "FTC Orders Novartis to Run Ads to Correct 'Misbeliefs' about Pill," *Wall Street Journal Online*, May 28, 1999, http://online.wsj.com.

57. A study evaluating the effects of a corrective advertising order against STP oil additive determined that corrective advertising action in this case worked as intended: False beliefs were corrected without injuring the product category or consumers' overall perceptions of the STP Corporation. See Kenneth L. Bernhardt, Thomas C. Kinnear, and Michael B. Mazis, "A Field Study of Corrective Advertising Effectiveness," *Journal of Public Policy & Marketing* 5 (1986), 146–62. This article and the one by Mazis in the previous endnote are important reading for anyone interested in learning more about corrective advertising.

58. J. Craig Andrews, Scot Burton, and Jeremy Kees, "Is Simpler Always Better? Consumer Evaluations of Front-of-Package Nutrition Symbols," *Journal of Public Policy & Marketing* 30 (fall 2011), 175–190.

59. "Warning Letter," regarding Yaz, NDA #21-676, 21–873, 22–045, to Bayer Healthcare Pharmaceuticals, Inc., U.S. Food & Drug Administration, October 3, 2008, 1–7; and Natasha Singer, "A Birth Control Pill That Promised Too Much," *New York Times*, February 10, 2009, http://www.nytimes.com/2009/02/11/business/11pill.html?_r=1& ref=business& pagewanted=print.

60. Dorothy Cohen, *Legal Issues in Marketing Decision Making*, Cincinnati, OH: South-Western, 1995, 173.

61. "Pizza Hut Inc. v. Papa John's International, Inc., Papa John's USA, Inc.," U.S. Court of Appeals, 5th Circuit, file no. 00-10071, September 19, 2000, 1–38.

62. Apryl Duncan, "Better Pizza? Bigger Lawsuit," About.com Advertising, http://advertising.about.com/od/foodrelatedadnews/a/papajohns.htm?p=1 (accessed May 27, 2010).

63. "Pizza Hut Inc. v. Papa John's International, Inc., Papa John's USA, Inc.," 33.

64. Andrew J. Strenio, Jr., "The FTC in 1988: Phoenix or Finis?" *Journal of Public Policy & Marketing* 7 (1988), 21–39.

65. Jean J. Boddewyn, "Advertising Self-Regulation: True Purpose and Limits," *Journal of Advertising* 18, no. 2 (1989), 19–27.

66. Jean J. Boddewyn, "Advertising Self-Regulation: Private Government and Agent of Public Policy," *Journal of Public Policy & Marketing* 4 (1985), 129–41.

67. Avery M. Abernethy and Jan LeBlanc Wicks, "Self-regulation and Television Advertising: A Replication and Extension," *Journal of Advertising Research* 41 (May/June 2001), 31–37; Avery M. Abernethy, "Advertising Clearance Practices of Radio Stations: A Model of Advertising Self-Regulation," *Journal of Advertising* 22 (September 1993), 15–26; Herbert J. Rotfeld, Avery M. Abernethy, and Patrick R. Parsons, "Self-Regulation and Television Advertising," *Journal of Advertising* 19

(December 1990), 18–26; and Eric J. Zanot, "Unseen but Effective Advertising Regulation: The Clearance Process," *Journal of Advertising* 14, no. 4 (1985), 44–51, 59.

68. Eric J. Zanot, "A Review of Eight Years of NARB Casework: Guidelines and Parameters of Deceptive Advertising," *Journal of Advertising* 9, no. 4 (1980), 20.

69. "Iron Kids Bread," *NAD Case Reports*, August 1994, 90–91.

70. "Tyson Foods Inc.," *NAD Case Reports*, May 4, 2010, Case #5172.

71. "Coastal Contacts, Inc.," *NAD Case Reports*, October 25, 2011, Case #5387.

72. Jim Guthrie, "Give Self-regulation a Hand," *Advertising Age*, October 15, 2001, 16.

73. Carolyn Y. Yoo, "Personally Responsible," *BizEd*, May/June 2003, 24.

74. O.C. Ferrell and Larry G. Gresham, "A Contingency Framework for Understanding Ethical Decision Making in Marketing," *Journal of Marketing* 49 (summer 1985), 87–96.

75. A provocative and informative discourse on the issue of consumer vulnerability is presented in N. Craig Smith and Elizabeth Cooper-Martin, "Ethics and Target Marketing: The Role of Product Harm and Consumer Vulnerability," *Journal of Marketing* 61 (July 1997), 1–20.

76. Sara Schaefer Munoz, "Nagging Issue: Pitching Junk to Kids," *Wall Street Journal Online*, November 11, 2003, http://online.wsj.com; for more specific categories (e.g., $1.6 billion on food and beverages to kids), see *Marketing Food to Children and Adolescents: A Review of Industry Expenditures, Activities, and Self-Regulation: A Report to Congress*, Federal Trade Commission, July 2008, 1–120.

77. For those who are interested in learning more about how children and teenagers are influenced by marcom messages, the following articles, all in the same issue of one journal, are must reading: Louis J. Moses and Dare A. Baldwin, "What Can the Study of Cognitive Development Reveal about Children's Ability to Appreciate and Cope with Advertising?" *Journal of Public Policy & Marketing* 24 (fall 2005), 186–201; Cornelia Pechmann, Linda Levine, Sandra Loughlin, and Frances Leslie, "Impulsive and Self-Conscious: Adolescents' Vulnerability to Advertising and Promotion," *Journal of Public Policy & Marketing* 24 (fall 2005), 202–21; and Peter Wright, Marian Friestad, and David M. Boush, "The Development of Marketplace Persuasion Knowledge in Children, Adolescents, and Young Adults," *Journal of Public Policy & Marketing* 24 (fall 2005), 222–33.

78. Laura Bird, "Gatorade for Kids," *Adweek's Marketing Week*, July 15, 1991, 4–5.

79. "Obesity Rates Among All Children in the U.S.," Centers for Disease Control and Prevention, http://www.cdc.gov/obesity/childhood/data.html (accessed July 15, 2011).

80. Joseph Pereira and Audrey Warren, "Coming Up Next …," *Wall Street Journal Online*, March 15, 2004, http://online.wsj.com.

81. Stephanie Thompson, "Campbell Aims Squarely at Kids with Push for Pastas and Soups," *Advertising Age*, May 31, 2004, 62.

82. Janet Whitman, "Subway Weighs Television Ads on Childhood Obesity," *Wall Street Journal Online*, June 16, 2004, http://online.wsj.com; and Bob Garfield, "Subway Walks Line between Wellness, Child Exploitation," *Advertising Age*, July 26, 2004, 29.

83. "U.S. Food Companies to Restrict Advertising Aimed at Children," *Wall Street Journal Online*, July 18, 2007, http://online.wsj.com; and Andrew Martin, "Kellogg to Phase Out Some Food Ads to Children," *New York Times*, June 14, 2007, http://www.nytimes.com.

84. Eben Shapiro, "Molson Ice Ads Raise Hackles of Regulators," *Wall Street Journal*, February 25, 1994, B1, B10.

85. Guideline 8 in the Industry Advertising Code. Published in an undated pamphlet distributed by the Department of Consumer Awareness and Education, Anheuser-Busch, Inc., St. Louis, MO.

86. Brian Steinberg and Suzanne Vranica, "Brewers Are Urged to Tone Down Ads," *Wall Street Journal Online*, June 23, 2003, http://online.wsj.com.

87. "Alcohol Radio Ads Still Air on Programs with Teen Audiences," *Wall Street Journal Online*, September 1, 2006, http://online.wsj.com.

88. Christopher Lawton, "Lawsuits Allege Alcohol Makers Target Youths," *Wall Street Journal Online*, February 5, 2004, http://online.wsj.com.

89. Stefan Fatsis and Christopher Lawton, "Beer Ads on TV, College Sports: Explosive Mix?" *Wall Street Journal Online*, November 12, 2003, http://online.wsj.com.

90. See, for example, Lawrence C. Soley, "Smoke-filled Rooms and Research: A Response to Jean J. Boddewyn's Commentary," *Journal of Advertising* 22 (December 1993), 108–109; Richard W. Pollay, "Pertinent Research and Impertinent Opinions: Our Contributions to the Cigarette Advertising Policy Debate," *Journal of Advertising* 22 (December 1993), 110–17; Joel B. Cohen "Playing to Win: Marketing and Public Policy at Odds over Joe Camel," *Journal of Public Policy & Marketing*, 19 (fall 2000), 155–67; Kathleen J. Kelly, Michael D. Slater, and David Karan, "Image Advertisements' Influence on Adolescents' Perceptions of the Desirability of Beer and Cigarettes," *Journal of Public Policy & Marketing* 21 (fall 2002), 295–304; Cornelia

Pechmann and Susan J. Knight, "An Experimental Investigation of the Joint Effects of Advertising and Peers on Adolescents' Beliefs and Intentions about Cigarette Consumption," *Journal of Consumer Research* 29 (June 2002), 5–19; Marvin E. Goldberg, "American Media and the Smoking-related Behaviors of Asian Adolescents," *Journal of Advertising Research* 43 (March 2003), 2–11; and Marvin E. Goldberg, "Correlation, Causation, and Smoking Initiation among Youths," *Journal of Advertising Research* 43 (December 2003), 431–40.

91. "Women's Magazines Are Urged to Stop Accepting Tobacco Ads," *Wall Street Journal Online*, June 6, 2007, http://online.wsj.com.

92. *Family Smoking Prevention and Tobacco Control Act*, HR 1256, June 22, 2009, 1–86.

93. J. Craig Andrews, Richard G. Netemeyer, Scot Burton, D. Paul Moberg, and Ann Christiansen, "Understanding Adolescent Intentions to Smoke: An Examination of Relationships among Social Influence, Prior Trial Behavior, and Antitobacco Campaign Advertising," *Journal of Marketing* 68 (July 2004), 110–23.

94. Ira Teinowitz, "Filmmakers: Give Ad-practice Shifts a Chance to Work," *Advertising Age*, October 2, 2000, 6; David Finnigan, "Pounding the Kid Trail," *Brandweek*, October 9, 2000, 32–38; and Betsy Spethmann, "Now Showing: Federal Scrutiny," *Promo*, November 2000, 17.

95. Scott Donaton, "Why the Kids Marketing Fuss? Here's Why Parents Are Angry," *Advertising Age*, October 16, 2000, 48.

96. "Fighting Ads in the Inner City," *Newsweek*, February 5, 1990, 46.

97. For further reading about these and other controversial cases, see Smith and Cooper-Martin, "Ethics and Target Marketing."

98. Dan Koeppel, "Insensitivity to a Market's Concerns," *Adweek's Marketing Week*, November 5, 1990, 25; "A 'Black' Cigarette Goes Up in Smoke," *Newsweek*, January 29, 1990, 54; and "RJR Cancels Test of 'Black' Cigarette," *Marketing News*, February 19, 1990, 10.

99. Laura Bird, "An 'Uptown' Remake Called Power-Master," *Adweek's Marketing Week*, July 1, 1991, 7.

100. "Fighting Ads in the Inner City."

101. For more discussion of this case, see Smith and Cooper-Martin, "Ethics and Target Marketing."

102. Paul W. Farris and Mark S. Albion, "The Impact of Advertising on the Price of Consumer Products," *Journal of Marketing* 44 (Summer 1980), 18.

103. For an insightful treatment of practitioners' views of advertising ethics, see Minette E. Drumwright and Patrick E. Murphy, "How Advertising Practitioners View Ethics," *Journal of Advertising* 33 (summer 2004), 7–24. For additional coverage of practitioners' views on advertising morality, see Jeffrey J. Maciejewski, "From Bikinis to Basal Cell Carcinoma: Advertising Practitioners' Moral Assessments of Advertising Content," *Journal of Current Issues and Research in Advertising* 27 (fall 2005), 107–15.

104. Ronald Berman, "Advertising and Social Change," *Advertising Age*, April 30, 1980, 24.

105. The interested reader is encouraged to review the following three articles for an extremely thorough, insightful, and provocative debate over the social and ethical role of advertising in American society. Richard W. Pollay, "The Distorted Mirror: Reflections on the Unintended Consequences of Advertising," *Journal of Marketing* 50 (April 1986), 18–36; Morris B. Holbrook, "Mirror, Mirror on the Wall, What's Unfair in the Reflections of Advertising?" *Journal of Marketing* 51 (July 1987), 95–103; and Richard W. Pollay, "On the Value of Reflections on the Values in 'The Distorted Mirror,'" *Journal of Marketing* (July 1987), 104–109. Pollay and Holbrook present alternative views of whether advertising is a "mirror" that merely reflects societal attitudes and values or a "distorted mirror" that is responsible for unintended and undesirable social consequences.

106. John E. Calfee and Debra Jones Ringold, "The 70% Majority: Enduring Consumer Beliefs about Advertising," *Journal of Public Policy & Marketing* 13 (fall 1994), 228–38.

107. Peter R. Darke and Robin J. B. Ritchie, "The Defensive Consumer: Advertising Deception, Defensive Processing, and Distrust," *Journal of Marketing Research* 44 (February 2007), 114–27.

108. Rich Thomaselli, "Vytorin Ad Shame Taints Entire Marketing Industry," *Advertising Age*, January 21, 2008, 1, 33.

109. Marian Friestad and Peter Wright, "The Persuasion Knowledge Model: How People Cope with Persuasion Attempts," *Journal of Consumer Research* 21 (June 1994), 1–31; and Marian Friestad and Peter Wright, "Persuasion Knowledge: Lay People's and Researchers' Beliefs about the Psychology of Advertising," *Journal of Consumer Research* 22 (June 1995), 62–74.

110. For an accessible treatment on the issue of automatic, or noncontrolled motivation and behavior, see John A. Bargh, "Losing Consciousness: Automatic Influences on Consumer Judgment, Behavior, and Motivation," *Journal of Consumer Research* 29 (September 2002), 280–285. See also John A. Bargh and Tanya L. Chartrand, "The Unbearable Automaticity of Being," *American Psychologist* 54 (July 1999), 462–479; Johan C. Karremans, Wolfgang Stroebe, and Jasper Claus, "Beyond Vicary's Fantasies: The Impact of Subliminal Priming and

Brand Choice," *Journal of Experimental Social Psychology* 42 (November 2006), 792–798.

111. Avery Johnson, "New Impotence Ads Draw Fire-Just Like Old Ones," *Wall Street Journal*, February 16, 2007, B1.

112. Terence A. Shimp and Elnora W. Stuart, "The Role of Disgust as an Emotional Mediator of Advertising Effects," *Journal of Advertising* 33 (spring 2004), 43–54.

113. Stephen B. Castleberry, Warren French, and Barbara A. Carlin, "The Ethical Framework of Advertising and Marketing Research Practitioners: A Moral Development Perspective," *Journal of Advertising* 22 (June 1993), 39–46. Indirectly, a similar argument is made in the following source that intimates that dishonesty is widespread in society: Nina Mazar and Dan Ariely, "Dishonesty in Everyday Life and Its Policy Implications," *Journal of Public Policy & Marketing* 25 (spring 2006), 117–26.

114. American Association of Advertising Agencies, "Code of Ethical Standards," http://www.aaaa.org/about/association/Pages/standardsofpractice.aspx (accessed July 19, 2011). See also the new ethics code from the Institute for Advertising Ethics, http://adage.com/article/news/advertisers-agencies-ethics-code-review/149464 (accessed July 19, 2011).

115. These issues were identified by Paula Fitzgerald Bone and Robert J. Corey, "Ethical Dilemmas in Packaging: Beliefs of Packaging Professionals," *Journal of Macro marketing* 12 (No. 1, 1992), 45–54. The following discussion is guided by this paper. The authors identified a fifth ethical aspect of packaging (the relationship between a package and a product's price) that is not discussed here.

116. J. Craig Andrews, Scot Burton, and Richard G. Netemeyer, "Are Some Comparative Nutrition Claims Misleading? The Role of Nutrition Knowledge, Ad Claim Type, and Disclosure Conditions," *Journal of Advertising*, 20 (fall 2000), 29–42.

117. For an interesting discussion of perceptual differences among packaging professionals, brand managers, and consumers on the issue of packaging ethics, see Paula Fitzgerald Bone and Robert J. Corey, "Packaging Ethics: Perceptual Differences among Packaging Professionals, Brand Managers and Ethically-interested Consumers," *Journal of Business Ethics* 24 (April 2000), 199–213.

118. For an insightful discussion of sales promotion practices and related consumer psychology that result in exaggerated expectations of winning, see James C. Ward and Ronald Paul Hill, "Designing Effective Promotional Games: Opportunities and Problems," *Journal of Advertising* 20 (September 1991), 69–81.

119. A special issue of the *Journal of Public Policy & Marketing* 19 (spring 2000) is devoted to privacy and ethical issues in online marketing. See the articles on pages 1 through 73 by the following authors: George R. Milne; Eve M. Caudill and Patrick E. Murphy; Mary J. Culnan; Joseph Phelps, Glen Nowak and Elizabeth Ferrell; Ross D. Petty; Anthony D. Miyazaki and Ana Fernandez; and Kim Bartel Sheehan and Mariea Grubbs Hoy.

120. "FTC Charges Deceptive Privacy Practices in Google's Rollout of Its Buzz Social Network," *FTC News*, March 30, 2011, http://www.ftc.gov/opa/2011/03/google.shtm.

121. Jeffrey P. Davidson, "The Elusive Nature of Integrity: People Know It When They See It, but Can't Explain It," *Marketing News*, November 7, 1986, 24.

122. Donald P. Robin and R. Eric Reidenbach, "Social Responsibility, Ethics, and Marketing Strategy: Closing the Gap between Concept and Application," *Journal of Marketing* 51 (January 1987), 44–58. In this context, two additional articles that discuss ethical responsibilities of marketing practitioners are Rhoda H. Karpatkin, "Toward a Fair and Just Marketplace for All Consumers: The Responsibilities of Marketing Professionals," *Journal of Public Policy & Marketing* 18 (spring 1999), 118–22; and Gene R. Laczniak, "Distributive Justice, Catholic Social Teaching, and the Moral Responsibility of Marketers," *Journal of Public Policy & Marketing* 18 (spring 1999), 125–29.

123. Based on Gene R. Laczniak and Patrick E. Murphy, "Fostering Ethical Marketing Decisions," *Journal of Business Ethics* 10 (1991), 259–71.

124. Dave Dolak, "Let's Lift the Human Spirit," *Brandweek*, April 28, 2003, 30.

2

PART

© Jorg Hackemann/Shuttersto

CHAPTERS

Fundamental IMC Planning Background and Decisions

Part 2 builds a foundation for understanding the nature and function of marketing communications and for marcom planning by providing practical and theoretical overviews of four fundamental marcom areas: (1) segmentation, targeting, and positioning; (2) communications and consumer behavior; (3) marcom persuasion; and (4) objective setting and budgeting. *Chapter 5* introduces segmentation, targeting, and positioning as key elements in effective marketing communications. The chapter focuses on the market segmentation process and four sets of audience-defining characteristics that influence how people respond to marcom programs: behaviorgraphics, psychographics, demographics, and geodemographics.

 Chapter 6 provides further foundation for targeting activities by examining both the communications process and essentials of consumer behavior. Consumer behavior is discussed from two different perspectives: (1) the consumer processing model (with rational, logical decisions) and (2) the hedonic/experiential model (with behavior driven by fun, fantasies, and feelings). Particular detail is applied to describing consumer information processing steps, including exposure, attention, comprehension, and learning of marcom messages.

 Chapter 7 extends the overview of communications and consumer behavior by discussing the role of persuasion (i.e., attitude change) in IMC. Special attention will be devoted to the major elements in persuasion to consider in marcom campaigns, as well as two important models of persuasion processes applied to marcom: (1) the Elaboration Likelihood Model and its motivation, ability, and opportunity to process elements, and (2) the Theory of Reasoned Action.

 Chapter 8 completes the treatment of fundamental marcom decisions by examining objective setting and budgeting. The importance of setting objectives is initially discussed via the hierarchy of marcom effects explaining how the choice of a marcom objective depends on where in the hierarchy (e.g., awareness or product trial) members of the target audience are located. Requirements for setting suitable marcom objectives are detailed. Then, the issue of whether marcom should be based on sales or presales (communication) objectives is addressed. Four practical budgeting methods conclude the chapter: (1) percentage-of-sales, (2) objective-and-task, (3) competitive parity, and (4) affordability.

Segmentation, Targeting, and Positioning

Positioning and "McBucks": Is McDonald's Becoming Starbucks?

When the name McDonald's comes to mind, most people might think of the golden arches, Ronald McDonald, french fries, Big Macs, and so on. Similarly, when you call to mind the chain of Starbucks stores, you probably think of strong-tasting coffee and expensive specialty drinks such as espressos, lattes, cappuccinos, and mochas. But what is your view of McDonald's now that it is selling specialty coffee drinks (lattes, cappuccinos, etc.), and how do you regard Starbucks now that it offers sandwiches and other non-dessert breakfast items?

Starbucks certainly has experimented in many stores with nontraditional breakfast items—food products typically associated more with fast food chains than with

© ZAK BRIAN/SIPA/Newscom

coffee shops. Perhaps of far greater interest is the move by McDonald's into specialty coffee drinks. McDonald's added specialty coffee drinks to the menus of all of its U.S. stores starting in 2009. Because quick service is and will continue to be mandatory to McDonald's success (in comparison to the more relaxed atmosphere at Starbucks), McDonald's uses push-button machines to produce specialty coffee drinks in a single step. These specialty beverages at McDonald's are priced about 50 cents less than at Starbucks.

Why did McDonald's move in this direction? Starbucks has been hugely successful in pioneering the mass distribution of specialty coffee drinks in the United States and beyond, and now the market is ripe for competitive efforts to capture market share. It is estimated that about 20 percent of Americans drink some form of espresso-based coffee daily, and the market is expected to grow at an annual rate of 4 percent for the next several years. On top of this, the profit margins for specialty coffees are extremely attractive in comparison to most of McDonald's menu items. The incentives were large for McDonald's to move in this direction. The president of McDonald's USA says that the objective is to transform his company into a beverage destination, and that McDonald's convenience, speed of service, and value will make that chain a formidable player in the specialty coffee business.

Initially, one major problem appeared in McDonald's thrust into this new business: Many franchise owners strongly opposed the initiative in view of the estimated $100,000 investment required to cover renovations and the cost of new equipment. Franchisees were concerned that there would be little customer interest in buying specialty coffee drinks at McDonald's and that it would take years for them to recoup their investment. On the other hand, corporate officials estimated that offering specialty coffee products would boost individual stores' annual revenue by approximately $125,000.

So far, it turns out that the specialty coffees are a success for McDonald's. As a Pew Research Center poll taken after installation of the coffees indicates, 43 percent of a national sample of adults would "rather live in a place with more McDonald's" compared to 35 percent who chose to "live in a place with more Starbucks" (the rest had no opinion or did not answer). As noted previously, the profit margin on the coffees is higher than food and McDonald's is undergoing a remake of their stores. This remodeling includes removing the red roofs, focusing on earth tones, eliminating fiberglass/steel chairs, installing more drive-through windows, and adding flat screen TVs and free Wi-Fi.

Since the beginning of 2010, however, Starbucks has been posting sales growth of 7 percent, compared with 3 percent at McDonald's. Yet, total McDonald's sales revenue was $24 billion in 2010 compared to $10.7 billion for Starbucks. Size certainly has its advantages in negotiating prices with suppliers, as McDonald's operating profit margin is 31 percent compared with 13.5 percent at Starbucks. Clearly, the battle is on and only time will tell if the two giant competitors are correct in their positioning strategies.

Sources: Janet Adamy, "McDonald's Is Poised for Lattes," March 1, 2007, *Wall Street Journal Online*; Ashley M. Heher, "Big Mac, Fries and a Latte?" November 19, 2007, *ABC News Online*; Michael Arndt, "The Great Divide: McDonald's vs. Starbucks," *Bloomberg Businessweek*, February 19, 2009, http://www.businessweek.com/the_thread/brandnewday/archives/2009/02/mcdonalds_captu.html; "McDonald's To Look Like Starbucks," *Huffington Post*, May 9, 2011, http://www.huffingtonpost.com/2011/05/09/mcdonalds-look-like-starbucks_n_859342.html?view=print; and Michael Brush, "McDonald's or Starbucks: Who Wins?" *MSN Money*, July 5, 2011, http://money.msn.com/investment-advice/mcdonalds-or-starbucks-who-wins-brush.aspx.

Introduction

This chapter expands the discussion of segmentation, targeting, and positioning that was introduced in Chapter 1. Recall that Chapter 1 provided a model of the marcom process and described various forms of "fundamental" and "implementation" decisions. The section on fundamental decisions concluded with the following mantra:

All marketing communications should be: (1) directed to a particular target market, (2) clearly positioned, (3) created to achieve a specific objective, and (4) undertaken to accomplish the objective within budget constraint.

The market segmentation process and targeting audiences can be considered the starting points for all marcom decisions. Thus, the purpose of this chapter is to describe how marcom practitioners go through the segmentation process and target prospective customers. Segmentation and targeting allow marketing communicators to deliver their messages precisely and prevent wasted coverage on people falling outside the targeted market.

This chapter focuses on four sets of segmentation bases or characteristics that singularly or in combination influence what people consume and how they respond to marketing communications: behavioral segmentation, psychographics, demographics, and geodemographics. Specifically, behavioral segmentation ("behaviorgraphics") represents information about the audience's behavior—in terms of past purchase behavior or online search activity—in a particular product category or set of related categories. Psychographics captures aspects of consumers' psychological makeup and lifestyles including their attitudes, values, and motivations. Demographics reflect measurable population characteristics such as age, income, and ethnicity. And geodemographics is based on demographic characteristics of consumers who reside within geographic clusters such as ZIP code areas and neighborhoods.

Subsequent sections are devoted to all four groups of audience-defining characteristics. First, however, it will be useful to distinguish the four general segmentation bases in terms of two considerations: (1) how easy or difficult it is to obtain data (i.e., *measure*) the characteristic on which a targeting decision is to be made, and (2) how *predictive* the characteristic is of consumer choice behavior. The graph presented in Figure 5.1 lays these two considerations out as the vertical

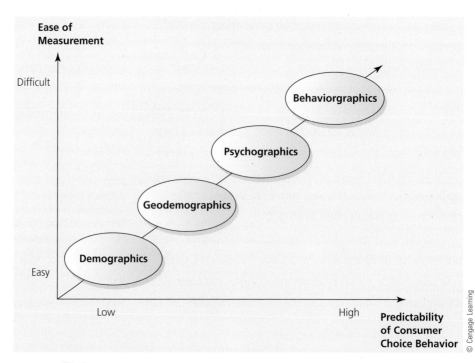

FIGURE 5.1 Classification of Four General Targeting Characteristics

(measurement ease) and horizontal (behavior predictability) dimensions. It thus can be seen that demographic data is relatively easy to obtain but that demographic information is the least predictive of consumer choice behavior. At the other extreme, behavioral segmentation data are relatively more difficult and/or expensive to procure, but are highly predictive of choice behavior. Geodemographic and psychographic data fall between these extremes.

The chapter then concludes with material about brand positioning. A brand's positioning represents the key feature, benefit, or image that it stands for in the target audience's collective mind. Brand communicators and the marketing team in general must identify a *positioning statement*, which is the central idea that encapsulates a brand's meaning and distinctiveness vis-a-vis competitive brands. Segmentation and targeting decisions affect positioning decisions, as they are made with respect to intended targets. Likewise, segmentation and targeting decisions are based on a clear idea of how brands are positioned and distinguished from competitive offering. A good example of such positioning strategy was found in recent brand decisions for McDonald's and Starbucks', described in the chapter opening *Marcom Insight*.

Segments and the Market Segmentation Process

A market segment is a group of customers who share a similar set of needs and wants.[1] For example, a Mountain Dew (www.mountaindew.com) campaign for its new beverage flavors, "Pitch Black" and "Supernova," might focus on young urban males ages 14 to 21 who enjoy skateboarding, alternative or "indie" music, snowboarding, Facebook, and YouTube videos. In general, the process of market segmentation is the act of dividing a market into *distinct groups of customers* who might require separate products and/or marketing mixes.[2] The segmentation process certainly can help with efficiently directing and accounting for marcom resources.

Following a consideration of customer needs and benefits sought, the following represent the *major steps in the market segmentation process*:[3]

1. **Market segmentation:**
   a. Identify bases (e.g., behavior, demographics) to segment the market
   b. Develop profiles of resulting segments
2. **Market targeting:**
   a. Develop measures of segment attractiveness
   b. Select the target segment(s)
3. **Market positioning:**
   a. Develop positioning for each target segment
   b. Develop marketing mix for each target segment

Most of the remaining discussion in this chapter will follow this process, yet will concentrate on the identification of appropriate bases or characteristics to segment the market for marcom programs, as well as the resulting profiles of these segments.

Segmentation Bases: Behaviorial Segmentation

Let us move forward 10 years and imagine that you are a successful entrepreneur who owns a really cool store located in a trendy area. Your establishment appeals primarily to professionals and white-collar workers. From the very start of your business five years ago, you have maintained impeccable records on every customer's purchases. You know precisely when they have purchased, what items they have selected, and how much they have spent. Now let us suppose that you are going to run a sale on a certain line of merchandise and will announce this sale via a combination of postal mail and e-mail. Although you could send postal announcements to all of your customers, you want to be more efficient in your selection so as not to waste money on reaching less viable prospects.

How would you make the targeting decision? In actuality, you have no need to target based on customers' demographic characteristics (say, by selecting just those between the ages of 25 and 39) or their psychographic profiles because you have an even better basis for making the selection decision. That is, you know whether they have made past purchases of the specific merchandise line that you are discounting. Thus, based on customers' past behavior profiles you know which people are likely to be responsive to a sale on items that they have or have not previously purchased. Accordingly, you send sales announcements to all customers who have previously purchased the merchandise in question to increase your return on investment (ROI).

The previous scenario describes the essence of behavior segmentation: i.e., this form of segmentation is based on how people behave (with respect to a product) rather than in terms of their attitudes and lifestyles (psychographics); their age, income, or ethnicity (demographics); or where they live (geodemographics). Yet, sometimes behavioral data does not exist. For example, marketers of truly innovative new products do not have past behavior information on which to identify the best prospective customers. Similarly, many manufacturers of products that are sold in retail outlets in developing countries where optical scanning machines are unavailable have no way of tracking customer purchase behavior. In contrast, mass marketers of CPG items (i.e., consumer package goods) do have detailed records on consumer purchase behavior that are available from firms that track— via optical scanners in supermarkets and other retail outlets—the specific items people purchase and the conditions under which purchases are made (e.g., with or without a coupon). Likewise, most B2B marketers have detailed records on customer purchase behavior and thus are in an ideal situation to target future communications toward "best" prospects based on their past purchasing patterns.

Online Behavioral Targeting

In addition to behavior-based segmentation in conventional retailing contexts, an even more ideal venue for this form of targeting is available online. Websites increasingly are tracking their users' online site-selection behavior so as to enable advertisers to serve targeted ads (e.g., Google AdWords). Ad network companies such as Audience Science and Tacoda (now part of AOL) track online users' surfing behaviors and provide this information to advertisers that wish to target prospective customers based on their online search behavior. (See Figure 5.2 for an illustration of online advertising process flows.) For example, suppose a manufacturer of golfing equipment (a company such as Calloway Golf Company) wishes to reach the best prospects for purchasing its newest driver—a club likely to cost $300 or more. Turning to a company such as Audience Science or Tacoda (AOL), Calloway would request the provider to identify prospective customers who spend a lot of time visiting golf-related websites. With knowledge of these individuals, it is technologically simple by attaching "cookie" files on computers that identify the computer's (i.e., user's) site-selection behavior. Then, ad servers (e.g., Double Click) place ads for Calloway's new driver on sites visited by these "golf surfers"—golf-related or otherwise. The essence of online behavioral targeting is thus a matter of directing online advertisements to just those individuals who most likely are interested—as indicated by their online site-selection behavior—in making a purchase decision for a particular product category.

American Airlines employed the service of Audience Science to identify best prospects for placing online ads. People who visited websites containing travel articles were pinpointed on the assumption that these individuals likely traveled

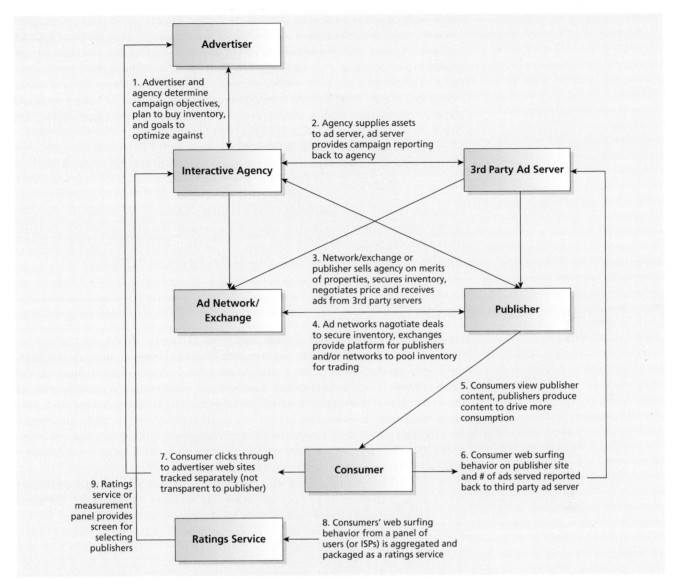

FIGURE 5.2 An Illustration of Online Ad Process Flows

Source: DeSilva + Phillps, LLC, "Online Ad Networks: Monetizing the Long Tail," March 2008, http://www.mediabankers.com/PDF/DeSilva+ Phillips Ad Networks White Paper 3 08.pdf, (accessed July 24, 2011), 1–15. Used with permission.

on business at least occasionally. Ads for American Airlines were then placed on the website of the *Wall Street Journal* (http://online.wsj.com) whenever individuals identified as business travelers visited this website. This behavioral targeting campaign enjoyed considerable success.[4]

To promote Aquafina Alive, a new brand of low-calorie vitamin-enhanced water, Pepsi-Cola employed the services of Tacoda (AOL) to identify the best websites for reaching health-conscious consumers. Tacoda (AOL), which tracks a network of 4,000 sites, followed for a month the traffic to websites featuring healthy lifestyles. Pop-up ads for Aquafina Alive were then placed on the best of these sites for reaching health-conscious people. The results of the ad campaign revealed that in comparison with previous campaigns, Pepsi realized a threefold increase in the number of people clicking on the Aquafina Alive ads.[5]

Privacy Concerns

As typically is the case, technological advances in marketing bring with them increased ability to serve consumers, but also at the risk of invading privacy. Applied in the context of online behavior targeting, Web surfers are increasingly more likely to be served with ads for products that are most relevant to their interests. However, this advantage comes at the expense that companies such as Audience Science and Tacoda (AOL) have access to our online search behavior *without our approval or knowledge*. On the plus side, to be targeted with only those ads that we are most likely interested in is a good thing. On the other side, who wants "Big Brother" overlooking what we do? Would you want someone observing, if they could, every TV program you viewed during the course of a year? Probably not. As always in life, there are trade-offs to make.

Since the mid-1990s, the Federal Trade Commission (FTC) has been involved in the oversight of privacy issues associated with behavioral targeting (also known as "behavioral advertising"). Following hearings on this topic, a set of four behavioral advertising principles was issued by the FTC staff in 2009:[6] (1) transparency and consumer control (i.e., regarding notice, consent, access of information collected), (2) security for data retained, (3) affirmative express consent (opt-in) for material changes to existing privacy promises, and (4) affirmative express consent (opt-in) for sensitive data (i.e., health, financial, children) for behavioral advertising.[7]

Psychographic Segmentation

Historically, marketers based their targeting decisions almost exclusively on their audiences' demographic characteristics—considerations such as the market's age, gender, income level, and race/ethnicity. Sophisticated practitioners eventually realized, however, that demographic information tells only part of the story about consumers' buying preferences, media-usage habits, and purchase behaviors. It is for this reason that marketing communicators also began investigating consumers' psychographic characteristics (attitudes, values, motivations, lifestyles, etc.) to obtain a richer understanding of how best to influence consumers to respond favorably to marcom efforts.

Consider, for example, how you might go about identifying target customers if you were marketing to prospective cruise-line travelers. Demographic information such as age and income undoubtedly would play some role in defining appropriate audiences; that is, you might expect somewhat older individuals (35-plus) and those with average or higher incomes to be prime prospects. But not everyone in the same age or income categories would be equally responsive to, say, advertisements for cruises to the Caribbean. Not all baby boomers and elderly consumers are good candidates for cruises; only those boomers and elders who are members of two particular psychographic segments—"pampered relaxers" and "global explorers"—are prime prospects for cruising.[8]

© Antonio Mo/Taxi/Getty Images

In general, **psychographics** refers to information about consumers' attitudes, values, motivations, and lifestyles as they relate to buying behavior in a particular product category. For example, a psychographic study of sports utility vehicles (SUVs) would assess the types of activities owners of SUVs participate in (e.g., camping and fishing, driving youth sports teams, tailgating at sporting events, hauling lawn care items and do-it-yourself

TABLE 5.1	Illustrative Statements Used in a Banking-Related Psychographic Study

- A local bank is more likely to lend me money.
- Bankers don't know as much as brokers about investments.
- I rely on a banker's advice about managing money.
- My debt is too high.
- I'd never consider an account at a bank that doesn't have an ATM.

- A long-term relationship with a bank is more important than price.
- All banks are the same.
- I prefer a fixed price for all services provided to me.
- I always shop around for the best deal.
- I enjoy going to the lobby to do my banking business.

- There is never enough time to study all the financial alternatives.
- I worry about saving enough money for the future.
- I'd rather invest in mutual funds than CDs.

Source: James W. Peltier, John A. Schibrowsky, Don E. Schultz, and John Davis, "Interactive Psychographics: Cross Selling in the Banking Industry," *Journal of Advertising Research* 42 (March/April 2002), Table 1. Reprinted from the *Journal of Advertising Research*, © 2002, by the Advertising Research Foundation.

building materials) and measure their values and attitudes toward issues related to owning or not owning an SUV (e.g., how much value they place on safety, their views toward the environment, and their need for control). This information would be useful in designing advertising messages and selecting appropriate media outlets.

Customized Psychographic Profiles

Table 5.1 presents a set of illustrative statements that were included in a psychographic study of consumers' banking practices. Survey respondents answered these statements in terms of how strongly they agreed or disagreed with each. Researchers then analyzed the results and, based on responses to these items, were able to categorize the 1,000 respondents into four psychographic groups—"worried traditionalists," "bank loyalists," "secured investors," and "thrifty bankers." It was determined that people classified into these groups differed substantially in terms of various banking behaviors.[9] Subsequent communications aimed at "worried traditionalists" emphasized safety and security, whereas rate of return received greater emphasis in communications targeted to "secured investors."

General Purpose Psychographic Profiles

In addition to psychographic studies that are customized to a client's particular needs, brand managers can purchase "off-the-shelf" psychographic data from services that develop psychographic profiles of people independently of any particular product or service. One of the best known of these is the Futures Company MindBase psychographic segmentation scheme. MindBase consists of 8 general segments and 32 specific subsegments. Table 5.2 summarizes the eight general MindBase segments and labels these with descriptive terms such as "I am Expressive," "I am Rock Steady," and "I am Sophisticated." Direct marketers and other marketing communicators can use these profiles for designing creative advertising campaigns that best match the attitudes, values, and lifestyles of their target audiences.

A second well-known psychographic segmentation scheme is Strategic Business Insights' (SBI) VALS™ system. The U.S. VALS segmentation scheme places American adult consumers into one of eight segments based on psychological characteristics that are related to purchase behavior and several key demographic variables such as age and household income. Japan VALS and U.K. VALS are available for understanding consumers in those countries. (You can determine your segmentation grouping by answering the questions on a survey available at www. strategicbusinessinsights.com/vals/presurvey.shtml.)

Figure 5.3 presents the eight VALS segments. The horizontal dimension in this figure represents individuals' *primary motivations*, whether in terms of their pursuit of ideals, their need for achievement, or drive to self-express. The vertical

TABLE 5.2	**MindBase Segments**

I am Expressive my motto is *Carpe Diem*
I live life to the fullest and I'm not afraid to express my personality. I'm active and engaged and I embody a true "live in the now" attitude with a firm belief that the future is limitless and that I can be or do anything I put my mind to.

I am Driven my motto is *Nothing Ventured, Nothing Gained*
I'm ambitious with a drive to succeed both personally and professionally. I think of myself as self-possessed and resourceful, and I'm determined to show the world I'm on top of my game in all I do, from career ambitions to family, home, and my social life.

I am At Capacity my motto is *Time Is of the Essence*
My life is very busy and I'm looking for control and simplification. I am a demanding and vocal consumer, and I'm looking for convenience, respect, and a helping hand so I can devote more of my time to the important things in life.

I am Rock Steady my motto is *Do the Right Thing*
I think of myself as a positive individual. I draw energy from my home and family. I'm dedicated to living an upstanding life and I listen to my own instincts in terms of making thoughtful decisions in my personal life and in the marketplace.

I am Down to Earth my motto is *Ease on Down the Road*
I'm cruising down life's path at my own pace, seeking satisfaction where I can. I'm looking to enhance my life, stretch myself to try new things, and treat myself through novel experiences and products along the way.

I am Sophisticated my motto is *Sense and Sensibility*
I am intelligent, upstanding, and I have an affinity for the finer things in life. I also have high expectations both for myself and for the companies I give my business. I am dedicated to doing a stellar job at work but I balance my career dedication with a passion for enriching experiences.

I Measure Twice my motto is *An Ounce of Prevention*
I'm a mature individual and I like to think of myself on a life path to actualization and fulfillment. I live a healthy, active life. I'm dedicated to ensuring that my future is both secure and highly rewarding and vitalized.

I am Devoted my motto is *Home Is Where the Heart Is*
I'm traditional and rooted in the comforts of home. Some would say my beliefs are conventional, but they make sense to me. I'm spiritual and content with my life. I like things the way they have always been and I don't need novelty for novelty's sake or newfangled technology.

Source: MindBase Segments © 2005 The Futures Company. Used with permission.

dimension reflects individuals' *resources* as based on their educational accomplishments, income levels, health, energy, and consumerism. For example, as seen in Figure 5.3, "Thinkers" and "Believers" both are motivated by the pursuit of ideals, but "Thinkers" have greater financial resources than "Believers." Similarly, both "Experiencers" and "Makers" are driven by the need for self-expression, but "Makers" have fewer resources than "Experiencers." Each of the eight segments in the VALS framework is now described.[10]

Innovators *are successful, sophisticated, take-charge people with high self-esteem. They have abundant resources, are very active consumers, and have cultivated tastes for upscale, niche products and services.*

Thinkers *are motivated by ideals. They are mature, satisfied, comfortable, and reflective people who value order, knowledge, and responsibility. They tend to be well educated and actively seek out information in the decision-making process. Thinkers are conservative, practical consumers; they look for durability, functionality, and value in the products they buy.*

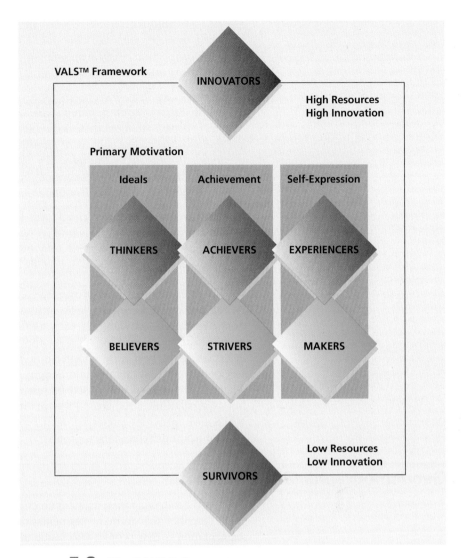

FIGURE **5.3** The 8 VALS Segments

Source: Strategic Business Insights (SBI); http://www.strategicbusinessinsights.com/vals. Reprinted with permission.

Believers, *like Thinkers, are motivated by ideals, yet have fewer resources. As consumers, Believers are predictable; they choose familiar products and established brands. They favor American products and are generally loyal customers.*

Achievers, *who are motivated by the desire for achievement, have goal-oriented lifestyles, and a deep commitment to career and family. Achievers live conventional lives, are politically conservative, and respect authority and the status quo. Image is important to Achievers; they favor established, prestige products and services that demonstrate success to their peers and value time-saving devices.*

Strivers *are trendy and fun loving. They are concerned about the opinions and approval of others. Money defines success for Strivers, who don't have enough of it to meet their desires. They favor stylish products that emulate the purchases of people with greater material wealth. Many see themselves as having a job rather than a career, and a lack of skills and focus often prevents them from moving ahead. As consumers, they are as impulsive as their financial circumstance will allow.*

Experiencers *are motivated by self-expression. As young, enthusiastic, and impulsive consumers, Experiencers quickly become enthusiastic about* *new possibilities but are equally quick to cool. They seek variety and excitement. Experiencers are avid consumers and spend a comparatively high proportion of their income on fashion, entertainment, and socializing. They want to look good and have "cool" stuff.*

Makers, *like Experiencers, are motivated by self-expression—building a house, raising children, fixing a car, or canning vegetables. Makers are practical people who have constructive skills and value self-sufficiency. They live within a traditional context of family, practical work, and physical recreation and have little interest in what lies outside that context. Makers are unimpressed by material possessions other than those with a practical or functional purpose. Because they prefer value to luxury, they buy basic products.*

Survivors *live narrowly focused lives. With few resources with which to cope, they often believe that the world is changing too quickly. They are comfortable with the familiar and are primarily concerned with safety and security. They are loyal to favorite brands, especially if they can purchase them at a discount.*

To determine the best prospective customer target for a product or service on the market, VALS users look at national surveys that have the VALS questionnaire embedded within it such as GFK MRI's Survey of American Consumers or develop custom surveys and include the VALS questionnaire. For determining the best early adopter target for a brand new innovative product or service (e.g., a new automobile design), a series of focus groups could be held where each group is composed of just one VALS type (e.g., one comprised of Innovators, another Achievers) for qualitative insights and preliminary feedback. VALS also provides preferred media of each type as well as the distinctive communication styles of each group.

Geodemographic Segmentation

The word *geodemographic* is a conjunction of *geography* and *demography*, which aptly describes this form of segmentation. The idea underlying geodemographic segmentation is that people who reside in similar areas, such as neighborhoods or postal ZIP code zones, also share demographic and lifestyle similarities and general marketplace behaviors. Several companies have developed services that delineate geographical areas into common groups, or clusters, wherein reside people with similar demographic and lifestyle characteristics. These companies (and their services, in parentheses) include CACI (ACORN), Donnelly Marketing (ClusterPlus), Experian (MOSAIC), Nielsen Claritas (PRIZMNE), and SBI (GeoVALS™). The following section describes Nielsen Claritas' PRIZMNE system of geodemographic profiling. Geodemographic clustering systems have been developed in many countries other than the United States, including Canada, most countries in Western Europe, some African countries, Australia, and Japan.[11]

PRIZMNE is an acronym in which PRIZM stands for Potential Rating Index by ZIP Markets and NE represents the "new evolution" of Nielsen Claritas's original segmentation system. The PRIZMNE classification system delineates every neighborhood in the United States into 1 of 66 clusters based on an analysis of neighborhoods' demographic characteristics. These characteristics include variables such as educational attainment, race/ethnicity, predominant age range, occupational achievement, and type of housing (e.g., owned versus rented). Sophisticated statistical analysis of these demographic characteristics has enabled Nielsen Claritas to identify 66 groups, or clusters, of neighborhoods that share similar demographic profiles. Each cluster is labeled with a colorful and descriptive term. Illustrative names include "Upper Crust," "Big Fish, Small Pond," "Bohemian Mix," "Country Casuals," "White Picket Fences," "Heartlanders," "Suburban Pioneers," and "City Roots." Let us briefly characterize two of these clusters to give you a sense of how the clusters are characterized.[12]

Bohemian Mix captures a collection of young, mobile urbanites who represent the nation's most liberal lifestyles. Bohemian Mixers are a blend of young singles and couples, students and professionals, Hispanics, Asian-Americans, African-Americans, and whites. They are disproportionately likely to be early adopters who are quick to attend the latest movie, frequent the newest nightclub, or adopt the most up-to-date laptop or microbrew. Bohemian Mix households represent nearly 2 percent of all U.S. households. The average occupant of a Bohemian Mix household is less than 35-years-old; has an income of about $57,000; likely is unmarried; rents an apartment or lives in a high-rise; is college educated; and is employed as a professional or in a white-collar position. He or she is not defined by any particular race or ethnicity.

Suburban Pioneers includes neighborhoods where occupants live eclectic lifestyles and includes a mix of young singles, recently divorced, and single parents who have moved into older, inner-ring suburbs. They reside in aging homes and garden-style apartment buildings. The mix of African-American, Latino, and white residents work in mostly blue-collar jobs and live a working-class lifestyle. The average occupant of Suburban Pioneer households is under age 55, earns an income around $33,000, and has a high school education or less. Just over 1 percent of U.S. households fall into this cluster.

Many major marketers use PRIZMNE, Donnelly's ClusterPlus, or another geodemographic clustering service to help them with important marcom decisions. Selecting geographical locales for narrowcasting television advertisements and identifying appropriate households for direct mailings are just two marcom decisions that are facilitated by the availability of geodemographic data. Needless to say, geodemographic data are extremely useful for other marketing purposes such as deciding where to locate new stores.

If you would like to know how the neighborhood in which you grew up or resided would be classified by the PRIZMNE system, enter "You Are Where You Live" into Google or another search engine put in your home neighborhood's five-digit ZIP code. Students in countries outside the United States should go online to identify whether your country has a PRIZM system in place. See the *Global Focus* insert for discussion of geodemographic segmentation and the use of smartphones throughout the world.

Demographic Segmentation

This section examines three major demographic aspects that have considerable relevance for marcom practitioners: (1) the age structure of the population (e.g., children, Generations X and Y, and baby boomers); (2) the changing household composition (e.g., the increase in the number of single-person households); and (3) ethnic population developments. The focus is, necessarily, exclusively on characteristics of the U.S. population. Although the same considerations are relevant elsewhere, the particulars are country specific. Interested readers from countries outside the United States can obtain detailed demographic information from a government agency that is equivalent to the U.S. Census Bureau (www.census.gov), which is a division of the Department of Commerce. (For example, in Spain, see the National Statistics Institute [www.ine.es/en/welcome_en.htm] and in China, the National Bureau of Statistics [www.stats.gov.cn/english]). Before examining features of the U.S. population, it will be helpful to place these topics in context by first examining population growth and geographic distribution of the world and U.S. populations.

At the time of this writing, the total population of human beings on the earth is estimated at approximately 6.95 billion people. (For a daily update on the projected world and U.S. populations, go to www.census.gov/main/www/popclock.

GLOBAL FOCUS

Geodemographics and Smartphone Use: It's Not What It Seems

Surprisingly, the *worldwide* percentage of mobile phone users with smartphones is currently only at 11 percent (2011) and expected to grow slowly to 17 percent by the year 2014. So, although it *seems* as if *everyone* has a smartphone, that is not the case worldwide. In North America, the United States is clearly the leader in smartphones with an estimate of 54 percent penetration by mobile phone users by the year 2014. However, both Italy (67 percent) and other countries in Western Europe (e.g., Spain, 64 percent) are expected to have higher penetration rates than the United States by 2014.

On average, the worldwide smartphone user is likely male, between the ages of 25 and 34, and twice as likely to make greater than $100,000 as nonusers. These statistics fit into the pattern of the "average demographic" for many using smartphones for business. Yet, although mobile Internet users in Spain are also primarily between 25 and 34 years, the youth unemployment rates approach 40 percent. So, here, *geo*demographics are important, as country or culture serve to interact with the common demographic characteristic of age. The morale of this new product adoption example is that if you are trying to use the same demographic globally, you may be missing important nuances in different countries or cultures.

© Oleksiy Maksymenko Photography/Alamy

Sources: "Canadian Mobile Subscriptions to Climb 20% by 2014; Smartphone Ownership and Mobile Ad Spending Also Rise," eMarketer Blog, June 10, 2010, http://www.emarketer.com/Article.aspx?R=1007747 (citing Cisco Systems Report, Feb. 9, 2009); Chris Quick, "With Smartphone Adoption on the Rise, Opportunity for Marketers is Calling," Nielsen Wire, September 15, 2009, http://blog.nielsen.com/nielsenwire/online_mobile/with-smartphone-adoption-on-the-rise-opportunity-for-marketers-is-calling; and "Mobile Advertising landscape in Europe," Experian Panorama, Summer 2011, http://www.experian.it/emea/2011-no05-mobile-advertising-landscape-europe.html.

© Bruce Rolff/Shutterstock.com

html.) The world population is expected to grow to approximately 8 billion people by the year 2025 and 9.5 billion by 2050. Table 5.3 provides a list of the world's 25 largest countries as of 2011; it can be seen that both China and India have populations exceeding 1 billion people with a huge drop-off to the next largest country—the United States—with an estimated population of approximately 311 million. (Please note that projections of population size vary somewhat depending on the source, because estimators use slightly different assumptions about fertility rates, longevity levels, and other factors that enter into the equation.)

A particularly interesting aspect of the U.S. population is the ancestral diversity of its residents. Known as a melting pot, the United States has attracted immigrants from throughout the world, thus making the country an amalgam of people whose ancestors had different cultures and backgrounds. Many immigrants to the United States now arrive from Latin America, Asia, and Eastern Europe, although historically most came from Western European countries. A report from *USA Today* charted the percentage of the U.S. population claiming their ancestral roots. The top ancestry group was German (15.2), followed by Irish (10.8), African-American (8.8), and English (8.7). The fifth group is

TABLE 5.3	World's 25 Largest Countries as of 2011			
Rank Country	**Population**	**Rank Country**	**Population**
1. China	1,336,718,015	14. Vietnam	90,549,390
2. India	1,189,172,906	15. Egypt	82,579,636
3. United States	311,050,977	16. Germany	81,471,834
4. Indonesia	245,613,043	17. Turkey	78,785,548
5. Brazil	203,429,773	18. Iran	77,891,220
6. Pakistan	187,342,721	19. Congo (Kinshasa)	71,712,867
7. Nigeria	165,822,569	20. Thailand	66,720,153
8. Bangladesh	158,570,535	21. France	65,102,719
9. Russia	138,739,892	22. United Kingdom	62,698,362
10. Japan	127,469,543	23. Italy	61,016,804
11. Mexico	113,724,226	24. Burma (Myanmar)	53,999,804
12. Philippines	101,833,938	25. South Africa	49,004,031
13. Ethiopia	90,873,739		

Source: U.S. Census Bureau, International Data Base, http://www.census.gov/ipc/www/idb/rank.php.

simply "American." Interestingly, slightly over 7 percent of the U.S. population now refer to themselves as a part of this "Americans" group, which is up from 5 percent in 1990.[13] In other words, many American residents do not acknowledge any particular ancestry—possibly in part due to pride and also in view of the hybrid character of Americans' ancestries.

The Changing Age Structure

One of the most dramatic features of the American population is its relentless aging. The median age of Americans was 28 in 1970, 30 in 1980, 33 in 1990, 36 in 2000, and is projected to reach 38 by 2025. Table 5.4 presents population figures distributed by age group. The following sections examine major age groupings of the U.S. population and the implications these hold for marcom efforts. Discussion proceeds from the youngest age cohort, preschoolers, to the elderly. First, however, it will be helpful to overview the epochal event—namely, the baby boom—that has affected future generations and the general trend toward an ever-aging population.

Demographers (people who study demographic trends) termed the birth of around 77 million Americans between 1946 and 1964 the **baby-boom** generation. This population-boom period following the end of World War II (in 1945) persisted for nearly two decades. Using 2012 as a point of reference, the youngest person classified as a "boomer" is 48, and the oldest baby boomer is 66. Effects of the baby boom (and subsequent bust) have been manifested in the following major population developments:

1. The original baby boomers created a mini baby boom as they reached child-bearing age. As shown in Table 5.4, the number of children and teenagers in the United States totaled about 84 million in 2010.
2. Due to a low birthrate from the mid-1960s through the 1970s (prior to the time when most baby boomers were of childbearing age), relatively few

TABLE 5.4	Population of the United States by Age Group, as of 2010	
Age	**Population (millions)**	**Percent of Total**
Children and Teens (<20)		
Under 5	21.10	6.8
5–9	20.89	6.7
10–14	20.40	6.6
15–19	21.77	7.0
Total	84.16	27.10
Young Adults (20–34)		
20–24	21.78	7.0
25–29	21.42	6.9
30–34	20.40	6.6
Total	63.60	20.30
Middle Agers (35–54)		
35–39	20.27	6.5
40–44	21.01	6.8
45–49	22.60	7.3
50–54	22.11	7.1
Total	85.99	27.70
Olders (55–64)		
55–59	19.52	6.3
60–64	16.76	5.4
Total	36.28	11.70
Elders (65–74)		
65–69	12.26	4.0
70–74	9.20	3.0
Total	21.46	7.00
The Very Old (75+)		
75–79	7.28	2.3
80–84	5.73	1.8
85+	5.74	1.8
Total	18.75	5.9
Total U.S. Population	310.23	100%

Source: Year Age Groups for the United States, Population Division, U.S. Census Bureau, July 22, 2011.

babies were born. There now are proportionately fewer young adults (ages 20 to 34) than there were in prior generations.

3. The number of "olders" (ages 55 to 64) has increased dramatically, totaling nearly 36 million Americans as of 2010. This maturing of the baby boomers is one of the most significant demographic developments marketers face.

Children and Teenagers

The group of young Americans age 19 and younger has fallen dramatically from 40 percent of the population in 1965 (during the baby-boom heyday) to slightly over 27 percent of the population in 2010. Yet this remains a substantial group, with over 84 million occupants. (See Table 5.4 for specific breakdowns by age group—i.e., under 5, 5 to 9, 10 to 14, and 15 to 19.)

Marketers typically refer to children ages 4 through 12 as "kids" to distinguish this cohort from toddlers and teenagers. Children in this broad grouping either directly spend or influence the spending of billions of dollars worth of purchases each year. Aggregate spending by kids or on behalf of this age group roughly doubled every decade in the 1960s, 1970s, and 1980s, and tripled in the 1990s.

Preschoolers Preschool-age children, age 5 or younger, represent a cohort that has grown substantially in recent years. As part of the "baby boomlet," more babies were born in the United States in 1990 (4.2 million) than at any time since the baby boom peak of 4.3 million babies born in 1957. Marketers of toys, furniture items, clothing, food, and many other products and services routinely appeal to the parents of these children, or, on occasion, directly to the kids themselves.

Elementary-school-age children This group includes children ages 6 to 11. These children directly influence product purchases and indirectly influence what their parents buy. Children in this group influence their parents' choice of clothing and toys and even the brand choice of products such as toothpaste and food products, as Figure 5.4 illustrates. Advertising and other forms of marketing communications aimed at young children, or their families, have increased substantially in recent years. Numerous new products annually hit the shelves to cater to kids' tastes. For example, Mattel, which is known for its line of Hot Wheels toy cars, has extended the brand into the area of marketing skateboards, snowboards, and extreme-sports apparel under the Hot Wheels name. The Walt Disney Company introduced the Disney Dream Desk PC, a computer and monitor combo where the monitor is shaped in the form of Mickey Mouse ears. Marketers are increasingly reaching these young consumers, especially girls, via online virtual communities. The Barbie Girls site, for example, has millions of registered users.[14] (To learn more about how children are socialized as consumers and develop understanding of advertising, the reader is encouraged to examine the articles identified in the following footnote.[15])

Tweens A category of children that marketers have dubbed "tweens"—not quite kids nor yet teenagers—is an age cohort actively involved in consumption. Tweens are usually classified as children between the ages of 8 and 12. Tweens generally have well-formed ideas about what brands they like and dislike and are largely influenced by their peers to own those products and brands that are considered "cool." Retailers such as Limited Too gear much of their marcom efforts at garnering tweens' growing desire for fashionable clothing items (www.limitedtoo.com).

An important study of tweens (including also some teens aged 13 and 14) examined their materialistic values and how these values relate to a variety of demographic variables, purchase-related behaviors, and involvement with advertisements and promotions.[16] A "youth materialism scale" (the YMS) consisted of 10 statements with response options ranging from "disagree a lot" to "agree a lot," including "I'd rather spend time buying things than doing almost anything else"; "I really enjoy going shopping"; and "When you grow up, the more

FIGURE **5.4** An Appeal to Preschoolers' Parents

money you have, the happier you are." A national sample of nearly 1,000 youths between the ages of 9 and 14 produced the following set of findings:

1. Boys are more materialistic than girls.
2. Youths from lower-income households are more materialistic.
3. Highly materialistic youths shop more frequently.
4. Highly materialistic youths show a greater interest in new products.
5. Highly materialistic youths are: (a) more likely to watch TV commercials, (b) more likely to ask parents to buy products because they've seen them on TV, (c) more responsive to celebrity endorsements, (d) more likely to exert pressure on their parents to purchase products, (e) inclined to want more spent on them for Christmas and birthdays, and (f) prone to like school less and to have somewhat poorer grades.

Teenagers Consumers in this age group, totaling in the United States over 25 million 13- to 19-year-olds, have tremendous earning power and considerable influence in making personal and household purchases.[17] Teenagers often are referred to as members of the *Millennial Generation, Millenials*, or *Generation Y* (in contrast to the generation that preceded it—Generation X—born between 1965 and 1981). Although there is no single definition of when people were born into the millennial generation, we will consider Generation Y as the generation of people who were born from 1982 to 1996. Thus, as of 2012, Gen Yers would include all people between the ages of 16 and 30, or more than 60 million Americans. The present discussion focuses just on the subset of teenagers who are members of this millennial generation.

A study by Teenage Research Unlimited, which follows teen trends and attitudes, estimated that American teenagers spend more than $159 billion annually.[18] Teenagers have purchasing influence and power far greater than ever, which accounts for the growth of marcom programs aimed at this group (see Figure 5.5). For example, Hewlett-Packard changed its back-to-school computer marketing strategy from efforts to appeal to parents with price-oriented ads placed in conventional media to the use of humor appeals placed in online media that reach teenagers.[19] For their older counterparts, the *IMC Focus* insert offers one illustration of a creative marcom initiative on Facebook.

FIGURE 5.5 An Appeal to Teenagers

IMC FOCUS

College Students: An Inviting Target for Odor-Fighting Products

Imagine the worst dorm room (or apartment) you ever encountered: A dirty, cluttered, smelly, disgusting space filled with uneaten food items, dirty clothes, empty beer bottles, and perhaps even a pet. Your dorm room (or apartment) is likely much cleaner and less smelly than the hypothetical "disaster" just described. Nonetheless, with immense pressures on your time and the likelihood of two or more students occupying the same room, it is probable that your room is not as clean or as odor-free as you may desire. Like millions of other college students, you are a good candidate for odor-fighting products while living in a dorm, fraternity/sorority building, or off-campus apartment.

One maker of such products, Procter & Gamble, has focused its marketing of Febreze line of products explicitly to college students, who, in the United States alone, number 18 million potential customers! Realizing that reaching college students via conventional mass media such as television and magazines would be too costly and ineffective, P&G

and its advertising agency opted for an online campaign using Facebook and postings to YouTube. An interactive online site (www.facebook.com/pages/Telling-Febreze-WHAT-STINKS/21606803968) was developed and housed within Facebook, and postings were made to YouTube ("I Tell Feberze What Stinks"). The site uses humor designed to appeal to college students, and includes features such as a video game (the "Dank Game") where players armed with a bottle of Febreze take aim at dirty laundry items. In addition to the online site, campus tours (posted to YouTube) were designed in which improvisational actors conducted interactive performances with students and queried them about things in their lives that stink. All in all, this campaign is a clever way to target a previously untapped group of consumers who represent a large and viable audience for Febreze products.

Source: Adapted and updated from Rupal Parekh, "Febreze Sniffs Out New Target: Dorm Dwellers," *Advertising Age*, October 29, 2007, 12.

Young Adults

Scholarly treatment of this age cohort, commonly referred to as Generation X (or Gen X), identifies it as Americans born between 1961 and 1981.[20] However, to avoid overlap with the baby boom generation (1946 to 1964) and Gen Y (1982 to 1996), it is convenient to define this age cohort as people born between 1965 and 1981. As of 2012, Gen X included over 65 million Americans in the age category from 31 to 47. Because Gen Xers were born immediately after the baby boom, which ended in 1964, this group also is referred to as *baby busters*.

One well-known marketing research firm has classified Gen Xers into four groups based on their attitudinal profiles: *Yup & Comers*, Bystanders, Playboys, and Drifters. *Yup & Comers* have the highest levels of education and income and account for approximately 28 percent of Gen Xers. They tend to focus on intangible rewards rather than material wealth and are confident about themselves and their futures. *Bystanders* represent nearly 37 percent of Gen Xers and consist predominantly of female African-Americans and Hispanics. Although their disposable income is relatively low, this subsegment of Gen Xers has a flair for fashion and loves to shop. *Playboys* is a predominantly white, male group accounting for almost 19 percent of the Gen X cohort. Playboys adhere to a "pleasure before duty" lifestyle and are self-absorbed, fun loving, and impulsive. *Drifters* constitute the smallest subset at 16 percent of Gen Xers. They are frustrated with their lives, are among the least educated, seek security and status, and choose brands that offer a sense of belonging and self-esteem.[21] Thus, Gen Xers are not a uniform group.

Middle-Aged and Mature Consumers

Although somewhat arbitrary, we can think of middle age as starting at age 35 and ending at 54, at which point maturity is reached. Actually, there is some disagreement over the dividing point between middle age and maturity. Sometimes a 65-and-over classification is used, because age 65 normally marks retirement. In this text we will use the U.S. Census Bureau's designation, which classifies **mature people** as those who are 55 and older.

Middle-aged As of 2010 there were roughly 86 million Americans between the middle ages of 35 and 54 (see Table 5.4). These individuals represent two generations of people: younger baby boomers and older Gen Xers. The following discussion focuses on baby boomers, or "boomers" for short, because Generation X already has been discussed.

As mentioned previously, the baby-boom generation encompassed approximately 77 million Americans born immediately after World War II in 1946 and through the year 1964. The baby boomers offer tremendous potential for many marketers. What makes boomers such an attractive target group is that they are relatively affluent and thus represent a good general target for second homes, quality vehicles, investments (insurance, real estate, and securities), travel, self-help products, cosmetic surgery, grown-up "toys" like golfing equipment, automobiles with convertible tops (the average convertible buyer is 50 years old),[22] and motorcycles—Harley-Davidson's best customers are middle-aged men, and the typical buyer is an average age of 46.[23] Given their relative affluence, baby boomers also represent an attractive target for a variety of "luxury" goods. For

example, appliance maker Whirlpool appeals to affluent boomers who want the very best appliance quality with a line of items named Whirlpool Gold. And luxury skin-care marketers have experienced revenue growth by introducing high-priced anti-aging products such as L'Oreal's Absolut.

Moreover, just because baby boomers are aging does not necessarily mean they are getting psychologically old or are significantly altering their consumption patterns from a younger age.[24] Rather, there are indications that baby boomers are retaining many of their more youthful consumption habits and, in a sense, are unwilling to change. For example, the rather dramatic increase in purchases of hair-color products by baby boomers reflects this tendency for boomers to prolong youth and to gravitate toward products that support their youth obsession. Manufacturers of health-care items, cosmetics, exercise machines, and food products have actively appealed to baby boomers' passion for remaining in youthful shape. Unfortunately, with their indulgent personalities, financial planning and retirement savings have not been a major priority with many boomers.

Mature Consumers Turning to mature consumers (also called seniors), in 2010 there were nearly 77 million U.S. citizens age 55 or older, representing approximately 25 percent of the total U.S. population. In other words, nearly one quarter of all Americans are senior citizens. Historically, many marketers have ignored mature consumers or have treated this group in unflattering ways by focusing on "repair kit products" such as dentures, laxatives, and arthritis remedies.[25] Not only are mature consumers numerous, but also they are relatively wealthier and more willing to spend as the economy improves. Mature Americans control nearly 70 percent of the net worth of all U.S. households.

People age 65 and older are particularly well off, having the highest discretionary income (i.e., income unburdened by fixed expenses) and the most assets of any age group. The number of people in this 65-plus age category is quite large, totaling about 40 million in 2010, which represents nearly 13 percent of the total population.

A variety of implications accompany marcom efforts directed at mature consumers. In advertising aimed at this group, it is advisable to portray them as active, vital, busy, forward looking, and concerned with looking attractive and being romantic. Advertisers now generally appeal to seniors in a flattering fashion such as using attractive models to represent clothing, cosmetics, and other products that had been the exclusive advertising domain of youthful models.

It is important to reiterate that just because mature consumers share a single commonality (i.e., age 55 or older), they by no means represent a homogeneous market segment. The results of a national mail survey of over 1,000 people age 55 and older led to the classification of seniors into four groups: Healthy Hermits, 38 percent; Ailing Outgoers, 34 percent; Frail Recluses, 15 percent; and Healthy Indulgers, 13 percent.[26] Brief descriptions follow.

- Healthy Hermits, although in good health, are psychologically withdrawn from society. They represent a good market for various services such as tax and legal advice, financial services, home entertainment, and do-it-yourself products. Direct mail, the Internet, and print advertising are the best media for reaching this group.
- Ailing Outgoers are diametrically opposite to Healthy Hermits. Although in poor health, they are socially active, health conscious, and interested in learning to do new things. Home health care, dietary products, planned retirement communities, and entertainment services are some of the products and services this group most desires. They can be reached via the Internet and through select mass media tailored to their positive self-image and active, social lifestyle.
- Frail Recluses are withdrawn socially and are in poor health. Various health and medical products and services, home entertainment, and domestic assistance services (e.g., lawn care) can be successfully marketed to this group via mass media advertising.
- Healthy Indulgers are vigorous, relatively wealthy, and socially active. They are independent and want the most out of life. Mature consumers in this group represent a good market for financial services, leisure/travel entertainment, clothes, luxury goods, and high-tech products and services. They are accessible via in-store promotions, direct mail, specialized print media, and the Internet.

The Ever-Changing American Household

A household represents an independent housing entity, either rental property (e.g., a single room or an apartment) or owned property (a mobile home, condominium, or house). As of 2010, there were approximately 117.5 million households in the United States, of which 78.8 million (67 percent) were family households (i.e., two or more related people occupying the household) and 38.7 million (33 percent) nonfamily households. The average household size across all 117.5 million American households was 2.6 people.[27]

Households are growing in number, shrinking in size, and changing in character. The traditional American family—that is, married couples with children younger than 18—represents less than one-third of all U.S. households, whereas in 1960 such families constituted nearly 50 percent. The number of new households has grown twice as fast as the population, whereas household size has declined. In 1950, families constituted nearly 90 percent of all households, whereas in 2010 fewer than 70 percent were family units.[28]

The changing composition of the American household has tremendous implications for marketing communicators, perhaps especially advertisers. Advertising has to reflect the widening range of living situations that exist. This is particularly true in the case of households with a single occupant. Singles and unrelated couples or friends living together represent a large and ever-growing group. Many advertisers make special appeals to the buying interests and needs of singles. For example, these food ads focus on needs such as ease and speed of preparation, maintenance simplicity, and small serving sizes. Reaching singles requires special media-selection efforts because singles tend not to be big prime-time television viewers but are skewed instead toward the late fringe hours (after 11 PM), are disproportionately more likely than the rest of the population to view cable television, go online, and are disproportionately heavy magazine readers. Many magazines cater to the interests of singles, and TV programs are produced to represent their actual or idealized lifestyles—programs such as *The Office, Gossip Girl, How I Met Your Mother, Two and a Half Men, Lost, Friends*, and *Seinfeld* (these latter three programs remain on TV in syndication but are no longer produced.)

Ethnic Population Developments

America has always been a melting pot. It became even more so in recent decades. The largest ethnic groups in the United States are Hispanics and African-Americans, and ethnic minorities now represent nearly 1 of 3 people in the United States. To initiate our discussion, based the U.S. Census Bureau's last census, the American population as of 2010 is distributed in the following fashion:[29]

White, not Hispanic	63.7%
Hispanic, of any race	16.3
Black, not Hispanic	12.2
Asians	4.7
Others*	3.1
Total	100%

*Includes American Indians, native Hawaiians, Pacific Islanders, native Alaskans, and people of mixed race.

Non-Hispanic whites' share of the U.S. population is projected to decline from 63.7 percent of the total population in 2010 to just 50 percent by 2050.[30] The implication is obvious: marketers and marketing communicators need to devise marcom strategies that meet ethnic groups' unique needs/wants because ethnicity plays an important role in directing consumer behavior.[31] Table 5.5 provides a picture of the

TABLE 5.5 **Ethnic Groups' Population Representation in the United States, 2000–2050 (in millions)**

Ethnic Group	2000	2010	2020	2030	2040	2050
African-American	35.82*	40.45	45.37	50.44	55.88	61.36
	(12.7%)	(13.1%)	(13.5%)	(13.9%)	(14.3%)	(14.6%)
Hispanic**	35.62	47.76	59.76	73.06	87.59	102.56
	(12.6%)	(15.5%)	(17.8%)	(20.1%)	(22.3%)	(24.4%)
Asian	10.68	14.24	17.99	22.58	27.99	33.43
	(3.8%)	(4.6%)	(5.4%)	(6.2%)	(7.1%)	(8.0%)
Total population (major ethnic groups)	82.12	102.45	123.12	146.1	171.5	197.4
	(29.1%)	(33.2%)	(36.7%)	(40.2%)	(43.7%)	(47.0%)
Total U.S. Population	282.13	308.94	335.81	363.58	391.95	419.85

*To be read: there were 35.82 million African-Americans in the United States as of 2000, which constituted approximately 12.7 percent of the total population.
**Includes Hispanics of any race.

Source: U.S. Census Bureau, 2004, "U.S. Interim Projections by Age, Sex, Race, and Hispanic Origin," http://www.census.gov/ipc/www/usinterimproj.

major ethnic groups' population representation in the United States from 2000 through 2050. The following sections provide more details for the three major ethnic groups: African-Americans, Hispanics (Latinos), and Asian-Americans.

African-Americans

Non-Hispanic African-Americans constitute approximately 40.5 million individuals as of 2010, or slightly more than 13 percent of the U.S. population (see Table 5.5). African-Americans are characterized more by their common heritage than by skin color—a heritage based on a beginning in slavery, a history of discrimination, limited housing opportunities, and, historically, only partial participation in many aspects of the majority culture.[32] Although this situation has changed for the better, there remain distinct differences between the majority white culture and blacks, differences that are manifest in the marketplace.

Four reasons explain why African-Americans are attractive consumers for many companies: (1) the average age of black Americans is considerably younger than that for whites; (2) African-Americans are geographically concentrated, with approximately three-fourths of all blacks living in just 16 states (California, Texas, Illinois, Louisiana, Alabama, Georgia, Florida, South Carolina, North Carolina, Maryland, Michigan, Ohio, Pennsylvania, Virginia, New York, and New Jersey); (3) African-Americans tend to purchase prestige and name-brand products in greater proportion than do whites; and (4) the total spending power of African-Americans is considerable, projected to be $1.1 trillion by 2012.[33]

These impressive figures notwithstanding, many companies make no special efforts to communicate with African-Americans. This is unwise because research indicates African-Americans are responsive to advertisements placed in black-oriented media and to ads that make personalized appeals by using African-American models and contexts with which they can identify, such as the advertisement in Figure 5.6. Major corporations are increasingly developing marcom programs for communicating with black consumers. By one account, some of the American corporations that do the best job in communicating with African-American consumers include Altria Group, Ford Motor, General Motors, Procter & Gamble, and Walmart.[34]

Although greater numbers of companies are realizing the importance of directing special marcom efforts to African-Americans, it is important to emphasize that black consumers do not constitute a single market any more than do whites. African-Americans exhibit diverse purchasing behaviors according to their lifestyles, values, and demographics. Therefore, companies must use different advertising media, distribution channels, advertising themes, and pricing strategies as they market to the various subsegments of the African-American population.

Hispanic Americans (Latinos)

The U.S. Latino[35] population grew from only 4 million in 1950 to a population of nearly 51 million in 2010 and now is America's largest minority with a slight edge over African-Americans in share of the total U.S. population.[36] From 2000 until 2010, U.S. Latino population grew by 43 percent compared to just 4.9 percent of non-Latinos.[37] Latinos in the United States will constitute about

Image courtesy of The Advertising Archives

FIGURE 5.6 African-American Models Appeal to African American Consumers

TABLE 5.6	Top 10 U.S. Hispanic Markets (estimates as of 2010)		
Rank	Metro Market	Hispanic Population	Hispanic % of Total Local Market Population
1	Los Angeles, CA	8,106,800	63.2
2	New York, NY	4,588,100	24.3
3	Houston, TX	2,063,900	34.7
4	Miami/Fort Lauderdale, FL	2,033,600	36.5
5	Chicago, IL	1,985,100	21.0
6	Dallas/Fort Worth, TX	1,846,900	29.0
7	San Francisco, CA	1,570,400	36.2
8	Phoenix/Prescott, AZ	1,455,200	34.7
9	San Antonio, TX	1,318,000	61.5
10	McAllen, TX	1,161,400	94.0

Sources: "Hispanic Fact Pack, 2010 Edition," *Advertising Age's Annual Guide to Hispanic Marketing and Media* (New York: Crain Communications Inc., July 26, 2010), 35; and "Table of U.S. Metropolitan Statistical Areas," Wikipedia, http://en.wikipedia.org/wiki/Table_of_United_States_Metropolitan_Statistical_Areas.

one quarter of the total population by 2050 (see Table 5.5) and presently constitute a population greater than that of Canada's entire population! The largest percentage of Latinos are Mexican Americans—about 63 percent—but large numbers of Puerto Rican Americans, Latin Americans from Central and South America, and Cuban Americans also reside in the United States.[38]

Hispanic Americans have historically been concentrated in relatively few states such as California, Texas, New York, Florida, Illinois, Arizona, and New Jersey. However, Latinos are becoming increasingly mobile and have begun to fan out from the few states in which they originally concentrated. Table 5.6 provides information pertinent to the top 10 Hispanic markets in the United States. Table 5.6 shows that Latinos represent the majority or near-majority of the total population in several large U.S. cities. In the Los Angeles metro area, for example, there are over eight million Latinos representing about 63 percent of that metro area's population.

Marketing communicators in the past devoted insufficient attention to Hispanic Americans, but their attention has increased substantially since the Census Bureau announced a 43 percent increase in the number of Hispanic Americans between 2000 and 2010. Yet, companies advertise to Latinos much less than their market size would justify. Research has shown that the frequency of Hispanics' appearances in television advertising is considerably less than their proportion of the population.[39] Many companies are increasingly shifting more of their budgets into media that reach Latino consumers, but it would appear that marketers in large part are underspending in efforts targeted toward this large and growing segment of the U.S. population.[40] One exception recently was Kraft, who had received a rating of just a "follower" by the Association of Hispanic Ad Agencies in 2009. So, in 2010, they tripled spending on Hispanic marketing, including a major effort on Kool-Aid. This campaign depicted the Kool-Aid Man mascot jumping into a pool shouting, "Donde esta la diversion, esta Kool-Aid" ("Where there's fun, there's Kool-Aid").[41]

Marketing communicators need to be aware of several important points when attempting to reach Latino consumers. Because a large percentage of Hispanic-Americans use primarily Spanish media, it is important to target messages to some (but not all) Latinos using Spanish-speaking media. A key in designing effective advertising for Hispanics is to advertise in their dominant language.[42] Because approximately half of Hispanic Americans speak only or mostly Spanish at home, reaching these consumers requires the use of Spanish.

Plain English isn't always enough.

With Spanish spoken in 90% of Hispanic homes* in the U.S., it could be very risky to deliver your advertising message only in English. As the leading Spanish-language broadcaster, nobody reaches this country's largest minority of 37 million Hispanics like the networks of Univision.

Don't let an opportunity this big slip by.

UNIVISION   TELEFUTURA   Galavisión

© Univision Communications Inc. *Nielsen Media Research, 2003 MRI Volume Estimates: Autumn '04

© Courtesy of Univision 2003

However, for Hispanics who are English dominant, as are many younger Latinos, it obviously makes greater sense to use English in advertising copy that reflects their values and culture.

It is important to recognize that Latinos do not represent a single, unified market. There are strong intraethnic differences among Cubans, Mexicans, and Puerto Ricans that necessitate unique appeals be directed to each Latino group. Moreover, as with all general groupings, there are huge differences within each group in terms of English-speaking ability, length of residence in the United States (and thus degree of acculturation), level of income, and so on.

Some prominent companies—Coca-Cola, Pepsi, Procter & Gamble, Sears, McDonald's, Dunkin' Donuts, Best Buy, Toyota, Anheuser-Busch, to name a few—are now investing heavily in Hispanic-oriented advertising and event sponsorships that reach Latinos in their local communities and often in celebratory moods. Sponsoring Cinco de Mayo events, for example, is beginning to take on the same proportion as putting commercial support behind St. Patrick's Day celebrations. For an interesting appeal to the Latino market, see the *IMC Focus* insert about the marketing of Clamato and a new brand of beer that contains Clamato juice, Chelada.

Asian-Americans

Asian-Americans in the United States represent many nationalities: Asian Indians, Chinese, Filipino, Japanese, Korean, Vietnamese, and others. Asian-Americans have been heralded as the newest "hot" ethnic market. The demographics support this optimistic outlook. In 2010, approximately 14 million Asians were living in the United States; that number will increase to over

---

IMC FOCUS

A Special Beverage for Latino Consumers, Clamato

Clamato, the name representing the conjoining of clam and tomato, is a tomato juice containing a hint of clam along with celery, onions, and spices. Many American consumers have never tried the product or dislike it due to the difficulty of drinking juice tinged with clams. Although available on supermarket shelves for over 25 years, the brand basically languished until its marketer, Mott's, concentrated its entire marketing budget on the Latino market. Why? Because some Latino consumers somehow have the impression that Clamato juice is an aphrodisiac. Although Mott's makes no claims as to Clamato's powers, advertising refers obliquely to the brand's appeal with the tagline "Clamato le pone sabor al momento" (Clamato adds flavor to the moment).

Leveraging this (mis)perception among Latino consumers, Mott's undertook an integrated campaign that involved TV and radio advertisements, outdoor signage, and in-store promotions in major Hispanic

markets. In a special appeal to Mexican Americans, who constitute about 70 percent of U.S. Latinos, Mott's developed a phone card promotion whereby cards with free minutes for calls to Mexico were given away when consumers purchased 64-ounce bottles of Clamato. These IMC efforts have driven a substantial sales increase since Mott's began the Hispanic initiative for Clamato.

And of further interest, Anheuser-Busch developed a brand named Chelada that consists of a mixture of Budweiser (or Bud Light) with Clamato juice along with salt and lime flavoring. These two new versions of Chelada—regular and light—will come in 24-ounce cans.

Sources: Adapted from Gabriel Sama, "Appeal of Clamato Isn't Just Its Taste," *Wall Street Journal Online*, October 21, 2003, http://online. wsj.com; and the section on Chelada is from BrewBlog, http://www. brewblog.com/brew/2007/02/ab_readies_chel.html (accessed November 9, 2007).

© Jim Barber/Shutterstock.com

33 million by 2050 (see Table 5.5). The largest Asian groups in the United States are of Chinese and Asian Indian descent, both with populations of about 2.5 million. According to census data, Asian-Americans on average are better educated, have higher incomes, and occupy more prestigious job positions than any other segment of American society.

It is important to emphasize that just as there is no single African-American or Hispanic market, there certainly is no single Asian-American market. Moreover, unlike other ethnic groups, such as Hispanics, who share a similar language, Asian-Americans speak a variety of languages. Among Asian nationalities there are considerable differences in product choices, brand preferences, and English-language skills.

Some firms have been successful in marketing to specific Asian consumers by customizing marketing programs to their values and lifestyles rather than merely translating Anglo programs. Mainstream marketers have available various media options for targeting Asian-Americans: Asian-language radio stations are now burgeoning in areas where large concentrations of Asian consumers live, and direct marketing via postal mail is an outstanding medium for micro-marketing to specific groups of Asian-Americans. Online sites also are a valuable medium for reaching Asian-American consumers in that they represent a disproportionately high group of online users compared to other Americans.

In summary, one has to be careful with the use of demographics in multicultural segmentation and targeting. For example, Facebook and other social media sites do not ask for race or ethnicity information on the profile. Moreover, Nielsen and CBS recently partnered to reduce a focus on age and gender in TV program information in favor of behavioral data.[43] Yet, unless you are looking at what *motivates* behavior, one may not fully understand the segment. For example, just taking behavior and grouping all Hispanics together is likely to ignore important intra-cultural variations.

Market Targeting

Once resulting segments are developed based on demographics, behavior, etc., then the question is whether or not these segments are attractive enough to be worth our attention. Five *criteria for segment effectiveness* (i.e., attractiveness) are suggested:[44]

1. **Measurable:** *the degree to which useful information exists on the segment.* For example, a company may not have measures of a very small segment's size, purchasing power, or other important characteristics. (This should not deter creative attempts to measure this however.)
2. **Substantial:** *the degree to which the segment is large enough and/or profitable to be worth attention.* There are notable exceptions to this: the Orphan Drug Act of 1983 facilitates the development and commercialization of prescription drugs by pharmaceutical firms to treat rare diseases.[45]
3. **Accessible:** *the degree to which a firm can focus their marketing efforts on the segment.* As most college students know, your time is limited and you represent a difficult market to reach. So, firms are especially glad to reach out to students with promotions on spring break, gift packs at dorms and rec centers, etc.
4. **Differentiable:** *the degree to which the segment is distinguishable and will respond differently to changes in marketing mix elements and programs.* If younger and older urban Asian-American men within one mile of a restaurant respond exactly the same to a sushi lunch special, they may not represent different segments.
5. **Actionable:** *the degree to which the programs can be formulated and implemented.* Sometimes, resources may not be available for a special marcom effort for a given segment.

Several alternatives for actually selecting the segments have been deemed attractive or effective. These target market strategies[46] include: (1) *undifferentiated marketing*, in which overall marketing mix is applied to the mass market (e.g., Model T Ford with one color and price for all Americans), (2) *differentiated marketing*, in which a separate marketing mix is applied to each separate segment (e.g., General Motors' separate divisions), or (3) *concentrated marketing*, in which one overall marketing mix is applied to one separate segment (e.g., Mercedes and high-end owners). Of course, other factors such as company resources, homogeneity of the market, and competition can affect one's choice of a given strategy.

Market Positioning in Practice: The Fundamentals

Brand positioning is an essential preliminary activity to developing a successful marcom program. By having a clear positioning statement, the brand management team is committed to conveying a consistent message in all forms of marcom messages.

Conceptually, the term *positioning* suggests two interrelated ideas. First, as previously defined, brand positioning represents the key feature, benefit, or image that a brand stands for in the target audience's mind. Second, the brand's meaning in consumers' memories stands in *comparison* to what they know and think about competitive brands in the product or service category (i.e., "positioning against" the competition).

Strategically and tactically, positioning is a short statement—even a word—that represents the message you wish to imprint in customers' minds.[47] This statement tells how your brand differs from and is superior to competitive brands. It gives a reason why consumers should buy your brand. For example, the following consumer associations might be paired with brands: Volvo (safety), GE (innovation), State Farm (good neighbor), Disney (family entertainment), McDonald's (convenience and fast food), and Starbucks (quality coffee). A good positioning statement should satisfy two requirements: (1) It should reflect a brand's *competitive advantage* (vis-a-vis competitive offerings in the same product category) and (2) it should *motivate* consumers to *action*.

To make the idea of positioning even more concrete, a brand's image (see Figure 5.7) consists of types, favorability, strength, and uniqueness of brand associations. Our focus for now will be limited to the *types* of brand associations. In Figure 5.7, types of associations include brand attributes, benefits, and an overall

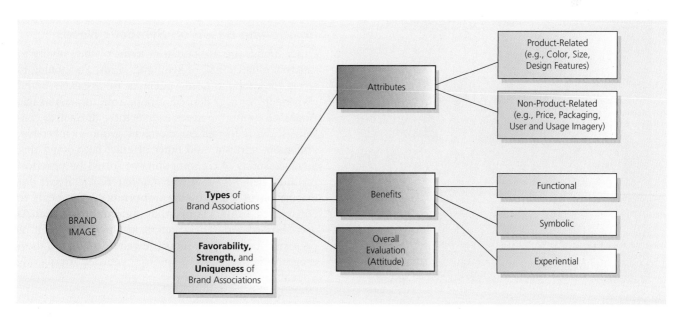

FIGURE 5.7 A Framework for Brand Positioning

Source: Adapted from Kevin Lane Keller, Conceptualizing, Measuring, and Managing Customer-Based Brand Equity, *Journal of Marketing* 57 (January 1993), 7.

evaluation of, or attitude toward, the brand. Brand *attributes* include product-related and non-product-related features. Non-product-related attributes would include, for example, a brand's price, consumer perceptions of the type of people who own the brand (user imagery), and the occasions when the brand would be appropriately used (usage imagery). Brand *benefits* consist of ways by which a brand satisfies customers' needs and wants and can be classified as functional, symbolic, or experiential. Generally speaking, we can position a brand by focusing on product *attributes* or *benefits*.

Benefit Positioning

As noted briefly in Chapter 2, positioning with respect to brand benefits can be accomplished by appealing to any of three categories of basic consumer *needs*: functional, symbolic, or experiential.[48] Upon a quick review of the consumer-based brand equity framework (refer again to Figure 5.7), you will see that these three categories are shown as a specific type of association termed *benefits*. Note that benefits are the need-satisfying features provided by brands.

Positioning Based on Functional Needs

A brand positioned in terms of functional needs attempts to provide solutions to consumers' current consumption-related problems or potential problems by communicating that the brand possesses specific benefits capable of solving those problems. Appeals to functional needs are the most prevalent form of brand-benefit positioning. Consumer goods marketers also regularly appeal to consumers' needs for convenience, safety, good health, cleanliness, and so on, all of which are functional needs that can be satisfied by brand benefits. For example, Rockport aired a commercial showing two girls wearing their comfortable Rockport shoes walking dogs on the steep hills of San Francisco. As another example, the Crocs brand (see Figure 5.8) appeals to consumers' desire for lightweight, comfortable, and odor-resistant footwear. The *IMC Focus* insert offers further details about this brand.

AP Images/Frank Augstein

Positioning Based on Symbolic Needs

Other brands are positioned in terms of their ability to satisfy nonfunctional, or symbolic, needs. Positioning in terms of symbolic needs attempts to associate brand ownership with a desired group, role, or self-image. Appeals to symbolic needs include those directed at consumers' desire for self-enhancement, group membership, affiliation, altruism, and other abstract need states that involve aspects of consumption not solved by practical product benefits. (See the *Global Focus* insert for discussion of the growing importance of appeals to consumers using claims that agricultural products are "fair traded.") Marketers in categories such as personal beauty products, jewelry, alcoholic beverages, cigarettes, and motor vehicles frequently appeal to symbolic needs.

Positioning Based on Experiential Needs

Consumers' experiential needs represent their desires for products that provide sensory pleasure, variety,

FIGURE 5.8 Croc Advertisement Illustrating Appeal to Functional Needs

IMC FOCUS

Not Lovely, but Successful

Crocs is a brand of footwear widely worn by young and old alike. Many people own multiple pairs of the somewhat clumsy-looking shoes that are made from a plastic-like foam resin. And for every product owner, there are several other people who wouldn't be caught dead wearing Crocs. Regardless of your personal view, the fact is that Crocs became a successful brand very quickly. The Colorado-based company was founded in 2002 by three friends who took frequent boating trips together. While sailing in the Caribbean on one occasion, one of the trio wore a pair of foam clogs he had purchased in Canada. Favorable response from others encouraged the three friends to start their own company to market a footwear item they named Crocs. They purchased the product from a Canadian company that had proprietary rights to the foam resin from which Crocs are formed. This resin, called Croslite, is lightweight, anti-bacterial, and foot-forming. After adding a strap to the back of the original clogs, the partners started selling Crocs at boat shows and at other events that attracted potential purchasers.

It wasn't long before word-of-mouth influence resulted in a rapid increase in sales and widespread distribution in many different types of retail outlets.

After realizing sales of only $1 million in 2003, by 2007 (and through 2009) Crocs generated sales of more than $800 million from shoes sold in over 40 countries! Much of the brand's success is due to its fulfilling consumers' functional needs for a comfortable and an easy-to-care-for footwear item—slip them on and hose them off when they get dirty. The brand's phenomenal achievements also can be attributed to creative marketing that has affiliated Crocs with universities, professional sports teams, and other high-equity associations. In a sense, when purchasing Crocs the consumer purchases a functional product that is laden with emotional connection to, say, your own university.

Sources: Based on Vivian Manning-Schaffel, "Crocs-Still Rocking," http://www.brandchannel.com, August 27, 2007; and Evelyn M. Rusli, "Crocs Is Still a Buy," http://www.forbes.com, November 12, 2007.

FIGURE 5.9 Dove Advertisement Illustrating Appeal to Experiential Needs

Source: DOVE® and A CHOCOLATE EXPERIENCE LIKE NO OTHER are registered trademarks of Mars, Incorporated. These trademarks are used with permission. Mars, Incorporated is not associated with Cengage Learning. The DOVE advertisement is printed with permission of Mars, Incorporated.

and, in a few product circumstances, cognitive stimulation. Brands positioned toward experiential needs are promoted as being out of the ordinary and high in sensory value (looking elegant, feeling wonderful, tasting or smelling great, sounding divine, being exhilarating, and so on) or rich in the potential for cognitive stimulation (exciting, challenging, mentally entertaining, and so on). The Dove advertisement in Figure 5.9 represents this brand's traditional positioning as an especially flavorful chocolate candy (Seduction by Chocolate). Consumers are promised the experience of tasting a special product ("A chocolate experience like no other").

It is important to recognize that brands often offer a mixture of functional, symbolic, and experiential benefits. Yet, it has been argued that successful positioning requires a communication strategy that entices a *single type* of consumer need (functional, symbolic, or experiential) rather than attempting to be something for everyone.[49]

Attribute Positioning

A brand can be positioned in terms of a particular attribute or feature, provided that the attribute represents a competitive advantage and can motivate customers to purchase that brand rather than a competitive offering. Product attributes, as shown in Figure 5.7, can be distinguished as either *product-related* or *non-product-related*.

Product-Related

Sleeker product design, superior materials, and more color options are just a few of the virtually endless attributes that can provide the foundation for positioning a brand. If your brand has a product advantage,

GLOBAL FOCUS

The Symbolism of Certifying Products as Fair Traded

Most consumers know that agricultural commodities often are imported from other countries rather than grown and harvested domestically. Yet, most people go to their local grocery stores or supermarkets with little awareness that agricultural workers in other countries often are paid dreadfully low wages and farm owners have difficulty earning a profit. Poor wage rates and minuscule profits, if not losses, are largely due to the economics of growing commodity products. Coffee, for example, is grown in Latin American countries such as Brazil and Colombia and also is harvested in African countries and, ever increasingly, Vietnam. In most years, coffee supply exceeds demand, and anyone familiar with basic economics knows that the effect of this imbalance is falling prices. Intense competition has forced prices and wages down to the point where growers have difficulty making a living and workers are hard-pressed to feed their families. On the other hand, low coffee prices benefit retailers and consumers in countries that import low-priced coffee. The situation, in other words, is not win-win but rather one where businesses and consumers in economically advantaged economies gain at the expense of growers and workers in developing economies. Is there a resolution to this imbalance? Perhaps there is; please read on.

The resolution is not the competitive marketplace, because the economics of supply-demand disequilibrium inevitably lead to further lowering of commodity prices. Hence, the only way possible for commodity growers and workers to receive higher profits and wages is some form of "artificial" intervention—that is, for forces other than the economics of supply and demand to come into play. This has happened, in fact, because many consumers in advanced economies are willing to pay higher prices so poor workers and growers are able to survive. These consumers have been given the label "LOHAS" consumers, which stands for "lifestyles of health and sustainability." About one-third of adults in the United States, or around 50 million people, are classified as LOHAS according to a recent study.

But even if a consumer is LOHAS inclined, how does one know which products to purchase? Increasingly, commodity products such as coffee, grapes, mangos, pineapples, and others are labeled with stickers bearing "Fair Trade Certified." This label means that workers in developing economies receive higher wages and benefits for their efforts than the supply-demand disequilibrium would normally dictate. Large retail chains such as McDonald's, Dunkin' Donuts, and Starbucks offer some fair-traded coffee, and many supermarkets are carrying more commodity products with the fair-trade label. Another label being used to signify fair trading is "Rainforest Alliance Certified." Procter & Gamble's coffee products carry this label.

The LOHAS movement reveals that consumers' symbolic needs—the sense of being fair and socially responsible—sometimes trump their functional need to pay the lowest possible prices. This form of altruism enables workers and farm owners in poor countries to sustain an existence and to continue to grow and harvest products their economies depend on. Fair trading achieves more of a win-win outcome than the rich-countries-win/poor-countries-lose situation previously prevailing.

Source: Adapted from Katy McLaughlin, "Is Your Grocery List Politically Correct?" *Wall Street Journal Online*, February 17, 2004. For additional information on fair trade and fair-traded products and organizations see http://en.wikipedia.org/wiki/Fair_trade and http://www.globalexchange.org.

flaunt it, especially if the advantage is something that consumers truly desire in the product category and will motivate them to action. For example, in an appeal to people who are concerned with product safety, the advertisement for the Toyota Highlander in Figure 5.10 claims that no other vehicle in the Highlander's category has more standard safety features. This is a distinct product-related positioning directed to consumers who are concerned about their personal safety and, perhaps especially, the well-being of "precious cargo" such as children and grandchildren.

Photography by Mark Ku

FIGURE **5.10** Highlander Advertisement Illustrating Product-Related Attribute Positioning

RALPH LAUREN

NEW YORK   LONDON   PARIS   HONG KONG   CHICAGO   PALO ALTO   DALLAS   BAL HARBOUR   PALM BEACH   BEVERLY HILLS

Image courtesy of The Advertising Archives

FIGURE 5.11 Ralph Lauren Advertisement Illustrating Positioning Based on User Imagery

Non-Product-Related: Usage and User Imagery

A brand positioned according to the image associated with how it is used, its *usage imagery*, depicts the brand in terms of specific, and presumably unique, usages that become associated with it. For example, advertisers sometimes position SUVs and passenger trucks in terms of their seemingly unique ability to go "off-road" and traverse rough terrain. Such advertisements create the impression that only the advertised brand is capable of forging streams, climbing hills, and navigating other tough-to-travel areas.

Brands also can be positioned in terms of the kind of people who use them. This *user imagery* thus becomes the brand's hallmark; the brand and the people who are portrayed as using it become virtually synonymous. Positioning a brand via user imagery thus amounts to associating the brand with icon-like representations of the kind of people who are portrayed in advertisements as typical users of the brand. Consider the Ralph Lauren advertisement in Figure 5.11. The ad says little about the wide line of apparel items carried by this retailer. Instead, the ad's most prominent feature is the attractive model who reflects Ralph Lauren's positioning of a typical owner of its merchandise.

Repositioning a Brand

There are points in a brand's life cycle where brand managers need to alter what the brand stands for in order to enhance the brand's competitiveness. Consider the following illustration of successful repositioning in a B2B context. MeadWestvaco Corporation is a leading global producer of packaging products, coated and specialty papers, and other items. One of its many products is a printing paper that was once branded under the name TexCover II. Although an excellent product providing consistent performance, TexCover II held just the fifth-largest market share in its category and generated annual revenues of less than $40 million. Because the brand was underperforming despite its excellent quality and reputation for dependable performance, an advertising agency, the Mobium Creative Group, was hired to pump up TexCover II's performance.

Known for their creative work, Mobium set about the task of repositioning the line of TexCover II printing paper. They made a major strategic shift by changing the brand name to the catchy name Tango and positioning the brand as "always performing." The name Tango is easy to remember, although it is not naturally related to the attributes or benefits of printing paper. They reinforced this positioning through a series of attention-gaining advertisements that cleverly illustrated the idea of "always performing" in a humorous and captivating manner. These marcom innovations resulted in a first-year revenue increase of 27 percent. Overall, Tango's total revenue increased $126 million on a marcom investment of only $2 million![50]

Marketing Mix Development

As noted in Chapter 1, integrated marketing communications consists of the coordination of each element in the promotion mix (e.g., advertising, sales promotion, social media, etc.) with each other, *and with the other elements of a firm's marketing mix*, such that they speak with one voice with the customer. So, the final step in the segmentation process is to apply the marketing mix elements to each segment, based on its prior positioning. For example, the Tango's new positioning campaign was no doubt coordinated with its price, product attributes, and location (place) availability options for B2B customers in ensuring its success.

Summary

This chapter has emphasized the importance of the segmentation process and targeting marcom messages. Determining how a brand's marcom efforts should be directed toward specific groups of consumers—based on behaviorial, psychographic, demographic, or geodemographic considerations—is the initial and most fundamental of all marcom decisions. All subsequent marcom decisions (positioning, setting objectives, and determining budgets) are inextricably intertwined with this initial, segmentation and targeting decision.

Perhaps the most diagnostic way to target consumers is to identify their past purchase behavior in the product category for which a brand manager is making a targeting decision. Armed with behavioral information about how customers have made decisions in the past, it is possible to project with considerable accuracy how they will behave in the future. Also, knowledge of consumers' online search behavior enables the targeting of advertisements for brands that match the characteristics of consumers who visit those sites. Even so, privacy concerns can continue to be an issue with online behavioral targeting.

Marketing communicators also segment customers using knowledge about their activities, interests, and opinions (or, collectively, their lifestyles) to better understand what people want and how they are likely to respond to advertising, direct mail, and other forms of marketing communications. The term *psychographics* describes this form of segmentation. Customized studies are conducted to identify psychographic segments directly applicable to the marketer's product category and brand, but syndicated research systems such as SBI's VALS system also provide useful information for making important marcom decisions. The VALS system classifies people into one of eight groups based on a combination of their self-orientation and resources.

Another basis for targeting consumers is geodemographics. This form of targeting basically identifies clusters of consumers who reside in neighborhoods where residents share similar demographic characteristics and related lifestyles. Donnelly's ClusterPlus and Nielsen Claritas' PRIZMNE are two well-known and respected clustering systems that identify meaningful groupings of geographical units such as ZIP code areas. The section on geodemographics covered the PRIZMNE and indicated that this clustering system delineates the population into 66 groups that are labeled with catchy names such as Bohemian Mix, Country Casuals, Suburban Pioneers, and City Roots. Geodemographic information is especially useful when making direct marketing decisions, selecting retail outlets, or spotting broadcast advertisements in select markets.

The next section of the chapter reviewed three major demographic developments: (1) the age structure of the U.S. population, (2) the changing American household, and (3) ethnic population developments. Some of the major demographic developments discussed include (1) the progressive aging of the U.S. population from an average age of 33 in 1990 to an expected average age of 38 by 2025, (2) the increase in the percentage of single American adults, and (3) the explosive growth of ethnic minorities, particularly Latinos.

This chapter concluded with the idea of brand positioning, described as representing the key feature, benefit, or image that a brand stands for in the target audience's collective mind. A positioning statement is the central idea that encapsulates a brand's meaning and distinctiveness vis-a-vis competitive brands. The chapter discussed three approaches to developing brand positions—appeals to functional, symbolic, and experiential needs of the target audiences.

Discussion Questions

1. In what sense is behavioral segmentation information about customers more diagnostic of their future purchase behavior than is, say, demographic information?

2. In your own words, explain how online behavioral targeting works.

3. In what sense is online behavioral targeting a potential invasion of privacy?

4. If you were to design a psychographic study for a new chain of lower-priced coffee stores that are planned to compete against Starbucks, what lifestyle characteristics (i.e., people's interests, values, and activities they participate in) might you consider as indicative of whether they might be interested in your new stores?

5. To which of the VALS segments do you belong? (Go to www.strategicbusinessinsights.com/vals/presurvey.shtml)

6. Having read the section on the size of the world and U.S. populations, update the figures presented in the text, which were current as of July 2011, by going to www.census.gov/main/www/popclock.html.

7. Demographers tell us that U.S. households are growing in number and shrinking in size. What specific implications do these changes hold for companies that manufacture and market products such as appliances, consumer electronics, and automobiles?

8. Most readers of this text fall either in the Gen X or Gen Y age categories. Just because you share this commonality with all other Gen Xers or Gen Yers, does this one piece of information about you and your cohorts represent a sufficient basis on which a marcom practitioner might aim its advertising efforts?

9. African-American, Latino, and Asian-American consumers do not signify three homogeneous markets; rather, they represent many markets composed of people who merely share a common ethnicity and/or language. Explain.

10. Explain the reasons for the relentless aging of the U.S. population, and discuss some implications this will have on marketing and marketing communications in the foreseeable future.

11. Assume you are brand manager of a food product that is consumed by all Americans—African-Americans, Caucasians, Hispanics, Asians, and others. You are considering running an extended advertising campaign on prime-time television that uses Latino actors and appeals to Latino consumers. Aside from cost considerations, what reservations might you have about this type of campaign?

12. When we discussed the mature market, it was noted that advertising aimed at this group should portray them as vital, busy, forward looking, and attractive or romantic. Interview several mature consumers and coalesce their views on how they perceive advertising directed at them and their peers. Your interview results along with those from fellow students should lead to an interesting class discussion.

13. What are your views on targeting products to kids (i.e., children between the ages of 4 and 12)? Aside from your personal views, discuss the issue of targeting to children from two additional perspectives: first, that of a brand manager who is responsible for the profitability of a child-oriented product, and second,

from the viewpoint of a regulatory agency or non-profit group in charge of protecting children. Imagine what each of these parties might say about the practice of targeting products to children.

14. Based on your personal background and using the VALS system, how would you categorize most of the adults with whom you and your family associate?

15. Identify magazine advertisements that reflect appeals to at least three of the eight VALS groups. Describe in as much detail as possible the neighborhood in which you were raised. Come up with a label (similar to the PRIZMNE cluster names) that captures the essence of your neighborhood.

16. In Chapter 2, you read about "leveraging" (refer to Figure 2.5) as one of the ways by which brand associations are created. Relate that discussion to the concept of imbuing a brand with meaning by pulling existing meaning from the "culturally constituted world."

17. How does your college or university position itself? If you were responsible for coming up with a new positioning, or repositioning, for your college or university, what would that be? Justify your choice.

18. How is your favorite brand of athletic footwear (Adidas, Nike, Reebok, etc.) positioned?

End Notes

1. Philip Kotler and Kevin Lane Keller, *Marketing Management*, 13th ed., Upper Saddle River, NJ: Pearson Prentice-Hall, 2009, 208.

2. Philip Kotler and Gary Armstrong, *Principles of Marketing*, 9th ed., Upper Saddle River, NJ: Prentice-Hall, 244–45.

3. Ibid, 245.

4. Kris Oser, "Targeting Web Behavior Pays, American Airlines Study Finds," *Advertising Age*, May 17, 2004, 8.

5. Emily Steel, "How Marketers Hone Their Aim Online," *Wall Street Journal Online*, June 19, 2007, http://online.wsj.com.

6. "FTC Staff Revises Online Behavioral Advertising Principles," *FTC News*, February 12, 2009, http://www.ftc.gov/opa/2009/02/behavad.shtm.

7. Ibid.

8. Carol M. Morgan and Doran J. Levy, "Targeting to Psychographic Segments," *Brandweek*, October 7, 2002, 18–19.

9. James W. Peltier, John A. Schibrowsky, Don E. Schultz, and John Davis, "Interactive Psychographics: Cross-Selling in the Banking Industry," *Journal of Advertising Research* 42 (March/April 2002), 7–22.

10. These descriptions are from http://www.strategicbusinessinsights.com/vals/ustypes.shtml (accessed July 24, 2011).

11. Michael J. Weiss, *The Clustered World: How We Live, What We Buy, and What It All Means About Who We Are*, Boston: Little, Brown and Company, 2000.

12. Nielsen Claritas PrizmNE Segments, http://www.tetrad.com/pub/documents/pnesegments.pdf (accessed July 22, 2011).

13. "A County-by-County Look at Ancestry," *USA Today*, July 1, 2004, 7A.

14. Emily Bryson York, "The Hottest Thing in Kids Marketing? Imitating Webkinz," *Advertising Age*, October 8, 2007, 38.

15. Deborah Roedder John, "Consumer Socialization of Children: A Retrospective Look at Twenty-Five Years of Research," *Journal of Consumer Research* 26 (December 1999), 183–213; Elizabeth S. Moore and Richard J. Lutz, "Children, Advertising, and Product Experiences: A Multimethod Inquiry," *Journal of Consumer Research* 27 (June 2000), 31–48; and *Marketing Food to Children and Adolescents: A Review of Industry Expenditures, Activities, and Self-Regulation, A Report to Congress*, FTC Staff Report, July 2008, http://www.ftc.gov/os/2008/07/P064504foodmktingreport.pdf.

16. Marvin E. Goldberg, Gerald J. Gorn, Laura A. Peracchio, and Gary Bamossy, "Understanding Materialism among Youth," *Journal of Consumer Psychology* 13, no. 3 (2003), 278–88.

17. For an academic treatment on the topic, see Sharon E. Beatty and Salil Talpade, "Adolescent Influence in Family Decision Making: A Replication with Extension," *Journal of Consumer Research* 21 (September 1994), 332–41; and Kay M. Palan and Robert E. Wilkes, "Adolescent-Parent Interaction in Family

Decision Making," *Journal of Consumer Research* 24 (September 1997), 159–69.

18. "TRU Projects Teens Will Spend $158 Billion in 2005," Teen Research Unlimited, December 15, 2005, http://tru-insight.com/pressrelease.cfm?page_id=378.

19. Beth Snyder Bulik, "Forget the Parents: HP Plans to Target Teenagers Instead," *Advertising Age*, July 30, 2007, 8.

20. William Strauss and Neil Howe, *Generations: The History of America's Future, 1584–2069,* New York: William Morrow and Company, Inc., 1991. For a less technical treatment written by an advertising practitioner, see Karen Ritchie, *Marketing to Generation X*, New York: Lexington Books, 1995.

21. Yankelovich Partners, cited in "Don't Mislabel Gen X," *Brandweek*, May 15, 1995, 32, 34.

22. Michelle Higgins, "Cushier Convertibles for Aging Boomers," *Wall Street Journal Online*, September 1, 2004, http://online.wsj.com.

23. Margaret G. Zackowitz, "Harley's Midlife Crisis," *National Geographic*, August 2003.

24. For an interesting discussion of subjective (versus chronological) age and its role in influencing consumer behavior, see George P. Moschis and Anil Mathur, "Older Consumer Responses to Marketing Stimuli: The Power of Subjective Age," *Journal of Advertising Research* 46 (September 2006), 339–46.

25. The expression "repair kit" is from Charles D. Schewe, "Marketing to Our Aging Population: Responding to Physiological Changes," *The Journal of Consumer Marketing* 5 (summer 1988), 61–73.

26. The research was performed by George P. Moschis and is reported in "Survey: Age Is Not Good Indicator of Consumer Need," *Marketing Communications*, November 21, 1988, 6. See also George P. Moschis and Anil Mathur, "How They're Acting Their Age," *Marketing Management* 2, no. 2 (1993), 40–50.

27. All statistics in this paragraph are from the U.S. Census Bureau, Current Population Survey, Table HH-1, Households by Type: 1940 to Present. Internet release date: November 2010 (Excel file).

28. http://www.census.gov/population/www/socdemo/hh-fam.html#ht., Table FM-1, Families by Presence of Own Children, Under 18: 1950 to Present, Internet release date: November 2010.

29. "Demographics: U.S. Population Totals, U.S. Census Bureau Data," Hispanic Fact Pack 2011, supplement to *Advertising Age*, July 25, 2011, 42.

30. Ibid.

31. See Douglas M. Stayman and Rohit Deshpande, "Situational Ethnicity and Consumer Behavior," *Journal of Consumer Research* 16 (December 1989), 361–71; and Cynthia Webster, "Effects of Hispanic Ethnic Identification on Marital Roles in the Purchase Decision Process," *Journal of Consumer Research* 16 (September 1994), 319–31.

32. This characterization is based on James F. Engel, Roger D. Blackwell, and Paul W. Miniard,

Consumer Behavior, 8th ed., Fort Worth: The Dryden Press, 1995, 647.

33. David Dodson, "Minority Groups Share of $10 Trillion U.S. Consumer Market Is Growing Steadily," University of Georgia, Selig Center for Economic Growth, July 31, 2007, http://www.terry.uga.edu/news/releases/2007/minority_buying_power_report.html.

34. Lisa Sanders, "How to Target Blacks? First, You Gotta Spend," *Advertising Age*, July 3, 2006, 19.

35. Hispanic is actually a government-invented term that encompasses people of Spanish or Latin American descent or Spanish-language background. Many people of Latin American descent prefer to be referred to as Latinos.

36. Matt Carmichael and Peter Francese, "Five Surprising Facts Marketers Should Know About 2010 Census," *Advertising Age*, April 4, 2011, http://adage.com/article/news/census-2010-surprising-facts-marketers/149692; and U.S. Census Bureau, 2004, "U.S. Interim Projections by Age, Sex, Race, and Hispanic Origin."

37. Ibid, Carmichael and Francese.

38. "Hispanic Population Growth," Hispanic Fact Pack," 2011 Edition, A Supplement to *Advertising Age*, July 25, 2011, 49.

39. "Hispanic Characters Remain Scarce on Prime-Time TV," *Wall Street Journal Online*, June 24, 2003, http://online.wsj.com.

40. Dana James, "Many Companies Underspend in Segment," *Marketing News*, October 13, 2003, 6.

41. Andrew Adam Newman, "Kraft Aims Kool-Aid Ads at a Growing Hispanic Market," *New York Times*, May 26, 2011, http://www.nytimes.com/2011/05/27/business/media/27adco.html?ref=business&pagewanted=print.

42. Sigfredo A. Hernandez and Larry M. Newman, "Choice of English vs. Spanish Language in Advertising to Hispanics," *Journal of Current Issues and Research in Advertising* 14 (fall 1992), 35–46.

43. Matthew Carmichael, "Where Does Multicultural Targeting Fit in a Diverse World?" *Advertising Age*, May 30, 2011, 1, 33.

44. Kotler and Keller, 228.

45. "Orphan Drug Act of 1983," Wikipedia, http://en.wikipedia.org/wiki/Orphan_Drug_Act_of_1983.

46. Philip Kotler, *Principles of Marketing*, Englewood Cliffs, NJ: Prentice-Hall, 1980, 311.

47. Kevin J. Clancy and Peter C. Krieg, Counter-Intuitive Marketing: Achieve Great Results Using Uncommon Sense, New York: Free Press, 2000, 110.

48. C. Whan Park, Bernard J. Jaworski, and Deborah J. MacInnis, "Strategic Brand Concept-Image Management," *Journal of Marketing* 50 (October 1986), 136. The following discussion of functional, symbolic, and experiential needs/benefits adheres to Park et al.'s conceptualizations.

49. For further discussion of this point, see ibid.

50. This description is based on Bob Lamons, "Marcom Proves Itself a Worthy Investment," *Marketing News*, Junc 9, 2003, 13.

CHAPTER 6

The Communications Process and Consumer Behavior

MARCOM INSIGHT

Everyday Consumer Habits Helping the World

Disorders and diseases linked to dirty hands (e.g., diarrhea) kill children in the world every 15 seconds, and 50 percent of these deaths could be prevented by handwashing with soap. So, an anthropologist, Dr. Val Curtis, director of the Hygiene Center at the London School of Hygiene and Tropical Medicine, contacted large multinational corporations (e.g., Procter & Gamble, Colgate-Palmolive, Unilever, etc.) to better understand how people develop good habits, like washing hands with soap.

Many of the companies surveyed by Dr. Curtis had invested millions of dollars into finding underlying cues in consumers' lives that they could use in introducing new products. For example, many of the everyday products we use—chewing gum, skin

© FRANCIS R. MALASIG/EPA/Newscom

moisturizers, disinfectant wipes and lotions, air fresheners, antiperspirants, teeth whiteners, fabric softeners, and vitamins—are a result of manufactured habits. For instance, since so-called "bad smells" occur too infrequently, researchers at P&G looked for regular everyday cues for which to pair with their Febreze odor freshener. The key they found was the very act of cleaning a room—with windows open and fresh wind— a cue that was then used in Febreze commercials.

Such tactics were important for Dr. Curtis and the Global Public-Private Partnership for Handwashing with Soap, and especially for a country like Ghana in West Africa. In Ghana, diarrhea accounts for 25 percent

Chapter Objectives

After reading this chapter, you should be able to:

1 Appreciate elements of the communications process.

2 Understand the nature of meaning and semiotics in marketing communications, and how that meaning is a constructive process involving the use of signs and symbols.

3 Describe marketing communicators' usage of three

forms of figurative language: simile, metaphor, and allegory.

4 Discuss the two perspectives that characterize how consumers process information: the consumer processing model (CPM) and the hedonic, experiential model (HEM).

5 Explain the eight stages of consumer information processing.

of all deaths in children under 5, and is among the top three causes of childhood morbidity. Approximately nine million episodes of disease could be prevented each year by simply washing hands with soap.

Dr. Curtis discovered that although most people (75 percent) sampled in Ghana claimed they used soap after restroom use, only 4 percent had actually done so. Studies showed soap use increased when they felt their hands were dirty, triggered by a feeling of disgust. So, the solution was to show mothers and children in ads walking out of bathrooms with a glowing purple stain on their hands that contaminated everything they touched, tapping into the feeling of disgust. The ads turned out to be successful: There was a 13 percent increase in soap use after using the

restroom and a 41 percent increase in using soap before eating.

Currently, the success in Ghana in understanding consumer habits has been transformed into the Global Handwashing Day, promoting handwashing with soap for over 200 million people in greater than 100 countries around the world. (At the time of this writing, October 15 is designated as this day: www.globalhandwashingday. org). The ultimate goal is to reduce worldwide deaths among children under the age of 5 by two-thirds by 2015.

Sources: Charles Duhigg, "Warning: Habits May Be Good for You," *New York Times*, July 13, 2008, 1, 6; Global Handwashing Day, http://www.globalhandwashingday.org (accessed August 3, 2011); Public-Private Partnership to Promote Handwashing in Ghana, http://www.globalhandwashingday.org/ppph_in_ghana.asp (accessed August 3, 2011); and Ghana's Hand Washing Campaign, http://www.globalhandwashingday.org/GHD_Video.asp (accessed August 3, 2011).

The Communications Process

The opening *Marcom Insight* touched on many aspects that are discussed in this chapter, including the communications process, the nature of meaning, meaning transfer (and different cultures), and the fundamentals of consumer behavior. We start the chapter with the communications process.

The word *communication* is derived from the Latin word *communis*, which means "common." That is, communication can be thought of as the process of establishing a commonness, or oneness, of thought between a message sender, such as an advertiser, and a receiver, such as a consumer.[1] Thus, for communications to occur, there must be a commonness of thought between sender and receiver—not just messages sent from sender to receiver. This implies a *sharing relationship* between sender and receiver, say, a social media site and a consumer.

Consider a situation in which a salesperson is delivering a presentation to a purchasing agent who appears to be listening, but is actually checking her smartphone. Contrary to what an observer might perceive, communication is *not* occurring because thought is not being shared. (As an aside, multi-tasking has greatly limited attention spans and reading comprehension in the last decade.[2]) Although sound waves are bouncing off the receiving eardrums, the purchasing agent is not actively hearing what the salesperson is saying. Both sender and receiver must be active participants in the same communication relationship for thought to be shared. Communication is something one does *with* another person, not *to* another person.

Elements in the Communication Process

All communication activities involve the following elements: (1) a *source*, who has a (2) *communication objective*, that is transformed into a (3) a *message*, that is delivered via a (4) *message channel*, to a (5) *target audience*, which experiences a (6) *communication outcome*. That outcome represents (7) *feedback* to the message source, although the entire process is subject to interference, interruptions, or, in general, (8) *noise*. Figure 6.1 displays this process, and each element is now briefly described.

Source. In marketing communications, the source is a communicator in some marcom capacity—an advertiser, salesperson, blogger, etc.—who has

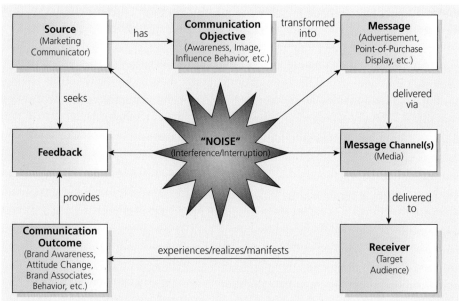

FIGURE 6.1 Elements in the Communication Process

GLOBAL FOCUS

Cultural Differences in Communication: High versus Low Context Cultures

Cross-cultural IMC can be challenging and misunderstandings are common! Marketers need to know the difference between high context and low context cultures in the design of ads, the use of gestures and non-verbal communications in personal selling, the design of social media sites, the use of in-store merchandising and packaging, running live events, and with many other marcom elements.

In *high-context cultures*, such as Mexico, Japan, and in the Middle East, large amounts of information are provided in a non-verbal manner (e.g., gestures, eye contact, touch, pauses, and facial expressions). Yet, clear differences exist with *low-context cultures*, such as Germany, Switzerland, the United Kingdom, and the United States, in which all meaning is explicitly provided in the message itself. For example, the use of a finger and a hand to indicate "come here please" is viewed as offensive and rude in some cultures (e.g., in Latin America) and Asians typically use the entire hand to point to something. Although touching a person's head is

considered friendly and affectionate in low context (Western) cultures, it is inappropriate in Asia where the head is considered sacred. In the Middle East, the left hand is reserved for bodily hygiene and should not be used to touch or transfer objects. In Muslim cultures, depicting touching between the genders is generally inappropriate.

Finally, in low context (Western) cultures, direct eye contact is viewed as being attentive and conveying honesty (e.g., the saying "look people in the eye" when talking). Yet, in Hispanic, Asian, Middle Eastern, and Native American cultures, eye contact is thought to be disrespectful and rude, especially among opposite genders.

Sources: "Cultural Differences in Non-verbal Communication," *Vermont Department of Health*, http://healthvermont.gov/family/toolkit/tools%5CF-6%20Cultural%20Differences%20in%20Nonverbal%20Communic.pdf (accessed November 5, 2011); "Cross-Cultural Communication Styles: High and Low Context," Communicaid Blog, February 12, 2011, http://blog.communicaid.com/cross-cultural-training/high-and-low-context; and "Spanish Culture and Non-Verbal Communication," http://www.spanishprograms.com/spanish-culture.htm (accessed November 5, 2011).

---

thoughts (ideas, sales points, etc.) to share with an individual customer/prospect or an entire target audience. The source *encodes* a message to accomplish a communication objective. Encoding is the process of translating thought into symbolic form. The source (e.g., ad copy writer, graphic artist) selects specific *signs* from a nearly infinite variety of words, sentence structures, symbols, and nonverbal elements to design a message that will communicate effectively with the target audience. (See the *Global Focus* insert about the differences in cross-cultural communication.)

Communication objective. As discussed in Chapter 2, the objectives of marcom efforts might include creating brand awareness, implanting positive associations in the consumer's memory as a basis for a positive brand image, and influencing behavior (action). Creating effective marketing communications requires that the communicator has a crystal clear idea of what should be accomplished.

Message. The message itself is a symbolic expression of what the communicator intends to accomplish. Advertisements, sales presentations, package designs, social media postings, and point-of-purchase signs are examples of forms of marcom messages.

Message channel. The message channel is the path through which the message moves from source to receiver. Television, radio, newspapers, magazines, the Internet, billboards, T-shirts, packages, point-of-purchase displays, signs painted on automobiles, and advertisements at movie theaters are just some of the more notable channels for delivering brand messages. Messages also are transmitted to customers directly via salespeople and indirectly via word of mouth communication from friends and family members.

Receiver. The receiver is the person or group of people (target audience) with whom the source attempts to share ideas. In marketing communications, receivers are the prospective and present customers of an organization's product or service. Decoding involves activities undertaken by receivers to interpret—or derive meaning from—marketing messages.

Communication outcome. The target audience experiences or realizes an outcome(s) in response to the message (or, more likely, a stream of messages) received from a brand communicator. The outcome will hopefully match the communicator's general objective and result in increased levels of brand awareness, more positive attitudes, or greater purchasing of the brand.

Feedback. Feedback allows the source a way of monitoring how accurately the intended message is being received and whether it is accomplishing its intended objective(s). As shown in Figure 6.1, feedback allows the source to determine whether the original message hit the target accurately or whether it needs to be altered. Using research-based feedback from their markets (e.g., ad copy tests), management can reexamine and often correct ineffective or misdirected marcom messages.

Noise. A message moving through a channel is subject to the influence of extraneous and distracting stimuli. These stimuli interfere with or interrupt reception of the message in its pure and original form. Such interference and distortion is called noise. Noise may occur at any stage in the communication process (see Figure 6.1). For example, at the point of message encoding, the sender may be unclear about what the message is intended to accomplish. A likely result is a poorly focused and perhaps even contradictory message rather than a message that is clear-cut and integrated. Noise also occurs in the message channel—a poor Internet connection, a crowded magazine page on which an advertisement is surrounded by competitive clutter, and a personal sales interaction that is interrupted repeatedly by texting and phone calls. Noise also can be present at the receiver/decoding stage of the process. An infant might cry during a television commercial and block out critical points in the sales message; passengers in an automobile might talk and not listen to a radio commercial; or the receiver simply may not possess the knowledge base needed to understand fully the promotional message. (See the *IMC Focus* insert for a study on "neural candy.")

"Neural Candy": Sounds in Advertising That We Can't Resist

If asked, most people would argue that they are too smart to be persuaded by advertising cues and messages. They are natural skeptics and say they do not pay attention to commercials and online ads. Yet, according to Martin Lindstrom in *Buyology*, neuromarketing research shows that certain aural (and other) cues can be especially appealing to consumers. Given that (according to Lindstrom) 83 percent of all advertising appeals rely on only one of our senses—sight—there is plenty of room to appeal to other ignored senses.

To determine what cues might appeal to our auditory sense, Lindstrom played recordings to consumers from McDonald's "I'm Lovin' It" jingle,

to birds chirping, to cigarettes being lit. The highest ranked sounds (based on enhanced recall, positive affect) was clearly that of a baby laughing, followed by a vibrating cell phone, ATM dispensing cash, steak sizzling on a grill, and a soda being popped and poured. Interestingly, most responded to sound cues when they were more subtle and better matched with the product in question. (Be sure to watch the video from the *Time* source link below.)

Sources: Jeffrey Kluger, "Neural Advertising: The Sounds We Can't Resist," *Time*, March 1, 2010, 43–45, http://www.time.com/time/magazine/article/0,9171,1966467-1,00.html; and Martin Lindstrom, *Buyology: Truth and Lies About What We Buy*, 2008, NY: Doubleday.

Marketing Communication and Meaning

Fundamental to the concept and practice of communication and positioning is the idea of *meaning*. This section discusses the nature of meaning using a perspective known as semiotics. Semiotics, broadly speaking, is the study of signs and the analysis of meaning-producing events.[3] The important point of emphasis is that the semiotics perspective sees meaning as a *constructive process*. That is, meaning is determined both by the message source's choice of communication elements and, just as importantly, by the receiver's unique social-cultural background and mind-set. Thus, meaning is not thrust upon consumers; rather, consumers are actively involved in constructing meaning from messages.

The fundamental concept in semiotics is the *sign*, the noun counterpart to the verb *signify*. (Singers sing; runners run; dancers dance; and signs signify!) Marketing communications in all its various forms uses signs in the creation of messages. When reading the word *sign*, you probably think of how this word is used on an everyday basis—such as road signs (stop, yield, danger, or directional signs), store signs, signs announcing a car or home for sale, and signs of less tangible concepts such as happiness (the happy face sign). The general concept of a sign encompasses these everyday notions, but includes

many other types of signs, including words, visualizations, tactile objects, and anything else that is perceivable by the senses and has the potential to communicate meaning to the receiver, who in semiotics terms is also referred to as an interpreter. For example, certain sounds (e.g., baby laughing) have been described as "neural candy," leading to outcomes such as enhanced recall and positive affect.[4]

Formally, a sign is something physical and perceivable that signifies something (the *referent*) to somebody (the *interpreter*) in some *context*.[5] The dollar sign ($), for example, is understood by many people throughout the world as signifying the currency of the United States (as well as the currencies of Australia, Canada, Hong Kong, New Zealand, and several other countries). The thumbs-up sign (Figure 6.2) signifies a positive reaction to or appraisal of an action or event. For example, movie critics sometimes signify that they like a new movie by displaying an upward thumb sign; or parents display the thumbs-up when their children perform well in artistic or athletic events. Interestingly, as indicated in the *Global Focus*, the upward thumb in the Middle East signifies an entirely different meaning than in the West; it represents a crass expression not unlike the middle-finger sign in the West. This difference in sign usage indicates that meaning is contained within the person and not the sign per se; in other words, meaning is both idiosyncratic and context dependent—meaning is *constructed*!

FIGURE 6.2 The Thumps-Up Sign

The Meaning of Meaning

Although we use signs to share meaning with others, the two terms (*signs* and *meanings*) are not synonymous.[6] Signs are simply stimuli that are used to evoke an intended meaning in another person. But words and nonverbal signs do not have meanings per se; instead, *people have meanings for signs*. Meanings are internal responses people hold for external stimuli. Many times people have different meanings for the same words, gestures, or symbols. For example, if one asks a retail clerk in the Southeast for a Coca-Cola ("Coke"), a likely response would be "What type of Coke do you want?" referring to *any* type of soft drink or soda—including Pepsi!

Consumers interpret a sign as intended when signs are common to both the sender's and the receiver's fields of experience. A field of experience, also called the *perceptual field*, is the sum total of a person's experiences that are stored in memory. Like a Venn diagram, the larger the overlap, or commonality, in their perceptual fields, the greater the likelihood that signs will be interpreted by the receiver/interpreter in the manner intended by the sender. Effective communication is severely compromised when, for example, marketing communicators use words, visualizations, or other signs that customers do not understand. This is especially problematic when developing communication programs for consumers in other cultures.

Up to this point, we have referred to meaning in the abstract. Now a definition is in order. Meaning can be thought of as the *thoughts and feelings* that are evoked within a person when presented with a sign in a particular *context*.[7] It should be clear that meaning is internal to an individual, subjective, and highly context dependent. Again, meaning is not imposed upon us, but rather is constructed by the interpreter of signs, such as consumers who are barraged daily with hundreds of advertisements and other marcom messages.

The Dimensions of Meaning

Although people learn meaning from individual signs, such signs (words) are rarely used independently of one another. Normally, they are placed in a certain series or order according to prescribed rules of grammar—which is known as *syntax*. Such syntax can elicit different meanings and we now describe four dimensions of meaning based on different orderings and content: denotative, connotative, structural, and contextual meaning.

Denotative meaning refers to exact or direct meaning, as expressed in sign-object relationships. This might be found in express ad claims, such as "Our car gets 100 miles per gallon." Words high in denotative meaning are words that are most strongly object-tied. In contrast, *connotative meaning* refers to implied or interpretative meaning in sign-object relationships. An example might be the use of puffery in an implied ad claim, such as "Our car gets great gas mileage." Words such as *great, good, dependable, quality, attractive*, etc. elicit different responses from different people.

Structural meaning provides understanding from simple sign-to-sign relationships. For example, if you saw a product claim, "Scope has $T_2 5^*$," most of us would probably not know what $T_2 5^*$ means. We can try to infer meaning from the structure; however, we really need greater context to help with the interpretation of the sign. So, *contextual meaning* provides a description of signs to aid in their interpretation. For example, the following provides added contextual meaning: "Scope has $T_2 5^*$. $T_2 5^*$ is a blend of active agents that provides better oral protection and refreshment." Offering the right contextual meaning to consumers who may be limited in their ability to interpret difficult marketing communications (e.g., owners' manuals, prescription drug leaflets, and credit card terms) due to literacy and other knowledge deficiencies should be an important issue for any marketer.

Meaning Transfer: From Culture to Object to Consumer

The culture and social systems in which marketing communications take place are loaded with meaning. Through the process of socialization, people learn cultural values, form beliefs, and become familiar with the physical cues representing these values and beliefs. The artifacts of culture are charged with meaning, which is transferred from generation to generation. For example, the Lincoln Memorial and Ellis Island are signs of freedom to Americans. To Germans, and many other people throughout the world, the now-crumbled Berlin wall signified oppression and hopelessness. Comparatively, yellow ribbons signify crises and hopes for hostage release and the safe return of military personnel. Pink ribbons signal support for breast cancer victims. Red ribbons have grown into an international symbol of solidarity on AIDS. The Black Liberation flag with its red, black, and green stripes—representing blood, achievement, and the fertility of Africa—symbolizes civil rights.

Marketing communicators, when in the process of positioning their brands, draw meaning from the *culturally constituted world* (i.e., the everyday world filled with artifacts such as the preceding examples) and transfer that meaning to their brands. Advertising is an especially important instrument of meaning transfer and positioning.[8]

When exposed to an advertisement (or any other form of marcom message), the consumer is not merely drawing information from the ad but is actively involved in assigning meaning to the advertised brand.[9] Stated alternatively, the consumer approaches advertisements as texts to be interpreted.[10] (Note that the term *text* refers to any form of spoken or written words and images, which clearly encompasses advertisements.)

As an example, consider an advertisement for the Honda Accord that was created some years ago when American consumers were suspicious of Japanese-made automobiles and perhaps even considered it un-American to buy something other than an American model. Shortly after the Honda Motor Company began producing automobiles in the United States, it undertook a print advertising campaign to convey that four out of five Accords sold in America are manufactured in the United States. Beyond stating this fact in the ad copy, the two-page advertisement presented large photos of five icons of American culture: a hamburger, cowboy boots, an oversized bicycle (not like the sleek, Asian or European racing bikes), a baseball, and a jazz ensemble. By associating itself with these well-known symbols of American consumer culture, Honda pulled meaning from the "culturally constituted world" of its target audience consumers, most of whom would immediately recognize the five icons as uniquely American. The obvious intent was subtly to convey the meaning to consumers that the Accord, embedded as it was among the five icons of American popular culture, is made in America and thus is itself American. If Honda's advertising agency had made such a claim in stark, verbal form ("Honda is an American automobile!"), most readers would have doubted the claim, fully realizing that the Honda is of Japanese origin. But by presenting the message at a nonverbal level and merely via association with American icons, consumers probably were somewhat inclined to accept the Honda Accord as at least quasi-American.

Consider also the two advertisements for V8 vegetable juice in Figure 6.3 that embed this brand in the context of health and fitness symbols—one ad showing bottles of V8 juice as ear plugs on a stethoscope and the other displaying multiple bottles of V8 juice arranged into the shape of a zipper. The suggestion is that V8, which is made with 100 percent vegetable juice, is good for the heart and also the waist. (We will ignore sodium levels for now!) Thus, once again we see an advertiser using well-known symbols to draw meaning from the "culturally constituted world" and attempt to transfer that meaning to the advertised brand.

The Use of Figurative Language in Marketing Communications

Symbol usage is widespread in marketing communications. A symbol relation is formed when an object (such as a brand) becomes a symbol of something else (a referent) when the object and referent have no prior intrinsic relationship but rather are arbitrarily or metaphorically related.[11] Prudential Insurance advertises itself as "The Rock" and portrays the company in the context of the Rock of Gibraltar. The rock metaphor symbolizes strength and security, which are good traits for an insurance company. Merrill Lynch (now part of Bank of America) features a bull in its advertising, undoubtedly because in financial circles the bull is a symbol of growth and prosperity. Nike has made famous the "swoosh" symbol to identify its brand and impart the notion of speed—a key performance

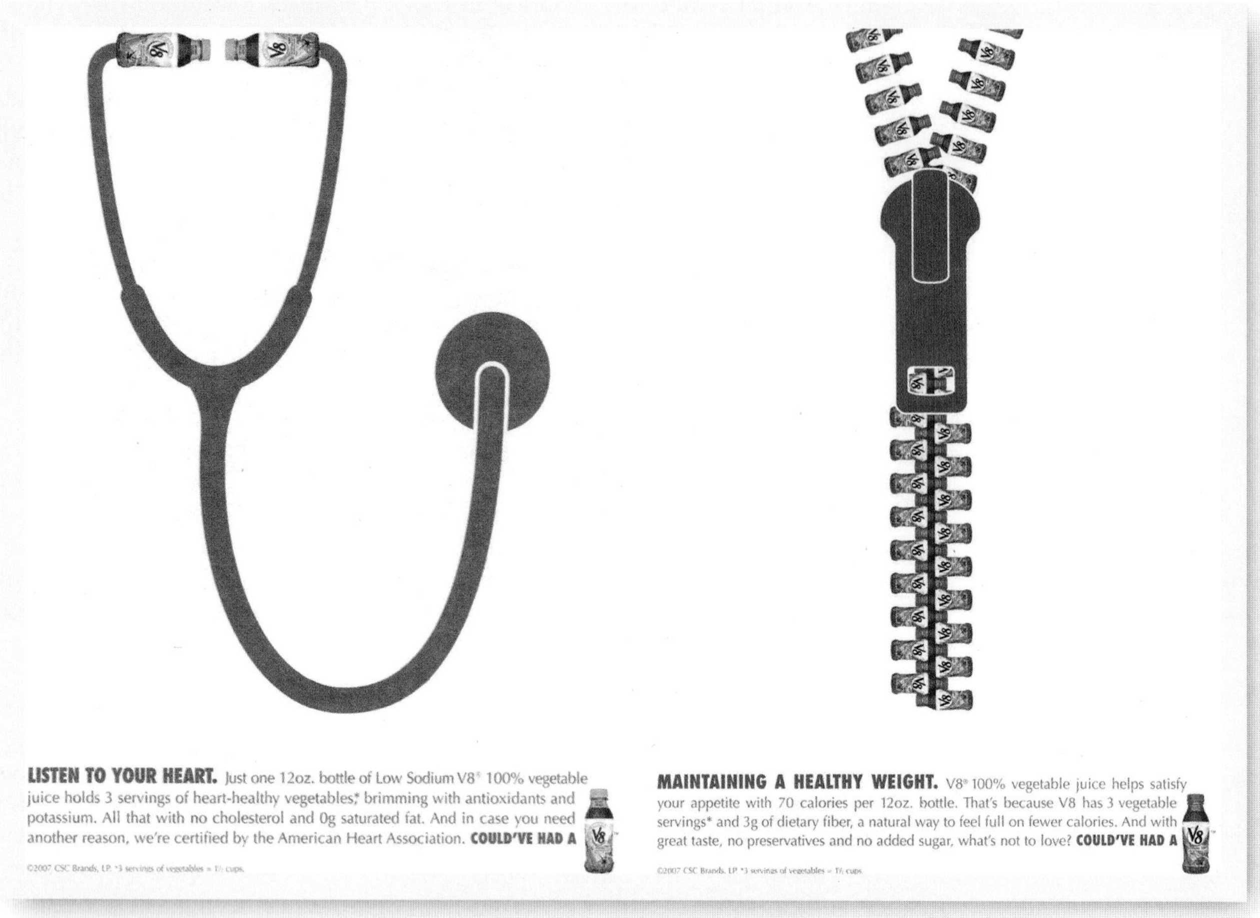

LISTEN TO YOUR HEART. Just one 12oz. bottle of Low Sodium V8® 100% vegetable juice holds 3 servings of heart-healthy vegetables,* brimming with antioxidants and potassium. All that with no cholesterol and 0g saturated fat. And in case you need another reason, we're certified by the American Heart Association. **COULD'VE HAD A** V8

©2007 CSC Brands, LP. *5 servings of vegetables = 2½ cups.

MAINTAINING A HEALTHY WEIGHT. V8® 100% vegetable juice helps satisfy your appetite with 70 calories per 12oz. bottle. That's because V8 has 3 vegetable servings* and 3g of dietary fiber, a natural way to feel full on fewer calories. And with great taste, no preservatives and no added sugar, what's not to love? **COULD'VE HAD A** V8

©2007 CSC Brands, LP. *3 servings of vegetables = 1½ cups.

FIGURE 6.3 Illustration of Contextual Meaning—V8 Advertisements

attribute, especially when this brand was introduced in the heyday of the jogging and road-running craze.

When establishing symbolic relations, marketing communicators often utilize *figurative*, or nonliteral, language. Figurative language involves expressing one thing (such as a brand) in terms normally used for denoting another thing (such as an idea or object) with which it may be regarded as analogous.[12] Three forms of figurative language used by marketing communicators are simile, metaphor, and allegory.[13]

Simile. Simile uses a comparative term such as *like* or *as* to join items from different classes of experience. "Love is like a rose" exemplifies the use of simile.[14] For many years, viewers of the soap opera *Days of Our Lives* have listened to the program open with the intonation of the simile: "Like sands through an hourglass, so are the days of our lives." A tourist advertisement for Jekyll Island, a popular resort on the coast of Georgia, illustrates one advertiser's use of simile in proclaiming: "Jekyll Island, Georgia. Like the tide, it draws you back again and again." Advertising slogans sometimes use simile, as illustrated in the advertisement in Figure 6.4 that likens using the Hydro 5 to feeling like it's a blast of hydration.

Metaphor. Metaphor differs from simile in that the comparative term (*as, like*) is omitted (love is a rose; she has a heart of gold; he is a prince, etc.). Metaphor applies a word or a phrase to a concept or object that it does not literally denote in order to suggest a comparison and to make the abstract more concrete. With metaphor, the qualities of one object or idea are transferred to another object such as a brand. Metaphors are widely used in advertising

It's like a blast of hydration.

Image courtesy of The Advertising Archives

FIGURE 6.4 Illustration of a Simile Usage

Image courtesy of The Advertising Archives

FIGURE 6.5 The Use of Metaphor—Budweiser

because they arouse and enliven the consumer's imagination, represent an effective yet economical (in terms of print space or broadcast time) way to create brand associations, and can enhance persuasion.[15] When used in advertising, metaphors create a picture in consumers' minds and tap into meaning shared both by the advertiser and consumer.[16] Metaphors may not accomplish their desired objective, however, if the metaphor is complicated or too abstract.[17]

Metaphors abound in advertisements. Advertising metaphors occur in verbal form, through visual representations, or by combining verbal and visual presentation. For example, all of the following advertising slogans have been used or are now being used: Wheaties is the "breakfast of champions"; Budweiser is the "king of beers" (Figure 6.5); and Pioneer is the "art of entertainment." In using metaphor, the advertiser hopes that by repeatedly associating its brand with a well-known and symbolically meaningful referent, the meaning contained in the referent will eventually transfer to the brand.

Consider the following illustrative uses of metaphor in advertisements. Figure 6.6 for Geico insurance associates a caveman (usually incapable of modern human understanding) with online insurance services "So easy a caveman can do it." An ad for Cheer laundry detergent uses a visual metaphor in comparing its ability to preserve

FIGURE 6.6 The Use of Metaphor—Geico

clothes from fading with a Mason jar's widely understood capacity for preserving food products from spoiling.

Allegory. Allegory, a word derived from a Greek term meaning *other-speak*, represents a form of *extended metaphor*. Allegorical presentation equates the objects in a particular text (such as the advertised brand in a television commercial) with meanings outside the text itself.[18] In other words, "allegory conveys meaning in a story-underneath-a-story, where something other than what is literally represented is also occurring."[19] In addition to the use of metaphor, another determining characteristic of allegorical presentation is *personification*.[20]

Through personification, the abstract qualities in a brand (its attributes or benefits) assume positive human characteristics. Current or past examples of allegorical characters in advertising include:

1. Mr. Clean, who personifies heavy-duty cleaning ability in the brand of cleaner whose package he adorns.
2. Mr. Goodwrench (General Motors), who exemplifies professional, efficient car service.
3. The Pillsbury dough boy, who signifies the joy of making (and eating) cookies and fond remembrances.
4. The Geico gecko (Figure 6.7), who exemplifies a smart-thinking spokesperson touting how much money you could be saving with Geico.
5. The Qantas koala bear personifies the CEO-type treatment one can expect to receive when flying Qantas business class for this Australian-based airline. The advertisement's body copy mentions several attractive

FIGURE 6.7 Illustration of Personification—The Geico Gecko

features of flying business class, but the "story beneath the story" is that the business-class passenger will be pampered in a fashion found for CEOs of major corporations.

Allegory often is used in promoting products that are difficult to advertise without upsetting, offending, or boring some audience members. Advertisers have found that using personifications (e.g., human-like animals or person-like product characters) makes advertising of these potentially offensive or mundane products more palatable to audiences. For example, the "successful," albeit much-criticized and now retired, advertising campaign for Camel cigarettes employed the camel personification known as Old Joe or Smooth Joe. Joe was the embodiment of hip. In the many executions of this campaign, Joe was always portrayed as a cool, adventurous, swinging-single-type character. The subtle implication was that smoking Camels was itself the with-it thing to do. Although there are distinct ethical issues associated with this campaign, there is no questioning its effectiveness. Two years after Old Joe's introduction, Camel shipments rose 11.3 percent and market share increased from 3.9 to 4.3 percent.[21] This may seem a pittance, but every share point in the cigarette industry amounts to sales in the hundreds of millions of dollars. The critics of smoking, especially concerning youth, were outraged by RJRT's advertising of Camel cigarettes; indeed, Joe Camel in its allegorical splendor became the rallying point around which criticism of tobacco advertising was based and restrictions were eventually imposed,[22] culminating in U.S. Food & Drug Administration oversight of the entire industry in 2011.[23]

Allegory certainly is not restricted to taboo products. Consider the advertising campaign for Chevron gasoline, online at www.chevroncars.com/meet. In this campaign, the vehicles are made to look human (called "anthropomorphizing") and in fact serve to personify the lifestyle of the intended market segment. Two such examples are Wendy Wagon, a green station wagon (Figure 6.8) and Pete Pickup, a blue pickup truck (Figure 6.9). Wendy Wagon is aimed at "soccer moms" who constantly are on the go, and Pete Pickup is directed at macho males who want a high-performing pickup truck. On the surface, this concept is an entertaining way of advertising a mundane gasoline product. Slightly below the surface, however, these examples are attempting to persuade consumers that the choice of Chevron gasoline reflects good judgment (she is the "winning wagon" because she visits Chevron; and, for him, "no task is too tough").

FIGURE 6.8 Illustration of Allegory—Chevron Characters

FIGURE 6.9 Illustration of Allegory—Chevron Characters

Behavioral Foundations of Marketing Communications

Marketing communicators direct their efforts toward influencing consumers' brand-related *beliefs, attitudes, emotional reactions*, and *choices*. Ultimately, the objective is to encourage consumers to choose "our" brand rather than a competitive offering. To accomplish this goal, marketing communicators design advertising messages, promotions, packages, brand names, sales presentations, and other forms of brand-related messages—all of which are designed to drive home the brand's meaning, or its positioning. This section focuses on the consumer's perspective by examining how individuals receive and are influenced by marcom messages.

The discussion is based on two different perspectives about how consumers process marcom information and ultimately use this information to choose from among the alternatives available in the marketplace. We will label these the *consumer processing model (CPM)* and the *hedonic, experiential model (HEM)*. From a consumer-processing perspective (CPM), information processing and choice are seen as rational, cognitive, systematic, and reasoned.[24] In the hedonic, experiential perspective (HEM), in contrast, emotions in pursuit of fun, fantasies, and feelings drive consumer processing of marcom messages and behavior.[25] Interestingly, each perspective is certainly not tied to a given type of product purchase (e.g., for a new car). For example, one free-spirited consumer (say, "Jack") may have purchased a metallic blue, Mazda Miata sports car on a whim after work (HEM perspective), whereas another ("Doug") may have spent considerable time in visiting dealers, online services (www.edmunds.com), his insurance agent, and talking with current owners before arriving at the very same car decision (CPM perspective).

A very important point needs to be emphasized before further discussing each framework: consumer behavior is much too complex and diverse to be captured perfectly by two extreme models. So, you should think of these as bipolar perspectives that anchor a continuum of possible consumer behaviors—ranging, metaphorically speaking, from the "icy-blue cold" CPM perspective to the "red-hot" HEM perspective (Figure 6.10). At the CPM end of the continuum is consumer behavior that is based on *pure reason*—cold, logical, and rational. At the HEM end is consumer behavior based on *pure passion*—hot, spontaneous, and perhaps even irrational. Between these extremes rests the bulk of consumer behavior, neither based totally on pure reason or pure passion.

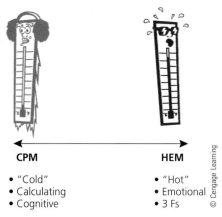

CPM

- "Cold"
- Calculating
- Cognitive

HEM

- "Hot"
- Emotional
- 3 Fs

© Cengage Learning

FIGURE 6.10 Comparison of the CPM and HEM Models

The Consumer Processing Model (CPM)

The following sections discuss consumer information processing in terms of a set of interrelated stages based on William McGuire's Stages of Information Processing.[26] Although the following stages are primarily a part of the CPM, we will deviate on occasion to discuss HEM departures from the traditional CPM perspective.

Stage 1: Being *exposed* to information

Stage 2: Paying *attention*

Stage 3: *Comprehending* attended information

Stage 4: *Agreeing* with comprehended information

Stage 5: *Retaining* accepted information in memory

Stage 6: *Retrieving* information from memory

Stage 7: *Deciding* from alternatives

Stage 8: *Acting* on the basis of the decision

Stage 1: Being Exposed to Information

The marketing communicator's fundamental task is to deliver messages to consumers, who, it is expected, will process the messages, understand the brand positioning, and, if the positioning is congenial with the consumer's preference structure, undertake the course of action advocated by the marketer. By definition, exposure simply means that consumers come in contact with the marketer's message (they see a magazine ad, hear a radio commercial, notice an Internet banner, text message, and so on). Although exposure is an essential preliminary step to subsequent stages of information processing, the mere fact of exposing consumers to the marketing communicator's message does not ensure the message will have any impact. Gaining exposure is a *necessary* but *insufficient* condition for communication success. Ultimate success generally depends on message quality and frequency. The preceding sentence added a qualifier in saying that ultimate success "generally" depends on message quality along with frequency because there is some evidence that simple repeated exposure to a message increases the likelihood that the receiver will judge that message to be true. This is termed the *truth effect* and is more consistent with the HEM perspective.[27]

In practical terms, exposing consumers to a brand's message is a function of two key managerial decisions: (1) providing a sufficient marcom budget and (2) selecting appropriate media and vehicles with which to present a brand message. In other words, a high percentage of a targeted audience will be exposed to a brand's message if adequate funds are allocated and wise choices of media outlets are made; insufficient budget and poor media selection invariably result in low levels of exposure.

Stage 2: Paying Attention

Laypeople use the expression "paying attention" in reference to whether someone is really listening to and thinking about what a speaker (such as a teacher) is saying, or whether his or her mind is wandering off into its own world of thought. For psychologists, the term *attention* means fundamentally the same thing. Attention, in its formal use, means to focus cognitive resources on and think about a message to which one has been exposed. Actually, consumers pay attention to just a small fraction of marcom messages. This is because the demands placed on our attention are great (we are virtually bombarded with advertisements and other commercial messages), but information-processing *capacity is limited*, leading to constraints on one's *opportunity to process* messages.[28] Effective utilization of limited processing capacity requires that consumers selectively allocate mental energy (processing capacity) only to messages that are *relevant and of interest to current goals*.

For example, once their initial curiosity is satisfied, most people who are *not* in the market for a new automobile, especially a luxury brand such as a Mercedes Benz, would pay zero attention to an ad listing detailed comments about the Mercedes Benz because the product has little relevance to them (i.e., *non-attention*). In contrast, in a first type of attention, people who are anxious to purchase a luxury automobile would likely devote *willful or conscious attention* (i.e., *voluntary attention*) to an advertisement for, say, a Mercedes Benz because it would hold a high level of involvement or relevance to their interests. Notice that "conscious attention" is emphasized in the previous sentence. This is to distinguish this deliberate, controlled form of attention from an *automatic* form of relatively superficial attention (i.e., *involuntary attention*) that occurs when, for example, an individual reacts to a loud noise even when the source of the noise holds little, if any, personal relevance.[29] A third type is *non-voluntary attention*, or spontaneous attention, in which the Mercedes Benz ad might offer *potential* interest—but not prior or willful interest, as found in voluntary attention.

How can attention selectivity be avoided? The short answer is that marketing communicators can most effectively gain the consumer's attention by creating messages that truly appeal to their needs for product-relevant information. The likelihood that consumers will pay attention to an advertisement or other form of marcom message also is increased by creating messages that are novel, spectacular, aesthetically appealing, eye catching, and so forth. In conclusion, attention is no easy task, as it is well known that *clutter* reduces message effectiveness.[30]

Stage 3: Comprehension of What Is Attended

To comprehend is to understand and create meaning out of stimuli and symbols. Communication is effective when the meaning, or positioning, a marketing communicator intends to convey matches what consumers actually extract from a message. The term *comprehension* often is used interchangeably with *perception*; both terms refer to *interpretation*. Because people respond to their perceptions of the world and not to the world as it actually is, the topic of comprehension, or perception, is one of the most important subjects in marketing communications.[31]

The perceptual process of interpreting stimuli is called perceptual encoding. Two main stages are involved. Feature analysis is the initial stage whereby a receiver examines the basic features of a stimulus (such as size, shape, color, and angles) and from this makes a preliminary classification. For example, we are able to distinguish a motorcycle from a bicycle by examining features such as size, presence of an engine, and the number of controls. The second stage of perceptual encoding, active synthesis, goes beyond merely examining physical features. The *context* or situation in which information is received plays a major role in determining what is perceived and interpreted, or, in other words, what meaning is acquired. Interpretation results from combining, or synthesizing, stimulus features with expectations of what should be present in the context in which a stimulus is perceived. For example, a synthetic fur coat placed in the window of a discount clothing store (the context) is likely to be perceived as a cheap imitation; however, the same coat, when attractively merchandised in an expensive boutique (a different context) might now be considered a high-quality, stylish garment.

The important point is that consumers' comprehension of marketing stimuli is determined by stimulus features and by characteristics of the consumers themselves. Expectations, needs, personality traits, past experiences, and attitudes toward the stimulus object all play important roles in determining consumer perceptions. Due to the subjective nature of the factors that influence our perceptions, comprehension is often idiosyncratic, or peculiar to each individual. A New Yorker's somewhat biased view in Figure 6.11 of other regions, states, and cities in the U.S. provides an example of selective perception.

A classic statement regarding the idiosyncratic nature of perception is offered in the following quote:

> *We do not simply "react to" a happening or to some impingement from the environment in a determined way (except in behavior that has become reflexive or habitual). We [interpret and] behave according to what we bring to the occasion, and what each of us brings to the occasion is more or less unique.*[32]

This quote is from an analysis of fan reaction to a heatedly contested football game between Dartmouth and Princeton Universities back in 1951. The game was highly emotional and arguments and fights broke out on both sides. Interestingly, fan reaction to the dirty play divided along team loyalties. Dartmouth fans perceived Princeton players as the perpetrators; Princeton fans considered

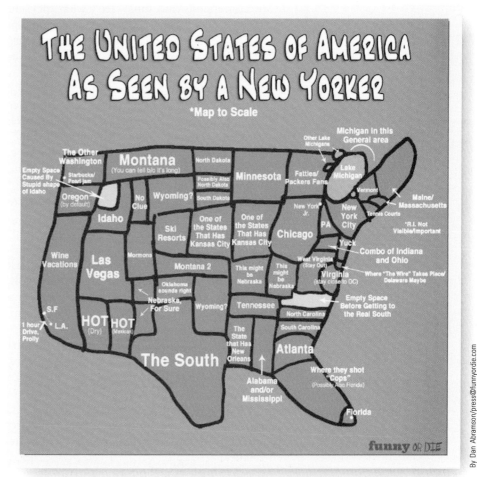

FIGURE **6.11** Humorous Illustration of Selective Perception

Dartmouth players to be at fault; that is, what fans experienced and how they interpreted events depended on their view of who were the "good guys." In short, our individual uniqueness conditions what we see!

An individual's *mood* also can influence one's perception of stimulus objects. Research has found that when people are in a good mood they are more likely to retrieve positive rather than negative material from their memories; are more likely to perceive the positive side of things; and, in turn, are more likely to respond positively to a variety of stimuli.[33] Advertisers are well aware of this, at least intuitively, when they use techniques such as humor and nostalgia to put message receivers in a good mood.

Finally, consumers with creative mind sets tend to be persuaded by ad claims (abstract or concrete) that are *in*compatible with their "mental construal" (i.e., abstract or concrete thinkers).[34] As the authors note, however, future research is needed to see if these ad claim construal effects work for more low-involved consumers.

Miscomprehension People sometimes *misinterpret* or *miscomprehend* messages so as to make them more consistent with their existing beliefs or expectations. This typically is done unconsciously; nonetheless, distorted perception and message miscomprehension are common. Miscomprehension of marcom messages occurs primarily for three reasons: (1) messages are themselves sometimes misleading or unclear, (2) consumers are biased by their own preconceptions and thus "see" what they choose to see, and (3) processing of advertisements often takes place under time pressures and noisy circumstances.

In a study of miscomprehension of three forms of televised communication, programming content, commercials, and public service announcements (PSAs), using a true/false question format with almost 3,000 consumers, the average miscomprehension rate was nearly 30 percent.[35] In ad copy tests involving misleading advertising, the use of control questions on items *not* appearing in the ads revealed a miscomprehension rate of about 10 to 15 percent.[36] Despite some differences in the communications and measures, the moral is clear: Marketing communicators cannot simply assume that consumers interpret messages in the manner intended. Rather, message testing is absolutely imperative before investing in print space, broadcast time, or other media outlets. Also, it is important that marcom messages be repeated so as to assure that most viewers and readers eventually understand the marketer's intended meaning.

Stage 4: Agreement with What Is Comprehended

A fourth information-processing stage involves the matter of whether the consumer *agrees with* (i.e., accepts) a message argument that he or she has comprehended. It is crucial from a marcom perspective that consumers not only comprehend a message but also that they agree with the message (as opposed to countering it or rejecting it outright). Comprehension alone does not ensure that the message will change consumers' attitudes or influence their behavior. Understanding that an advertisement is attempting to position a brand in a certain way is not tantamount to accepting that message. For example, we may clearly understand when a retailer advertises itself as providing outstanding service, but we would not agree with that positioning if we personally have experienced something less than this level of service from that retailer.

Although more information on agreement and persuasion (i.e., attitude change) is presented in Chapter 7, one's motivation, ability, and opportunity to process the message are critical factors in understanding agreement.[37] For example, under high levels of motivation, ability, and opportunity to process the message, message receivers tend to scrutinize message arguments leading to enduring positive or negative attitude change. Yet, if one is deficient in motivation, ability, *or* opportunity to process elements, peripheral cues to the message (e.g., attractive sources, pleasant music, nice scenery) may lead to more temporary positive or negative attitude change.

In the case when message arguments are scrutinized, agreement can depend on whether the message is *credible* (i.e., believable, trustworthy) and whether it contains information and appeals that are *compatible with the values* that are important to the consumer. For example, a consumer who is more interested in the symbolic implications of consuming a particular product than in acquiring functional value is likely to be persuaded more by a message that associates the advertised brand with a desirable group than one that talks about mundane product features. Using endorsers who are perceived as trustworthy is another means of enhancing message credibility. Structuring believable messages rather than making unrealistic claims can also boost credibility.

Stages 5 and 6: Retention and Search and Retrieval of Stored Information

These two information-processing stages, *retention* and *search and retrieval*, are discussed together because both involve *memory* factors.[38]

From a marcom perspective, memory involves the related issues of what consumers remember (recognize and recall) about marketing stimuli and how they access and retrieve information when in the process of choosing among product alternatives. The subject of memory is inseparable from the process of learning, so the following paragraphs first discuss the basics of memory, then examine learning fundamentals, and finally emphasize the practical application of memory and learning principles to marketing communications.

Elements of Memory In general, three competing models show how memory operates: (1) multiple store, (2) levels of processing, and (3) spreading activation.[39] In the *multiple store approach*, memory consists of long-term memory (*LTM*); short-term, or working, memory (*STM*); and a set of sensory stores (*SS*). Information is received by one or more sensory receptors (sight, smell, touch, and so on) and passed to an appropriate SS, where it is rapidly lost (within fractions of a second) unless attention is allocated to the stimulus. Attended information is then transferred to STM, which serves as the center for current processing activity by integrating information from the sense organs and from LTM. *Limited processing capacity* is the most outstanding characteristic of STM; individuals can process only a finite amount of information at any one time. An excessive amount of information will result in reduced recognition and recall. Furthermore, information in STM that is not thought about or rehearsed will be lost from STM in about 30 seconds or less.[40] (This may happen when you get a cell number from a friend, but then are distracted before you have an opportunity to enter it in your phone.)

Information is transferred from STM to LTM, which cognitive psychologists consider to be a virtual storehouse of unlimited information. (For example, it is likely that you remember the name of your first or primary grade teacher.) Information in LTM is organized into coherent and associated cognitive units, which are variously called *schemata, memory organization packets*, or *knowledge structures*. All three terms reflect the idea that LTM consists of associative links among related information, knowledge, and beliefs. A diagram of the concept of a knowledge structure is illustrated in Figure 6.12. This representation captures one baby-boomer's memory structure for the Volkswagen Beetle, a car she first owned during her college years in the late 1960s and repurchased recently to celebrate her 61st birthday.

In the *levels of processing approach* to memory, individuals have limited processing capacity that can be allocated to processing marcom messages.[41] Specifically, this capacity can be allocated to yield various levels of processing from simple sensory analysis (e.g., the brand logo is big and red) to more complex semantic and cognitive elaborations (e.g., relating the brand to other experiences in memory). Arguably, the lower-level, sensory analysis would require less allocation of capacity than higher and deeper levels (e.g., semantic understanding). It is then argued that the level of processing attained determines the future retention of information. Thus, with levels of processing, the focus is on increasing capacity allocated, rather than on separate memory stores.

Spreading activation theory proposes that links between concepts (e.g., nutrients, diet-disease relationships) in memory are a function of the strength or importance of each link between such concepts.[42] When a concept is primed (e.g., by a "no cholesterol" claim), activation is spread to an expanding set of links in the network (e.g., inferences that the advertised brand is "low fat" or "will not lead to heart disease"). However, this activation process is weakened the further it travels outward in the network. The spreading activation approach is based on only one memory store, rather than multiple stores.

In the CPM perspective, marketing communicators continually attempt to alter consumers' long-term memories, or knowledge structures, by facilitating consumer *learning* of information that is compatible with the marketer's interest. Under the HEM approach, learning can be *low involving* in nature. As depicted in Figure 6.13, a person's drive (hunger) can lead to a simple

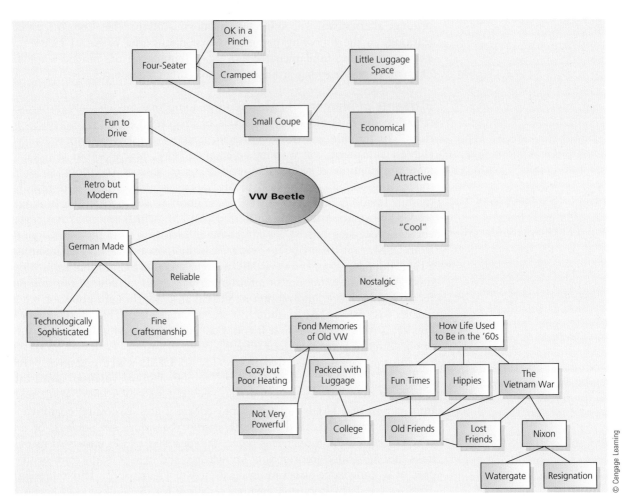

© Cengage Learning

FIGURE **6.12** Consumer's Knowledge Structure for the Volkswagen Beetle

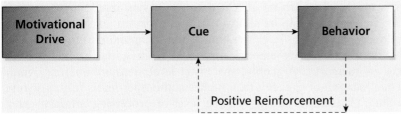

FIGURE **6.13** Low Involvement Learning

Source: Based on *Basic Marketing*, 8e, by E.J. McCarthy and W.D. Perreault, © 1984 Richard D. Irwin, Inc.

recognition of a cue (pizza aroma) to a response (wandering into a pizza shop and eating). If the response is positive (satisfaction from the pizza), then it is likely to serve as a reinforcement and one would return to the cue and behavior when the drive (hunger) reoccurs. This type of HEM learning is similar to classical conditioning with the pairing of cues (brands) in triggering the desired behavior.

Types of CPM Learning Two primary types of CPM learning are relevant to marcom efforts.[43] One form is *strengthening of linkages* between the marketer's brand and some feature or benefit of that brand. Metaphorically, the marketing communicator wishes to build mental "ropes" (rather than flimsy strings) between a brand and its positive features and benefits. The objective is, in other words, to position the brand's essence securely in the consumer's memory. In general, linkages are strengthened by *repeating* claims, being *creative* in conveying a product's features, and presenting claims in a *concrete* fashion. For example, the ad for Philadelphia Extra Light cream cheese (Figure 6.14) compares this brand to a feather and also connects it with an image of an opening of the heavens as concrete metaphorical representations that the brand is as light in fat content (only 6 percent fat) as the

FIGURE 6.14 Illustration of an Effort to Strengthen a Linkage between a Brand and Its Benefits

proverbial feather and that it is "heavenly" good. The marketers of Philadelphia Extra Light cream cheese have attempted to build the strong linkage in consumers' minds that although this is a healthy brand it nonetheless tastes good.

Marketing communicators might facilitate a second form of learning by *establishing entirely new linkages*. Returning to our discussion of brand equity back in Chapter 2, the present notion of establishing new linkages is equivalent to the previously discussed idea of enhancing brand equity by building strong, favorable, and perhaps unique associations between the brand and its features and benefits. Hence, the terms *linkage* and *association* are interchangeable in this context. Both involve a relation between a brand and its *features and benefits that are stored in a consumer's memory*.

Search and Retrieval of Information Information that is learned and stored in memory only impacts consumer choice behavior when it is searched and retrieved. Retrieval is facilitated when a new piece of information is linked, or associated, with another concept that is itself well known and easily accessed. This is precisely what the brand management and ad agency team for Philadelphia Extra Light cream cheese has attempted to accomplish by using a feather as a metaphorical representation that the brand is light in fat content. It is much easier for people to retrieve the concrete idea of a feather as emblematic of lightness than it is to salvage from memory the abstract semantic concept that Philadelphia Extra Light cream cheese is low fat.

The Use of Concretizing and Imagery Concretizing and imagery are used extensively in marketing communications to facilitate both consumer learning and retrieval of brand information. Concretizing is the process of providing more concrete (versus abstract) information for consumers to process, as it is easier for them to remember and retrieve tangible rather than abstract information. Concrete claims about a brand are more perceptible, palpable, real, evident, and vivid. Here are a few illustrations.

1. The makers of Anacin tablets needed a concrete way to present that brand as "strong pain relief for splitting headaches." The idea of splitting headaches was concretized by showing a hard-boiled egg splitting with accompanying sound effects.
2. Tinactin, a treatment for athlete's foot, concretized its relief properties by showing a person's pair of feet literally appearing to be on fire, which is then extinguished by applying Tinactin.
3. To convey the notion that Purina Hi Pro dog food will recharge an active dog and keep it running, a magazine ad portrayed the brand in the form of a battery—doing a better job of conveying the notion of recharging visually than found with the more abstract claim in the ad's body copy.

Underlying some of the above illustrations is the notion of imagery. Imagery is the representation of sensory experiences in short-term, or working, memory—including visual, auditory, and other sensory experiences.[44] When presented with the following words: *smartphone*, *snowboard*, *beach*, and *standard deviation*, the first three are likely to have evoked distinct images in your mind. However, unless you just covered standard deviation in class, it is less likely that this will elicit an image in your mind. What can marketers do to elicit imagery? Three strategies are possible: (1) use visual or pictorial stimuli (Figure 6.15), (2) present concrete verbal stimuli, and (3) provide imagery instructions.[45] (This latter tactic is not used extensively in marcom, although it occurs in radio ads.)

According to dual-coding theory, pictures are represented in memory in verbal as well as visual form, whereas words are less likely to have visual representations.[46] In other words, pictures and visuals (versus words) are better remembered because pictures are especially able to elicit mental images. Research has shown that information about product attributes is better recalled when the information is accompanied with pictures than when presented only as prose.[47] The value of pictures is especially important when verbal information is itself low in imagery.[48]

Consumer researchers have found that people remember significantly greater numbers of company names when the names are paired with meaningful pictorials. For example, the name "Jack's Camera Shop" is better remembered when the store name is presented along with a jack playing card shown holding a movie camera to its eye.[49] Many marketing communicators use similar pictorials, as can be proven by perusing the yellow pages of any city telephone directory and by surfing the Internet. Recently, studies have shown that the use of other non-visual, sense information (aural "candy" cues—such as babies' laughing,[50] or product scents[51]) can improve recall. Yet, in general, if one knows too much, as with extremely knowledgeable consumers, this actually can result in false recall memory.[52]

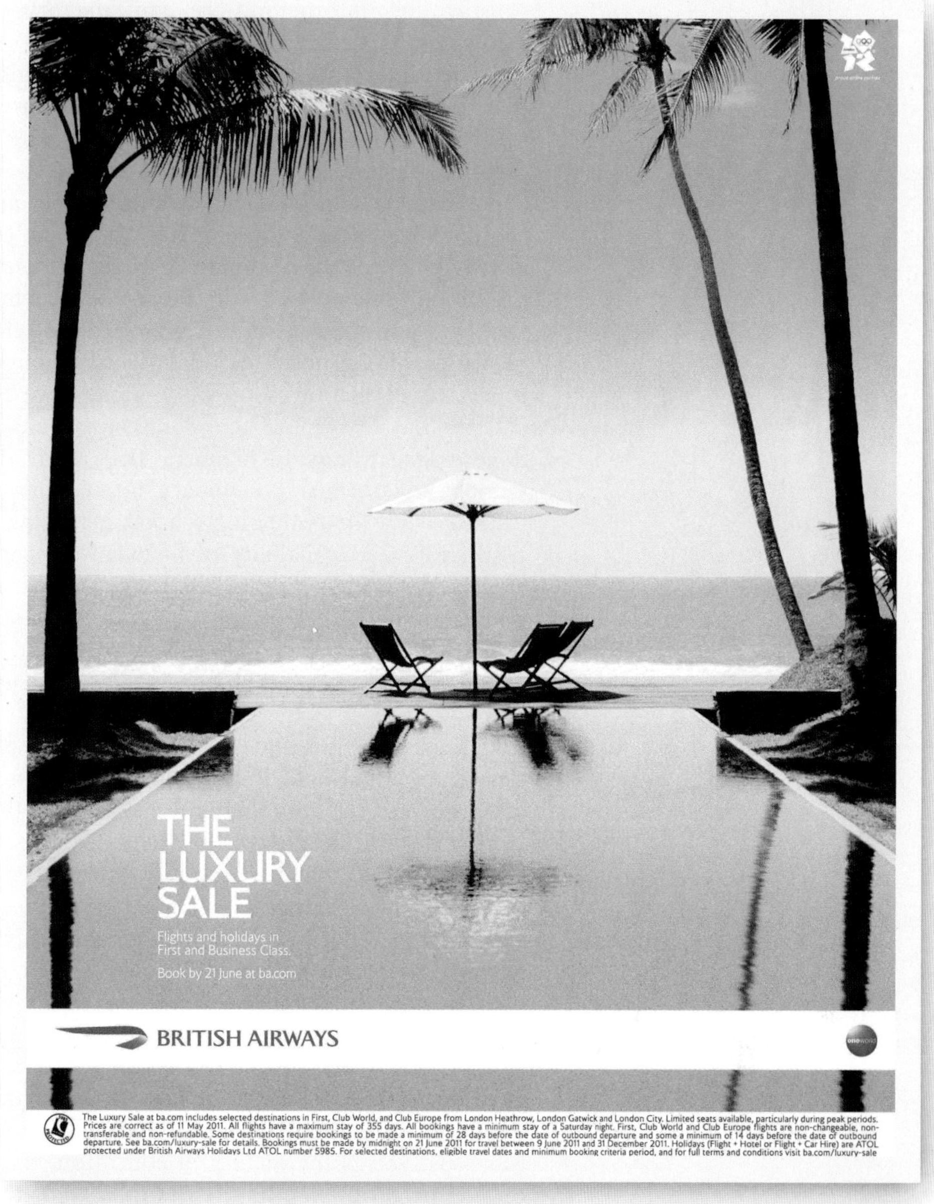

Image courtesy of The Advertising Archives

FIGURE 6.15 Illustration of Visual Imagery

Stage 7: Deciding among Alternatives

The six preceding stages have examined how consumers receive, encode, and store information that is pertinent to making consumption choices. Stored in consumers' memories are numerous information packets for different consumption alternatives. This information is in the form of bits and pieces of *knowledge* (e.g., Coca-Cola is a brand of soft drinks), specific *beliefs* (e.g., Coca-Cola is sweet tasting), and attitudes (e.g., I like Coca-Cola).

The issue for present discussion is this: When contemplating a purchase from a particular product category, how does a consumer decide which brand to choose? The simple answer is that she or he simply selects the "best" brand. However, it is not always clear what the best brand is, especially when considering that the consumer likely has stored in long-term memory a wide variety of information (facts, beliefs, attitudes, etc.) about each brand in his or her consideration set. Some of the information is positive, and some negative; occasionally the information is contradictory; oftentimes the information is incomplete.

The following discussion provides some insight into how consumers react in this situation. It will become clear that consumers often resort to simplifying strategies, or *heuristics*, to arrive at decisions that are at least satisfactory if not perfect. We now examine one of the most important decisions we will ever make, namely, which college or university to attend.

For some of you, there really was no choice—you went to a school you had always planned on attending, or perhaps your parents insisted on a particular institution. Others, especially those of you who work full- or part-time or have family responsibilities, may have selected a school purely as a matter of convenience or affordability; in other words, you really did not seriously consider other institutions. But some of you may have actively evaluated several or many colleges and universities before making a final choice. The process was probably done in the following manner: You received information from a variety of schools and formed preliminary impressions of these institutions; you established criteria for evaluating schools (academic reputation, distance from home, cost, curricula, availability of financial assistance, quality of athletic programs, etc.); you formed weights regarding the relative importance of these various criteria; and you eventually integrated this information to arrive at the all-important choice of which college to attend. Now, let's use this example to understand better the different types of heuristics and the terminology that follows.

The simplest of all decision heuristics is what is called affect referral.[53] With this strategy, the individual simply calls from memory his or her attitude, or affect, toward relevant alternatives and picks that alternative for which the affect is most positive. In the college decision, for example, you may have always liked most the school that you chose to attend (e.g., due to summer camps, sporting events, family influence)—therefore, your affect for it was much stronger than was that for other institutions. In general, this type of choice strategy would be expected for frequently purchased items where risk is minimal.

Consider, by comparison, the use of a compensatory heuristic. In this situation, for a given alternative (college), the strength of one attribute (e.g., education) offsets (or compensates for) the weakness of another attribute (e.g., social life). Thus, *trade-offs* among attitudes are being made. Returning to the college choice decision, other illustrative trade-offs might concern tuition cost versus the quality of education, the size of school versus the quality of athletic programs, or the desirability of the school versus its proximity or distance from home. In general, when applying principles of compensation, the chosen alternative probably is not the best in terms of all criteria; rather, its superiority on some criteria offsets (or compensates for) its lesser performance on other criteria.[54] In short, the consumer typically cannot have it all unless she or he is willing to pay super-premium prices to obtain *crème de la crème* brands.

In contrast to compensatory choice behavior, consumers use a variety of so-called noncompensatory heuristics. With a noncompensatory heuristic, one attribute does *not* compensate for another one. Rather, a series of simple decision rules are used. For example, under a conjunctive model, the consumer establishes minimum cutoffs (e.g., a "7" out of "10") on *all* attributes considered. For instance, using the college choice example, for a given college to be considered, it has to meet or exceed the minimum cutoffs (e.g., a "7" out of "10") on academic quality *and* cost *and* social life. Under the disjunctive model, for an alternative to be considered, it only has to meet or exceed the minimum cutoffs *on just one* of the attributes (e.g., academic quality *or* cost *or* social life.) So, as you might surmise, the disjunctive model is not as discriminating as a conjunctive model. The last noncompensatory heuristic example is the lexicographic model.

Under the lexicographic model, attributes (e.g., academic quality, cost, social life) are first ranked. Then, the alternative (college) that is the best on the highest ranked attribute (e.g., academic quality) is selected. In case of a tie, the alternatives (colleges) would be evaluated on the next highest-ranked attribute (e.g., cost). Of course, a combination of heuristics, or *phased strategies*, might be used as well.

Stage 8: Acting on the Basis of the Decision

It might seem that consumer choice behavior operates in a simple, lockstep fashion. This, however, is not necessarily the case. *People do not always behave in a manner consistent with their preferences.*[55] A major reason is the presence of events, or *situational factors*, that disrupt, inhibit, or otherwise prevent a person from following through on his or her intentions. Situational factors are especially prevalent in the case of low-involvement consumer behavior. Stock-outs, price-offs, in-store promotions, and shopping at a different store are just some of the factors that lead to the purchase of brands that are not necessarily the most preferred and that would not be the predicted choice based on some heuristic, such as affect referral.

What all this means for marketing communicators is that all aspects of marketing (as discussed in Chapter 1) must be coordinated and integrated in order to get consumers to act favorably toward the marketer's offering. Also, perhaps one uses an elaborate compensatory model in trading off attributes in a college choice (e.g., academic quality, cost, social life), and one arrives at a choice, only to have another situational issue (e.g., boyfriend, girlfriend) become the deciding factor.

A CPM Wrap-Up

A somewhat detailed account of consumer information processing has just been presented. As noted in the introduction, the CPM perspective provides an appropriate description of consumer behavior when that behavior is deliberate, thoughtful, or, in short, highly cognitive. No doubt, some important consumer behavior is of this nature. Then again, much behavior also is motivated by emotional, hedonic, and experiential considerations. Therefore, we need to consider the HEM perspective and the implications this model holds for marketing communicators and brand positioning.

The Hedonic, Experiential Model (HEM)

It again is important to emphasize that the *rational* consumer processing model (CPM) and the hedonic, experiential model (HEM) are *not* mutually exclusive. Indeed, there is impressive evidence that individuals use both of these rational and experiential processes operating interactively with one another, with their relative influence based on the situation and the amount of emotional involvement. For example, research shows the greater the emotional involvement, the greater the influence of experiential processes.[56] Therefore, the HEM model probably better explains how consumers process information when they are carefree and happy and confronted with positive outcomes.[57]

Whereas the CPM perspective views consumers as pursuing such objectives as "obtaining the best buy," "getting the most for their money," and "maximizing utility," the HEM viewpoint recognizes that people often consume products for fun, fantasies, or feelings, or in the pursuit of amusement or sensory stimulation.[58] Product consumption from the hedonic perspective results from the *anticipation* of having fun, fulfilling fantasies, or having pleasurable feelings. Comparatively, choice behavior from the CPM perspective is based on the thoughtful evaluation that the chosen alternative will be more functional and provide better results than the alternatives.

The differences between the HEM and CPM perspectives hold meaningful implications for marcom practice. Whereas verbal stimuli and rational arguments designed to position a brand and to affect consumers' product knowledge and beliefs are most appropriate in CPM-oriented marcom efforts, the HEM approach emphasizes nonverbal content or emotionally provocative words and is intended to generate images, fantasies, and positive emotions and feelings. For example, the Subaru Outback, a four-wheel drive vehicle, can attribute much of its success in America to an advertising campaign that used Paul Hogan (a.k.a. Crocodile Dundee) as the spokesperson for the brand by capitalizing on his image as a fearless, charming, and down-to-earth hero from the Australian Outback. This famous advertising campaign achieved success for the Subaru Outback by creating an emotional connection between consumers and the brand.[59]

The advertisement for the Nissan Altima Coupe (Figure 6.16) is an example of the HEM approach to advertising. This advertisement provides little information about product attributes and functional benefits other than to say "True performance." Rather, the ad in its striking simplicity appeals directly to the

FIGURE 6.16 Illustration of an HEM-Oriented Advertisement

emotions of fun and exhilaration by shaping mini-versions of the Nissan Altima Coupe into the form of a running shoe.

The prior discussion and examples have emphasized advertising, but it should be apparent that the differences between the CPM and HEM perspectives apply as well to other forms of marketing communications. A salesperson, for example, may emphasize product features and tangible benefits in attempting to make a sale (CPM approach), or he or she may attempt to convey the fun, fantasies, and pleasures that prospective customers can enjoy with product ownership. Successful salespeople know how to adapt their presentations to different customers—it is hoped, of course, that they are doing it honestly and maintaining standards of morality.

Finally, no single positioning strategy, whether aimed at CPM or HEM processing, is effective in all instances. What works best depends on the specific nature of the product category, the competitive situation, and the character and needs of the target audience. Returning to the fundamentals of positioning in Chapter 5, brands can be positioned to appeal to *functional* needs, which is congenial with the CPM perspective, or to *symbolic* or *experiential* needs, which is more harmonious with the HEM approach.

Summary

Communication is the process of establishing a commonness or oneness of thought between sender and receiver. The process consists of the following elements: a source that encodes a message to achieve a communication objective; a channel that transmits the message; a receiver who decodes the message and experiences a communication outcome; noise, which interferes with or disrupts effective communication at any of the previous stages; and a feedback mechanism that affords the source a way of monitoring how accurately the intended message is being received and whether it is accomplishing its objective.

Signs are used to share meaning, but signs and meaning are not synonymous. Meaning represents people's internal responses toward signs. Meaning is acquired through a process whereby stimuli (signs in the form of words, symbols, etc.) become associated with physical objects and evoke within individuals responses that are similar to those evoked by the physical objects themselves. Marketing communicators use a variety of techniques to make their brands stand for something, to embellish their value, or, in short, to give them meaning. This can be accomplished by relating the brand to a symbolic referent that has no prior intrinsic relation to the brand (forging a symbol relation). Simile, metaphor, and

allegory are forms of figurative language that perform symbolic roles in marketing communications.

This chapter also describes the fundamentals of consumer choice behavior. Two relatively distinct perspectives on choice behavior are presented: the consumer processing model (CPM) and the hedonic, experiential model (HEM). The CPM approach views the consumer as an analytical, systematic, and logical decision maker. According to this perspective, consumers are motivated to achieve desired goals. The CPM process involves being exposed to, attending to, encoding, retaining, retrieving, and integrating information so that a person can achieve a suitable choice among consumption alternatives. The HEM perspective views consumer choice behavior as resulting from the pursuit of fun, fantasy, and feelings. Thus, some consumer behavior is based predominantly on emotional considerations rather than on objective, functional, and economic factors.

The distinction between the CPM and HEM views of consumer choice is an important one for marketing communicators. The techniques and creative strategies for affecting consumer choice behavior clearly are a function of the prevailing consumer orientation. Specific implications and appropriate strategies are emphasized throughout the chapter.

Discussion Questions

1. Discuss the nature and importance of feedback. In what ways do marketing communicators receive feedback from present and prospective customers?
2. A reality of communication is that the same sign often means different things to different people. The red ribbon, for example, means different things to different groups. Provide a good example from your own personal experience in which the same sign might have differential meaning for diverse people. What are the general implications for marketing communications?

3. Some magazine advertisements show a picture of a product, mention the brand name, but have virtually no verbal content except, perhaps, a single statement about the brand. Locate an example of this type and explain what meaning you think the advertiser is attempting to convey. Ask two friends to offer their interpretations of the same ad, and then compare their responses to determine the differences in meaning that these ads have for you and your friends. Draw a general conclusion from this exercise.

4. How can a marketing communicator (such as an advertiser or salesperson) reduce noise when communicating a product message to a customer?

5. The famous Geico gecko commercial humanized a gecko by using personification. The gecko was given a cockney British accent and explained how cheap Geico insurance would be. Explain how this ad illustrates allegorical presentation in advertising.

6. Provide two examples of the use of metaphor in magazine advertisements.

7. When discussing exposure as the initial stage of information processing, it was claimed that gaining exposure is a necessary but insufficient condition for success. Explain.

8. Explain why attention is highly selective and what implication selectivity holds for brand managers and their advertising agencies.

9. Most marketing communications environments are cluttered. Explain what this means and provide several examples. Do not restrict your examples just to advertisements.

10. Explain each of the following related concepts: perceptual encoding, feature analysis, and active synthesis. Using a packaged good of your choice (i.e., a product found in a supermarket, drug store, or mass-merchandise outlet), explain how package designers for your brand have used concepts of feature analysis in designing the package.

11. In what sense would attending a Saturday afternoon college football game represent an hedonic- or experiential-based behavior?

12. Figure 6.12 presents one consumer's knowledge structure for the VW Beetle. Construct your knowledge structure for this vehicle. Then, illustrate your knowledge structure for the one automobile that you most covet owning.

13. Find a commercial that is an application of allegory using personification. What is your interpretation of the commercial? Is there a story told underneath the superficial commercial story?

14. Online advertisements must draw attention away from consumers' primary goals for using the Internet, namely, entertainment and informational pursuits. Expose yourself to some current online ads and then identify and describe at least three specific techniques that online advertisers use to ensure attention. What are the strengths and limitations of each technique?

End Notes

1. Wilbur Schramm, *The Process and Effects of Mass Communication*, Urbana, IL: University of Illinois Press, 1955, 3.

2. Laura L. Bowman, Laura E. Levine, Bradley M. Waite, and Michael Gendron, "Can Students Really Multitask? An Experimental Study of Instant Messages While Reading," *Computers & Education*, 54 (May), 2010, 927–31.

3. For in-depth treatments of semiotics in marketing communications and consumer behavior, see David Glen Mick, "Consumer Research and Semiotics: Exploring the Morphology of Signs, Symbols, and Significance," *Journal of Consumer Research* 13 (September 1986), 196–213; Eric Haley, "The Semiotic Perspective: A Tool for Qualitative Inquiry," in *Proceedings of the 1993 Conference of the American Academy of Advertising*, ed. Esther Thorson, Columbia, MO: The American Academy of Advertising, 1993, 189–96; and Birgit Wassmuth et al., "Semiotics: Friend or Foe to Advertising?" in *Proceedings of the 1993 Conference of the American Academy of Advertising*, ed. Esther Thorson, Columbia, MO: The American Academy of Advertising, 1993, 271–76. For interesting applications of a semiotic analysis, see Morris B. Holbrook and Mark W. Grayson, "The Semiology of Cinematic Consumption: Symbolic Consumer Behavior in Out of Africa," *Journal of Consumer Research* 13 (December 1986), 374–81; Edward F. McQuarrie and David Glen Mick, "On Resonance: A Critical Pluralistic Inquiry into Advertising Rhetoric," *Journal of Consumer Research* 19 (September 1992), 180–97; Linda M. Scott, "Understanding Jingles and Needledrop: A Rhetorical Approach to Music in Advertising," *Journal of Consumer Research* 17 (September 1990), 223–36; and Teresa J. Domzal and Jerome B. Kernan, "Mirror, Mirror: Some Postmodern Reflections on Global Advertising," *Journal of Advertising* 22 (December 1993), 1–20. For an insightful treatment on "deconstructing" meaning from advertisements and other marketing communications, see Barbara B. Stern, "Textual Analysis in Advertising Research: Construction and Deconstruction of Meanings," *Journal of Advertising* 25 (fall 1996), 61–73.

4. Jeffrey Kluger, "Neural Advertising: The Sounds We Can't Resist," *Time*, March 1, 2010, 43–45.

5. This description is based on John Fiske, *Introduction to Communication Studies*, New York: Routledge, 1990; and Mick, "Consumer Research and Semiotics," 198.

6. The subsequent discussion is influenced by the insights of David K. Berlo, *The Process of Communication*, San Francisco: Holt, Rinehart & Winston, 1960, 168–216.

7. This interpretation is adapted from Roberto Friedmann and Mary R. Zimmer, "The Role of Psychological Meaning in Advertising," *Journal of Advertising* 17, no. 1 (1988), 31; and Robert E. Klein III and Jerome B. Kernan, "Contextual Influences on the Meanings Ascribed to Ordinary Consumption Objects," *Journal of Consumer Research* 18 (December 1991), 311–24.

8. Grant McCracken, "Culture and Consumption: A Theoretical Account of the Structure and Movement of the Cultural Meaning of Consumer Goods," *Journal of Consumer Research* 13 (June 1986), 74.

9. For further discussion, see Grant McCracken, "Advertising: Meaning or Information," in *Advances in Consumer Research*, vol. 14, ed. Melanie Wallendorf and Paul F. Anderson, Provo, UT: Association for Consumer Research, 1987, 121–24.

10. Edward F. McQuarrie and David Glen Mick, "Visual Rhetoric in Advertising: Text-Interpretive, Experimental, and Reader-Response Analyses," *Journal of Consumer Research* 26 (June 1999), 37–54; and Linda M. Scott, "The Bridge from Text to Mind: Adapting Reader-Response Theory to Consumer Research," *Journal of Consumer Research* 21 (December 1994), 461–80.

11. Jeffrey F. Durgee, "Richer Findings from Qualitative Research," *Journal of Advertising Research* 26 (August/September 1986), 36–44.

12. Kristine Bremer and Moonkyu Lee, "Metaphors in Marketing: Review and Implications for Marketers," *Advances in Consumer Research* 24 (Provo, UT: Association for Consumer Research, 1997), 419. For additional discussion of figurative language and its role in persuasion, see William J. McGuire, "Standing on the Shoulders of Ancients: Consumer Research, Persuasion, and Figurative Language," *Journal of Consumer Research* 27 (June 2000), 109–14.

13. The following discussion is based on writings by Barbara B. Stern: "Figurative Language in Services Advertising: The Nature and Uses of Imagery," in *Advances in Consumer Research*, vol. 15, ed. Michael J. Houston, Provo, UT: Association for Consumer Research, 1987, 185–90; "How Does an Ad Mean? Language in Services Advertising," *Journal of Advertising* 17, no. 2 (1988), 3–14; "Medieval Allegory: Roots of Advertising Strategy for the Mass Market," *Journal of Marketing* 52 (July 1988), 84–94; and "Other-Speak: Classical Allegory and Contemporary Advertising," *Journal of Advertising* 19, no. 3 (1990), 14–26.

14. Stern, "Figurative Language in Services Advertising."

15. Donna R. Pawlowski, Diane M. Badzinski, and Nancy Mitchell, "Effects of Metaphors on Children's Comprehension and Perception of Print Advertisements," *Journal of Advertising* 27 (summer 1998), 86–87. See also McGuire, "Standing on the Shoulders of Ancients."

16. Nancy A. Mitchell, Diane M. Badzinski, and Donna R. Pawlowski, "The Use of Metaphors As Vivid Stimuli to Enhance Comprehension and Recall of Print Advertisements," in *Proceedings of the 1994 Conference on the American Academy of Advertising*, ed., Karen Whitehill King, Athens, GA: The American Academy of Advertising, 1994, 198–205.

17. Susan E. Morgan and Tom Reichert, "The Message is in the Metaphor: Assessing the Comprehension of Metaphors in Advertisements," *Journal of Advertising* 28 (winter 1999), 1–12.

18. Stern, "How Does an Ad Mean? Language in Services Advertising," 186.

19. Stern, "Other-Speak: Classical Allegory and Contemporary Advertising," 15.

20. Stern, "Medieval Allegory: Roots of Advertising Strategy for the Mass Market," 86. (Stern also recognizes moral conflict as an additional characteristic but notes that moral conflict is less relevant to the use of allegory in advertising than in its historical application. See Stern, "Other-Speak: Classical Allegory and Contemporary Advertising.")

21. Laura Bird, "Joe Smooth for President," *Adweek's Marketing Week*, May 20, 1991, 20–22.

22. For discussion of issues related to tobacco advertising effectiveness and subsequent ad restrictions, see Richard W. Pollay et al., "The Last Straw? Cigarette Advertising and Realized Market Shares Among Youths and Adults, 1979–1993," *Journal of Marketing* 60 (April 1996), 1–16; and Sandra E. McKay, Mary Jane Dundas, and John W. Yeargain, "The FDA's Proposed Rules Regulating Tobacco and Underage Smoking and the Commercial Speech Doctrine," *Journal of Public Policy & Marketing* 15 (fall 1996), 296–302. See especially Joel B. Cohen, "Charting a Public Policy for Cigarettes," in *Marketing and Advertising Regulation: The Federal Trade Commission in the 1990s*, eds. Patrick E. Murphy and William L. Wilkie, Notre Dame, IN: University of Notre Dame Press, 1990, 234–54.

23. *Family Smoking Prevention and Tobacco Control Act* (110 U.S.C. §§ 900-302), June 22, 2009, 1–83.

24. What is being called the *consumer processing model* (CPM) is more conventionally called the *consumer information processing* (CIP) model. CPM is chosen over CIP for two reasons: (1) It is nominally parallel

to the HEM label and thus simplifies memory, and (2) the term *Information* is too limiting inasmuch as it implies that only verbal claims (information) are important to consumers and that other forms of communications (e.g., nonverbal statements) are irrelevant. This latter point was emphasized by Esther Thorson, "Consumer Processing of Advertising," *Current Issues & Research in Advertising* 12, ed. J. H. Leigh and C. R. Martin, Jr., Ann Arbor: University of Michigan, 1990, 198–99.

25. Elizabeth C. Hirschman and Morris B. Holbrook, "Hedonic Consumption: Emerging Concepts, Methods, and Propositions," *Journal of Marketing* 46 (summer 1982), 92–101; and Morris B. Holbrook and Elizabeth C. Hirschman, "The Experiential Aspects of Consumption: Consumer Fantasies, Feelings, and Fun," *Journal of Consumer Research* 9 (September 1982), 132–40.

26. William J. McGuire, "Some Internal Psychological Factors Influencing Consumer Choice," *Journal of Consumer Research* 4 (March 1976), 302–19. See also James B. Bettman, *An Information Processing Theory of Consumer Choice*, Reading, MA: Addison-Wesley, 1979, 1.

27. Scott A. Hawkins and Stephen J. Hoch, "Low-Involvement Learning: Memory without Evaluation," *Journal of Consumer Research* 19 (September 1992), 212–25. See also the *mere exposure* or *familiarity effect* (in which people tend to develop a preference for things merely because they are familiar with them), Robert B. Zajonc, "Attitudinal Effects of Mere Exposure," *Journal of Personality and Social Psychology* 9 (1968, 2, Pt.2): 1–27.

28. Rajeev Batra and Michael L. Ray, "Situational Effects of Advertising Repetition: The Moderating Influence of Motivation, Ability, and Opportunity to Respond," *Journal of Consumer Research* 12 (March 1986), 432–45; and Richard E. Petty and John T. Cacioppo, *Communication and Persuasion: Central and Peripheral Routes to Attitude Change*, New York, NY: Springer-Verlag, 1986.

29. For an excellent treatment of this distinction as well as a broader perspective on factors determining consumer attention, comprehension, and learning of advertising messages, see Klaus G. Grunert, "Automatic and Strategic Processes in Advertising Effects," *Journal of Marketing* 60 (October 1996), 88–102.

30. Paul Surgi Speek and Michael T. Elliott, "The Antecedents and Consequences of Perceived Advertising Clutter," *Journal of Current Issues and Research in Advertising* 19 (fall 1997), 39–54. In addition to being disliked by consumers, advertising clutter has also been shown to have undesirable effects for the advertising community, at least in the case of magazine circulation. See Louisa Ha and Barry R. Litman, "Does Advertising Clutter Have Diminishing and Negative Returns?" *Journal of Advertising* 26 (spring 1997), 31–42.

31. A thorough discussion of comprehension processes is provided by David Glen Mick, "Levels of Subjective Comprehension in Advertising Processing and Their Relations to Ad Perceptions, Attitudes, and Memory," *Journal of Consumer Research* 18 (March 1992), 411–24.

32. Albert H. Hastorf and Hadley Cantril, "They Saw a Game: A Case Study," *Journal of Abnormal & Social Psychology* 49 (1954), 129–34.

33. Alice M. Isen, Margaret Clark, Thomas E. Shalker, and Lynn Karp, "Affect, Accessibility of Material in Memory, and Behavior: A Cognitive Loop," *Journal of Personality and Social Psychology* 36 (January 1978), 1–12; and Meryl Paula Gardner, "Mood States and Consumer Behavior: A Critical Review," *Journal of Consumer Research* 12 (December 1985), 281–300.

34. Xiaojing Yang, Tortsen Ringberg, Huiwang Mao, and Laura A. Peracchio, "The Construal (In)compatibility Effect: The Moderating Role of a Creative Mind-Set," *Journal of Consumer Research* 38 (December 2011), forthcoming.

35. Jacob Jacoby and Wayne D. Hoyer, "Viewer Miscomprehension of Televised Communication: Selected Findings," *Journal of Marketing* 46 (fall 1982), 12–26.

36. J. Craig Andrews and Thomas J. Maronick, "Advertising Research Issues from FTC Versus Stouffer Foods Corporation," *Journal of Public Policy & Marketing*, 14 (fall 19995), 301–309.

37. Ibid, Batra and Ray; Ibid, Petty and Cacioppo.

38. Several valuable sources for technical treatments of memory operations are available in the advertising and marketing literatures. See Bettman, "Memory Functions," *An Information Processing Theory of Consumer Choice*, chap. 6; James B. Bettman, "Memory Factors in Consumer Choice: A Review," *Journal of Marketing* 43 (spring 1979), 37–53; Andrew A. Mitchell, "Cognitive Processes Initiated by Advertising," in *Information Processing Research in Advertising*, ed. R. J. Harris, Hillsdale, NJ: Lawrence Erlbaum Associates, 1983, 13–42; Jerry C. Olson, "Theories of Information Encoding and Storage: Implications for Consumer Research," in *The Effect of Information on Consumer and Market Behavior*, ed. A. A. Mitchell, Chicago: American Marketing Association, 1978, 49–60; Thomas K. Srull, "The Effects of Subjective Affective States on Memory and Judgment," in *Advances in Consumer Research*, vol. 11, ed. T. C. Kinnear, Provo, UT: Association for Consumer Research, 1984; and Kevin Lane Keller, "Advertising Retrieval Cues on Brand Evaluations," *Journal of Consumer Research* 14 (December 1989), 316–33.

39. James R. Bettman, "Memory Factors in Consumer Choice: A Review," *Journal of Marketing* 43 (spring 1979), 37–53.

40. Richard M. Shiffrin and R. C. Atkinson, "Storage and Retrieval Processes in Long-Term Memory," *Psychological Review* 76 (March 23, 1969), 179–93.

41. Fergus I.M. Craik and Robert S. Lockhart, "Levels of Processing: A Framework for Memory Research," *Journal of Verbal Learning and Verbal Behavior* 11, 671–84.

42. Allan M. Collins and Elizabeth F. Loftus, "A Spreading Activation Theory of Semantic Processing," *Psychological Review* 82 (6), 407–28.

43. Andrew A. Mitchell, "Cognitive Processes Initiated by Advertising," in *Information Processing Research in Advertising*, ed. R.J. Harris, Hillsdale, NJ: Lawrence Erlbaum Associates, 1983, 13–42.

44. Kathy A. Lutz and Richard J. Lutz, "Imagery-Eliciting Strategies: Review and Implications of Research," in *Advances in Consumer Research*, vol. 5, ed. H. Keith Hunt, Ann Arbor, MI: Association for Consumer Research, 1978, 611–20.

45. Ibid, Lutz and Lutz, 611–20.

46. Allan Paivio, "Mental Imagery in Associative Learning and Memory," *Psychological Review* 76 (May 1969), 241–63; and John R. Rossiter and Larry Percy, "Visual Imaging Ability as a Mediator of Advertising Response," in *Advances in Consumer Research*, vol. 5, ed. H. Keith Hunt, Ann Arbor: Association for Consumer Research, 1978, 621–29.

47. Michael J. Houston, Terry L. Childers, and Susan E. Heckler, "Picture-Word Consistency and the Elaborative Processing of Advertisements," *Journal of Marketing Research* 24 (November 1987), 359–69.

48. H. Rao Unnava and Robert E. Burnkrant, "An Imagery-Processing View of the Role of Pictures in Print Advertisements," *Journal of Marketing Research* 28 (May 1991), 226–31.

49. Kathy A. Lutz and Richard J. Lutz, "The Effects of Interactive Imagery on Learning: Application to Advertising," *Journal of Applied Psychology* 62 (August 1977), 493–98.

50. Kluger, "Neural Advertising," 43–45.

51. Aradhna Krishna, May O. Lwin, and Maureen Morrin, "Product Scent and Memory," *Journal of Consumer Research* 37 (June 2010), 57–67.

52. Ravi Mehta, Joandra Hoegg, and Amitav Chakravarti, "Knowing Too Much: Expertise-Induced False Recall Effects in Product Consumption," *Journal of Consumer Research* 38 (October 2011), forthcoming.

53. Peter L. Wright, "Consumer Choice Strategies: Simplifying vs. Optimizing," *Journal of Marketing Research* 11 (February 1975), 60–67.

54. The best known illustration of compensation in consumer behavior is Fishbein and Ajzen's theory of reasoned action, which states that one's attitude toward performing an action is the sum of one's beliefs regarding the outcomes of the action weighed by one's evaluation of those outcomes. Further discussion of this can be found in the next chapter.

55. Martin Fishbein and Icek Ajzen, *Beliefs, Attitude, Intention, and Behavior: An Introduction to Theory and Research*, Reading, MA: Addison Wesley, 1975.

56. Veronika Denes-Raj and Seymour Epstein, "Conflict between Intuitive and Rational Processing: When People Behave against Their Better Judgment," *Journal of Personality and Social Psychology* 66, no. 5 (1994), 819–29.

57. Ibid.

58. Hirschman and Holbrook, "Hedonic Consumption."

59. For a fascinating discussion of the Subaru Outback advertising campaign, see Sal Randazzo, "Subaru: The Emotional Myths behind the Brand's Growth," *Journal of Advertising Research* 46 (March 2006), 11–17.

CHAPTER 7

The Role of Persuasion in Integrated Marketing Communications

MARCOM INSIGHT Can We Be Persuaded to Overcome Bad Habits? The Cell-Free Club

Persuasion can be challenging. By definition, it is an effort by people (e.g., marketing communicators) to change one's attitude or behavior. It can be especially difficult when it involves overcoming bad habits, such as excessive cell phone or smartphone use, smoking, drug and alcohol addictions, eating disorders, gambling, 24/7 social media use (Facebook, Twitter), and so on.

For instance, always being connected can have its disadvantages, as many can attest. A recent article by humor writer Joel Stein documents the many ways in which bad things can happen with excessive cell phone use. Many interviewed for the story comment that they cannot remember close friends' phone numbers or appointments

© Kirill P/Shutterstock.com

anymore without checking their cell. Also, it seems as if *everyone* owns one, as a frequent world traveler (a deputy editor with *Conde Nast*) notes: "In India, even the yak herders and rickshaw drivers have cell phones."

Others have noticed a decline in meaningful conversations and communications, especially with those who are not in your inner circle. Several managers note a lack of attention and focus in important meetings, when colleagues miss opportunities to contribute because they are glancing at email or leaving the room to make a call. Interestingly, Jonathan Reid, Dean of the College of Arts & Sciences at the University of LaVerne, noticed recently in Israel (and elsewhere) that many of the phones are

Chapter Objectives

After reading this chapter, you should be able to:

1 Understand the nature and role of attitudes in marketing communications, different hierarchy of effects models, and under what conditions that attitudes should predict behavior.

2 Appreciate the role of persuasion in marketing communications.

3 Explain the tools of influence from the marketing communicator's perspective.

4 Discuss the five important factors of persuasion: message strength, peripheral cues, receiver involvement, receiver initial position, and communication modality.

5 Understand the elaboration likelihood model (ELM) and its implications for marketing communications.

6 Understand practical marketing communications efforts that enhance consumers' motivation, opportunity, and ability to process messages.

7 Explain the theory of reasoned action (TORA) and basic attitude, preference, and behavior change strategies.

used as status symbols. Reid recounted that "I was sitting at a very nice restaurant and two men were sitting there with beautiful women and they were on their phones. Do they have something better on the other line?"

So how does one use persuasion to reduce cell-phone addiction? One possibility is showing the behavior of credible and (somewhat) well-known celebrity sources that are (as Stein puts it) part of a very exclusive club—the "cell-free club." It is hoped that addicts will emulate the behavior of this club that has received public notoriety, and includes Warren Buffett, Mikhail Prokhorov (Russian billionaire who owns the Brooklyn Nets), and Travis Smiley (host of a weekly PBS talk show and a national radio show). At his cell-free company (The Smiley Group), Mr. Smiley has noticed a return to more productive conversations and work.

Other techniques such as *anti-branding* have been used on occasion to aid persuasion from bad habits. For example, the National Youth Anti-Drug Media Campaign has employed such anti-branding techniques successfully, through "Parents. The Anti-Drug" (www.theantidrug.com) and "Above the Influence" (www.abovetheinfluence.com). Other anti-branding efforts have been used in state anti-tobacco campaigns (e.g., FACT; Fight Against Corporate Tobacco, www.fightwithfact.com), rallying teens against corporate tobacco efforts.

Additional efforts to fight bad habits and addictions include evaluating where an affected person fits in the "stages of change" toward quitting—pre-contemplation, contemplation, preparation, action, or maintenance—and in turn, designing the right programs and communications to fit the appropriate stage. Finally, understanding a communication's response efficacy (e.g., will this advocated solution solve my problem?) and self-efficacy (e.g., will this solution work for me? Can I do this myself?) are important aspects in the success of persuasive attempts to change behavior. Calls to action and other self-help communications (e.g., 1-800-QUIT-NOW to be placed on U.S. cigarette packages) can aid persuasive attempts via self-efficacy.

In this chapter, we examine major factors accounting for persuasion in marketing communications: receiver initial position, peripheral cues (e.g., source effects), message strength, communication modality, and receiver involvement. Many of these important factors were key issues in the success of the examples and campaigns noted above.

Sources: Joel Stein, "The Cell-Free Club: America's Most Exclusive Club," *Bloomberg Businessweek*, August 9, 2010, 78–79, http://www.businessweek.com/print/magazine/content/10_33/b4191077620370.htm; Vanessa Harmatz, "The Importance of Branding in the National Anti-Drug Media Campaign," *Social Marketing Quarterly* 10 (summer 2004), 59–61; James O. Prochaska, John C. Norcross, and Carlo C. DiClemente, *Changing for Good.* New York: Harper Collins, 1994; R.W. Rogers, "A Protection Motivation Theory of Fear Appeals and Attitude Change," *Journal of Psychology* 91, 93–114; and R.W. Rogers, "Cognitive and Physiological Processes in Fear Appeals and Attitude Change: A Revised Theory of Protection Motivation," in *Social Psychophysiology*, J. Cacioppo and R. Petty, eds. New York: Guilford Press, 1993.

The Nature and Role of Attitudes

What Is an Attitude?

Attitudes are hypothetical constructs; they cannot be seen, touched, heard, or smelled. Because attitudes cannot be observed, a variety of perspectives have developed over the years in attempting to describe and measure them.[1] The term attitude will be used here to mean a general and somewhat enduring positive or negative feeling toward, or evaluative judgment of, some person, object, or issue.[2] Of course, for our purposes, brands are the attitude object of primary interest.

Beyond this basic definition are three other notable features, namely, that attitudes (1) are learned, (2) are relatively enduring, and (3) influence behavior.[3] Consider the following examples of people's attitudes that express feelings and evaluations with varying degrees of intensity: "I like Diet Mountain Dew"; "I really like the initiatives undertaken by Doctors Without Borders"; "I don't like LeBron James"; "I really like Lady Gaga and Katy Perry"; or "I really like my Burton snowboard." All of these attitudes are learned and likely will be retained until there is some strong reason to change them. Moreover, it can be expected that the holders of these attitudes would behave consistently with their evaluations—drinking Diet Mountain Dew, supporting Doctors Without Borders with a donation, questioning LeBron James' move to the Miami Heat, attending a concert for Lady Gaga or Katy Perry, or buying a new Burton snowboard or boots, and so on.

The preceding description focuses on feelings and evaluations, or what is commonly referred to as the affective component ("I like ___"); this is generally what is referred to when people use the word *attitude*. However, attitude theorists recognize two additional components, cognitive and conative.[4] The cognitive component refers to a person's beliefs (i.e., knowledge and thoughts) about an object or issue ("our basketball team is ranked first in their conference"; "talking on cell phones is dangerous while driving"; or "BMW automobiles are well engineered"). The conative component represents one's behavioral tendency, or predisposition to act, toward an object. In consumer-behavior terms, the conative component represents a consumer's intention to purchase a specific item. Generally speaking, attitudes predispose people to respond to an object, such as a brand, in a consistently favorable or unfavorable way.[5] Thus, for example, people who like the idea of reducing addictive cell phone use (as described in the opening *Marcom Insight*) are more likely to engage in programs or activities to reduce this behavior than others who do not embrace this idea.

Hierarchies of Effects

The *high involvement hierarchy* (also known as the "standard learning hierarchy") shows a clear progression under high involvement from initial cognition to affect to conation.[6] An individual becomes aware of an object, such as a new brand, then acquires information and forms beliefs about the brand's ability to satisfy consumption needs (cognitive component). Beliefs are integrated, and feelings toward and evaluations of the product are developed (affective component). On the basis of these feelings and evaluations, an intention is formed to purchase or not to purchase the new product (conative component).

Other alternative "hierarchies of effect" have been postulated, including the *low involvement hierarchy* from minimal cognition to conation (and actual behavior) and then to affect.[7] For example, a student may have heard of San Pellegrino Limonata (i.e., a sparkling lemon water in a distinctive package) from a friend, notice it near a checkout counter, buy and consume it, and then form a feeling about it later. Although the high involvement hierarchy and low involvement hierarchy have received substantial support, other hierarchies have been suggested, such as *dissonance-attribution* (conation → affect → cognition) and *integrative models* (e.g., the Integrative Information Response Model in Chapter 8) that depend on moderators such as involvement.[8]

Using Attitudes to Predict Behavior

Marketing researchers regularly measure consumer attitudes with expectations of being able to accurately predict how consumers will behave. The issue is not whether attitudes predict behavior, but rather, *when* attitudes will accurately predict behavior.[9] Quite often, researchers will complain that for some reason the attitudes measured in their study did not impact behavior. However, in fact, it may have been a matter of not taking into account two important determinants in predicting behavior from attitudes. These two major determinants are: (1) measurement specificity and (2) having direct (versus indirect) experience with the object of the attitude measurement.

Measurement Specificity

A fundamental problem in attitudinal research has been invalid data resulting from the measurement of attitudes and behavior at *different levels of specificity*. Four components of any overt behavior should be considered in order to obtain specific and accurate measures of attitudes. "TACT" consists of (1) the *target* of the behavior, (2) the specific *action*, (3) the *context* in which the behavior occurs, and (4) the *time* when it occurs.[10] For example, if one asks, "What is your attitude toward obtaining (action) an MBA degree (target)?" It is likely that the type of responses will vary considerably, as well as the resulting correlations of these attitudes with actually obtaining such a degree. However, with added specificity of context and time (e.g., "What is your attitude toward obtaining [action] an MBA degree [target] at Marquette University [context] after graduation [time]?"), it is likely that the strength of attitude-behavior relationships will improve.

The Role of Direct Experience

A series of experiments in psychology (e.g., using puzzle game experiences) clearly demonstrated that attitudes based on direct experience (e.g., with the game prior to playing) predicted (playing) behavior better than attitudes based on indirect experience (with just verbal descriptions of puzzles).[11] In another experiment using direct (versus indirect) experience with a cheese-filled pretzel, and then a task to read ads about the pretzels, the results indicated significantly higher levels of attitude-behavior consistency for the direct experience subjects than for the indirect-experience ones.[12] Thus, it is very important in attitude and behavior studies to make sure that respondents are screened for direct experience with the target object (e.g., brand or product).

Persuasion in Marketing Communications

The foregoing discussion of attitudes provides us with useful concepts as we turn now to the strategic issue of how marketing communicators influence customers' attitudes and behaviors through persuasive efforts. Salespeople attempt to convince customers to purchase one product rather than another. Advertisers appeal to consumers' intellect (CPM approach discussed in Chapter 6) or to their fantasies and feelings (HEM approach). Brand managers use online coupons, samples, rebates, and other types of promotions to induce consumers to try their products and to purchase them now rather than later.

Persuasion is the essence of marketing communications. Marketing communicators—along with people in other persuasion-oriented roles (e.g., parents, teachers, theologians, politicians)—attempt to guide people toward the acceptance of (or change to) some belief, attitude, or behavior by using reasoning and emotional appeals.

The Ethics of Persuasion

At times, marketing communicators' persuasion efforts may be undeniably unethical. Shrewd operators have at times misled the unsuspecting and credulous into buying products or services that are never delivered. Elderly consumers, for example, are occasionally hustled into making advance payments for household repairs (e.g., roof repairs) that are never performed. Historically, unscrupulous realtors sold useless swamp land in Florida to unsuspecting retirees who thought they were acquiring prized real estate. Currently, telemarketers and e-mail solicitors sometimes get our attention under the pretense that they are conducting marketing research or representing a charitable cause and then try to sell us something. So, yes, sometimes persuasion by some marketing communicators is unethical. However, it is the *practice* of persuasion that can be noble or deplorable. Nothing is wrong with persuasion per se; it is the practitioners of persuasion who sometimes are at fault. To adapt an old adage: Don't throw the persuasion baby out with the bath water; just make sure the water is clean.

Tools of Influence: The Persuader's Perspective

Persuaders in all capacities of life use various persuasion tools, which have evolved throughout the millennia to influence people. They are widely understood by many persuaders, if only tacitly. Persuadees, such as consumers, learn these tactics—again, if only tacitly—and form knowledge, or schemas, about persuaders' persuasive intent. A well-known persuasion researcher coined the catchy phrase *schemer schema* to capture the idea that people form rather strong and stable intuitive theories about marketers' efforts to influence their actions.[13]

Social psychologist Robert Cialdini has spent much of his professional career studying the persuasive tactics used by car dealers, insurance salespeople, fund-raisers, waiters, and other persuasion practitioners. His studies, involving both fieldwork (as car salesperson, fund-raiser, etc.) and laboratory research, have identified six tools of influence that cut across persuasion practices. (Note: These are what he *observed*; not all may be viewed as passing an ethics test.) Tools that he observed are: (1) reciprocation, (2) commitment and consistency, (3) social proof, (4) liking, (5) authority, and (6) scarcity.[14]

Before discussing these influence tools, it is important to note that these tactics work because much of our behavior occurs in a rather automatic, noncontrolled, and somewhat mindless fashion. Due to limitations on our information processing capacities (as discussed in Chapter 6) and time pressures, we often make judgments and choices without giving a great deal of thought to the matter (i.e., engaging in scripted behavior in response to a trigger). Cialdini called this "click-whirr" behavior. That is, something triggers a response (click), and then an autonomic, scripted behavior follows (whirr).

Reciprocation

As part of the socialization process in all cultures, people acquire a norm of reciprocity. As children we learn to return a favor with a favor, to respond to a nicety with another nicety. Knowing this, marketing communicators sometimes give gifts or samples with hopes that customers will reciprocate by purchasing products. We see this with in-store sampling of food items in supermarkets. Anyone who has ever attended a Tupperware party (or other product party of this sort) knows that the hostess often distributes free gifts at the beginning with designs that attendees will reciprocate with big purchases. College students are encouraged to make application for another credit card after being baited by an offer for a free T-shirt emblazoned with their university's logo.

This happens not only with individual consumers, but also in B2B marketing interactions. For example, pharmaceutical companies hold dinner meetings with physicians. A sales rep invites a small group of physicians to dinner at an expensive restaurant; exposes them to a product presentation before dinner; wines and dines them; then, afterwards, presents them with, say, a $100 "honorarium" for having given their time and attention. Research shows that

80 percent of dinner meetings produce increased sales of the presented brand. Click-whirr: "Something nice was done for me; I should return the favor."[15]

You would be correct if you are thinking that reciprocation tactics do not always work. Sometimes we "see through" the tactic and realize that the nicety is not really a sincere offering but rather a come-on to get us to respond in kind. (In addition, many purchasing agents, federal employees, etc. are subject to rules of ethics regarding limits on accepting gifts from suppliers and customers.) Certainly, the effectiveness of a tactic is contingent on the circumstances: Whether and when a tactic is effective depends on the persuasion circumstances and the characteristics of the persuader and persuadee. As a student of marketing communications, it is strongly recommended that you incorporate this "it depends" thinking into your understanding of marketing practices.

With regard to reciprocation, this tactic is most effective when the persuadee perceives the gift giver as honest and sincere. Party plans like the Tupperware parties typify this situation in that the persuader (the host or hostess) is often friendly with the persuadees who attend.

Commitment and Consistency

After people make a choice (a commitment), there often is a strong tendency to remain faithful to that choice. Consistency is a valued human characteristic. We admire people who are consistent in their opinions and actions. We sometimes feel ashamed of ourselves when we say one thing and do something different. Hence, the marketing communicator might attempt to "click-whirr" the consumer by getting him or her to commit to something (commitment is the click, or trigger) and then hope that the consumer will continue to act in a manner consistent with this commitment.

Consider the tactic often used by automobile salespeople. They might obtain the consumer's commitment to a price or specific model and then say they have to get their sales manager's approval. At this point, the consumer has psychologically committed to buying the car. The salesperson, after supposedly taking the offer to the sales manager, returns and declares that the manager would not accept the price. Nevertheless, the consumer, now committed to owning the car, will often increase the offer. In the trade, this is referred to as lowballing the consumer, a tactic that is widespread because it is effective (albeit not entirely ethical).

When would you expect commitment and consistency to be most effective in marketing communications? (Think first before reading on.) Again, the apparent sincerity of the persuader would play a role. The tactic is unlikely to work when it is obviously deceitful and self-serving. From the persuadee's perspective, it would be expected that consumers are most likely to remain consistent when they are highly involved in their choices. In other words, it is hard not to be consistent when a great amount of thought and psychological energy have gone into a choice.

Social Proof

What do I do? How should I behave? The principle of social proof is activated in circumstances where appropriate behavior is somewhat unclear. Not knowing exactly what to do, we take leads from the behavior of others; their behavior provides social proof of how we should behave. For example, suppose someone asks you for a charitable donation. The appropriate amount to give is unclear, so you might ask the fund-raiser what amount others are giving and then contribute a similar amount. (Or, the fund-raiser will tell you who has given and an average amount.) As discussed in Chapter 3, new-product developers sometimes encourage widespread adoption by giving new products to opinion leaders and trendsetters, who, it is expected, will provide social proof for others to adopt the same behavior. In general, we are most likely to accept the actions of others as correct "when we are unsure of ourselves, when the situation is unclear or ambiguous, when uncertainty reigns."[16]

Game-winning pass.
Ever since I was a kid, my mom
and coach taught me that to play my best,
I need to fuel up to play 60. And one of
the best ways to do that is with milk. Even
now that I'm a Super Bowl champion,
milk's still part of my game plan.
Make it part of yours.

got milk?

whymilk.com/aaronrodgers

RODGERS
12

Eat Right.
Get Active.
Make a Difference.
FUEL UP
play 60
FuelUpToPlay60.com

NFL PLAYERS

© AP Images/PRNewsFoto/MilkPEP

FIGURE 7.1 The Role of Liking–A Milk Mustache Ad

Liking

This influence tactic deals with the fact that we are most likely to adopt an attitude or undertake an action when a likable person promotes that action. There are various manifestations of likability. Two of the more prominent in marketing communications are physical attractiveness and similarity. Research (described in detail in a Chapter 11 dealing with specific message characteristics) has shown that people respond more favorably to others whom they perceive as like themselves and physically attractive. This explains why models in advertising, individuals on magazine covers, and celebrity endorsers are typically attractive people to whom consumers can relate and like. The advertisement presented as Figure 7.1 shows a celebrity (Green Bay Packers' Aaron Rodgers) who has been used in the ongoing "Milk Mustache" advertising campaign undertaken by the National Fluid Milk Processing Promotion Board. These celebrities (including the animated Kermit and the late Curly Howard of the Three Stooges) appeal to various demographic categories and different consumer groups.

Authority

Most people are raised to respect authority figures (parents, teachers, coaches, etc.) and to exhibit a sense of duty toward them. It therefore comes as no surprise that marketing communicators sometimes appeal to authority. Because marketers cannot invoke the same types of sanctions as real authority figures (e.g., parents withholding allowances), appeals to authority in the marketplace typically use surrogates of real authority figures. For example, advertisers sometimes use medical authorities to promote their products' virtues. Broadcasters often air infomercials that devote 30-minute programs to weight loss, skin care, exercise equipment, hair-restoration products, and other items of this sort. Frequently, these products are endorsed by medical doctors, entertainers, and athletes, upon whose authority the consumer is promised the product will perform its function. The Federal Trade Commission's Endorsement and Testimonial Guides discuss misleading situations in which consumer experiences are presented as "typical" (and maybe not) and the need for disclosure of material connections (e.g., payment, free goods) to endorsers that is not expected by consumers.[17]

Scarcity

This influence tactic is based on the principle that things become more desirable when they are in great demand but short supply. Simply put, an item that is rare or becoming rare is more valued. Salespeople and advertisers use this tactic when encouraging people to buy immediately with appeals such as "Only a few are left," "We won't have any more in stock by the end of the day," and "They're really selling fast."

The theory of psychological reactance helps explain why scarcity works.[18] This theory suggests that people react against any efforts to reduce their freedom of choice. Removed or threatened freedoms and choices are perceived as even more desirable than previously. Of course, appeals to scarcity are not always effective. But if the persuader is credible and legitimate, then an appeal may be effective.

Perhaps nowhere in the world is scarcity more used as an influence tactic than in Singapore. In the Hokkien dialect of Chinese, the word *kiasu* means "fear of losing out." Singaporeans, according to a lecturer in the philosophy department at the National University, will take whatever they can secure, even if they are not sure they really want it.[19] The majority of Singaporeans apparently share a herd mentality—no one wants to be different, and most conform to what others do. Marketers, needless to say, have exploited this cultural characteristic of Singapore to sell all types of products. For example, a Singaporean automobile dealership, announced that it was moving its location and offered for sale 250 limited-edition BMW 316i models, priced at $78,125 for a manual transmission and $83,125 for automatic. All 250 models were sold within four days, and the dealer was forced to order another 100, which were quickly sold even though delivery was unavailable for months.

THE INFLUENCE PROCESS: THE PERSUADEE'S PERSPECTIVE

The persuasive efforts by two advertisers will serve to illustrate the following discussion. In the advertisement for Rinaldi "ToBe Healthy" Pasta Sauce (see Figure 7.2), several reasons and arguments are presented to convince consumers that this Rinaldi brand represents a healthy choice in the selection of a pasta sauce. The American Heart Association seal, brand name "ToBe Healthy," and several positive, nutrient content claims (e.g., 64mg. DHA Omega 3, gluten free, cholesterol free, only 290-330mg. sodium, a good source of Vitamin A) all help to make the clear the impression that the brand is healthy and nutritious. On the other hand, the Rosetta Stone advertisement (Figure 7.3) says virtually nothing (at least in words) about their language programs. This ad's minimalist text simply states "More than words. Possibilities." The prominent and attractive couple sharing a set of headphones cleverly connects the Rosetta Stone language programs with being able to meet someone attractive who speaks a different language. As noted in the *Global Focus* insert, such creativity and use of meaningful imagery is especially important in global campaigns.

These contrasting persuasive efforts highlight the fact that there are many different ways in which to use persuasion. The following section identifies five factors that are fundamental in the persuasion process.[20] Three factors (message arguments, peripheral cues, and communication modality) deal with persuasion vehicles under the marketing communicator's control. The other two (receiver involvement and initial position) apply to persuadee characteristics.

Message Arguments

The strength or quality of message arguments is often the major determinant of whether and to what extent persuasion occurs. Consumers are much more likely to be persuaded by convincing and believable messages than by weak arguments, especially under a message of high involvement. It may seem strange, then, that much advertising fails to present substantive information or compelling arguments. One reason is that the majority of advertising, particularly television commercials, is for product categories (like soft drinks) in which inter-brand differences are modest or virtually

FIGURE **7.2** Argument-Based Persuasion

FIGURE 7.3 Emotion-Based Persuasion

nonexistent. Another reason for advertising that promotes images rather than presents facts is that emotion, as discussed in Chapter 6, plays a key role in driving consumer choice. Ad copy testing of message argument strength is important.

Peripheral Cues

A second major determinant of persuasion is the presence of cues that are peripheral to the primary message arguments. These peripheral cues include such elements as background music, attractive sources, scenery, and graphics. For example, one may not be interested in a language program per se, but the attractive sources in the Rosetta Stone ad may draw one's attention to the ad. As explained in a later section, under certain conditions these peripheral

GLOBAL FOCUS

Ad Persuasion for Global Public Causes

One of the more challenging issues in persuasion is to make your advertising come to life, connect with your audience, and to be distinctive from the thousands of other appeals out there. This can be an even greater challenge when one has to communicate and persuade across several different languages and cultures (e.g., pan-European campaigns) and for public causes (e.g., energy conservation, wildlife preservation) that are competing for funds with other well-publicized issues. Such competing global campaigns for public causes include AIDS, domestic abuse, natural disasters, homelessness, hygiene, anti-drug and anti-smoking appeals, energy conservation, anti-pollution, wildlife conservation, hunger, protecting rain forests, global warming, driving safety, children's rights, among others.

Fortunately, the "Ads of the World" site (http://adsoftheworld.com and then select "public interest" under "industry") provides thousands of creative ads for many different categories, media, and countries that serve as inspiration for persuasive ad design. Two recent examples in the public interest area include work by Leo Burnett Brussels on energy conservation and by Ogilvy Paris for the World Wildlife Federation. Both campaigns provide creative and vivid images to better connect and persuade their diverse audiences across Europe and do so by avoiding lengthy ad copy.

Source: Ads of the World, http://adsoftheworld.com (accessed November 5, 2011).

cues may play a more important role than message arguments in determining the outcome of a persuasive effort.

Communication Modality

A third important moderator of persuasion is the mode of communication, whether television, radio, social media, or magazines, etc. Experiments have shown that a likable communicator is more persuasive when presenting a message via broadcast media, whereas an unlikable source is more persuasive when the communication is written.[21] The reason for this phenomenon is that people pay closer attention to the quality of message arguments when processing written rather than broadcast messages.

Receiver Involvement

The personal relevance that a communication (e.g., an advertisement) has for a receiver is a critical determinant of the extent and form of persuasion.[22] Highly involved consumers (i.e., those for whom an advertisement is most relevant) are motivated to process message arguments when exposed to marketing communications, whereas uninvolved consumers are likely to exert minimal attention to message arguments and perhaps to process only peripheral cues. The upshot is that involved and uninvolved consumers have to be persuaded in different ways (which is detailed fully in a following section that presents an integrated model of persuasion).

Receiver's Initial Position

Scholars agree that persuasion results not from external communication per se but from the self-generated thoughts (e.g., cognitive responses) that people produce in response to persuasive efforts. Persuasion, in other words, is self-persuasion, or, stated poetically, "thinking makes it so."[23] These self-generated thoughts include both cognitive and emotional responses. These responses are directed at message arguments and executional elements or may involve emotional reactions and images related to using the advertised brand (e.g., "Coca-Cola. Live Positively." to emphasize volunteerism and public causes).[24]

There are two primary forms of cognitive responses: support arguments and counterarguments.[25] These responses are subvocal rather than vocalized; they are the thoughts elicited spontaneously in response to advertisements and other persuasive efforts. Support arguments occur when a receiver agrees with a message argument. For example, a consumer with beginning heart disease reading the Rinaldi advertisement may respond favorably to several copy points made about nutrients that may serve to help reduce further damage to his or her heart. Counterarguments arise when the receiver challenges a message claim. Another person with hypertension reading the same Rinaldi ad may express concern that at almost 14 percent of their daily value of sodium (330 mg. of 2400 mg.), this Rinaldi brand may have more sodium per serving than they are willing to consume. This "counterarguer," in other words, does not agree with the message arguments even though he or she fully comprehends the advertiser's claims. (Recall from Chapter 6 the concept of *agreement*—stage 4 in the CPM process—and understand that counterarguing represents a form of subvocal disagreement.)

Whether a persuasive communication accomplishes its objectives depends on the balance of cognitive and emotional responses. If counterarguments outnumber supportive arguments, it is unlikely that many consumers will be convinced to undertake the course of action advocated. On the other hand, marketing communications can successfully persuade consumers if more supportive than negative arguments are registered or if emotional responses are predominantly positive. Other types of cognitive and emotional responses include *source bolstering* (positive source) and *source derogation* (negative source) thoughts.

An Integrated Model of Persuasion

The several factors overviewed now are combined into a coordinated theory of persuasion. Figure 7.4 presents a model of alternative mechanisms, or "routes," by which persuasion occurs. This explanation is based on psychologists Petty and Cacioppo's *elaboration likelihood model (ELM)*, work by psychologist Chaiken, marketing scholars Batra and Ray, and marketing scholars' MacInnis and Jaworski's integrative framework.[26]

It should be clear by this point in the chapter that there is no single mechanism by which persuasion occurs. Instead, there are a variety of possibilities in understanding the concept of elaboration. Elaboration refers to the mental activity in response to a message such as an advertisement. People elaborate on a message when they think about what the message is saying, evaluate the arguments in the message, engage in mental imagery when viewing pictures, and perhaps react emotionally to some of the claims. In other words, elaboration involves an application of cognitive resources in response to a marcom message. To merely look at an online commercial with a blank stare, for example, does not involve elaboration. However, elaboration is engaged when one views, say, a different commercial—a commercial that is personally relevant—and thinks about the people in the commercial and their similarity to one's own family or friends and how the advertised product may indeed fit into one's consumption lifestyle.

Whether and to what extent a person engages in elaboration depends on that person's motivation, ability, and opportunity to process a marketing message's selling claims. Motivation is high when a message relates to a person's present consumption-related goals and needs and is thus relevant to that individual. Generally speaking, consumers are more motivated to process messages the more involved they are in the subject matter of a message. Opportunity involves the matter of whether it is physically possible for a person to process a message; opportunity is restricted when, among other reasons, a message is presented too quickly, the sound is too low, or an individual is distracted. Ability concerns whether a person is familiar with message claims and has the necessary skills (e.g., literacy, knowledge) to help comprehend them. Consumers on occasion

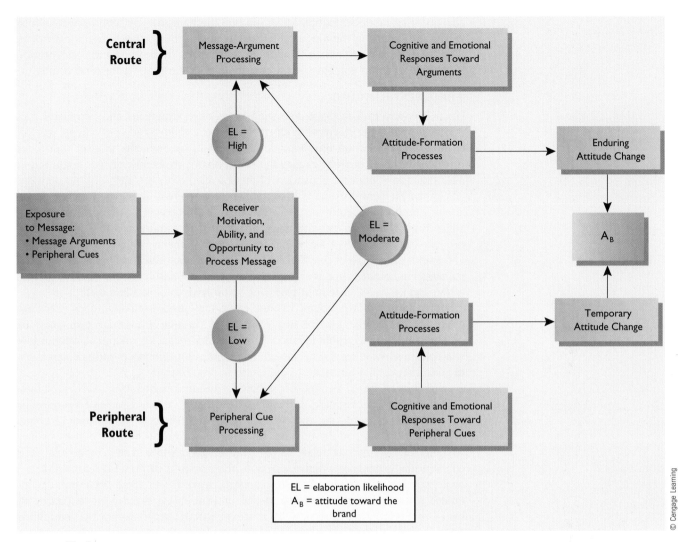

Central Route } Message-Argument Processing

Cognitive and Emotional Responses Toward Arguments

EL = High

Exposure to Message:
• Message Arguments
• Peripheral Cues

Receiver Motivation, Ability, and Opportunity to Process Message

EL = Moderate

Attitude-Formation Processes

Enduring Attitude Change

A_B

EL = Low

Attitude-Formation Processes

Temporary Attitude Change

Peripheral Route } Peripheral Cue Processing

Cognitive and Emotional Responses Toward Peripheral Cues

EL = elaboration likelihood
A_B = attitude toward the brand

© Cengage Learning

FIGURE **7.4** An Integrated Model of Persuasion

are motivated, yet are unable to process certain message claims (e.g., with pre-scription drug claims).

Together, these three factors (*motivation, opportunity*, and *ability*, or *MOA* for short) determine each individual's elaboration likelihood for a particular message. *Elaboration likelihood (EL)* represents the chance or prospect that a message receiver will elaborate on a message by thinking about and reacting to it and comparing it with his or her preexisting thoughts and beliefs regarding the product category, the advertised brand, and perhaps competitive brands. When all three MAO elements are high, elaboration on the message is likely high. We can envision an *elaboration likelihood continuum* ranging from a low likelihood at one end to a high likelihood at the other.

The elaboration likelihood is low when the MOA factors are low or even when only one of the MAO elements is deficient. This would be the case when a consumer has the ability and opportunity to process an ad, but he or she is not interested in the advertised product (hence low motivation). In many mar-ketplace situations, consumers' ELs for messages are at a moderate level rather than being low or high. Note in Figure 7.4 that three EL levels (EL = High, Moderate, or Low) are shown in circles extending from the box labeled Receiver Motivation, Ability, and Opportunity to Process Message.

In general, the strength of one's elaboration likelihood will determine the type of process by which attitudes toward the advertised brand will be formed or changed. The model in Figure 7.4 shows two mechanisms—or "routes"—by which persuasion occurs: at the top, a central route, and at the bottom, a peripheral route. Also, there exists an implicit dual route that results from a moderate elaboration likelihood level and combines features of both the central and peripheral routes.

The Central Route

Upon exposure to a message consisting of message arguments and peripheral cues (see Figure 7.4), the receiver's level of motivation, ability, and opportunity will determine the elaboration likelihood level. When EL is high, the receiver will focus predominantly on message arguments rather than peripheral cues (see Figure 7.4). This situation defines the activation of the so-called central route.

When the central route is activated, the receiver will listen to, watch, or read about a brand's attributes and benefits but will not necessarily accept them at face value. Rather, because the consumer is motivated to acquire information about the product category, she or he will react to the arguments with subvocal cognitive and emotional responses (see Figure 7.4). The consumer may accept some of the arguments but counterargue with others. She or he may also emit emotional reactions to the arguments—"That's not true!" or "You have to be kidding me!"

The nature of the cognitive and emotional processing—whether predominantly favorable (supportive arguments and positive emotional responses) or predominantly unfavorable (counterarguments and negative emotional reactions)—will determine whether the persuasive communication influences attitudes and also the direction of that influence.

In emotion-based persuasion, when a consumer is highly involved in a message such as a TV commercial, there is a tendency to relate aspects of the message to his or her personal situation (e.g., a campaign directed at persuading young adults not to drink and drive). The consumer may vicariously place himself or herself into the commercial, relate to the product and people in the commercial, and empathically experience positive emotions (e.g., a sense of pride, relief, confidence) or negative emotions (e.g., anguish, reactance, fear). Under these circumstances, attitudes toward the advertised brand (A_b in Figure 7.4) stand a good chance of being changed in the direction of the experienced emotion—positive emotional reactions leading to positive brand attitudes and negative reactions leading to negative attitudes. Also, because the consumer's elaboration likelihood is high, any attitude change under the central route will be relatively enduring.

The second central-route attitude-formation process, message-based persuasion, results from processing message arguments. When consumers are sufficiently motivated, able, and have the opportunity to process a message's specific arguments, their cognitive responses are likely to lead to changes in beliefs about the advertised brand or changes in evaluations of the importance of brand attributes and benefits. The end result is an enduring change in attitudes toward the brand. An example of message-based persuasion is found in General Electric's Advantium oven campaign in the following *IMC Focus*.

The Peripheral Route

When the MOA factors—motivation, opportunity, and ability (see Figure 7.4)—are at low levels, a different route of persuasion is involved. (Note: Only one of the MAO elements needs to be deficient for this route to be possible.) For example, when a consumer is not motivated to attend and comprehend message arguments, their elaboration likelihood on message content is low. Yet, she or he may nonetheless attend to the message's peripheral features. The peripheral route is shown at the bottom of Figure 7.4, where attention focuses on processing peripheral cues rather than message arguments.

Peripheral cues involve elements of a message that are *unrelated* (and hence peripheral) to the primary selling points in the message. For example, such peripheral cues might include background music, scenery, or attractive models in a commercial. In the case of a presentation by a salesperson, peripheral cues

IMC FOCUS

Faster Than a Microwave Oven; Better Than a Conventional Oven

Imagine that you want to bake a potato and have a choice between a conventional or microwave oven. The conventional oven will take a long time (at least an hour), but the potato will come out well cooked on the inside and crisp on the outside. In a microwave oven, the potato will be baked in less than 30 minutes, but it will not have that crisp, scrumptious exterior. Thus, the choice of oven in which to prepare the potato requires a trade-off between speed of cooking (the microwave oven wins hands down) and delectability of the finished potato (the conventional oven is the clear winner). What if there were an alternative, an oven that provides the quick-cooking ability of a microwave and the better-tasting result from a conventional oven?

Too good to be true? Well that was the challenge faced by the General Electric (GE) company in its marketing of the Advantium oven. The Advantium oven uses white-hot halogen bulbs in combination with microwave energy to cook foods as much as eight times faster than conventional ovens. The food tastes as good as if it

were cooked in a conventional oven (in comparison to what one gets with microwave cooking) and comes out beautifully browned. GE somehow had to convince consumers that they could "eat their cake and have it too"—that is, that the Advantium oven can cook in microwave time, but the food is as good as from a conventional oven.

To alter beliefs it was critical that consumers actually experienced products cooked in an Advantium oven so they could learn for themselves that fast cooking and good tasting are not mutually exclusive benefits. Cooking demonstrations by retailers (followed by taste-testing by consumers) were important to assure people that it was possible to prepare items quickly that taste great.

Sources: "Fast & Simple Advantium Ovens" (www.geappliances.com/products/introductions/advantium), accessed August 23, 2011; Adapted from Steve Kruschen, "Speedcooking Now Easier Than Ever with GE Profile Advantium 120 Oven" (www.mrgadget.com/hitechhome01/advantium120.html); and Matt Murray, "Marketing Fast and Costly Oven Poses a Tricky Challenge for GE," October 18, 1999 (http://interactive.wsj.com/articles/SB940195016585656673.htm).

© Jim Barber/Shutterstock.com

could include that individual's physical appearance, how he or she is dressed, his or her accent, and so on.

Having focused on a peripheral cue (and not the message arguments), a consumer may experience thoughts or emotions in response to the cue ("The music is exhilarating"; "What a beautiful dress"; or "The scenery is gorgeous"). These cognitive and emotional responses toward the peripheral cues might produce a temporary attitude change toward the advertisement itself and/or the advertised brand.[27] Classical conditioning provides one account of how attitudes toward a brand (A_b) are formed via the peripheral route.

Classical Conditioning of Attitudes

Perhaps you are familiar with the experiments in which the famous Russian scientist, Ivan Pavlov, trained dogs to salivate on hearing a bell ring. Pavlov accomplished this canine response by establishing a systematic relationship between the bell and a desirable object (to dogs) such as meat powder, which by itself was able to make dogs salivate. Trial after trial, dogs would hear a bell ring and then would be presented with meat powder. In this situation, meat powder was an unconditioned stimulus (US), and salivation was an unconditioned response (UR). By repeatedly pairing the bell (a conditioned stimulus, or CS) with the meat powder, the bell by itself eventually caused the dog to salivate. The dog, in other words, had been trained to emit a conditioned response (CR) upon hearing the bell ring. The dog had learned that the bell regularly preceded meat powder, and thus the ringing bell caused the dog to predict that something desirable—the meat powder—was forthcoming.

Something similar to this happens when consumers process peripheral cues. For example, brand advertisements that include adorable babies, attractive people, and majestic scenery can elicit positive emotional reactions. Think of these peripheral cues as analogous to meat powder (US), the emotional reactions as similar to the dog's salivation (UR), and the advertised brand as similar to the bell in Pavlov's experiments (CS). The emotion contained in the cue may become associated with the brand, thereby influencing consumers to like the brand more than they did prior to viewing the commercial. Through their repeated association, the CS (advertised brand) comes to elicit a conditioned response (CR) similar to the unconditioned response (UR) evoked by the US itself (the peripheral cue).[28]

Temporary versus Enduring Attitude Change

According to the ELM, people experience only temporary attitude change when persuaded via the peripheral route in comparison to the relatively enduring change experienced under the central route. Thus, in circumstances in which receivers think about and process message arguments (i.e., when the elaboration likelihood is high and the central route is invoked), attitudes that are formed will be relatively enduring compared to attitudes formed via the peripheral route. Moreover, these central route attitudes will be comparatively stronger, more accessible, and more resistant to change.

Comparatively, when the elaboration likelihood is low (e.g., because the message is not relevant), peripheral route attitude change may still occur due to peripheral cues, but will be only temporary unless consumers are exposed continuously to the peripheral cue. There is some evidence, however, that the use of peripheral cues in advertising can influence attitudes and even shape choice behavior so long as the advertised brand is not dominated by a competitive brand that is superior with respect to all pertinent choice criteria.[29]

Dual Routes

The central and peripheral paths represent endpoints on a continuum of persuasion strategies and are not intended to imply that persuasion is an either-or proposition. In other words, in many cases there is a combination of central and peripheral processes operating simultaneously.[30] This is shown in Figure 7.4 when the MOA factors produce a moderate elaboration likelihood level. In this instance, which no doubt captures many situations in marketing communications, consumers use peripheral cues to determine how much thinking to do about the message.

Enhancing Consumers' Motivation, Opportunity, and Ability to Process Advertisements

There is no single way to influence people to form favorable attitudes toward brands or to act in ways marketing communicators desire. Rather, the appropriate influence strategy depends both on *consumer characteristics* (their motivation, opportunity, and ability to process marcom messages) and on *brand strengths*. If consumers are interested in learning about a product (with the necessary MAO elements), and a company's brand has clear advantages over competitive brands, then the appropriate persuasion tactic is obvious: *design a message telling people explicitly why your brand is superior*. The result should be equally clear: Consumers likely will be swayed by your arguments, which will lead to a relatively enduring attitude change and a strong chance they will select your brand over competitive offerings.[31]

The reality, however, is that brands in most product categories are similar, so consumers generally are not anxious to devote mental effort toward processing messages that provide little new information. Thus, the marketing communicator, faced with this double whammy (only slightly involved consumers and a me-too brand), has to find ways to enthuse consumers sufficiently such that they will listen to or read the communicator's message. Hence, strategies to enhance or appeal to the MOA factors (motivation, opportunity, and ability) inherent in consumers will likely increase communication effectiveness. Figure 7.5 provides a framework for the following discussion of how marketing communicators can enhance the MOA factors.[32] (Note, however, that one's MAO to process the message does not exist within the message, but rather is *within the individual* and how they in turn react to the message.) Each of six strategies in Figure 7.5 now will be discussed and illustrated with examples.

Motivation to Attend to Messages

Figure 7.5 shows that one of the communicator's objectives is to increase the consumer's motivation to attend to the message and to process brand information. This section discusses just the attention component; the following section will consider the processing element.

As you will recall from Chapter 6, two major forms of attention are voluntary and involuntary attention.[33] Voluntary attention is willful or prior attention to a message due to its perceived relevance pertinent to our needs (e.g., intent to purchase an advertised product). Conversely, involuntary attention

I. **Enhance Consumers' MOTIVATION to ...**

  A. **Attend to the message by ...**

- Appealing to hedonic needs (appetite appeals, sex appeals)
- Using novel stimuli (unusual pictures, different ad formats, large number of scenes)
- Using intense or prominent cues (action, loud music, colorful ads, celebrities, large pictures)
- Using motion (complex pictures; edits and cuts)

  B. **Process brand information by ...**

- Increasing relevance of brand to self (asking rhetorical questions, using fear appeals, using dramatic presentations)
- Increasing curiosity about the brand (opening with suspense or surprise, using humor, presenting little information in the message)

II. **Enhance Consumers' OPPORTUNITY to ...**

  A. **Encode information by ...**

- Repeating brand information
- Repeating key scenes
- Repeating the ad on multiple occasions

  B. **Reduce processing time by ...**

- Creating Gestalt processing (using pictures and imagery)

III. **Enhance Consumers' ABILITY to ...**

  A. **Access knowledge structures by ...**

- Providing a context (employing verbal framing)

  B. **Create knowledge structures by ...**

- Facilitating exemplar-based learning (using concretizations, demonstrations, and analogies)

FIGURE 7.5 Enhancing Consumers' Motivation, Opportunity, and Ability to Process Brand Information

Source: Adapted from Deborah J. MacInnis, Christine Moorman, and Bernard J. Jaworski, "Enhancing and Measuring Consumers' Motivation, Opportunity, and Ability to Process Brand Information from Ads," *Journal of Marketing 55* (October 1991), 36.

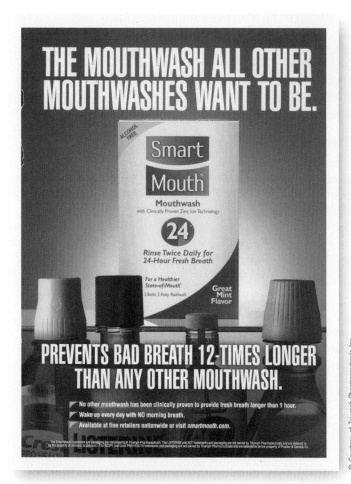

FIGURE 7.6 An Appeal to Informational Needs

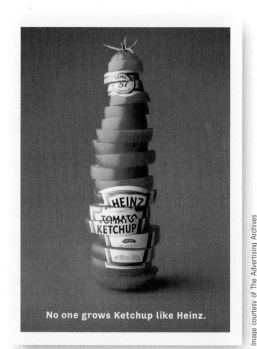

FIGURE 7.7 Using Novelty to Attract Attention

occurs automatically or involuntarily due to an intruding stimulus (e.g., due to the use of attention-gaining techniques) rather than by the consumer's inherent interest in the topic. Novel stimuli, intense or prominent cues, complex pictures, and, in the case of broadcast ads, edits and cuts of the sort seen with YouTube-like videos are some of the techniques used to attract attention that otherwise would not be given.

Appeals to Informational and Hedonic Needs

Under high elaboration likelihood (EL), consumers can be attracted to those stimuli that serve their *informational needs* by supplying relevant facts and figures. As an illustration, consider the advertisement in Figure 7.6 for Smart Mouth mouthwash. The ad informatively points out that this brand "prevents bad breath 12-times longer than any other mouthwash" and also supplies other pertinent details that provide reasons for consumers to consider purchasing this brand. (This advertisement uses a technique described later in the text as an *indirect comparison*.)

Especially in the case of low elaboration likelihood (EL), *hedonic needs* can be satisfied when consumers attend to messages that make them feel good and serve their pleasure needs (e.g., by using children, fun scenes with friends, romantic appeals). Similarly, advertisements for appetizing food products are especially likely to be noticed when people are hungry. So, many restaurants and fast-food marketers advertise on the radio during the after-work rush hour when this may happen. Needless to say, the best time to reach consumers with a message is just at the time they are experiencing a need for the product category in which the brand resides.

Use of Novel Stimuli

There are innumerable ways marketing communicators use novelty to attract involuntary attention. In general, novel messages are *unusual*, *distinctive*, *unpredictable*, and *somewhat unexpected*. Such stimuli tend to produce greater attention than those that are familiar and routine. This can be explained by the behavioral concept of *human adaptation*. People adapt to the conditions around them: As a stimulus becomes more familiar, people become desensitized to it. Psychologists refer to this as *habituation*. For example, if you drive past a billboard daily, you likely notice it less on each occasion. If the billboard were removed, you probably would notice it was no longer there. In other words, *we notice by exception*.

Examples of novelty abound. For example, Figure 7.7 is an advertisement for Heinz ketchup that employs an eye-catching graphic showing the Heinz bottle as a layer of tomato slices capped off with a stem attached. The copy at the ad's bottom brings clarity to the bottle graphic when claiming that "No one grows Ketchup like Heinz."

Use of Intense or Prominent Cues

Intense and prominent cues (those that are louder, more colorful, bigger, brighter, etc.) increase the probability of attracting attention. This is

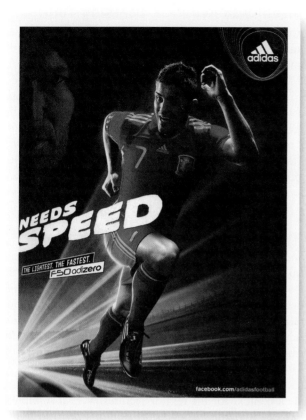

FIGURE 7.8 Using Intensity to Attract Attention

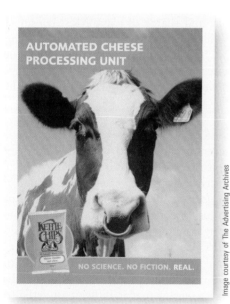

FIGURE 7.9 Using Prominence to Attract Attention

because it is difficult for consumers to avoid such stimuli, leading to *involuntary attention.*

Advertisements, too, utilize intensity and prominence to attract attention. For example, the Adidas ad in Figure 7.8 with Spain's David Villa makes an effective use of light rays to help demonstrate the speed of Adidas' soccer (futbol) shoes. Kettle Chips (see Figure 7.9) creatively uses a cow to draw attention to the brand and to convey the point that Kettle Chips are made with real cheese.

Using Motion

Advertisers sometimes employ motion to both attract and direct consumer attention to the brand name and to pertinent ad copy. Falling objects (e.g., a flipping coin), people appearing to be running, and automobiles in motion are some of the techniques used in print ads to attract attention. The advertisement for Excedrin Migraine pills (see Figure 7.10) portrays a sense of movement and also conveys that Excedrin users will start receiving relief in just 30 minutes—an active butterfly (post-usage) released from a state of cocoon-like dormancy (pre-usage).

Motivation to Process Messages

Enhanced processing motivation means that the ad receiver has increased interest in reading or listening to the ad message to determine what it has to say that might be of relevance. Increased processing motivation has been shown to strengthen the impact of brand attitudes on purchase intentions.[34] To accomplish enhanced motivation, marketing communicators can do two things: (1) enhance the *relevance* of the brand to the consumer and (2) enhance *curiosity* about the brand. Methods for enhancing brand relevance include using *fear appeals* (discussed later in the text), employing *dramatic presentations* to increase the significance of the brand to consumers' self-interests, and raising *rhetorical questions* (e.g., with figurative language) that activate consumer interest in the advertised brand.[35]

Using *humor,* presenting *little information* in the message (and thereby encouraging the consumer to think about the brand), or opening a message with *suspense or surprise* can enhance curiosity about a brand. The ad for Viva paper towels (see Figure 7.11) uses an element of *suspense* (a spaghetti and meatball plate precariously perched on the edge of a cabinet) to attract the reader's attention.

Opportunity to Encode Information

Marketing messages have no chance of effectiveness unless consumers comprehend information about the brand and incorporate it with product information in their existing memory structure. Thus, the communicator's goal is to get consumers to *encode* information and to make it as simple and quick as possible for them to do so. The secret to facilitating encoding is *repetition,* especially under low involvement—a common occurrence. In this sense, the marketing communicator should repeat brand information, repeat key scenes, and repeat the advertisement on multiple occasions.[36] Through repetition consumers have an increased opportunity to encode the important information the communicator wishes to convey. This is why we see advertisements repeated night after night on TV, sometimes to excess. But, advertisers know that repetition is required to get their point across, especially when consumers are not as involved in the message.

FIGURE 7.10 Using Motion to Attract Attention

FIGURE 7.11 Using Suspense to Enhance Processing Motivation

Opportunity to Reduce Processing Time

Opportunity to process is further enhanced if the communicator takes extra measures to *reduce the time* required of the consumer to read, listen to, and ultimately discern the meaning of a marcom message. The use of pictures and imagery create a form of total-message processing (or *gestalt*) whereby the consumer can readily encode the totality of the message rather than having to process information bit by bit or to think much about what the advertiser is claiming. Consider the advertisement in Figure 7.12 for NyQuil Cold & Flu medicine. The image of a comfortable bed placed in a teaspoon conveys the gestalt impression that a teaspoon of NyQuil promotes a "great night's sleep."

Ability to Access Knowledge Structures

A brand-based *knowledge structure* represents the associative links in the consumer's long-term memory between the brand and thoughts, feelings, and beliefs about that brand. In general, people are most able to process new information that relates to something they already know or understand. In general, the marketing communicator's task is to enable consumers either to *access* existing knowledge structures or to *create* new knowledge structures.

To help with access, marketing communicators need to provide a context for the text or pictures. *Verbal framing* is one way of providing a context. This means that pictures in an ad are placed in the context of, or framed with, appropriate words or phrases to aid understanding. In an advertisement for DuPont's Teflon brand of scratch-resistant coatings, attention is drawn to the incongruous image of a skillet filled with copper wiring, tacks, and shards of glass. Most consumers believe that nonstick skillets can be easily damaged when scratched with sharp objects. The limited copy simply points out that DuPont Teflon coatings are scratch resistant and encourages readers to visit their website (http://teflon.com) for further information.

Ability to Create Knowledge Structures

Sometimes marketing communicators need to *create* knowledge structures for information they want consumers to have about their brands. This is accomplished by facilitating *exemplar-based learning*. An *exemplar* is a specimen or model of a particular concept or idea. By using concretizations, demonstrations, or analogies, the marketing communicator can facilitate learning by appealing to exemplars. Consider, for example, the concept of product freshness dates (i.e., the final date for which the product remains fresh). We all know what freshness means, but it can be a rather abstract concept that is difficult to verbalize. In order to demonstrate this, Diet Pepsi's brand managers used exemplars of products that people routinely inspect for freshness (squeezing an orange, pinching a loaf of bread). Then, by analogy, the point was made that consumers should check Diet Pepsi cans to ensure that the contents are not outdated. The advertisement for Hidden Valley Ranch dressing (see Figure 7.13) uses the analogy that this brand is like the proverbial "icing on the cake" that enhances the taste of vegetables—just like cake icing improves the taste of cake.

FIGURE 7.12 Using a Gestalt to Reduce Processing Time

FIGURE 7.13 Using Analogy to Create a Knowledge Structure

Source: HIDDEN VALLEY® is a registered trademark of The HV Food Products Company. Used with permission. © 2012, The HV Food Products Company. Reprinted with permission. Photographer: Eric Tucker

Concretizations

Concretizing, which was discussed in Chapter 6, is used extensively in advertising to facilitate both consumer learning and retrieval of brand information. Concretizing is based on the straightforward idea that it is easier for people to remember and retrieve *tangible* rather than abstract information. Claims about a brand are more concrete (versus abstract) when they are made perceptible, palpable, real, evident, and vivid. Concretizing is accomplished by using concrete words and examples. For example, the advertisement for Hellmann's (see Figure 7.14) shows a jar of Hellmann's Extra Light mayonnaise that has become so thin its label is falling down, thereby concretizing the tacit claim that this brand is a good choice for managing weight.

Section Summary

The foregoing discussion has emphasized that advertisers, along with other marketing communicators, benefit from enhancing consumers' motivation, opportunity, and ability to process marketing messages. A variety of communication devices enables advertisers to achieve their goals in the hopes of influencing consumers' brand-related attitudes, purchase intentions, and, ultimately, their behavior. We conclude the chapter with a well-known theory of persuasion and several strategies to change attitudes, preferences, and behavior.

The Theory of Reasoned Action (TORA)

The message-based persuasion process described previously has been fully developed in the well-known *theory of reasoned action (TORA)*. This theory proposes that all forms of planned and reasoned behavior (versus unplanned, spontaneous, impulsive behavior) have two primary determinants: attitudes and normative influences.[37] Many of you may have learned about this theory in a psychology or consumer behavior course, so rather than explain the entire theory, the present discussion will describe just the attitudinal component.[38]

Attitude formation according to TORA can best be described in terms of the following equation.

$$A_{Bj} = \sum_{i=1}^{n} b_{ij} \cdot e_i \qquad (7.1)$$

where:

A_{Bj} = *attitude* toward a particular brand (brand j)

b_{ij} = the *belief*, or expectation, that owning brand j will lead to outcome i

e_i = the positive or negative *evaluation* of the ith outcome

A consumer's attitude toward a brand (or, more technically, toward the act of owning and consuming the brand) is determined by his or her *cognitive structure* (i.e., the beliefs regarding the outcomes, or consequences, of owning the brand multiplied by the evaluations of those outcomes). Outcomes (expressed in Equation 7.1 as $i = 1$ through n, where n is typically fewer than 7) involve those aspects of product ownership (e.g., a running shoe) that the consumer either desires to obtain (e.g., getting in shape, improving

FIGURE **7.14** Using Concretization to Aid Learning

one's race time) or to avoid (e.g., knee or foot injuries, abnormal shoe wear). Consumers approach benefits and avoid detriments.

Beliefs (the b_{ij} term in Equation 7.1) are the consumer's subjective probability assessments, or expectations, regarding the likelihood that performing a certain act (e.g., buying brand j—Nike Air Max running shoe) will lead to a certain outcome. In theory, the consumer who is in the market for a product has a separate belief associated with each potential outcome for each shoe brand he or she is considering buying, and it is for this reason that the belief term in Equation 7.1 is subscripted both with an i (referring to a particular outcome) and j (referring to a specific brand).

Because all outcomes are not equally important or determinant of consumer choice, we need to introduce a term that recognizes this influence differential. This term is the evaluation component, e_i, in Equation 7.1. Evaluations represent the value, or importance, that consumers attach to consumption outcomes (e.g., getting into shape, improving race times, avoiding foot injury). It is important to note that outcome evaluations apply to the product category in general and are not brand specific. It is for this reason that we need only a single subscript, i, to designate evaluations and not also a j as in the case of beliefs.

In summary, Equation 7.1 and the attitude formation process under TORA results from the integration (see the summation symbol in the equation) of beliefs regarding individual outcomes of brand ownership multiplied by their evaluation. This integration is referred to as the brand's "cognitive structure." Attitudes toward a brand are more positive when a brand is perceived favorably with respect to valued outcomes and less positive when a brand is perceived unfavorably on these outcomes.

Attitude Change Strategies

With Equation 7.1 in mind, we can identify three strategies that marketing communicators employ in attempting to change consumer attitudes: (1) changing beliefs, (2) altering outcome evaluations, or (3) introducing a new outcome into the evaluation process.[39]

The first attitude-change strategy attempts to bolster attitudes by *influencing brand-related beliefs*, which thus explains the term *"belief change"* to characterize this strategy. This strategy *"operates"* on the b_{ij} term from Equation 7.1. Consider the following marcom efforts to influence consumers' beliefs:

1. Many American consumers consider the BMW to be an automobile that is excessively expensive to maintain. Accordingly, a campaign was introduced to advertise BMW as "the car that tunes itself."[40]
2. When you think of safety, what automobile comes to mind? If you're like most people, the car that occurred to you probably is a Volvo. Knowing this fact, marketers at Swedish-made Saab undertook a major ad campaign to put Saab in a safety class with Volvo. In an effort to enhance consumers' belief regarding Saab's safety, print ads included copy lines such as "Safety marries performance. They elope"; "If Saab makes the safest cars in Sweden, and Sweden makes the safest cars in the world …"[41]

A second attitude-change strategy is to *influence existing evaluations* (the e_i term in Equation 7.1). This evaluation-change strategy involves getting consumers to reassess a particular outcome associated with brand ownership and to

Image courtesy of The Advertising Archives

alter their evaluations of the outcome's value. For example, Tylenol advertised the fact that, unlike some competitive brands of pain reliever, it contains no caffeine. Thus, it placed more weight/value on a negative product outcome on which their brand performed especially well.

A third strategy used by marketing communicators to change attitudes is what we might call an *add-an-outcome strategy*. The objective is to get consumers to judge brands in a product category in terms of a new product benefit on which "our" brand fares especially well. For example, Tropicana reformulated its Pure Premium orange juice with a newly patented calcium source called FruitCal—a highly soluble form of calcium.[42] The advertising campaign that trumpeted this product reformulation attempted to modify the way consumers evaluate orange juice by focusing on a purchase consideration—calcium—that most consumers had never before considered when making a brand selection from the orange juice category.

A number of other food product companies touted the same source-of-calcium benefit as did Tropicana, so eventually this product feature lost some its differentiating luster. To regain a health-claim advantage over other food products, Tropicana several years later began an advertising campaign claiming that orange juice is a natural source of potassium, a mineral that can reduce the risk of high blood pressure and strokes.[43] Hence, reducing the risk of high blood pressure and strokes represents a potent new outcome that consumers typically do not think of when considering a product such as orange juice. Nutrition claims such as these have enabled Tropicana to build its premium orange juice in the number 3–selling grocery brand in the United States, behind only Coca-Cola and Pepsi.

Changing Preferences and Behavioral Modification Strategies

A preference is a behavioral tendency that exhibits itself in how a person acts toward an object.[44] Preferences can be both cognitively and affectively based.[45] Marketing communicators' efforts at changing preferences by appealing to cognitions may meet with failure if the preferences have an affective basis. Furthermore, even when a preference is primarily cognitive-based, affect may become independent of the cognitive elements that were originally its basis.[46] Thus, the only way to influence some strongly held preferences may be by using methods that have direct emotional impact (e.g., graphic visual warnings shown to smokers with entrenched beliefs).

In addition to emotional conditions, marketers use a variety of other methods to change consumer preferences (and behavior) that do not require changing cognitions. These *behavioral modification methods* include various forms of classical and operant conditioning, modeling, and ecological modification.[47] For example, shaping is one application by which marketers attempt to shape certain behaviors through a process of changing preceding conditions and behaviors. Coupons, loss leaders, special deals, and free-trial periods are all examples to help shape future consumer behavior.

Vicarious learning, or modeling, is an attempt to change preferences and behavior "by having an individual observe the actions of others ... and the consequences of those behaviors."[48] In a Ryder commercial using the tagline, "Either Rent Ryder or It's Wrong," a fully air-conditioned and spotless Ryder rental truck passes a broken-down and un-air-conditioned U-Haul truck in the desert, demonstrating the use of vicarious learning.

Summary

Marketing communications in its various forms (advertising, social media, personal selling, direct marketing, and so on) involves efforts to persuade consumers by influencing their attitudes and ultimately their behavior. This chapter describes the role and nature of attitudes and different hierarchies by which they are formed and changed. From the marketing communicators' perspective, attitude formation and change represent the process of persuasion. The role of measurement specificity and direct experience is discussed in trying to predict behavior from attitude measures. Persuasion efforts on the part of the persuader are next described and illustrated, including six influence tactics: reciprocity, commitment and consistency, social proof, liking, authority, and scarcity.

The nature of persuasion is discussed with particular emphasis on an integrated framework called the elaboration likelihood model (ELM). Two alternative persuasion mechanisms are described: a central route, which explains enduring persuasion under conditions when the receiver is motivated, able, and has the opportunity (MAO) to process the message; and a peripheral route, in which one MAO elements may be deficient, yet a peripheral cue may account for short-term persuasion. In this context, three attitude-formation processes are described: emotion-based persuasion, message-based persuasion,

and classical conditioning. The first two are mechanisms for attitude change under the central route, whereas classical conditioning is a peripheral-route process.

A treatment is then given to practical efforts to enhance consumers' motivation, opportunity, and ability to process marketing messages. This section includes descriptions and illustrations of marcom efforts to heighten consumers' motivation to attend and process messages, measures to augment consumers' opportunity to encode information and reduce process time, and techniques used to increase consumers' ability to access knowledge structures and create new structures.

A final topic covered is the theory of reasoned action (TORA) found in persuasion research and basic attitude, preference, and behavior change strategies.

Discussion Questions

1. Explain the cognitive, affective, and conative attitude components. Provide examples of each using your attitude toward the idea of personally pursuing a career in selling and sales management. Contrast the high involvement (standard learning) hierarchy with that of the low involvement one.

2. Distinguish between message arguments and peripheral cues as fundamental determinants of persuasion. Provide several examples of each from actual television commercials or other advertisements.

3. Receiver involvement is the fundamental determinant of whether people may be persuaded through a central or a peripheral route. Explain.

4. There are three general strategies for changing attitudes. Explain each, using, for illustration, consumers' attitudes toward a fast-food chain of your choice (McDonald's, Burger King, KFC, etc.).

5. Assume that your target audience is composed of people who can afford to purchase a "hybrid" automobile such as the Chevy Volt, Honda's Insight, or Toyota's Prius. (Note: Hybrid automobiles are high-mileage cars that combine efficient gasoline engines with electric motors powered by batteries.) Assume that your target audience is composed of people who have negative attitudes toward hybrid vehicles. Using material from the chapter, how would you attempt to change their attitudes if you were the advertising agency responsible for this campaign? Be specific. Do the same for all-electric vehicles, such as the Nissan Leaf.

6. Have you personally experienced unethical persuasive efforts from marketing communicators? Under what circumstances would you most expect to find unethical marketing communications, and when would unethical communications most likely be effective in marketing? Draw upon the integrated model of persuasion (e.g., ELM, see Figure 7.4) in forming your answer.

7. In the discussion of the influence tactic of reciprocation, you were introduced to the concept of

contingency, or "it-depends," thinking. What "it-depends" factors best explain when the scarcity tactic would and would not be effective?

8. Assume that you are on the fundraising committee for a non-profit institution. Explain how in this situation you could use each of the six influence tactics discussed in the text. Be specific.

9. Describe the similarity between the concept of elaboration and active synthesis, which was explained in the prior chapter.

10. Locate two advertisements that illustrate exemplar-based learning and provide detailed explanations as to how specifically your chosen advertisements facilitate exemplar-based learning.

11. Pretend you are in charge of advertising for an online retailer. You know that consumers have positive evaluations for the convenience of online shopping but many are distrustful of unknown retailers and of giving out credit card numbers online. Using material from this chapter, explain how you would attempt to change consumers' attitudes about the risks of online shopping. Visit several actual online retailers and describe instances where the retailers have addressed consumers' risk perceptions.

12. Visit the Internet sites of approximately five brands that appeal to you. Based on the framework in Figure 7.5, identify at least one example of each of the following efforts to enhance consumers' MOA factors: Locate an effort to increase consumers' motivation to process brand information. Identify an Internet advertisement that attempts to enhance consumers' opportunity to encode information. Find an advertisement that uses an exemplar to assist consumers in either accessing or creating a new knowledge structure.

13. The opening *Marcom Insight* posed this question: Can we be persuaded to overcome bad habits? What is your viewpoint on this matter? Please back up your position with appropriate content from the chapter.

14. Identify two magazine advertisements of your choice, presumably involving brands/products that hold some interest for you. With each advertisement, indicate what you consider to be its message arguments and peripheral cues. Then explain why you regard these as message arguments/peripheral cues.

15. Construct an illustration to demonstrate your understanding of Equation 7.1. Identify three brands in a product category that is personally relevant. Then specify four "outcomes" (i.e., benefits and detriments) pertinent to that category. Next, assign a numerical value from 1 to 5 to each outcome, where 1 equals "virtually no importance" and

5 equals "extreme importance." Then assign a value from 1 to 5 to represent your beliefs regarding how well each of the three brands satisfies each of the four outcomes. In assigning your beliefs, treat 1 as indicating that the brand performs very poorly on this outcome, 5 as indicating the brand performs extremely well, and 2-through-4 reflecting increasingly positive performance.

16. Assume that all outcomes ($i = 1...n$ outcomes) are equally important to consumers in a particular product category. If this were so, how would you adjust the attitude model in Equation 7.1 to capture the attitude-formation process?

End Notes

1. A number of major theories of attitudes and attitude-change processes have developed over the last half-century. Seven particularly significant theories are reviewed in Richard E. Petty and John T. Cacioppo, *Attitudes and Persuasion: Classic and Contemporary Approaches*, Dubuque, IA: Wm. C. Brown Company, 1981. For another review, see Richard E. Petty, Rao H. Unnava, and Alan J. Strathman, "Theories of Attitude Change," in *Handbook of Consumer Behavior*, ed. T. S. Robertson and H. H. Kassarjian, Englewood Cliffs, NJ: Prentice-Hall, 1991, 241–80.

2. This definition adheres to Petty and Cacioppo, *Attitudes and Persuasion*, 7, and also reflects the concept of attitude popularized by Fazio and his colleagues. See, for example, Russell H. Fazio, Jeaw-Mei Chen, Elizabeth C. McDonel, and Steven J. Sherman, "Attitude Accessibility, Attitude-Behavior Consistency, and the Strength of the Object-Evaluation Association," *Journal of Experimental Social Psychology* 18, 1982, 339–57. On a technical note, the definition makes no distinction between what some authors properly consider to be the distinct constructs of *affect* (or feeling states) and *attitude* (or evaluative judgments). For discussion, see Joel B. Cohen and Charles S. Areni, "Affect and Consumer Behavior," in *Handbook of Consumer Behavior*, ed. T. S. Robertson and H. H. Kassarjian, Englewood Cliffs, NJ: Prentice-Hall, 1991, 188–240.

3. Daniel J. O'Keefe, *Persuasion: Theory and Research*, Newbury Park, Calif.: Sage Publications, 1990, 18.

4. See, for example, Richard P. Bagozzi, Alice M. Tybout, C. Samuel Craig, and Brian Sternthal, "The Construct Validity of the Tripartite Classification of Attitudes," *Journal of Marketing Research* 16 (February 1979), 88–95; and Richard J. Lutz, "An Experimental Investigation of Causal Relations among Cognitions, Affect, and Behavioral Intention," *Journal of Consumer Research* 3 (March 1977), 197–208.

5. This is the classic viewpoint of attitude popularized by Gordon W. Allport, "Attitudes," in *A Handbook of Social Psychology*, ed. C. A. Murchinson, Worcester, MA: Clark University Press, 1935, 798–844.

6. Michael L. Ray, "Marketing Communications and the Hierarchy of Effects," in *New Models for Mass Communication Research*, ed. Peter Clarke, Beverly Hills, CA: Sage Publishing, 1973, 147–76.

7. Ibid. For further discussion, also see Thomas E. Barry, "The Development of the Hierarchy of Effects," in *Current Issues and Research in Advertising*, ed. James H. Leigh and Claude R. Martin, Jr., Ann Arbor: Division of Research, Graduate School of Business, University of Michigan, 1987, 251–96.

8. Demetrios Vakratsas and Tim Ambler, "How Advertising Works: What Do We Really Know?" *Journal of Marketing* 63 (January 1999), 26–43; Ibid, Ray.

9. D.T. Regan and R.H. Fazio, "On the Consistency between Attitudes and Behavior: Look to the Method of Attitude Formation," *Journal of Experimental Psychology*, 13 (1977), 28–45; see also Deborah L. Roedder, Brian Sternthal, and Bobby J. Calder, "Attitude-Behavior Consistency in Children's Responses to Television Advertising," *Journal of Marketing Research*, 20 (November 1983), 337–49.

10. Martin Fishbein and Icek Ajzen, Belief, Attitude, Intention, and Behavior: An Introduction to Theory and Research (Reading, MA: Addison-Wesley, 1975), 369–70; and Icek Ajzen and Martin Fishbein, *Understanding Attitudes and Predicting Social Behavior*, Englewood Cliffs, NJ: Prentice-Hall, 1980, 34–35.

11. R.H. Fazio, M.P. Zanna, and J. Cooper, "Direct Experience and Attitude-Behavior Consistency: An Information Processing Analysis," *Personality and Social Psychology Bulletin*, 4 (winter 1978), 48–52; and R.H. Fazio and M.P. Zanna, "On the Predictive Validity of Attitudes: The Roles of Direct Experience and Confidence," *Journal of Personality*, 40 (June 1977), 228–43.

12. Robert E. Smith and William R. Swinyard, "Attitude-Behavior Consistency: The Impact of Product Trial Versus Advertising," *Journal of Marketing Research*, 20 (August 1983), 257–67.

13. Peter Wright, "Schemer Schema: Consumers' Intuitive Theories about Marketers' Influence Tactics," in *Advances in Consumer Research* 13, ed. Richard J. Lutz, Provo, UT: Association for Consumer Research, 1985, 1–3. An elaborate and thorough discussion of consumers' persuasion knowledge is provided by Marian Friestad and Peter Wright, "The Persuasion Knowledge Model: How People Cope with Persuasion Attempts," *Journal of Consumer Research* 21 (June 1994), 1–31. An empirical demonstration of consumers' persuasion knowledge vis-à-vis that of advertising researchers is available in Marian Friestad and Peter Wright, "Persuasion Knowledge: Lay People's and Researchers' Beliefs about the Psychology of Advertising," *Journal of Consumer Research* 22 (June 1995), 62–74.

14. Cialdini actually discusses seven influence tactics, but the seventh, instant influence, cuts across all the others and need not be discussed separately. Also, he refers to influence tactics as "weapons" of influence. Because the term *weapons* implies that the persuadee is an adversary, we prefer instead the term *tools* insofar as many modern marketing practitioners view their customers as participants in a long-term relation-building process and not as adversaries or victims. The following sections are based on Cialdini's insightful work. See Robert B. Cialdini, *Influence: Science and Practice*, 2nd ed., Glenview, IL: Scott, Foresman, 1988.

15. "Pushing Drugs to Doctors," *Consumer Reports*, February 1992, 87–94. See also David Evans, "Pfizer Broke the Law by Promoting Drugs for Unapproved Uses," *Bloomberg News*, November 9, 2009, http://www.bloomberg.com/apps/news?pid=newsarchive&sid=a4yV1nYxCGoA.

16. Cialdini, Influence: Science and Practice, 123.

17. Federal Trade Commission, "Guides Concerning the Use of Endorsements and Testimonials in Advertising," *Code of Federal Regulations* 16 Part 255 (October 5, 2009), http://www.ftc.gov/os/2009/10/091005revisedendorsementguides.pdf.

18. Jack W. Brehm, *A Theory of Psychological Reactance*, New York: Academic Press, 1966. See also Mona Clee and Robert Wicklund, "Consumer Behavior and Psychological Reactance," *Journal of Consumer Research* 6 (March 1980), 389–405.

19. Ian Stewart, "Public Fear Sells in Singapore," *Advertising Age*, October 11, 1993, I8. Singaporeans even make fun of themselves regarding their kiasu behavior. "Mr. Kiasu" is a popular comic book character, and a small cottage industry has sprung up around the character.

20. These factors are identified and discussed in J. Craig Andrews, *Tests of the Elaboration Likelihood Model Involving Persuasive Marketing Communication*, Ph.D. Dissertation, Columbia, SC: University of South Carolina, 1985, 7–12.

21. Shelly Chaiken and Alice H. Eagly, "Communication Modality as a Determinant of Persuasion: The Role of Communicator Salience," *Journal of Personality and Social Psychology*, vol. 45 (August 1983), 241–256.

22. For a discussion of different advertising involvement concepts, effects, and measures, see J. Craig Andrews, Srinivas Durvasula, and Syed H. Akhter, "A Framework for Conceptualizing and Measuring the Involvement Construct in Advertising Research," *Journal of Advertising* 19 (4), 1990, 27–40.

23. Richard M. Perloff and Timothy C. Brock, "'And Thinking Makes It So': Cognitive Responses to Persuasion," in *Persuasion: New Directions in Theory and Research*, ed. M. E. Rioloff and G. R. Miller, Beverly Hills, CA: Sage Publications, 1980, 67–99. See also Robert E. Burnkrant and H. Rao Unnava, "Effects of Self-Referencing on Persuasion," *Journal of Consumer Research* 22 (June 1995), 17–26.

24. Deborah J. MacInnis and Bernard J. Jaworski, "Information Processing from Advertisements: Toward an Integrative Framework," *Journal of Marketing* 53 (October 1989), 8.

25. Peter L. Wright, "The Cognitive Processes Mediating the Acceptance of Advertising," *Journal of Marketing Research* 10 (February 1973), 53–62. Also see Amitava Chattopadhyay and Joseph W. Alba, "The Situational Importance of Recall and Inference in Consumer Decision Making," *Journal of Consumer Research* 15 (June 1988), 1–12.

26. Petty and Cacioppo, *Attitudes and Persuasion*; Shelly Chaiken, "Heuristic Versus Systematic Information Processing and the Use of Source Cues Versus Message Cues in Persuasion," *Journal of Personality and Social Psychology*, 39, 752–66; Richard E. Petty and John T. Cacioppo, *Communication and Persuasion: Central and Peripheral Routes to Attitude Change*, New York, NY, Springer-Verlag, 1986; Rajeev Batra and Michael L. Ray, "Situational Effects of Advertising Repetition: The Moderating Influence of Motivation, Ability, and Opportunity to Respond," *Journal of Consumer Research* 12 (March 1986), 432–45; and MacInnis and Jaworski, "Information Processing from Advertisements." For applications of ELM predictions, see Richard E. Petty, John T. Cacioppo, and David W. Schumann, "Central and Peripheral Routes to Advertising Effectiveness: The Moderating Role of Involvement," *Journal of Consumer Research* 10 (September 1983), 135–46; J. Craig Andrews and Terence A. Shimp, "Effects of Involvement, Argument Strength, and Source Characteristics on Central and Peripheral Processing of Advertising," *Psychology & Marketing* 7 (fall 1990), 195–214; and Paul W. Miniard, Sunil Bhatla, Kenneth R. Lord, Peter R. Dickson, and H. Rao Unnava, "Picture-Based Persuasion Processes and the Moderating Role of Involvement," *Journal of Consumer Research* 18 (June 1991), 92–107. Another integrative framework is provided by Joan Meyers-Levy and Prashant Malaviya, "Consumers'

Processing of Persuasive Advertisements: An Integrative Framework of Persuasion Theories," *Journal of Marketing* 63 (Special Issue 1999), 45–60.

27. For a thorough review of research involving the attitude toward the ad construct, see Scott B. MacKenzie and Richard J. Lutz, "An Empirical Examination of the Structural Antecedents of Attitude Toward the Ad in an Advertising Pretesting Context," *Journal of Marketing* 53 (April 1989), 48–65.

28. For a more detailed account of classical conditioning, see Terence A. Shimp, "Neo-Pavlovian Conditioning and Its Implications for Consumer Theory and Research," in *Handbook of Consumer Behavior*, ed. T. S. Robertson and H. H. Kassarjian, Englewood Cliffs, NJ: Prentice-Hall, 1991, 162–87.

29. Paul W. Miniard, Deepak Sirdeshmukh, and Daniel E. Innis, "Peripheral Persuasion and Brand Choice," *Journal of Consumer Research* 19 (September 1992), 226–39.

30. Petty and Cacioppo, *Communication and Persuasion*, 206; see also an indirect demonstration of this in a series of experiments conducted by Michael Tuan Pham, "Cue Representation and Selection Effects of Arousal on Persuasion," *Journal of Consumer Research* 22 (March 1996), 373–87.

31. Petty and Cacioppo, *Attitudes and Persuasion*. See also Richard E. Petty, Rao H. Unnava, and Alan J. Strathman, "Theories of Attitude Change," in *Handbook of Consumer Behavior*, ed. T. S. Robertson and H. H. Kassarjian, Englewood Cliffs, NJ: Prentice Hall, 1991, 241–80.

32. The ensuing discussion is based on the work of Deborah J. MacInnis, Christine Moorman, and Bernard J. Jaworski, "Enhancing and Measuring Consumers' Motivation, Opportunity, and Ability to Process Brand Information from Ads," *Journal of Marketing* 55 (October 1991), 32–53.

33. James R. Bettman, Mary Frances Luce, and John W. Payne, "Constructive Consumer Choice Processes," *Journal of Consumer Research* 25 (December 1998), 193; and Daniel Kahneman, *Attention and Effort*, Englewood Cliffs, NJ: Prentice Hall, 1973.

34. Scott B. MacKenzie and Richard A. Spreng, "How Does Motivation Moderate the Impact of Central and Peripheral Processing on Brand Attitudes and Intentions?" *Journal of Consumer Research* 18 (March 1992), 519–29.

35. For reading on the role and effectiveness of rhetorical questions in advertising, see a series of articles by Edward F. McQuarrie and David Glen Mick: "Figures of Rhetoric in Advertising Language," *Journal of Consumer Research* 22 (March 1996), 424–38;

"Visual Rhetoric in Advertising: Text Interpretive, Experimental and Reader Response Analyses," *Journal of Consumer Research* 26 (June 1999), 37–54; and "Visual and Verbal Rhetorical Figures under Directed Processing versus Incidental Exposure to Advertising," *Journal of Consumer Research* 29 (March 2003), 579–87. See also Rohini Ahluwalia and Robert E. Burnkrant, "Answering Questions about Questions: A Persuasion Knowledge Perspective for Understanding the Effects of Rhetorical Questions," *Journal of Consumer Research* 31 (June 2004), 26–42.

36. For a fascinating article on the role of advertising repetition, see Prashant Malaviya, "The Moderating Influence of Advertising Context on Ad Repetition Effects: The Role of Amount and Type of Elaboration," *Journal of Consumer Research* 34 (June 2007), 32–40.

37. Martin Fishbein and Icek Ajzen, *Belief, Attitude, Intention, and Behavior: An Introduction to Theory and Research*, Reading, MA: Addison-Wesley, 1975; and Icek Ajzen and Martin Fishbein, *Understanding Attitudes and Predicting Social Behavior*, Englewood Cliffs, NJ: Prentice-Hall, 1980.

38. The normative structure of the theory concerns the influence that important others (i.e., referent groups: friends, family, coaches) have on our intentions and behavior (as measured by normative beliefs) multiplied by the motivation to comply with those important others.

39. Richard J. Lutz, "Changing Brand Attitudes through Modification of Cognitive Structure," *Journal of Consumer Research* 1 (March 1975), 49–59.

40. Fara Warner, "BMW Ads Challenge Maintenance Myth," *Advertising Age*, June 20, 1994, 5.

41. Jim Henry, "Saab Takes on Volvo, BMW in First Campaign Via Martin," *Advertising Age*, August 18, 1997, 4.

42. Elizabeth Jensen, "New Juice Ad Touts Calcium without the Chalky Undertaste," *Wall Street Journal Interactive Edition*, August 15, 1997.

43. Betsy McKay, "PepsiCo's Tropicana to Claim Its Juice Has Cardiac Benefit," *Wall Street Journal Interactive Edition*, October 31, 2000.

44. Robert B. Zajonc and Hazel Markus, "Affective and Cognitive Factors in Preferences," *Journal of Consumer Research* 9 (September 1982), 123–31.

45. Ibid.

46. Ibid.

47. Walter R. Nord and J. Paul Peter, "A Behavioral Modification Perspective on Marketing," *Journal of Marketing* 44 (spring 1980), 36–47.

48. Ibid., p. 40.

CHAPTER 8

Objective Setting and Budgeting

Cavemen, Geckos, Flo, Mayhem, Magic Jingles, and the Insurance Industry Ad Brawl

You likely have seen TV commercials advertising Geico, one of the major companies that sell automobile insurance. You may recall Geico's commercials with a talking, Australian-accented gecko. And who could forget those ads that featured sophisticated cavemen who were insulted—in a parody on political correctness—by "insensitive" offenders who implied that using Geico.com was "so easy, a caveman could do it." Although both the gecko and cavemen commercials can be judged effective in terms of their creativity, that is not the issue that will be emphasized in this section. Instead, we focus on the vast amount of *money* budgeted by Geico for

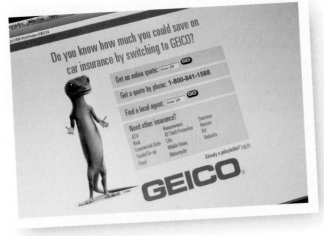

these TV commercials and the amount of success achieved.

The top four automobile insurance companies—State Farm, Allstate, Progressive, and Geico—compete in a highly aggressive environment where price wars to lure new customers are common. Using clever and frequent advertising and spokespeople are alternate routes by which competitors in this industry fight over new customers (e.g., State Farm's "Magic Jingle" ads, Allstate's "Mayhem" campaign, Progressive's Flo, and Geico's gecko and cavemen). Geico, despite having the third-largest market share, has been the leading advertiser among these top-four automobile insurance providers.

1 Understand the process of marcom objective setting and the requirements for good objectives.

2 Appreciate the hierarchy-of-marcom effects model and its relevance for setting marcom objectives.

3 Discuss the Integrated Information Response Model and how it helps determine the integration of advertising and direct product experience under different levels of involvement.

4 Comprehend the role of sales as a marcom objective and the logic of vaguely right versus precisely wrong thinking.

5 Know the relation between a brand's share of market (SOM) and its share of voice (SOV) and the implications for setting an advertising budget.

6 Understand the various rules of thumb, or heuristics, that guide practical budgeting.

Indeed, in 2009, Geico invested slightly over $827 million in advertising—which was over $300 million more than any of its competitors. Much of this spending can be attributed to Warren Buffett, who made Geico a subsidiary of his Berkshire Hathaway Corporation.

This massive investment has paid dividends for Geico. It now enjoys a very high level of advertising awareness—over 97 percent of surveyed consumers indicate that that they have heard of the Geico brand, which is tied with Allstate (with their "Mayhem" campaign), and the more traditional market share leader, State Farm. The nearest competitor in terms of ad awareness is State Farm at 80 percent. But, beyond creating awareness, Geico is the only brand in the auto insurance category to obtain double-digit growth in brand share, a climb of approximately 13 percent in its share of total auto insurance business. Also, Geico is the top brand in terms of new-customer acquisition. Needless to say, these impressive gains by Geico have prompted State Farm and Allstate to elevate their own levels of advertising spending.

The Geico case illustrates unmistakably that creative advertising backed with a sufficient advertising budget can accomplish various marcom objectives such as increasing awareness, attracting new customers, and boosting market share.

Sources: Adapted from E.J. Schultz, "How the Insurance Industry Got into a $4 Billion Ad Brawl," *Advertising Age*, February 21, 2011, http://adage.com/article/news/insurance-industry-s-4-billion-advertising-brawl/148992; and Mya Frazier, "Geico's Big Spending Pays Off, Study Says," *Advertising Age*, June 26, 2007, http://adage.com.

Introduction

Returning again to the model of the marcom process provided in Chapter 1, you will recall that the framework described various forms of "fundamental" and "implementation" decisions. We continue with this theme as it relates specifically to advertising objective setting and budgeting. These activities, along with segmentation, targeting, and positioning (see Chapter 5), are the bedrock of all subsequent marcom decisions. Marcom strategy built on a weak foundation is virtually guaranteed to fail. Intelligent objectives and an adequate budget are critical for success. Let us not forget the mantra introduced in Chapter 1:

All marketing communications should be (1) directed to a particular target market, *(2) clearly* positioned, *(3) created to achieve a* specific objective, *and (4) undertaken to accomplish the objective* within budget constraint.

This chapter culminates the discussion of fundamental marcom decisions by examining objective setting and budgeting. Both topics have been treated in the past mostly from the perspective of advertising rather than marcom in general. However, these issues are similar regardless of the form of marketing communications.

Finally, this chapter argues that objective setting and budgeting decisions must be formal and systematic rather than haphazard. Both topics represent key decisions that set the stage for the "implementation" of the choice of messages, media, mixture of marcom elements, and message continuity (or momentum), as introduced in Chapter 1.

Setting Marcom Objectives

Marcom objectives are general outcomes that the various marcom elements try to achieve individually or collectively. (Note that when one adds magnitude [e.g., increase of 10 percent] and scope of time [e.g., at the end of the first quarter], objectives become goals.[1]) Objectives provide the foundation for all remaining decisions. Later chapters detail more specific objectives that each component of the marcom mix is designed to accomplish; for present purposes we will introduce an illustrative set of general objectives for communicators. Alongside each objective, in parentheses, are the marcom tools most suitable for accomplishing that objective:

- Facilitate the successful introduction of new brands (brand naming and packaging, advertising, sales promotions, word-of-mouth buzz generation, point-of-purchase [POP] displays, and social media).
- Build sales of existing brands by increasing the frequency of use, the variety of uses, other quantity purchased (advertising and sales promotions).
- Inform the trade (wholesalers, agents or brokers, and retailers) and consumers about brand improvements (personal selling and trade-oriented advertising).
- Create brand awareness (advertising, social media, packaging, and POP messages).
- Enhance a brand's image (brand naming and packaging, advertising, social media, event sponsorship, cause-oriented marketing, and marketing-oriented public relations [PR]).
- Generate sales leads (advertising).
- Persuade the trade to handle the manufacturer's brands (trade-oriented advertising and personal selling).
- Stimulate point-of-purchase sales (brand naming and packaging, POP messages, and external store signage).

- Increase customer loyalty (advertising, social media, and sales promotions).
- Improve corporate relations with special interest groups (marketing-oriented PR).
- Offset bad publicity about a brand or generate good publicity (marketing-oriented PR and social media).
- Counter competitors' communications efforts (advertising and sales promotions).
- Provide customers with reasons for buying immediately instead of delaying a purchase (advertising, social media and sales promotions).

The objectives that marketing communications in its various forms must accomplish are varied, but regardless of the substance of the objective, there are three major reasons why it is essential that objectives be established *prior to* making the all-important implementation decisions regarding message selection, media determination, and how the various marcom elements should be mixed and maintained:[2]

1. *Achieving management consensus:* The process of setting objectives literally forces top marketing executives and marcom personnel to agree on a brand's marcom strategy for a given planning period, as well as the tasks it is to accomplish for a specific brand. As such, objectives provide a formalized expression of management consensus.
2. *Guiding subsequent marcom decisions:* Objective setting guides the budgeting, message, and media aspects of a brand's marcom strategy. Objectives determine how much money should be spent and suggest guidelines for the kinds of message strategy and media choice needed to accomplish a brand's marketing communications objectives.
3. *Providing standards:* Objectives provide standards against which results can be measured. As will be detailed later, good objectives set precise, quantitative yardsticks of what a marcom program hopes to accomplish. Subsequent results can then be compared with these standards to determine whether the effort accomplished what it was intended to do.

The Hierarchy of Marcom Effects

A full appreciation of marcom objective setting requires that we first look at the process of communications from the customer's perspective. The general idea of the hierarchy-of-effects model studied in the last chapter is appropriate for accomplishing this understanding. The hierarchy framework reveals that the choice of marcom objective depends on the target audience's degree of experience with the brand prior to commencing a marcom campaign.[3]

Based on the idea of the hierarchy-of-effects, the various marcom elements must advance consumers through a series of psychological stages in order to be successful. A variety of hierarchy models have been formulated, all of which are predicated on the idea that the marcom elements, if successful, move people from an initial state of unawareness about a brand to eventually purchasing that brand.[4] Intermediate stages in the hierarchy represent progressively closer steps to brand purchase. The hierarchy of marcom effects in Figure 8.1 goes a step further by establishing brand loyalty as the top step on the ladder.[5]

The meaning of each of these stages, or hierarchy steps, is best understood by examining an actual advertisement. Consider the ad in Figure 8.2 for a brand called Pegetables. A quick glance at this ad indicates that this product somehow is related to pets. On closer reading one can see that the brand name, Pegetables, represents a combination of the "p" in pet and the word "vegetables" without the "v"—in other words, vegetables for pets.

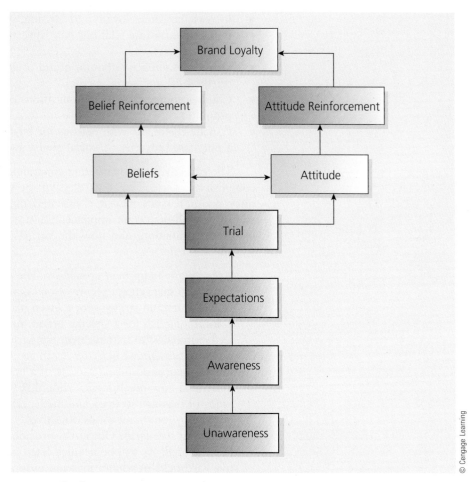

FIGURE **8.1** Hierarchy of Marcom Effects

Advancing Consumers from Unawareness to Awareness

When first introduced to the market, consumers were initially unaware of Pegetables' existence and of its special features (many no doubt remain unaware). The initial marcom objective, therefore, is to make consumers aware that there is a product such as Pegetables. In general, creating awareness is essential for new or unestablished brands. Of all the marcom tools, advertising (via mass media, social media, etc.) generally is the most effective and efficient method for quickly creating brand awareness. Sometimes advertising agencies place excessive emphasis on building brand awareness by creating zany ads with offbeat humor or using blatant sex appeals. However, please read the *IMC Focus*, which describes a case where creating awareness did not assure that consumers will move further up the hierarchy toward purchasing the brand and potentially becoming loyal repeat purchasers.

Creating an Expectation

Mere brand name awareness generally is insufficient to get people to buy a brand, particularly when consumers already possess a solution to a consumption-related problem or remain unaware that a solution is available. Advertising and other marcom elements must instill in consumers an expectation of what product benefit(s) they will obtain from buying and experiencing a brand. It should be noted that an expectation from the consumer's perspective is based on how the brand has been positioned, which was the subject of Chapter 5.

The positioning for Pegetables is a promise to consumers that it is a delicious-tasting and nutritious snack for dogs that is made with real vegetables (see the corn-, carrot-, and celery-shaped items). To the extent consumers

FIGURE **8.2** Advertisement Illustrating Hierarchy of Marcom Effects

This Cat(fight) Is a Dog

In response to diet fads eschewing the intake of carbohydrates (e.g., the Atkins and South Beach diets) that were highly popular during the early 2000s, the Miller Brewing Company undertook an aggressive advertising campaign by comparing Miller Lite against Anheuser-Busch's Bud Light. Using humorous but hard-hitting TV ads, Miller Lite's advertisements attempted to persuade consumers that that brand should be their preferred choice because it contains only one-half the carbohydrate content of Bud Light. This campaign had a substantial impact on Miller Lite's market share, which rose while Bud Light's share declined.

But prior to this particular ad campaign, Miller had attempted to boost sales of Miller Lite by running a campaign with blatant sex appeal. The campaign was dubbed "Catfight" based on the campaign's initial spot in which two scantily clad women fought and shed clothing over whether Miller Lite tastes great or is less filling. A series of additional spots presented sexy women in confrontational scenes arguing over Miller Lite's relative merits. The campaign generated considerable buzz as well as controversy for its treatment of women as sex objects.

However, of primary relevance in the context of the present discussion is the fact that, although brand awareness of Miller Lite increased during the Catfight campaign, actual sales declined by 3 percent. In a meeting with financial analysts who track the performance of Miller's various brands, the president of Miller Lite had this to say about the ad campaign: "Awareness is not the problem, but actual [purchase] consideration is the problem and challenge and opportunity. We want to ensure that the [advertising] spend we put behind the brand is leading toward actual consideration and not just continuing to build awareness."

Source: Hillary Chura, "Miller Loses 'Catfight,' Buzz Doesn't Lift Lite," *Advertising Age*, June 2, 2003, 3, 51. Copyright Crain Communications Inc., 2003. Used with permission.

The Miller Lite Catfight Girls

develop this expectation, they may undertake trial purchases of Pegetables to learn for themselves (based on whether their pets seem to enjoy the product) whether it lives up to its promise.

Encouraging Trial Purchases

Sales promotions and advertisements sometimes work together to encourage trial purchases (i.e., a first purchase), often by influencing consumers to switch from brands they currently are purchasing. Because most advertisements can simply hope to entice, enthuse, and whet one's appetite—or, in general, create expectations—a more compelling mechanism is required for generating trial purchases. Sales promotions ideally fit this role for marketing communications. Free samples and coupons are particularly effective devices for getting consumers to try new brands of packaged goods. In the case of expensive durable products, major price discounts and rebate offers are effective in encouraging a form of trial behavior such as test-driving automobiles.

Forming Beliefs and Attitudes

Upon trying a brand for the first time, the consumer will form beliefs about its performance. With respect to Pegetables, the beliefs may be thoughts such as, "My dog really likes these snacks, and, because they are made with real vegetables, they must be good for him." These beliefs, in turn, form the basis for developing an overall attitude toward the brand. Beliefs and attitudes are mutually reinforcing, as illustrated by the double-headed arrow linking these two elements in Figure 8.1. If Pegetables lives up to the pet owner's expectations, the attitude toward that brand most likely will be positive; however, the attitude can be expected to be somewhat ambivalent or even negative if the brand fails to satisfy the expected benefit that motivated the trial purchase.

Reinforcing Beliefs and Attitudes

Brand-specific beliefs and attitudes are formed as the *outcome from firsthand product usage experience*. Then, subsequent marketing communications merely serve to reinforce the consumers' beliefs and attitudes that resulted from trying the product. In Figure 8.1 this is referred to as belief reinforcement and attitude reinforcement. The reinforcement objective is accomplished when a marketing communicator sticks with a particular promise and promotes this point repeatedly.

Accomplishing Brand Loyalty

As long as the brand continues to satisfy expectations and a superior brand is not introduced, the consumer may become a brand-loyal purchaser. (Note, as discussed in Chapter 2, *brand loyalty* is the consumer's commitment to continue using or advocating a brand.) This is the ultimate objective, because, as has been mentioned, it is much cheaper to retain present customers than it is to prospect continuously for new ones.[6]

Brand loyalty is the top rung on the hierarchy of marcom effects (see Figure 8.1). Loyalty is not a guaranteed outcome, however. Strong brand loyalty occasionally develops. For example, some consumers always purchase the same brand of cola, toothpaste, shampoo, or even automobile. In many other instances, however, the consumer never forms a strong preference for any brand. Rather, the consumer continually shifts his or her allegiance from one brand to the next, constantly trying, trying, and trying but never developing a strong commitment to any particular brand.

It is interesting to note, however, that the various marcom elements may be in conflict toward the goal of accomplishing brand loyalty. Whereas advertising has the desirable long-run effect of making consumers less price sensitive and more brand loyal, sales promotions (e.g., online coupon offers) can actually reduce loyalty by effectively "training" consumers to be price sensitive and thus inclined to switch among brands to avail themselves of price discounts.[7]

The Integrated Information Response Model

The preceding traditional view of the hierarchy of effects has been criticized at times because it suggests a single response pattern (i.e., cognition → affect → conation). However, the pattern in the traditional hierarchy only applies in instances of *high-involvement behavior*, in which the purchase decision is important to the consumer and has significant risks associated with it. A more comprehensive model is needed to capture fully the diversity of purchase decisions and consumer behavior in response to advertising.

The integrated information response model (see Figure 8.3) provides this needed comprehensiveness.[8] The model takes its name from the idea that consumers *integrate information* from two sources—advertising and direct product usage experience—in forming attitudes and purchase intentions toward products and brands. Therefore, in Figure 8.3, two *information sources* are available to the consumer: *advertising* and one's own *direct experience* in using the product or brand. *Information acceptance* (due to factors such as source credibility) ranges between low and high levels. Extending from information acceptance are *cognitions*, shown in Figure 8.3 as either lower- or higher-order beliefs. Lower-order beliefs represent the consumer's mere awareness or recognition of the brand and/or claims that it possesses some feature or benefit. For example, after seeing the ad for Pegetables (Figure 8.2), a dog owner may simply take away that the multicolored brand name is a combination of pet and vegetables. This knowledge is a lower- rather than higher-order belief because merely registering what an advertiser has said is not the same as experiencing the product actually doing what the ad said it would.

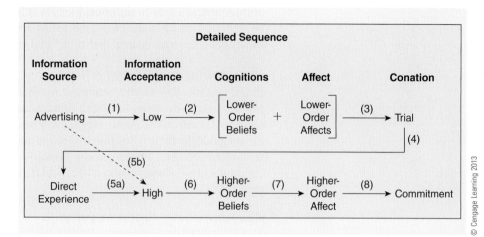

FIGURE **8.3** Integrated Information Response Model

Higher-order beliefs, which result from direct product experience (or under high involvement), represent the consumer's acceptance that a brand does in fact do (or fail to do) what the advertiser has claimed. (For example, if you used Pegetables for your pet, you then could experience via your pet the product's nutritious advantages.) *Affect* is also shown to be lower- or higher-order. Lower-order affect is a little more than a favorable (or unfavorable) disposition about a brand after learning about it, for example, in an advertisement. For instance, one consumer's response to learning about Pegetables might be "That's a great idea! It seems like an easy way to give my pet nutritious vegetables." Higher-order affect, on the other hand, represents the consumer's actual feelings toward the product after using it. For example, "I really believe Pegetables provides the antioxidants, protein, fiber, calcium and vitamins my pet needs!" Finally, *conation* ranges from a one-time trial purchase (as with an inexpensive packaged good) all the way to a commitment to regularly use the product or brand as part of one's lifestyle. Based on this terminology, we now present three response patterns or routes to advertising that are implied by the model.

Pattern 1: Cognition → Affect → Commitment

The pattern of cognition to affect to commitment is the traditional (high involvement) hierarchy-of-effects model previously described. This is shown in Figure 8.3 by the dashed arrow from advertising to high information acceptance (path 5b) and then, in turn, to higher-order beliefs (path 6), to higher-order affect (path 7), and ultimately to commitment (path 8).

This pattern is applicable when consumers fully accept advertising message claims (under high involvement), form attitudes toward the advertised brand, and become firmly committed to purchasing the advertised product. It is important to note that this *high-involvement* pattern has the potential of impacting higher-order beliefs and affect without trial or direct experience, similar to the central route to persuasion studied in the previous chapter.

Pattern 2: (Minimal) Cognition → Trial → Affect → Commitment

This sequence from (minimal) cognition to trial to affect to commitment is captured in Figure 8.3 by the flow of solid arrows from advertising to low information acceptance (path 1), on through lower-order beliefs and lower-order affect (path 2), then to trial (path 3), and ultimately to commitment as a function of direct experience and the higher-order beliefs and affect that result (paths 5a through 8).

This response pattern typifies *low-involvement learning*. When consumers are passive learners of information (as typically the case with most products), higher-order affect results only *after* one has acquired direct (or first-hand) experience using a product. A true attitude (i.e., higher-order affect) typically follows rather than precedes direct product usage experience. Thus, actual product usage experience (e.g., eating a food, drinking a beverage, or using a smartphone) is extremely informative and convincing, whereas merely learning from advertising (under low involvement) about how a product is supposed to taste or perform may be far less revealing.

The initial (minimal) thoughts from a TV commercial (e.g., candy bar's brand name) represent lower-order beliefs and initial impressions represent lower-order affect. This lower-order beliefs and impressions are tentatively held awaiting support or refutation based on actual product usage. First-hand knowledge (e.g., after actual use) will help guide and form higher-order affect and commitment.

Pattern 3: Cognition → Trial → Trial → Trial ...

This pattern from cognition to multiple trials is implicit in Figure 8.3 and suggests that in the case of relatively homogeneous product categories there may be no such thing as higher-order affect either before or after direct usage experience. In such instances, consumers simply switch brands consistently and may never form a preference or commitment. This may happen with fellow students who simply purchase soap or shampoo solely on low price or what is available. So, in some cases like response pattern 3, long-term commitment or brand loyalty is not assured.

Section Summary

It should be apparent from this discussion of marcom's hierarchy of effects that the objective for a brand's marcom program at any point in time depends on where in the hierarchy consumers are located and their relative involvement level in processing the communication. Although individual consumers inevitably will be at different levels of the hierarchy, the issue is one of where most consumers are located. For example, if research reveals that the vast majority of the target audience remains unaware of the brand, then creating awareness is of uppermost importance. If, however, most members of the target audience know of the brand but are unclear what it stands for, then the marcom task becomes one of designing messages that build an expectation capable of motivating consumers to try the brand. Involvement levels of the target market are also important in understanding different response patterns or routes taken in the integrated information response model.

Requirements for Setting Suitable Marcom Objectives

A marcom objective is a specific statement about a planned execution in terms of what a marcom program is intended to accomplish at a point in time. That objective is based on knowledge of where on the hierarchy of effects members of the target audience are located; knowledge of the current, or anticipated, competitive situation in the product category; and the problems that the brand must confront or the opportunities that are available.

The specific content of a marcom objective depends entirely on the brand's unique situation and current details about competition (e.g., as those provided by marketing research). We can, however, describe the requirements that all good objectives must satisfy. Let us start by clarifying that not all objectives are well stated. Consider the following examples:

> *Example A: The objective next business quarter for Brand X is to realize increased sales.*

> *Example B: The objective next business quarter for Brand X is to elevate overall brand awareness from the present level of 60 percent to 80 percent.*

These extreme examples differ in two important respects. First, example B is obviously more specific. Second, whereas example A deals with a sales objective, example B involves a presales goal (increase awareness). The sections that

- Include a precise statement of who, what, and when
- Be quantitative and measurable
- Specify the amount of change
- Be realistic
- Be internally consistent
- Be clear and in writing

FIGURE **8.4** Criteria That Good Marcom Objectives Must Satisfy

© Cengage Learning

follow describe the specific criteria that good objectives must satisfy.[9] We will return to examples A and B in the process of presenting these criteria, which are listed in Figure 8.4.

Objectives Must Include a Precise Statement of Who, What, and When

Objectives must be stated in precise terms in moving them toward a goal. At a minimum, objectives should specify the target audience (who), indicate the specific communication stage—such as awareness level—to be accomplished (what), and indicate the relevant time frame over which the objective is to be achieved (when). For example, the marcom campaign for Pegetables (Figure 8.2) might move a general objective (awareness) into a goal with the following examples: (1) "Within four months from the beginning of the advertising campaign, research should show that 25 percent of all dog owners are aware of the Pegetables name"; (2) "Within six months from the beginning of the campaign, research should show that at least 50 percent of the target audience who now are aware of the Pegetables name know that this brand is a vegetable-based snack treat for dogs"; or (3) "Within one year from the beginning of the campaign, at least 5 million households should have tried Pegetables."

Returning to the two hypothetical objectives (A versus B), example B represents the desired degree of specificity and, as such, would give brand managers a meaningful goal and benchmark to direct their efforts for assessing whether the marcom campaign has accomplished its objective. Example A, by comparison, is much too general. Suppose sales have actually increased by 2 percent during the course of the campaign. Does this mean the campaign was successful because sales have in fact increased? If not, how much increase is necessary for the campaign to be regarded as a success?

Objectives Must Be Quantitative and Measurable

This requirement demands that ad objectives be stated in quantitative terms so as to be measurable. A nonmeasurable objective for Pegetables would be a vague statement such as, "Marketing communications should enhance consumers' knowledge of Pegetables." This objective lacks measurability because it fails to specify the product benefit of which consumers are to possess knowledge.

Objectives Must Specify the Amount of Change

In addition to being quantitative and measurable, objectives must specify the amount of change they are intended to accomplish in moving toward goals. Example A (to increase sales) fails to meet this requirement. Example B (to increase awareness from 60 percent to 80 percent) is satisfactory because it clearly specifies that anything less than a 20 percent awareness increase would be considered unsuitable performance.

Objectives Must Be Realistic

Unrealistic objectives are as useless as having no objective at all. An unrealistic objective is one that cannot be accomplished in the time allotted to the proposed marcom campaign. For example, a brand that has achieved only 15 percent consumer awareness during its first year on the market could not realistically expect a small marcom budget to increase the awareness level to, say, 45 percent next year. Several years ago, the Beecham Company sued their marketing research agency, Yankelovich Clancy Shuman, because Yankelovich's initial (erroneous) forecast had predicted a share for Delicare (a cold-water wash detergent) to be between 45 percent and 52 percent when in fact it only reached 17 percent.[10] The moral is that although it is essential to have accurate and timely information to guide decisions, it also is important to speak up in meetings when information may not be realistic given the environment (e.g., consumer, cultural, competitive, supplier, technological, regulatory, and market situations).

Objectives Must Be Internally Consistent

Objectives set for a particular element of a marcom program must be compatible (internally consistent) with objectives set for other marcom components. It would be incompatible for a manufacturer to proclaim a 25 percent reduction in sales force while simultaneously stating that the advertising and sales promotion objective is to increase retail distribution by 20 percent. Without adequate sales force effort, it is doubtful that the retail trade would give a brand more shelf space.

Objectives Must Be Clear and in Writing

For objectives to accomplish their purposes of fostering communication and permitting evaluation, they must be stated clearly and in writing so that they can be disseminated to marcom personnel who will be held responsible for seeing that the objectives are accomplished.

Should Marcom Objectives Be Stated in Terms of Sales?

We can broadly distinguish two types of marcom objectives: sales versus pre-sales objectives. *Pre-sales objectives* are commonly referred to as *communication objectives*, with the term *communication* derived from efforts to communicate outcomes that will increase the target audience's brand awareness, enhance their attitudes toward the brand, shift their preference from competitors' brands to our brand, and so on. Comparatively, using *sales* as the goal for a particular advertising campaign means that the marcom objective literally is to increase sales by a specified amount. Marcom practitioners and educators have traditionally rejected the use of sales as an appropriate objective. However, a relatively recent perspective asserts that influencing sales should *always* be considered as the ultimate objective of any marcom effort. The following discussion first presents the traditional view on this matter (favoring a pre-sales, or communications, objective) and then introduces the "heretical" (opposite) position (preferring a sales objective).

The Traditional View

This view asserts that using sales as the objective for a branded product's marcom effort is unsuitable for two major reasons. First, a brand's sales volume during any given period is the consequence of a host of factors in addition to advertising, sales promotions, and other elements of the marcom program. These include the prevailing economic climate, competitive activity, and all the marketing mix variables used by a brand—its price level, product quality, distribution strategy, and so forth. It is virtually impossible, according to the traditional view, to determine precisely the role advertising or other marcom elements have had in influencing sales in a given period, because marketing communications is *just one of many possible determinants* of a brand's sales volume.

A second reason that sales response is claimed to represent an unsuitable marcom objective is that marcom's effect on sales is typically delayed, or *lagged*. For example, advertising during any given period does not necessarily influence sales in the current period but may influence sales during later periods. On the one hand, advertising for a particular automobile model this year may have a limited effect on some consumers' purchasing behavior because these consumers are not presently in the market for a new automobile. On the other hand, this year's advertising can influence consumers to select the advertised model next year when they *are* in the market. Thus, advertising may have a decided influence on consumers' brand awareness, product knowledge, expectations, attitudes, and, ultimately, purchase behavior, but this influence may not be evident during the period when the effect of advertising on sales is measured.

Advocates of the traditional view thus argue that it is misguided to use sales as the goal for a particular marcom effort. Their view, fundamentally, is that it is idealistic to set sales as the objective because marcom's exact impact on sales cannot be accurately assessed.

The Heretical (Opposite) View

Conversely, some marcom authorities contend that marketing communicators should always state objectives in terms of sales or market share gains and that failure to do so is a cop-out. The logic of this nontraditional, or heretical, view is that marcom's purpose is not just to create brand awareness, convey copy points, influence expectations, or enhance attitudes, but also ultimately to generate sales. Thus, according to this position it is always possible to measure, if only vaguely and imprecisely, marcom's effect on sales. Pre-sales, or communication, objectives such as increases in brand awareness are claimed to be "precisely wrong," in contrast to sales measures that are asserted to be "vaguely right."[11] These positions are depicted in Figure 8.5. Basically, an argument can be made that a sales objective ultimately is the right objective. However, communication objectives (e.g., awareness, comprehension) are more accurately measured, as sales can be a function of many factors. The impact of advertising on sales is more vaguely measured.

An Accountability Perspective (A Synthesis)

There is no simple resolution as to whether the traditional or heretical view is more correct. However, there are some situations in which sales (direct) objectives may be more appropriate, including weekly advertising by retailers, direct response advertising (focusing on behavior), sales promotion advertising (e.g., free-standing inserts with coupon bar codes), and business-to-business advertising (e.g., with fewer customers than with consumer advertising).

One thing is certain, however, companies, their chief executives, and financial officers are increasingly demanding greater *accountability* from marcom programs. Increasing pressure has been placed on agencies to develop campaigns that produce bottom-line results—increases in sales, in market share, and higher returns on investment (ROI). Although it is difficult to measure the

Objective-Setting Issue	Alternative Possibilities
• Choice of Objective	Chosen objective is *Right* or *Wrong*
• Accuracy of Measurement	Accuracy is *Precise* or *Vague* (i.e., Imprecise)

© Cengage Learning

FIGURE **8.5** The Logic of Vaguely Right versus Precisely Wrong Thinking

precise effect marketing communications have on sales, in a climate of increased demands for accountability, it is essential that advertisers and other marketing communicators measure, as best they can, whether the marketing communications program during a particular financial period has increased a brand's sales, market share, and ROI.

Importantly, this is *not* to say that efforts should not also be made to assess whether marcom affects pre-sales goals such as improving brand awareness, driving home copy points, and augmenting attitudes and intentions. The point, instead, is that the measurement of effects should *not stop* with these measures. Awareness, for example, is a suitable substitute for sales only if there is a direct transformation of enhanced awareness levels into increased sales. This, unfortunately, is rarely the case. A marcom campaign may increase brand awareness by a substantial amount but have limited impact on sales (recall the discussion of the Miller Lite "Catfight" ad campaign in the *IMC Focus* insert). As such, brand managers should not permit agencies to mislead them into thinking that a campaign has been successful just because brand awareness has improved.

Returning to the hierarchy of marcom effects, increased awareness will lead to sales gains only if other rungs on the ladder have been traversed. In sum, the assessment of effectiveness should include, but not be restricted to, pre-sales goals. Setting sales as the objective of a marcom campaign ensures that this ultimate goal will not be neglected.

Marcom Budgeting

Establishing a budget is, in many respects, one of the most important marcom decisions. Budgeting is a critical decision as marcom endeavors such as advertising are typically very expensive. (The substantial investment in marketing communications is illustrated in the *Global Focus* insert, which identifies advertising spending by the top-20 global marketers.) Moreover, the implications of spending too little or too much are considerable. If too little is invested in marketing communications, sales volume will not achieve its potential and profits will be lost. If too much is spent, unnecessary expenses will reduce profits.

Of course, the dilemma brand managers face is determining what spending level is "too little" or how much is "too much." As with most marketing and business decisions, the "devil is in the doing!" Budgeting is not only one of the most important marcom decisions, but also it is one of the most complicated. This challenge will be demonstrated in the following discussion of how—in theory—advertising budgets should be set if the objective is to maximize profits.

Budgeting in Theory

Budgeting for advertising or other marcom elements is, in theory, a simple process, provided one accepts the premise that the best (optimal) level of any investment is the level that *maximizes profits*. This assumption leads to a simple rule for establishing advertising budgets: *Continue to invest in advertising as long as the marginal revenue from that investment exceeds the marginal cost.*

Some elaboration is needed on this clear-cut rule. According to basic economics, marginal revenue (MR) and marginal cost (MC) are the *changes* in the total revenue and total cost, respectively, that result

GLOBAL FOCUS

The Top-20 Global Marketers' Advertising Spending

Advertising expenditures around the globe are enormous. As shown in the following list, the top-20 global marketers alone recently spent over $53 billion on advertising in one year. These are all well-known companies whose products and services are available around the world. The huge American company, Procter & Gamble, leads the way with global advertising expenditures exceeding $8.6 billion, but even the smallest advertiser among these top 20 (Walt Disney) spent over $1.4 billion advertising its services.

Rank	Advertiser	Headquarters	Ad Spend (in $ millions)
1	Procter & Gamble Co.	Cincinnati, OH	$8,679
2	Unilever	London, U.K./Rotterdam, Netherlands	6,033
3	L'Oreal	Clichy, France	4,560
4	General Motors Corp.	Detroit, MI	3,268
5	Nestle	Vevey, Switzerland	2,615
6	Coca Cola Co.	Atlanta, GA	2,442
7	Toyota Motor Co.	Toyota City, Japan	2,305
8	Johnson & Johnson	New Brunswick, NJ	2,251
9	Reckitt Benckiser	Berkshire, U.K.	2,237
10	Kraft Foods	Northfield, IL	2,118
11	McDonald's Corp.	Oak Brook, IL	2,076
12	Ford Motor Corp.	Dearborn, MI	2,057
13	Volkswagen	Wolfsburg, Germany	1,938
14	Pfizer	New York, NY	1,827
15	Sony Corp.	Tokyo, Japan	1,715
16	GlaxoSmithKline	Brentford, U.K.	1,630
17	Danone Group	Paris, France	1,611
18	Mars, Inc.	McLean, VA	1,587
19	PepsiCo	Purchase, NY	1,550
20	Walt Disney Co.	Burbank, CA	1,440

Source: "Top 20 Global Marketers," *Advertising Age*, Spring 2011, 3.

from a change in a business factor (such as advertising) that affects the levels of total revenue and cost. The profit-maximization rule is a matter of straightforward economic logic: Profits are maximized at the point where MR = MC. At any investment level below this point (where MR > MC), profits are not maximized because at a higher level of advertising investment more profit remains to be earned. Similarly, at any level above this point (where MC > MR), there is a marginal loss. In practical terms, this means that advertisers should continue to increase their advertising investments as long as every dollar of investment yields more than a dollar in revenue.

It is evident from this simple exercise that setting the advertising budget is a matter of answering a series of *if-then* questions—*if* $X are invested in advertising, *then* what amount of revenue will be generated? Because budgets are set before the actual observance of how sales respond to advertising, this requires that the if-then questions be answered *before the fact*. (Analogously, this would be equivalent to predicting how many fish one will catch on a given day based simply on knowing the number of lures in that person's fishing box.) But this is where the complications begin. To employ the profit-maximization rule for budget setting, the advertising decision maker must know the *sales-to-advertising response function* for every brand for which a budgeting decision will be made. Because such knowledge is rarely available, theoretical (profit-maximization) budget setting is an ideal that is generally impractical in the real world of advertising decision making. To appreciate this point fully we need to elaborate on the concept of a sales-to-advertising (S-to-A) response function.

The sales-to-advertising response function refers to the relationship between money invested in advertising and the response, or output, of that investment in terms of revenue generated. As with any mathematical function, the S-to-A function maps the relationship between an "output" (in this case, sales revenue) to each meaningful level of an "input" (advertising expenditures). Table 8.1 demonstrates a hypothetical S-to-A response function by listing a series of advertising expenditures and the corresponding revenue yielded at each ad-expenditure level. Marginal costs, revenues, and profits also are presented (columns C through E).

Consider that our hypothetical decision maker is contemplating spending anywhere between $1,000,000 and $5,000,000 in advertising a brand during a particular period. Column A in Table 8.1 lists a range of possible advertising expenditures that increase in $500,000 increments starting at $1,000,000 and ending at $5,000,000. Assume that it is somehow possible to know precisely how much revenue will be generated at each level of advertising. Column B presents the various levels of sales in response to advertising. If you were to graph the relation between columns A and B, you would see that sales respond slowly to advertising until ad expenditures increase above $2,000,000, at which point sales revenue jumps considerably, especially at $3,000,000 invested in

TABLE 8.1	Hypothetical Sales-to-Advertising Response Function			
(A) Advertising Expenditures ($)	(B) Sales Response ($)	(C) Marginal Cost ($)	(D) Marginal Revenue ($)	(E) Marginal Profit (MR – MC)
1,000,000	5,000,000	NA	NA	NA
1,500,000	5,750,000	500,000	750,000	250,000
2,000,000	6,500,000	500,000	750,000	250,000
2,500,000	7,500,000	500,000	1,000,000	500,000
3,000,000	10,000,000	500,000	2,500,000	2,000,000
3,500,000	10,600,000	500,000	600,000	100,000
4,000,000	11,100,000	500,000	500,000	0
4,500,000	11,500,000	500,000	400,000	–100,000
5,000,000	11,800,000	500,000	300,000	–200,000

advertising. Thereafter, sales response to advertising tapers off substantially. It is easy to determine the level of marginal profit by simply subtracting the marginal cost at each level of advertising from the corresponding marginal revenue. The point of profit maximization is realized at an advertising investment of $4,000,000 where MR = MC = $500,000. Any ad investment below that amount continues to yield marginal profit, whereas any investment above $4,000,000 results in a marginal loss. Thus, as previously noted, profits are maximized at the point where MR = MC.

If in fact marcom personnel could accurately estimate the S-to-A response function (columns A and B in Table 8.1), then setting the advertising budget to maximize profits would represent the proverbial "piece of cake." However, because the S-to-A response function is influenced by a *multitude of factors* (such as the creativity of advertising execution, the intensity of competitive advertising efforts, the overall quality of the brand's marketing mix, the state of the economy at the time advertising is undertaken, etc.), and not solely by the amount of advertising investment, it is difficult to know with any certainty what amount of sales a particular level of advertising expenditure will generate.

Hence, if an S-to-A response function is unknown prior to when a budgeting decision is made, then a total revenue curve cannot be constructed. In turn, marginal revenue cannot be derived at each level of ad investment. Thus, applying profit-maximization budgeting requires information that rarely is available. Necessarily, marcom budget setters turn to more practical approaches for establishing budgets—methods that do not assure profit maximization but that are easy to work with and have the semblance, if not the substance, of being "correct."

Budgeting in Practice

Given the difficulty of accurately predicting sales response to advertising, companies typically set budgets by using judgment, applying experience with analogous situations, and using rules of thumb, or *heuristics*.[12] Although criticized because they do not provide a basis for advertising budget setting that is directly related to the profitability of the advertised brand, these heuristics continue to be widely used.[13] The practical budgeting methods most frequently used by both B2B companies and consumer goods firms in the United States, Europe, and even in China are the percentage-of-sales, objective-and-task, competitive parity, and affordability methods.[14]

Percentage-of-Sales Budgeting

In using the percentage-of-sales method, a company sets a brand's advertising budget by simply establishing the budget as a fixed percentage of *past* (e.g., last year's) or *anticipated* (e.g., next year's) sales volume. Assume, for example, that a company has traditionally allocated 3 percent of anticipated sales to advertising and that the company projects next year's sales for a particular brand to be $100,000,000. Its advertising budget would thus be set at $3,000,000.

A survey of the top 100 consumer goods advertisers in the United States found that slightly more than 50 percent employ the percentage-of-anticipated-sales method and 20 percent use the percentage-of-past-sales method.[15] This is expected, because budget setting should logically correspond to what a company expects to do in the future rather than being based on what it accomplished in the past.

What percentage of sales revenue do most companies devote to advertising? Actually, the percentage is highly variable. For example, among approximately 200 different types of products and services, the highest percentage of sales devoted to advertising in a recent year was the wood household furniture industry, which invested 18.4 percent of sales to advertising. Some other categories with double-digit advertising-to-sales ratios were transportation services (16.9 percent); distilled and blended liquor (16.8 percent); food products (11.9 percent); rubber and plastic footwear (11.7 percent); and dolls and stuffed toys (10.9 percent). Most product categories average less than 5 percent advertising-to-sales ratios. In fact, the average advertising-to-sales ratio across nearly 200 categories of B2C and B2B products and services was *3.1 percent.*[16]

Criticism of Percentage-of-Sales Budgeting The percentage-of-sales method is frequently criticized as being illogical. Critics argue that the method reverses the logical relationship between sales and advertising. That is, the true ordering between advertising and sales is that advertising causes sales, meaning that the level of sales is a function of advertising: *Sales = f (Advertising).* Contrary to this logical relation, implementing the percentage-of-sales method amounts to reversing the causal order by setting advertising as a function of sales: *Advertising = f (Sales).*

By this logic and method, when sales are anticipated to increase, the advertising budget also increases; when sales are expected to decline, the budget is reduced. Applying the percentage-of-sales method leads many firms to reduce advertising budgets during economic downswings. However, rather than decreasing the amount of advertising, it may be wiser during these times to increase advertising to prevent further sales erosion. When used blindly, the percentage-of-sales method is little more than an arbitrary and simplistic rule of thumb substituted for what needs to be a sound business judgment. Used without justification, this budgeting method is another application of precisely wrong (versus vaguely right) decision making, as was discussed in the context of setting marcom objectives.

In practice, most sophisticated marketers do not use percentage of sales as the sole budgeting method. Instead, they employ the method as an initial pass, or first cut, for determining the budget and then alter the budget forecast depending on the objectives and tasks to be accomplished, the amount of competitive ad spending, and the availability of funds.

The Objective-and-Task Budgeting Method

The objective-and-task method is generally regarded as the most sensible and defendable advertising budgeting method. In using this method, advertising planners specify clear objectives for the advertising, identify the tasks the advertising must perform to reach these objectives, and then set the budget accordingly. The role is typically identified in terms of a communication objective (e.g., increase brand awareness by 20 percent), but could be stated in terms of expected sales volume or market share (e.g., increase market share from 15 to 20 percent).

The objective-and-task method is the advertising budget procedure used most frequently by both B2C and B2B companies. Surveys have shown that over 60 percent of consumer goods companies and 70 percent of B2B companies use this budgeting method.[17] The following steps are involved when applying the objective-and-task method:[18]

1. The first step is to establish specific *marketing objectives* that need to be accomplished, such as sales volume, market share, and profit contribution.

   Consider the marketing and advertising challenge in the United States that faced Volkswagen (VW). Although this once-vaunted automobile company had achieved huge success in the 1960s and 1970s with its VW Beetle, by the mid-1990s VW was confronted with what

© picturesbyrob/Alamy

perhaps was its final opportunity to recapture the American consumer, who had turned to other imports and domestic models because VW had not kept up with what Americans wanted.[19] Sales of its two leading brands, the Golf and Jetta, had dropped by about 50 percent each compared with sales in prior years. VW's marketing objective (not to be confused with its specific advertising objective, which is discussed next) was to increase sales of the Golf and Jetta models substantially and its overall share of the U.S. automobile market—from a low of only about 21,000 Golfs and Jettas to a goal of selling 250,000 VW models in the near future.

2. The second step in implementing the objective-and-task method is to assess the *communication functions* that must be performed to accomplish the overall marketing objectives.

   VW had to accomplish two communication functions to realize its rather ambitious marketing objective. First, it had to increase consumers' awareness of the Golf and Jetta brand names substantially, and, second, it had to establish an image for VW as a company that offers "honest, reliable, and affordable cars." In short, VW had to enhance the Golf's and Jetta's brand equities.

3. The third step is to *determine advertising's role in the total communication mix* in performing the functions established in step 2.

   Given the nature of its products and communication objectives, advertising was a crucial component in VW's mix.

4. The fourth step is to establish specific advertising goals in terms of the levels of *measurable communication response* required to achieve marketing objectives.

   VW might have established goals such as increase awareness of the Jetta from, say, 45 to 75 percent of the target market; and expand the percentage of survey respondents who rate VW products as high quality from, say, 15 to 40 percent. Both objectives are specific, quantitative, and measurable.

5. The final step is to *establish the budget* based on estimates of expenditures required to accomplish the advertising goals.

   In view of VW's challenging objectives, the decision was made to invest approximately $100 million in an advertising campaign in hopes of gaining higher brand awareness, enhancing the company's image among American consumers, and, ultimately, substantially increasing sales of VW products. The chief executive officer of VW's advertising agency explained that the advertising challenge was "to come up with hard, clear, product-focused ads that give car buyers the kind of information they need to make an intelligent choice."

In sum, the objective-and-task method of advertising budgeting is aptly named in that it is based on first establishing a clear *objective* that advertising (or another marcom element) is designed to accomplish, and then identifying the *tasks* that advertising must perform in order to achieve the designated objective. The overall advertising budget can then be determined by calculating the amount of money needed to accomplish the identified tasks. This is a more systematic process than applying a simple formula (e.g., percentage of sales) or using more arbitrary techniques.

Budgeting via the Competitive Parity Method

The competitive parity method sets the budget by examining what competitors are doing. A company may learn that its primary competitor is devoting 10 percent of sales to advertising and then adjust its percentage of advertising for its own brand. Armed with information on competitors' spending, a company may decide not merely to match but also to exceed the expenditures that competitors are committing to advertising. This is precisely what Geico did (see *Marcom Insight* at beginning of chapter) when it decided to vastly outspend its competitors in the auto insurance industry in order to attract new users and build market share. Interestingly, research has shown that companies that spend heavily on advertising can signal to customers that their brands are of high quality.[20]

The importance of paying attention to what competitors are spending on advertising (or on any other marcom element) cannot be overemphasized. For example, the share of market (SOM) and share of voice (SOV) metrics, and their relationships, are important competitive tools. These measures relate to a single product category and consider each brand's revenues and advertising expenditures during, say, a fiscal year compared to the total revenues and ad expenditures in the category. The ratio of one brand's revenue to total category revenue is that brand's SOM. Similarly, the ratio of a brand's advertising expenditures (its "ad spend") to total category advertising expenditures is that brand's SOV.

SOV and SOM generally are correlated: Brands having larger SOVs also generally realize larger SOMs. For example, Tables 8.2 and 8.3 list the advertising expenditures, the SOVs, and the SOMs for the top-5 wireless phone brands (see Table 8.2) and the top-5 beer brands (see Table 8.3) in one recent year. The correlation between the shares of market and voice for these brands is apparent; that is, brands with larger shares of market typically have larger shares of voice. This does not mean, however, that SOV causes SOM. In fact, the relationship between SOV and SOM is bidirectional: A brand's SOV is partially responsible for its SOM. At the same time, brands with larger SOMs can afford to achieve higher SOVs, whereas smaller-share brands are limited to relatively small SOVs.

TABLE 8.2	Advertising Spend, SOV, and SOM for Top-5 Wireless Phone Providers		
Carrier	**Ad Spend (in $ million)**	**SOV**	**SOM**
Verizon	$1,851	32.12%	31.9%
AT&T	1,605	27.85	29.8
Sprint Nextel	1,239	21.50	16.8
T-Mobile	513	8.90	11.8
MetroPCS	83	1.44	2.3
Top 5	5,292	91.84	92.7
Industry Totals	$5,762	100.00%	100.00%

Note: SOV and SOM do not sum to 100 because the data include just the top-5 wireless phone providers. Column totals may not reflect rounding.

Source: Reprinted with permission from the December 20, 2010 special edition of *Advertising Age*. Copyright, Crain Communications Inc., 2010.

TABLE 8.3	Advertising Spend, SOV, and SOM for Top-5 Beer Marketers		
Marketer	Ad Spend (in $ million)	SOV	SOM
Anheuser-Busch InBev	$528	42.27%	49.0%
MillerCoors	417	33.39	29.6
Crown Imports	75	6.00	5.1
Heineken	139	11.13	4.1
Pabst Brewing Co.	3	0.24	2.7
Top 5	1,163	93.11	90.5
Industry Totals	$1,249	100.00%	100.00%

Note: SOV and SOM do not sum to 100 because the data include just the top-5 beer marketers. Column totals may not reflect rounding.

Source: Reprinted with permission from the December 20, 2010 special edition of *Advertising Age.* Copyright, Crain Communications Inc., 2010.

The SOM-SOV relationship is a jousting match of sorts between competitors. If large market share brands reduce their SOVs to levels that are too low, they are vulnerable to losing market share to aggressive competitors (such as Sprint Nextel in Table 8.2). Conversely, if competitors with relatively small market shares (such as Heineken in Table 8.3) become too aggressive, the leading marketers (Anheuser-Busch and MillerCoors) may be forced to increase their advertising expenditures to offset the challenge.

Four General SOM/SOJ Situations   Figure 8.6 provides a framework for evaluating whether a brand should increase or decrease its advertising expenditures in view of its share of market (horizontal axis) and of the competitor's share of voice (vertical axis).[21] Although numerous possible relations are in this two-dimensional space, we can simplify the discussion by considering just four general situations, which in Figure 8.6 are the quadrants, or cells, labeled

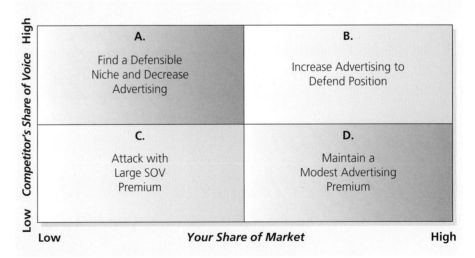

FIGURE 8.6   The SOV Effect and Ad Spending Implications

Source: Reprinted by permission of Harvard Business Review, from, "Ad Spending: Growing Market Share," by James C. Schoer (January-February 1990), p. 48. © 1990 by the Harvard Business School Publishing Corporation; all rights reserved.

A, B, C, and D. Advertising budgeting implications for each situation are as follows:

- *Cell A:* In this situation, your company's SOM is relatively low and your competitor's SOV is relatively high. Crown Imports (Corona, Pacifico, St. Pauli) in Table 8.3 exemplifies this situation when compared with Anheuser-Busch and MillerCoors. The recommendation is that the advertiser should consider decreasing ad expenditures and find a niche that can be defended against other small-share brands.
- *Cell B:* Your SOM in this situation is relatively high and your competitor has a high SOV. This characterizes Anheuser-Busch in Table 8.3 vis-à-vis MillerCoors. Anheuser-Busch probably should increase its advertising expenditures to defend its present market share position. Failure to do so likely would result in a share loss to these aggressive competitors.
- *Cell C:* In this situation, your SOM is low and your competitor's SOV also is low. Sprint Nextel and T-Mobile in Table 8.2 appear to occupy such a relationship. The general recommendation in such a situation is to attack the low-SOV competitor aggressively with a *large SOV premium* vis-à-vis that competitor. This appears to be the tact that Sprint Nextel has taken by spending more than double that of T-Mobile. In other words, this is a good opportunity to wrest market share from a moribund or complacent competitor.
- *Cell D:* In this situation, you have the attractive position of holding a high market share, but your competitor is nonaggressive and has a relatively low SOV. Hence, it is possible for you to retain your present large share by *maintaining only a modest advertising spending premium* over your competitor.

These are guidelines for determining a brand's advertising budget rather than hard-and-fast rules. The general point to stress is that advertising budgets—as well as budgets for all other marcom elements—must be set with knowledge of what competitors are doing.[22] This is because the opportunity for growth in market share or the challenge to maintain an existing share position depends in large part on the quality and effectiveness of competitive efforts. Moreover, brand managers should generally set budgets on a market-by-market basis rather than nationally because the competitive warfare actually takes place in the individual, localized markets.

The Role of Competitive Interference It is essential to set advertising budgets with an eye to the actions of competitors. This is especially important given that a brand's advertising must compete for the consumer's recall with the advertising from competitive brands, a situation of potential *competitive interference*. If "your" brand were the only one advertising in a particular product category, it probably could get by with a substantially smaller ad budget than what is necessitated when competitors also are aggressively advertising their brands. Merely increasing advertising expenditures does *not* guarantee a substantial impact on augmenting a brand's sales volume.[23]

There are reasons to expect that established brands in a product category are less susceptible to the interference from competitive advertising than are less established and relatively unfamiliar brands. This explains why established brands' SOMs tend to exceed their advertising SOVs, whereas unestablished brands' SOVs often exceed their SOMs.[24] Unfamiliar brands that compete in an environment of advertising clutter are, in effect, at a competitive disadvantage in conveying their points of uniqueness vis-à-vis established brands, although even established brands suffer from the effects of competitive interference.[25] It follows that because relatively small-share brands are disadvantaged by competitive advertising, they need to avoid heavily cluttered, traditional media and perhaps turn to alternative marcom tools—such as using event marketing, viral marketing and other buzz-generating methods, or any of a number of non-traditional (alternative) advertising media.

Overcoming competitive interference is not just a matter of spending more but rather one of *spending more wisely*. A psychological theory called the encoding variability hypothesis explains how advertisers can be smarter spenders.[26] (The term *encoding* refers to transferring information into memory.) The encoding variability hypothesis contends that people's memory for information is enhanced when multiple *pathways*, or connections, are created between the object to be remembered and the information about that object. For advertising, this can include (1) varying the advertising *message* itself and (2) varying the advertising *media* in which the message is placed.

Budgeting via the Affordability Method

In the so-called affordability method, a firm spends on advertising only those funds that remain after budgeting for everything else. In effect, when this "method" is used, advertising, along with other marcom elements, are relegated to a position of comparative insignificance (vis-à-vis other investment options) and are implicitly considered relatively unimportant to a brand's present success and future growth. Sometimes marcom funds are in short supply due to extreme sales slowdowns. At such times, product and brand managers behave rationally when severely cutting back on their advertising spending or other marcom investments. Yet, in many competitive marketing situations it is a good idea that marcom personnel fight the tendency of financial planners to treat marcom expenditures as an unnecessary evil. The challenge is for brand managers to demonstrate that advertising and other marcom initiatives do, in fact, produce results. Absent compelling evidence, it is understandable when financial officials allocate funds for advertising as a virtual afterthought.

Section Summary

Most advertising budget setters combine two or more methods rather than depending exclusively on any one heuristic. For example, an advertiser may have a fixed percentage-of-sales figure in mind when starting the budgeting process but subsequently adjust this figure in light of anticipated competitive activity, funds availability, and other considerations.

Moreover, brand managers often find it necessary to adjust their budgets during the course of a year, keeping expenditures in line with changing conditions in the marketplace. Many advertisers operate under the belief that it is logical to spend most heavily on advertising and on other marcom elements during periods when marketplace circumstances and the competitive situation warrant heavy expenditures. Rather than spending based on a fixed budget that was predetermined months in advance, it makes greater to sense to adjust the budget to accommodate current circumstances.

Summary

This chapter detailed marcom objective setting and budgeting. Advertising objective setting depends on the pattern of consumer behavior and information that is involved in the particular product category. Toward this end, an introductory section presented a hierarchy-of-effect model of how consumers respond to marcom messages and discussed the implications for setting objectives. The integrated information response model was discussed, demonstrating how consumer involvement levels dictate whether one relies more on advertising information (under high involvement) or their own product trial experience in processing advertising (under low involvement). Requirements for developing effective objectives were discussed. A final section described the arguments both promoting and opposing the use of sales volume as the basis for setting objectives.

The chapter concluded with an explanation of the marcom budgeting process. The budgeting decision is one of the most important decisions and also one of the most difficult. The complication arises with the difficulty of determining the sales-to-advertising response function. In theory, budget setting is a simple matter, but the theoretical requirements are generally unattainable in practice.

For this reason, practitioners use various rules of thumb (heuristics) to assist them in arriving at satisfactory, if not optimal, budgeting decisions. Percentage-of-sales budgeting and objective-and-task methods are the dominant budgeting heuristics, although maintaining competitive parity and not exceeding funds' availability are other relevant considerations when setting budgets.

Discussion Questions

1. It can be argued that creating an expectation is the most important function many advertisements and other marcom messages perform. Provide examples of two online advertisements that illustrate advertisers' attempts to create expectations. Offer explanations of what expectations the advertisers are attempting to forge in their audiences' minds.

2. Chapter 5 was devoted to the topic of marcom segmentation, targeting, and positioning. Offer an explanation of the similarity between the concepts of positioning and creating expectations.

3. Apply the hierarchy of marcom effects framework (see Figure 8.1) to explain the evolution of a relationship between two people, beginning with dating and culminating in a wedding.

4. Repeat question 3, but use a relatively obscure brand as the basis for your application of Figure 8.1. Along the lines of the Pegetables illustration (see Figure 8.2), identify a relatively unknown brand and explain how marcom efforts must attempt to move prospective customers through the various hierarchy stages.

5. Interview several other students on a recent purchase of theirs. Applying the principles of the Integrated Information Response Model (see Figure 8.3), which response pattern did they use—high involvement, low involvement, or continual switching?

6. What reasons can you give for certain industries investing considerably larger proportions of their sales in advertising than other industries?

7. Compare the difference between precisely wrong and vaguely right advertising objectives. Give an example of each.

8. Some critics contend that the use of the percentage-of-sales budgeting technique is illogical. Explain.

9. Explain how an advertising budget setter could use two or more budgeting heuristics in conjunction with one another.

10. In your own words, explain why it is extremely difficult to estimate sales-to-advertising response functions.

11. Established brands' shares of market tend to exceed their advertising shares of voice, whereas unestablished brands' SOVs often exceed their SOMs. Using the concept of competitive interference as your point of departure, explain these relationships.

12. Construct a picture to represent your understanding of how the encoding variability hypothesis applies in an advertising context. Use an actual brand for illustration purposes.

End Notes

1. Philip Kotler and Kevin Lane Keller, *Marketing Management*, 14th ed., Boston, MA: Prentice Hall, 2012, 50.

2. Charles H. Patti and Charles F. Frazer, *Advertising: A Decision-Making Approach*, Hinsdale, IL: Dryden Press, 1988, 236.

3. Some claim that hierarchy models poorly represent the advertising process. See William M. Weilbacher, "Point of View: Does Advertising Cause a 'Hierarchy of Effects?'" *Journal of Advertising Research* 41 (November–December 2001), 19–26; William M. Weilbacher, "Weilbacher Comments on 'In Defense of Hierarchy of Effects,'" *Journal of Advertising Research* 42 (May–June 2002), 48–49; and William M. Weilbacher, "Point of View: How Advertising Affects Consumers," *Journal of Advertising Research* 43 (June 2003), 230–34. For an alternative view, see Thomas E. Barry, "In Defense of the Hierarchy of Effects: A Rejoinder to Weilbacher," *Journal of Advertising Research* 42 (May–June 2002), 44–47. Although the hierarchy model attributes excessive influence to advertising per se, the model does represent a reasonable representation of the effects that all marcom elements have working collectively.

4. For thorough discussions, see Demetrios Vakratsas and Tim Ambler, "How Advertising Works: What Do We Really Know," *Journal of Marketing* 63 (January 1999), 26–43; Thomas E. Barry, "The Development of the Hierarchy of Effects: An Historical Perspective," *Current Issues and Research in Advertising*, vol. 10, ed. James H. Leigh and Claude R. Martin, Jr., Ann Arbor: Division of Research, Graduate School of Business Administration, University

of Michigan, 1987, 251–96; Ivan L. Preston, "The Association Model of the Advertising Communication Process," *Journal of Advertising*, 11(2), 1982, 3–15; and Ivan L. Preston and Esther Thorson, "Challenges to the Use of Hierarchy Models in Predicting Advertising Effectiveness," in *Proceedings of the 1983 Convention of the American Academy of Advertising*, ed. Donald W. Jugenheimer, Lawrence, KS: American Academy of Advertising, 1983.

5. Adapted from Larry Light and Richard Morgan, *The Fourth Wave: Brand Loyalty Marketing*, New York: Coalition for Brand Equity, American Association of Advertising Agencies, 1994, 25.

6. For further reading on the nature and role of brand loyalty, see Richard L. Oliver, "Whence Consumer Loyalty?" *Journal of Marketing* 63 (special issue 1999), 33–44; and Arjun Chaudhuri and Morris B. Holbrook, "The Chain of Effects from Brand Trust and Brand Affect to Brand Performance: The Role of Brand Loyalty," *Journal of Marketing* 65 (April 2001), 81–93.

7. Carl F. Mela, Sunil Gupta, and Donald R. Lehmann, "The Long-Term Impact of Promotion and Advertising on Consumer Brand Choice," *Journal of Marketing Research* 34 (May 1997), 248–61.

8. Robert E. Smith and William R. Swinyard, "Information Response Models: An Integrated Approach," *Journal of Marketing* 46 (winter 1982), 81–93.

9. The following discussion is influenced by the classic work on advertising planning and goal setting by Russell Colley. His writing, which came to be known as the DAGMAR approach, set a Standard for advertising objective setting. See Russell H. Colley, *Defining Advertising Goals for Measured Advertising Results*, New York: Association of National Advertisers, 1961.

10. Philip Gendall and Don Esslemont, "Market Research: What It Can and Can't Do," *Marketing Bulletin*, 1992, 3, 63–66.

11. Leonard M. Lodish, *The Advertising and Promotion Challenge: Vaguely Right or Precisely Wrong?*, New York: Oxford University Press, 1986, chap. 5.

12. Gary L. Lilien, Alvin J. Silk, Jean-Marie Choffray, and Murlidhar Rao, "Industrial Advertising Effects and Budgeting Practices," *Journal of Marketing* 40 (January 1976), 21.

13. J. Enrique Bigné, "Advertising Budgeting Practices: A Review," *Journal of Current Issues and Research in Advertising* 17 (fall 1995), 17–32; and Fred S. Zufryden, "How Much Should Be Spent for Advertising a Brand?" *Journal of Advertising Research* (April/May 1989), 24–34.

14. The extensive use of the percentage-of-sales and objective-and-task methods in an industrial context has been documented by Lilien et al., "Industrial Advertising Effects," while support in a consumer context is provided by Kent M. Lancaster and Judith A.

Stern, "Computer-Based Advertising Budgeting Practices of Leading U.S. Consumer Advertisers," *Journal of Advertising*, 12(4), 1983, 6. A thorough review of the history of advertising budgeting research is provided in Bigné, "Advertising Budget Practices." For information on advertising budgeting in China, see Gerard Prendergast, Douglas West, and Yi-Zheng Shi, "Advertising Budgeting Methods and Processes in China," *Journal of Advertising*, 35(3), 2006, 165–76.

15. Lancaster and Stern, "Computer-Based Advertising."

16. These data are based on research by Schonfeld & Associates and published by that company in "Advertising Ratios & Budgets," 2006.

17. Charles H. Patti and Vincent J. Blasko, "Budgeting Practices of Big Advertisers," *Journal of Advertising Research* 21 (December 1981), 23–29; and Vincent J. Blasko and Charles H. Patti, "The Advertising Budgeting Practices of Industrial Marketers," *Journal of Marketing* 48 (fall 1984), 104–10. See also C. L. Hung and Douglas C. West, "Advertising Budgeting Methods in Canada, the UK and the USA," *International Journal of Advertising*, 10(3), 1991, 239–50.

18. Adapted from Lilien et al, "Industrial Advertising and Budgeting," 23.

19. This description is based on Kevin Goldman, "Volkswagen Has a Lot Riding on New Ads," *Wall Street Journal*, January 31, 1994, B5.

20. Tim Ambler and E. Ann Hollier, "The Waste in Advertising Is the Part That Works," *Journal of Advertising Research* 44 (December 2004), 375–89. See also Amna Kirmani, "The Effect of Perceived Advertising Costs on Brand Perceptions," *Journal of Consumer Research* 17 (September 1990), 160–71.

21. Adapted from James C. Schroer, "Ad Spending: Growing Market Share," *Harvard Business Review* 68 (January/February 1990), 48. See also John Philip Jones, "Ad Spending: Maintaining Market Share," *Harvard Business Review* 68 (January/February 1990), 38–42.

22. For a slightly different perspective on how the relationship between competitors affects ad budgeting, see Boonghee Yoo and Rujirutana Mandhachitara, "Estimating Advertising Effects on Sales in a Competitive Setting," *Journal of Advertising Research* 43 (September 2003), 310–21.

23. Leonard M. Lodish, Magid Abraham, Stuart Kalmenson, Jeanne Livelsberger, Beth Lubetkin, Bruce Richardson, and Mary Ellen Stevens, "How T.V. Advertising Works: A Meta-Analysis of 389 Real World Split Cable T.V. Advertising Experiments," *Journal of Marketing Research* 32 (May 1995), 125–39.

24. Jones, "Ad Spending: Maintaining Market Share."

25. Robert J. Kent and Chris T. Allen, "Competitive Interference Effects in Consumer Memory for

Advertising: The Role of Brand Familiarity," *Journal of Marketing* 58 (July 1994), 97–105; and Robert J. Kent, "How Ad Claim Similarity and Target Brand Familiarity Moderate Competitive Interference Effects in Memory for Advertising," *Journal of Marketing Communications* 3 (December 1997), 231–42. For evidence that established brands suffer from competitive interference, see Anand Kumar and Shanker Krishnan, "Memory Interference in Advertising: A Replication and Extension," *Journal of Consumer Research* 30 (March 2004), 602–11.

26. H. Rao Unnava and Deepak Sirdeshmukh, "Reducing Competitive Ad Interference," *Journal of Marketing Research* 31 (August 1994), 403–11.

© Jorg Hackemann/Shuttersto

3

PART

CHAPTERS

Advertising Management and New Media Choices

Part 3 includes nine chapters that examine advertising management and new media choices (e.g., mobile advertising, social media). *Chapter 9* presents the role and importance of advertising and functions that it performs. The advertising management process and role of advertising agencies is then provided.

Chapter 10 describes the creative aspects of the ad management process, including the creative brief, alternative creative styles, means-end chaining, and ad strategy.

Chapter 11 examines the role of endorsers in advertising ("source effects") and different message appeals in advertising. Coverage includes how endorser credibility, attractiveness, and power operate, as well as how message appeals to fear, humor, music, etc. work.

Chapter 12 provides an analysis of traditional advertising media with attention to evaluating the unique characteristics, recent changes, and strengths/ weaknesses of four major media: newspapers, magazines, radio, and television.

Chapter 13 discusses the use of online advertising as a media choice, including the online ad process and the dramatic growth of mobile advertising. The chapter examines privacy and online behavioral targeting, as well as metrics for online ad effectiveness.

Chapter 14 describes the many different social media choices marketers face, including communication (e.g., social networking with Facebook, Twitter), collaboration (e.g., social news, wikis), and entertainment and multimedia options (e.g., media platforms, livecasting). Advantages and disadvantages of social media are discussed, as well as successful social media campaigns. The chapter concludes with recent consumer trends and issues in social media (e.g., privacy, addiction) and measurement choices.

Chapter 15 covers direct (response) advertising and "other" advertising media, such as yellow-pages advertising, videogame advertising, brand placements in movies and other media, cinema advertising, and other alternative media. The chapter describes where direct response advertising fits into overall direct marketing strategies.

Chapter 16 describes four media planning and analysis topics: target audience selection, objective specification, media-vehicle selection, and media-buying activities.

Chapter 17 presents the many different techniques to assess ad message effectiveness, discussing industry standards for message research, and the types of information a brand management team and its ad agency desire.

CHAPTER 9

Overview of Advertising Management

The Story of "Mad Man," the "Elvis of Advertising"

Perhaps no one has attracted as much attention in the advertising agency business as Alex Bogusky, described affectionately as both "Mad Man" (a takeoff from the popular *Mad Men* TV series about advertising in the 1960s) and "The Elvis of Advertising." Alex Bogusky is a designer, marketer, author, and consumer advocate; and once was a creative director, ad executive, and principal of the ad agency Crispin, Porter + Bogusky (CP+B). He also was the chief creative director at MDC Partners (CP+B's parent company).

Bogusky's meteoric rise to the top of the ad industry began as the sixteenth employee at Crispin Porter in 1989. He became creative director of the agency in five years, partner in 1997, and co-chairman in 2008. Along the way, he

© Peter Yang/AUGUST

pushed creative boundaries with some of the most memorable, outlandish, and ambitious campaigns in advertising. These include the successful Truth anti-smoking campaign, the Mini Cooper car ads (placing Minis atop SUVs), Burger King's ads "Subservient Chicken" and "The King," and VW's "unpimp my ride" campaign with "Helga" and "Wolfgang." During his time, CP+B's success was attributed to four of their non-traditional principles: (1) *get close* to the client's customers, (2) *fire clients* that are not a good match, (3) *be media neutral*, and (4) "*risky is good.*"

Based on his creative successes, Bogusky was inducted into the American Advertising Federation's Hall of Achievement in 2002. He received an honorary PhD from the University

1 Understand the magnitude of advertising and the percentage of sales revenue companies invest in this marcom tool.

2 Appreciate that advertising can be extraordinarily effective but that there is risk and uncertainty when investing in this practice.

3 Discuss advertising's effect on the economy, including resolving the advertising = market power and advertising = information viewpoints.

4 Recognize the various functions that advertising performs.

5 Explore the advertising management process from the perspective of clients and their agencies.

6 Understand the functions agencies perform and how they are compensated.

7 Explore the issue of when investing in advertising is warranted and when disinvesting is justified.

8 Examine advertising elasticity as a means for understanding the contention that "strong advertising is a deposit in the brand equity bank."

of Colorado in 2009 and was awarded "Creative Director of the Decade" by *Adweek* magazine in their "Best of 2000s" issue.

Then, in 2008, Bogusky released his new book, *The 9-Inch "Diet": Exposing the Big Conspiracy in America*, which protested fast-food corporations' supersize tendencies. (The nine-inch reference was the average diameter of a dinner plate in 1970; it is now a third larger.) As one would expect, the book did not go over well with CP+B clients Burger King and Domino's.

Since retiring from CP+B and MDC Partners in 2010, Bogusky has become a consumer advocate on his blog post ("Fearless Revolution") and web TV show ("Fearless TV"). He advocates a ban on children's advertising (especially fast food), and emphasizes transparency, sustainability, democracy, and collaboration among businesses and consumers. With a partner in 2010, he launched COMMON, a network for combining and launching social ventures under a unified brand.

Some have argued that the ad agency business has moved beyond "big names" like Bogusky, due to digital content in which programmers, designers, and the technology itself should all receive credit. Yet, creative directors certainly guide and continue to make important contributions to this process. In Alex Bogusky's case, there is certainly no mistaking the independence, critical thinking, risk taking, and consumer advocacy that he embraced in his very successful run in a somewhat traditional and predictable agency business. No doubt that this "Mad Man" and "Advertising's Elvis" will be missed.

Sources: Susan Berfield, "Mad Man," *Bloomberg Businessweek*, August 2, 2010, 60–63; Danielle Sachs, "Alex Bogusky, Advertising's Elvis. Tells Fast Company Why He Quit MDC and the Ad Biz," *FastCompany.com*, July 1, 2010, http://www.fastcompany.com/ 1665887/alex-bogusky-resign-mdc; "Alex Bogusky," *Wikipedia*, http://en.wikipedia.org/wiki/Alex_Bogusky (accessed September 2, 2011); Daniel Kiley, "The Craziest Ad Guys in America," *Businessweek*, May 22, 2006, 72–80; Maureen Morrison, "A Bad Week for Crispin," *Advertising Age*, March 3, 2011, 1, 23; and Creative X, "The Industry Doesn't Need a Bogusky," *Advertising Age*, January 17, 2011, http://adage.com/print/148251.

Introduction

This chapter introduces the first major IMC tool—advertising—and presents the fundamentals of advertising management. An initial section looks at the magnitude of advertising in the United States and elsewhere. The second major section examines the advertising management process, advertising's effect on the economy, the functions of advertising, and the role of advertising agencies. A concluding section provides a detailed discussion of the arguments favoring investments in advertising and counterarguments regarding circumstances when it is advisable to disinvest. This section also explores the concept of advertising elasticity and compares it with price elasticity to determine the circumstances when a brand manager should either increase advertising expenditures or reduce prices.

First, however, it will be useful to define the topic of this and the subsequent chapters specifically so as to make a clear distinction between advertising and other forms of marketing communications.

> *Advertising is a paid, mediated form of communication from an identifiable source, designed to persuade the receiver to take some action, now or in the future.*[1]

The word *paid* in this definition distinguishes advertising from a related marcom tool—public relations—that secures unpaid space or time in media due to the news value of the public relations content. The expression *mediated communication* is designed to distinguish advertising, which typically is conveyed (mediated) via print and electronic media, from person-to-person forms of communication, including personal selling, word of mouth, and (usually) social media. Finally, the definition emphasizes that advertising's purpose is to *influence action*, either presently or in the future. The idea of influencing action is in keeping with the fifth key IMC feature presented in Chapter 1: The ultimate objective of any form of marketing communications is to eventually affect behavior rather than merely its precursors such as the levels of consumers' brand awareness and the favorability of their attitudes toward the advertised brand.

Companies that sell their brands to final consumers undertake most advertising activities (*B2C advertising*). Consumer packaged goods companies (e.g., Procter & Gamble, General Mills, Kraft Foods) are especially heavy advertisers in the B2C arena, but service providers (e.g., wireless telephone service) and consumer durables (e.g., automobiles) are heavy advertisers as well. Some companies that sell directly to other companies rather than to consumers also are heavy advertisers (*B2B advertising*). Much of their advertising takes place in trade magazines that appeal to the special interests of practitioners who are prospects for the B2B advertiser's products. Interestingly, however, B2B advertisers also use traditional consumer media (e.g., television) to reach audiences that do not typically subscribe to trade publications. For example, Parker Hannifin, an industrial firm that manufactures hoses, valves, and other such products, placed advertising for their products on cable television programs that appeal to engineers, the target audience for the company's products. These included TLC's *Junkyard Wars* (a program showing clever people building machines from discarded items) and the History Channel's *Modern Marvels* (a program focusing on technology feats). The campaign was designed to increase engineers' awareness of the Parker Hannifin name when a valve- or hose-purchasing need arose.

Interestingly, the campaign used humor to convey its point, which is a relatively atypical appeal in B2B advertising (see an example from an advertising agency in Figure 9.1). In one TV spot, for example, two engineer-type characters are seated at a sushi bar and appear to be flirting with two attractive women at the other end of the bar. As one of the women uses chopsticks to lift a piece of sushi to her lips, an engineer asks his colleague, "Do you see what I see?" And the other responds, "Oh yeah." This brief dialogue is punctuated

An image is a
terrible thing to waste.

Don't let this happen to yours.

LIVING THE UNEXPECTED

www.mccom.com 972.480.8383

Advertising Public Relations Internet Marketing Image Interventions

FIGURE 9.1 Example of the Use of Humor in B2B Advertising

by the scene changing to a research lab where a robotic arm is shown lifting a lobster out of a tank. The connection between the sushi bar scene and the research lab is made clear when the campaign's tagline appears on the screen: "Engineers see the world differently." Parker Hannifin's campaign celebrates engineers and engineering feats, and in so doing hopes to increase the odds that real (not TV) engineers will be more likely to recommend the use of the company's products.[2]

The Magnitude of Advertising

Advertising expenditures in the United States were estimated to have exceeded $300 billion in 2010.[3] This amount approaches $1,000 in advertising for each of the approximately 312 million men, women, and children living in the United States. Ad spending in the United States has for many years averaged approximately 2.2 percent of the country's gross domestic product.[4] Needless to say, advertising in the United States is serious business!

Advertising spending is also considerable in other major industrialized countries, but not nearly to the same magnitude as in the United States. Global ad spending outside the United States totaled approximately $500 billion in 2010.[5] It is notable that ad spending in developing countries—particularly the so-called BRIC nations (Brazil, Russia, India, and China)—is growing at a much more rapid rate than in the United States and elsewhere around the globe.[6] See the *Global Focus* insert for a discussion of consumers' trust in advertising around the globe and how advertising-related trust compares with consumers' trust in information received from fellow consumers.

Several companies in the United States spend more than $2 billion annually to advertise their goods and services. Recently, Procter & Gamble spent

GLOBAL FOCUS

Which Source of Product Information Do Consumers Most Trust?

Nielsen, an influential global marketing research firm, conducts an online survey biannually that assesses consumer attitudes toward a wide variety of marketing-related issues. A recent survey queried Internet users about their trust in various sources of product and service information. More than 26,000 participants from 47 countries around the world were asked to indicate how much they trusted information received from 15 different sources, including traditional ad media (TV, newspapers, magazines, and radio), online ads, and recommendations from other consumers.

The percentages of respondents indicating that they somewhat trusted or completely trusted each source of information are as follows:

Recommendations from consumers	90%
Consumer opinions posted online	70%
Brand websites	70%
Editorial content (e.g., newspaper article)	69%
Brand sponsorships	64%
Television	62%
Newspapers	61%
Magazines	59%
Billboards/outdoor advertising	55%
Radio	55%
E-mail I signed up for	54%
Ads before movies	52%
Search engine ads	41%
Online banner ads	33%
Text ads on mobile phone	24%

The results of this survey are abundantly clear: Global consumers have greater faith in information from fellow consumers than from traditional ad media, and even less so from online ads and mobile ads (although this has been increasing since 2007). Overall trust in advertising, regardless of source,

varies greatly across countries. Filipinos and Brazilians were the most trusting of all forms of advertising (tied at 67 percent trust), whereas Italians (32 percent) and Danes (28 percent) were the least trusting. The top five and bottom five countries in terms of trust in advertising are as follows:

Top Five	
Philippines	67%
Brazil	67%
Mexico	66%
South Africa	64%
Taiwan	63%

Bottom Five	
Latvia	38%
Germany	35%
Lithuania	34%
Italy	32%
Denmark	28%

It is apparent from these findings that consumers vary widely around the globe in terms of their trust (or lack of trust) in different sources of product and service information. It comes as little surprise that information received from other consumers is the most trusted inasmuch as we actively select such information in comparison to advertisements that typically are thrust upon us whether or not we are interested in receiving such information. Especially surprising is the wide differential among countries in terms of their faith in advertising. The low levels of trust among European consumers are particularly intriguing.

Sources: The Nielsen Company, "Nielsen Global Online Survey," April 2009; and "Trust in Advertising: A Global Nielsen Consumer Report," October 2007.

TABLE 9.1	Top 25 Spenders in U.S Advertising, 2010		
Rank	Company	Headquarters	Ad Expenditures ($ million)
1	Procter & Gamble Co.	Cincinnati, OH	$4,614.7
2	AT&T	Dallas, TX	2,989.0
3	General Motors Corp.	Detroit, MI	2,869.0
4	Verizon Communications	New York, NY	2,451.0
5	American Express Co.	New York, NY	2,222.6
6	Pfizer	New York, NY	2,124.1
7	Walmart Stores	Bentonville, AR	2,055.3
8	Time Warner	New York, NY	2,044.3
9	Johnson & Johnson	New Brunswick, NJ	2,026.5
10	L'Oreal	Clichy, France	1,978.8
11	Walt Disney Co.	Burbank, CA	1,931.7
12	J.P. Morgan Chase & Co.	New York, NY	1,916.7
13	Ford Motor Co.	Dearborn, MI	1,914.9
14	Comcast Corp.	Philadelphia, PA	1,852.5
15	Sears Holdings Corp.	Hoffmann Estates, IL	1,778.6
16	Toyota Motor Corp.	Toyota City, Japan	1,735.7
17	Bank of America Corp.	Charlotte, NC	1,552.6
18	Target Corp.	Minneapolis, MN	1,508.0
19	Macy's	Cincinnati, OH	1,417.0
20	Sprint Nextel Corp.	Overland Park, KS	1,400.0
21	Unilever	Rotterdam/London, U.K.	1,379.2
22	Anheuser Busch InBev	Leuven, Belgium/St. Louis, MO	1,357.9
23	Berkshire Hathaway	Omaha, NE	1,343.6
24	News Corp.	New York, NY	1,319.5
25	J.C. Penney Co.	Plano, TX	1,317.0

Source: "100 Leading National Advertisers," *Advertising Age*, June 20, 2011, 10. Copyright Crain Communications Inc., 2011. Used with permission.

$4.62 billion advertising its products in the United States; AT&T, $2.99 billion; General Motors, $2.87 billion; Verizon, $2.45 billion; Pfizer, $2.12 billion; Walmart, $2.06 billion; Time Warner $2.04 billion; Johnson & Johnson, $2.03 billion; and L'Oreal, $1.98 billion.[7] Table 9.1 lists these firms along with others that constitute the 25 top-spending U.S. advertisers in a recent year. Although not listed in the top 25, even the U.S. government (ranked number 28) advertised to the tune of $1.11 billion. The government's advertising goes to such efforts as drug control, the U.S. Postal Service, Amtrak rail services, anti-smoking campaigns, and military recruiting.

Advertising-to-Sales Ratios

In 2011, the average advertising-to-sales ratio across nearly 200 categories of B2C and B2B products and services was *3.28 percent*. That is, on average, the advertising spend for companies in the United States is slightly over 3 cents out of every dollar of sales revenue. (These advertising expenditures are for traditional measured media advertising.) Table 9.2 provides greater detail by illustrating ad-to-sales ratios for companies that compete in three industries—retail,

TABLE 9.2	Advertising-to-Sales Ratios for Select Product Categories		
Industry and Company	**U.S. Sales Revenue ($ million)**	**U.S. Measured Media Advertising ($ million)**	**Ad/Sales Ratio (%)**
Retail			
Walmart stores	313,054	903	<0.1
Macy's	23,877	890	3.7
Sears	39,795	702	1.8
Target	66,325	650	1.0
Home Depot	61,019	448	0.7
J.C. Penney	18,571	414	2.2
Lowe's	47,754	390	0.8
Kohl's	18,571	340	1.8
Gap	10,612	322	3.0
Best Buy	37,142	267	0.7
Category Average			**0.6**
Restaurants			
McDonald's	32,391	888	2.7
Subway	10,616	429	4.0
Starbucks	9,064	43	0.5
Burger King	8,703	301	3.5
Wendy's	8,341	283	3.4
Taco Bell	6,933	275	4.0
Dunkin' Donuts	5,632	115	2.0
Pizza Hut	5,380	217	4.0
KFC	4,694	206	4.4
Applebee's	4,333	147	3.4
Category Average			**1.5**
Movie Studios			
Time Warner	1,923	694	36.1
Viacom	1,733	455	26.3
News Corp.	1,638	442	27.0
Walt Disney	1,479	362	24.5
Sony	1,342	468	34.9
Comcast	961	495	51.5
Summit Entertainment	528	127	24.1
Lions Gate	518	201	38.8
Overture Films	85	51	60.0
Weinstein Co.	85	32	37.7
Category Average			**33.8**

Source: Adapted from "Market Leaders," *Advertising Age*, June 20, 2011, 20–22.

restaurants, and movie studios. Advertising as a percentage of sales for these select product categories ranges from a low of less than 0.1 percent for Walmart Stores in the retail industry to a high of 60 percent for Overture Films under movie studios.

Perusal of this table also reveals that some smaller competitors in each industry typically invest relatively larger percentages of their sales revenues in advertising. In most cases, this is because companies with smaller market shares generally have to spend relatively heavily on advertising in order to be competitive, and thus the ad-to-sales ratios are higher because the sales base is relatively small compared with bigger competitors. A final notable observation is that the category average ad-to-sales ratio for movie studios, at 33.8 percent, is substantially higher than the corresponding averages for the other product categories. This is because movies often are sold less on the basis of "product performance" and more in terms of image, which requires greater advertising support to convey the desired impression. This is also true for other high ad-to-sales ratio categories, such as personal care products and toys. For some companies with low ad-to-sales ratios, price (e.g., for Walmart) or brand recognition/word-of-mouth (e.g., for Starbucks) may be more important than advertising.

Advertising Effects Are Uncertain

Advertising is costly and its effects often uncertain. It is for these reasons that many companies think it appropriate at times to reduce advertising expenditures or to eliminate advertising entirely. Marketing managers—and perhaps especially chief financial officers—sometimes consider it unnecessary to advertise when their brands already are enjoying great success. Companies find it particularly seductive to pull funds out of advertising during economic downturns—every dollar not spent on advertising is one more dollar added to the bottom line. For example, during the economic downturn in 2001 and the impending recession late that year—propelled in part by the economic fallout from the terrorist attacks on the World Trade Center and the Pentagon—advertising expenditures in the United States declined between 4 and 6 percent. Declines of this magnitude had not been seen in the United States since the Great Depression of the late 1920s and early 1930s.[8] Following a brief recovery after 2001, ad spending plunged again: 10.2 percent in 2009 during the brunt of another recession. Although spending recovered in 2010 (an 8.8 percent increase), an uncertain economy and employment outlook put pressure on 2011 ad budgets.[9]

Such behavior implicitly fails to recognize that advertising is not just a current expense (as the term is used in accounting parlance) but rather is an investment. Although businesspeople fully appreciate the fact that building a more efficient production facility is an investment in their company's future, many of these same people often think that advertising can be dramatically reduced or even eliminated when financial pressures call for cost-cutting measures. However, an ex-chief executive officer at Procter & Gamble—one of the world's largest advertisers—drew the following apt analogy between advertising and exercise:

> *If you want your brand to be fit, it's got to exercise regularly. When you get the opportunity to go to the movies or do something else instead of working out, you can do that once in a while—that's [equivalent to] shifting funds into [sales] promotion. But it's not a good thing to do. If you get off the regimen, you will pay for it later.*[10]

This viewpoint is captured further in the advice of a vice president at Booz Allen Hamilton, a major consulting agency, when asked what great companies such as Procter & Gamble, Kellogg, General Mills, Coca-Cola, and PepsiCo have in common. All these companies, in his opinion, are aware that *consistent investment spending* is the key factor underlying successful advertising. "They do not raid their budgets to ratchet earnings up for a few quarters. They know that advertising should not be managed as a discretionary variable cost."[11] This point should remind you of our discussion in Chapter 1 regarding the importance of establishing momentum for marcom efforts. Advertising momentum is like exercise. Stop exercising and you will lose conditioning and probably gain weight. Stop advertising and your brand likely will lose some of its equity and market share as well.

Advertising's Effect on the Economy

There are two divergent schools of thought on advertising's economic role: (1) *advertising = market power* and (2) *advertising = information*. Table 9.3 summarizes these two different perspectives.[12]

Advertising = Market Power

Advertising equals market power is a more negative view of advertising's impact on the economy. It argues that advertising yields marketing power in being able to *differentiate physically homogenous products*. It follows from the view that advertising will foster brand loyalty, thereby encouraging customers to be less price sensitive than they would in the absence of advertising. In turn, entry barriers are increased; in order to enter an industry (i.e., beverage, brewing), new firms must spend relatively more (than established forms) on advertising to overcome existing brand-loyalty patterns. It follows that established brands are relatively insulated from potential rivals and have discretionary power to increase prices and influence the market in other ways. According to the advertising = market power position, the result is that firms charge higher prices than they would in the absence of advertising and are able to earn excessive profits.

TABLE 9.3	Two Schools of Thought on Advertising's Role in the Economy	
	Advertising = Market Power	**Advertising = Information**
Advertising	Advertising affects consumer preferences and tastes, changes product attributes, and differentiates the product from competitive offerings	Advertising informs consumers about product attributes and does not change the way they value those attributes
Consumer-Buying Behavior	Consumers become brand loyal, less prices sensitive, and perceive fewer substitutes for advertised brands	Consumers become more price sensitive and buy best "value;" only the relationship between price and quality affects elasticity for a given product
Barriers to Entry	Potential entrants must overcome established brand loyalty and spend relatively more on advertising	Advertising makes entry possible for new brands because it can communicate product attributes to consumers
Industry Structure and Market Power	Firms are insulated from market completion and potential rivals; concentration increases, leaving firms with more discretionary power	Consumers can compare competitive offerings easily and competitive rivalry is increased; efficient firms remain, and as the inefficient leave, new entrants appear; the effect on concentration is ambiguous
Market Conduct	Firms can charge higher prices and are not as likely to compete on quality or price dimensions; innovation may be reduced	More-informed consumers put pressures on firms to lowers prices and improve quality; innovation is facilitated via new entrants
Market Performance	High prices and excessive profits accrue to advertisers and give them even more incentive to advertise their products; output is restricted compared to conditions of perfect competition	Industry prices are decreased; the effect on profits due to increased competition and increased efficiency is ambiguous

Source: Paul W. Farris and Mark S. Albion, "The Impact of Advertising on the Price of Consumer Products," *Journal of Marketing*, vol. 44, Summer 1980, p. 18. Journal of Marketing by American Marketing Association; American Marketing Society; National Association of Marketing Teachers. © 1980. Reproduced with permission of American Marketing Association in the format Republish in a textbook via Copyright Clearance Center.

Advertising = Information

The advertising = information perspective provides an antithesis (opposite view) to the market power position. It is a more positive view and argues that by informing consumers about product attributes and benefits, advertising increases consumers' price sensitivity and their ability to obtain the best value. Barriers to entry for new firms are reduced because advertising enables these new firms to communicate important product attributes and advantages to consumers. In turn, advertising allows consumers to easily compare competitive offerings, leading to increased competitive rivalry. Product innovation is aided via new entrants, and quality is improved. Furthermore, prices are forced downward because consumers, informed by advertising, put pressure on firms to lower prices.

A Synthesis

The world is never as simple and straightforward as these two opposite views of advertising would lead us to believe. Neither view is entirely correct or adequate by itself. Critics of the advertising = market power view contend that a number of factors other than advertising (e.g., superior product quality, better packaging efficient distribution) also account for brand loyalty and price insensitivity.[13] Thus, advertising is not the sole market force responsible for a firm's market power. Also, the impact of advertising in one period rarely is limited to an impact on sales in the next period.

Similarly, advertising does not possess all the virtues that advocates of the advertising = information school would lead us to believe. Critics of this view contend that advertising goes beyond merely providing consumers with information; in fact, it can influence consumers' relative preferences for different product attributes. It follows from this contention that advertising may create the same undesirable consequences in some situations (e.g., market concentration, price insensitivity, entry barriers, etc.) claimed by the advertising = market power advocates.

In sum, advertising's macroeconomic role is neither all good nor all bad. The exact role varies from situation to situation, and generalizations are ill-advised. On balance, advertising has negative economic effects (as claimed by the market power school) to the extent that only one or a few advertisers in a given market situation possess differential advantages over competitors in terms of advertising spending ability or effectiveness. However, when any one competitor's advertising efforts can be countervailed by other advertising, the positive economic effects of advertising (as claimed by the information school) outweigh the negative.[14]

Advertising Functions

Many business firms as well as not-for-profit organizations do have faith in advertising. In general, advertising is valued because it is recognized as performing five critical communications functions: (1) informing, (2) influencing, (3) reminding and increasing salience, (4) adding value, and (5) assisting other company efforts.[15]

Informing

One of advertising's most important functions is to publicize brands.[16] That is, advertising makes consumers aware of new brands, educates them about a brand's distinct features and benefits, and facilitates the creation of positive brand images. Because advertising is an efficient form of communication capable of reaching mass audiences at a relatively low cost per contact, it facilitates the introduction of new brands and increases demand for existing brands, largely by increasing consumers' *top-of-mind awareness (TOMA)* for established brands in mature product categories.[17] Advertising performs another valuable

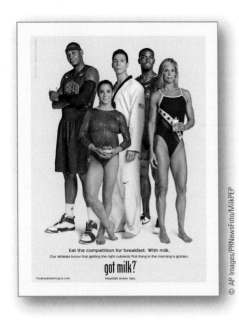

Eat the competition for breakfast. With milk.
Our athletes know that getting the right nutrients first thing in the morning is golden.

got milk?

Nourish every day.

© AP Images/PRNewsFoto/MilkPEP

information role—both for the advertised brand and the consumer—by teaching new uses for existing brands. This practice, termed *usage expansion advertising*, is typified by the following illustrations:[18]

- Campbell's soup, which is typically eaten for lunch and during other informal eating occasions, was advertised as being suitable for eating during formal family dinners or even at breakfast.
- Gatorade, which originally was used during heavy athletic activity, was advertised for replenishing liquids during flu attacks.
- Special K, a breakfast cereal, was advertised for afternoon or late-night snacking.
- Hidden Valley Ranch Dressing was placed in frozen grocery sections when consumers began using it on frozen foods, such as pizza, vegetables, and chicken wings.

Influencing

Effective advertising influences prospective customers to try advertised products and services. Sometimes advertising influences *primary demand*—that is, building demand for an entire product category. Examples include collective efforts by companies in funding campaigns for the California Milk Processor Board ("Milk Mustache" campaign) and the Florida Orange Growers Association. More frequently, advertising attempts to build *secondary demand*, the demand for a company's brand. Advertising by both B2C and B2B companies provides consumers and customers with reasoned arguments and emotional appeals for trying one brand versus another. The *IMC Focus* insert describes the inaugural national TV advertising campaign the Starbucks specialty coffee chain undertook in an attempt to influence consumers to purchase specialty coffees at that chain's stores rather than elsewhere.

Reminding and Increasing Salience

Advertising keeps a company's brand fresh in the consumer's memory. When a need arises that is related to the advertised product, the influence of past advertising makes it possible for the advertiser's brand to come to the consumer's mind as a purchase candidate. This has been referred to as making a brand more *salient*; that is, enriching the memory trace for a brand such that the brand comes to mind in relevant choice situations.[19] Effective advertising also increases the consumer's interest in mature brands and thus the likelihood of purchasing brands that otherwise might not be chosen.[20] Advertising has been demonstrated, furthermore, to influence brand switching by reminding consumers who have not recently purchased a brand that the brand is available and that it possesses favorable attributes.[21] Finally, as noted in Chapter 8, simple reminder cues (e.g., water dripping on an ice-cold beer in a print ad) may be important, especially for consumers under low involvement processing.

Adding Value

There are three basic ways by which companies can add value to their offerings: innovating, improving quality, and altering consumer perceptions. These three value-added components are completely interdependent as astutely captured in the following quote:

> *Innovation without quality is mere novelty. Consumer perception without quality and/or innovation is mere puffery. And both innovation and quality, if not translated into consumer perceptions, are like the sound of the proverbial tree falling in the empty forest.*[22]

Advertising adds value to brands by influencing perceptions. Effective advertising causes brands to be viewed as more elegant, more stylish, more prestigious,

IMC FOCUS

A National Advertising Effort for Starbucks

Starbucks, the famous chain of specialty coffee stores, was founded in Seattle in 1971, although it was not until 1987 that any expansion beyond Seattle occurred. In less than 40 years, the chain grew from a single store to now more than 11,000 U.S. locations and 6,000 more in other countries. Although there were cutbacks in 2008, Starbucks' store growth in the United States is ambitious, to say the least, with new-store additions exceeding 1,500 each year. Some analysts contend that Starbucks has reached a saturation point and cannot sustain the continual addition of large numbers of new stores, but executives at Starbucks counter that demand for specialty coffees remains largely untapped and that there is considerable potential for additional growth. (You may recall in Chapter 5 the discussion of McDonald's entry into the specialty coffee business, which seemingly supports the view that much latent demand remains to be fulfilled.)

It is questionable whether Starbucks will be able to achieve its ambitious growth plans and maintain sales levels in existing stores. That is, although the addition of new Starbucks outlets likely will add to the overall level of Starbucks' corporate revenue and profit, existing stores may experience lost volume from customers shifting their purchases to new Starbucks outlets—the net effect being that incremental revenues and profits may not be proportionate to the number of new stores being added. What can Starbucks do to achieve its ambitious growth plans while maintaining proportionate sales volume at all of its stores?

Historically, Starbucks' growth was achieved with low levels of advertising and mostly via the power of word of mouth—satisfied customers telling other people, who in turn further spread the word, and so on. But, by late 2007, Starbucks executives determined that they would have to increase the level of advertising effort and the company launched its first national television advertising campaign in November 2007. The idea was to sustain store growth and with the objective of reaching out to a broader audience that had not previously experienced Starbucks.

This move into TV advertising reflects a significant development for a company that heretofore was able to grow at a double-digit rate without advertising at the level undertaken by most businesses that compete in the retail food and beverage business. Currently, Starbucks spends approximately $94 million on media advertising— outspent by 2 to 8 times by rivals such as McDonald's. Yet, their efficient advertising combined with steady price points and complementary food items appears to have paid off. Starbucks passed Wendy's and Burger King in 2011 to be the number 3 restaurant chain based on sales, behind only McDonald's and Subway.

Sources: Janet Adamy, "At Starbucks, Too Many, Too Quick?" *Wall Street Journal*, November 15, 2007, B1; Janet Adamy, "Starbucks Turns to TV in Bid to Boost Results," *Wall Street Journal*, November 16, 2007, Al 4; Starbucks Timeline and History, http://www.starbucks.com/aboutus/timeline.asp (accessed December 30, 2007); Julie Jargon, "Coffee Talk: Starbucks Chief on Prices, McDonald's Rivalry," *Wall Street Journal* (online edition), http://online.wsj.com/article/SB10001424052748704076804576180313111969984.html (accessed September 9, 2011); Maureen Morrison, "Starbucks Hits No. 3 Despite Limited Ad Spending," *Advertising Age*, May 2, 2011, http://adage.com/article/news/starbucks-hits-3-limited-ad-spending/227316; and "Starbucks," *Wikipedia*, http://en.wikipedia.org/wiki/Starbucks (accessed September 9, 2011).

© Jim Barber/Shutterstock.com

of higher quality, and so on. Indeed, research involving over 100 brands drawn from five nondurable products (e.g., paper towels and shampoo) and five durable products (e.g., televisions and cameras) has demonstrated that greater ad spending influences consumers to perceive advertised brands as higher in quality.[23] Effective advertising, then, by influencing perceived quality and other perceptions, can lead to increased market share and greater profitability.[24] Recent examples of brands adding value abound. For example, cereals (e.g., Cheerios, Special K) now tout their heart healthiness. Also, new auto technology has allowed companies to offer state-of-the art hybrids or all-electric vehicles (e.g., Chevy's Volt, Nissan's Leaf).

By adding value, advertising can generate for brands more sales volume, revenue, and profit and reduce the risk of unpredictable future cash flows. In finance parlance, all of this can be captured in the concept of *discounted cash flow (DCF)*.

By making a brand more valuable, advertising generates incremental DCF. One advertising practitioner eloquently captured advertising's value-adding role with this claim: "Advertising builds brands. Brands build the business. Let the discounted cash flow!"[25] And, in a world of accountability, it is absolutely imperative that advertising deliver positive financial results. It has even been demonstrated that firms that invest greater percentages of their sales revenues in advertising can reduce the risk that their stock values will fall during a period of general declines in stock market valuations.[26]

Assisting Other Company Efforts

Advertising is just one member of the marcom team. Advertising's primary role is at times to facilitate other marcom efforts. For example, advertising may be used as a vehicle for delivering coupons and sweepstakes and attracting attention to these and other promotional tools. Another crucial role is to assist sales representatives. Advertising pre-sells a company's products and provides salespeople with valuable introductions prior to their personal contact with prospective customers. Sales effort, time, and costs are reduced because less time is required to inform prospects about product features and benefits. Moreover, advertising legitimizes or makes more credible the sales representative's claims.[27]

Advertising also enhances the effectiveness of other marcom tools. For example, consumers can identify product packages in the store and more readily recognize a brand's value following exposure to advertisements for it on television or in a magazine. Advertising also can augment the effectiveness of price deals. Customers are known to be more responsive to retailers' price deals when retailers advertised that fact compared to when retailers offer a deal absent any advertising support.[28]

The Advertising Management Process

In general, advertising management can thus be thought of as the process of creating ad messages, selecting media in which to place the ads, and measuring the effects of the advertising efforts: messages, media, and measures. This process usually involves at least two parties: the organization that has a product or service to advertise, the *client*, and the independent organization that is responsible for creating ads, making media choices, and measuring results, the *agency*. The following sections first examine advertising management from the client's perspective and then the agent's. Because most advertising is undertaken for specific brands, the client typically is represented by an individual who works in a brand- or product-management position. This individual and his or her team are responsible for marcom decisions that affect the brand's welfare.

Managing the Advertising Process: The Client Perspective

Figure 9.2 graphically illustrates the advertising management process, which consists of three sets of interrelated activities: advertising strategy, strategy implementation, and assessing ad effectiveness.

Formulating and Implementing Advertising Strategy

Advertising strategy formulation involves four major activities (see the top box in Figure 9.2). The first two, setting objectives and devising budgets, were described in Chapter 8 when discussing these activities in the context of all marcom elements. Message creation, the third aspect of formulating advertising strategy, is the subject of Chapters 10 and 11. The fourth element, media strategy, the topic of Chapters 11 through 16, involves the selection of media categories and specific vehicles to deliver advertising

Advertising Strategy
- Setting Objectives
- Formulating Budgets
- Creating Ad Messages
- Selecting Ad Media and Vehicles

↓

Strategy Implementation

↓

Assessing Ad Effectiveness

© Cengage Learning

FIGURE 9.2 The Advertising Management Process

messages. (The term *vehicle* is used in reference to, say, the specific TV program in which an advertisement is to be placed—TV is the medium, the program [e.g., *It's Always Sunny in Philadelphia*, *Grey's Anatomy*, *The Office*, or *Entourage*] is the vehicle.)

Implementing Advertising Strategy

Strategy implementation deals with the tactical, day-to-day activities that must be performed to carry out an advertising campaign. For example, whereas the decision to emphasize television over other media is a strategic choice, the selection of specific types of programs and times at which to air a commercial is a tactical implementation matter. Likewise, the decision to emphasize a particular brand benefit is a strategic message consideration, but the actual way the message is delivered is a matter of creative implementation. This text focuses more on strategic than tactical issues.

Measuring Advertising Effectiveness

Assessing effectiveness is a critical aspect of advertising management—only by evaluating results is it possible to determine whether objectives are being accomplished. This often requires that baseline measures be taken before an advertising campaign begins (to determine, for example, what percentage of the target audience is aware of the brand name) and then afterward to determine whether the objective was achieved. Because research is fundamental to advertising control, Chapter 17 explores a variety of measurement techniques that are used for evaluating advertising effectiveness.

The Role of Advertising Agencies

Message strategies and decisions most often are the joint enterprise of the companies that advertise (the clients) and their advertising agencies. This section examines the role of advertising agencies and describes how agencies are organized. Table 9.4 lists the top 25 advertising agencies in the United States according to revenue. Two observations are pertinent. First, all of these agencies were at one time independent businesses; now, due to mergers and acquisitions, most are owned by large marketing organizations such as Omnicom Group (New York), WPP Group (London), Interpublic Group (New York), Publicis Groupe (Paris), and Havas (Suresnes, France). Second, it is apparent that most of the major U.S. ad agencies are located in New York City, which for many years has been the world's major advertising center. Needless to say, there literally are thousands of ad agencies throughout the United States and worldwide, although most generate revenues only a small fraction of those shown in Table 9.4.

To appreciate why a company would use an ad agency, it is important to recognize that businesses routinely employ outside specialists: lawyers, financial advisors, management consultants, tax specialists, and so on. By their very nature, these "outsiders" bring knowledge, expertise, and efficiencies that companies do not possess within their own ranks. Advertising agencies can provide great value to their clients by developing highly effective and profitable advertising campaigns. The relationship between ad agency and client sometimes lasts for decades. Of course, client–agency relationships also can be short lived and volatile if the client evaluates the agency as underperforming and failing to enhance the equity and market share of the client's brand. Research has demonstrated that agencies are fired shortly after clients experience declines in their brands' market shares.[29]

In general, advertisers have three alternative ways to perform the advertising function: use an in-house advertising operation, purchase advertising services on an as-needed basis from specialized agencies, or select a full-service advertising agency. First, a company can choose *not* to use an advertising agency but rather maintain its own *in-house advertising operation*. This necessitates employing an advertising staff and absorbing the overhead required to maintain the staff's operations. Such an arrangement is unjustifiable unless a company does a large amount of continual advertising. Even under these conditions, most businesses instead choose to use the services of advertising agencies.

TABLE 9.4	Top 25 U.S. Advertising Agencies in Ad Revenue, 2010		
Rank	**Agency**	**Headquarters**	**Ad Revenue ($ millions)**
1	McCann Erickson Worldwide [Interpublic]	New York, NY	$457
2	BBDO Worldwide [Omnicom]	New York, NY	450
3	JWT [WPP]	New York, NY	356
4	Y&R [WPP]	New York, NY	304
5	DDB Worldwide Communications Group [Omnicom]	New York, NY	264
6	TBWA Worldwide [Omnicom]	New York, NY	260
7	Leo Burnett Worldwide/Arc [Publicis]	Chicago, IL	255
8	DraftFCB [Interpublic]	Chicago, IL/New York, NY	239
9	Saatchi & Saatchi [Publicis]	New York, NY	214
10	Grey Worldwide [WPP]	New York, NY	191
11	Euro RSCG Worldwide [Havas]	New York, NY	185
12	Deutsch [Interpublic]	New York, NY	172
13	Richards Group	Dallas, TX	170
14	Ogilvy & Mather Worldwide [WPP]	New York, NY	168
15	Publicis [Publicis]	New York, NY/Paris, France	168
16	Hill Holliday [Interpublic]	Boston, MA	166
17	Campbell-Ewald [Interpublic]	Warren, MI	157
18	Crispin, Porter, & Bogusky [MDC Partners]	Miami, FL/Boulder, CO	145
19	Goodby, Silverstein & Partners [Omnicom]	San Francisco, CA	143
20	Wieden+Kennedy	Portland, OR	139
21	Martin Agency [Interpublic]	Richmond, VA	137
22	Doner	Southfield, MI	133
23	RPA	Santa Monica, CA	111
24	Zimmerman Advertising [Omnicom]	Ft. Lauderdale, FL	105
25	Mullen [Interpublic]	Boston, MA	93

Source: "Top 25 Advertising Agencies in the U.S.," *Advertising Age*, April 25, 2011, 30. Most revenue amounts have been estimated. Where appropriate, each agency's parent company is shown in brackets. Copyright Crain Communications Inc., 2011. Used with permission.

A second way for a client to accomplish the advertising function is to *purchase advertising services a la carte*. That is, rather than depending on a single full-service agency to perform all advertising and related functions, an advertiser may recruit the services of a variety of firms with particular specialties in distinct aspects of advertising, including creative work, media selection, advertising research, direct response advertising, digital, search engine, and so on. This arrangement's advantages include the ability to contract for services only when they are needed, thus yielding potential cost efficiencies. On the downside, specialists (so-called *boutiques*) sometimes lack financial stability and may be poor in terms of cost accountability.

Third, *full-service advertising agencies* perform at least four basic functions for the clients they represent: (1) creative services, (2) media services, (3) research services, and (4) account management. They also may be involved in the advertiser's total marketing process and, for a fee, perform other marcom functions, including sales promotion, publicity, package design, strategic marketing planning, and sales forecasting. Why would an advertiser want to employ the services of a full-service agency? The primary advantages include acquiring the services of specialists with in-depth knowledge of advertising and obtaining negotiating leverage with the media. The major disadvantage is that some control over the advertising function is lost when it is performed by an agency rather than in house. Nonetheless, brand managers frequently utilize the services of full-service ad agencies because these agencies understand their clients' businesses and are capable of producing equity-enhancing advertising campaigns. Understanding the client's business and "good chemistry" between client and agency are the two primary reasons cited by managers for choosing a particular ad agency partner.[30]

Creative Services

Advertising agencies have staffs of copywriters, graphic artists, and creative directors who create advertising copy and visualizations. Advertising agencies on occasion create brilliant advertising campaigns that enhance brand equity and increase a brand's sales volume, market share, and profitability. Often, however, advertisements are not sufficiently clever or novel to break through the clutter of surrounding advertising.

Media Services

This unit of an advertising agency is charged with selecting the best advertising media for reaching the client's target market, achieving ad objectives, and meeting the budget. *Media planners* are responsible for developing overall media strategy (where to advertise, how often, when, etc.), and *media buyers* then procure specific vehicles within particular media that media planners have selected and clients have approved. The complexity of media buying requires the use of sophisticated analysis and continual research of changing media costs and availability. Experts in media and vehicle selection are able to make more effective decisions than are brand managers on the client side who have no particular expertise in media and vehicle selection.

Research Services

Full-service advertising agencies employ research specialists who study their clients' customers' buying habits, purchase preferences, and responsiveness to advertising concepts and finished ads. Focus groups, mail intercepts, ethnographic studies by trained anthropologists, and acquisition of syndicated research data are just some of the services agencies' research specialists perform. These specialists are sometimes referred to as *account planners*.

Account Management

This facet of a full-service advertising agency provides the mechanism to link the agency with the client. Account managers act as liaisons so that the client does not need to interact directly with several different service departments and specialists. In most major advertising agencies, the account management department includes account executives and management supervisors. *Account executives* are involved in tactical decision making and frequent contact with brand managers and other client personnel. Account executives are responsible for seeing that the client's interests, concerns, and preferences have a voice in the advertising agency and that the work is being accomplished on schedule. Account executives report to *management supervisors*, who are more involved in actually getting new business for the agency and working with clients at a more strategic level. Account executives are groomed for positions as management supervisors.

Agency Compensation

There are three basic methods by which clients compensate agencies for services rendered: (1) receiving commissions from media, (2) being compensated based on a fee system, and (3) earning compensation based on outcomes.

1. *Commissions from media* for advertisements aired or printed on behalf of the agency's clients provided the primary form of ad agency compensation in the past. Historically, U.S. advertising agencies charged a standard commission of 15 percent of the gross amount of billings.[31] To illustrate, suppose the Creative Advertising Agency buys $200,000 of space in a certain magazine for its client, ABC Company. When the invoice for this space comes due, Creative would remit payment of $170,000 to the magazine ($200,000 less Creative's 15 percent commission); bill ABC for the full $200,000; and retain the remainder, $30,000, as revenue for services rendered. The $30,000 revenue realized by Creative was, in the past, regarded as fair compensation to the agency for its creative expertise, media-buying insight, and ancillary functions performed in behalf of its client, ABC Company.

   The 15 percent compensation system has, as one may suppose, been a matter of some controversy between client marketing executives and managers of advertising agencies. The primary area of disagreement is whether 15 percent compensation is too much (the marketing executives' perspective) or too little (the ad agencies' perspective). The disagreement has spurred the growth of alternative compensation systems. Indeed, today just a fraction of advertisers still pay a 15 percent commission. Although there are alternatives to the commission system, it probably will not vanish entirely. Rather, a reduced commission system, by which the ad agency is compensated with a flat fee that is less than 15 percent, has experienced increased usage.

2. The most common compensation method today is a *labor-based fee system*, by which advertising agencies are compensated much like lawyers, tax advisors, and management consultants; that is, agencies carefully monitor their time and bill clients an hourly fee based on time commitment. This system involves price negotiations between advertisers and agencies such that the actual rate of compensation is based on mutual agreement concerning the worth of the services rendered by the advertising agency.

3. *Outcome- or performance-based programs* represent the newest approach to agency compensation. Ford Motor Company, for example, uses a compensation system whereby it negotiates a base fee with its agencies to cover the cost of services provided and additionally offers incentive payments that are tied to brand performance goals such as targeted revenue levels. Procter & Gamble (P&G) employs a sales-based model whereby ad agencies are compensated based on a percentage of sales that a P&G brand obtains. The agency's compensation rises with sales gains and falls with declines. Needless to say, this incentive-based system encourages, indeed demands, agencies to use whatever IMC programs are needed to build brand sales. P&G's best interest (growth in brand sales and market share) and the agency's best interest (increased compensation) are joined by this compensation system in a hand-in-glove fashion. In another example, Coca-Cola's pay-for-performance model for agencies ranges from nothing more than recouped costs for poor performance to profit margins as high as 30 percent based on outcome targets.[32] Ultimately, the success of outcome-based programs will depend on demonstrating that advertising and other marcom efforts agencies initiate do indeed translate into enhanced brand performance.[33]

Ad-Investment Considerations

Thus far, we have introduced the topic of advertising, presented facts illustrating its magnitude, discussed its functions, provided an overview of the advertising management process from the client's perspective, and described the functioning and compensation of advertising agencies. It is important to ask now whether the billions of dollars invested in advertising are warranted. More precisely, when is it justifiable to invest in advertising, and when is it appropriate to disinvest?

Let us first examine a few equations that will put things into focus. These equations deal with the relations among sales volume (or simply volume), sales revenue (or simply revenue), and profit.

$$\text{Profit} = \text{Revenue} - \text{Expenses} \tag{9.1}$$
$$\text{Revenue} = \text{Price} \times \text{Volume} \tag{9.2}$$
$$\text{Volume} = \text{Trial} + \text{Repeat} \tag{9.3}$$

We see first with Equation 9.1 that a brand's profit during any accounting period—such as a business quarter or an entire year—is a function of its revenue minus expenses. Because advertising is an expense, total profit during an accounting period can be increased by reducing advertising expenses. At the same time, an undesirable effect of reducing advertising is that revenue may decline because fewer units can be sold or the price per unit has to be reduced in the absence of adequate advertising support (see Equation 9.2). We can further note from Equation 9.3 that sales volume (i.e., number of units sold) is obtained by a combination of recruiting more *trial*, or first-time, users to a brand and encouraging users to continue purchasing the brand—that is, to remain *repeat* purchasers.

Whether one chooses to invest or disinvest in advertising depends largely on expectations about how advertising will influence a brand's sales volume (Equation 9.3) and revenue (Equation 9.2). Let us look at arguments first for investing and then for disinvesting.

The Case for Investing in Advertising

In terms of profitability, investing in advertising is justified only if the incremental revenue generated from the advertising exceeds the advertising expense. In other words, if the advertising expense is $X, then over the long term (i.e., not necessarily immediately) revenue attributable to the advertising must be more than $X to justify the investment. On what grounds might one expect that the revenue will exceed the advertising expense? In terms of Equation 9.3, it might be expected that effective advertising will attract new triers to a brand and encourage repeat purchasing. (Obviously, advertising is not the only marcom tool able to generate trial and repeat purchasing; indeed, sales promotions perform both roles in conjunction with advertising.) Thus, effective advertising should build sales volume by enhancing brand equity—both by increasing brand awareness and by enhancing brand image (recall the discussion in Chapter 2).

Equation 9.2 shows that the other determinant of revenue besides sales volume is the unit price at which a brand is sold. Advertising has the power to enhance a brand's perceived quality and thus the ability of brand managers to charge higher prices; that is, consumers are willing to pay more for brands they perceive as higher quality. Taken together, then, the case for investing in advertising is based on the belief that it can increase profitability by increasing sales volume, enabling higher selling prices, and thus increasing revenue beyond the incremental advertising expense.

The Case for Disinvesting

As previously noted, firms often choose to reduce advertising expenditures either when a brand is performing well or during periods of economic recession. This is a seductive strategy because a reduction in expenses, everything else held constant, leads to increased profits (Equation 9.1). But is "everything else held constant" when advertising budgets are cut or, worse yet, severely slashed? The implicit assumption is that revenue (and revenue's constituent elements, volume and price) will *not* be affected adversely when ad budgets are diminished. However, such an assumption is based on the naive premise that past advertising will continue to affect sales volume positively, even when advertising in the current period is curtailed or reduced. The assumption also is somewhat illogical. On the one hand, it presumes that past advertising will carry over into the future to maintain revenue; on the other hand, it neglects to acknowledge that the absence of advertising in the present period will have an adverse effect on revenues in subsequent periods!

Which Position Is More Acceptable?

The profit effect of reducing advertising expenses is relatively certain: For every dollar not invested in advertising, there is a dollar increase in short-term profit—assuming, of course, that the reduction in advertising does not adversely affect revenue. It is far less certain, however, that maintaining or increasing advertising expenditures will increase profits. This is because it is difficult to know with certainty whether advertising will build brand volume or enable higher prices; either outcome or both will lead to increased revenues. Yet, and it is a *big* yet, most sophisticated companies are willing to place their bet on advertising's ability to boost revenues and thus enhance profits from the *revenue-increase side* rather than from the *expense-reduction side*.

A Deposit in the Brand Equity Bank

The reason many marketing executives continue to invest in advertising, even during economic downturns, is because they believe advertising will enhance a brand's equity and increase sales. You will recall from the discussion in Chapter 2 that marcom efforts enhance a brand's equity by creating brand awareness and forging favorable, strong, and perhaps unique associations in the consumer's memory between the brand and its features and benefits. When advertising and other forms of marketing communications create unique and positive messages, a brand becomes differentiated from competitive offerings and is relatively insulated from future price competition.

Advertising's long-term role has been described in these terms: "Strong advertising represents a deposit in the brand equity bank."[34] This clever expression nicely captures the advertising challenge. It also correctly notes that not all advertising represents a deposit in the brand equity bank, only advertising that is *strong*—that is, different, relevant, held in high esteem, and memorable (e.g., positive knowledge).

Advertising versus Pricing Elasticity

Returning more directly to the issue of investing or disinvesting in advertising, we have to grapple with the following challenge: What are the alternative ways by which brand managers can grow their brands' sales volume, revenue, and profits? Increasing advertising is one option; reducing price—via outright price cuts or through promotional dealing—is another. Which option is more promising? The answer requires we have a common measure, or metric, for comparing the effects of increasing advertising versus decreasing prices. The concept of *elasticity* provides just such a metric.

Elasticity, as you will recall from a basic economics or marketing course, is a measure of how responsive the demand for a brand is to changes in marketing variables such as price and advertising. We can calculate elasticity coefficients for price (E_P) and advertising (E_A), respectively, based on the following equations:

E_P = Percentage change in quantity demanded ÷ Percentage change in price (**9.4**)

E_A = Percentage change in quantity demanded

    ÷ Percentage change in advertising (**9.5**)

© Keith Morris/Alamy

To illustrate these concepts, consider the situation faced by a recent college graduate, Aubrey, who sells T-shirts imprinted with thematic messages. (Students well familiar with the concept of elasticity are encouraged to skip this basic treatment and resume reading the subsection titled "Average Price and Advertising Elasticities.")

Aubrey has being doing a pretty good business but thinks he can increase revenues and profits by lowering the price at which he sells imprinted T-shirts. (The *law of inverse demand* says that sales volume, or quantity, typically increases when prices are reduced, and vice versa.) Last week (we refer to this as week 1), Aubrey priced his product at $10 each and sold 1,500 shirts (P1 = $10; Q1 = 1,500). He decided the following week, week 2, to reduce the price to $9, and then sold 1,800 shirts (P2 = $9; Q2 = 1,800). Applying Equation 9.4, we quickly see that the percentage change in quantity demanded is 20 percent. That is, (1,800 − 1,500) ÷ 1,500 = 20 percent. Thus, with an 11 percent decrease in price—that is, (10 − 9) ÷ 9—he realized a 20 percent increase in quantity sold. The price elasticity (E_P) expressed as an absolute value is 1.82 (i.e., 20 ÷ 11). (Refer to Equation 9.4 to see how the elasticity coefficient for price, E_P, is calculated.) Aubrey was pleased with this result because total revenue in week 2 was $16,200 (P2 × Q2 = $9 × 1,800 = $16,200) compared with the $15,000 revenue obtained in week 1 ($10 × 1,500). Thus, although he reduced the price of T-shirts, he enjoyed an 8 percent increase in revenue—that is, ($16,200 − $15,000) ÷ $15,000.

Now consider that rather than reducing price, Aubrey decided to increase the amount of advertising from week 1 to week 2. Suppose that in week 1 he had spent $1,000 advertising in the local newspaper. As before, he obtained $15,000 revenue in week 1 from selling 1,500 T-shirts at a price of $10 each. Suppose in week 2 he increased the level of advertising to $1,500 (a 50 percent increase over week 1) and sold 1,600 shirts at $10 each. In this case, the percentage change in quantity demanded is 6.67 percent. That is, (1,600 − 1,500) ÷ 1,500 = 6.67 percent. This increase in quantity sold was enjoyed with a 50 percent increase in ad expenditures. Thus, applying Equation 9.5, the advertising elasticity (E_A) is 6.67 ÷ 50 = 0.133. Whereas Aubrey received $15,000 in week 1 revenue (P1 = $10; Q1 = 1,500), revenue increased in week 2 by $1,000 (P2 = $10; Q2 = 1,600). This increased revenue ($1,000) was obtained with a $500 increase in advertising, so Aubrey enjoyed a $500 increase in profit—not a bad week's work for a young entrepreneur!

Average Price and Advertising Elasticities An interesting question is whether increases in advertising can be justified, especially when compared with the alternative possibility of merely reducing prices. We know a lot about advertising and price elasticities. An important study determined that the average price and advertising elasticities for 130 brands of durable and nondurable products were 1.61 and 0.11, respectively.[35] In another study of 751 ad elasticity coefficients, the average short-term ad elasticity was 0.12 and was higher for durable goods, early stages in the life cycle, yearly (versus quarterly) data, and for gross rating points (GRPs) as opposed to monetary values.[36] (Also, we should note that the price elasticity is presented here as an absolute value, although technically it should have a negative sign insofar as price increases typically result in volume decreases and price decreases result in volume increases.) A price elasticity of 1.61 is interpreted as meaning that a 1 percent reduction in price leads to a 1.61 percent increase in sales volume; similarly, the ad elasticity coefficient of 0.11 indicates that a 1 percent increase in ad expenditures increases volume by just 0.11 percent.

Hence, sales volume is about 14.6 times (1.61 ÷ 0.11) more responsive, on average, to changes in price than to changes in advertising. For just durable goods, the average price and advertising elasticities are 2.01 and 0.23, which indicates that sales volume for these goods is, on average, 8.7 times more responsive to price discounts than advertising increases. Comparatively, for nondurable goods, the average price and advertising elasticities are 1.54 and 0.09, respectively, indicating that, on average, sales volume is 17 times more responsive to price cuts than advertising increases.

What's a Manager to Do? Do these results indicate that brand managers should always discount prices and never increase advertising? Absolutely not! As you have learned from this text and elsewhere, every situation is unique. Pat answers ("This is how you should do it.") are flat out wrong and misleading! Every brand does not experience the same price and advertising elasticities as presented here. "On average," as used in our discussion, means that some brands are at the average, whereas others are above or below the average; there is, in other words, a distribution of elasticity coefficients around the average. In general, we can consider four combinations of advertising and price elasticities. For each situation we will identify the appropriate strategy for increasing profit, whether to increase advertising or to reduce price:[37]

- *Situation 1: Maintain the status quo.* Consider a situation where consumers have well-established brand preferences such as during the decline stage of a product's life cycle or in established niche markets. In a market such as this, demand would not be very price elastic or advertising elastic; consequently, profits would be maximized by basically adhering to the status quo and maintaining the present price and advertising levels. In short, facing a situation such as this, brand managers should neither discount prices nor increase levels of advertising.
- *Situation 2: Build image via increased advertising.* In a situation where demand is more advertising elastic than price elastic, it is advisable to spend relatively more on advertising increases than price discounts. This situation is likely for new products, luxury goods, and products characterized by symbolism and imagery (cosmetics, designer labels in apparel and home furnishings, expensive brands of distilled spirits, etc.). The profit-increasing strategy in a situation such as this is to build a brand's image by increasing advertising.
- *Situation 3: Grow volume via price discounting.* This third situation is characterized by mature consumer goods markets where consumers have complete information about most brands in the category and brand switching is frequent. Because brands are little differentiated, the market is more price than advertising elastic. Profit increases are obtained more from price discounts than advertising investments.
- *Situation 4: Increase advertising and/or discount prices.* This is a situation where the market is both price elastic and advertising elastic. This would be expected when brands in the product category are inherently differentiable (cereals, automobiles, appliances, etc.) and for products that are seasonal (e.g., lawn products, seasonal clothing, and special holiday gift items). In situations such as these, informative advertising can influence consumers' beliefs about product attributes (e.g., Scotts fertilizer is longer-lasting than competitive brands), but because brands are similar, consumers also are eager to compare prices.

Given knowledge of the price and advertising elasticities that exist in a particular situation, it is possible to determine mathematically whether it is more profitable to increase advertising or discount price. The mathematics is beyond the scope of this text, but the interested reader is referred to additional sources.[38] It is hoped that this section conveyed the point that the choice to invest (increase) or disinvest (decrease) in advertising can be made only after determining the relative advertising and price elasticities that confront a brand in a particular market situation. Also, it should be cautioned that price can have a more immediate and direct impact on sales than advertising. Moreover, every brand has a unique situation in how it might respond to changes in advertising and/or price.

Ad Spending, Advertising Elasticity, and Share of Market

The effect of advertising for a brand on its sales volume, revenue, and market share—that is, its proportional representation of total product category revenue—is determined both by how much it spends relative to other brands in the category (its share of voice, or SOV) and how effective its advertising is. It was mentioned earlier that *strong* advertising is a deposit in the brand equity bank. Full appreciation of this statement requires that we explore the concept of advertising "strength." We have, in fact, a measure of advertising strength, and that measure is the familiar concept we've been discussing, namely, *advertising elasticity*. Table 9.5 presents real data for the top ten U.S. beer brands from a recent year as a basis for illustrating advertising elasticity and the concept of strength. However, before proceeding, it is necessary to introduce a final equation, Equation 9.6.

$$\text{SOM}_i = A_i^e \bigg/ \sum_{j=1}^{n} A_j^e \qquad (9.6)$$

Equation 9.6 indicates that a brand's predicted market share (i.e., the SOM for the ith brand in a product category) depends on its level of advertising (A_i) raised to the power of its advertising elasticity (e) in comparison to the total level of advertising for all brands in the category (brands $j = 1$ to n, where n is the total number of brands in the category) raised to the power of their elasticity coefficients.[39] Table 9.5 brings this formulation to life with a straightforward example drawn from the U.S. beer industry.

TABLE 9.5 The Effect of Advertising Elasticity on Brands Share of Market

Beer Marketer	Ad Spend ($ million) (A)	Hypothetical Elasticity Coefficients (B)	(A) ^ (B)* (C)	Predicted SOM (1) (D)	(A) ^ (B)† (E)	Predicted SOM (2) (F)
Anheuser Busch	$555	0.11	2.00	13.57%	2.00	13.11%
MillerCoors	394	0.11 or 0.15	1.93	13.09	2.45	16.06
Crown Imports	78	0.11	1.62	10.99	1.62	10.62
Heineken	139	0.11	1.72	11.67	1.72	11.27
Pabst	3	0.11	1.13	7.67	1.13	7.40
Diageo (Guinness)	12	0.11	1.31	8.89	1.31	8.58
N. American Breweries	5	0.11	1.19	8.07	1.19	7.80
Boston Beer Co.	33	0.11	1.47	9.97	1.47	9.63
D.G. Yuengling & Son	2	0.11	1.08	7.33	1.08	7.08
Mark Anthony (Mike's)	10	0.11	1.29	8.75	1.29	8.45
Column Sums	$1,231	NA	14.74	100%	15.26	100%

*Assumes elasticity coefficients for all 10 beer marketers are equal at 0.11.
†Assumes that MillerCoors' elasticity coefficient is 0.15, whereas all other marketers' elasticities remain at 0.11.

Source: "Top 10 Beer Marketers," *Advertising Age*, June 20, 2011, 22. Copyright Crain Communications Inc., 2011. Used with permission.

The first column of data, column A, indicates the advertising expenditures in a recent year for each of the top 10 U.S. beer companies. For example, Anheuser-Busch InBev spent a total of $555 million to advertise its flagship brands, Budweiser, Bud Light, Stella Artois, etc. Total ad expenditures among these 10 marketers exceeded $1.2 billion. Column B makes the simplifying assumption that advertising for every beer company is equally strong (or equally weak), as indicated by identical elasticity coefficients of 0.11, which, as pointed out previously, is the average advertising elasticity across many consumer products. Note that two coefficients are presented for MillerCoors, either 0.11 or 0.15. We explain later why two coefficients are shown for this particular brand.

In column C, the ad spend is raised to the power of the elasticity coefficient, with the symbol ^ indicating a power function. For example, Anheuser Busch InBev's ad spend of $555 million raised to the power of 0.11 equals 2.00, and MillerCoors' spend raised to the same power equals 1.93. Each value in Column C, one for each of the 10 beer marketers, is the numeric equivalent to the A_i^e term in Equation 9.6. The summation of all of the values in column C is 14.74, which represents the numerical counterpart to the summation term in Equation 9.6, namely $\sum A_j^e$.

Thus, following Equation 9.6, each value in column C is divided by the summation of all values to yield, in column D, predicted market shares for each of the 10 beer brands. Of course, Equation 9.6 makes the simplifying assumption that advertising is the sole determinant of market share. If that were the case, then the market shares in column D should correlate strongly with actual market shares. In fact, although not shown in Table 9.5, the correlation between actual and predicted market shares equals 0.80, which indicates that advertising is an important determinant of market shares in the beer industry.

Column E provides a new set of values that have been derived by assuming that all elasticity coefficients remain equal at 0.11 with the exception of Miller-Coors, which now is assumed to be 0.15. The assumption, in other words, is that MillerCoors advertising is "stronger" than its competitors', due perhaps to more creative advertising content or a novel and compelling ad message. If this in fact were the case, then predicted market shares would look like those in column F. Note carefully that MillerCoors predicted market share has increased by almost 3 share points (from 13.09 in column D to 16.06 in column F), whereas the shares for all other beers have declined. MillerCoors gain (due to hypothetically superior advertising) has come at the expense of its competitors.

In sum, this exercise has shown how it is possible to translate the idea of advertising "strength" into numerical values by capitalizing on the concept of advertising elasticity. Equation 9.6 is based on the simplifying assumption that advertising alone influences market share. Yet, simplification aside, it enables us to see the effect of creating better, more creative, and stronger advertising vis-a-vis competitors' efforts can lead to increased market shares. The following two chapters will go into much greater detail in developing the concept of advertising creativity and ad message strategies.

Summary

This chapter offered an introduction to advertising. First, advertising was defined as a paid, mediated form of communication from an identifiable source that is designed to persuade the receiver to take some action, either now or in the future. We then looked at the magnitude of advertising in the United States and elsewhere. For example, U.S. ad expenditures totaled approximately $300 billion in 2010, and global ad spending outside the United States in 2010 was estimated to total approximately $500 billion. Also discussed in this context were advertising-to-sales ratios for several illustrative product categories.

Next explored was advertising's role in the economy—and resolving the debate between the adverting = market power versus advertising = information perspectives. Then, the functions advertising performs, which include informing, influencing, reminding and increasing salience, adding value, and assisting other company efforts were presented. Following this, the advertising management process was examined from the perspectives of clients. The role of advertising agencies then was discussed, and methods of compensation were reviewed.

A concluding section provided a detailed discussion of the arguments favoring investment in advertising and counterarguments regarding circumstances when it is advisable to disinvest. In the context of this discussion, considerable attention was devoted to the issue of advertising versus pricing elasticities. We pointed out that sales volume is about 14.6 times more responsive, on average, to changes in price than to changes in advertising. Although this would seem to suggest that revenue is best grown by reducing prices rather than increasing ad spending, the point was made that not all advertisers are "average" and not all advertising situations are the same. Moreover, oftentimes, pricing has a more immediate and direct effect on sales than does advertising. Thus, whether increasing advertising or reducing price is a better strategy depends entirely on the situation facing each particular product category and competitor in that category. In conclusion we examined the role of advertising expenditures and elasticity coefficients in determining market shares.

Discussion Questions

1. Describe circumstances when each of the five advertising functions described in the chapter might be more important than the others.
2. Advertising is said to be "a deposit in the brand equity bank," but only if the advertising is "strong." Explain.
3. Provide an example of usage expansion advertising other than those illustrated in the chapter.
4. Present arguments for and against using advertising agencies. Are there lessons to learn from the experiences of Alex Bogusky (CP+B), featured in the *Marcom Insight*?
5. Ad agency compensation is increasingly turning to performance- or outcome-based compensation. Explain how this form of ad agency compensation works and why it potentially is superior to alternative methods of compensating ad agencies.
6. Using Equations 9.1 through 9.3, explain the various means by which advertising is capable of influencing a brand's profitability.
7. In the context of the discussion of price and advertising elasticities, four situations were presented by comparing whether price or advertising elasticity is stronger. Situation 2 was characterized as "build image via increased advertising." In your own terms, explain why in this situation it is more profitable to spend relatively more on advertising rather than reduce a brand's price.
8. Research results were presented showing that sales volume is about 14.6 times more responsive, on average, to changes in price than to changes in advertising. Explain exactly what this means for the manager of a brand who is considering whether to grow sales by increasing advertising expenditures or lowering the price.
9. Data in this same section indicated that nondurable goods (versus durables) are relatively more responsive to price cuts than advertising increases. Offer an explanation for this differential.
10. Show your understanding of Equation 9.4 and the data presented in Table 9.5 by constructing a spreadsheet (using, for example, Microsoft Excel) and altering the elasticity coefficients for different beers. For example, just as MillerCoors' elasticity coefficient was changed from 0.11 to 0.15 while holding all the others constant at 0.11, you may want to vary the coefficient for, say, Heineken.

End Notes

1. Jef I. Richards and Catharine M. Curran, "Oracles on 'Advertising': Searching for a Definition," *Journal of Advertising* 31 (summer 2002), 63–77.
2. Timothy Aeppel, "For Parker Hannifin, Cable TV Is the Best," *Wall Street Journal Online*, August 7, 2003, http://online.wsj.com.
3. Based on estimates of measured media advertising by Kantar Media and unmeasured media advertising by *Advertising Age*, as summarized and reported in "Advertising," Wikipedia, http://en.wikipedia.org/wiki/Advertising (accessed September 14, 2011).
4. Bradley Johnson, "Consumers Cite Past Experience as the No. 1 Influencer When Buying," *American Demographics*, November 20, 2006, 21.
5. The global advertising estimate is from "Advertising," Wikipedia.
6. Steve King, "Ad Spending in Developing Nations Outpaces Average," *Advertising Age*, June 18, 2007, 23.
7. "100 Leading National Advertisers," *Advertising Age*, June 20, 2011, 10.
8. Laurel Wentz and Mercedes M. Cardona, "Ad Fall May Be Worst Since Depression," *Advertising Age*, September 3, 2001, 1, 24.
9. Bradley Johnson, "100 Leading National Advertisers," *Advertising Age*, June 20, 2011, 8.
10. Jennifer Lawrence, "P&G's Artzt on Ads: Crucial Investment," *Advertising Age*, October 28, 1991, 1, 53.
11. Bernard Ryan, Jr., *It Works! How Investment Spending in Advertising Pays Off*, New York: American Association of Advertising Agencies, 1991, 11.

12. The following discussion closely follows the excellent review in Paul W. Farris and Mark S. Albion, "The Impact of Advertising on the Price of Consumer Products," *Journal of Marketing* 44 (summer 1980), 17–35. Note: a commonly accepted measure of market concentration or *market power* is HHI or the Herfindahl-Hirschman Index. The HHI is calculated by squaring the market share of each firm competing in the market and then summing the resulting numbers. For example, for a market consisting of four firms with shares of 30, 30, 20, and 20 percent, the HHI is 2,600 (302 + 302 + 202 + 202 = 2,600). Markets in which the HHI is between 1,000 and 1,800 points are considered to be moderately concentrated, and those in which the HHI is in excess of 1,800 points are considered concentrated. Transactions that increase the HHI by more than 100 points in concentrated markets presumptively raise antitrust concerns under the Horizontal Merger Guidelines issued by the U.S. Department of Justice and the Federal Trade Commission.

13. Ibid, 19.

14. Kent M. Lancaster and Gordon E. Miracle, "How Advertising Can Have Largely Anticompetitive Effects in One Sector But Largely Procompetitive Effects in Another," University of Illinois Working Paper No. 7, Urbana, IL, November 1979.

15. These functions are similar to those identified by the noted advertising pioneer James Webb Young. For example, "What Is Advertising, What Does It Do," *Advertising Age*, November 21, 1973, 12.

16. The idea of publicizing brands is based on the ideas of Andrew Ehrenberg and colleagues who regard advertising as a form of creative publicity. See Andrew Ehrenberg, Neil Barnard, Rachel Kennedy, and Helen Bloom, "Brand Advertising as Creative Publicity," *Journal of Advertising Research* 42 (August 2002), 7–18.

17. Giles D'Souza and Ram C. Rao, "Can Repeating an Advertisement More Frequently than the Competition Affect Brand Preference in a Mature Market?" *Journal of Marketing* 59 (April 1995), 32–42. See also A. S. C. Ehrenberg, "Repetitive Advertising and the Consumer," *Journal of Advertising Research* (April 1974), 24–34; and Stephen Miller and Lisette Berry, "Brand Salience versus Brand Image: Two Theories of Advertising Effectiveness," *Journal of Advertising Research* 28 (September/October 1998), 77–82.

18. The term *usage expansion advertising* and the examples are from Brian Wansink and Michael L. Ray, "Advertising Strategies to Increase Usage Frequency," *Journal of Marketing* 60 (January 1996), 31–46; and Ryan Flinn, "Clorox Growth Hinges on Ranch-Dipped Pizza, Scented Trash Bags," *Bloomberg News*, November 11, 2010, http://www.bloomberg.com/news/print/2010-11-11/clorox-growth-hinges-on-ranch-dipped-pizza-scented-trash-bags.html.

19. Ehrenberg et al., "Brand Advertising as Creative Publicity," 8.

20. Karen A. Machleit, Chris T. Allen, and Thomas J. Madden, "The Mature Brand and Brand Interest: An Alternative Consequence of Ad-Evoked Affect," *Journal of Marketing* 57 (October 1993), 72–82.

21. John Deighton, Caroline M. Henderson, and Scott A. Neslin, "The Effects of Advertising on Brand Switching and Repeat Purchasing," *Journal of Marketing Research* 31 (February 1994), 28–43.

22. *The Value Side of Productivity: A Key to Competitive Survival in the 1990s*, New York: American Association of Advertising Agencies, 1989, 12.

23. Sridhar Moorthy and Hao Zhao, "Advertising Spending and Perceived Quality," *Marketing Letters* 11 (August 2000), 221–34.

24. *The Value Side of Productivity*, 13–15. See also, Larry Light and Richard Morgan, *The Fourth Wave: Brand Loyalty Marketing*, New York: Coalition for Brand Equity, American Association of Advertising Agencies, 1994, 25.

25. Jim Spaeth, "Lost Lessons of Brand Power," *Advertising Age*, July 14, 2003, 16.

26. Leigh McAlister, Raji Srinivasan, and MinChung Kim, "Advertising, Research and Development, and Systematic Risk of the Firm," *Journal of Marketing* 71 (January 2007), 35–48.

27. The synergism between advertising and personal selling does not always equate to a one-way flow from advertising to personal selling. In fact, one study has demonstrated a reverse situation, in which personal sales calls sometimes pave the way for advertising. See William R. Swinyard and Michael L. Ray, "Advertising-Selling Interactions: An Attribution Theory Experiment," *Journal of Marketing Research* 14 (November 1977), 509–16.

28. Albert C. Bemmaor and Dominique Mouchoux, "Measuring the Short-Term Effect of In-Store Promotion and Retail Advertising on Brand Sales: A Factorial Experiment," *Journal of Marketing Research* 28 (May 1991), 202–14.

29. Mukund S. Kulkarni, Premal P. Vora, and Terence A. Brown, "Firing Advertising Agencies," *Journal of Advertising* 32 (Fall 2003), 77–86.

30. Kate Maddox, "It's So Good To Be Understood," *BtoB*, January 15, 2007, 25.

31. The 15 percent rate was for advertisements placed in newspapers and magazines, and on television and radio. The discount paid to advertising agencies for outdoor advertising has historically been slightly higher at 16.67 percent.

32. Jeremy Mullman and Natalie Zmuda, "Coke Pushes Pay-for-Performance Model," *Advertising Age*, April 27, 2009, 1, 34.

33. A theoretical treatment of outcome-based compensation programs is provided by Deborah F. Spake, Giles D'Souza, Tammy Neal Crutchfield, and Robert

M. Morgan, "Advertising Agency Compensation: An Agency Theory Explanation," *Journal of Advertising* 28 (fall 1999), 53–72.

34. John Sinisi, "Love: EDLP Equals Ad Investment," *Brandweek*, November 16, 1992, 2.

35. Raj Sethuraman and Gerard J. Tellis, "An Analysis of the Tradeoff between Advertising and Price Discounting," *Journal of Marketing Research* 28 (May 1991), 160–74. A recent study reveals that the average price elasticity based on an analysis of over 1,800 elasticity coefficients is even larger than previously thought. In fact, compared to Sethuraman and Tellis's estimated price elasticity of –1.61, this more complete and recent study yielded a mean price elasticity coefficient of –2.62. See Tammo H. A. Bijmolt, Harald J. van Heerde, and Rik G. M. Pieters, "New Empirical Generalizations on the Determinants of Price Elasticity," *Journal of Marketing Research* 42 (May 2005), 141–56.

36. Raj Sethuraman, Gerald J. Tellis, and Richard Biesch, "How Well Does Advertising Work? Generalizations from Meta-Analysis of Brand Advertising Elasticities," *Journal of Marketing Research* 48 (June 2011), 457–71.

37. Adapted from Sethuraman and Tellis 1991, ibid, especially Figure 1, p. 163, and the surrounding discussion.

38. See ibid, p. 164.

39. This formulation is based on an Internet posting by Gerard Tellis on ELMAR-AMA, June 4, 2003, http://elmar.ama.org.

CHAPTER 10

Effective and Creative Ad Messages

Perhaps the Greatest TV Commercial of All Time

Most people would agree that TV commercials are generally of average quality, not especially bad or good. Some commercials, although relatively few, are so dreadful that we are immediately turned off. At the opposite end of the ad-quality continuum are a small number of exceptionally good commercials. One such commercial, for Apple's Macintosh computer, aired on a single occasion 28 years ago. Many advertising pundits consider it to be the best advertising execution of all time.

Apple Computers had just developed the world's most user-friendly computer and needed breakthrough advertising to introduce its new Macintosh brand, which was a revolution in computing technology. Steve Jobs, the co-founder of Apple, who was only 29 at the time of the Macintosh introduction, instructed his

Image Courtesy of The Advertising Archives

advertising agency, Chiat/Day, to create an explosive television commercial that would portray the Macintosh as a truly revolutionary machine. The creative people at Chiat/Day faced a challenging task, especially since Macintosh's main competitor was the powerful and much larger "Big Blue" (IBM). (In 1984, Dell, Hewlett-Packard, and other personal computer brands were nonexistent. It was only Apple versus IBM in the personal desktop computer business, and IBM was the well-established leader known for its corporate computers.) However, Chiat/Day produced a commercial in which IBM was obliquely caricatured as the much despised and feared institution reminiscent of the Big Brother theme in George Orwell's book *1984*. (In the book, political power is controlled by Big Brother, and individual dignity and

Chapter Objectives

After reading this chapter, you should be able to:

1 Appreciate the factors that promote effective, creative, and "sticky" advertising.

2 Describe the features of a creative brief.

3 Explain alternative creative styles of advertising messages.

4 Understand the concept of means-end chains and their role in advertising strategy.

5 Appreciate the MECCAS model, laddering techniques, and their role in guiding message formulation.

6 Recognize the role of corporate image and issue advertising.

freedom are superseded by political conformity.) The one-minute commercial created in this context, dubbed "1984," was run during the Super Bowl XVIII on January 22, 1984, and was never repeated on commercial television. This was not because it was ineffective; to the contrary, its incredible word-of-mouth-producing impact negated the need for repeat showings.

> The commercial … opens on a room of zombie-like citizens staring at a huge screen where Big Brother is spewing a relentless cant about "information purification … unprincipled dissemination of facts" and "unification of thought."
>
> Against this ominous backdrop, a woman in athletic wear [a white jersey top and bright red running shorts, which was the only primary color in the commercial] runs in and hurls a sledgehammer into the screen, causing a cataclysmic explosion that shatters Big Brother. Then the message flashes on the TV screen: "On January 24th, Apple Computer will introduce Macintosh. And you'll see why 1984 won't be like '1984.'"

This remarkable advertising is considered by some to be the greatest TV commercial ever made. It attracted immediate attention; it broke through the clutter of the many commercials aired during the Super Bowl; it was memorable; it was discussed by millions of people; and, ultimately, it played an instrumental role in selling truckloads of Macintosh computers. Moreover, it created a unique image at the time for the Mac (short for Macintosh) as described adroitly by one observer.

> The Mac is female. Conversely, IBM must be male. IBM is not just male, it is Big Brother male. And Apple is not just female, but New Female. She is strong, athletic, independent, and, most important, liberated. After all, that's what the young athlete is all about. She is, in terms of the 1980s, empowerment and freedom.

Certainly, times have changed since 1984 with a positioning to all demographics (e.g., male and female), and Apple has seen a significant boost in sales of Macs. This shift has been attributed, in part, to their creative advertising and success of the iPod, iPhone, and iPad, a halo effect in which satisfied iPod, iPhone, or iPad owners purchase more Apple equipment. From 2001 to 2008, Mac sales increased continuously on an annual basis. Apple reported worldwide sales of 3.36 million Macs during the 2009 holiday season. As of mid-2011, Macintosh continues to enjoy large market share increases in the United States, growing from 7.3 percent of all computer shipments in 2010 to 9.3 percent in 2011.

Sources: Based on Bradley Johnson, "The Commercial, and the Product, That Changed Advertising," *Advertising Age*, January 10, 1994, 1, 12–14; Bob Garfield, "Breakthrough Product Gets Greatest TV Spot," *Advertising Age*, January 10, 1994, 14; "The Most Famous One-Shot Commercial Tested Orwell, and Made History for Apple Computer," *Advertising Age*, November 11, 1996, A22; James B. Twitchell, *20 Ads That Shook the World: The Century's Most Groundbreaking Advertising and How It Changed Us All*, New York: Crown Publishers, 2000, 190; and "Macintosh," Wikipedia, http://en.wikipedia.org/wiki/Macintosh (accessed September 21, 2011).

Introduction

Advertisers in most product categories generally operate in an advertising context where audiences are continually bombarded by advertisements. This state of affairs, referred to as advertising *clutter*, means that ad messages must be creative to gain the receiver's attention and accomplish even more ambitious goals such as enhancing brand images and motivating prospects to purchase advertised products. The present chapter, which is the first of two to examine the message aspect of advertising, addresses questions such as these: What is advertising creativity? What makes for an effective and successful advertising message? What is required for an advertisement to have lasting impact? How can understanding consumer values lead to the production of effective advertisements? What are the different types of creative styles, and when and why is each used?

Suggestions for Creating Effective Advertising

We turn now to the issue of how advertising agencies and clients work together to develop effective advertising campaigns. No simple answer is possible, but toward this end we first must attempt to understand the meaning of *effective advertising*. It is easy, in one sense, to define effective advertising: Advertising is effective if it accomplishes the advertiser's objectives. This perspective defines effectiveness from the *output side*, or in terms of what it accomplishes. It is much more difficult to define effective advertising from an *input perspective*, or in terms of the composition of the advertisement itself. There are many viewpoints on this issue. For example, a practitioner of direct-mail advertising or social media probably has a different opinion about what constitutes effective advertising than would Steve Hayden, the inspirational source and copy writer behind the "1984" Macintosh commercial that was described in the chapter-opening *Marcom Insight*.

Although it is impractical to provide a singular, all-purpose definition of what constitutes effective advertising, it is possible to first talk about general characteristics.[1] At a minimum, and from a strategic and practical point of view, effective advertising satisfies the following considerations:

1. *It extends from sound marketing strategy.* Advertising can be effective only if it is compatible with other elements of an integrated and well-orchestrated marcom strategy. For example, as established in Chapter 1, all marcom tools must be integrated and "speak" with a single voice.

2. *Effective advertising takes the consumer's view.* Advertising must be stated in a way that relates to the consumer's—rather than the marketer's—needs, wants, and values. In short, effective advertising *connects* with the target audience by reflecting keen insight into what consumers are looking for when making brand-selection decisions in specific product categories. For example, several years ago, when Northwest Airlines (now part of Delta) pulled out of Milwaukee as a hub, frequent flyers were quite upset. Yet, Midwest Airlines (now part of Frontier) filled the void by offering nearly 40 direct flights to major destinations from Milwaukee each day. Midwest's advertising campaign then showed consumers on pogo sticks hopping around a map of the United States, depicting all of their competitors with non-direct flights. Midwest remained Milwaukee's "hometown airline" and leader in market share for almost 25 years. In general, an advertising practitioner who specializes in creative thinking has stated the issue in these terms: "Consumers don't want to be bombarded with ads—they want to be inspired by ideas that will change their lives. Ads create transactions. Ideas create transformations. Ads reflect our culture, ideas imagine our future."[2]

3. *It finds a unique way to break through the clutter.* Advertisers continually compete for the consumer's attention. Gaining attention is no small task considering the massive number of print advertisements, broadcast commercials, Internet ads, social media feeds, and other sources of information consumers

see daily. Indeed, the situation in television advertising has been characterized as "audiovisual wallpaper"—a sarcastic implication that consumers pay about as much attention to commercials as they do to the detail in their wallpaper after seeing it for years.[3]

4. *Effective advertising never promises more than it can deliver.* This point speaks for itself, both with respect to ethics and in terms of smart business sense. Consumers learn when they have been deceived and will resent the advertiser. Effective advertising promises no more than the advertised product is capable of delivering.

5. *It prevents the creative idea from overwhelming the strategy.* The purpose of advertising is to inform, inspire, and ultimately sell products; the purpose is not to be creative merely for the sake of being clever. For example, a famous, long-running ad campaign for Miller Lite used well-recognized sports celebrities, yet the creative use of these celebrities did not overshadow the main ad claim of "Tastes Great, Less Filling." Regarding creativity, it is argued, although perhaps unfairly, that advertising agencies place excessive emphasis on winning awards at the various annual ceremonies the ad industry conducts—for example, the Cannes Lions International Advertising Festival in France, the London International Advertising Awards, and the Clio Awards in the United States.

Qualities of Successful Advertising

Several years ago, the noted advertising scholar and visionary, Herbert Krugman, cited what he believed were three important ingredients of successful advertising: (1) information, (2) rational stimulus ("reason why"), and (3) emphasis.[4] He noted that few ads boasted all three elements. The first, *information*, refers to whether the advertiser has important news to share with the world (i.e., newsworthiness). For example, the American Dental Association's endorsement of Crest toothpaste in 1960 was an important piece of news advertised by Procter & Gamble and helped assure their market leadership position for many years. Second, the *rational stimulus* or "reason why" usually occurs under high involvement (e.g., due to a prior need or product search) and often motivates a scrutiny of message-relevant arguments in seeking the "reason why" one should purchase or consider the advertised brand. The third ingredient, *emphasis*, focuses on repeating a single theme or aspect of the product. Although ideal under low involvement (and as a reminder to purchase), it easily can lead to irritation and "ad wearout" if overdone. Yet, for many items for which consumers do not value as being important in their lives, emphasizing a single theme may bring the item to one's "top of mind" awareness when shopping.

What Exactly Does Being "Creative" and "Effective" Mean?

An argument can be made that "effective" or successful advertising is usually being creative with a purpose. Certainly, the notion of effective advertising can vary from culture to culture. In the United Kingdom, a premium may be placed on being different, humorous, or out-of-the ordinary in differentiating campaigns from the mass of mediocre advertising.

In the United States, creative advertising is viewed more often as being "effective" in that the creativity has a purpose. That is, upon determining the specific tasks, or objectives that an advertising campaign must accomplish, it is the challenge of the advertising team—the advertising agency along with the client—to develop advertising executions that connect with the target audience, cut through the clutter, and position the brand optimally in view of the brand's strengths relative to competitive brands. Importantly, the focus is on the original objectives for the campaign (e.g., ROI).

Certainly, it is easier to give examples of creative advertising than to offer a universal definition. Consider the following three examples of unique and creative messaging: (1) the E*TRADE baby campaign showing that online investment

© AP Images/PRNewsFoto/Kia Motors America

trading with E*TRADE is so easy, a baby could do it; (2) the Kia Soul's dancing hamsters' campaign ("Share Some Soul"); and (3) Nike's "Back 4 The Future" shoe campaign, featuring actors from the original *Back to the Future* movies. (The first campaign was run on Super Bowls from 2008 to 2011, whereas the last two examples were some of the top viral ads for 2011.)[5]

Jazz musician Charlie Mingus described creativity about as well as it can be described: "Creativity is more than just being different. Anybody can play weird, that's easy. What's hard is to be simple as Bach. Making the simple complicated is commonplace, making the complicated simple, awesomely simple, that's creativity."[6] The following section discusses several elements found in "creative" ads.[7]

Creativity: The CAN Elements

Although identifying advertising creativity is challenging, there is some agreement that "creative" ads share three common features: connectedness, appropriateness, and novelty. These are the "CAN" elements.[8]

Connectedness

Connectedness addresses whether an advertisement reflects *empathy*, creates a bond, and is relevant with the *target audience's* basic needs and wants as they relate to making a brand-choice decision in a product category. For example, if competitive price and speed of delivery are paramount to corporate purchasing agents, then ads that reflect these motivations *are* connected.

Appropriateness

Appropriateness means that an advertisement must provide information that is pertinent to the *advertised brand* relative to other brands in the product category. An advertisement is appropriate to the extent that the message is on target for delivering the brand's positioning strategy and capturing the brand's relative strengths and weaknesses vis-a-vis competitive brands. Appropriate ads also are coherent in the sense that all message elements work in concert to deliver a singular, unambiguous message.

Novelty

Novel ads are unique, fresh, and unexpected. They differ from consumers' expectations of a typical ad for a brand in a particular product category. Novelty draws consumers' attention to an ad so that they engage in more effortful information processing, such as attempting to comprehend the meaning of the advertised brand. Unoriginal advertising is unable to break through the competitive clutter and grab the consumer's attention.

Advertising agencies sometimes develop ads that are unique, different, unexpected, and weird. Yet, novel advertisements can be considered creative only if they also are connected and appropriate. Such ads CAN be effective!

Getting Messages to "Stick"

Beyond being creative, advertisers want their advertising to "stick." Sticky ads are ads for which the audience comprehends the advertiser's intended message; they are remembered, and they change the target audience's brand-related opinions or behavior.[9] Such ads have *lasting impact*: they stick.

What are the features of sticky messages in general? We now describe six common features of messages that tend to stick—that is, have relatively lasting impact.[10]

Simplicity

Sticky advertisements are both *simple* and *profound*. An advertisement can be said to be simple when it represents the brand's core idea or key positioning statement (i.e., the advertising execution is stripped to its critical essence and captures the key element that needs to be communicated). Simple advertisements are *appropriate* in the sense of the term's CAN elements of creativity usage.

Unexpectedness

Sticky advertisements generate interest and curiosity when they deviate from audience members' expectations. As the marketplace is cluttered with commercial messages, communicators must overcome consumers' natural tendency to attend selectively only those messages that are relevant to their goals. Note the similarity of unexpectedness to the *novelty* element in the list of creative CAN features. Sticky messages also are creative. As depicted earlier, hamsters dancing to party music (in the Kia Soul campaign) is clearly unexpected by viewers.

Concreteness

Sticky ideas possess concrete images as compared to abstract representations. As discussed in further detail in Chapter 6, advertisers "concretize" their messages to facilitate both consumer learning and retrieval of brand information. *Concretizing* is based on the straightforward idea that it is easier for people to remember and retrieve concrete versus abstract information. Concretizing is accomplished by using tangible, substantive (i.e., concrete) words and demonstrations. For example, a marketer of pickup trucks demonstrates concreteness when visually showing the truck lugging a huge load versus an abstract claim of just being "tough."

Credibility

Sticky advertisements are *believable*. They have a sense of authority and provide reasons why they should be accepted as fact. For example, the American Dental Association seal of approval for cavity prevention was advertised in Crest campaigns in the 1960s, which aided Crest's market leadership position for years. Chapter 11 discusses in greater detail the nature and importance of credibility when describing the role of celebrity endorsers.

Emotionality

People care about ideas that generate emotions and tap into feelings. For example, fun and upbeat commercials (e.g., E*TRADE baby, Kia Soul dancing hamsters) may generate positive feelings and affect in the form of happiness, joy, cheerfulness, amusement, and other favorable emotions. In general, advertisers can get people to care about their brands by appealing to emotions that are relevant to the product category in which the advertised brand competes.

Storytelling

The sixth element of sticky messages is telling stories. By definition, stories have plots, characters, and settings—all features of which are contained in the long-running ad campaign for Subway restaurants based on the real-life character named Jared.[11] Subway's advertising agency has used Jared's story as the basis for its campaign touting that Subway sandwiches can promote weight loss. At one point in his life, Jared weighed in excess of 400 pounds and had a 60-inch waist. Following a hospital visit after experiencing chest pains, his physician father warned him that he might not live past 35 unless he undertook a dramatic weight loss regimen. This got Jared's attention, and he proceeded to develop his own, all-Subway diet consisting of eating a foot-long veggie sub for lunch and a six-inch turkey sub for dinner. This diet, along with increased exercise, resulted in Jared's losing nearly 250 pounds. To make a long story short, the Subway chain eventually learned of Jared's personal diet and built an advertising campaign around his story. This story is inspiring, and it obviously has stuck with thousands of consumers who now believe that Subway sandwiches are healthier than the fare at other fast-food restaurants.

To sum up, sticky messages are those that have lasting impact. The elements of sticky messages are Simplicity, Unexpectedness, Concreteness, Credibility, Emotionality, and Storytelling, or SUCCESs.[12]

Illustrations of Creative and Sticky Advertising Executions

In addition to the highly creative (and effective!) advertisement presented in the chapter opening *Marcom Insight* insert, the following examples illustrate individual advertisements and advertising campaigns that, in the authors' opinion, register high marks on the CAN facets of creativity and the SUCCESs elements of stickiness.

Miss Clairol: "Does She ... or Doesn't She?"

Imagine yourself employed as a copywriter in a New York advertising agency in 1955. You have just been assigned creative responsibility for a product that heretofore (as of 1955) had not been nationally marketed or advertised. The product: hair coloring. The brand: Miss Clairol. Your task: devise a creative strategy that will convince millions of American women to purchase Miss Clairol hair coloring—at the time called Hair Color Bath. This challenge occurred, by the way, in a cultural context where it was considered patently inappropriate for respectable women to smoke in public, wear long pants, or color their hair.

The person actually assigned this task was Shirley Polykoff, a copywriter for the Foote, Cone & Belding agency. At the time of the Miss Clairol campaign, there was no hair-coloring business. Women were even ashamed to color their own hair due to social disapproval and because at-home hair color often turned out looking unnatural. A product that provided a natural look stood a strong chance of being accepted, but women would had to be convinced that an advertised hair-coloring product would, in fact, give them that highly desired natural look.

Shirley Polykoff explains the background of the famous advertising line that convinced women Miss Clairol would produce a natural look.

> *In 1933, just before I was married, my husband had taken me to meet the woman who would become my mother-in-law. When we got in the car after dinner, I asked him, "How'd I do? Did your mother like me?" and he told me his mother had said, "She paints her hair, doesn't she?" He asked me, "Well, do you?" It became a joke between my husband and me; anytime we saw someone who was stunning or attractive we'd say, "Does she, or doesn't she?" Twenty years later [at the time she was working on the Miss Clairol account], I was walking down Park Avenue talking out loud to myself, because I have to hear what I write. The phrase came into my mind again. Suddenly, I realized, "That's it. That's the campaign." I knew that [a competitive advertising agency] couldn't find anything better. I knew that immediately. When you're young, you're very sure about everything.*[13]

The advertising line "Does she ... or doesn't she?" actually was followed with the tagline "Hair color so natural only her hairdresser knows for sure!" The headline attracted the reader's attention, whereas the tagline promised a conclusive benefit: The product works so well that only an expert would recognize that her hair color was not her actual color. This brilliant advertising persuaded millions of American women to become product users and led to dramatically increased sales of Miss Clairol.[14] In terms of the six stickiness elements, this campaign performs extremely well with respect to at least five of these features: simplicity, concreteness, credibility, emotionality, and storytelling.

Absolut Vodka

Imported brands of vodka were virtually nonexistent in the United States until the early 1980s. Three brands (Stolichnaya from Russia, Finlandia from Finland, and Wybrowa from Poland) made up less than 1 percent of the total U.S. vodka market. Absolut vodka from Sweden—a country previously not associated with vodka—was introduced to the United States in 1980. In addition to having a great name (suggesting the unequivocally best, or *absolute*, vodka), the brand's most distinguishing feature was a unique bottle—crystal clear with an interesting shape.

With a small budget and the capability of advertising only in print media (broadcast advertising of beer, wine, and distilled spirits was not permitted), the brand's advertising agency, TBWA, set about the task of rapidly building brand awareness. The agency's brilliant idea was simply to feature a full-page shot of the bottle with a two-word headline: The first word would always be the brand name, Absolut, used as an adjective to modify a second word that (1) described the brand (e.g., Absolut Perfection); (2) characterized its consumer (e.g., Absolut Sophisticate); or (3) associated the brand with positive places, people, or events (e.g., Absolut Barcelona). Literally hundreds of print ads were executed over the next quarter century, and Absolut rose to the top in the vodka industry, only to be knocked off its perch by the early 2000s when luxury brands such as Grey Goose, Ketel One, and many others were introduced. (A website with illustrations of Absolut's print ads is available at www.absolutad.com.) The campaign was discontinued in 2007 and replaced with another campaign titled "In an Absolut World." The rationale for discontinuing the earlier, famous campaign is presented in the *Global Focus* insert. This campaign performs especially well on the simplicity aspect of the SUCCESs model.

GLOBAL FOCUS

Why Dump an Extraordinarily Successful Ad Campaign?

Absolut's bottle-oriented print advertising campaign included some 1,500 print executions and extended over 25 years, with one brilliant ad followed by another. The campaign was extremely effective for a number of years, but the vodka industry changed, and by the 1990s there were literally dozens of premium vodka brands that competed with Absolut. Absolut no longer was *the* superpremium brand, and the advertising simply wore out—or perhaps, alternatively, the people in charge of the advertising grew tired of creating one "Absolut This" ad followed by the next "Absolut That" ad. Also, research conducted in nine countries indicated that consumers had become less involved with the bottle campaign and were no longer inspired by it.

A new campaign titled "In an Absolut World" was introduced in 2007 to replace the famous bottle campaign. The new campaign presents images of what it would be like to live in an ideal, Absolut world. In one execution, for example, pregnant men are portrayed alongside their elated wives. Another (and controversial) execution in Mexico showed "in an Absolut world" what the United States–Mexican border and map would look like before the Mexican-American War in 1848. In another execution, police and protesters are shown "fighting"—not with guns and clubs, but with pillows! The message conveyed is that Absolut is the ideal brand of vodka for this ideal world. Whereas the original bottle campaign was restricted to print advertising, this new campaign is appropriate for various media, including television and the Internet.

Sources: Jeremy Mullman, "Why Absolut Said Bye-Bye to the Bottle," *Advertising Age*, May 28, 2007, 3, 28; Keith McArthur, "Absolut Vodka Maker Replaces Iconic Ad Campaign," http://great-ads.blogspot.com/2007/04/absolut-vodka-maker-replaces-iconic-ad.html (accessed January 2, 2008).

The Aflac Duck

Until the early 2000s, a supplementary insurance company named the American Family Life Assurance Company (Aflac) was anything but a household name. In fact, that was the problem: Despite having invested heavily in advertising for a number of years, most consumers had never heard the name Aflac or little remembered it. Aflac's chief executive officer and chairperson knew that a creative advertising campaign was needed to generate the necessary level of *brand awareness*. Hired for this purpose was, at the time, a little known ad agency—the Kaplan Thaler Group.

Just days before the deadline for the new campaign, a member of the creative team took a long walk during his lunch break and started voicing out loud the name "Aflac." After repeating the name over and over, it dawned on him that he sounded like a quacking duck. With great excitement he returned to his office and, along with his creative teammate, quickly wrote the first spot for an Aflac commercial featuring the now-famous "spokesduck" (Figure 10.1). This creative insight initiated one of advertising's most heralded ad campaigns debuting in CNN's Millennium Special and subsequently running on every major college football game. Incorporated seamlessly into dialogue about supplemental insurance in each ad execution, the unnoticed duck exclaimed, "Aflac!!" in response to questions such as "What is supplemental insurance? What is it called?" The ad campaign registered incredible results from its inception and increased Aflac's brand identity from 10 percent to more than 90 percent![15]

Today, the Aflac Duck continues to score with consumers and businesses. With research showing that as long as the duck continues to find himself in the most unlikely scenarios, he will continue to resonate with consumers and enhance Aflac's image.[16] This campaign performs extremely well with respect to creativity, and with at least two of the stickiness elements: simplicity and concreteness.

Can your insurance do this?

Can your insurance do this?

FIGURE 10.1 Illustrations of the Aflac Adverting Campaign with the "Spokesduck"

Nike Shoes

Sports shoe and apparel company, Nike of Beaverton, Oregon, and its Portland-based advertising agency, Wieden+Kennedy, are known for their original and often captivating advertising. This was typified when Wieden+Kennedy created an absorbing campaign for Nike. Professional athletes were shown in various executions playing hockey, volleyball, baseball, bowling, boxing, and so on. You might be wondering, What is the big deal? Hundreds of commercials for sporting goods have done the same thing. The brilliance in these ads was the creative juxtaposition of famous athletes with sports other than those for which they are known. For example, in Nike's "What If" commercial, tennis player Andre Agassi was portrayed playing baseball; quarterback Michael Vick was shown as a hockey player par excellence; seven-time Tour de France winner Lance Armstrong was portrayed as an accomplished boxer; tennis player Serena Williams was shown making a vicious serve in volleyball; and baseball pitcher Randy Johnson looked like a professional bowler. As with other Nike commercials, this campaign made the nuanced point that Nike, like the famous athletes who endorse its products, is somehow special and out of the ordinary.[17] These advertisements score well on several SUCCESs elements: simplicity, unexpectedness, concreteness, and emotionality.

Making an Impression

Advertising that is creative and purposeful oftentimes is effective as well. Yet, such advertising must make a relatively lasting impact on consumers. This means getting past the clutter from other advertisements, activating attention, and giving consumers something to remember about the advertised product. In other words, advertising must make an *impression*. Advertising can have different types of impressions on a consumer. Research with television commercials has identified a structured, well-defined hierarchy of impressions that includes five major types of advertising impressions.[18] From the most basic to the highest level, here is the hierarchy:

Brand name. The easiest and most likely take-away from a commercial that viewers retain in memory is the brand name. Consumers often remember little else but what brand was being advertised.

Generics. The second most typical impression consists of generics. The generics represents the major selling claim associated with the advertised brand (e.g., Haagen-Dazs claims to have the purest and finest ice cream ingredients in the world; General Electric focuses on imagination at work; Walmart claims that you will save money and live better).

Attitudinal response (feelings). Next in the impression hierarchy is the generation of an attitudinal response or feelings.[19] Television commercials and online videos (e.g., from YouTube, Tumblr) can evoke a variety of positive and negative feelings. Positive feelings might include reactions such as pride, excitement, warmth, tenderness, amazement, confidence, humor, and so on. Negative feelings might include fear, boredom, sadness, anger, disgust, and irritation.

Commercial specifics. Retention of commercial specifics is the fourth most frequent form of impression. Commercial specifics involve the elements in the execution of the advertisement such as the spokesperson or endorser (e.g., Aaron Rodgers or Chris Bosh in "Milk Mustache" print ads), the music (e.g., "Party Rock Anthem" by LMFAO in Kia Soul's dancing hamsters commercial), the overall situation (e.g., an emotional ad for Hallmark greeting cards), and characters (e.g., Geico's gecko, Progressive's Flo, and actors in Allstate's "Mayhem" commercials).

Specific sales message. The last or highest level of an impression viewers retain is the specific sales message. However, repeated exposures and persistence during the course of an advertising campaign can enable (at least part of) a sales message to retained as a "generic" element. For example, a long-running campaign for Paul Masson wines used the confident and "larger than life" actor Orson Welles. Initially, Welles was the most outstanding impression. But, over time, consumers retained the specific sales message (i.e., "Paul Masson will not be sold before its time.").

Advertising Plans and Strategy

Advertising plans provide the framework for the systematic execution of advertising strategies. An advertising plan evaluates a brand's advertising history, proposes where the next period's advertising should head, and justifies the proposed strategy for maintaining or improving a brand's competitive situation.

To put an advertising plan into action requires (1) careful evaluation of customer behavior related to the brand, (2) detailed evaluation of the competition, and (3) a coordinated effort to tie the proposed advertising program to the brand's overall marcom strategy. (Note: one's advertising plan should be closely tied and an integral part of the overall marketing plan for the firm.[20]) In turn, advertising strategy is what the advertiser says about the brand being advertised. It involves the development of an advertising message that communicates the brand's value proposition—i.e., its primary benefit or how it can solve the consumer's problem.

A Five-Step Program

Developing an advertising strategy requires that the advertiser and its agency undertake a formal process, such as the following five-step program:[21]

1. Specify the key fact from the consumer's point of view.
2. State the primary problem from the marketer's point of view.
3. State the communications objective.
4. Implement the creative message strategy (creative platform).
5. Establish mandatory requirements.

Each step in the ad strategy process will be illustrated by considering an advertising campaign undertaken by E*TRADE, a leading online brokerage firm reporting total revenue of $2.4 billion in 2010.[22] From 2008 through 2011, E*TRADE aired perhaps some of the most memorable Super Bowl (and other) commercials by Grey Advertising (NY) featuring a smart-talking baby whose theme was that trading online with E*TRADE was so easy a baby could do it. The series of highly rated and funny commercials included Trading Baby, Clown, Golf, Lottery, Singing Baby, Tears, First Class, Barbershop, Girlfriend, Time Out, Documentary, Solitary, Cat, and Tailor. The implication was clear; it was so easy to invest and trade online using E*TRADE that anyone could do it.

Step 1: Specify the Key Fact

The key fact in an advertising strategy is a single-minded statement from the *consumer's point of view*. It identifies why consumers are or are not purchasing the product, service, or brand or are not giving it proper consideration.

In the case of E*TRADE, research revealed that consumers perceived online trading as somewhat risky and tough to do.[23] So, an important objective for the campaign was to persuade consumers that investing online (particularly with E*TRADE) was easy to conduct.[24]

Step 2: State the Primary Problem

Extending from the key fact, this next step is to state the problem from the *marketer's point of view*. The primary problem may be an image issue, a product perception view, or competitive weakness, to name a few.

For E*TRADE, it was a crowded competitive marketplace, with strong competition from Charles Schwab, TD Ameritrade, Fidelity, and Scotttrade. As E*TRADE was a no-frills online broker (like TD Ameritrade), it was important to justify their value with consumers and differentiate themselves from competition.

Step 3: State the Communications Objective

This step is a straightforward statement about *what effect the advertising is intended to have on the target market*.

E*TRADE's advertising with the smart-talking baby (actually the voice of Pete Holmes, a comedian who has appeared on Comedy Central) had three primary communications objectives focusing on consumer awareness. The first objective is to acknowledge that investing is tough—but that it can be easy online with E*TRADE. Second, that E*TRADE offers value versus the other brokerages. The third objective is that "you the consumer" are in the driver's seat with E*TRADE.

Step 4: Implement the Creative Message Strategy (i.e., the Creative Platform)

The creative message strategy, sometimes called the *creative platform*, represents the internal workings of the overall advertising strategy. The creative platform for a brand is summarized into a single statement classed a *value proposition* (previously discussed in this text) or *positioning statement*. A positioning statement (or "take away" or "net impression") is the single most important idea that a brand is intended to stand for in consumers' minds. It also takes into account how competitors have positioned their brands. These consumer thoughts and feelings about our brand should stand out in comparison to competitive offerings and should motivate the customer or prospect to try our brand. The *creative platform* consists of (1) defining the target market, (2) identifying the primary competition, (3) choosing the positioning statement, and (4) offering reasons why.

Define the Target Market   You will recall from discussion in Chapter 5 that the target market for a brand's advertising strategy and related marketing programs can be defined in terms of demographics, geodemographics, psychographics, or product usage (behavioral) characteristics.

E*TRADE's target markets consist of both individual and corporate investors categorized by their trade frequency and income: mass affluents (more than 30 trades per quarter, over \$50,000 in assets); main street investors (less than 30 trades per quarter, less than \$50,000 in assets); active traders (more than 30 trades per quarter regardless of total assets); and corporate clients (2,500 firms in over 100 countries).[25]

Identify the Primary Competition   Who are the primary competitors in the segment the brand is attempting to tap, and what are their advantages and disadvantages? Answering this question enables an advertiser to know exactly how to position a brand against consumers' perceptions of competitive brands.

The primary competitors for E*TRADE are Charles Schwab, TD Ameritrade, Fidelity, and Scotttrade. Although both Charles Schwab and TD Ameritrade both advertise modestly at the national level (versus E*TRADE), TD Ameritrade is a major competitor occupying the similar "no frills" online investor space as E*TRADE.

Offer Reasons Why   The "reasons why" are the facts supporting the positioning statement. In some instances, advertisers back up advertising claims with factual information that is relevant, informative, and interesting to consumers. Other times, the initial appeal or premise may be more emotional or psychological, hopefully driving traffic to a website or social media location with greater detail. In some instances, advertisers turn to celebrities, authority figures, or other experts to offer support to the implicit advertising promise.

E*TRADE's promise in the talking baby commercials is that online investing with E*TRADE is so easy that a baby could do it. (The Solitary and Time Out commercials actually show the baby doing this on his smartphone!)

Step 5: Mandatory Requirements

The final step in developing an advertising strategy involves the mandatory requirements that must be included in an ad. These include those imposed by corporate officers as a matter of policy and tradition, or due to regulatory requirements in some instances (e.g., side effects and warnings listed for prescription drugs). Non-regulatory requirements usually include the corporate slogan and/or logo and a standard tag line at the bottom of a print ad or end of a commercial. (See the *IMC Focus* for a discussion of advertising slogans.) Other requirements include the corporate website and/or social media sites (Facebook, Twitter) and QR (quick response) codes for smartphone scanning to link with brand information.

Constructing a Creative Brief

Perhaps the most important document in the development of an ad campaign and its execution is the creative brief. The creative brief is the "blueprint," or guide, that links the advertising strategy with the execution of the ad campaign. All key parties (e.g., account executive, client, creative director) must approve the brief before the campaign is developed and launched. So, the work of copywriters and other creatives is directed by the brief, channeling their efforts toward a solution that will serve the interests of the client. (Sometimes, other parties are involved, such as key retailers.) Although creative briefs vary in terms specificity, and from agency to agency, most briefs would include answers to the following questions:[26]

Advertising Objectives

The initial question that must be addressed is: *Why are we advertising?* The answer requires a brief explanation regarding why the advertising agency is being asked to perform a certain advertising job. What is it that the client wishes to achieve with the campaign? This usually includes a specification of the primary and secondary objectives for the campaign. For example, the purpose may be to launch a new brand, gain back lost sales from a competitor, or introduce a new version of an established product.

Target Audience

Who are we talking to? This is a *precise* description of the primary and secondary target markets. With knowledge of the behaviorgraphic, psychographic, demographic, or geodemographic characteristics of the intended customer (see Chapter 5), creatives have a specific target at which to direct their efforts.

Motivations, Thoughts, and Feelings

What are the motivations of the target audience? What do they currently think and feel about our brand? Here is where research and account planning are needed as the foundation for the advertising job. The advice here is to perform research *prior* to developing creative advertisements. With the assistance of account planners in interpreting research results, ad creatives are then prepared to design research-based advertising that speaks to the target audience in terms of their known thoughts and feelings about the brand rather than relying on mere suppositions. Sure, effective ads can be created absent any formal research (recall the Aflac ad and how it came about); however, the odds of success are much improved if formal research precedes creative activity.

What do we want the target audience to think or feel about the brand, and why should they think this way? This guideline simply reminds everyone what the client wants the advertising to accomplish. It calls for a short statement about the crucial feelings or thoughts that the advertisement should evoke in its intended audience. For example, the ad might be designed to move the audience emotionally, to make them feel deserving of a better lifestyle, or to get them to feel anxious about a currently unsafe course of behavior. Is there a current perception that needs to be changed? For example, if a large number of consumers in the target market consider the brand overpriced, how can we change that perception and convince them that the brand actually is a good value due to its superior quality? Knowing this, creatives can then design appropriate advertisements to achieve that objective. Given multiple objectives, it is desirable to prioritize them from most to least important and to focus on the most important objective.

Also, although not a typical practice in the ad industry when constructing creative briefs, it is helpful to indicate not only what objectives are to be accomplished, but also how achievement of these objectives will be measured. By specifying measures in advance, client and agency are on the proverbial same page when follow-up research is performed to assess whether the advertising campaign has actually accomplished what it was designed to do.[27]

Brand Positioning and Personality

What is the brand positioning and brand personality that we want to project? Copywriters are reminded that their creative work must reflect the brand's positioning statement. The brand management team must clearly articulate the brand's meaning and personality, or what it is to stand for in the audience's collective mind. Also, the creative brief might suggest to the advertising agency a slogan the client wants to use for the brand or request ideas from the agency for alternative slogans that might be used. The *IMC Focus* presents a number of well-known ad slogans and also provides information about consumers' ability to identify brand slogans correctly.

Primary Outcome or "Take Away"

What is the single most important thing that we want our target audience to take away from our advertising? Beyond thoughts and feelings, this guideline focuses on the "take away," "net impression," or "generics" (i.e., major selling claim) that you want the target audience to recognize or recall. Thus, measurement via copy tests on these factors is important in gauging the success of this guideline.

What do we want the target audience to do? This guideline may focus on the specific *outcome(s)* that the advertising campaign is designed to achieve in the target audience. For example, the advertising might be intended to get prospects to request further information, to go online to participate in a sweepstake or contest, to contact a salesperson, or to go to a retail outlet within the next week to take advantage of a limited-time sales opportunity.

Other Details and Mandatories

Some agencies also include specifics in the brief about the exact message, media, deadlines, and budget for the campaign. There usually are mandatories listed, such as the brand website, brand logo, social media sites (e.g., Facebook, Twitter), QR codes, and/or toll-free or local contact numbers.

How Well Do You Know Advertising Slogans?

Slogans, or taglines, have always played an important role in advertising. Effective slogans encapsulate a brand's key positioning and value proposition and provide consumers with a memory tag for distinguishing one brand from another. Some slogans have been used with success for decades, as evidenced in the following list (A) of what some would regard as the top slogans of modern marketing. See if you can match the slogan with its company. (Answers are provided on the next page.)

These famous slogans aside, it appears that current advertising slogans may be less effective, certainly less memorable, than are these famous slogans. A survey of 500 people determined that only 5 percent could correctly identify even half of the slogans in use by 29 advertisers. Only 3 of 29 slogans were correctly identified by more than 50 percent of the surveyed respondents. The following table (B) presents the slogans, the companies or brands using the slogans, and the percentages of correct identification.

(A)

Slogan		Company	
1. "A diamond is forever."	6. "Good to the last drop."	A. Maxwell House (1915)*	F. Morton Salt (1911)
2. "Just do it."	7. "Breakfast of Champions."	B. Wheaties (1935)	G. Clairol (1964)
3. "The pause that refreshes."	8. "Does she … or doesn't she?"	C. Wendy's (1984)	H. Coca-Cola (1929)
4. "Tastes great, less filling."	9. "When it rains it pours."	D. De Beers (1950)	I. Avis (1962)
5. "We try harder."	10. "Where's the beef?"	E. Miller Lite (1974)	J. Nike (1988)

*Slogan's date of inception

(B)

Company or Brand	Slogan	Percentage Correct Identification	Company or Brand	Slogan	Percentage Correct Identification
Allstate	"You're in good hands."	87%	Coca-Cola	"Real."	5%
State Farm	"Like a good neighbor."	70	Dr Pepper	"Be you."	5
Walmart	"Always low prices. Always."	67	General Electric	"Imagination at work."	5
General Electric	"We bring good things to life."	39	Heineken	"It's all about the beer."	4
Sprite	"Obey your thirst."	35	Michelob Ultra	"Lose the carbs. Not the taste."	4
Taco Bell	"Think outside the bun."	34	Sears	"Good life. Great price."	4
McDonald's	"I'm loving it."	33	Chrysler	"Inspiration comes standard."	3
Capital One	"What's in your wallet?"	27	Corona	"Miles away from ordinary."	3

Company or Brand	Slogan	Percentage Correct Identification	Company or Brand	Slogan	Percentage Correct Identification
Gatorade	"Is it in you?"	19	Arby's	"What are you eating today?"	2
Chevrolet	"An American revolution."	17	Miller	"Good call."	1
J.C. Penney	"It's all inside."	15	Buick	"The spirit of American style."	1
Nissan	"Shift."	12	Kmart	"Right here, right now."	1
Toyota	"Get the feeling."	11	Staples	"That was easy."	0
Budweiser	"True."	10	Wendy's	"It's better here."	0
Sierra Mist	"Yeah, it's kinda like that."	6			

Sources: The table of matching slogans is from Deborah L. Vence, "The Test of Time," *Marketing News*, December 15, 2004, 8–9. The table with 29 brand slogans is from Becky Ebenkamp, "Slogans' Heroes, Zeroes," *Brandweek*, October 25, 2004, 17. See also, "Can You Name the Slogan That Matches the Brand Logo?" Sporcle.com, http://www.sporcle.com/games/gloucester/match-the-brand-logo-to-slogan- (accessed September 21, 2011).

(A) Answers: 1, D; 2, J; 3, H; 4, E; 5, I; 6, A; 7, B; 8, G; 9, F; 10, C.

Means-End Chaining and Laddering

The notion of a means-end chain provides a useful framework for understanding the relationship between consumers or customers and advertising messages. A means-end chain represents the linkages among brand *attributes*, the *consequences* obtained from using the brand and "consuming" the attributes, and the *personal values* that the consequences reinforce.[28] These linkages represent a means-end chain because the consumer sees the brand and its attributes, the consumption of which has consequences, as the *means* for achieving a valued end state resulting from these consequences. Schematically, the means-end chain is as follows:

$$[\text{Attributes} \rightarrow \text{Consequences}] \rightarrow \{\text{Values}\}$$
$$[\text{Means}] \qquad \rightarrow \{\text{End}\}$$

Attributes are features or aspects of advertised brands. In the case of automobiles, for example, attributes include price, gas mileage, engine performance, aesthetic features, and so on. Consequences are what consumers hope to receive (*benefits*) or avoid (*detriments*) when consuming brands. Increased status, convenience, performance, safety, and resale value are positive consequences associated with automobiles (benefits), whereas breakdowns, mishandling, and poor resale value are negative consequences that consumers wish to avoid (detriments). In the case of large-screen plasma TVs, screen size and resolution are product attributes leading to consequences such as remarkably clear images vis-a-vis old-fashioned TVs (benefit) but also high energy consumption (detriment) versus TVs based on LED technology (light-emitting diodes).

In sum, the important thing to appreciate is that attributes reside in brands, whereas consumers experience consequences as a result of brand acquisition and usage. Together, brand attributes and the consequences of consuming these attributes are the *means* whereby people achieve valued *ends*.

Values represent those enduring beliefs people hold regarding what is important in life.[29] They pertain to end states that people desire in their lives, they transcend specific situations, and they guide selection or evaluation of behavior.[30]

In general, values determine the relative desirability of consequences and serve to organize the meanings for products and brands in consumers' cognitive structures.[31]

Values represent the starting point, the catalyst, and the source of motivation for many aspects of human behavior. Consumer behavior, like other facets of behavior, involves the pursuit of valued states, or outcomes. Brand attributes and their consequences are not sought per se, but rather are desired as means to achieving valued end states. From the consumer's perspective, the *ends* (values) drive the *means* (attributes and their consequences). Let us now examine more fully the values that energize human behavior.

The Nature of Values

Psychologists have conducted extensive research on values and constructed numerous value typologies. This chapter takes the view that 10 basic values adequately represent the important human values people in a wide variety of culturally diverse countries share. Table 10.1 lists these 10 values.[32] Research identified these values based on studies conducted in 20 culturally diverse countries: Australia, Brazil, Estonia, Finland, Germany, Greece, Holland, Hong Kong, Israel, Italy, Japan, New Zealand, China, Poland, Portugal, Spain, Taiwan, the United States, Venezuela, and Zimbabwe. People in these countries shared the same values, each of which is now briefly described:[33]

1. *Self-direction.* Independent thought and action is the defining goal of this value type. It includes the desire for freedom, independence, choosing one's own goals, and creativity.
2. *Stimulation.* This value derives from the need for variety and achieving an exciting life.
3. *Hedonism.* Enjoying life and receiving pleasure are fundamental to this value type.
4. *Achievement.* Enjoying personal success through demonstrating competence according to social standards is the defining goal of this value type. Being regarded as capable, ambitious, intelligent, and influential are different aspects of the achievement value.
5. *Power.* The power value entails the attainment of social status and prestige along with control or dominance over people and resources (wealth, authority, social power, and recognition).
6. *Security.* The essence of this value type is the longing for safety, harmony, and the stability of society. This value includes concern for personal and family safety and even national security.
7. *Conformity.* Self-discipline, obedience, politeness, and, in general, restraint from actions and impulses that are likely to upset or harm others and violate social norms are at the root of this value type.

TABLE 10.1	Ten Universal Values	
1. Self-direction		6. Security
2. Stimulation		7. Conformity
3. Hedonism		8. Tradition
4. Achievement		9. Benevolence
5. Power		10. Universalism

Source: Reprinted from *Advances in Experimental Social Psychology*, Vol. 25, Shalom H. Schwartz, "Universals in the Content and Structure of Values: Theoretical Advances and Empirical Tests in 20 Countries," 1992, 1–65, with permission from Elsevier.

8. *Tradition.* This value encompasses respect, commitment, and acceptance of the customs that one's culture and religion impose.
9. *Benevolence.* The motivational goal of benevolence is the preservation and enhancement of the welfare of one's family and friends. It includes being honest, loyal, helpful, a true friend, and loving in a mature manner.
10. *Universalism.* Universalism represents individuals' motivation to understand, appreciate, tolerate, and protect the welfare of all people and of nature. It incorporates notions of world peace, social justice, equality, unity with nature, environmental protection, and wisdom.

Which Values Are Most Relevant to Advertising?

The 10 values just presented are apt descriptions of human psychology around the world. It is important to note, however, that they apply to *all* aspects of life and not to consumer behavior per se. Consequently, all 10 values may *not* be equally important to consumers and thus not equally applicable to advertisers in their campaign-development efforts.

If you are like us, you will have concluded that the first six values—self-direction through security—apply to many advertising and consumption situations, whereas the last four are less typical drivers of much consumer behavior. These latter four values certainly are applicable under select advertising situations (e.g., advertising efforts by nonprofit organizations such as churches and charitable organizations) and perhaps even more so in the East than in the West, but they may not typify usual consumer behavior for most products and services. Therefore, self-direction, stimulation, hedonism, achievement, power, and security are the valued end states that drive the bulk of consumer behavior and thus are the objectives to which advertisers might appeal.

Advertising Applications of Means-End Chains: The MECCAS Model

The creation of effective advertisements demands that brand managers possess a clear understanding of what people value from product categories and specific brands. Because consumers differ in what they value from a particular brand, it is meaningful to discuss values only at the *market segment* level. A brand advertiser, armed with knowledge of segment-level values, is in a position to know what brand attributes and consequences to emphasize to a particular market segment as the means by which that brand can help consumers achieve a valued end state. A formal model, called MECCAS—standing for <u>m</u>eans-<u>e</u>nd <u>c</u>onceptualization of <u>c</u>omponents for <u>a</u>dvertising <u>s</u>trategy—provides a procedure for applying the concept of means-end chains to the creation of advertising messages.[34]

Table 10.2 presents and defines the various levels of the MECCAS model. Note that the components include a *value orientation, brand consequences* and *brand attributes*, and a *creative strategy and leverage point* that provide the structure for presenting the advertising message and the means for tapping into or activating the value orientation.[35] The *value orientation* represents the consumer value or end level on which the advertising strategy focuses and can be thought of as the *driving force* behind the advertising execution. Every other component is geared toward achieving the end level, so this should be the starting point in ad strategy.

The following sections apply the MECCAS framework in analyzing five advertisements, one for five of the first six values shown in Table 10.1. It is important to note that these applications are the authors' post hoc interpretations. It is unknown whether the advertisers in these cases actually performed formal means-end analyses in developing their ads. Nonetheless, these analyses will provide an enhanced understanding of how the means-end logic (attributes → consequences → values) can be translated into the design of actual advertisements.

TABLE 10.2	A MECCAS Model Conceptualization of Advertising Strategy	
Component	**Definition**	
Value orientation ↑	The end level (value) to be focused on in the advertising; it serves as the driving force for the advertising execution.	
Brand consequences ↑	The major positive consequences, or benefits of using the brand, that the advertisement verbally or visually communicates to consumers.	
Brand attributes ↑	The brand's specific attributes or features that are communicated as a means of supporting the consequence(s) of using the brand.	
Creative strategy and leverage point	The overall scenario for communicating the value orientation and the manner (leverage point) by which the advertisement will tap into, reach, or activate the key value that serves as the ad's driving force.	

Source: Adapted from Thomas J. Reynolds and Jonathan Gutman, "Advertising Is Image Management," *Journal of Advertising Research* 24 (February/March 1984), 27–36. Reprinted with permission from *Journal of Advertising Research*, © 1984, by the Advertising Research Foundation.

Self-Direction and Rolex Watches

Self-direction includes the desire for freedom, independence, and choosing one's own goals. The value orientation serving as the driving force in the Rolex advertisement (Figure 10.2) is an unadorned appeal to consumers' need to reject conformity (see the ad's headline "Breaking the Rules"), which represents an appeal to those consumers who desire to choose freely and be unconstrained by the dictates of social pressures.

Hedonism and Steak

Fundamental to the hedonism value is enjoying life and receiving pleasure. The ad in Figure 10.3 shows a mouth-watering photo of steak, a product much enjoyed by most nonvegetarians. The catchy head-line—"There's no such thing as a chicken knife"—intimates that only steak, unlike chicken, is worthy of having a utensil named for it. The advertiser, The Beef Checkoff Program, is clearly appealing to people's desire to enjoy one of life's little pleasures.

Achievement and Home Depot

In an appeal to competence and accomplishment—the elements of achievement—the advertisement in Figure 10.4 tells a little story (recall the storytelling component of the SUCCESs framework) based on a typical customer's triumph in remodeling her home. Amy, with the implied assistance of Home Depot's personnel, proved "just how much she really can handle" and overcame others' doubts that remodeling her home "would be too much for a single mom to handle." This Home Depot ad represents an un-mistakable appeal to the value consumers' place on achieving home-improvement goals.

Power and the Hummer Alpha

As a valued end state, power entails the attainment of social status and prestige along with control or domi-nance over people and resources (e.g., authority, social power, and recognition). The ad in Figure 10.5 for the MG ZR refers to this high-performance vehicle as "high in caffeine" and "maximum strength." The

Image courtesy of The Advertising Archives

FIGURE 10.2 MECCAS Illustration for Self-Direction Value

THERE'S NO SUCH THING AS A CHICKEN KNIFE.

FIGURE 10.3 MECCAS Illustration of Hedonism Value

Everyone said it would be too much for a single mom to handle. But Amy bought the old house anyway. Then she went to her Home Depot® and learned how to hang cabinets. She repainted, tore out floors, added on a room, and finished the entire attic. Herself. And she proved just how much she really can handle.

See Amy's story, and others, at homedepot.com/truestories.

You can do it. We can help.™

FIGURE 10.4 MECCAS Illustration for Achievement Value

body visual, which provides the ad's leverage point, suggests that prospective purchasers—skewed males, no doubt—also will have a "high caffeine" or exhilarating experience in driving the MG ZR. The insinuation is that the vehicle is fast and powerful and so is its owner. This ad subtly conveys to potential purchasers of MG ZRs that they also will be perceived as hard charging, tough, rigorous, and powerful individuals, and will attain status and prestige from their acquisition of this vehicle.

Security and Neosporin

Personal and family safety are aspects of the security value pertinent to the ownership and consumption of many products. An advertisement for Neosporin antibiotic ointment uses the storytelling method in its implicit suggestion that even very small cuts and scrapes might lead to serious infection. The story describes Neosporin's attributes and states that it provides better protection against serious infection than other brands. The leverage point for the valued end state of security is apparent in the visual of a healthy child embracing her mother, who declares "I will never leave another cut untreated."

Identifying Means-End Chains: The Method of Laddering

Laddering is a research technique that has been developed to identify linkages between attributes (A), consequences (C), and values (V). The method is termed *laddering* because it leads to the construction of a hierarchy, or ladder, of relations between a brand's attributes and consequences (the means) and consumer values (the end). Laddering involves in-depth, one-on-one interviews that typically last 30 minutes to more than one hour. In contrast to surveys, laddering attempts to get at the root or deep reasons why individual consumers buy certain products and brands.[36]

An interviewer first determines which attributes the interviewee feels are most important in the product category and, from there, attempts to identify the linkages in the interviewee's mind from attributes to consequences and from consequences to abstract values. In conducting a laddering interview, the interviewer refers the interviewee to a specific attribute and then, through directed probes, attempts to detect how the interviewee links that attribute with more abstract consequences and how the consequences are linked with even more abstract values. After linkages for the first attribute are exhausted, the interviewer moves on to the next salient attribute, and then the next, until all important attributes have been explored; this typically ranges from three to seven attributes. Probing is accomplished with questions such as the following:[37]

- Why is that particular attribute important to you?
- How does that help you out?
- What do you get from that?
- Why do you want that?
- What happens to you as a result of that?

Image courtesy of The Advertising Archives

FIGURE **10.5** MECCAS Illustration of Power Value

Let us illustrate the method of laddering with the advertisement for the Home Depot in Figure 10.4. Imagine that an interviewer asks a consumer why it is important to her to perform do-it-yourself household improvements. Her response is, "I don't want to have to depend on anyone." A follow-up probe by the interviewer ("How does that help you out?") results in this consumer claiming that "it is important that I have a nice home, and I can't afford to pay for someone else to repair it." In response to a prompt of "Why is that important to you?" she comments, "I want my parents to be proud of me. I want them to know that I can raise their grandchildren by myself and that I will provide a nice home for them."

We see in this hypothetical description that doing her home improvements is ultimately linked to the achievement value and the resulting satisfaction from having proud parents. The advertisement in Figure 10.4 apparently is based on the view that there is a market segment of consumers like Amy who want to improve their homes and thus realize their ambitions, achieve recognition, and perhaps make others—as well as themselves—proud of their accomplishments.

Practical Issues in Identifying Means-End Chains

In conclusion, the important point to remember about the MECCAS approach is that it provides a systematic procedure for linking the advertiser's perspective (i.e., a brand with attributes that have desirable and undesirable consequences) with the consumer's perspective (the pursuit of products and brands to achieve desired end states, or values). Effective advertising does not focus on product attributes and consequences per se; rather, it is directed at showing how the advertised brand will benefit the consumer and enable him or her to achieve what he or she most desires in life—self-determination, stimulation, hedonism, and the other values listed in Table 10.2. Also, means-end chaining (relying on consumer behavior) via laddering (based on marketing research) and its application in MECCAS (via advertising), offers a valuable inter-disciplinary approach among these related elements in helping to meet consumer needs through advertising.

All said, it is important to note that the means-end approach and the method of laddering are not without critics. The primary criticisms are several: First, some claim that the laddering method "forces" interviewees to identify hierarchies among attributes, consequences, and values that may actually not have existed before the interview and absent the interviewer's directive probes. Second, some suggest that consumers may possess clear-cut linkages between attributes and consequences but not necessarily between consequences and values. Finally, some criticize laddering on grounds that the ultimate hierarchy constructed is a crude aggregation of A → C → V chains from multiple individuals into a single chain that is assumed to represent all consumers in the target audience.[38]

These criticisms are not unfounded, but the reality is that all methods for creative strategy development in advertising have their imperfections. The value of laddering is that it forces advertisers to identify how consumers relate product attributes to more abstract states such as benefits and values. This systematic approach thereby ensures that advertising emphasis will be placed on communicating benefits and implying valued end states rather than focusing on attributes per se. It is likely for some product categories and particular brands that consumers do not possess clear linkages between brand consequences and values. So, although the means-end chain may entail only A → C links rather than the full set of A → C → V links, the systematic laddering procedure serves its purpose by encouraging creative personnel to focus on product benefits rather than attributes.

Alternative Styles of Creative Advertising

By the very nature of advertising and the process that goes into message development, there are innumerable ways to devise creative advertisements.[39] Several relatively distinct creative styles have evolved over the years and represent the bulk of contemporary advertising.[40] Table 10.3 summarizes six styles and groups them into three categories: product category dominance, functionally oriented, and symbolically or experientially oriented.

You may recall the discussion of brand concept management in Chapter 2 in which distinctions were made among functional, symbolic, and experiential needs or benefits. These same distinctions are maintained in the present explanation of different styles of creative advertising. The *category-dominance strategies* (generic and preemptive in Table 10.3) do not necessarily use any particular type of appeal to consumers, but are designed to achieve an advantage over competitors in the same product category. *Functionally oriented* advertising appeals to consumers' needs for tangible, physical, and concrete benefits. *Symbolically or experientially oriented* advertising strategies are directed at psychosocial needs.

Finally, it is important to note that, as is the case with most categorization schemes, the alternative styles covered in the following sections sometimes have fuzzy borders when applied to specific advertising executions. In other words, distinctions are sometimes very subtle rather than perfectly obvious, and a particular advertising execution may simultaneously use multiple creative approaches. For example, a *positioning strategy* might use a combination of the unique selling proposition (USP) (with distinct benefits) to preempt competition, with such depictions labeled in a perceptual brand map.

Generic Creative Style

The generic style or strategy uses a straightforward product claim with no assertion of brand superiority (e.g., "Soup is good food," "Orange juice is not for breakfast anymore."). Thus, an advertiser employs a generic style when making a claim that any company that markets a brand in that product category could make. Again, the advertiser makes *no* attempt to differentiate its brand from competitive offerings or to claim superiority. This strategy is most appropriate for a brand that *dominates a product category*. In such instances, the firm making a generic claim will enjoy a large share of any primary demand stimulated by advertising.

For example, Campbell's dominates the prepared-soup market in the United States, selling nearly two-thirds of all soup. So any generic advertising that increases overall soup sales naturally benefits Campbell's. This strategy explains the "Soup is good food" campaign used by Campbell's in years past. Campbell's followed this campaign with another one that simply declared, "Never underestimate the power of soup." Along similar lines, AT&T's "Reach out and touch someone" campaign, which encouraged more long-distance calling, was a wise strategy in light of this company's one-time grip on the long-distance

TABLE 10.3	Styles of Creative Advertising	
Category-Dominance Orientation	**Functional Orientation**	**Symbolic or Experiential Orientation**
• Generic • Preemptive	• Unique selling proposition (USP)	• Brand image • Resonance • Emotional

© Cengage Learning 2013

telephoning market. (Intense competition weakened that grip, yet interestingly, AT&T's share of the wireless market continues to increase.)

Preemptive Creative Style

The preemptive style, a second category-dominance technique, is employed when an advertiser makes a generic-type claim but does so with an *assertion of superiority*. This approach is most often used by advertisers in product or service categories where there are few, if any, functional differences among competitive brands. Preemptive advertising is a clever strategy when a meaningful superiority claim is made first and therefore precludes competitors from saying the same thing. Any branch of the military service could claim that they enable recruits to "be all you can be," but no other branch could possibly make such a claim after the Army adopted this phrase as its unique statement. In another example, the huge JP Morgan Chase, which was the result of the merger of Chase Manhattan and Chemical Banks, undertook a $45 million advertising campaign shortly after the merger that referred to Chase as "the Relationship Company." In clear recognition of the value of preemption, the chief marketing officer for Chase justified the campaign by stating, "the idea is to stamp that word [*relationship*] on our brand enough to preempt the use of it by anyone else in the category."[41]

In another instance, the maker of Visine eyedrops advertised that this brand "gets the red out." All eyedrops are designed to get the red out, but by making this claim first, Visine made a dramatic statement that the consumer will associate only with Visine. No other company could subsequently make this claim for fear of being labeled a mimic. Another clever preemptive campaign was introduced by Nissan Motor with its clever preemptive claim touting the Maxima as the "four-door sports car." Of course, all sedans have four doors, but Maxima preempted sports car status with this one clever claim. Its sales immediately increased by 43 percent over the previous year despite a price increase.[42]

Unique Selling Proposition Creative Style

With the unique selling proposition (USP) style, an advertiser makes a superiority claim based on a unique product attribute that represents a *meaningful, distinctive consumer benefit*. The main feature of USP advertising is identifying an important difference that makes a brand unique and then developing an advertising claim that competitors either cannot make or have chosen not to make. The translation of the unique product feature into a relevant consumer benefit provides the USP. The USP approach is best suited for a company with a brand that possesses a relatively lasting competitive advantage, such as a maker of a technically complex item or a provider of a sophisticated service.

There are numerous examples of the USP style. The Gillette Sensor razor used a USP when claiming that it is "the only razor that senses and adjusts to the individual needs of your face." NicoDerm CQ's USP was contained in the claim that this product is the only nicotine patch "you can wear for 24 hours." An Allegra advertisement included a USP in its claim that "only Allegra has fexofenadine for effective nondrowsy relief of seasonal allergy symptoms." Prescription drug Flonase used a comparative advertising method (more of which is discussed in Chapter 11) in claiming that only it—but not Zyrtec, Clarinex, Claritin, or Allegra—is "approved [by the Food and Drug Administration] to relieve nasal symptoms caused by indoor allergies, outdoor allergies and nonallergic irritants." Dyson vacuum cleaners were promoted as the only brand "not to lose suction." Wet Ones hands and face wipes promoted their brand as the only wipe that is alcohol and fragrance free.

In many respects the USP style is *the* optimum creative technique, because it gives the consumer a clearly differentiated reason for selecting the advertiser's brand over competitive offerings. If a brand has a truly meaningful advantage over competitive offerings, then advertising should exploit that advantage. The only reason USP advertising is not used more often is that brands in many product categories are pretty much at parity with one another. They have no unique physical advantages to advertise and therefore are forced to use strategies favoring the more symbolic, psychological end of the strategy continuum.

Brand Image Creative Style

Whereas the USP strategy is based on promoting physical and functional differences between the advertiser's brand and competitive offerings, the brand image style, a symbolic or experiential orientation, involves *psychological* rather than physical differentiation. Advertising attempts to develop an image or identity for a brand by associating the brand with *symbols*. In imbuing a brand with an image, advertisers draw meaning from the culturally constituted world (that is, the world of artifacts and symbols) and transfer that meaning to their brands. In effect, the well-known properties of the everyday world come to reside in the unknown properties of the advertised brand.[43]

Developing an image through advertising amounts to creating a *distinct identity* or *personality* for a brand. This image is especially important for brands that compete in product categories in which (arguably) there is little physical differentiation and all brands are relatively similar (bottled water, soft drinks, blue jeans, etc.). Thus, Pepsi at one time was referred to as the soft drink for the "new generation." Mountain Dew has consistently presented itself as a "cool" brand for teens who favor a somewhat alternative lifestyle. Absolut vodka, as previously discussed, has regularly associated itself with positive images that serve to enhance the brand's reputation for hipness.

Brand image advertising is *transformational* (versus informational) in character. That is, transformational advertising associates the experience of using an advertised brand with a unique set of psychological characteristics that typically would *not* be associated with the brand experience to the same degree without exposure to the advertisement. Such advertising is transforming (versus informing) by virtue of endowing brand usage with a particular experience that is different from using any similar brand. As the result of repeated advertising, the brand becomes associated with its advertising and the people, scenes, or events in those advertisements.[44]

Transformational advertisements contain two notable characteristics: (1) they make the experience of using the brand richer, warmer, more exciting, or more enjoyable than what would be the case based solely on an objective description of the brand and (2) they connect the experience of using the brand so tightly with the experience of the advertisement that consumers cannot remember the brand without recalling the advertising experience. E*TRADE and the smart talking baby; Geico and the gecko; Progressive and "Flo"; and Nike with its swoosh, sports celebrities, and cool college football uniforms are examples.

Resonance Creative Style

When used in an advertising context, the term *resonance* is analogous to the physical notion of noise resounding off an object. In a similar fashion, an advertisement resonates (*patterns*) the audience's life experiences. A resonant advertising strategy, one that is symbolic or experiential orientated, extends from psychographic research and structures an advertising campaign to pattern the prevailing lifestyle orientation of the intended market segment.

Resonant advertising does *not* focus on product claims or brand images, but rather seeks to present circumstances or situations that find counterparts in the real or imagined experiences of the target audience. Advertising based on this strategy attempts to match "patterns" in an advertisement with the target audience's stored experiences. For example, Unilever's Dove brand of soap introduced a campaign that associated the brand with "real" women (e.g., Figure 10.6)—that is, actual women rather than models who

Image courtesy of The Advertising Archives

FIGURE 10.6 Illustration of Resonance Creative Strategy

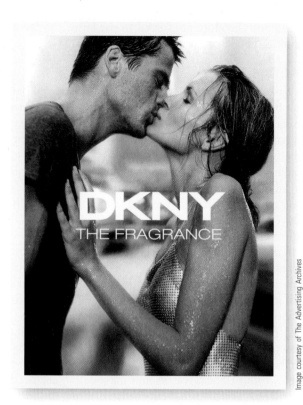

Image courtesy of The Advertising Archives

FIGURE 10.7 Illustration of Emotional Creative Strategy

are depicted in ads without any imperfections. The imperfections of real women resonate with the target audience, which better identifies with a few flaws because it is real and not manufactured.

Emotional Creative Style

Emotional (or affective) advertising is the third form of symbolically or experientially oriented advertising. Much contemporary advertising aims to reach the consumer at a visceral level through the use of emotional strategy. Many advertising practitioners and scholars recognize that products often are bought on the basis of emotional factors and that appeals to emotion can be very successful if used appropriately and with the right brands. The use of emotion in advertising runs the gamut of positive and negative emotions, including appeals to romance, nostalgia, compassion, excitement, joy, fear, guilt, disgust, and regret. Chapter 11 treats several of these emotionally charged appeals in detail.

Although the emotional strategy can be used when advertising virtually any brand, emotional advertising seems to work especially well for product categories that naturally are associated with emotions (foods, jewelry, insurance, cosmetics, fragrances, fashion apparel, etc.). For example, the advertisement for DKNY fragrance (Figure 10.7) is an obvious appeal to romance.

Section Summary

We have discussed six general creative styles and categorized them as category-dominance, functional, or symbolic/experiential oriented. These alternatives help to understand the different approaches available to advertisers and the factors influencing the choice of creative style. However, we should note that because there is some unavoidable overlap, it is possible that an advertiser may consciously or unconsciously use two or more styles simultaneously. For example, a New York agency found that ads containing a combination of functional and psychological appeals outperformed the functional-only ads by a substantial margin.[45]

An important final take away is that the choice of creative strategy for advertising a particular brand is determined by three key considerations: (1) What are the target audience's needs and motivations related to the product category? (2) What are the brand's strengths and weaknesses relative to competitive brands in the category? and (3) How are competitors advertising their brands?

Corporate Image and Corporate Issue Advertising

The type of advertising discussed to this point is commonly referred to as *brand-oriented advertising*. Such advertising focuses on a specific brand and attempts ultimately to influence consumers to purchase the advertiser's brand.

Another form of advertising, termed *corporate advertising*, focuses not on specific brands, but on a corporation's overall image or on economic or social issues relevant to the corporation's interests. This form of advertising is prevalent.[46] Consistent spending on corporate advertising can serve to boost a corporation's equity, much in the same fashion that brand-oriented advertising represents a deposit in the brand equity bank. Two somewhat distinct forms of corporate advertising are discussed in the following sections: (1) image advertising and (2) issue, or advocacy, advertising.[47]

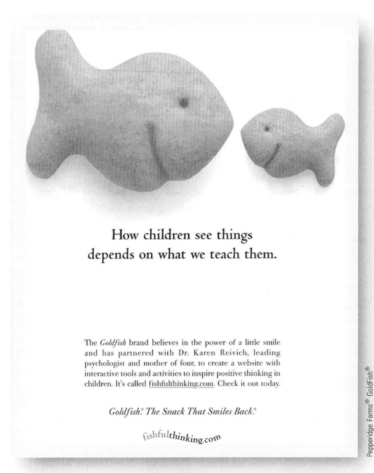

How children see things
depends on what we teach them.

The *Goldfish* brand believes in the power of a little smile
and has partnered with Dr. Karen Reivich, leading
psychologist and mother of four, to create a website with
interactive tools and activities to inspire positive thinking in
children. It's called fishfulthinking.com. Check it out today.

Goldfish. *The Snack That Smiles Back.*

fishfulthinking.com

Pepperidge Farms® Goldfish®

FIGURE **10.8** Illustration of Corporate Image Advertising

Corporate Image Advertising

Corporate image advertising attempts to (1) increase a firm's name recognition, (2) establish goodwill for the company and its products, or (3) identify itself with some meaningful and socially acceptable activity. This type of corporate advertising is concerned with creating favorable images among audiences such as consumers, stockholders, employees, suppliers, and potential investors. Such advertising asks for no specific action from the target audience(s) other than a favorable attitude toward the corporation and passive approval for the company's activities.[48] For example, a General Motors advertisement for hybrid-powered buses did not promote any specific General Motors vehicle but rather, like other corporate image advertisements, attempted to enhance the company's image by associating it with fuel efficiency and conservation. The ad in Figure 10.8 reflects another illustration of corporate social responsibility advertising. In this example, the Goldfish® brand has developed a program called Fishful Thinking™ to help moms inspire optimism and positive thinking in children. By aligning with a higher order purpose, the Goldfish® brand is positioning itself well to deepen its relationship with consumers.

In general, research has found that executives regard name identity and image building to be the two most important functions of corporate advertising.[49] Corporate image advertising is directed at more than merely trying to make consumers feel good about a company. Companies are increasingly using the image of their firms to enhance sales and financial performance.[50] Research has shown that a positive corporate image can favorably affect consumers' product evaluations, especially when the purchase decision is risky.[51] Corporate advertising that does not contribute to increased sales and profits is difficult to justify in today's climate of accountability.

Corporate Issue (Advocacy) Advertising

The other form of corporate advertising is issue, or advocacy, advertising. When using issue advertising, a company takes a position on a *controversial social issue of public importance* with the intention of swaying public opinion.[52] It does so in a manner that supports the company's position and best interests while expressly or implicitly challenging the opponent's position and denying the accuracy of their facts.[53] Imagine, for example, a major petroleum company undertaking an advertising campaign that challenges the economic prudence and energy efficiency of the fledgling corn-based ethanol industry. Such advocacy would serve the corporation's purposes if it convinced the voting populace and their representatives that special funding to prop up the ethanol industry is unjustified.

Issue advertising is a topic of considerable controversy.[54] Business executives are divided on whether this form of advertising represents an effective allocation of corporate resources. Critics question the legitimacy of issue advertising and challenge its status as a tax-deductible expenditure. Because further discussion of these points is beyond the scope of this chapter, the interested reader is encouraged to review the sources contained in the last endnote.[55]

Summary

This chapter examined creative advertising and presented a number of illustrations of creative advertising campaigns. An important initial question asked, what are the general characteristics of effective advertising? Discussion pointed out that effective advertising must (1) extend from sound marketing strategy, (2) take the consumer's view, (3) break through the competitive clutter, (4) never promise more than can be delivered, and (5) prevent the creative idea from overwhelming the strategy. Some qualities of successful advertising included newsworthiness, appeals to the rational stimulus ("reason why"), and emphasis of a single theme. A following section described three characteristics that advertisements must satisfy to be considered truly creative (connectedness, appropriateness, and novelty). This was followed by a discussion of the elements that advertisements must manifest in order to achieve "stickiness," that is, the ability to have lasting impact on consumers. These characteristics are simplicity, unexpectedness, concreteness, credibility, emotionality, and storytelling. The successive levels of ad impressions (brand name, "generics," feelings, commercial specifics, and specific sales message) were then presented. Next, the steps in advertising strategy and creative brief elements were discussed.

The chapter then turned to the concept of means-end chains and the MECCAS framework (means-end conceptualization of components for advertising strategy) that can be used in developing advertising and campaigns. Means-end chains and MECCAS models provide bridges between product attributes and the consequences to the consumer of realizing product attributes (the means) and the ability of these consequences to satisfy consumption-related values (the end). MECCAS models provide an organizing framework for developing creative ads that simultaneously consider attributes, consequences, and values.

The next major subject covered in this chapter was the alternative forms of creative advertising that are in wide use. Six specific creative styles—generic, preemptive, unique selling proposition, brand image, resonance, and emotional—were described and examples given.

The final subject discussed was corporate advertising. A distinction was made between conventional brand-oriented strategy and advertising that focuses on facilitating corporate goodwill, enhancing a corporation's overall image, and advocating matters of economic or social significance that are relevant to a corporation. Two forms of corporate advertising, image and issue (advocacy) advertising, were described.

Discussion Questions

1. The *Marcom Insight* described the famous Macintosh Computer advertisement and characterized it as perhaps the single greatest commercial in advertising history. Without using any of the examples presented in this chapter, identify several commercials that you regard as truly "great" advertising. Be sure to explain why you consider these commercials great.

2. Early in the chapter when discussing how effective advertising must take the consumer's view, the following quotation was presented: "Consumers don't want to be bombarded with ads—they want to be inspired by ideas that will change their lives. Ads create transactions. Ideas create transformations. Ads reflect our culture, ideas imagine our future." What, in your opinion, does this quote mean?

3. When discussing the concept of advertising novelty, the chapter stated that novelty is a necessary, but insufficient condition for advertising creativity. Explain what this means.

4. In context of the section on "sticky" advertisements, provide three examples of advertisers' efforts to concretize their advertisements. Television commercials would be a good source of ideas. Explain the specific elements in your chosen commercials that illustrate concreteness.

5. Analyze three magazine advertisements in terms of which of the SUCCESs elements each ad satisfies.

6. In your view, which of the SUCCESs elements are most important? Offer an explanation and then rank the six elements from most to least important in terms of their ability to achieve message stickiness.

7. When discussing the creative advertising style known as unique selling proposition, or USP, it has been claimed that in many respects the USP style is *the* optimum creative technique. Explain whether you agree or disagree with this assertion.

8. Several examples of brand image advertisements were offered in the chapter. Identify two additional examples of advertisements that appear to be using the brand image, or transformational, creative style.

9. One requirement for effective advertising is the ability to break through competitive clutter. Explain what this means, and provide several examples of advertising methods that successfully accomplish this.

10. Select a magazine or newspaper advertisement and apply the MECCAS model to interpret the ad. Describe what you consider to be the ad's value orientation, its leverage point, and so on.

11. Explain the differences between the USP and brand image creative styles, and indicate the specific conditions under which each is more likely to be used. Provide one illustration of each creative style, using examples other than those used in the text.

12. Select two advertising campaigns that have been on television for some time. Describe in detail what you think their creative message styles are.

13. Using the laddering procedure that was described in the chapter, select a product category of your choice, interview one individual, and construct that person's hierarchical map, or ladder, for *two* product attributes that are important to that person. Use the types of probing questions listed in the chapter to see how this individual mentally connects the product attributes with consequences, and how, in turn, these consequences extend into valued end states. Be persistent!

14. Some critics contend that advocacy, or issue, advertising should not be treated as a legitimate tax-deductible expenditure. Present and justify your opinion on this matter.

End Notes

1. The following points are a mixture of the authors' views and perspectives presented by A. Jerome Jewler, *Creative Strategy in Advertising*, Belmont, CA: Wadsworth, 1985, 7–8; and Don E. Schultz and Stanley I. Tannenbaum, *Essentials of Advertising Strategy*, Lincolnwood, IL: NTC Business Books, 1988, 9–10.

2. Joey Reiman, "Selling an Idea for $1 Million," *Advertising Age*, July 5, 2004, 15.

3. Stan Freberg, "Irtnog Revisited," *Advertising Age*, August 1, 1988, 32.

4. Herbert E. Krugman, "What Makes Advertising Effective?" *Harvard Business Review* 53 (March–April 1975), 96–103.

5. "The Top 10 Viral Video Ads Chart," *Visible Measures*, http://visiblemeasures.com/adage (accessed September 27, 2011).

6. Lou Centlivre, "A Peek At the Creative of the '90s," *Advertising Age*, January 18, 1988, 62.

7. For interesting discussion on creativity and the creative process in advertising, review the following sources: Jaafar El-Murad and Douglas C. West, "The Definition and Measurement of Creativity: What Do We Know?" *Journal of Advertising Research* 44 (June 2004), 188–201; Vincent J. Blasko and Michael P. Mokwa, "Paradox, Advertising and the Creative Process," in *Current Issues and Research in Advertising*, ed. J. H. Leigh and C. R. Martin, Jr. (Ann Arbor: Graduate School of Business Administration, University of Michigan, 1989), 351–66; and Jaco Goldenberg, David Mazursky, and Sorin Solomon, "Creative Sparks," *Science* 285 (September 1999), 1495–96. These three elements represent the author's perspective along with a blending of research evidence from these sources: Scott Koslow, Sheila L. Sasser, and Edward A. Riordan, "What Is Creative to Whom and Why? Perceptions in Advertising Agencies," *Journal of Advertising Research* 43 (March 2003), 96–110; and Swee Hoon Ang, Yih Hwai Lee, and Siew Meng Leong, *Journal of the Academy of Marketing Science* 35 (June 2007), 220–32.

8. Lou Centlivre, "A Peek at the Creative of the '90s," *Advertising Age*, January 18, 1988, 62.

9. Chip Heath and Dan Heath, *Made to Stick*, New York: Random House, 2007.

10. The following discussion of all six features is adapted from Heath and Heath, *Made to Stick*.

11. This description is based on ibid., p. 218 ff.

12. This acronym is not original to this text but rather is attributable to ibid.

13. Based on an interview by Paula Champa in "The Moment of Creation," *Agency*, May/June 1991, 32.

14. For additional reading on this famous advertisement, see Twitchell, *20 Ads That Shook the World*, 118–25.

15. Linda Kaplan Thaler and Robin Koval, *Bang! Getting Your Message Heard in a Noisy World*, New York: Currency Doubleday, 2003, 24.

16. Lisa Sanders, "AFLAC CMO Says: Shut the Duck Up," *Advertising Age*, February 19, 2007, 1, 63.

17. Some of the ideas for this description are inspired by the eloquent comments of Bob Garfield in his review of the Nike commercials, *Advertising Age*, April 5, 2004, 37.

18. Dave Vadehra, "Making a Lasting Impression: What Viewers Remember Leads to 'Outstanding' Commercials," *Advertising Age*, April 25, 1983, M-4, M-38; see also Demetrios Vakratsas and Tim Ambler, "How Advertising Works: What Do We Really Know?" *Journal of Marketing* 63 (January 1999), 26–43.

19. See David A. Aaker, Douglas M. Stayman, and Richard Vezina, "Identifying Feelings Elicited by Advertising," *Psychology & Marketing* 5 (Spring 1988), 1–16.

20. A marketing plan is the written document that summarizes what the firm has learned about the marketplace, and how it plans to reach its marketing objectives, programs, budgets, and controls. It serves to direct and coordinate the marketing efforts for the firm. See Philip Kotler and Kevin Lane Keller, *Marketing Management*, 14th ed., Boston, MA: Prentice-Hall, 2012, 54.

21. Adapted from Don E. Schultz, Dennis Martin, and William P. Brown, *Strategic Advertising Campaigns*, Lincolnwood, IL: NTC Business Books, 1987, 240–45.

22. E*TRADE Financial (ETFCD), http://www.wikinvest.com/stock/E*TRADE_Financial_(ETFCD) (accessed September 27, 2011).

23. Ibid.

24. Ibid.

25. Ibid.

26. Adapted from the Fitzgerald & Co. Agency (Atlanta, GA) and Ogilvy Worldwide (New York, NY).

27. Don E. Schultz brought this idea to the author's attention in "Determine Outcomes First to Measure Efforts," *Marketing News*, September 1, 2003, 7.

28. See Thomas J. Reynolds and Jerry C. Olson, *Understanding Decision Making: The Means-End Approach to Marketing and Advertising Strategy,* Mahwah, NJ: Erlbaum, 2001. See also Jonathan Gutman, "A Means-End Chain Model Based on Consumer Categorization Processes," *Journal of Marketing* 46 (spring 1982), 60–72; Thomas J. Reynolds and Jonathan Gutman, "Advertising Is Image Management," *Journal of Advertising Research* 24 (February/March 1984), 27–36; Thomas J. Reynolds and Jonathan Gutman, "Laddering Theory, Method, Analysis, and Interpretation," *Journal of Advertising Research* 28 (February/March 1988), 11–31; and Thomas J. Reynolds and Alyce Byrd Craddock, "The Application of MECCAS Model to the Development and Assessment of Advertising Strategy: A Case Study," *Journal of Advertising Research* 28 (April/May 1988), 43–59.

29. For further discussion of cultural values, see Lynn R. Kahle, Basil Poulos, and Ajay Sukhdial, "Changes in Social Values in the United States during the Past Decade," *Journal of Advertising Research* 28 (February/March 1988), 35–41; Sharon E. Beatty, Lynn R. Kahle, Pamela Homer, and Shekhar Misra, "Alternative Measurement Approaches to Consumer Values: The List of Values and the Rokeach Value Survey," *Psychology and Marketing* 2, no. 3 (1985), 181–200; Wagner A. Kamakura and Jose Afonso Mazzon, "Value Segmentation: A Model for the Measurement of Values and Value Systems," *Journal of Consumer Research* 18 (September 1991), 208–18; and Wagner A. Kamakura and Thomas P. Novak, "Value-System Segmentation: Exploring the Meaning of LOV," *Journal of Consumer Research* 19 (June 1992), 119–32.

30. Shalom H. Schwartz, "Universals in the Content and Structure of Values: Theoretical Advances and Empirical Tests in 20 Countries," *Advances in Experimental Social Psychology* 25 (1992), 4.

31. J. Paul Peter and Jerry C. Olson, *Consumer Behavior: Marketing Strategy Perspectives*, Homewood, Ill: Irwin, 1990.

32. Schwartz, "Universals in the Content and Structure of Values." Another value typology that has been validated across 30 countries is available in Simeon Chow and Sarit Amir, "The Universality of Values:

Implications for Global Advertising Strategy," *Journal of Advertising Research* 46 (September 2006), 301–14.

33. These descriptions are based on ibid., 5–12.

34. Jerry Olson and Thomas J. Reynolds, "Understanding Consumers' Cognitive Structures: Implications for Advertising Strategy," in *Advertising and Consumer Psychology*, ed. L. Percy and A. Woodside, Lexington, MA: Lexington Books, 1983, 77–90.

35. The language used in Table 10.3 is adapted from that employed in the various writings of Gutman, Reynolds, and Olson such as those cited in endnote 32. It is the authors' opinion that the present terminology is more user friendly without doing a disservice to the original MECCAS conceptualization.

36. Brian Wansink, "Using Laddering to Understand and Leverage a Brand's Equity," *Qualitative Market Research: An International Journal* 6(2), 111–18.

37. Thomas J. Reynolds, Clay Dethloff, and Steven J. Westberg, "Advancements in Laddering," in Thomas J. Reynolds and Jerry C. Olson, *Understanding Decision Making*, 91–118.

38. See John R. Rossiter and Larry Percy, "The a-b-e Model of Benefit Focus in Advertising," in Thomas J. Reynolds and Jerry C. Olson, *Understanding Decision Making*, 183–213; and Joel B. Cohen and Luk Warlop, "A Motivational Perspective on Means-End Chains," in Thomas J. Reynolds and Jerry C. Olson, *Understanding Decision Making*, 389–412.

39. A good review of the literature along with the presentation of an insightful message strategy model are provided by Ronald E. Taylor, "A Six-Segment Message Strategy Wheel," *Journal of Advertising Research* 39 (November/December 1999), 7–17.

40. The following discussion represents an adaptation of Charles F. Frazer, "Creative Strategy: A Management Perspective," *Journal of Advertising* 12, no. 4 (1983), 36–41. For other perspectives on creative strategies, see Henry A. Laskey, Ellen Day, and Melvin R. Crask, "Typology of Main Message Strategies for Television Commercials," *Journal of Advertising* 18(1), 1989, 36–41; and Taylor, "A Six-Segment Message Strategy Wheel."

41. Terry Lefton, "Cutting to the Chase," *Brandweek*, April 7, 1997, 47.

42. This description is based on "Four-Door Sports Car," *1990 Winners of the Effie Gold Awards: Case Studies in Advertising Effectiveness,* New York: American Marketing Association of New York and the American Association of Advertising Agencies, 1991, 124–31.

43. Grant McCracken, "Culture and Consumption: A Theoretical Account of the Structure and Movement of the Cultural Meaning of Consumer Goods," *Journal of Consumer Research* 13 (June 1986), 74.

44. Christopher P. Puto and William D. Wells, "Informational and Transformational Advertising: The

Differential Effects of Time," in *Advances in Consumer Research*, vol. 11, ed. Thomas C. Kinnear, Provo, Utah: Association for Consumer Research, 1984, 638–43. See also David A. Aaker and Douglas M. Stayman, "Implementing the Concept of Transformational Advertising," *Psychology & Marketing* 9 (May/June 1992), 237–53.

45. Kim Foltz, "Psychological Appeal in TV Ads Found Effective," *Adweek*, August 31, 1987, 38. Note that this research referred to rational rather than functional appeals, but rational is essentially equivalent to functional.

46. David W. Schumann, Jan M. Hathcote, and Susan West, "Corporate Advertising in America: A Review of Published Studies on Use, Measurement, and Effectiveness," *Journal of Advertising* 20 (September 1991), 35–56. This article provides a thorough review of corporate advertising and is must reading for anyone interested in the topic. For evidence of the increase in corporate advertising, see Mercedes M. Cardona, "Corporate-Ad Budgets at Record High: ANA Survey," *Advertising Age*, April 27, 1998, 36.

47. This distinction is based on a classification by S. Prakash Sethi, "Institutional/Image Advertising and Idea/Issue Advertising as Marketing Tools: Some Public Policy Issues," *Journal of Marketing* 43 (January 1979), 68–78. Sethi actually labels the two subsets of corporate advertising as "institutional/image" and "idea/issue." For reading ease, they are shortened here to image versus issue advertising.

48. Ibid.

49. Charles H. Patti and John P. McDonald, "Corporate Advertising: Process, Practices, and Perspectives (1970-1989)," *Journal of Advertising* 14(1) (1985), 42–49.

50. Lewis C. Winters, "Does It Pay to Advertise to Hostile Audiences with Corporate Advertising?" *Journal of Advertising Research* 28 (June/July 1988), 11–18.

51. Zeynep Gürhan-Canli and Rajeev Batra, "When Corporate Image Affects Product Evaluations: The Moderation Role of Perceived Risk," *Journal of Marketing Research* 41 (May 2004), 197–205.

52. Bob D. Cutler and Darrel D. Muehling, "Advocacy Advertising and the Boundaries of Commercial Speech," *Journal of Advertising* 18(3) (1989), 40.

53. Sethi, "Institutional/image Advertising," 70.

54. For discussion of the First Amendment issues surrounding the use of advocacy advertising, see Cutler and Muehling, "Advocacy Advertising and the Boundaries of Commercial Speech"; and Kent R. Middleton, "Advocacy Advertising, The First Amendment and Competitive Advantage: A Comment on Cutler & Muehling," *Journal of Advertising* 20 (June 1991), 77–81.

55. Louis Banks, "Taking on the Hostile Media," *Harvard Business Review* (March/April 1978), 123–130; Barbara J. Coe, "The Effectiveness Challenge in Issue Advertising Campaigns," *Journal of Advertising* 12(4), (1983), 27–35; David Kelley, "Critical Issues for Issue Ads," *Harvard Business Review* (July/August 1982), 80–87; and Ward Welty, "Is Issue Advertising Working?" *Public Relations Journal* (November 1981), 29. For an especially thorough and insightful treatment of issue advertising, particularly with regard to the measurement of effectiveness, see Karen F. A. Fox, "The Measurement of Issue/Advocacy Advertising," in *Current Issues and Research in Advertising*, vol. 9, ed. James H. Leigh and Claude R. Martin, Jr. (Ann Arbor: Division of Research, Graduate School of Business Administration, University of Michigan, 1986), 61–92.

CHAPTER 11

Endorsers and Message Appeals in Advertising

You might recall viewing television advertisements in which Apple's Mac computer was compared with non-Macs, those simply referred to as PCs. In a series of executions for Apple's "Get a Mac" campaign, a relatively hip guy (actor Justin Long, who starred in the movies *Accepted, He's Just Not That into You*, and *Dodgeball*) is shown wearing clothing that could be described as cool office casual and personified the Mac. Comparatively, a nerdish, bumbling character (actor John Hodgman from the *Daily Show*) dressed in more formal business clothing embodied the generic PC. In every execution of this campaign, the cool Mac character put down the nerdish PC person and implied superiority of the Mac computer.

© JM5 WENN Photos/Newscom

This campaign was successful in the United States based on the number of different advertising executions that were run over an extended period. Interestingly, however, Apple had to alter the campaign substantially when introducing it to the Japanese market. First, whereas direct comparisons are commonplace in U.S. advertising, Japanese consumers are put off by the use of a confrontational style of advertising, which is considered to be rude, immodest, and lacking class. Second, in an interesting cultural reversal, the formal clothing style worn by the PC character in the American version of this advertising campaign is evaluated more positively in Japan in comparison to the office-casual clothing worn by the person who personified the Mac computer.

1 Describe the role of endorsers in advertising.

2 Explain the requirements and receiver processing modes for an effective endorser.

3 Appreciate the factors that enter into the endorser-selection decision.

4 Discuss the role of Q Scores in selecting celebrity endorsers.

5 Describe the role of humor in advertising.

6 Explain the logic underlying the use of appeals to fear in advertising.

7 Understand the nature of appeals to guilt in advertising.

8 Discuss the role of sex appeals, including the downside of such usage.

9 Explain the meaning of subliminal messages and symbolic embeds.

10 Appreciate the role of music in advertising.

11 Understand the function of comparative advertising and the considerations that influence the use of this form of advertising.

Given these cultural differences between the United States and Japan, advertising for Apple's Mac computer required change before introduction to the Japanese market. For the Japanese versions, friendly banter between the Mac and PC characters replaced the more confrontational form of U.S. advertising. Instead of having the actors wear clothes that cast the PC character as nerdish and the Mac person as office cool, the Japanese version made a more subtle distinction by having the PC personality wear office attire and the Mac individual wear weekend clothing. Mac also gave PC a nickname, *waaku*, which is a good-natured Japanese version of the word "work."[1]

Two of the issues touched on here—the use of humor and the application of comparative advertising—are among the many topics covered in this chapter. As will become evident, these factors can depend on different audience characteristics, such as culture, gender, age, prior beliefs, etc.

Introduction

In most viewing situations, in order to be effective, advertising must break through the clutter and sufficiently motivate the audience to pay attention and engage in higher-order processing of ad messages. Effective advertising, as Chapter 10 notes, is usually creative, and creative ads tend to be connected, appropriate, and novel (the CAN elements).

This chapter presents some of the common approaches used in creating advertising messages. The first major section examines the widespread use of endorsers in advertising. Following sections are devoted to five types of messages that are prevalent in advertising: (1) humor, (2) appeals to fear, (3) appeals to guilt, (4) sex appeals, and (5) subliminal messages. The chapter concludes with reviews of music's role in advertising and the pros and cons of using comparative advertisements.

Where possible, an attempt is made to identify *generalizations* about the creation of effective advertising messages. Generalizations, however, are not the same as scientific laws or principles. Such generalizations (rather than laws or principles) are drawn because it is virtually impossible to identify advertising approaches that are effective across all products, services, and situations. Thus, the effectiveness of any message format depends on conditions such as the nature of the competition, the character of the product, the degree of brand equity and market leadership, the advertising environment, and the extent of consumer involvement. Throughout the text we emphasize the importance of an "it depends" mind-set, and this way of thinking certainly applies to this chapter.

The Role of Celebrity Endorsers in Advertising

Advertised brands frequently receive endorsements from a variety of popular public figures. It has been estimated that approximately one-sixth of ads worldwide feature celebrities.[2] In addition to celebrity endorsements, products receive the explicit or tacit support of noncelebrities, also known as *typical-person endorsers*. The following discussion is limited to celebrity endorsers.

Television stars, movie actors, famous athletes, and even dead personalities are widely used to endorse brands. Advertisers and their agencies are willing to pay huge salaries to celebrities who are liked and respected by target audiences and who will, it is hoped, favorably influence consumers' attitudes

© PETER MUHLY/AFP/Getty Images

and behavior toward the endorsed brands. For the most part, such investments are justified. For example, stock prices have been shown to rise when companies announce celebrity endorsement contracts[3] and to fall when negative publicity reaches the media about a celebrity who endorses one of the company's brands.[4] Although some research shows that celebrity endorsers produce an increase in readership of print ads (i.e., 9.4 percent),[5] other research shows a negative shift on sales for TV ads containing celebrities (i.e., –1.4 percent).[6] The latter negative finding is argued to be driven by the use of celebrities on top of bad creative messages from advertisers and not the fault of celebrities per se.[7] Yet, lists of the

TABLE 11.1	Top Endorsement Incomes of American Athletes, 2011		
Rank	**Athlete**	**Sport**	**Endorsement Earnings**
1	Tiger Woods	Pro golf	$60,000,000
2	Phil Mickelson	Pro golf	$57,000,000
3	LeBron James	NBA basketball	$30,000,000
4	Dale Earnhardt Jr.	NASCAR	$22,000,000
5	Jeff Gordon	NASCAR	$18,000,000
6	Peyton Manning	NFL football	$15,000,000
7 (tie)	Kevin Durant	NBA basketball	$14,000,000
7 (tie)	Kevin Garnett	NBA basketball	$14,000,000
7 (tie)	Dwyane Wade	NBA basketball	$14,000,000
10 (tie)	Dwight Howard	NBA basketball	$12,000,000
10 (tie)	Jimmie Johnson	NASCAR	$12,000,000
12 (tie)	Tom Brady	NFL football	$10,000,000
12 (tie)	Kobe Bryant	NBA basketball	$10,000,000
12 (tie)	Derek Jeter	Major league baseball	$10,000,000
15	Jim Furyk	Pro golf	$9,000,000
16 (tie)	Albert Pujols	Major league baseball	$8,000,000
16 (tie)	Amar'e Stoudemire	NBA basketball	$8,000,000
18 (tie)	Brett Favre	NFL football	$7,000,000
18 (tie)	Eli Manning	NFL football	$7,000,000
20	Carmelo Anthony	NBA basketball	$6,000,000

Source: Adapted from Jonah Freedman, "The 50 Highest-Earning American Athletes," *SI.com*, http://sportsillustrated.cnn.com/specials/fortunate50-2011/index.html (accessed October 21, 2011).

"most negative" or "most annoying" celebrities abound, with some studies showing negative impacts on sales ("sink") to range from −24 percent (Donald Trump) to −30 percent (Tiger Woods) in a given year.[8]

However, top celebrities continue to receive enormous payments for their endorsement services. For example, although his off-course troubles plagued golfer Tiger Woods and reduced his endorsement deals by $40 million from 2007, he still earned $60 million from multiple companies, including Nike and Electronic Arts (EA). To put this amount of money in perspective, a person earning a not-so-paltry annual income of $250,000 would have to work 240 years at that salary to earn as much as Tiger Woods received in a single year from his endorsement activities. Table 11.1 lists the endorsement incomes of America's top endorsement-earning athletes.

Source Attributes and Receiver Processing Modes

Based on extensive research, and as presented by the social psychologist Herbert Kelman, three basic source attributes contribute to a source's (e.g., an endorser's) effectiveness: (1) *credibility*, (2) *attractiveness*, and (3) *power*.[9] Each attribute involves a different mechanism by which the source (e.g., endorser) affects consumer attitudes and behavior. As described in Table 11.2, credibility operates through internalization, attractiveness via identification, and power through compliance.

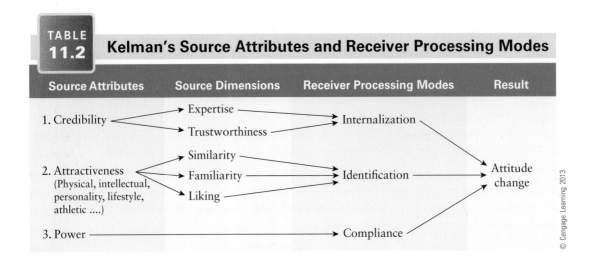

TABLE 11.2 Kelman's Source Attributes and Receiver Processing Modes

Source Attributes	Source Dimensions	Receiver Processing Modes	Result
1. Credibility	Expertise, Trustworthiness	Internalization	Attitude change
2. Attractiveness (Physical, intellectual, personality, lifestyle, athletic ....)	Similarity, Familiarity, Liking	Identification	
3. Power		Compliance	

© Cengage Learning 2013

Credibility: The Process of Internalization

In its most basic sense, *credibility* refers to the tendency to believe or trust someone. When an information source, such as an endorser, is perceived as credible, audience attitudes are changed through a psychological process called *internalization*. (This process resembles the central route to persuasion studied in Chapter 7.) Internalization occurs when the receiver accepts the source's position on an issue as his or her own. An internalized attitude tends to be maintained even if the source of the message is forgotten or if the source switches to a different position.[10]

Two important dimensions of source credibility are expertise and trustworthiness. Expertise refers to the perceived knowledge, experience, or skills possessed by a source as they relate to the communications topic. Expertise is a perceived rather than an absolute phenomenon. Whether a source is indeed an expert is unimportant; all that matters is how the target audience perceives the source. For example, an endorser who is perceived as an expert on a given subject is more persuasive in changing audience opinions pertaining to his or her area of expertise than an endorser who is not perceived as an expert.

Marketing communications use a variety of techniques in attempting to convey source expertise. Salespersons often receive extensive training so that they are very knowledgeable of their company's products. Some social media sites (e.g., LinkedIn) allow for personal recommendations for those seeking employment. Advertisers frequently show products being used in situations that imply that the product is technologically advanced, or has superior quality or performance. Moreover, athletic professionals are often used as brand spokespeople, such as David Beckham, Serena and Venus Williams, Danica Patrick, Dwyane Wade, Kobe Bryant, Derek Jeter, Michael Jordan, and Aaron Rodgers. (Note: The Federal Trade Commission Guidelines for Advertising Endorsers, Testimonials, and Bloggers should be consulted.[11])

Trustworthiness refers to the perceived honesty, integrity, and believability of a source. Although expertise and trustworthiness are not mutually exclusive, often a particular source may be perceived as highly trustworthy, but not especially expert. The degree of honesty or trustworthiness of a source depends primarily on the audience's perception of the source's *intent*. If consumers believe that a source (e.g., an endorser) is motivated purely by self-interest, that source will be less persuasive than someone regarded as having nothing to gain by endorsing the brand.

A celebrity earns the audience's trust through the life he or she lives professionally (on the screen, on the sports field, in public office, etc.) and personally, as revealed to the general public via the mass media. Advertisers capitalize on the value of trustworthiness by selecting endorsers who are widely regarded as being honest, believable, and dependable people.[12] In general, endorsers must establish that they are not attempting to manipulate the audience and that they are objective in their presentations. By doing so, they establish themselves as trustworthy and, therefore, credible. Also, although this represents more of a peripheral effect, an endorser has a greater likelihood of being perceived as trustworthy the more he or she matches the audience in terms of distinct demographic characteristics.[13]

Advertisers have used "candid" interviews in ads with real (i.e., "everyday" or "typical") spokespeople in order to increase trustworthiness. With the use of real or typical spokespeople, the audience is likely to perceive greater objectivity and less self-interest as the advertisers' intent. In fact, advertised products that match the consumers' actual (versus desired or ideal) self tend to have the greatest impact on emotional brand attachment.[14]

Attractiveness: The Process of Identification

Source attractiveness consists of three related dimensions: *similarity*, *familiarity*, and *liking*. That is, a source (e.g., an endorser) is considered attractive to receivers if they share a sense of similarity or familiarity with the source or if they like the source regardless of whether the two are similar in any respect. (For example, we like Dwyane Wade a lot, but we are very different. He is a young, wealthy, and incredibly talented basketball player. We are both over 40, not very wealthy, and have lost whatever little basketball talent we used to have.)

Persuasion occurs through the identification process when receivers find something in the source that they like and consider attractive. This does not mean simply physical attractiveness, but includes any number of virtuous characteristics that consumers may perceive in an endorser: intellectual skills, personality properties, lifestyle characteristics, athletic prowess, and so on. When receivers perceive a source to be attractive, they are very likely to adopt the beliefs, attitudes, behaviors, interests, or preferences of the source. For example, a tagline for a famous Michael Jordan Gatorade commercial, showing kids imitating his moves, said, "I want to be like Mike." That is, when consumers perceive a celebrity endorser to be attractive, they identify with the endorser and are likely to adopt the endorser's attitudes, behaviors, interests, or preferences. Yet, these beliefs and attitudes are not as durable as found under credibility; that is, they are maintained only as long as the endorser maintains the beliefs or attitudes.

Power: The Process of Compliance

According to Kelman, the source attribute of *power* works through the psychological process of *compliance*. Compliance occurs when an individual is persuaded by an advertised source because they hope to achieve a favorable reaction or approval from this source. More specifically, this underlying process works through compliance with the *perceived* rewards and punishments from the source. Although this is not as likely to occur with mass media advertising, such processes may take place through personalized direct advertising materials, personal selling appeals, and/or social media messages. These perceptions are more likely when there is an imbalance of power; for example, when a small supplier wishing to work with a large, "big box" retailer receives personal communication from the retailer.

Practical Issues in Selecting Celebrity Endorsers

Advertising executives use a variety of factors in selecting celebrity endorsers. The following appear to be the most important: (1) celebrity and audience matchup, (2) celebrity and brand matchup, (3) celebrity credibility, (4) celebrity attractiveness, (5) cost considerations, (6) a working ease or difficulty factor, (7) an endorsement saturation factor, and (8) a likelihood-of-getting-into-trouble factor.[15]

Celebrity and Audience Matchup

The first question a brand manager must pose when selecting an endorser is, "Will the target market positively relate to this endorser?" Derrick Rose, LeBron

James, Kevin Durant, Kobe Bryant, Dwyane Wade, and other National Basketball Association (NBA) superstars who endorse basketball shoes match up well with the predominantly teenage audience who aspire to slam dunk, block shots, intercept passes, and sink 25-foot jump shots. Yao Ming (a recently retired NBA basketball player) matches well with the growing number of Chinese youth who also aspire to basketball stardom. And Serena Williams (tennis star and fashion devotee) matches well with young women of all races who admire an athlete who is both highly competent and attractive physically and otherwise.

Celebrity and Brand Matchup

Advertising executives require that the celebrity's behavior, values, appearance, and decorum be compatible with the image desired for the advertised brand. For example, the chief marketing officer at cosmetics firm Elizabeth Arden explained the choice of supermodel and actress Catherine Zeta-Jones in these terms: "Catherine has [a] great career and family, she's a mom, and she has a timeless beauty, which is exactly the image we want to project."[16]

If a brand has a competitive edge image in conveying that it overcomes all obstacles or limitations, then the celebrity endorser should personify this competitive strength. For example, athletic shoemaker Nike signed NBA players LeBron James, Kobe Bryant, Dwyane Wade, Kevin Durant, Carmelo Anthony, and Amar'e Stoudemire to endorse its brand because they all are competitive individuals with unmistakable talent. Comparatively, a brand intentionally casting itself with a "bad boy" image would select entirely different endorsers. Again using current and former NBA stars, Allen Iverson and Vince Carter (and perhaps Dennis Rodman or even Kobe) may fit well with this latter image. Suppose a brand manager wished to enhance a brand's equity by portraying the brand as incomparable in terms of durability, dependability, and consistency. Who better to personify these characteristics than, say, Cal Ripken, the Baltimore Orioles baseball player who played in 2,632 consecutive baseball games prior to retiring. See the *Global Focus* insert for discussion of why China's Li Ning Co., the leading Chinese athletic-shoe brand, chose a relatively unknown NBA player, Damon Jones, to endorse Li Ning shoes.

Celebrity Credibility

A celebrity's credibility is a primary reason for selecting a celebrity endorser. People who are trustworthy and perceived as knowledgeable about the product category are best able to convince others to undertake a particular course of action. This partially explains why most products that had been recommended by Oprah Winfrey obtained success virtually overnight.

Celebrity Attractiveness

In selecting celebrity spokespeople, advertising executives evaluate different aspects that can be lumped together under the general label *attractiveness*. As discussed earlier, attractiveness is multifaceted and includes more than physical attractiveness. It also is important to note that advertising executives generally regard attractiveness as less important than credibility and endorser matchup with the audience and the brand. The ongoing "Milk Mustache" ads for the "Got Milk?" campaign have utilized endorser "attractiveness" for many years.

Cost Considerations

How much it will cost to acquire a celebrity's services is an important consideration but one that should not dictate the final choice. Everything else held constant, a less costly celebrity will be selected over a more costly alternative. Yet, brand managers must attempt to calculate the alternative returns on investment given multiple options of celebrities who would appropriately fit with a brand's desired image and its target market.

GLOBAL FOCUS

Two Unknowns (to most Americans) Connect in China

You possibly have never heard of Li Ning, which is the largest supplier of sports shoes in China. (Readers who are familiar with Li Ning likely gained this familiarity from the company's presence as a sponsor of the 2008 Summer Olympics held in China.) Unless you are a big fan of the National Basketball Association, you may also be unaware of a basketball player named Damon Jones—who, at the time of this writing, was a guard for a professional team in Puerto Rico, but who since 1998 also has played for 10 NBA teams, including the Milwaukee Bucks twice!

Li Ning produces shoes and sportswear mostly for the Chinese market. Its major shoe lines are the Flying Armor series of basketball shoes and Flying Feather running shoes. With sales less than $1 billion, but growing rapidly, Li Ning executives desired to further grow the brand and to offset the rapid gains in China from global brands Nike and Adidas. The company selected an obvious tactic for achieving this goal, namely, using an NBA player at the time—Damon Jones—to endorse the brand. NBA basketball is very popular in China, due in large part to the success of Yao Ming and upstart Chinese players such as Yi Jianlian. In fact, the NBA considers China to be its second-largest market.

Why choose Damon Jones to endorse the Li Ning brand in China? The Li Ning advertising slogan is *yiqie jie you keneng*, which translates as "anything is possible." Damon Jones's career as an NBA player matches well with Li Ning's slogan. Jones was an undrafted player who worked extremely hard first to get into the league and then to stay there. His career demonstrates to young basketball fans that hard work enables unexpected achievement—anything is possible! However, there were other factors in play in the choice of Damon Jones to endorse the Li Ning brand. Perhaps most important, as a relatively small company, Li Ning could not afford that huge cost it would have incurred to pay for an NBA superstar's endorsement. Moreover, Li Ning wanted an endorser who was "hungry" for a shoe contract, who would willingly travel to China with some regularity, would happily meet with Chinese youth and demonstrate his skills while wearing Li Ning shoes and apparel items, would reflect a positive image, and would otherwise interact with the brand without being a "hassle factor." Damon Jones satisfied all criteria, and the relationship between Li Ning and Jones has worked well for both parties.

Sources: Stephanie Kang and Geoffrey A. Fowler, "Li Ning Wanted an NBA Endorser, And Damon Jones Needed a Deal," *Wall Street Journal*, June 24, 2006, Al; "Li Ning Company Limited," http://en.wikipedia.org/wiki/Li-Ning_Company_Limited (accessed January 16, 2008); and Damon Jones, Wikipedia, http://en.wikipedia.org/wiki/Damon_Jones (accessed October 21, 2011).

Working Ease or Difficulty Factor

Some celebrities are relatively easy to work with, whereas others may be difficult—stubborn, noncompliant, arrogant, temperamental, inaccessible, or otherwise unmanageable. Brand managers and their advertising agencies would prefer to avoid the "hassle factor" of dealing with individuals who are unwilling to flex their schedules, hesitant to participate with a brand outside of celebrity-restricted bounds, or otherwise difficult. For example, jeanswear maker Tarrant Apparel Group filed a civil suit against pop singer Jessica Simpson on grounds that she "would not pose for photos nor provide photographs to promote" the line of apparel that carried her name.[17] Although Simpson matched well with the brand and with the brand's target market, it appears that the endorsement relationship failed because she was difficult to work with.

Saturation Factor

Another key consideration, certainly not as important as the previous factors but one that nonetheless has to be evaluated, is the number of other brands the celebrity is endorsing. If a celebrity is overexposed—that is, endorsing too many products—his or her perceived credibility may suffer.[18] Tiger Woods, who may be the most impactful (and controversial) endorser in the history of advertising endorsements, at one time tried to intentionally limit the number of brands he endorsed (e.g., Nike and EA Sports).[19] However, he did approach the "saturation point" with advertising overexposure during a Screen Actors Guild strike a number of years ago.

The Trouble Factor

The potential that a celebrity may get into trouble is a matter of considerable concern to brand managers and ad agencies. Suppose a celebrity is convicted of a crime or has his or her image blemished in some way during the course of an advertising campaign. What are the potential negative implications for the endorsed brand? Frankly, there are no simple answers to this provocative question, although researchers are beginning to explore the issue in a sophisticated fashion.[20]

Many advertisers and advertising agencies are reluctant to use celebrity endorsers. Their concern is not without justification. Consider some of the celebrity-related incidents making news in recent years and during past decades: (1) Pro golfer Tiger Woods, the top athlete endorser of all time ($100 million in 2007), was involved in a very public infidelity scandal in November 2009. He subsequently lost five major endorsers: AT&T, Accenture, Tag Heuer, Gatorade, and Gillette; yet, he retained Nike and Electronic Arts. His per year endorsement revenue plummeted to $60 million in 2011, yet he *still* led all athlete endorsers. (2) Basketball player Kobe Bryant was convicted, although subsequently acquitted, of a rape charge in Colorado. Shortly thereafter, McDonald's Corporation refused to renew Bryant as a spokesperson, as did a much smaller Italian company that makes Nutella chocolate-hazelnut spread. Bryant made a relatively swift comeback with endorsement income of $16 million in 2007 (putting him in sixth place); yet that has recently declined to $10 million (twelfth place in Table 11.1). (3) Swimmer and Olympic gold-medalist Michael Phelps was arrested on a DUI (driving under the influence) charge after returning from the Olympics in Athens. (4) Track star Marion Jones's reputation was tarnished by an investigation and subsequent conviction that she had used performance-enhancing drugs. (5) Record-setting homerun hitter Barry Bonds was accused of using performance-enhancing drugs (as were a number of other Major League Baseball players). (6) Boxer Mike Tyson—an active endorser before a series of mishaps—was convicted on a rape charge and served a prison sentence (not to mention the fact that he bit a chunk out of opponent Evander Holyfield's ear during a match following his prison sentence). (7) Actress Cybill Shepherd had a lucrative endorsement deal with the beef industry, but embarrassed the industry by revealing to the press that she avoided eating beef. (8) Ex-football player and actor O. J. Simpson (a major Hertz endorser) was indicted for, but not convicted of, murder. (9) Britney Spears, Lindsey Lohan, and Paris Hilton have frequently been in the news on charges of alcohol and drug abuse. (10) Professional quarterback Michael Vick was arrested, convicted, and imprisoned for participating in a dog-fighting ring. Although he has been reinstated in the NFL since his release, his endorsement money level has not rebounded from the $7 million he earned in 2007.

Due to the risks of such incidents after the consummation of multimillion-dollar celebrity endorsement contracts, there has been increased scrutiny in selecting celebrity endorsers.[21] An alternative is to use the "endorsements" of celebrities who are no longer living (e.g., Jackie Robinson, Marilyn Monroe). Dead celebrities are well known and respected by consumers in the target audiences to whom they appeal, and their use in advertising is virtually risk free because they cannot engage in behaviors that will sully their reputations and brands they promote. Another risk-free option is the use of *spokescharacters* (the Aflac duck, the Pillsbury Doughboy, Geico's gecko, etc.) in lieu of human endorsers who are susceptible to pratfalls that tarnish images of the brands with which endorsers are associated.[22]

The Role of Q Scores

The selection process of high-priced celebrities is facilitated with Performer Q Scores that are commercially available from a New York–based firm called Marketing Evaluations (www.qscores.com). For reasons that we will discuss shortly, the Q in Q Score signifies quotient.

Marketing Evaluations obtains Q Scores for over 1,800 public figures (entertainers, athletes, and other famous people) by mailing questionnaires to a representative national panel of 1,800 individuals. Participants are asked two straightforward questions for each public figure: (1) Have you heard of this person? (a measure of *familiarity*); and (2) if so, do you rate him or her poor, fair, good, very good, or one of your favorites? (a measure of *popularity*). The calculation of each performer's Q score, or *quotient*, is accomplished by determining the percentage of panel members who respond that a particular performer is "one of my favorites" and then dividing that number by the percentage who indicate that they have heard of that person. In other words, *the popularity percentage is divided by the familiarity percentage, and the quotient is that person's Q Score.* This rating simply reveals the proportion of a group that is familiar with a person and who regard that person as one of their favorites.

For example, assume that a study by Marketing Evaluations determines that 90 percent of panel participants indicate that they are familiar with Britney Spears and that 15 percent consider her a favorite. Hence, Britney's Q Score (which is expressed without a decimal point) is reported as 17 (i.e., 15 divided by 90 is roughly 17). Comparatively, assume in this same survey that Brad Pitt had an extremely high Q Score of 58, which was obtained by dividing the 55 percent of respondents who considered him one of their favorites by the 95 percent who were familiar with him. It comes as little surprise that advertisers have not flocked to Britney to sign her up to endorse their products, whereas many advertisers would select Brad as their brand endorser if he were so inclined.

Q Scores provide useful information to brand managers and advertising agencies, but there is more to selecting a celebrity to endorse a brand than simply scouring through the pages of Q Scores. Subjective judgment ultimately comes into play in determining whether a prospective celebrity endorser matches well with the brand image and its intended target market.

The Role of Humor in Advertising

Politicians, actors and actresses, public speakers, professors, and indeed all of us at one time or another use humor to create a desired reaction. Advertisers also turn to humor in the hopes of achieving various communication objectives—gaining attention, guiding consumer comprehension of product claims, influencing attitudes, enhancing recall, and, ultimately, creating customer action. The use of humor in advertising is extensive, representing approximately 25 percent of all television advertising in the United States and more than 35 percent in the United Kingdom.[23]

A study based on a sampling of television advertisements from four countries (Germany, Korea, Thailand, and the United States) determined that humorous advertisements in all of these countries generally involve the use of *incongruity resolution*.[24] Humor in U.S. magazines and radio advertising also typically employs incongruity resolution.[25] Incongruity exists when the meaning of an ad is not immediately clear. Baffled by the incongruity, the consumer is provoked to understand the ad's meaning and resolve the incongruity. When the meaning is eventually determined—as, for example, when the humor in an ad is detected—a feeling of surprise is experienced, and it is this sensation of surprise that generates a humorous response.[26] In turn, this humorous response can elicit a favorable attitude toward the advertisement and perhaps toward the advertised brand itself.[27]

FIGURE **11.1** The Use of Humor in Advertising

The E*TRADE commercial depicted in Figure 11.1 illustrates the use of humor in television advertising. This commercial, as part of a long-running campaign, uses a smart-talking baby to tell everyone that you need to take control of your finances with the online investment firm E*TRADE. The incongruity is that the baby is dressed in golf attire in the clubhouse telling his golf partner Frank to take control of his finances ("Frank's trying not to pay me my winnings from the skins beat-down I just issued him because his 401k is tanking"). They also argue about the baby moving the ball on the course, but the implied point of the commercial is that investing with E*TRADE to control your finances is so easy a baby could do it.[28]

Whether humor is generally effective and what kinds of humor are most successful are matters of some debate among advertising practitioners and scholars.[29] Advertising agency executives consider humor to be especially effective for purposes of *attracting attention* to an advertisement and *creating brand awareness*.[30] Some evidence indicates that humor serves to influence consumers' attitudes toward advertisements positively, which, in turn, affects their attitudes favorably toward the advertised brands; however, this chain of influence (humor → attitude toward the advertisement → attitude toward the advertised brand) is most likely to occur only when consumers are weakly motivated to process the more substantive message points in the advertisement.[31] Research on the effects of humor leads to the following tentative generalizations (with noted cautions and exceptions below):[32]

- Humor is an effective method for attracting attention to advertisements.
- Humor can elevate consumers' recall of message points in advertisements.[33] (Yet, caution is suggested in situations in which receivers are laughing so hard that message points are forgotten.)
- Humor enhances liking of both the advertisement and the advertised brand.
- Humor does not necessarily harm comprehension and may in fact increase memory for advertising claims if the humor is relevant to the advertised brand.[34] (Yet, it has the same caution to not overrun the ad with humor so that the comprehension is lost.)
- Humor does not offer an advantage over nonhumor at increasing persuasion. (Yet, peripheral route persuasion under low involvement may occur.)
- Humor does not enhance source credibility. (However, as was the case with VW Beetle's famous "Think Small" print ad campaign, making fun of one's own brand may increase trustworthiness, a key dimension of source credibility.)
- The nature of the product affects the appropriateness of using humor. Specifically, humor is used more successfully with established rather than new products. Humor also is more appropriate for products that are more feeling oriented, or experiential, and those that are not very involving (such as inexpensive consumer packaged goods).

When used correctly, *and in the right circumstances* (as noted previously), humor can be an extremely effective advertising technique. A complication of using humor in advertising is that humorous appeals *vary in their effectiveness across demographic groups and even among individuals*. For example, men and women are not equally attentive to humorous ads.[35] In addition to demographic differences, research evidence also shows that humorous ads are more effective than nonhumorous ads *only when consumers' evaluations of the advertised brand are already positive.* When prior evaluations are negative toward the advertised brand, humorous ads have been shown to be less effective than non-humorous ads.[36] This finding has a counterpart in interpersonal relations: When you like someone, you are more likely to consider his or her attempt at humor to be funny than if you do not like that person. Finally, research shows that individuals who have a higher *need for humor* (i.e., the tendency to seek out amusement, wit, and nonsense) are more responsive to humorous ads than are those with a lower need on this personality trait.[37]

In sum, humor in advertising can be an extremely effective device for accomplishing a variety of marketing communications objectives. Nonetheless, advertisers should *proceed cautiously* when contemplating the use of humor. First, the effects of humor can differ due to differences in audience characteristics—what strikes some people as humorous is not at all funny to others.[38] Second, the definition of what is funny in one country or region of a country is not necessarily the same in another. Finally, a humorous message may be so distracting to an audience that receivers ignore the message content. Thus, advertisers should carefully research their intended market segments before venturing into humorous advertising.

Appeals to Consumer Fears

Marketing communicators employ a variety of techniques to enhance consumers' information-processing motivation, opportunity, and ability. As would be expected, the appeal to fear is especially effective as a means of enhancing motivation. The unfortunate fact is that consumers live in a world where the threat of terrorism is ever present, natural disasters occur occasionally such as horrific tsunamis, hurricanes, and tornadoes, and crime and health-related problems abound. It is estimated that nearly 56 million Americans suffer from irrational fears and that anxiety disorders afflict approximately 18.1 percent of adults.[39]

Although there are ethical issues with its use, advertisers (and public health officials) attempt to motivate consumers to process information and to take action by appealing to their fears. Appeals to fears in marcom (e.g., with warnings) tend to identify the negative consequences of either: (1) *not using the advertised brand* or (2) *engaging in unsafe behavior* (such as drinking and driving, smoking, using drugs, eating unhealthy foods, driving without seat belts, text messaging while driving, and engaging in unprotected sex).[40]

Fear Appeal Logic

The underlying logic is that appeals to consumer fears will stimulate audience involvement with a message and thereby promote acceptance of message arguments. The appeal to consumer fears may take the form of *social disapproval* or *physical danger.* For example, mouthwashes, deodorants, toothpastes, and other products appeal to fears when emphasizing the social disapproval we may suffer if our breath is not fresh, our underarms are not dry, our teeth are not perfectly white, and so on. Smoke detectors, automobile tires, unsafe sex, driving under the influence of alcohol and other drugs, and being uninsured are a sampling of products and themes used by advertisers to induce fear of physical danger or impending problems. Health-care ads frequently appeal to fears, and advertising agencies justify the use of these appeals with logic such as, "Sometimes you have to scare people to save their lives."[41]

According to the Protection Motivation Theory,[42] in addition to the *perceived threat* of the fear appeal and its *severity*, it is important to gauge the *perceived response efficacy* of the (marcom) action to reduce the negative behavior (i.e., is it perceived to work by the audience?). Also, the audience's *perceived self-efficacy* in taking the action can be just as essential (i.e., do they perceive that *they* [themselves] have the ability to take the action?). For example, research on the effectiveness of anti-smoking advertising indicates that social disapproval risks of smoking often resonate more strongly with adolescents than do long-term health consequences of smoking.[43]

Appropriate Intensity

Aside from the basic ethical issue of whether fear should be used at all, the fundamental issue for advertisers is determining *how intense* the threat should be. Should the advertiser employ a slight threat merely to get the consumer's attention, or should a heavy threat be used so the consumer cannot possibly miss the point the advertiser wishes to make? Early theoretical work proposed an inverted-U between fear intensity and persuasiveness—predicting the greatest persuasion under moderate threat levels.[44] However, this theory has *not* received consistent support.[45] Rather, considerable evidence suggests a positive linear relationship, with stronger levels of fear-arousing conditions associated with greater message acceptance.[46] In a review (i.e., a meta-analysis) of more than 100 fear appeal articles, it was concluded that "the stronger the fear aroused by a fear appeal, the more persuasive it is."[47]

In general, it appears that the degree of threat intensity that is effective in evoking fear in an audience depends in large part on (1) *how much relevance* a topic has for an audience and (2) whether there is an objective solution (i.e., "a way out") for the fear created. Regarding the first issue, the greater the relevance, the lower the threat intensity that is needed to activate a response. In other words, people who are highly involved in a topic can be motivated by a relatively "light" appeal to fear, whereas a more intense level of threat is required to motivate uninvolved people.[48] In the case of the second point, fear appeals with a clear solution (e.g., an 800 number help line) tend to lead to objective adaptive action taken, whereas increasing fear without a solution tends to lead to maladaptive outcomes (e.g., increase anxiety).[49]

To illustrate the relation between threat intensity and issue relevance, let us compare a low-threat advertising campaign for Michelin tires with the much more intense appeal of advertisements designed to discourage drinking and driving. A low level of threat to evoke fear, with a baby surrounded by tires, is all that is needed to create fear, because safety for their children is the most relevant concern for most parents. Yet, by comparison, more intense appeals to fear are needed to impress on high schoolers the risk in which they place themselves and their friends when drinking/text messaging and driving.[50] Similar results are found with tobacco warnings, as the more graphic the visual depiction on tobacco packages, the greater are smoker intentions to quit.[51]

The Related Case of Appeals to Scarcity

Advertisers and other persuasion agents appeal to scarcity when emphasizing in their messages that things become more desirable when they are in great demand but short supply.[52] Salespeople and advertisers use this tactic when encouraging people to buy immediately with appeals such as "Only a few are left," "We won't have any more in stock by the end of the day," and "They're really selling fast."

The theory of psychological reactance helps explain why scarcity works.[53] This theory suggests that people react against any efforts to reduce their freedom or choices. Removed or threatened choices are perceived as even more desirable than previously. Of course, appeals to scarcity are not always effective. But, if the persuader is credible and legitimate, then an appeal may indeed be effective.

Perhaps nowhere in the world is scarcity more used as an influence tactic than in Singapore. In the Hokkien dialect of Chinese, the word *kiasu* means the "fear of losing out." Singaporeans, according to a lecturer in the philosophy department at National University, will take whatever they can secure, even if they are not sure they really want it.[54] Many Singaporeans apparently share a herd mentality—no one wants to be different. Marketers, needless to say, have exploited this cultural characteristic to sell all types of products. For example, a Singapore automobile dealership announced that it was moving its location and offered for sale 250 limited-edition BMW 316i models, priced at $78,125 for a manual transmission and $83,125 for an automatic. All 250 models were sold within four days, and the dealer was forced to order another 100, which were quickly sold even though delivery was unavailable for months.

Appeals to Consumer Guilt

Like appeals to fear, appeals to guilt attempt to trigger negative emotions. People feel guilty when they break rules, violate their own standards or beliefs, or behave irresponsibly.[55] Advertisers and other marketing communicators appeal to guilt and attempt to persuade prospective customers by asserting or implying that feelings of guilt can be relieved by using the promoted product.[56] An analysis of a broad spectrum of magazines revealed that about 1 of 20 ads contains an appeal to guilt.[57] Consider, for example, a magazine advertisement for Veterinary Pet Insurance, a company that sells insurance for the coverage of unexpected pet accidents or illness. The headline surrounding the photo of a sad-looking dog puts the pet owner on a guilt trip when stating, "[Your pet] will never know you can't afford the treatment. But you will." This advertisement represents an appeal to anticipatory guilt. If the ad works as designed, consumers will purchase pet insurance as a way of allaying guilt feelings.

Evidence, albeit limited, suggests that appeals to guilt are *ineffective* if advertisements containing guilt appeals *lack credibility* or advertisers are perceived as having *manipulative intentions*. When ads are perceived as lacking credibility or attempting to manipulate the receiver, feelings of guilt are mitigated rather than increased.[58]

The Use of Sex in Advertising

Whereas the previous two sets of advertising appeals—to fear and guilt—are fundamentally negative (i.e., people generally avoid these two emotions), the use of sex in advertising appeals to something that people generally approach rather than avoid. Depending on the culture, sex appeals in advertising are used frequently and with increasing explicitness. Whereas the use of such explicit sex was unthinkable not many years ago, it now represents part of the advertising landscape.[59] The trend is not restricted to the United States; indeed, sexual explicitness is more prevalent and more overt elsewhere—for example, in Brazil and certain European countries.

What Role Does Sex Play in Advertising?

Actually, it has several potential roles.[60] First, sexual material in advertising acts to attract and hold attention for a longer period, often by featuring attractive models in provocative poses.[61] This is called the *stopping-power role of sex*. An advertising campaign for Three Olives vodka typifies this role. Each execution in this campaign portrays an attractive, seductively posed female model in a huge martini glass. Placed conspicuously beside the model-filled martini glass is a rhetorical question (rhetorical questions may prompt MOA factors discussed in Chapter 7): "What's in your martini?" There is a clear double entendre in this question, on the one hand suggesting that Three Olives should be the vodka in your glass, and, on the other, intimating that by drinking Three Olives one is likely to attract beautiful women.

A second potential role is to *enhance recall* of message points. Research suggests, however, that sexual content or symbolism will enhance recall *only if it is appropriate to the product category and the creative advertising execution*.[62] Sexual appeals produce significantly better recall when the advertising execution has an appropriate relationship with the advertised product.[63]

A third role performed by sexual content in advertising is to *evoke emotional responses*, such as feelings of arousal and even lust.[64] These reactions can increase an ad's persuasive impact, with the opposite occurring if the ad elicits negative feelings such as disgust, embarrassment, or uneasiness.[65] The advertisement for the Three Olives brand of vodka described previously probably was designed to arouse feelings in the target audience of predominantly young and middle-aged men. The appeal to lust is typified by a Diet Coke television commercial that was aired in the 1990s in which a group of voyeuristic women is shown watching with palpable pleasure from their office building a sexy worker at a nearby construction site taking off his shirt and then opening a Diet Coke.

Sexual content stands little chance of being effective unless it is directly relevant to an advertisement's primary selling point. When used appropriately, and accounting for cultural and demographic differences, however, sexual content may be capable of eliciting attention, enhancing recall, and creating a favorable association with the advertised product.

The Potential Downside of Sex Appeals in Advertising

Evidence suggests that the use of explicit sexual illustrations in advertisements may interfere with consumers' processing of message arguments and reduce message comprehension.[66] Moreover, many people can be offended by advertisements that portray women (and men) as brainless sex objects.

A TV advertisement for Miller Lite beer (dubbed "Catfight") during NFL games several years ago perhaps typifies the questionable use of sexual content in advertising. (This ad is discussed in the *IMC Focus* in Chapter 8.) The ad portrayed two attractive women literally ripping each other's clothes off in a swimming pool and later in wet cement as they supposedly fought over whether Miller Lite beer was "better tasting" or "less filling." The ad certainly raised distinct ethical issues about advertising propriety. In general, the use of sex in advertising is a matter of concern to people and advertising regulators throughout the world.[67] As noted previously, its use can be demeaning and, for this reason, should be used cautiously.

Subliminal Messages and Symbolic Embeds

The word *subliminal* refers to the presentation of stimuli at a speed or visual level that is *below the conscious threshold of awareness*. One example is self-help audiotapes (such as tapes to help one quit smoking) that play messages at a decibel level indecipherable to normal hearing. Stimuli that are imperceptible by the conscious senses may nonetheless be perceived subconsciously. This possibility has generated considerable concern from advertising critics and has fostered much speculation from researchers. Although it is highly unlikely that advertisers use subliminal methods, surveys have shown that a large percentage of Americans believe advertisers do use them.[68] Representatives of the advertising community strongly disavow using subliminal advertising.[69]

The original outcry concerning subliminal advertising occurred over 55 years ago in response to a researcher who claimed to have increased the sales of Coca-Cola and popcorn in a New Jersey movie theater by using subliminal messages. At five-second intervals during the movie *Picnic*, subliminal messages saying "Drink Coca-Cola" and "Eat Popcorn" were said to have appeared on the screen for a mere 1/3,000 second. Although the naked eye could not possibly have seen these messages, the researcher, James Vicary, claimed that sales of Coca-Cola and popcorn increased 58 percent and 18 percent, respectively.[70] Although Vicary's research is not scientifically valid because he failed to use proper experimental procedures, the study nonetheless raised public concerns about subliminal advertising and led to congressional hearings.[71] Federal legislation in the United States was never enacted, but since then subliminal advertising has been the subject of concern by advertising critics, a matter of embarrassment for advertising practitioners, and an issue of curiosity to advertising scholars.[72]

The fires of controversy were fueled again in the 1970s and 1980s with the publication of three provocatively titled books: *Subliminal Seduction, Media*

Sexploitation, and *The Clam Plate Orgy*.[73] The author of these books, Wilson Key, claimed subliminal advertising techniques are used extensively and have the power to influence consumers' choice behaviors.

Why It Is Unlikely That Subliminal Advertising Works

Many advertising practitioners and marcom scholars discount Key's arguments and vehemently disagree with his conclusions. Part of the difficulty in arriving at clear answers as to who's right and who's wrong comes from the fact that commentators differ in what they mean by subliminal advertising. In fact, there are three distinct forms of subliminal stimulation. A first form presents *visual stimuli* at a very rapid rate by means of a device called a *tachistoscope* (say, at 1/3,000 second as in Vicary's research). A second form uses *accelerated speech in auditory messages*. The third form involves *embedding hidden symbols* (such as sexual images or words) in print advertisements.[74]

Is there evidence to support subliminal advertising (especially embedding)? Despite a few limited studies on the issue, a variety of practical problems prevent embedding from being effective in a realistic marketing context.[75] Perhaps the major reason why embedding in advertising has little effect is because the images have to be concealed to preclude consumers' detection. Because the majority of consumers devote little time and effort in processing advertisements, a weak stimulus means that most consumers would not be influenced much.[76]

Even if consumers do attend to and encode embeds under natural advertising conditions, there remains serious doubt that this information would have sufficient impact to affect brand choice behavior. Standard (supraliminal) advertising information itself has difficulty influencing consumers. How could subliminal information possibly be any more effective?

The following quote sums up the research evidence on subliminal advertising. Please note that the quote acknowledges that *subliminal perception* is a bona fide phenomenon (i.e., research has demonstrated that people *are* capable of perceiving stimuli in the absence of conscious awareness of those stimuli), but the weak effects of subliminal stimuli are nullified under actual market circumstances where many brands compete for the consumer's attention at the point of purchase.

> *A century of psychological research substantiates the general principle that more intense stimuli have a greater influence on people's behavior than weaker ones. While subliminal perception is a bona fide phenomenon, the effects obtained are subtle and obtaining them typically requires a carefully structured context. Subliminal stimuli are usually so weak that the recipient is not just unaware of the stimulus but is also oblivious to the fact that he/she is being stimulated. As a result, the potential effects of subliminal stimuli are easily nullified by other ongoing stimulation in the same sensory channel or by attention being focused on another modality. These factors pose serious difficulties for any possible marketing application.*[77]

From Timothy E. Moore, "Subliminal Advertising: What You See Is What You Get," 46 (2) pp. 38–47. *Journal of Marketing*, 1982.

A Unique Situation Where Subliminal Stimuli May Influence Brand Choice

Much human behavior is *not* under conscious control, but rather, occurs virtually *automatically* (i.e., without cognitive intervention). Capitalizing on this aspect of human psychology, communicators may be able to employ a technique called *subliminal priming* to affect consumers' brand choices. In brief, subliminal priming involves presenting people with single words or images at a speed that is below the conscious threshold. These words/images can activate, or prime, people's knowledge, beliefs, stereotypes, or other cognitions.

These cognitions, in turn, are capable of influencing individuals' behavior under the right conditions. In particular, for subliminal priming to be effective, the primed topic must be compatible with the individual's current need states, motivations, or goals. In other words, one cannot be subliminally induced to act in a certain way unless he or she has a need to act in that way.[78] For example, individuals who are primed with words such as *generous*, *help*, and *give*—all relating to generosity—will not automatically contribute money to a charitable cause unless they have an inherent desire to help others. (That is, are they in the "market to act"?) Moreover, a primed need does not remain an active driver of judgments and behavior over the long run, but is limited in its length of influence. Thus, point-of-purchase advertising (e.g., in-store radio programming) may provide an opportune (and perhaps unethical) medium for subliminally priming consumers into purchasing particular brands.

The foregoing discussion may have presented the reader with mixed signals: On the one hand, it was claimed that embeds in advertising likely are unable to influence consumer choice behavior. Then, on the other hand, the previous discussion has suggested that the use of subliminal primes might work. As pointed out early in the chapter as well as elsewhere in the text, the only proper conclusion is that subliminal advertising probably is ineffective under most circumstances, although the possibility remains that it is capable of influencing consumer choice behavior under limited conditions of subliminal priming. The *IMC Focus* describes a study that used subliminal priming and demonstrated that, in this limited context, it is capable of influencing brand choice.

The Functions of Music in Advertising

Music has been an important component of the advertising landscape virtually since the beginning of recorded sound. Jingles, background music, popular tunes, and classical arrangements are used to attract attention, convey selling points, set an emotional tone for an advertisement, and influence listeners' moods. Well-known entertainers, nonvocal musical accompaniment, and unknown vocalists are used extensively in promoting everything from fabric softeners to automobiles. Recent examples of songs featured in commercials include LMFAO's "Party Rock Anthem" for the Kia Soul ("dancing hamsters") campaign, Elvis Presley's "Devil in Disguise" featured in Nissan Altima ads, "Rescue Me" (by Mr. Little Jeans) in the Honda CRV campaign, and "Hey Soul Sister" (by Train) for Samsung's 3D LED TV ads.[79]

Many advertising practitioners and scholars regard music as capable of performing a variety of useful communications functions. For example, music (combined with creative material) can be so positive and addicting that viewers may be more than willing to share the ad virally with others—as was the case with over one million views of the Kia Soul commercial. Other functions include *attracting attention* to commercial messages, *putting consumers in a positive mood* while hearing or viewing these messages, making them *more receptive to message arguments*, and even *communicating meanings about advertised brands*.[80] Consider, for example, the use of music in a famous Pepsi advertisement. While the famous Hank Williams song, "Your Cheatin' Heart," plays in the background, a Coke deliveryman is seen approaching a Pepsi cooler that is adjacent to his own Coca-Cola cooler. The delivery man is shown sneaking a look at the Pepsi cooler, opening it, and then removing a can of Pepsi—at which time dozens of Pepsi cans cascade to the floor with a huge noise, much to the deliveryman's embarrassment. The commercial's key point is that Pepsi is so good that even a Coke employee will switch loyalty.

A brief review for an important research study on the role of music demonstrates the influence it can have when placed in an advertising context.[81] This study used classical conditioning in an effort to influence study participants' preferences for a ballpoint pen.[82] As you may recall from a course in psychology or consumer behavior, an *unconditioned stimulus (US)* is something in the environment that naturally evokes pleasant feelings or thoughts in people. For example, babies, puppies, spring flowers, and the first snowfall of the season engender positive feelings in most people. A *conditioned stimulus (CS)* is one that is emotionally or cognitively

Subliminal Priming and Brand Choice

Imagine that you have been asked to participate in a study at your university. Upon arriving at the study location, the experimenter informs you and fellow participants that the study entails a *visual detection task*. She explains that you will be presented with 25 separate images on a computer screen and that each image consists of a string of capital Bs (BBBBBBBBB). She further notes that on occasion the string of Bs will contain a single lowercase *b* such as BBBBbBBBB. Your task is to be viligant and to identify how many of the 25 strings of capital Bs contain a small b.

Researchers in the Netherlands used this research procedure to disguise the purpose of a study that actually involved a form of subliminal advertising. Research participants saw not only 25 strings of capital Bs intermingled occasionally with small b's, but also, unbeknownst to them, separate images of *subliminally primed words* that appeared on the screen prior to the images containing strings of Bs. The primed words were on the computer screen for the extremely short duration of only 23 milliseconds (i.e., 23/1,000 second). The researchers wondered whether subliminally priming participants with an actual brand name would subsequently influence them to choose that brand at the end of the experimental session.

As typical in an experiment, approximately half of the participants were assigned to a "treatment" group and the other half were assigned to a "control" group. All participants participated in the identical visual detection task. However, "treatment group" participants were primed on multiple occasions with the brand name "Lipton Ice," whereas "control group" participants were primed an equal number of times with "Npeic Tol," which is a non-word that contains the same letters as in Lipton Ice.

The experiment involved an additional study feature: Prior to participating in the visual detection task and before being exposed to primed words, half of the participants ate a salty food item that made them extremely thirsty (the "thirsty condition"), whereas the other half did not consume this salty item ("non-thirsty condition").

Following the visual detection task, participants were asked to indicate which of two beverages they would prefer to drink—either Lipton Ice tea or Spa Rood, a Dutch brand of mineral water. The researchers predicted that participants who were primed with the words *Lipton Ice* would be much more likely to choose that brand, but only if they were in the "thirsty condition."

The research results bore out the researchers' prediction. Specifically, about 85 percent of participants in the "thirsty condition" who received the Lipton Ice prime selected the Lipton Ice brand when given the choice between it and Spa Rood. Comparatively, only 20 percent of participants in the "thirsty condition" who received the Npeic Tol prime selected Lipton Ice. Although participants in the "non-thirsty condition" who received the Lipton Ice prime were more likely to select Lipton Ice than were those participants who received the Npeic Tol prime, the difference in choosing Lipton Ice (about 54 percent versus 32 percent) was far less than the difference for those participants in the "thirsty condition" (80 percent versus 20 percent).

Findings from this study make it clear that subliminally primed words are capable of influencing consumer choice behavior under *ideal conditions*, namely, when brand choice closely follows exposure to subliminally primed words. Additional research is needed to determine whether this effect will occur under more realistic marketplace conditions, such as when exposure to brand-name primes and brand choice are *not* close in time, and for actual shopping conditions when consumers are exposed to numerous brands and are forced to make many decisions. The present research can thus be considered intriguing but not definitive with respect to the question of whether subliminal priming "works" under natural marketplace conditions.

Source: Adapted from Johan C. Karremans, Wolfgang Stroebe, and Jasper Claus, "Beyond Vicary's Fantasies: The Impact of Subliminal Priming and Brand Choice," *Journal of Experimental Social Psychology* 42 (November 2006), 792–798.

Note: This description is a simplification of this research and only describes one of the two studies performed by the researchers.

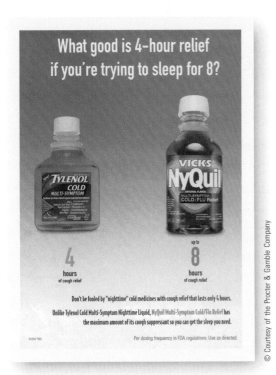

© Courtesy of the Procter & Gamble Company

FIGURE 11.2 Illustration of a Direct Comparison Advertisement

© Courtesy of Allegra

FIGURE 11.3 Illustration of an Indirect Comparison Advertisement

neutral prior to the onset of a conditioning experiment. In simple terms, classical conditioning is achieved when the pairing of US and CS results in a transfer of feeling from the US (music in the present case) to the CS (the ballpoint pen).

Experimental participants in this study were informed that an advertising agency was trying to select music for use in a commercial for a ballpoint pen. Participants then listened to music while they viewed slides of the pen. The positive US for half the participants was music from the movie *Grease*, and the negative US for the remaining participants was classical Asian Indian music. This research demonstrated that the simple association between the music and the pen influenced product preference: Nearly 80 percent of the participants exposed to the *Grease* music chose the advertised pen, whereas only 30 percent of the participants exposed to the Asian Indian music chose the advertised pen.[83]

The Role of Comparative Advertising

The practice in which advertisers directly or indirectly compare their products against competitive offerings and claim superiority is called comparative advertising. Comparative ads vary both with regard to the explicitness of the comparisons and with respect to whether the target of the comparison is named or referred to in general terms.[84] In some countries (e.g., Belgium, Hong Kong, and Korea) it is illegal to use comparative advertising; and with the exception of the United States and Great Britain, advertising comparisons are used infrequently in those countries where they are legal.[85]

To better appreciate comparative advertising, it will be useful to examine a couple of examples. The ad in Figure 11.2 for Vicks NyQuil compares itself *directly* against competitor Tylenol Cold Multi-Symptom Nighttime Liquid. The ad indicates that Vicks NyQuil offers up to eight hours of cough relief in comparison to Tylenol's four hours of relief.

Consider now the indirect comparison advertisement for Allegra in Figure 11.3. Without mentioning any competitive brands, this ad shows graphically and in its copy that a dose of Allegra "lasts up to 4 times longer than one dose of most OTC [over-the-counter] allergy medicines."

Is Comparative Advertising More Effective?

In deciding whether to use a comparative advertisement or a more conventional noncomparative format, an advertiser must address questions such as the following:[86]

- How do comparative and noncomparative advertisements match up in terms of impact on brand awareness, consumer comprehension of ad claims, and credibility?
- Do comparative and noncomparative ads differ with regard to effects on brand preferences, buying intentions, and purchase behavior?
- How do factors such as consumer brand preference and the advertiser's market share influence the effectiveness of comparative advertising?
- Under what specific circumstances should an advertiser use comparative advertising?

Researchers have performed numerous studies that have examined the processes by which comparative advertising operates, the results it produces, and how its effects contrast with those from noncomparative ads.[87] Findings are at times inconclusive, depending on the study context. Lack of definitive results is expected, however, because advertising is a complex phenomenon that varies from situation to situation in terms of executional elements, audience demographics, media characteristics, and other factors.

Considerations Dictating the Use of Comparative Advertising

Situational Factors

Characteristics of the audience, media, message, company, and product all play important roles in determining whether comparative advertising will be more effective than noncomparative advertising. For example, comparative advertisements seem to be evaluated *less* favorably by people holding a prior preference for the comparison brand (the brand that the advertised brand is compared against) than by those without a prior preference for that brand. Also, receivers should be under relatively higher levels of involvement, and thus paying attention to the ad. Otherwise, confusion between the two brands compared is likely.

Distinct Advantages

Comparative advertising is particularly effective for promoting brands that possess distinct advantages relative to competitive brands.[88] When a brand has a distinct advantage over competitive brands, comparative advertising provides a powerful method to convey this advantage. The advertisement for Vicks NyQuil (Figure 11.2) typifies this situation. Relative to noncomparative advertising, comparative advertising has also been shown to increase the perceived similarity between a challenger brand in a product category and the category leader.[89] However, research also has demonstrated that indirect comparative advertisements can be more effective than direct comparative ads in certain circumstances. One study found that direct comparison ads are more effective than indirect comparative ads in positioning a brand as superior to a *specific* competitive brand, but indirect comparative ads were better at positioning a brand as superior to *all brands in the category*.[90]

The Credibility Issue

The effectiveness of comparative advertising increases when comparative claims are made to appear more credible. There are three ways to accomplish this: (1) have an independent research organization support the superiority claims, (2) present impressive test results to back up the claims, and (3) use a trusted endorser as the spokesperson.

Assessing Effectiveness

Because comparative advertisements make claims for an advertised brand relative to another brand and because consumers encode this comparative information in a relative fashion, measurement techniques in assessing the effectiveness of comparative advertising are most sensitive when questions are *worded in a relative fashion*. That is, for maximal sensitivity, the question context, or wording, should match the consumer's encoding mind-set. For example, with reference to the Vicks NyQuil advertisement (Figure 11.2), two *alternative* questions could be framed to ascertain whether consumers perceive Vicks NyQuil as an effective brand in providing cough relief: (1) How likely is it that the cough-relief effects of Vicks NyQuil are long lasting? (*nonrelative* framing) or (2) How likely is it that Vicks NyQuil provides longer-lasting cough relief than Tylenol Cold Multi-Symptom? (*relative* framing). Research has shown that relative framing does a better job of assessing consumers' beliefs after their exposure to comparative advertisements.[91]

Summary

This chapter discussed two general topics. The first major section dealt with the role of endorsers in advertising. The Kelman source attribute model (credibility, attractiveness, power) provided an important framework for understanding how sources (such as endorsers) may or may not be effective through underlying processes, such as internalization, identification, and compliance. The following factors appear to be the most important ones brand managers use in actually selecting celebrity endorsers: (1) celebrity and audience matchup, (2) celebrity and brand matchup, (3) celebrity credibility, (4) celebrity attractiveness, (5) cost considerations, (6) working ease or difficulty factor, (7) endorsement saturation factor,

and (8) likelihood-of-getting-into-trouble factor. Discussion of celebrity endorsers indicates that endorsers have an influence on consumers via the attributes of credibility and attractiveness. Credibility functions via the process of internalization, whereas attractiveness operates through an identification mechanism.

Finally, several sections were devoted to a variety of message appeals in advertising. Widely used advertising techniques discussed in this chapter include humor, appeals to fear, appeals to guilt, sex appeals, subliminal messages, the use of music, and comparative advertisements. Discussion covered empirical research and indicated the factors involved in selecting each of these message elements.

Discussion Questions

1. Using the concepts of attractiveness, expertise, and trustworthiness, explain what makes Tiger Woods an effective or ineffective endorser. Do the same for LeBron James, Alex Rodriguez, Aaron Rodgers, Derek Jeter, David Beckham, and Maria Sharapova.

2. Presented early in the chapter was a quote from philosopher Alfred North Whitehead stating, "Seek simplicity and distrust it." What does this quote mean in terms of the effectiveness of particular advertising appeals, such as the use of humor?

3. Attractiveness as an attribute of endorsers includes but is not restricted to physical attractiveness. Many would regard British soccer star David Beckham (of *Bend It Like Beckham* fame) as attractive. In what ways, other than physical attractiveness, might he be considered attractive?

4. Considering the likelihood-of-getting-into-trouble factor, identify three entertainment or sports celebrities that you, as a brand manager, would be reluctant to have endorse your brand for fear they would get into some sort of trouble.

5. NBA superstar Michael Jordan for many years endorsed Hanes underwear, among many other brands. Suppose you were brand manager for Hanes and had to come up with a replacement for Mr. Jordan. Who would you select? Justify the rationale behind your choice.

6. Infomercials are long commercials that generally last from 30 to 60 minutes. These commercials typically air during fringe times and frequently promote products such as diet aids, balding cures, and exercise products. These infomercials often use endorsements from physicians and other health professionals to buttress claims about the promoted brand's efficacy. Using concepts from this chapter, explain why health professionals are used in this form of advertising.

7. You have probably seen a number of public service announcements along the lines of those described in the fear appeals section to discourage drinking and

driving. In your opinion, is this form of advertising effective in altering the behavior of people your age? Be specific in justifying your answer.

8. The fear of getting AIDS should be relevant to many college students. Accordingly, would you agree that a relatively weak fear appeal should suffice in influencing students to either abstain from sexual relations or practice safe sex? If you disagree, then how can you reconcile your disagreement with the degree-of-relevance explanation?

9. Identify three or four products for which you feel appeals to guilt might be a viable approach to persuading consumer acceptance of a brand. What kinds of products do not lend themselves to such appeals? Explain why you feel these products would be inappropriate.

10. Consumers occasionally find television commercials humorous and enjoyable. Some advertising pundits claim that such commercials may capture attention but are frequently ineffective in selling products. What is your viewpoint on this issue? Justify your position.

11. Identify two or three YouTube videos with brands that you consider humorous. Is the use of humor appropriate for the brands advertised in these videos and given their likely target audiences? Justify your responses.

12. Identify several TV commercials or magazine ads that use sex appeal. Describe each advertisement and then explain whether an appeal to sex is appropriate or inappropriate for the brand.

13. Comment on the following allegation: "There is too much use of sex in advertising."

14. The article titled "Understanding Jingles and Needledrop: A Rhetorical Approach to Music in Advertising" (see endnote 80) suggests that music in commercials communicates specific meanings to listeners and viewers. In other words, music "speaks" to people by conveying a sense of speed, excitement, sadness, nostalgia, and so on. Identify two commercials in which music communicates a specific

emotion or other state or action to consumers, and identify this emotion, state, or action.

15. Photocopy or save one or two examples of comparative advertisements from magazines. Analyze each

ad in terms of why you think the advertiser used a comparative-advertising format and whether you think the advertisement is effective. Justify your position.

End Notes

1. Based on Geoffrey A. Fowler, Brian Steinberg, and Aaron O. Patrick, *Wall Street Journal*, March 1, 2007, B1.
2. Erin White, "Found in Translation?" *Wall Street Journal Online*, September 20, 2004, http://online.wsj.com.
3. Jagdish Agrawal and Wagner A. Kamakura, "The Economic Worth of Celebrity Endorsers: An Event Study Analysis," *Journal of Marketing* 59 (July 1995), 56–62.
4. Therese A. Louie, Robert L. Kulik, and Robert Johnson, "When Bad Things Happen to the Endorsers of Good Products," *Marketing Letters* 12 (February 2001), 13–24.
5. "Despite Risks, Celebrity Endorsers Raise Print Advertising Awareness," *GfK MRI Starch Advertising Research Press Release*, February, 23, 2011, http://www.gfkmri.com/assets/PR/GfKMRI_022311PR_CelebrityEndorsers.htm.
6. Peter Daboll, "Celebrities in Advertising Are Almost Always a Big Waste of Money," *Advertising Age*, January 12, 2011, http://adage.com/print/148174.
7. Ibid, Daboll.
8. Ibid.
9. For a classic treatment of the subject, see Herbert C. Kelman, "Processes of Opinion Change," *Public Opinion Quarterly* 25 (spring 1961), 57–78. For a more current treatment, see Daniel J. O'Keefe, *Persuasion Theory and Research*, Newbury Park, CA: Sage, 1990, chap. 8. For a recent discussion of the various processes by which a message source, such as a celebrity, influences consumers, see Yong-Soon Kang and Paul M. Herr, "Beauty and the Beholder: Toward an Integrative Model of Communication Source Effects," *Journal of Consumer Research* 33 (June 2006), 123–30.
10. Richard E. Petty, Thomas M. Ostrom, and Timothy C. Brock, eds., *Cognitive Responses in Persuasion*, Hillsdale, NJ: Lawrence Erlbaum Associates, 1981, 143.
11. "FTC Publishes Final Guides Governing Endorsements, Testimonials: Changes Affect Testimonial Advertisements, Bloggers, Celebrity Endorsements," Federal Trade Commission News Release, October 5, 2009, http://www.ftc.gov/opa/2009/10/endortest.shtm.
12. It has been demonstrated, however, that under select conditions, a less trustworthy, although expert, source may be more effective than an equally expert but more trustworthy source. This is because people tend to elaborate more on persuasive arguments presented by less (versus more) trustworthy sources and form attitudes that both are held more strongly and are relatively more resistant to change. See Joseph R. Priester and Richard E. Petty, "The Influence of Spokesperson Trustworthiness on Message Elaboration, Attitude Strength, and Advertising Effectiveness," *Journal of Consumer Psychology* 13, no. 4 (2003), 408–21.
13. Rohit Deshpande and Douglas Stayman, "A Tale of Two Cities: Distinctiveness Theory and Advertising Effectiveness," *Journal of Marketing Research* 31 (February 1994), 57–64.
14. Lucia Malar, Harley Krohmer, Wayne D. Hoyer, and Bettina Nyffenegger, "Emotional Brand Attachment and Brand Personality: The Relative Importance of the Actual and the Ideal Self," *Journal of Marketing* 75 (July 2011), 35–52.
15. Two studies have addressed this issue: B. Zafer Erdogan, Michael J. Baker, and Stephen Tagg, "Selecting Celebrity Endorsers: The Practitioner's Perspective," *Journal of Advertising Research* 41 (May/June 2001), 39–48; and Alan R. Miciak and William L. Shanklin, "Choosing Celebrity Endorsers," *Marketing Management* 3 (winter 1994), 51–59.
16. Christine Bittar, "Cosmetic Changes Beyond Skin Deep," *Brandweek*, May 17, 2004, 20.
17. Teri Agins, "Jeans Maker Tarrant Sues Singer Jessica Simpson," *Wall Street Journal*, April 12, 2006, B3.
18. Carolyn Tripp, Thomas D. Jensen, and Les Carlson, "The Effects of Multiple Product Endorsements by Celebrities on Consumers' Attitudes and Intentions," *Journal of Consumer Research* 20 (March 1994), 535–47.
19. Rich Thomaselli, "Dream Endorser," *Advertising Age*, September 25, 2006, 1, 37.
20. For example, see Therese A. Louie and Carl Obermiller, "Consumer Response to a Firm's Endorser (Dis)Association Decisions," *Journal of Advertising* 31 (winter 2002), 41–52; Louie, Kulik, and Johnson, "When Bad Things Happen"; Brian D. Till and Terence A. Shimp, "Endorsers in Advertising: The Case of Negative Celebrity Information," *Journal of Advertising* 27 (spring 1998), 67–82; and R. Bruce Money, Terence A. Shimp, and Tomoaki Sakano, "Celebrity Endorsements in Japan and the United States: Is Negative Information All That Harmful?" *Journal of Advertising Research* 46 (March 2006), 113–23.
21. Richard Tedesco, "Sacked," *Promo*, September 2007, 22–31.
22. Judith A. Garretson and Scot Burton, "The Role of Spokescharacters as Advertisement and Package Cues in Integrated Marketing Communications," *Journal of Marketing* 69 (October 2005), 118–32.
23. Marc Weinberger and Harlan Spotts, "Humor in U.S. versus U.K. TV Advertising," *Journal of*

Advertising 18, no. 2 (1989), 39–44. For further discussion of differences between American and British advertising, see Terence Nevett, "Differences between American and British Television Advertising: Explanations and Implications," *Journal of Advertising* 21 (December 1992), 61–71.

24. Dana L. Alden, Wayne D. Hoyer, and Chol Lee, "Identifying Global and Culture-Specific Dimensions of Humor in Advertising: A Multinational Analysis," *Journal of Marketing* 57 (April 1993), 64–75.

25. Harlan E. Spotts, Marc G. Weinberger, and Amy L. Parsons, "Assessing the Use and Impact of Humor on Advertising Effectiveness: A Contingency Approach," *Journal of Advertising* 26 (fall 1997), 17–32; and Karen Flaherty, Marc G. Weinberger, and Charles S. Gulas, "The Impact of Perceived Humor, Product Type, and Humor Style in Radio Advertising," *Journal of Current Issues and Research in Advertising* 26 (spring 2004), 25–36.

26. Josephine L. C. M. Woltman Elpers, Ashesh Mukherjee, and Wayne D. Hoyer, "Humor in Television Advertising: A Moment-to-Moment Analysis," *Journal of Consumer Research* 31 (December 2004), 592–98.

27. For a formal theoretical account, see Dana L. Alden, Ashesh Mukherjee, and Wayne D. Hoyer, "The Effects of Incongruity, Surprise and Positive Moderators on Perceived Humor in Television Advertising," *Journal of Advertising* 29 (summer 2000), 1–16.

28. Differences in the use of humor across advertising media are demonstrated in Marc G. Weinberger, Harlan Spotts, Leiand Campbell, and Amy L. Parsons, "The Use and Effect of Humor in Different Advertising Media," *Journal of Advertising Research* 35 (May/June 1995), 44–56.

29. A thorough review of the issues is provided in two valuable reviews: Paul Surgi Speek, "The Humorous Message Taxonomy: A Framework for the Study of Humorous Ads," *Current Issues and Research in Advertising*, vol. 3, ed. J. H. Leigh and C. R. Martin Jr. (Ann Arbor: Graduate School of Business Administration, University of Michigan, 1991), 1–44; and Marc G. Weinberger and Charles S. Gulas, "The Impact of Humor in Advertising: A Review," *Journal of Advertising* 21 (December 1992), 35–59.

30. Thomas J. Madden and Marc G. Weinberger, "Humor in Advertising: A Practitioner View," *Journal of Advertising Research* 24, no. 4 (1984), 23–29.

31. Yong Zhang and George M. Zinkhan, "Responses to Humorous Ads," *Journal of Advertising* 35 (winter 2006), 113–28.

32. Based, in part, on Weinberger and Gulas, "The Impact of Humor in Advertising: A Review," 56–57, as well as on more recent research.

33. Thomas W. Cline and James J. Kellaris, "The Influence of Humor Strength and Humor-Message Relatedness on Ad Memorability," *Journal of Advertising* 36 (spring 2007), 55–68.

34. For discussion on this point, see H. Shanker Krishnan and Dipankar Chakravarti, "A Process Analysis of the Effects of Humorous Advertising Executions on Brand Claims Memory," *Journal of Consumer Psychology* 13, no. 3 (2003), 230–45.

35. Thomas J. Madden and Marc G. Weinberger, "The Effects of Humor on Attention in Magazine Advertising," *Journal of Advertising* 11, no. 3 (1982), 4–14.

36. Amitava Chattopadhyay and Kunal Basu, "Humor in Advertising: The Moderating Role of Prior Brand Evaluation," *Journal of Consumer Research* 27 (November 1990), 466–76.

37. Thomas W. Cline, Moses B. Altsech, and James J. Kellaris, "When Does Humor Enhance or Inhibit Ad Responses? The Moderating Role of the Need for Humor," *Journal of Advertising* 32 (fall 2003), 31–46; and Cline and Kellaris, "The Influence of Humor Strength and Humor-Message Relatedness on Ad Memorability."

38. See Yong Zhang, "Responses to Humorous Advertising: The Moderating Effect of Need for Cognition," *Journal of Advertising* 25 (spring 1996), 15–32; also, Flaherty, Weinberger, and Gulas, "The Impact of Perceived Humor, Product Type, and Humor Style in Radio Advertising."

39. "Any Anxiety Disorders Among Adults," National Institute of Mental Health, http://www.nimh.nih.gov/statistics/1ANYANX_ADULT.shtml (accessed May 8, 2012).

40. Please note that there is a related advertising form referred to as "shock advertising" that does not appeal to fear per se but that deliberately intends to startle and even offend its audience. Tentative research on this topic has demonstrated that shock advertising is perhaps even better than appeals to fear in activating attention and encouraging the audience to engage in message-relevant behaviors. See Darren W. Dahl, Kristina D. Frankenberger, and Rajesh V. Manchanda, "Does It Pay to Shock? Reactions to Shocking and Nonshocking Advertising Content among University Students," *Journal of Advertising Research* 43 (September 2003), 268–80.

41. This is a quote from Jerry Della Femina, a well-known advertising agency executive and former copywriter. Cited in Emily DeNitto, "Healthcare Ads Employ Scare Tactics," *Advertising Age*, November 7, 1994, 12.

42. Ronald W. Rogers, "Cognitive and Psychological Processes in Fear Appeals and Attitude Change: A Revised Theory of Protection Motivation," in *Social Psychophysiology: A Source Book*, John Cacioppo and Richard Petty, eds., New York: Guilford Press, 1983, 153–76; see also John F. Tanner, Jr., James B. Hunt, and David R. Eppright, "The Protection Motivation Model: A Normative Model of Fear Appeals," *Journal of Marketing* 55 (July 1991), 36–45.

43. Cornelia Pechmann, Guangzhi Zhao, Marvin E. Goldberg, and Ellen Thomas Reibling, "What to Convey in Antismoking Advertisements for Adolescents: The Use of Protection Motivation Theory to Identify Effective Message Themes," *Journal of Marketing* 67 (April 2003), 1–18.

44. I. L. Janis and S. Feshbach, "Effects of Fear-Arousing Communications," *Journal of Abnormal and Social Psychology* 48, no. 1 (1953), 78–92; and M. L. Ray and W. L. Wilkie, "Fear: The Potential of an Appeal Neglected by Marketing," *Journal of Marketing* 34, no. 1 (1970), 34–62.

45. K. Witte and M. Allen, "A Meta-Analysis of Fear Appeals: Implications for Effective Public Health Campaigns," *Health Education & Behavior* 27, no. 5 (2000), 591–615.

46. Ibid, Witte and Allen.

47. Ibid, 601; for a review of warning communications, see J. Craig Andrews, "Warnings and Disclosures" (Chapter 15) in *Communicating Risks and Benefits: An Evidence-Based User's Guide*, Baruch Fischhoff, Noel T. Brewer, and Julie S. Downs, eds., Silver Spring, MD: U.S. Food & Drug Administration, 2011, 149–61.

48. Peter Wright, "Concrete Action Plans in TV Messages to Increase Reading of Drug Warnings," *Journal of Consumer Research* 6 (December 1979), 256–69. For an explanation of the psychological mechanism by which fear-intensity operates, see Punam Anand Keller and Lauren Goldberg Block, "Increasing the Persuasiveness of Fear Appeals: The Effect of Arousal and Elaboration," *Journal of Consumer Research* 22 (March 1996), 448–59.

49. H. Leventhal, "Findings and Theory in the Study of Fear Communications," in *Advances in Experimental Social Psychology*, ed. L. Berkowitz, ed. vol. 5, New York: Academic Press, 1970, 119–86.

50. For further reading on the use of appeals to fear in anti-drinking and driving campaigns, see Karen Whitehill King and Leonard N. Reid, "Fear Arousing Anti-Drinking and Driving PSAs: Do Physical Injury Threats Influence Young Adults?" *Current Issues and Research in Advertising*, vol. 12, ed. J. H. Leigh and C. R. Martin, Jr., Ann Arbor: Graduate School of Business Administration, University of Michigan, 1990, 155–75. Other relevant articles on fear appeals include John F. Tanner, James B. Hunt, and David R. Eppright, "The Protection Motivation Model: Normative Model of Fear Appeals," *Journal of Marketing* 55 (July 1991), 36–45; Tony L. Henthorne, Michael S. LaTour, and Rajan Natarajan, "Fear Appeals in Print Advertising: An Analysis of Arousal and Ad Response," *Journal of Advertising* 22 (June 1993), 59–70; and James T. Strong and Khalid M. Dubas, "The Optimal Level of Fear-Arousal in Advertising: An Empirical Study," *Journal of Current Issues and Research in Advertising* 15 (fall 1993), 93–99.

51. Jeremy Kees, Scot Burton, J. Craig Andrews, and John Kozup, "Understanding How Graphic Pictorial Warnings Work on Cigarette Packaging," *Journal of Public Policy & Marketing* 29 (fall 2010), 265–76.

52. Robert B. Cialdini, *Influence: Science and Practice*, 4th ed., Boston: Allyn & Bacon, 2001.

53. Jack W. Brehm, *A Theory of Psychological Reactance*, New York: Academic Press, 1966. See also Mona Clee and Robert Wicklund, "Consumer Behavior and Psychological Reactance," *Journal of Consumer Research* 6 (March 1980), 389–405.

54. Ian Stewart, "Public Fear Sells in Singapore," *Advertising Age*, October 11, 1993, 18. Singaporeans even make fun of themselves regarding their kiasu behavior. "Mr. Kiasu" is a popular comic book character, and a small cottage industry has sprung up around the character.

55. Carroll E. Izard, *Human Emotions*, New York: Plenum, 1977.

56. Robin Higie Coulter and Mary Beth Pinto, "Guilt Appeals in Advertising: What Are Their Effects?" *Journal of Applied Psychology* 80 (December 1995), 697–705; and Bruce A. Huhmann and Timothy P. Brotherton, "A Content Analysis of Guilt Appeals in Popular Magazine Advertisements," *Journal of Advertising* 26 (summer 1997), 35–46.

57. Huhmann and Brotherton, "A Content Analysis of Guilt Appeals in Popular Magazine Advertisements," 36.

58. June Cotte, Robin A. Coulter, and Melissa Moore, "Enhancing or Disrupting Guilt: The Role of Ad Credibility and Perceived Manipulative Intent," *Journal of Business Research* 58 (March 2005), 361–68.

59. A content analysis of magazine advertising indicates that the percentage of ads with sexual content had not changed over a two-decade period. What changed, however, was that sexual illustrations had become more overt. See Lawrence Soley and Gary Kurzbard, "Sex in Advertising: A Comparison of 1964 and 1984 Magazine Advertisements," *Journal of Advertising* 15, no. 3 (1986), 46–54.

60. For a variety of perspectives on the role of sex in advertising, see Tom Reichert and Jacqueline Lambiase, eds., *Sex in Advertising: Perspectives on the Erotic Appeal*, Mahwah, NJ: Lawrence Erlbaum, 2003.

61. Robert S. Baron, "Sexual Content and Advertising Effectiveness: Comments on Belch et al. (1981) and Caccavale et al. (1981)," in *Advances in Consumer Research*, vol. 9, ed. Andrew Mitchell, Ann Arbor, MI: Association for Consumer Research, 1982, 428.

62. Larry Percy, "A Review of the Effect of Specific Advertising Elements upon Overall Communication Response," in *Current Issues and Research in Advertising*, vol. 2, ed. J. H. Leigh and C. R. Martin, Jr., Ann Arbor: Graduate School of Business Administration, University of Michigan, 1983, 95.

63. David Richmond and Timothy P. Hartman, "Sex Appeal in Advertising," *Journal of Advertising Research* 22 (October/November 1982), 53–61.

64. Michael S. LaTour, Robert E. Pitts, and David C. Snook-Luther, "Female Nudity, Arousal, and Ad Response: An Experimental Investigation," *Journal of Advertising* 19, no. 4 (1990), 51–62.

65. Baron, "Sexual Content and Advertising Effectiveness," 428.

66. Jessica Severn, George E. Belch, and Michael A. Belch, "The Effects of Sexual and Nonsexual Advertising Appeals and Information Level on Cognitive Processing and Communication Effectiveness," *Journal of Advertising* 19, no. 1 (1990), 14–22.

67. A study of consumers in Denmark, Greece, New Zealand, and the United States revealed consistent criticism of sexist role portrayals. See Richard W. Pollay and Steven Lysonski, "In the Eye of the Beholder: International Differences in Ad Sexism Perceptions and Reactions," *Journal of International Consumer Marketing* 6, vol. 2 (1993), 25–43.

68. Three surveys have demonstrated this fact. For the most recent review of these surveys, see Martha Rogers and Kirk H. Smith, "Public Perceptions of Subliminal Advertising: Why Practitioners Shouldn't Ignore This Issue," *Journal of Advertising Research* 33 (March/April 1993), 10–18.

69. Martha Rogers and Christine A. Seiler, "The Answer Is No: A National Survey of Advertising Industry Practitioners and Their Clients about Whether They Use Subliminal Advertising," *Journal of Advertising Research* 34 (March/April 1994), 36–45.

70. This description is adapted from Martin P. Block and Bruce G. Vanden Bergh, "Can You Sell Subliminal Messages to Consumers?" *Journal of Advertising* 14, no. 3 (1985), 59.

71. Vicary himself acknowledged that the study that initiated the original furor over subliminal advertising was based on too small an amount of data to be meaningful. See Fred Danzig, "Subliminal Advertising—Today It's Just Historic Flashback for Researcher Vicary," *Advertising Age*, September 17, 1962, 42, 74.

72. For example, see Sharon E. Beatty and Del I. Hawkins, "Subliminal Stimulation: Some New Data and Interpretation," *Journal of Advertising* 18, no. 3 (1989), 4–8.

73. Wilson B. Key, *Subliminal Seduction: Ad Media's Manipulation of a Not So Innocent America*, New York: Signet, 1972; *Media Sexploitation*, New York: Signet, 1976; and *The Clam Plate Orgy: And Other Subliminal Techniques for Manipulating Your Behavior*, New York: Signet, 1980. Key has since written *The Age of Manipulation: The Con in Confidence, the Sin in Sincere*, New York: Holt, 1989.

74. For a sophisticated treatment of visual imagery and symbolism in advertising (although not dealing with subliminal advertising per se), see Linda M. Scott, "Images in Advertising: The Need for a Theory of Visual Rhetoric," *Journal of Consumer Research* 21 (September 1994), 252–73.

75. Ronnie Cuperfain and T. K. Clarke, "A New Perspective of Subliminal Perception," *Journal of Advertising* 14, no. 1 (1985), 36–41; Myron Gable, Henry T. Wilkens, Lynn Harris, and Richard Feinberg, "An Evaluation of Subliminally Embedded Sexual Stimuli in Graphics," *Journal of Advertising* 16, no. 1 (1987), 26–31; and William E. Kilbourne, Scott Painton, and Danny Ridley, "The Effect of Sexual Embedding on Responses to Magazine Advertisements," *Journal of Advertising* 14, no. 2 (1985), 48–56.

76. For discussion of the practical difficulties with implementing subliminal advertising and the questionable effectiveness of this advertising technique, see Timothy E. Moore, "Subliminal Advertising: What You See Is What You Get," *Journal of Marketing* 46 (spring 1982), 41; and Joel Saegert, "Why Marketing Should Quit Giving Subliminal Advertising the Benefit of the Doubt," *Psychology & Marketing* 4 (summer 1987), 107–20.

77. Moore, "Subliminal Advertising: What You See Is What You Get," 46.

78. For an accessible treatment on the issue of automatic, or noncontrolled motivation and behavior, see John A. Bargh, "Losing Consciousness: Automatic Influences on Consumer Judgment, Behavior, and Motivation," *Journal of Consumer Research* 29 (September 2002), 280–85. See also John A. Bargh and Tanya L. Chartrand, "The Unbearable Automaticity of Being," *American Psychologist* 54 (July 1999), 462–79.

79. The music identified in these commercials was found from Squidoo, http://www.squidoo.com/TV_commercial_music and from YouTube, http://www.youtube.com (accessed October 22, 2011).

80. Very good reviews of music's various advertising functions are available in Gordon C. Bruner II, "Music, Mood, and Marketing," *Journal of Marketing* 54 (October 1990), 94–104; Linda M. Scott, "Understanding Jingles and Needledrop: A Rhetorical Approach to Music in Advertising," *Journal of Consumer Research* 17 (September 1990), 223–36; Deborah J. MacInnis and C. Whan Park, "The Differential Role of Characteristics of Music on High and Low-Involvement Consumers' Processing of Ads," *Journal of Consumer Research* 18 (September 1991), 161–73; James J. Kellaris and Robert J. Kent, "The Influence of Music on Consumers' Temporal Perceptions: Does Time Fly When You're Having Fun?" *Journal of Consumer Psychology* 1, no. 4 (1992), 365–76; James J. Kellaris, Anthony D. Cox, and Dena Cox, "The Effect of Background Music on Ad Processing: A Contingency Explanation," *Journal of Marketing* 57 (October 1993), 114–25; James

J. Kellaris and Robert J. Kent, "An Exploratory Investigation of Responses Elicited by Music Varying in Tempo, Tonality, and Texture," *Journal of Consumer Psychology* 2, no. 4 (1993), 381–402; Kineta Hung, "Framing Meaning Perceptions with Music: The Case of Teaser Ads," *Journal of Advertising* 30 (fall 2001), 39–50; Michelle L. Roehm, "Instrumental vs. Vocal Versions of Popular Music in Advertising," *Journal of Advertising Research* 41 (May/June 2001), 49–58; Rui (Juliet) Zhu and Joan Meyers-Levy, "Distinguishing between the Meanings of Music: When Background Music Affects Product Perceptions," *Journal of Marketing Research* 42 (August 2005), 333–45; and Steve Oakes, "Evaluating Empirical Research into Music in Advertising: A Congruity Perspective," *Journal of Advertising Research* 47 (March 2007), 38–50.

81. Gerald J. Gorn, "The Effects of Music in Advertising on Choice Behavior: A Classical Conditioning Approach," *Journal of Marketing* 46 (winter 1982), 94–101.

82. Technically, this study is better characterized as an evaluative conditioning study rather than an application of classical (Pavlovian) conditioning. For review of evaluative conditioning, see Bryan Gibson, "Can Evaluative Conditioning Change Attitudes toward Mature Brands? New Evidence from the Implicit Association Test," *Journal of Consumer Research* 35 (June 2008), 178–88.

83. A replication of this study failed to obtain supporting evidence, thereby calling into question the ability to generalize from Gorn's prior research. See James J. Kellaris and Anthony D. Cox, "The Effects of Background Music in Advertising," *Journal of Consumer Research* 16 (June 1989), 113–18.

84. See Darrel D. Muehling, Donald E. Stem, Jr., and Peter Raven, "Comparative Advertising: Views from Advertisers, Agencies, Media, and Policy Makers," *Journal of Advertising Research* 29 (October/November 1989), 38–48.

85. Naveen Donthu, "A Cross-Country Investigation of Recall of and Attitude toward Comparative Advertising," *Journal of Advertising* 27 (summer 1998), 111–22.

86. These questions are adapted from Stephen B. Ash and ChowHou Wee, "Comparative Advertising: A Review with Implications for Further Research," in *Advances in Consumer Research*, vol. 10, ed. R. P. Bagozzi and A. M. Tybout, Ann Arbor, MI: Association for Consumer Research, 1983, 374.

87. A sampling of significant comparative advertising research includes the following: Cornelia Droge and Rene Y. Darmon, "Associative Positioning Strategies through Comparative Advertising: Attribute versus Overall Similarity Approaches," *Journal of Marketing Research* 24 (November 1987), 377–88; Cornelia Pechmann and David W. Stewart, "The Effects of Comparative Advertising on Attention, Memory, and Purchase Intentions," *Journal of Consumer Research* 17 (September 1990), 180–91; Cornelia Pechmann and S. Ratneshwar, "The Use of Comparative Advertising for Brand Positioning: Association versus Differentiation," *Journal of Consumer Research* 18 (September 1991), 145–60; Cornelia Pechmann and Gabriel Esteban, "Persuasion Processes Associated with Direct Comparative and Noncomparative Advertising and Implications for Advertising Effectiveness," *Journal of Consumer Psychology* 2, no. 4 (1993), 403–32; Randall L. Rose, Paul W. Miniard, Michael J. Barone, Kenneth C. Manning, and Brian D. Till, "When Persuasion Goes Undetected: The Case of Comparative Advertising," *Journal of Marketing Research* 30 (August 1993), 315–30; Shailendra Pratap Jain, Bruce Buchanan, and Durairaj Maheswaran, "Comparative versus Noncomparative Advertising: The Moderating Impact of Prepurchase Attribute Verifiability," *Journal of Consumer Psychology* 9, no. 4 (2000), 201–12; Shi Zhang, Frank R. Kardes, and Maria L. Cronley, "Comparative Advertising: Effects of Structural Alignability on Target Brand Evaluations," *Journal of Consumer Psychology* 12, no. 4 (2002), 303–12; Michael J. Barone, Kay M. Palan, and Paul W. Miniard, "Brand Usage and Gender as Moderators of the Potential Deception Associated with Partial Comparative Advertising," *Journal of Advertising* 33 (spring 2004), 19–28; and Dhruv Grewal, Sukuman Kavanoor, Edward F. Fern, Carolyn Costley, and James Barnes, "Comparative versus Noncomparative Advertising: A Meta-Analysis," *Journal of Marketing* 61 (October 1997), 1–15.

88. Terence A. Shimp and David C. Dyer, "The Effects of Comparative Advertising Mediated by Market Position of Sponsoring Brand," *Journal of Advertising* 7, no. 3 (1978), 13–19.

89. Gerald J. Gorn and Charles B. Weinberg, "The Impact of Comparative Advertising on Perception and Attitude: Some Positive Findings," *Journal of Consumer Research* 11 (September 1984), 719–27.

90. Paul W. Miniard, Michael J. Barone, Randall L. Rose, and Kenneth C. Manning, "A Further Assessment of Indirect Comparative Advertising Claims of Superiority Over All Competitors," *Journal of Advertising* 35 (winter 2006), 53–64.

91. Rose, Miniard, Barone, Manning, and Till, "When Persuasion Goes Undetected: The Case of Comparative Advertising"; and Paul W. Miniard, Randall L. Rose, Michael J. Barone, and Kenneth C. Manning, "On the Need for Relative Measures When Assessing Comparative Advertising Effects," *Journal of Advertising* 22 (September 1993), 41–57. For an alternative explanation of why relative framed messages are more effective, see Zhang, Kardes, and Cronley, "Comparative Advertising: Effects of Structural Alignability on Target Brand Evaluations."

MARCOM INSIGHT Has TV Advertising Lost Its Effectiveness? Or Has It Simply Changed Its Look?

Television as an advertising medium has undergone rather dramatic changes in the past decade or so. The average television household (via cable or satellite) now has literally hundreds of TV channels from which to choose. This means that advertisements simply do not reach the large numbers of consumers they once did. In fact, the decline in ratings for network TV affiliates began in the mid-1980s (prime-time household [HH] rating average = 44.8) and has declined steadily over the years (e.g., 25.6 in 2009). Beyond this audience fragmentation, people have many more entertainment options to distract them from watching TV, including social media, smartphones, tablets, etc. Complicating matters for advertisers, the number of TV households owning digital video recorders (DVRs) has increased to nearly 40 percent, and the owners of these devices

© PSL Images/Alamy

often use them to skip completely or fast-forward through commercials. Finally, the cost of TV advertising remains high, which means that ads placed on television must be effective in order to yield a positive return on investment (ROI).

Some studies have concluded that TV advertising is declining in effectiveness. Over three quarters of the Association of National Advertisers executives are of the opinion that traditional TV advertising has declined in effectiveness, and many intended to reduce their TV advertising budgets. A study conducted by McKinsey & Company reports that ad spending on prime-time TV over the past decade and a half increased by nearly 40 percent while the number of viewers decreased by about 50 percent, the result being a much higher cost per viewer reached. A final report by Deutsche Bank presented data showing that a high percentage of the TV

1 Describe the four major traditional advertising media (newspapers, magazines, radio, and television).

2 Discuss the strengths and weakness for each of the following major traditional advertising media: newspapers, magazines, radio, and television.

3 Describe how each of these traditional media choices has changed with the appearance of new media options (e.g., social media, online advertising).

4 Appreciate the research methods that are used for each ad medium to determine the size of the audience exposed to advertising vehicles.

advertisements for 23 mature brands (e.g., Coca-Cola Classic, Campbell's soup, Heinz ketchup) in the consumer packaged goods (CPG) category do not yield positive ROIs. Newer brands were more likely to yield positive ROIs. (Yet, that new brands perform better than mature brands should come as no surprise in that TV advertising generally is effective only when the advertising is persuasive and provides distinctive, newsworthy information, such as when introducing new brands.)

Yet, there are many counterarguments to the purported decline of TV advertising. First, the fragmentation of media has made TV more valuable, and in demand, as the explosion of options has reduced the supply of ad space that can reach millions at once. In turn, this has increased prime-time cost of TV ads by 17 percent in the last year. Recently, ad dollars are argued to be flowing toward two poles—TV and the Internet. Media experts indicate that TV does a great job in helping consumers become aware of (and understand) the advantages of different brands, whereas the Internet excels in taking your order once you know what you want. Second, rather than "killing TV," social media is actually becoming more integrated with TV content via tweets, posts, and check-ins. During the Bravo Network's final episode of the third season of the *Real Housewives of New York City*, thousands of viewers simultaneously used the interactive feature, Talk Bubble, on the Bravo website, as well as mobile-based voting on smartphones, and now there is an iPad app for the show. A recent Nielsen study found

consumers now spend on average 3 hours and 41 minutes each month watching TV and simultaneously browsing the Interent. Also, 86 percent of U.S. mobile users watch TV on their devices. Apps such as GetGlue, IntoNow, Showtime Social, and Shazam have helped consumers watch live TV through their digital devices. Finally, even with challenges facing Google with acquiring and delivering TV content, the full integration of smart TVs with Internet compatibility is being launched by efforts such as Google TV.

The takeaway from all of these trends is that even though traditional TV has been under fire, the delivery of its content has changed dramatically from previous years. It continues to be an important consideration for advertisers in capturing multi-screen audiences.

Sources: Bill Gorman, "Where Did the Primetime Broadcast TV Audience Go?" *TV by the Numbers*, April 12, 2010, http://tvbythenumbers.zap2it.com/2010/04/12/where-did-the-primetime-broadcast-tv-audience-go/47976; Robert Seidman, "DVR Penetration Grows to 39.7% of Households, 42.2% of Viewers," *TV by the Numbers*, March 23, 2011, http://tvbythenumbers.zap2it.com/2011/03/23/dvr-penetration-grows-to-39-7-of-households-42-2-of-viewers/86819; "TV Ads Losing Power, Survey Shows," *Wall Street Journal*, March 23, 2006, B2; Abbey Klaassen, "Major Turnoff: McKinsey Slams TV's Selling Power," *Advertising Age*, August 7, 2006, 1, 33; Jack Neff, "TV Doesn't Sell Package Goods," *Advertising Age*, May 24, 2004, 1, 30; Jessica E. Vascellaro and Sam Schechner, "TV Lures Ads But Viewers Drop Out," *Wall Street Journal*, September 21, 2011, B1, B2; Kunur Patel and Irina Slutsky, "Is Social Media Killing TV?" *Advertising Age*, April 18, 2011, 4; Felix Gillette, "For Bravo, One Screen Isn't Enough," *Bloomberg Businessweek*, November 8–14, 2010, 43–44; Katherine Bouhret, "Using Another Screen to Interact with the TV," *Wall Street Journal*, December 21, 2011, D2; and "Google Embarks on a Career in Television," *Wall Street Journal*, November 21, 2011, C10.

Introduction

This chapter focuses on the four major mass advertising media: newspapers, magazines, radio, and television. Separate sections focus on each of these four major media, with primary emphasis devoted to exploring each medium's strengths and limitations and to explaining the research methods that are used for measuring the number of people who are exposed to advertising vehicles within each medium.

Measured media advertising in the United States in these four traditional media outlets is estimated to reach $120.9 billion by the end of 2012. (Current estimates are approximately $300 billion for *all* media—measured *and* unmeasured—as indicated in Chapter 9.) Television commanded nearly 51 percent of these total expenditures, radio approximately 19 percent, newspapers about 17 percent, and magazines (including business-to-business) approximately 13 percent.[1]

In terms of 2010 net U.S. media revenue (for the 100 leading media companies), broadcast TV and cable TV increased 14 percent and 8 percent from the previous year, respectively, radio rose 5.7 percent, whereas magazines declined 0.8 percent and newspapers were down 5.1 percent.[2] U.S. employment showed a 31 percent increase (July 2009 to July 2011) for Internet media companies, whereas decreases were evident for magazine companies (–7.1 percent), broadcast TV (–0.3 percent), cable TV (–0.6 percent), and radio (–4.8 percent). There has been a 29 percent decline in newspaper positions since 2007.[3]

Some Preliminary Comments

It is important to recognize that no advertising medium is always best. The value or worth of a medium depends on the circumstances confronting a brand at a particular time: consumer behavior, the advertising objective, the target market toward which this objective is aimed, and the available budget. An analogy will clarify this point. Suppose someone asked you, "What type of restaurant is best?" You likely would have difficulty offering a single answer because you would recognize that what is best depends on your particular needs on a specific occasion (e.g., speed of service—McDonald's; ambiance—a classy Italian restaurant).

The same is true of advertising media. Which medium is "best" depends entirely on consumer preferences, the advertiser's objectives, the creative needs, the competitive challenge, and the budget available. The best medium, or combination of media, is determined by conducting a careful examination of the advertised brand's needs and resources.

The following presentation of ad media progresses in the following order: first covered are the two print media, newspapers and magazines. Then examined are the broadcast media, radio and television. TV receives the most in-depth treatment because it commands the greatest amount of advertising dollars and because ongoing developments in this medium are the most dynamic.

Newspapers

Newspapers reach approximately 48 million U.S. households during the week and about 49 million on Sundays.[4] For either print or online versions, 41 percent of all adults in the United States read a daily newspaper, and about 46 percent read a Sunday newspaper.[5] Newspapers historically were the leading advertising medium, but television and radio both surpassed newspapers as mediums that receive the greatest amount of advertising expenditures. This is partially attributable to the fact that newspaper readership has been on a constant decline for years. However, many newspapers (e.g., *New York Times*) have attempted to expand their readership with digital subscriptions, with

© Lourens Smak/Alamy

unlimited access to the newspaper's website and applications (apps) for access on smartphones and tablets.[6] Print subscribers are offered Internet access to digital delivery as well.

Local advertising is clearly the mainspring of newspapers. However, newspapers have become more active in their efforts to increase national advertising. The Newspaper Advertising Bureau (NAB), a nonprofit sales and research organization, has facilitated these efforts. The NAB offers a variety of services that assist both newspapers and national advertisers by simplifying the task of buying newspaper space and by offering discounts that make newspapers a more attractive medium.

Buying Newspaper Space

A major problem in the past when buying newspaper space, especially for advertisers that purchased space from newspapers in many cities, was that newspaper page size and column space varied, which prevented an advertiser from preparing a single advertisement to fit every newspaper. So, the advertising industry adopted a standardized system known as the Standardized Advertising Unit (SAU) system, which enables advertisers to purchase any one of *56 standard ad sizes* to fit the advertising publishing parameters of all U.S. newspapers.

Under this system, advertisers prepare advertisements and purchase space in terms of column widths and depth in inches. There are six column widths:

1 column:	2 1/16 inches
2 columns:	4 1/4 inches
3 columns:	6 7/16 inches
4 columns:	8 5/8 inches
5 columns:	10 13/16 inches
6 columns:	13 inches

Space *depth* varies in size from 1 inch to 21 inches. Thus, an advertiser can purchase an ad as small as 1 inch by 2 1/16 inches or as large as 13 inches by 21 inches, with numerous in-between combinations of widths and depths. A chosen size for a particular advertisement can then be run in newspapers throughout the country. Space rates can be compared from newspaper to newspaper and adjusted for circulation differences. For example, in 2010, the daily SAU column-inch rate for the *St. Petersburg (FL) Times* (circulation: 239,700) was $640, whereas the same rate in the competitive *Tampa (FL) Tribune* (circulation: 145,000) was $435.[7] On the surface, the *Tribune* is cheaper than the *Times*, but when adjusted to a per-thousand-readers basis, the cost per thousand (CPM) of procuring a column inch in the *Times* is approximately $2.67 (i.e., $640 ÷ 239.7), compared with a CPM of about $3.00 (i.e., $435 ÷ 145) for the *Tribune*. Hence, it is actually slightly cheaper, on a CPM basis, to advertise in the *Times*. Of course, the advertiser must observe audience characteristics, newspaper image, and other factors when making an advertising decision rather than considering only cost.

The choice of an advertisement's position must also be considered when buying newspaper space. Space rates apply only to advertisements placed ROP (*run of press*), which means that the ad appears in any location, on any page, at the discretion of the newspaper. Premium charges may be assessed if an advertiser has a preferred space positioning, such as at the top of the page in the financial section. Premium charges, if assessed, are negotiated between the advertiser and the newspaper.

Newspaper Advertising's Strengths and Limitations

As with all advertising media, newspaper advertising has various strengths and limitations (see Table 12.1).

Newspaper Advertising's Strengths

Because people read newspapers for news, they are in the *right mental frame to process advertisements* that present news of store openings, new products, sales, and so forth.

Mass audience coverage, or broad reach, is a second strength of newspaper advertising. Coverage is not restricted to specific socioeconomic or demographic groups but rather extends across all strata. However, newspaper readers on average are more economically upscale than television viewers. College graduates are more likely to read a newspaper than the population at large. Because economically advantaged consumers are comparatively light TV viewers, newspaper advertising provides a relatively inexpensive medium for reaching these consumers. Special-interest newspapers also reach large numbers of potential consumers. For example, the vast majority of college students read a campus newspaper. A survey revealed that 71 percent of college students had read at least one of the last five issues of their college newspaper.[8]

Flexibility is perhaps the greatest strength of newspapers. National advertisers can adjust copy to match the specific buying preferences and peculiarities of localized markets. Local advertisers can vary copy through in-paper inserts targeted to specific ZIP codes. In addition, advertising copy can be placed in a newspaper section that is compatible with the advertised product. Retailers of wedding accessories advertise in the bridal section, providers of financial services advertise in the business section, sporting goods stores advertise in the sports section, and so forth. A second facet of newspaper flexibility is that this medium enables advertisers to design ads of many different sizes (56 in total); few size or length options are possible in other mass media.

The *ability to use detailed copy* is another of newspaper advertising's strengths. Detailed product information and extensive editorial passages are used in newspaper advertising to an extent unparalleled by any other medium.

Timeliness is the final significant strength of newspaper advertising. Short lead times (the time between placing an ad and having it run) permit advertisers to tie in advertising copy with local market developments or newsworthy events.

TABLE 12.1	Newspaper Advertising's Strengths and Limitations	
Strengths	**Limitations**
Audience in appropriate mental frame to process messages	Clutter
	Not a highly selective medium
Mass audience coverage	Higher rates for occasional advertisers
Flexibility	Mediocre reproduction quality
Ability to use detailed copy	Complicated buying for national advertisers
Timeliness	Changing composition of readers
	Declining readership

Advertisers can develop copy or make copy changes quickly and thereby take advantage of dynamic marketplace developments.

Newspaper Advertising's Limitations

Clutter is a problem in newspapers, as it is in all of the other major media. A reader perusing a newspaper is confronted with many ads, all of which compete for the reader's limited time and only a subset of which receive the reader's attention. It is noteworthy, however, that a national survey of consumers revealed that they perceived newspapers as being significantly less cluttered with advertisements than television, radio, and magazines.[9]

A second limitation of newspaper advertising is that newspapers are *not a highly selective medium*. Newspapers are able to reach broad cross sections of people but, with few exceptions (such as campus newspapers), are unable to reach specific groups of consumers effectively. Media specialists consider newspapers to fare poorly in comparison to network television in efficiently targeting specific audiences.[10]

Occasional users of newspaper space (such as national advertisers who infrequently advertise in newspapers) pay higher rates than do heavy users (such as local advertisers) and have difficulty in securing preferred, non-ROP positions. In fact, newspapers' price lists (called *rate cards*) show higher rates for national than local advertisers.

Newspapers generally offer a *mediocre reproduction quality*. Although color photos, etc. have been incorporated, in a relative sense, newspapers are not generally known to enhance a product's perceived quality, elegance, or snob appeal, as can magazines and television.

Buying difficulty is a particularly acute problem in the case of the national advertiser who wishes to secure newspaper space in multiple markets. On top of the high rates charged to national advertisers, each newspaper must be contacted individually. Fortunately, as mentioned previously, the NAB has made great strides toward facilitating the purchase of newspaper space by national advertisers.

Another problem with newspaper advertising involves the *changing composition of newspaper readers*. Although most everyone used to read a daily newspaper, readership has declined progressively during the past generation. The most faithful newspaper readers are individuals aged 45 and older, but the large and attractive group of consumers aged 30 to 44 are reading daily newspapers less frequently than ever.

Perhaps the major problem is that *readership of printed newspapers has declined substantially*. However, it is noteworthy that all major newspapers have created online sites that have attracted readers who do not pay for printed newspapers. Hence, actual readership of newspapers—the combination of electronic and print readership—can be considerably higher than many reported circulation levels for printed newspapers. Newspaper companies are increasing their advertising revenues by including search engines on their online sites and then charging for advertisements that pop up alongside search results.[11]

Magazines

Although considered a mass medium, there are literally thousands of special-interest magazines, both consumer- and business-oriented, that appeal to audiences that manifest specific interests and lifestyles. In fact, Standard Rate and Data Service (now known simply as SRDS Media Solutions), a company that tracks information for the magazine industry (as well as for most other media), identifies well over 3,000 consumer print magazines (and 5,000 digital ones) in dozens of specific categories, such as automotive (e.g., *Motor Trend*); general editorial (e.g., the *New Yorker*); sports (e.g., *Sports Illustrated*); and women's fashions, beauty, and grooming (e.g., *Glamour*). In addition to consumer magazines, thousands of other publications are classified as business magazines. Advertisers obviously have numerous options when selecting magazines to promote their products either to consumers or to businesspeople. Advertisers and media planners turn to SRDS (www.srds.com) to

© AP Images/Paul Sakuma

obtain information on standardized ad rates, contact information, reader profiles, and other information, which facilitates media planning and buying.

Buying Magazine Space

A number of factors influence the choice of magazine vehicles in which to advertise. Most important is selecting magazines that reach the type of people who constitute the advertiser's target market. However, because the advertiser typically can choose from several alternative vehicles to satisfy the target market objective, cost considerations also play an extremely important role.

Advertisers interested in using the magazine medium can acquire a wealth of demographic data about the composition of a magazine's readership. This information is provided in each magazine's *media kit* that is made available to ad agencies and prospective advertisers. Media kits can be found online for many magazines. For example, Figure 12.1 presents the demographic profile for *Golf Digest* magazine based on data presented by Condé Nast, which is

	Audience (in thousands)	Composition (%)	Index
Total Audience	6,245	100%	100
Age			
18–34	1,405	23%	74
35–44	1,096	18	98
45–54	1,190	19	98
55–64	1,262	20	132
65+	1,291	21	123
Median Age	50.4		
Education			
Graduated College+	2,874	46%	169
Attended College+	4,659	75	135
Occupation			
Top Management	973	16%	177
Professional/Managerial	1,797	29	128
Household Income (HHI)			
$100,000+	2,861	46%	182
$ 75,000+	3,907	63	161
$ 50,000+	5,060	81	140
Median HHI	$93,749		

FIGURE **12.1** *Golf Digest*'s Demographic Profile

Source: Condé Nast, September 2011, http://www.gdmediakit.com/reader_profile.pdf. (accessed December 1, 2011).

the owner of this magazine and many others. The median age of *Golf Digest*'s readership is 50.4 with a median household income of $93,749. It is apparent that this magazine has its greatest appeal among older, economically prosperous consumers.

Also presented in Figure 12.1 are specific breakdowns by age, education, occupation, and household income. For each demographic grouping, the first column contains audience size expressed in thousands, the second column presents percentage breakdowns for each demographic subgroup that represent that subgroup's composition of *Golf Digest*'s total audience, and the last column indexes each percentage against that group's proportionate population representation. For example, 18 percent of *Golf Digest*'s readers fall in the age group of 35–44, 46 percent graduated college, 29 percent are employed in professional and managerial positions, and 46 percent have household incomes of $100,000 or more. As mentioned, the last column in Figure 12.1 indexes each subgroup's composition of *Golf Digest*'s readership against that group's proportionate population representation. For example, the 18–34 age group composes only 23 percent of *Golf Digest*'s total audience, which is substantially below that group's proportionate representation in the total population. This underrepresentation is reflected in the 18–34 age group having an index of only 74. Comparatively, the 65+ age group (i.e., retirees who have a lot of time to play golf and read golf magazines) constitutes 21 percent of *Golf Digest*'s total audience, but the high index of 123 reflects that this age group reads this particular magazine disproportionately more than its population representation.

Media kits also provide prospective advertisers with pertinent cost information in the form of *rate cards*. A partial rate card for *Sports Illustrated* magazine is presented in Figure 12.2. This card includes advertising rates for different page sizes (full page, two-thirds page, half page, one-third page, etc.), and for four-color and black-and-white (B&W) ads. For example, an advertiser would pay $370,500 to place a full-page, four-color ad in *Sports Illustrated* on a one-time (open) rate basis. However, as is typical in magazines' price policies, cumulative discounts are available based on the number of pages advertised in *Sports Illustrated* during 12 consecutive months. Cumulative quantity discounts provide clear incentives for advertisers to remain with a particular magazine.

Although every magazine has its own media kit, advertisers and their agencies do not have to contact each magazine to obtain them. SRDS compiles media kits and then makes them available (of course, for a fee) to advertisers and their agencies. Also, rate cards can be obtained online by simply conducting a search such as inputting "Sports Illustrated rate card" into Google. Information for each magazine (or *book* as they are referred to in the advertising industry) includes editorial features, rates, readership profiles, circulation, and contact information.

	4-Color	B&W
Full Page	$370,500	$240,900
2/3 Page	$308,800	$200,800
1/2 Page	$259,400	$168,700
1/3 Page	$166,800	$108,500
Second Cover Spread	$852,200	N/A
Third Cover	$407,600	N/A
Back Cover	$481,700	N/A

FIGURE **12.2** Partial Rate Card for *Sports Illustrated* (Rate base = 3,150,000)

Source: *Sports Illustrated* Rate Card #69, effective January 10, 2011, http://www.simediakit.com/ media/property/download/ratecard/Sports%20Illustrated%202011%20Rate%20Card.pdf. (accessed December 1, 2011).

Advertisers use the CPM measure (i.e., cost to reach 1,000 readers of an issue) to compare different magazine buys. (See also Chapter 16 for CPM calculations. The "M" in CPM is the Roman numeral for a thousand.) CPM information for each magazine is available from two syndicated magazine services: GfK Mediamark Research Inc. (MRI) and Experian Simmons (formerly Simmons Market Research Bureau) (SMRB or simply "Simmons"). These services provide CPM figures for general reader categories (e.g., total men) and also break out CPMs for subgroups (e.g., men ages 18 to 49, male homeowners). These more specific subgroupings enable the advertiser to compare different magazine vehicles in terms of cost per thousand for reaching the target market (CPM-TM) rather than only in terms of gross CPMs. Cost-per-thousand data are useful in making magazine vehicle selection decisions, but many other factors must be taken into account.

Magazine Advertising's Strengths and Limitations

Magazine advertising too has both strengths and limitations, depending on the advertisers' needs and resources (see Table 12.2).

Magazine Advertising's Strengths

Some magazines reach *very large audiences*. For example, magazines like *Better Homes & Gardens, Reader's Digest, Sports Illustrated*, and *Time* have total audiences that exceed 29 million readers.

However, the ability to pinpoint specific audiences (termed *selectivity*) most distinguishes magazine advertising from other media. If a potential market exists for a product, there most likely is at least one periodical that reaches that market. Selectivity enables an advertiser to achieve effective, rather than wasted, exposure. This translates into more efficient advertising and lower costs per 1,000 target customers.

Magazines are also noted for their *long life*. Unlike other media, magazines often are used for reference and kept for weeks around the home (and in barber shops, and beauty salons, and dentists' and doctors' offices, etc.). Magazine subscribers sometimes pass along their copies to other readers, further extending a magazine's life.

In terms of qualitative considerations, magazines as an advertising medium are exceptional with regard to elegance, quality, beauty, prestige, and snob appeal. These features result from the *high level of reproduction quality* and from the surrounding editorial content that often transfers to the advertised product. For example, food items advertised in *Bon Appétit* always look elegant, furniture items in *Better Homes & Gardens* look tasteful, and clothing items in *Cosmopolitan* and *Gentlemen's Quarterly* (GQ) appear especially fashionable.

TABLE 12.2	Magazine Advertising's Strengths and Limitations
Strengths	**Limitations**
Some magazines reach large audiences	Not intrusive
Selectivity	Long lead times
Long life	Clutter
High reproduction quality	Somewhat limited geographic options
Ability to present detailed information	Variability of circulation patterns by market
Ability to convey information authoritatively	
High involvement potential	

© Cengage Learning

Magazines are also a particularly good source for providing *detailed product information* and for conveying this information with a *sense of authority*. That is, because the editorial content of magazines often includes articles that themselves represent a sense of insight, expertise, and credibility, the advertisements carried in these magazines convey a similar sense of authority, or correctness.

A final and especially notable feature of magazine advertising is its creative ability to get consumers *involved in ads* or, in a sense, to attract readers' interest and to engage them to think about the advertised brands. This ability is due to the self-selection and reader-controlled nature of magazines compared with more intrusive media such as radio and television. For example, issues of *Runner's World* routinely offer novice runners tips for steadily increasing their mileage and not giving up, yet also provide experienced marathoners details on the right marathons to enter to qualify for the Boston Marathon.

Magazine Advertising's Limitations

Several limitations are associated with magazine advertising (see Table 12.2). First, unlike TV and radio, which by their very nature infringe on the attention of the viewer and listener, magazine advertising is *not intrusive*; readers control their exposure to a magazine ad.

A second limitation is *long lead times*. In newspapers and the broadcast media, it is relatively easy to change ad copy on fairly short notice and in specific markets. Magazines, by comparison, have long closing dates that require advertising materials to be on hand for weeks in advance of the actual publication date. For example, for four-color ads the closing dates for the following sampling of magazines are shown in parentheses: *Better Homes & Gardens* (10 weeks), *Cosmopolitan* (8 weeks), *Sports Illustrated* (5 weeks), and *Time* (4 weeks).[12]

As with other advertising media, *clutter* is a problem with magazine advertising. In certain respects clutter is a worse problem with magazines than, say, television, because readers can become engrossed in editorial content and skip over advertisements.

Magazine advertising also provides *fewer geographic options* than do other media, although some large circulation magazines such as *Sports Illustrated* provide considerable selectivity. For example, *Sports Illustrated* offers advertising rates for seven key regions, all 50 states, and 33 metropolitan areas. An advertiser could choose to advertise in *Sports Illustrated* only in the northeastern edition, say, and in so doing pay $57,200 for a full-page, four-color ad. Comparatively, the same ad in a slightly larger market such as in the western edition would cost $62,000.[13]

A final limitation of magazine advertising is *variability in circulation patterns* from market to market. *Rolling Stone* magazine, for example, is read more in metropolitan than rural areas. Hence, advertisers who are interested, say, in reaching young men would not be very successful in reaching nonmetropolitan readers. This would suggest placing ads in one or more magazines other than *Rolling Stone*, which would up the total cost of the media buy. Radio, TV, or both might better serve the advertiser's needs and provide more uniform market coverage.

Magazine Audience Measurement

When selecting magazine vehicles, it is critical for advertisers to know the audience size candidate magazines reach. Determining the size of a particular magazine's readership might seem a simple task that merely involves tallying the number of subscribers to a magazine. Unfortunately, it is more complicated than this because several factors make subscription counting an inadequate way of determining a magazine's readership: First, magazine subscriptions are collected through a variety of intermediaries, making it difficult to obtain accurate lists of who subscribes to which magazines. Second, magazines often are purchased from newsstands, supermarkets, and other retail outlets rather than through subscriptions, thus completely eliminating knowledge of who purchases which magazines. Third, magazines that are available in public locations such as doctors' offices, barber shops, and beauty salons are read by numerous people and not just the subscriber. Finally, individual magazine subscribers often share issues with other people.

For these reasons, the number of subscriptions to a magazine and the number of people who actually read the magazine are not equivalent. Fortunately, two previously mentioned services—MRI and Simmons—specialize in measuring magazine readership and determining audience size. These companies offer very similar, yet competitive, services.

In brief, both services take large, national probability samples and query respondents to identify their media consumption habits (e.g., which magazines they read) and determine their purchase behaviors for an extensive variety of products and brands. Statisticians then employ inference procedures to generalize sample results to the total population. Advertisers and media planners use the readership information along with detailed demographic and product and brand usage data to evaluate the absolute and relative value of different magazines.

Advantages aside, not all is perfect in the world of magazine audience measurement due to three notable problems: (1) respondents to readership surveys are asked to rate numerous magazines (as well as many vehicles in other media), which can lead to fatigue and hasty or faulty responses; (2) sample sizes often are small, especially for small-circulation magazines, which leads to high margins of sampling error when generalizing to the total population; and (3) sample composition may be unrepresentative of audience readership.[14] Also, because these two readership services use different research methods, their results often are discrepant. Consider, for example, Simmons' versus MRI's estimates for the following large-circulation magazines: *Better Homes & Gardens* (43.69 million readers estimated by Simmons versus 39.26 million readers estimated by MRI), *Cosmopolitan* (20.90 million versus 18.45 million), and *National Geographic* (44.75 million versus 30.88 million).[15] In percentage terms and using the smaller estimate as the base, these differences are 11.3, 13.3, and 44.9 percent, respectively. Media planners thus confront the challenge of determining which service is right or whether both are wrong in their estimates of audience size.[16]

Using Simmons and MRI Reports

Despite these problems, media planners must make the most of the audience estimates and readership profiles Simmons and MRI generate. Both companies produce annual reports of product and brand usage data and provide detailed media information. Using imported beer/ale as an illustration, Table 12.3 provides a pared-down report that will be useful for explaining the construction and interpretation of Simmons and MRI reports.[17] Your library may subscribe to an electronic version of either a Simmons or MRI database. If so, you should access a recent report and inspect the vast amount of information that is provided in these reports.

MRI and Simmons reports are structurally equivalent to the data contained in Table 12.3. Each of the detailed tables in these reports present cross-tabulations of demographic segments by product or brand usage. Table 12.3 presents usage of imported beer/ale delineated by age groupings, educational status, geographic region, and Internet and TV quintiles (which will be explained subsequently). (For simplicity, all subsequent references to imported beer/ale will be shortened to imported beer.) The table is to be interpreted as follows:

1. The first row (*Total*) shows the occurrence of imported beer purchases in the total U.S. population. Thus, of the 228,112,000 adults living in the

TABLE 12.3	Illustration of a MRI Report for Imported Beer/Ale (based on all adults indicating whether they have drunk imported beer/ale within the last six months)				
	Total '000	A Proj '000	B % Across	C % Down	D Index
Total	228,112	45,910	20.1	100.0	100
Age 18–24	28,815	5,898	20.5	12.8	102
Age 25–34	40,710	10,503	25.8	22.9	128
Age 35–44	41,552	10,241	24.6	22.3	122
Age 45–54	44,605	9,078	20.4	19.8	101
Age 55–64	34,456	6,522	18.9	14.2	94
Age 65+	37,973	3,668	9.7	8.0	48
Educ: graduated college plus	61,723	17,899	29.0	39.0	144
Educ: attended college	63,819	12,254	19.2	26.7	95
Educ: graduated high school	70,358	11,252	16.0	24.5	79
Educ: did not graduate HS	32,211	4,505	14.0	9.8	69
Educ: postgraduate	21,647	6,550	30.3	14.3	150
Educ: no college	102,570	15,757	15.4	34.3	76
Census Region: Northeast	41,697	10,902	26.1	23.7	130
Census Region: South	84,310	13,905	16.5	30.3	82
Census Region: Midwest	50,012	8,555	17.1	18.6	85
Census Region: West	52,092	12,547	24.1	27.3	120
TV (total) Quintile I (Heavy)	45,631	6,566	14.4	14.3	71
TV (total) Quintile II	45,623	8,507	18.6	18.5	93
TV (total) Quintile III	45,605	10,387	22.8	22.6	113
TV (total) Quintile IV	45,628	10,336	22.7	22.5	113
TV (total) Quintile V (Light)	45,626	10,113	22.2	22.0	110
Internet Quintile I (Heavy)	45,635	10,905	23.9	23.8	119
Internet Quintile II	45,621	11,439	25.1	24.9	125
Internet Quintile III	45,618	10,948	24.0	23.8	119
Internet Quintile IV	45,619	6,939	15.2	15.1	76
Internet Quintile V (Light)	45,618	5,678	12.4	12.4	62

Source: MRI Reporter, Fall 2010.

United States at the time of data collection, 45,910,000 (see column A), or 20.1 percent (see column B, % *Across*), drank imported beer at least once within the last six months.

2. Each set of detailed entries shows the estimate in four different ways (denoted as columns A, B, C, and D) for the product category (imported beer in this case) and the specified population grouping:

   a. *Column A* presents the estimate of *total product users* (expressed in thousands). Note carefully that Table 12.3 presents data in thousands, shown as '000, so the value of 45,910 in the top row stands for

45,910,000 drinkers of imported beer. Of the 45,910,000 total drinkers of imported beer, 5,898,000 are in the 18–24 age category, 10,503,000 in the 24–34 age group, and so on.

b. *Column B (% Across)* reflects each subgroup's proportionate representation with respect to the total number of product users in the product category. For example, of the 28,815,000 people in the 18–24 age group (see the value under the Total column), MRI estimates that 5,898,000 in that subgroup are imported beer drinkers. Thus, the percent across values in Column B (20.5 percent in this case) simply represents the proportionate representation of each value under column A compared with its corresponding value under the Total column.

c. *Column C (% Down)* represents the percentage of product users in each demographic subgroup compared with the total number of product users. For example, 5,898,000 of the 45,910,000 total drinkers of imported beer are in the 18–24 age group. This age group thus represents 12.8 percent of the total number of imported beer drinkers. Note that each value in column C (*% Down*) is calculated by dividing the column A value for a particular row by the total value in column A (i.e., 45,910,000).

d. *Column D (Index)* is a measure of a particular demographic group's proportionate product consumption compared with the total population's proportionate product consumption. For example, 20.1 percent of all American adults are at least occasional imported beer drinkers. Comparatively, 20.5 percent of consumers in the 18–24 age group are imported beer drinkers (these two figures, 20.1 and 20.5 percent, respectively, are shown in Column B, *% Across*). The index values in Column D reflect this relationship. Hence, the index value for consumers aged 18–24 is calculated as follows: $(20.5 \div 20.1) \times 100 = 102$. This index indicates that people in the 18–24 age group are 2 percent *more likely* than the general population to drink imported beer. Comparatively, older consumers in the 55–64 age group with an index of 94 $[(14.2 \div 18.9) \times 100 = 94]$ are 6 percent *less likely* than the general population, with an index of 100, to drink imported beer.

All in all, the index numbers for age groups indicate that imported beer consumption generally declines with increasing age. Similarly, the index numbers based on educational attainment (see Table 12.3) indicate that people who have graduated college and those with postgraduate degrees are disproportionately more likely to drink imported beer. Comparatively, individuals with high school degrees and those who did not graduate high school are disproportionately less likely to drink imported beer.

Does this mean that imported beer marketers should cater only to younger consumers and those with higher education and neglect the others? Probably not. For example, although people ages 45 to 54 (index = 101) are proportionately less likely than the younger age groups to consume imported beer, there are, nonetheless, a total of approximately nine million people in this age group who do consume imported beer. It thus would make little sense to disregard such a large number of consumers simply because the index number is only slightly more than 100. Although prudent imported beer marketers would not neglect these older consumers, the index numbers in Table 12.3 suggest that less media emphasis, or weight, should be directed at older consumers than the weight targeted at the younger consumers.

Turning to the Internet and TV data in Table 12.3, notice under the Total column that the total number of American adults (228,112,000) has been divided into five basically equal-sized groups (quintiles) based on their Internet and TV usage. Hence, Quintile I represents the heaviest Internet users and the heaviest TV viewers, whereas Quintile V represents the lightest Internet users and lightest TV viewers. Column D in Table 12.3 reveals that heavier Internet users are more likely to be drinkers of imported beer (index numbers of 119 and 125 for Quintiles I and II) and that imported beer consumption declines in the lighter Internet quintiles (Quintiles IV and V). Conversely, heavy TV viewers (Quintiles I and II) are disproportionately less likely than the lighter viewer quintiles to consume imported beer. How might an advertiser use these data?

In using media data supplied in MRI and Simmons reports, the advertiser must weigh various pieces of information to make intelligent use of these reports. Evidence indicates that media planners too often use MRI and Simmons data in a simplistic manner that fails to utilize fully all information provided by these reports.[18] The tendency is to focus excessively on the index numbers contained in Column D. Although the index numbers reflect a subgroup's proportionate product-usage representation compared with the total population's product usage, the index numbers fail to tell the whole story.

It is essential to go beyond the index numbers and consider each demographic subgroup's total size and potential for growth in using the product category. Thus, for example, although Americans who have only a high school education drink imported beer proportionately less than those who have graduated college (index numbers of 79 for high school grads versus 144 for college grads; see Table 12.3), the number of high-school-only grads (70,358,000) is considerably larger than the number of college grads (61,723,000). Hence, an imported beer advertiser should not neglect people who have not graduated college, but rather might cultivate this market by developing advertisements that appeal to their lifestyles and advertising in media vehicles that are particularly effective in reaching them.

Customized Magazines

Discussion to this point has focused on magazines that are published by companies whose primary business is creating and distributing magazines (i.e., magazine publishers). However, there has been a major development in recent years wherein marketers of specific brands are developing newsletters and magazines that focus on their brands and issues related to these brands and the interests of brand purchasers. These customized magazines are distributed free of charge to brand users either online in electronic form ("e-zines") or in printed form.

One of the primary purposes for brand marketers to create customized magazines is to reach out to existing brand users and to create a bond that will result in increased levels of *customer loyalty*. For example, *Lexus Magazine* is distributed to owners of Lexus automobiles. The magazine, both in printed and electronic forms, provides useful and entertaining information related to travel, insider tips about the Lexus, and other topics and achieves a high level of readership. This customized magazine is distributed throughout the world, with the North American version alone having a circulation of 800,000 per issue.[19]

Customized publishing is definitely on the rise and is capturing a growing percentage of many companies' marcom budgets. In fact, one survey revealed that customized publishing accounts for nearly one-fourth of the total money that companies allocate for marketing, advertising, and communications.[20] Customized magazines thus represent a valuable marcom tool for reaching and maintaining the loyalty of a brand's existing customers. Customized magazines do not replace advertisements placed in traditional (i.e., noncustomized) magazines because advertisements placed in traditional magazines reach prospective customers as well as current brand users. Nonetheless, customized magazines have a unique role in a brand's overall marcom program, especially as a means of maintaining a continuous dialogue with current brand users.

One other recent change has been linking magazine content to tablets (e.g., iPad, Kindle, Nook) and mobile devices.[21] Although ensuring reader engagement has been an issue with digital delivery of content, many reported deals (e.g., with *Sports Illustrated*, *Time*, *Fortune*), as well as the Audit Bureau of Circulation, have recognized that digital subscriptions will count to the subscriber base.[22]

Radio

Radio is a nearly ubiquitous medium: There are 14,503 commercial radio stations in the United States; almost 100 percent of all homes have radios; most homes have several; virtually all cars have a radio; more than 50 million radios are purchased in the United States each year; and radio in the United States reaches slightly over 93 percent of all people age 12 or older.[23] These impressive figures indicate radio's strong potential as an advertising medium. Although radio has always been a favorite of local advertisers, regional and national advertisers have increasingly recognized radio's advantages as an ad medium.

Buying Radio Time

Radio advertisers are interested in reaching target customers at a reasonable expense while ensuring that the station format is compatible with a brand's image and its creative message strategy. Several considerations influence the choice of radio vehicle. *Station format* (classical, urban, rock, country, top-40, tejano, news/talk, etc.) is a major consideration. Certain formats are obviously most appropriate for particular products and brands.

A second consideration is the *choice of geographic areas to cover*. National advertisers buy time from stations whose audience coverage matches the advertiser's geographic areas of interest. This typically means locating stations in preferred metropolitan statistical areas (MSAs) or in so-called areas of dominant influence (ADIs), which number approximately 200 in the United States and correspond to the major television markets.

A third consideration in buying radio time is the *choice of daypart*. Radio dayparts include the following:

Morning drive:	5 AM to 10 AM
Midday:	10 AM to 3 PM
Afternoon drive:	3 PM to 7 PM
Evening:	7 PM to Midnight
Late night:	Midnight to 7 AM

Rate structures vary depending on the attractiveness of the daypart; for example, morning and afternoon drive times are more expensive than midday and late-night dayparts. Information about rates and station formats is available in Spot Radio Rates and Data, a source published by SRDS Media Solutions.

Radio Advertising's Strengths and Limitations

This section examines the advantages and also explores some of the problems with radio advertising (see the summary in Table 12.4).

TABLE 12.4	Radio Advertising's Strengths and Limitations	
Strengths		**Limitations**
Ability to reach segmented audiences		Clutter
Intimacy		No visuals
Economy		Audience fractionalization
Short lead times		Buying difficulties
Transfer of imagery from TV		
Use of local personalities		

Radio Advertising's Strengths

The first major strength of radio is that it is second only to magazines in its *ability to reach segmented audiences*. An extensive variety of radio programming enables advertisers to pick specific formats and stations to be optimally compatible with both the composition of their target audience and their creative message strategies. Radio can be used to pinpoint advertisements to specific groups of consumers: teens, Hispanics, sports fanatics, news addicts, jazz enthusiasts, political conservatives, and so on. As noted earlier, there are over 14,500 commercial radio stations in the United States, and these stations are formatted to cater to special listening interests.

A second major advantage of radio advertising is its *ability to reach prospective customers on a personal and intimate level*. Local store merchants and radio announcers can be extremely personable and convincing. Their messages sometimes come across as if they are personally speaking to each audience member. A top-level advertising agency representative metaphorically described radio as a "universe of private worlds" and a "communication between two friends."[24] In other words, people select radio stations in much the same way that they select personal friends. Therefore, it has a real potential to increase consumers' engagement with advertisements placed in this medium.

Economy is a third advantage of radio advertising. In terms of target audience CPM, radio advertising is considerably cheaper than other mass media. Over the past several decades, radio's CPM has increased less than any other advertising medium.

Another relative advantage of radio advertising is a *short lead time*. Because radio production costs are typically inexpensive and scheduling deadlines are short, copy changes can be made quickly to take advantage of important developments and changes in the marketplace (e.g., a sudden weather change and weather-related products, changing inventory levels, special events, and holidays).

A very important advantage of radio advertising is its *ability to transfer images from television advertising*. A memorable television advertising campaign that has been aired frequently effects in consumers a mental association between the sight and sound elements in the commercial. This mental image (i.e., imagery) can then be transferred to a radio commercial that uses the TV sound or some adaptation of it.[25] For example, Corona beer's TV commercial with a couple relaxing with the sounds of the ocean nearby is easily transferable to radio. Also, the advertiser effectively gains the advantage of TV advertising at the lower cost of radio. By using a combination of TV and radio advertising, the advertiser is able to achieve higher levels of reach and frequency than would be achieved if the entire budget were invested exclusively in television advertising.

A final strength of radio advertising is its ability to avail itself of the reputations and the sometimes bigger-than-life persona of *local personalities*. Radio personalities in local markets are often highly respected and admired, and their endorsement of, say, a retail establishment can serve to enhance that establishment's image and drive purchases to the store.

Radio Advertising's Limitations

Radio's foremost limitation, one it shares with other ad media, is that it is *cluttered* with competitive commercials and other forms of noise, chatter, and interference. Radio listeners frequently switch stations, especially on their car radios, to avoid commercials.[26] The irritation of having to listen to one commercial after another partially explains why many people have turned to iPods and other brands of portable digital-audio players as an alternative to radio listening. The iPod's growing popularity has been shown, in fact, to correlate with reduced radio ratings. So-called AQH ratings, which measure the number of people tuned to radio during an average quarter hour (AQH) as a percentage of the population, fell by almost 6 percent during a recent five-year period, with the ratings decline among the college-aged demographic (18–24) even greater at 11 percent.[27]

A second limitation is that radio is the only major medium that is *unable to employ visualizations*. However, radio advertisers attempt to overcome the medium's visual limitation by using sound effects and choosing concrete words to conjure up mental images in the listener. It is important to note that many advertising campaigns use radio as a supplement to other media rather than as a stand-alone medium. This reduces radio's task from creating visual images to reactivating images that already have been created by ads placed in visual media—television, the Internet, and magazines. In contrast, information-based advertising campaigns do not necessarily require visualizations, and radio under such circumstances is fully capable of delivering brand-based information—for example, a mortgage company's interest rate, a special sale at a local department store, or the location of an automobile repair shop.

A third problem with radio advertising results from a high degree of *audience fractionalization*. Selectivity is a major advantage of radio advertising, but at the same time the advertiser is unable to reach a diverse audience because each radio station and program has its own unique set of audience demographics and interests.

A final limitation is the *difficulty of buying radio time*. This problem is particularly acute in the case of the national advertiser that wishes to place spots in different markets throughout the country. With over 14,500 commercial radio stations operating in the United States, buying time is complicated by unstandardized rate structures that include a number of combinations of fixed and discount rates. One prospect that may offset this problem is the growth of the fledgling satellite radio industry. Companies such as Sirius XM Satellite Radio can broadcast nationally (even internationally) and thus offer advertisers an opportunity to reach large audiences and pay a single rate for the purchased airtime. As of 2009, Sirius XM had a total of over 19 million subscribers.[28]

Radio Audience Measurement

Radio audiences are measured both nationally and locally. Arbitron is the major company at both the national and the local levels involved with measuring radio listenership and audience demographics. At the *national level*, Arbitron owns a service that goes by the acronym RADAR, which stands for Radio's All Dimension Audience Research. The RADAR service produces radio-listening estimates by recruiting 70,000 individuals age 12 and older, who, during a one-week period, make diary entries that identify their daily listening behavior, including the radio stations they listened to, the time of day they listened to each station, and their location when they listened (e.g., in the car, at home, or at work). RADAR's research provides ratings estimates for network radio programming and audience demographic characteristics. Advertisers use this information to select network programming that matches their intended target audiences.

At the *local level*, there used to be two major research services that measured radio audience sizes: Birch Scarborough Research and Arbitron. However, in the early 1990s Birch discontinued operations, leaving Arbitron the sole supplier of local radio ratings data. Arbitron measures listening patterns in over 250 markets located throughout the United States. Arbitron researchers obtain data in each market from 250 to 13,000 randomly selected individuals age 12 or older. Respondents are

© Cengage Learning 2013

compensated for maintaining *diaries* of their listening behavior for a seven-day period. Subscribers to the Arbitron service (thousands of radio stations, advertisers, and agencies) receive reports that detail people's listening patterns, station preferences, and demographic breakdowns. This information is invaluable to advertisers and their agencies for purposes of selecting radio stations whose listener compositions match the advertiser's target market.

Arbitron is in the process of attempting to get away from the paper-diary method of data collection by having people carry pager-like meters throughout the day that pick up inaudible codes in broadcast signals. This data-collection method, called the *Portable People Meter*, currently is being deployed in the top 48 radio markets in the United States.[29]

Television

Television is practically ubiquitous in the United States and throughout the rest of the industrialized world. Television sets are present in slightly more than 98.9 percent of all American households, which amounted to 115.9 million TV households in the United States as of 2011.[30] As an advertising medium, television is uniquely personal and demonstrative, yet it is also expensive and subject to considerable competitive clutter. Consumers consider television the most cluttered of all ad media.[31]

Before elaborating on television's specific strengths and weaknesses, it first will be instructive to examine two specific aspects of television advertising: (1) the different programming segments, or so-called dayparts; and (2) the alternative outlets for television commercials (network, spot, syndicated, cable, and local).

Television Programming Dayparts

Advertising costs, audience characteristics, and programming appropriateness vary greatly at different times of the day. As with radio, these times are referred to as *dayparts*. There are seven TV dayparts, with the following shown for Eastern Standard Time:

Early morning:	5 AM to 9 AM
Daytime:	9 AM to 4 PM
Early fringe:	4 PM to 7 PM
Prime access:	7 PM to 8 PM
Prime time:	8 PM to 11 PM
Late fringe:	11 PM to 2 AM
Overnight:	2 AM to 5 AM

The three major dayparts are daytime, fringe time, and prime time, each of which has its own strengths and weaknesses.

Daytime

The period that begins with the early morning news shows and extends to 4:00 PM is known as *daytime*. Early daytime appeals first to adults with news programs and then to children with special programs designed for them. Afternoon programming—with its special emphasis on soap operas, talk shows, and financial news—appeals primarily to people working at home, retirees, and, contrary to the stereotype, even young men.[32]

Fringe Time

The period preceding and following prime time is known as *fringe time*. Early fringe starts with afternoon reruns and is devoted primarily to children but becomes more adult oriented as prime time approaches. Late fringe appeals chiefly to young adults.

TABLE 12.5	Average Prime-Time Audience (in millions) for Six Major Networks	
Network	**Estimated Viewers (in millions)**	
CBS	12.86	
ABC	9.99	
Fox	9.39	
NBC	7.30	
Univision	3.59	
CW	2.08	
Total	45.21	

Source: Robert Seidman, "Weekly Network Ratings," ten weeks ending November 27, 2011, http://tvbythenumbers.zap2it.com/2011/11/30/2011-12-season-fox-cbs-still-tied-in-adults-18-49-ratings-through-week-10-ending-november-27-2011/112175 (accessed December 20, 2011).

Prime Time

The period between 8:00 PM and 11:00 PM (or between 7:00 PM and 10:00 PM in some parts of the United States) is known as *prime time*. The best and most expensive programs are scheduled during this period. Audiences are largest during prime time. Table 12.5 indicates the average prime-time audience size for the six major U.S. networks at the end of 10 weeks in the fall of 2011. The audience sizes range from 12.86 million viewers on average for CBS down to 2.08 million average viewers for The CW Network. Interestingly, the total audience size these six major networks garnered during this one week is approximately 45 million; comparatively, the total audience size during 1994 and 1995 was just over 62 million. This decline of about 27 percent reflects the continuing trend wherein network TV is capturing smaller audiences, whereas cable TV's audience base continues to grow.[33]

The networks naturally charge the highest rates for prime-time advertising. Popular prime-time programs sometimes reach as many as 20 million U.S. households. Advertisers pay dearly to reach the large numbers of households highly popular prime-time programs deliver. For example, the fabulously successful *American Idol* singing-competition program had charged advertisers over $600,000 for a single 30-second commercial. With the exception of *American Idol*, the 10 highest-priced programs for the Fall 2010 television season are shown in Table 12.6, where it can be seen that the cost for a single 30-second commercial placed on these programs ranges from a low of $204,806 (*Dancing with the Stars*) to a high of $415,000 (*Sunday Night Football*). Note that these advertising prices are for just the 10 most expensive TV programs. Most 30-second commercials broadcast on prime-time TV during the fall 2010 season were in the range of $50,000 to $200,000, with the same programs priced higher for the spring 2011 season.

Network, Spot, Syndicated, Cable, and Local Advertising

Television messages are transmitted by local stations, which are either locally owned cable

© Photo by FOX via Getty Images

TABLE 12.6

The 10 Highest-Priced TV Programs Fall 2010 (price per 30-second commercial)

Program	Network	Price
Sunday Night Football	NBC	$415,000
Glee	Fox	$272,694
Family Guy	Fox	$259,289
The Simpsons	Fox	$253,173
House	Fox	$226,180
Grey's Anatomy	ABC	$222,113
The Office	NBC	$213,617
Desperate Housewives	ABC	$210,064
Two and a Half Men	CBS	$206,722
Dancing with the Stars	ABC	$204,806

Source: Brian Steinberg, "Simon Who? 'Idol' Spots Still Priciest in Prime Time," *Advertising Age*, October 10, 2010, http://adage.com/article/ad-age-graphics/american-idol-spots-priciest-prime-time/146495.

television systems or affiliated with the five commercial networks (ABC, CBS, NBC, Fox, Univision, and The CW) or with an independent cable network (such as TBS, the Turner Broadcasting System). This arrangement of local stations and networks allows for different ways of buying advertising time on television.

Network Television Advertising

Companies that market products nationally often use network television to reach potential customers throughout the country. The advertiser, typically working through an advertising agency, purchases desired time slots from one or more of the networks and advertises at these times on all local stations that are affiliated with the network. The cost of such advertising depends on the time of day when an ad is aired, the popularity of the television program in which the ad is placed, and the time of year. The average cost for all 30-second prime-time television commercials during the first three quarters of 2009 were: first quarter (January–March), $94,800; second quarter (April–June), $86,000; and third quarter (July–September), $59,800.[34]

Network television advertising, although expensive in terms of per-unit cost, can be a cost-efficient means to reach mass audiences. Consider a 30-second commercial that costs $300,000 and reaches 15 percent of the 115.2 million American households with TV sets, or about 17.28 million households. Although $300,000 is a lot to pay for 30 seconds of commercial time, reaching 17.28 million households means that the advertiser would have paid approximately only $17.36 to reach every 1,000 households.

Network advertising is inefficient, and in fact unfeasible, if the national advertiser chooses to concentrate efforts only on select markets. For example, some brands, although marketed nationally, are directed primarily at consumers in certain geographic locales.

Spot Television Advertising

The national advertiser's alternative to network advertising is *spot advertising*. As the preceding discussion suggests, this type of advertising is placed (spotted) only in selected markets.

Spot advertising is particularly desirable when a company rolls out a new brand market by market before it achieves national distribution, when a marketer needs to concentrate on particular markets due to poor performance in these markets or aggressive competitive efforts, or when a company's product distribution is limited to one or a few geographical regions. Also, spot advertising is useful even for those advertisers who use network advertising, but need to supplement the national coverage with greater amounts of advertising in select markets that have particularly high brand potential.

Syndicated Advertising

Syndicated programming occurs when an independent company—such as Disney-ABC Domestic Television Company and Sony Pictures Television—sells a TV show to as many network-affiliated or cable television stations as possible. Because an independent firm markets syndicated programs to individual television stations, the same syndicated program will appear on, say, NBC stations in some markets and on ABC or CBS stations in other markets. Syndicated programs are either original productions (e.g., *Curb Your Enthusiasm*, *Entourage*) or shows that first appeared on network television and are subsequently shown as reruns (e.g., *Friends*, *Seinfeld*).

Cable Advertising

Unlike network television, which is free to all TV owners, cable television requires users to subscribe (pay a fee) to a cable service and have their sets specially wired to receive signals via satellite or other means. Although cable television has been available since the 1940s, only in recent decades have advertisers turned to cable as a valuable advertising medium. Growing numbers of major national companies now advertise on cable TV. Cable television's household penetration increased from less than 25 percent of all households in 1980 to a current level of about 90.6 percent of U.S. households with television sets.[35] Advertising spending on cable TV is climbing steadily.

Cable advertising is attractive to national advertisers for several reasons. First, because cable networks focus on narrow areas of viewing interest (so-called *narrow casting*), advertisers are able to reach more finely targeted audiences (in terms of demographics and psychographics) than when using network, syndicated, or spot advertising. Indeed, cable stations are available to reach almost any imaginable viewing preference. A brand marketer can select cable stations that appeal to a variety of specific viewing interests such as cooking and eating (Food Network); golfing (Golf Channel); sports in general (ESPN, ESPN2, and Fox Sports Network); music entertainment (Country Music Television, MTV, and VH1); nature, science, and animal life (Animal Planet, Discovery Channel, and National Geographic Channel); general education (the History Channel and Travel Channel); and so forth.

A second reason that cable advertising appeals to national advertisers is that high network advertising prices and declining audiences have compelled advertisers to experiment with media alternatives such as cable. A third factor behind cable advertising's growth is the demographic composition of cable audiences. Cable subscribers are more economically upscale and younger than the population as a whole. By comparison, the heaviest viewers of network television tend to be somewhat economically downscale. It is little wonder that the relatively upscale characteristics of cable viewers have great appeal to many national advertisers.

Local Television Advertising

National advertisers historically dominated television advertising, but local advertisers have turned to television in ever greater numbers. Local advertisers often find that the CPM advantages of television, along with the ability to demonstrate products, justify the TV medium. Many local advertisers are using cable stations to an unprecedented degree. In fact, the growth rate in local cable advertising is faster than other ad media.[36]

Television Advertising's Strengths and Limitations

Like the other forms of media, advertising on television has a number of strengths and limitations (see the summary in Table 12.7).

Television Advertising's Strengths

Beyond any other consideration, television possesses the unique capability to *demonstrate a product in use*. No other medium can reach consumers simultaneously through auditory and visual senses. Viewers can see and hear a product being used, identify with the product's users, and imagine using the product.

Television also has *intrusion value* unparalleled by other media; that is, television advertisements engage one's senses and attract attention even when one would prefer not to be exposed to an advertisement. In comparison, it is much easier to avoid a magazine or newspaper ad by merely flipping the page, or to avoid a radio ad by changing channels. But it is often easier to sit through a television commercial rather than attempting to avoid it either physically or mentally. Of course, as will be discussed shortly, remote controls and digital video recorders have made it easier for viewers to avoid television commercials via zipping and zapping.

A third relative advantage of television advertising is its combined *ability to provide entertainment and generate excitement*. Advertised products can be brought to life or made to appear even bigger than life. Products advertised on television can be presented dramatically and made to appear more exciting and less mundane than perhaps they actually are.

Television also has the unique ability to *reach consumers one on one*, as is the case when a spokesperson or endorser touts a particular product. Like a sales presentation, the interaction between spokesperson and consumer takes place on a personal level.

More than any other medium, television is able to *use humor* as an effective advertising strategy. As discussed in Chapter 11, many of the most memorable commercials are those using a humorous format.

In addition to its effectiveness in reaching ultimate consumers, television advertising also is *effective with a company's sales force and its retailers* (a.k.a., "the trade"). Salespeople find it easier to sell new or established brands to the trade when a major advertising campaign is planned. The trade has added incentive to increase merchandise support (e.g., through advertising features and special display space) for a brand that is advertised on television.

| TABLE 12.7 | Television Advertising's Strengths and Limitations |

Strengths	Limitations
Demonstration ability	Rapidly expanding cost
Intrusion value	Erosion of viewing audiences
Ability to generate excitement	Audience fractionalization
One-on-one reach	Zipping and zapping
Ability to use humor	Clutter
Effective with sales force and trade	
Ability to achieve impact	

© Cengage Learning

The Rising Cost of Super Bowl Advertising

The Super Bowl football game, which pits the winners of the National and American Football Conferences of the National Football League, is for many Americans the most important sporting event of the year. Super Bowl Sunday, which occurs annually in late January or early February, has been described as the third- or fourth-largest "holiday" celebrated in America. People throw parties and consume large quantities of food and drink while watching the clash of professional football teams. This event is one of the few remaining television spectaculars that can be described as mass television. The sponsoring TV network is able to command top prices for 30-second commercials because advertisers know they can reach well over 100 million people with an advertisement placed during this single program. In fact, the 2012 Super Bowl (between the New England Patriots and the New York Giants who won the game) attracted an average of 111.3 million viewers, which made this the highest-viewed Super Bowl up to this time.

Year	Price (adjusted for inflation to 2000 dollars)	Rating (% of U.S. TV households tuned to Super Bowl)	Year	Price (adjusted for inflation to 2000 dollars)	Rating (% of U.S. TV households tuned to Super Bowl)
1967	$216,665	23.0%	1990	$ 922,800	39.0
1968	267,362	36.8	1991	1,012,041	41.9
1969	316,901	36.0	1992	982,466	40.3
1970	347,264	39.4	1993	1,013,529	45.1
1971	306,311	39.9	1994	1,046,356	45.5
1972	353,493	44.2	1995	1,130,577	41.3
1973	401,645	42.7	1996	1,207,967	46.0
1974	373,957	41.6	1997	1,288,224	43.3
1975	352,286	42.4	1998	1,374,172	44.5
1976	378,515	42.3	1999	1,654,742	40.2
1977	460,604	44.4	2000	2,100,000	43.3
1978	488,888	47.2	2001	2,050,000	41.1
1979	526,868	47.1	2002	1,824,380	40.4
1980	575,030	46.3	2003	2,172,801	40.7
1981	614,707	44.4	2004	2,144,750	41.4
1982	615,995	49.1	2005	2,210,400	43.4
1983	691,968	48.6	2006	2,268,500	41.6
1984	746,246	46.4	2007	2,128,618	42.6
1985	800,651	46.4	2008	2,364,390	43.3
1986	864,644	48.3	2009	2,413,555	42.0
1987	872,117	45.8	2010	2,349,168	45.0
1988	873,880	41.9	2011	2,320,598*	46.0
1989	937,923	43.5	2012	2,656,345*	47.0

*The actual costs of Super Bowl advertising for every year from 2002 to 2008 were deflated to 2000 dollars using the Gross Domestic Product Deflator Inflation Calculator, http://cost.jsc.nasa.gov/inflateGDP.html. The 2009 to 2012 numbers were calculated using International Monetary Fund Deflation figures, http://www.imf.org. Values for the remaining years (from 1967 to 2001) were already calculated from the 2001 source materials presented in the source documentation.

Advertising rates have more than doubled in 16 years, from $1,130,577 in 1995 to $2,656,345 in 2012 (both cost figures have been adjusted for inflation to 2000 dollars). The following table provides detailed statistics for every Super Bowl from its inception in 1967 through 2012. Note that the prices for each year have been adjusted for inflation and are presented in constant 2000 dollars. For example, the actual price of a 30-second commercial during Super Bowl XLV in 2012 was $3,500,000, which, when adjusted for inflation, amounts to $2,656,345 in 2000 dollars. Interestingly, because the number of TV households grows annually, Super Bowl XLVI in 2012 had the largest number of Super Bowl viewers of all time, but its rating of 47 is much lower than the record-high rating of 49.1 almost 30 years ago in 1982.

Sources: Brian Steinberg, "Super Bowl Busts Ratings Records on 'The Greatest Day Ever' for Fox," *Advertising Age*, February 11, 2008, 21; Claire Atkinson, "Super Bowl: It's a Big (Ad) Deal," *Advertising Age*, January 3, 2005, 10 (ratings for 2002–2004 are provided in this source; all other ratings are from the following sources); Richard Linnett and Wayne Friedman, "No Gain," *Advertising Age*, January 15, 2001, 43; and Wayne Friedman, "Second Down," *Advertising Age*, September 3, 2001, 3, 22. The 2005 rating is from "Super Bowl Ratings Down from '04," *CBSNews.com*, February 7, 2005, http://www.cbsnews.com. The 2009 to 2011 pricing: "Kantar Media Reports Super Bowl Spending Reached $1.62 Billion Over The Past 10 Years," *Kantar Media*, January 18, 2011, http://kantarmediana.com; and "Super Bowl Ad: Is $3 million worth it?", *CNNMoney*, February 3, 2011, http://money.cnn.com. The 2009 to 2011 rating sources: "Super Bowl Gives NBC 42.0 Rating, Record 98.7 Million Viewers," *Sports Business Daily*, February 3, 2009, http://sportsbusinessdaily.com; "CBS Sports Coverage of Super Bowl XLIV Is Most-Watched Program In Television History," *TV by the Numbers*, February 8, 2010, http://tvbythenumbers.zap2it.com; and "Eli, Eli, Eli! Super Bowl XLVI is Most-Watched Television Show in U.S. History," *TV by the Numbers*, February 6, 2012, http://tvbythenumbers.zap2it.com/2012/02/06/eli-eli-eli-super-bowl-xlvi-is-most-watched-television-show-in-u-s-history/118826.

The greatest relative advantage of television advertising, however, is its *ability to achieve impact*; that is, to activate consumers' awareness of ads and enhance their receptiveness to sales messages.

Television Advertising's Limitations

As an advertising medium, television suffers from several distinct problems. First, and perhaps most serious, is the *rapidly escalating advertising cost*. The cost of network television advertising has more than tripled over the past two decades. A dramatic illustration of this is the increasing cost of buying advertising time during the Super Bowl. In 1975 a 30-second commercial cost $110,000. By 2012, the average price for placing a 30-second ad on Super Bowl XLV was $3.5 million! (For more on Super Bowl advertising, see the *IMC Focus*.) In addition to the cost of buying airtime, it is costly to produce television commercials. The average cost of making a national 30-second commercial was $324,000 in a recent year.[37]

A second problem is the *erosion of television viewing audiences*. Syndicated programs, cable television, the Internet, and other leisure and recreational alternatives have diminished the number of people viewing network television. The five major networks' share of television audiences during prime time fell from over 90 percent around 1980 to just about 60 percent today. Program ratings have consistently fallen over the past 40 years. Whereas the most popular programs used to have ratings in the 50s (meaning that more than 50 percent of all television households were tuned in to these programs), the top-rated programs now rarely obtain a rating of 20.

Today it is uncommon for a show to have a rating above 15. For example, the 10 top-rated programs during the week of March 12, 2012, are shown in Table 12.8. The highest-rated program, *American Idol* (Wednesday broadcast), had a rating of 10.7, and the last-ranked program (*The Bachelor*) with a rating of only 6.7.[38] Ratings on network television continue to slide.

There also has been substantial *audience fractionalization*. Advertisers cannot expect to attract large homogeneous audiences when advertising during any particular program due to the great amount of program selection now available to television viewers.

Fourth, when watching TV programs, viewers spend much of their time *switching from station to station*, zapping or zipping commercials. Zapping

TABLE 12.8 — Top-10 Prime-Time Broadcast TV Programs

Rank*	Program	Network	Rating**	Viewers (000)***
1	*American Idol-Wednesday*	FOX	10.7	18,384
2	*American Idol-Thursday*	FOX	9.4	16,021
3	*Voice*	NBC	8.4	14,515
4	*NCIS*	CBS	8.2	12,978
5	*CSI*	CBS	7.5	11,706
6	*Criminal Minds*	CBS	7.3	11,427
6	*NCIS: Los Angeles*	CBS	7.3	11,334
8	*60 Minutes*	CBS	6.9	10,800
9	*Missing*	ABC	6.8	10,603
10	*Bachelor: After Final Roses*	ABC	6.7	9,866

*Based on household rating percentage from Nielsen Media Research's National People Meter sample for the week of March 12, 2012.

**Ratings are the percentage of TV homes in the United States tuned into television.

***Total viewers include all persons over the age of two.

Source: "Top Ten Broadcast TV Programs for the Week of March 12, 2012," Nielsen Media Research, http://www.nielsen.com/us/en/insights/top10s/television.html (for current week) (accessed April 19, 2011).

occurs when viewers switch to another channel when commercials are aired, prompting one observer to comment (only partially with tongue in cheek) that the remote control "zapper" is the greatest threat to capitalism since Karl Marx.[39] Research reveals that perhaps as much as one-third of the potential audience for a TV commercial may be lost to zapping.[40] Although zapping is extensive, one intriguing study presented evidence suggesting that commercials that are zapped are actively processed prior to being zapped and may have a more positive effect on brand purchase behavior than commercials that are not zapped.[41]

In addition to zapping, television viewers also engage in zipping. Zipping takes place when ads that have been recorded along with program material using a *digital video recorder* (of the TiVo variety) are fast-forwarded (zipped through) when the viewer watches the prerecorded material. Research has shown that zipping is extensive.[42] DVRs from companies such as TiVo and ReplayTV allow viewers to fast-forward past commercials by simply pushing a skip button that fast-forwards in 30-second intervals, which, by no coincidence, is the standard length of a TV commercial.

It is estimated that current DVR penetration in U.S. households is 37 percent, which means that over 42 million households had DVRs as of 2011.[43] Many DVR owners use the technology to fast-forward through commercials or skip them altogether. One study found that nearly 60 percent of male viewers skip commercials and an even greater percentage of female viewers, nearly 70 percent, do the same.[44] Fast-forwarding through commercials is particularly high (upward of 75 percent) when programs are prerecorded for later viewing; however, fast-forwarding of commercials drops considerably (to below 20 percent) when people watch live programs.[45] Thus, one might conclude that commercials are more likely to be watched during live programs, which perhaps explains why programs such as *American Idol* command such premium prices. Yet, Nielsen counters that in homes that have DVRs, and among young viewers (18- to 49-year-olds), ratings for prime-time commercials rise by 44 percent when playback within three days is counted (i.e., with "C3 ratings," standing for "commercial live + 3 days").[46]

Moreover, research from Procter & Gamble suggests that consumers fast-forwarding through ads with DVRs recall those ads at about the same level as do people who see the ad at normal speed in real time.[47] Nonetheless, other indicators of advertising effectiveness (feelings of warmth, likeability, overall persuasion) may be negatively affected when fast-forwarding, such that "TiVo-ing" is likely to diminish commercial effectiveness.

Given the reality of Tivo-ing—i.e., viewers fast-forwarding through commercials—advertisers are devising techniques to diminish this behavior. For example, during a broadcast of *Mythbusters*, a brief ad for Guinness beer included a scene where one character in the ad asked another whether it is a myth that a bottle of Guinness contains only 125 calories. After being told that the calorie count is accurate, a voice-over declared: "*Mythbusters*, sponsored by Guinness."[48]

Finally, whereas DVRs allow consumers to *time-shift* their TV viewing—i.e., allowing people to record programs and view them whenever convenient—there is another technology that provides consumers with further *control* over TV viewing. In particular, the *Slingbox* enables individuals to *place-shift* their viewing of live TV programs. This technology is described in the *Global Focus* insert.

GLOBAL FOCUS

Place-Shifting TV Viewing

Suppose you, as an American citizen, are working in Europe (or Asia, or wherever) and that you miss watching live broadcasts of your favorite college or professional athletic team. These programs are not, of course, televised live in London, Paris, Madrid, Tokyo, or anywhere else you may be located. You could have a family member back in the States send you a recording, but watching a game several days after it has been played is not nearly as enjoyable as seeing it in real time. What's a fan to do?

A solution is a device called the *Slingbox*. To explain how the *Slingbox* works, let us assume that you are a graduate of Boston College with an MBA from Columbia University. Having specialized in international business, your first job takes you to Barcelona, Spain, where you work for an American company that has offices located around the globe. You love your job and the excitement of living in Barcelona, but every Saturday in the fall you miss watching your beloved BC Eagles play football. The solution is the *Slingbox*, a device that weighs two pounds and costs less than $200.

Here's how you could watch live broadcasts of Boston College football games using the *Slingbox* technology. First, you could have your father back in

Massachusetts connect a newly purchased *Slingbox* to his TV. He would then connect the *Slingbox* to his computer network/router. Dad would mail you the software for the *Slingbox* (called SlingPlayer), and you would load this software on your computer or even on a Windows-enabled mobile phone. That done, you are now prepared to watch live broadcasts of your BC football team in Barcelona or anywhere else in the world where you have Internet connection.

It should be obvious that the *Slingbox* enables place-shifting anywhere, whether in another city in your home state or across the globe. Importantly, the *Slingbox* technology reflects another move in the direction of consumers' gaining increasing control over TV viewing. Sling Media also has launched sling.com, an online video destination, where users can go to watch clips, TV, shows, films, news, sports, etc. *Slingbox* users (and those with mobile platforms) can connect to sling.com as well. All in all, control continues to shift from marketers to consumers.

Sources: Sling Media, http://www.slingmedia.com (accessed March 9, 2008); Abbey Klaassen, "Why This Box Changes Everything," *Advertising Age*, June 5, 2006, 1, 49; "Slingbox," Wikipedia, http://en.wikipedia.org/Slingbox (accessed December 4, 2011).

Clutter is a fifth serious problem with television advertising. Clutter refers to the growing amount of nonprogram material, including public service messages and promotional announcements for stations and programs, but especially commercials. In fact, out of every broadcast hour of prime-time television, nonprogram content ranges slightly over 15 minutes among the major TV networks, or more than 25 percent of the time.[49] As noted earlier, consumers perceive television to be the most cluttered of all major advertising media. Clutter has been created by the network's increased use of promotional announcements to stimulate audience viewing of heavily promoted programs and by advertisers' increased use of shorter commercials. Whereas 60-second commercials once were prevalent, the duration of the vast majority of commercials today is only 30 or 15 seconds.[50] The effectiveness of television advertising has suffered from the clutter problem, which creates a negative impression among consumers about advertising in general, turns viewers away from the television set, and perhaps reduces advertising recognition and recall.[51]

Infomercials

Introduced to television in the early 1980s, the long commercial, or infomercial, is an alternative to the conventional, short form of television commercial. By comparison, infomercials are full-length commercial segments that typically last 28 to 30 minutes and combine product news and entertainment. Infomercials account for nearly one-fourth of the programming time for most cable stations. Marketers' increased use of infomercials extends from two primary factors: First, technologically complicated products and those that require detailed explanations benefit from the long commercial format. Second, the infomercial format is in lockstep with increasing demands for marketing accountability insofar as most orders obtained from infomercials occur within 24 hours or so after an infomercial is aired.[52]

In the early years, infomercials were restricted primarily to unknown companies selling skin-care products, balding treatments, exercise equipment, and other such products. However, the growing respectability of this form of advertising has encouraged a number of consumer goods companies to promote their brands via infomercials. Well-known infomercial users include Avon, Braun, Clairol, Chrysler, Eastman Kodak, Estée Lauder, Hoover, Pioneer, Procter & Gamble, and Sears.

Courtesy of Square One Entertainment, Inc.

Numerous advertisers have found infomercials on television to be an extremely effective tool for moving merchandise. This long-form commercial is apparently here to stay. Although consumers have complaints with infomercials (e.g., that some make false claims and are deceptive),[53] this form of long commercial appears to be especially effective for consumers who are brand and price conscious and who highly value shopping convenience.[54] Recent success stories for brands on infomercials and direct response TV ads include: Rosetta Stone, ShamWow, Snuggie, Proactiv, Time-Life, Swivel Sweeper, PedEgg, and Nutrisystem, among others, especially during recessionary periods.[55]

Brand Placements in Television Programs

Brand managers and network television executives have responded to consumers' zipping and zapping behavior by borrowing from the movie industry and finding a way to circumvent TV viewers' fondness for avoiding commercials. Have you noticed brands appearing more often in television programs? This is not by chance; rather, brand managers are paying to get prominent placements for their brands, precisely as they have done in placing their products in movies (e.g *Talladega Nights*). The widely viewed *Survivor* program epitomizes the use of product placements, perhaps to the point where TV viewers now realize that the brands placed in *Survivor* episodes are little more than thinly disguised commercials. The ever-present display of Coca-Cola on the set of *American Idol* is yet another instance of brand placement as commercial message.

Compared with movie placements, brand appearances in TV programs have the advantages of (1) much larger audiences; (2) more frequent exposure; and (3) global reach, especially when programs are rerun around the world under syndication.[56]

Brand placements on TV can be very effective provided the brand is displayed in a context that appropriately matches the brand's image. The downside with placements in TV programs is that brand managers relinquish the full control available to them by comparison when providing the final approval for TV commercials. Interestingly, the more people feel a sense of connection with a TV program—that is, they identify with a program's characters, issues, and images—the higher their recall of brands that are placed in that program.[57] This obviously implies that TV programs that create a heightened sense of connectedness among their audiences are more effective vehicles in which to place brands in comparison to programs that fail to achieve high levels of connectedness.

Recent Developments in TV Advertising

In combatting declines in ratings, and movement of ad dollars online and to social media, the television industry is rolling out *addressable ads* and *interactive TV*. Addressable ad technology allows TV commercials to be targeted to individual homes and is projected to total $1.5 billion by 2015.[58] In the setup for DIRECTV, the advertiser specifies what homes they would be interested in by demographic choices (e.g., income, gender, geography). The household's DIRECTV set-top box will then "vote" (i.e., match) the most appropriate commercial for that household. In soliciting household data from third parties, households will be assigned a code (as opposed to the set-top box ID). Yet, addressable ads and interactive ads (enabling viewers to request more information) face challenges of a wide range of cable, satellite, and telecom providers, as well as many different set-top boxes, etc.[59]

One of the more interesting developments, mentioned in the *Marcom Insight*, is the link between social media (Twitter, Facebook, and Talk Bubble) and TV programs or "Social TV." As Mark Ghuneim, the CEO of Trendrr (a social media tracking company), indicates, "Social buzz does tend to signal tune-in intent. People who are socially engaged with a show this week are much more likely to also tune in next week."[60] Conversely, declining social engagement for the TV program *Glee* later signaled a decline of 200,000 fewer Tweets and Nielsen ratings declining 29 percent for the show.[61]

Television Audience Measurement

As noted earlier, a 30-second commercial on prime-time television for national airing can cost as much as $3,500,000 (for a Super Bowl spot in 2012) or less than $100,000. Of course, the cost of advertising on spot television (i.e., non-national) is considerably cheaper because the market covered is much smaller. Also, advertising on cable stations and syndicated programs typically is cheaper than on network TV, again due to smaller audience sizes. Whatever the case, the reason for the disparity in commercial costs is *ratings*. Generally speaking, higher-rated programs command higher prices. Because prices and ratings go hand in hand, the accurate measurement of program audience size—the basis on which ratings are determined—is a critically important, multimillion-dollar industry. Advertising researchers continually seek ways to measure more accurately the size of TV program audiences. The following discussion will distinguish network (national) and local audience measurement. Inherent in this distinction is whether audience-size data are collected via electronic technology (i.e., with people meters) or paper diaries.

National (Network) Audience Measurement: Nielsen's People Meter Technology

The people meter, by Nielsen Media Research, represents perhaps the most important and controversial research innovation since the advent of television audience measurement.[62] Nielsen uses the people meter technology by outfitting a national sample of households with TV set-top boxes that require consumers to punch a button to record their viewing. Twenty-five thousand households (of 115.9 million TV households in the United States as of 2011) are currently included in Nielsen's sample. The box has eight buttons for family members and two additional buttons for visitors (see Figure 12.3). A family member (or visitor) is requested to push his or her designated numerical button each time he or she selects a particular program. The meter automatically records which programs are being watched,

FIGURE **12.3** Nielsen People Meter

which family members are in attendance, and how many households are watching. These data are then statistically extrapolated to all households to arrive at estimates of each program's ratings on a given occasion, such as *American Idol* on a particular Tuesday. Information from each household's people meter is fed daily into a central computer via telephone lines, although typically only about 80 percent of the 25,000 households actually transmit data to Nielsen.[63] This viewing information is then combined with each household's demographic profile to provide a single source of data about audience size and composition.

You might be wondering, why would anyone take the time to push a button on every occasion they sit down to watch TV? In actuality, some portion of the participating households and household members probably are *not* especially faithful in pushing their button(s) to identify they are viewing TV (e.g., children). However, because Nielsen compensates participating households—up to $600 for a two-year period—many participants feel obligated to perform the task.

People meters likely are here to stay in one form or another, and probably so is the controversy surrounding their use. The major networks, which pay Nielsen more than $10 million annually for its data, are growing increasingly critical of Nielsen's data. They claim that Nielsen undercounts major segments of the population, especially young people and viewers watching TV outside the home.

Local Audience Measurement: Nielsen's Diary Panels

The 25,000 households on which Nielsen's network audience measurement is based are scattered around the United States. For example, in the city where both of the authors has lived (Columbia, South Carolina—a metropolitan area with over 767,000 residents, 405,670 TV households [0.35 percent of the United States], and the number 78th TV market in the United States[64]), there may be only 88 or fewer households that are included in Nielsen's national sample. Obviously, there are many more households represented in much larger markets (New York City, Los Angeles, Chicago, etc.), but fewer in smaller markets. Considering just Columbia, South Carolina, for illustration, it should be obvious that the estimated 88 or so households included as part of Nielsen's national people meter sample are far too few to draw statistically reliable estimates of TV viewing in the Columbia market.

Given this statistical fact, Nielsen has used an alternative data collection procedure for estimating TV program ratings in local markets. Nielsen has, since the 1950s, used *paper diaries* to collect information regarding audience viewing habits and the composition of households that view particular programs. Paper diaries of TV viewing behavior are filled out by a sample of 375,000 households from local markets throughout the United States. Each of these households completes a 20-page diary four times a year—February, May, July, and November, which are the months known in the TV industry as "sweep" periods. Randomly selected households in 210 markets throughout the United States fill out the diaries, which are delineated for each day of the week into 15-minute chunks. Participating households identify which household member(s) watch which TV programs during each 15-minute chunk.[65] You might be thinking, who would take the time to record their viewing behavior faithfully? Needless to say, this measurement system is imperfect because some participating households do not carefully record who watched what. Further, over 10 percent of households return diaries with substantial sections blank or containing illegible entries due to poor handwriting.

Local Audience Measurement: Nielsen's Local People Meters

It is for these reasons that the TV industry has insisted on a superior method of measuring viewing behavior in local markets. Enter the *local people meter technology*. Local people meters (LPMs) are the same devices Nielsen uses for its national audience measurement. Compared to paper diaries, which collect crucial viewing and demographic information only during the four sweep months, LPMs provide media buyers with daily feedback about audience size and composition for particular programs.

LPMs are currently available in 25 major markets, with plans to reach 56 markets total—representing approximately 70 percent of all TV households in the United States—e.g., Boston, Chicago, Los Angeles, New York, San Francisco, Dallas-Fort Worth, Detroit, Philadelphia, Atlanta, and Washington, D.C.[66] Currently, of the 210 local markets, 25 are served by the LPMs, 31 are measured by set meters and diaries, and the remaining 154 by paper diaries alone.[67] In fact, Nielsen is expected to soon eliminate the antiquated paper diary method, which was developed when there were just three major TV networks in the United States.[68] With multiple networks and numerous cable stations, the diary method of recording TV viewing has outlived its original purpose. In markets where people meters are available, it has been shown that more young adults (18- to 34-year-olds) view TV than the diary method indicates. This is because young adults are too busy to fill out paper diaries as conscientiously as older adults.[69]

Measuring Away-from-Home Viewers (and Listeners)

Needless to say, much radio listening and TV viewing occurs outside the home. For example, millions of college students listen to radios and watch TV in their dorms, but the traditional Arbitron and Nielsen measuring systems do not include this group in their samples. Likewise, people often consume radio and TV while at bars and restaurants; when they are exercising in gyms; while working in offices, stores, and factories; and so on. Yet, the traditional Arbitron (radio) and Nielsen (TV) systems miss these out-of-home listening and viewing experiences. It is for this reason that Arbitron and Nielsen undertook a collaborative effort starting in 2005 to measure people's radio listening and television viewing when they are away from home.[70] As previously mentioned, this data was captured by the portable people meter—a pager-like device that can detect embedded codes in radio and TV programs at any location. Unfortunately, the collaborative effort was discontinued by Nielsen for TV in 2006.[71]

Challengers to Nielsen

Nielsen is often criticized for its monopoly powers because it has been the only major service involved with estimating national and local TV audiences. However, a company called TNS Media Research started competing with Nielsen in 2008. TNS collects viewing data from 100,000 set-top boxes that are available from subscribers to DIRECTV.[72] This much larger sample of households in comparison with Nielsen's sample size is expected to yield estimates of TV viewing that are more statistically reliable. Moreover, TNS's set-top box data will provide second-by-second information about TV viewing (compared with Nielsen's minute-by-minute data) and will include data pertaining to TV commercial viewing as well as program viewing.

Another recent competitor is Rentrack and its "TV Essentials" service that also uses TV set-top boxes to collect TV ad viewing from 14,000 households.[73] These alternatives to Nielsen offer an exciting prospect for some advertisers who have doubts about the accuracy of Nielsen's estimates of TV program and commercial viewing.

Summary

Excluding out-of-home advertising (covered in Chapter 22), online and mobile advertising (covered in Chapter 13), and social media (covered in Chapter 14), there are four major media available to media planners: newspapers and magazines (print media), and radio and television (broadcast media). Each medium has unique qualities with strengths and weaknesses. This chapter provided a detailed analysis of each medium. Newspapers provide mass audience coverage and reach readers who are in the appropriate mental frame to process messages. But, newspapers suffer from high clutter, limited selectivity, and declining readership, among other limitations. Magazines enable advertisers to reach selective audiences and to present detailed information in an involving manner. This medium lacks intrusiveness, however, and also experiences considerable clutter. Radio also has the ability to reach segmented audiences and is economical. Clutter and the lack of visuals are notable weaknesses. Finally, television is an intrusive medium that is able to generate excitement, demonstrate brands in use, and achieve impact. Television advertising suffers from clutter, audience fractionalization, and high cost.

In addition to examining each medium's strengths and limitations, the chapter also examined how media space and time are purchased. Another major focus was the measurement of audience size and composition for each medium. Specific coverage included Mediamark Research Inc. and the Simmons Market Research Bureau for magazine measurement, the Arbitron service for radio audience measurement (and portable people meters [PPMs]), and Nielsen Media Research for TV audience measurement. Detailed discussion of Nielsen's people meter system—including their use for national audience measurement and use of the local people meters (LPMs)—was provided, along with mention of its historical paper diary method for measuring local audiences.

Discussion Questions

1. What are the advantages and disadvantages of cable television advertising? Why are more national advertisers turning to cable television as a viable advertising medium? How is social media (Twitter, Facebook, etc.) becoming integrated into TV viewing?

2. Assume you are brand manager for a new product line of book bags designed for college students. These bags come in each university's school colors and are imprinted with the school's mascot. Assume you have $5 million to invest in a two-month magazine advertising campaign (July and August). Which magazines would you choose for this campaign? Justify your choices.

3. Assume you are a manufacturer of various jewelry items. Graduation rings for high school students are among the most important items in your product line. You are in the process of developing a media strategy aimed specifically at high school students. With an annual budget of $10 million, what media and specific vehicles would you use? How would you schedule the advertising over time?

4. Examine a copy of the most recent Spot Radio Rates and Data available in your library and compare the advertising rates for three or four of the radio stations in your hometown or university community.

5. Pick your favorite clothing store in your university community (or hometown) and justify the choice of one radio station that the clothing store should select for its radio advertising. Do not feel constrained by what the clothing store may be doing already; focus instead on what you think is most important. Be certain to make explicit all criteria used in making your choice and all radio stations considered.

6. Magazine A is read by 11,000,000 people and costs $52,000 for a full-page, four-color advertisement. Magazine B reaches 15,000,000 readers and costs $68,000 for a full-page, four-color advertisement. Holding all other factors constant, in which magazine would you choose to advertise and why?

7. Go online and see if you can locate a current (as of January of the present year) rate card for your favorite magazine. Carefully study this rate card and summarize your observations regarding price differentials for, say, black-and-white ads versus four-color ads of the same page size. (If you cannot locate a rate card for your favorite magazine, find one for your next favorite, and so on.)

8. Radio is the only major medium that is nonvisual. Is this a major disadvantage? Thoroughly justify your response.

9. In your opinion, will portable digital-audio players (e.g., Apple's iPod) eventually replace radio?

10. One marketer made the following assertion: "Infomercials are junk. I wouldn't waste my money advertising on this medium." What is your response to her contention?

11. Members of the advertising community often claim that people meters are flawed. What are some of the reasons why people meters may not yield precise information about the number of households tuned into a specific television program or provide accurate demographic information of the people who actually do view a particular program?

12. Locate a recent SMRB or MRI publication in your library and select a product large numbers of consumers use (soft drinks, cereal, candy bars, etc.). Pick out the index numbers for the 18–24, 25–34, 35–44, 45–54, 55–64, and 65 and older age categories. Show how the index numbers were calculated. Also, identify some magazines that would be especially suitable for advertising to the heavy users of your selected product category.

13. With the following data, fill in the empty blanks:

	Total '000	A '000	B % Across	C % Down	D Index
All Adults	218,289	35,144	16.1	100.0	100
Age 18–24	28,098	6,285	____	____	____
Age 25–34	39,485	10,509	____	____	____

14. Based exclusively on the data in question 13, if you were an advertiser deciding whether to advertise your brand just to people ages 18 to 24, just to the 25-to-34 age group, or to both age groups, what would be your decision? Provide a detailed rationale for your decision.

15. Why, in your opinion, is viewership of cable TV growing rather dramatically at the expense of network TV?

16. What effect, in your view, will digital video recorders (of the TiVo variety) have on television advertising effectiveness, say, 10 years from now?

17. Discuss how multitasking among TV viewing (e.g., smartphones, social media) has affected how people watch program content. How can this best be measured?

18. What are your thoughts about brand placements in TV programs? Do you find these placements irritating or do you accept them as simply part of the programming landscape? Do you think they influence your attitudes toward advertised brands and purchase behavior?

19. Offer your thoughts about the likelihood that portable people meters (PPMs) will serve to track people's listening and viewing behaviors effectively when they are away from home. Should Nielsen have taken advantage of this technology for measuring TV viewing?

End Notes

1. These are estimated expenditures for 2012 published in *Marketer's Guide to Media 2011*, vol. 34, New York: Prometheus Global Media, 12.
2. "2010 Revenue by Sector" (100 Leading Media Companies 2011), *Advertising Age*, October 3, 2011, 52.
3. Bradley Johnson, "100 Leading Media Companies," *Advertising Age*, October 3, 2011, 45.
4. *Marketer's Guide to Media*, 2011, 191.
5. Ibid.
6. "NY Times Subscriptions: Frequently Asked Questions," http://www.nytimes.com/subscriptions/Multiproduct/lp5558.html (accessed December 4, 2011).
7. These circulation levels and rates are from ibid, 179.
8. Emily Steel, "Big Media on Campus," *Wall Street Journal*, August 9, 2006, B1.
9. Michael T. Elliott and Paul Surgi Speek, "Consumer Perceptions of Advertising Clutter and Its Impact across Various Media," *Journal of Advertising Research* 38 (January/February 1998), 29–41.
10. Karen Whitehill King, Leonard N. Reid, and Margaret Morrison, "Large-Agency Media Specialists' Opinions on Newspaper Advertising for National Accounts," *Journal of Advertising* 26 (summer 1997), 1–18. This article indicates that ad agencies consider newspapers less effective as an advertising medium in most all respects compared with network television.
11. Julia Angwin and Joe Hagan, "As Market Shifts, Newspapers Try to Lure New, Young Readers," *Wall Street Journal*, March 22, 2006, A1.
12. *Marketer's Guide to Media 2011*, 158–61.
13. *Sports Illustrated* rate card #69, http://www.simediakit.com/media/property/download/ratecard/Sports%20Illustrated%202011%20Rate%20Card.pdf, effective January 10, 2010.
14. Stephen M. Blacker, "Magazines Need Better Research," *Advertising Age*, June 10, 1996, 23; and Erwin Ephron, "Magazines Stall at Research Crossroads," *Advertising Age*, October 19, 1998, 38.
15. *Marketer's Guide to Media 2011*, 166–68.
16. For additional information on magazine audience measurement, see Thomas C. Kinnear, David A. Horne, and Theresa A. Zingery, "Valid Magazine

Audience Measurement: Issues and Perspectives," in *Current Issues and Research in Advertising*, ed. James H. Leigh and Claude R. Martin, Jr., Ann Arbor: Division of Research, Graduate School of Business, University of Michigan, 1986, 251–70.

17. The following information is based on the *Mediamark Reporter* (GfK Mediamark Research Inc., Fall 2010).

18. Kevin J. Clancy, Paul D. Berger, and Thomas L. Magliozzi, "The Ecological Fallacy: Some Fundamental Research Misconceptions Corrected," *Journal of Advertising Research* 43 (December 2003), 370–80, especially 377–79.

19. Sandy Blanchard, "Marketers on Custom Media," *Advertising Age*, January 29, 2007, C10. For the Lexus Magazine, see https://secure.drivers.lexus.com/lexusdrivers/magazine/home.do (accessed December 20, 2011).

20. "Custom Media 07," *Advertising Age*, January 29, 2007, C1; see also the Custom (Media) Content Council, http://www.customcontentcouncil.com (accessed December 20, 2011).

21. Mark Walsh, "Mobile Devices Boost Magazine Subscriptions," *Media Post News*, November 21, 2011, http://www.mediapost.com/publications/article/162779/mobile-devices-boost-magazine-subscriptions.html.

22. David Carr, "Now to Sell Advertisers on Tablets," *New York Times*, May 8, 2011, http://www.nytimes.com/2011/05/09/business/media/09carr.html?pagewanted=all.

23. *Marketer's Guide to Media 2011*, 72.

24. Burt Manning, "Friendly Persuasion," *Advertising Age*, September 13, 1982, M8.

25. For further reading on the nature and value of imagery in advertising, see Paula Fitzgerald Bone and Pam Scholder Ellen, "The Generation and Consequences of Communication-Evoked Imagery," *Journal of Consumer Research* 19 (June 1992), 93–104; Darryl W. Miller and Lawrence J. Marks, "Mental Imagery and Sound Effects in Radio Commercials," *Journal of Advertising* 21 (December 1992), 83–93; and Laurie A. Babin and Alvin C. Burns, "Effects of Print Ad Pictures and Copy Containing Instructions to Imagine on Mental Imagery That Mediates Attitudes," *Journal of Advertising* 26 (Autumn 1997), 33–44.

26. A thorough study of this behavior was conducted by Avery M. Abernethy, "The Accuracy of Diary Measures of Car Radio Audiences: An Initial Assessment," *Journal of Advertising* 18, no. 3 (1989), 33–39.

27. Abbey Klaassen, "iPod Threatens $20B Radio-ad Biz," *Advertising Age*, January 24, 2005, 1, 57.

28. "Sirius XM," Wikipedia, http://en.wikipedia.org/wiki/Sirius_satellite_radio (accessed December 20, 2011).

29. "New Age for Radio—Electronic Audience Measurement with the Portable People Meter™ System," Arbitron, http://www.arbitron.com/portable_people_meters/ppm_service.htm (accessed December 20, 2011).

30. *Marketer's Guide to Media 2011*, 23.

31. Elliott and Speek, "Consumer Perceptions of Advertising Clutter and Its Impact across Various Media."

32. Cynthia M. Frisby, "Reaching the Male Consumer by Way of Daytime TV Soap Operas," *Journal of Advertising Research* 42 (March/April 2002), 56–64.

33. Statistics in this paragraph are from two sources: Robert Seidman, "Weekly Network Ratings," ten weeks ending November 27, 2011, http://tvbythenumbers.zap2it.com/2011/11/30/2011-12-season-fox-cbs-still-tied-in-adults-18-49-ratings-through-week-10-ending-november-27-2011/112175; and Nielsen Media Research as reported in "Stiff Competition: TV Has Seen Better Days," *Marketing News*, December 15, 2004, 8.

34. *Marketer's Guide to Media*, 29.

35. Ibid., 52.

36. Ellen Sheng, "Local Cable Advertising Heats Up as Viewership Further Fragments," *Wall Street Journal Online*, December 15, 2004, http://online.wsj.com.

37. "Results of 4As 2010 TV Production Cost Survey," http://www.aaaa.org/news/bulletins/Pages/tvprod_112311.aspx (accessed December 20, 2011).

38. "Top Ten Broadcast TV Programs for the Week of March 12, 2012," Nielsen Media Research, http://www.nielsen.com/us/en/insights/top10s/television.html (for current week) (accessed April 19, 2011).

39. "The Toughest Job in TV," *Newsweek*, October 3, 1988, 72; and Dennis Kneale, "'Zapping' of TV Ads Appears Pervasive," *Wall Street Journal*, April 25, 1988, 21.

40. John J. Cronin, "In-Home Observations of Commercial Zapping Behavior," *Journal of Current Issues and Research in Advertising* 17 (fall 1995), 69–76.

41. Fred S. Zufryden, James H. Pedrick, and Avu Sankaralingam, "Zapping and Its Impact on Brand Purchase Behavior," *Journal of Advertising Research* 33 (January/February 1993), 58–66.

42. John J. Cronin and Nancy E. Menelly, "Discrimination vs. 'Zipping' of Television Commercials," *Journal of Advertising* 21 (June 1992), 1–7.

43. Steve McClellan, "TV Ads Are Less Effective, Survey Says," *Adweek.com*, February 20, 2008 (accessed March 8, 2008).

44. "Study: DVR Users Skip Live Ads, Too," *Brandweek*, October 18, 2004, 7.

45. Erwin Ephron, "Live TV Is Ready for Its Closeup," *Advertising Age*, March 22, 2004, 19.

46. Brian Stelter, "The Myth of Fast-Forwarding Past the Ads," *New York Times*, December 20, 2010, http://www.nytimes.com/2010/12/21/business/media/21adco.html.

47. Jack Neff, "P&G Study: PVR Ad Recall Similar to TV," *Advertising Age*, March 17, 2003, 4.

48. Suzanne Vranica, "New Ads Take on TiVo," *Wall Street Journal*, October 5, 2007, B4.

49. Andrew Green, "Clutter Crisis Countdown," *Advertising Age*, April 21, 2003, 22.

50. For an interesting article that compares the effectiveness of 15- and 30-second commercials, see Surendra N. Singh and Catherine A. Cole, "The Effects of Length, Content, and Repetition on Television Commercial Effectiveness," *Journal of Marketing Research* 30 (February 1993), 91–104.

51. Whether advertising clutter has adverse effects on brand name recall and message memorability is a matter of some dispute. For somewhat different accounts, see Tom J. Brown and Michael L. Rothschild, "Reassessing the Impact of Television Advertising Clutter," *Journal of Consumer Research* 20 (June 1993), 138–46; Robert J. Kent and Chris T. Allen, "Does Competitive Clutter in Television Advertising 'Interfere' with the Recall and Recognition of Brand Names and Ad Claims?" *Marketing Letters* 4, no. 2 (1993), 175–84; Robert J. Kent and Chris T. Allen, "Competitive Interference in Consumer Memory for Advertising: The Role of Brand Familiarity," *Journal of Marketing* 58 (July 1994), 97–105; and Robert J. Kent, "Competitive Clutter in Network Television Advertising: Current Levels and Advertiser Response," *Journal of Advertising Research* 35 (January/February 1995), 49–57.

52. Jim Edwards, "The Art of the Infomercial," *Brandweek*, September 3, 2001, 14–18.

53. Paul Surgi Speck, Michael T. Elliott, and Frank H. Alpert, "The Relationship of Beliefs and Exposure to General Perceptions of Infomercials," *Journal of Current Issues and Research in Advertising* 14 (spring 1997), 51–66.

54. Research has indicated that infomercial shoppers are impulsive; see Naveen Donthu and David Gilliland, "Observations: The Infomercial Shopper," *Journal of Advertising Research* 36 (March/April 1996), 69–76. There is countervailing evidence that challenges the claim that infomercial shoppers are particularly impulsive; see Tom Agee and Brett A. S. Martin, "Planned or Impulse Purchases? How To Create Effective Infomercials," *Journal of*

Advertising Research 41 (November/December 2001), 35–42.

55. Jack Neff, "Amid Cutbacks, ShamWow Marches On," *Advertising Age*, March 3, 2009, http://adage.com/article/news/downturn-worsens-drtv-picks-slack-media/135403.

56. Rosellina Ferraro and Rosemary J. Avery, "Brand Appearance on Prime-Time Television," *Journal of Current Issues and Research in Advertising*, 22 (fall 2000), 1–16.

57. Cristel Antonia Russell, Andrew T. Norman, and Susan E. Heckler, "The Consumption of Television Programming: Development and Validation of the Connectedness Scale," *Journal of Consumer Research* 31 (June 2004), 150–61.

58. Suzanne Vranica, "Targeted TV Ads Set for Takeoff," *Wall Street Journal*, December 20, 2010, B1, B7.

59. Brian Steinberg, "Does Anyone Under 30 Watch Live TV These Days?" *Advertising Age*, September 27, 2010, 46.

60. Simon Dumenco, "So Why Do Networks Seem to Care So Much About Social TV?" *Advertising Age*, October 3, 2011, 22.

61. Ibid, 22.

62. For a technical analysis of the reliability of people-meter measurement, see Roland Soong, "The Statistical Reliability of People Meter Ratings," *Journal of Advertising Research* 28 (February/March 1988), 50–56.

63. Emily Nelson and Sarah Ellison, "Nielsen's Feud with TV Networks Shows Scarcity of Marketing Data," *Wall Street Journal Online*, October 29, 2003, http://online.wsj.com.

64. *Marketer's Guide to Media 2011*, 37.

65. These details are from Brooks Barnes, "For Nielsen, Fixing Old Ratings System Causes New Static," *Wall Street Journal Online*, September 16, 2004, http://online.wsj.com.

66. "The Local People Meter–The Game Changer," *The Cab*, http://www.thecab.tv/main/cablenetworks/localmeasurement/peoplemeters/index.shtml (accessed December 21, 2011).

67. Gary Holmes, "More Second Thoughts on Set-Top-Box Measurement," *MediaPost*, December 13, 2011, http://mediapost.com/publications/article/164137.

68. Abbey Klaassen, "Down with Diaries: Nielsen Modernizes," *Advertising Age*, June 19, 2006, 8.

69. Monica M. Clark, "Nielsen's 'People Meters' Go Top 10," *Wall Street Journal*, June 30, 2006, B2.

70. Joan Fitzgerald, "Evaluating Return on Investment of Multimedia Advertising with a Single-Source

Panel: A Retail Case Study," *Journal of Advertising Research* 44 (September/October 2004), 262–70.

71. Katy Bachman, "Agency, TV Execs Question Nielsen's Dropping PPM Deal," *Adweek*, March 6, 2006, http://www.adweek.com/news/advertising/agency-tv-execs-question-nielsens-dropping-ppm-deal-84338.

72. Stephanie Kang, "TNS Aims to Take Bite Out of Nielsen," *Wall Street Journal*, January 31, 2008, B8.

73. Janet Stilson, "Rentrak's Influence Growing In Ratings Wars," *TV News Check*, December 13, 2011, http://www.tvnewscheck.com/article/2011/12/13/56019/rentraks-influence-growing-in-ratings-wars.

Online and Mobile Advertising

Mobile Headache: The Excitement and Challenges of Mobile Advertising

A recent interview with five advertising executives revealed that although mobile advertising can be challenging (some calling it a "mobile headache"), its allure is overwhelming based on its global reach, integration, and consumer utility. In fact, ad spending on mobile in the United States currently is at $1.1 billion and is expected to grow to over $2.5 billion by 2014. As noted by the executives, mobile advertising is an excellent media choice to aid horizontal IMC (e.g., moving from short message service [SMS] texts to the Web to applications [apps] to games to social media and back to building brands, such as Coca-Cola, Hewlett Packard, Walmart, etc.). It also provides an excellent international platform in helping with revenue growth, cost reduction, and customer satisfaction. For example, Hewlett-Packard's mobile effort currently is in 71 countries

© Oleksiy Maksymenko Photography/Alamy

with important devices, such as the ePrint app allowing one to print from a mobile phone in other countries. Consumer utility also is enhanced with mobile marketing by providing an "answer in their hand" in the form of store maps, deals, shopping lists, meal planners, etc.

Yet, the industry execs readily acknowledge that *more* mobile apps (e.g., a new "Angry Birds" game) do not necessarily represent *better* apps, as they may not fit into a consumer's lifestyle or a company's IMC strategy. Moreover, a corporate "cookie cutter" approach in not likely to work in every country, as there are many different intermediaries and carriers from country to country. Many execs also point out that this is not an IT-driven media (with long, 3-year lead times on programs). Rather, there are rapid, 30-day program cycles, often driven by consumer

Chapter Objectives

After reading this chapter, you should be able to:

1   Appreciate the magnitude, nature, and potential for online and mobile advertising.

2   Describe how the online advertising process works.

3   Understand the various forms of online advertising: search engine advertising, display or banner ads, rich media, websites and sponsorships, blogs and podcasts, e-mail advertising, mobile advertising, and advertising via behavioral targeting.

4   Describe the nature of mobile advertising: its forms (e.g., short message services, location-based services), benefits and costs, and strategies.

5   Understand the issues associated with privacy and online behavioral targeting.

6   Appreciate the importance of measuring online advertising effectiveness and the various metrics used for this purpose.

desires and marketing initiatives. Finally, many note that to move into the mobile space means that they have to make difficult decisions in moving money from other traditional areas (e.g., newspapers, magazines).

Recently, *Advertising Age* made three important suggestions to maximize retail mobile marketing. First, companies should make their website "mobile friendly." Most consumers seek out brand information from websites, not from apps. Yet, 79 percent of Google's largest advertisers do not have a mobile optimized site (e.g., with Quick Response or other bar coding). Second, *Advertising Age* suggests to watch out for "scan and scram shoppers"; that is, shoppers who scan barcodes in stores but make

purchases elsewhere. One way to combat this activity is to match competitor prices in the stores. Finally, *Advertising Age* recommends having a tablet-optimized app or site. Companies must develop high-quality, catalog-type efforts that allow consumers to drag and drop items directly into an online shopping cart. So, from the above discussion, it can be seen that mobile advertising represents an exciting, but ever-changing and challenging option for many advertisers.

Sources: Kunur Patel, "Mobile Headaches: Execs Tackle Difficult but Enticing Medium," *Advertising Age*, October 3, 2011, 36; "Mobile Marketing 2011," *Advertising Age*, Digital Issue (Fall), September 19, 2011, section pullout; and Kathryn Koegel, "Three Tips to Maximize Retail Mobile Marketing," *Advertising Age*, November 28, 2011, 4.

Introduction

When consumers have access to marketing communications online, it helps perform many marketing functions for companies, including building demand, conducting transactions, filling orders, providing customer service, and serving as a versatile advertising medium. However, this chapter is *not* about online marketing or e-commerce in general, but rather is restricted to *online advertising* and *mobile advertising* functions. As you are probably aware, the exact role of online advertising is in a state of flux: New technologies are continually emerging, and marketers are experimenting with varied uses of online communications. This chapter's objective is to overview most aspects of online advertising (including mobile advertising), hoping that students will fully appreciate both the changes occurring and the uncertainties of what exactly the future might bring. Certainly, as described in the discussion of mobile advertising in the *Marcom Insight*, online advertising media will continue to draw advertising dollars from the traditional ad media.

Traditional advertising media, those covered in the previous chapter (television, radio, magazines, and newspaper), have served advertisers' needs for generations. Over the past few decades, however, there have been increased efforts on the part of advertisers and their agencies to locate new media that are less costly, less cluttered, and potentially more effective than the established media. For years, some observers have gone so far as to claim that traditional advertising is on its deathbed.[1] The contention is that online advertising is superior to traditional media because it provides consumers with virtually full control over the commercial information they choose to receive or avoid. The Internet is claimed to be a better communications medium due to its versatility and superiority at targeting customers.[2] Most agree, however, that online advertising is nothing more than a potentially key element of IMC programs; it is not a replacement for conventional media.[3]

Dating back just to 1994, the "World Wide Web" has become an important advertising medium. Although at the time of this writing, the Internet commands only about 17 percent ($28.5 billion) of U.S. major media advertising revenue, total online advertising spending in the United States is expected to reach $40.5 billion by 2014.[4] Perhaps the most dramatic indicator of the growth of online advertising is the fact that the total digital advertising revenue (e.g., from search companies such as Google and Yahoo!) generated in 2010 was greater than the combined prime-time ad revenues of the four major U.S. television networks.[5] Many firms, both business-to-consumer (B2C) and business-to-business (B2B), continue to shift larger percentages of their total marcom budgets to online advertising.

Online Advertising: Benefits and Costs

Several benefits or key features of online advertising include individualization, interactivity, immediate publishing, and cost efficiency.[6] *Individualization* refers to the fact that the online user has control over the flow of information. This feature leads, in turn, to the ability to target advertisements and promotions that are relevant to the consumer. *Interactivity*, which is intertwined with individualization, allows for users to select the information they perceive as relevant and for brand managers to build relationships with customers via two-way communications. For example, the user can choose to devote one second or 15 minutes to a message. He or she is, for all intents and purposes, engaged in a "conversation" with the commercial message at a subvocal level. A request for additional information occurs with the push of a button, the touch of a screen, or the click of a mouse.[7] Another benefit or feature is the *immediate publishing* of information and content, not limited by geography or time, as found with other media choices. It also tends to be a very *cost-efficient* media choice. For example, the minimum charge to advertise based on keyword searches on Google is a cost per click (CPC) of 0.01, or a cost to reach one thousand views (or impressions) (CPM) of 0.25, both requiring just a minimum $10 payment to begin.[8]

Advertising online is not without its disadvantages. Some of these include potential user distraction or interruptions, an extremely wide range of choices, international coordination, rapid change, very short lead times, and making tough IMC choices internally. For example, whereas the TV viewer is casually watching TV programs and advertisements in a relaxed mood (leaning back, so to speak), the online user is goal-driven usually and on a mission to obtain information (leaning forward). Thus, banner ads, pop-ups, and unsolicited e-mail messages may simply represent a *distraction or interruption* to what the user is trying to do online.[9] Also, the Internet as a medium for advertising is *not* homogeneous; rather, there are a *wide variety of different choices* of online advertising. These can range from e-mail and display or banner advertisements, which typically offer relatively little opportunity or desire for interaction, to ads encountered when one actively searches a topic (referred to as search engine ads that appear as sponsored links when one conducts a Google search), which generate more interaction. As noted in the *Marcom Insight*, the *coordination of international online ad placement* (e.g., with mobile advertising) can be a "headache," as one is dealing usually with a multitude of providers, carriers, and consumer devices. Next, obviously, this medium is undergoing *rapid change*. Some areas are cooling off (e.g., e-mail advertising is predicted to stay a steady percentage of online advertising), whereas other areas continue at a breakneck speed (e.g., amount spent on mobile advertising is to double in three years).[10] As also noted in the *Marcom Insight*, extremely short lead times (e.g., 30-day program cycles) can arise for online ad placement often driven by short-term consumer desires. Finally, many companies are making tough IMC choices internally in the movement of ad dollars from more traditional media areas (with vested interests internally) to online ad formats. This also has required new thinking on adjusting traditional tradeoffs for media planning, such as reach and frequency, as online strategy may be more about optimizing frequency over time with more targeted placement efforts online.[11]

From the above discussion, it should be obvious that no medium is perfect for all purposes. Rather, it is very important to figure out what the consumer need and/or problem is first, and then apply the right mix of IMC elements to the issue.[12] Finally, as you may recall from Chapter 1, all marketing communications should be (1) directed to a particular *target market*, (2) clearly *positioned*, (3) created to achieve a *specific objective*, and (4) undertaken to accomplish the objective *within budget constraint*.

The Online Advertising Process

Many parties are involved in online advertising process, from the advertiser to the final consumer viewing the ad online, and to the ratings services measuring the impact of the ad. Figure 13.1 depicts the process flows in an illustration of the online advertising process. (You may recall this figure from Chapter 5 that we used for the purposes of discussing online behavioral targeting.)

For illustration, the process might begin with an advertiser (California Travel & Tourism Commission) contacting an interactive agency (e.g., R/GA, AKQA, Tribal DDB) with the campaign objectives and a plan to buy ad inventory online. Next, the agency might supply the ad materials (video, banners, etc.) to a third-party server (e.g., Atlas, Google's DoubleClick) who either contacts a publisher directly (e.g., Lonely Planet, Travel Channel) or works with an ad network/exchange (e.g., Google, Microsoft, Time Warner/AOL). The ad network is an intermediary between the publisher and advertiser or ad agency that helps to sell inventory, especially to small- to mid-sized publishers.[13] These ad networks are important, as the top 100 publishers sell only 40 percent of inventory through direct means.[14] Also, it is argued that total campaign costs are better managed with the use of ad networks.[15] In the balance of ad objectives (e.g., page views per CPM, CPC, or cost-per-order or -action [CPA]) versus

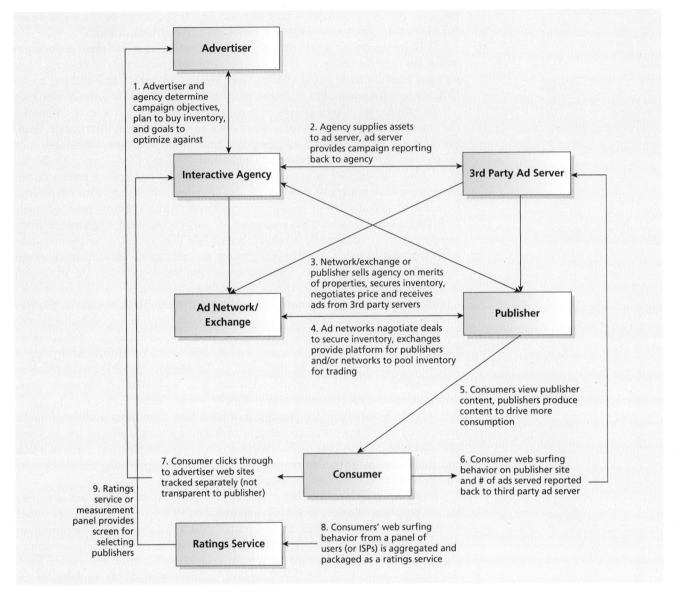

FIGURE **13.1** The Online Advertising Process

Source: DeSilva + Phillps, LLC, "Online Ad Networks: Monetizing the Long Tail," March 2008, http://www.mediabankers.com/PDF/ DeSilva+Phillips Ad Networks White Paper 3 08.pdf, (accessed July 24, 2011), 1–15. Used with permission.

cost, the advertiser or agency will use a service such as ComScore or Nielsen Monitor-Plus to screen potential publisher outlets against demographics or other aspects of the target audience. The delivery of the actual ads to viewers may be based on the *content* of the ad visited (e.g., delivered via Google AdSense) or based on *behavior* (from cookie tracking files for sites visited on the computer) delivered by services such as Tacoda (AOL) or Revenue Science.[16] This latter approach allows for an advertiser to target individual computers (as a proxy for people). (This topic is discussed further in the section on privacy.) Of course, the advertiser (California Travel & Tourism Commission) could work directly with social media sites as well (e.g., Facebook, YouTube, Twitter).

Online Advertising Formats

Online advertisers use a variety of advertising formats with unique characteristics. Table 13.1 lists the various forms of online advertising that are described in this chapter. Of course, all forms of online advertising are not equal in terms of ad expenditures, nor are all forms equally effective.[17] The major form of online advertising is search engine advertising (SEA) commanding 48 percent of all

TABLE 13.1	Online Advertising Formats

- Search Engine Advertising
  - Keyword-Matching Advertising
  - Content-Targeted Advertising
- Display or Banner Ads
- Rich Media
  - Pop-Ups
  - Interstitials
  - Superstitials
  - Video Ads
- Websites and Sponsored Sites
- Blogs and Podcasts
  - Blogs
  - Podcasts
- E-mail Advertising
  - Opt-in versus Spam
  - E-zines
- Mobile Advertising
- Advertising via Behavioral Targeting

© Cengage Learning 2013

Internet advertising; whereas e-mail advertising represents only 0.8 percent.[18] However, the fattest growing is mobile advertising, projected to increase 131 percent from 2011 to 2014.[19]

The following sections examine the major forms of online advertising. It is important to appreciate that any sweeping and definitive claims would be inappropriate, because online advertising and its subcategories are so new, dating back at most less than two decades. Oftentimes some categories (e.g., mobile advertising) are changing almost weekly!

Search Engine Advertising

In general, search engine advertising (SEA) refers to a method of placing online advertisements on Web pages that show results from search engine queries.[20] Search advertisements usually are targeted to match key search terms (called *keywords*) entered on search engines, such as Google, Yahoo!, Bing, Yelp!, or Baidu (in China). eMarketer—one of the leading publishers of data, analysis, and insights on digital marketing—has estimated that by 2014, search engine advertising will grow to $18.84 billion from $13.59 currently.[21]

It should be noted that SEA is realizing that Internet search engines include a variety of well-known services that people use when seeking information as they perform what can be referred to as *natural searches*—for example, one enters the expression "inexpensive book bags" when searching online for items of this sort. Google, Yahoo!, and Bing (Microsoft) are the best known and most frequently used search engines. Google is far and away the most dominant search engine, with over 64 percent of U.S. searches and almost the same worldwide.[22]

Another critical element of SEA is that this form of advertising attempts to place messages in front of people precisely when their natural search efforts indicate they apparently are interested in buying a particular good or service.

In this context, an insightful statement in media planning is that advertising achieves its effectiveness "through a chance encounter with a ready consumer."[23]

A key (and probably the most important) feature of SEA is keywords. Keywords are specific words and short phrases that describe the nature, attributes, and benefits of a marketer's offering. For example, suppose a consumer was performing an online search to locate a really specific product such as a navy blue sports coat. In performing a natural search for such an item, one consumer might input the expression "navy blue sports coat," another consumer may simply input "blue blazer," yet another may enter "dress jacket." In other words, there are many ways to search for the same item. If we enter "navy blue sports coat" into the Google search line, about 64,000 matches are returned. Of most relevance to the present discussion, the top of the Google results page lists three highlighted *sponsored* links and eight sponsored links on the right side of the page. These links are for companies that pay Google to advertise their websites. For example, two of the links are for well-known retailers, Brooks Brothers (www.brooksbrothers.com) and Macy's (www.macys.com). Clicking through to the websites for these two companies reveals that both retailers offer multiple products for sale, of which navy blue sports coats are just one of many. Note that a future attempt to repeat this search would undoubtedly yield different results.

Now, from the perspective of a company that sells sports coats, it would be useful to have an ad for its product appear whenever consumers enter into a search engine any expression that might relate to navy blue sports coats. In other words, when natural search results are returned by Google, Yahoo!, Bing, or any other search engine, companies would like to have their websites listed as sponsored links. In our previously mentioned example of "navy blue sports coat," nearly 64,000 results were returned. Each Google page lists only 10 links and most people will look at maybe only five pages. This means that thousands of potential items—including your company's listing—would never be seen unless it appeared somewhere on the first five pages of search results. Because advertising is all about increasing the odds that ready consumers will have a "chance encounter" with your ad (not just any ad), your task as an online advertiser is to increase these odds. Sponsored links to natural searches serve beautifully to accomplish this objective. The foregoing description can be summarized in the series of steps listed in Figure 13.2.

Purchasing Keywords and Selecting Content-Oriented Websites

There actually are two forms of search engine advertising available to online advertisers. One form, as described already, is *keyword search* (also called *keyword matching*), and the other involves placing ads on content-oriented websites that provide appropriate contexts in which to advertise a particular type of product. Each form of SEA is described using Google's advertising services. Google is selected for illustration because it is by far the leading search engine and commands over 64 percent of all Internet searches.[24]

Step 1: Prospective purchasers of a specific good or service perform natural search using one or more search engines to locate that item.

Step 2: Matches to Internet shopper's search are generated by Google or another search engine.

Step 3: Alongside the matches are sponsored links that correspond to the keyword(s) entered by the shopper.

Step 4: These sponsored links appear because companies offering the searched item purchased corresponding keywords from the search engine company.

Step 5: Shoppers may click through to a sponsored website and purchase a desired item or, at least, consider this website for future purchases.

FIGURE **13.2** The Role of Keywords in Increasing the Odds That Consumers Will Encounter Your Ad

© Cengage Learning

Keyword-Matching Advertising

To become a sponsored link to Internet shoppers' search results, interested advertisers must bid for and purchase keywords from search engine services such as Google. For example, the obvious keywords that a sports coat advertiser might employ to attract consumers to its website would include terms and phrases such as "sports coats," "blazers," "blue blazer," "blue sports coat," "blue sports jacket," "wool sports coat," "moderately priced blazers," and so forth.

Google has a keyword advertising program called AdWords. (Interested students can learn more about AdWords by reviewing its demonstration at http:// adwords.google.com.) In AdWords, prospective advertisers bid for keywords by indicating how much they are willing to pay each time an Internet shopper clicks on their website when it appears as a sponsored link. The cost per click (CPC) varies by country. In the United States, the cost ranges from one penny per click to as much as advertisers are willing to pay as a function of keyword quality. The higher an advertiser's bid, the more prominent the placement of the advertiser's sponsored link. That is, the highest bidder per keyword receives the top placement; the second-highest bidder, the second placement; and so on. However, recent research suggests that although click-through rate (CTR) is best with top placement, greater purchase intentions (i.e., conversion rates) tend to occur with a *lower* placement, suggesting a recency bias.[25]

When purchasing keywords, advertisers also indicate the top amount they are willing to budget each day. So for example, if an advertiser is willing to pay only 20 cents per CPC for a particular keyword and specifies a daily budget limit of $300, then that advertiser could receive a maximum of 1,500 click-throughs to its website on a given day for just that one keyword.

The keyword advertiser also can specify the country where ads are to be sponsored and particular local areas where ads are to be targeted. For example, advertisers of services provided in local communities are interested in reaching only people located in particular communities and surrounding areas. Google's AdWords program also provides advertisers with performance reports that indicate which keywords are generating the most click-throughs and how much each keyword costs on average. Advertisers can then decide to drop usage of underperforming keywords or rebid how much they are willing to pay to use these words or phrases.

Content-Targeted Advertising

In addition to its AdWords service, Google has another program called AdSense. With this program, Google enables online advertisers to run ads on websites other than Google's own site. Advertisers specify the sites on which they want their ads to appear rather than picking keywords that are tied to online surfers' natural search behavior (as described previously for the AdWords program). Advertisers pay Google to run ads on selected websites, and then Google pays these websites (or "content network partners") about 68 percent of the revenue generated from advertisers.[26] In a sense, Google operates as an ad agency placing ads on other websites, taking as commission about 32 percent of the revenue and allowing the content-oriented websites to earn the bulk of the ad-placement cost. Recently, Google added "Google Instant" that immediately offers search results for the first keystroke.[27] This is argued to benefit brands attached to a first letter keyword, and increasing the impressions for such searches.

Cost control efforts aid advertisers using SEA.[28] For example, campaigns can begin slowly to test effectiveness of keywords and texts (e.g., $20 to $40 per day) before scaling up (e.g., $1,000 per day). *Negative* keywords (to avoid ads) can be helpful. For example, "Microsoft Windows" could be used as a negative keyword if one was selling replacement windows for buildings and wished to avoid "Microsoft Windows" from appearing. Finally, correct word order and location-specific searches can help in the use of SEA.

In summary, SEA with programs such as Google's AdWords, Google's AdSense, and Google Instant provide Internet advertisers ways to place their ads in places where prospective customers are searching and thus to increase the odds of encountering ready consumers. The advantages are clear (cost efficiency, pinpointed targeting, and quick and easy assessment of ad effectiveness), yet SEA is not without problems.

SEA Problems

The major problem with search engine advertising, especially the keyword-matching variety, is click fraud. Click fraud occurs when a competitor or other party poses as a legitimate user and clicks on a sponsored link repeatedly in order to bias advertising effectiveness. Using a computer to commit click fraud is a felony in many jurisdictions (e.g., California), especially involving malicious clicking to deplete a competitor's ad budget.[29] Recall that advertisers pay for sponsored links on a cost-per-click basis, and that advertisers specify an upper limit on how much they are willing to budget daily. You may further recall that at 20 cents per click and with a daily limit of $300, the advertiser can achieve a total of only 1,500 click-throughs on a given day. A competitor could repeatedly click on a sponsored link until the 1,500 limit is reached, thus preventing any legitimate click-throughs. As such, our hypothetical advertiser would receive zero benefit from its modest investment.

In addition to competitors engaging in click fraud, this practice also takes place when employees of content-oriented websites repeatedly click on advertised websites to increase the revenue a search engine such as Google pays to them. Again, advertisers suffering from fraudulent click-throughs receive no benefit from their advertising. So-called *bot* software programs (short for robot) have been used to click on ads automatically and repeatedly, thereby generating substantial revenue for websites and wasting advertisers' honest investment that is intended to enhance their brand images and drive sales.

Estimates of click fraud's magnitude range from 5 percent to 20 percent.[30] The magnitude of the problem prompted a top executive at Google to describe click fraud as "the biggest threat to the Internet economy" and to encourage that something be done as quickly as possible to curtail the problem before it threatens the SEA business model.[31] The solution comes in the form of companies that specialize in click-fraud detection. The service these companies provide has been described as follows: "Click fraud detection technology identifies and alerts companies to suspicious activity while it is happening, allowing paid search managers to stall ads running on keywords where the abuse is happening, preventing further budget loss."[32]

Click fraud notwithstanding, it remains that SEA is generally a highly effective form of online advertising, and click fraud is simply a cost of doing business. Most authorities believe that the return on investment from SEA is unmatched by other forms of online marcom.

Display or Banner Ads

One popular advertising format in the Internet's short advertising history has been the static advertisement known as a display, or banner ad. Banner ads, a staple of online advertising, are static ads—somewhat analogous to print ads placed in magazines and newspapers—that appear on frequently visited websites. Currently, this format is second (to search engine advertising) in ad dollars spent online at $6.56 billion and is expected to grow to $8.63 billion by 2014.[33] Yet, this growth is tempered by recent arguments that brand managers would prefer greater "engagement" (via social media) rather than the static ad banners.[34]

Click-Through Rates

Click-through rates (CTRs) to banner ads are very low, averaging less than 0.3 percent. (Note: Click-through means that an Internet user, upon clicking a banner ad, is directed to the advertiser's website.) Banner ads for B2B companies receive somewhat higher CTRs than do those for B2C companies.[35] In other words, online users pay attention and solicit information from only a small percentage of all the Internet banner ads to which they are exposed. (Remember, exposure is necessary for but not equivalent to attention. Exposure merely indicates that the consumer has had a chance to see an advertisement.) Although the mere exposure to a banner ad can have some value in enhancing brand awareness, low CTRs reduce the effectiveness of banner ads.

Research has found that CTRs are a function of *brand familiarity*, with brands that consumers know best receiving substantially higher CTRs than unfamiliar brands.[36] Importantly, but not particularly surprisingly, this same research revealed that CTRs decrease with multiple exposures to banner ads for familiar brands, whereas the rates increase with more exposures to ads for unfamiliar brands. New and relatively unknown brands thus need to produce a banner-ad media schedule that allows for multiple exposures. Established brands, conversely, may not experience increased CTRs with multiple exposures.

This, however, does not necessarily imply that established brands do not benefit from banner advertising. On the contrary, such brands may achieve increasing levels of *brand awareness*—culminating in top-of-mind awareness, or TOMA, even though consumers choose not to click through to the brand's website. (Recall the discussion of brand awareness in Chapter 2.) Banner advertising, along with other communications elements in an IMC program, can serve to facilitate increasing levels of brand awareness and thus enhance brand equity. Moreover, beyond merely enhancing brand equity, research evidence indicates—contrary to popular belief—that exposure to banner ads has a significant effect on actual purchase behavior.[37] That is, more exposure to banner ads leads to increased probability of purchasing online advertisers' products and services.

Standardization of Banner-Ad Sizes

The Internet Advertising Bureau (IAB), a leading trade association in the online advertising industry, facilitated standardization of banner sizes. The IAB endorsed seven online ad formats, labeled Internet marketing units (IMUs). These seven IMUs compare with the earlier full banner, which was 468×60 pixels (28,080 square pixels).

Table 13.2 contrasts the IMUs against this original full banner. This table makes it clear that the IMUs are generally *considerably larger* than the original full banner ad. It is likely that the larger ad sizes increase attention and thus CTRs. A study conducted by a research firm for the IAB determined that the skyscraper and large rectangle IMUs were more than three to six times as effective in increasing brand awareness and favorable message associations as the 468×60 standard banner IMU.[38]

TABLE 13.2 Types and Sizes of Internet Marketing Units (IMUs)

Type and Size of IMU (pixel size)	Square Pixels	Size Differential versus Full Banner
Full Banner (468×60)	28,800	--
Skyscraper (120×600)	72,000	156%
Wide Skyscraper (160×600)	96,000	242
Rectangle (180×150)	27,000	−4
Medium Rectangle (300×250)	75,000	167
Large Rectangle (336×280)	94,080	235
Vertical Rectangle (240×400)	96,000	242
Square Pop-Up (250×250)	62,500	123

Rich Media: Pop-Ups, Interstitials, Superstitials, and Video Ads

It was only a matter of time before Internet advertisers began using online formats that were more dynamic than banners in their use of motion, sights, and sounds. This form of online advertising is referred to as *rich media*, and includes pop-up ads, interstitials, superstitials, and video advertisements. In other words, the relatively dull and inanimate form of banner advertising has naturally progressed to the attention-gaining, albeit sometimes annoying, animated form of online advertising. Some of these rich media formats might even be compared to the low-budget ads on cable TV that use fast-talking salespeople, elevated noise levels, and dynamic movements to gain viewers' attention. Surprisingly, contextual targeted online ads (e.g., matched display) are only marginally more effective on purchase intentions than obtrusive online ads (e.g., pop-ups)—even though viewers often complain about such ads.[39]

Let us briefly distinguish rich media formats. Pop-up ads appear in a separate window that materializes on the screen, seemingly out of nowhere, while a selected Web page is loading. Pop-ups remain until they are manually closed. Interstitials—based on the word *interstitial*, which describes the space that intervenes between things—are, by comparison, ads that appear between (rather than within, as is the case with pop-ups) two content Web pages. Both pop-up ads and interstitials are obtrusive, but in different ways. The difference between pop-ups and interstitials is more than trite, as described compellingly in this quote:

> *First, unlike pop-ups, interstitials do not interrupt the user's interactive experience because they tend to run while the user waits for a page to download. Users, however, have less control over interstitials because there is no "exit" option to stop or delete an interstitial, which is common among pop-ups. In other words, with interstitials, users have to wait until the entire ad has run.[40]*

Superstitials are short, animated ads that play over or on top of a Web page. Finally, online video ads are audiovisual ads that range in length from 15 seconds to several minutes. With more households having access to broadband connection to the Internet, video ads are now feasible—unlike with a dial-up connection, which was much too slow in downloading audiovisual files.

The various forms of rich media, although often a source of irritation, are effective attention getters. Internet advertisers, like advertisers in all other media, have to fight through the clutter to find ways to attract and hold the online user's attention. Bigger ads, ads popping up, and ads that offer sounds, animation, and movement are just some of the ways that have been devised to accomplish these objectives. These formats are more eye-catching and memorable than are standard (i.e., static) banner ads and yield higher CTRs.

However, in their effort to gain attention, rich media advertising formats also greatly annoy Internet users. One study determined that whereas only about 10 percent of respondents indicate they are "very annoyed" with TV ads, over 80 percent of these respondents revealed considerable annoyance with pop-ups.[41] Advertisers have accordingly reduced their use of pop-up ads, although interstitials, superstitials, and video ads are widely used. The growing importance of video ads warrants a separate section.

Video Ads and Webisodes

One of the fastest-growing forms of online advertising is video ads, including so-called *Webisodes*, which are video ads that run as a series of episodes on websites. As noted earlier, video ads are audiovisual ads that are compressed into manageable file sizes and range in length from 15 seconds to several minutes.

© Jeff Greenberg/Alamy

Research firm eMarketer predicts that online video advertising will grow to nearly $7.15 billion by 2015 from $2.16 billion currently.[42]

Consider, for example, local video online advertising developed by Mixpo (www.mixpo.com) for the well-known restaurant IHOP (International House of Pancakes). The objective for this local video online campaign was to maintain IHOP's rank as the number 1 family dining restaurant in the United States. Mixpo was able to take IHOP's national TV commercial and transform it into 1,400 customized video ads for 31 different local markets. The local online video campaign resulted in 14.9 million impressions, over 195,000 views, and a 1.73 percent "engagement rate" (i.e., views, interactions, and clicks divided by impressions).[43] For another example of video advertising, see the *IMC Focus*, which describes Johnson & Johnson's use of animated Webisodes to promote its brand of baby lotion.

Web Videos for Johnson's Baby Lotion

Johnson's Baby Lotion is an established brand that has been on the market since 1942. Referred to as the "Pink brand" in reference to the package color, Johnson's Baby Lotion competes in a product category that amasses nearly $1 billion annual sales, with Johnson's capturing about half of the market. Interestingly, Johnson's has not invested much in advertising the brand for a number of years. The last TV commercial for the Pink brand was in 1990, and the last print advertising was in 1991. The company's rationale for not advertising the brand is that sales have grown steadily without advertising. In recent years, however, competition has intensified in the baby-care market with the addition of several new competitors. A new advertising push to protect the Pink brand's market share was thus justified.

Although television advertising has been a mainstay for many of Johnson's brands, for the Pink brand the company chose not to advertise extensively on TV but turned instead to online advertising using a series of animated Webisodes.

This choice was based on Johnson's belief that the Internet is a main source of information for young parents seeking baby-care advice. Based on research it has done on mothers and their babies, Johnson's is promoting its baby lotion brand as a means for parents to develop deeper bonds with their babies. The animated Webisodes (now available on YouTube at www. johnsonsbaby.com/bonding-tip-a-mothers-touch) feature images of mothers touching and massaging their babies. The message conveyed to viewers is that Johnson's Baby Lotion plays a meaningful role in enhancing the emotional bond between mother and child. To drive traffic to the website that carries the Webisodes, Johnson's placed a series of ads on parent-focused websites.

Sources: Adapted from Emily Steel, "J&J's Web Ads Depart from TV Formula," *Wall Street Journal*, February 12, 2008, B3; http://www. johnsonsbaby.com/bonding-tip-a-mothers-touch (accessed January 5, 2012).

© Jim Barber/Shutterstock.com

Websites and Sponsored Sites

A company's website is an advertisement for the company. However, beyond being a form of advertising, websites represent a venue for generating and transacting exchanges between organizations their customers. Websites can be considered the centerpiece of companies' online advertising efforts, with other advertising formats (e.g., paid searches, banners, e-mail) simply serving to drive traffic to their websites. Affiliated or sponsored sites are also an option for some marketers. On the affiliate site there.com (www.there.com), visitors can create their own avatar and interact with brands such as Scion, K-Swiss, Coca-Cola, and NBC Universal.

A brand's website is an invaluable advertising medium for conveying information about the brand, its character, and its promotional offerings. Perhaps the major difference between websites and other online ad formats is that users seek out websites in a *goal-oriented fashion* (e.g., to learn more about a company or brand, to play a game, or to register for a contest), whereas other online formats typically are "stumbled upon accidentally."[44] Research has shown, for example, that half of all new-vehicle buyers visit websites prior to going to automobile dealerships; moreover, people who visit these websites spend, on average, about five hours online shopping for new vehicles.[45] Another study demonstrated that site visitations for newly released movies play a prominent role in predicting box office performance. Specifically, the greater the number of unique (not repeat) visits to a new movie's website, the more people actually see the movie in a cinema.[46]

A small-town retailer was fond of saying that "merchandise well displayed is half sold," implying, of course, that attractively displayed items capture the shopper's attention and invite purchase.[47] The same advice applies to website construction: Attractive and user-friendly sites invite usage and revisits. Forrester Research, an organization well known in the area of Internet research, examined the websites of 259 B2C companies and 60 B2B firms. Forrester's research determined that text legibility is a major problem with the websites of both B2C and B2B companies. In fact, only 17 percent of the B2B sites and 20 percent of the B2C sites provided legible text.[48]

There is some tentative evidence that Web pages designed with relatively simple backgrounds (i.e., with minimal color and animation) might be preferred

to more complex pages. A study using a state lottery as the focal website learned that the most complex background produced the least favorable attitudes toward the advertised service and the weakest purchase intentions.[49]

Because consumers visit websites with the objective of acquiring useful information or being entertained, it follows that websites are of most value when they fulfill consumers' goal-seeking needs by providing useful information rather than attempting to dazzle with excessive graphic cleverness. The architect's advice that "form follows function" certainly applies to the website as an online advertising tool. It has been demonstrated, for example, that the background color of a Web page affects the perceived speed of a download; that is, more relaxing colors (such as blue and green) are perceived to download more quickly than exciting colors (such as red and yellow).[50]

Blogs and Podcasts

This section describes two interrelated forms of communication—blogs and podcasts—that can play a prominent role in marcom programs for brands both B2B and B2C companies promote. (Social media is covered in Chapter 14.)

Blogs

Web logs, or blogs for short, are, in a manner of speaking, "everyman's" way of communicating with others and establishing digital communities wherein individuals, mostly of like mind, can exchange their views on issues of personal relevance. It is in this context that products and brands are sometimes discussed. It is here where companies can endeavor to further enhance the equity of their brands by building brand awareness and enhancing (or protecting) their brand images. The importance of blogs to businesses has been stated in a direct and convincing fashion in the pages of *BusinessWeek* magazine:

> *Go ahead and bellyache about blogs. But you cannot afford to close your eyes to them, because they're simply the most explosive outbreak in the information world since the Internet itself. And they're going to shake up just about every business—including yours. It doesn't matter whether you're shipping paper clips, pork bellies, or videos of Britney in a bikini, blogs are a phenomenon that you cannot ignore, postpone, or delegate. Given the changes barreling down upon us, blogs are not a business elective. They're a prerequisite.*[51]

Much of the appeal of blogs is that a company can communicate directly with prospective customers, who in turn can become active communicators through their own posted comments.

The reality of blogging is that thousands of blogs individuals create often discuss companies and their brands in a more negative tone. It is for this reason that companies can learn a great amount about what is being said about their brands by monitoring and analyzing conversations that take place on blogs. Nielsen BuzzMetrics is one of a number of research companies that, for a fee, track and analyze what is being said in the blogosphere about a company or about its brands and competitive brands (e.g., see www.nmincite.com).[52] Another company, VML, developed a program named Seer to track influential bloggers and to monitor comments about companies and their brands. For example, shortly after Adidas introduced its Predator brand of soccer shoes in Europe, customers began noticing the colors of the shoe leather were quickly fading. Based on feedback from the Seer program, VML informed the German maker of Adidas that people were complaining about the leather, which prompted Adidas' marketing team to notify customers that the shoes' leather should be treated before wearing them.[53] This rapid feedback from the Seer program averted what could have become a virtual epidemic of negative word of mouth.

Blogs as an Advertising Format

Brand marketers can develop their own blogs or simply place advertisements on blogs that are appropriate for the advertiser's brand. For example, Google offers a service that enables small ads to be placed on blog sites. Only after a blog visitor clicks on the ad is revenue generated. Advertisers can turn to vendors such as Blogads (www.blogads.com), which is a network of blogs that accept advertising; the network matches advertisers with appropriate blogs at which to place their advertisements. Advertisers purchase ads through Blogads on a weekly or monthly basis, with costs varying based on the popularity of the blog.

Although the numbers indicate that blogging is growing exponentially (e.g., Huffington Post, TechCrush, and Mashable are some leading blog sites), this does *not* necessarily mean that blogs represent a viable advertising medium. The value of blogs to their producers and consumers is the community created and the opportunity for a free and honest exchange of ideas. Because advertising is often perceived as less than fully objective and an intrusion, the purpose for producing and consuming blogs—that is, as a form of "citizen journalism"—may be antithetical with using blogs as an advertising vehicle. At the present time it is questionable whether blogs will represent a major advertising opportunity. The CEO of an organization that is dedicated to online advertising, the Interactive Advertising Bureau, cautions that "it's too soon to gauge blog's relevance as a stand-alone ad medium."[54]

Podcasts

Whereas traditional blogs are written documents, podcasting is an audio version of blogging. Podcasts are MP3 audio files that are available for free online and are accompanied by written blogs. Search engine PodNova (www.podnova.com) lists more than 90,000 podcast programs that are arranged alphabetically under virtually any topic one might contemplate.[55]

Podcasting is a way of publishing sound files to the Internet, allowing users to subscribe to a feed and receive new audio files automatically. In effect, podcasters self-produce radio-type programs. Consumers subscribe to podcasts using a special form of so-called aggregator software that periodically checks for and downloads new content, which then is playable on computers and digital audio players. Podcasting enables advertisers to target messages to consumers who share similar lifestyle characteristics as revealed by their self-selection to particular podcasts.[56] Numerous companies have created podcasts for communicating with present and prospective customers about their brands. For example, General Motors' podcasts feature interviews with company executives who discuss the company's newest cars. Nestle's Purina brand of pet foods offers podcasts called "Animal Advice" that provide useful information to pet owners. Johnson & Johnson created a podcast for its Acuvue brand of contact lenses involving a series of episodes about teenage life called "Download with Heather & Jonelle."[57]

E-mail Advertising

With millions of people online and the numbers increasing each year, it is little wonder that marketing communicators have turned to e-mail as a viable advertising medium. Yet, due to online spam, and better online ad options (e.g., social media), the amount of ad spending in this area has stayed constant at approximately $240 million.[58] As with any other advertising medium, there is no such thing as a single type of e-mail message; they appear in many forms, ranging from pure-text documents to more sophisticated versions that use all the audiovisual powers of the Internet. Often firms send e-mail messages and encourage recipients to pass along the messages to their personal distribution list of other people. See the *Global Focus* insert for an application of e-mail advertising designed to build buzz.

Nescafé's Viral E-mail Effort in Argentina

Café con Leche, which is a mixture of coffee with milk, is sold by Nescafé in Argentina and some other countries. Given a very small budget for marketing the brand in Argentina, it was necessary for Nescafé to come up with a clever marcom strategy. The plan devised involved the use of e-mails to create brand buzz. Users of Café con Leche who were known to be technology savvy and frequent forwarders of e-mail messages were recruited. The request made of these men and women, all in the 25-to-45 age group, was to pass along a commercial message for Café con Leche to at least 15 other people. The spot focused on two young women who were preparing an iced coffee with Café con Leche. Also included was a link to a website containing a virtual kitchen. Visitors to the site could click on ingredients located in cupboards and a refrigerator while following recipes to create coffee shakes with ice cream and to mix Café con Leche with rum or other ingredients. The intent, of course, was to increase user involvement with the brand and to demonstrate its variety of uses.

Within only a month of the launch of the campaign, the e-mail message was forwarded 100,000 times. Moreover, upward of 20 percent of visitors to the website responded to a survey by providing information about the brand and its uses. Beyond this specific application, which was unique at the time for Argentina, one may question why anyone would be willing to forward e-mail messages to other people. The fact is that all Internet users receive e-mails that encourage us to pass them along to others. Why are people willing to pass messages along? Research has determined that the major motives for passing e-mail messages along are because people enjoy doing so and find it entertaining and possibly of help to others.

Sources: Charles Newbery, "Nescafé Builds Buzz via Viral E-Mail Effort," *Advertising Age*, May 2, 2005, 24; Joseph E. Phelps, Regina Lewis, Lynne Mobilio, David Perry, and Niranjan Raman, "Viral Marketing or Electronic Word-of-Mouth Advertising: Examining Consumer Responses and Motivations to Pass Along E-mail," *Journal of Advertising Research* 44 (December 2004), 333–48.

E-mail can be an effective marcom tool for delivering advertising messages and providing sales incentives to mass audiences or to smaller targeted groups. However, this form of online communications has been spoiled somewhat by marketers sending junk mail in a practice known as "spamming." Conservative estimates are that approximately two-thirds of all commercial e-mail messages represent spam,[59] although some day-to-day tracking estimates run as high as 72 percent or more.[60] Too many messages are sent, and too many represent spam rather than messages received from companies for whom the recipient has some interest. "Unspoiling" e-mail advertising is possible only by gaining recipients' permission to send them e-mail ads.

Opt-In E-mailing versus Spam

Imagine, for example, that a hypothetical consumer is interested in purchasing a digital camera and visits a website that appeared when she conducted a Google search for "digital cameras." While logged into this website, she received a query asking whether she would be interested in receiving more information about photographic equipment. She replied, "Yes," and provided her e-mail address as well as other information. The website electronically recorded her "permission granted" and, unknown to the unsuspecting shopper, sold her name and e-mail address to a broker that specializes in compiling lists. This list broker, in turn, sold her name and e-mail address to companies that market photographic equipment and supplies. Our hypothetical Internet user's name and e-mail address eventually appeared on a variety of lists, and she received numerous unsolicited e-mail messages for photographic equipment and supplies.

The solution to this problem is opt-in, or permission granted, e-mail. Opt-in e-mailing is the practice of marketers asking for and receiving consumers' permission to send them messages on particular topics. The consumer has agreed, or opted in, to receive messages on topics of interest rather than receiving messages that are unsolicited. In theory, opt-in e-mailing serves both the marketer's and the consumer's interests. However, frequency and quantity of e-mail messages can become intrusive as more and more companies have access to your name and areas of interest. Consumers feel especially violated when the e-mail messages deal with topics that are irrelevant or only tangential to their primary interests.

Anti-spam legislation under the rubric CAN-SPAM has been passed in the United States, and regulations against unsolicited e-mail are even more stringent in Europe. The spam problem represents a bothersome intrusion for consumers and also presents an economic cost to legitimate marketers that use commercial e-mail messages as an honest way of conducting business. In an effort to curtail spamming, the Federal Trade Commission has recommended to Congress a rewards program that pays anywhere from $100,000 to $250,000 as incentives for people to turn in spammers.[61] Yet, research using time series analysis has shown no significant impact of the CAN-SPAM legislation on spamming behavior.[62]

Phishing

Perhaps even more troubling than spam is a related illegal e-mailing practice known as phishing. Phishing takes place when criminals send e-mail messages appearing to be from legitimate corporations and direct recipients to phony websites that are designed to look like companies' actual websites. These phony websites attempt to extract personal data from people such as their credit card and ATM numbers. Pronounced like fishing, the practice of phishing has the same intent—to cast line with hopes of hooking some suckers. Not only are consumers injured when their identities are stolen but also brand equity suffers when thieves masquerade as legitimate businesses.

E-mail Magazines (E-zines)

A growing form of e-mail advertising, briefly described in the prior chapter, known as *e-zines*, or sponsored e-mail, is the distribution of free magazine-like publications. These publications originally focused on trendy issues such as entertainment, fashion, and food and beverages, but e-zines have since broadened in their content and appeal. Most e-zines include a relatively small number of ads that link readers to the websites of stores and brands. In order to boost the credibility of their publications, e-zine editors clearly identify advertisements and avoid mentioning advertisers' products in editorial copy.[63] E-zines enable advertisers to reach highly targeted audiences and to deliver credible advertising messages that are clearly designated as such.

Mobile Advertising

Mobile, or cellular, phones are nearly ubiquitous. It is estimated that by 2015 there will be more than 4.85 billion mobile phones around the world, which will represent a mobile phone for almost 67 percent of all the people on Earth.[64] As noted in the *Marcom Insight*, U.S. mobile ad spending will increase from $1.1 billion currently to $2.55 billion in 2014, including mobile display, search, messaging, and video categories.[65] As noted by mobile device users, GPS access and social media use are the most valued specific features (beyond the obvious general messaging and talking).[66] Other specific mobile device features mentioned are downloading and playing music, Web browsing, playing games, check-ins, sending feedback to companies, and making mobile payments.

Until the mid-2000s, Americans had used their mobile phones primarily as talking devices. Yet, European and Asian consumers have used these phones for transmitting text messages for years and Americans have followed suit. Short Message System (SMS) allows users to send and receive text messages on their mobile phones of up to 160 characters in length. Multimedia Messaging Service (MMS) is a more advanced technology that permits transmitting messages along with graphics and sound. In a sense, the mobile phone is emerging into what amounts almost to a small laptop computer. Indeed, mobile phones are being dubbed the *third screen*, meaning that TV (the first screen), computers (the second screen), and now mobile phones are common audiovisual devices for receiving information, entertainment, and advertisements.

The growing numbers of mobile phone users indicate considerable potential for advertisers to reach people through these devices. (See the *Global Focus* insert about mobile phone ads in India.) Younger consumers are especially viable targets. It is estimated that about 75 percent of teens ages 12 to 17 use their cell phones for text messaging on a regular basis and 25 percent of teens have a smartphone.[67]

Perhaps the more important issue, however, is whether people *want* to be contacted by advertisers. Because mobile phones are highly personal items (i.e., they go with us everywhere and often are in constant contact with our bodies),

GLOBAL FOCUS

Mobile Phone Advertising in India

India is a huge country with over one billion citizens, many of whom live in villages and lack access to newspapers and television. However, mobile phone usage is increasing at an incredible rate, with millions of new subscribers every month. There probably is no place in the world that is riper for mobile phone advertising than India. This is attributable to two major factors: (1) many Indians, particularly those living in villages, lack access to major media, and (2) mobile call rates in India are extremely low with a one-minute call costing less than one cent.

Of course, most Indian citizens earn less than $3 a day, so even one cent per minute of mobile phone usage is not a trivial charge. One prospect for further reducing the cost of mobile phone usage is to subsidize calls through advertising. Although this may seem a dramatic move to people in other

countries, this is precisely how television operates in countries such as the United States—advertising subsidizes the cost of TV viewing!

India's cellular network reaches 700 million subscribers, far more than the current 97 million regular Internet users. Because mobile phones reach millions of people who cannot be reached via mainstream media or the Internet, the growth potential for mobile phone advertising in India is unparalleled. India's experience with mobile phone advertising may serve as a model for this form of advertising elsewhere around the world.

Sources: Eric Bellman and Tariq Engineer, "India Appears Ripe for Cellphone Ads," *Wall Street Journal*, March 10, 2008, B3; and Nilanjana S. Roy, "Mobile Phones Offer Indian Women a Better Life," *New York Times*, May 22, 2012, http://www.nytimes.com/2012/05/23/world/asia/23iht-letter23.html.

many critics of mobile advertising (as well as advertisers themselves) are concerned that unwanted messages represent an *invasion of privacy*. Feeling invaded, recipients of undesired advertisements may immediately delete the intruding item and harbor negative feelings toward the offending advertiser—"How dare you send me a message for a product or service about which I have absolutely no interest!"

In addition to privacy invasion, a few are skeptical about mobile advertising's future on the grounds that advertising is antithetical to the reasons that people own mobile phones in the first place. The argument, in other words, is that people own mobile phones for reasons of enhancing time utilization and increasing work-related productivity while away from the workplace or home, and the last thing they want while using these devices is to receive unwanted, interrupting advertising messages. Another potential issue is that the small screens on mobile phones limit the space for presenting creative advertising messages.

Yet, mobile advertising has been growing at tremendous pace and it can help with enhancing brand awareness, loyalty, customer satisfaction, sales promotions (e.g., contests, deals), and local retail IMC efforts. It also is a medium in which companies are testing new marketing ideas. For example, in 2011, Buick, Disney, Delta, and T-Mobile started using "Google Goggles" to help consumers directly link ad messages with tangible benefits.[68] Google Goggles allows consumers to take pictures of brands, ads, and other objects with their mobile phones (like a bottle of wine) and then links the picture to a Google search for more information on the brand, ad, or object. As shown, a picture taken of a bottle of wine leads to a Google Goggles' product search for that specific brand. Thus, advertisers can produce ads with images recognized by Google Goggles' software on smartphones. For example, a Buick print ad could, when photographed, lead to a dedicated website via a quick response (QR) code.[69]

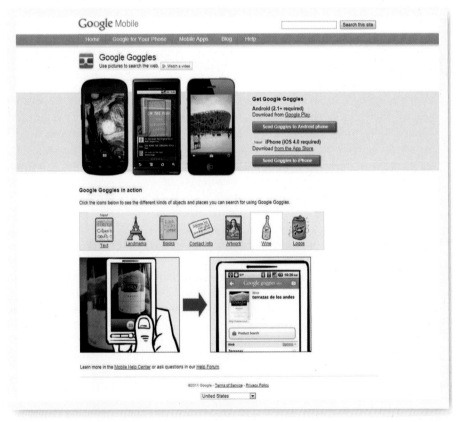

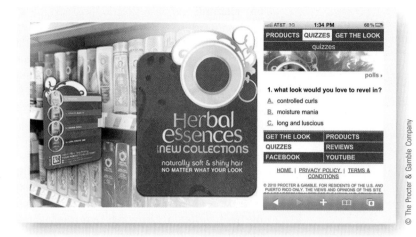

© The Procter & Gamble Company

Also in 2011, Mobile Marketer cited several top mobile ad campaigns, including Clairol Herbal Essence utilizing Microsoft Tag efforts, and the Unilever Dove Men × Care iAd campaign.[70] Clairol Herbal Essence rolled their mobile ad campaign out using Microsoft Tags (2D barcode) on shelf talkers in 53,000 retail stores to help shoppers determine which hair products would be best for them. The tag is scanned by smartphones and offered added information on products, hair styling quizzes, and links to YouTube clips on hair styling. As another successful example, Unilever used its Dove Men+Care brand to initiate a mobile iAd campaign (via the iPad) during the 2011 NCAA Men's Division I Basketball Championship. It shared motivating stories (linked to the brand) from basketball celebrities, such as Magic Johnson, Bobby Hurley, and John Thompson III.[71]

As noted in the *Marcom Insight* in Chapter 1, mobile devices have advanced to the point of providing a multitude of location-based services (e.g., check-ins, coupons, promotional links) via Foursquare, Google, and Facebook. Placed-based scanning via mobile devices is revolutionizing grocery shopping (e.g., with Scan It! at Giant and Stop and Shop stores). Perhaps the most interesting venture is that of Goggle Wallet, turning the mobile device into an electronic payment mechanism. So, even with privacy issues, the mobile platform is arguably the most exciting and creative of the online ad formats.

Advertising via Behavioral Targeting and Privacy Issues

The essence of online *behavioral targeting* is a matter of directing online advertisements to just those individuals who most likely are interested—as indicated by their online site-selection behavior—in making a purchase decision for a particular product category. Unlike content-oriented SEA, where the advertiser must pay for every person who has an opportunity to see the advertiser's message, with behavioral targeting *only those consumers known to be interested in a particular product or service* would receive ads from a marketer that employs behavioral targeting. By being selective, advertisers are able to place ads on many more websites than they could afford when employing a relatively indiscriminate content-oriented campaign. Many argue that behavioral targeting takes Internet advertising to a level higher than SEA provides. In fact, one practitioner has dubbed behavioral targeting "search [engine advertising] on steroids."[72]

Online advertisers, like the savvy conventional advertisers who preceded them, have turned increasingly to customer targeting as a means of increasing click-through rates and converting "clickers" into purchasers. With improved tracking technology, it has become possible to determine more about online surfers' (or at least the computers') consumer behavior and then to tailor the specific ads to which surfers (i.e., the computers) are exposed. This is accomplished with electronic files (called *cookies*) that track users' (i.e., the computers') online behavior. (For an accessible explanation of Internet cookies, see www.cookiecentral.com/c_concept.htm.) Online advertisers use cookies to direct ads that are compatible with Internet users' product-usage interests.

Courtesy of Golf Fitness Magazine, Inc.

For example, when a golf lover clicks on an ad for a golf magazine, that click is recorded. Once that golfer goes online again (to any Internet site), an ad server detects the cookie, and adds a golf-related banner to the website. That way, advertisers can isolate that customer as a golfer and sell targeted advertising related to golf.

As always with any form of advertising, behavioral targeting is not without disadvantages. The most notable is that this form of targeting can be viewed as *an invasion of people's privacy*. Simply, many people feel violated knowing that their Web-search behavior is being closely tracked.[73] Recently, the "Do Not Track Me Online Act" was introduced as legislation in both the U.S. House and Senate.[74] Yet, at the time of this writing, neither has passed. Self-regulatory efforts have increased, including the provision of the "Advertising Option Icon," that shows consumers information about vendors, information collected, and opt-out options.[75] However, many frustrated consumers have taken efforts into their own hands, with 4.5 million downloads in 2011 of anti-tracking software, such as Ghostery, AdBlock Plus, and Tracker Block.[76]

Measuring Internet Ad Effectiveness

A variety of firms offer measurement and analysis of online audiences, advertising, video, social media, and online behavior (e,g., Nielsen Net View, ComScore, Compete). Most of these services use a paid panel of Internet users and measure unique audience visits, page views, time spent, loyalty, demographic information, and consumer behavior.

With the conventional media (TV, radio, magazines, and newspapers) as a benchmark, one can readily appreciate that online advertisers have precisely the same measurement concerns: How many people clicked through a particular Web ad? What are the demographic characteristics of these people? How many visited a particular website? What actions were taken following click-throughs or site visits? Is this form of online advertising yielding a suitable return on investment?

Metrics for Measuring Internet Ad Performance

The word *metric* refers, in general, to a unit of measurement. As applied in the present context, the issue is one of which particular indicators are most appropriate for assessing the effectiveness of websites and ads placed on these sites. In actuality, a wide variety of metrics are used because advertisers have different measurement objectives and because formats for advertising online are highly varied. There are at least four general objectives, as follows, for assessing online advertising effectiveness and (in parentheses) a variety of

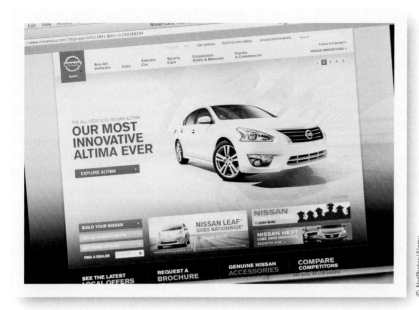

metrics that can be used to indicate whether the objective has been accomplished.[77]

1. The exposure value or popularity of a website or online ad (e.g., number of users exposed to an ad, number of unique visitors, and click-through rate)
2. The ability of a site to attract and hold users' attention and the quality of customer relationships (e.g., average time per visit, number of visits by unique visitors, and average interval between user visits)
3. The usefulness of websites (e.g., proportion of repeat visitors)
4. The ability to target users (e.g., profile of website visitors and visitors' previous website search behavior)

It should be apparent that many metrics are used to assess the effectiveness of websites and the ads placed on those sites. A brief discussion is now devoted to just three widely used metrics: click-through rates, cost per thousand impressions, and cost per action.

Click-through rates (CTR), as mentioned several times already, simply represent the percentage of people who are exposed to, say, an Internet-delivered ad and actually clicked their mouse on it. The click-through percentage has continued to decline, especially for banner ads, and many in the advertising community have become disenchanted with this metric—although some claim that banner ads can have a positive effect on brand awareness even if Internet users do not click through to learn more about the advertised brand.

Cost per thousand impressions (CPM) is a simple alternative to click-through rates that assesses how much (on a per-thousand-impressions basis) it costs to place an online ad. The only information the CPM metric reveals is what it costs (again, on a per-thousand-impressions basis) to have an ad come into potential contact with the eyeballs of Internet users. This measure captures Internet users' opportunity to see (OTS) an ad but provides no information about the actual effect of an advertisement.

Use of the CPM metric is beginning to give way to the *cost-per-action* (CPA) metric. The action in cost-per-action refers to determining the number of users who actually visit a brand's website, register their names on the brand's site, or purchase the advertised brand. Many advertisers prefer to pay for Internet advertising on a CPA rather than a CPM basis. The terms of purchasing Internet advertising on a CPA basis vary greatly, with higher prices paid for actions involving actual purchases or actions closer to purchase (such as registering for free samples of a brand) compared with merely clicking on, say, a banner ad. However, given that advertisers are interested in achieving specific results, especially increased sales of their brands, they are willing to pay more for metrics, indicating that desired results have been achieved (i.e., CPA metrics) than for those, such as CTR, that merely promise the possibility of achieving desired results.

In summary, it should be apparent that there is no such thing as perfect measurability—for the Internet or for any other advertising medium. The difficulty of determining an ad medium's effectiveness is illustrated, in the extreme, by the following set of questions: "Consider the Nike logo on Kobe Bryant's shoes or the University of Oregon football uniforms: Does it make you more likely to buy some of the company's products? If so, would you admit it in a survey? Would you admit it to yourself? Would you even know it?"[78]

Summary

This chapter has covered a variety of online advertising media with a special emphasis on mobile advertising. Figure 13.1 explained the overall online advertising process and the major parties involved. Table 13.1 structured the discussion by identifying specific forms of online advertising. Spending on online advertising (especially mobile advertising) is growing at an exponential rate in the United States as well as elsewhere around the globe. In comparison to most other advertising media, the Internet possesses the two key features of *individualization* and *interactivity*. These features allow users to control the information they receive and the amount of time and effort devoted to processing advertising messages.

The bulk of the chapter discussed various forms of online advertising media. First discussed, search engine advertising (SEA) commands the largest online advertising investment at about 48 percent of all online ad expenditures. The fundamental concept underlying SEA is that advertisements can be located where consumers and B2B customers are searching. In other words, SEA increases the odds of encountering the ready consumer. Two forms of SEA are widely used: keyword matching and placing ads on content-oriented websites that match the advertiser's offering.

Next, display, or banner, ads were examined, which are a popular form of online advertising, although click-through rates are notoriously low. Because CTRs to displays are small, online advertisers have turned to new technology and larger ad sizes to attract the online surfer's attention. Rich-media formats such as pop-ups, interstitials, superstitials, and video ads have experienced increased usage due to their ability to engage online viewers. The downside of rich-media ads is that online users may find them intrusive and annoying at times. Websites were considered the centerpiece of companies' online advertising efforts, with other advertising formats (e.g., paid searches, banners, and e-mail) serving to drive traffic to companies' sites. Web logs (blogs) were described as a potential advertising vehicle, but one with an uncertain future because users' reasons for blogging may be antithetical to the role and purpose of advertising. The ubiquity of blogs, including the radio-type version known as podcasts, makes this an attractive prospect for advertisers, but only time will tell whether advertising on blogs and podcasts is an economically viable option.

E-mail advertising was once a widely used form of online advertising, although excessive spamming has compromised the effectiveness of this format. Permission-based, or opt-in, e-mail is an effort to legitimize the use of e-mail advertising, but many consumers simply do not like being advertised to online. E-mail magazines (e-zines) represent a more acceptable advertising medium because ads are clearly labeled for what they are, which explains why this form of sponsored e-mail is on the rise.

Perhaps the fastest-growing sector of online advertising is that of mobile advertising. Very creative and exciting uses of this online option include location-based check-ins, ability to scan shelf tags and quick response (QR) codes, and use as an electronic payment system.

Behavioral targeting is a final form of online advertising discussed in this chapter. This form of advertising directs ads just to those individuals who most likely are interested in purchasing a particular good or service as indicated by their past online site-selection behavior. Behavioral targeting takes online advertising to a level higher than even SEA. Yet, privacy concerns remain with many in the form of recently proposed "do not track" legislation and millions of consumers downloading anti-tracking software.

The final topic discussed was measuring online ad effectiveness. The choice of metrics for measuring the effectiveness of online advertising is somewhat of a "moving target" due to the dynamic nature of online advertising and the many formats available to advertisers for reaching prospective customers online. Three specific measures for measuring ad performance were described: click-through rates (CTR), cost per thousand impressions (CPM), and cost per action (CPA). This last measure is growing in usage because advertisers are interested in achieving particular results—e.g., influencing people to purchase products—and this is precisely what the CPA measures.

Discussion Questions

1. As noted in the text, some observers have gone so far as to claim that traditional advertising is on its deathbed and will eventually be supplanted by online advertising. What are your views on this?

2. Based on your experiences, what do you believe are the key benefits and costs with online advertising? Are these consistent with the text?

3. The text described the online user as being in a "leaning-forward" mind-set compared with, say, the TV viewer who is "leaning back." Explain what this means and why the distinction is advantageous or problematic for online advertisers.

4. Describe your typical response behavior to online ads. That is, do you often click on banner ads? What's your reaction to pop-ups, interstitials, superstitials, and online videos?

5. Can banner ads be effective if less than 0.3 percent of all people click through them?

6. Do you believe that online companies' use of cookies invades your privacy? Would you favor legislation that prevents the use of this technology? If such a law were passed, what would be the downside from the consumer's perspective?

7. Have you personally downloaded ad-blocking software onto your computer? What are the implications of this practice if millions of consumers had ad-blocking software loaded on their computers and other digital devices?

8. The following set of questions was mentioned in the chapter in reference to the Nike logo on Kobe Bryant's basketball shoes or the University of Oregon football uniforms: Does it make you more likely to buy some of the company's products? If so, would you admit it in a survey? Would you admit it to yourself? Would you even know it? What implications do these questions (and their answers) hold for measuring Internet advertising effectiveness?

9. The Cookie Central website (www.cookiecentral. com) is dedicated to explaining exactly what cookies are and what they can do. Visit this site and present a discussion on how cookies can be and are used to compile lists for behavioral targeting purposes.

10. What has been your personal experience with e-mail advertising? Are you part of any opt-in lists whereby you receive regular (say weekly) e-mail messages? What proportion of the e-mail messages do you receive on a daily basis that you would consider spam?

11. One virtue of e-mail advertising is that different messages for the same product or service can be mailed to various customer groups that differ with respect to pertinent buyographic, demographic, or other characteristics. This ability to "mass customize" messages should increase marcom effectiveness, yet a cynic might look at this practice as a bit deceptive—somehow saying different things about your product to different audiences seems misleading. What is your view on this?

12. E-mail advertising is claimed to be very effective for viral marketing purposes—that is, buzz generation. This is accomplished by requesting an e-mail recipient to forward the message to a friend. Present your views on the effectiveness of the e-mail viral marketing practice. In other words, explain what makes e-mail buzz generation effective or not.

13. Behavioral targeting was characterized as search engine advertising on steroids. Explain what the practitioner who used this clever expression had in mind.

14. From the perspective of an advertiser for a low-involvement, packaged-goods product such as cereal, compare and contrast the strengths and weaknesses of the two forms of search engine advertising: keyword-matching versus content-targeted advertising.

15. What, in your view, is the potential of using blogs as an advertising medium?

16. What, in your view, is the potential of using mobile devices as an advertising medium? What else could be done with this option?

End Notes

1. Roland T. Rust and Richard W. Oliver, "Notes and Comments: The Death of Advertising," *Journal of Advertising* 23 (December 1994), 71–77. See also Roland T. Rust and Sajeev Varki, "Rising from the Ashes of Advertising," *Journal of Business Research* 37 (November 1996), 173–81.

2. For example, Rafi A. Mohammed, Robert J. Fisher, Bernard J. Jaworski, and Aileen M. Cahill, *Internet Marketing: Building Advantage in a Networked Economy*, Newyork: McGraw-Hill, 2002, 370.

3. Ibid., 375; and Jonah Bloom, "Dedicated Social-Media Silos? That's the Last Thing We Need," *Advertising Age*, June 8, 2009, 11.

4. "Digital Fast Facts 2011," *Advertising Age*, Digital Issue (section pullout), February 28, 2011.

5. "2010 Revenue by Sector," *Advertising Age*, 100 Leading Media Companies 2011 Issue, October 3, 2011, 52.

6. Mohammed et al., *Internet Marketing: Building Advantage in a Networked Economy*, 371; "Online Advertising," Wikipedia, http://en.wikipedia.org/wiki/Online_advertising (accessed March 3, 2011); and "The Internet," *Marketer's Guide to Media 2011*, 34 (North Hollywood, CA: Prometheus Global Media, 2011), 261–62.

7. For more formal treatments of the concept of interactivity, see the following sources: Yuping Liu and L. J. Shrum, "What Is Interactivity and Is It Always Such a Good Thing? Implications of Definition, Person, and Situation for the Influence of Interactivity on Advertising Effectiveness," *Journal of Advertising* 31 (winter 2002), 53–64; Sally J. McMillan and Jang-Sun Hwang, "Measures of Perceived Interactivity: An Exploration of the Role of Direction of Communication, User Control, and Time in Shaping Perceptions of Interactivity," *Journal of Advertising* 31 (fall 2002), 29–42; and Yuping Liu, "Developing a Scale to Measure the Interactivity of Websites," *Journal of Advertising Research* 43 (June 2003), 207–16. For an especially complete treatment of interactivity in Internet advertising, see Grace J. Johnson, Gordon C. Bruner II, and Anand Kumar, "Interactivity and Its Facets Revisited: Theory and Empirical Test," *Journal of Advertising* 35 (winter 2006), 35–52.

8. *Marketer's Guide to Media 2011*, 273.

9. The ideas in this paragraph are adapted from Terry Lefton, "The Great Flameout," *The Industry Standard*, March 19, 2001, 75–78.

10. "Digital Fast Facts 2011," *Advertising Age*, Digital Issue (section pullout), February 28, 2011.

11. Ted McConnell, "In Online Advertising, Brands Shouldn't Equate Frequency and Blind Repetition; Proper Context and Timing Matter," *Advertising Age*, September 19, 2011, 72.

12. Jonah Bloom, "Want to Restore Marketers' Faith? Embrace Agnosticism," *Advertising Age*, September 24, 2007, 16.

13. "Online Ad Networks: Monetizing the Long Tail," DeSilva + Phillips, LLC, New York, NY, March 2008, 1–15.

14. DeSilva + Phillips, 3.

15. Ibid, 5.

16. Ibid, 6.

17. Research has demonstrated that attitudes toward Internet ad formats are positively related to attitudes toward advertisements that are carried within these formats. See Kelli S. Burns and Richard J. Lutz, "The Function of Format," *Journal of Advertising* 35 (spring 2006), 53–63.

18. "Digital Fast Facts 2011," *Advertising Age*, Digital Issue, February 28, 2011, section pullout.

19. "Mobile Marketing 2011," *Advertising Age*, Digital Issue (Fall), September 19, 2011, section pullout.

20. "Search Advertising," Wikipedia, http://en.wikipedia.org/wiki/Search_advertising (accessed January 4, 2012).

21. "Digital Fast Facts 2011."

22. Ibid.

23. Carol Krol, "Search Draws Big Spending," *BtoB's Interactive Marketing Guide*, 2008, 19.

24. "Search Engine Marketing Shows Strength as Spending Continues on a Growth Track against Doom and Gloom Economic Background," Sempo Press Release, March 17, 2008, http://www.sempo.org/?page=pr_20080317.

25. Ashish Agarwal, Kartik Hosanagar, and Michael D. Smith, "Location, Location, Location: An Analysis of Position in Online Advertising Markets," *Journal of Marketing Research* 48 (December 2011), 1057–73.

26. "Google Form 10-Q, Q2 2010," July 15, 2010.

27. Michael Learnmonth, "What Google Instant Means for Marketers: More Ad Impressions," *Advertising Age*, September 13, 2010, 1, 32.

28. "Search Advertising," Wikipedia, http://en.wikipedia.org/wiki/Search_advertising (accessed January 5, 2012).

29. California Penal Code, Sections 484-502.9, http://www.leginfo.ca.gov/cgi-bin/displaycode?section=pen&group=00001-01000&file=484-502.9 (accessed January 5, 2012).

30. Kevin J. Delaney, "Google to Target Brands in Revenue Push," *Wall Street Journal Online*, April 25, 2005.

31. Ibid.

32. Lisa Wehr, "Click Fraud Detection Gives Instant Protection," *btobonline.com*, February 12, 2007, 17.

33. "Digital Fast Facts 2011."

34. "Look Ahead 2012," *Advertising Age*, January 2, 2012, 14.

35. Ritu Lohtia, Naveen Donthus, and Edmund K. Hershberger, "The Impact of Content and Design Elements on Banner Advertising Click-through Rates," *Journal of Advertising Research* 43 (December 2003), 410–18.

36. Micael Dahlen, "Banner Advertisements through a New Lens," *Journal of Advertising Research* 41 (July/August 2001), 23–30.

37. Puneet Manchanda, Jean-Pierre Dubé, Khim Yong Goh, and Pradeep K. Chintagunta, "The Effect of Banner Advertising on Internet Purchasing," *Journal of Marketing Research* 43 (February 2006), 98–108.

38. "Interactive Advertising Bureau/Dynamic Logic Ad Unit Effectiveness Study," Interactive Advertising Bureau, March/June 2001, http://www.iab.net.

39. Catherine Tucker and Avi Goldfarb, "Online Display Advertising: Targeting and Obtrusiveness," *Marketing Science* 30 (May–June 2011), 389–404.

40. Shelly Rodgers and Esther Thorson, "The Interactive Advertising Model: How Users Perceive and Process Online Ads," *Journal of Interactive Advertising* 1 (fall 2000), http://jiad.org/article5.

41. Jack Neff, "Spam Research Reveals Disgust with Pop-up Ads," *Advertising Age*, August 25, 2003, 1, 21.

42. "Online Video Market 2011," *Advertising Age*, Digital (Fall) Issue, September 19, 2011, section pullout.

43. "Case Study IHOP: Video Day Makes Every Day an IHOP Day," Mixpo.com, Cox Digital Solutions, http://dynamicvideoad.mixpo.com/docs/Mixpo_Case Study_IHOP_2011.pdf, June 2011, 1–2.

44. Shelly Rodgers and Esther Thorson, "The Interactive Advertising Model: How Users Perceive and Process Online Ads." *Journal of Interactive Advertising* 1 (fall 2000), http://www.jiad.org/article5.

45. Jean Halliday, "Half Hit Web before Showrooms," *Advertising Age*, October 4, 2004, 76.

46. Fred Zufryden, "New Film Website Promotion and Box-Office Performance," *Journal of Advertising Research* 40 (January/April 2000), 55–64.

47. The first author learned this advice from his dear late father, Aubrey Shimp, who worked in retailing for many years. He is not sure whether this was his own wisdom or whether it can be attributed to another source.

48. Mary Morrison, "Usability Problems Plague B-to-B Sites," *BtoB's Interactive Marketing Guide*, 2007, 10.

49. Julie S. Stevenson, Gordon C. Bruner II, and Anand Kumar, "Webpage Background and Viewer Attitudes," *Journal of Advertising Research* 40 (January/April 2000), 29–34. See also Gordon C. Bruner II, and Anand Kumar, "Web Commercials and Advertising Hierarchy-of-Effects," *Journal of Advertising Research* 40 (January/April 2000), 35–42. The latter article involves research using a non-student sample and provides interesting refinement concerning the role of Web page complexity.

50. Gerald J. Gorn, Amitava Chattopadhyay, Jaideep Sengupta, and Shashank Tripathi, "Waiting for the Web: How Screen Color Affects Time Perception," *Journal of Marketing Research* 41 (May 2004), 215–25.

51. Stephen Baker and Heather Green, "Blogs Will Change Your Business," *BusinessWeek*, May 2, 2005, 57.

52. Allison Enright, "Listen, Learn," *Marketing News*, April 1, 2007, 25–29.

53. Aaron O. Patrick, "Tapping into Customers' Online Chatter," *Wall Street Journal*, May 18, 2007, B3.

54. Kate Fitzgerald, "Blogs Fascinate, Frighten Marketers Eager to Tap Loyalists," *Advertising Age*, March 5, 2007, S-4.

55. Paul Gillin, "Podcasting, Blogs Cause Major Boost," *B2B's Interactive Marketing Guide*, 2007, 30.

56. Albert Maruggi, "Podcasting Offers a Sound Technique," *Brandweek*, May 2, 2005, 21.

57. David Kesmodel, "Companies Tap Podcast Buzz to Sell Contact Lenses, Appliances," *Wall Street Journal*, June 30, 2006, B1.

58. "Digital Fast Facts 2011."

59. "DoubleClick's 2004 Consumer E-mail Study," DoubleClick, October 2004, http://www.doubleclick.com.

60. See "Spam Data," BarracudaCentral.Org, http://www.barracudacentral.org/data/spam (accessed January 6, 2012).

61. "FTC Recommends Bounty to Nab Spammers," *Wall Street Journal Online*, September 16, 2004, http://online.wsj.com.

62. Alex C. Kigerl, "CAN SPAM Act: An Empirical Analysis," *International Journal of Cyber Criminology* 3 (December 2009), 566–89.

63. Elizabeth Weinstein, "Retailers Tap E-Zines to Reach Niche Audiences," *Wall Street Journal Online*, April 28, 2005, http://online.wsj.com.

64. "Mobile Marketing 2011."

65. Ibid.

66. Ibid.

67. Olivia B. Waxman, "Texting 1, 2, 3: Schools Test 'Bring Your Own Technology' Programs," *Time Techland*, May 2, 2012, http://techland.time.com/2012/05/02/texting-1-2-3-schools-test-bring-your-own-technology-programs.

68. Todd Wasserman, "5 Innovative Mobile Marketing Campaigns," Mashable.com, March 8, 2011, http://mashable.com/2011/03/08/mobile-marketing-campaigns.

69. Ibid.

70. Giselle Tsirulnik, "Top 10 Mobile Advertising Campaigns in Q1," *Mobile Marketer*, April 20, 2011, http://www.mobilemarketer.com/cms/news/advertising/9747.html.

71. Ibid.

72. Richard Karpinski, "Behavioral Targeting," *Intelligence*, spring 2004, 16.

73. For reading on privacy and ethical issues in online marketing, see the special issue of the *Journal of Public Policy & Marketing* 19 (spring 2000), 1–73.

74. Christine Birkner, "Marketing in 2011: Looking Back Means Looking Ahead," *Marketing News*, December 30, 2011, 16–19.

75. Ibid, 18–19.

76. Byron Acohido, "Consumers Turn to Do-Not-Track Software to Maintain Privacy," *USA Today*, December 29, 2011, http://www.usatoday.com/tech/news/story/2011-12-29/internet-privacy/52274608/1.

77. Subodh Bhat, Michael Bevans, and Sanjit Sengupta, "Measuring Users' Web Activity to Evaluate and Enhance Advertising Effectiveness," *Journal of Advertising* 31 (fall 2002), 97–106. This source identified a fifth objective that is not listed here (co-marketing success).

78. Rob Walker, "The Holy Grail of Internet Advertising, the Ability to Measure Who Is Clicking on the Message, Is Under Assault," *New York Times*, August 27, 2001, C4.

Is Facebook Becoming Passé?

With 1 billion active users, $4.27 billion in revenue, and *Fortune* 500 companies rushing to establish a presence, Facebook *appears* to be as strong as ever as the leading social networking site in the world. In the United States, the number of active users (at 190 million) is larger than the recent record number of viewers for the Super Bowl (111 million). Moreover, Mark Zuckerman, Facebook's CEO and founder, says that reaching a billion members is "almost a guarantee."

Yet, there now appears to be some cracks in the armor of Facebook, such that some have predicted "Facebook Fatigue" for some consumers, and have described Facebook advertising as "The Media World's Black Hole." For consumers, some ad executives have predicted Facebook's popularity to fade as a result of "IPO + privacy issues + your grandma joining + one redesign too many + general social network fatigue = Fonzie on waterskiis." (The "Fonzie" analogy refers to a desperate *Happy Days* episode to reverse a drop in ratings and featured a gimmick with Fonzie jumping a shark on water skis.) As consumers now spend 23 percent of their online time on Facebook, and an average of seven hours a month on the social networking site (equal to AOL, Yahoo!, and Google combined), some ad executives predict wearout. Moreover, teens, who drove the initial Facebook growth, are increasingly moving to other social network options (e.g., Twitter, Google$^+$), as parents, grandparents, neighbors, parents, friends, etc. try to "friend them" on Facebook.

© PSL Images/Alamy

1 Describe what exactly is meant by "social media."

2 Discuss the advantages and disadvantages of social media compared to traditional media choices.

3 Explain some of the major social media categories and different social media brands (e.g., Facebook, Twitter, Google⁺, LinkedIn) within those categories (e.g., Communication—social networking).

4 Provide examples of some successful social media campaigns and how these were integrated into a company's IMC efforts.

5 Explain the privacy issues and other major concerns with social media.

6 Understand how social media effectiveness is best measured and what metrics are used.

For more savvy advertisers, there are concerns about what consumers are actually experiencing on Facebook as well. An *Advertising Age* article recently made an analogy between Facebook and its new timeline change with a crowded version of your favorite restaurant or bar (e.g., they used Paddy's Pub from the TV program *It's Always Sunny in Philadelphia*). For example, your entire life history is now listed on the restaurant or bar walls, there are too many jukeboxes (e.g., Spotify's Facebook site), too many attempts to get more sponsors or partners, and you are spending way too much time in the restaurant or bar. Moreover, all the servers or bartenders are now gossips about your trusted personal information (e.g., Facebook's recent privacy problems).

Currently, click-through rates for Facebook ads are well below industry averages and are falling. Yet, Facebook's ad revenue continues to increase just because Facebook is getting larger. This may be analogous to Theodore Levitt's warning in his famous article, "Marketing Myopia," that a major self-deceiving condition for companies is to assume you are in a growth industry simply due to an expanding population or audience.

Interestingly, Facebook has to deal with the actual reason people go to their site in the first place—to visit with friends and post relevant and fun material. Visitors usually are not looking to "bond" with advertisers or brands. However, increasingly, personal information

about Facebook activity (e.g., posts, reading an article offsite via a Facebook app, listening to music via the Facebook Spotify site) creeps back via ads on Facebook's user sites. And, as people spend more time on Facebook, and the number of users grows, advertisers (and media companies) have fewer (and shorter) opportunities to access consumers *off* Facebook. So, consumers and advertisers may be wondering—*are we a patron/client or a hostage* of this massive social network? Certainly, only time will tell if "marketing myopia" visits Facebook. Right now, consumers and advertisers may feel a bit trapped as they may believe they do not have any other viable options.

Sources: "Facebook: Key Facts," http://newsroom.fb.com (accessed October 4, 2012); "Facebook," *Wikipedia*, http://en.wikipedia.org/wiki/Facebook (accessed July 9, 2012); Brian Womack, "Facebook Revenue Will Reach $4.27 Billion, eMarketer Says," *Bloomberg Businessweek*, September 20, 2011, http://www.bloomberg.com/news/print/2011-09-20/facebook-revenue-will-reach-4-27-billion-emarketer-says-1-.html; Suzanne Vranica, "*&%@#! and Other Ad Trends for 2012," *Wall Street Journal*, January 4, 2012, B6; Brad Stone, "Sell Your Friends," *Bloomberg Businessweek*, September 27, 2010, 64–72; Robert Seidman, "Super Bowl XLV Breaks Viewing Record, Averages 111 Million Viewers," *TV by the Numbers*, http://tvbythenumbers.zap2it.com/2011/02/07/super-bowl-xlv-poised-to-break-viewing-records-ties-1987-with-highest-overnight-ratings-ever/81684 (accessed December 6, 2011); Simon Dumenco, "Why Facebook is Becoming the Media World's Black Hole," *Advertising Age*, October 2, 2011, http://adage.com/print/230157; "November 2011—Top U.S. Web Brands," *Nielsen Wire*, December 30, 2011, http://blog.nielsen.com/nielsenwire/online_mobile/november-2011-top-u-s-web-brands; Martha Irvine, "Teens Migrating to Twitter—Sometimes for Privacy," *Yahoo! Finance*, January 29, 2012, http://finance.yahoo.com/news/teens-migrating-twitter-sometimes-privacy-170206041.html; and Theodore Levitt, "Marketing Myopia," *Harvard Business Review*, vol. 38, July–August 1960, 45–56.

Introduction

So, what exactly is "social media"? One concise definition is that social media represents web-based and mobile technology used to turn communication into interactive dialogue.[1] Alternatively, business firms may refer to social media as "consumer generated media."[2] The overall idea of social media is to integrate technology and social interactions to create value for users. In doing so, this often will help to solve consumer problems (e.g., with needed brand communication dialogue, multimedia file sharing, advertising, and blogging). Certainly, one main advantage of social media is its role in establishing two-way communication in place of the traditional one-way media efforts.

Social Media Background and Landscape

A review of social media statistics reveals an impressive rise of this online venue as a tool for IMC, with nearly 80 percent of active Internet users now visiting social networks and blogs.[3] Social networking now represents more than 22 percent of all time spent online in the United States.[4] Of the top 10 websites in the United States, Facebook had the highest "engagement" (i.e., time spent) for visitors with nearly seven hours spent on the site per month (14 minutes per day).[5] (Interestingly, 10 other countries beat this statistic, with Israel coming in on top at over 11 hours per month.[6]) Of course, the idea is to make sure that such visitors also are engaging with your brand or company, as Coca-Cola has done with a consumer-generated Facebook site with over 53 million "friends" (www.facebook.com/coca-cola). As noted in the *Marcom Insight*, Facebook is the "Goliath" of social media, with 1 billion users and 156 million unique visitors per month.[7]

Yet, other social media options are just as impressive. The social network Twitter, which enables users to send and read other users' messages (up to 140 characters) called tweets, only took 3 years, 2 months, and 1 day from the first tweet to reach the billionth tweet.[8] It now can take just a minimum of one week for users to send one billion tweets and, on average, there are now 50 million tweets sent per day![9]

One would think most of the growth of social media usage is from a younger demographic category (e.g., those 18 to 49 years of age). However, this is not the case, as users over the age of 55 are driving most of this expansion via mobile device access to social media.[10] No doubt, this has caused some embarrassment on the part of teens and young adults sometimes not wanting to accept "friend requests" from parents and grandparents!

Figure 14.1 provides a quick synopsis of the "Social Media Landscape," showing the top social media brands. First, as one will quickly surmise, the development and enhancement of brand equity is an important challenge in the social media world. Literally *hundreds* of social media brands are in this crowded space. As mentioned in Chapter 2, brand identification and differentiation activities require additional thought and strategy with this explosion of social media names, such as Bebo, Doof, Friendfeed, Meembo, Ning, Orkut, Phorum, Pogo, Plurk, and Twitxr. The social media brands in Figure 14.1 can be generally organized in a clockwise fashion from collaboration tools (publish, share, and discuss) to communication modes (social networks and microblogs) to multimedia and entertainment options (lifestream, livecast, virtual worlds, social games, and massively multiplayer online [MMO] games). Students are likely familiar with some of the following social media brands listed in the figure: collaboration (Wikipedia, Digg, YouTube, Flickr, Slideshare, and Pinterest), communication (Facebook, Twitter, MySpace, LinkedIn, and Skype), and multimedia and entertainment (Friendfeed, Yahoo! Live, and Kongregate). For a more comprehensive list, see Table 14.1 later in this chapter.

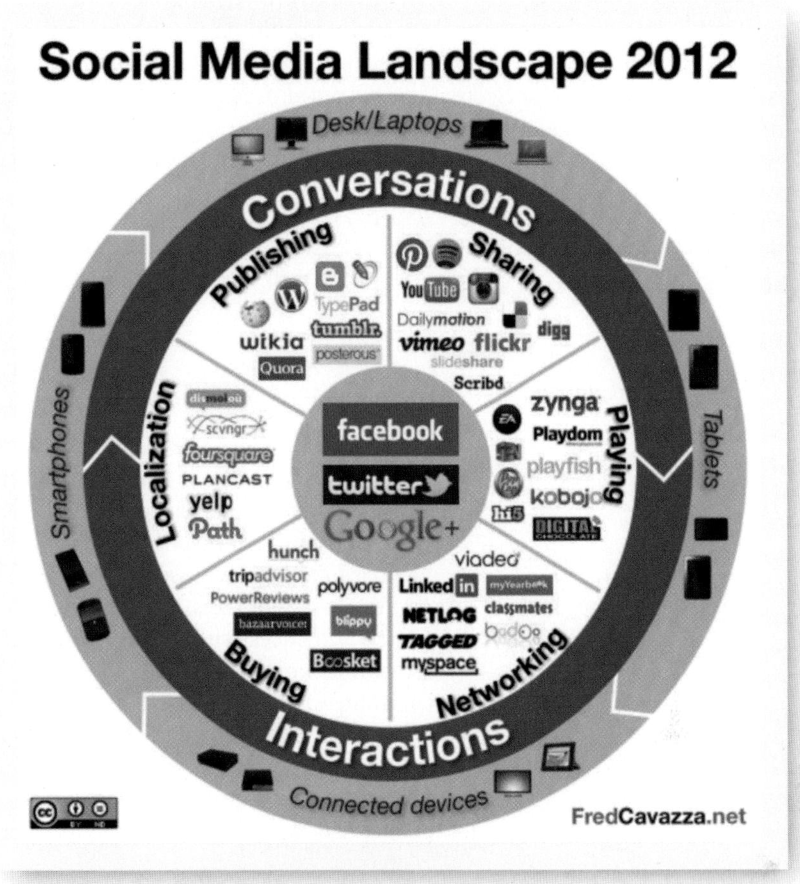

FIGURE **14.1** Social Media Landscape

Comparisons with Traditional Media

As presented in Chapter 12, traditional ad media includes television, radio, magazines, and newspapers. In contrast, social media are quite distinct from traditional media in that they can be launched inexpensively and are accessible to all with Internet access, whereas traditional media may require substantial resources (e.g., a $1 million TV commercial) to publish advertising information. We now examine five points of comparison between social media and traditional media choices:[11]

- *Reach*: Both can offer scale—reaching global audiences—but traditional media are more centralized in organization, production, and dissemination, whereas social media rely on consumer-generated content and thus are more decentralized in terms of production and usage (e.g., YouTube).
- *Accessibility*: Depending on the country, the means of production for traditional media are government and/or privately owned. However, social media options (e.g., Facebook, Twitter, WordPress) are generally available to everyone at little or no cost if there are no country-specific restrictions.
- *Usability*: With traditional media production, it usually requires more specialized skills and training. In contrast, although there is a need for some digital expertise, in theory, anyone with online access can operate the means for social media production.
- *Immediacy*: The time lag, due dates, and press dates for traditional media can be quite long (and in some countries, subject to a lottery and other

restrictions). In comparison, any delay in social media is usually due to the participant. No doubt, traditional media are trying to bridge this gap with electronic solutions (e.g., apps, software).

- *Permanence*: Once created, traditional media cannot be altered (e.g., once a magazine ad is distributed, it cannot be changed). However, with social media, changes can be made immediately and "on the fly," if needed, with editing.

Social Media Advantages and Disadvantages

As a relatively new set of options for advertisers and consumers, social media (e.g., social networking, blogging, wikis, collaboration, virtual worlds) has had its share of ever-evolving advantages and disadvantages. Some current advantages include:

- *Flexibility*: The use of social media offers tremendous flexibility in marketing and advertising planning, with the ability to quickly modify postings, ads, and blogs in response to competitive and industry changes.
- *Reach options*: Increased targeting via demographics, web visits, and posted preferences and likes has helped with the ability of advertisers to reach small audiences with social media. At the same time, the scale of some social networking sites (e.g., Facebook, Twitter) allows advertisers to reach extremely large audiences as well.
- *Consumer engagement*: With consumer-generated content, it helps to ensure engagement in sites such as YouTube, Flickr, Facebook, Twitter, Pinterest, etc., as well as brands and companies featured on these sites. Online panel data has long shown the link between online advertising and purchase behavior.[12]
- *Two-way dialogue*: Consumer feedback; new brand and product ideas; and pricing, location, and promotion modifications can all be gleaned from social media sites. Tracking social network and blog data (via sentiment analysis—i.e., contextual polarity of comments) can help in this regard.
- *Integration and ability to drive traffic*: An ad that is placed on a social media site (e.g., YouTube), if well done, can turn viral and drive traffic to other sites (via QR, or quick response codes) and to retail stores and other brand promotions.
- *Improved metrics and research*: Measurement of the impact of social media has come a long way. For example, companies such as Radian6 offer detailed tracking results in dashboards displaying sentiments, share of voice and conversations, and brand tracking versus the industry and competitors. Others, such as comScore, offer audience measurement statistics though their panel, such as monthly brand impressions (i.e., total exposures) and the overall weight of a brand campaign (e.g., gross rating points [GRPs] as a function of the percentage *reached* at least once and the *frequency* of times reached).
- *Cost effectiveness*: Compared to placing a $200,000, 30-second ad (or $3.5 million for the 2012 Super Bowl), placing an ad on Facebook (with price based on cost per click or cost per views/impressions) or a free upload on YouTube is certainly more cost effective.

Yet, just as importantly, marketers and advertisers should be prepared for social media's disadvantages:

- *Privacy and censorship*: These issues have occurred repeatedly with social network sites, such as Facebook and Twitter. For instance, Facebook Places allowed users to tag other friends from sites for which they were never there.[13] Recently, Twitter allowed greater censorship of tweets in some countries than users desired.[14] Google recently standardized their privacy policy and also has fought a long-running battle with Chinese authorities over censorship of content.

- *Lost productivity, addiction, and fatigue*: With an average of seven hours per month spent by U.S. Facebook users on average, many companies worry that employees working on social media projects will experience lost productivity. In fact, there have been cases (in general) of social media addiction, burnout, or fatigue.

- *Meaningless comments and babble*: The original Twitter prompt of "What are you doing?" was changed in 2009 to "What's happening?" in part to upgrade the content of 40 percent of tweets that were categorized as "pointless babble."[15]

- *Hackers and fraud*: Social media sites have been hacked at times and there have been instances of fraud.[16] Such attempts may be seemingly innocent posts such as "Hey—check out this link FREE IPAD!" but instead may be delivering malware searching for personally identifiable information.

- *Dealing with negative (viral) comments*: Marketers have to have a "thick skin" at times in using social media, in that negative comments and other embarrassing situations concerning the brand or company may spread like wildfire virally. Public relations and internal marketing efforts can be important in light of such unfortunate situations in seriously addressing such comments and not just resorting to deleting negative posts.

Social Media Categories and Brands

Table 14.1 categorizes most of the major social media brands around three prominent categories: communication, collaboration, and entertainment and multimedia. In addition, a global traffic ranking of these social media brands by Alexa (www.alexa.com) is provided in parentheses, with a "1" indicating the top site out of 1,000 sites raked by Alexa.

Social Networking

Social networking sites such as Facebook, MySpace, Twitter, and Second Life have signed up an estimated one billion people around the globe who interact with "friends," share opinions and information, and create online communities of people who have similar interests and wish to share their experiences with others. It comes as little surprise that marketers have tapped into the celebrated social networking sites or have created their own social networks as a mechanism for communicating with consumers about their brands. In this chapter, we now highlight two of the more prominent social networking venues—Facebook and Twitter.

Facebook

Facebook has certainly come a long way from its "humble" beginnings as Mark Zuckerman's project ("Facemash") as a college sophomore in 2003. At Harvard, he acquired photos from the online facebooks of nine private dorm houses, and then placed two photos side-by-side, asking users to choose the "hotter" person.[17] Although the site was quickly shut down a few days later by Harvard administrators, he expanded on the initial project for an art history class by uploading 500 Augustan images to a website and then allowing students to share notes.[18] This initial project then evolved at Harvard into "the facebook," allowing students to share photos and post other information.

Fast forward to February 2012, and following the attraction of established investors along the way,[19] Facebook filed for an initial public offering (IPO) estimated to value the social network between $50 and $125 billion, depending on

TABLE 14.1	Ranking of Social Media Sites*		
Communication	**Collaboration**	**Entertainment and Multimedia**
Blogs	*Business*	*Game Sharing*
Blogger (47)	Central Desktop	Armor Games
Blogspot (7)		Kongregate
LiveJournal (104)	*Content Management*	**Miniclip (548)**
TypePad (243)	e107	Newgrounds
Vox	**Drupal (451)**	
WordPress (18)	Plone	*Media Platforms*
Xanga	**WordPress (18)**	**Break.com (911)**
		DailyMotion (101)
Microblogs	*Visual Collaboration*	**Hulu (220)**
Foursquare (806)	Creately	**Metacafe (389)**
Plurk		**MySpace (154)**
Twitter (9)	*Document Management*	**Nico Nico Douga (Japan) (168)**
Tumblr (38)	Docs.com (Microsoft)	Veoh
	Dropbox.com (252)	VEVO
Advertising	**Google Docs (1*)**	**Vimeo (113)**
SocialVibe		**YouTube (3)**
	Social Bookmarking	
Events	**Delicious (398)**	*Virtual Worlds*
Eventful	folkd	Active Worlds
The Hotlist	**Google Reader (1*)**	**Battle.net (World of Warcraft) (521)**
Meetup.com (553)	**StumbleUpon (128)**	Second Life
Upcoming		The Sims Online
Yelp (190)	*Social Navigation*	
	Trapster	*Livecasting*
Aggregators	Waze	blip.tv
Twine		**Justin.tv (612)**
Netvibes	*Social News*	Livestream
	Chime.In	**Skype (165)**
Advocacy and Fundraising	**Digg (189)**	**Ustream (581)**
Causes	Newsvine	**YouTube (3)**
Kickstarter	NowPublic	
hitRECord	**Reddit (115)**	*Music*
IndieGoGo		Bandcamp
Jumo	*Wikis*	**Groove Shark (632)**
	Pbworks	The Hype Machine
Social Networking	Wetpaint	**Last.fm (674)**
Bebo	**Wikia (177)**	ccMixter
CyWorld (Korea)	Wikidot	**MySpace Music (154)**

TABLE 14.1	Ranking of Social Media Sites* (*continued*)	
Communication	**Collaboration**	**Entertainment and Multimedia**
Diaspora	Wikimedia (155)	Pandora Radio (352)
Facebook (2)	Wikinews	SoundClick
Google+ (1*)	**Wikipedia.org (6)**	**SoundCloud (349)**
Hi5 (926)	Wikispaces	Spotify
Hyves (Netherlands)		
IRC		*Photography and Art*
LinkedIn (13)		**deviantArt (130)**
Mixi (Japan) (207)		**Flickr (43)**
MySpace (154)		**Imgshack (149)**
Netlog (Belgium)		**Photobucket (153)**
Ning (345)		**Picasa (1*)**
Orkut (Google) (171)		SmugMug
RenRen (China) (100)		
Tagged (288)		*Presentation Sharing*
Tuenti (Spain) (915)		Prezi
XING (Germany) (293)		**scribd (275)**
Yammer		**Slideshare (204)**
		Reviews and Opinions
		ask.com (52)
		Askville (Amazon)
		cNet (83)
		Customer Lobby
		Ehow (147)
		eopinions.com
		MouthShut.com
		Quora (937)
		WikiAnswers (194)
		Yahoo! Answers (4*)
		Yelp (190)

Sites are listed in alphabetical order by category. All numbers in parenthesis show the social media site's Alexa global traffic ranking as of January 2012 and is based on the previous three-month period. Alexa rankings are a metric derived from a combination of a website's reach (unique visitors) and page views per unique visitor. Bolded social media websites are prominent websites in the top 1,000 sites per Alexa.

*Note that certain websites are comprised of multiple subdomains (e.g., plus.google.com). Alexa rankings for these websites will reflect the overall Alexa ranking of the primary domain (in this case www.google.com), which includes all of that site's traffic. Thus, rankings for individual offerings like Google+ and Yahoo! Answers will reflect overall Google and Yahoo! Traffic respectively.

Source: Based on data from http://www.alexa.com (accessed January 26, 2012).

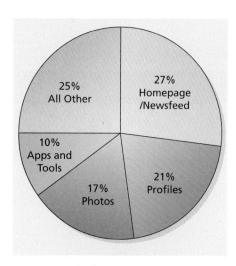

FIGURE 14.2 Share of Time Spent on Facebook.com by Content Section

Source: comScore Mediabuilder, U.S., May 2011. Used by permission of comScore.

estimates of future ad (and other) revenue.[20] Unlike other companies operating on the Web, Facebook is profitable (up 65 percent last year) and its sales revenue has now reached $4.27 billion. At this point, sources of revenue include social gaming (at 15 percent, with partners such as Zynga) and the remaining revenue from online ads.[21] The latter component currently drives the revenue, as the number of ads delivered on the site grew 42 percent and average price 18 percent from 2010 to 2011.[22] This growth is attributed in the IPO filing to a vast trove of information users post based on age, location, gender, education, work history, specific interests, or using the "like" button.[23] For instance, over 53 million users are now fans (have "liked") of Coca-Cola's main Facebook site (www.facebook.com/coca-cola).

The consumer engagement statistics for Facebook are equally impressive, with 1 billion active users for which 50 percent check their site daily.[24] The average user has 130 friends (equating with just four degrees of separation from thousands) and 600 million use their mobile devices to access Facebook.[25] Finally, mainstream marketers have taken notice (as partners), with more than seven million apps and websites now integrated with Facebook.[26]

Online ("engagement") ads still drive Facebook's revenue; such ads appear live on the right side of the user's page, footnoted by the number of friends who have "liked" or interacted with the ad. Oftentimes, these are based on the user's demographics, online interests, and other "likes" posted. If a user "likes" a brand, future company ads may appear inside the user's news feed. As noted in Figure 14.2, 27 percent of consumer engagement on Facebook is on the user's homepage and news feed, followed by profile viewing (21 percent), photo viewing (17 percent), and use of apps and tools (10 percent).[27] Importantly, the news feed (via fans who "like" a brand and the friends of fans) offers the greatest opportunity to engage consumers on Facebook. In general for all Facebook ads, click-throughs are only 0.1 percent compared to Google search ads at 10 percent. However, if a user sees that a friend "likes" an ad, they are 30 percent more likely to recall the ad's message.[28] This really points to the value of trusted, viral messages and the "long tail" of social media networks such as Facebook.

Recently, to bolster ad revenue beyond unpaid mentions in a user's news feed, Facebook has been promoting "sponsored stories" for advertisers. These stories allow advertisers to pay Facebook to more prominently highlight real status updates or "like" activity from users to friends as part of the news feed.[29] Traditional unpaid displays of posts to users (i.e., *non*-sponsored stories) have decreased, as content that used to live for a day now lives only minutes on a news feed.[30] In contrast, the "sponsored stories" leverage word-of-mouth campaigns en mass online.[31]

One aspect of Facebook that has escaped many is that, although it was developed and grown in the United States, 81 percent of current users are in countries outside of the United States and Canada.[32] Of course, operating in other countries can have its share of rewards and challenges, as noted in the *Global Focus*.

Twitter

Established in 2006, Twitter is an online social networking and micro-blogging service that allows users to send and read text-based posts (called tweets) for up to 140 characters.[33] These posts are displayed on a user's profile page and users may subscribe to other author tweets, known as a "following," with subscribers known as "followers." The service has gained worldwide popularity with over 500 million users, of which 100 million are active logging in once a month, and 50 million check-ins every day.[34] Initially, Twitter's early adopters tended to be in the 35-to-54 age category; however, teens have been increasingly joining due to privacy issues associated with Facebook (e.g., parents, grandparents).[35] Also, there are global differences, as Twitter is confirmed by comScore to be the largest social media network in Japan, with Facebook coming in second.[36] Revenue from Twitter is estimated to be $140 million.[37]

The Great Firewall: China's Social Media Clones

The great irony for many U.S. social media companies is that although China has the world's largest Internet market (477 million users), such companies essentially have been blocked from having a presence there. As Facebook considers such an entry, they face many of the same obstacles that have impeded other U.S. online giants, such as Google, eBay, and Twitter. These include government protectionism, censorship, strong local competition, a late entrance, a lack of market and consumer knowledge, and intellectual property issues. So, although Facebook has experienced tremendous growth in other Asian markets (e.g., India, Indonesia, Philippines), handling China's restrictions for handling sensitive user data and censorship of data will be a challenge for Facebook.

Currently, strong Chinese competition exists from local social networking sites such as Renren ("Everybody's Website"), established in 2005 by graduates of the University of Delaware. With over 31 million active monthly users, and compliance with Chinese content regulations (via monitoring sensitive keywords), Renren is perceived to be the local Chinese leader. It is popular among youth and college students, has a "like" button, and location-service called Renren Places (similar to Facebook Places).

LinkedIn's Chinese counterpart is "Ushi," with 250,000 business members; Twitter's is Sina's "Weibo" and sells ads on its site; Google's search engine clone is "Baidu," with revenue of $1.2 billion; Foursquare's Chinese version is "Jiepang," with 910,000 users for this location-based service; and YouTube's identical twin is "Youku," which is also the "Hulu of China," delivering TV programs online. So, as dominant as social media brands such as Facebook, LinkedIn, Twitter, Foursquare, and YouTube are in the United States and throughout the world, they still have their work cut out for them competing in China—with the world's largest online population.

Sources: Normandy Madden,"What Will Facebook Find If It Ventures Into China?" *Advertising Age*, June 13, 2011, 12, 14; Loretta Chao, "Renren Changes Key User Figure Before IPO," *WSJ Online*, April 29, 2011, http://online.wsj.com/article/SB1000142 405274870472930457628690321755560.html; "Behind the Great Firewall," *Advertising Age*, June 13, 2011, 12; and Renren Corporate Information, http://www.renren-inc.com/en/info/management.html, February 4, 2012.

No doubt, Twitter has gone through some challenges and growing pains. As alluded to earlier, a content analysis study by Pear Analytics in 2009 of 2,000 U.S. tweets revealed that 40 percent contained "pointless babble," 38 percent were "conversational," 9 percent had "pass-along value," 6 percent were categorized as "self-promotion," 4 percent were "spam," and 4 percent were labeled as "news."[38] (Note: categories do not total 100 percent due to rounding.) Although a follow-up is needed, Twitter may have corrected this starting in late 2009 by changing their prompt from "What are you doing?" to "What's happening?"

Certainly, one way that Twitter has benefitted consumers is through the complaint process—similar to the strategy used by musician Dave Carroll with his YouTube complaint song "United Breaks Guitars,"[39] Twitter has offered some measure of relief for many disgruntled consumers when normal channels have not helped. For example, when travelers initially were denied frequent flyer miles and actual seats (for a disabled passenger) on Delta and JetBlue airlines, respectively, they only found aid for their problems via Twitter.[40]

As opposed to taking action on Twitter, most users are active followers of other Twitter users. So, what exactly are most consumers following on Twitter? It would *seem* that most Twitter followers are enamored with celebrities; after all, Lady Gaga leads the celebrity pack with 11.6 followers, Justin Bieber with 11 million, Britney Spears has 8.5 million, Katy Perry with 8.3 million, and Kim Kardashian also with 8.3 million.[41] Also, some have argued that the dramatic increase in Twitter popularity can be traced to 2009 when many celebrities opened accounts. There even have been arguments at times that celebrities (and other popular brands) should receive a commission for building followers and social networking sites!

Yet, a recent study in the United Kingdom indicates that brands were 50 percent more popular than celebrities as to "likes" and "followings" online.[42] If that is the case, just what is being shown and promoted in brand Twitter posts and links? A recent content analysis study of 44 global brands' use of Twitter revealed that human personality is often interjected—by using human spokespeople, personal pronouns and verbs in the imperative form in texts, and brand names and re-directing cues in tweets.[43] We will examine in a later section just how advertisers can use options such as Promoted Tweets, Promoted Trends, and Promoted Accounts to increase consumer engagement with brands.

IMC FOCUS

Pinterest: Fast and Furious Growth, yet Potential Legal Issues

When considering the major players in the social media world, there is Facebook for finding friends, Twitter for sharing messages, and now Pinterest for sharing photos and images. Pinterest's growth since its development in late 2009 and launch in 2010 has been nothing short of "fast and furious," by being the quickest site ever to break through 10 million unique users in the United States. Although this torrid pace has cooled a bit, Pinterest boasts 11.7 current unique users in the United States, 83 percent of which are female.

As originally developed and launched by founder Ben Silbermann, Pinterest began as an invitation-only beta test. Its essence is that it allows users to create and manage theme-based image collections (e.g., events, interests, hobbies) through a pin-board-style photo sharing website. In addition to pinning images to a board, these images can be "repinned" by other Pinterest users—often spreading virally online. In fact, many users have claimed to be addicted to it, as one can scroll down through an endless array of photos and images. In comparison to Facebook, Pinterest is viewed by its users as a refuge from relationship status, check-ins from restaurants, pictures of kids, and being bombarded by other people's oversharing of "uninteresting and annoying experiences."

Many companies have been enjoying increased traffic from Pinterest postings of their brands and products. For example, brands like the e-commerce website Boticca use Pinterest as a virtual storefront for driving customers to their website. Users inbound from Pinterest are estimated to spend $180, compared to $85 spent from Facebook users.

Yet, legal issues may be on the horizon for Pinterest. Some photographers have complained about copyright violations of their work posted on Pinterest. Under fair use, copyrighted work can be used without permission if someone is commenting on it, criticizing it, reporting on it, teaching about it, or conducting research. Unfortunately, just repinning it does not fit one of these categories. In *Kelly v. Arriba Soft Corporation*, a search engine firm won the case versus a photographer because it used thumbnail images rather than the full image of the work. Yet, Pinterest uploads the entire image from the original source. To combat any copyright issues, there is currently a strong disclaimer on the Pinterest site for its users, as well as allowing copyright holders to (1) request that content be removed from the Pinterest site and (2) opt out of having images being pinned from their own site. Thus far, no major copyright lawsuits have emerged against Pinterest, but this is something to monitor.

Sources: Mark W. Smith, "How to use Pinterest's pinboard for the Web," *USAToday Tech*, January 17, 2012, http://www.usatoday.com/tech/news/story/2012-01-17/how-to-pinterest-mark-smith/52615856/1; Lydia Dishman, "Why Pinterest Is So Addictive," Fastcompany.com, February 16, 2012, http://www.fastcompany.com/1816603/why-pinterest-is-so-addictive; Alyson Shontell, "A Non-Geek's Guide To Pinterest, The Biggest Internet Hit Since Facebook," Business insider.com, February 27, 2012, http://articles.businessinsider.com/2012-02-27/tech/31103115_1_social-media-gilt-groupe-formspring; Alyson Shontell, "A Lawyer Who Is Also A Photographer Just Deleted All Her Pinterest Boards Out Of Fear," Businessinsider.com, February 28, 2012, http://articles.businessinsider.com/2012-02-28/tech/31106641_1_repinning-copyright-entire-image; and "Pinterest," Wikipedia, http://en.wikipedia.org/wiki/Pinterest (accessed July 18, 2012).

Successful Social Media Campaigns

This section offers a review of some of the more successful social media and networking campaigns since social networking became a reality in the mid-2000s. However, as noted in Chapter 10, there certainly can be debate as to what one considers being "successful," "effective," and "creative." Yet, most (if not all) of these campaigns have been cited in the advertising media as especially creative and engaging, have won awards, or have performed extremely well on metrics (e.g., impressions, actions, ROI). Importantly, as we mentioned in Chapter 1, integration with other IMC elements is critical (via links, feeds, viral networking) in order to try to offer multiple "touch points" with a single, overall message. The campaigns are now presented in alphabetical order.

Alamo Rent-a-Car's "Ultimate Escapes." Jeff Bullas, author of one of the largest social media blogs (www.jeffbullas.com), cites Alamo Rent-a-Car as one of the "Five Cool Facebook Campaigns" for 2011.[44] The sweepstakes campaign was titled, "The Alamo Ultimate Escape," and asked Facebook users to write about their ultimate escape to win $5,000 toward a vacation. The original objectives were to increase Facebook "likes," build an e-mail database, create customer loyalty, and sell rentals with deals and specials on display. The contest has increased the number of "likes" by over 5,000 since its beginning and clearly is on its way to achieving its other obejctives.[45]

Beats Electronics "Humble Beginnings." Beats Electronics was founded in 2006 by legendary artist Dr. Dre and Jimmy Iovine, CEO of Interscope Geffen A&M Records who wanted to develop a new type of headphones with the capability to capture the full spectrum of sound that artists experience in professional recording studios.[46] Their Facebook page offers emotional and inspiring content (also featured on YouTube) that records musicians' stories of their "Humble Beginnings." To access the stories, visitors need to "like" the page, thereby increasing brand loyalty. However, the page is not as much about selling as it is connecting with visitors on an emotional level.[47]

Blendtec's "Will it Blend?" Web videos on YouTube for the Blendtec Total Blender show the kitchen blender destroying just about everything from a baseball to an iPad. Judges from Forbes.com unanimously ranked this series of destructive shorts as one of the best-ever social media campaigns. The home sales of Blendtec's blenders have increased 700 percent since the start of the campaign in November 2006.[48]

© Photo by Anthony Behar/FilmMagic/Getty Images

Burger King's "Subservient Chicken." The Burger King irreverent campaign developed by Crispin, Porter + Bogusky (CP + B) to promote the chain's TenderCrisp sandwich has had a guy in a chicken suit taking fans' commands on the Web since 2004.[49] According to the ad agency, the website, where a participant can still type in commands like "moonwalk" and "make a sandwich" and watch the chicken obey the order, received 15 million hits in the first five days. This campaign also was listed as one of Forbes.com's best-ever social media campaigns.

Burger King's "Whopper Sacrifice." Beginning in 2008, this Burger King campaign was not afraid to ask the tough question: "What do you love more, your friends or the Whopper?" The Facebook application bribed consumers to "unfriend" 10 people from their Facebook friends list in exchange for a free burger. Ad agency Crispin, Porter + Bogusky says the application terminated some 234,000 "friendships." Ultimately, Facebook decided that letting its users know that they had been let go contradicted its business plan, and the application itself was sacrificed. Yet, Forbes.com gave the campaign one of its best-ever awards due to its creativity.[50]

Evian's "Roller Babies." The *Guinness Book of World Records* says this YouTube megahit, which features computer-generated babies on roller skates breakdancing and backflipping, is the most viewed online ad in history. This one is purely about the numbers, with the effort from Euro RSCG in Paris receiving more than 54,000 comments and tweets to date, as well as more than 60 million views.[51]

Craftsman Tools "Neighborhood Park Renovation." Craftsman Tools ran a social marketing campaign on Facebook that asked users to post a photo of a park in their area that could really use a renovation. The winning park was to receive a $10,000 makeover and the user who posted the photo receives a set of Craftsmen tools. The objectives for this contest included engagement with the target market, local social marketing, and increasing sales of Craftsmen tools.[52]

Mattel's Barbie and MGA Entertainment's Bratz Online Dolls. In appeals to reach 8- to 12-year-old girls, both Mattel Inc.'s Barbie and MGA Entertainment Inc.'s Bratz created separate social networking sites in 2007—Barbiegirls.com and Be-Bratz.com. The Be-Bratz.com site, for example, is accessible only after purchasing a special Bratz doll that is equipped with a USB key. Users choose a screen name and their own online dolls (as "avatars") that can be tailored to their tastes, including "buying" clothing for their avatars in an online store with virtual currency that

Image courtesy of The Advertising Archives

is earned by playing games online. Participants can also customize their own online rooms and chat with other users.[53]

National Geographic's "Remembering 9/11." The National Geographic Channel tapped into deeply held emotions with its Facebook Campaign titled "Remembering 9/11: Where Were You?" Those posting on this site are able to tell their story and enter their location on that day into an interactive map that also lists other people's locations and stories. As of January 2012, the original goals of network exposure and engagement are being met with a fan count increasing from 551,000 to 587,000 in just a few days.[54]

Nike's "Write the Future." This 2010 soccer FIFA world cup, three-minute video features soccer royalty (e.g., the United Kingdom's Wayne Rooney) in a frenetically-paced look at the ultimate what-if scenarios, with fates revolving around a blocked pass or a lightning strike.[55] The video was launched initially only on Facebook and generated nine million views. After it posted on YouTube (www.youtube.com/watch?v=lSggaxXUS8k), it lead to 21 million viewers. The video—developed by Wieden+Kennedy Amsterdam—won a 2010 Grand Prix Award in the film category at Cannes.[56]

Graubunden Tourism's "Obermutten Goes Global." Recently, *Advertising Age* cited Graubunden Tourism's "Obermutten Goes Global" Facebook campaign as one of the best in 2011. The story is about a public relations strategy to boost awareness (and tourism, etc.) for a tiny Swiss town named Obermutten. The campaign invited Facebook fans to "like" the town and, in turn, the fans' pictures were posted on the town's physical community bulletin board. When they ran out of space, the photos had to be posted on the walls of local barns! The campaign ended up with Obermutten fans from 32 countries and generated $2.4 million in media stories from a budget of only $10,800.[57]

Old Spice's "Smell Like a Man, Man." Procter & Gamble's Old Spice was just another guy's scented deodorant brand in 2010 with an entertaining spokesperson (Isaiah Mustafa) on TV commercials. This was until the brand's ad agency Wieden+Kennedy put Mustafa online and invited fans to use Twitter, Facebook, and social media to pose all types of questions that he answered quickly.[58] Based on the many questions from fans (and some celebrities), Mustafa responded in more than 180 Web videos produced in just a few days. This real-time, social media effort was the first of its kind, and recognized as among some of the best-ever social media campaigns by Forbes.com and a panel of experts.

Olla Condoms' "Unexpected Babies." Brazilian agency Age Isobar's unusual campaign for Olla Condoms in 2011 on Facebook targeted young men who received mysterious friend requests from babies who happened to have the young man's same name, followed by "Jr." The profile then featured a link to the brand's website.[59]

SMELL LIKE A MAN, MAN.
Old Spice

Image courtesy of The Advertising Archives

Pepsi's "Refresh." The Pepsi "Refresh" campaign began in 2010 and plans to award a total of $20 million in grants to individuals, businesses, and non-profits to promote new ideas that would have a positive impact on their community, state, or the nation. The rules state that the first 1,000 ideas proposed each month will be considered for a share of $1.3 million available each month.[60] The application process had social media links, did not require grant writing skills, and began with the prompt "What Do You Care About?" This social marketing initiative has impacted an estimated 1.4 million lives (www.refresheverything.com) and is a Forbes.com award winner for one of the best-ever social media campaigns.

Philippines Department of Tourism's "It's More Fun in the Philippines." A slogan "It's More in the Philippines" went viral after the campaign (developed by BBDO Guerrero Manila) encouraged Filipinos and other fans of the country to post their own additions of what "is more fun in the Philippines." Some of the consumer-generated content can be found in the link in the endnotes and offers some creative twists and images that play on the ad slogan and text.[61] These include images that play on the words "commuting" (showing paddling in a kayak), "tailgating" (with a picture of a diver following a shark's tail), "social climbing" (displaying tourists on a mountain above the clouds), etc.

Procter & Gamble's "People's Choice" and "Capressa" networking sites. In 2007, Procter & Gamble (P&G) created two social networking sites that enabled consumers to learn from one another and to share their experiences. P&G's "The People's Choice" site focused on entertainment and allows consumers to share their views on matters such as reality TV programs, entertainers, musicians, and so on. (P&G also sponsors the popular "People's Choice Awards" each year.) P&G's second social networking site, "Capessa," targeted women who wished to interact on matters such as health, weight loss, and pregnancy. In spirit with the nature of social networks and participants' strong desire not to be inundated with marketing messages, P&G did not commercialize either site with ad messages, although occasional pop-up ads appeared from P&G ads already run on Yahoo![62]

Stella Artois UK's "DVD Film Contest." Stella Artois UK sponsored a popular contest in which after a user "likes" their Facebook page, they were prompted to answer a question about a film from a DVD given away on the page. After answering the question, users provided a phone number and e-mail address for a chance to win either a free film DVD or a collection of 40. Brand exposure, engagement, and loyalty all increased dramatically as a result of the campaign.[63]

Common Objectives and Themes for These Successful Social Media Campaigns

Several common objectives and themes can be found in these successful social media campaigns. First, some have an objective to *enhance public relations*, as displayed quite effectively in the "Obermutten Goes Global" Facebook campaign. Others may wish to share their own (and consumers') *creativity, humor, or other ad executions*, as found with "It's More Fun in the Philippines," "Will it Blend?," "Unexpected Babies," "Roller Babies," and "Subservient Chicken" campaigns. Some successful social media campaigns stress *deals and contests* for their fans, such as with "Whopper Sacrifice," "DVD Film Contest," and "Ultimate Escape." As found with the "Smell Like a Man, Man," "People's Choice," and "Capressa" campaigns, at times, the objective is to engage consumers in *dialogue and two-way communication* to uncover brand insights and ideas. Other social media campaign objectives include *launching causes, sponsorships or events* (e.g., with "Write the Future," "Refresh," "Neighborhood Park Renovation"), *introducing new products* ("Subservient Chicken"), or just having *fun with interactive games, virtual worlds, and avatars* (e.g., with Barbie, Bratz, or Subservient Chicken). Finally, others are able to successfully *elicit consumer-generated stories* about the brand, product category ("Humble Beginnings"), or important issues in society or events in history ("Remembering 9/11"). We now turn our attention to what critics consider to be key factors in general in the success of social media campaigns and why.

Factors That "Work" in Social Media Campaigns and Why

Perhaps the most important suggestion by critics and experts in social media is to encourage or elicit *storytelling about the brand*.[64] The Intel-Toshiba "Inside" campaign brought Facebook users into the creation process and engaged them in an evolving social film about the film's lead character. Facebook users' posts and videos influenced the plotline and helped the character escape from a room where a mysterious kidnapper had trapped her. In general, and based on research tracking 83 blogs over six months, such social media stories or narratives can be quite effective when advertisers and brands are congruent with the social media site or forum in allowing for co-production of messages and meanings, rather than forced amplification of marketer themes.[65]

A second important suggestion is to *step into the real world*. This statement means to try to connect and engage consumers through empathy, understanding, and openness with real-life issues in social media campaigns.[66] As an example, Heinz "Get Well Soup" from the U.K. agency We Are Social allowed Facebook users to send personalized cans of soup to sick friends. Such approaches tend to enhance the personal relevance of social media messages.[67]

A third recommendation is to *evolve with your customers in being social and human*. This statement means admitting mistakes at times and accepting criticism on social networking sites. This can go a long way to enhancing trustworthiness, an important dimension of source credibility. As noted by *Advertising Age*, Pfizer's Chapstick needed to do this (instead of deleting negative posts) based on critical comments regarding a model's compromising position when searching for lip balm.[68] We now turn our attention to how to organize social media efforts.

Organizing Social Media Efforts

In today's fast-paced digital world, numerous social media positions have been listed in job postings, such as social media strategists, social media planners, social media buyers, social media coordinators, and so forth. Moreover, there are efforts to establish social media departments and social media agencies recently. Yet, others, such as former *Advertising Age* Editor Jonah Bloom, have argued that such social media activities should be integrated with other IMC work. As he observed in a humorous fashion:

> *Every time an apparently foreign object [e.g., social media] is identified in adland, it seems the inhabitants split, roughly speaking, into two parties—those who fear the foreign body and those who are excited by it. The excited annex the object and create their own nation around it. The fearful homelanders breathe a sigh of relief and go back to doing whatever they were doing....*[69]

> Jonah Bloom, "Dedicated Social-Media Silos? That's the Last Thing We Need," Advertising Age, June 8, 2009, 11. Copyright Crain Communications Inc., 2009. Used with permission.

Bloom aptly observed that this annexing and "nation building" has been occurring in advertising for many decades. For instance, before social media it was digital media. Before digital media, it was direct marketing. Decades ago, Bloom notes that the same separation process occurred with television and radio several years before it. The danger with the annexation and nation building is that important data-driven processes and analytics can be separated mainstream IMC strategy within agencies. Thus, Bloom's point is that social media is not a "box to be ticked or a department to be manned or even a campaign to be launched."[70] Rather, it is just one of the many possible tools that might be applied and integrated to help better solve consumer or societal problems.

How to Advertise on Social Networks

This section examines how to advertise on social networks, with specific attention to the leading social networks: Facebook and Twitter. We discuss the type of ads that can appear on these sites, as well as the process to advertise, and current issues.

As explained by comScore, there are several choices (some paid and other paid) when advertisers seek to create impressions (i.e., the number of times an ad has been shown on a site) on Facebook:[71]

- *Page Publishing*: These are unpaid impressions appearing on the fan page wall and may appear in the news feed of a fan or friend of a fan.

- *Stories about Friends*: These also are unpaid impressions, but are when a friend actively engages with a brand (e.g., Amy "likes" Southwest Airlines). This information becomes visible either on a friend's wall or in the news feed and may appear to fans and friends of fans.
- *Sponsored Stories*: These are paid impressions that are similar to Stories about Friends, but are described as being actively distributed more broadly and appear in the right-hand column to fans and friends of fans.
- *Ads with Social*: These are branded and paid impressions that come directly from advertisers with a social message that appears to friends of fans (e.g., Roger Tison likes Southwest Airlines at the bottom of the ad).

Facebook provides interested advertisers with a set of five steps for "promoting their business with ads on Facebook."[72] The first step is to *identify goals* (e.g., awareness, sales, fans). Second, they suggest *targeting the right people* (via location, language, education, work, age, gender, birthday, relationships, "likes," friend of fans, or fans). Third, advertisers are encouraged to *design engaging ads* by including the business name and key information, clear actions to take, a simple eye-catching image, and targeting different groups. Fourth, there are decisions to make in *managing ad budget*. These include whether they are using cost per click (CPC) or cost per impression (CPM), the amount for each click, and the maximum amount (budget) they are willing to pay each day. Finally, advertisers are told to *review and improve* via an "ad manager" that provides metrics. Such metrics include impressions, clicks, targeted reach, reach, social reach (i.e., the percent who saw an ad or sponsored story with names of friends who liked it, RSVPed to an event, or used an app), and connections (those actually liking such ads). Audience details and effectiveness over time also are tracked.

In the case of Twitter, advertisers face fewer key options compared to Facebook, including Promoted Tweets, Promoted Trends, and Promoted Accounts.[73] More specifically, a "Promoted Tweet" is a tweet first sent and promoted to followers, then appears in search results when a user searches for a keyword the advertiser has bid on. The advertiser only pays when a user completes an *engagement action*, such as rewteeting, clicking on, or "favoriting" the Promoted Tweet. The "Prompted Trend" allows an advertiser to be listed, align themselves, and offer conversation for a certain hashtag (#) or trend (e.g., a recent hurricane). Finally, the "Promoted Account" is similar to a Facebook "like," in that advertisers are hoping to have a "follow" ("like") for ads/brands placed in Twitter profile that are suggested to other accounts as "Who to follow." These followers (and retweets) are important in offering the "long tail" for Twitter brand information, similar to the value of "Fans" and "Friends of Fans" on Facebook.

There have been critics of current advertising procedures on Twitter, as some argue that Twitter could do more a better job of targeting (e.g., by location) and that many accounts do not have any followers.[74] For instance, if one wanted to target urban, 20-year-old males with a coupon (e.g., envisioned as a "Groupon + Twitter" promotion), it currently would not be possible. One issue in the targeting debate is the fact that Twitter profiles are typically very short and privacy concerns found with other social networks can play a part. However, when promoting important new information or relevant ads, Twitter promoted tweet campaigns have done far better than the average 3 to 5 percent engagement actions noted above. For example, engagement actions for recent tweets for the VW Beetle redesign (at 52 percent), Google Instant product launch (at 38 percent), and bringing the "Old Spice Guy" out of retirement (at 36 percent) were all above-average engagement action levels.[75] The real overriding issue for Twitter and advertisers is where and when to interrupt the flow of tweets to integrate relevant ad messages, if at all.

One tough issue for social media networks (such as Facebook and Twitter) is that their average CPM (cost per 1,000 impressions) is only 56 cents, compared to a $2.43 average for the Internet at large.[76] Some of the reasons for depressed pricing is due to the oversupply of ad page views and that much of the social media advertising (e.g., on Facebook) is small and oriented toward text.

Privacy and Other Concerns

Over the years, social media networks have faced many complaints of breaches of privacy policies with their users, including a series of miscues by Facebook. Before we examine some of these specific privacy issues, it is important to consider the four *general privacy principles* applied to one's personal information for all advertising and marketing activities, namely, notice, consent, access (to information), and security. We now will detail many of the reported privacy issues associated with the notification and changes to Facebook's privacy policy over the years.

Several changes to Facebook's privacy policy began in 2009 and 2010, such as third-party data tracking firms (e.g., Google's Double Click and Yahoo Inc.'s Right Media) receiving Facebook users' names or identification numbers tied to personal profile information without proper notification to the users.[77] Later in August 2010, Facebook launched their Facebook Places location-based service that provided a voluntary check-in for users at locations, such as retail stores, etc. However, it initially was allowing friends to tag each other in location check-ins even though the other person may not physically be at the location or even aware of the check-in.[78] This was corrected later to an opt-in, whereby the tagged friend could click "not now" or accept the friend's check-in. (Users selecting "not now" might continue to receive annoying requests until a change is made in the privacy profile.) In October 2010, it was found that popular Facebook apps (Farmville, Phrases, Texas HoldEm, etc.) were transmitting personally identifiable information to advertisers and tracking firms.[79] Finally, privacy critics have voiced concerns over Facebook's sponsored stories that allows advertisers to buy and republish Facebook messages that users post about brands (e.g., with a check-in at a local retail store) when a user clicks the site's "like" button.[80]

Many of these (and other) privacy issues eventually drew the attention of the Federal Trade Commission (FTC), who specifically detailed the following privacy policy concerns for Facebook in a November 2011 FTC complaint and agreement with the firm:[81]

- In December 2009, Facebook changed its website so certain information that users may have designated as private—such as their Friends List—was made public. They did not warn users that this change was coming, or get their approval in advance.
- Facebook represented that third-party apps that users installed would have access only to user information that they needed to operate. In fact, the apps could access nearly all of users' personal data—data the apps did not need.
- Facebook told users they could restrict sharing of data to limited audiences—for example with "friends only." In fact, selecting "friends only" did not prevent their information from being shared with third-party applications their friends used.
- Facebook had a "Verified Apps" program and claimed it certified the security of participating apps—but it did not.
- Facebook promised users that it would not share their personal information with advertisers—but it did.
- Facebook claimed that when users deactivated or deleted their accounts, their photos and videos would be inaccessible. But Facebook allowed access to the content, even after users had deactivated or deleted their accounts.
- Facebook claimed that it complied with the U.S.–EU Safe Harbor Framework that governs data transfer between the United States and the European Union—but it did not.

Thus, in November 2011, Facebook agreed to settle Federal Trade Commission charges that it deceived consumers by telling them they could keep their information on Facebook private, and then repeatedly allowing it to be shared and made public.[82] Another recent issue is with respect to security, as hackers have attacked social networks such as Facebook and Twitter.[83] In sum, balancing the privacy (and security) of your users with the needs of advertisers and data tracking firms is indeed a serious undertaking that requires continual vigilance.

Other Social Media Network Concerns

A new study conducted by the International Center for Media & the Public Agenda (ICMPA) asked 200 students at the University of Maryland to abstain from using all media for 24 hours.[84] After their 24 hours of abstinence, the students were then asked to blog on private class websites about their experiences: to report their successes and admit to any failures. In aggregate, the students wrote over 110,000 words—the same number as a 400-page novel. According to researchers, students describe their feelings in abstaining from using media in literally the same terms associated with drug and alcohol *addiction*; that is, in terms of withdrawal, frantic craving, being very anxious, extremely antsy, miserable, jittery, and crazy. Most of the comments regarded not being able to check social networking sites and mobile devices.

Other social media network debates have centered on exactly *how young* should users be allowed on such sites. Or, in other words, should 9-year olds really be on Facebook?[85] Currently, according to *Consumer Reports*, an estimated five million Facebook users are 10 or younger.[86] The argument against early use is that logic and sophisticated reasoning is not really activated until high school, and therefore, younger children may not realize when one of their posts is inappropriate. Certainly, there have been many reports of cyber-bullying at young ages. On the other side, some researchers argue that it is important to avoid blanket judgments about online communication and social media.[87] That is, online communication is argued to have a positive aspect in the socialization process, by establishing identities and independence. No doubt, questions such as "How is this social media network going to interact with my child's personality?" should be asked.[88]

Measurement of Social Media Campaigns

A recent survey of 1,000 online businesses indicates that companies continue to struggle with measuring the return on investment (ROI) of social media efforts.[89] In the survey, 41 percent of the companies report they do not have a ROI measure for *any* of the money spent on social media. Just 8 percent can determine the ROI of *all* of what they spend on social media. Part of the problem is *not* that there is dearth of metrics and firms—because there are many of both. Rather, the constant stream of (usually "count") data on social media creates the "illusion of precision."[90] What is desired is to offer audiences specific metrics (more on this below), providing a more in-depth assessment of the impact of social media campaigns. These can take a while to build (e.g., comScore studies taking from 6 months to 2 years[91]) and metrics (in general) can cost from $1,000 per month to $100,000 a year.

Many firms and metrics exist for measurement of social media. For example, firms such as Google Analytics and Omniture can offer standard metrics such as unique visitors, time spent on site, total time per users, frequency of visits, depth of visit, and conversions. Other social media monitoring firms include Radian6, Evolve24, Nielsen Buzz Metrics (which at one time offered "blog pulse" that tracked keyword statistics for thousands of blog sites), Collective Intellect, Alexa, Compete, and comScore, among others. As many offer different tools and metrics, perhaps the most important question is to *determine what one's objectives* (e.g., increasing unique visitors? fans? conversions? impressions? gross rating points?) *are for the social media campaign*. For instance, maybe one is interested in traffic rankings based on reach (unique visitors) and page views per unique visitor—so Alexa (www.alexa.com; see Table 14.1) may be the choice. Or, based on recruited panelists, one be interested in audience profile data, including media exposure, search term usage, cross-shopping, conversions, and competitive behaviors among different audience segments—so Compete (www.compete.com) or comScore (www.comscore.com) might be the selection.

Also, many statistics can be gleaned directly from the social media site itself. For example, Facebook offers an *EdgeRank Score* that is an algorithm that Facebook uses to determine which of a page's statuses the page's online community will see in their news feed.[92] The algorithm is calculated as:

EdgeRank Score = Affinity * Weight * Time Decay

The *affinity score* is based on the number of number of times that you send a friend messages and check their profile; a greater number of messages and checks leads to a higher affinity score. A *weight* is then assigned to each type of interaction. Pictures carry the highest weight score, followed by comments and then by "likes." Finally, *time decay* reflects the fact that the older the interaction, the less important it becomes. The EdgeScores are categorized as follows: 0–6 is below average, 7–13 is average, 14–19 is above average, and scores above 20 are excellent.[93] Other researchers have taken the idea of measuring influential users a step further in developing an approach to determine which users have significant effects on the activities of others using the longitudinal records of members' log-in activity.[94]

Other companies, such as Radian6 (www.radian6.com), offer detailed social media tracking resulting in summary dashboards displaying sentiments (i.e., the polarity of a text in social media), share of voice (e.g., brand mentions versus competitors), and share of conversations (e.g. brand versus industry). Such summary dashboards offer a convenient summary of the social media impact of one's brand versus competitors.

A final example involves the use of comScore's Social Essentials measurement service based on a two-million-member global panel of Internet users.[95] comScore provides audience measure statistics though their panel, such as monthly brand impressions (i.e., total exposures) and the overall weight of a brand campaign (e.g., gross rating points [GRPs] as a function of the percentage reached at least once and the frequency of times reached). This information is provided in Table 14.2 from comScore for Starbucks, Southwest Airlines, and Bing for May 2011. In the case of Starbucks, if one divides the number of total impressions (in thousands; 17,098) by the number of unique exposed fans (in thousands; 6,314) this equals the average frequency of exposures (2.7) in May.

TABLE 14.2 Unpaid Brand Impressions on Facebook

	Exposed Fans (000)	Impressions (000)	Total U.S. Reach	Total Internet Reach	Frequency	Total U.S. GRPs*
Fans						
Starbucks	6,314	17,098	2.1%	2.9%	2.7	5.7
Southwest	917	2,924	0.3%	0.4%	3.2	1.0
Bing	1,221	3,670	0.4%	0.6%	3.0	1.2
Friends						
Starbucks	10,630	35,267	3.5%	4.9%	3.3	11.6
Southwest	1,123	2,994	0.4%	0.5%	2.7	1.0
Bing	2,208	4,441	0.7%	1.0%	2.0	1.5

*Final GRPs may vary slightly due to rounding.

Source: comScore's "The Power of Like," p. 14. Used by permission of comScore.

The total U.S. reach (2.1) (dropping the percentage) times the frequency (2.7) equals the total U.S. gross rating points (GRPs) of 5.7. These figures are important in that they can enable some comparability with other digital campaigns, as well as some data for comparison with cross-media campaigns.

As the social media world will undoubtedly change and evolve, so will social media metrics. The challenge is to go beyond the temptation of relying on simple counts (e.g., our brand has 39 million fans!) and move toward audience specific data that can be compared with other media options. A social media content manager recently made three very insightful suggestions about the nature of social media measurement.[96] First, social media is the vehicle—not the destination. So, social media is just an IMC tool that requires consistent attention and integration with other IMC tools. Second, listen to the discussions generated by social media channels and learn how these can benefit every department in the organization. Finally, IMC performance metrics are media agnostic. That is, the focus should not be on forcing social media (or a certain social media presence). Rather, it is applying the right IMC tools to help solve consumer and social problems.

Summary

This chapter presented material on perhaps the most exciting and ever-growing and changing tool found in IMC today, that is, social media. We first describe exactly what "social media" means. We then discuss the advantages and disadvantages of this evolving media option compared to traditional media choices. Many of the major social media categories and different social media brands (e.g., Facebook, Twitter, Google⁺, Pinterest, LinkedIn) within those categories (e.g., Communication—social networking) are then presented with special attention paid to Facebook and Twitter social networks. Then, 19 of some of the best social media campaigns of all time are presented. We then discuss organizational issues associated with social media, as well as how to advertise on social media networks. Privacy and other major areas of concern are described and then followed by an in-depth discussion of current metrics used in evaluation the return on investment (ROI) for investments in social media campaigns.

Discussion Questions

1. Based on your own experiences with social media (e.g., Facebook, Twitter, MySpace, YouTube, WordPress, Pinterest, LinkedIn), what do you consider to be its major advantages and disadvantages?

2. As mentioned in the *Marcom Insight*, critics of Facebook have likened it to your once favorite and cozy restaurant or bar now becoming very crowded, with more gimmicks to keep you there, many changes to the décor, and servers and bartenders who are now gossips. Do you agree with this analogy? What do you think is the future for Facebook?

3. An examination of Figures 14.1 and Tables 14.1 suggests a very crowded brand space in the social media world. Provide specific ideas and suggestions as to how some of the newer social media brands can better identify themselves and differentiate themselves from competition.

4. One possible disadvantage of using social media may be that a firm's public mistake or "faux pas" with consumers goes viral—reaching millions of consumers the next day. Explain how you would respond, especially from a public relations perspective.

5. How would you go about advertising on Facebook? Twitter? Other social media? Compare how this differs from other traditional media (e.g., television, radio, magazines, newspapers).

6. Describe how posting items on Facebook has affected your privacy. Has this also occurred for tweets on Twitter? (If you are not on these sites, sample a roommate or friend.) How should advertisers balance the need for collecting such information with their targeting efforts?

7. Do you agree with major social networking sites (e.g., Facebook, Twitter) allowing for the censorship of content in certain countries? If you answer "no," will that affect such sites' profitability and growth in allowing for almost identical competitors (e.g., Ren-Ren) in these countries?

8. Select one of your favorite brands. Discuss how you would use social marketing to drive traffic to your other IMC elements in an integrated campaign. What do you consider to be some of the more effective techniques mentioned with the successful social media campaigns mentioned in the chapter?

9. How should social media be organized within agencies and firms? Do you think it should be set up as a separate department?

10. Discuss what you consider to be the measure of the success and effectiveness of social media. Should it be share of voice? Share of conversation? Sentiments? Brand mentions versus the industry or competitors? Audience characteristics, such as impressions and gross rating points (reach × frequency)? Cost per impression or view? Cost per click? Cost per engagement or action?

End Notes

1. "Social Media," Wikipedia, http://en.wikipedia.org/wiki/Social_media (accessed January 18, 2012).

2. "Social Media."

3. "Facebook Statistics," http://www.facebook.com/press/info.php?statistics (accessed January 22, 2012, before Facebook's IPO); see also Facebook Fact Sheet, February 4, 2012, http://newsroom.fb.com/content/default.aspx?NewsAreaId=22.

4. "November 2011 - Top U.S. Web Brands," Nielsen-Wire, December 30, 2011, http://blog.nielsen.com/nielsenwire/online_mobile/november-2011-top-u-s-web-brands (accessed February 18, 2012).

5. Ibid.

6. "Social Networking is the Most Popular Online Activity," Social Networking Watch, December 26, 2011, http://www.socialnetworkingwatch.com/2011/12/social-networking-is-the-most-popular-online-activity.html.

7. "Facebook Key Facts," http://newsroom.fb.com (accessed October 4, 2012); and "Facebook Statistics," http://newsroom.fb.com/content/default.aspx?NewsAreaId=22 (accessed July 9, 2012).

8. "#numbers," Twitter Blog, March 14, 2011, http://blog.twitter.com/2011/03/numbers.html.

9. Ibid.

10. Claire Cain Miller, "Who's Driving Twitter's Popularity? Not Teens," *New York Times*, August 25, 2009, http://www.nytimes.com/2009/08/26/technology/internet/26twitter.html.

11. "Social Media."

12. Kevin J. Delaney, "Second Look: Once Wary Industry Giants Embrace Internet Advertising," *Wall Street Journal*, April 17, 2006, A1, A12.

13. Geoffrey A. Fowler, "Facebook Fights Privacy Concerns," *Wall Street Journal*, August 21–22, 2010, B1, B6.

14. David Crary, Twitter's New Censorship Plan Rouses Global Furor, Associated Press, January 28, 2012, http://finance.yahoo.com/news/Twitter-new-censorship-plan-apf-293577013.html.

15. "Twitter Study," Pear Analytics, August 2009, 1–13, http://www.pearanalytics.com/blog/wp-content/uploads/2010/05/Twitter-Study-August-2009.pdf (accessed January 29, 2012).

16. Geoffrey A. Fowler, Shayndi Raice, Amir Efrati, "Spam Finds New Target," *Wall Street Journal*, January 4, 2012, B1, B2.

17. Laura Locke, "The Future of Facebook," *Time* (New York), July 17, 2007; and Alan J. Tabak, "Hundreds Register for New Facebook Website," *The Harvard Crimson* (Cambridge, MA). February 9, 2004.

18. Tabak, Ibid.

19. Daniel Gross, "Facebook's Rise From Start-Up to Establishment," Yahoo! Finance, February 2, 2012, http://ca.finance.yahoo.com/blogs/daniel-gross/facebook-rise-start-establishment-220928408.html.

20. Geoffrey A. Fowler and Shayndi Raice, "Advertisers' Free Ride on Facebook May End," *Wall Street Journal*, February 3, 2012, B1, B7.

21. Shayndi Raice, "Facebook Sets Historic IPO," *Wall Street Journal*, February 2, 2012, A1, A2.

22. Ibid.

23. Ibid.

24. "Facebook Statistics," http://newsroom.fb.com/content/default.aspx?NewsAreaId=22 (accessed July 9, 2012); see also Facebook Key Facts, October 2, 2012, http://newsroom.fb.com/content/default.aspx?NewsAreaId=22.

25. Ibid.

26. Ibid.

27. Andrew Lipman, Graham Mudd, Mike Rich, and Sean Bruich, "The Power of Like," comScore, July 26, 2011, 8.

28. Brad Stone, "Sell Your Friends," *Bloomberg Businessweek*, September 27, 2010, 64–72.

29. Geoffrey A. Fowler and Shayndi Raice, "Advertisers' Free Ride on Facebook May End," *Wall Street Journal*, February 3, 2012, B1, B7.

30. Some critics have noted that the trend toward "Sponsored Stories" and paid space is due to overcrowding of ads and the need to have more "creative" methods to capture revenue to feed Facebook's growth; see Dumenco.

31. "Advertisers' Free Ride on Facebook May End."

32. Facebook Fact Sheet, February 4, 2012, http://newsroom.fb.com/content/default.aspx?NewsAreaId=22.

33. "Twitter," Wikipedia, http://en.wikipedia.org/wiki/Twitter (accessed February 12, 2012).

34. Ibid, "Twitter" (accessed October 3, 2012); and Chris Taylor, "Twitter Has 100 Million Active

Users," *Mashable.com*, http://mashable.com/2011/09/08/twitter-has-100-million-active-users (accessed February 12, 2012).

35. Claire Cain Miller, "Who's Driving Twitter's Popularity? Not Teens," *New York Times*, August 25, 2009, http://www.nytimes.com/2009/08/26/technology/internet/26twitter.html; and *Irvine, Yahoo! Finance* 2012.

36. Jay Yarrow, "There's Only One Place In The World Where Twitter Is Bigger Than Facebook," *Business Insider*, January 6, 2012, http://www.businessinsider.com/theres-only-one-place-in-the-world-where-twitter-is-bigger-than-facebook-2012-1#ixzz1mD3JBCK7.

37. "Hacker Exposes Private Twitter Documents," *Bits* (*New York Times* blog), July 15, 2009, http://bits.blogs.nytimes.com/2009/07/15/hacker-exposes-private-twitter-documents/?hpw.

38. "Twitter Study," Pear Analytics.

39. See http://www.youtube.com/watch?v=5YGc4zOqozo (accessed October 29, 2012) for Dave Carroll's complaint song, "United Breaks Guitars." As of October 2012, it had 12.5 million viewers.

40. Scott McCartney, "The Airlines' Squeaky Wheels Turn to Twitter," *Wall Street Journal*," October 28, 2010, D1, D5.

41. "Google + Gaga = Tweet Deal," *Wall Street Journal*, July 15, 2001, C10.

42. Matt Rhodes, "Brands 50% More Popular Than Celebrities in Social Media," FreshNetworks Blog, October 31, 2010, http://www.freshnetworks.com/blog/2010/10/brands-more-popular-than-celebrities-in-social-media.

43. Eun Sook Kwon and Yongjun Sung, "Follow Me! Global Marketers' Twitter Use," *Journal of Interactive Marketing*, 12, no.1), fall 2011, 4–16.

44. Jeff Bullas, "5 Cool Creative Facebook Marketing Campaigns," Jeff Bullas Blog, August 9, 2011, http://www.jeffbullas.com/2011/08/09/5-creative-facebook-marketing-campaigns.

45. Ibid.

46. Jeff Bullas, "5 Cool Creative Facebook Marketing Campaigns," August 9, 2011.

47. Ibid.

48. Victoria Taylor, "The Best-Ever Social Media Campaigns," *Forbes*, August 17, 2010, http://www.forbes.com/2010/08/17/facebook-old-spice-farmville-pepsi-forbes-viral-marketing-cmo-network-social-media_slide_11.html.

49. Victoria Taylor, "The Best-Ever Social Media Campaigns."

50. Ibid.

51. Ibid.

52. Jeff Bullas, "5 Cool Creative Facebook Marketing Campaigns," August 9, 2011.

53. This description is based on Nicholas Casey, "Online Popularity Contest Next in Barbie-Bratz Brawl," *Wall Street Journal*, July 23, 2007, B1.

54. Jeff Bullas, "5 Cool Creative Facebook Marketing Campaigns," August 9, 2011.

55. Teressa Iezzi, "Nike's "Write the Future" Wins Grand Prix at Cannes," Fast Company Co-Create Blog, 2010, http://www.fastcocreate.com/1679203/nike-write-the-future-wins-film-grand-prix-at-cannes (accessed February 13, 2012).

56. Ibid.

57. Ann-Christine Diaz, "Facebook 101: Is Your Brand Worth A Like?" *Advertising Age*, January 5, 2012, 6.

58. Victoria Taylor, "The Best-Ever Social Media Campaigns."

59. "Olla Condoms: Unexpected Babies," *Advertising Age*, December 5, 2011, 22.

60. Victoria Taylor, "The Best-Ever Social Media Campaigns"; and Sean Ryan, "This Side Up Campaign Competing for $250,000 Grant from Pepsi Refresh Project," *Richmond Biz Sense*, November 10, 2010, http://www.richmondbizsense.com/2010/11/10/this-side-up-campaign-competing-for-250000-grant-from-pepsi-refresh-project.

61. Paul Jamez, "25 Things That Are More Fun in the Philippines," *BuzzFeed*, January 2012, http://www.buzzfeed.com/pauljamez/25-things-that-are-more-fun-in-the-philippines-2kjh (accessed February 14, 2012); and "It's More Fun in the Philippines," *Advertising Age*, January 16, 2012, 23.

62. This description of P&G's social networking sites is based on Lisa Cornwell, "P&G Launches Two Social Networking Sites," *Marketing News*, February 1, 2007, 21.

63. Jeff Bullas, "5 Cool Creative Facebook Marketing Campaigns," August 9, 2011.

64. Diaz, January 30, 2012, 6.

65. Robert V. Kozinets, Kristine de Valck, Andrea C. Wojnicki, and Sarah J. S. Wilner, "Networked Narratives: Understanding Word-of-Mouth Marketing in Online Communities," *Journal of Marketing*, 74 (March 2010), 71–89.

66. Sampad Swain, "Branding 2.0 & Social Media," January 5, 2009, http://managementchords.blogspot.com; and Diaz, 6.

67. Diaz, 6.

68. Ibid.

69. Jonah Bloom, "Dedicated Social-Media Silos? That's the Last Thing We Need," *Advertising Age*, June 8, 2009, 11.

70. Ibid.

71. Andrew Lipsman, Graham Mudd, Mike Rich, and Sean Bruich, "The Power of Like," comScore, July 26, 2011, 4–5.

72. "How to Promote Your Business with Ads [on Facebook]" http://www.facebook.com/business/ads/www.facebook.com/ads/manage (accessed February 16, 2012).

73. John E. Lincoln, "How to Advertise on Twitter: Promoted Tweets, Promoted Trends and Promoted

Accounts," Search Engine Optimization (SEO), Inc. (blog), August 22, 2011, http://www.seoinc.com/seo-blog/how-to-advertise-on-twitter.

74. Irina Slutsky, "Ad Growing Pains for Twitter," *Advertising Age*, April 4, 2011, 1, 88.

75. Michael Learmonth, "#Winning on Twitter: The Top 10 Promoted Tweets," *Advertising Age*, May 9, 2011, 4.

76. Edmund Lee, "Social Networks Sink Online-Ad Pricing," *Advertising Age*, July 12, 2010, 1, 20.

77. Emily Steel and Jessica E. Vascellaro, "Facebook, MySpace Confront Privacy Loophole," *Wall Street Journal*, May 10, 2010, http://online.wsj.com/article/SB10001424052748704513104575256701215465596.html.

78. Geoffrey A. Fowler, "Facebook Fights Privacy Concerns," *Wall Street Journal*, August 21–22, 2010, B1, B6.

79. Emily Steel and Geoffrey Fowler, "Facebook in Privacy Breach," *Wall Street Journal*, October 18, 2010, A1, A2.

80. Geoffrey Fowler, "Facebook Friends Used in Ads," *Wall Street Journal*, January 26, 2011, B9.

81. "Facebook Settles FTC Charges That It Deceived Consumers by Failing to Keep Privacy Promises," Federal Trade Commission News, November 29, 2011, http://ftc.gov/opa/2011/11/privacysettlement.shtm.

82. Ibid.

83. Geoffrey A. Fowler, Shayndi Raice, Amir Efrati, "Spam Finds New Target," *Wall Street Journal*, January 4, 2012, B1, B2.

84. Rick Nauert, "New College Addiction: Social Media, Facebook, or Friends?" Psych Central, April 23, 2010, http://psychcentral.com/news/2010/04/23/new-college-addiction-social-media-facebook-or-friends/13108.html.

85. Bonnie Rochman, "Very Early Adopters. Should 9-Year-Olds Really Be on Facebook?" *Time*, June 27, 2011, 60.

86. Ibid.

87. Perri Klass, M.D., "Seeing Social Media More as Portal Than as Pitfall," *New York Times*, January 9, 2012, http://www.nytimes.com/2012/01/10/health/views/seeing-social-media-as-adolescent-portal-more-than-pitfall.html.

88. Ibid.

89. Graham Charlton, "Companies Continue to Struggle with Social Media Measurement: Report," E-Conultancy.com (blog), November 18, 2011, http://econsultancy.com/us/blog/8307-companies-continue-to-struggle-with-social-media-measurement-report.

90. Bob Barocci, "The Illusion of Precision: The Future of Media Measurement," *Advertising Age*, January 16, 2012, 12; and "Facebook IPO Will Be Watershed If Company Can Demystify Metrics," *Advertising Age*, January 2, 2012, 13.

91. Michael Brito, "Measuring Social Media," http://www.britopian.com (social media blog), September 1, 2010.

92. Ralph Paglia, "Do You Know Your Facebook Edge-Rank Score?" *Social Media Today*, June 2, 2012, http://socialmediatoday.com/ralphpaglia/302536/do-you-know-your-facebook-edgerank-score.

93. Ibid.

94. Michael Trusov, Anand V. Bodapati, and Randolph E. Bucklin, "Determining Influential Users in Internet Social Networks," *Journal of Marketing Research*, 47 (August 2010), 643–58.

95. Andrew Lipman, Graham Mudd, Mike Rich, and Sean Bruich, "The Power of Like," comScore, July 26, 2011, 4, 14.

96. This is attributed to Hal Thomas, content manager at BFG Communications and mentioned in a blog by Erica Swallow, "Measuring Social Media ROI: 3 Things to Consider," Mashable, November 15, 2011, http://mashable.com/2011/11/15/social-media-roi-measure.

CHAPTER 15

Direct Marketing and Other Media

During a Recession, ShamWow Marches On

During recent recessionary periods (e.g., 2007–2011), direct response TV advertising (DRTV) has flourished. Typically, DRTV takes two basic forms: *long form* (half hour or hour-long segments explaining a product in detail, known as an infomercial) or *short form* (30-, 60-, or 120-second commercials asking viewers for an immediate response). Such short-form DRTV commercials are best for products under $30 that are easily and quickly understood, often operating on a limited budget.

Although some have experienced problems over the years, many famous personalities have

been developed (or used in) DRTV sales pitches, such as Anthony Robbins, Billy Blanks (Tae Bo), Cher, Chuck Norris, George Forman (grills), fitness guru Jack LaLanne, inventor and salesperson Ron Popeil, Tony Little (Gazelle elliptical glider), Anthony Sullivan (Swivel Sweeper), Billy Mays (OxiClean), Dan Marino, Richard Simmons, Matthew Lesko (free government money), Susan Powter (Stop the Insanity), and Vince Offer (ShamWow). The short form 60- and 120-second DRTV spots often using such celebrities have been doing extremely well in recession periods.

Although traditional TV advertisers pull back significantly

Chapter Objectives

After reading this chapter, you should be able to:

1 Explain direct marketing and the reasons underlying its growth.

2 Describe the characteristics of direct-response advertising.

3 Discuss the distinctive features of direct-mail advertising.

4 Appreciate the role of database marketing, data mining, and lifetime-value analysis.

5 Discuss the advantages and disadvantages of outbound and inbound telemarketing.

6 Explain the value of other media options, including brand placements, yellow pages advertising, video game advertising (advergaming), and other "alternative" media.

during economic downturns, the short-form DRTV advertisers have been quick to replace them. For example, in the midst of a recent recession period in 2008, DRTV advertisers spent $172.1 million in advertising Rosetta Stone, $44.6 million in pitching ShamWow, $23.6 million for PedEgg, and $7.7 million in advertising the Swivel Sweeper.

Such DRTV ads can be cost effective, as the pitchmen usually work for royalties, the ads can cost only $50,000 in test markets (or $1 per 1,000 viewers on late-night cable), and TV production costs are as little as $5,000. Not every segment of DRTV is recession-proof, though, as larger-ticket items (e.g., Nautilus BowFlex) and continuity plans (e.g., NutriSystem) have seen sales declines. But for less expensive products, short-form DRTV has been a blessing for companies. For example, during the same recession years mentioned above, Snuggie sold 4 million units, while PedEgg had sales of 24 million units. Even in tight budgetary periods, a smart shifting of ad dollars (e.g., to short-form DRTV ads), coupled with creative appeals often found in direct response advertising, can help weather the economic storm.

Sources: "Direct Marketing," Wikipedia, http://en.wikipedia.org/wiki/Direct_marketing (accessed February 20, 2012); Timothy R. Hawthorne, "When and Why to Consider Infomercials," Hawthorne Direct, February 1998, http://freefastcharger.com/tim_hawthorne_articles/?post=when_why_to_consider_infomercials (accessed February 20, 2012); and Jack Neff, "Amid Cutbacks, ShamWow Marches On," *Advertising Age*, March 23, 2009, 1, 14.

Introduction

Some of our prior chapters emphasized the traditional advertising media (television, magazines, newspapers, and radio), as well as new media choices such as online and mobile advertising and social media. Historically, traditional ad media have been used to reach *mass audiences* and have been judged in terms of cost efficiencies. Advertising in mass media creates brand awareness, conveys product information, and builds or reinforces a brand's image. Marketers of brands such as Rosetta Stone, Nautilus, and many others (see *Marcom Insight*) are turning increasingly to direct advertising and database marketing to fine-tune their customer selection, better serve customer needs, and fulfill their own needs by achieving advertising results that can be measured by actual sales response. Mass-media advertising and direct marketing efforts are components of well-designed integrated marketing communications efforts.

This chapter covers the related topics of direct marketing and database marketing, which collectively include direct-response advertising, direct mail, telemarketing, and direct selling (discussed briefly). Then, other "alternative media" are introduced. An overview of direct marketing now is provided before turning to each specific topic.

Direct Marketing

At its onset, direct marketing was considered a specialty form of marketing and advertising appropriate only for products and services offered by book publishers, correspondence schools, and marketers of inexpensive gadgets and cheap clothing. Today, however, most *Fortune 500* firms are enthusiastic users of databases and direct-marketing initiatives, in addition to online and social media efforts. Indeed, direct marketing continues to a major contributor to the U.S. and global economy.

Precisely what is direct marketing? The Direct Marketing Association, a trade group whose members practice various forms of direct marketing, offers the following definition:

> Direct marketing is an *interactive system* of marketing which uses *one or more advertising media* to effect a *measurable response* and/or transaction *at any location.*[1]

Note the italicized features of this definition. First, direct marketing involves *interactive marketing* in that it entails personalized communications between marketer and prospect. Second, direct marketing involves *one or more media* (for instance, direct mail with telephone follow-up marketing; social media with e-mail). Third, direct marketing via media such as direct mail and online advertising allows for relatively greater *measurability of response* in comparison to indirect media such as television advertising. It is easier to measure because purchase responses to direct marketing: (1) typically are more immediate than responses to mass-media advertising and (2) can be tracked to specific customers in response to specific marketing efforts. Finally, direct marketing takes place at a *variety of locations*—online, by phone, at a kiosk, by mail, or by personal visits.

You now have a general understanding of direct marketing; however, the terminology of direct marketing might be confusing to some because the word *direct* is used in several different ways: direct marketing, direct-response advertising, direct mail, and direct selling. Figure 15.1 provides a framework to help clarify the distinctions among these various *direct* words. As shown by Figure 15.1, the total marketing process consists of indirect and direct marketing, with the latter being split into its various forms.

Indirect marketing includes the use of intermediaries in the channel of distribution; examples include distributors or dealers in business-to-business marketing and retailers in consumer-goods marketing. Indirect marketing is what

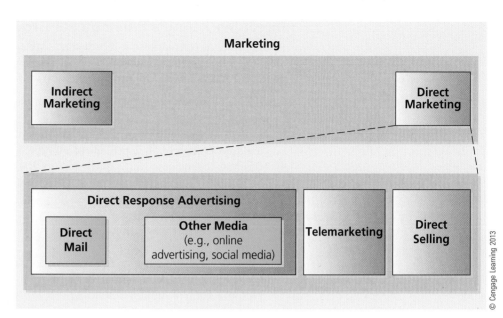

© Cengage Learning 2013

FIGURE **15.1** Distinctions among Various "Direct" Concepts

typically comes to mind when one thinks of marketing. However, there has been substantial growth in various forms of direct or interactive home shopping whereby consumers make catalog purchases, engage in online shopping, or order from home-shopping television networks. Many manufacturers now routinely bypass retailers and sell directly to consumers, referred to as *disintermediation.*[2] Dell Computer, for example, became the leading marketer of desktop computers (now second to Hewlett Packard) by exclusively selling its products directly to consumers without retailer intervention.

The marketer's purpose with *direct marketing* is to establish a relationship with a customer in order to initiate an immediate and measurable response. Direct marketing is accomplished using direct-response advertising (via direct mail and cataloging, online marketing, social media), telemarketing, and direct selling.

Direct response advertising involves the use of any of several media to transmit messages that encourage buyers to purchase directly from the advertiser. *Direct mail* is an important direct-advertising medium, but it is certainly not the only one. Direct-response advertising also uses television, online websites, social media, magazines, and other media with the intent of creating immediate action from customers. *Telemarketing,* another important form of direct marketing, includes making outbound calls from telephone salespersons and handling inbound orders, inquiries, and complaints from present or prospective customers. *Direct selling* is the use of salespeople (for example, Avon, Amway, Mary Kay, and Tupperware representatives) to sell directly to the final consumer. Direct selling often, but not always, uses *multi-level marketing* (i.e., salespeople are paid for selling and for sales made by people they recruit or sponsor) rather than *single-level marketing* (i.e., in which a salesperson is paid only for sales they make themself). Direct selling will be further discussed in Chapter 23.

Finally, direct marketing really relies on the practice of *database marketing.* Database marketing (DBM), which is used both by indirect and direct marketers, is a process in which companies collect information on consumers, analyze it to predict who will buy, and then develop tailored marketing messages to those consumers.[3] Typical databases include customers' past purchase details ("behavioral" data) and other types of relevant information (demographic, geographic, and psychographic data). The information also is used to establish long-term communication relationships with consumers.[4] Although database marketing and direct marketing are *not* equivalent, the increased sophistication of database marketing has been largely responsible for the growing use and effectiveness of direct marketing.

Direct Marketing's Phenomenal Growth

At one time, direct marketing represented a relatively small part of most companies' marketing efforts. However, direct marketing now is an enormous enterprise, as reflected in the following statistics:[5]

- U.S. sales revenues attributable to direct marketing reached almost $1.8 trillion in 2010.
- In 2010, marketers spent $153.3 billion on direct marketing, accounting for approximately 54.2 percent of all ad expenditures in the United States.
- Business-to-business (B2B) marketers in 2010 produced sales of $332.4 billion from telephone marketing. Direct marketing expenditures for B2B marketers in 2010 totaled $74.6 billion, or about 49 percent of all direct-marketing expenditures.
- For 2010, direct marketing accounted for 8.3 percent of the U.S. gross domestic product.
- There are 1.4 million direct marketing employees in the United States, with direct-marketing sales supporting another 8.4 million jobs. In total, this accounts for 9.8 million U.S. jobs.

Lester Wunderman, the famous direct-marketing practitioner who coined the expression "direct marketing," had this to say: "Direct marketing, today, is scientific, accountable, versatile, multi-dimensional and growing faster than any other form of advertising."[6]

A variety of factors help to explain direct marketing's growth. Fundamental *societal changes* (e.g., intensified time pressures, increased use of smartphones and credit cards) have created an opportunity for the convenience of direct-marketed products and services. Direct marketing provides shoppers with an easy, convenient, and relatively hassle-free way to buy.

Major advances in *technology and database management* have made it possible for companies to maintain large databases containing millions of prospects and customers. For example, Netflix, the movie-rental business, has a database of over 35 million households for both streaming- and DVD-rentals, and Kraft General Foods has a list of more than 30 million users of its products.

In addition to the growth of consumer-oriented direct marketing, applications of direct marketing by business-to-business marketers also have experienced tremendous expansion. B2B expenditures on direct marketing (predominantly telephone sales and direct mail) are estimated to grow by 4.9 percent from 2009 to 2014, for total expenditures of $92.1 billion in 2014.[7] Table 15.1 displays all of the major categories of direct marketing with their ad expenditures and sales estimated for 2014 by the Direct Marketing Association, as well as their percentage growth calculated for 2009–2014.

A major reason for this trend is the rising cost of personal sales calls, which on average can be $500 per call.[8] As a result, telemarketing and direct mail have actually replaced the sales force in some companies, whereas in others, direct marketing is used to supplement the sales force's efforts by building goodwill, generating leads, and opening doors for salespeople. Online selling, telemarketing, and other forms of direct marketing provide attractive options for firms who either prefer to avoid the huge expense of a traveling sales force or desire to supplement sales-force effort with supportive marketing communications to expand markets.

Direct-Response Advertising

As shown in Figure 15.1, direct-response advertising includes direct mail and other media (e.g., online advertising, social media). As found in Table 15.1, direct mail is by far the dominant direct-response advertising medium, but some direct-response advertising is placed in conventional mass media (newspapers,

TABLE 15.1	Ad Expenditure and Sales Estimates for Direct-Marketing Categories			
	Ad Expenditures 2014 (est.) (billions)	Ad Expenditure Yearly Growth 2009–2014 (%)	Sales 2014 (est.) (billions)	Sales Yearly Growth 2009–2014 (%)
Telephone Marketing	41.5	1.00	343.5	0.50
Direct Mail (Non-Catalog)	34.5	3.30	534.5	3.70
Direct Response TV	26.9	6.80	174.4	6.30
Direct Mail (Catalog)	18.6	4.30	135.1	4.10
Internet Search	18.5	10.60	404.7	10.70
Internet Display	10.9	8.70	209.0	8.30
Direct Response Magazine	7.7	3.00	77.8	2.60
Direct Response Newspaper	7.6	−3.00	90.2	−3.90
Internet Other	6.7	13.20	114.2	13.90
Direct Response Radio	4.1	4.40	33.5	3.90
Other	3.4	6.80	23.1	6.70
Social Networking	2.3	14.70	29.8	15.90
Commercial E-mail	1.1	13.10	40.5	9.20
Insert Media	1.1	5.30	12.2	5.10
Mobile	0.8	29.10	10.4	37.50
Total	$185.7	4.50%	$2232.9	5.10%

Source: Data from *DMA 2010 Statistical Fact Book*, pp. 2–5. New York, NY: Direct Marketing Association.

magazines, and television—e.g., infomercials; see *Marcom Insight*). In general, three distinct features characterize direct-response advertising: (1) it makes a *definite offer*; (2) it contains *all the information necessary for the prospect to make a decision*; and (3) it includes a *response device* (coupon, phone number, web link, or some combination) to facilitate immediate action.[9]

An illustration of direct-response advertising can be found in the advertisement in Figure 15.2 for Nutrisystem's Success Plan. This ad satisfies the requirements of a direct-response advertisement in its appeal (primarily) to women who read Sunday newspaper inserts. For example, the ad provides prospective customers with interesting background information, a celebrity testimonial (Marie Osmond), and solid reasons to consider purchasing this weight-loss menu plan. The ad also offers readers a convenient mechanism to finalize their purchase in the form of a toll-free 888 number. In addition, a special 40 percent discount offer and a free gift (protein shake each day) help motivate purchasers to try the Nutrisystem weight-loss menus. All of these characteristics make it easy for consumers to order, essential for direct marketing.

In general, the direct advertiser's objective is to select a medium (or multiple media) that provides maximum ability to segment the market at a reasonable cost. Effective direct-response media selection demands that the marketer clearly define a target market. Consider, for example, the direct-response ad for DIRECTV's satellite service (see Figure 15.3). One target market for the DIRECTV satellite service consists of urban households, interested in sports programming, and frustrated with local cable service ("Don't Settle for Cable"). Advertisements for this product are placed in Sunday newspaper inserts in major markets throughout the United States, in addition to other media outlets.

FIGURE **15.2** Illustration of Direct Response Advertising

Direct Mail

Chapter 13 discussed online advertising in its various forms, including e-mail and mobile advertising. This section of the chapter includes detailed coverage of direct-mail advertising that is *not* online (i.e., it occurs through postal services). These advertisements take many forms, including letters, postcards, programs, calendars, folders, online and offline catalogs, DVDs, order blanks, price lists, and menus.

At least four factors account for the widespread use of direct mail by B2B as well as B2C marketers. First, rising costs of television advertising and increasing audience fragmentation have led many advertisers to reduce investments in the television medium. Second, direct mail enables unparalleled targeting of messages to desired prospects. Why? Because, according to one expert, it is "a lot better to talk to 20,000 prospects than 2 million suspects."[10] Third, increased emphasis on measurable advertising results has encouraged advertisers to use that medium—namely, direct mail—that most clearly identifies how many prospects purchased the advertised product. Fourth, many consumers have

FIGURE 15.3 Another Illustration of Direct Response Advertising

favorable attitudes toward mail advertisements and would be disappointed if they could not get direct-mail offers and catalogs.

Illustrations of Successful Direct-Mail Campaigns

Three examples of highly successful direct-mail campaigns are described. One involves a B2B product, one a consumer-packaged good, and the third a consumer durable. (For a fourth illustration, see the *Global Focus* insert.)

The Caterpillar 414E Industrial Loader Campaign

Caterpillar (or Cat for short) manufacturers and sells an extensive line of heavy equipment products. Cat built the 414E industrial loader to help compete with John Deere in the Southwest United States. They needed a marcom program that would make a strong impression on its dealers. The solution was to create

GLOBAL FOCUS

How a Major Production Mistake Turned into a Huge Direct-Mailing Success

The "major production mistake" that the title above refers to involves the Glenmorangie Distillery, which is located in the Highlands of Scotland. One of Glenmorangie's brands is Ardbeg—a single malt whisky distilled in Islay, which is a small island west of the Scottish mainland. Due to a mistake committed by a production employee who pulled the wrong lever, two of Glenmorangie's brands—Ardbeg and Glen Moray—were accidentally blended together—resulting in an inferior-blended Scotch whisky from the mixture of two single malt brands. The initial course of action facing Glenmorangie's executives was simply to suffer a huge economic loss and destroy the 15,000 bottles of what seemed to be a useless product. Could anything else be done?

Rather than destroy 15,000 bottles, creative thinking led to the decision to market the "production mistake" as a unique new brand. The new brand of blended whisky, which actually was quite good, was named Serendipity—a name (based on well-known legend) that means "good luck in making unexpected and fortunate discoveries."[11]

A direct-mail campaign (termed "Pity to Waste It") was developed to market Serendipity. A mailer was distributed to a list of 30,000 loyal Ardbeg drinkers. A booklet described Glenmorangie's production mistake and asked recipients to sign an "official pardon," which actually was an order form for Serendipity. The campaign was hugely successful. The mailing generated a 23 percent response rate and brought in sales of nearly $1 million at a cost of only $100,000. This was a one-time mistake that generated a handsome economic gain for the Glenmorangie Company rather than a huge loss, which attests to the power of creativity and the effective use of direct mail.

Source: Adapted from Michael Raveane, "How the STORY Agency Turned a Major Mistake into a Marketing Masterpiece," *Deliver Magazine*, December 2007, 25–27.

a special event for the new 414E loader and then to promote that event via a direct-mail campaign just prior to a NASCAR race. The objective was to have Cat dealers—the 414E's target market—construct a racecourse using the new 414E machine, allowing dealers to learn firsthand the versatility of this new product. Upon construction, dealers were invited to race small vehicles (called dune buggies) on the newly constructed racecourse.

Direct-mail pieces (as part of the "Eat My Dirt" campaign) were distributed to 1,700 dealers, who were informed that they would have an opportunity to use the new 414E to build a racecourse and then to race dune buggies over it. The 414E campaign drew a hugely successful 18 percent response compared to the normal range of 1 to 3 percent for direct-mail pieces. As a result, Caterpillar sold 28 of the 414E machines, some priced as high as $75,000; the Eat My Dust promotion cost less than $100,000. In other words, selling just two machines offset the total cost of the direct-mail campaign and the racecourse event, with the remaining sales of 26 machines contributing to Caterpillar's bottom line. By any standard, this was a hugely successful campaign.[12]

The Stacy's Pita Chip Campaign

The Boston-based Stacy's Pita Chip Company was a successful operation, but its business was largely limited to the New England region. In an effort to expand its distribution nationwide, Stacy's needed a successful yet affordable marcom program. Budget limitations made it impossible for Stacy's to use mass media such as TV advertising, so a direct-mail campaign was undertaken instead. The clever campaign they developed focused on the company's name, Stacy's. With the aid of outside companies that specialize in direct marketing, Stacy's was able to identify the names and addresses of 133,000 people named Stacy located throughout the United States.

Each of the 133,000 Stacys was mailed a cardboard carton with gold lettering reading: "To Stacy, From Stacy." Product samples of five pita chip products were enclosed (e.g., Stacy's cinnamon sugar, Stacy's parmesan garlic) along with a $1 coupon and a postcard that enabled recipients to request free samples for a designated friend. The mailing also encouraged recipients to deliver a form letter to their local grocery store asking deli managers to stock Stacy's products. As a result, Stacy's Chief Marketing Officer (CMO) indicated that a large amount of publicity was generated at an expense much less than what a single 30-second TV commercial would have cost the company.[13]

The Saab 9-5 Campaign

The Saab 9-5 represented Saab's first entry in the luxury category and was designed to compete against well-known high-equity brands, including Mercedes, BMW, Volvo, Lexus, and Infiniti. A total of 200,000 consumers, including 65,000 current Saab owners and 135,000 prospects, were targeted via multiple direct mailings with the objective of encouraging them to test-drive the 9-5. Mailings provided prospects with brand details and made an appealing offer for them to test-drive the 9-5. Names of the most qualified prospects were then fed to dealers for follow-up.

Saab's advertising agency designed four mailings: (1) an initial mailing announced the new Saab 9-5, provided a photo of the car, and requested recipients to complete a survey of their automobile purchase interests and needs; (2) a subsequent qualification mailing provided respondents to the first mailing with product information addressing their specific purchase interests (performance, safety, versatility, etc.) and offered a test-drive kit as an incentive for returning an additional survey; (3) a third mailing included a special issue from *Road & Track* magazine that was devoted to the Saab 9-5's product development process; and (4) a final test-drive kit mailing extended an offer for recipients to test-drive the 9-5 for three hours and also provided an opportunity for prospects to win an all-expenses-paid European driving adventure (through Germany, Italy, and Sweden) as incentive for test-driving the 9-5.

An outbound telemarketing campaign followed the direct mailings. Telephone calls were made to all people who responded to the initial mailings as well as to all prospects who had auto leases or loans that were expiring. These callings reinforced the European test-drive offer and set up times for local dealers to call back to schedule test-drives. The direct marketing effort for the 9-5 was fabulously successful. Of the 200,000 initial prospects contacted by the introductory mailing, 16,000 indicated interest in test-driving the 9-5 (an 8 percent response rate), and more than 2,200 test-drives were scheduled.[14]

Direct Mail's Distinctive Features

Direct-mail expenditures are quite large. In the United States alone, more than $45 billion is annually invested direct mailing.[15] These expenditures include B2B as well as B2C direct mailings. Direct mail offers five distinctive features as compared to mass forms of advertising: targetability, measurability, accountability, flexibility, and efficiency:

- *Targetability.* Direct mail is capable of targeting a precisely defined group of people. For example, Saab's advertising agency selected just 200,000 current Saab owners and prospects.
- *Measurability.* It is possible with direct mail to determine exactly how effective the advertising effort was because the marketer knows how many mailings were sent and how many people responded. This enables ready calculations of cost per inquiry and cost per order. As previously noted, more than 2,200 consumers signed up for test-drives of the Saab 9-5. Proprietary dealer sales data reveal how many of the initial 200,000 mailings resulted in purchases.
- *Accountability.* Direct mail simplifies accountability because results can be readily demonstrated (as in the case of the Saab 9-5), and brand managers can justify budget allocations to direct mail.
- *Flexibility.* Effective direct mail can be produced relatively quickly (compared with a TV commercial), so it is possible for a company to launch a direct-mail campaign that meets changing circumstances (e.g., with high inventory). Direct mail also offers the advantage of testing communications ideas on a small-scale basis quickly and out of the view of competitors. Direct mail also is flexible in the sense that it has no constraints in terms of form, color, or size (other than those imposed by cost and practical considerations).
- *Efficiency.* Direct mail makes it possible to direct communications efforts just to a highly targeted group, such as the 200,000 consumers who received mailings for the Saab 9-5. The cost-efficiency resulting from such targeting is considerable compared with mass-advertising efforts.

An alleged disadvantage of direct mail is its expense. On a cost-per-thousand (CPM) basis, direct mail typically is more expensive than other media. For example, the CPM for a particular mailing may be as high as $200 to $400, whereas a magazine's CPM might be as low as $4. However, compared with other media, direct mail is much less wasteful and will usually produce the highest percentage of responses. Thus, on a *cost-per-order basis*, direct mail is often a better bargain.

Perhaps the major problem with direct mail is that many people consider it excessively intrusive and invasive of privacy. Consumers are accustomed to receiving massive quantities of mail and so have been "trained" to accept the voluminous amount of direct mail received. (The average consumer receives 24.7 pieces of direct mail per week.[16]) Often, it is not the amount of mail that concerns most people, but the fact that virtually any business or other organization can readily obtain their names and addresses.

Who Uses Direct Mail and What Functions Does It Accomplish?

All types of marketers use direct mail as a strategically important advertising medium. Packaged goods companies such as Nestlé Purina, Kraft Foods, Gerber Products, Sara Lee, Quaker Oats, and Procter & Gamble are some of the primary users of direct mail. Direct mailing by firms such as these is especially valuable for introducing new brands and distributing product samples. In addition, financial firms, local supermarkets, publishers, and mail-order firms all make extensive use of direct mail.

Research and practical experience indicate that direct-mail campaigns can achieve the following functions:[17] (1) increase sales and usage from current customers; (2) sell products and services to new customers; (3) build traffic at a specific retailer or website; (4) stimulate product trial with promotional offers and incentives; (5) generate leads for a sales force; (6) deliver product-relevant information and news; (7) gather customer information that can be used in building a database; and (8) communicate with individuals in a relatively private manner and thereby minimize the likelihood of competitive detection.

The Special Case of Catalogs and Audiovisual Media

Catalogs

Cataloging is a huge enterprise, with more than 13.5 billion catalogs distributed annually in the United States.[18] Of the more than 12,500 catalog listings in the United States, 84 percent have an online version.[19] Certainly, cataloging is highly effective, as revealed by the findings from one study indicating that (1) more than two-thirds of catalog recipients visit the catalog company's website, (2) sales to catalog recipients are over 150 percent greater on average compared to consumers not receiving a catalog, and (3) catalog recipients buy more items on average and spend more money than do non-recipients.[20]

From the marketer's perspective, catalog selling provides an efficient and effective way to reach prime prospects. From the consumer's perspective, shopping by catalog offers several advantages: (1) catalog shopping saves time because people do not have to find parking spaces and deal with in-store crowds; (2) catalog buying appeals to consumers who are fearful of shopping due to concerns about crime; (3) catalogs allow people the convenience of making purchase decisions at their leisure and away from the pressure of a retail store; (4) the availability of toll-free (800, 855, 866, 877, and 888) numbers and online websites, credit-card purchasing, and liberal return policies make it easy for people to order from catalogs; (5) consumers are confident purchasing from catalogs because merchandise quality and prices often are comparable, or even superior, to what is available in stores; and (6) guarantees are attractive. Illustrative of this last point, consider the policy of L.L. Bean, the famous retailer from Maine:

All of our products are guaranteed to give 100 percent satisfaction in every way. Return anything purchased from us at any time if it proves otherwise. We will replace it, refund your purchase price or credit your credit card, as you wish. We do not want you to have anything from L.L. Bean that is not completely satisfactory.

Although catalog marketing is pervasive, the sales growth rate had subsided (from 2004 to 2009, there was a -2.6 percent loss) for several reasons: First, industry observers note that the novelty of catalog scanning had worn off for many consumers. Second, as typically is the case when a product or service reaches maturity, the costs of catalog marketing had increased dramatically. A primary reason is that firms have incurred the expenses of developing more attractive catalogs and compiling better mailing lists in an effort to outperform their competitors. Costs have been further strained by third-class postal rate increases in recent years and sharp increases in paper prices. Yet, as noted in Table 15.1, sales are expected to grow 4.1 percent from 2009 to 2014, primarily due to online versions of catalogs.[21]

Audiovisual Advertising

This form of direct advertising involves the use of videotapes, CDs, or DVDs to present advertising messages. Video advertising is both more effective and less expensive than print advertising delivered via direct mail, and consumers are less likely to throw away an unsolicited audiovisual message than they are a brochure or other printed material. Moreover, such an approach serves as an attractive alternative to promoted Web links (e.g., YouTube), as such material can be more permanent and of better quality than many Web links to advertising.

Consider the use of audiovisual advertising by a tourist destination. When a prospective tourist requests information, a disc could be mailed out that would contain the sights (video and pictures) and sounds (music, wildlife, ocean waves, etc.) of the area and would present this information in a newsworthy and entertaining fashion. CDs and DVDs also have considerable potential in the area of B2B marketing. Audiovisual presentations of new products can be mailed to prospective customers, who are encouraged to call for additional information or to arrange a personal sales visit.

The Use of Databases

Successful direct mailing requires available computer databases and the *address-ability* inherent in these databases. That is, databases enable contacts with present or prospective customers who can be accessed by companies whose databases contain direct mail and e-mail addresses along with other demographic information. Thus, direct advertising tries to create individual relationships with each prospective customer. The following analogy aptly pits direct mail (also referred to as "addressable media") against broadcast media: "Broadcast media send communications; addressable media send and receive. Broadcasting targets its audience much as a battleship shells a distant island into submission; addressable media initiate conversations."[22]

An up-to-date database provides firms with a number of assets, including the ability (1) to direct advertising efforts to those individuals who represent the best prospects for a company's products or services, (2) to offer varied messages to different groups of customers, (3) to create long-term relationships with customers, (4) to enhance advertising productivity, and (5) to calculate the lifetime value of a customer or prospect. Due to the importance of customer lifetime value, the following section focuses on this fifth database asset.

Lifetime-Value Analysis

A key feature of database marketing is the need to consider each address contained in a database from a lifetime-value perspective. That is, each present or prospective customer is viewed as not just an address but also as a *long-term asset*. Customer lifetime value is the *net present value* (NPV) of the profit that a company stands to realize on the average new customer during a given number of years. This concept is best illustrated using the data in Table 15.2.

Assume that a small specialty retailer has a database of 1,000 customers (see the intersection of row A and Year 1 column in Table 15.2). The following analysis

TABLE 15.2	Customer Lifetime-Value Analysis				
	Year 1	**Year 2**	**Year 3**	**Year 4**	**Year 5**
Revenue					
A Customers	1,000	400	180	90	50
B Retention rate	40%	45%	50%	55%	60%
C Average yearly sales	$150	$150	$150	$150	$150
D Total revenue	$150,000	$60,000	$27,000	$13,500	$7,500
Costs					
E Cost percentage	50%	50%	50%	50%	50%
F Total costs	$75,000	$30,000	$13,500	$6,750	$3,750
Profits					
G Gross profit	$75,000	$30,000	$13,500	$6,750	$3,750
H Discount rate	1	1.2	1.44	1.73	2.07
I NPV profit	$75,000	$25,000	$9,375	$3,902	$1,812
J Cumulative NPV profit	$75,000	$100,000	$109,375	$113,277	$115,088
K Lifetime value per customer	$75.00	$100.00	$109.38	$113.28	$115.09

© Cengage Learning

illustrates how the average customer's NPV can be calculated over a time frame of five years.[23] First, the *retention rate* (see row B) indicates the likelihood that people will remain customers of this particular retailer over the course of five years. It is assumed that 40 percent of 1,000 customers in Year 1 will continue to be customers in Year 2 (i.e., 400 customers; see intersection of row A, Year 2 column); 45 percent of these 400 customers, or 180 customers, will remain into Year 3; 50 percent will remain in Year 4; and 55 percent will remain in Year 5.

Row C indicates that the *average yearly sales* in years 1 through 5 are constant at $150. That is, customers on average spend $150 at this particular retail establishment. Thus, the *total revenue*, row D, in each of the five years is simply the product of rows A and C. For example, the 1,000 customers in Year 1 who spend on average $150 produce $150,000 of total revenue; the 400 customers in Year 2 generate $60,000 in total revenue; and so on.

Row E reflects the cost of selling merchandise to the store's customers. For simplification it is assumed that the cost is 50 percent of revenue. *Total costs* in each year, row F, are thus calculated by multiplying the values in rows D and E. *Gross profit*, row G, is calculated by subtracting total costs (row F) from total revenue (row D).

The *discount rate*, row H, is a critical component of NPV analysis and requires some discussion. The discount rate reflects the idea that money received in future years is not equivalent in value to money received today. This is because money received today, say $100, can be immediately invested and begin earning interest. So, $100 received in the future, say in three years, is worth less than the same amount received today. Some adjustment is needed to equate the value of money received at different times. This adjustment is called the *discount rate* and can be expressed as:

$$D = (1 + i)^n$$

where D is the discount rate, i is the interest rate, and n is the number of years before the money will be received. The discount rate given in row H of Table 15.2

assumes an interest rate of 20 percent. Thus, the discount rate in Year 3 is 1.44 because the retailer will have to wait two years (from Year 1) to receive the profit that will be earned in Year 3. That is:

$$(1 + 0.2)^2 = 1.44$$

The *NPV profit*, row I, is determined by taking the reciprocal of the discount rate (i.e., $1 \div D$) and multiplying the gross profit, row G, by that reciprocal. For example, in Year 3, the reciprocal of 1.44 is 0.694, which implies that the present value of $1 received two years later is only about $0.69 at an interest rate of 20 percent. Thus, the NPV of the $13,500 gross profit to be earned in Year 3 is $9,375. (You should perform the calculation for years 4 and 5 to ensure that you understand the derivation of NPV. Recall that the reciprocal of a particular value, such as 1.44, is calculated by dividing that value into 1.)

The *cumulative NPV* profit, row J, simply sums the NPV profits across the years. This summation reveals that the cumulative NPV profit to our hypothetical retailer, who had 1,000 customers in Year 1, of whom 50 remain after five years, is $115,088. Finally, row K, the *lifetime value per customer*, shows the average worth of each of the 1,000 people who were customers of our hypothetical retailer in Year 1. The average lifetime value of each of these customers, expressed as NPV over a five-year period, is thus $115.09.

Based on our example, the key issue is this: What can a marketer do to enhance the average customer's lifetime value? There are five ways to augment lifetime value:[24]

1. Increase the *retention rate*. The more customers a firm has and the longer they are retained, the greater the lifetime value. It therefore makes sense for marketers and advertisers to focus on retention rather than just acquisition. Database marketing is ideally suited for this purpose because it enables regular communication with customers (via blogs, frequency programs, social media, etc.) to build relationships, important in customer relationship management (CRM) practices today.
2. Increase the *referral rate*. Positive relations created with existing customers can influence others to become customers through positive word of mouth.
3. Enhance the *average purchase volume per customer*. Existing customers can be encouraged to purchase more of a brand. Product satisfaction and capable management of customer relations are means to building the base of loyal customers.
4. Cut *direct costs*. By altering the channel of distribution via direct marketing efforts, a firm may be able to cut costs and hence increase profit margins.
5. Reduce *marketing communications costs*. Effective database marketing can lead to meaningful reductions in marcom expenses because direct advertising often is more productive than mass-media advertising.

Types of Mailing Lists

Success with direct mail depends on the quality of mailing lists contained in a company's database. There are two broad categories of lists: internal (house lists) and external (public lists, including house lists of other companies and complied lists). House lists are based on a company's own internal list of present or prospective customers. As noted previously, Netflix has a list of over 35 million households in its database. Because house lists contain the names of customers who previously responded to a company's offering, they are generally more valuable than external lists.

The external list comes in two forms. The first, house lists of other companies, is bought by a firm to promote its own products. These lists are effective because they comprise the names of people who have responded to another related company's direct-response offer. The greater the similarity of the products offered by both the buyer and the seller of the list, the greater the likelihood that the purchased list will be effective.

Compiled lists, the second type of external list, include lists purchased from another company (a "compiler") that specializes in list compilation. Examples of list compilers are infoUSA, Dun & Bradstreet (ZapData), Experian, and Acxiom. They combine raw data from sources, such as local yellow page and white page directories, public government state data, association data, and other publishing to make a comprehensive marketing list. List brokers can provide the right match between the company's needs and the thousands of lists on the market.

Compiled lists are not as desirable as house lists, however, for two important reasons. The first is because they do not contain information about the willingness of a person to purchase the specific item by mail. Second, the individuals or companies included on the list may have had to pay a fee to belong to an association representing the primary source for some lists. Therefore, it is very important to ask compilers about exactly how the lists provided were compiled in the first place.

The Practice of Data Mining

Databases can be massive in size with millions of addresses and dozens of variables for each database entrant. With the availability of specialized software, companies can mine their databases for the purpose of learning more about customers' buying behavior. The goal of data mining is to discover hidden facts contained in databases. Sophisticated data miners look for revealing relations among the variables contained in a database for purposes of using these relationships to better target prospective customers, develop cooperative marketing relations with other companies, and otherwise better understand who buys what and when, how often, and along with what other products and brands they make their purchases.

Consider, for example, a credit card company that mines its huge database and learns that its most frequent and largest-purchase users are disproportionately more likely than the average credit card user to vacation in exotic locations. The company could use this information to design a promotional offering that has an exotic vacation site as the grand prize. As another example, suppose a furniture chain mining its database learns that families with two or more children rarely make major furniture purchases within two years of buying a new automobile. Armed with this information, the chain could acquire automobile purchase lists and then direct advertisements to households that have not purchased a new automobile for two or more years.

Another use of databases is to segregate a company's customer list by the *recency* (R) of a customer's purchase, the *frequency* (F) of purchases, and the *monetary value* (M) of each purchase. Companies typically assign point values to accounts based on these classifications. Each company has its own customized procedure for point assignment (i.e., its own *R-F-M formula*), but in every case more points are assigned to more recent, more frequent, and more expensive purchases. The R-F-M system offers tremendous opportunities for database mining and mail targeting. For example, a company might choose to send out free catalogs (or a link to online catalogs) only to accounts whose point totals exceed a certain amount.

Outbound and Inbound Telemarketing

As noted in Table 15.1, telephone marketing is a dominant form of direct advertising expenditures with an estimated $41.5 billion to be spent by 2014, and is third in direct marketing sales estimated to be $344 billion in 2014.[25]

Telemarketing entails both outbound telephone usage to sell products over the phone or perform other marketing functions (e.g. arranging test drives for the Saab 9-5) and inbound telephone marketing efforts that are directed at taking orders and servicing customers.

Outbound Telemarketing

Many companies use the telephone to support or even replace their conventional sales forces. Telemarketing uses outbound calls from salespeople for purposes of: (1) opening new accounts; (2) qualifying advertising leads; and (3) servicing existing business, including reorders and customer service. Outbound telemarketing is integrated with advertising, direct mail, websites, catalog sales, and face-to-face selling.

Who Should Use Outbound Telemarketing?

Telemarketing is not appropriate for all sales organizations. The following eight factors should be considered when evaluating the suitability of introducing a telephone sales force.[26]

1. An initial consideration is an evaluation of the *importance of face-to-face contact*. The more essential it is, the less appropriate is outbound telemarketing.
2. A second consideration is *geographical concentration*. Telephone selling may represent an attractive alternative to in-person selling if customers are highly dispersed. If, however, customers are heavily concentrated (such as apparel makers in Manhattan or automobile manufacturers in Detroit), minimal travel time is required and personal selling is probably preferable.
3. *Economic considerations* involving average order size and total potential should be estimated to determine the cost effectiveness of in-person sales. In cases of small and marginal accounts, customers may be served more economically by telephone.
4. A fourth area for evaluation is *customer decision criteria*. Telephone sales may be sufficient if price, delivery, and other quantitative criteria are paramount, but in-person sales may be essential in instances where product quality, dealer reputation, and service are uppermost in importance.
5. A fifth factor is the *number and type of decision makers* typically involved in purchasing a company's product. Face-to-face contact is typically necessary when several decision makers are involved, using different buying criteria—e.g., when an industrial engineer, a purchasing agent, and a financial representative all contribute to a purchase decision.
6. Another consideration is the *nature of the purchase*. Routine purchases (such as office supplies) can be handled easily by phone, whereas purchases of more complex products will likely require face-to-face interactions.
7. The *status of the major decision maker* is a seventh consideration. The telephone is acceptable for buyers, purchase agents, and engineers but probably not for owners, presidents, and vice presidents.
8. A final consideration is an evaluation of the *specific selling tasks* that telemarketing is or is not capable of performing. For example, telephone representatives may be particularly effective for prospecting and postsale follow-ups, whereas in-person sales effort is needed for the intervening sales task—preapproach, approach, presentation, objection handling, and closing.

Inbound Telemarketing
Toll-Free (800, 855, 866, 877, 888 Numbers)

Toll-free numbers ("800 numbers") are virtually everywhere. Every time you open a magazine, turn on the television, or pick up a newspaper, you read or

FIGURE 15.4 Prominent Display of a Toll-Free Number

hear, "Call 1-800-XXX-XXXX." An 800-number telecommunication program uses an incoming WATS (wide area telecommunication service) telephone system to encourage potential customers to request product or service information, place direct orders, express complaints or grievances, request coupons or other sales-promotion materials, and inquire about the nearest dealers or outlets. For example, the consumer receives a direct mailing from Omaha Steaks and, attracted by an enticing offer ("Save $128") and some free gifts, places an order via the 800 number that is prominently displayed at the bottom of the ad (see Figure 15.4).

Customer-service representatives who receive 800 calls can provide immediate responses to requests for merchandise and product information and can handle complaints. Additionally, representatives can record callers' names and addresses to initiate immediate follow-ups by sending promotional materials. Also, the effectiveness of an advertising campaign can be measured quickly. The advent of sophisticated call-center technology (called ACDs for automatic call distributor) has substantially facilitated and improved incoming telephone service. Interestingly, with 400,000 agents, the Philippines has now surpassed India as the major call center destination for this estimated $150 billion global industry.[27]

Pay-Per-Call (900 Numbers)

The Pay-Per-Call, or 900 number, service was introduced by AT&T to permit callers, who pay a fee, to phone a central number and register an opinion on a particular issue. The 900 service is the only national communication medium that can accept simultaneous calls by large numbers of people at a flat rate. The first major use of the Dial-It service was during the Carter-Reagan presidential debate in 1980, when over 700,000 people spent 50 cents each to call a 900 number and register their opinions about who won the debate. Since then, use of 900-number telemedia activity has decreased substantially, primarily due to toll-free number expansion and online services. Also, many unethical and unscrupulous efforts have dominated 900-number usage; leading to oversight (e.g., prominent disclosures) by the Federal Trade Commission.

Major Telemarketing Regulation

The Federal Trade Commission in 1995 introduced the Telemarketing Sales Rule (TSR) to regulate against untoward telemarketing practices. The key provisions of

TABLE 15.3	Key Provisions of the Telemarketing Sales Rule

Telemarketers must:

- Initially identify themselves, their business, and the goods or services they are selling to the customer.

- Tell customers the odds of winning any prizes while explaining that no purchase or payment is necessary to win them.

- Clearly and completely explain their offerings and their price(s), payment terms, and the customer's financial commitment by placing a telephone order.

- Obtain and tape record customer's express oral authorization for a sale before checking account debiting.

- Maintain complete employment records; all advertising, marketing, and promotional materials (including telemarketing scripts); and for contests, lists of the names and addresses of all prize winners and descriptions of those prizes valued at $25 or more.

- Identify, maintain lists of, and comply with rules regarding customers who request that they not be contacted again by telemarketers.

Telemarketers must not:

- Assist or facilitate deceptive or abusive telemarketing acts.

- Launder credit cards (i.e., illegally use credit information obtained for one sale toward another unauthorized transaction).

- Use threats, intimidation, or profane or obscene language toward customers.

- Call customers before 8 A.M. or after 9 P.M. (local time zones).

© Cengage Learning 2013

the rule are listed in Table 15.3. In addition, in 2003, the Federal Trade Commission (with the Federal Communications Commission) initiated the National Do Not Call Registry, based on a Congressional mandate (and revision later in 2007), allowing consumers to register (only once) to maintain their phone numbers on a do-not-call list. As of 2011, approximately 210 million U.S. households were on this list.[28] Cell phone numbers need not be included on the registry to avoid unsolicited calls. FCC regulations prohibit telemarketers from calling a cellular phone number with an automatic dialer.

Placing one's number on the National Do Not Call Registry will stop most, but not all, unsolicited calls. However, there are exceptions, including if one has a business line, calls from political organizations, non-profit organizations, companies for which one has an existing business relationship (up to 18 months after his or her last purchase, payment, or delivery), and bill collection agencies (during reasonable hours).[29] Yet, a person can specifically ask the company not to call again.

Other Media

Table 15.4 lists "other" advertising media covered in this chapter and usually are used in a supplementary capacity to support IMC programs that place primary emphasis on advertising. Yet, there are times when these "other" media may serve in a stand-alone capacity. For example, some brands—especially for younger segments—may require only an "advergaming" campaign to achieve success or use the "other" media solely when their budgets cannot afford traditional ad media.

TABLE 15.4	Framework for Various Forms of "Other" Advertising Media

- Brand Placements
- Yellow-Pages Advertising
- Video-Game Advertising (Advergaming)
- Cinema Advertising
- A Collection of Alternative Ad Media

© Cengage Learning 2013

Brand Placements

Brand placement (sometimes referred to as "product placement") is a marketing strategy whereby an advertiser promotes a brand by placing it *within the context* (i.e., in a program scene or story) of a selected medium (e.g., a TV, film, online, or gaming program).[30] (The term *branded entertainment* includes brand placement, as well as event and sponsorship marketing, also covered in Chapter 21.) It has been estimated that brand-placement spending in the United States amounted to around $3.6 billion in 2009, with TV placements accounting for approximately 70 percent of these expenditures.[31] Yet, total amount of brand placements actually declined 2.8 percent in 2009, after posting a 27.1 percent growth rate from 2004 to 2009.[32] On the other hand, the total value of both paid and non-paid brand placements remains strong ($7.35 billion) and is expected to grow. Readers are referred to the chapter endnotes for a growing list of research studies on brand placement.[33]

In comparison with traditional mass-media advertising, brand placements in movies, TV programs, etc. have certain distinct advantages and disadvantages. First, in terms of advantages, brand placements generally are less intrusive than advertisements and thus less likely to be avoided. Second, because consumers often dislike blatant marketing appeals, brand placements are less likely to be summarily rejected as just another persuasive attempt. Third, when a brand is appropriately connected with the plot or characters of a movie (or TV program, song, etc.), there is a strong potential for the placement to augment a brand's image and to build an emotional connection with the target audience. Finally, a prominent placement can create a memorable association serving to enhance consumers' memories (recognition and recall) of a brand and possible selection from among competitive options.

On the downside, marcom practitioners lose some control of how their brands are positioned when movie and TV directors decide how exactly brands are placed in an entertainment event. Another disadvantage of brand placements is the difficulty of measuring their effectiveness and their ROI. Finally, prices of brand placements are spiraling upward, and many brand managers consider the cost unreasonably high. For example, 79 percent of major marketers surveyed in a poll the Association of National Advertisers conducted believe branded-entertainment deals are overpriced.[34]

In sum, brand placements offer many potential advantages, but these do not come free of cost. We now discuss brand placements in movies and in TV programs.

Brand Placements in Movies

Brand placements in movies date back to the 1940s, yet the frequency is greater now than ever. It is virtually impossible to attend a movie without seeing various well-known brands (e.g., Apple, Coca-Cola, Ford, Nike, and Sony)

appearing in these movies. In fact, it is likely that a record was set with 97 brands placed in the 2006-released movie, *Talladega Nights: The Ballad of Ricky Bobby* (a satire about NASCAR racing featuring Will Farrell). Some of the featured brands in the movie were ACDelco, Advanced Auto Parts, Bennigan's, Budweiser, Checkers, Chevrolet, Coca-Cola, Domino's Pizza, ESPN, FedEx, Fig Newton, Food Lion, Ford, FOX, Goodyear, GQ, Halliburton, Hardee's, Havoline, Honda, Huffy Bicycle Company, Hummer, Jim Beam, Kentucky Fried Chicken, Kodak, Lowe's, Lucky Charms, M&M's, Mac Tools, McDonald's, Miller, Mobil, Mopar, Motorola, MTV, NASCAR, NBC, Nextel, Old Spice, Pepsi, Perrier, Pontiac, Powerade, PUMA, QVC, Rally's Hamburgers, Shake 'N Bake, Sharpie, Sony VAIO, SPEED Channel, Sprint, Subway, Sunoco, Taco Bell, TAG Heuer, Target, Tide, Tylenol, United Auto Workers (UAW), Waffle House, Walmart, Winnebago, and Wonder Bread! Interested readers can see the brands that are featured in your favorite films by going to the following website: www.brandchannel.com/brandcameo_films.asp. This source has been tracking brand placements in movies since the early 2000s and identifies which brands are placed in the most films. For example, in 2011, Apple was the brand placed in the most films (17), followed by a three-way tie for Chevrolet (9), Dell (9), and Ford (9).

Do brand placements work? There is some evidence that brand awareness and recall increase with more prominent placements.[35] Also, in a study of 928 brand placements in 159 films, researchers found an inverted-U effect between brand stock returns and time (in days).[36] That is, returns gradually increased to a point (16 days after release date), followed by a price stabilization and decline. One caveat to the short-term success of brand placements is that overexposing brands in the same film reduced stock returns.

In general, it would seem that advertisers have little to lose and much to gain when using this form of supplemental marketing communications. The typical price for a brand placement ranges from as low as $25,000 to into the millions.[37] Several factors determine how much a brand placement is worth and thus how much it should cost a brand marketer to place a brand in a particular movie.[38] A first determinant is the amount of time the brand gets on screen. Placements in which a brand is in the foreground of a scene and in which the brand logo is clearly seen are more valuable to a brand and lead to higher prices than when the brand is in the background and the logo is difficult to detect. Second, brand placements are more valuable (and priced higher) when characters in the movie use the brand and perhaps mention it and exclaim its virtues. A third determinant of a placement's value is whether the brand appears during an important plot point in the movie (if it does, the placement is worth more).

Based on a large global study that a major advertising media company conducted (with over 11,000 interviews with consumers from 20 countries), younger consumers appear to be the most responsive to brand placements in movies.[39] Compared to older age groups, 16-to-24-year-olds were the most likely to notice brand placements in movies (57 percent) and to consider trying the brands seen in films (41 percent). Perhaps the most interesting finding was the difference across countries in the percentages of consumers saying they would try a brand if they saw it in a film. The percentages for a subset of countries were Mexico (53 percent), Singapore (49 percent), India (35 percent), Hong Kong (33 percent), the United States (26 percent), Finland (14 percent), Denmark (14 percent), the Netherlands (9 percent), and France (8 percent). Consumers from the latter four countries objected to brand placements because they felt they interfered with the film-making process.

Brand Placements in TV Programs

The topic of brand placements in TV programs was briefly mentioned in Chapter 12 when discussing television as a mass-advertising medium. A few additional comments are appropriate at this time. Brand placements in TV programs are prevalent. In fact, a study of prime-time TV programs determined that brands are placed in these programs an average of once every three minutes.[40] Brand-placement spending on television is even greater than in movies, accounting for perhaps as much as 70 percent of total brand-placement expenditures across all media outlets. The substantial increase in brand placements on TV has been associated with the growth of reality television programming. Programs such as *American Idol, Survivor*, and *The Apprentice* represent near-perfect contexts in which to place brands and provide brand managers with an alternative form of exposure to the traditional 30-second commercial. Of course, brand placements are not limited just to reality shows; they can be observed on most successful TV programs. Even reruns of TV sitcoms are being digitally remastered to include brands in scenes where they did not exist when initially produced.[41]

Advertising Age has cited some of the "best" and "worst" brand placements in TV shows. At the top of the list of the "best" included 1,000 Pontiac Solstice roadster cars sold in just 14 minutes following an episode of *The Apprentice* based on contestants designing a brochure for the Solstice.[42] Following the program, viewers could visit the Pontiac website to print out a certificate to order one of the first 1,000 ones built. At the other end, one of the "worst" also appeared in *The Apprentice* in which Domino's Pizza paid $1 million to sponsor competing teams developing and selling their new meatball pizza.[43] Donald Trump, the show's host, then appeared in an ad for Domino's meatball pizza during the program. Unfortunately, a competitor, Papa John's, was able to appear in a competing 30-second ad during the NBC program selling their own meatball pizza!

Yellow-Pages Advertising

The "yellow pages" (www.yellow.com) represent a major advertising medium that consumers turn to when they are seeking a product or service supplier and are prepared to make a purchase. The online and print versions of the yellow pages together have produced annual global revenues exceeding $23 billion; yet they have a current negative revenue growth rate of –1.5 percent.[44] One reason for this decline is a reduced reliance on *print* directories. However, it is estimated that future digital (online) growth will soon offset declines in print revenues. By 2015, 53 percent of global yellow pages revenues will be digital, compared with just 29 percent in 2011.[45] Over 7,000 localized yellow-pages directories are distributed annually to hundreds of millions of consumers. There are more than 4,000 headings for different product and service listings. Local businesses place the majority of yellow-pages ads, but national advertisers also are frequent users of the yellow pages. For example, in a recent year, the following national companies all invested over $20 million advertising in the yellow pages: ServiceMaster ($51 million), U-Haul ($38 million), State Farm Insurance ($35 million), Budget, and Ryder ($20.5 million).[46]

At the consumer level, an estimated 60 percent of all American adults use the yellow pages at least once in a typical week. The heaviest yellow-pages users tend to fall most in the 25-to-49 age category, are college educated, and have relatively high household incomes ($60,000 and up).[47] Some of the major reasons people use yellow pages include saving time spent shopping around for information, saving energy and money, finding information quickly, and learning about products and services. Yet, no doubt, consumers have other choices online (e.g., Google searches) even versus online yellow-page options.

Video-Game Advertising (a.k.a. Advergaming)

Brand managers and marcom practitioners are continually seeking ways to get their messages before difficult-to-reach consumers such as young men. Electronic games (video games) provide an excellent advertising medium for this purpose. These games typically are available on game consoles (e.g., Xbox 360) or online, and marketers either customize their own games or incorporate their brands into existing games. The producers of video games now routinely pursue tie-ins with brand marketers, who pay for advertising space within the games. It is estimated that U.S. video-game advertising totaled about $1 billion in 2010, and that worldwide spending on advergaming will reach $7.2 billion by 2016.[48] It is easy to understand why video games represent a potentially valuable ad medium, considering that popular games sell millions of units, and users of these games play for an average of 40 hours before growing tired of them.[49] In the United States, approximately 190 million households will use a next-generation video-game console in 2012, with 80 percent of these households playing online.[50] Recent brain research has revealed that video-game users tend to be better at multitasking, decision making, and creativity than non-users.[51] (For further details about characteristics of game players, see the *IMC Focus* insert.)

Measuring Video-Game Audiences

Although growing at a reasonably rapid rate, expenditures on advergaming are small in comparison to those on TV and other mass media. Nevertheless, Nielsen (of TV ratings fame) has developed a service called Nielsen GamePlay Metrics to measure video-game audiences. Nielsen tracks game usage through an audience panel of 12,000 U.S. homes. Employing a small monitor (somewhat akin to the set-top boxes used in TV measurement), Nielsen is able to measure game-playing behavior and to capture key demographics of players.[52]

Profile of the Video-Gaming Community

Research firm NPD and the Entertainment Software Association have studied video gamers to better understand who plays games and where and what games they play. Here are some of the key findings from their research:

Total amount spent—In 2010, total consumer spending on gaming content, accessories, and hardware was $25.1 billion.

Gender—Women comprise slightly over 42 percent of the total video-game audience.

Income—The average household income for online gamers ranges between $35,000 and $75,000.

Age and usage—The single largest age group of gamers is aged 18 to 49 (53 percent), although five years ago it was kids ages 6 to 12. The average gamer today is 34 years old, and has been playing video games for 12 years, often up to 18 hours per week.

Console ownership—Xbox 360 owners are disproportionately more likely to play games online than any other console owners, and, at an average of 7.1 hours per week, Xbox 360 owners spend more time playing games online than any other group of console owners.

Type of games sold—The top five video games sold in 2010: (1) *Call of Duty: Black Ops*, (2) *Madden NFL 11*, (3) *Halo: Reach*, (4) *New Super Mario Bros.*, and (5) *Red Dead Redemption*. The top five computer games sold in 2010: (1) *Starcraft II: Wings of Liberty*, (2) *World of Warcraft: Cataclysm Expansion Pack*, (3) *The Sims 3*, (4) *World of Warcraft: Wrath of the Lich King Expansion Pack*, and (5) *Civilization 5*.

Sources: Based on Robert Lee Hotz, "When Gaming is Good for You," *Wall Street Journal*, March 6, 2012, D1, D12; and Beth Snyder Bulik, "Who Is Today's Gamer? You Have No Idea," *Advertising Age*, May 14, 2007, 28.

Cinema Advertising

In addition to placements of brands in movies, the movie theater is another option for placing advertising messages.[53] Expenditures on cinema advertising in the United States amounted to over $658 million in 2010, a 13 percent increase from the previous year.[54] Research has demonstrated that cinema advertisements that appear prior to a featured film do *not* antagonize consumers.[55]

Younger consumers, those in the 12-to-24 demographic, are more positively disposed toward cinema advertising than older individuals, making this an attractive option for brand marketers.[56] The prospect that cinema advertising has a bright future is perhaps best evidenced by Nielsen Media Research, which offers Nielsen Cinema, an in-theater audience measurement service that cinema companies and advertisers use for buying and selling cinema advertising.

Potpourri of Alternative Advertising Media

There is a medley of creative alternative media, all of which have minor but potentially useful roles to play *as part of* an integrated marcom program. For example, Figure 15.5 is an advertisement from the 3M Company, suggesting that Post-it Notes can be used as a powerful ad medium reaching potential customers day after day, note after note. Figure 15.6 is a photo taken at a professional football stadium (the Carolina Panthers stadium in Charlotte, North Carolina), showing a cup holder emblazoned with an advertisement for Coca-Cola.[57]

Courtesy of 3M

FIGURE 15.5 3M's Post-It Notes as an Advertising Medium

Courtesy of Terence A. Shimp

FIGURE 15.6 A Football Stadium's Cup Holders as an Advertising Medium

Why let space go to waste when it can be sold as an advertising outlet? Consider, for example, the space available on the sides of the many garbage trucks that daily navigate city streets. The maker of Glad trash bags put a message saying "New York City tough" on 2,000 New York City garbage trucks and 450 street sweepers. During a two-month advertising period, Glad's ad campaign generated about 17 million impressions (i.e., gross rating points) and boosted the brand's citywide market share by 2 percentage points.[58]

Advertisers have even turned to restroom space as a venue to convey their messages. For example, Axe deodorant from Unilever has been advertised in public restrooms in major U.S. markets (especially in bars).[59] An enterprising firm called The Fruit Label Company has used apples and other fruits and vegetables to carry mini-ads for movies and other products. Levi Strauss & Co. advertised Levi's 501 jeans on the back covers of *Marvel* and *DC* comics, an excellent medium because these two comic-book companies combined sell more than 10 million copies of their comic books every month. The comics provided Levi Strauss & Co. with an outlet for reaching the notoriously difficult-to-reach segment of boys ages 12 to 17.

Another interesting ad medium is skywriting. A company named Skytypers—with bases in California, Florida, and New York—"writes" sky messages in the form of white cloud formations. At a U.S. Open tennis tournament in Flushing Meadows, New York, tennis patrons saw messages for brands such as Heineken, Dunkin' Donuts, and Geico. A message of 25 to 30 letters costs between $25,000 and $30,000 and could be seen by upwards of 2.5 million people in the 400-square-mile area surrounding the site of the U.S. Open.[60]

Finally, even the human body has been used as an advertising medium. A British company has paid students the equivalent of about $8 an hour to walk up and down busy streets with their foreheads temporarily imprinted with brand names. The company has a group of about 1,000 students who are willing to serve as walking billboards. Tattoo advertising also has appeared in the United States. Dunkin' Donuts ran a forehead tattoo promotion in conjunction with the National Collegiate Athletic Association (NCAA) March Madness basketball tourney. One hundred students from 10 universities in Massachusetts, Illinois, Georgia, and Florida earned between $50 and $100 per day to walk around their campuses with the Dunkin' Donuts logo temporarily tattooed on their foreheads.[61]

In conclusion, this brief discussion of alternative media was intended merely to demonstrate that virtually any blank surface can be converted into a creative space for an advertisement. However, advertisers must be mindful of the advice about IMC presented in Chapter 1: Contact brand users wherever and whenever possible, use all appropriate touch points to convey messages to increase brand awareness, and be sure to integrate messages so they speak with a single voice. Multiple media are to little avail if their messages are inconsistent or possibly even conflicting.

© PRNewsFoto/Newscom

Summary

This chapter has examined a variety of advertising media used in direct marketing. Figure 15.1 helped differentiate among key "direct" terms, such as *direct marketing*, *direct response advertising*, *direct mail*, and *direct selling*. Direct mail received the most extensive coverage in view of its widespread usage and huge investment in this medium. The functions and advantages and disadvantages of cataloging, and inbound and outbound telemarketing also were examined.

Direct (response) advertising is increasingly viewed as a critical component of successful IMC programs. Indeed, for many firms direct advertising is the cornerstone of their communications efforts. The increased sophistication of database marketing has been largely responsible for the growing use and effectiveness of direct advertising. Major advances in computer technology have made it possible for companies to maintain large databases containing millions of prospects and customers. This can enable the calculation of a customer's lifetime value and help to build long-term relationships with consumers. Sophisticated data mining can look for interesting relationships used to target prospective customers, develop cooperative marketing relations, and otherwise better understand who buys what, and when, how often, and along with what other products and brands they purchase.

The chapter then examined "other media," such as brand placements in movies and in TV programs. These placements provide advertisers with an opportunity to reach consumers in a rather subtle fashion and to portray brands positively by connecting them with entertainment plots and characters.

Yellow-pages advertising and video-game advertising (also known as advergaming) also received coverage in the chapter. The yellow pages (online as well as in print) are virtually a must for local advertisers in their quest to attract prospective customers and repeat purchases. Advergaming is a rapidly growing form of advertising that can provide marketers with tailored and tough-to-reach segments who are avid gamers.

Another interesting development in the search for alternative advertising media is the recent growth of cinema advertising. Most theaters now show commercials before presenting the featured movie. These ads often are the same ones shown on TV. The appeal of this medium is that it captures the attention of a young demographic group that can be difficult to reach via traditional media. Moreover, when shown prior to the commencement of the feature film, cinema advertising is viewed as less disruptive when compared to TV commercials.

The final section includes a medley of alternative advertising media (i.e., advertising options that generally are used to supplement mainstream media rather than to carry the full advertising load). The discussion included forms of advertising, such as placing ads on garbage trucks, advertising in restrooms, and using airplanes to skywrite ads.

Discussion Questions

1. Explain the differences among direct marketing, direct-response advertising, direct mail, and direct selling.

2. Why has direct marketing enjoyed such rapid growth in recent years?

3. Refer to the ad for DIRECTV's satellite system (see Figure 15.3). Assume the manufacturer of this product chose to use direct mail to sell the product in addition to advertising it in magazines. Explain how you, as a chief marketing officer (or brand manager) for this company, would acquire a mailing list. What characteristics of businesses would you select in generating the list? Be specific.

4. What should government regulators (e.g., Federal Trade Commission) do to prevent telemarketing abuses? What kind of prohibitions, if any, should be placed on telemarketing? Should there be any changes to the "do not call list" procedures? Should there be a "do not track list" for online marketing? How might it work?

5. Conduct 5 to 10 interviews with nonstudent adults regarding their personal experiences with and evaluations of telemarketing. Are they hassled often? Do they mind having telephone salespeople call them? What specific complaints do they have?

6. Virtually any space is a potential medium for a marketer's advertisement. Identify several novel forms of advertising media that go beyond the "other" media described in this chapter. Describe the target for each of these novel media, and offer an explanation as to why, in your opinion, each novel medium is effective or ineffective.

7. Can you recall any prominent brand placements in movies you have seen lately? What were these placements? Were the products "positioned" in positive or negative contexts? How successful, in your opinion, were these placements?

8. Describe your use, if any, of yellow-pages advertising in recent weeks.

9. Provide two illustrative variables that a catalog marketer of men's or women's clothing (your choice) might include in its database.

10. Assume you are a direct marketer for a line of merchandise imprinted with the logos of major universities. These items are targeted to the fans and supporters of university athletic programs. Detail how you would compile an appropriate mailing list, one that would reach people who are most likely to purchase the logo merchandise. Use your college or university for illustration.

11. Following is a lifetime-value analysis framework similar to that presented in the chapter.

Perform the calculations necessary to complete row K:

	Year 1	Year 2	Year 3	Year 4	Year 5
Revenue					
A Customers	2,000	—	—	—	—
B Retention rate	30%	40%	55%	65%	70%
C Average yearly sales	$250	$250	$250	$250	$250
D Total revenue	—	—	—	—	—
Costs					
E Cost percentage	50%	50%	50%	50%	50%
F Total costs	—	—	—	—	—
Profits					
G Gross profit	—	—	—	—	—
H Discount rate	1	1.15	—	—	—
I NPV profit	—	—	—	—	—
J Cumulative NPV profit	—	—	—	—	—
K Lifetime value per customer	—	—	—	—	—

12. Assume that, 10 years after graduating from your university or college, you are appointed to your school's Athletics Oversight Committee. The chair of the committee suggests that it would be useful to know the lifetime value of the average basketball season-ticket holder. Describe how you might go about estimating the average ticket holder's lifetime value over the first five years starting with the year that he or she first purchases season tickets. Refer to Table 15.2 to assist you with this analysis. Make whatever assumptions you deem necessary and then conduct the analysis. Using a spreadsheet program such as Microsoft Excel would obviously facilitate your analysis.

13. What are your views on advergaming? Respond by commenting about this advertising practice both from the perspective of advertisers and from the viewpoint of game players.

14. Brand placements in movies and in TV programs represent a subtle, even covert, way to present a brand message. Traditional advertising, by comparison, is, in a manner of speaking, "in your face." One therefore could argue that traditional advertising is a more honest form of communications than the practice of branded entertainment. What are your views on this? Might one argue that brand placements are even a bit deceitful?

15. Visit www.brandchannel.com/brandcameo_films.asp and identify a movie that you either have seen or you are at least familiar with. Examine the brands that have been placed in that movie and comment on why you think these brands chose to be placed in that particular movie.

16. Given the chapter's discussion of "alternative" forms of ad media (on garbage trucks, in restrooms, on people, etc.) and the implication that any unused space is a potential advertising medium, identify two "spaces" advertisers are not currently using that could be used for placing ad messages. What kinds of brands would advertise on each of your suggested spaces, and what would be an appropriate target audience for such messages? Do you think this form of advertising is appropriate?

17. What is your reaction to advertisements in movie theaters that precede featured films? Does such advertising disturb you, or do you find it perfectly acceptable?

End Notes

1. *Fact Book on Direct Response Marketing*, New York: Direct Marketing Association, Inc., 1982, xxiii. Italics added.

2. For an insightful and thorough discussion of interactive home shopping (IHS), see Joseph Alba, John Lynch, Barton Weitz, Chris Janiszewski, Richard Lutz, Alan Sawyer, and Stacy Wood, "Interactive Home Shopping: Consumer, Retailer, and Manufacturer Incentives to Participate in Electronic Marketplaces," *Journal of Marketing* 61 (July 1997), 38–53.

3. Jonathan Berry, John Verity, Kathleen Kerwin, and Gail DeGeorge, "A Potent New Tool for Selling: Database Marketing," *Businessweek*, September 5, 1994, 56–57.

4. For more information about database marketing, see Don E. Schultz, "The Direct/DataBase Marketing Challenge to Fixed-Location Retailing," in *The Future of U.S. Retailing: An Agenda for the 21st Century*, ed. Robert A. Peterson, New York: Quorum Books, 1992, 165–84.

5. "DMA Releases Statistical Fact Book," Press Release, Direct Marketing Association, March 1, 2011, http://www.the-dma.org/cgi/disppressrelease?article=1474.

6. Lester Wunderman, "Excerpts from New Frontiers in Direct Marketing IV," *Direct Connection* (Newsletter of the Direct Marketing Educational Foundation, winter 1993–1994), 6.

7. *DMA 2010 Statistical Fact Book*, New York: Direct Marketing Association, January 2010, 3.

8. Philip Kotler and Kevin Lane Keller, *Marketing Management*, 14th ed. (Boston: Prentice Hall), 2012, 426; see also Tom Reilly, "How Much Does a Sales Call Really Cost?" *Manufacturing Works* (blog), November 19, 2011, http://manufacturing-works.com/sales_bytes/2010-11-19.php.

9. Bob Stone, "For Effective Direct Results," *Advertising Age*, March 28, 1983, M32.

10. Don Schultz as quoted in Gary Levin, "Going Direct Route," *Advertising Age*, November 18, 1991, 37.

11. http://wordnetweb.princeton.edu/perl/webwn?s=serendipity.

12. This description is adapted from Jeff Borden, "Eat My Dust," *Marketing News*, February 1, 2008, 20–22.

13. This description is adapted from Anne Stuart, "Do You Know Stacy?" *Deliver Magazine*, May 2007, 25–27.

14. Information for this description was provided by the marketing communication agency responsible for the campaign, The Martin Agency, Richmond, VA.

15. *DMA 2010 Statistical Fact Book*, 2.

16. Ibid, 17.

17. See also "Benefits of Direct Mail," United States Postal Service, https://www.usps.com/business/direct-mail-benefits.htm (accessed March 5, 2012).

18. *DMA 2010 Statistical Fact Book*, 43.

19. Ibid, 51.

20. "Direct Mail Perks Up Online Traffic, and Sales," December 14, 2007, http://delivermagazine.com.

21. *DMA 2010 Statistical Fact Book*, 4.

22. Robert C. Blattberg and John Deighton, "Interactive Marketing: Exploiting the Age of Addressability," *Sloan Management Review* (fall 1991), 5.

23. There are more sophisticated approaches to lifetime-value analysis, but this example contains all the elements essential to understanding the fundamentals of the approach.

24. Arthur M. Hughes, *Strategic Database Marketing* (Chicago: Probus, 1994), 17; see also arguments for considering "willingness to spend" (WTS) in addition to customer lifetime value in Phillip E. Pfeifer and Anton Ovchinnikov, "A Note on Willingness to Spend and Customer Lifetime Value for Firms with Limited Capacity," *Journal of Interactive Marketing*, 25 (2011), 178–89.

25. *DMA 2010 Statistical Fact Book*, 2, 5.

26. Hubert D. Hennessey, "Matters to Consider before Plunging into Telemarketing," *Marketing News*, July 8, 1983, 2.

27. Vikas Bajaj, "A New Capital of Call Centers," *New York Times*, November 25, 2011, http://www.nytimes.com/2011/11/26/business/philippines-overtakes-india-as-hub-of-call-centers.html?pagewanted=all; and Cheryl Arcibal, "Philippines Still Top BPO Destination – Consulting Firm," GMA Network, October 4, 2007, http://www.gmanetwork.com/news/story/63053/economy/companies/philippines-still-top-bpo-destination-consulting-firm.

28. "FTC Issues The FY 2011 National Do Not Call Registry Data Book; Nearly 210 Million Phone Numbers on Do Not Call List," FTC Press Release, November 30, 2011, http://ftc.gov/opa/2011/11/dnc.shtm.

29. "National Do Not Call Registry: Information for Businesses," Federal Trade Commission, 2003,

https://www.donotcall.gov/faq/faqbusiness.aspx (accessed March 11, 2012).

30. Adapted from "Global Branded Entertainment Marketing Forecast 2010–2014: Executive Summary," 4th ed., 2010, PQ Media, 1–11.

31. "Global Branded Entertainment Marketing Forecast 2010–2014: Executive Summary," 2010, 11; and Patricia Odell, "Star Struck," *Promo*, April 2007, 16–21.

32. "Global Branded Entertainment Marketing Forecast 2010–2014: Executive Summary," 2010, 11.

33. For example, see Ekaterina V. Karniouchina, Can Uslay, and Grigori Erenburg, "Do Marketing Media Have Life Cycles? The Case of Product Placement in Movies," *Journal of Marketing* 75 (May 2011), 27–48; Cristel Antonia Russell and Barbara B. Stern, "Consumers, Characters, and Products: A Balance Model of Sitcom Product Placement Effects," *Journal of Advertising* 35 (spring 2006), 7–22; Siva K. Balasubramanian, James A. Karrh, and Hemant Patwardhan, "Audience Response to Product Placements: An Integrative Framework and Future Research Agenda," *Journal of Advertising* 35 (fall 2006), 115–42; Cristel Antonia Russell and Michael Belch, "A Managerial Investigation into the Product Placement Industry," *Journal of Advertising Research* 45 (March 2005), 73–92; and Cristel Antonia Russell, "Investigating the Effectiveness of Product Placements in Television Shows: The Role of Modality and Plot Connection Congruence on Brand Memory and Attitude," *Journal of Consumer Research* 29 (December 2002), 306–18. For coverage of practitioners' views on brand placement, see James A. Karrh, Kathy Brittain McKee, and Carol J. Pardun, "Practitioners' Evolving Views on Product Placement Effectiveness," *Journal of Advertising Research* 43 (June 2003), 138–49.

34. Abbey Klaasen, "Marketers Fear Being Fleeced at Corner of Madison and Vine," *Advertising Age*, March 28, 2005, 3, 124.

35. Ibid. See also, Emma Johnstone and Christopher A. Dodd, "Placements as Mediators of Brand Salience within a UK Cinema Audience," *Journal of Marketing Communications* 6 (September 2000), 141–58; and Alain d'Astous and Francis Chartier, "A Study of Factors Affecting Consumer Evaluations and Memory of Product Placements in Movies," *Journal of Current Issues and Research in Advertising* 22 (fall 2000), 31–40.

36. Ekaterina V. Karniouchina, Can Uslay, and Grigori Erenburg, "Do Marketing Media Have Life Cycles? The Case of Product Placement in Movies," *Journal of Marketing* 75 (May 2011), 27–48.

37. Pola B. Gupta and Kenneth R. Lord, "Product Placement in Movies: The Effect of Prominence and Mode on Audience Recall," *Journal of Current Issues and Research in Advertising* 20 (spring 1998), 47–60.

38. Adapted from Brian Steinberg, "Product Placement Pricing Debated," *Wall Street Journal Online*, November 19, 2004, http://online.wsj.com.

39. Emma Hall, "Young Consumers Receptive to Movie Product Placements," *Advertising Age*, March 29, 2004, 8.

40. Carrie La Ferle and Steven M. Edwards, "Product Placement: How Brands Appear on Television," *Journal of Advertising* 35 (winter 2006), 65–86.

41. Patricia Odell, "Rewriting Placement History," *Promo*, March 2005, 8.

42. Marc Graser and T.L. Stanley, "Brand Integration: Lessons from Madison & Vine," *Advertising Age*, October 3, 2005, 12.

43. Ibid.

44. BIA Kelsey News Release, December 6, 2011, http://www.biakelsey.com/Company/Press-Releases/111206-BIAKelsey-Estimates-2011-Global-Yellow-Pages-Revenues-at-$23.4-Billion.asp.

45. Joel J. Davis, "Section Five: Consumer Dynamics," *Understanding Yellow Pages*, http://www.ypa-academics.org/UYPII/section5.html.

46. Joel J. Davis, "Section One: Industry Overview," *Understanding Yellow Pages*, http://www.ypa-academics.org/UYPII/section1.html.

47. Ibid; For consumer yellow-pages usage behavior and graphic design studies, Avery M. Abernethy and David N. Laband, "The Customer Pulling Power of Different-sized Yellow Pages Advertisements," *Journal of Advertising Research* 42 (May/June 2002), 66–72; Karen V. Fernandez and Dennis L. Rosen, "The Effectiveness of Information and Color in Yellow Page Advertising," *Journal of Advertising* 29 (summer 2000), 61–73; and Gerald L. Lohse and Dennis L. Rosen, "Signaling Quality and Credibility in Yellow Pages Advertising: The Influence of Color and Graphics on Choice," *Journal of Advertising* 30 (summer 2001), 73–85.

48. "DFC Intelligence Forecasts Global Advertising in Video Games to Reach $7.2 billion in 2016," September 13, 2011, DFC Intelligence, http://www.dfcint.com/wp/?p=315.

49. Kenneth Hein, "Getting in the Game," *Brandweek*, February 17, 2004, 26–28.

50. "Video Game Statistics," http://grabstats.com/statcategorymain.asp?StatCatID=13 (accessed March 9, 2012).

51. Ibid.

52. Nick Wingfield, "Nielsen Tracker May Benefit Videogames as Ad Medium," *Wall Street Journal*, July 26, 2007, B2.

53. For an interesting conceptual treatment of cinema advertising, see Joanna Phillips and Stephanie M. Noble, "Simply Captivating: Understanding Consumers' Attitudes toward the Cinema as an Advertising Medium," *Journal of Advertising* 36 (spring 2007), 81–94.

54. Richard Verrier, "Cinema Advertising Spending Jumps 13% in 2010," *Los Angeles Times (blog)*, March 28, 2011, http://latimesblogs.latimes.com/entertainmentnewsbuzz/2011/03/cinema-advertising-spending-movie-theater.html.

55. Diane Williams and Bill Rose, "The Arbitron Cinema Advertising Study 2007: Making Brands Shine in the Dark," http://www.arbitron.com/downloads/cinema_study_2007.pdf (accessed April 22, 2008).

56. Ibid.

57. The first author includes this photo in honor of his late, great friend, John Kuhayda, and to his dear wife Patty and family. John was the embodiment of integrity and loyalty. Every moment we spent together was one of joy. His "dash" was too short but full of substance and character. He will always be my Padna, the Champ.

58. Jack Neff, "Trash Trucks: A New Hot Spot for Ads," *Advertising Age*, February 5, 2007, 8.

59. Lisa Sanders, "More Marketers Have to Go to the Bathroom," *Advertising Age*, September 20, 2004, 53.

60. Michael Applebaum, "Look, Up in the Sky: Brands!" *Brandweek*, September 13, 2004, 42.

61. Details about the British campaign and that for Dunkin' Donuts are from Arundhati Parmar, "Maximum Exposure," *Marketing News*, September 15, 2003, 6, 8.

CHAPTER 16

Advertising Media: Planning and Analysis

The cost of placing a 30-second commercial on the National Football League Super Bowl increased from $400,000 in 1984 to $3.5 million in 2012, which equates to approximately $116,667 per second. However, because the audience for the Super Bowl is enormous, totaling over 111.3 million American TV households, advertisers during the Super Bowl extravaganza justify the expense on grounds that the cost of reaching potential customers is reasonable.[1] In fact, nearly one-third of American consumers watch the Super Bowl. A breakdown of the average age for Super Bowl viewers shows 17 percent of children age 2–11, 26.5 percent of those age 12–17, 34.4 percent of the

© AP Images/Chrysler Group LLC

18–49 age group, 37.5 percent of 25–54, and 36.9 percent of people 55 and older. Super Bowl advertisers further justify their decision to advertise during the Super Bowl on the basis that consumers are much more engaged when viewing this program than they typically are when watching other TV programs.

Nevertheless, one may question whether the sizable investment in this television extravaganza can be justified, especially considering that 30-second spots on the top-rated prime-time television programs sell for a fraction of that cost, typically in the range of $100,000–$350,000. Media planners at a company that specializes in media selection questioned

Chapter Objectives

After reading this chapter, you should be able to:

1 Describe the major factors used in segmenting target audiences for media planning purposes.

2 Explain the meaning of reach, frequency, gross rating points, target rating points, effective reach, and other media concepts.

3 Discuss the logic of the three-exposure hypothesis and its role in media and vehicle selection.

4 Describe the use of the efficiency index procedure for media selection.

5 Distinguish the differences among three forms of advertising allocation: continuous, pulsed, and flighted schedules.

6 Explain the principle of recency and its implications for allocating advertising expenditures over time.

7 Perform cost-per-thousand calculations.

8 Review the application of media planning software and actual media plans.

whether the Super Bowl represented a prudent buy and proposed another way to spend the amount of money equivalent to purchasing a 30-second Super Bowl spot. They developed an alternative media plan that consisted of (1) buying advertising time on all network programs aired at the same time on Tuesday evening; (2) securing advertising time on all network programs aired at the same time on Sunday evening (e.g., Sunday night movies); and (3) purchasing a final single spot from the Fox network's Saturday night programming. (The Tuesday and Sunday night buys are called "roadblocks" because advertising purchased on all network programs aired simultaneously acts as a roadblock to ensure that all consumers viewing TV at this time will be exposed to the brand's advertising.) This alternative media plan was able to secure 13 prime-time advertising spots, or a total time of 6.5 minutes, compared with purchasing a single 30-second ad on the Super Bowl. Comparative GRPs (gross rating points, detailed later in the chapter) for the Super Bowl media buy and the alternative plan are as follows.

Whereas a single 30-second ad on the Super Bowl provided 40 GRPs based on the 18-to-49 age group, 42 GRPs based on the 25-to-54 group, and so on, the equivalently priced 13 spots yielded considerably more GRPs. For example, for all adults ages 25 to 54, the 78 GRPs from the 13 prime-time spots were 86 percent greater than the 42 GRPs generated by the Super Bowl advertisement.

Thus, one can conclude that advertisers should not advertise on the Super Bowl but rather would be better served by investing their advertising money elsewhere. Correct? Not necessarily! One also needs to factor in the all-important issue of advertising impact. People react with a relatively unenthusiastic response to advertisements placed during the programs contained in the alternative (13-spot) media buy. Comparatively, advertisements placed during the Super Bowl are, like the program itself, a special event. For example, Clint Eastwood's appearance in the 2012 Super Bowl commercial for Chrysler, "Halftime in America," was viewed by critics as dramatic and having an impact on the audience. So, consumers look forward to new, dramatic ads and product launches and often go online and talk about the ads well after the Super Bowl is over. In fact, evidence indicates that people enjoy watching TV commercials during the Super Bowl. One survey determined that a sample of viewers indicated that they prefer viewing the ads to watching the game. Since journalists comment about Super Bowl advertisements in magazines and newspapers, and consumers share their own views online and in social media, advertisers receive a secondary form of brand contact. In short, all advertising does not have equivalent impact. When planners are buying advertising media, considerations, often subjective, other than mere comparisons of cost and rating points have to be factored into the decision.

Sources: Robert Seidman, "Eli, Eli, Eli! Super Bowl XLVI is Most-Watched Television Show in U.S. History," *TV By the Numbers*, February 6, 2012, http://tvbythenumbers.zap2it.com/2012/02/06/eli-eli-eli-super-bowl-xlvi-is-most-watched-television-show-in-u-s-history/118826; Bradley Johnson, "CFOs Cringe At Price, But Bowl Delivers the Masses," *Advertising Age*, January 29, 2007, 8; Rob Frydlewicz, "Missed Super Bowl? Put Your Bucks Here," *Advertising Age*, January 30, 1995, 18; and Joe Mantese, "Majority Prefer Super Bowl Ads, Socializing vs. the Game Itself," *MediaDailyNews*, February 7, 2005.

Introduction

Several of the previous chapters have examined the message component of advertising strategy. Although effective messages are essential for successful advertising, these messages are of little use unless advertising media are selected that will effectively reach the intended target audience.[2] Chapter 12 examined the traditional print and broadcast media—magazines, newspapers, television, and radio. Chapter 13 focused on online media, while Chapter 14 explored social media. Chapter 15 examined direct marketing, direct response advertising, and alternative ad media (e.g., product placements in movies and cinema advertising). This chapter goes beyond an examination of media choices and is devoted to strategic considerations of media planning and buying. The present chapter describes the media planning process and the various factors that go into selecting media.

Some Useful Terminology: Media versus Vehicles

Advertising practitioners distinguish between advertising media and vehicles. Media are the general communication methods that carry advertising messages—that is, television, magazines, newspapers, and so on. Vehicles are the specific broadcast programs or print choices in which advertisements are placed. For example, television is a specific medium, and *NCIS*, *CBS Evening News*, *Two and a Half Men*, and *Sunday Night Football* are vehicles for carrying television advertisements. Magazines are another medium, and *Time*, *Bloomberg's Businessweek*, *Ebony*, and *Cosmopolitan* are vehicles in which magazine ads are placed. Each medium and each vehicle has a set of unique characteristics and virtues. Advertisers attempt to select those media and vehicles that are most compatible with the advertised brand in reaching its target audience affordably and conveying the intended message. The *Global Focus* insert provides an online source for obtaining useful information about media vehicles in countries around the world. Be sure to visit this website to see the wealth of available information.

Messages and Media: A Hand-in-Glove Relation

Advertising message and media considerations are inextricably related. Media and messages represent a hand-in-glove relationship, where each must be

GLOBAL FOCUS

Searching for Media Options Around the Globe

Suppose you are interested in learning about news media in any city or state in the United States. Perhaps your interest goes beyond the United States and you wish to know what news media and advertising outlets may be available in most any city in the world. How would you learn, for example, what newspapers are available in Moscow, or what TV stations exist in Madrid? Fortunately, there is an independent site on the Internet named the Kidon Media-Link (www.kidon.com/media-link) that makes this information available. Kidon's website provides direct links to various news sources, which represent potential advertising outlets. Go to the Kidon Media-Link homepage, select the continent where a city of interest is located, identify the country, navigate to the desired city, and then inspect available media. Up-to-date news is provided at the media outlets available in that city. It is worth your time to access www.kidon.com and learn more about this interesting resource that provides direct links to global media.

Source: © Cengage Learning

compatible with the other. It has been said that advertising creatives "can't move until they deal with a media strategist."[3] Creatives and media specialists must team up to design advertisements that effectively and efficiently deliver the right brand concept to the intended target audience. Advertising practitioners agree that reaching a specific audience effectively is the most important consideration in selecting advertising media.[4] Advertisers are placing more emphasis than ever on media planning, and media planners have achieved a level of unparalleled stature.[5] This is because an advertising message can be effective only when placed in the media and vehicles that best reach the target audience at a justifiable expense.

The choice of media and vehicles is, in many respects, the most complicated of all marketing communications decisions due to the variety of decisions that must be made. In addition to determining which general media categories to use (television, radio, magazines, newspapers, outdoor, online, or alternative media), the media planner must also pick specific vehicles within each medium and decide how to allocate the available budget among the various media and vehicle alternatives. Moreover, consumers may be interested in interacting with programs (and ads) on multiple screens (e.g., smartphones, TV, gaming consoles, computers) at the same time (see *IMC Focus*). Additional decisions involve choosing geographical advertising locations and determining how to distribute the budget over time. The complexity of media selection is made clear in the following commentary:

> *An advertiser considering a simple monthly magazine schedule, out of a pool of 30 feasible publications meeting editorial environment and targeting requirements, must essentially consider over one billion schedules when narrowing the possibilities down to the few feasible alternatives that maximize campaign goals within budget constraints. Why over one billion possible schedules? There are two outcomes for each monthly schedule, either to use a particular publication or not to do so. Therefore, the total number of possible schedules equals two raised to the 30th power (i.e., $2^{30} = 1,073,741,800$) ... Now imagine how the options explode when one is also considering 60 prime time and 25 daytime broadcast television network programs, 22 cable television networks, 16 radio networks, 4 national newspapers, and 3 newspaper supplements, with each vehicle having between 4.3 [i.e., the average number of weeks in a month] and perhaps as many as 20 or more possible insertions per month.*[6]

Selecting and Buying Media and Vehicles

As discussed in Chapter 9, traditional full-service advertising agencies usually have been responsible for both creating advertising messages for their clients' brands and planning and buying media time and space in which to place those messages. However, a dramatic change has occurred in the manner in which media planning is performed. An event that rocked the advertising industry in 2000 was General Motors' (GM) decision to consolidate in a single company its media planning and buying for its many automobile brands. Whereas in the past media planning and buying took place in each advertising agency that represented each GM brand, *all* media planning was done in a single company under an organization referred to as "GM Planworks" until 2009. This unit handled media planning amounting annually to approximately $3 billion. By consolidating media planning and buying, GM achieved significant cost savings for its various brands.[7] However, in 2009, GM changed its focus and re-integrated the GM account with Publicis' Starcom MediaVest Group (SMG); then moved it to Aegis Carat in 2012 in an effort to increase efficiencies and even further cut costs.[8]

Other major corporations have tried to follow GM's experiment in "unbundling" media planning from creative services. Unilever moved its $700 million U.S. media buying clout from its various ad agencies to a single media

IMC FOCUS

A Multi-Screen Media World

One night in June 2010, 2.6 million viewers were on the Bravo Network watching the final episode of the *Real Housewives of New York City*. As housewife LuAnn was singing a "cringe-worthy" single, *Money Can't Buy You Class*, 13,000 viewers soon went to Bravo's website to use an interactive feature called Talk Bubble and to interact with fellow viewers. The site's tools allowed them to share jokes on Twitter, update their Facebook page, and follow a "Tweet Heat" graphic that grouped the viewer's collective views about the show (e.g., "Stop Singing!").

Nielsen research has shown that consumers now spend an average of over 3 hours and 41 minutes per month both watching TV and browsing online simultaneously, and that almost 60 percent of TV viewers engage in 2-screen viewing. In Europe, multi-screen viewers are found to be more educated, affluent, brand loyal, and are greater brand advocates compared to the average adult viewer.

In general, screen convergence is not viewed as cannibalization by many media advertisers and critics, as smartphones, TV, gaming consoles, and computers each have different benefits and personalities for users. Research has also shown that multi-screen viewing of the same ad can increase aided awareness scores and post-ad actions. However, measurement that marries the different systems from traditional panels to third-party data (e.g., video across TV, smartphones, games, computer websites) can be challenging. Nielsen's recent Online Campaign Ratings (OCR) (e.g., with

gross rating points to be covered later in the chapter) is attempting to measure, for example, how many people saw a campaign ad in three different dimensions: (1) only on TV, (2) only online, and (3) on both. Such unified metrics in a multi-screen media world can only help with what is already a difficult and challenging job in media planning and buying.

© Rex Features via AP Images

Sources: Felix Gillette, "For Bravo, One Screen Isn't Enough," *Bloomberg Businessweek*, November 8–14, 2010, 43–44; Anita Caras, "What's On Their Screens," Microsoft Advertising White Paper, 2010, http://advertising.microsoft.com/europe/WWDocs/User/Europe/ResearchLibrary/ResearchReport/6.%20Multi-screen%20Whitepaper.pdf (accessed March 14, 2012); Shelly Palmer, "Nielsen Tackles Inertia in Multiscreen Ad Space," Screenplaysmag.com (blog), January 30, 2012, http://www.screenplaysmag.com/2012/02/02/nielsen-tackles-inertia-in-multiscreen-ad-space.

© Jim Barber/Shutterstock.com

buyer. Likewise, Kraft Foods consolidated its $800 million North American media planning and buying account into a single media planner and buyer.

Traditional full-service advertising agencies have criticized these moves. They claim that creative services and media planning go hand in hand, and that the symbiotic relationship between these services is damaged when ad agencies are relegated to just creating ad messages while independent firms are fully responsible for planning media selection. A top official of a major ad agency had this to say:

> *You can't keep compartmentalizing each aspect of an account. Many of the insights we get come from the media side, and that informs the creative side and vice versa. I have a hard time believing that [ad agencies] can be as effective without that kind of close relationship.*[9]

The chief executive officer of a media planning company presented a counterperspective.

> *Separating media buying and planning [from creative] can be beneficial to clients who work in a multi-brand environment. Even though GM has different car lines, with different goals and strategies, there's something to be said for bringing all the planning operations together into one centralized location. It gives them an opportunity to apply learning and strategic thinking across the portfolio in a way that's faster and more efficient.*[10]

There obviously are arguments on both sides of the issue, yet the proverbial genie is now out of the bottle. The historical role of the all-powerful full-service advertising agency has diminished. Perhaps of greatest significance is that this development accentuates the importance of the media planning aspect of the advertising process. Creating effective advertising messages is critical, but it is essential also that these messages be placed in the right media and vehicles.

The Media-Planning Process

Media planning is the design of a strategy that shows how investments in advertising time and space will contribute to the achievement of marketing objectives. The challenge in media planning is determining how best to *allocate* the fixed advertising budget for a particular planning period among ad media, across vehicles within media, and over time. As shown in Figure 16.1, media planning involves coordinating three levels of strategy: marketing, advertising, and media strategy. The overall *marketing strategy* (consisting of target market identification and marketing mix selection) provides the impetus and direction for the choice of both advertising and media strategies. The *advertising strategy*—involving advertising objectives, budget, and message and media strategies—thus extends naturally from the overall marketing strategy.

For illustration purposes, let us consider an advertising campaign for the Smart Car. As background, the Smart Car entered the U.S. market as the "Fortwo" in early 2008. It is the cousin of the European Smart Car that has been available since the late 1990s and has already sold more than 770,000 in 36 countries.[11] The Smart Car is a vehicle with two seats that also has reasonable luggage space contained in a body that is 8 feet and 10 inches long.[12] Prices for different 2012 U.S. Smart Car models range from less than $12,490 for the Coupe to over $17,690 for the Passion Cabriolet convertible.[13]

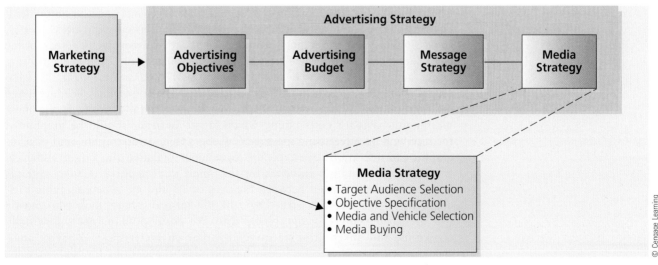

FIGURE 16.1 Model of the Media-Planning Process

© Darren Brode/Shutterstock.com

In other countries (as well as in the United States), the Smart Car has appealed to urban dwellers who need a small car for parking in the tight spaces that are common in larger cities and also those who desire a relatively inexpensive and gas-efficient vehicle. We also might assume that prospective customers are cosmopolitan, environmentally conscious, and adventuresome. In addition, the media strategy for the Smart Car naturally must extend from Smart USA's (a division of Daimler AG's Mercedes-Benz brand) strategy to sell, for example, approximately 30,000 Smart Cars at retail in 2012.

Media strategy is inextricably related to the other aspects of advertising strategy (see Figure 16.1). Let us assume that the Smart Car has a $15 million advertising budget for 2012, which equates to $500 advertising per each of the 30,000 cars expected to be sold in 2012. Suppose further that the objective is to create brand awareness for the Smart Car among targeted consumers and to convey the image of a convenient, fuel-efficient, and adventurous car. Advertising strategy decisions simultaneously impose constraints on media strategy (e.g., $15 million is the maximum amount that could be spent on the 2012 Smart Car campaign) and provide direction for media selection.

The media strategy itself consists of four sets of interrelated activities (see again Figure 16.1):

1. Selecting the target audience
2. Specifying media objectives
3. Selecting media categories and vehicles
4. Buying media

We now will examine the first three actions in greater detail.

Selecting the Target Audience

Effective media strategy requires, first, that the target audience be pinpointed. Failure to define the audience precisely results in wasted exposures; that is, some nonpurchase candidates are exposed to advertisements, whereas prime candidates are missed. Four major types of information are used in segmenting target audiences for media strategy purposes: (1) behavioral data, (2) geographic data, (3) demographics, and (4) lifestyle/psychographics. Product usage information (behavioral data), when available, generally provides the most meaningful basis for determining which target audience should be pinpointed for receiving an advertising message.[14] Geographic, demographic, and psychographic considerations are typically combined to define the target audience. For example, the target audience for the Smart Car might be defined in terms such as: men and women between the ages of 18 and 49 (a demographic variable), who have incomes exceeding $50,000 (also demographic), who mostly live in urban centers (geographic), who are cosmopolitan, environmentally conscious, and adventuresome (psychographic characteristics). A target audience defined in such specific terms has obvious implications for both message and media strategy.

Specifying Media Objectives

The next media-planning consideration involves specifying the *objectives* that an advertising schedule is designed to accomplish during the planned advertising period. Media planners, in setting objectives, confront issues such as: (1) what proportion of a target audience do we want to reach with our advertising message during a specified period, (2) with what frequency do we need to expose the audience to our message during this period, (3) how much total advertising is necessary to accomplish the first two objectives, (4) how should we allocate the advertising budget over time, (5) how close to the time of purchase should the target audience be exposed to our advertising message, and (6) what is the most economically justifiable way to accomplish the other objectives?

Practitioners have technical terms they associate with each of these six objectives: (1) *reach*, (2) *frequency*, (3) *weight*, (4) *continuity*, (5) *recency*, and (6) *cost*. The following sections treat each objective as a separate matter. A later section addresses their interdependence.

Reach

Advertising managers and media specialists generally regard reaching specific audiences efficiently as the most important consideration when selecting media and vehicles.[15] The issue of reach deals with getting an advertising message heard or seen by the targeted audience. More precisely, reach represents the *percentage of the target audience* that is exposed, *at least once*, during a specified time frame to the *vehicles* in which our advertising message is inserted. The time frame the majority of media planners use is a *four-week period*. (Thus, there are 13 four-week media-planning periods during a full year.) Some media specialists also use the single week as the planning period.

Regardless of the length of the planning period, reach represents the percentage of all target customers who have an *opportunity to see or hear* the advertiser's message one or more times during this time period. (Advertising people use the expression *opportunity to see*, or *OTS*, to refer to all advertising media, whether visual or auditory.) Advertisers never know for sure (before advertising) whether members of their target audiences will actually see or hear an advertising message. Advertisers only know to which media vehicles the target audience is exposed. From these vehicle exposure data, it then can be inferred that people have had an opportunity to see the advertising message carried in the vehicles.

Other terms media planners use for describing reach are *1+* (read "one-plus"), *net coverage*, and *unduplicated audience*. (Both "net coverage" and "unduplicated audience" refer to the *absolute* number in the target audience reached.) Later it will become clear why these terms are related to *reach*.

Determinants of Reach

Several factors can increase the reach that is achieved with a particular media schedule: (1) use multiple media, (2) diversify vehicles within each medium, and (3) vary the dayparts in the case of radio and TV advertising.

Generally speaking, more prospective customers are reached when a media schedule allocates the advertising budget among *multiple media* rather than to a single medium. For example, if the Smart Car were advertised only on network television, its advertisements would reach fewer people than if it also were advertised on cable TV, in magazines, online, on the radio, and in national newspapers. If an advertiser were to advertise a brand only in, say, newspapers, it would miss 40 percent of the adult population in the United States which does not regularly read a daily newspaper. Likewise, advertising only on select TV programs would miss people who do not view those particular programs. Hence, using multiple media increases the odds of reaching a greater proportion of the target audience. In general, the more media options used, the greater the chances that an advertising message will come into contact with people whose media habits differ.

A second factor influencing reach is the *number and diversity of media vehicles used*. For example, if Smart Car's media planners were to choose to advertise this automobile in, say, just a single magazine (e.g., *Cosmopolitan*) rather than in a variety of magazines, the advertising effort would reach far fewer consumers. Using *Cosmopolitan* as an example, if Smart Car were advertised only in that particular magazine, the ad campaign would fail to reach all people in the target audience who do *not* read that magazine.

Third, *diversifying the dayparts* used to advertise a brand can increase reach. For example, network television advertising during prime time and cable television advertising during fringe times would reach more potential automobile purchasers than advertising exclusively during prime time.

In sum, reach is an important consideration when developing a brand's media schedule. Advertisers wish to reach the highest possible proportion of the target audience that the budget permits. However, reach by itself is an inadequate objective for media planning because it tells nothing about *how often* target customers need to be exposed to the brand's advertising message for it to accomplish its goals. Therefore, frequency of advertising exposures must also be considered.

Frequency

Frequency signifies the number of times, on average, during the media-planning period that members of the target audience are exposed to the media *vehicles* that carry a brand's advertising message. Frequency actually represents a media schedule's *average frequency*, but media people use the term *frequency* as a shorthand way of referring to average frequency.

To better understand the concept of frequency and how it relates to reach, consider the simplified example in Table 16.1. This example provides information about 10 hypothetical members of the target audience for the Smart Car and their exposure to *Cosmopolitan* magazine over four consecutive weeks. (We are assuming for purposes of this simplified example that *Cosmopolitan* is the sole vehicle used for advertising the Smart Car.) Audience member A, for example, is exposed to *Cosmopolitan* on two occasions, weeks two and three. Member B is exposed to *Cosmopolitan* all four weeks. Member C is never exposed to this magazine during the four-week period. Member D is exposed three times, in weeks one, three, and four, and so on for the remaining six members of Smart Car's audience. Notice in the last column of Table 16.1 that for each week, only 5 of 10 households (50 percent) are exposed to *Cosmopolitan* and thus have an opportunity to see an advertisement for the Smart Car placed in this advertising vehicle. This reflects the fact that a single vehicle (in this case, *Cosmopolitan*) rarely reaches the full target audience.

The Concept of Frequency Distribution

Presented at the bottom of Table 16.1 are the frequency distribution and summary reach and frequency statistics for the Smart Car's media Schedule. A *frequency distribution* represents the percentage of audience members (labeled "Percentage *f*" in Table 16.1) who are exposed *f* times (where *f* = 0, 1, 2, 3, or 4) to the *Cosmopolitan* magazine and thus have an opportunity to see ads for the Smart Car carried in that magazine. The cumulative frequency column (labeled "Percentage *f*+") indicates the percentage of the 10-member audience that has been exposed *f* or more times to *Cosmopolitan* magazine during this four-week period (again, *f* = 0, 1, 2, 3, or 4).

For example, the percentage exposed at least two times is 70 percent. Note carefully that for any value of *f*, the percentage in the Percentage *f*+ column simply represents the summation from the Percentage *f* column of that value plus all greater values. Reading from the Percentage *f* column in Table 16.1, you

TABLE 16.1	Hypothetical Frequency Distribution for the Smart Car Advertised in *Cosmopolitan* Magazine

Week	A	B	C	D	E	F	G	H	I	J	Total Exposures
							Target Audience Member				
1		X		X	X		X		X		5
2	X	X			X		X		X		5
3	X	X		X				X		X	5
4		X		X		X	X			X	5
Total Exposure	2	4	0	3	2	1	3	1	2	2	

Summary Statistics

Frequency Distribution (*f*)	Percentage *f*	Percentage *f*+	Audience Members
0	10%	100%	C
1	20	90	F, H
2	40	70	A, E, I, J
3	20	30	D, G
4	10	10	B

Reach (1+ exposures) = 90

Frequency = 2.2

GRPs = 200

© Cengage Learning

will see that the percentage of target audience members exposed exactly two times is 40 percent (namely, audience members A, E, I, and J). The percentage exposed exactly three times is 20 percent (members D and G) and the percentage exposed four times is 10 percent (member B). Hence, the cumulative percentage of audience members exposed two or more times (i.e., the percentage *f*+ when *f* = 2) is 70 percent (40 + 20 + 10 = 70).

We now are in a position to illustrate how both reach and frequency are calculated. It can be seen in Table 16.1 that 9 (i.e., the net coverage or unduplicated audience) of the 10 audience members for the Smart Car advertisement have been exposed to one or more ads during the four-week advertising period. (Reading from the Percentage *f*+ column, with *f* = 1, it can be seen that the 1+ cumulative percentage is 90.) This figure, 90 percent, represents the *reach* for this advertising effort. Note that advertising practitioners drop the percent sign when referring to reach and simply refer to the number. In this case, reach equals 90.

Frequency is the average of the frequency distribution. In this situation, frequency equals 2.22. That is, 20 percent are reached one time, 40 percent are reached two times, 20 percent are reached three times, and 10 percent four times. Or, arithmetically, average frequency (or simply, frequency) equals:

$$\frac{(1 \times 20) + (2 \times 40) + (3 \times 20) + (4 \times 10)}{90} = \frac{200}{90} = 2.22 \qquad (16.1)$$

This hypothetical situation thus indicates that 90 percent of the Smart Car's target audience is reached by the advertising schedule and that they are exposed an average of 2.2 times during the four-week advertising schedule in *Cosmopolitan*. This value, 2.2, represents this simplified media schedule's frequency. (The exact frequency is 2.22; however, media practitioners conventionally round frequency figures to a single decimal place.) Note carefully that the sum of all frequencies (the numerator in the previous calculation) is divided by the reach figure to obtain frequency (reach = 90).

Weight

A third objective involved in formulating media plans is determining how much advertising volume (termed *weight* by practitioners) is required to accomplish advertising objectives. Different metrics are used in determining an advertising schedule's weight during a specific advertising period. This section describes three weight metrics: gross ratings, target ratings, and effective ratings. First, however, it will be useful to explain the meaning of ratings.

What Are Ratings?

The concept of ratings has a unique meaning in the advertising industry unlike its everyday meaning. When people typically use the word *rating*, they are referring to a judgment about something. For example, a movie (or a restaurant, CD, etc.) might be rated on a five-star scale from terrible (= 1 star) to wonderful (= 5 stars). However, in the context of advertising, the term *ratings* refers to the percentage of an audience that has an *opportunity to see* an advertisement placed in that vehicle.

Let us illustrate the meaning of ratings, using television as an example. As of 2012, there were approximately 114.7 million households in the United States who had television sets.[16] Therefore, a single rating point during this period represents 1 percent of all television households, or 1,147,000 households.

Suppose, for sake of example, that during one week in 2012 a TV program named *NCIS* had roughly 18 million households tuned in. *NCIS* ratings during that week would thus be 15.7 (i.e., 18 ÷ 114.7), which would indicate in a straight-forward fashion that 15.7 percent of all TV households viewed *NCIS* during this one weekly episode in 2012. This, quite simply, is the meaning of ratings. It is important to recognize that the concept of ratings applies to all media and vehicles, not just to television and TV programs.

© Photo by John Shearer/WireImage/Getty Images

Gross Rating Points (GRPs)

Notice at the bottom of Table 16.1 that Smart Car's ad schedule in *Cosmopolitan* yields 200 GRPs. Gross rating points (GRPs) reflect the weight that a particular advertising schedule has delivered. The term *gross* is the key. GRPs indicate the total coverage, or *duplicated audience*, exposed to a particular advertising schedule. Compare these terms with the terms given earlier for the absolute number of those reached—that is, *net coverage* and *unduplicated audience.*

Returning to our hypothetical example of an ad for the Smart Car in *Cosmopolitan*, the reach was 90, meaning that 9 of the 10 households in our mini-audience were exposed to at least a single issue of *Cosmo* magazine. (Again, the "9" is the net coverage or unduplicated audience.) The gross rating points in this example amount to 200 GRPs because audience members were exposed multiple times (2.22 times on average) to the vehicles that carried the Smart Car ad during the four-week ad schedule.

It should be apparent from this discussion that GRPs represent the arithmetic product of reach times frequency.

$$\text{GRPs} = \text{Reach}(R) \times \text{Frequency}(F)$$
$$= 90 \times 2.22$$
$$= 200$$

By simple algebraic manipulation the following additional relations are obtained:

$$R = \text{GRPs} \div F$$
$$F = \text{GRPs} \div R$$

In other words, with knowledge of any two pieces of information from among R, F, and GRPs, it is easy to calculate the third by simple mathematical derivation.

Determining GRPs in Practice

In advertising practice, media planners make media purchases by deciding how many GRPs are needed to accomplish established objectives. However, because the frequency distribution and reach and frequency statistics are unknown before the fact (i.e., at the time when the media schedule is determined), media planners need some other way to determine how many GRPs will result from a particular schedule.

There is, in fact, a simple way to make this determination. GRPs are ascertained by simply summing the ratings obtained from the individual vehicles included in a prospective media schedule. Remember, gross rating points are nothing more than *the sum of all vehicle ratings in a media schedule*. For example, during the week of February 27, 2012, the 10 most highly rated TV programs were as follows:

Program	Network	Household Rating
NCIS	CBS	11.3
American Idol—Thursday	Fox	10.8
American Idol—Wednesday	Fox	10.1
NCIS: Los Angeles	CBS	9.9
American Idol Tues Special	Fox	9.4
Voice	NBC	8.7
NASCAR Daytona 500 Mon	Fox	8.0
Criminal Minds	CBS	7.8
NASCAR Daytona 500 BNS	Fox	7.5
Two and a Half Men	CBS	7.5

Source: "Nielsen Top 10 TV Ratings: Prime Broadcast Network TV Programs – United States," Nielsen Media Research, week of February 27, 2012, http://www.nielsen.com/us/en/insights/top10s/television.html (accessed March 12, 2012). Copyrighted information of Nielsen, licensed for use herein.

Suppose by chance that an advertiser had placed a single ad on each of these TV programs during the week of February 27, 2012. This being the case, the advertiser would have accumulated 91 GRPs when advertising in these particular programs ($11.3 + 10.8 + \cdots + 7.5 = 91.0$). In short, the gross ratings generated by a particular media schedule simply equals the *sum of the individual ratings* obtained across all vehicles included in that schedule.

Target Rating Points (TRPs)

A slight but important variant of GRPs is the notion of target rating points. Target rating points (TRPs) adjust vehicle ratings to reflect just those individuals *who match the advertiser's target audience*. Returning to the Smart Car example, let us assume that the advertising target for this model is primarily people between the ages of 18 and 49 who have incomes of $50,000 or more and generally reside in urban areas. Considering the 10 TV programs listed previously, assume that, for simplicity, only 30 percent of the total audience exposed to each of these programs actually match Smart Car's target market. Hence, although placing a single ad in each of these programs yields 91 *gross* rating points, this same schedule produces only 31.4 *target* rating points (i.e., $91 \times 0.3 = 27.3$).

It should be obvious from this simple illustration that GRPs represent some degree of wasted coverage because some audience members fall outside the target audience the advertiser wishes to reach. Comparatively, target rating points, TRPs, represent a better indicator of a media schedule's *non-wasted weight*. GRPs equal *gross* weight, some of which is wasted; TRPs equal *net* weight, none of which is wasted.

The Concept of Effective Reach

Alternative media schedules are usually compared in terms of the number of GRPs (or TRPs) that each generates. A greater number of GRPs (or TRPs) does not necessarily indicate superiority, however. Consider, for example, two alternative media plans that require the exact same budget. We will refer to these plans as plan X and plan Z. Plan X generates 95 percent reach and an average frequency of 2.0, thereby yielding 190 GRPs. (Note again that *reach* is defined as the proportion of the audience exposed one or more times to advertising vehicles during the course of a typical four-week campaign.) Plan Z provides for 166.4 GRPs from a reach of 52 percent and a frequency of 3.2.

Which plan is better? Plan X is clearly superior in terms of total GRPs and reach, but Plan Z has a higher frequency level. If the brand in question requires a greater number of exposures for the advertising to achieve effectiveness, then Plan Z may be superior even though it yields fewer GRPs. By the way, the same comparison would apply as well if this example were in terms of TRPs rather than GRPs.

It is for the reason suggested in the preceding comparison that many advertisers and media planners have become critical of the GRP and TRP concepts, contending that "[these concepts] rest on the very dubious assumption that every exposure is of equal value, that the 50th exposure is the same as the tenth or the first."[17] Although the GRP and the TRP metrics remain very much a part of media planning, the advertising industry has turned away from the exclusive use of "raw" advertising weight toward a concept of media *effectiveness*.[18] The determination of media effectiveness takes into consideration *how often* members of the target audience have an opportunity to be exposed to advertising messages for the focal brand. Media practitioners often use the terms *effective reach* and *effective frequency* interchangeably to capture the idea that an effective media schedule delivers a sufficient but not excessive number of ads to the target audience. Although either term is acceptable, hereafter we will simply refer to *effective reach*.

Effective reach is based on the idea that an advertising schedule is effective only if it does not reach members of the target audience *too few* or *too many* times during the media scheduling period, which, as noted previously, is typically a four-week period. In other words, there is a theoretical optimum range of exposures to an advertisement with minimum and maximum limits. But what constitutes too few or too many exposures? This, unfortunately, is one of the most complicated issues in all of advertising. The only statement that can be made with certainty is, "It depends!"

It depends, in particular, on considerations such as the level of consumer awareness of the advertised brand, its market share, the audience's degree of loyalty to the brand, message creativity and novelty, and the objectives that advertising is intended to accomplish for the brand. In fact, high levels of weekly exposure to a brand's advertising may be unproductive for loyal consumers because of a leveling off of ad effectiveness.[19] Specifically, brands with higher market shares and greater customer loyalty typically require *fewer* advertising exposures to achieve minimal levels of effectiveness. Likewise, it would be expected that distinctive advertising campaigns require *fewer* exposures to accomplish their objectives. The higher up the hierarchy of effects the advertising is attempting to move the consumer, the *greater* the number of exposures needed to achieve minimal effectiveness. For example, fewer exposures probably would be needed merely to make consumers aware that there is a brand named Smart Car than would be required to convince them that although Smart Car is small it is relatively safe.

How Many Exposures Are Needed?

It follows from the foregoing discussion that the minimum and maximum numbers of effective exposures can be determined only by conducting sophisticated research. Because research of this nature is time-consuming and expensive, advertisers and media planners generally have used rules of thumb in place of research in determining exposure effectiveness. Advertising industry thinking on this matter has been heavily influenced by the so-called three-exposure hypothesis, which addresses the *minimum* number of exposures needed for advertising to be effective. Its originator, an advertising practitioner named Herbert Krugman, argued that a consumer's initial exposure to a brand's advertising initiates a response of "What is it?" The second exposure triggers a response of "What of it?" And the third exposure and those thereafter are merely reminders of the information that the consumer already has learned from the first two exposures.[20]

This hypothesis, which was based on little empirical data and a lot of intuition, has virtually become gospel in the advertising industry. Many advertising practitioners have interpreted the three-exposure hypothesis to mean that media schedules are *ineffective* when they deliver average frequencies of *fewer than three exposures* to the advertising vehicle in which a brand's advertisement is placed.

Although there is some intuitive appeal to the notion that frequencies of fewer than three are insufficient, this interpretation of the three-exposure hypothesis is too literal and also fails to recognize that Krugman's hypothesis had in mind three exposures to an advertising *message* and not three exposures to vehicles carrying the message.[21] The difference is that vehicle exposure, or what we previously referred to as *opportunity to see (OTS)* an ad, is *not* tantamount to advertising exposure. For example, a viewer of a TV program will probably miss some of the commercials placed during a 30- or 60-minute program or will be inattentive to some of those that are aired.

Aside from this general misunderstanding of the three-exposure hypothesis, it must also be recognized that no specific number of minimum exposures—whether 3, 7, 17, etc.—is absolutely correct for all advertising situations. It cannot be overemphasized that what is effective (or ineffective) for one product or brand may not necessarily be so for another. "There is no magic number, no comfortable '3+' level of advertising exposures that works, even if we refer to advertising exposure rather than OTS."[22]

Effective Reach Planning in Advertising Practice

The mostly widely accepted view among media planners is that *fewer than 3 exposures* during a four-week media schedule is generally considered ineffective, whereas *more than 10 exposures* during this period is considered excessive. The range of effective reach, then, can be thought of as *3 to 10 exposures* during a designated media-planning period.

The use of effective reach rather than gross rating points as the basis for media planning can have a major effect on overall media strategies. In particular, effective reach planning generally leads to using *multiple media* rather than depending exclusively on television, which is often the strategy when using the GRP metric. Prime-time television is especially effective in terms of generating high levels of reach (1+ exposures), but may be deficient in terms of achieving effective reach (3+ exposures). Thus, the use of effective reach as the decision criterion often involves giving up some of prime-time television's reach to obtain greater frequency (at the same total cost) from other media.

This is illustrated in Table 16.2, which compares four media plans involving different combinations of media expenditures from an annual advertising budget of $25 million.[23] Plan A allocates 100 percent of the $25 million budget to network television advertising, plan B allocates 67 percent to television and 33 percent to network radio, plan C splits the budget between network television and magazines, and plan D allocates 67 percent to television and 33 percent to outdoor advertising.

Notice first that plan A (the use of 100 percent TV) leads to the lowest levels of reach, effective reach, frequency, and GRPs. An even (50/50) split of TV and magazines (plan C) generates an especially high level of reach (91 percent), whereas combinations of TV with radio (plan B) and TV with outdoor advertising (plan D) are especially impressive in terms of frequency, GRPs, and the percentage of consumers exposed three or more times.

More to the point, notice that the TV-only plan compared with the remaining plans yields far fewer GRPs and considerably fewer effective rating points (ERPs). (Note that in Table 16.2 ERPs equal the product of effective reach, or 3+ exposures, times frequency; plan A, for example, yields 81 ERPs, i.e., 29 × 2.8 = 81.2.) Plan D, which combines 67 percent TV with 33 percent outdoor advertising, is especially outstanding in terms of the numbers of GRPs and ERPs generated. This is because outdoor advertising is seen frequently as people travel to and from work and participate in other activities.

Should we conclude from this discussion that plan D is the best and that plan A is the worst? Not necessarily. Clearly, the impact from seeing one

TABLE 16.2 Alternative Media Plans Based on a $25 Million Annual Budget and Four-Week Media Analysis

	Plan A: TV (100%)	Plan B: TV (67%), Radio (33%)	Plan C: TV (50%), Magazines (50%)	Plan D: TV (67%), Outdoor (33%)
Reach (1+ exposures)	69%	79%	91%	87%
Effective reach (3+ exposures)	29%	48%	53%	61%
Frequency	2.8	5.5	3.2	6.7
GRPs	193	435	291	583
ERPs	81	264	170	409
Cost per GRP	$129,534	$57,471	$85,911	$42,882
Cost per ERP	$308,642	$94,697	$147,059	$61,125

billboard advertisement is generally far less than being exposed to a captivating television commercial. This illustration points out a fundamental aspect of media planning: *subjective factors* also must be considered when allocating advertising dollars. Superficially, the numbers do favor plan D. However, judgment and past experience may favor plan A on the grounds that the only way to advertise this particular product effectively is by presenting dynamic action shots of people consuming and enjoying the product. Only television could satisfy this requirement. Other media (radio, magazines, and outdoor advertising) may be used to complement the key message TV ads drive home. (The strengths and limitations of each of these ad media are discussed in the following chapter.)

It is useful to return again to a point established in Chapter 8: *It is better to be vaguely right than precisely wrong.* Reach, frequency, effective reach, GRPs, TRPs, and ERPs are precise in their appearance but, in application, if used blindly, may be precisely wrong.

An Alternative Approach: Frequency Value Planning

Advertising scholars have proposed an alternative approach to the three-exposure doctrine.[24] The objective of *frequency value planning* is to select that media schedule (from a set of alternative schedules) that generates the most exposure value per GRP—or, stated differently, the objective is to select that media schedule that provides a "bigger bang for the buck." Frequency value planning is an approach that attempts to get the most out of an advertising investment in the sense of selecting the most *efficient* advertising schedule. The following implementation steps are involved:

Step 1. Estimate the *exposure utility* for each level of vehicle exposure, or OTS, that a schedule produces.[25] Exposure utility represents the worth, or value, of each additional opportunity for audience members to see an ad for a brand during the period of an advertising schedule. Table 16.3 lists OTSs from 0 to 10+ and their corresponding exposure utilities. (Note that these utilities are not invariant across all situations but have to be determined uniquely for each brand-advertising situation.) It can be seen that 0 vehicle exposures has, of course, an exposure utility of 0. One exposure adds the greatest amount of utility, assumed here to be 0.50 units; a second OTS contributes 0.13 additional units of utility (for an overall utility of 0.63); a third exposure contributes 0.09 more units to the second exposure (for an overall utility of 0.72 units); a fourth exposure adds 0.07 units of utility to the third exposure; and so on. One can

TABLE 16.3	Exposure Utilities for Different OTS Levels	
OTS		**Exposure Utility**
0		0.00
1		0.50
2		0.63
3		0.72
4		0.79
5		0.85
6		0.90
7		0.94
8		0.97
9		0.99
10+		1.00

readily see that this utility function reflects decreasing marginal utility with each additional OTS. At an OTS of 10, the maximum utility of 1.00 is achieved. Hence, this illustration proposes that OTSs in excess of 10 offer no additional utility. By graphing the utilities in Table 16.3, one can readily see that the function is nonlinear and concave to the origin. In other words, each additional exposure contributes decreasing utility.

Step 2. Estimate the *frequency distribution* of the various media schedules that are under consideration. Computer programs, such as the program discussed later in the chapter, are available for this purpose. Table 16.4 shows the distributions for two alternative media schedules. Reading in Table 16.4 from column B (Schedule 1) and column D (Schedule 2), it can be seen that 15 percent of the target audience is estimated to be exposed zero times to Schedule 1 (8 percent exposed zero times to Schedule 2), 11.1 percent of the target audience is estimated to be exposed exactly one time to Schedule 1 (21.0 percent are exposed one time to Schedule 2), 12.5 percent of the audience exposed exactly two times to Schedule 1 (17.6 percent to Schedule 2), 13.2 percent three times to Schedule 1 (13.6 percent to Schedule 2), and so on.

Step 3. Estimate the *OTS value at each OTS level.*[26] Entries in the *OTS value* columns in Table 16.4 (column C for Schedule 1, column E for Schedule 2) are calculated at each OTS level (OTS = 1, 2, 3, ..., 10+) by simply taking the arithmetic product of the Exposure Utility at each OTS level times the Percentage of Target column. Hence, at an OTS of one exposure, the exposure value is $0.5 \times 11.1 = 5.55$ for Schedule 1 and $0.5 \times 21.0 = 10.5$ for Schedule 2. At an OTS of two exposures, the exposure value is $0.63 \times 12.5 = 7.875$ (Schedule 1) and $0.63 \times 17.6 = 11.088$ (Schedule 2), and so on.

Step 4. Determine the *total value across all OTS levels.* After calculating the value at each OTS level, the *total value* is obtained by simply summing the individual exposure values $(5.55 + 7.875 + 9.504 + \cdots + 10.5 = 66.481$ for

TABLE 16.4 Frequency Distributions and Valuations of Two Media Schedules

OTS	Schedule 1			Schedule 2	
	(A) Exposure Utility	(B) Percentage of Target	(C) OTS Value (A × B)	(D) Percentage of Target	(E) OTS Value (A × D)
0	0.00	15.0%	0.000	8.0%	0.000
1	0.50	11.1	5.550	21.0	10.500
2	0.63	12.5	7.875	17.6	11.088
3	0.72	13.2	9.504	13.6	9.792
4	0.79	11.0	8.690	10.9	8.611
5	0.85	8.4	7.140	8.6	7.310
6	0.90	6.3	5.670	6.6	5.940
7	0.94	5.0	4.700	5.2	4.888
8	0.97	3.9	3.783	3.9	3.783
9	0.99	3.1	3.069	3.0	2.970
10+	1.00	10.5	10.500	1.6	1.600
Total Value			66.481		66.482
GRPs			398.6		333.8
Index of Exposure Efficiency (Value/GRPs)			0.167		0.199

Schedule 1; 10.5 + 11.088 + 9.792 + ⋯ + 1.6 = 66.482 for Schedule 2, which is virtually identical to that for Schedule 1).

Step 5. Develop an *index of exposure efficiency*. This index is calculated by dividing each schedule's *total value* by the number of GRPs produced by that schedule. Total GRPs are determined from the data in Table 16.4 in the same way they were identified earlier from the data in Table 16.1. Specifically, Schedule 1's total of 398.6 GRPs (see bottom of Table 16.4) is calculated as (1 × 11.1) + (2 × 12.5) + (3 × 13.2) + ⋯ + (10 × 10.5). (You should ensure that you understand this by calculating the GRPs for Schedule 2.) The index of exposure efficiency for Schedule 1 is 0.167 (i.e., 66.481 ÷ 398.6), whereas the index value for Schedule 2 is 0.199 (i.e., 66.482 ÷ 333.8).

What can be concluded from these calculations? With higher index values representing greater *efficiency*, it should be clear that Schedule 2 in Table 16.4 is the more efficient media schedule. That is, Schedule 2 has a higher efficiency index than Schedule 1 because Schedule 2 accomplishes an equivalent exposure value (66.482 versus 66.481), but with fewer GRPs and hence less expense. Moreover, whereas Schedule 1 reaches a high percentage of the target audience 10 or more times (i.e., 10+ OTS = 10.5 percent), Schedule 2 focuses more on reaching the audience at least one time rather than wasting expenditures on reaching the audience 10 or more times. The 1+ OTS for Schedule 2 equals 92 percent, compared with Schedule 1's 1+ OTS of 85 percent.

Although this method of frequency value planning is theoretically sounder than the three-exposure heuristic, the latter is embedded in advertising practice whereas the former was introduced more recently. The implication is not that this newer procedure should be dismissed out of hand; the point, instead, is that advertising practice has not as yet widely adopted the approach. It is only fair to note that the difficulty with implementing frequency value planning is in estimating exposure utilities, such as those presented in Table 16.3. There simply is no easy way to estimate exposure utilities, which is why many media planners prefer to employ rules of thumb.

Continuity

Continuity involves the matter of how advertising is allocated during the course of an advertising campaign. The fundamental issue is this: Should the media budget be distributed uniformly throughout the period of the advertising campaign, should it be spent in a concentrated period to achieve the most impact, or should some other schedule between these two extremes be used? As always, the determination of what is best depends on the specifics of the situation. In general, however, a uniform advertising schedule may suffer from too little advertising weight at any one time. A heavily concentrated schedule, in contrast, can suffer from excessive exposures during the advertising period and a complete absence of advertising at all other times.

Advertisers have three general alternatives related to allocating the budget over the course of the campaign: *continuous, pulsing,* and *flighting* schedules. Figure 16.2 shows how advertising allocations might differ from month to month for a dairy company depending on the use of continuous, pulsing, or flighting schedules. Assume the annual advertising budget available to this marketer is $3 million.

Continuous Schedule

In a continuous advertising schedule, an equal or relatively equal number of ad dollars are invested throughout the campaign. The illustration in panel A of Figure 16.2 shows an extreme case of continuous advertising in which the advertiser allocates the $3 million advertising budget in equal amounts of exactly $250,000 for all 12 months.

Such an advertising allocation would make sense only if dairy products were consumed in essentially equal quantities throughout the year. However,

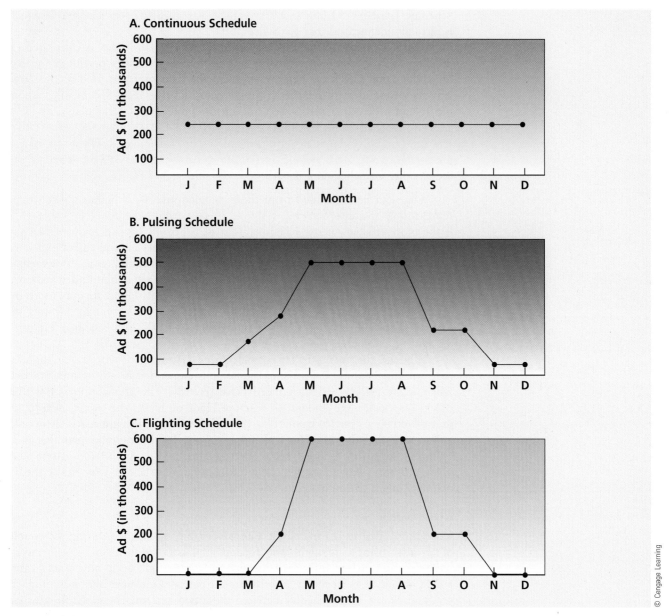

FIGURE **16.2** Continuous, Pulsing, and Flighting Advertising Schedules for a Brand of Ice Cream

consumption is particularly high during May, June, July, and August when people increasingly eat ice cream, which is an especially important product in this company's product line and one for which sales are especially sensitive to advertising support. This calls for a *discontinuous* allocation of advertising dollars throughout the year.

Pulsing

In a pulsing advertising schedule, some advertising is used *during every period* of the campaign, but the amount of advertising varies from period to period. In panel B of Figure 16.2, a pulsing schedule for this dairy company shows that its advertising is especially heavy during the high ice cream-consumption months of May through August (spending $500,000 each month), but the company nonetheless advertises in every month throughout the year. The minimum advertising expenditure is $50,000 even in the relatively low ice cream-sales months of January, February, November, and December.

Flighting

In a flighting schedule, the advertiser varies expenditures throughout the campaign and allocates *zero* expenditures in some months. As demonstrated in panel C of Figure 16.2, the dairy company allocates $600,000 to each of the four high ice cream-consumption months (May through August), $200,000 each to moderate ice cream-consumption months (April, September, and October), but $0 to the five low-consumption months (January, February, March, November, and December). To help remember this, a flighted schedule, just like the flight of a plane or bird, must come "down to the ground" (i.e., zero expenditures) at some point in the yearly campaign.

Recency Planning (a.k.a. The Shelf-Space Model)

Some advertising practitioners argue that flighted and pulsed advertising schedules are necessitated by the tremendous increases in media costs, especially the expense of network television advertising as few advertisers can afford to advertise consistently and heavily throughout the year. Also, discontinuous advertising (i.e., pulsing or flighting) goes hand in hand with the goal of achieving effective reach (3+) during any advertising period in which a brand manager chooses to have an advertising presence.

However, the logic of discontinuous scheduling has been challenged strongly by a New York media specialist named Erwin Ephron. Ephron and his supporters assert that the advertising industry has failed to prove the value of the effective reach (3+) criterion for allocating advertising budgets and that this dubious criterion leads inappropriately to flighted allocations. Ephron has formulated an argument favoring continuous advertising that he terms the *principle of recency*, also called the *shelf-space model*.[27] Because flighting is an on-and-off advertising proposition, by analogy, if retail shelves were out of stock for that brand during various times throughout the year, it could affect brand sales adversely.

The **recency principle**, or *shelf-space model*, is built on three interrelated ideas: (1) that consumers' *first exposure* to an advertisement for a brand is the most powerful; (2) that advertising's primary role is to influence brand choice, and that advertising does indeed influence choice for the *subset of consumers who are in the market* for the product category at the time a brand in that category advertises; and (3) that achieving a *high level of weekly reach* for a brand should be emphasized over acquiring heavy frequency. Let us examine all three ideas.

The Powerful First Exposure

Empirical evidence (albeit somewhat tentative) has demonstrated that the first exposure to advertising has a greater effect on sales than do additional exposures.[28] (The utility function given previously in Table 16.3 also uses the logic that the first exposure has the greatest impact.) The empirical evidence mentioned above is based on single-source data, when a single household is exposed to brand advertising and also provides demographic and brand purchase data at the same time. The research produced provocative findings based on an extensive study of 142 brands representing 12 product categories (detergents, bar soaps, shampoos, ice cream, peanut butter, ground coffee, etc.). In the study, it was demonstrated that the first advertising exposure for these brands generated the highest proportion of sales and that additional exposures added very little to the first.[29]

Influencing Brand Choice

The concept of recency planning is based on the idea that consumer needs determine advertising effects. Advertising is especially effective when it occurs *close to the time when consumers are in the market for a particular product*. There is, in other words, a window of advertising opportunity for capturing the consumer's selection of the advertised brand versus other brands in the product category. "Advertising's job is to influence the purchase. Recency planning's job is to place the message in that window."[30]

The logic, in other words, is that a brand can achieve greater sales volume by reaching more consumers a single time during an advertising period (a reach objective) rather than reaching fewer consumers more often (a frequency objective). Also, the advertising budget is not necessarily lower with recency planning; rather, the budget is allocated differently than is a flighted advertising budget. In particular, recency planning allocates the budget over more weeks throughout the year and invests less weight (fewer GRPs or TRPs) during the weeks in which advertising is undertaken. Recency planning uses *one week*, rather than four weeks, as the planning period and attempts to reach as many target consumers as possible in as many weeks as the budget will permit.

Optimizing Weekly Reach

Accordingly, it can be argued that media planners should devise schedules that are geared toward providing a continuous (or near continuous) presence for a brand with the objective of optimizing *weekly reach* rather than effective reach as embodied in the three-exposure hypothesis.

The logic of recency planning can be summarized as follows:

1. Contrary to the three-exposure hypothesis, which has been interpreted to mean that advertising must *teach* consumers about brands (therefore requiring multiple exposures), the recency principle, or shelf-space model, assumes that the role of advertising is *not* to teach but to influence consumers' *brand selection*. "Unless it's a new brand, a new benefit, or a new use, there is not much learning involved."[31] Hence, the purpose of most advertising is to remind us of, reinforce, or evoke earlier messages rather than to teach consumers about product benefits or uses.

2. With the objective of influencing brand selection, advertising must therefore reach consumers when they are ready to buy a brand. The purpose of advertising by this logic is to "rent the shelf" so as to ensure a brand presence close to the time when consumers make purchase decisions. *Out of sight, out of mind* is a key advertising principle.

3. Advertising messages are most effective when they are *close to the time of purchase*, and a single advertising exposure is effective if it reaches consumers close to the time when they are making brand-selection decisions.

4. The cost effectiveness of a single exposure is approximately *three times greater* than the value of subsequent exposures.[32]

5. Thus, rather than concentrating the advertising budget to achieve multiple exposures only at select times throughout the year, planners should allocate the budget to *reach more consumers more often*.

6. In a world without budget constraints, the ideal advertising approach would be to achieve a weekly reach of 100 (i.e., to reach 100 percent of the target audience at least one time) and to sustain this level of reach for all 52 weeks of the year. Such a schedule would yield 5,200 weekly reach points. Because most advertisers cannot afford to sustain such a constant level of advertising, the next best approach is to *reach as high a percentage of the target audience as possible for as many weeks as possible*. This goal can be accomplished by (1) using 15-second TV commercials as well as more expensive 30-second spots; (2) spreading the budget among cheaper media (e.g., radio) rather than spending exclusively on television advertising; and (3) buying cheaper TV programs (e.g., cable, syndicated) rather than exclusively prime-time network programs. All of these strategies free up advertising dollars and permit an advertising schedule that will reach a high percentage of the target audience continuously rather than sporadically.

Toward Reconciliation: It Depends!

The concept of scheduling media to achieve a continuous rather than sporadic presence has considerable appeal. However, no single approach is equally effective for all brands. The logic of recency planning recognizes this when suggesting (in the first point previously) that for new brands, new benefits, or different ways of using a brand, the advertising objective indeed may be to teach rather than merely remind. Another advertising executive summarized the issue well.

We've always believed that the first exposure is the most powerful, yet we don't want to have hard and fast rules. Every brand is a different situation. The leader in a category has different frequency needs than a competitor with less market share. It's not fair to say every brand has the same need for frequency.[33]

So, what works best depends on the specific circumstances facing a brand. If the brand is *mature* and well established, then effective weekly reach (the shelf-space model) is probably an appropriate way to allocate the advertising budget. Conversely, if the brand is *new*, or if *new benefits or uses* for the brand have been developed, or if the advertising *message is complex*, then the budget should be allocated in a manner that achieves the frequency necessary to teach consumers (e.g., with flighting) about brand benefits and uses.

Cost Considerations

Media planners attempt to allocate the advertising budget in a cost-efficient manner subject to satisfying other objectives. One of the most important and universally used indicators of media efficiency is the cost-per-thousand criterion. Cost-per-thousand (CPM) (the M represents the Roman numeral for 1,000) is the cost of reaching 1,000 people who are readers, viewers, or listeners of the media vehicle. The measure can be refined to mean the cost of reaching 1,000 members of the target audience, excluding those people who fall outside the target market. This refined measure is designated CPM-TM.

CPM and CPM-TM are calculated by dividing the cost of an advertisement placed in a particular advertising vehicle by the vehicle's total-market reach (CPM) or by its target-market reach (CPM-TM):

$$\text{CPM} = \text{Cost of ad} \div \text{Number of } \textit{total} \text{ contacts reached}$$
$$(\text{expressed in thousands})$$

$$\text{CPM-TM} = \text{Cost of ad} \div \text{Number of } \textit{target market} \text{ contacts reached}$$
$$(\text{expressed in thousands})$$

The term *contacts* is used here to represent any type of advertising audience (television viewers, magazine readers, radio listeners, etc.) that is reached by a single advertising placement in a particular vehicle.

Illustrative Calculations

To illustrate how CPM and CPM-TM are calculated, consider the following unconventional advertising situation. During Saturday football games at a major university, a local airplane advertising service flies messages on a trailing device that extends behind the plane. The cost is $500 per message. The football stadium holds 80,000 fans and is filled to capacity every Saturday. Hence, the CPM in this situation is $6.25, which is the cost per message ($500) divided by the number of people in thousands (80) who potentially are exposed to (i.e., have an opportunity to see, or OTS) an advertising message trailing from the plane.

Now assume that a new student bookstore uses the airplane advertising service to announce its opening to the approximately 20,000 students who are typically in attendance at each game. Because the target market in this instance is only a fraction of the total audience, CPM-TM is a more appropriate cost-per-thousand statistic. CPM-TM in this instance is $25 ($500 ÷ 20)—which of course is four times higher than the CPM statistic because the target audience is one fourth the size of the total audience.

To further illustrate how CPM and CPM-TM are calculated, suppose an advertiser promoted its brand on the reality program *American Idol*, and that during a particular week *American Idol*'s Nielsen rating is 16.2, meaning that viewers in approximately 18.3 million households had an OTS for any commercial aired on that program. At a cost of $780,000 for a 30-second commercial on Tuesday evening airings of *American Idol* during the 2008 season, the CPM is as follows:

$$\text{Total viewership} = 18,273,600 \text{ households}$$
$$\text{Cost of 30-second commercial} = \$780,000$$
$$\text{CPM} = \$780,000 \div 18,273.6$$
$$= \$42.68$$

If we assume that the advertised brand's target market consists only of girls and women between the ages of 13 and 34 and that this submarket represents 60 percent of the total audience—or 10,964,160 girls and women who view *American Idol*—then the CPM-TM is

$$\text{CPM-TM} = \$780,000 \div 10,964.16 = \$71.14$$

Use with Caution!

The CPM and CPM-TM statistics are useful for comparing the *cost-efficiency* of different advertising vehicles. They must be used cautiously, however, for several reasons. First, these are measures of cost-efficiency—not of effectiveness. A particular vehicle may be extremely efficient but totally ineffective because it (1) reaches the wrong audience (if CPM is used rather than CPM-TM) or (2) is inappropriate for the product category and the brand advertised. By analogy, a Smart Car is undoubtedly more efficient in terms of miles per gallon than a large SUV but may be less effective for one's purposes.[34]

A second limitation of CPM and CPM-TM measures is their *lack of comparability across media*. As is emphasized in the following chapter, the various media perform unique roles and are therefore priced differently. A lower CPM for radio does not mean that buying radio time is better than buying a more expensive (CPM-wise) television schedule.

Finally, CPM statistics can be misused unless vehicles within a particular medium are compared on the same basis. For example, the CPM for an advertisement placed on daytime television is lower than that for a prime-time program, but this represents a case of comparing apples with oranges. The proper comparison would be between two daytime programs or between two prime-time programs rather than across dayparts. Similarly, it would be inappropriate to compare the CPM for a black-and-white magazine ad with a four-color magazine ad unless the two ads are considered equal in terms of their ability to present the brand effectively.

The Necessity of Making Trade-Offs

We have now discussed various media-planning objectives—reach, frequency, weight, continuity, recency, and cost—in some detail. Each was introduced without direct reference to the other objectives. It is important to recognize, however, that these objectives are actually somewhat at odds with one another. That is, given a fixed advertising budget (e.g., $15 million for the Smart Car), the media planner cannot simultaneously optimize reach, frequency, and continuity objectives. Trade-offs must be made because media planners operate under the constraint of fixed advertising budgets. Hence, optimizing one objective (e.g., minimizing CPM or maximizing GRPs) requires the sacrifice of other objectives. This simply is due to the mathematics of constrained optimization: Multiple objectives cannot simultaneously be optimized when constraints (like limited budgets) exist.

With a fixed advertising budget, the media planner can choose to maximize reach or frequency but not both. With increases in reach, frequency is sacrificed and vice versa: if you want to reach more people, you cannot reach them as often with a *fixed* advertising budget; if you want to reach them more often, you cannot reach as many. In another sense, the brand manager faced with an advertising budget constraint (which always is the case), must decide whether frequency is more important (the three-exposure hypothesis) or reach is more imperative (the recency principle).

Thus, each media planner must decide what is best given the particular circumstances surrounding the advertising decision facing his or her brand. For example, if one needs to *teach* consumers about new brands, new uses, or complex messages, then achieving *effective reach* (3+ exposures) and *repetition* are particularly important. However, for established brands that already are well known by consumers, the advertising task is simply one of *reminding* consumers about the brand, best achieved by maximizing *reach*.

Media-Scheduling Software

On top of the difficult task of making intelligent tradeoffs among sometimes opposing objectives (reach, frequency, etc.), there literally are thousands, if not millions, of possible advertising schedules that could be selected depending on how the various media and media vehicles are combined. Fortunately, this daunting task is facilitated by the availability of computerized models to assist media planners in selecting media and vehicles (e.g., with Telmar's ADPlus/InterMix Software). These models essentially attempt to optimize an objective function (e.g., selecting a schedule that yields the greatest level of reach or the highest frequency), subject to satisfying constraints such as not exceeding the upper limit on the advertising budget. A computer algorithm (a problem-solving computer program) searches through the possible solutions and selects the specific media schedule that optimizes the objective function and satisfies all specified constraints.

For illustration purposes, let us assume that a media planner has decided to invest $6.5 million in a one-month safety advertising campaign entitled "Esuvee," that will focus on young men in trying to reduce the almost 10,000 SUV rollover crashes in the United States.[35] The budget will be allocated between television and magazine advertising, with $4.5 million to be invested on the former during the introductory month and another $2 million to be spent on the latter. (To simplify the discussion, only the magazine component of the media schedule is described.) Assume further that the target market for the Esuvee Safety Campaign consists of men between the ages of 18 and 49, who have incomes exceeding $45,000 and who are outdoor-oriented.

Using a computerized media-scheduling program to select the "best" magazine vehicles from a large set of magazine options would entail the following steps:

Step 1. Develop a *media database*. This initial aspect of media planning involves three activities: (1) identify prospective advertising vehicles, (2) specify their ratings, and (3) determine individual vehicle cost. Table 16.5 illustrates the essential information contained in the media database for the Esuvee.

Step 2. Select the *criterion for optimizing the media schedule*. Media-schedule optimization alternatives include maximizing reach (1+), effective reach (3+), frequency, and GRPs. In the illustration to follow, *maximizing reach* has been selected as the optimizing criterion for the Esuvee Campaign's one-month introductory magazine campaign.

Source: "How Do You Ride? What Everyone Needs to Know about SUV Safety." Used with permission from Peppercom Strategic Communications.

TABLE 16.5	Media Database for the Esuvee Safety Campaign		
Magazine	**Rating**	**4C/Open Cost***	**Maximum Insertions†**
American Hunter	5.7	$ 49,040	1
American Rifleman	10.1	60,915	1
Bassmaster	6.3	38,063	1
Car & Driver	17.6	187,269	1
Ducks Unlimited	3.0	37,390	1
ESPN Magazine	17.6	216,320	2
Field & Stream	13.6	115,800	1
Game & Fish	5.7	38,185	1
Guns & Ammo	12.5	38,570	1
Hot Rod	11.9	92,020	1
Maxim	14.1	253,845	1
Men's Fitness	10.4	71,095	1
Men's Health	16.4	177,575	1
Motor Trend	14.0	165,065	1
North American Hunter	9.2	39,400	1
Outdoor Life	9.7	67,000	1
Sporting News	6.5	52,219	2
Sports Illustrated	34.5	352,800	4

*4C/open stands for a full-page, four-color ad purchased without a quantity discount. Cost information is from *Marketers Guide to Media*, 34, New York, NY: Prometheus Global Media, 2011, 159–161, 173–177.
†Maximum insertions are based on how frequently a magazine is published. *Sports Illustrated* is published weekly, which would enable one ad in each of the weeks during the four-week scheduling period. With the exception of *ESPN Magazine* and *Sporting News*, which are published every other week, all other magazines under consideration are published monthly.

Step 3. Specify *constraints*. These include (1) determining a *budget constraint* for the media planning period, and (2) identifying *the maximum number of ad insertions for each vehicle*. The introductory one-month magazine budget constraint has been set at $2 million. The computer algorithm is being "told," in other words, to select magazines that maximize reach for an expenditure not to exceed $2 million.

In addition to the overall budget constraint, magazine-insertion constraints also are identified in Table 16.5. The purpose of these insertion constraints is to assure that the optimum solution does not recommend inserting more ads in a particular publication than can be run during the four-week scheduling period. As can be seen in Table 16.5, with only three exceptions (*ESPN Magazine, Sporting News*, and *Sports Illustrated*), all remaining magazines are issued only once per month. Hence, the maximum number of insertions for most of the magazines in Table 16.5 is constrained to "1," although up to "2" ads each will be permitted in *ESPN Magazine* and *Sporting News* and up to "4" ads in *Sports Illustrated*. Although advertisers sometimes run multiple ads for a brand in the same magazine issue, the simplifying assumption made here is that not more than one ad for the Esuvee Safety Campaign should be placed in any particular magazine per issue.

Step 4. The final step is to seek out the optimum media schedule according to the specified objective function and subject to satisfying the budget and number-of-insertion constraints. The following illustration reveals how this is accomplished.

Hypothetical Illustration: A One-Month Magazine Schedule for the Esuvee Safety Campaign

Let us assume that a media planner for the Esuvee Safety Campaign is in the process of choosing the optimal four-week schedule from among magazines considered appropriate for reaching men ages 18 to 49 who have household incomes of $45,000 or greater, and are outdoor-oriented (i.e., they like to hunt, fish, cycle, camp, enjoy sports, etc.). Based on 2010 U.S. Census data, there are approximately 68,904,000 million male Americans aged 18 to 49, representing approximately (with rounding) 62 percent of all adult males. Also based on 2010 U.S. Census data, approximately 38.4 million males *18 and older* earn $45,000 or greater. On the assumption that only 62 percent of this group satisfies the Esuvee Campaign's age target of males *18 to 49* who earn $45,000 or more, the target market is reduced to 23,768,224 prospective customers for the Esuvee Safety Campaign (i.e., 0.619852×38.345 million). Then, if one assumes almost 75 percent (i.e., 0.7436331) of the group would be outdoor-oriented, the final target market for our example would be 17,674,840 (with rounding). All subsequent planning is based on this estimate.

The Esuvee Safety Campaign Database

The media planner has prepared a database consisting of 18 magazines considered suitable for reaching the target audience (see again Table 16.5). These magazines were selected because they are read predominantly by male readers, engaging in outdoor activities such as hunting, fishing, and sports, and having household incomes of $45,000 or greater.

The second key input was magazine ratings. Ratings (see the second column in Table 16.5) were determined by dividing each magazine's audience size by the size of Esuvee Safety Campaign's target market, which, as indicated, is estimated as 17.7 million potential customers.[36] Next, costs (the third column) were designated according to the price each magazine charged for a one-time placement of a full-page, four-color advertisement. Finally, maximum insertions (the last column) were based on each magazine's publication cycle. As noted previously, 15 of the 18 magazines are published once per month, whereas *ESPN Magazine* and *Sporting News* are published bimonthly and *Sports Illustrated* is published weekly. Hence, only one ad each can be placed during the four-week period in 15 of the magazines, whereas it is possible to place up to two ads each in *ESPN Magazine* and *Sporting News* and up to four ads in *Sports Illustrated.*

The Objective Function and Constraints

The information in Table 16.5 was input into Telmar's ADPlus (InterMix) computerized media scheduling program.[37] With this information, the program was instructed to maximize reach (1+) without exceeding a budget of $2 million for this four-week introductory magazine advertising campaign.

The Optimal Schedule

Had advertisements been placed in all 18 magazines listed in Table 16.5 (including multiple insertions in *ESPN Magazine, Sporting News*, and *Sports Illustrated*, that were permissible), the total advertising cost would have amounted to over $2.5 million. This amount would have been unacceptable, because a $2 million budget constraint was imposed on magazine advertising. It thus was necessary to select from these magazines such that the budget constraint was met and the goal to maximize reach was satisfied. This is precisely what media-scheduling algorithms accomplish.

Given 18 magazines with different numbers of maximum insertions in each, there are numerous combinations of magazines that could be selected. However, in a matter of seconds, the scheduling algorithm identified the single combination of magazines that would maximize reach for an expenditure of $2 million or less. The solution is displayed in Table 16.6.

TABLE 16.6	ADPlus Magazine Schedule for the Esuvee Safety Campaign

| | | Frequency (f) Distributions | | | |
| | | Vehicle | | Message | |
	f	%f	%f+	%f	%f+
XYZ Ad Agency	0	35.1	100.0	63.4	100.0
Esuvee Safety Campaign	1	16.7	64.9	9.5	36.6
March 2012	2	9.6	48.2	7.1	27.1
Target: 17,674,840	3	8.7	38.6	5.8	20.0
Males/18–49/$45K HHI/Outdoor	4	8.6	30.0	4.6	14.3
Message/Vehicle = 52.5%	5	7.6	21.4	3.4	9.7
	6	5.8	13.8	2.5	6.3
	7	3.8	8.0	1.6	3.8
	8	2.2	4.2	1.0	2.2
	9	1.1	2.0	0.6	1.1
	10+	0.5	0.5	0.3	0.3

| | Summary Evaluation | |
	Vehicle	Message
Reach (1+)	64.9%	36.6%
Effective reach (3+)	38.6%	20.0%
Gross rating points (GRPs)	232.2	121.9
Average frequency (f)	3.6	3.3
Gross impressions (000s)	41,041.0	21,546.5
Cost-per-thousand (CPM)	$48.67	$92.71
Cost-per-rating point (CPP)	$8,603	$16,386

Vehicle List (14)	Rating	GRPs	Ad Cost	CPM-MSG	Ads	Total Cost	Mix
Guns & Ammo	12.5	12.5	$ 38,570	$ 33.25	1	$ 38,570	1.9%
North American Hunter	9.2	9.2	39,400	46.15	1	39,400	2.0
American Rifleman	10.1	10.1	60,915	65.00	1	60,915	3.0
Bassmaster	6.3	6.3	38,063	65.11	1	38,063	1.9
Game & Fish	5.7	5.7	38,165	72.19	1	38,165	1.9
Men's Fitness	10.4	10.4	71,095	73.67	1	71,095	3.6
Outdoor Life	9.7	9.7	67,000	74.44	1	67,000	3.4
Hot Rod	11.9	11.9	92,020	83.33	1	92,020	4.6
Sporting News	6.5	13.0	52,219	86.58	2	104,438	5.2
Field & Stream	13.6	13.6	115,800	91.76	1	115,800	5.8
American Hunter	5.7	5.7	49,040	92.72	1	49,040	2.5
Sports Illustrated	34.5	103.5	352,800	110.20	3	1,058,400	53.0
Car & Driver	17.6	17.6	187,269	114.67	1	187,269	9.4
Ducks Unlimited	3.0	3.0	37,390	134.31	1	37,390	1.9
Totals		232.2		$ 92.71	17	$1,997,585	100.0%

Table 16.6 shows that the optimal schedule consists of three ads in *Sports Illustrated*, two ads in *Sporting News*, and one each in 12 other magazines. (Four magazines—*ESPN Magazine*, *Maxim*, *Men's Health*, and *Motor Trend*—were not included in the final solution. Perusal of Table 16.5 reveals that these magazines are relatively expensive in view of the ratings delivered.) The total cost of this schedule is $1,997,585, which is under the specified upper limit of $2 million by $2,415. Note that the inclusion of any single additional advertisement would have exceeded the imposed budget limit. The least expensive magazine of the four that is not included is *Motor Trend* at a cost of $165,065. Had an advertisement been placed in this magazine (or in *ESPN Magazine Maxim* or *Men's Health*), the total cost would have exceeded the budget constraint of $2 million. The solution in Table 16.6 is *the* optimum solution for maximizing reach subject to satisfying the budget constraint.

Interpreting the Solution

Let us carefully examine the data in Table 16.6. Notice first that the information in the upper-left corner provides details about the media schedule (ad agency, campaign, target size and description, and message-to-vehicle ratio). This message-to-vehicle ratio is shown in Table 16.6 to equal 52.5 percent. This value represents the likelihood that consumers who are exposed to the magazine vehicle *also* will be exposed to the advertising message within it. The expectation is that 52.5 percent of consumers exposed to any particular magazine in the Esuvee Safety Campaign's schedule will actually attend to an Esuvee safety ad inserted in these magazines. This ratio, although a rough estimate, was obtained from a survey of media directors who were asked to identify the message-to-vehicle rations they use for different media categories.[38] The corresponding rations for television, radio, and newspapers have been estimated at 32 percent, 16 percent, and 16 percent, respectively.[39] These certainly can be imperfect estimates, not necessarily applicable to every situation (e.g., Super Bowl, World Cup).

The next pertinent information to observe in Table 16.6 is the *frequency distribution* for the vehicle and for the message. Conceptually these are identical, but the percentages in the message distribution are lower for the reasons described in the previous paragraph. For the *vehicle frequency distribution*, recall the earlier discussion (see Table 16.1) of the 10-household market for the Smart Car advertised in *Cosmopolitan* magazine. It will be helpful to review the concepts of (1) exposure level (f); (2) frequency distribution, or percentage of audience exposed at each level of f (Percentage f); and (3) cumulative frequency distribution (Percentage $f+$). When f equals zero, the Percentage f and Percentage $f+$ values in Table 16.6 are 35.1 and 100, respectively. This is to say that the 35.1 percent of the 17.7 million target audience members for the Esuvee Safety Campaign will *not* be exposed to any of the 14 magazines that made it into the optimal solution and that are listed at the bottom of Table 16.6. The cumulative frequency when f equals zero is of course 100—that is, 100 percent of the audience members will be exposed zero or more times to magazine vehicles in Esuvee Safety Campaign's four-week advertising schedule.

Note further that Percentage f and Percentage $f+$ are 16.7 and 64.9 when f equals 1. That is, the computer program estimates that 16.7 percent of the target audience will be exposed to *exactly* one of the 14 magazines, and 64.9 percent of the audience will be exposed to one or more of the magazines during this four-week period. Note carefully under the summary evaluation in the middle of Table 16.6 that vehicle *reach* equals 64.9 percent. With reach defined as the percentage of the target audience exposed one or more times (i.e., 1+), the level of reach is determined merely by identifying the corresponding value in the Percentage $f+$ column, which, when f equals 1, is 64.9 percent. It should also be clear that because 35.1 percent of the audience is exposed zero times, the complement of this value (100 − 35.1 = 64.9 percent) is the percentage of the audience exposed one or more times—that is, the percentage of the audience reached.

Therefore, this optimum schedule yields a *vehicle reach* of 64.9, which is the maximum level of reach that any combination of the 18 magazines included in the database (see Table 16.5) could achieve within a budget constraint of $2 million.

This optimal schedule produces 232.2 *GRPs*. These GRPs, by the way, are calculated by multiplying the ratings for each magazine by the number of ads placed in that magazine and then summing [(*Guns & Ammo* = 23.5 × 1) + (*North American Hunter* = 9.2 × 1) + ... (*Ducks Unlimited* = 3.0 × 1) = 232.2 GRPs].

Further, this magazine schedule is estimated to reach the audience an average of 3.6 times (see *average frequency* under the summary evaluation in Table 16.6). Having defined earlier that frequency equals GRPs ÷ reach, you can readily calculate that the level of frequency equals 232.2 ÷ 64.9 = 3.5778, which is rounded in Table 16.6 to 3.6.

Effective reach (i.e., 3+) is 38.6 percent. That is, nearly 39 percent of the total audience is exposed to three or more vehicles. This value is obtained from the frequency distribution at the top of Table 16.6 by reading across from $f = 3$ to the corresponding *Percentage f+* column.

The *cost-per-thousand (CPM)* is $48.67. This value is calculated as follows: (1) audience size is 17,674,840; (2) 64.9 percent—or approximately 11,470,971 of the audience members—are reached by the schedule of magazines shown in Table 16.6; (3) each person reached is done so on average 3.5778 times (in Table 16.6, frequency is presented only to a single decimal point and is rounded up to 3.6); (4) the number of gross impressions, which is the number of people reached multiplied by the average number of times they are reached, is thus 41,041,000 (see summary evaluation in Table 16.6); (5) the *total cost* of this media schedule is $1,997,585 (see the bottom of the Total Cost column in Table 16.6); and (6) therefore, the CPM is $1,997,585 ÷ 41,041 = $48.67.

Finally, the *cost-per-rating point (CPP)* is $8,603. This is calculated simply by dividing the total cost by the number of GRPs produced (i.e., $1,997,585 ÷ 232.2 GRPs).

Does Table 16.6 present a good media schedule? In terms of reach, the schedule is the best possible one that could have been produced from the combinations of 18 magazines that were input into the media scheduling algorithm and subject to a $2 million budget constraint. No other combination from among these magazines could have exceeded this schedule's reach of 64.9 percent. Note carefully, however, that this *opportunity to see (OTS)* the ad for the Esuvee Safety Campaign is not tantamount to having actually seen the ad. Indeed, under the *message* frequency distribution, the ad message for the Esuvee Safety Campaign is estimated to reach only 36.6 percent of the audience one or more times. Such a result would be inadequate were it not for the fact (as noted earlier) that television advertising is to be run simultaneously with the magazine schedule. The combination of these media can be expected to produce much more impressive numbers and to achieve the Esuvee Safety Campaign introductory advertising objectives.

There's No Substitute for Judgment and Experience

It is critical to emphasize that media models such as what has just been illustrated do not make the ultimate scheduling decision. All they can do is efficiently perform the calculations needed to determine which single media schedule will optimize some objective function such as maximizing reach or GRPs. Armed with the answer, it is up to the media planner to determine whether the media schedule satisfies other, non-quantitative objectives such as those described in the following chapter.

Review of Media Plans

Now that fundamental issues in media scheduling have been identified, it will be useful to consider several actual media plans—Diet Dr Pepper, the Saab 9-5, and for two brands of Olympus cameras.

The Diet Dr Pepper Plan

An award-winning advertising campaign for Diet Dr Pepper that the Young & Rubicam advertising agency developed illustrates a media schedule for a consumer packaged good.[40] Although this is not a current schedule, the fundamentals are as applicable now as when the schedule was implemented.

Campaign Target and Objectives

The target audience for Diet Dr Pepper consisted primarily of adults ages 18 to 49 who were present or prospective diet soft-drink consumers. The objectives for the Diet Dr Pepper ad campaign (titled "The Taste You've Been Looking For") were as follows:

1. To increase Diet Dr Pepper sales by 4 percent and improve its growth rate to at least 1.5 times that of the diet soft-drink category.
2. To heighten consumers' evaluations of the key product benefit and image factors that influence brand choice in this category: it is refreshing, tastes as good as regular Dr Pepper, is a good product to drink at any time, and is a fun brand to drink.
3. To enhance those key brand-personality dimensions that differentiate Diet Dr Pepper from other diet drinks—particularly that Diet Dr Pepper is a unique, clever, fun, entertaining, and interesting brand to drink.

Creative Strategy

The creative strategy for Diet Dr Pepper positioned the brand as "tasting more like regular Dr Pepper." This was a key claim based on research revealing that nearly 60 percent of initial trial users of Diet Dr Pepper were motivated by the desire to have a diet soft drink that tasted like regular Dr Pepper. The cornerstone of the campaign entailed the heavy use of 15-second commercials, which historically had not been used by major soft-drink brands, Coca-Cola and Pepsi-Cola; they preferred the entertainment value of longer commercials. The aggressive use of 15-second commercials enabled Diet Dr Pepper to convey its key taste claim ("Tastes more like regular Dr Pepper") and differentiate the brand from competitive diet drinks. Moreover, by employing cheaper 15-second commercials, it was possible to buy considerably more commercial spots and hence achieve greater weekly reach (recall the prior discussion of the shelf-space model), to obtain greater frequency, and to generate more weight for the same advertising budget. Diet Dr Pepper's advertising expenditures for the year totaled $20.3 million.

Media Strategy

The advertising schedule for Diet Dr Pepper generated a total of 1,858 GRPs, with a cumulative *annual* reach of 95 and frequency of 19.6. These media-weight values were accomplished with the national media plan summarized as a flowchart in Table 16.7.

Each of the 12 months and the week-beginning dates (Mondays) are listed across the top of the chart. Table entries reflect the GRPs each TV vehicle achieved for each weekly period based on targeted adults in the age category 18 to 49. The first entry, a 41 for the *NFL Championship Games*, indicates that placing advertisements for Diet Dr Pepper during the football games televised the week beginning January 17 produced 41 gross rating points. Ten additional

TABLE 16.7 — Media Plan for Diet Dr Pepper

ADULTS 18–49 GRPs	JAN					FEB					MAR				APR				MAY					JUN		
SPORTS	27	3	10	17	24	31	7	14	21	28	7	14	21	28	4	11	18	25	2	9	16	23	30	6	13	20
NFL Championship Games				41																						
Road to the Superbowl					10																					
FOX "Game of the Week"																										
NBC "Game of the Week"																										
NBC Thanksgiving Game																										
ABC *Monday Night Football*																										
4Q Sports Total				41	10																					
SEC Championship Game																										
SEC-CFA Regular Game																										
SEC Thanksgiving Game																										
SEC Local/Conference Fee																										
SEC Sponsorship Total																										
TOTAL SPORTS				41	10																					
EVENTS																										
McDonald's Golf Classic																				1						
Daytime Emmy Awards																						23				
Country Music Awards																			32							
Garth Brooks Special																			12							
Michael Bolton Sponsorship																										
May Event Print																					17		18			
JC Penney LPGA Golf																										
Harvey Penick Special																							1			
Diners Club Golf																										
TOTAL EVENTS																			61	18	17	41	1			
CONTINUITY																										
Prime			53			53					53	54		34	35			35			35					35
May Event Prime Scatter																			29	28						
Late Night			6		5						5				3				3		4					
Syndication				14		14					13				8			8			8					8
Cable				13		14					14				11			11			11					
TOTAL CONTINUITY			86	126	15	86	81				85	68		56	57			54	86	28	86	58				43
Integration-to-date																										
Total Diet Plan			86	126	15	86	81				85	68		56	57			54	147	46	103	127	59			43
A18–49 GRPs/Week																										
Amount Over Budget																										
A18–49 GRPs/Month			227					167				238				167					477				102	
A18–49 GRPs/Quarter							632													746						

GRPs were garnered by placing an ad on the *Road to the Super Bowl* program that aired during the week of January 24.

Note that the Diet Dr Pepper media plan consisted of (1) placing advertisements during professional and college football games (SEC stands for

TABLE 16.7	**Media Plan for Diet Dr Pepper (*continued*)**

ADULTS 18–49 GRPs	JUL					AUG					SEP			OCT						NOV				DEC		
	27	4	11	18	25	1	8	15	22	29	5	12	19	26	3	10	17	24	31	7	14	21	28	5	12	19
SPORTS																										
NFL Championship Games																										
Road to the Superbowl																										
FOX "Game of the Week"														28							24			25		
NBC "Game of the Week"																13					22			20		
NBC Thanksgiving Game																							22			
ABC *Monday Night Football*																22			20	10		24				25
4Q Sports Total														28		35			20	10	46	24	22	45		25
SEC Championship Game																								33		
SEC-CFA Regular Game															8											
SEC Thanksgiving Game																							6			
SEC Local/Conference Fee																										
SEC Sponsorship Total															8								6	33		
TOTAL SPORTS														28	8	35			20	10	46	24	28	78		25
EVENTS																										
McDonald's Golf Classic																										
Daytime Emmy Awards																										
Country Music Awards																										
Garth Brooks Special																										
Michael Bolton Sponsorship																										
May Event Print																										
JC Penney LPGA Golf																										
Harvey Penick Special																										
Diners Club Golf																										
TOTAL EVENTS																										
CONTINUITY																										
Prime	25					25					26															
May Event Prime Scatter																										
Late Night																										
Syndication																										
Cable																										
TOTAL CONTINUITY	25					25					26															
Integration-to-date																										
Total Diet Plan	25					25					26			28	8	35			20	10	46	24	28	78		15
A18–49 GRPs/Week																										
Amount Over Budget																										

A18–49 GRPs/Month	JUL	AUG	SEP	OCT	NOV	DEC
	75	51	52	91	108	103
A18–49 GRPs/Quarter	178			302		

Southeastern Conference); (2) sponsoring various special events (e.g., the *Country Music Awards* and golfing events); and (3) continuously advertising during prime time, on late-night television (e.g., *David Letterman*), on syndicated programs, and on cable stations.

At the bottom of Table 16.7 is a summary of GRPs broken down by week (e.g., 86 GRPs during the week beginning January 10), by month (e.g., 227 GRPs during January), and by quarter (e.g., 632 GRPs produced during the first quarter, January through March). It can be seen that the media schedule was *flighted* insofar as advertisements were placed during approximately two-thirds of the 52 weeks with no advertising during the remaining weeks. In sum, the media schedule was designed to highlight Diet Dr Pepper during special events and to maintain continuity throughout the year with prime-time network ads and less expensive support on syndicated and cable programming.

Saab 9-5's Media Plan

The 9-5 model represented Saab's entry in the luxury category and was designed to compete against well-known high-equity brands, including Mercedes, BMW, Volvo, Lexus, and Infiniti.[41] Despite being a unique automobile company—with a respected background in airplane manufacturing—Saab had done relatively little to enhance its brand image in the United States. Saab suffered from a low level of consumer awareness and a poorly defined brand image.

Campaign Target and Objectives

Prior to the introduction of the 9-5 model, Saab's product mix had historically attracted younger consumers. Achieving success for its new luxury sedan required that the advertising appeal to upscale families and relatively affluent older consumers.

The introductory advertising campaign was designed to achieve the following objectives: (1) generate excitement for the new 9-5 model line; (2) increase overall awareness for the Saab name; (3) encourage consumers to visit dealers and test-drive the 9-5; and (4) produce retail sales of 11,000 units of the 9-5 during the introductory year.

Creative Strategy

The Saab 9-5 was positioned as a luxury automobile capable of delivering an ideal synthesis of performance and safety. Creative advertising executions portrayed Saab as a premium European luxury manufacturer and were designed to have a hint of mystery and wit. An intensive media campaign was needed to deliver the creative executions and achieve the company's three advertising objectives.

© AP Images/Jennifer Graylock

Media Strategy

An integrated media campaign was designed to generate high levels of reach and frequency among the target group of older and financially well-off consumers and ultimately to sell at retail 11,000 Saab 9-5 vehicles. The media schedule is presented in Table 16.8. It first will be noted that TV advertising started in January, which was before the 9-5's introduction in April. Network and cable TV advertising ran from mid-January through early February and then again throughout May following the 9-5's introduction. Notice that the initial network TV campaign accumulated 74 GRPs for each of three weeks (the weeks beginning

TABLE 16.8 Media Plan for the Saab 9-5

	JAN				FEB				MAR					APR				MAY					JUN			
	29	5	12	19	26	2	9	16	23	2	9	16	23	30	6	13	20	27	4	11	18	25	1	8	15	22
Network TV					74 wk														95 wk							
Network Cable					40 wk														60 wk							
Magazines																										
Newspapers																										
USA Today																										
3 PBW (2X)														1X		1X										
SPBW (1X)															1X											
PBW (12X)																										
T Page (58X)		1X		1X	1X	1X		1X		2X	2X	2X	2X	2X	2X	2X	2X	2X	1X	1X		1X		1X		1X
1/4 PBW (8X)												4X	2X	2X												
Wall Street Journal																										
3 PBW (2X)														1X		1X										
SPBW (1X)															1X											
PBW (12X)																										
4 col x 14" (63X)		1X	1X		1X	1X	1X		1X	2X	2X	2X	2X	2X	2X	2X	2X	2X	1X	1X	1X	1X	1X	1X	1X	1X
4 col x 8" (8X)												2X	4X	2X												
Interactive																										

	JUL				AUG					SEP				OCT				NOV					DEC			
	29	6	13	20	27	3	10	17	24	31	7	14	21	28	5	12	19	26	2	9	16	23	30	7	14	21
Network TV																										
Network Cable																										
Magazines																										
Newspapers																										
USA Today																										
3 PBW (2X)																										
SPBW (1X)																										
PBW (12X)														1X	3X	2X					3X	1X	2X			
T Page (58X)		1X	1X	1X	1X	1X	1X	1X	1X	1X	1X	1X	2X	1X		1X	2X	2X	2X.	2X		1X	1X	2X	2X	1X
1/4 PBW (8X)																										
Wall Street Journal																										
3 PBW (2X)																										
SPBW (1X)																										
PBW (12X)														1X	2X	2X	1X				2X	1X	2X	1X		
4 col x 14" (63X)	1X	2X	1X	1X	1X	1X	1X	1X	1X	1X		1X	2X	1X	1X	1X	1X	2X	2X	2X	1X	1X	1X	1X	2X	1X
4 col x 8" (8X)																										
Interactive																										

Legend:

1X, 2X, etc. = Number of insertions per week placed in *USA Today* or WSJ (1X = one insertion, 2X - two insertions, etc.)
3 PBW = 3 pages black & white magazine ad
SPBW = Spread page black & white (ad runs across 2 pages like a centerfold)
PBW = 1 page black & white
T Page = An odd shaped add placement
1/4 PBW = 1/4 page black & white
Interactive = Internet banner ad placed on *the Wall Street Journal Interactive Edition*

January 19, January 26, and February 2) and that accompanying advertising on cable TV amassed 40 GRPs for each of these same three weeks. Following the 9-5's introduction, the May television schedule accumulated 95 and 60 GRPs, respectively, on network and cable TV. Or, in other words, a total of 620 television GRPs [(95 × 4) + (60 × 4)] were purchased in May.

Table 16.8 further reveals that magazine advertising for the Saab 9-5 started in late January and continued for the remainder of the year without interruption. Magazines used to reach Saab's designated market for the 9-5 included automotive magazines (e.g., *Car & Driver* and *Road & Track*), sports publications (e.g., *Ski* and *Tennis*), home magazines (e.g., *Martha Stewart Living* and *Architectural Digest*), business magazines (e.g., *Money*, *Forbes*, and *Working Women*), and general interest publications (e.g., *Time* and *New York Magazine*). National newspaper advertising in *USA Today* and the *Wall Street Journal* also ran throughout the year. Finally, Internet banner ads ran continuously throughout the introductory year. In sum, this was a highly successful media plan that achieved its objectives and led to a successful introduction of the Saab 9-5 luxury automobile.

Olympus Camera Media Plan

The camera business has become increasingly competitive and diverse with new players entering the industry on a regular basis.[42] Where at one time it was primarily Kodak, Canon, Olympus, and Nikon that dominated the industry, firms such as Sony and others compete for the buying public's camera purchases. The modern camera industry is now one of sophisticated digital consumer electronics rather than simply point-and-click devices. To transition the company's camera business into the broader world of consumer electronics successfully, executives at Olympus realized the company would need to implement a marcom program that would change both consumer and retailer perceptions of Olympus—a change from the belief that Olympus is merely a point-and-click camera maker to the perception that it is a major player in designer electronics. The shift began in earnest when Olympus asked The Martin Agency to develop a media campaign for introducing its two new brands, the Stylus Verve and the m:robe.

Campaign Objectives

The first product, Stylus Verve, had all of the features of Olympus's flagship Stylus Digital line, but was uniquely designed and available in six colors. To make the jump even more substantial, Olympus introduced a wholly new product to the market several years ago, the m:robe—a combination MP3 player and camera. The Martin Agency's job was to create a media plan that would serve to introduce the Stylus Verve and the m:robe successfully and simultaneously to facilitate the shift in marketplace perceptions that Olympus was a maker of designer electronics items and not merely cameras.

The Strategy

A high-impact, event-driven media strategy was developed to meet these objectives. Overall, the idea was to place the Olympus message in media that people talk about, that generate buzz, that yield free media coverage, that have longevity, and that are influential. Moreover, it was important that the selected media reach both men and women and be suitable for Olympus's key, fourth-quarter selling season running from October through December.

Media and Vehicles

TV programs were selected to deliver high viewership and to satisfy the criteria previously mentioned. Considered especially suitable were high-impact and widely viewed programs that aired only once a year. Ads for the Stylus Verve were placed in programs such as the *World Series*, the *American Music Awards*, *Macy's Thanksgiving Day Parade*, and *Dick Clark's Rockin' New Year's Eve*.

The m:robe was launched in the ultimate high-profile program, the *Super Bowl*, followed by *The Grammys*. Network cable added frequency and continuity to the network TV schedule. Ad placements on cable channels E! and ESPN complemented and extended the entertainment and sporting events. The addition of programs such as *Sex and the City* and *Friends* rounded out the TV schedule and further served to generate buzz for the Verve and m:robe.

In addition to TV spots, magazine issues such as *People*'s "Sexiest Man Alive," *Sports Illustrated*'s "Sportsman of the Year," and *Time*'s "Person of the Year" carried four-page gatefold ads for the Stylus Verve. These special magazine issues reach millions of consumers who were exposed to ad messages in a positive context. Moreover, these special issues have a "life of their own" when people talk, for example, about whether they agree with *People*'s choice of the sexiest man alive. As part of the m:robe launch, the biggest magazine issue of the year, *Sports Illustrated*'s "Swimsuit" edition, was utilized, along with *Rolling Stone*'s "Richest Rock Stars" issue, a perfect tie in with the music aspect of the product.

Out of home (OOH) also played a role using a combination of impact units purchased within four key Olympus markets and in-theater advertising in the top-25 markets. Impactful OOH units were selected based on high-traffic areas, as well as proximity to key Olympus retailers. A five-week flight of in-theater advertising starting Thanksgiving weekend capitalized on the heavy holiday movie traffic. Additionally, an online element of highly visible brand placements and sponsorships was developed for both the Stylus Verve and the m:robe. The chosen sites had to be contextually relevant for the target and included high-traffic areas on the Web featuring entertainment and sporting events—for example, E! Online for entertainment and Fox Sports for its coverage of World Series baseball and the National Football League.

The online advertising element for the m:robe brand went beyond just website advertising. With the m:robe propelling Olympus into the consumer electronics category, the online element needed to express the m:robe experience and help define its points of differentiation from competitive brands while helping support ad placements during the Super Bowl. To achieve these objectives, a nonbranded interactive website was developed featuring the "pop-locking" (robotic) dance moves that would later be viewed as the focus of the Olympus Super Bowl spots. The interactive website allowed users to make the website characters pop lock or see themselves pop lock by uploading a picture of their head to the site. This website was passed along to friends and family, getting picked up on blogs and other websites in the process.

Table 16.9 presents a flowchart of the integrated media plan for Olympus's Stylus Verve and m:robe brands. Because the plan was not bought specifically in terms of generating designated levels of gross ratings, no point totals are presented. Note the diversity of media used (sponsored events, national TV, print, online, in-theater, and OOH) and the various vehicles used in each medium.

Results

The Stylus Verve advertising campaign launched during the U.S. Tennis Open in August and concluded with New Year's. During this period, unaided awareness of Olympus increased by 23 percent. The advertising also contributed to an increase in consumers believing that Olympus was trendy and innovative. The m: robe launch raised awareness of Olympus as a player in the digital music category from 0 percent to 5 percent, which was on par with the more established iRiver brand; moreover, 20 percent of the respondents to an advertising tracking study indicated that they believe Olympus offers good quality features. This compares favorably with Apple's iPod score of 17 percent on this same feature. Retailer perceptions were also greatly influenced when the Super Bowl media buy was announced as part of m:robe's product launch at the annual Consumer Electronic Show, generating press coverage in *USA Today* and the *Wall Street Journal*.

TABLE 16.9	Media Plan for Olympus's Stylus Verve and m:robe Brands

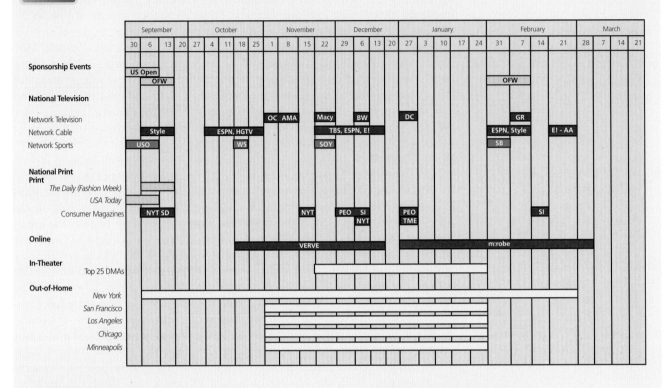

Television Event Programs

US Open on CBS
Style Network - Fashion Week Coverage (September and February)
ESPN: NFL and high-profile programming
HGTV: High-profile prime and weekend day
World Series Game #3
The OC Premiere
American Music Awards
Macy's Parade
Sports Illustrated Sportsman of the Year on FOX
Barbara Walter's 25 Most Intruiging People
Dick Clark's Rockin New Year's Eve
Super Bowl coverage on ESPN
Super Bowl
Grammy Awards
Academy Awards on E!
TBS: *Seinfeld, Friends, Everybody Loves Raymond,* and *Sex and the City*
ESPN: NFL and high-profile programming
E! / Style bonus: Entertainment/high-profile programming

Newspapers and Consumer Magazines

NYT = *New York Times*
SD = *Time Style & Design*
PEO = *People Magazine*
SI = *Sports Illustrated*
TME = *Time Magazine*

© Cengage Learning

Summary

Selection of advertising media and vehicles is one of the most important and complicated of all marketing communications decisions. Media planning must be coordinated with marketing strategy and with other aspects of advertising strategy. The strategic aspects of media planning involve four steps: (1) selecting the target audience toward which all subsequent efforts will be directed; (2) specifying media objectives, which typically are stated in terms of reach, frequency, gross rating points (GRPs), or effective rating points (ERPs); (3) selecting general media categories and specific vehicles within each medium; and (4) buying media.

A variety of factors influence media and vehicle selection; most important are target audience, cost, and creative considerations. Media planners select media vehicles by identifying those that will reach the designated target audience, satisfy budgetary constraints, and be compatible with and enhance the advertiser's creative message. There are numerous ways to schedule media insertions over time, but media planners have typically used some form of pulsed or flighted schedule whereby advertising is on at times, off at others, but never continuous. The principle of recency, also referred to as the shelf-space model of advertising, challenges the use of flighted advertising schedules and purports that weekly efficient reach should be the decision criterion of choice because it ensures that advertising will be run at the time when consumers are making brand selection decisions.

The chapter provided detailed explanations of the various considerations media planners use in making advertising media decisions, including the concepts of reach, frequency, gross rating points, effective rating points, and cost and continuity considerations. Media vehicles within the same medium are compared in terms of cost using the cost-per-thousand criterion.

The chapter included a detailed discussion of a computerized media-selection model (Telmar's ADPlus Inter-Mix software). This model requires information about vehicle cost, ratings, maximum number of insertions, and a budget constraint and then maximizes an objective function subject to that budget. Optimization criteria include maximizing reach (1+), effective reach (3+), frequency, or GRPs.

The chapter concluded with descriptions of media plans for Diet Dr Pepper, the Saab 9-5, and the Stylus Verve and m:robe brands of Olympus cameras.

Discussion Questions

1. Why is target audience selection the critical first step in formulating a media strategy?
2. Compare and contrast TRPs and GRPs as media selection criteria.
3. Contrast the term reach with its related terms net coverage and unduplicated audience.
4. A television advertising schedule produced the following vehicle frequency distribution:

f	Percentage f	Percentage $f+$
0	31.5	100.0
1	9.3	68.5
2	7.1	59.2
3	6.0	52.1
4	5.2	46.1
5	4.6	40.9
6	4.1	36.3
7	3.7	32.2
8	3.4	28.5
9	3.1	25.1
10+	22.0	22.0

   a. What is the reach for this advertising schedule?
   b. What is the effective reach?
   c. How many GRPs does this schedule generate?
   d. What is the frequency for this schedule?

5. Assume that the TV advertising schedule in Question 4 cost $2 million and generated 240 million gross impressions. What are the CPM and CPP?
6. A publication issue called the *100 Leading National Advertisers* in *Advertising Age* is an invaluable source for determining how much money companies invest in advertising. Go to your library and find the most recent version of this issue. Identify the advertising expenditures and the media used in advertising the following companies: Apple, General Mills, Nike, and Walt Disney Company.
7. With reference to the three-exposure hypothesis, explain the difference between three exposures to an advertising message versus three exposures to an advertising vehicle.
8. When an advertiser uses the latter, what implicit assumption is that advertiser making?

9. Describe in your own words the fundamental logic underlying the principle of recency (or what also is referred to as the shelf-space model of advertising). Is this model always the best model to apply in setting media allocations over time?
10. A TV program has a rating of 17.6. With approximately 114.7 million television households in the United States as of 2012, what is that program's CPM if a 30-second commercial costs $600,000? Now assume that an advertiser's target audience consists only of people ages 25 to 54, which constitutes 62 percent of the program's total audience. What is the CPM-TM in this case?
11. Which is more important for an advertiser: maximizing reach or maximizing frequency? Explain in detail.
12. Reach will be lower for an advertised brand if the entire advertising budget during a four-week period is devoted to advertising exclusively on a single program than if the same budget is allocated among a variety of TV programs. Why?
13. Following are the ratings and number of ad insertions on five cable TV programs designated as C1 through C5: C1 (rating = 7, insertions = 6); C2 (rating = 4, insertions = 12); C3 (rating = 3, insertions = 20); C4 (rating = 5, insertions = 10); and C5 (rating = 6, insertions = 15). How many GRPs would be obtained from this cable TV advertising schedule?
14. Assume that in Canada there are 14 million TV households. A popular TV program, *Hockey Night in Canada*, aired at 6 PM and had a *rating* of 5.7 and a 10 *share*. At the 6 PM airtime, how many TV sets were tuned into this or another program? (Hint: Ratings are based on total households, whereas share is based on just the households that have their TV sets on at a particular time, in this case at 6 PM. Because the numerator value remains constant in both the calculation of ratings and share values, by simple algebraic manipulation you can determine from the rating information the number of households with their sets on.)

End Notes

1. Super Bowl XLVI, which resulted in underdog New York Giants beating the New England Patriots, drew a record audience with more than 111.3 million viewers. With a cost of $3.5 million per 30-second commercial, this equates to a cost-per-thousand (CPM) of $31.45. Information on audience size is from Robert Seidman, *TV By the Numbers*, February 6, 2012.

2. Some in the media have viewed it exactly the opposite; that is, don't blame the messenger (i.e., media) for poor ROI, blame the message (i.e., uninspired creativity); see Jack Neff, "Why Marketers Shouldn't Always Blame the Media," *Advertising Age*, September 27, 2010, 10.

3. Thom Forbes, "Consumer Central: The Media Focus Is Changing—And So Is the Process," *Agency*, winter 1998, 38.

4. Karen Whitehill King and Leonard N. Reid, "Selecting Media for National Accounts: Factors of Importance to Agency Media Specialists," *Journal of Current Issues and Research in Advertising* 19 (fall 1997), 55–64.

5. Kate Maddox, "Media Planners in High Demand," *BtoB*, November 8, 2004, 24; and Ave Butensky, "Hitting the Spot," *Agency*, winter 1998, 26.

6. Kent M. Lancaster, "Optimizing Advertising Media Plans Using ADOPT on the Microcomputer," working paper, University of Illinois, December 1987, 2–3. (Note that in the last line of this quote Lancaster actually used 30 rather than 20 possible insertions. We have changed it to 20 so as not to create confusion with the earlier reference to "30 feasible publications.")

7. Laura Freeman, "Taking Apart Media," *Agency*, winter 2001, 20–25.

8. Stephen Williams, "GM Parks $3 Billion Media Account at Carat," *Advertising Age*, January 24, 2012, http://adage.com/article/agency-news/gm-parks-3-billion-media-account-aegis-carat/231699.

9. *Agency*, 22.

10. Ibid., 23.

11. Roland Jones, "Smart's Fortwo Aiming for Big U.S. Sales," MSNBC.com, November 21, 2007, http://www.msnbc.msn.com/id/21882844.

12. Jared Gall, "First Drive: 2008 Smart Fortwo, Previews," *Car and Driver*, November, 2007, http://www.caranddriver.com/reviews/2008-smart-fortwo-first-drive-review.

13. Smart USA, http://www.smartusa.com (accessed March 10, 2012).

14. Henry Assael and Hugh Cannon, "Do Demographics Help in Media Selection?" *Journal of Advertising Research* 19 (December 1979), 7–11; and Hugh M. Cannon and G. Russell Merz, "A New Role for Psychographics in Media Selection," *Journal of Advertising* 9, no. 2 (1980), 33–36, 44.

15. Karen Whitehill King, Leonard N. Reid, and Wendy Macias, "Selecting Media for National Advertising Revisited: Criteria of Importance to Large-Company Advertising Managers," *Journal of Current Issues and Research in Advertising* 26 (spring 2004), 59–68.

16. "Nielsen Estimates Number of U.S. Television Homes to be 114.7," *Nielsen Wire* (blog), May 3, 2011, http://blog.nielsen.com/nielsenwire/media_entertainment/nielsen-estimates-number-of-u-s-television-homes-to-be-114-7-million.

17. A quote from advertising consultant Alvin Achenbaum cited in B. G. Yovovich, "Media's New Exposures," *Advertising Age*, April 13, 1981, S7.

18. One study found that more than 80 percent of advertising agencies use effective reach as a criterion in media planning. See Peggy J. Kreshel, Kent M. Lancaster, and Margaret A. Toomey, "How Leading Advertising Agencies Perceive Effective Reach and Frequency," *Journal of Advertising* 14, no. 3 (1985), 32–38.

19. Gerard J. Tellis, "Advertising Exposure, Loyalty, and Brand Purchase: A Two-Stage Model of Choice," *Journal of Marketing Research* 25 (May 1988), 134–44.

20. Herbert E. Krugman, "Why Three Exposures May Be Enough," *Journal of Advertising Research* 12, no. 6 (1972), 11–14.

21. This point is made especially forcefully by Hugh M. Cannon and Edward A. Riordan, "Effective Reach and Frequency: Does It Really Make Sense?" *Journal of Advertising Research* 34 (March/April 1994), 19–28.

22. Ibid., 24.

23. Adapted from "The Muscle in Multiple Media," *Marketing Communications*, December 1983, 25.

24. Cannon and Riordan, "Effective Reach and Frequency," 25–26. The following illustration is adapted from this source.

25. The original authors of this procedure referred to it as exposure value rather than exposure utility, but this use of *value* gets confused with a later use of *value*.

26. A procedure for estimating these values is available in Hugh M. Cannon, John D. Leckenby, and Avery Abernethy, "Beyond Effective Frequency: Evaluating Media Schedules Using Frequency Value Planning," *Journal of Advertising Research* 42 (November/December 2002), 33–47.

27. Erwin Ephron, "More Weeks, Less Weight: The Shelf-Space Model of Advertising," *Journal of Advertising Research* 35 (May/June 1995), 18–23. See also Ephron's various writings archived at his website, Ephron on Media (http://www.ephrononmedia.com).

28. Ibid., 5–18. See also John Philip Jones, "Single-Source Research Begins to Fulfill Its Promise," *Journal of Advertising Research* 35 (May/June 1995), 9–16; Lawrence D. Gibson, "What Can One TV Exposure Do?" *Journal of Advertising Research* 36 (March/April 1996), 9–18; and Kenneth A. Longman, "If Not Effective Frequency, Then What?" *Journal of Advertising Research* 37 (July/August 1997), 44–50.

29. Jones, "Single-Source Research Begins to Fulfill Its Promise." Despite these findings, which have had considerable impact on the advertising community, there is some counterevidence suggesting that Jones's research results are not solely the result of advertising exposure but in fact are correlated with sales promotion activity. In other words, what may appear to be the exclusive impact of successful advertising may actually be due at least in part to a brand's sales promotion activity (such as couponing or cents-off dealing) that takes place at the same time that advertising for the brand is running on television. Until research evidence is more definitive on this matter, a reasonable conclusion is that Jones's measure of advertising effectiveness is interesting and suggestive of the findings, yet more may be needed in the way of proper experimental or statistical controls for sales promotions, price changes, and other potential determinants of a brand's sales volume. For counterperspectives to Jones's claims, see Gary Schroeder, Bruce C. Richardson, and Avu Sankaralingam, "Validating STAS Using BehaviorScan," *Journal of Advertising Research* 37 (July/August 1997), 33–43. For another challenge, see Gerard J. Tellis and Doyle L. Weiss, "Does TV Advertising Really Affect Sales? The Role of Measures, Models, and Data Aggregation," *Journal of Advertising* 24 (fall 1995), 1–12.

30. Erwin Ephron, "What Is Recency?" Ephron on Media, http://www.ephrononmedia.com.

31. Ephron, "More Weeks, Less Weight: The Shelf-Space Model of Advertising," 19.

32. Ibid., 20.

33. A quote from Joanne Burke, senior vice president worldwide media research director, TN Media, New York, in Laurie Freeman, "Effective Weekly Planning Gets a Boost," *Advertising Age*, July 24, 1995, S8, S9.

34. This analogy is adapted from Charles H. Patti and Charles F. Frazer, *Advertising: A Decision-Making Approach*, Hinsdale, IL: Dryden Press, 1988, 369.

35. The "Esuvee" name was actually used in a national safety campaign a few years ago that was aimed at young drivers to educate them about SUV driving safety (see http://www.youtube.com/watch?v=MZ7bcUrjNIk). Because SUVs have a higher center of gravity than passenger cars, there is a greater risk of rollover resulting from speeding, abrupt maneuvers, aggressiveness, and so on. For more about the campaign, see "Esuvee.com: New SUV Safety Campaign," *Road & Travel* magazine, 2005, http://www.roadandtravel.com/safetyandsecurity/2005/esuvee.htm (accessed March 16, 2012).

36. To construct Table 16.5, magazine audience sizes were based on the larger of the estimated audience sizes provided by Simmons and MRI. Figures were obtained from *Marketer's Guide to Media: 2011*, vol. 34, New York: Prometheus Global Media, 2011, 173–77. Because many of the readers of these magazines do not satisfy the income requirement of $45,000 or are not within the 18–49 age category targeted for the Esuvee Safety Campaign, each magazine's total audience size was arbitrarily reduced by 50 percent prior to being divided by the target audience size of 17,674,840.

37. The program is ADPlus, which was developed by Kent Lancaster and is distributed by Telmar Information Services Corp., 470 Park Ave. South, 15th Floor, New York, NY 10016 (phone: 212-725-3000). It should be noted that ADPlus is available from Telmar under the name InterMix. Newer versions of ADPlus ("InterMix"), may generate somewhat different solutions than are presented here (see Table 16.6). So, the results presented in Table 16.6 are for illustration purposes only and are intended simply to explain how the various media diagnostics (reach, frequency, etc.) are generated. The authors appreciate the help of Mr. Jeffrey Wieland, Account Executive, Telmar Information Services Corp. (Los Angeles) with Table 16.6.

38. Kent M. Lancaster, Peggy J. Kreshel, and Joya R. Harris, "Estimating the Impact of Advertising Media Plans: Media Executives Describe Weighting and Timing Factors," *Journal of Advertising* 15 (September 1986), 21–29, 45.

39. Kent Lancaster, *ADPlus for Multi-media Advertising Planning* (Gainesville, FL: Media Research Institute, Inc., 1990), 18.

40. The following descriptions are based on a summary of a Diet Dr Pepper's advertising campaign prepared by Young & Rubicam. Appreciation for these materials is extended to Chris Wright-Isak and John T. O'Brien.

41. Appreciation is extended to Dr. Jack Lindgren of the University of Virginia for facilitating our access to this media plan and to the Martin Agency (Richmond, VA) for making this plan available. The description provided herein is an adaptation of the Martin Agency's media plan for the Saab 9-5.

42. Appreciation is extended to Dr. Lauren Tucker of the Martin Agency (Richmond, VA) for facilitating our access to this media plan. We also greatly appreciate the assistance of Ms. Lori Baker of the Martin Agency in providing us with the plan discussed in this section. The description provided herein is an adaptation of the plan provided by Ms. Baker in April 2005.

CHAPTER 17

Measuring Ad Message Effectiveness

Lessons in Ad Copy Testing and Tracking: The National Youth Anti-Drug Media Campaign

In general, there are *four stages in advertising research*: (1) copy development, (2) a rough stage, (3) copy testing (i.e., pretesting), and (4) tracking (i.e., posttesting). In copy development, initial ideas are developed from points on the creative brief discussed in Chapter 10 and screened in focus groups. Then, the final (or nearly final) ads are copy tested by consumers in the target market. Finally, after appearing in the media, the ads are tracked using surveys usually measuring ad recall, attitudes, intentions, and behavioral (e.g., sales) data.

In addition, a very important issue in ad research is whether your ad *caused* an intended outcome (e.g., sales, behavioral change). This calls for an evaluation of *causality* (e.g., Did X

IS IT REALLY FUN IF YOU DON'T REMEMBER?
Live above drugs and alcohol, live **abovetheinfluence.com** ⬆

© The National Youth Anti-Drug Media Campaign (www.AbovetheInfluence.com)

[the ad] cause Y [a targeted behavior]?) and requires three conditions to be met: (1) X should vary with Y, (2) X should come before Y, and (3) the need to eliminate alternative explanations for Y.

Perhaps one of the best examples of the ad research stages and the notion of causality is that of the National Youth Anti-Drug Media Campaign (NYADMC). As briefly noted in Chapter 1, due to increases in adolescent drug use in the 1990s, the White House's Office of National Drug Control Policy (ONDCP) launched the largest public health ad campaign in U.S. history (see www.whatsyouranti drug.com and www.abovethe influence.org for current sites). Beginning in 1995, an average of $180 million was spent each year, mostly on national TV ads

1 Explain the rationale and importance of ad message research.

2 Discuss the different stages of ad message research.

3 Describe the various research techniques used to measure consumers' recognition and recall of advertising messages.

4 Illustrate measures of emotional reactions to advertisements.

5 Explain the role of persuasion measurement, including pre- and posttesting of consumer preferences.

6 Discuss the meaning and operation of single-source measures of advertising effectiveness.

focusing on resistance skills, peer intervention, negative consequences, and modeling positive behaviors. (Important online messages and public relations efforts also were made.) In addition to parents, the primary targets for the campaign were adolescents aged 12- to 17-years-old. (See Figure 17.1 for the ONDCP research process.) For Stages 1 and 2 of the ad research process, input from behavioral and creative briefs, the Partnership for a Drug Free America (PDFA), behavioral change experts, and adolescent drug surveys ("Monitoring the Future"), all served to aid the creative development of the ads. These ad ideas and themes then were presented in rough form (e.g., storyboards) and subjected to "formative creative evaluation panels" (i.e., focus groups) of youth, parents, and multicultural youth panels (Hispanic, African American, Asian, and American Indian) across the United States.

Following the finalization of the anti-drug ads (developed from pro bono work by agencies recruited by the PDFA), a rigorous copy testing procedure was used in testing youth and parents in Stage 3 of the ad research process. For each ad tested in the youth copy tests, the sample consisted of 200 African American, 200 Caucasian, and 200 Hispanic youth, split 50/50 on

grade (grades 7–8 vs. grades 9–10) and 50/50 on gender. For each ethnic group and grade, 50 youths were randomly assigned to either the test group (i.e., they see the anti-drug ad) or a non-exposure control group (i.e., they do not see the anti-drug ad). (Parents with at least one child in grades 7–10 were tested following the same procedure, yet with only 100 per ethnic group.)

The sample sizes were selected to detect differences of 10 percent or more between test and control groups with a power of 0.80, a 95 percent confidence level ($p \leq 0.05$), and an observed within-group variance of 0.6. The copy tests only allowed those spots that significantly increased anti-drug beliefs and/or reduced intentions to use drugs versus control groups to appear in the televised media. The use of the control groups is very important in eliminating other alternative explanations for the beliefs and intention results, a key element in establishing causality. Other important measures, such as opened-ended and diagnostic items (believability, attention, argument strength) also were taken.

In Stage 4, a set of researchers later tracked the effects of the campaign on anti-drug beliefs, intentions to use drugs, and actual use over time. Unfortunately for the researchers, no baseline (beginning) control measures specific to the campaign were taken. (Copy testing and tracking experts were assigned to the campaign after it started.) So, the next "best" measure was to use ad recall, separating it into those with high and low ad recall scores, a proxy for lower and higher ad exposure. Researchers surveyed approximately 6,000 adolescents annually in their homes after the campaign began, with the same adolescents surveyed four times. Ninety-four percent of the youths reported seeing the ads, with a median frequency of 2 to 3 ads per week. Because the lower and higher ad exposure groups may have differed in their prior drug use, the researchers used covariates (e.g., sensation seeking) to try to control for or factor out these effects. In the end, the tracking study found mixed effects and concluded that the campaign was ineffective and perhaps counterproductive. On the positive side, as the campaign progressed, anti-drug beliefs increased (yet without a control group, it could not be concluded that the campaign caused this trend). On the negative side, higher recall of the ads sometimes predicted greater intent to use one year later.

However, it was unclear whether these negative effects can be tied to the campaign itself. For example, research shows that advertising effects usually occur within days or weeks—not a year later. Moreover, *reverse causality* may have occurred such that adolescents who already formed an intent to use based on risk factors (or were using) paid more attention to the anti-drug ads (and maintained their intent due to the risk factors). An independent measure of ad exposure unrelated to the viewer's intent (e.g., ad GRPs) might have been considered. Better yet, a true baseline no-exposure group or control group not exposed to the ads (and matched to the test group) would have been preferred.

Recent research has shown more positive effects of the campaign on targeted groups (e.g., lower rates of use for eighth-grade girls), and for all adolescents when combined with in-school community interventions. Yet, the overall lesson for the evaluation of major ad campaigns, such as NYADMC, is that (1) careful planning with experts is important before the campaign is launched, (2) control groups for both baseline exposure (tracking) and in the case of copy testing are critical, (3) screening for the affected target markets should be conducted, and (4) a consideration of all possible IMC "touch points" helps (e.g., in addition to national TV ads, one might consider in-school programs, public relations, social media, and so forth).[1] Certainly, the NYADMC had many (but not all) of these elements and provides a great model for discussion in the development and evaluation of major advertising campaigns.

Sources: Robert Denniston, "Planning, Implementing, and Managing an Unprecedented Government-Funded Prevention Communications Initiative," *Social Marketing Quarterly*, 10 (summer 2004), 7–12; Diane Foley and Cornelia Pechmann, "The National Youth Anti-Drug Media Campaign Copy Test System," *Social Marketing Quarterly*, 10 (summer 2004), 34–42; Cornelia Pechmann and Craig Andrews, "Copy Test Methods to Pretest Advertisements," in *Wiley Encyclopedia of Marketing*, Jagdish Sheth and Naresh K. Maholtra, Editors- In-Chief (vol. 4, *Advertising and Integrated Marketing Communications*, Michael A. Belch and George E. Belch, eds.), West Sussex, UK: John Wiley & Sons, Ltd., 2011, 54–62; "National Youth Anti-Drug Media Campaign," Communication Strategy Statement Supplement, Office of National Drug Control Policy: Washington, DC, August 2001, 1–27; Robert Hornik, Lela Jacobsohn, Robert Orwin, Andrea Plesse, and Graham Kalton, "Effects of the National Youth Anti-Drug Media Campaign," *American Journal of Public Health*, 98 (12), 2008, 2229–36; Cornelia Pechmann and J. Craig Andrews, "Methodological Issues and Challenges in Conducting Social Impact Evaluations" in *Scaling Social Impact: New Thinking*, Paul N. Bloom and Edward Skloot, eds., New York: Palgrave Macmillan, 2010, 217–34; Leendert Marinus Koyck, *Distributed Lags and Investment Analysis*, Amsterdam: North Holland Publishers, 1954; Christopher S. Carpenter and Cornelia Pechmann, "Exposure to the Above the Influence Antidrug Advertisements and Adolescent Marijuana Use in the United States, 2006–2008," *American Journal of Public Health*, 101 (May 2011), 948–54; and Michael D. Slater, Kathleen J. Kelly, Frank R. Lawrence, Linda R. Stanley, and Maria Leonora G. Comello, "Assessing Media Campaigns Linking Marijuana Non-Use with Autonomy and Aspirations: Be Under Your Own Influence and ONDCP's Above the Influence," *Prevention Science*, vol. 12 (online), 2011, 12–22.

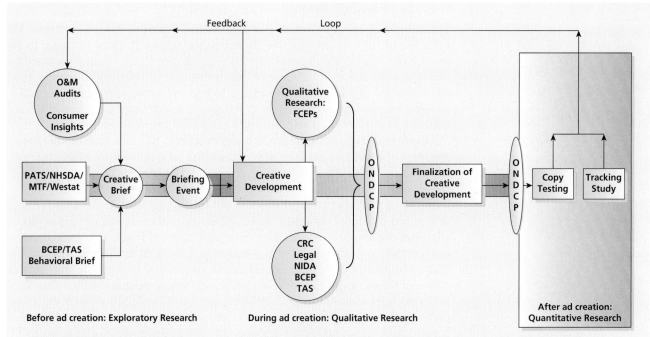

KEY: O&M: Ogilvy & Mather, BCEP: Behavioral Change Expert Panel, PDFA: Partnership for a Drug-Free America, PATS: Partnership Attitude Tracking Study, FCEP: Formative Creative Evaluation Panel, CRC: Creative Review Committee, MTF: Monitoring the Future, NIDA: National Institute on Drug Abuse, TAS: Target Audience Specialist, NHSDA: National Household Survey on Drug Abuse

FIGURE **17.1** National Youth Anti-Drug Media Campaign Advertising Development/Research Process
Source: Office of National Drug Control Policy (ONDCP).

Introduction to Advertising Research

Chapter 10 examined the role of advertising creativity and Chapter 11 explored the role of endorsers and forms of advertising executions (e.g., humor and fear appeals). A well-defined value proposition is the key to advertising effectiveness, but there are many different types of creative advertising strategies (e.g., USP, brand image, and generic) and different message strategies that can accomplish the intended marcom objectives described in Chapter 8.

At the same time, the brand management team is responsible for researching whether proposed advertisements stand a good chance of being successful *prior* to investing money in printing or airing ads. It would, in other words, be presumptuous at best or even foolhardy to assume that a proposed advertisement will be successful absent any research-based evidence. Yet, in your future marketing or advertising careers, you will likely hear colleagues give dismissive reactions to testing in that "we already know that" or "I know this ad will [or won't] work," or "we already tested that in another region." Unfortunately, such thinking avoids finding out exactly what *consumers* (not work colleagues) in your region *really* think about your brand or advertising. Moreover, the demand for *accountability* that is prevalent throughout business (recall the discussion in Chapter 2) necessitates that ads be tested before they are placed in media and then again during or after the period in which they have been printed or broadcast.

Sound business practice requires that efforts be made to determine whether advertising expenditures are justified, especially considering that it may cost up to $500,000 (on average) to produce a national TV ad campaign. Accordingly, a significant amount of time and money are spent on testing message effectiveness. This chapter surveys some of the most important techniques used in the advertising research business.

It Is Not Easy or Inexpensive

Measuring message effectiveness is a difficult and expensive task. Nonetheless, the value gained from undertaking the effort typically outweighs the drawbacks. In the absence of formal research, most advertisers would not know whether proposed ad messages are going to be effective or whether ongoing advertising is doing a good job, nor could they know what to change to improve future advertising efforts. Advertising research enables management to increase advertising's contribution toward achieving marketing goals and yielding a reasonable return on investment.

Contemporary message research traces its roots to the nineteenth century, when measures of recall and memory were obtained as indicators of print advertising effectiveness.[2] Today, most national advertisers would not even consider airing a television commercial or placing a magazine advertisement without testing it first. A survey of the largest advertisers and advertising agencies in the United States determined that more than 80 percent of the respondents from each group pretest television commercials before airing them on a national basis.[3] Interestingly, these commercials typically are tested in a preliminary form rather than as finished versions. The purpose of testing commercials in rough form is to enable an economic means of screening out bad ideas at significantly lower expense than is necessitated in developing finished commercials.[4] Research has shown that results from testing prefinished commercials closely parallel those from tests performed on finalized commercials.[5] (The *IMC Focus* describes the various prefinished forms in which TV commercials typically are tested.) Finally, even with digital (online) media, in which there can be major context- and content-specific differences, approximately 75 percent of advertisers routinely test some digital ads during development.[6]

What Does Advertising Research Involve?

Advertising research encompasses a variety of purposes, methods, measures, and techniques. Broadly speaking, we can distinguish between two general forms of ad research: measures of *media effectiveness* and those of *message effectiveness*. Chapters 12 to 16 (especially Chapter 12) addressed the matter of media effectiveness; the present chapter focuses exclusively on measuring message effectiveness.

Achieving brand awareness, conveying copy points, influencing attitudes, creating emotional responses, and affecting purchase choices are the various foci of message research. In short, message research is undertaken to test the effectiveness of advertising messages. (Message research also is called *copy research*, or *copy testing*, but these terms are too limiting inasmuch as message research involves testing all aspects of advertisements, not just the verbal copy material.) For example, as shown in the *Marcom Insight*, tracking the overall effects of a campaign on beliefs, attitudes, intentions, and behavior usually is part of message research evaluation.

As mentioned in the *Marcom Insight*, there are four stages at which ad message research is usually conducted: (1) at the copy development stage; (2) at the "rough" stage (i.e., in prefinished form such as animatics and photomatics; see the *IMC Focus*); (3) at the final production stage, but prior to placing the ad in magazines, on TV, or in other media (i.e., pretesting with copy tests); and (4) after the ad has been run in media (i.e., posttesting with tracking studies).[7] In other words, advertising research involves both *pretesting* messages during developmental stages (prior to actual placement in advertising media) and *posttesting* messages for effectiveness after they have been aired or printed. Pretesting is performed to eliminate ineffective ads before they are ever run, whereas posttesting is conducted to determine whether messages have achieved established objectives.

Sometimes research is done under natural advertising conditions (e.g., field studies) and other times in simulated or laboratory situations. Measures of effectiveness range from paper-and-pencil instruments (such as attitude scales) to physiological devices (e.g., pupillometers that measure eye movement). It should be clear that there is no single encompassing form of message research. Rather, measures of advertising effectiveness are as varied as the questions that advertisers and their agencies want answered.

IMC FOCUS

Testing TV Commercials in Prefinished Form

An advertising agency works from a creative brief that has been developed in conjunction with the client-side brand management team. As described in Chapter 10, the creative brief is a document designed to inspire copywriters by channeling their creative efforts toward a solution that will serve the interests of the client. The creative brief also represents an informal pact between client and advertising agency that secures agreement on what an advertising campaign is intended to accomplish. Among other features, the creative brief identifies the brand positioning, the overall marketing strategy for the brand, and a statement of the brand's key value proposition. Working from this brief, copywriters and other agency personnel develop two or more creative executions that are considered suitable for accomplishing agreed-on objectives. However, rather than immediately producing a finished commercial, which can easily cost $500,000 or more, it is practical and cost-efficient to test the advertising concept in a prefinished form. There are five prefinished forms that are tested in television commercial research. The form furthest removed from a finished commercial is the storyboard, whereas the other forms become more like a produced commercial as we progress from the animatics form to the liveamatics version. Each is briefly described here.

1. *Storyboards*: This prefinished version presents a series of key visual frames and the corresponding script of the audio. The sequence of visual frames is literally pasted on a poster-type board, hence the storyboard name. The storyboard version, unlike a dynamic commercial, is completely static. Drawings of people replace the actual actors or celebrities who ultimately will appear in

the finished commercial. Testing of storyboards often is done in focus group settings with small groups of consumers.

2. *Animatics*: This is a film or videotape of a sequence of drawings with simultaneous playing of audio to represent a proposed commercial. The animatic version maintains the primitive nature of the storyboard but incorporates an element of dynamism by videotaping the sequence of drawings.

3. *Photomatics*: A sequence of photographs is filmed or videotaped and accompanied by audio to represent a proposed commercial. This version is increasingly realistic because photographs of real people are displayed rather than, as in the case of storyboards or animatics, merely shown as drawn renderings of real people.

4. *Ripomatics* (also called steal-o-matics): Footage is taken from existing commercials and spliced together to represent the proposed commercial. Hence, the ripomatics version captures the realism of an actual commercial but does not entail the huge expense associated with filming an original commercial.

5. *Liveamatics*: This prefinished version entails filming or videotaping live talent to represent the proposed commercial. This version is the closest to a finished commercial, but it does not fully represent the actual settings or talent that will be used in the finished commercial.

Sources: Adapted from David Olson, "Principles of Measuring Advertising Effectiveness," American Marketing Association, http:// www.marketingpower.com (accessed October 14, 2004); and Karen Whitehill King, John D. Pehrson, and Leonard N. Reid, "Pretesting TV Commercials: Methods, Measures, and Changing Agency Roles," *Journal of Advertising* 22 (September 1993), 85–97.

Industry Standards for Message Research

Although message-based research is prevalent, much of it is not of the highest caliber. Sometimes it is unclear exactly what the research is attempting to measure, measures often fail to satisfy the basic requirements of sound research, and results occasionally have little to say about whether tested ads stand a good chance of being effective.

Members of the advertising research community have been mindful of these problems and have sought a higher standard of performance from advertising researchers. U.S. advertising agencies formulated a major document, called Positioning Advertising Copy Testing (PACT), to remedy the problem of mediocre or flawed advertising research. The document is directed primarily at television advertising, but is relevant to the testing of advertising in all media.

The PACT document consists of nine message-testing principles.[8] More than mere pronouncements, these principles represent useful guides to how advertising research should be conducted. (Note that the developers of the PACT principles referred to copy testing rather than message research. The following descriptions retain the use of copy testing, although as noted previously, message research is a more apt label.)

Principle 1

A good copy testing system needs to provide measurements that are *relevant to the advertising objectives*. The specific objective(s) that an advertising campaign is intended to accomplish (such as creating brand awareness, influencing brand image, or creating warmth) should be the first consideration in determining the methods to assess advertising effectiveness. For example, if the objective for a particular advertising campaign is to evoke strong emotional reactions from viewers, a measure of brand awareness would likely be insufficient for determining if the message succeeded in accomplishing its objective.

Principle 2

A good copy testing system *requires agreement about how the results will be used in advance of each specific test*. Specifying the use of research results before data collection ensures that all parties involved (advertiser, agency, and research firm) agree on the research goals and reduces the chance of conflicting interpretations of test results. This principle's intent is to encourage the use of decision rules or action standards that, before actual testing, establish the test results that must be achieved for the test advertisement to receive full media distribution.

Principle 3

A good copy testing system provides *multiple measurements* because single measurements are generally inadequate to assess the totality of an ad's performance. The process by which advertisements influence customers is complex, so multiple measures are more likely than single measures to capture the various advertising effects.

Principle 4

A good copy testing system is based on *a model of human response to communications*—the reception of a stimulus, the comprehension of the stimulus, and the response to the stimulus. Because advertisements vary in the impact they are intended to achieve, a good copy testing system is capable of answering questions that are patterned to the underlying model of behavior. For example, if consumers purchase a particular product for primarily emotional reasons, then message research should use a suitable measure of emotional response rather than simply measuring recall of copy points. It is interesting to note that message research has historically focused excessively on the rational, cognitive aspect of human behavior and devoted insufficient attention to emotions and feelings—factors that are increasingly being recognized by scholars and practitioners as just as important, if not more influential, than cognition in driving consumer behavior.[9] A later discussion will discuss the role of emotionality in advertising and in message-based advertising research.

Principle 5

A good copy testing system allows for consideration of *whether the advertising stimulus should be exposed more than once*. This principle addresses the issue of whether a single test exposure (showing an ad or commercial to consumers only once) provides a sufficient test of potential impact. Because multiple exposures are often required for advertisements to accomplish their full effect, message research should expose a test ad to respondents on two or more occasions when the communications situation calls for such a procedure.[10] For example, a single-exposure test is probably insufficient to determine whether an advertisement successfully conveys a complex benefit. Conversely, a single exposure may be adequate if an advertisement is designed solely to create name awareness for a new brand.

Principle 6

A good copy testing system recognizes that a more finished piece of copy can be evaluated more soundly; therefore, a good system requires, at minimum, that *alternative executions be tested in the same degree of finish*. Test results typically vary depending on the degree of finish, as, for example, when testing a photomatic or ripomatic version of a television commercial (see the *IMC Focus*). Sometimes the amount of information lost from testing a less-than-finished ad is inconsequential; sometimes it is critical.

Principle 7

A good copy testing system *provides controls to avoid the bias normally found in the exposure context*. The context in which an advertisement is contained (e.g., the clutter or lack of clutter in a magazine) will have a substantial impact on how the ad is received, processed, and accepted. For this reason, copy testing procedures should attempt to duplicate the eventual context of an advertisement or commercial.

Principle 8

A good copy testing system takes into account *basic considerations of sample definition*. This typically requires that the sample be representative of the target audience to which test results are to be generalized and that the sample size be sufficiently large to permit reliable statistical conclusions.

Principle 9

Finally, a good copy testing system can *demonstrate reliability and validity*. Reliability and validity are basic requirements of any research endeavor. As applied to message research, a reliable test yields *consistent* results each time an advertisement is tested, and a valid test *assesses what it is intended to assess* (e.g., being predictive of marketplace performance).

The foregoing principles establish a high set of standards for the advertising research community and should be viewed as mandatory if advertising effectiveness is to be tested in a meaningful way.

What Do Brand Managers and Ad Agencies Want to Learn from Message Research?

Message research is needed to provide *diagnostic information* about an advertisement's equity-enhancing and sales-expanding potential for brands (pretesting research) and to determine whether finalized advertisements actually accomplished these objectives (posttesting research).

It is important to note that members of the advertising community have attempted for many years to figure out which measures of advertising best predict advertising effectiveness. Particularly notable is a major study funded by the influential Advertising Research Foundation (ARF) that evaluated which of 35 different measures best predict the sales effectiveness of television commercials.[11] Although representing a heroic effort, results from ARF's Copy Research Validity Project are both inconclusive and controversial.[12] Probably the only definitive conclusion that can be made is that *no one measure is always most appropriate or universally best*. Each brand-advertising situation requires a careful assessment of the objectives that advertising is intended to accomplish and then the use of research methods that are appropriate for determining whether these objectives have been accomplished.

Given the scope of advertising research techniques in use, it would be impossible in this chapter to provide an exhaustive treatment. Literally dozens of methods for measuring message effectiveness have appeared over the years, and many companies specialize in measuring advertising effectiveness—firms such as the GfK Mediamark Research & Intelligence (MRI), the (former) Bruzzone Research Company, Millward Brown, Ameritest, Gallup & Robinson, Mapes and Ross, Ipsos ASI, comScore ARS, nViso, and so on.

Two General Forms of Message Research

Broadly speaking, message research comes in two general forms: qualitative and quantitative. We first will describe qualitative research somewhat briefly and then devote primary attention to quantitative methods. This is not because the latter is more important; rather, the simple fact is that quantitative research has dominated in the ad industry and has a more established history of use in comparison to qualitative procedures.

Qualitative Message Research

This form of research is called *qualitative* because it is not based on producing numerical results and statistical analyses related to advertising copy and people's responses to that copy. Rather, qualitative research is concerned with generating insights into and interpretations of those advertising elements that influence people's responses to advertisements. Focus groups represent one form of qualitative ad research. For example, panels of (usually 6 to 10) focus group participants are presented with a storyboard version of a proposed new commercial, and then, with the probing of an experienced moderator, are urged to share their thoughts and feelings about the commercial.

More sophisticated forms of qualitative advertising research seek to better understand the meaning consumers derive from advertisements and the mental models that drive their thinking and behavior. One such method is *ethnographic research*. This form of research requires that advertising researchers fully immerse themselves into the study of the role that products and brands play in people's lives. Ethnography relies less on asking large samples of people questions about their opinions and beliefs and more on in-depth *observations* of the behavior of a small number of consumers. Ethnographers observe people's behavior in their homes or in other natural habitats where consumption and sometimes production of goods and services takes place. In addition to observing natural consumer behavior, ethnographic researchers also perform in-depth interviews with consumers to learn about their consumption behavior and the forces, such as advertising, that influence that behavior. Indeed, as explained in the following *Global Focus*, such observational techniques can be important due to differences in how consumers interact with and use brands around the world.[13]

The Zaltman Metaphor Elicitation Technique (ZMET)

A specific form of ethnographic research is the Zaltman Metaphor Elicitation Technique (ZMET).[14] This technique is based on several underlying premises, such as the fact that most human communication involves *nonverbal elements* (pictures, scenes, and music), that people's thoughts and feelings occur nonverbally as images, and that metaphors are the key mechanism for tapping into people's thoughts and feelings.[16] (A *metaphor* is based on the idea that people understand and experience things in terms of other things. For example, we refer to someone as having "eagle eyes" to mean he or she has keen sight; we sometimes characterize products as "lemons" to suggest they are fatally flawed. Hence, "eagle eyes" and "lemons" are metaphors that stand for something else.) Metaphors serve to reveal people's thoughts and shape them as well. By understanding the metaphors people use when thinking about brands, it is possible to apply this insight in developing advertising copy that resonates with people's brand-relevant thoughts and feelings.

Jack Daniels Old No. 7 and Global Ad Research

In the early 2000s due to lackluster U.S. sales, Brown-Forman decided to expand internationally with its famous Jack Daniels Old No. 7 brand. To do so, they conducted a series of consumer and trade focus groups, as well as hands-on tasting research, to better determine the right approach to selling their American whiskey in numerous countries and cultures around the world. This research certainly has paid off, as nearly one-half of Jack Daniels's business is now from overseas (in 135 countries), with 20 percent of the 3.5 million visits to their website (now in 14 languages) being from outside the United States.

Even though the company is known for their consistent focus in ads on its small-town, nineteenth-century Lynchburg, Tennessee home and roots ("pop. 361"), and images of nineteenth-century hillbillies in straw hats, exactly *how* this image is communicated in different countries and cultures varies a great deal. For example, the British relish the handcrafted, small-town story often appearing in London subways, but many young and successful Chinese and Indian consumers have moved from the poorer countryside, and do not want to see these sorts of images. In India and China, the iconic black-and-white bottle is featured, leaving the Lynchburg story to be discovered on its website or on concert displays. This international flexibility is enhanced by *not* featuring customers or celebrities in Jack Daniels ads (other than Jack Daniels and nineteenth-century Lynchburg citizens). According to global managers, this strategy leaves the brand accessible to leather-clad bikers and schoolteachers, and whether they are in St. Petersburg, Russia, or St. Petersburg, Florida.

Focus group research for Jack Daniels with younger Taiwanese men shows that ad images depicting the purity of the water from Tennessee's limestone shelf and charcoal filtering are important, given water purity problems in places where they had grown up. Other research reveals that in Japan, it is customary for a dinner group of 4 to 5 to split a bottle of Jack Daniels. Yet, in Australia, they prefer to drink at home, leading to the creation of a popular packaged mix called "Jack and Cola," selling over 1 million cases.

However, in the United Kingdom, research indicates that most people prefer to have bartenders mix their Jack Daniels, whereas in Spain, it is consumed straight. In China, many prefer mixing it with green tea.

So, onsite research, tastings, and education are critical for Jack Daniels in its strategy around the world. This effort has many Moscow consumers at clubs preferring Jack Daniels to vodka or the more familiar Scotch whiskey. (See the accompanying Russian Jack Daniels ad with his picture above the headline translated as "Happy Birthday, Mister Jack!"[15]) In China, research and careful positioning has made Jack Daniels close to being the number-one, best-selling whiskey.

Sources: Adapted from Matthew Swibel, "Drinking to the Dollar," *Forbes*, April 18, 2005, http://www.forbes.com/forbes/2005/0418/152.html; David Kiley, "Jack Daniels' International Appeal," *Businessweek*, October 10, 2007, http://www.businessweek.com/innovate/content/oct2007/id20071010_651037.htm; and Jiang Jingjing, "Spirited Competition," *China Daily*, October 10, 2007, http://www.chinadaily.com.cn/bw/2007-10/10/content_6155721.htm.

The details about how a ZMET is implemented are beyond the scope of this text. (Refer to the articles cited in endnote 14 for specifics.) However, the important takeaway from this brief discussion is that qualitative research such as the Zaltman Metaphor Elicitation Technique can be invaluable as input into developing advertising copy. Thus, unlike the quantitative techniques that follow, ZMET is used as a basis for developing advertising copy rather than for testing that copy.

Quantitative Message Research

Quantitative message research is concerned with measuring the effects an advertisement may have (pretest research) or has had (posttest research). The following sections discuss some of the more popular methods national advertisers use. It first is important to realize that some advertisers—especially smaller companies and organizations—do *not* conduct any advertising research, in either testing proposed advertising copy or testing ads that have been printed or aired in the form of, say, finished newspaper ads or TV commercials. The excuse given is that there is not sufficient time or funding to perform the research. Frankly, this is a bit lame given that the cost of making a mistake (for example, airing bad commercials) is far greater than the cost in terms of both time and money of testing ad copy. We would go so far as to say that no ad should ever be placed in media prior to conducting at least *some* research, although more formal research is preferable (e.g., see *Marcom Insight*).

A second preliminary point that will set the stage for the detailed presentation of quantitative message research methods is contained in this quote:

> *Measurement is the first step that leads to control and eventually to improvement. If you can't measure something, you can't understand it. If you can't understand it, you can't control it. If you can't control it, you can't improve it.*[17]

The point is that advertising research is crucial in order to measure the effects that advertisements have so that improvements can be made on a continual basis.

What exactly does quantitative message research measure? To address this question, it will be helpful to return to one of the previously discussed copy testing principles. PACT principle 4 stated that a good copy testing measurement system is based on a model of human response to communications. In other words, before determining precisely what to measure, it is important to know which types of responses advertising is capable of eliciting. What hierarchy of effects might advertising have? Well, advertisements can have a variety of effects beyond initial exposure, including the following: (1) creating brand awareness; (2) teaching prospective customers about brand features and benefits; (3) forging emotional connections with people; (4) influencing purchase-relevant beliefs and positively (or negatively!) affecting attitudes toward advertised brands; (5) shifting people's preferences from one brand to another; and, ultimately, (6) encouraging trial and repeat purchase behavior.

As a matter of convenience (and some necessary simplification), we will categorize message research into four groups of measures: (1) recognition and recall, (2) emotional reactions, (3) persuasion, and (4) sales response. The intent is to provide a representative sampling of the primary measurement techniques that brand managers and their ad agencies use for measuring advertising effectiveness. These general categories and the specific measures contained within each category are summarized in Table 17.1.

In brief, measures of *recognition and recall* assess whether advertising has successfully influenced brand awareness and influenced brand-related thoughts and feelings. Measures of *emotional reaction* provide indicators of whether advertisements have emotionally aroused consumers. Measures of *persuasive impact* represent pre-behavioral indicators of whether an advertisement is likely to influence purchase intentions and behavior. Finally, measures of *sales response* determine whether an advertising campaign has affected consumers' purchases of an advertised brand.

TABLE 17.1	Illustrative Message Research Methods

Measures of Recognition and Recall

- GfK MRI's Starch Ad Readership Studies (magazines)
- Bruzzone tests (TV)
- Day-after recall testing (TV)

Measures of Emotional Reactions

- BBDO Emotional Measurement System
- Facial imaging technology
- Brain imaging (fMRI)
- Self-reports
- Physiological tests

Measures of Persuasion

- Ipsos ASI Next*TV method
- comScore ARS' Share of Choice method

Measures of Sales Response (single-source systems)

- Symphony IRI Group's BehaviorScan
- Nielsen's ScanTrack

Measures of Recognition and Recall

After exposure to an advertisement, consumers may experience varying degrees of awareness, the most basic of which is simply noticing an ad without processing specific elements. Advertisers intend, however, for consumers to heed specific parts, elements, or features of an ad and associate those with the advertised brand. Recognition and recall both represent elements of consumers' memories for advertising information, but *recognition measures*, which can be equated with multiple-choice test questions, tap a more superficial level of memory compared with *recall measures*, which are similar to essay questions.[18] It also will be noted from the discussion of brand equity in Chapter 2 that recognition is a lower level of brand awareness than recall. Thus, brand managers want consumers not only to recognize a brand name and its attributes or benefits, but also to recall this information freely from memory without cues or reminders. Yet, some ad experts counter that recognition is quite useful as it is a better measure of forgetting than traditional measures of recall.[19]

Several commercial research firms provide advertisers with information on how well their ads perform in terms of generating awareness, which typically is assessed with recognition or recall measures. Three services are described in the following sections: GfK MRI's Starch Ad Readership Studies (magazine recognition), Bruzzone tests (television recognition primarily), and day-after recall tests (television recall).[20]

Starch Ad Readership Studies

Starch Ad Readership Studies, a testing service of a company named GfK Mediamark Research & Intelligence (MRI), measures the primary objective of a *magazine ad*—that is, to be seen and read. Starch examines reader awareness of advertisements in consumer magazines and business publications. Approximately 118,000 advertisements for over 3,000 issues are studied annually, involving more than 180 national publications. Sample sizes range from 100 to 150 individuals per issue, with most interviews conducted in respondents' homes or, in the case of business publications, in offices or places of business. Interviews are conducted during the early life of a publication. Following a suitable waiting period after the appearance of a publication to give readers an opportunity to read or look through their issue, interviewing commences and continues for a full week (for a weekly publication), two weeks (for a biweekly), or three weeks (for a monthly publication).

Starch interviewers locate eligible readers of each magazine issue studied. An *eligible reader* is one who has glanced through or read some part of the issue prior to the interviewer's visit and who meets the age, sex, and occupation requirements set for the particular magazine. Once eligibility is established, interviewers turn the pages of the magazine, inquiring about each advertisement being studied. Respondents are first asked, "Did you see or read any part of this advertisement?" If a respondent answers "Yes," a prescribed questioning procedure is followed to determine the respondent's awareness of various parts of the ad (illustrations, headlines, etc.). Respondents are then classified as *noted, associated, read-some,* or *read-most* readers according to these specific definitions:[21]

- *Noted* is the percentage of people interviewed who remembered having previously seen the advertisement in the issue being studied.
- *Associated* is the percentage of people interviewed who not only noted the ad, but also saw or read some part of it that clearly indicated the name of the brand or advertiser.
- *Read some* is the percentage of people interviewed who read any part of the ad's copy.
- *Read most* is the percentage of people interviewed who read half or more of the written material in the ad.

For each magazine advertisement that has undergone a Starch analysis, indices are developed for that ad's noted, associated, read-some, and read-most scores. Two sets of indices are established: One index compares an advertisement's scores against the average scores for *all ads* in the magazine issue (called the Issue Index), and the second (called the Adnorm Index) compares an advertisement's scores against other ads in the *same product category* as well as with the same size (e.g., full-page) and color classifications (e.g., four-color). Thus, an advertisement that achieves an average value receives an index of 100. By comparison, a score of 130, for example, would mean that a particular ad scored 30 percent above comparable ads, whereas a score of 75 would indicate it scored 25 percent below comparable ads.

Figure 17.2 illustrates a Starch Advertising Research Report for an Amazon Kindle advertisement from a recent issue of *Time* magazine. This Amazon Kindle ad contains some body copy under a picture of the e-reader Kindle with a catchy headline, "Bring some romance into her life." The Starch Ad Readership scores for this ad reflect that 67 percent of the respondents remembered having previously seen (or *noted*) the ad, 64 percent *associated* it, 64 percent *read some* of it, and 45 percent *read most* of the body copy contained in this ad. (For readers who are experienced with the Starch procedure, note that Starch used to attach little yellow labels on advertisements years ago to indicate these percentages, but it no longer affixes these labels; rather, scores are provided in the separate report, as seen in Figure 17.2.)

As another example, a José Cuervo Especial tequila ad shows a man and a woman in wet bathing suits in a romantic embrace. It attracts attention and perhaps creates an emotional bond with the brand, even though only a small bottle of the tequila is shown in one corner of the ad. Containing virtually no body copy other than a three-word headline, "PURSUE YOUR DAYDREAMS," this ad's noted, associated, read-some, and read-most scores also were quite good, at 58, 54, 39, and 39 percent, respectively.

A basic assumption of the Starch procedure is that respondents in fact do remember whether they saw a particular ad in a specific magazine issue. The Starch technique has sometimes been criticized because in so-called *bogus ad*

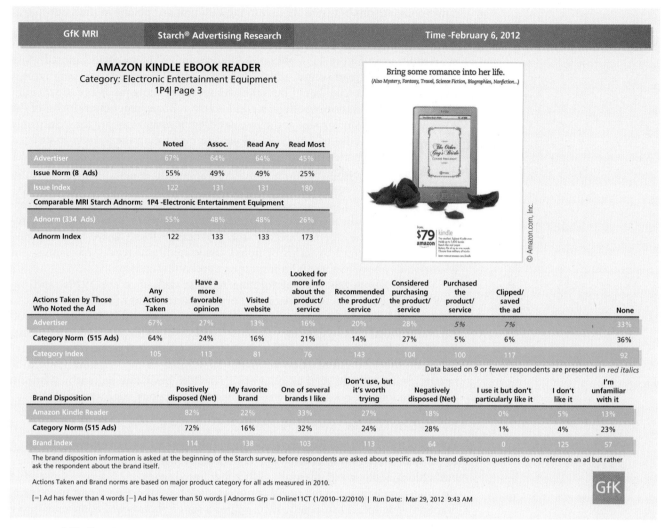

FIGURE 17.2 Starch Advertising Research Report

studies (i.e., studies that use prepublication or altered issues), respondents report having seen ads that actually never ran. The company that conducts Starch studies does not consider such studies valid and claims that the bogus studies have not adhered to proper procedures for qualifying issue readers and questioning respondents. Research demonstrates that when properly interviewed, most respondents are able to identify the ads they have seen or read in a specific issue with a high degree of accuracy; according to this research, false reporting of ad noting is minimal.[22] Recent research with eye tracking equipment (showing attention via "fixations" on ad elements) indicates that attention to ads predicted the ad-noted measure and attention to the brand predicted the association measure.[23] Yet, attention to the ad text did not predict the read-most scores. Also, consumers overclaimed ad recognition with larger pictorials, smaller-sized brands, and larger text in ads. Based on their evidence, the researchers argue for an adjustment to bias in recognition test scores based on the proportion of consumers who would fixate on the ad or its elements five times or more.[24]

Due to the inherent frailties of people's memories, it is almost certain that Starch scores do *not* provide exact percentages, but rather are biased to some degree by people reporting they have seen or read an ad when in fact they have not. Another potential source of bias is people reporting they have *not* seen an ad when, in fact, they have. Nonetheless, it is not exact scores that are critical, but rather comparisons between scores among different ads placed in the same magazine issue (Issue Index) or comparisons for the same type of ad placed in different magazines for the same product category (Adnorm Index). For example, the Amazon Kindle ad in Figure 17.2 obtained Adnorm Index scores of 122 (noted), 133 (associated), 133 (read some), and 173 (read most). These indices mean that this ad performed 22 percent better than the average noted score (an index of 100 indicates an average-performing ad; hence 122 − 100 = 22 percent better) for all of the advertisements of similar size and color in different magazines for the "electronic equipment entertainment" category, 33 percent better than the average associated score, 33 percent better than the average read-some score, and 73 percent better than the average read-most score. It is obvious that this ad performed well above average, especially for the read-most category. Comparatively, the Adnorm indices for the José Cuervo Especial tequila ad discussed earlier are 107 (noted), 108 (associated), 105 (read some), and 229 (read most). Compared to similarly sized advertisements for the alcohol category, the provocative José Cuervo ad performed slightly above average in terms of noted, associated, and read-some scores, but dramatically above average with respect to its read-most score.

Because Starch has been performing these studies since the 1920s, and has compiled a wealth of baseline data, or norms, advertisers and media planners can make informed decisions concerning the relative merits of different magazines and informed judgments regarding the effectiveness of particular advertisements. Recently, GfK MRI has offered "Starch Digital," a syndicated service that measures the readership and effectiveness of *digital advertising* in top consumer magazine brands. Starch Digital releases data on a monthly basis aggregated by platform or medium (tablets, e-readers, or in electronic reproductions, such as Zinio).

Bruzzone Tests

For years, the Bruzzone Research Company (BRC) provided advertisers with a test of consumer *recognition* of television commercials that have aired along with their evaluations of these commercials. (BRC also tested magazine advertisements, but the discussion here is limited to TV commercials. The tests are now part of the firm, StartSampling Inc.) Historically, BRC mailed a set of photoboard commercials to a random sample of households and encouraged responses by providing a nominal monetary incentive. Starting in the late 1990s, BRC's data collection turned to the Internet and away from mailed distribution, as testing commercials online proved more efficient, less costly, and equally valid to the mailing procedure.[25]

In its standard testing procedure, BRC e-mails 15 commercials to a sample of online users. For each tested commercial, respondents first see this question: "Do you remember seeing this commercial on TV?" This question is followed by a series of six key scenes from the commercial and corresponding script. Immediately below the six-scene presentation are three response options: "Yes," "No," and "Not Sure." Respondents who respond "Yes" (that they do remember seeing this commercial) continue answering a series of questions about the commercial. (Those who answer "No" or "Not Sure" skip to the next tested commercial.) Importantly, anything that identifies the advertiser (such as mentioning the brand name in the script) is removed, so that those who noticed the commercial can indicate whether they remember the name of the advertised brand. (For an interesting demonstration of BRC's online testing procedure, go to www.bruzzone-research.com/demo_surveys2.htm.)

An example of an illustrative Bruzzone test is a Taco Bell commercial titled "Carne Asada Taquitos."[26] This 30-second commercial first aired during a Super Bowl and was tested by BRC shortly after the airing. The commercial focuses on two lions chitchatting about Taco Bell's new (at the time) grilled steak taco, or, in Spanish, *carne asada taquitos*. The commercial is humorous in a low-key fashion, and is somewhat engaging and enjoyable.

The Bruzzone testing procedure first requests respondents to indicate whether they recalled seeing this commercial. Respondents subsequently are asked to indicate how interested they are in the commercial and how it makes them feel about the advertised brand (Taco Bell's grilled steak taco). Respondents also are requested to describe their feelings by checking any of 27 adjectives that, in their opinion, characterize the commercial—items such as amusing, appealing, believable, clever, and so on. Following these ratings, respondents indicate whether it is appropriate for the advertiser (Taco Bell, in this case) to air this commercial. They then make known how much they liked the commercial (from "Liked it a lot" to "Disliked it a lot") and whether they remember which brand was being advertised.

Because BRC has performed hundreds of such tests (BRC tested nearly 800 ads aired during the Super Bowls leading up to this commercial), it has established norms for average commercial performance against which a newly tested commercial can be compared. BRC's Advertising Response Model (ARM) links responses to the 27 descriptive adjectives to consumers' attitudes toward both the advertisement (attitude toward the ad) and the advertised product (attitude toward the product), and ultimately to the overall impact of the ad (overall impact). Figure 17.3 presents the ARM analysis for Taco Bell's "Carne Asada Taquitos" commercial.

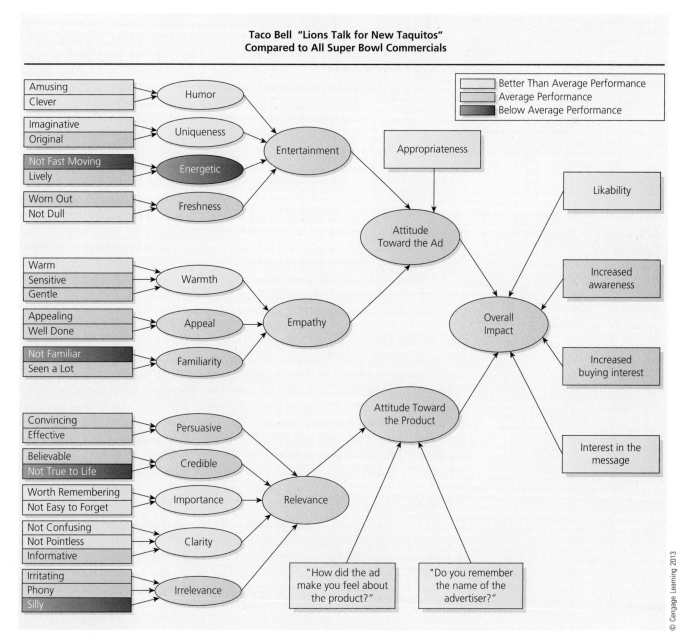

© Cengage Learning 2013

FIGURE 17.3 Advertising Response Model (ARM) for the "Carne Asada Taquitos" Commercial

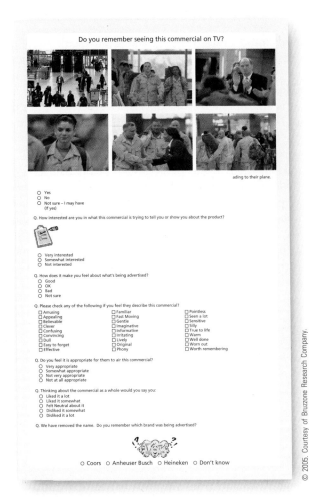

Do you remember seeing this commercial on TV?

ading to their plane.

○ Yes
○ No
○ Not sure – I may have
   (If yes)

Q. How interested are you in what this commercial is trying to tell you or show you about the product?

○ Very interested
○ Somewhat interested
○ Not interested

Q. How does it make you feel about what's being advertised?
○ Good
○ OK
○ Bad
○ Not sure

Q. Please check any of the following if you feel they describe this commercial?

☐ Amusing   ☐ Familiar   ☐ Pointless
☐ Appealing   ☐ Fast Moving   ☐ Seen a lot
☐ Believable   ☐ Gentle   ☐ Sensitive
☐ Clever   ☐ Imaginative   ☐ Silly
☐ Confusing   ☐ Informative   ☐ True to life
☐ Convincing   ☐ Irritating   ☐ Warm
☐ Dull   ☐ Lively   ☐ Well done
☐ Easy to forget   ☐ Original   ☐ Worn out
☐ Effective   ☐ Phony   ☐ Worth remembering

Q. Do you feel it is appropriate for them to air this commercial?
○ Very appropriate
○ Somewhat appropriate
○ Not very appropriate
○ Not at all appropriate

Q. Thinking about the commercial as a whole would you say you:
○ Liked it a lot
○ Liked it somewhat
○ Felt Neutral about it
○ Disliked it somewhat
○ Disliked it a lot

Q. We have removed the name. Do you remember which brand was being advertised?

○ Coors   ○ Anheuser Busch   ○ Heineken   ○ Don't know

© 2005. Courtesy of Bruzzone Research Company.

FIGURE 17.4 Key Scenes and Questions from BRC's Test of the "Thanking the Troops" Commercial

Notice first in the upper-right corner the color coding for this analysis. Specifically, adjectives coded in *yellow* indicate that the commercial performed better than average (compared to BRC norms), words coded in *light blue* reveal average performance, and those adjectives coded in *red* indicate below-average performance. A review of Figure 17.3 shows that the Taco Bell commercial scored above average on indicators of humor, uniqueness, warmth, importance, and clarity. At the same time, the ad performed below average on energy (it was an intentionally subdued ad). Moving from left to right on Figure 17.3, it further can be seen that the ad performed at just an average level in terms of entertainment value, empathy, and relevance. As a result, the ad scored at just an average level (based on Bruzzone norms) in terms of both attitude toward the ad and attitude toward the product. The result was a Super Bowl commercial whose overall impact was in the average range for the dozens of Super Bowl commercials that Bruzzone tested in that year.

By comparison, consider another commercial sponsored by Anheuser-Busch titled "Thanking the Troops." Perusal of the six key scenes in Figure 17.4 reveals that this commercial involves an airport setting in which passengers awaiting flights give a standing ovation to U.S. troops who are in route to their plane. Figure 17.5 presents the ARM analysis for this commercial. The "Thanking the Troops" commercial scored above average on indicators of uniqueness, freshness, warmth, persuasiveness, credibility, importance, and clarity. At the same time, the ad performed below average on energy and humor (it obviously was not intended to be energetic or humorous). Moving from left to right in Figure 17.5, it further can be seen that the ad performed at just an average level in terms of entertainment value but, as expected, above average in terms of empathy and relevance. As a result, the ad scored above average in terms of both attitude toward the ad and attitude toward the product, and the commercial's overall impact was above average. This was a highly effective commercial by Bruzzone standards, and in view of the emotional impact also a highly "watchable" ad.

Day-After Recall Testing

Beginning in 1952, and for decades after, perhaps the most popular method for testing consumer recall of TV commercials was the "Burke Day-After Recall Test." Although no longer used by Burke, Inc., the day-after recall test serves as the model for many other recall tests. For example, Gallup & Robinson and Mapes and Ross are two well-known research companies that provide recall testing of ads placed in *print media*. Also, Ipsos ASI is a research firm that is particularly notable for testing consumer recall of *television commercials*. We first review the day-after recall procedure used by Burke and then examine the Ipsos ASI testing method.

Day-After Recall Test

Burke's Day-After Recall (DAR) procedure tested commercials that had been aired as part of normal television programming. The day after the first airing of a commercial, Burke's telephone staff conducted interviews with a sample of consumers. The sample included individuals who watched the program in which the commercial was placed and who were physically present at the time the commercial was aired. These individuals receive a product or brand cue, are asked if they saw the test commercial in question, and then are asked to recall all they can about it.

For each tested commercial, Burke reported findings as (1) *claimed-recall scores*, which indicate the percentage of respondents who recall seeing the ad;

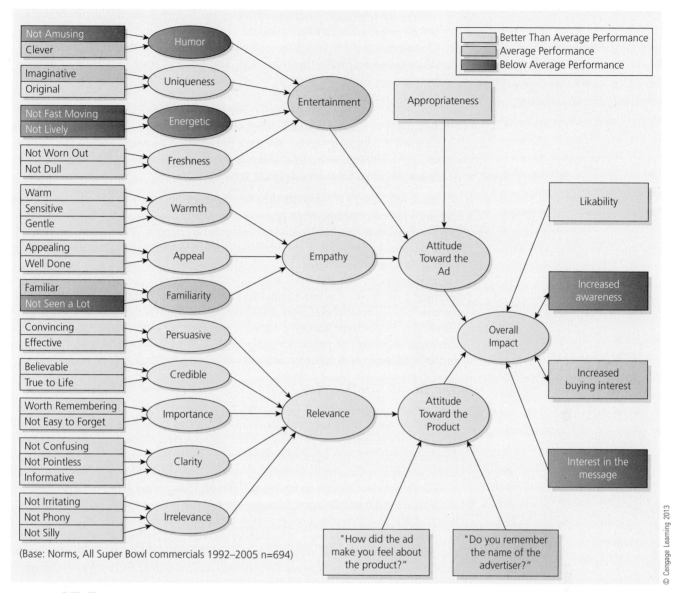

FIGURE 17.5 Advertising Response Model (ARM) for the "Thanking the Troops" Commercial

and (2) *related-recall scores*, which indicate the percentage of respondents who accurately describe specific advertising elements. These scores, along with verbatim statements of respondents, aided advertisers' decisions to air the commercial nationally, revise it first, or to drop it altogether.

The Ipsos ASI Next*TV® Method

Ipsos is a French company that purchased ASI Market Research, an American company. This international firm (which goes by Ipsos ASI, The Advertising Research Company) performs advertising research in more than 50 countries. One of its most important advertising research services is the Next*TV® method. This method tests both the ability to recall and persuasive nature of television commercials using the following procedure:

1. The company recruits consumers by informing them that their task, if they agree to participate, is to evaluate a television program. This is actually a disguise because the real purpose of the research is to evaluate consumer responses to advertisements that are embedded in a TV program.

2. The company mails to a national sample of consumers a videotape that contains a 30-minute TV program (such as a situation comedy); embedded

within are television commercials. This procedure essentially replicates the actual prime-time viewing context.

3. Consumers are instructed to view the program (and, implicitly, the embedded advertising) from the videotape. The viewing context is thus actual, in-home viewing, the same as when consumers view any television advertisement under natural viewing conditions.

4. One day after viewing the videotaped TV program (and advertisements), Ipsos ASI personnel contact sampled consumers and measure their reactions to the TV program (in concert with the original disguise) and to the advertisements, which, of course, is the primary objective.

5. Ipsos ASI then measures message recall.

Ipsos ASI Next*TV® employs the same basic methodology around the world. The in-home videotape methodology provides a number of advantages. First, the in-home exposure makes it possible to measure advertising effectiveness in a natural environment. Second, by embedding test advertisements in actual programming content, it is possible to assess the ability of TV commercials to break through the clutter, gain the viewer's attention, and influence message recallability and persuadability. Third, by measuring recall one day after exposure, Ipsos ASI can determine how well tested commercials are remembered after this delay period. Fourth, the videotape technology allows the use of representative national sampling. Finally, by providing several alternative measures of persuasion, the Next*TV® method allows brand managers and their ad agencies to select the measures that best meet their specific needs.

The Recall Controversy

Considerable controversy has surrounded the use of recall as an indicator of advertising effectiveness.[27] For example, Coca-Cola executives reject recall as a valid measure of advertising effectiveness because, in their opinion, recall simply measures whether an ad is received but not whether the message is accepted.[28] It also is known that measures of recall are biased in favor of younger consumers. This is to say that recall scores deteriorate with age progression.[29] Third, there is mounting evidence that the recall scores generated by advertisements are not predictive of sales performance; that is, regardless of which measure of recall is used, the evidence suggests that sales levels do not increase with increasing levels of recallability.[30] Finally, there is some evidence that recall testing significantly *understates the memorability* of commercials that employ *emotional or feeling-oriented themes* and is biased in favor of rational or thought-oriented commercials.[31] Research has even demonstrated a negative correlation between how well consumers recall ads and how much they like them.[32]

In closing this section, it is important to note that no single measure of advertising effectiveness is perfect for every situation. As we now discuss, measures in addition to recall (and recognition) also should be obtained.

Measurement of Emotional Reactions

Researchers have increasingly recognized that advertisements that positively influence receivers' feelings and emotions can be extremely successful. This is because consumer behavior is governed not by reason alone—or even primarily by reason—but also by gut feelings and emotions. Indeed, some brands are virtually loved because they connect with consumers by creating a strong emotional bond.

Given the importance of emotions in consumer behavior and the trend toward more advertising directed at emotions, there has been a corresponding increase in efforts to measure consumers' emotional reactions to advertisements.[33] This is fully justified considering research has shown that ads that are better liked—often because they elicit positive emotions—are more likely to be remembered and to persuade.[34]

Advertising researchers can use the following ways to measure consumers' emotional responses to advertisements: (1) BBDO's Emotional Measurement System; (2) facial recognition technology; (3) brain imaging (fMRI); (4) self-report

FIGURE 17.6 BBDO Emotional Measurement System and Photos Reflecting Disgust and Happiness

measures; and (5) physiological measures. Most of the following discussion is based on physiological measures, but a brief discussion is devoted to the first four.

BBDO's Emotional Measurement System

An interesting approach to measuring consumers' emotional reactions to ads is the use of photos to reflect different emotions. This nonverbal procedure originally was devised by the BBDO Worldwide ad agency years ago to measure reactions to TV commercials, because they had found that many people find it difficult to articulate their feelings. For example, words may not be readily available to express how we feel, or we may be reluctant to share our true feelings out of embarrassment.

BBDO spent three years testing hundreds of photos and refining its nonverbal procedure. This research culminated in a final collection of 53 photos that represent 26 universal emotional reactions: shame, fear, happiness, disgust, and so on. (See Figure 17.6 for similar examples.) The Emotional Measurement System is simple to use. After consumers have been exposed to a test commercial, they are given the deck of 53 photos and asked to set aside any or all of the photos that reflect how they felt after viewing the commercial. The frequency with which the 150 to 600 respondents choose a photo is then recorded, and a perceptual map is constructed. The perceptual map provides a vivid graphical representation of emotions that reflect a set of tested commercials and provides a convenient way to show how different commercials compare against one another based on the emotions they evoke.[35]

FIGURE 17.7 nViso Tracks Facial Muscles

Facial Imaging Technology

Recently, 3D Facial Imaging Technology has been used in capturing and interpreting emotions as they occur, in easy-to-implement procedures. With nViso's facial imaging technology, only a web browser and webcam is needed to test consumer emotional reactions to commercials and other marketing communication.[36] For example, nViso can send a TV commercial to a respondent's computer and then the webcam captures the most transitory of micro-expressions as they view the commercial. The nViso technology tracks 43 facial muscles in real time (see Figure 17.7) with an algorithm based on a facial coding system that translates these facial expressions into emotions such as happiness, surprise, fear, anger, disgust, sadness, etc.

In a different application of facial imaging technology, Kraft recently launched a new sampling machine for Jell-O Temptations in New York and Chicago that uses facial imaging to determine if the recipient is an adult or a child.[37] (The sample is only dispensed to adults, the intended target market.) Kraft also is working to determine if the recipient is smiling when receiving their sample!

Neuroscience and Brain Imaging

Brain imaging is another relatively new technique in advertising research. Brain imaging applies knowledge from the field of *neuroscience* and uses a functional Magnetic Resonance Imaging (fMRI) device to detect changes in blood oxygenation and flow that occur in response to neural activity. When a brain area is more active, it consumes more oxygen to meet this increased demand, which increases blood flow to the active area. Greater blood flow into emotional centers of the brain indicates increased amounts of emotional response to advertisements. (As a reminder, you may recall reading the *IMC Focus* in Chapter 2 that described a neuroscience test of why consumers prefer Coca-Cola over Pepsi.)

This form of measurement is not without limitations and is in its infancy as it relates to understanding emotional reactions to advertisements. Much work remains before advertising researchers can be confident that the results from fMRI provide reliable and valid tests of consumers' emotional reactions to advertisements. Nevertheless, some interesting marketing applications beyond advertising include its use in studying trade-offs in decision making, trust toward brands and companies, how consumers view price cues, and insight into sales negotiations.[38]

Self-Report Measurement

A fourth method widely used to determine consumers' emotional responses to advertisements is self-report measurement. Consumers' emotional reactions in response to advertisements are measured by asking them to self-report their feelings. Both verbal and visual self-reports are used for this purpose.[39] With *verbal self-reports*, researchers ask consumers to rate their emotional reactions to a particular advertisement on conventional rating scales. For example, respondents might be asked to indicate their degree of agreement or disagreement with a statement such as: "This ad gave me a warm feeling." *Visual self-reports*, in contrast, use cartoon-like characters to represent different emotions and emotional states. For each emotion that an advertisement might elicit, consumers select one of several cartoon characters to reflect their emotional reaction to the advertisement. Imagine, for example, that a researcher might use "smiling faces" varying in their degree of smiling to assess the strength of consumers' emotional reactions to a particular advertisement.

Physiological Testing

The fifth general method for measuring consumers' emotional responses to advertisements is physiological testing that measures any of several autonomic responses to advertisements. *Autonomic responses* occur in the autonomic nervous system, which consists of the nerves and ganglia that furnish blood vessels, the heart, the eyes, smooth muscles, and glands. Because individuals have little voluntary control over the autonomic nervous system, researchers use changes in physiological functions to indicate the actual, unbiased amount of arousal resulting from advertisements. Such responses include facial expressions, sweating, and heart rate.[40] Psychologists have concluded that these physiological functions are indeed sensitive to psychological processes of concern in advertising.[41]

As an example, consider the case of the previously described José Cuervo Especial advertisement that promotes the advertised brand by placing it in the context of a young couple in a provocative embrace along with the suggestive headline, "Pursue your daydreams." During pretesting of this ad, some people may respond that they really find it appealing. Others, when asked what they think of it, may indicate that they dislike the ad because they consider it too provocative and gratuitous. Still others may even feign aggravation to make (what they perceive to be) a favorable impression on the interviewer. Thus, measures of physiological arousal can help prevent self-monitoring of feelings and biased responses to standard paper-and-pencil measures.

The Galvanometer

The galvanometer (also referred to as the *psychogalvanometer*) is a device for measuring *galvanic skin response*, or GSR. (*Galvanic* refers to electricity produced by a chemical reaction.) When some element in an advertisement activates the consumer's autonomic nervous system, a physical response occurs in the sweat glands located in the palms and fingers. These glands open to varying degrees depending on the intensity of the arousal, and skin resistance drops when the sweat glands open. By sending a very fine electric current through one finger and out the other and completing the circuit through a galvanometer, testers are able to measure both the degree and the frequency with which an advertisement activates emotional responses.

There is evidence that GSR is a valid indicator of the amount of warmth an advertisement generates.[42] Many companies have found the galvanometer to be a useful tool for assessing the potential effectiveness of advertisements, direct-mail messages, package copy, and other marcom messages. Advertising research practitioners who use the galvanometer claim that it is a *valid* predictor (see PACT principle 9) of an advertisement's ability to *motivate* consumer purchase behavior.[43] Indeed, in recognition of the galvanometer's ability to reveal an advertisement's motivational properties, practitioners also refer to GSR research as the Motivational Response Method, or MRM. A recent application of GSR research to facial muscles (e.g., smiling, frowning) has shown that although television and radio advertising evoked positive emotion about equally, television advertising (vs. radio) tended to generate slightly higher negative emotional reactions.[44]

The Pupillometer

Using a device called a pupillometer, pupillometric tests in advertising are conducted by measuring respondents' pupil dilation as they view a television commercial or focus on a printed advertisement. Respondents' heads are in a fixed position to permit continuous electronic measurement of changes in pupillary responses. Responses to specific elements in an advertisement are used to *suggest* positive reaction (greater dilation) or negative reaction (smaller relative dilation). Although not unchallenged, some scientific evidence since the late 1960s suggests that pupillary responses are correlated with people's arousal to stimuli and perhaps even with their likes and dislikes.[45]

Eye Tracking

Eye tracking is a methodology in which viewers are asked to look at an ad during which a sensor aims a harmless beam of infrared light at the eye. The beam then follows the movement of the eye and shows the exact spot in the ad on which the viewer is focusing. The eye movement is typically divided into fixations and saccades, when the eye gaze pauses in a certain position (a fixation) and when it moves to another position (a saccade).[46] The resulting series of fixations and saccades (with direction, length of time, and sequence elements) is called a *scanpath* and can be labeled on the ad in question. Applications of eye tracking have included TV ads, print ads, online ads, brand logos, packaging, e-mail, and even fast-forwarding through commercials.[47] Recent eye tracking research has shown that dense features in ads tend to hurt brand attention and ad attitude, whereas creative design features tend to enhance brand attention, comprehension, and ad attitude.[48]

Other physiological measures tied to advertising over the years include voice-pitch analysis (VOPAN; measuring the tightness of vocal chords) and binocular rivalry (beaming one ad to one eye and another to the second), among others. One caution that is very important with the use of physiological measures is that although they may give an indication of overall arousal or engagement, they may not necessarily always indicate the true *valence* (i.e., the positive or negative direction) of this arousal or engagement. For example, even a "smile" may not always indicate a true positive emotion (e.g., some NBA players' react with a "smile" when called for a foul).

Measures of Persuasion

Measures of persuasion are used when an advertiser's objective is to influence consumers' attitudes toward and preference for the advertised brand. Firms that perform this type of research include, among others, Ipsos ASI and comScore ARS. The following sections describe the Ipsos ASI Next*TV® method and comScore ARS' Share of Choice method. More discussion is devoted to the latter advertising research procedure because comScore ARS has done a particularly outstanding job in documenting its commercial service.

The Ipsos ASI Next*TV® Method

This method was described in detail when previously discussing measures of ad recall. In brief, the Next*TV® method involves having a sample of consumers view videotapes of TV programs in their homes, and embedded in these programs are TV commercials. The day after consumers have viewed the program and commercials, researchers call them back and measure both their ability to recall the commercials and whether they have been persuaded. Persuasion is measured by assessing consumers' attitudes toward advertised brands, their shift in brand preferences, and their brand-related buying intentions.

The comScore ARS Share of Choice Method

comScore ARS is one of the most active message-testing research suppliers in the world. This company tests individual selling propositions, completed television commercials, and other marcom messages. Commercials are tested at varying stages of completion ranging from rough-cut (e.g., animatics or photomatics) to finished form. For many years, the testing procedure was called the "ARS Persuasion method," where ARS stands for Advertising Research System and it produced "ARS Persuasion scores." Recently, comScore has changed the name to the "Share of Choice" method and "Share of Choice" scores. The ARS (Share of Choice) testing procedure is as follows:

> *Commercials are exposed in regular ARS test sessions to [800 to 1,000] men and women [aged 16+] drawn randomly from [eight] metropolitan areas and invited to preview typical television material. Each test commercial and other unrelated commercials are inserted into the television programs. While at the central location, a measurement of ARS Persuasion is made by obtaining brand preferences before and after exposure to the programs. The ARS Persuasion measure is the percent of respondents choosing the test product over competition after exposure to the TV material minus the percent choosing the test product before exposure.*[49]

In other words, comScore ARS' Share of Choice method first has respondents indicate which brands they would prefer to receive from various product categories if their names were selected in a drawing to win a "basket" of free items (the *premeasure*). Among the list of products and brands is a "target brand" for which, unbeknown to respondents, they subsequently will be exposed to a commercial that is being tested. After exposure to a television program, within which is embedded the test commercial, respondents again indicate which brands they would prefer to receive if their names were selected in a drawing (the *postmeasure*). The Share of Choice score simply represents the postmeasure percentage of respondents preferring the target brand minus the premeasure percentage who prefer that brand (see the following equation). A positive score indicates that the test commercial has shifted preference *toward* the target brand and reinforced brand preference among pre-choosers.

$$\text{Share of Choice Score} = \text{Post \% for target brand} - \text{Pre \% for target brand} \qquad (17.1)$$

comScore ARS has tested over 40,000 commercials, and from these tests it has established—albeit not without challenge[50]—that its Share of Choice scores predict the magnitude of actual sales performance when commercials are aired. That is, higher-scoring commercials generate greater sales volume and larger market share gains.

Predictive Validity of Share of Choice Scores

Based on the results of 332 commercials that were tested in seven countries—including Belgium, Germany, Mexico, and the United States—principals at comScore ARS have demonstrated how Share of Choice scores relate to changes in market share.[51] A total of 148 brands (some with multiple commercials tested) representing 76 product categories were involved in the analysis. All 332 commercials were tested under the procedures described previously, and then market-share levels under actual in-market circumstances were compared during a period after advertising commenced for the brands versus a period prior to any advertising. Thus, the key issue is whether Share of Choice scores accurately predict the magnitude of market-share gain (or loss) following advertising. That is, are the scores generated from the comScore ARS laboratory testing predictive of actual marketplace performance? This obviously is a validity issue as described previously under PACT principle 9. Results from these 332 tests are presented in Table 17.2. This global validation revealed that Share of Choice scores are predictive of market-share changes, yielding, in fact, a high correlation coefficient ($r = 0.71$) and an impressive coefficient of determination ($r^2 = 0.51$).

TABLE 17.2 Share of Choice Scores and In-Market Results

Share of Choice Score Range	Average Share Change	Percentage of Ads Achieving Share-Point Difference of:			
		0.0+	0.5+	1.0+	2.0+
<2.0	−0.2	47%	12%	2%	0%
2.0−2.9	0.0	53	19	6	0
3.0−3.9	0.5	80	46	26	6
4.0−6.9	0.8	80	58	33	9
7.0−8.9	1.6	100	87	56	36
9.0−11.9	2.2	100	97	72	49
12.0+	5.4	100	100	94	83

Source: "Summary of the ARS Group's Global Validation and Business Implications 2004 Update," June 2004, 17. Reprinted with permission.

To understand fully what these results reveal, let us carefully examine the first row in Table 17.2. This row includes all commercials that received very low (less than 2.0) Share of Choice scores, and implies that commercials scoring less than 2.0 are probably incapable of driving market-share gains. In fact, as shown under the "Average Share Change" column, commercials scoring less than 2.0 on the Share of Choice measure experienced, on average, *losses* of 0.2 market-share points. Looking at the next four columns reveals that for those commercials yielding Share of Choice scores of less than 2.0, only 47 percent were able to maintain market share or yield some small incremental growth. Comparatively, 53 percent (i.e., 100 – 47) of these low-scoring commercials actually suffered market-share losses! Moreover, only 2 percent of these low-scoring commercials generated gains of one full market-share point or more, and none experienced gains of two or more share points.

At the other extreme, 100 percent of the highly effective commercials (i.e., those with Share of Choice scores of 12.0 or higher) yielded positive share gains. Indeed, all 100 percent of these high-performance commercials produced gains of 0.5 share points or better, with 94 percent yielding gains of at least 1.0 share point, and 83 percent providing gains of at least 2.0 share points. The average gain in market-share points for commercials receiving Share of Choice scores of 12.0+ was an impressive 5.4.

Let us examine one additional row of data, specifically, that for commercials receiving Share of Choice scores in the middle range of 4.0 to 6.9. Commercials in this range yielded an average gain of 0.8 market-share points. Eighty percent of the commercials in this range either maintained or increased their brands' market shares, with 58 percent of the commercials yielding share gains of 0.5 share points or greater, 33 percent producing gains of 1.0 full share point or more, and 9 percent generating gains of 2.0 or more share points. Entries for the other ranges can be interpreted in a similar fashion.

It is apparent from these 332 test cases that Share of Choice scores are valid predictors of in-market performance. In sum, the higher the Share of Choice score, the greater the likelihood that a tested commercial will produce positive sales gains when the focal brand is advertised under real-world, in-market conditions. This global study thus informs advertisers that they should not place advertising weight behind commercials that have tested poorly. Table 17.2 reveals, in fact, that commercials with a 2.0 or lower Share of Choice score most likely will *not* produce a positive share gain, and that a large percentage (i.e., 100 – 53 = 47 percent) of those scoring in the 2.0 to 2.9 range also are likely to suffer share losses. It is only when commercials test in the 3.0 to 3.9 range or higher that meaningful share gains can be anticipated.

comScore ARS has, of course, a vested interest in reporting that its testing system provides accurate predictions of marketplace performance; nonetheless, the fact that articles authored by comSocre ARS' principals have been published in peer-reviewed journals (e.g., the *Journal of Advertising Research*) authenticates their conclusions. Moreover, advertising scholars have provided independent endorsement of the Share of Choice technique.[52]

Measures of Sales Response (Single-Source Systems)

Determining the sales impact of advertising is—as discussed in Chapters 2, 8, and 9—a most difficult task. However, research procedures now are capable of assessing the effects an advertising campaign has on a brand's sales—especially in the case of consumer packaged goods (CPG).

So-called single-source systems (SSSs) have evolved to measure the effects of advertising on sales. SSSs became possible with the advent of three technological developments: (1) *electronic television meters*, (2) *optical laser scanning* of universal product codes (UPC symbols), and (3) *split-cable* technology.

Single-source systems gather purchase data from panels of households using optical scanning equipment and merge them with household demographic characteristics and, most important, with information about causal marketing variables, such as advertisements, that influence household purchases. The following sections describe two major single-source systems: ACNielsen's Scan-Track and Symphony IRI Group's BehaviorScan.

ACNielsen's ScanTrack

There are two very interesting characteristics of ScanTrack's data-collection procedure. First, and most important, ScanTrack collects purchase data by having its hundreds of panel households (the Homescan Consumer Panel) use *handheld scanners*. These scanners are located in panel members' homes. Upon returning from a shopping trip, ScanTrack panelists are directed to record purchases of *every bar-coded product purchased*, regardless of the store where purchased—a major grocery chain, independent supermarket, mass merchandiser, or wholesale club.[53]

A second distinguishing characteristic of ScanTrack is that panel members also use their handheld scanners to enter any coupons used and to record all store deals and in-store features that influenced their purchasing decisions. Each panel member transmits purchases and other data to Nielsen every week by calling a toll-free number and holding up the scanner to a phone, which records the data via a series of electronic beeps. ACNielsen's ScanTrack has provided advertisers and their agencies with invaluable information about the short- and long-term effects of advertising.

SymphonyIRI Group's BehaviorScan

Founded as Information Resources, Inc. ("IRI"), SymphonyIRI Group pioneered single-source data collection when it introduced its BehaviorScan service a generation ago. SymphonyIRI Group (hereafter referred to as "IRI") operates BehaviorScan panel households in five markets around the United States: Pittsfield, Massachusetts; Eau Claire, Wisconsin; Cedar Rapids, Iowa; Midland, Texas; and Grand Junction, Colorado. (IRI also has BehaviorScan panels in many other countries.) These small cities were chosen because they are located far enough from television stations that residents must depend on *cable TV* to receive good reception. Moreover, grocery stores and drugstores in these cities are equipped with optical scanning devices that read UPC symbols from packages and thereby record exactly which product categories and brands panel household members purchase.

In each market, approximately 3,000 households are recruited to participate in a BehaviorScan panel, and about one-third of these households are equipped with electronic meters attached to TV sets. Panel members are eligible for prize drawings as remuneration for their participation. Because each BehaviorScan household has an identification card that is presented at the grocery store check-out on every shopping occasion, IRI knows precisely which items each household purchases by merely linking up optically scanned purchases with ID numbers. (Starting in 2002, IRI also began supplying panel members with handheld scanners to record purchases in stores other than traditional grocery stores, such as mass merchandise outlets and supercenters. This enabled IRI's BehaviorScan procedure to provide coverage of all retail outlets, as does ACNielsen's ScanTrack method.)

Panel members also provide IRI with detailed demographic information, including family size, income level, number of televisions owned, the types of newspapers and magazines read, and who in the household does most of the shopping. (Please note that ACNielsen's ScanTrack procedure also collects this type of information.) IRI then combines all these data into a *single source* and thereby determines which households purchase which products and brands and how responsive they are to advertising and other purchase-causing variables.

Thus, single-source data consist of (1) household demographic information; (2) household purchase behavior; and (3) household exposure to (or, more technically, the opportunity to see) new television commercials that are tested under real-world, *in-market* test conditions.

The availability of cable TV enables IRI (with the cooperation of cable companies and advertisers) to intercept a cable signal before it reaches households, *split the signal*, and send different advertisements to two panels of households (test versus control). Hence, the split-cable feature and optically scanned purchase data enable IRI to know which commercial each household had an opportunity to see and how much of the advertised brand the household purchases.

Weight versus Copy Tests

SymphonyIRI Group's BehaviorScan procedure enables testing of television commercial effectiveness. Two types of tests are offered: weight tests and copy tests. For both, a test commercial is aired in, say, two BehaviorScan markets for up to a full year. With *weight tests*, panel households are divided into test and control groups. The identical commercial is transmitted to both groups, but the number of times the commercial is aired (its so-called "weight") is varied between the groups during the course of the test period. Any difference between the groups' aggregate purchase behavior for the tested brand is obviously attributable to the advertising weight differential between the two groups.

The second form of testing, *copy tests*, holds the amount of weight constant but varies commercial content. That is, a test group is exposed during the course of the testing period to a new commercial, whereas a control group has an opportunity to see either a public service announcement (PSA) or an old commercial for the same brand inserted in place of the new commercial. Regardless of the type of test, aggregating purchase data across all households in each of the two groups simplifies determining whether differences in advertising copy or weight generate differences in purchase behavior.

The Testing Procedure

To better understand how BehaviorScan's single-source data can be used to show the relationship between advertising and sales activity, consider a situation in which a manufacturer of a new snack food is interested in testing the effectiveness of a television commercial promoting this brand. BehaviorScan would do the following: (1) select, say, two markets in which to conduct the test (perhaps Midland, Texas, and Grand Junction, Colorado); (2) stock the manufacturer's brand in all grocery stores and perhaps drugstores located in these markets; (3) selectively broadcast a new commercial for the brand using special split-cable television so approximately one-half of the panel members in each market are exposed either to the new commercial or to PSAs; (4) record electronically (via optical scanners) grocery purchases all panel members made; and (5) compare the purchase behavior of the two groups of panel members who were exposed either to the new commercial or to PSAs.

If the advertising is effective, a greater proportion of the panel members exposed to the test commercial should buy the promoted item than those only exposed to the PSAs. The percentage of panel members who make a trial purchase of the advertised brand would thereby indicate the effectiveness of the new television commercial, and the percentage that make a repeat purchase would indicate how much the brand is liked.

In sum, single-source systems of advertising measurement (ACNielsen's ScanTrack and SymphonyIRI's BehaviorScan) enable brand managers and their advertising agents to determine whether advertisements do more than just increase brand awareness, facilitate message recall, influence consumers' brand-related attitudes, or achieve other prebehavioral goals. Beyond this, single-source systems address the critical issue of whether an advertising campaign has actually driven increases in brand sales and augmented the brand's market share.[54]

Some Major Conclusions about Television Advertising

The extensive testing that comScore ARS has performed has played a significant role in understanding of the strengths and limitations of television advertising. Four major conclusions can be drawn with respect to what it takes for television advertising to enhance a brand's sales performance and market share growth successfully: (1) ad copy must be distinctive, (2) ad weight without persuasiveness is insufficient, (3) the selling power of advertising wears out over time, and (4) advertising works quickly if it works.[55]

Conclusion 1—All Commercials Are Not Created Equal: Ad Copy Must Be Distinctive

Research by comScore ARS has shown that commercials having *strong selling propositions* are distinctive and thereby tend to achieve higher Share of Choice scores. What determines whether a commercial has a strong selling proposition? Research indicates that any differentiating information concerning a new brand or a new feature of an existing brand gives a selling proposition a significantly higher chance of a superior score.[56] Although commercials for new brands and those with new features are more persuasive on average, advertising for established brands also can be very persuasive via *brand differentiation*—that is, by distinguishing the advertised brand from competitive offerings and providing consumers with a distinctive reason to buy it.[57] The photoboard version of a Mentadent ProCare toothbrush television commercial (Figure 17.8) illustrates an advertisement that obtained a high Share of Choice score of 11.2 because the ad contained the strong selling proposition that this toothbrush has a flexible handle that allows gentle brushing.

The foregoing discussion has illustrated a key advertising principle: Effective advertising must be persuasive and distinctive; it must possess a strong selling proposition. Appreciation of this point necessitates rigorous testing of proposed advertisements prior to committing any media dollars to their airing or printing (i.e., "Test before you air or print!").

Evidence from Frito-Lay's Copy Tests

To test the effectiveness of television commercials for its various salted snack and cookie brands, marketing researchers and brand managers at Frito-Lay commissioned SymphonyIRI Group to perform 23 split-panel experiments in BehaviorScan markets over a four-year period.[58] All 23 experiments were copy (versus weight) tests that involved comparing one group of households who were exposed to advertising for a Frito-Lay brand (advertising households) against another group that had no opportunity to see the advertising (control households). Each of the 23 tests was conducted in at least two BehaviorScan markets and lasted a full year. In addition to the advertising versus no-advertising condition, Frito-Lay's BehaviorScan tests also were classified in terms of (1) whether the tested brand was a new brand (e.g., SunChips was new at the time of the test) or an established brand (e.g., Ruffles); and (2) whether sales for the brand were relatively large (e.g., Doritos) or small (e.g., Rold Gold).

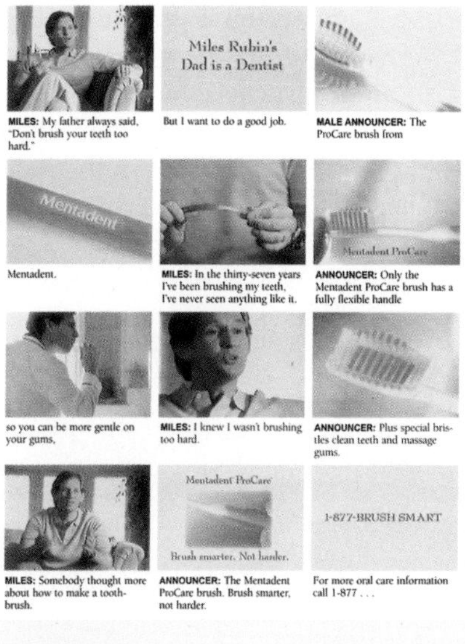

The objective in conducting these tests was to determine whether sales volume would be greater in households exposed to advertisements for Frito-Lay brands versus those households that had no opportunity to be exposed to these television commercials. Results from the 23 Frito-Lay BehaviorScan tests are summarized in Table 17.3.

The first notable observation from Table 17.3 is that advertising for 57 percent of the 23 tested brands generated significant increases in sales volume during the one-year test duration. (Although not

FIGURE 17.8 Illustration of a Commercial with a Strong Selling Proposition

© Church & Dwight Co., Inc., Princeton, New Jersey

© Photodisc/Getty Images

shown in Table 17.3, the average gain in sales volume between the advertising versus no-advertising household panels was 15 percent across the 12 advertisements that yielded significant sales increases.) A second key finding shown in Table 17.3 is that advertising for the small sales-volume brands was much more effective in driving sales gains than was advertising for the large brands. In fact, of the 12 small brands tested, 83 percent, or 10 brands, experienced significant increases in sales as a result of their one-year advertising efforts. A third important finding is that advertising for 88 percent of the new brands generated significant sales gains, whereas only 40 percent of the established brands resulted in sales gains from advertising.

The 23 BehaviorScan tests of Frito-Lay brands reveal that advertising is not always effective; indeed, it was effective in only slightly more than one half of the tests. Importantly, this research supports the finding that advertising is effective only when it provides distinctive, newsworthy information, such as when introducing new brands or line extensions.

Conclusion 2—More Is Not Necessarily Better: Weight Is Not Enough

As noted in Chapter 16, an important measure of campaign weight is *gross rating points*, or *GRPs*—equal to the product of reach × frequency. More frequent airing of a TV commercial implies greater advertising weight, or more GRPs. Obviously, advertising weight and spending also correlate—the more weight, the higher the cost.

We now consider a second important conclusion about advertising effectiveness—that the amount of advertising weight invested in a brand does *not* by itself provide a good predictor of sales performance. That is, merely increasing ad weight (e.g., GRPs) does not directly translate into better performance for a brand. Advertising copy *must also be distinctive and persuasive* (as previously established) for advertising to have a positive impact on a brand's sales and market share. An advertising practitioner perhaps said it best when stating that "airing ineffective advertising is like being off air; it just costs more."[59]

This conclusion receives support from a landmark study that analyzed numerous tests based on BehaviorScan single-source data. A well-known advertising scholar and his colleagues determined that when advertisements are

TABLE 17.3	BehaviorScan Tests of Advertising Effectiveness for 23 Frito-Lay Brands		
	Established Brands	**New Brands**	**Total**
Large Brands	13% (n = 8)*	67% (n = 3)	27% (n = 11)
Small Brands	71 (n = 7)	100 (n = 5)	83 (n = 12)
Total	40 (n = 15)	88 (n = 8)	57 (n = 23)

© Cengage Learning 2013

*Table entries are to be interpreted as follows: A total of 8 (out of 23) tests involved large, established brands. Of the 8 tests conducted with this particular combination of brands, only 1 test, or 13 percent, detected a statistically significant increase in sales volume in those households exposed to advertising compared to the noadvertising control households.

unpersuasive, there is no more likelihood of achieving sales volume increases even when doubling and tripling TV advertising weight.[60]

The virtual independence between advertising weight and sales is clearly demonstrated in Table 17.4. The results presented in this table are based on studies using single-source data for various brands of CPGs. The data in Table 17.4 are derived from *weight tests* whereby two panels of households had an opportunity to see the identical commercial for a particular brand, but the amount of spending, or weight, was varied between the two panels. These households' subsequent purchases of the advertised brand are later compared based on purchase data acquired via optical scanning devices in grocery stores.

Table 17.4 presents data from 20 weight tests, each involving an actual market-place examination of advertising's influence on the sales of a branded grocery product. In each test, there are two key features of the advertising effort. First is the number of GRPs, or weight, used to advertise the brand. This is expressed in Table 17.4 as the *weight difference* between the two panels of households. A difference of zero would mean that an identical amount of advertising

TABLE 17.4   Relations among Advertising Weight, Persuasion Scores, and Sales

Test Number	Weight Difference	Share of Choice Score	Sales Difference
1	334 GRPs	–1.3	NSD*
2	4,200	0.6	NSD
3	406	1.8	NSD
4	1,400	2.6	NSD
5	695	2.7	NSD
6	800	2.8	NSD
7	2,231	3.5	NSD
8	1,000	3.6	NSD
9	900	3.7	NSD
10	1,800	4.0	NSD
11	947	4.2	NSD
12	820	4.3	NSD
13	1,364	4.4	NSD
14	1,198	4.4	NSD
15	583	5.9	SD†
16	1,949	6.7	SD
17	580	7.0	SD
18	778	7.7	SD
19	1,400	9.0	SD
20	860	9.3	SD

*NSD: Purchases of the advertised brand were *not* significantly different between the two split-cable panels at a 90 percent confidence level.

†SD: Purchases of the advertised brand were significantly different between the two split-cable panels at a 90 percent confidence level.

Source: Margaret Henderson Blair, "An Empirical Investigation of Advertising, Wearin, and Wearout," *Journal of Advertising Research* 27 (December 1987/January 1988), 45–50. Reprinted with permission from the *Journal of Advertising Research*, © 1987, by the Advertising Research Foundation.

weight (in terms of GRPs) was aired during the test period to both groups of households, whereas a positive weight difference indicates that one group was exposed to more commercials for the brand than was the other group. The second key advertising feature is the Share of Choice score that the test commercial obtained in each test. These scores range from a low of −1.3 (test 1) to a high of 9.3 (test 20). Finally, for each reported test, the last column indicates whether a statistically significant sales difference occurred between the two panels.

Thus, test 8, for example, shows a weight difference of 1,000 GRPs between the two panels. However, the tested commercial in this case received a below-average Share of Choice score of 3.6. Given this combination of a heavy weight difference between the two panels and a relatively unpersuasive commercial, the result was no significant difference (NSD) in sales between the two panels of households at the end of the full-year testing period. In other words, heavy advertising weight was unable to compensate for an unpersuasive commercial.

Now let us examine test 15. The weight difference between the two panels of households amounted to 583 GRPs, but the new commercial in this test received a Share of Choice score of 5.9. The result: A significant difference (SD) in sales was recorded when the tested brand was advertised with a moderately persuasive commercial.

Table 17.4 also demonstrates that no significant sales differences are obtained even in instances of huge weight differences such as in tests 2 (a 4,200 GRP difference) and 7 (a 2,231 GRP difference). These two tests corresponded (at the time of the research) with annual ad expenditures of $21 and $11 million, yet no differential sales response materialized after a full year. Comparatively, notice in tests 15 through 20 that significant sales differences *are* observed even when the weight differences are relatively small compared with the weight differences in tests 2 and 7. Hence, it can be concluded that the primary determinant of sales differences in these tests was the *persuasiveness* of the tested commercials. *Whenever the Share of Choice score was 5.9 or greater*, significant sales differences were detected at the end of the test; in all instances in which the Share of Choice score was below 5.9, no significant sales differences were obtained.

Thus, the implication is that persuasiveness, and not mere ad weight, is the prime determinant of whether an ad campaign will translate into improved sales performance. Investing advertising in unpersuasive commercials is akin to throwing money away. Advertising weight is important, but only if a commercial presents a persuasive story![61]

Campbell Soup Company Findings

Research that comScore ARS conducted for the Campbell Soup Company provides additional evidence regarding the importance of commercial persuasiveness.[62] Figure 17.9 presents the results of comScore ARS' testing of various commercials for an undisclosed Campbell Soup Company brand, which we will assume to be Prego spaghetti sauce. Note that the horizontal axis is broken into 18 four-week periods, and that the vertical axis of the graph depicts this brand's market shares. The graph shows that Prego's market share during the first four-week period was 19.6.

Notice next that a new commercial (titled "Tastes Great 30," with the *30* signifying a 30-second commercial) was aired during the second four-week period. This commercial, when comScore ARS tested it, received a Share of Choice score of 5.8. Shortly after airing this new commercial, Prego's market share jumped from 19.6 to 21.4—an increase of nearly 2 share points. Thereafter, Prego's market share varied from a low of 20.4 (period 5) to a high of 21.5 (period 4). Then in period 7, when a new commercial started airing ("Beauty Shot Revised 15"), Prego's market share jumped by an incredible 4.5 share points to 25.4.

Notice how this result correlates to the strength of the new commercial, which obtained a Share of Choice score of 10.0. Over the next several months, the market share for Prego fell to 22.0 (period 14). Then in period 15 another new commercial began airing ("Beauty Shot Poolout 2 15"). This commercial, which obtained a Share of Choice score of 10.9, immediately increased Prego's

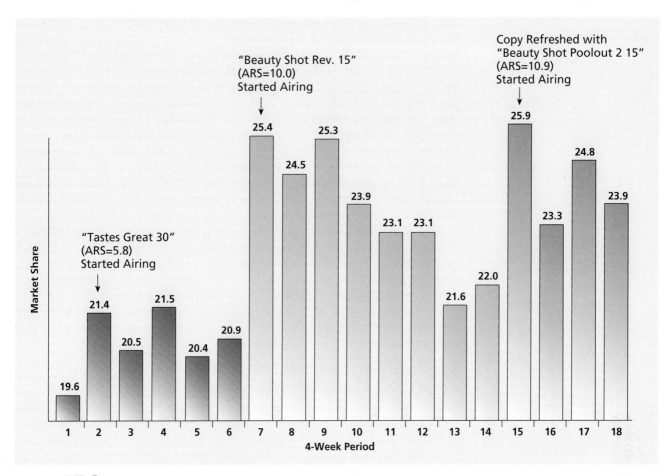

FIGURE 17.9 The Role of Sales-Effective Advertising for an Undisclosed Campbell Soup Brand

Source: Used with permission from the ARS Group.

sales to a 25.9 market share. By period 18 the share had declined to a 23.9, but compared with the initial share of 19.6 in period 1, this still represented a gain of 4.3 share points in slightly more than a year—a substantial market-share gain by any standard in an established product category. These results indicate that persuasive commercials can have a rather dramatic effect in increasing market share.

The Relationship between Media Weight and Creative Content

Beyond results from comScore ARS, important research from the academic front has provided further insight into the conditions under which additional advertising weight does or does not increase a brand's sales.[63] This research program tested 47 actual TV commercials that were drawn from a variety of mature product categories for familiar brands (i.e., brands in categories such as frozen entrees, snack chips, and long-distance dialing services). Each of the 47 commercials was classified as to whether its tone and content primarily included (1) *rational information* (i.e., commercials conveying details about product features and benefits); (2) *heuristic appeals* (i.e., commercials employing credible or trustworthy endorsers, and those using pictures or music to convey brand information); or (3) *affectively based cues* (i.e., commercials using warmth appeals, captivating scenery, and likable music—all of which can generate positive emotions).

The researchers examined the sales results of *weight tests* for these 47 commercials and tested whether the heavy weight differences between groups of consumers exposed to higher- or lower-levels of advertising weight led to significant sales differences between test and control groups. (The higher-weight groups were exposed to anywhere from 50 to 100 percent more commercials for a particular brand during the test period.) Further and importantly, they also tested whether the effect of weight on sales varied as a function of advertising content. In short, then, the issue these researchers addressed was whether greater advertising weight uniformly drives increased sales or whether the effect of increased advertising weight *depends* on the type of creative content in a commercial.

The very important finding from this research is that increased advertising weight led to significant increases in sales for consumers exposed to greater amounts of advertising weight *only* for commercials using *affectively based cues*. For commercials employing rational information or heuristic appeals, no significant sales gains were realized when the amount of advertising weight was increased substantially. It seems, then, that commercials using affectively based cues respond positively to greater advertising weight because this type of commercial evokes positive feelings in consumers; comparatively, commercials containing rational information or heuristic appeals grow tiresome more quickly and may even turn consumers off with repeated showings.

It is important to realize that this research included only commercials drawn from mature product categories and included only familiar brands. The results possibly do not generalize to commercials for new product categories or new brands in mature categories. In either event, heavy advertising weight thrown behind informative advertisements (i.e., those supplying rational information or using heuristic appeals) may *not* serve very well to drive sales. Conversely, putting more weight behind ads using affectively based cues (i.e., emotional ads) may well increase sales rather substantially.

Conclusion 3—All Good Things Must End: Advertising Eventually Wears Out

Another important lesson learned from the previous presentation of the Campbell's Prego case, and supported by abundant other evidence, is that advertising ultimately *wears out* and therefore must be periodically refreshed to maintain or increase a brand's sales.[64] Academic and practitioners' research has convincingly demonstrated that with the accumulation of GRPs for a brand, the persuasive power of that brand's advertising declines over time.[65] This is referred to as wearout, the result of which is diminished effectiveness of advertising as GRPs accumulate over time. Interestingly, *familiar brands* (i.e., those for which consumers have direct usage experience or have learned about the brand via information from marcom messages) have been shown to wear out more slowly than unfamiliar brands.[66] This suggests that stronger brands—that is, those with greater equity (recall discussion in Chapter 2)—can continue to use creative executions for a longer period of time, need to refresh advertising less frequently, and thus obtain a bigger bang for the advertising buck. The old saying that "knowledge begets knowledge" has a counterpart in this context: "success begets more success." Familiar brands that possess greater brand equity enjoy increased marcom effectiveness by postponing the onset of advertising wearout.

The moral from conclusion 3 is that it is important to retest commercials periodically (using, for example, the Share of Choice measurement) to determine how much persuasive power remains in a commercial. When the persuasive power falls into the 3.0 to 3.9 range or even below (see Table 17.2), it probably is time to replace the commercial with a new or revised execution.

Conclusion 4—Do Not Be Stubborn: Advertising Works Quickly or Not at All

Due to the difficulty of precisely determining what effect advertising has on sales, in many instances advertisers initiate an advertising campaign and then stick with it for an extended period. Even though there may be no initial evidence that advertising is moving the sales dial, there is a tendency among some advertisers to "hang in there," hoping that with repeated exposures (increased weight) the advertising will eventually achieve positive results. Thoughts such as "Let's not drop the campaign too quickly" or "We just have to be patient" often are applied to sustain a questionable advertising campaign.

Insight into the issue of how long advertisers should stick with an ad campaign is available from the previously discussed findings from Frito-Lay's series of 23 BehaviorScan copy tests. Although not apparent in Table 17.3, a fourth notable result from the Frito-Lay BehaviorScan testing is that in all 12 (of 23) cases where advertisements for Frito-Lay brands drove significant sales increases, the effects occurred within the first six months. More dramatically, in 11 of the 12 tests with significant sales gains, the increased sales occurred within *the first three months*! When advertising works, it works relatively quickly or not at all.

Note that although there is some virtue to being patient, there is a difference between being patient and stubborn. Sometimes advertisers have to accept the fact that an advertising campaign simply is not driving sales increases. The economic concept of *sunk costs* is relevant in this context. That concept, in particular, informs us that decisions should not be made with respect to past expenditures but in terms of future prospects. That is, strive not to throw good money after bad.

Summary

Although difficult and often expensive, measuring message effectiveness is essential for advertisers to better understand how well their ads are performing and which changes they need to make to improve performance. Message-based research evaluates the effectiveness of advertising messages. Dozens of techniques for measuring advertising effectiveness have evolved over the years. The reason for this diversity is that advertisements perform various functions and multiple methods are needed to test different indicators of advertising effectiveness.

GfK MRI's Starch Ad Readership Studies, Bruzzone tests, and ("Burke") day-after recall tests are techniques for measuring recognition and recall. Some measures to capture emotions include BBDO's Emotional Measurement System, facial imaging technology, brain imaging, and self-report items. Physiological measures, such as galvanic skin response and pupil dilation, also are used to assess emotional arousal advertisements activate. The Ipsos ASI Next*TV® method is a videotape, in-home system for measuring consumer reactions to television commercials. The comScore ARS "Share of Choice" method is used to measure preference shifts employing a pre- and post-measurement of consumer preference for a brand before and after they have seen the brand's advertisement.

The impact of advertising on actual purchase behavior is measured with single-source data collection systems (SymphonyIRI Group's BehaviorScan and Nielsen's ScanTrack) that obtain optical-scanned purchase data from household panels and then integrate them with television-viewing behavior and other marketing variables.

No single technique for measuring advertising effectiveness is ideal, nor is any particular technique appropriate for all occasions. The choice of technique depends on the specific objective an advertising campaign is intended to accomplish. Moreover, multiple measurement methods are usually preferable to single techniques to answer the many questions involved in attempts to assess advertising effectiveness.

The final major section presented conclusions about TV commercial effectiveness based on substantial research on advertising persuasiveness, advertising weight, creative copy, and links to meaningful sales gains. Four major conclusions are drawn: (1) ad copy must be distinctive in order to drive sales gains; (2) more advertising weight does not necessarily equate to increased sales; (3) advertising eventually wears out; and (4) if advertising is going to work, it will achieve its positive effect relatively quickly.

Discussion Questions

1. It is desirable that measurements of advertising effectiveness focus on sales response rather than on some precursor to sales, yet measuring sales response to advertising is typically difficult. What complicates the measurement of sales response to advertising? To answer this question, please return to Chapter 8 and the section on using sales as an objective for marcom programs, as well as the *Marcom Insight* in this chapter.

2. PACT principle 2 states that a good copy testing system should establish how results will be used in advance of each copy test. Explain the specific meaning and importance of this copy testing principle. Construct an illustration of an anticipated result lacking a sufficient action standard and one with a suitable standard.

3. What's the distinction between the pre- and post-testing forms of advertising research? Which in your

opinion is more important? Be sure to justify your response.

4. The Bruzzone test is based on a measure of recognition in comparison to day-after recall testing, which, of course, is based on a recall measure. Present an argument as to why the Bruzzone recognition measurement might be more appropriate than the recall measurement in attempting to determine the effectiveness of television commercials. To facilitate your discussion, consider the difference between multiple-choice testing (a form of recognition measurement) and essay testing (a form of recall measurement).

5. Offer your interpretation of the following quote presented earlier in the chapter: "If you can't measure something, you can't understand it. If you can't understand it, you can't control it. If you can't control it, you can't improve it."

6. If you were an account executive in an advertising agency, what would you tell clients to convince them to use (or not to use) the GfK MRI Starch Ad Readership Studies?

7. A test of television advertising effectiveness BehaviorScan performs will cost you, as brand manager of a new brand of cereal, over $250,000. Why might this be a prudent investment in comparison to spending $50,000 to perform an awareness study?

8. Assume that several years from now, after you have graduated college and begun a career, you open your mail one day and find a letter from SymphonyIRI Group requesting you to become a BehaviorScan panel member. Would you have any reservations about agreeing to do this? Assume that the letter is from ACNielsen, instead of SymphonyIRI, requesting your participation in ScanTrack. What would be your reservations, if any, in this case?

9. Select three recent television commercials for well-known brands, identify the objective(s) each appears to be attempting to accomplish, and then propose a procedure for how you would go about testing the effectiveness of each commercial. Be specific.

10. Television commercials are tested in various stages of completion, including storyboards, animatics, photomatics, ripomatics, liveamatics, and finished commercials (see *IMC Focus*). What reservations might you have concerning the ability to project results from testing prefinished commercials to actual marketplace results with real commercials? Be specific and refer to the PACT principles where appropriate.

11. What are your thoughts about the value (or lack of value) of using measures of physiological response such as the galvanometer?

12. Turn to Table 17.2 and inspect the row in that table having a Share of Choice score range of 7.0 to 8.9. With that particular row in mind, interpret the entries under each of the four columns of share-point differences. For example, what is the specific interpretation of 56 percent under the column heading 1.0+?

13. Compare and contrast the Ipsos ASI Next*TV® measure with comScore ARS' Share of Choice method.

14. In the context of the discussion of single-source data, explain the difference between weight tests and copy tests. Illustrate your understanding of the difference between these two types of tests by designing a hypothetical weight test and then a copy test for the same brand.

15. With reference to Frito-Lay's copy tests in Table 17.3, the results reveal that of the 23 commercials tested, only 57 percent of the tests generated significant differences in sales between the split panels tested. Assume that Frito-Lay's results are applicable to television advertising in general. What is your general conclusion from this key finding?

16. Offer an explanation as to why, in general, increasing advertising weight is an insufficient means of increasing brand sales.

17. Explain your understanding of why in the case of mature products with familiar brands greater advertising weight is effective in increasing sales only when affective cues are used in advertising the brand.

18. In your opinion, why do commercials for familiar brands with strong equities wear out less rapidly than is the case for unfamiliar brands?

End Notes

1. For a comprehensive review of issues associated with the evaluation of major advertising campaigns affecting public health, see the following: Joel B. Cohen, "Charting a Public Policy Agenda for Cigarettes," in *Marketing and Advertising Regulation: The Federal Trade Commission in the 1990s*, Patrick E, Murphy and William L. Wilkie, eds., Notre Dame. IN: University of Notre Dame, 1990, 234–54; Robert C. Hornik, "Epilogue: Evaluation Design for Public Health Communications Programs," in *Public Health Communication: Evidence for Behavior Change*, R.C. Hornik, ed., Mahwah, NJ: Lawrence Erlbaum, 2002, 385–405; and Cornelia Pechmann and J. Craig Andrews, "Methodological Issues and Challenges in Conducting Social Impact Evaluations" in *Scaling Social Impact: New Thinking*, Paul N. Bloom and Edward Skloot, eds., New York: Palgrave Macmillan, 2010, 217–34.

2. Karen Whitehill King, John D. Pehrson, and Leonard N. Reid, "Pretesting TV Commercials: Methods, Measures, and Changing Agency Roles," *Journal of Advertising* 22 (September 1993), 85–97.

3. Ibid.

4. John Kastenholz, Charles Young, and Tony Dubitsky, "Rehearse Your Creative Ideas in Rough Production to Optimize Ad Effectiveness." Paper presented at the Advertising Research Foundation Convention, New York City, April 26–28, 2004.

5. Ibid.

6. Jack Neff, "Copy Testing Coming to Digital Marketing," *Advertising Age*, February 28, 2011, 18.

7. This description is based on Allan L. Baldinger in the *Handbook of Marketing Research: Uses, Misuses, and Future Advances*, Rajiv Grover and Marco Vriens, eds., Thousand Oaks, CA: Sage, 2006; see also Cornelia Pechmann and Craig Andrews, "Copy Test Methods to Pretest Advertisements," 54.

8. Material for this section is extracted from the PACT document, which is published in its entirety in the *Journal of Advertising* 11, no. 4 (1982), 4–29.

9. See, for example, Bruce F. Hall, "A New Model for Measuring Advertising Effectiveness," *Journal of Advertising Research* 42 (April 2002), 23–31.

10. Herbert E. Krugman, "Why Three Exposures May Be Enough," *Journal of Advertising Research* 12 (December 1972), 11–14.

11. Russell I. Haley and Allan L. Baldinger, "The ARF Copy Research Validity Project," *Journal of Advertising Research* 31 (March/April 1991), 11–32.

12. John R. Rossiter and Geoff Eagleson, "Conclusions from the ARF's Copy Research Validity Project," *Journal of Advertising Research* 34 (May/June 1994), 19–32.

13. Various articles devoted to ethnographic advertising research are covered in an issue of the *Journal of Advertising Research* 46 (September 2006). See in this issue Jane Fulton Suri and Suzanne Gibbs Howard, "Going Deeper, Seeing Further: Enhancing Ethnographic Interpretations to Reveal More Meaningful Opportunities for Design," 246–50; Eric J. Arnould and Linda L. Price, "Market-Oriented Ethnography Revisited," 251–62; and Gwen S. Ishmael and Jerry W. Thomas, "Worth a Thousand Words," 274–78.

14. Gerald Zaltman and Robin Higie Coulter, "Seeing the Voice of the Customer: Metaphor-Based Advertising Research," *Journal of Advertising Research* 35 (July/August 1995), 35–51; and Robin A. Coulter, Gerald Zaltman, and Keith S. Coulter, "Interpreting Consumer Perceptions of Advertising: An Application of the Zaltman Metaphor Elicitation Technique," *Journal of Advertising* 30 (winter 2001), 1–21.

15. The authors thank a colleague, Professor Peter Toumanoff, Department of Economics, Marquette University, for this translation.

16. Zaltman and Coulter, "Seeing the Voice of the Customer: Metaphor-Based Advertising Research."

17. A quote attributable to H. James Harrington, chairman of the board of Emergence Technology Ltd., as presented in Amy Miller and Jennifer Cioffi, "Measuring Marketing Effectiveness and Value: The Unisys Marketing Dashboard," *Journal of Advertising Research* 44 (September 2004), 238.

18. For an in-depth discussion of the differences between recognition and recall measures, see Erik du Plessis, "Recognition versus Recall," *Journal of Advertising Research* 34 (May/June 1994), 75–91. For additional reading on advertising recognition and its relation to advertising factors (such as ad likeability), see Jens Nördfalt, "Track to the Future? A Study of Individual Selection Mechanisms Preceding Ad Recognition and Their Consequences," *Journal of Current Issues and Research in Advertising* 27 (spring 2005), 19–30. For further discussion of the distinction between recognition and recall as separate aspects of memory, see James H. Leigh, George M. Zinkhan, and Vanitha Swaminathan, "Dimensional Relationships of Recall and Recognition Measures with Selected Cognitive and Affective Aspect of Print Ads," *Journal of Advertising* 35 (spring 2006), 105–22.

19. Herbert E. Krugman, "What Makes Advertising Effective?" *Harvard Business Review*, (March–April 1975), 96–103.

20. For further details on other services, see David W. Stewart, David H. Furse, and Randall P. Kozak, "A Guide to Commercial Copytesting Services," in *Current Issues and Research in Advertising*, James H. Leigh and Claude R. Martin, Jr., eds., Ann Arbor: Division of Research, Graduate School of Business, University of Michigan, 1983, 1–44; and Surendra N. Singh and Catherine A. Cole, "Advertising Copy Testing in Print Media," in *Current Issues and Research in Advertising*, James H. Leigh and Claude R. Martin, Jr., eds., Ann Arbor: Division of Research, Graduate School of Business, University of Michigan, 1988, 215–84.

21. These definitions are available in any Starch Ad Readership Report. For more information on the Starch Ad Readership Studies, students are encouraged to visit http://www.gfkmri.com/Products/Starch.aspx. We appreciate the help of Ms. Wendy Goodman, Analyst/Copywriter, GfK Mediamark Research & Intelligence, LLC for current Starch information and the research report.

22. D. M. Neu, "Measuring Advertising Recognition," *Journal of Advertising Research* 1 (1961), 17–22. For an alternative view, see George M. Zinkhan and Betsy D. Gelb, "What Starch Scores Predict," *Journal of Advertising Research* 26 (August/September 1986), 45–50.

23. Anocha Aribarg, Rik Pieters, and Michel Wedel, "Raising the BAR: Bias Adjustment of Recognition Tests in Advertising," *Journal of Marketing Research*, 47 (June 2010), 387–400.

24. Ibid, 398.

25. Donald E. Bruzzone, "Tracking Super Bowl Commercials Online," *ARF Workshop Proceedings*, October 2001, 35–47.

26. Appreciation for this illustration is extended to Mr. R. Paul Shellenberg, former director of sales (and now with StartSampling Inc.), and Mr. Donald E. Bruzzone, former president, of Bruzzone Research Company, Alameda, California. The Bruzzone test is now part of the firm, StartSampling Inc.

27. The value of commercial recall testing has been questioned by Joel S. Dubow, "Point of View: Recall Revisited: Recall Redux," *Journal of Advertising Research* 34 (May/June 1994), 92–106.

28. "Recall Not Communication: Coke," *Advertising Age*, December 26, 1983, 6.

29. Joel S. Dubow, "Advertising Recognition and Recall by Age—Including Teens," *Journal of Advertising Research* 35 (September/October 1995), 55–60.

30. Leonard M. Lodish et al., "How T.V. Advertising Works: A Meta-Analysis of 389 Real World Split Cable T.V. Advertising Experiments," *Journal of Marketing Research* 32 (May 1995), 135. See also John Philip Jones and Margaret H. Blair, "Examining 'Conventional Wisdoms' about Advertising Effects with Evidence from Independent Sources," *Journal of Advertising Research* 36 (November/December 1996), 42.

31. John J. Kastenholz and Chuck E. Young, "The Danger in Ad Recall Tests," *Advertising Age*, June 9, 2003, 24; Jack Honomichl, "FCB: Day-After-Recall Cheats Emotion," *Advertising Age*, May 11, 1981, 2; and David Berger, "A Retrospective: FCB Recall Study," *Advertising Age*, October 26, 1981, S36, S38.

32. John Kastenholz, Chuck Young, and Graham Kerr, "Does Day-After Recall Testing Produce Vanilla Advertising?" *Admap*, June 2004, 34–36; and Lisa Sanders and Jack Neff, "Copy Tests Under Fire from New Set of Critics," *Advertising Age*, June 9, 2003, 6.

33. Judie Lannon, "New Techniques for Understanding Consumer Reactions to Advertising," *Journal of Advertising Research* 26 (August/September 1986), RC6–RC9; and Judith A. Wiles and T. Bettina Cornwell, "A Review of Methods Utilized in Measuring Affect, Feelings, and Emotion in Advertising," in *Current Issues and Research in Advertising*, ed. James H. Leigh and Claude R. Martin, Jr., Ann Arbor: Division of Research, Graduate School of Business, University of Michigan, 1991, 241–75.

34. Steven P. Brown and Douglas M. Stayman, "Antecedents and Consequences of Attitude toward the Ad: A Meta-Analysis," *Journal of Consumer Research* 19 (June 1992), 34–51; Haley and Baldinger, "The ARF Copy Research Validity Project"; and David Walker and Tony M. Dubitsky, "Why Liking Matters," *Journal of Advertising Research* 34 (May/June 1994), 9–18.

35. "Ad-testing Technique Measures Emotions," *Marketing News*, April 16, 1990, 9; and Gary Levin, "Emotion Guides BBDO's Ad Tests," *Advertising Age*, January 29, 1990, 12.

36. nViso 3D Facial Imaging Technology, 2012, http://www.nviso.ch/technology.html (accessed March 31, 2012).

37. Bruce Horovitz, "New Sampling Machine Can Gauge Your Age and Sex," *USA Today*, December 14, 2011, http://www.usatoday.com/money/industries/food/story/2011-12-13/face-recogniton-sampling-machine/51890500/1.

38. See William Hedgecock and Akshay R. Rao, "Trade-Off Aversion as an Explanation for the Attraction Effect: A Functional Magnetic Resonance Imaging Study," *Journal of Marketing Research*, 46 (February 2009), 1–13; and Nick lee, Amanda J. Broderick, and Laura Chamberlain, "What is 'Neuromarketing'? A Discussion and Agenda for Future Research," *International Journal of Psychophysiology*, 36, 2007, 199–204.

39. For in-depth discussion of self-report measures of emotions, see Karolien Poels and Siegfried Dewitte, "How to Capture the Heart? Reviewing 20 Years of Emotion Measurement in Advertising," *Journal of Advertising Research* 46 (March 2006), 18–37.

40. See ibid. for in-depth treatment.

41. Paul J. Watson and Robert J. Gatchel, "Autonomic Measures of Advertising," *Journal of Advertising Research* 19 (June 1979), 15–26.

42. For an especially thorough and insightful report on the galvanometer, see Priscilla A. LaBarbera and Joel D. Tucciarone, "GSR Reconsidered: A Behavior-Based Approach to Evaluating and Improving the Sales Potency of Advertising," *Journal of Advertising Research* 35 (September/October 1995), 33–53.

43. Ibid.

44. James Peacock, Scott Purvis, and Richard L. Hazlett, "Which Broadcast Medium Better Drives Engagement? Measuring the Powers of Radio and Television with Electromyography and Skin-Conductance Measurements," *Journal of Advertising Research*, (December 2011), 578–85.

45. For a detailed discussion of pupil dilation and other physiological measures, see Joanne M. Klebba, "Physiological Measures of Research: A Review of Brain Activity, Electrodermal Response, Pupil Dilation, and Voice Analysis Methods and Studies," in *Current Issues and Research in Advertising*, James H. Leigh and Claude R. Martin, Jr., eds., Ann Arbor: Division of Research, Graduate School of Business, University of Michigan, 1985), 53–76. See also John T. Cacioppo and Richard E. Petty, *Social Psychophysiology*, New York: The Guilford Press, 1983.

46. "Eye Tracking," Wikipedia, http://en.wikipedia.org/wiki/Eye_tracking (accessed March 31, 2012).

47. See Matthew Creamer, "Don't Look Now, But Ogilvy is Eyeballing You," *Advertising Age*, July 4,

2005, 8; and S. Adam Brasel and James Gips, "Breaking Through Fast-Forwarding: Brand Information and Visual Attention," *Journal of Marketing*, 72 (November 2008), 31–48.

48. Rik Pieters, Michel Wedel, and Rajeev Batra, "The Stopping Power of Advertising: Measures and Effects of Visual Complexity," *Journal of Marketing*, 74 (September 2010), 48–60.

49. Anthony J. Adams and Margaret Henderson Blair, "Persuasive Advertising and Sales Accountability: Past Experience and Forward Validation," *Journal of Advertising Research* 32 (March/April 1992), 25. Note: This quotation actually indicated that 1,000 respondents are drawn from four metropolitan areas. However, subsequent company newsletters and reports indicate that 800 to 1,000 respondents are randomly selected from eight metropolitan areas.

50. Leonard M. Lodish, "J. P. Jones and M. H. Blair on Measuring Advertising Effects—Another Point of View," *Journal of Advertising Research* 37 (September/October 1997), 75–79; see also Joshua Ziliak, "Advertising Engagement: Giving Creative Credit Where Credit is Due," *comScore Voices*, September 7, 2011, http://blog.comscore.com/2011/09/advertising_engagement_giving_1.html.

51. The ARS Group, Evansville, IN, "Summary of the ARS Group's Global Validation and Business Implications 2004 Update," June 2004. Note that an earlier validation study the ARS Group undertook was published in the following source: Margaret Henderson Blair and Michael J. Rabuck, "Advertising Wearin and Wearout: Ten Years Later: More Empirical Evidence and Successful Practice," *Journal of Advertising Research* 38 (September/October 1998), 1–13.

52. For example, John Philip Jones, "Quantitative Pretesting for Television Advertising," in *How Advertising Works: The Role of Research*, John Philip Jones, ed., Newbury Park, CA: Sage Publications, 1998, 160–69.

53. Information for this description is from Andrew M. Tarshis, "The Single Source Household: Delivering on the Dream," *AIM* (a Nielsen publication) 1, no. 1 (1989).

54. For a recent review, see Scott Koslow and Gerald R. Tellis, "What Scanner-panel Data Tell Us About Advertising: A Detective Story with a Dark Twist," *Journal of Advertising Research*, (March 2011), 87–100.

55. These conclusions are based on Margaret Henderson Blair and Karl E. Rosenberg, "Convergent Findings Increase Our Understanding of How Advertising Works," *Journal of Advertising Research* 34 (May/June 1994), 35–45. Of course, other research by practitioners and academics converge on these general conclusions.

56. Scott Hume, "Selling Proposition Proves Power Again," *Advertising Age*, March 8, 1993, 31.

57. Lee Byers and Mark Gleason, "Using Measurement for More Effective Advertising," *Admap*, May 1993, 31–35.

58. Dwight R. Riskey, "How T.V. Advertising Works: An Industry Response," *Journal of Marketing Research* 34 (May 1997), 292–93. For more complete reporting on the effectiveness of TV advertising, see Lodish et al, "How T.V. Advertising Works: A Meta-Analysis of 389 Real World Split Cable T.V. Advertising Experiments," *Journal of Marketing Research* 32 (May, 1995), 125–39; and Leonard M. Lodish et al., "A Summary of Fifty-Five In-Market Experimental Estimates of the Long-Term Effect of TV Advertising," *Marketing Science* 14, no. 3 (1995), G133–G140.

59. The quote is from Jim Donius as cited in Don Bruzzone, "The Top 10 Insights about Measuring the Effect of Advertising," *Bruzzone Research Company Newsletter*, October 28, 1998, principle 8.

60. Lodish et al, "How T.V. Advertising Works," 128.

61. Compared with the results presented in Table 17.4, research by Lodish et al. does not demonstrate a strong relationship between commercial persuasiveness and sales. See Table 11 in "How T.V. Advertising Works," 137.

62. Adams and Blair, "Persuasive Advertising and Sales Accountability."

63. Deborah J. MacInnis, Ambar G. Rao, and Allen M. Weiss, "Assessing When Increased Media Weight of Real-World Advertisements Helps Sales," *Journal of Marketing Research* 39 (November 2002), 391–407.

64. Lodish et al.'s findings also support this conclusion. See "How T.V. Advertising Works."

65. For review, see Connie Pechmann and David W. Stewart, "Advertising Repetition: A Critical Review of Wearin and Wearout," *Current Issues and Research in Advertising* 11 (1988), 285–330; David W. Stewart, "Advertising Wearout: What and How You Measure Matters," *Journal of Advertising Research* 39 (September/October 1999), 39–42; Blair and Rabuck, "Advertising Wearin and Wearout"; and MacInnis, Rao, and Weiss, "Assessing When Increased Media Weight of Real-World Advertisements Helps Sales."

66. Margaret C. Campbell and Kevin Lane Keller, "Brand Familiarity and Advertising Repetition Effects," *Journal of Consumer Research* 30 (September 2003), 292–304.

PART

4

© Jorg Hackemann/Shutterstock

Sales Promotion Management

Part 4 includes three chapters that cover trade- and consumer-oriented sales promotions. *Chapter 18* overviews sales promotions by defining the term, explaining the focus of promotional efforts, presenting the reasons for the rapid growth of sales promotions versus advertising, and describing the tasks that sales promotion can and cannot accomplish. The chapter also examines trade-oriented promotions, describing the most widely used forms of trade promotions and discussing forward buying, diverting, and manufacturer-oriented everyday low pricing. Account-specific marketing also receives prominent treatment. The chapter concludes with a discussion of nine empirical generalizations about trade and consumer promotions.

Two forms of consumer-oriented sales promotions, sampling and couponing, are the focus of *Chapter 19*. Prior to this discussion, however, all consumer sales promotions are categorized on the basis of the primary brand management objective (trial, repeat purchases, or reinforcing brand image) and consumer reward (immediate or delayed) intended for the promotion. Then, the different forms of sampling programs and three major sampling initiatives are discussed (targeting, innovative distribution methods, and sampling's ROI). The second topic in Chapter 19, couponing, includes treatment of the different forms of coupons, recent trends in couponing (e.g., group coupons), the economic implications of couponing, and the process of coupon redemption and misredemption.

Chapter 20 continues coverage of consumer-oriented promotions by examining various promotions other than sampling and couponing. Each of the following promotional programs receives coverage: premiums, price-off promotions, bonus packs, promotional games, rebates/refunds, and sweepstakes/contests. The chapter then discusses how consumer panel data (e.g., penetration rate, purchase size, purchase frequency) can be used to evaluate consumer sales promotions. It then concludes with a three-step procedure for evaluating sales promotion ideas and suggestions for how to conduct a postmortem analysis of promotions that have already "run."

CHAPTER 18

Sales Promotion Overview and the Role of Trade Promotion

MARCOM INSIGHT

It's a Matter of Power—Nike Versus Foot Locker

A theme presented throughout this chapter is that the role of sales promotions, especially trade-oriented promotions, is largely a function of the relative *power* between manufacturers and retailers. Power, in a dictionary sense, describes the strength, might, or force that one entity has relative to another. In the marketplace, power involves the ability of one channel member to command or control another with increased economic or noneconomic (e.g., informational) resources. Weak trade partners have terms of sale imposed on them; more powerful partners can, at the

© Susan Van Etten

extreme, dictate terms of sale. Walmart, for example, is a mega-powerful retailer that is well known for commanding its suppliers to produce products that meet Walmart's price and nonprice requirements.

An incident in the athletic footwear industry illustrates another application of power; a major power clash between two industry giants—Nike, a manufacturer, and Foot Locker, a retailer. This collision occurred when the CEO of Foot Locker became infuriated at Nike's rigid terms of sale being imposed on Foot Locker (and other retail buyers) in both the selection of which of

1. Understand the nature and purpose of sales promotions.
2. Know the factors that account for the increased investment in promotions, especially those that are trade oriented.
3. Recognize the tasks that promotions can and cannot accomplish.
4. Appreciate the objectives of trade-oriented promotions and the factors critical to building a successful trade promotion program.
5. Explain the various forms of trade allowances and the reasons for their use.
6. Be aware of forward buying and diverting and how these practices emerge from manufacturers' use of off-invoice allowances.
7. Appreciate the role of everyday low pricing (EDLP) and pay-for-performance programs as means of reducing forward buying and diverting.
8. Understand nine empirical generalizations about promotions.

Nike's shoes Foot Locker would carry in its stores and how the shoes would be priced. Due to its industry dominance and power position, Nike requires retailers to buy all types of Nike shoes, not just the particular models that retailers deem most appropriate for their clientele. Also, Nike provides retailers lower markups on Nike shoes in comparison to the markups permitted by other athletic footwear makers.

Angered by Nike's rigid terms and power politics, Foot Locker's CEO announced it would cut Nike orders by 15 to 25 percent per year, or between $150 million and $250 million annually. How did Nike respond to Foot Locker's power play? On the one hand, Nike could relax its rigid terms so as to appease Foot Locker and prevent the huge loss of business. On the other hand, Nike could respond in kind by making its own power move. The latter is what happened: Nike slashed its planned shipments to Foot Locker by $400 million (40 percent of the previous year's shipments) and withheld its most highly demanded shoes from being sold in Foot Locker stores. One power move trumped by another! A former Foot Locker executive noted that

Foot Locker's CEO made the mistake of thinking that Nike is as dependent on his company as Foot Locker is reliant on Nike. "They've taught Foot Locker a lesson they'll never forget."

Ironically, *too much* promotion and built-up demand for certain Nike shoes has created recent problems for Foot Locker. A launch of one of Nike's debut NBA Galaxy, glow-in-the-dark, All-Star sneakers at Foot Locker stores throughout the Southeast had to be suspended due to too many unruly shoppers fighting to get the new shoes. One suspected reason for the out-of-control demand was Nike's decision not to sell the shoe online. No doubt, the balance of power between manufacturers and retailers, and the delicate relationship working as "business partners," both represent important aspects of successful marketing.

Sources: Maureen Tkacik, "In a Clash of the Sneaker Titans, Nike Gets Leg Up on Foot Locker," *Wall Street Journal Online*, May 13, 2003, http://online.wsj.com; and Bruce Horovitz, Doug Staglin, and Carolyn Pesce, "Foot Locker Halts Events After Riots Over Nike Sneaker," *USA Today*, February 24, 2012, http://www.usatoday.com/news/nation/story/2012-02-24/nike-sneaker-riot/53235360/1.

Introduction

The objective of this chapter and the two that follow is to provide a thorough introduction to sales promotion's role in the overall marcom function. This chapter introduces the topic of sales promotions and then examines the role of trade-oriented promotions. The following two chapters extend this introduction by analyzing promotion's job in influencing the actions of consumers.

The Nature of Sales Promotion

By definition, sales promotion (or simply promotion) refers to *all promotional activities* (excluding advertising, public relations, personal selling, direct marketing, and online marketing/social media) that *stimulate short-term behavioral responses* from (1) consumers, (2) the trade (e.g., distributors, wholesalers, or retailers), and/or (3) the company's sales force. Sales promotion can refer to any *incentive* manufacturers, retailers, and even not-for-profit organizations use that serve to change a brand's perceived price or value *temporarily*. Manufacturers use promotions to induce the *trade* (e.g., off-invoice allowance) or *consumers* (e.g., a coupon or sample) to buy a brand or to encourage the manufacturer's *sales force* to sell it aggressively. Sales promotions aimed at a company's own sales force might focus on motivation techniques (e.g., sales contests, bonuses, meetings in attractive locations) and/or training tools (e.g., sales aids, training materials, point-of-purchase displays). Retailers use promotional incentives to encourage consumers to shop at this store, buy a certain brand this week, purchase larger quantities, etc. And not-for-profit organizations employ promotions to encourage people to increase their donations to worthy causes and to donate now rather than later.

It should be noted that promotions involve incentives (allowances, rebates, sweepstakes, coupons, premiums, and so on) that are additions to—not substitutes for—the basic benefits a purchaser typically acquires when buying a particular product or service. Also, the target of the incentive is the trade, consumers, sales force, or all three parties. Finally, the incentive changes a brand's perceived price or value, but *only temporarily*. This is to say that a sales promotion incentive for a particular brand applies to a single purchase or perhaps several purchases during a period, but not to every purchase a trade customer or consumer would make over an extended time.

In contrast to advertising, which typically is relatively long term in nature and best suited to enhancing buyer attitudes and aiding brand equity, promotion is more *short-term oriented* and capable of influencing *behavior* (versus just attitudes or intentions). Promotion has the character of urgency in its injunction to *act now* because tomorrow is too late.[1] It has the power to influence behavior because it offers the buyer superior value in the short term and can make buyers feel better about the buying experience.[2]

Although consumer packaged goods (CPG) companies are the most common users of promotions, all types of companies use promotional incentives. For example, restaurants may make use of online group coupons (e.g., Groupon, Living Social) that are activated when a certain number of people sign up for the offer. Online companies may offer free shipping for orders above a certain monetary amount. Furniture stores often provide free gifts when selected items are purchased. Athletic teams use a variety of promotions to attract fans and to encourage their return. (See the *IMC Focus* for an interesting history of some successful and not-so-successful baseball promotions.) And automobile companies regularly offer rebates and cheap financing to attract purchasers.[3]

Baseball Promotions: The Good, The Bad, and The Ugly

Baseball, throughout its history, provides many examples of successful and less-than-successful promotions aimed at bringing in fans to the ballpark, increasing viewership of games at home, or enhancing the sponsor's brand. Our first successful promotion ("The Good") involved Taco Bell, Fox's airing of the 2007 World Series, and Major League Baseball (MLB). A total of $5.6 million (including free airtime for Taco Bell) was spent in advertising a national free taco giveaway for October 30, 2007 if there was one stolen base in the World Series that year. Red Sox rookie Jacoby Ellsbury complied by stealing second base in the bottom of the fourth inning in the second game of the Series. The total cost of the free tacos was under $1 million, with the doubling of positive blog posts, immediate sales increases, and public relations value viewed as "priceless."

In past years, 3,000 or so seats in the Los Angeles Dodger stadium's right-field pavilion often sat empty, even when admission to these seats was priced at just $6 to $8. As another example of "The Good," their solution was to give fans seated in this stadium's section the opportunity to eat as much food as desired at no cost. The incentive worked, as more Dodger fans than ever chose seats in the right-field pavilion—and at an increased price of $20 or more per seat! The all-you-can-eat section opened 1.5 hours before game time and closed 2 hours after the start of the game. If one excluded drink consumption, fans in the right-field pavilion consumed on average 2.5 hot dogs, 1 bag of peanuts or popcorn, and 1 plate of nachos per game. (There are obvious critics of this promotion though due to obesity problems in the United States.)

"The Bad" includes a promotion run by True Value Hardware and the MLB on April 7, 1997 in which souvenir baseballs and coupons were given to fans at opening day games in most major league ballparks. Unfortunately, in Milwaukee and Kansas City, fans immediately threw the balls on the field. It was so bad in the Milwaukee Brewers game that fans were throwing the balls at their own players, the game was stopped three times, and Brewers manager Phil Garner had to plead with fans to stop so they would not end up forfeiting the game (that they eventually won).

The first of "The Ugly" promotions is for "Ten Cent Beer Night" at Cleveland's Municipal Stadium on June 4, 1974. This promotion attempted to fill the stands for the struggling Indians' franchise. Yet, it resulted in fireworks and other items thrown from the stands, fans running on the field, a bench-clearing brawl with Texas manager Billy Martin fully involved, and a forfeit in favor of the Texas Rangers.

In the spirit of many stunts and promotions by owner Bill Veeck of the Chicago White Sox, a "Disco Demolition Night" was held in Chicago's Comiskey Park on July 12, 1979, and is our second of "The Ugly" promotion examples. Veeck invited fans to bring their unwanted disco records to a doubleheader against the Detroit Tigers in exchange for cheaper admission and a chance to see their records exploded on the field between games. Unfortunately, after the demolition, fans poured onto the field (see picture below), tore down batting cages, and started fires. The White Sox had to forfeit the second game and the field was almost unplayable for the remainder of the season.

The morale of the history of baseball promotions is that although they can be quite successful, things can go very wrong if the execution of the promotion is not well developed and thought out.

© AP Images/Fred Jewell

Sources: Adam Thompson and Jon Weinbach, "Free Eats Sell Bad Ballpark Seats," *Wall Street Journal*, May 16, 2007, B1; "5 Corporate Promotions That Ended in (Predictable) Disaster," Cracked.com, July 2, 2009, http://www.cracked.com/article_17479_5-corporate-promotions-that-ended-in-predictable-disaster.html; "MLB Notes: New Rule to Keep Fans from Having a Ball at the Stadium," *Las Vegas Sun*, April 8, 1997, http://www.lasvegassun.com/news/1997/apr/08/mlb-notes-new-rule-to-keep-fans-from-having-a-ball; and Emily Bryson York, "Why Taco Bell's World Series Play was a Steal," *Advertising Age*, October 29, 2001, 3, 56.

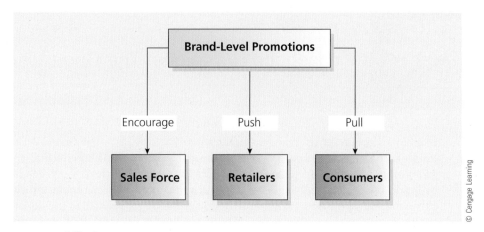

FIGURE **18.1** Brand-Level Promotion Targets

Finally, in an unconventional, yet increasingly practiced, form of promotion by not-for-profit organizations, a major state university wrote letters to hundreds of high school students who had been named National Merit Semi-finalists and offered four-year tuition, on-campus housing their freshman year, scholarship money up to $3,000, and a free laptop if they enrolled and attained a finalist status as a National Merit Scholar.

Promotion Targets

Three groups—a manufacturer's sales force, retailers, and consumers—are targets of sales promotional efforts (see Figure 18.1). First, trade- and consumer-oriented sales promotions provide the manufacturer's sales force with the necessary tools and motivation for enthusiastically selling to wholesale and retail buyers. That is, salespeople have an incentive to put special selling empha-sis behind promoted brands.

A second target of sales promotion efforts is the trade, including wholesalers but especially retailers. Various types of allowances, discounts, contests, and ad-vertising support programs are used in a forward thrust from manufacturers to trade accounts (referred to as *push* efforts) that provide retailers with reasons for stocking, displaying, advertising, and perhaps placing the promoted brand on a price-discounted deal. Third, the use of consumer-oriented promotions (e.g., coupons, samples, premiums, cents-off deals, sweepstakes, and contests) serves to *pull* a brand through the channel by providing consumers with a spe-cial reason to purchase a promoted brand on a trial or repeat basis. Sometimes a pull strategy is preferred when there may be some reluctance for the trade to stock a manufacturer's item.

Increased Budgetary Allocations to Promotions

Advertising spending as a percentage of total marketing communications expen-ditures has declined in recent years, whereas promotion spending has steadily increased. Advertising expenditures as a proportion of companies' total marcom budgets used to average over 40 percent. However, beginning about 30 years ago and continuing today, media advertising's portion of the average marcom budget has fallen to just about one-quarter. In fact, although there are year-to-year changes, Kantar Retail and other CPG industry sources estimate that trade promotions (including account-specific marketing, discussed later in the chapter) *on average* command 50 percent of total U.S. marcom expenditures, consumer advertising achieves 25 percent of the total, and consumer promotions capture the remaining 25 percent.[4] Why have firms shifted money from advertising and into promotions, especially trade-oriented promotions? The following section examines the major reasons underlying this shift.

Factors Accounting for the Shift

Several factors account for why brand managers have shifted budgetary allocations increasingly toward a greater proportion of trade promotions. However, before we describe the reasons for this shift, it will be beneficial to review the concepts of push and pull marketing strategies that encourage channel members (the trade) to handle and merchandise brands and to persuade consumers to purchase them.

Push involves a forward thrust of effort, metaphorically speaking, whereby a manufacturer directs personal selling, advertising, and trade-oriented promotions to wholesalers, distributors, and retailers. Through this combination of sales influence, advertising, and, perhaps especially, promotions in the form of allowances and other deals, manufacturers "push" channel members to increase their inventories of the manufacturer's brand versus competitive brands. Pull, in contrast, entails a backward tug, again speaking metaphorically, from consumers to retailers. This tug, or "pull," is the result of a manufacturer's successful advertising and consumer promotion efforts that encourage consumers to prefer, at least in the short term, the manufacturer's brand versus competitive offerings.

Table 18.1 illustrates the differences between push- and pull-oriented promotional strategies based on two companies' allocations of $30 million among different promotional activities. Company X emphasizes a *push strategy* by allocating most of its promotional budget to personal selling and trade promotions aimed at retail customers. Company Y uses a *pull strategy* by investing the vast majority of its budget in consumer advertising.

It is important to recognize that pushing and pulling are *not* mutually exclusive activities. Both efforts occur simultaneously. Manufacturers promote to consumers (creating pull) and to trade members (accomplishing push). The issue is not which strategy to use but rather which to emphasize.

Historically, at least through the 1970s, the emphasis was on promotional pull (such as Company Y's budget in Table 18.1). Manufacturers advertised heavily, especially on network television, and literally forced retailers to handle their brands by creating consumer demand for those heavily advertised items. However, over the past generation, pull-oriented

TABLE 18.1	**Push and Pull Strategies**	
	Company X (PUSH)	**Company Y (PULL)**
Personal Selling to Retailers	$13,500,000	$6,000,000
Sales Promotion to Retailers	12,000,000	150,000
Advertising to Retailers	2,400,000	300,000
Advertising to Consumers	1,800,000	20,550,000
Sales Promotion to Consumers	300,000	3,000,000
TOTAL	$30,000,000	$30,000,000

TABLE 18.2	Developments Underlying the Growth in Promotions

- Shift in balance of power from manufacturers to retailers
- Increased brand parity and price sensitivity
- Reduced brand loyalty
- Splintered mass market and reduced media effectiveness
- Emphasis on short-term results in corporate reward structures
- Responsive consumers

© Cengage Learning 2013

marketing has become less effective due in large part to the splintering of the mass media and audience fractionalization, as discussed in Chapter 12. Along with this reduced effectiveness has come an increase in the use of push-oriented sales promotion practices (such as Company X's budget in Table 18.1).

Increased investment in sales promotion, especially trade-oriented promotions, has gone hand in hand with the growth in push marketing. Major developments that have given rise to sales promotion are summarized in Table 18.2 and discussed hereafter. These developments are interdependent rather than separate and distinct. Therefore, there is no particular order of importance implied by the listing in Table 18.2.

Balance-of-Power Shift to Retailers

Until roughly 1980, national manufacturers generally were more powerful and influential than the supermarkets, drugstores, mass merchandisers, and other retailers that carried manufacturers' brands. The reason was twofold. First, manufacturers were able to create consumer pull by virtue of heavy network television advertising, thus effectively requiring retailers to handle their brands whether retailers wanted to or not. Second, retailers did little research of their own and, accordingly, were dependent on manufacturers for information such as whether a new product would be successful. A manufacturer's sales representative could convince a buyer to carry a new product using test-market results suggesting a successful product introduction (e.g., with information from Nielsen, Symphony IRI).

The balance of power began shifting when network television dipped in effectiveness as an advertising medium and, especially, with the advent of optical scanning equipment and other technologies that provided retailers with current information about product movement. Armed with a steady flow of data from optical scanners, retailers now know virtually on a real-time basis which brands are selling and which advertising and promotion programs are working. Retailers no longer need to depend on manufacturers for data. Instead, retailers use the facts they now possess to demand terms of sale rather than merely accepting manufacturers' terms.

The consequence for manufacturers is that for every promotional dollar used to support retailers' advertising or merchandising programs, one less dollar is available for the manufacturer's own advertising. Needless to say, retailers are not always more powerful than manufacturers, as indicated in the *Marcom Insight* where a manufacturer (Nike) was more powerful than its recalcitrant retailer (Foot Locker) and accordingly dictated the terms of sale.

Increased Brand Parity and Price Sensitivity

In earlier years, when truly new products were being offered to the marketplace, manufacturers could effectively advertise unique advantages over competitive offerings. As product categories have matured, however, most new offerings represent only slight changes from those already on the market, thus resulting, more often than not, in greater similarities between competitive brands. With fewer distinct product differences, consumers have grown more reliant on price and price incentives (discounts, coupons, cents-off deals, refunds, etc.) as ways of differentiating parity brands. Because concrete advantages are often difficult to obtain, both manufacturers and retailers have turned increasingly to promotion to achieve temporary advantages over competitors.

Consumers are especially price sensitive during periods of economic downturns and the presence of recessionary or inflationary forces. It is then that we see all forms of discounts and price-reducing incentives being used, such as automobile manufacturers offering 0 percent financing and home builders offering prospective homeowners the opportunity to purchase new homes without making down payments.

Reduced Brand Loyalty

Consumers probably are less loyal than they once were. This is partly because brands have grown increasingly similar, thereby making it easier for consumers to switch among brands. Also, marketers have effectively trained consumers to expect that at least one brand in a product category will always be on deal with a coupon, cents-off offer, or refund; thus, many consumers rarely purchase brands other than those on deal. (The term deal refers to any form of sales promotion that delivers a price reduction to consumers. Retailer discounts, manufacturer cents-off offers, and the ubiquitous coupon are the most common forms of deals.)

One team of researchers investigated the impact that deal promotions have on consumers' price sensitivity using eight years of data for a nonfood brand in the CPG category. These researchers determined that price promotions make consumers *more price sensitive in the long run.* Moreover, increased use of price promotions serves, for all intents and purposes, to "train" consumers to search for deals. Nonloyal consumers are especially likely to be conditioned by marketers' use of price deals.[5] Research also reveals that the use of coupons by brands in the mature liquid detergent category (brands such as Wisk, Era, and Bold) resulted in increased consumer price sensitivity and reduced brand loyalty.[6]

The upshot of heightened dealing activity is that marketers have created a "monster" in the form of consumers' desire for deals. Reduced loyalty and increased brand switching have resulted, requiring more dealing activity to feed the monster's insatiable appetite. A major international study conducted in Germany, Japan, the United Kingdom, and the United States investigated the effects of price-related promotions (such as

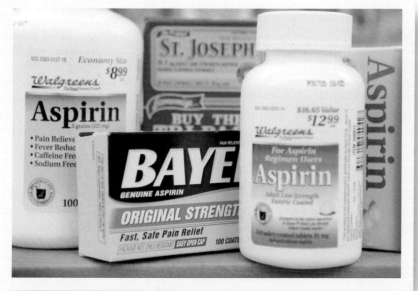

© Scott Olson/Getty Images

© iStockphoto.com/101dalmatians

cents-off deals and coupons) on a brand's sales after a promotional period is over. The dramatic finding from this research, which examined dozens of brands in 25 CPG categories, is that these promotions have virtually *no impact* on a brand's long-term sales or on consumers' repeat buying loyalty. No strong aftereffects occurred because extra sales for the promoted brands came almost exclusively from a brand's long-term customer base. In other words, the people who normally buy a brand are the ones who are most responsive to the brand's price promotion. Thus, price promotions effectively serve to induce consumers to buy on deal what they would have bought at regular prices anyway. In sum, although price-related promotions typically result in immediate and huge sales spikes, these short-term gains generally do not positively influence long-term brand growth.[7]

Splintering of the Mass Market and Reduced Media Effectiveness

Advertising efficiency is directly related to the degree of homogeneity in consumers' consumption needs and media habits. The greater their homogeneity, the less costly it is for mass advertising to reach target audiences. However, as consumer lifestyles have diversified and advertising media have narrowed in their appeal, mass-media advertising's efficiency has weakened. On top of this, advertising effectiveness has declined with simultaneous increases in ad clutter and escalating media costs. These combined forces have influenced many brand managers to devote proportionately larger budgets to promotions at the expense of advertising.

Short-Term Orientation and Corporate Reward Structures

Sales promotions go hand in hand with the brand management system, which is the dominant organizational structure in CPG firms. The reward structure in firms organized along brand manager lines emphasizes *short-term sales response* rather than slow, long-term growth. In other words, brand managers' performances are assessed on an annual basis or even quarter-by-quarter. And sales promotion is incomparable when it comes to generating quick sales response. This is important, as sales promotions are often tied by brand managers to Nielsen panel data outcomes (e.g., generating trial, encouraging repeats), explored in greater detail in Chapter 20. In fact, the majority of packaged-good brand sales are associated with some kind of promotional deal.[8]

Consumer Responsiveness

A final force that explains the shift toward sales promotion at the expense of advertising is that consumers respond favorably to money-saving opportunities and other value-adding promotions. Consumers would not be responsive to promotions unless there was something in it for them—and there is. All promotion techniques provide consumers with rewards (benefits, incentives, or inducements) that encourage certain forms of behavior brand managers desire. These rewards, or benefits, are both utilitarian and hedonic.[9] Consumers using sales promotions receive *utilitarian*, or functional, benefits of (1) monetary savings (e.g., when using coupons); (2) reduced search and decision costs (e.g., by simply availing themselves of a promotional offer and not thinking about other alternatives); and (3) improved product quality, because price reductions allow consumers to buy superior brands they might not otherwise purchase.

Consumers also obtain *hedonic* (i.e., nonfunctional) benefits when taking advantage of sales promotion offers, including (1) a sense of being a wise shopper when taking advantage of sales promotions;[10] (2) a need for stimulation and variety when, say, trying brands they otherwise might not purchase if it were not for attractive promotions; and (3) entertainment value when, for example, consumers compete in promotional contests or participate in sweepstakes.

A Consequence of the Increase: A Shift in Accounting Rules

In view of the major increase in sales promotions over the past 30 years, especially trade-oriented promotions, the organization responsible for establishing accounting standards in the United States—the Financial Accounting Standards Board (FASB)—reexamined how sales promotion expenditures should be handled on business organizations' income statements. Promotion expenditures historically were treated in exactly the same fashion as advertising expenditures, as *current expenses* that were deducted from top-line revenue. However, a unit of FASB called the Emerging Issues Task Force proposed new accounting regulations (EITF 00-14 and 00-25) that went into effect in late 2001.[11] EITF 00-14 and 00-25 require that those sales promotions used as a form of price discount—including promotions directed to retailers (e.g., off-invoice and slotting allowances, discussed later in this chapter) as well as to consumers (e.g., couponing expenditures and loyalty programs)—must now be treated as *reductions in sales revenue.*

Table 18.3 presents simplified income statements to illustrate the effect of this accounting change. Under the "new" (post-EITF 00-14 and 00-15) accounting procedure and assuming identical expenditures, the bottom-line profit would remain at $7 million. Notice in Table 18.3, however, that the difference between the "old" and "new" procedures is in the amount recorded for the top-line revenue—specifically, $50 million under the "old" procedure compared to $42 million for the "new" procedure ($50 million sales minus $8 million promotion expenditures).

TABLE 18.3	Illustration of "Old" and "New" Accounting Procedure	
	"Old" Accounting Procedure	**"New" Accounting Procedure**
Revenue	$50,000,000	$42,000,000
Cost of Goods Sold	20,000,000	20,000,000
G&A Expenses	10,000,000	10,000,000
Sales Promotion	8,000,000	NA*
Advertising	5,000,000	5,000,000
Total Expenses	43,000,000	35,000,000
Pretax Profit	$ 7,000,000	$ 7,000,000

*The $8,000,000 spent on sales promotions has been deducted from the top line.

You might think that this is no big deal because the change in accounting procedures really has had no impact on the bottom-line figure. The significance of the change, however, is that it better reflects "true" levels of sales revenue, which was the intent of the FASB's regulations. When sales promotions represent little more than a price discount, the amount of discount should not be treated as revenue, which under the old accounting system served to inflate actual revenue and to mislead financial analysts, stockholders, and other parties regarding a firm's actual revenue generation. Moreover, sales forces compensated on the basis of top-line results were overcompensated because revenue itself was overstated. Hence, under the new accounting rules, price-discounting promotions are appropriately treated as direct reductions from sales revenue rather than as indirect expense reductions.

This change in accounting standards is not a trivial development in terms of managerial behavior with respect to allocating marcom budgets. Knowing that every dollar of price-discounting promotion is immediately deducted from the revenue line, brand managers might be motivated to allocate relatively more money into advertising or into other forms of sales promotions other than price discounts.

What Are Sales Promotions' Capabilities and Limitations?

Trade and consumer promotions are capable of accomplishing certain objectives and not others. Table 18.4 summarizes these "can" and "cannot" capabilities, each of which is then discussed.[12]

What Promotions Can Accomplish

Promotions cannot work wonders, but they are well suited to accomplishing the following tasks.

TABLE 18.4 Tasks That Promotions Can and Cannot Accomplish

Sales Promotions *Can*
- Stimulate sales force enthusiasm for a new, improved, or mature product
- Invigorate sales of a mature brand
- Facilitate the introduction of new products to the trade
- Increase on- and off-shelf merchandising space
- Neutralize competitive advertising and sales promotions
- Obtain trial purchases from consumers
- Hold current users by encouraging repeat purchases
- Increase product usage by loading consumers
- Preempt competition by loading consumers
- Reinforce advertising

Sales Promotions *Cannot*
- Compensate for a poorly trained sales force or for a lack of advertising
- Give the trade or consumers any compelling long-term reason to continue purchasing a brand
- Permanently stop an established brand's declining sales trend or change the basic nonacceptance of an undesired product

Stimulate Sales Force Enthusiasm for a New, Improved, or Mature Product

Personal selling has many exciting and challenging aspects; there also are times when the job can become dull, monotonous, and unrewarding. Imagine what it would be like to call on a customer repeatedly if you never had anything new or different to say about your brands or the marketing efforts that support them. Maintaining enthusiasm would be difficult, to say the least. Exciting sales promotions give salespeople persuasive ammunition when interacting with buyers; they revive enthusiasm and make the salesperson's job easier and more enjoyable.

For example, Fiat Automobiles of Brazil had redesigned its Marea sedan and station wagon and was looking for an exciting promotion to motivate dealer salespeople and to encourage prospective customers to test-drive the Marea. The aspect of the promotional program aimed at salespeople involved "mystery shoppers" trained by Fiat who visited dealerships to test salespeople and managers on their technical knowledge of the Marea and their customer service skills. Salespeople and managers judged as having impeccable knowledge and sales skills received cash prizes. Additionally, each month, top-performing salespeople and managers earned additional cash prizes. At the campaign's end, top performers received paid vacations to Brazil's luxurious Comandatuba Island. The promotion was judged an incredible success.[13]

Invigorate Sales of a Mature Brand

Promotions can invigorate sales of a mature brand that requires a shot in the arm. Promotions cannot, however, reverse the sales decline for an undesirable product or brand.

Consider, for example, a promotion Bazooka bubble gum undertook in Latin America, where, as in the United States, Bazooka bubble gum is wrapped with a Bazooka Kid comic strip. The character in this comic strip is known to children in Argentina, Paraguay, and Uruguay as El Pibe Bazooka. Bazooka commanded over 40 percent of the gum market in these countries, but its share had fallen by more than 10 share points due to an onslaught of competitors. The maker of Bazooka gum, Cadbury, turned to its promotion agency for ideas to offset competitive inroads. The agency devised a promotion that temporarily replaced El Pibe Bazooka with Secret Clues that, when placed under a decoder screen, would reveal keys to "Bazooka Super Treasure." More than 150 million Secret Clues hit the market, and three million decoder screens were made available to kids through magazine and newspaper inserts and at candy stands and schools. After buying Bazooka and placing a Secret Clue under a decoder screen, kids learned immediately whether they would receive instant-win prizes such as T-shirts, soccer balls, and school bags. Kids could also enter a Super Treasure sweepstakes by mailing in 10 proofs of purchase. Top prizes included multimedia computers for winners and their schools along with stereo systems, TVs, bicycles, and other attractive items.

Consumer response was so overwhelming that Bazooka

© Jay Paul/Bloomberg via Getty Images

experienced distribution problems within several weeks of initiating the promotion. Bazooka sales increased by 28 percent and gained back about seven share points. This successful promotion demonstrates the power of sales incentives that catch the imagination of a receptive target market. Kids were encouraged to buy Bazooka gum to win instant prizes and to purchase the brand repeatedly to become eligible for very attractive sweepstakes awards.[14]

Facilitate the Introduction of New Products to the Trade

To achieve sales and profit objectives, marketers continually introduce new products and add new brands to existing categories. Promotions to wholesalers and retailers are typically necessary to encourage the trade to handle new offerings, which practitioners refer to as *stock-keeping units*, or SKUs. In fact, many retailers refuse to carry additional SKUs unless they receive extra compensation in the form of off-invoice allowances, display allowances, and slotting allowances. (Each of these forms of allowances is discussed later in the chapter.)

Increase On- and Off-Shelf Merchandising Space

Trade-oriented promotions, often in conjunction with consumer promotions, enable a manufacturer to obtain extra shelf space or more desirable space temporarily. This space may be in the form of extra facings on the shelf or off-shelf space in a gondola or an end-of-aisle display.[15]

Neutralize Competitive Advertising and Sales Promotions

Sales promotions can effectively offset competitors' advertising and promotion efforts. For example, one company's 50-cent coupon loses much of its appeal when a competitor simultaneously comes out with a $1 coupon. As previously described, Bazooka's promotion in Argentina, Paraguay, and Uruguay offset competitors' promotions and won back lost market share.

Obtain Trial Purchases from Consumers

Marketers depend on free samples, coupons, and other sales promotions to encourage trial purchases of new brands. Many consumers would never try new products or previously untried brands without these promotional inducements. Consider the following creative promotion that was extraordinarily successful in introducing a new line of lightbulbs in England.

Although consumers worldwide use massive quantities of lightbulbs, many people consider the brand name not all that important when selecting lightbulbs, because they assume that lightbulbs are essentially commodities—one bulb is as good (or bad) as the next. Against this perception, Philips Lighting attempted to create a differential advantage for its brand when introducing the Softone line of colored bulbs. Philips attempted to build demand for its Softone line—especially among younger families, who might become loyal product users for years.

A promotion agency (with a $2 million budget) developed a program based on what it described as a "ludicrously simple idea." Certain households were selected to receive bags, each of which contained an information brochure, a coupon, and a brief questionnaire. A response sheet inside a bag left at a household asked recipients if they were interested in receiving a free bulb and, if so, which of seven colors they wanted. Interested households were instructed to hang the bag with the completed questionnaire on their outside doorknob. That same evening, distribution crews inspected each household's response sheet and slipped the preferred-color lightbulb into the bag.

A total of two million bags were distributed. Of these, 700,000 households requested a free bulb—for a response rate of 35 percent. Follow-up surveys revealed that over 50 percent of bulb recipients actually used the bulbs. A total of 160,000 coupons were redeemed, which at 8 percent is a high redemption level. Sales in the six-month period following this special promotion doubled the prior average. Moreover, a subsequent bag distribution campaign was three times more efficient than the inaugural effort by focusing on neighborhoods near key retail accounts. This simple program illustrates how creative and strategically sound promotions can generate trial purchase behavior.[16]

Hold Current Users by Encouraging Repeat Purchases

Brand switching is a fact of life all brand managers face. The strategic use of certain forms of promotion can encourage at least short-run repetitive purchasing. Premium programs, refunds, sweepstakes, and various continuity programs (all described in Chapter 20) are useful promotions for encouraging repeat purchasing.

Increase Product Usage by Loading Consumers

The effect of many deal-oriented promotions is to encourage consumer *stockpiling*—that is, to influence consumers to purchase more of a particular brand than they normally would to take advantage of the deal. Research has found that when readily stockpiled items (e.g., canned goods, paper products, and soap) are promoted with a deal, purchase quantity increases—or stated alternatively, the consumption rate accelerates—by a substantial magnitude in the short term.[17]

This practice prompts a critical question: Do these short-term increases from consumer stockpiling actually lead to *long-term* consumption increases of the promoted product category, or do they merely represent *borrowed future sales*? An important study found that price promotions do *not* increase category profitability, but simply serve to shift short-term sales revenue from one brand to another. That is, sales gains in the short term induced by consumer stockpiling were offset by reduced demand in the long term.[18] Yet, it is cautioned that this finding is based on research involving a single product—a nonfood item (likely a household cleaning brand)—that may or may not be generalizable to other product categories.

Other researchers, however, have provided tentative evidence that establishes the conditions when the practice of loading might have positive long-term effects. These researchers determined that loading does increase consumers' product usage, especially when *usage-related thoughts about a product are vivid in the consumer's memory*. For example, people will not necessarily consume more soup just because they have stockpiled above-average quantities. However, if soup is on their minds (due to an advertising campaign touting soup's versatility), consumption is likely to increase. Also, products that are regularly *visible* (such as perishable items placed in the front of the refrigerator) are likely to be used frequently if consumers have stockpiled them.[19]

This finding receives additional support from research that has examined the impact of consumer inventory levels on the amount of usage for two product categories, ketchup and yogurt. Researchers predicted that consumption of yogurt would be more sensitive to inventory level because unlike ketchup, yogurt can be consumed at different times of the day and under a variety of circumstances (with meals, as a snack, etc.). Their results supported this expectation as the amount of yogurt consumption, but not ketchup, was influenced by the quantity of yogurt available in consumers' refrigerators—more yogurt, more (than normal) consumption; more ketchup, no more (than normal) consumption.[20]

Although no simple conclusion is currently available, the empirical evidence suggests that marketer's price-oriented deals that encourage stockpiling promote increased long-term consumption for some product categories but not others. There are at least two conditions when increased consumption occurs from stockpiling: First, when stockpiled products are *physically visible* to consumers as well as *perishable*, the effect may be to encourage increased short-term consumption without stealing sales from future periods. Second, consumers seem to increase their consumption rate of stockpiled products when the product is *convenient to consume* compared with when it requires preparation. Hence, it would be expected that snack foods would be consumed more rapidly when larger quantities are available in the household than would, say, a product such as pasta that has to be prepared.[21]

Conversely, the use of price deals that lead consumers to stockpile products like ketchup and household cleaning products may simply serve to increase product purchasing in the short term without increasing long-term consumption. Consumers, in effect, stockpile these items when they go on deal but do not increase normal product usage. Thus, we would tentatively conclude that price dealing is a useful *offensive weapon* (that is, for purposes of increasing total consumption) only for items such as yogurt, cookies, and salty snacks, whereas products such as ketchup should be price promoted only for *defensive reasons* such as offsetting competitive efforts that attempt to steal market share.

Preempt Competition by Loading Consumers

When consumers are loaded with one company's brand, they are temporarily out of the marketplace for competitive brands. Hence, one brand's promotion serves to preempt sales of competitive brands.[22]

Reinforce Advertising

A final can-do capability of sales promotion is to reinforce advertising. A well-coordinated sales promotion effort can greatly strengthen an advertising campaign.

The relationship between advertising and promotion is two way. On the one hand, an exciting promotion can reinforce advertising's impact (e.g., a free-standing newspaper insert for a coupon also has advertising surrounding it). On the other hand, advertising is increasingly being used as a communications mechanism for delivering promotional offerings. It is estimated, in fact, that upwards of one-third of all media advertisements (TV, print, online, etc.) carry a promotional message.[23] The growing importance of promotion-oriented advertising is evidenced by the fact that promotion agencies are increasingly responsible for creating advertisements—a role historically of the traditional full-service advertising agency.

What Promotions Cannot Accomplish

As with other marketing communications elements, there are limits to what sales promotions are capable of accomplishing. Particularly notable are the following three limitations.

Inability to Compensate for a Poorly Trained Sales Force or for a Lack of Advertising

When suffering from poor sales performance or inadequate growth, some companies consider promotion to be the solution. However, promotions will provide at best a temporary fix if the underlying problem is due to a poor sales force, a lack of brand awareness, a weak brand image, or other maladies that only proper sales management and advertising efforts can overcome.

Inability to Give the Trade or Consumers Any Compelling Long-Term Reason to Continue Purchasing a Brand

The trade's decision to continue stocking a brand and consumers' repeat purchasing are based on continued satisfaction with the brand, which results from meeting profit objectives (for the trade) and providing benefits (for consumers). Promotions cannot compensate for a fundamentally flawed or mediocre brand unless the promotions offset the flaws by offering superior value to the trade and consumers.

Inability to Permanently Stop an Established Brand's Declining Sales Trend or Change the Basic Nonacceptance of an Undesired Product

Declining sales of a brand over an extended period indicate poor product performance or the availability of a superior alternative. Promotions cannot reverse the basic nonacceptance of an undesired brand. A declining sales trend can be reversed only through product improvements or perhaps an advertising campaign that breathes new life into an aging brand. Promotions used in combination with advertising efforts or product improvements may reverse the trend, but sales promotion by itself would be a waste of time and money when a brand is in a state of permanent decline.

Problems with an Excessive Emphasis on Sales Promotion

As a short-term incentive, it is generally acknowledged that there can be three major problems with an *excessive* emphasis on sales promotions; that is, it can (1) diminish the image of the product, (2) diminish brand loyalty, and/or (3) actually reduce consumption. For example, consumers (and store managers) obsessed with a sales promotion game and obtaining and monitoring winning pieces may not even consider the quality or appeal of the restaurant chain's food offering the game. Or, a grocery store manager may be so obsessed with winning a manufacturer's trade contest offering a new TV that they are not even interested in the manufacturer's new items being introduced.

The Role of Trade Promotions

With the shift in power from manufacturers to retailers, and with brands from competitive manufacturers becoming increasingly indistinct and numerous, retailers have pressured the manufacturers that supply them to provide attractive price discounts and other forms of promotional dollars as well.

Consider the case of Clorox. Several years ago, the Clorox Company acquired a firm named First Brands. One of First Brands' most important products was the line of plastic items (wraps and bags) under the Glad brand name. Clorox thought it could quickly boost sales of Glad products because First Brands had previously invested virtually nothing in media advertising behind the brand, relying instead almost exclusively on consumer promotions (primarily coupons) and heavy trade promotion spending. Clorox's strategy was to cut Glad's consumer and trade promotions for two years and to invest heavily in mass-media advertising. Much to the disappointment of Clorox's marketing management, competitors did not follow. How did retailers react? They withdrew merchandise support, and Glad sales fell dramatically—as did Clorox's stock price, which dropped by about 20 percent in the two years after acquiring First Brands.[24]

With declining market share and a sagging stock price, Clorox responded in the only way it could: It returned to couponing and trade promotion spending. As previously noted, the power of retailers continues to grow relative to that of manufacturers. As one observer noted, "Without unique products and strong advertising, package-goods brands have little choice but to pay up to maintain shelf space, especially as consolidation makes retailers more powerful."[25]

Trade Promotions' Scope and Objectives

As cited earlier, trade promotions represent over half of every manufacturer dollar invested in advertising and promoting new and existing products. Manufacturers' trade promotions are directed at wholesalers, distributors, retailers, and other marketing intermediaries (rather than at consumers). A manufacturer's consumer-oriented advertising and promotions are likely to fail unless trade promotions have succeeded in influencing channel intermediaries to stock adequate quantities. The special incentives manufacturers offer to their distribution channel members are expected to be passed through to consumers in the form of price discounts offered by retailers, often stimulated by advertising support and special displays. As we will see later, however, this does not always occur.

Even though trade promotions do not always work as intended, manufacturers have legitimate objectives for using trade-oriented promotions.[26] These objectives include the following:

1. Introducing new or revised products
2. Increasing distribution of new packages or sizes
3. Building retail inventories
4. Maintaining or increasing the manufacturer's share of shelf space
5. Obtaining displays outside normal shelf locations
6. Reducing excess inventories and increasing turnover
7. Achieving product features in retailers' advertisements
8. Countering competitive activity
9. Selling as much as possible to final consumers

Ingredients for a Successful Trade Promotion Program

To accomplish these myriad objectives, several ingredients are critical to building a successful trade promotion program.[27]

Financial Incentive

A manufacturer's trade promotion must offer retailers increased profit margins, increased sales volume, or both. For example, some grocers might average only a razor-thin 1.0 to 1.5 percent profit margin. Therefore, manufacturer trade promotions should take this into account.

Correct Timing

Trade promotions are appropriately timed when they are (1) tied in with seasonal events during a time of growing sales (such as candy sales during Valentine's Day, Halloween, and Christmas); (2) paired with a consumer-oriented sales promotion; or (3) used strategically to offset competitive promotional activity.

Minimize the Retailer's Effort and Cost

The more effort and expense required, the less likely it is that retailers will cooperate in a program they see as benefiting the manufacturer but not themselves. One notable example was Kohler Company's smart use of its "Remodeling America" mobile idea center that traveled to be on site at plumbing supply and do-it-yourself outlets in the United States.

Quick Results

The most effective trade promotions generate immediate sales or increases in store traffic. (As you will see in the next chapter, instant gratification is an important motivator of consumer responses to consumer-oriented promotions. This same motive applies to retailers as well.)

Improve Retailer Performance

Promotions are effective when they help the retailer do a better selling job or improve merchandising methods as, for example, by providing retailers with improved displays. The notion of account-specific marketing or co-marketing (to be discussed later) lies at the heart of trying to improve retailer performance.

Trade Allowances

Manufacturers use trade allowances to reward retailers for performing activities in support of the manufacturer's brand. These allowances, also called *trade deals* (and communicated through "deal sheets"), encourage retailers to stock the manufacturer's brand, discount the brand's price to consumers, feature it in advertising, or provide special display or other point-of-purchase support.

By using trade allowances, manufacturers hope to accomplish two interrelated objectives: (1) increase retailers' purchases of the manufacturer's brand, and (2) augment consumers' purchases of the manufacturer's brand from retailers. The latter is based on the expectations that consumers are receptive to price reductions and that retailers will actually pass along to consumers the discounts they receive from manufacturers.

These expectations do not always become reality. Retailers often take advantage of allowances without performing the services for which they receive credit. In fact, a study of trade promotion spending by the Nielsen Company revealed that fewer than one-third of surveyed manufacturers rated the value they received from trade promotion as "good" or "excellent."[28] Moreover, the vast majority of retailers think that trade promotions should serve to increase sales and profits of entire product categories without concern for whether a manufacturer's specific brand benefits from the trade promotion.[29] Industry-wide, Procter & Gamble (P&G) has claimed that only 30 percent of trade promotion money actually reaches the consumer in the form of lower prices, while 35 percent is lost in inefficiencies and 35 percent winds up in the retailer's pocket.[30]

There is, in short, a substantial rift between manufacturers and retailers over the matter of which party trade promotions are intended to benefit. Manufacturers use trade promotions to advance their brands' sales and profit performance. Retailers, in contrast, tend to regard trade dollars as an opportunity for increasing their profit margins and thus boosting bottom lines. This schism is easy to understand because parties to economic transactions often have conflicting objectives yet depend on each other for success.

Major Forms of Trade Allowances

There are three major forms of trade allowances: (1) off-invoice allowances, (2) bill-back allowances, and (3) slotting allowances.[31] As we will see in the following discussion, manufacturers use off-invoice and bill-back allowances by choice, but retailers impose slotting allowances.

Off-Invoice Allowances

The most frequently used form of trade allowance is an off-invoice allowance, which represents a manufacturer's temporary price reduction to the trade on a particular brand. Off-invoice allowances are, as the name suggests, deals offered periodically to the trade that permit retailers to *deduct a fixed amount from the invoice*—merely by placing an order during the period which the manufacturer is "dealing" a brand. In offering an off-invoice allowance, the manufacturer's sales force informs retail buyers that a discount of, say, 15 percent can be deducted from the invoice amount for all quantities purchased during the specified deal period. Many CPG manufacturers provide off-invoice allowances at regularly scheduled intervals, which for many brands is one 4-week period during every 13-week business quarter. This means that many brands are on off-invoice deals approximately 30 percent of the year.

A manufacturer in using an off-invoice allowance does so with the expectation that retailers will purchase more of the manufacturer's brand during the deal period than they normally would and, to sell off excess inventories rapidly, *will pass the deals on to consumers in the form of reduced prices*—which thus should spur consumers' purchasing of the manufacturer's price-reduced brand.

However, as previously stated, retailers do not always comply with this expectation and, in fact, are typically not contractually bound to pass along discounted prices to consumers. Rather, retailers receive an off-invoice allowance (of, say, 15 percent) when purchasing the manufacturer's brand, but often they do not discount their selling prices to consumers or they reduce prices by substantially less than the full 15 percent.[32] Although P&G cited a lower estimate, many manufacturers estimate that retailers pass through to consumers only about one-half of the trade funds they provide to retailers.

We will discuss two undesirable offshoots of off-invoice allowances later—forward buying and diverting—but first it will be useful to discuss the other two major forms of trade allowances, bill-back and slotting allowances.

Bill-Back Allowances

Retailers receive allowances for featuring the manufacturer's brand in advertisements (bill-back ad allowances) or for providing special displays (bill-back display allowances). As the expression indicates, retailers do *not* deduct bill-back allowances directly from the invoice by virtue of ordering products (as is the case with off-invoice allowances), but rather must earn the allowances *by performing designated advertising or display services* on behalf of the manufacturer's brand. The retailer effectively bills (i.e., charges) the manufacturer for the services rendered, and the manufacturer pays an allowance to the retailer for the services received.

To illustrate, assume that the sales force for the Campbell Soup Company informs retailers that during October they will receive a 5 percent discount on all cases of V8 juice purchased during this period, provided they run newspaper advertisements in which V8 juice is prominently featured. With proof of having run feature ads in newspapers, retailers then would bill Campbell Soup for a 5 percent advertising allowance. Similarly, Campbell Soup's sales force could offer a 2 percent display allowance whereby retailers could receive an additional 2 percent discount on all purchases of V8 juice during the deal period for displaying V8 juice in prime locations.

Slotting Allowances

Slotting allowances are the fees manufacturers of both consumer packaged goods and durables pay retailers for access to the slot, or location, that the retailer must make available in its distribution center (e.g., warehouse) to accommodate the manufacturer's new brand. This form of trade allowance applies specifically to the situation where a manufacturer attempts to get one of its brands—typically a new brand—accepted by retailers.[33] Also called a *stocking allowance* or *street money*, a slotting allowance is not something manufactures of branded products choose to offer retailers. On the contrary, *retailers impose slotting allowances on manufacturers.* Retailers demand this fee of manufacturers supposedly to compensate them for added costs incurred when taking a new brand into distribution and placing it on the shelf. It should be obvious that manufacturers and retailers hold differing views regarding the appropriateness and value of the slotting-allowance practice.[34] The following discussion examines many of the key issues.[35]

When first used back in the 1960s, slotting allowances compensated retailers for the real costs of taking on a new stock-keeping unit, or SKU. The cost at that time averaged $50 per SKU per account. However, slotting allowances now can cost as much as $25,000 to $40,000 per item per store—although most slotting fees are much lower than this—and represent a healthy profit margin for retailers.[36] You probably are thinking, "This sounds like bribery." You also may be wondering, "Why do manufacturers tolerate slotting allowances?" Let's examine each issue.

First, slotting allowances are indeed a form of bribery. The retailer that demands slotting allowances denies the manufacturer shelf space unless the manufacturer is willing to pay the up-front fee—the slotting allowance—to acquire that space for its new brand. Second, manufacturers tolerate slotting allowances because they are confronted with a classic dilemma: Either they pay the fee and eventually recoup the cost through profitable sales volume, or they refuse to pay the fee and in so doing accept a fate of not being able to introduce new brands successfully.

In certain respects, slotting allowances *are* a legitimate cost of doing business and, in fact, can serve to increase marketplace efficiency rather than being anti-competitive.[37] When, for example, a large multi-store supermarket chain takes on a new brand, it may incur several added expenses. These expenses arise because the chain must make space for that new brand in its distribution center, create a new entry in its computerized inventory system, possibly redesign store shelves, and notify individual stores about the new SKU. In addition to these expenses, the chain takes the risk that the new brand will fail. This is a likely result in the grocery industry, where at least half of all new brands are failures. Thus, slotting allowances provide retailers with what effectively amounts to an insurance policy against the prospect that a brand will fail.

It is questionable, however, whether the actual expenses retailers incur are anywhere near the slotting allowances they charge. Large manufacturers can afford to pay slotting allowances because their volume is sufficient to recoup the expense. However, manufacturers of brands with small consumer franchises are frequently unable to afford these fees. Smaller manufacturers thus are placed at a competitive disadvantage when attempting to gain distribution for their new products.

How, you might be wondering, are retailers able to impose expensive slotting fees on manufacturers? The reason is straightforward: As noted earlier in the chapter, the balance of power has shifted away from manufacturers and toward retailers. Power means being able to call the shots, and increasing numbers of retailers are doing this. Also, CPG manufacturers have hurt their own cause by introducing thousands of new brands each year, most of which are trivial variants of existing products rather than distinct new offerings with meaningful profit opportunities for wholesalers and retailers. As such, every manufacturer competes against every other manufacturer for limited shelf space, and slotting allowances are simply a mechanism retailers use to exploit the competition among manufacturers. Furthermore, many grocery retailers find it easy to rationalize slotting allowances on the grounds that their net profit margins in selling groceries are minuscule (typically 1 percent to 1.5 percent) and that slotting allowances enable them to earn returns comparable to those manufacturers earn.

Further understanding of the rationale and dynamics underlying slotting allowances is possible by making a comparison with apartment prices in any college community. When units are abundant, different apartment complexes compete aggressively with one another and rental prices are forced downward to the benefit of students. But when apartments are scarce (which is typical in most college communities), prices often are inflated. The result: You may be forced to pay exorbitant rent to live in a second-rate, albeit conveniently located, apartment. The same is true regarding retailer slotting fees.

What can a manufacturer do to avoid paying slotting allowances? Sometimes nothing. But powerful manufacturers such as Procter & Gamble (P&G) and Kraft, for example, are less likely to pay slotting fees than are weaker national and particularly regional manufacturers. Retailers know that P&G's and Kraft's new brands probably will be successful because P&G and Kraft invest substantially in research to develop meaningful new products; spend heavily on advertising to create consumer demand for these products; and use extensive consumer promotions (e.g., sampling and couponing) to create strong consumer pull for their brands. Another way to avoid paying slotting allowances is simply to refuse to pay them and, if need be, to accept the consequence of being refused shelf space by some, if not most, retail chains.

In the final analysis, the issue of slotting allowances is extremely complicated. Manufacturers have legitimate reasons for not wanting to pay slotting allowances, but retailers have justification for charging them. Can both sides be right? Is the practice of slotting allowances a case of free-market competition working at its best, or at its worst? Simple answers are unavailable because the "correct" answer depends largely on which perspective—manufacturer's or retailer's—one takes on the matter.[38]

In the middle of this battle are government regulators, who have the responsibility of ensuring that the practice of slotting allowances does not reduce competition or harm consumers by forcing them to pay higher prices or limiting their options because smaller manufacturers are unable to gain shelf space for their new products. One regulatory agency, the Bureau of Alcohol, Tobacco, Firearms and Explosives, passed a ruling that prohibits the use of slotting fees in the marketing of alcohol products.[39] However, no prohibitions exist for the many other product categories where slotting allowances are charged. Although the Federal Trade Commission continues to investigate whether slotting allowances need to be regulated, it has not issued any regulation against retailers charging the fees.[40] In the meantime, slotting allowances remain for manufacturers an additional cost of introducing new products and an additional source of revenue for retailers. The power struggle goes on!

The Special Case of Exit Fees *(Deslotting Allowances)* Whereas slotting allowances represent a form of entry fee for getting a new brand into a grocery chain's distribution center, some retail chains charge manufacturers a fee for having unsuccessful brands removed from their distribution centers. These exit fees could just as well be called *deslotting allowances*. Here is how they operate: When introducing a new brand to a retail chain, the manufacturer and chain enter into a contractual arrangement. This arrangement stipulates the average volume of weekly product movement during a specified period that must be achieved for the manufacturer's brand to be permitted to remain in the chain's distribution center. If the brand has not met the stipulated average weekly movement, the chain will issue a deslotting charge. This charge, or exit fee, is intended to cover the handling costs for the chain to remove the item from its distribution center.

This practice may seem to be a marketplace application of the old saying about having salt rubbed into a wound. However, it really represents the fact that retailers, especially in the supermarket industry, no longer are willing to pay for manufacturers' new-product mistakes. There clearly is some economic logic to deslotting charges because these charges are another form of insurance policy to protect retail chains from slow-moving and unprofitable brands. To continue the apartment-rental analogy, a deslotting charge operates in much the same fashion as the stipulation between apartment owner and tenant regarding property damage. If the tenant damages an apartment, the apartment owner is fully justified in forfeiting all or part of the tenants' rental deposit. As such, the deposit provides the apartment owner with an insurance policy against potential negligence. This is precisely how an exit fee, or deslotting charge, operates.

GLOBAL FOCUS

Supermarket Slotting Fees Migrate to China

The slotting fee, a payment for a space (or "slot") in a grocer's warehouse, has been a staple of doing business in U.S. supermarkets since the 1960s. The arguments made by retailers for its use are well-known; that is, to try to offset an onslaught of manufacturer items often introduced with a lack of research and promotion leading ultimately to predicted failure in stores. Yet, such fees have drawn the scrutiny at times of the U.S. Federal Trade Commission (and Department of Justice) due to potential price discrimination issues in that not all manufacturers pay ("offer") the same slotting fees (in theory) to all grocers. In reality, and due to scale, larger manufacturers are better able to pay such fees than smaller- or medium-sized firms and such fees are hard to prove because they often are conducted orally and in private.

Like a virus spreading around the globe, slotting fees have emerged in many countries, including China in the 1990s. The large French retailer Carrefour entered China in 1995 with a slotting fee model to aid revenues, as well as mitigating cost increases. Yet, in 2003, a major dispute between the Shanghai Seed and Nut Roasters Association (SSNRA) and Carrefour China ensued over a multitude of fees charged by Carrefour, and 10 members of the SSNRA stopped selling to the 34 Carrefour stores in China.

Although the dispute was later resolved, a menu of some of the following slotting fees charged by Carrefour China received wide coverage in the Chinese media: (1) French holiday celebration (because Carrefour is headquartered in France): 100,000 Renminbis (RMBs) per year (1 RMB now is equivalent to 0.16 USD); (2) Chinese holiday celebration: 300,000 RMBs per year; (3) "grand opening" of new store: 10,000 to 20,000 RMBs per store; (4) store maintenance fee: 10,000 to 20,000 RMBs per year; (5) in-store advertising: 2,340 RMBs per store per ad (with 34 Carrefour stores in China, each store with an average of 10 ads a year, the total cost averaged 795,600 RMBs per year); (6) entrance fee for new items: 1,000 RMBs for each new product in each store; (7) wholesale discount: 8 percent of the sales; (8) service fee: 1.5 to 2 percent of the sales; (9) consulting fee: about 2 percent of the sales; (10) shelf space management fee: 2.5 percent of the sales; (11) fine for late delivery: 0.3 percent per day; (12) breakage:

Carrefour does not pay for damaged products; (13) returned products: about 3 to 5 percent; (14) tax refunding: 5 to 6 percent; and (15) lower wholesale price fine and refunding of price difference (i.e., suppliers have to pay Carrefour a fine if Carrefour finds lower [wholesale] prices for the same products in other supermarkets.) In 2010, Carrefour received much attention for reportedly charging more than 20 kinds of fees to Master Kong, a major Chinese instant noodle company. The number of fees (and amount) was reportedly much higher than those charged by Walmart, one of Carrefour's major competitors.

So, in December 2011, it was no surprise that the Chinese government unveiled a plan for cleaning up the escalating national problem of slotting fees. It would affect large-scale supermarkets with the following characteristics: (1) the largest store is more than 6,000 square meters, (2) the number of stores is more than 20, and (3) the total revenue in 2010 exceeds more than two billion RMB. The "Supermarket Charges" regulation specifies that (1) any *promotional fees* (e.g., for printing posters, launching promotional activities, placing ads, etc.) be expressly stipulated in the agreement with the supermarkets, and (2) any *noncompliant charges* are forbidden (e.g., renewal agreement fees, barcode fees, store decoration fees, celebration and store opening fees, sale rebate fees and returns irrelevant to sales goals, any other irrelevant fee to the promotion service). In 2012, the enforcement plan includes (1) self-reporting by the supermarkets, (2) joint investigations (by local agencies), and (3) corrective actions by government agencies. The Shanghai High People's Court issued an interpretation of a previous slotting fee case to note exceptions based on vendor volume allowances, promotional fees, and channels fees for the number and size of chain stores. Only time will tell to see if China is able to reign in this global "virus" to a greater extent than other countries around the world.

Sources: Richard Gibson, "Space War: Supermarkets Demand Food Firms' Payments Just to Get on the Shelf," *Wall Street Journal*, November 1, 1988, A1, A19; Hao Wang, "Slotting Allowances and Retailer Market Power," *Journal of Economic Studies*, 33 (1), 2006, 68–77; Shi Jing, "Carrefour Downs Shutters in Foshan," *China Daily*, January 14, 2011, http://europe.chinadaily.com.cn/business/2011-01/14/content_11853047.htm; and "China Cracks Down on Supermarket Charges by Large-Scale Retailers," McDermott Will & Emery, March 13, 2012, http://www.mwe.com/China-Cracks-Down-on-Supermarket-Charges-by-Large-Scale-Retailers-03-13-2012/?PublicationTypes=80ca8ee8-02a5-4d6c-bb51-fe2194cf5ea2.

Undesirable Consequences of Off-Invoice Allowances: Forward Buying and Diverting

Now that we have reviewed the three major forms of trade allowances—off-invoice, bill-back, and slotting allowances—we return to the first form of allowance and discuss the undesirable consequences that result from a manufacturer's use of off-invoice allowances.

Manufacturers' off-invoice allowances make considerable sense in theory, but in practice many retailers do not perform the services necessary to earn the allowances they receive from manufacturers. Large retail chains are particularly likely to take advantage of manufacturers' allowances without passing the savings along to consumers. A major reason is that large chains, unlike smaller chains, can merchandise their own *private brands* (or store brands). Because private brands can be sold at lower prices than manufacturers' comparable brands, large chains are able to use private brands to satisfy the needs of price-sensitive consumers while selling manufacturers' brands at their normal prices and pocketing the trade allowance as extra profit.

A second major problem with manufacturers' off-invoice allowances is that they often induce retailers to stockpile products to take advantage of the temporary price reductions. *Forward buying* and *diverting* are two interrelated practices retailers, especially those in the grocery trade, use to capitalize on manufacturers' trade allowances. Table 18.5 illustrates these practices.[41]

Forward Buying

As earlier noted, manufacturers' trade allowances are typically available for four weeks of each business quarter (which translates to about 30 percent of the year). During these deal periods, retailers buy larger quantities than needed for

---

TABLE 18.5	Illustration of Forward Buying and Diverting

1. In preparation for a huge promotional event in 2013 surrounding the Cinco de Mayo celebration of Mexican independence on May 5, Beauty Products Inc.—a hypothetical manufacturer of personal-care products—extends an *off-invoice offer* to grocery chains in the Los Angeles area. This promotion is a 15 percent off-invoice allowance on all orders placed for SynActive shampoo (a hypothetical brand) during the week beginning April 3, 2013, and extending through the week beginning April 24, 2013.

2. Assume that FB&D Supermarkets of Los Angeles (a hypothetical chain) orders 15,000 cases of SynActive—many more cases than it typically would sell in its own stores during any four-week period. Beauty Products Inc. has offered the 15 percent off-invoice allowance to FB&D Supermarkets with the expectation that FB&D will reduce SynActive's retail price to consumers by as much as 15 percent during the week of Cinco de Mayo festivities.

3. FB&D sells at the discounted price only 3,000 of the 15,000 cases purchased. (The remaining cases include some that are forward bought and some that will be diverted.)

4. FB&D resells 5,000 cases of SynActive at a small profit margin to Opportunistic Food Brokers—a company that services grocery retailers throughout the West. (This is the practice of *diverting*.)

5. FB&D later sells the remaining 7,000 cases of SynActive to shoppers in its own stores but at the regular, full price. (These 7,000 cases represent *forward buys*.)

normal inventory and warehouse the excess volume, thereby avoiding purchasing the brand at its full price during the remaining 70 percent of the year when a deal is not offered. Retailers often purchase enough products on one deal to carry them over until the manufacturer's next regularly scheduled deal. This is the practice of forward buying, which, for obvious reasons, is also called *bridge buying*—the amount of inventory purchased during one deal period bridges all the way to the next deal period.

When a manufacturer marks down a product's price by, say, 15 percent, retail chains commonly stock up with a 10- to 12-week supply. A number of manufacturers sell 80 percent to 90 percent of their volume during the occasions (approximately 30 percent of the year) when they are on deal. It is estimated that forward buying costs manufacturers between 0.5 percent and 1.1 percent of retail prices, which translates into hundreds of millions of dollars annually.[42]

Retailers employ mathematical models that enable them to estimate the profit potential from a forward buy and the optimum number of weeks of inventory to purchase. The models take into consideration the amount of savings from a deal and then incorporate into their calculations the various added costs from forward buying. These added costs include warehouse storage expenses, shipping costs, and the cost of tying up money in inventory when that money could be used to earn a better return in some other manner. Retailers, when forward buying, balance savings from reduced purchasing costs against the added expenses of the kind just noted.

It may appear that forward buying benefits all parties to the marketing process, but this is not the case. First, as previously mentioned, a substantial portion of retailers' savings from forward buying often are not passed on to consumers. Second, forward buying leads to increased distribution costs because wholesalers and retailers pay greater carrying charges by holding inventories of large quantities of forward-bought items. In fact, the average grocery product takes up to 12 weeks from the time a manufacturer ships it until it reaches retail store shelves. This delay obviously is not due to transit time but rather reflects storage time in wholesalers' warehouses and retailers' distribution centers from stockpiling surplus quantities of forward-bought items. Third, manufacturers experience reduced margins due to the price discounts they offer and the increased costs they incur.

A notable case in point is the situation that confronted Campbell Soup Company with massive forward buying of its chicken noodle soup when that product was placed on trade deal. As much as 40 percent of its annual chicken noodle soup production was sold to wholesalers and retailers in just six weeks when this product was on deal. Because wholesalers and retailers forward-bought chicken noodle soup in large quantities, Campbell had to schedule extra work shifts and pay overtime to keep up with the accelerated production and shipping schedules. After years of falling prey to forward buying, Campbell implemented a *bill-and-hold program* whereby it invoices (bills) the retailer as soon as the retailer places a forward-bought order but delays shipping (holds) the order until the retailer requests desired quantities. This program smoothed out Campbell's production and shipping schedules by allowing retailers to purchase large amounts at deal prices while delaying shipments until inventory was needed. The bill-and-hold program has not eliminated forward buying, but the negative consequences for Campbell Soup Company have been reduced.

Diverting

Diverting occurs when a manufacturer restricts a deal to a *limited geographical area* rather than making it available nationally. As described in Table 18.5, a brand of shampoo named SynActive is available only in Los Angeles as part of the city's Cinco de Mayo festivities. The hypothetical manufacturer illustrated in Table 18.5 (Beauty Products Inc.) intends for only retailers in the Los Angeles area to benefit from the deal. However, retailers (such as FB&D Supermarkets in Table 18.5) engage in diverting by buying abnormally large quantities at the deal price and then selling off, at a small profit margin, the excess quantities through food brokers in *other higher-priced geographical areas*. (Those in finance would label diverting an application of *arbitrage* behavior.)

Retailers blame manufacturers for offering irresistible deals and argue that they must take advantage of the deals in any way legally possible to remain competitive with other retailers. Manufacturers could avoid the diverting problem by placing brands *on national deal only*. This solution is more ideal than practical, however, since regional marketing efforts are expanding, and local deals and regional marketing go hand in hand. Further complicating the problem is that products intended for foreign markets sometimes are diverted back into a domestic market.

There are other negative consequences of diverting. First, product quality potentially suffers due to delays in getting products from manufacturers to retail shelves. For example, Tropicana requires its chilled juices to be stored between 32 and 36 degrees. If unrefrigerated for a few hours because of careless diverting practices, the product can go bad, and consumers may form negative impressions of the brand. A second and potentially more serious problem could result from product tampering. In the event of product tampering, it would be difficult, if not impossible, to identify exactly where a diverted brand may have been shipped.

Don't Blame Retailers

The preceding discussion has perhaps made it seem that retailers are villains when engaging in the practices of forward buying and diverting. This would be an unfair representation of retail buyers, who are simply taking advantage of an opportunity that is provided by manufacturers offering attractive trade deals. One retail executive explains his company's forward buying and diverting in this fashion: "We are very aggressive when it comes to buying at the best price. We have to be. If we don't, somebody else will."[43]

Efforts to Rectify Trade Allowance Problems

Because trade allowances spawn inefficiencies, create billions of added dollars in distribution costs, are often economically unprofitable for manufacturers, and perhaps inflate prices to consumers, a variety of efforts have been undertaken to alter fundamentally the way business is conducted, especially in the grocery industry.[44] The following sections are devoted to three practices some manufacturers undertake to minimize the negative effects of offering trade allowances: everyday low pricing, pay-for-performance programs, and account-specific marketing.

Everyday Low Pricing (EDLP)

Manufacturers lose billions of dollars every year to inefficient and ineffective trade deals stemming from the trade's practice of forward buying and diverting. It is for this reason that the powerful P&G, under the leadership of then-CEO Edwin Artzt, undertook a bold move in the 1990s to reduce the undesirable effects of retailers' forward buying and diverting. P&G introduced a new form of pricing called *everyday low pricing*, or EDLP, which the company also refers to as *value pricing*—signifying its desire to compete on the basis of providing product values and not mere price savings. Because some retailers also practice everyday low prices, we will distinguish between "back-door" EDLP manufacturers use from the "front-door" variety retailers practice.[45] Our interest is with the back-door variety of EDLP, which for clarity's sake we label EDLP(M) to stand for manufacturers' use of EDLP.

EDLP(M) is a form of pricing whereby a manufacturer charges the same price for a particular brand day in and day out. In other words, rather than charging high-low prices—that is, regular, or "high," prices for a period followed by off-invoice, or "low," prices for a shorter period—EDLP(M) involves charging the same price over an extended period. Because no off-invoice allowances are offered the trade under this pricing strategy, wholesalers and retailers have no reason to forward buy or divert. Hence, their profit is made from selling merchandise rather than from buying it.

How Has P&G Fared?

Researchers examined the effects of P&G's value pricing initiative over the first six years of its implementation.[46] The analysis encompassed a total of 24 product categories and 118 brands in these categories. From the year prior to P&G's implementation of EDLP through the first six years of the practice, P&G's advertising expenditures and net prices both increased by approximately 20 percent. During this same period, its expenditures on trade deals decreased by nearly 16 percent, and coupon spending was reduced by about 54 percent.

What was the effect of these changes? P&G lost about 18 percent market share on average across the 24 product categories analyzed. Value pricing clearly was a disaster for P&G, right? In actuality it was not. Although P&G suffered a significant decline in market share (due largely to competitors' retaliatory increases in promotional deals while P&G was cutting its own dealing activity), at the same time its overall profits increased by virtue of cutting trade deals and coupon activity and increasing net prices.[47] This pattern of reduced sales and market shares, yet higher profits, also occurred for P&G's value pricing program in Europe.[48] It could be argued that it is unwise ever to relinquish market share; however, in the final analysis, giving up market share can be justified if the share that remains generates greater profitability than what was obtained with a larger but less profitable share. Over the long haul, the bottom line (profits) is a more telling indicator of firm success than is the top line (sales).

Of course, not all products are a good fit for a *national* value pricing plan, as there can be tremendous variation in price competition from one region to the next. In fact, P&G has created cheaper versions of products (e.g., Tide Naturals) in developing and lower-priced markets (e.g., India, China).[49]

What Have Other Manufacturers Done?

Manufacturers less powerful than P&G have found it difficult to convert to a pure system of everyday low pricing. Even P&G has experienced resistance and has deviated from pure EDLP pricing with some brands such as laundry detergents. Three major reasons account for why many retailers resist manufacturers' EDLP initiatives. First, those retailers that established distribution infrastructures necessary to practice forward buying have resisted EDLP(M).[50] Second, there is some evidence that EDLP(M) benefits the manufacturers that price their products in this fashion more than it does the retailers that pay EDLP(M) rather than high-low prices. Finally, it also has been argued that EDLP(M) takes some of the excitement out of retailing. With EDLP(M), the retailer charges the same price to consumers day after day. Comparatively, with high-low pricing, there are periods when retailers can advertise attractive price savings, which breaks the monotony of never varying the retail price. Although in the long term the consumer realizes no savings from high-low pricing, in the short term it may be exciting to receive an appealing discount.

Pay-for-Performance Programs

As noted earlier, many trade promotions, especially in the grocery industry, are unprofitable for manufacturers because they merely shift future buying to the present when the trade engages in forward buying and diverting. Manufacturers, accordingly, have a strong incentive to devise an alternative system to the traditional off-invoice allowance. One such system is so-called *pay-for-performance programs*.

Consider the case of Nestlé and why that company shifted trade spending in this direction. Nestlé marketing officials were fed up with blowing trade dollars that served little useful purpose. Accordingly, new contracts with retailers were drawn up and emphasized the minimum duties retailers' would have to perform to receive Nestlé's trade dollars, duties such as reducing retail prices for a specified period of time, featuring Nestlé's brands in retailers' circulars, and providing special displays. Retailers failing to meet Nestlé's contractual requirements became ineligible to receive promotional funds, or, at the extreme, Nestlé simply withdrew its brands from noncomplying retailers' stores.

Rewarding Selling Rather Than Buying

As the name suggests, pay-for-performance is a form of trade allowance that rewards retailers for performing the primary function that justifies a manufacturer's offering a trade allowance—namely, selling increased quantities of the manufacturer's brand to consumers. Pay-for-performance programs are designed to *reward retailers for selling the manufacturer's brand supported with a trade allowance rather than for merely buying the brand at an off-invoice price.*

One form of pay-for-performance programs is called *scanner-verified trade promotions* or *scan downs*. (There are other pay-for-performance programs, such as those tied to loyalty marketing data.[51]) The "scan down" name is based on the idea that retail sales volume for a trade-supported brand is recorded via optical scanning devices at the point of sale. Scan downs entail three key facets:[52]

1. A manufacturer agrees with a retailer on a period during which the retailer receives an allowance for all quantities of a promoted brand that are sold to consumers at the designated deal price (e.g., an item that regularly sells to consumers at $1.99 per unit is to be reduced to $1.79).
2. The retailer's own scanning data verify the exact amount of the promoted brand that has been sold during this period at the deal price (e.g., 5,680 units at $1.79 each).
3. The manufacturer pays the retailer quickly, say within five days, at the designated allowance for the quantity sold. The manufacturer then reimburses the retailer for the reduced margin in selling a certain number of units (e.g., 5,680 units at a reduced margin of $0.20, or $1,136) and compensates the retailer for the amount of the trade allowance (e.g., 5,680 units at $0.05 each, or $284.00; thus, the manufacturer would mail a check to the retailer totaling $1,420).

A Win-Win-Win Situation

Scanner-verified programs provide an incentive to the retailer only for the items sold at discount to consumers during the agreed-on time period. Thus, unlike off-invoice allowances, manufacturers using scan downs do not pay for allowances where no benefit is received. Rather, manufacturers compensate retailers only for those items that are sold to consumers at discounted prices. Hence, this form of pay-for-performance program benefits all parties: consumers, retailers, and manufacturers. Consumers win by receiving reduced prices; retailers win by obtaining allowances for moving increased quantities of manufacturers' promoted brands; and manufacturers win by increasing sales of their brands, if only temporarily. By comparison, when using off-invoice allowances, manufacturers have no assurance that the off-invoice allowances given to retailers will be passed on to consumers.

The technological infrastructure is available in the United States (as well in most other economically developed countries) to support this form of trade promotion, and well-known companies such as Nielsen and Symphony Information Resources Inc. make it possible by serving, for a fee, as scanning agents. Scanning agents profit from performing the following functions:

© Justin Kase zsixz/Alamy

(1) collecting scanner data from retailers, (2) verifying the amount of product movement that meets the manufacturer's promotional requirements and warrants compensation, (3) paying the retailer, and (4) collecting funds from the manufacturer along with a commission for services rendered.

Customizing Promotions: Account-Specific Marketing

Account-specific marketing, also called *co-marketing*, is a descriptive term that characterizes promotional and advertising activity that a manufacturer *customizes* to specific retail accounts. With off-invoice programs, a manufacturer's promotion dollars are anything but customized to the needs of specific retail accounts—they are offered to *all* customers. In contrast, account-specific marketing directs promotion dollars to specific retail customers and develops in concert with the retailer advertising and promotion programs that simultaneously serve the manufacturer's brand, the retailer's volume and profit requirements, and the consumer's needs. Local radio tie-in advertising and loyalty programs using retailers' shopper databases are especially popular account-specific practices.

Some Examples

When introducing its expensive Photosmart photography system—a photo-scanning-and-printing system for home computers—Hewlett-Packard (HP) developed co-marketing arrangements with a small number of retailers. HP selected prime consumer prospects in each retailer's trade area and mailed invitations that appeared to be from the retailer, not HP. Prospective purchasers were invited to see an in-store demonstration and receive a chance to win a free Photosmart system.

An illustration from the CPG category is Hormel Foods' account-specific effort with the SPAM® Family of Products (the canned-meat product). To boost sales and to lure new consumers to the brand, Hormel Foods introduced the "SPAM Stuff" continuity program. Following in the footsteps of Kool-Aid and Pepsi, both of which had previously launched "stuff" programs, Hormel Foods offered consumers points toward the acquisition of free items (such as

© CB2/ZOB WENN Photos/Newscom

beanbag characters, boxer shorts, mouse pads, mugs, and T-shirts) with each purchase of SPAM products. In addition to offering "freebies" to encourage consumers to try SPAM products, Hormel Foods developed some account-specific programs to draw the trade's attention to the brand. Retailers were given SPAM advertising materials for their advertising flyers. They also received local advertising support for promoting SPAM on the radio and in newspapers. To further excite retailer participation, Hormel Foods offered one supermarket per region with a "SPAM Day" promotion for the best in-store display. Winning stores received "SPAM-wear" for employees and customers, free SPAMBURGER hamburgers grilled in the store's parking lot, and personal appearances by SPAM Cans characters. Silly as it may seem, programs like this often encourage retailers to devote greater attention to a brand (e.g., provide increased display space) and to entice consumers to purchase the brand more regularly.

What Does the Future Hold?

Account-specific marketing is a relatively recent innovation. First introduced by marketers in the packaged goods field, the practice eventually spread to companies that manufacture and market soft goods (e.g., apparel items) and durable items such as the HP Photosmart system. Because account-specific marketing requires a lot of effort in both development and implementation and is costly, interest among packaged goods companies already has peaked.[53] However, because powerful retailers benefit from well-designed account-specific programs, co-marketing is here to stay.

Generalizations about Promotions

The foregoing discussion has referred to research evidence regarding how promotions work and the objectives accomplished. Researchers—especially during the past two decades—have vigorously studied the functioning and effectiveness of sales promotions. These empirical efforts have enabled researchers to draw some tentative conclusions. These conclusions, more formally termed *empirical generalizations*, represent consistent evidence regarding different facets of promotion performance. Nine empirical generalizations are noteworthy (see Table 18.6).[54]

Generalization 1: Temporary retail price reductions substantially increase sales—but only in the short term

The evidence is clear that temporary retail price reductions generally result in substantial increases in short-term sales. These short-term sales increases are termed *sales spikes*. These spikes generally occur, however, at the expense of some reduction in consumer purchases of the promoted brand either preceding or following the promotional period.[55] Moreover, the effects of retail price

TABLE 18.6 **Nine Empirical Generalizations about Promotions**

1. Temporary retail price reductions substantially increase sales.
2. The greater the frequency of deals, the lower the height of the deal spike.
3. The frequency of deals changes the consumer's reference price.
4. Retailers pass through less than 100 percent of trade deals.
5. Higher-market-share brands are less deal elastic.
6. Advertised promotions can result in increased store traffic.
7. Feature advertising and displays operate synergistically to influence sales of discounted brands.
8. Promotions in one product category affect sales of brands in complementary and competitive categories.
9. The effects of promoting higher- and lower-quality brands are asymmetric.

Source: Adapted from Robert C. Blattberg, Richard Briesch, and Edward J. Fox, "How Promotions Work," *Marketing Science* 14, no. 3 (1995), G122–G132.

promotions are *short lived*. For example, one study examined price promotions for various brands in the soup and yogurt categories—the former representing a storable product and the latter a perishable—and found that the effect these promotions had on consumers' purchase likelihood, brand choice, and purchase quantity lasted only a matter of several weeks and did not alter consumers' long-term purchase behavior.[56]

Generalization 2: The greater the frequency of deals, the lower the height of the deal spike

When manufacturers and retailers offer frequent deals, consumers learn to anticipate the likelihood of future deals, and thus their responsiveness to any particular deal is diminished. Infrequent deals generate greater spikes, whereas frequent deals generate less dramatic sales increases. The psychology underlying this generalization is straightforward: When deals are frequently offered, the consumer's *internal reference price* (i.e., the price the consumer expects to pay for a particular brand) is lowered, thus making the deal price less attractive and generating less responsiveness than would be the case if the deal were offered less frequently.

Generalization 3: The frequency of deals changes the consumer's reference price

A corollary to the preceding generalization is that frequent deals tend to reduce consumers' price expectation, or reference price, for the deal-offering brand. This lowering of a brand's reference price has the undesirable consequence of lowering the brand's equity and thus the seller's ability to charge premium prices. Taken together, Generalizations 2 and 3 indicate that excessive dealing has the undesirable effects of both reducing a brand's reference price and diminishing consumer responsiveness to any particular deal.

Generalization 4: Retailers pass through less than 100 percent of trade deals

As previously described, manufacturers' trade deals, which typically are offered to retailers in the form of off-invoice discounts, are not always passed on to consumers. Although a manufacturer offers, say, a 15 percent off-invoice allowance, perhaps only 50 percent of retailers (or even fewer) will extend this allowance to consumers as lower retail prices. There is no legal obligation for retailers to pass through trade discounts. Retailers choose to pass along discounts only if their profit estimates lead them to the conclusion that greater profits can be earned from passing discounts to consumers rather than from directly "pocketing" the discounts. It is for this reason that manufacturers increasingly are implementing *pay-for-performance programs* that require retailers to perform specific services (e.g., provide special display space for a deal-offering brand) in order to receive discounts.

Generalization 5: Higher-market-share brands are less deal elastic

Suppose that a brand's price is reduced at retail by 20 percent and that sales volume increases by 30 percent. This would represent an *elasticity coefficient* of 1.5 (i.e., 30 ÷ 20), a value indicating that the increase in the quantity demanded is proportionately one and one-half times greater than the reduction in price. Generalization 5 suggests that for brands holding larger market shares, the deal elasticity coefficient generally is *smaller* than for smaller-share brands. The reason is straightforward: Smaller-share brands have proportionately more customers to gain when they are placed on deal, whereas larger-share brands have fewer remaining customers. As a result, larger-share brands when placed on deal gain "less bang for the promotional buck" compared with smaller-share brands.

Generalization 6: Advertised promotions can result in increased store traffic

Research suggests that store traffic generally benefits from brand-dealing activity. When exposed to a retailer's advertising featuring brands on deal, some consumers will switch stores, if only temporarily, to take advantage of attractive deals from stores other than those in which they most regularly shop.

Retailers refer to this temporary store-switching behavior as consumer "cherry picking," an apt metaphor. Interestingly, research has demonstrated that cherry-picking shopping behavior increases with increases in family size, when the head of household is a senior citizen, when a family does not have a working woman in the household, and with decreases in family income. All of these variables suggest that cherry-picking is greater when the *opportunity cost* of visiting multiple stores is reduced—for example, it is less costly in terms of time expenditure for a retired senior citizen to visit multiple stores to avail him- or herself of price discounts than it is for a younger, employed person.[57] This same research further revealed that cherry pickers save on average approximately 5 percent per item across all purchases. However, with gasoline prices again increasing at a rapid rate (as of 2012), net savings from cherry picking will undoubtedly decline as they must burn gas traveling from store to store to obtain deals.

Generalization 7: Feature advertising and displays operate synergistically to influence sales of discounted brands

When brands are placed on price deal, sales generally increase (see Generalization 1). When brands are placed on price deal and are advertised in the retailers' advertised features, sales increase even more (see Generalization 6). When brands are placed on price deal, are feature advertised, and receive special display attention, sales increase substantially more. In other words, the combined effects of advertising and display positively interact to boost a dealt brand's retail sales.

Generalization 8: Promotions in one product category affect sales of brands in complementary and competitive categories

An interesting thing often happens when a brand in a particular product category is promoted—namely, sales for brands in complementary and competitive categories are affected. For example, when Tostitos tortilla chips are promoted, sales of complementary salsa brands likely increase. Conversely, sales of brands in the competitive potato chip category could be expected to decrease as consumers' tortilla-chip purchases temporarily reduce their purchases of potato chips.

Generalization 9: The effects of promoting higher- and lower-quality brands are asymmetric

When a *higher*-quality brand is promoted, say, via a substantial price reduction, there is a tendency for that brand to attract switchers and thus steal sales from lower-quality brands.[58] However, a *lower*-quality brand on promotion is proportionately less likely to attract switchers from higher-quality brands. That is, switching behavior is *asymmetric*—the proportion of switchers drifting from low- to high-quality brands, when the latter is on deal, is higher than the proportion moving in the other direction when a low-quality brand is on deal.[59]

Summary

Sales promotion was introduced in this first of three chapters devoted to the topic. The precise nature of sales promotion was described. Promotion was explained as having three targets: the trade (wholesalers, distributors, and retailers), consumers, or a company's own sales force. The chapter proceeded to discuss the reasons for a significant trend toward increased investment in promotions vis-a-vis advertising. This shift is part of the movement from pull- to push-oriented marketing (and representing mostly trade promotion), particularly in the case of consumer package goods companies (CPGs). Underlying factors include a balance-of-power transfer from manufacturers to retailers, increased brand parity and growing price sensitivity, reduced brand loyalty, splintering of the mass market and reduced media effectiveness, a growing short-term orientation, and favorable consumer responsiveness to sales promotions.

The chapter also detailed the specific tasks that promotions can and cannot accomplish. For example, promotions cannot give the trade or consumers compelling long-term reasons to purchase. However, promotions are ideally suited for generating trial-purchase behavior, facilitating the introduction of new products, gaining shelf space for a brand, encouraging repeat purchasing, and performing a variety of other tasks.

Following this general introduction, the chapter presented the topic of trade-oriented sales promotions and described its various forms. Trade-oriented promotions represent on average over 50 percent of CPG companies' promotional budgets. These programs perform a variety of objectives. Trade allowances, or trade deals, are offered to retailers for performing activities that support the manufacturer's brand. Manufacturers find allowance promotions attractive for several reasons: they are easy to

implement, can successfully stimulate initial distribution, are well accepted by the trade, and can increase trade purchases during the allowance period. However, two major disadvantages of trade allowances, especially of the off-invoice variety, are that retailers often do not pass them along to consumers and they may induce the trade to stockpile a product in order to take advantage of the temporary price reduction. This merely shifts business from the future to the present. Two prevalent practices in current business are forward buying and diverting. Another form of trade deal, called a slotting allowance, applies to new-product introductions. Manufacturers of grocery products typically are required to pay retailers a slotting fee for the right to have their product carried by the retailer. Exit fees, or deslotting charges, are assessed to manufacturers whose products do not achieve prearranged levels of sales volume.

To reduce forward buying and diverting, some manufacturers have revised their method of pricing products. P&G is most notable in this regard for introducing what it calls value pricing, or what others refer to as everyday low pricing by a manufacturer, or EDLP(M). This method of pricing eliminates the historical practice of periodically offering attractive trade deals and instead charges the same low national price at all times. Another major development in the grocery industry that is aimed at curtailing forward buying and diverting is the implementation of pay-for-performance programs, which also are called scanner-verified systems, or scan downs. With this method of trade allowance, retailers are compensated for the amount of a manufacturer's brand that they sell to consumers, rather than according to how much they purchase from the manufacturer (as is the case with off-invoice allowances).

Discussion Questions

1. The term *promotional inducement* has been suggested as an alternative to sales promotion. Explain why this term is more descriptive than the established one.
2. Describe the factors that have accounted for sales promotion's rapid growth. Do you expect a continued increase in the use of promotion throughout the following decade?
3. Why, in your opinion, is the Internet a good medium for offering sales promotions to consumers?

How has social media helped to provide sales promotions to consumers?
4. Explain in your own words the meaning of push- versus pull-oriented promotional strategies. Using an illustration of a well-known supermarket brand of your choice, explain which elements of this brand's marcom mix embody push and which embody pull.
5. Assume you are the chief marketing officer of a large, well-known CPG company (e.g., P&G, Unilever, or Johnson & Johnson). What steps might

you take to restore a balance of power favoring your company in its relations with retailers?

6. Are promotions able to reverse a brand's temporary sales decline or a permanent sales decline? Be specific.

7. How can a manufacturer's use of trade- and consumer-oriented promotions generate enthusiasm and stimulate improved performance from the sales force?

8. Generalization 5 in the chapter claimed that higher-market-share brands are less deal elastic. Construct a realistic example to illustrate your understanding of this empirical generalization.

9. Generalization 8 asserted that promotions in one product category affect sales of brands in complementary and competitive categories. Tostitos tortilla chips were used as an example of this generalization. Provide examples of two additional brands and the complementary and competitive product categories that likely would be affected by promotions for your two illustrative brands.

10. Assume you are the marketing manager of a company that manufactures a line of paper products (tissues, napkins, etc.). Your current market share is 7 percent, and you are considering offering retailers an attractive bill-back allowance for giving your

brand special display space. Comment on this promotion's chances for success.

11. In your own words, explain the practices and problems of forward buying and diverting. Also, describe the advantages and disadvantages of bill-and-hold programs.

12. Assume you are a buyer for a large supermarket chain and that you have been asked to speak to a group of marketing students at a nearby university. During the question-and-answer session following your comments, a student makes the following statement: "My father works for a grocery product manufacturer, and he says that slotting allowances are nothing more than a form of larceny!" How would you defend your company's practice to this student?

13. Explain why selling private brands often enables large retail chains to pocket trade deals instead of passing their reduced costs along to consumers in the form of lower product prices.

14. In your own words, explain why EDLP(M) pricing diminishes forward buying and diverting. Can EDLP(M) be challenging to implement?

15. From your perspective, discuss how pay-for-performance programs, or scan downs, would, if widely implemented, virtually eliminate forward buying and diverting.

End Notes

1. Jacques Chevron, "Branding and Promotion: Uneasy Cohabitation," *Brandweek*, September 14, 1998, 24.

2. Pierre Chandon, Brian Wansink, and Gilles Laurent, "A Benefit Congruency Framework of Sales Promotion Effectiveness," *Journal of Marketing* 64 (October 2000), 65–81; and Robert M. Schindler, "Consequences of Perceiving Oneself as Responsible for Obtaining a Discount: Evidence for Smart-Shopper Feelings," *Journal of Consumer Psychology* 7, no. 4 (1998), 371–92.

3. A study of rebate programs concluded that automobile manufacturers' frequent use of rebates positively impacts revenue in the short run but has a negative effect on profits in the long run. See Koen Pauwels, Jorge Silva-Risso, Shuba Srinivasan, and Dominique M. Hanssens, "New Products, Sales Promotions, and Firm Value: The Case of the Automobile Industry," *Journal of Marketing* 68 (October 2004), 142–56.

4. These estimates are based on Al Heller, "Why Is Trade Promotion Spending Increasing?" CPGmatters, July 2011, http://www.cpgmatters.com/TradeMarketing0711.html; "2009 PROMO Industry Trends Report," PROMO, December 1, 2009,

http://chiefmarketer.com/09-industry-trends-report/index.html; and Betsy Spethman, "Is Promotion a Dirty Word?" PROMO, March 2001, http://chiefmarketer.com/mag/marketing_promotion_dirty_word.

5. Carl F. Mela, Sunil Gupta, and Donald R. Lehmann, "The Long-Term Impact of Promotion and Advertising on Consumer Brand Choice," *Journal of Marketing Research* 34 (May 1997), 248–61.

6. Purushottam Papatla and Lakshman Krishnamurthi, "Measuring the Dynamic Effects of Promotions on Brand Choice," *Journal of Marketing Research* 33 (February 1996), 20–35.

7. A. S. C. Ehrenberg, Kathy Hammond, and G. J. Goodhardt, "The After-Effects of Price-Related Consumer Promotions," *Journal of Advertising Research* 34 (July/August 1994), 11–21.

8. Robert C. Blattberg and Scott A. Neslin, "Sales Promotion: The Long and the Short of It," *Marketing Letters* 1, no. 1 (1989), 81–97.

9. Chandon, Wansink, and Laurent, "A Benefit Congruency Framework of Sales Promotion Effectiveness," 65–81. The following discussion of benefits is based on a typology these authors provided. See

Table 1 on pages 68–69. Another insightful perspective along similar lines is provided in Figure 2 of Kusum L. Ailawadi, Scott A. Neslin, and Karen Gedenk, "Pursuing the Value-Conscious Consumer: Store Brands versus National Brand Promotions," *Journal of Marketing* (January 2001), 71–89.

10. Research indicates that consumers who take advantage of promotional deals feel good about themselves for being "smart shoppers" and that these feelings are particularly strong when consumers have a sense of being personally responsible for availing themselves of a deal. See Schindler, "Consequences of Perceiving Oneself as Responsible for Obtaining a Discount: Evidence of Smart-Shopper Feelings."

11. Jack Neff, "Accounting by New Rules," *Advertising Age*, July 15, 2002, 4.

12. This discussion is guided by Charles Fredericks, Jr., "What Ogilvy & Mather Has Learned about Sales Promotion," *The Tools of Promotion* (New York: Association of National Advertisers, 1975); and Don E. Schultz and William A. Robinson, *Sales Promotion Management*, Lincolnwood, IL: NTC Business Books, 1986, chap. 3.

13. "A Real Gasser," *Promo*, January 2002, 27.

14. Amie Smith and Al Urbanski, "Excellence x 16," *Promo*, December 1998, 136.

15. A *facing* is a row of shelf space. Brands typically are allocated facings proportionate to their profit potential to retailers. Manufacturers must pay for extra facings by offering display allowances or providing other inducements that increase the retailer's profit.

16. "Adventures in Light Bulbs," *Promo*, December 2000, 89.

17. Chakravarthi Narasimhan, Scott A. Neslin, and Subrata K. Sen, "Promotional Elasticities and Category Characteristics," *Journal of Marketing* 60 (April 1996), 17–30. See also Sandrine Macé and Scott A. Neslin, "The Determinants of Pre- and Postpromotion Dips in Sales of Frequently Purchased Goods," *Journal of Marketing Research* 41 (August 2004), 339–50.

18. Carl F. Mela, Kamel Jedidi, and Douglas Bowman, "The Long-Term Impact of Promotions on Consumer Stockpiling Behavior," *Journal of Marketing Research* 35 (May 1998), 250–62.

19. Brian Wansink and Rohit Deshpande, "Out of Sight, Out of Mind: Pantry Stockpiling and Brand-Usage Frequency," *Marketing Letters* 5, no. 1 (1994), 91–100.

20. Kusum L. Ailawadi and Scott A. Neslin, "The Effect of Promotion on Consumption: Buying More and Consuming It Faster," *Journal of Marketing Research* 35 (August 1998), 390–98.

21. Pierre Chandon and Brian Wansink, "When Are Stockpiled Products Consumed Faster? A Convenience-Salience Framework of Postpurchase Consumption Incidence and Quantity," *Journal of Marketing Research* 39 (August 2002), 321–35.

22. For an empirical analysis of this effect, see Kusum L. Ailawadi, Karen Gedenk, Christian Lutzky, and Scott A. Neslin, "Decomposition of the Sales Impact of Promotion-Induced Stockpiling," *Journal of Marketing Research* 44 (August 2007), 450–67.

23. Betsy Spethmann, "Value Ads," *Promo*, March 2001, 74–79.

24. Jack Neff, "Clorox Gives in on Glad, Hikes Trade Promotion," *Advertising Age*, November 27, 2000, 22.

25. Ibid.

26. These objectives are adapted from a consumer promotion seminar conducted by Ennis Associates and sponsored by the Association of National Advertisers (New York, undated). See also Chakravarthi Narasimhan, "Managerial Perspectives on Trade and Consumer Promotions," *Marketing Letters* 1, no. 3 (1989), 239–51.

27. Schultz and Robinson, *Sales Promotion Management*, 265–66.

28. "ACNielsen Study Finds CPG Manufacturers and Retailers Increasing Their Use of Category Management Tools," Nielsen, May 3, 2004, http://us.nielsen.com/news/20040503.shtml.

29. This study is by Cannondale Associates as reported in Christopher W. Hoyt, "You Cheated, You Lied," *Promo*, July 1997, 64.

30. Zachary Schiller, "Not Everyone Loves a Supermarket Special," *Bloomberg Businessweek*, February 17, 1992, http://www.businessweek.com/archives/1992/b325246.arc.htm.

31. For a slightly different classification, see Miguel I. Gómez, Vithala R. Rao, and Edward W. McLaughlin, "Empirical Analysis of Budget and Allocation of Trade Promotions in the U.S. Supermarket Industry," *Journal of Marketing Research* 44 (August 2007), 410–24.

32. For a technical treatment regarding the profit implications of a retailer's decision to pass through a manufacturer's allowance, see Rajeev K. Tyagi, "A Characterization of Retailer Response to Manufacturer Trade Deals," *Journal of Marketing Research* 36 (November 1999), 510–16.

33. The term *slotting allowances* was originally used only with reference to new products, but the term has over time become a catchall expression for all efforts by manufacturers to gain retailer support for its brands. The term is used here in its original sense.

34. These differences are placed in stark contrast in Table 3 of William L. Wilkie, Debra M. Desrochers, and Gregory T. Gundlach, "Marketing Research and Public Policy: The Case of Slotting Fees," *Journal of Public Policy & Marketing* 21 (fall 2002), 275–88.

35. For a more complete treatment of the issue, including the presentation of survey results from both manufacturers and retailers, see Paul N. Bloom, Gregory T. Gundlach, and Joseph P. Cannon, "Slotting Allowances and Fees: Schools of Thought and the Views of Practicing Managers," *Journal of Marketing* 64 (April 2000), 92–108.

36. Paula Fitzgerald Bone, Karen Russo France, and Richard Riley, "A Multifirm Analysis of Slotting Fees," *Journal of Public Policy & Marketing* 25 (fall 2006), 224–37.

37. For a thorough and sophisticated treatment of the economic issues surrounding slotting allowances, see K. Sudhir and Vithala R. Rao, "Do Slotting Allowances Enhance Efficiency or Hinder Competition," *Journal of Marketing Research* 43 (May 2006), 137–55.

38. See Wilkie, Desrochers, and Gundlach, "Marketing Research and Public Policy" for further discussion of the economic and, especially, public policy issues associated with the practice of slotting allowances.

39. For an insightful discussion, see Gregory T. Gundlach and Paul N. Bloom, "Slotting Allowances and the Retail Sale of Alcohol Beverages," *Journal of Public Policy & Marketing* 17 (fall 1998), 173–84.

40. See David Balto, "Recent Legal and Regulatory Developments in Slotting Allowances and Category Management," *Journal of Public Policy & Marketing* 21 (fall 2002), 289–94.

41. This illustration is adapted from Zachary Schiller, "Not Everyone Loves a Supermarket Special," *Businessweek*, February 17, 1992, 64.

42. Robert D. Buzzell, John A. Quelch, and Walter J. Salmon, "The Costly Bargain of Trade Promotion," *Harvard Business Review* 68 (March/April 1990), 145.

43. Jon Berry, "Diverting," *Adweek's Marketing Week*, May 18, 1992, 22.

44. An insightful demonstration of why trade allowances are unprofitable is provided in Magid M. Abraham and Leonard M. Lodish, "Getting the Most out of Advertising and Promotion," *Harvard Business Review* 68 (May/June 1990), 50–60.

45. For discussion of everyday low pricing by retailers, see Stephen J. Hoch, Xavier Dreze, and Mary E. Purk, "EDLP, Hi-Lo, and Margin Arithmetic," *Journal of Marketing* 58 (October 1994), 16–27.

46. Kusum L. Ailawadi, Donald R. Lehmann, and Scott A. Neslin, "Market Response to a Major Policy Change in the Marketing Mix: Learning from Procter & Gamble's Value Pricing Strategy," *Journal of Marketing* 65 (January 2001), 44–61.

47. This conclusion is based on profit estimations made in ibid., 57.

48. Dagmar Mussey, "Value Pricing in Europe Backfires for P&G, Barilla," *Advertising Age*, January 13, 1997, http://adage.com/article/news/marketing-pricing-backfires-p-g-barilla-europe/69523.

49. Melanie Linder, "Trail of Tiers: How Procter & Gamble Made Cheap, New Products to Buck the Recession," CNNMoney, May 10, 2010, http://money.cnn.com/2010/05/06/news/companies/Proctor_Gamble_cheaper_products.fortune.

50. Kenneth Craig Manning, "Development of a Theory of Retailer Response to Manufacturers' Everyday Low Cost Programs" (Ph.D. dissertation, University of South Carolina, 1994).

51. Mark Hamstra, Elliot Zwiebach, and Jon Springer, "Retailers See Fewer Opportunities for Forward Buys," *Supermarket News*, May 10, 2011, http://supermarketnews.com/retail-amp-financial/retailers-see-fewer-opportunities-forward-buys.

52. Kerry E. Smith, "Scan Down, Pay Fast," *Promo*, January 1994, 58–59; and "The Proof Is in the Scanning," *Promo*, February 1995, 15.

53. Betsy Spethmann, "Wake Up and Smell the Co-Marketing," *Promo*, August 1998, 43–47.

54. The following discussion is based on the outstanding synthesis of the literature provided by Robert C. Blattberg, Richard Briesch, and Edward J. Fox, "How Promotions Work," *Marketing Science* 14, no. 3 (1995), G122–G132. The order of generalizations presented here is adapted from Blattberg et al.'s presentation. Please refer to this article for the specific studies on which the generalizations are based.

55. Harald J. van Heerde, Peter S. H. Leeflang, and Dick R. Wittink, "The Estimation of Pre- and Postpromotion Dips with Store-Level Scanner Data," *Journal of Marketing Research* 37 (August 2000), 383–95.

56. Koen Pauwels, Dominique M. Hanssens, and S. Siddarth, "The Long-Term Effects of Price Promotions on Category Incidence, Brand Choice, and Purchase Quantity," *Journal of Marketing Research* 39 (November 2002), 421–39.

57. Edward J. Fox and Stephen J. Hoch, "Cherry-Picking," *Journal of Marketing* 69 (January 2005), 46–62.

58. What appears to be an asymmetric effect due to brand quality may actually be due to market share. That is, smaller-market-share brands, which in many

product categories are of lower quality, can attract more brand switchers compared to larger-market-share brands simply because small-share brands have proportionately greater numbers of consumers to attract from large-share brands than the latter have to recruit from small-share brands (see Generalization 5). For evidence on this issue, see Raj Sethuraman and V. Srinivasan, "The Asymmetric Share Effect: An Empirical Generalization on Cross-Price Effects," *Journal of Marketing Research* 39 (August 2002), 379–86.

59. For a review of interesting experimental research on this issue, see Stephen M. Nowlis and Itamar Simonson, "Sales Promotions and the Choice Context as Competing Influences on Decision Making," *Journal of Consumer Psychology* 9, no. 1 (2000), 1–16.

CHAPTER 19

Consumer Sales Promotion: Sampling and Couponing

Groupon: A New Model for Couponing

This past year, consumers received 305 billion coupons, primarily through freestanding-inserts (FSIs) in Sunday newspapers, in-store handouts, direct mail, magazines, and in- or on-pack delivery. Given that almost 90 percent of all coupons distributed are FSIs, with an average redemption rate close to 1.0 percent, it is no wonder that only 3.5 billion (about 1.2 percent) of all coupons are redeemed.

To counter this apathy and inefficiency with coupons, and to appeal to more tech-savvy consumers, Groupon (derived from "group coupon") was launched in November 2008 in Chicago. Groupon was the first "deal-of-the-day" website (www. groupon.com),

© Scott Olson/Getty Images

offering discounted gift certificates from local or national companies. Currently, Groupon serves 500 local markets in 44 countries, such as the United States, Canada, Mexico, most of Europe, South America, and Southeast Asia (including India and China). Groupon's major U.S. competitor is Living Social, with Google and Facebook considering, but not yet launching, competing services.

Groupon's marketing strategy is that it offers one "Groupon" per day in each of its local markets. When a certain number of consumers sign up for the offer (the "tipping point"), it becomes available to all. If this predetermined number is not reached, the deal is not offered to anyone. Groupon keeps approximately 50 percent of the money the customer pays

1 Appreciate the objectives and classification of consumer-oriented sales promotions.

2 Recognize that many forms of promotions perform different objectives for marketers.

3 Know the role of sampling, the forms of sampling, and the trends in sampling practice.

4 Be aware of the role of couponing, the types of coupons, and the developments in couponing practice.

5 Understand the coupon redemption process and misredemption.

6 Appreciate the role of promotion agencies.

for the coupon. For example, a $100 dinner at a fine restaurant could be purchased by the consumer for $50 though Groupon. Then, Groupon and the restaurant would split the $50, with the restaurant receiving $25 from Groupon.

With Groupon, retailers are not required to pay upfront costs. In order to find the right retailer at the local level, Groupon relies on its sales staff to thoroughly research each city. They also find businesses with outstanding online reviews and use social media sites (e.g., Facebook) to further promote services. Customers who sign up for Groupon receive a daily e-mail to see if they are interested in a product or service offer, many of which focus on health, fitness, and beauty. In 2010, the company was expected to make $1 billion in sales—faster than any company ever. Due to its success, Groupon launched an initial public offering (IPO) in November 2011.

Sounds like a great business idea—right? (You may be saying to yourself, "Why didn't I think of that!") Yet, nothing is that simple with marketing strategy, especially in the volatile area of e-commerce. After revenue doubled to over $500 million in the fourth quarter of 2011, Groupon posted a $37 million loss in the first quarter of 2012. Problems emerged after their financial executives failed to set aside enough money for customer refunds. (Any unredeemed daily deal can be returned within the first seven days after purchase for a refund.) Groupon had more customers seeking refunds than expected due to a greater number of higher-priced deals offered. Moreover, critics have challenged Groupon's basic strategy on at least three points: (1) successful deals might swamp a small business with too many customers, (2) the deals merely attract one-time bargain hunters, and (3) an estimated seven of eight deals suggested by merchants are rejected. Of course, Groupon is working to overcome these criticisms as their sales staff continues to provide the best match of a deal between customers and retailers. Groupon certainly changed how couponing has been conducted for many years in the United States.

Sources: "NCH Annual Topline, U.S. CPG Coupon Facts Report For Year-End 2011," January 2012, 1–30; Bari Weiss, "Groupon's $6 Billion Gambler," *Wall Street Journal*, December 20, 2010, http://online.wsj.com/article_email/SB10001424052748704828104576021481410635432-lMyQjAxMTAwMDEwODExNDgyWj.html; Geoff Williams, "Groupon's Andrew Mason: The Unlikely Dealmaker," *Small Business* (blog), August, 9, 2010, http://smallbusiness.aol.com/2010/08/09/groupons-andrew-mason-the-unlikely-dealmaker/1#c29811638; Jamie Dunham, "Marketing to Women: Groupon or Groupoff? 10 Facts You Need To Know," *The Lipstick Economy* (blog), October 8, 2010, http://jamiedunham.wordpress.com/2010/10/08/marketing-to-women-groupon-or-groupoff-10-facts-you-need-to-know; Shayndi Rice, "Growing Pains at Groupon," *Wall Street Journal*, February 9, 2012, B1; Shayndi Rice and John Letzing, "Groupon Reveals Weak Controls," *Wall Street Journal*, March 31–April 1, 2012, A1, A6; Doris Hajewski, "Eateries Aren't Always Groupon Groupies," *Milwaukee Journal Interactive*, April 3, 2011, http://www.jsonline.com/business/119159609.html; Garett Sloane, "Groupon Hurt by Lack of Repeat Biz," *New York Post*, January 3, 2012, http://www.nypost.com/p/news/business/daily_deal_downer_BD1cnhAMIlINGF8bU6qOeP; and Groupon, http://www.groupon.com/cities (accessed April 16, 2012).

Introduction

Building on Chapter 18, which introduced the general topic of sales promotions and then focused on trade-oriented promotions, this chapter exclusively covers consumer-oriented promotions. The practices of sampling and couponing receive primary attention in this chapter; the subsequent chapter then explores additional forms of consumer-oriented promotions.

Before proceeding, it is appropriate to reiterate some advice that was provided in Chapter 1 with the following mantra:

> *All marketing communications should be (1) directed to a particular* target market, *(2) clearly positioned, (3) created to achieve a* specific objective, *and (4) undertaken to accomplish the objective* within budget constraints.

Thus, in the context of consumer promotions, target marketing and brand positioning continue to be the starting points for all decisions. With precise target and clear positioning, brand managers are prepared to specify the objective a particular promotion program is designed to accomplish. Managers also must work to ensure that promotion spending does not exceed their brands' budget limitations.

Why Use Consumer Promotions?

In almost every product category, whether durable products or consumer packaged goods (CPGs), several brands are available to wholesalers and retailers (the trade) to choose among and for consumers ultimately to select or reject for personal or family consumption. As a brand manager, your objective is to get your brand adequately placed in as many retail outlets as possible and to ensure that the brand moves off the shelves with frequency sufficient to keep retailers satisfied with its performance and to achieve your own profit objectives. This requires you to first have consumers try your brand and then, hopefully, become regular purchasers.

Unfortunately, your competitors have identical goals regarding the trade, activating consumer trial purchases, and achieving purchase regularity from the same consumers you also covet. Their gain is your loss. It is a vicious zero-sum game in the battle for trade customers and final consumers.

Certainly, advertising can help in flying above the day-to-day action found with sales promotions engaged in fighting off the competition and engaging in hand-to-hand battle. Advertising alone is insufficient; promotion by itself is inadequate. Yet, together they can make a formidable opponent.

So, why use consumer promotions? The short response is that promotions are used because they accomplish objectives that advertising by itself cannot. Consumers often need to be induced to buy now rather than later, to buy your brand rather than a competitor's, to buy more rather than less, and to buy more frequently. Sales promotions are uniquely suited to achieving these objectives. Whereas advertising can make consumers aware of your brand and shape a positive image, promotions serve to consummate the transaction.

Before proceeding, a final preliminary point is in order. You may have already experienced many types of sales promotions (e.g., coupons, samples, sweepstakes, games, rebates) that will be discussed in this chapter. Yet, it is our wish that you study the material in these two chapters with the goal of really understanding *why* the various types of promotions are used and which unique objectives each is designed to accomplish. Sophisticated brand managers do not simply reach into a "bag" and pick out any promotional tool as if the multiple forms of promotions are completely interchangeable. Rather, each is chosen to accomplish strategic objectives to a degree better than alternative options, given the budget constraint.

Brand Management Objectives and Consumer Rewards

What objectives do brand managers hope to accomplish by using consumer-oriented promotions, and why are consumers receptive to samples, coupons, contests, sweepstakes, cents-off offers, and other promotional efforts? Answers to these interrelated questions will provide us with a useful framework for understanding why particular forms of promotions are useful in view of the goal(s) that must be accomplished for a brand at a given point in time.

Brand Management Objectives

The overarching objective of consumer-oriented promotions is to promote increased sales (*sales promotion = promoting sales*). Secondary to this overall goal, and in concert with trade-oriented promotions (the subject of the previous chapter), consumer promotions are capable of achieving various sales-influencing objectives for the brand:[1]

- Gaining trade support for increased quantities of our brand during a limited period and providing superior display space for our brand during this period
- Reducing brand inventory for a limited period when inventories have grown to an excessive level due to slow sales, economic conditions, or effective competitive actions caused
- Providing the sales force with increased motivation during a promotional period to gain greater distribution for our brand, better display space, or other preferential treatment vis-à-vis competitive brands
- Protecting our customer base against competitors' efforts to lure them away
- Introducing new brands to the trade and to consumers
- Entering new markets with established brands
- Promoting trial purchases among consumers who have never tried our brand or achieving retrial from those who have not purchased our brand recently
- Rewarding present customers for continuing to purchase our brand
- Encouraging repeat purchasing of our brand and reinforcing brand loyalty
- Enhancing our brand's image
- Increasing advertising readership
- Facilitating the process of continually expanding the contact information in our database

As can be seen, consumer promotions are used to accomplish a variety of objectives during a specified time period, with the ultimate goal of driving increased sales of our brand. Consumer promotions, when done effectively, can serve to gain the trade's support, inspire the sales force to improve performance, and, most important for present purposes, motivate consumers to commit a trial purchase of our brand and, ideally, to purchase it with greater frequency and perhaps even in larger quantities.

To simplify matters, the discussion of specific forms of consumer-oriented promotions in this and the following chapter focus primarily on objectives directed at *influencing consumer behavior* rather than initiating trade or sales-force action. We will focus on three important and general categories of objectives: (1) generating purchase trial and retrial, (2) encouraging repeat purchases, and (3) reinforcing brand images.

Some sales promotions (such as samples and coupons) are used primarily with the objective of influencing consumers to *try or retry a brand*. A brand manager employs these promotional tools to prompt nonusers to try a brand for the first time or to encourage retrial from prior users who have not purchased the brand for perhaps extended periods. At other times, managers use promotions to hold onto their current customer base by rewarding them for continuing to purchase the promoted brand or loading them with a stockpile of the manufacturer's brand so they do not switch to another brand in the short run. This is sales promotions' *repeat-purchase objective*. (These promotions usually are located in, on, or near the product.) Sales promotions also can be used for *image reinforcement purposes*. For example, the careful selection of the right premium object or appropriate sweepstakes prize can serve to bolster a brand's image.

Consumer Rewards

Consumers would not be responsive to sales promotions unless there was something in it for them—and, in fact, there is. All promotion techniques provide consumers with rewards (benefits, incentives, or inducements) that *encourage certain forms of behavior* brand managers desire. These rewards, or benefits, are both utilitarian and hedonic.[2]

Consumers who respond to sales promotions receive various *utilitarian*, or functional, benefits: (1) obtaining monetary savings (e.g., when using coupons); (2) reducing search and decision costs (e.g., by simply availing themselves of a promotional offer and not having to think about other alternatives); and (3) obtaining improved product quality made possible by a price reduction that allows consumers to buy superior brands they might not otherwise purchase. Consumers also obtain *hedonic* benefits when taking advantage of sales promotion offers: (1) accomplishing a sense of being a wise shopper when taking advantage of sales promotions; (2) achieving a need for stimulation and variety when, say, trying a brand one otherwise might not purchase if it were not for an attractive promotion; (3) obtaining entertainment value when, for example, the consumer competes in a promotional contest or participates in a sweepstakes; (4) being viewed as "tech-savvy," for example, with a smartphone coupon; and (5) socializing with others on a deal with a group coupon. Consumer promotions also perform an informational function by influencing consumer beliefs about a brand—for example, by suggesting the brand is of higher quality than previously thought because it is co-promoted with another brand that is widely regarded as being high quality.[3]

The rewards consumers receive from sales promotions sometimes are immediate, while at other times they are delayed. An *immediate reward* is one that delivers monetary savings or some other form of benefit as soon as the consumer performs a marketer-specified behavior. For example, you potentially obtain immediate pleasure when you try a free food item or beverage that has been sampled in a supermarket or a club store such as Costco or Sam's Club. *Delayed rewards* are those that follow the behavior by a period of days, weeks, or even longer. For example, you may have to wait six or eight weeks before a mail-in premium item can be enjoyed, if it arrives at all (e.g., a NCAA Final Four T-shirt for several soda bottle tops).

Generally speaking, consumers are more responsive to immediate rewards than they are to delayed rewards. Of course, this is in line with the natural human preference for immediate gratification.

Classification of Promotion Methods

Table 19.1 presents a six-cell typology that was constructed by cross-classifying the two forms of consumer rewards (immediate versus delayed) with the three objectives for using promotions (generating trial purchases, encouraging repeat purchases, and reinforcing brand image).

Cell 1 in Table 19.1 includes four promotion techniques—samples, instant coupons, shelf-delivered coupons, and mobile phone coupons—that encourage *trial or retrial purchase behavior* by providing consumers with an *immediate reward*. The reward is either monetary savings, in the case of instant coupons, or a free product, in the case of samples.

Optical scanner-delivered coupons, media- and mail-delivered coupons, online coupons, social (group) coupons, and free-with-purchase premiums—all found in **cell 2**—are some of the techniques that generate consumer *trial/retrial*

TABLE 19.1	Major Consumer-Oriented Promotions		
Consumer Reward	**Brand Management Objective**		
	Generating Trial and Retrial	**Encouraging Repeat Purchases**	**Reinforcing Brand Image**
Immediate	**Cell 1** • Samples (19*) • Instant coupons (19) • Shelf-delivered coupons (19) • Mobile phone coupons (19)	**Cell 3** • Price-offs (20) • Bonus packs (20) • In-, on-, and near-pack premiums (20) • Games (20)	**Cell 5** (No Promotions Match Cell 5's Conditions)
Delayed	**Cell 2** • Scanner-delivered coupons (19) • Media- and mail-delivered coupons (19) • Online coupons (19) • Social (group) coupons (19) • Mail-in and online premiums (20) • Bounce-back coupons (19) • Free-with-purchase premiums (20)	**Cell 4** • In- and on-pack coupons (19) • Rebates and refunds (20) • Continuity programs (20)	**Cell 6** • Self-liquidating premiums (20) • Sweepstakes and contests (20)

© Cengage Learning

*Indicates the chapter, either Chapter 19 or 20, in which this form of sales promotion is covered.

yet *delay the reward*. Coupons along with samples are the topics of the present chapter, whereas premiums and other forms of consumer-oriented promotions are covered in the following chapter.

Cells **3** and **4** contain promotional tools that are intended to encourage *repeat purchases* from consumers. Marketing communicators design these techniques to reward a brand's existing customers and to keep them from switching to competitive brands—in other words, to encourage repeat purchasing. *Immediate reward tools*, in **cell 3**, include price-offs; bonus packs; in-, on-, and near-pack premiums; and games. *Delayed reward techniques*, listed in **cell 4**, include in- and on-pack coupons, refund and rebate offers, and continuity programs.

Building a *brand's image* is primarily the task of advertising; however, sales promotion tools may support advertising efforts by reinforcing a brand's image. By nature, these techniques are *incapable of providing consumers with an immediate reward*; therefore, **cell 5** is vacant. **Cell 6** contains self-liquidating premiums and two promotional tools, contests and sweepstakes, that, if designed appropriately, can reinforce or even strengthen a brand's image in addition to performing other tasks.

It is important to reemphasize that the classification of promotional tools in Table 19.1 is necessarily simplified. First, the table classifies each technique with respect to the *primary objective* it is designed to accomplish. Note, however, that promotions are capable of accomplishing more than a single objective. For example, bonus packs (cell 3) are classified as encouraging repeat purchasing, but first-time triers also occasionally purchase brands that offer extra volume and represent a good value. The various forms of coupons located in cells 1 and 2 are designed primarily to encourage triers or retriers and to attract switchers from other brands. In actuality, however, current purchasers redeem most coupons, not new buyers. In other words, although intended to encourage trial purchasing and switching, coupons can also invite repeat purchasing by rewarding present customers for continuing to purchase "our" brand.

Note also that two of the promotional tools in Table 19.1, *coupons* and *premiums*, are found in more than one cell. This is because these techniques achieve different objectives depending on the specific form of delivery vehicle. Coupons delivered through most media (newspapers, magazines, and online) or in the mail offer a form of delayed reward, whereas instant coupons that are peeled from a package at the point of purchase or instantly on a smartphone offer an immediate reward. Similarly, premium objects that are delivered in, on, or near a product's package provide an immediate reward, whereas those requiring mail delivery yield a reward only after some delay.

Sampling

Most practitioners agree that sampling is the premier sales promotion device for generating trial usage. Sample distribution is almost a necessity when introducing truly new products that can afford this form of promotion. Sampling is effective because it gives consumers an opportunity to experience a new brand personally. It allows an active, hands-on interaction rather than a passive encounter, as is the case with the receipt of promotional techniques such as coupons. A recent survey indicated that over 90 percent of consumers said they would buy a new brand if they liked a sample of the brand and considered its purchase price acceptable.[4]

By definition, sampling includes any method used to deliver an actual- or trial-sized product to consumers. The vast majority of manufacturers use sampling as part of their marcom programs to generate trials and leverage trade support. Companies use a variety of methods and media to deliver samples:

Photo Courtesy of Intel Corporation

- *Direct mail:* Samples are mailed to households targeted by demographic characteristics or in terms of geodemographics (as discussed in Chapter 4).
- *Newspapers and magazines:* Samples often are included in magazines and newspapers, which represent cost-efficient forms of sampling for reaching a mass audience. For example, Viva is a brand that competes with Bounty, Brawny, and other brands in the paper towel category, where annual sales exceed $2 billion. Viva is premium priced due to its higher quality. To convince consumers that the higher price is justified, consumers needed to actually touch Viva towels. To get samples of Viva into the hands of consumers, sheets were stitched into issues of two magazines, *Reader's Digest* and *Every Day with Rachel Ray.*[5]
- *Door-to-door sampling by distribution crews:* This form of sampling allows considerable targeting and possesses advantages such as lower cost and short lead times between when a brand manager requests sampling and when the sampling company ultimately delivers the samples. Companies that specialize in door-to-door sampling target household

Smart Sampling Machines Tell Kids to Scram

The food and beverage industry spends approximately $1 billion each year on product sampling. Getting the right sample to the right person is very important to CPG firms like Kraft, with billion-dollar brands, including Nabisco, Oscar Mayer, and Cadbury.

So, enter the iSample vending machine developed by Intel that can detect facial age (and gender) with a special camera that scans a user's face and determines if they are an adult or a child. The reason for this age bias is that Kraft is dispensing samples of mousse-like Temptations by Jell-O, the brand's first product aimed exclusively for adults. So far, Kraft selected two busy locations for the iSample machine and initial rollout: the Shedd Aquarium in Chicago and South Street Seaport in New York City.

If Intel's audience impression metric (AIM) software in the iSample machine detects a child (yet not with 100 percent certainly), an alarm sounds off and displays the following visual warning:

ATTENTION
CHILD DETECTED
Sorry, kid. You're too young to
appreciate indulgence like this.
Please step away, so the grownups
can get their free treat.

If an adult is detected, he or she is instructed to text a code or swipe a barcode with a smartphone. Once authenticated, one of six flavors selected (e.g., key lime pie, strawberry shortcake) is then dispensed. The mobile activation ensures that no one receives more than one sample per day. The iSample machine does not capture individual photos or videos, nor does it store phone numbers. However, data about what customers like (based on age and gender) is collected.

The future is bright for the iSample machine and AIM software. For example, retailers also can see if a sample recipient is smiling after they receive the item. Other similar machines have electronic menu screens (e.g., with recipe options for grilling and tailgating) and can detect based on demographics who is selecting different options. Adidas used AIM to feature a large video touch panel displaying different shoe types according to whether the person touching the screen was male or female. Harley-Davidson (H-D) created a specially designed electronic sign in a Toronto dealership to track if more women were in the store, and if so, H-D would place more saleswomen in the showroom. Intel's technology also can detect if the consumer is wearing a logo or can measure their dwell time on ads, screens, and other marketing stimuli. As long as one's information privacy is assured, this use of advanced technology in sampling (and other marketing efforts) can only aid its efficiency and effectiveness as an important IMC tool.

Sources: Bruce Horovitz, "New Sampling Machines Can Gauge Your Age and Sex," *USA Today*, December 14, 2011, http://www.usatoday.com/money/industries/food/story/2011-12-13/face-recogniton-sampling-machine/51890500/1; Leo Kelion, "Intel and Kraft's iSample Vending Kiosks Study Shoppers," *BBC News*, December 26, 2011, http://www.bbc.co.uk/news/technology-16323437; Nick Carbone, "Scram, Kids: New Vending Machine Dispenses Pudding to Adults Only, *Time* (blog), December 27, 2011, http://newsfeed.time.com/2011/12/27/scram-kids-new-vending-machine-dispenses-pudding-to-adults-only; and Emily Jed, "Kraft Vending Machine Dispenses Free Jell-O Samples; Tells Kids to Scram," *Vending Times*, 52 (1), January 2012, http://www.vendingtimes.com/ME2/dirmod.asp?sid=754303A430C54C2AA236B18E2C06AB17&nm=Vending+Features&type=Publishing&mod=Publications%3A%3AArticle&mid=8F3A7027421841978F18BE895F87F791&tier=4&id=227250540CB74BA5918370908BB108CA.

selection to fit the client's needs. Samples can be distributed just in blue-collar neighborhoods, in Hispanic areas, or in any other locale where residents match the sampled brand's target market.

- *On- or in-pack sampling:* This method uses the *package of another product* to serve as the sample carrier. A key requirement of this form of sampling is that the sampled brand and the carrier brand must be complementary with respect to their benefits, target audience characteristics, and image.
- *High-traffic locations and events:* Shopping centers, movie theaters, airports, and special events offer valuable forums for sample distribution. More will be said about this form of sampling in a later discussion of creative forms of sampling.
- *Sampling at unique venues:* Brand managers and their promotion agencies sometimes choose unique locations for sampling products that are especially

appropriate for people at a certain stage of life, referred to as life's change points. Sampling to college students at the beginning of a new school year (e.g., in dorms, rec centers) is one illustration of *change-point sampling*. Marriage offices are another change-point for reaching newlyweds. Newlywed kits containing various products are sometimes presented to couples when they apply for marriage licenses. The rationale for this sampling location is that newlyweds in the United States spend in excess of $70 billion for their households in the first year after marriage.[6]

- *In-store sampling:* Demonstrators provide product samples in grocery stores and other retail outlets for trial while consumers are shopping. It is understandable that in-store sampling is the most frequent form of sampling as it offers samples to consumers where and when their purchase decisions can be influenced most immediately.[7] Although there can be "moochers," research shows that about 60 percent of grocery shoppers sample products on trial, and 37 percent go on to buy the item.[8] A toy store such as Toys "R" Us, for example, would be an appropriate outlet for reaching moms and kids; beaches, concerts, and sporting events are excellent venues for delivering samples to teens and young adults. And fast-food restaurants—such as KFC, McDonald's, Sonic, and Wendy's—have turned to sampling as a means for introducing new menu items.[9]

- *Online sampling:* Brand managers are increasingly distributing samples online. They typically employ the services of companies that specialize in online sample delivery such as startsampling.com and thefreesite.com These and other specialized companies serve as online sampling portals for the CPG companies they represent. Interested consumers enter these sampling sites and register to receive free samples for brands that interest them. Samples are then mailed in a timely fashion. Because mailing represents a major cost element, it is estimated that online sampling costs are perhaps three times greater than sampling in stores or at special events.[10] The justification for this added expense is that people who go online to request particular samples generally are really interested in those brands—and eventually may purchase them—in comparison, say, to people who receive a sample at an event.

One recent and successful sampling campaign for Campbell's V8 Fusion + Tea products was conducted almost entirely on Facebook. The campaign gave Facebook followers who "friend" the V8 Fusion page a chance to receive one of the 1,000 samples of V8 V-Fusion + Tea given out each Monday. The Facebook page had a thermometer indicating how many samples were left in the week's quota out of 1,000. Yet, it turns out that most had

been given away to fans within hours of being placed online. Campbell's also provided a small number of samples directly through Facebook ads and at high-traffic locations (e.g., Rockefeller Plaza).[11]

Major Sampling Practices

Historically, many sampling efforts were unsophisticated and wasteful. In particular, there was a tendency to use mass-distribution outlets in getting sampled products in the hands of as many people as possible. Sophisticated sampling now insists on three prudent practices: (1) targeting rather than mass distributing samples, (2) using innovative distribution methods where appropriate, and (3) undertaking efforts to measure sampling's return on investment.

Targeting Sample Recipients

Sampling services that specialize in precision distribution (targeting) have emerged in recent years. For example, one sampling specialist aims for children under the age of 8 by distributing samples at zoos, museums, and other locations that appeal to young children and their parents. It also reaches children and teens (ages 9 to 17) at venues such as little league baseball fields, movie theaters, and skating centers. Suppose you wanted to reach preteens and preschool-age children with free samples. This could be accomplished by distributing sample packs at stores such as Toys "R" Us, the advantage of which has been described in these terms:

> When you're giving your product to customers in Toys "R" Us, you can bet with 99 percent accuracy you're reaching families with children under 12 or grandparents with grandchildren that age. You don't have that kind of certainty of reach with other [forms of marketing communications].[12]

Male high school students represent one of the most inaccessible markets because they are not particularly heavy television viewers or magazine readers. A company that specializes in targeted sample distribution developed a program that connected with teenage males by distributing gift packages of product samples (such as shaving cream, razors, mouthwash, and candy) at tuxedo rental shops. Recipients picked up their sample pack when they arranged to rent a prom tuxedo.

Samples are distributed to young adults (ages 18 to 24) at colleges and universities, malls, beaches, and concerts. Airports, shopping centers, and high-density retail districts are good sites for homing in on adults ages 25 to 54. Newlyweds, as mentioned previously, receive free samples when applying for marriage licenses.

How might you reach urban residents? A company that specializes in delivering samples to African-Americans and Latinos has established a network of several thousand African-American and Latino churches in which samples are distributed. Ministers in these churches often present sample bags to members of the congregation. This company also distributes samples to urban residents through a large network of beauty salons and barber shops.[13]

A final illustration of targeted sampling involves the distribution of Benadryl anti-itch cream conducted a few years ago by Warner-Lambert, then makers of Benadryl (since merged under the Pfizer name). Warner-Lambert wanted to develop a sampling program that would contact victims of itching caused by mosquito bites, heat rash, poison ivy, and so on. The objective was to approach prospective consumers at "point-of-itch" locations where they would be most receptive to learning about the virtues of Benadryl. The company considered sampling at retail lawn-and-garden departments but eliminated that prospect as not quite satisfying its point-of-itch objective. It eventually came up with the clever idea of sampling at KOA Kampground locations where people camp, enjoy the outdoors, and … itch. Twenty-five million people visit KOA Kampgrounds every year. During a two-summer period Warner-Lambert distributed six million Benadryl samples to 550 campgrounds, thereby achieving effective and cost-efficient sample distribution.[14]

All of these illustrations indicate that almost any group of consumers can be selectively sampled. The only limitation to targeted sampling is the absence of creativity!

Using Creative Distribution Methods

Companies are applying numerous creative ways to get sample merchandise into the hands of targeted consumers. To sample Cetaphil skin-care products, "pop-up shops" (temporary store-like facilities) were set up in three major cities: Atlanta, Chicago, and New York. Visitors to the "stores" received free hand massages with Cetaphil and also were invited to spin a wheel of fortune to take their chance at winning Cetaphil products such as skin cleanser and moisturizing lotion and cream. Over 250,000 samples of Cetaphil products were sampled during this promotional event, and to encourage subsequent purchasing visitors received a coupon worth $1 off any Cetaphil product.[15]

Progresso Soup, marketed by The Pillsbury Company (now owned by General Mills), employed a fleet of "Soupermen" to deliver cups of hot soup from backpack dispensers to consumers in cold-weather cities such as Cleveland, Chicago, Detroit, and Pittsburgh. From October through March, sampling teams visited consumers in these cities at sporting events, races, outdoor shows, and other locales—all of which represented ideal locations for getting consumers to try cups of hot Progresso soup.

Guinness Import Company sampled its unique beer using tractor trailers equipped with dozens of taps. These trailers traveled to Irish music festivals in cities such as New York, Chicago, and San Francisco. Guinness invested in the trailers because it regards hands-on sampling at special events as a good opportunity to create a unique brand usage experience and to avoid the clutter of mass-media advertising.

The famous Ben & Jerry's Homemade ice cream (now part of Unilever) offers another illustration of creative sampling. Requiring the event to match Ben & Jerry's upscale, pastoral image, the promotion planners created an "Urban Pasture" motif complete with cow mannequins, banners, lounge chairs, live bands, and, of course, free ice cream. The event toured 13 major U.S. cities, including Boston, Chicago, Los Angeles, and New York. The "Urban Pasture" set up in each city included a main stage, from which music was played, and sports and entertainment celebrities hosted ice-cream-scooping matches, with the winner at each tour stop receiving the opportunity to select a charity to receive an attractive donation—clearly in line with the brand's philanthropic image. Each "pasture" was up for a single day, but sampling crews remained in each city for at least an additional week during which time they sampled Ben & Jerry's ice cream from cow-bedecked buses.[16]

The promotion agency for Nivea for Men skin-care products devised a clever method to sample their product. Street teams distributed samples of Nivea products at almost 800 rail and subway stations across the United States. The brand enjoyed a 100 percent increase in sales in large part due to this creative sampling program.[17]

The marketers of EBoost, an immunity and energy booster, required a unique way to sample this brand so as to distinguish it from competitive offerings. The sampling solution was to distribute samples of EBoost to hotel guests—by placing samples on bedside tables and pillows or in bathrooms, or by handing out samples at check-in. Hotel sampling not only benefited EBoost but also the participating hotels that added value for their customers when giving away samples of a desirable product.[18] Managers of many brands other than EBoost have also enjoyed success in distributing samples in hotels.

Finally, if you were brand manager of a line of toilet tissue and thought sampling would benefit the brand, how would you provide consumers with free samples? Obviously, many of the traditional sampling methods would be inappropriate due to the high cost of sending out, say, millions of rolls of tissue. Brand managers

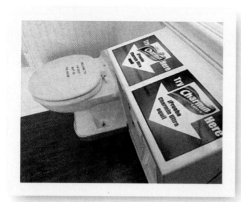

Courtesy of Procter & Gamble. Used with permission.

FIGURE 19.1 Sampling Charmin via a Fleet of Tractor Trailers

of P&G's Charmin brand faced precisely this challenge. They had tried various sampling methods without success, but then someone hit upon the idea of sampling Charmin at outdoor events. The company manufactured a fleet of tractor-trailer mounted bathrooms (see Figure 19.1) and conducted the Charmin Potty Palooza tour at events such as state fairs and Oktoberfests. Each trailer was equipped with running water, wallpapered walls, faux-wood floors, Charmin toilet tissue, and various samples of P&G's other brands—Safeguard soap, Bounty paper towels, and Pampers diapers—along with changing tables. As described by Charmin's brand manager, "[Toilet tissue] is a category that consumers don't think much about. To break through that and understand the benefits of Charmin Ultra, you really need to try it." P&G's research indicated a 14 percent increase in Charmin sales among people who used P&G's Potty Palooza facilities.[19]

Estimating Return on Investment

As previously detailed in Chapter 2, marketing communicators are increasingly being held accountable for their decisions. Chief financial officers, senior marketing executives, and other corporate leaders are demanding evidence that investments in advertising and promotions can be justified by the profits they return. Return on investment (ROI) is a tool that can be used to assess whether an investment in a sampling program is cost justified. Table 19.2 lays out the straightforward steps in applying an ROI analysis to a sampling investment.[20] Please read carefully the systematic procedure described in Table 19.2.

When Should Sampling Be Used?

Promotion managers use sampling to induce consumers to try either a brand that is new or one that is moving into a different market. Although it is important to encourage trial usage for new brands, sampling is not appropriate for all new or improved products. Ideal circumstances include the following:[21]

1. When a new or improved brand is either *demonstrably superior* to other brands or when it has *distinct relative advantages* over brands that it is intended to replace. If a brand does not possess superiority or distinct advantages, it probably is not economically justifiable to give it away.

2. When the product concept is so innovative that it is *difficult to communicate by advertising alone.* For example, Procter & Gamble sampled its new line of olestra-made Fat Free Pringles to lunchtime crowds in 20 major cities. The brand management team knew that consumers had to experience for themselves that this fat-free version of Pringles tasted virtually the same as regular Pringles chips. The earlier examples of sampling V8 Fusion + Tea, Ben & Jerry's Homemade ice cream, and Charmin toilet tissue further illustrate the need to sample products when advertising is insufficient for conveying the fundamental brand message. In general, sampling enables consumers to learn about product advantages that marketers would have difficulty convincing them of via advertising alone. (See the *Global Focus* insert for an application of this principle in China.)

3. When promotional budgets *can afford to generate consumer trial quickly.* If generating quick trial is not essential, then cheaper trial-impacting promotional tools such as coupons should be used.

TABLE 19.2	Calculating the ROI for a Sampling Investment

- **Step 1:** *Determine the total cost of sampling,* which includes the cost of the sample goods plus the costs of distribution—mailing, door-to-door distribution, and so on. Assume, for example, that the cost of distributing a trial-sized unit is $0.60 and that 15,000,000 units are distributed; hence, the total cost is $9 million.

- **Step 2:** *Calculate the profit per unit* by determining the average number of annual uses of the product and multiplying this by the per-unit profit. Assume, for example, that on average six units of the sampled product are purchased per year and that the profit per unit is $1. Thus, each user promises the company a profit potential of $6 when they become users of the sampled brand.

- **Step 3:** *Calculate the number of converters* needed for the sampling program to break even. (Converters are individuals who after sampling a brand become users.) Given the cost of the sampling program ($9 million) and the profit potential per user ($6), the number of conversions needed in this case to break even is 1,500,000 (i.e., $9 million divided by $6). This number represents a 10 percent conversion rate just to break even (i.e., 1,500,000 divided by 15,000,000).

- **Step 4:** *Determine the effectiveness of the sampling.* For a sampling to be successful, the conversion rate must exceed the break-even rate with gains in the 10 to 16 percent range. In this case, this would mean a minimum of 1,650,000 people must become users after trying the sampled brand (i.e., 1,500,000 times 1.1) to justify the sampling cost and yield a reasonable profit from the sampling investment.

© Cengage Learning

GLOBAL FOCUS

Introducing Oreos to China

Kraft Foods' Oreo cookies are one of the most popular dessert items in American grocery stores, with millions of packages sold weekly. Oreos are available in many other countries, but sales in China never achieved anywhere close to the volume enjoyed in the United States. As it turns out, Chinese consumers are not big cookie eaters, and Oreos are quintessentially an American cookie. After being on the Chinese market for a decade, Kraft's market research revealed that American-style Oreos were too sweet for the Chinese palate and that the price was too high. The options were obvious: either discontinue marketing Oreos in China or reformulate the product. Kraft chose the latter option and reformulated Oreos to be less sweet and less expensive. Interestingly, Kraft abandoned the circular sandwich version of Oreos, which did not resonate favorably with Chinese consumers, and replaced it with a chocolate-covered *wafer* filled with vanilla and chocolate cream.

Convincing Chinese consumers to try the new Oreo wafer was perhaps an even more challenging task than coming up with a suitable replacement for the American-style Oreo cookie. Although advertising was useful for making Chinese consumers aware of the new Oreo wafer, advertising alone would be insufficient to persuade Chinese consumers that Oreos taste good. Sampling clearly was required. The approach Kraft took for distributing product samples involved recruiting and training 300 college students to become Oreo brand ambassadors. These student ambassadors rode the streets of Beijing on bicycles and gave Oreo samples to more than 300,000 consumers. Oreo wafers quickly became the best-selling cookie in China, and Kraft doubled its Oreo revenue in that country.

Source: Adapted from Julie Jargon, "Kraft Reformulates Oreo, Scores in China," *Wall Street Journal,* May 1, 2008, B1.

© Bruce Rolff/Shutterstock.com

Sampling Problems

There are several problems with sampling. First, it is expensive. Second, the postal service or other distributors can mishandle mass mailings of samples. Third, samples distributed door to door or in high-traffic locations may suffer from wasted distribution and not reach the hands of the best potential customers. Fourth, in- or on-package sampling excludes consumers who do not buy the carrying brand. Fifth, in-store sampling often fails to reach sufficient numbers of consumers to justify its expense.

A sixth problem with samples is that consumers may misuse them. Consider the case of Sun Light dishwashing liquid, then a product of Lever Brothers (now Unilever). This product, which smells like lemons, was extensively sampled a number of years ago to more than 50 million households. Unfortunately, nearly 80 adults and children became ill after consuming the product, having mistaken the dishwashing liquid for lemon juice! According to a Lever Brothers' marketing research director at the time of the sampling, there is always a potential problem of misuse when a product is sent to homes rather than purchased with prior product knowledge at a supermarket.[22]

A final sampling problem, pilferage, can result when samples are distributed through the mail. This occurred in Poland shortly after the Iron Curtain separating Eastern from Western Europe was literally and symbolically demolished with the fall of Communist dominion in the East. P&G mailed 580,000 samples of Vidal Sassoon Wash & Go shampoo to consumers in Poland, the first ever mass mailing of free samples in that country. The mailing was a big hit—so big, in fact, that about 2,000 mailboxes were broken into. The shampoo samples, although labeled "Not for sale," turned up on open markets and were in high demand at a price of 60 cents each. P&G paid nearly $40,000 to the Polish Post, Poland's mail service, to deliver the samples. In addition to the cost of distribution, P&G paid thousands more to have mailboxes repaired.[23]

Due to its expense and because of waste and other problems, the use of sampling fell out of favor for a period of time as many marketers turned to less expensive promotions (e.g., couponing). However, with the development of creative solutions and innovations (e.g., the iSample machine used by Kraft), brand managers and their promotion agencies have again become enthusiastic about sampling. Sampling has become more efficient in reaching specific target groups, its results are readily measurable, and the rising costs of media advertising have increased its relative attractiveness.

Couponing

A coupon is a promotional device that rewards consumers for purchasing the coupon-offering brand by providing cents-off or dollars-off savings, which typically range from a low of 30¢ to $2 or more, depending on the price of the couponed item (see Figure 19.2). For example, Maxwell House coffee offered a coupon for $1 for a variety of its coffee products.

Coupons are delivered through newspapers; magazines; freestanding inserts; direct mail; in or on packages; online (including social group coupons); mobile phone; and at the point of purchase by package, shelf, and electronic delivery devices. Not all delivery methods have the same objective. *Instant coupons* (that is, those that can be peeled from packages or received on a smartphone at the point of purchase) provide immediate rewards to consumers and encourage trial purchases as well as repeat buying from loyal consumers (see Table 19.1). *Mail- and media-delivered coupons* delay the reward, although they also generate trial purchase behavior. Before discussing these specific coupon delivery modes in detail, it first will be instructive to examine pertinent developments in coupon use.

FIGURE 19.2 Illustration of Coupon Offers

Couponing Background

Approximately 305 billion coupons are distributed annually in the United States,[24] and coupon promotions cost U.S. marketers about $5.4 billion annually.[25] Nearly all CPG marketers issue coupons. The use of coupons is not, however, restricted to packaged goods. For example, General Motors Corporation mailed coupons valued as high as $1,000 to its past customers in hopes of encouraging them to purchase new cars. Surveys indicate that a majority of all American consumers (78.3 percent) use coupons at least on occasion per year, with redemption levels increasing during periods of economic downturns and declining when the economy is bustling.[26] Research has established that consumers vary greatly in terms of their *psychological inclination* to use coupons and that this coupon proneness is predictive of actual coupon redemption behavior. That is, some consumers are more inclined to use coupons because they are thriftier and receive greater psychological pleasure from saving money.[27]

Although vastly more coupons are distributed in the United States than elsewhere, *redemption rates* (the percentage of all distributed coupons that are taken to stores for price discounts) are higher in most other countries. However, couponing in some countries is virtually nonexistent or in the fledgling stage. For example, in Germany the government limits the face value of coupons to 1 percent of a product's value, which effectively eliminates couponing in Germany for low-priced CPGs. Only a small amount of couponing occurs in France because the few chains that control the retail grocery market in that country generally oppose the use of coupons. Couponing activity in Japan is in the early stages following the lifting of government restrictions.

Coupon Distribution Methods

The method of coupon distribution brand managers prefer is the *freestanding insert* (FSI). FSIs, which are inserts in Sunday newspapers, account for 89.4 percent of all coupons distributed in the United States.[28] The other media for coupon distribution are handouts at stores (4.2 percent), direct mail (2.3 percent), magazines (1.5 percent), in- and on-packages (1.1 percent), newspapers (1.0 percent), the Internet (0.2 percent), and all other methods of distribution (0.3 percent).[29] These percentages vary slightly from year to year, but FSIs have dominated coupon distribution for a number of years.

Another major trend in coupon distribution has been the establishment of cooperative coupon programs. These are programs in which a service distributes coupons for a single company's multiple brands or brands from multiple companies. Two such service companies—Valassis and News America's SmartSource service—are responsible for distributing the billions of FSI coupons in separate inserts in newspapers around the United States. Both Valassis and SmartSource distribute coupons every Sunday throughout the year and represent literally hundreds of different brands and companies. Procter & Gamble, the leading issuer of FSIs, has its own FSI insert program (P&G brandSAVER) that is distributed in Sunday newspapers every week. Valpak Direct Marketing Systems is a cooperative program for distributing coupons by direct mail.

Coupon Cost

The extensive use of couponing has not occurred without criticism. Some critics contend that coupons are wasteful and may actually increase prices of consumer goods. Whether coupons are wasteful and inefficient is debatable, but it is undeniable that coupons are an expensive proposition. For a better understanding of coupon costs, consider the case of a coupon with a $1 face value. (The *face value* is the amount paid to the consumer when he or she redeems the coupon at a retail checkout when purchasing the brand for which the coupon is offered.) The actual cost of this coupon is considerably more than $1. In fact, the actual cost, as shown in Table 19.3, is substantially more at $1.64. As can

TABLE 19.3	**Full Coupon Cost**	
1. Face value		$1.00
2. Distribution and postage cost		0.45
3. Handling charge		0.08
4. Consumer misredemption cost		0.07
5. Internal preparation and processing cost		0.02
6. Redemption cost		0.02
Total Cost		$1.64

Source: Adapted and updated from an analysis performed by the McKinsey & Co. Consulting firm.

be seen from the table, the major cost element is the face value of $1 that is deducted from the purchase price. But the marketers offering this coupon incur several other costs: (1) a hefty distribution and postage charge (45 cents), (2) a handling fee that is paid to retailers for their trouble (8 cents), (3) a misredemption charge resulting from fraudulent redemptions (estimated at 7 cents), (4) internal preparation and processing costs (2 cents), and (5) a redemption cost (2 cents). The actual cost of $1.64 per redeemed coupon is 64 percent greater than the face value of $1. Assume a marketer distributes 40 million of these FSI coupons and that 2 percent, or 800,000, are redeemed. The total cost of this coupon "drop" would thus amount to $1,312,000. It should be apparent that coupon activity requires substantial investment to accomplish desired objectives.

Obviously, programs that aid in reducing costs, such as cooperative couponing and online delivery (especially to smartphones), are eagerly sought. Coupons are indeed costly, some are wasteful, and other promotional devices may be better. However, the extensive use of coupons suggests either that there are a large number of incompetent brand managers or that superior promotional tools are not available or are economically infeasible. The latter explanation is more reasonable, with more efficient technological solutions on the horizon.

Is Couponing Profitable?

There is evidence that those households most likely to redeem coupons are also the most likely to buy the brand in the first place. Moreover, most consumers revert to their pre-coupon brand choice immediately after redeeming a competitive brand's coupon.[30] Hence, when consumers who redeem would have bought the brand anyway, the effect of couponing, at least on the surface, is merely to increase costs and reduce the per-unit profit margin. However, the issue is more involved than this. Although most coupons are redeemed by *current brand users*, competitive dynamics force companies to continue offering coupons to *prevent consumers from switching* to other brands that do offer coupons or other promotional deals.

Couponing is a fact of life that will remain an important part of marketing in North America and elsewhere. The real challenge for promotion managers is to seek ways to increase couponing profitability, to target coupons to consumers who may not otherwise purchase their brands, and to reward consumers for remaining loyal to their brands.

The following sections describe the major forms of couponing activity, the objectives each is intended to accomplish, and the innovations designed to increase couponing profitability. The presentation of couponing delivery methods follows the framework presented earlier in Table 19.1. Table 19.4 presents a summary of comparative redemption rates for major coupon distribution methods.

TABLE 19.4	Coupon Redemption Rates by Distribution Method	
Rank	**Method**	**Redemption Rates (%)**
1	Instant redeemable	19.5%
2	Internet (home printed)	18.0
3	Shelf pad (on shelf)	10.2
4	Bounceback (est.)	10.0
5	Mobile phone (est.)	10.0
6	Electronic shelf	9.1
7	Instant redeemable (cross ruff)	8.2
8	On pack	5.0
9	In pack	4.4
10	Electronic checkout (est.)	4.0
11	Direct mail*	3.5
12	Handout in-store/Away	3.2
13	Magazine	1.3
14	Freestanding insert (FSI)**	1.0
15	Newspaper ROP	0.7

*Direct mail represents the highest redemption rate for all mass-delivered (mail, media) coupons.
**FSIs represent 89.4 percent of all coupons distributed.

Source: NCH Marketing Services, Inc., Coupon Facts Report Year-End 2011; Coupon Resources, Inmar (CMS), etc. 2007–2010 data.

Point-of-Purchase Couponing

As will be described later in the context of point-of-purchase communications (see Chapter 22), approximately 76 percent of purchase decisions are made while shoppers are in the store. It thus makes sense to deliver coupons at the point where decisions are made. Point-of-purchase coupons come in four forms: instant, shelf-delivered, electronically delivered by optical scanner, and mobile phone coupons.

Instantly Redeemable Coupons

Most coupon distribution methods have delayed impact on consumers because the coupon is received in the consumer's home and held for a period of time before it is redeemed. *Instantly redeemable coupons* (IRCs) are peelable from the package and are designed to be removed by the consumer and redeemed at checkout when purchasing the brand carrying the coupon. This form of coupon represents an immediate reward that can spur the consumer to trial purchase the promoted brand (see cell 1 in Table 19.1). Instant coupons provide a significant price reduction and an immediate point-of-purchase incentive for consumers.

Although the instant coupon is a minor form of couponing, it has emerged in recent years as an alternative to price-off deals (in which every package must be reduced in price). The redemption level for instant coupons is considerably higher than the level for other couponing techniques. As noted in Table 19.4, whereas the dominant couponing method (FSIs) generates an average redemption level of approximately 1.0 percent (i.e., on average about 10 out of every

1,000 households that receive FSIs actually redeem them at stores), the average redemption rate for instant coupons has been estimated to be 19.5 percent.[31] One would think that most purchasers would remove instant coupons at the time of purchase so as to receive the savings, but it is obvious that the majority does not take advantage of these instant coupons.

A study compared the effectiveness of instantly redeemable coupons against free-standing inserts in generating sales for a brand of body wash. The FSI coupons and IRCs had 50-cent or $1 face values. Each coupon type and value combination (that is, 50-cent FSI coupon, $1 FSI coupon, 50-cent IRC, or $1 IRC) was placed on the body wash brand in each of two markets for a two-month period. Recorded sales data revealed that the IRCs outperformed FSI coupons of equal value. Moreover, the 50-cent IRC increased sales volume by 23 percent more than the $1 FSI coupon![32] This obviously is a counterintuitive finding that requires explanation.

A spokesperson for the research company said his company had no idea why the 50-cent IRC outperformed the $1 FSI coupon. However, research from the academic front offers an answer. One study found that a 75-cent coupon was not considered any more attractive than a 40-cent coupon.[33] A more directly relevant study determined that higher-value coupons *signal higher prices* to consumers.[34] This is especially true when consumers are *unfamiliar with a brand*. In this situation, high coupon values may scare off consumers by suggesting, or signaling, that these brands are expensive.

Perhaps the $1 FSI coupon for the body wash implied to prospective customers that the brand must be high priced or it could not otherwise justify offering such an attractive coupon. This being the case, they would not have removed the FSI coupon for later redemption. Comparatively, the 50-cent IRC was available to consumers at the point of purchase where the brand's actual price was also available. They had no reason to expect a high price; rather, they saw an opportunity to receive an attractive discount by simply peeling the coupon and presenting it to the clerk when checking out.

Ironically, higher-valued coupons may attract primarily current brand users who know the brand's actual price and realize the deal the attractive coupon offers, whereas a higher-valued coupon may discourage potential switchers from other brands if to them it signals a high price. This, of course, is particularly problematic with FSIs, which are received away from the point of purchase and, as a matter of practicality, include only the coupon value but not the brand's regular price. Such is not the case, however, with IRCs.

It would be unwise to draw sweeping generalizations from this single study based on only one product category (body wash), but the intriguing finding suggests that IRCs are capable of outperforming FSIs. Only with additional research will we know whether this finding holds up for other products.

Shelf-Delivered Coupons

Shelf-delivered coupon devices are attached to the shelf alongside coupon-sponsoring brands. A red device (referred to as the "instant coupon machine") is the best known among several shelf-delivered couponing services. Consumers interested in purchasing a particular brand can pull a coupon from the device and redeem it when checking out. The average redemption rate for shelf-delivered coupons is approximately 9 to 10 percent.[35]

© Susan Van Etten

Scanner-Delivered Coupons

There are several electronic systems for dispensing coupons at the point of purchase. Best known among these is an electronic checkout service from Catalina Marketing Corporation that is available in thousands of stores nationwide. Catalina offers two programs, one called Checkout Coupon and the other Checkout Direct. The *Checkout Coupon* program delivers coupons based on the particular brands a shopper has purchased. Once the optical scanner records that the shopper has purchased a competitor's brand, a coupon from the participating manufacturer is dispensed. By targeting competitors' customers, Catalina's Checkout Coupon program ensures that the manufacturer will reach people who buy the product category but are not currently purchasing the manufacturer's brand. The redemption rate is approximately 4 percent.[36]

Catalina's other couponing program, *Checkout Direct*, enables marketers to deliver coupons only to consumers who satisfy the coupon-sponsoring manufacturer's specific targeting requirements. The Checkout Direct program allows the coupon user to target consumers with respect to their purchase pattern for a particular product (e.g., direct coupons only to consumers who purchase toothpaste at least once every six weeks) or based on the amount of product usage (e.g., deliver coupons only to heavy users of the product). When shoppers who satisfy the coupon-sponsor's requirement make a purchase (as indicated by their loyalty or credit card), a coupon for the sponsoring brand is automatically dispensed for use on the shopper's next purchase occasion.

Frito-Lay used the Checkout Direct system to increase trial purchases when it introduced the Baked Lay's brand. Frito-Lay's brand managers targeted super-heavy users of healthier snack foods such as its own Baked Tostitos. Based on optical scanner data that records and stores consumers' past purchase data, the Checkout Direct system was programmed to issue coupons for Baked Lay's only to those consumers who purchased "better-for-you" snacks at least eight times during the past 12 months. When these consumers checked out, the scanner triggered a coupon for Baked Lay's. In excess of 40 percent of the coupons were redeemed, and the repeat-purchase rate was a very impressive 25 percent.[37]

Both Catalina programs are used to encourage trial purchasing or to induce retrial among those consumers who have not purchased a particular brand for a period of time. However, because coupons are distributed to consumers when they are checking out of a store and cannot be used until their next visit, the reward is *delayed*—unlike the instant or shelf-delivered coupons. Nevertheless, these scanner-delivered couponing methods are effective and cost-efficient because they provide a way to target coupon distribution carefully. Targeting, in the case of Checkout Coupon, is directed at competitive-brand users and, in the case of Checkout Direct, is aimed at users who satisfy a manufacturer's prescribed product-usage requirements.

© AP Images/Marketwire

Mobile Phone Coupons

The use of mobile phones to aid grocery shopping is of interest to 40 percent of consumers. So far, St. Louis–based grocer Shop N' Save is partnering with aisle411, a mobile-based navigation service, to offer shoppers an application (i.e., "app") to quickly find items and suggest coupon promotions on their phones. Others, such as grocers D'Agostino, Marsh, and Shop Rite, are working with a Cellfire application to merge digital coupons with store-based loyalty programs. (Cellfire is just one of many mobile phone organizations attempting to use phones [i.e., "third screen"] to distribute coupons and perform other marcom tasks.) In addition, Massachusetts-based Stop & Shop is rolling out its next phase of self-scanning, called ScanIt! Mobile. This app allows shoppers to use their own smartphones to scan groceries and redeem targeted coupons. In general across the United States, grocers are working to add optical scanners, upgrade software, and train cashiers to take advantage of mobile phone couponing. This certainly appears to be a major technological boost for shoppers that is expanding quickly.[38]

Mail- and Media-Delivered Coupons

These coupon-delivery modes initiate trial purchase behavior by offering consumers *delayed* rewards. Mail-delivered coupons represent about 2.3 percent of all manufacturer-distributed coupons. Mass-media modes (newspapers and magazines) are clearly dominant, carrying about 90 percent of all coupons—the bulk of which is in the form of FSIs in Sunday newspapers.

Mail-Delivered Coupons

Marketers typically use mail-delivered coupons to introduce new or improved products. Mailings can be either directed at a broad cross section of the market or targeted to specific geodemographic segments. Mailed coupons achieve the highest household penetration.

Coupon distribution via magazines and newspapers reaches fewer than 60 percent of all homes, whereas mail can reach as high as 95 percent. Moreover, direct mail achieves the highest redemption rate (3.5 percent) of all mass-delivered coupon techniques.[39] There also is empirical evidence to suggest that direct-mail coupons increase the amount of product purchases, particularly when coupons with higher face values are used by households that own their homes, have larger families, and are more educated.[40]

The major disadvantage of direct-mailed coupons is that they are relatively expensive compared with other coupon-distribution methods. Another disadvantage is that direct mailing is especially inefficient and expensive for brands enjoying a high market share. This is because a large proportion of the coupon recipients may already be regular users of the coupon brand, thereby defeating the primary purpose of generating trial purchasing. The inefficiencies of mass mailing account for the rapid growth of efforts to target coupons to narrowly defined audiences such as users of competitive brands.

FSIs and Other Media-Delivered Coupons

As earlier noted, approximately 89.4 percent of all coupons distributed in the United States are via FSIs in Sunday newspapers. The cost per thousand for FSIs is only about 50 to 60 percent of that for direct-mail coupons, which largely explains why FSIs are the dominant coupon-delivery mode. Another advantage of FSIs is that they perform an extremely important reminder function for the consumer who peruses the Sunday inserts, clips coupons for brands he or she intends to buy in the coming week, and then redeems these at a later date.[41] Finally, there is some evidence that FSIs also perform an advertising function. That is, when perusing the Sunday inserts, consumers are exposed to FSI "advertisements" and are somewhat more likely to purchase promoted brands even without redeeming coupons.[42] This comes as no great surprise because FSI coupons often are eye-catching "advertisements."

Research has shown that attractive pictures in FSIs are particularly effective when viewers of the FSI are loyal to a brand other than the one featured in the FSI. In this situation, consumers, loyal as they are to another brand, are not motivated to process arguments about a nonpreferred brand featured in the FSI. Hence, the use of attractive pictures (versus message arguments) is necessary to increase the odds that consumers will clip the FSI coupon.[43]

In addition to FSIs, coupons also are distributed in magazines and as part of the regular (noninsert) newspaper page. Redemption rates for coupons distributed in magazines and newspapers average about 1 percent.[44] A second problem with magazine- and newspaper-delivered coupons is that they do not generate much trade interest. Also, coupons delivered via magazines and newspapers are particularly susceptible to misredemption. The latter issue is so significant to all parties involved in couponing that it deserves a separate discussion later.

Finally, some coupons are known as *bounce-back coupons* in that they are requested by consumers via toll-free numbers or online. These coupons are then sent directly to consumers in the mail (i.e., they "bounce-back" to consumers). Their redemption rate has been estimated to be about 10 percent (see Table 19.4).

In- and On-Pack Coupons

In- and on-pack coupons are included either inside a product's package or as part of a package's exterior. This form of couponing should not be confused with the previously discussed instant, or peelable, coupon. Whereas IRCs are removable at the point of purchase and redeemable for that particular item while the shopper is in the store, an in- or on-pack coupon cannot be removed until it is in the shopper's home to be redeemed on a subsequent purchase occasion. This form of couponing thus affords consumers with a *delayed* reward that is designed more for encouraging repeat than trial purchases (see cell 4 in Table 19.1).

A coupon for one brand often is promoted by another brand. For example, General Mills promoted its brand of granola bars by placing cents-off coupons in cereal boxes. Practitioners call this practice *crossruffing*, a term borrowed from bridge and bridge-type card games where partners alternate trumping one another when they are unable to follow suit.

Although marketers use crossruffing to create trial purchases or to stimulate purchase of products, such as granola bars, that are not staple items, in- and on-pack coupons the *same brand* carries are generally intended to *stimulate repeat purchasing*. That is, once consumers have exhausted the contents of a particular package, they are more likely to repurchase that brand if an attractive inducement, such as a cents-off coupon, is available immediately. A package coupon has *bounce-back value*, so to speak. An initial purchase, the bounce, may stimulate another purchase, the bounce back, when an appealing inducement such as an in-package coupon is made available.[45] (This term should not be confused with the "bounce-back coupon" previously discussed.)

A major advantage of in- and on-pack coupons is that there are virtually *no distribution costs*. Moreover, redemption rates are much higher because brand users receive most of the package-delivered coupons. The average redemption rate for in-pack coupons is around 4.4 percent, whereas the redemption rate for on-pack coupons is 5 percent.[46] Limitations of package-delivered coupons are that they offer delayed value to consumers, do not reach nonusers of the carrying brand, and do not leverage trade interest due to the delayed nature of the offer.

Online and Social Group Couponing

A number of Internet sites now distribute coupons. Although representing a very small percentage of all coupons distributed (less than 1 percent), online couponing is growing in popularity, and redemption rates now stand at 18 percent. Consumers usually print the coupons on their home (or work) printers (although smartphones can accept or redeem these instantly, as noted above). Then, as with other modes of coupon delivery, consumers redeem the printed coupon along with the purchased item at checkout.

Allowing consumers to print their own coupons creates considerable potential for *fraud* because it leaves open the possibility that consumers will manipulate the face value and print multiple copies. Moreover, computer-savvy criminals download coupon files and scan coupons into their computers, and then change the bar codes, dates, amounts, and even the sponsoring brand.[47] To avoid this problem, some online couponing services allow the consumer to select the brands for which he or she would like to receive coupons, and then actual coupons are mailed. Certainly, the advent of mobile phone coupons can help reduce such problems, including delays, for consumers.

Finally, as described in detail in the *Marcom Insight*, social group coupons from Groupon and Living Social (among others) have exploded onto the coupon scene in the last several years. In contrast to the "tipping point," the minimum number to activate a purchased coupon from Groupon, Living Social offers a free deal if the coupon recipient can sign up three of their friends after purchase. For Groupon, estimated redemptions rates range from 78 to 82 percent *once the coupon is purchased*.[48] Readers are encouraged to revisit the *Marcom Insight* for additional information on Groupon.

The Coupon Redemption Process and Misredemption

Coupon misredemption is a widespread problem. The best way to understand how misredemption occurs is to examine the redemption process. A graphic of the process is presented in Figure 19.3.

The Process

The process begins with a manufacturer distributing coupons to consumers via FSIs, direct mail, or any of the other distribution modes previously described (see *path A* in Figure 19.3). Consumers collect coupons, take them to the store, and present them to a checkout clerk, who subtracts each coupon's face value from the shopper's total purchase cost (see *path B*). For the shopper to be entitled to the coupon discount, certain conditions and restrictions must be met: (1) he or she must buy the merchandise specified on the coupon in the size, brand, and quantity directed; (2) only one coupon can be redeemed per item; (3) cash may not be given for the coupon; and (4) the coupon must be redeemed before the expiration date. (Some coupon misredemption occurs because consumers present coupons that do not meet these requirements.)

Retailers, in turn, redeem the coupons they have received to obtain reimbursement from the manufacturers that sponsored the coupons. Retailers typically hire another company, called a *clearinghouse*, to sort and redeem the coupons in return for a fee (see *path C*). Clearinghouses, acting on behalf of a number of retail clients, consolidate coupons before forwarding them. Clearinghouses maintain control by ensuring that their clients sold products legitimately in the amounts they submitted for redemption.

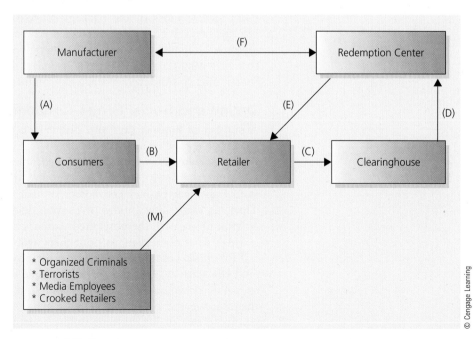

FIGURE 19.3 Coupon Redemption and Misredemption Process

Clearinghouses forward the coupons to *redemption centers* (see *path D*), which serve as agents of coupon-issuing manufacturers. A redemption center pays off on all properly redeemed coupons (see *path E*) and then is compensated for its services by the manufacturer (see *path F*). If a center questions the validity of certain coupons, it may go to its client, a manufacturer, for approval on redeeming suspected coupons.

The system is not quite as clear-cut as it may appear from this description. Some large retailers act as their own clearinghouses, some manufacturers serve as their own redemption centers, and some independent firms offer both clearinghouse and redemption-center services.

However, regardless of the specific mechanism by which a coupon is ultimately redeemed (or misredeemed), the retailer is reimbursed for the amount of the face value paid to the consumer and for payment of a handling charge, which currently in the United States is 8 cents per coupon. Herein rests the potential for misredemption: An unscrupulous person could earn $1.08 from redeeming a coupon that has a face value of $1. One thousand such misredeemed coupons would produce earnings of $1,080. Exacerbating the potential for misredemption is the fact that many coupons now have face values worth $1 or more.

The Consequences

Estimates of the misredemption rate range from a low of 15 percent to a high of 40 percent. Many brand managers have assumed a 20 to 25 percent rate of misredemption when budgeting for coupon events. However, it is likely that past estimates of coupon misredemption have been inflated; it now appears that fraudulent coupon redemption is, on average, closer to 3 or 4 percent rather than the 20 to 25 percent assumed previously.[49] Although imposing tighter controls at all stages of the coupon redemption process has reduced the magnitude of misredemption, a 3 to 4 percent misredemption level nevertheless represents millions of dollars lost by manufacturers.

The Participants

How does misredemption occur and who participates in it? Misredemption occurs at every level of the redemption process. Sometimes *individual consumers* present coupons that have expired, coupons for items not purchased, or coupons for a smaller-sized product than that specified by the coupon. Consumers also on occasion electronically alter the barcodes on computer-generated coupons to receive larger discounts than coupon-offering manufacturers intended.

Some *clerks* take coupons to the store and exchange them for cash without making a purchase. At the store level, *retailer managers* may boost profits by submitting extra coupons in addition to those redeemed legitimately. A dishonest retailer can buy coupons on the black market, age them in a clothes dryer (or even in a cement mixer) so that they appear to have been handled by actual consumers, combine them with legitimate coupons, and then mail in the batch for redemption. In fact, this happened in the case of 53 independent grocers who had fraudulently cashed in $1 million from submitting aged coupons stolen from newspapers that were discovered with narcotics by Miami police in 1986. U.S. Postal Inspectors (with the help of a clearinghouse) devised a fake coupon, "Broach" bug spray, to help catch the retailers.[50]

Shady *clearinghouses* engage in misredemption by combining illegally purchased coupons with real ones and certifying the batch as legitimate. Texas-based International Outsourcing Services, the largest coupon clearinghouse in the United States, was indicted in federal court in 2007 for allegedly defrauding CPG companies in the amount of $250 million over a

Courtesy of United Postal Service

nine-year period.[51] In another case of clearinghouse fraud, the branch manager of International Data's Memphis office was convicted in 2004 for defrauding companies of more than $50 million.[52]

Perhaps the major source of coupon misredemption is large-scale *professional misredeemers* (see *path M*, standing for misredemption, in Figure 19.3). These professional misredeemers either: (1) recruit the services of actual retailers to serve as conduits through which coupons are misredeemed or (2) operate phony businesses that exist solely for the purpose of redeeming huge quantities of illegal coupons. Illegal coupons typically are obtained by removing FSIs from Sunday newspapers.

The following examples illustrate organized misredemption efforts. The proprietor of Wadsworth Thriftway store in Philadelphia illegally submitted in excess of 1.5 million coupons valued at more than $800,000.[53] The top three executives of the Sloan's Supermarket in New York were indicted for their role in a 20-year operation that led to $3.5 million in coupon misredemption.[54] Another Philadelphian acted as a liaison between charities, from which he purchased coupons in bulk, and a supermarket employee, who submitted them for repayment by manufacturers or their redemption centers. The middleman earned $200,000 from the couponing scam before he was arrested.[55] Five operators of Shop n' Bag supermarkets in Philadelphia bought nearly 12 million coupons for only 20 to 30 percent of their face value and then redeemed them prior to being arrested.[56] And finally, according to the *New York Post*, Mideastern terrorists misredeemed perhaps up to $100 million by funneling illegally redeemed coupons through minimarts and Hispanic bodegas.[57]

The Role of Promotion Agencies

As discussed in Chapter 7, brand managers typically employ advertising agencies to create advertising messages, buy advertising media, and perform other services related to a brand's advertising function. Although less known than their ad agency counterparts, brand managers also hire specialized promotion agencies to help formulate promotion strategies and implement tactical programs.

Assume, for example, that a brand manager believes that a new brand needs to be sampled in trial-sized bottles to facilitate high levels of trial-purchase behavior. The promotion also will include coupons in the box containing the trial-size sample. Further, an introductory advertising campaign in magazines will include an attractive sweepstakes offer to draw attention to the ad and enhance consumer involvement with the brand. The brand manager determines that it will be best to use the services of a promotion agency that can expertly design a sampling program that efficiently targets sample distribution to young consumers and a sweepstakes program that would appeal to this age group.

The Rise of the Online Promotion Agency

In addition to conventional promotion agencies, which traditionally have emphasized programs using off-line media and in-store distribution, there is a new generation of promotion agencies that emphasize online promotions. The Internet has become an increasingly important venue for conducting promotions. (See *Promo* magazine's Sourcebook for a listing of these at http://directory.promomagazine.com, including AMP, Inmar, Market Resources, Inc., and Ventura Associates.) Coupons, sweepstakes offers, online promotional games, free sample offerings, and online continuity programs are just some of the promotions that are virtually ubiquitous online. These programs are effective because they enable marketers to target promotions to preferred consumers, to deliver the programs relatively inexpensively, and to measure results with greater precision than what is possible with other marketing programs. Promotion agencies are a valuable resource for brand managers in both planning strategically sound promotions and carrying through their implementation.

Summary

This chapter focused on consumer-oriented promotions. The many sales promotion tools available to marketers are classified in terms of whether the reward offered to consumers is immediate or delayed and whether the manufacturer's objective is to achieve trial impact, encourage repeat purchases, or reinforce brand images. Then, specific sales promotion techniques are classified as falling into one of six general categories (see Table 19.1).

The first and most critical requirement for a successful sales promotion is that it be based on clearly defined objectives. Second, the program must be designed with a specific target market in mind. It should also be realized that many consumers, perhaps most, desire to maximize the rewards gained from participating in a promotion while minimizing the amount of time and effort invested. Consequently, an effective promotion, from a consumer-response perspective, must make it relatively easy for consumers to obtain their rewards, and the size of the reward must be sufficient to justify the consumers' efforts. A third essential ingredient for effective sales promotions is that programs must be developed with the interests of retailers in mind—not just those of the manufacturer.

The bulk of the chapter was devoted to two of the major forms of consumer-oriented sales promotions: sampling and couponing. It was pointed out that sampling is the premier promotion for generating trial usage of a new brand. The various methods of distributing samples were presented, and it was emphasized that regardless of distribution method, three practices are necessary for sampling success: (1) targeting rather than mass distributing samples, (2) using innovative distribution methods where appropriate, and (3) undertaking efforts to measure sampling's return on investment. The specific circumstances when sampling is appropriately used were discussed, and various problems with sampling were identified.

The second major type of promotion, couponing, was described in terms of the magnitude of usage and types of distribution methods (via free standing inserts [FSIs], direct mail, optical scanners, at the point of purchase, mobile phones, online, etc.). The growing role of online couponing was identified. A major section described the coupon-redemption process and in this context discussed the act of coupon misredemption.

Discussion Questions

1. Why are immediate (versus delayed) rewards more effective in inducing the consumer behaviors a brand marketer desires? Use a specific, concrete illustration from your own experience to support your answer.

2. One of the major trends in product sampling is selective sampling of targeted groups. Assume you work for a company that has just developed a candy bar that tastes almost as good as other candy bars but has far fewer calories. Marketing research has identified the target market as economically upscale consumers, ages primarily 25 to 54, who reside in suburban and urban areas. Explain specifically how you might selectively sample your new product to approximately two million such consumers.

3. Compare and contrast sampling and media-delivered coupons in terms of objectives, consumer impact, and overall roles in marketing communications strategies.

4. A packaged goods company plans to introduce a new bath soap that differs from competitive soaps by virtue of a distinct new fragrance. Should sampling be used to introduce the product?

5. A manufacturer of golf balls introduced a new brand that supposedly delivered greater distance than competitively priced balls. However, in accordance with restrictions the governing body that regulates golf balls and other golfing equipment and accessories established, this new ball when struck by a driver travels on average only a couple of yards farther than competitive brands. The manufacturer identified a list of three million golfers and mailed a single golf ball to each. In view of what you have learned about sampling in this chapter, comment on the advisability of this sampling program.

6. Present your personal views concerning the number of coupons distributed annually in the United States. Is widespread couponing in the best interest of consumers?

7. Rather than offering discounts in the form of coupons, why don't brand managers simply reduce the prices of their brands?

8. Using Table 19.3 as a rough guide, calculate the full cost per redeemed coupon given the following facts: (1) face value = 75 cents, (2) 20 million coupons distributed at $7 per thousand, (3) redemption rate = 3 percent, (4) handling cost = 8 cents, and (5) misredemption rate = 5 percent.

9. Go through a Sunday newspaper and select three FSIs. Analyze each in terms of what you think are the marketer's objectives in using this particular promotion. Do not restrict your chosen FSIs to just those offering coupons.

10. Assume you are brand manager of Mountain State Bottled Water. This new brand competes in a product category with several well-known brands. Your

marketing communications objective is to generate trial purchases among predominantly younger and better-educated consumers. Propose a promotion that would accomplish this objective. Assume that your promotion is purely experimental and that it will be undertaken in a small city of just 250,000 people. Also assume that: (1) you cannot afford product sampling; (2) you will not advertise the promotion; and (3) your budget for this experimental promotion is $5,000. What would you do?

11. Describe your recent experiences with either group coupons (e.g., Groupon, Living Social) or mobile phone coupons. (Consult a friend if needed.) Have these technological changes helped spark your interest in couponing? The brands or services purchased? Discuss any problems experienced with the new methods.

12. A concluding section of the chapter indicated that promotion agencies have become an increasingly important resource for brand managers in planning and executing promotional programs. One could argue that the fees brand managers pay for the services of promotion agencies might better be spent elsewhere—for example, on increased advertising levels. Present arguments both in favor of and in opposition to hiring promotion agencies.

End Notes

1. Although the following discussion is based mostly on the first author's prior writing and thinking on the topic, these points are influenced by descriptions obtained from various practitioners.

2. Pierre Chandon, Brian Wansink, and Gilles Laurent, "A Benefit Congruency Framework of Sales Promotion Effectiveness," *Journal of Marketing* 64 (October 2000), 65–81. The following discussion of benefits is based on a typology provided by these authors. See their Table 1 on pages 68–69.

3. The idea that consumer promotions perform an informational role receives prominent attention in Priya Raghubir, J. Jeffrey Inman, and Hans Grande, "The Three Faces of Consumer Promotions," *California Management Review* 46 (summer 2004), 23–42.

4. "Secret Weapon," *Promo*, December 2007, 44.

5. Jack Neff, "Viva Viva! K-C Boosts Brand's Marketing," *Advertising Age*, June 11, 2007, 4, 41.

6. Sarah Ellison and Carlos Tehada, "Young Couples Starting Out Are Every Marketer's Dream," *Wall Street Journal Online*, January 30, 2003, http://online.wsj.com.

7. For an interesting study of food sampling in grocery stores, see Stephen M. Nowlis and Baba Shiv, "The Influence of Consumer Distractions on the Effectiveness of Food-Sampling Programs," *Journal of Marketing Research* 42 (May 2005), 157–68.

8. Gabriella Stern, "With Sampling, There is Too a Free Lunch," *Wall Street Journal*, March 11, 1994, B1, B6.

9. Kate MacArthur, "Give It Away: Fast Feeders Favor Freebies," *Advertising Age*, June 18, 2007, 10.

10. Dan Hanover, "We Deliver," *Promo*, March 2001, 43–45.

11. Brian Quinton, "V-8 Fusion Opts for Facebook as Sampling Channel," *Promo*, July 22, 2010, http://chiefmarketer.com/networks/v-8-fusion-opts-facebook-sampling-channel.

12. "Sampling Wins Over More Marketers," *Advertising Age*, July 27, 1992, 12.

13. Lafayette Jones, "A Case for Ethnic Sampling," *Promo*, October 2000, 41–42.

14. David Vaczek, "Points of Switch," *Promo*, September 1998, 39–40.

15. Patricia Odell, "Firsthand Experience," *Promo*, May 2007, 19.

16. Betsy Spethmann, "Branded Moments," *Promo*, September 2000, 83–98.

17. Lorin Cipolla, "Instant Gratification," *Promo*, April 2004, AR35.

18. Amy Johannes, "Room Service," *Promo*, February 2008, 38–40.

19. Jack Neff, "P&G Brings Potty to Parties," *Advertising Age*, February 17, 2003, 22.

20. Glenn Heitsmith, "Gaining Trial," *Promo*, September 1994, 108; and "Spend a Little, Get a Lot," *Trial and Conversion III: Harnessing the Power of Sampling Special Advertising Supplement,* New York: Promotional Marketing Association, Inc., 1996–1997, 18.

21. Charles Fredericks, Jr., "What Ogilvy & Mather Has Learned about Sales Promotion," *The Tools of Promotion*, New York: Association of National Advertisers, 1975. Although this is an older source, the wisdom still holds true today.

22. Lynn G. Reiling, "Consumers Misuse Mass Sampling for Sun Light Dishwashing Liquid," *Marketing News*, September 3, 1982, 1, 2.

23. Maciek Gajewski, "Samples: A Steal in Poland," *Advertising Age*, November 4, 1991, 54.

24. Different organizations arrive at varying estimates of actual coupon distribution numbers. For example, see "NCH Annual Topline, U.S. CPG Coupon Facts Report For Year-End 2011," January 2012, 3.

25. This estimate is based on 3.5 billion coupons redeemed in 2011 times and average face value of $1.54. See "NCH Annual Topline, U.S. CPG Coupon Facts Report For Year-End 2011," 9, 13.

26. Jack Neff, "Coupons are Hot, But are They a Bargain for Brands?" *Advertising Age*, July 11, 2011, 10; and Peter Meyers, "Coupons to the Rescue," *Promo*, April 2008, 63.

27. Donald R. Lichtenstein, Richard G. Netemeyer, and Scot Burton, "Distinguishing Coupon Proneness from Value Consciousness: An Acquisition-Transaction Utility Theory Perspective," *Journal of Marketing* 54 (July 1990), 54–67. For a detailed treatment of factors that influence consumers' coupon-redemption behavior, see also Banwari Mittal, "An Integrated Framework for Relating Diverse Consumer Characteristics to Supermarket Coupon Redemption," *Journal of Marketing Research* 31 (November 1994), 533–44. See also Judith A. Garretson and Scot Burton, "Highly Coupon and Sales Prone Consumers: Benefits beyond Price Savings," *Journal of Advertising Research* 43 (June 2003), 162–72.

28. "NCH Annual Topline, U.S. CPG Coupon Facts Report For Year-End 2011," 8.

29. Ibid.

30. "Coupons are Hot, But are They a Bargain for Brands?" 10; and Kapil Bawa and Robert W. Shoemaker, "The Effects of a Direct Mail Coupon on Brand Choice Behavior," *Journal of Marketing Research* 24 (November 1987), 370–76.

31. "NCH Annual Topline, U.S. CPG Coupon Facts Report For Year-End 2011," 17.

32. "Checkout: Instant Results," *Promo*, October 1998, 75.

33. Kapil Bawa, Srini S. Srinivasan, and Rajendra K. Srivastava, "Coupon Attractiveness and Coupon Proneness: A Framework for Modeling Coupon Redemption," *Journal of Marketing Research* 34 (November 1997), 517–525.

34. Priya Raghubir, "Coupon Value: A Signal for Price?" *Journal of Marketing Research* 35 (August 1998), 316–24.

35. "NCH Annual Topline, U.S. CPG Coupon Facts Report For Year-End 2011," 17; and Russ Bowman and Paul Theroux, *Promotion Marketing*, Stamford, Conn.: Intertec Publishing Corporation, 2000, 24.

36. Bowman and Theroux, Ibid.

37. "When the Chips Are Down," *Promo Magazine Special Report*, April 1998, S7.

38. Deena Amato-McCoy, "Four Technologies to Watch in 2012," Grocery Headquarters, January 4, 2012, http://www.groceryheadquarters.com/2012/01/four-technologies-to-watch-in-2012; "How Retailers Like Starbucks are Using QR Codes ad Mobile Coupons," TXTin (blog), March 27, 2011, http://txtin.com/news/how-retailers-like-starbucks-are-using-qr-codes-and-mobile-coupons; and Alice Z. Cuneo, "Package-goods Giants Roll Out Mobile Coupons," *Advertising Age*, March 10, 2008, 3, 26.

39. "NCH Annual Topline, U.S. CPG Coupon Facts Report For Year-End 2011," 17.

40. Kapil Bawa and Robert W. Shoemaker, "Analyzing Incremental Sales from a Direct Mail Coupon Promotion," *Journal of Marketing Research* 53 (July 1989), 66–78.

41. Erwin Ephron, "More Weeks, Less Weight: The Shelf-Space Model of Advertising," *Journal of Advertising Research* 35 (May/June 1995), 18–23.

42. Srini S. Srinivasan, Robert P. Leone, and Francis J. Mulhern, "The Advertising Exposure Effect of Free Standing Inserts," *Journal of Advertising* 24 (spring 1995), 29–40.

43. France Leclerc and John D. C. Little, "Can Advertising Copy Make FSI Coupons More Effective?" *Journal of Marketing Research* 34 (November 1997), 473–84.

44. "NCH Annual Topline, U.S. CPG Coupon Facts Report For Year-End 2011," 17.

45. For a technical analysis of the role of crossruffing, see Sanjay K. Dhar and Jagmohan S. Raju, "The Effects of Cross-Ruff Coupons on Sales and Profits," *Marketing Science* 44 (November 1998), 1501–16.

46. "NCH Annual Topline, U.S. CPG Coupon Facts Report For Year-End 2011," 17.

47. Karen Holt, "Coupon Crimes," *Promo*, April 2004, 23–26, 70; and Jack Neff, "Internet Enabling Coupon Fraud Biz," *Advertising Age*, October 20, 2003, 3.

48. Ron Dicker, "The Most Expensive Groupon? The One You Forget to Redeem," *AOL Daily Finance*, October 22, 2011, http://www.dailyfinance.com/2011/10/22/the-most-expensive-groupon-the-one-you-forget-to-redeem.

49. "A Drop in the Crime Rate," *Promo*, December 1997, 12.

50. Arnold Markowitz, "Police Invitation Nets 53 Suspects in Coupon-Cashing Fraud Scheme," *Miami Herald*, March 13, 1986, 1A, 20A.

51. Jack Neff, "Package-goods Players Just Can't Quit Coupons," *Advertising Age*, May 14, 2007, 8.

52. "Pushing Back the Tide," *Promo*, April 2006, 81.

53. Cecelia Blalock, "Another Retailer Nabbed in Coupon Misredemption Plot," *Promo*, December 1993, 38.

54. Ibid.

55. Cecelia Blalock, "Tough Sentence for Coupon Middle Man," *Promo*, June 1993, 87.

56. "Clipped, Supermarket Owners Charged with Coupon Fraud," *Promo*, May 1997, 14.

57. "Report: Coupon Scams Are Funding Terrorism," *Promo*, August 1996, 50. This issue was also the subject of testimony before the Senate Judiciary Technology, Terrorism, and Government Information Subcommittee, February 24, 1998.

CHAPTER 20

Consumer Sales Promotion: Premiums and Other Promotions

Whopper Sacrifice: Is an Online Premium Offer Worth 10 Friends?

One of the most talked about, creative, and quirky online premium offers in years was Burger King's "Whopper Sacrifice" developed by the Crispin, Porter + Bogusky ad agency. To earn an "Angry Whopper," visitors to the Whopper Sacrifice Facebook app had to "defriend" 10 Facebook friends to receive a coupon for the offer. In just a week, the Whopper Sacrifice app generated 25,000 coupons with 234,000 friends removed from Facebook user pages. As the Angry Whopper retail price was $3.69, customers were trading each deleted friend for 37 cents worth of a burger and bun.

One student with more than 200 Facebook friends remarked, "It's a good excuse to get rid of old girlfriends and their families on my account and get a Whopper

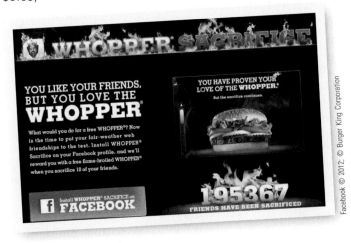

out of it." Yet, in a follow-up e-mail, the student admitted that it was hard defriending people, and that he got stuck at seven. He started questioning, "Do I like one-tenth of a Whopper more than the information these people could one day post on Facebook?"

The Whopper Sacrifice premium offer process worked as follows. First, the Facebook user would go the Whopper Sacrifice Facebook app site that would show 10 of their friends and ask them to "click on a friend to begin the sacrifice." Once a user would click on a friend, the app responded with "watch the sacrifice" and then showed a picture of their friend being burned. The user is then told, "You liked (your friend). You love the Whopper." (At this point, the friend is told

1 Understand the role of premiums, the types of premiums, and the developments in premium practice.

2 Recognize the role of price-off promotions and bonus packages.

3 Be aware of the role of rebates and refund offers.

4 Know the differences among sweepstakes, contests, and games, and the reasons for using each form of promotion.

5 Understand the role of continuity promotions.

6 Appreciate retailer-driven promotions.

7 Evaluate the potential effectiveness of sales promotion ideas, and appraise the effectiveness of completed promotional programs.

in the news feed that the user defriended them for a Whopper.) When the user reached 10 people defriended, they received an online coupon for the Angry Whooper.

Burger King relied on viral distribution and did not consult Facebook with this unique premium offer. Unfortunately, because Facebook explicitly says it will not inform users about friend removal, Facebook disabled the Whopper Sacrifice page after only a week. However, this was not before the 25,000 Angry Whopper coupons were requested with user contact information, as well as enormous buzz and press, making Whopper Sacrifice an extremely "successful" online premium offer for Burger King.

Crispin, Porter + Bogusky has been behind other quirky, yet successful stunts for Burger King, including the BK King; "Flame," a hamburger-scented body spray; "Whopper Virgins," a series of blind taste tests between the BK Whopper and McDonald's Big Mac in Romania and Thailand; and "Whopper Freakout," in which certain BK restaurants removed the Whopper from their menus and videotaped consumer responses for commercials. No doubt, the quirky Whopper Sacrifice offer was "successful" due to its viral nature and publicity value. Yet, the contact information provided (including Facebook "likes") can be invaluable for further database and marketing efforts. As such, creative sales promotions can work as fully integrated marketing communication programs for the brand.

Sources: Jenna Wortham, "The Value of a Facebook Friend? About 37 Cents," *New York Times* (blog), January 9, 2009, http://bits.blogs. nytimes.com/2009/01/09/are-facebook-friends-worth-their-weight-in-beef; and Brian Morrissey, "Whopper Sacrifice Ends," *Adweek*, January 15, 2009, http://www.adweek.com/news/technology/whopper-sacrifice-ends-98062.

Introduction

This chapter picks up where Chapter 19 left off and discusses major forms of consumer-oriented promotions other than sampling and couponing. To frame the subsequent discussion again, Table 19.1 is repeated in this chapter as Table 20.1.

The presentation proceeds as follows: first discussed is the use of product *premiums* (cells 2, 3, and 6 in Table 20.1); second, *price-off promotions* (cell 3); third, *bonus packs* (cell 3); fourth, *games* (cell 3); fifth, *rebates and refunds* (cell 4); sixth, *continuity programs* (cell 4); and seventh, *sweepstakes and contests* (cell 6). Three additional topics will follow the discussion of specific promotional tools: (1) overlay and tie-in promotions, (2) retailer-driven promotions, and (3) techniques for evaluating sales promotion ideas and conducting postmortem analyses.

It is important to emphasize again that each of the various promotional techniques covered in this chapter performs a unique role and is therefore appropriately used to achieve limited objectives. This chapter conveys each tool's role and identifies, where appropriate, unique limitations or problems associated with using each tool. It will be useful to review Table 20.1 before studying the various types of promotions.

Premiums

Broadly defined, premiums are articles of merchandise or services (e.g., travel) manufacturers offer as a form of gift to *induce action* on the part of consumers and possibly also retailers and the sales force. Our focus in this chapter is on premiums' consumer-oriented role. Premiums represent a versatile promotional tool and—depending on the type of premium offer—are able to generate trial purchases, encourage repeat purchasing, and reinforce brand images. Brand

TABLE 20.1	**Major Consumer-Oriented Promotions**		
	Brand Management Objective		
Consumer Reward	**Generating Trial and Retrial**	**Encouraging Repeat Purchases**	**Reinforcing Brand Image**
Immediate	**Cell 1** • Samples (19*) • Instant coupons (19) • Shelf-delivered coupons (19) • Mobile phone coupons (19)	**Cell 3** • Price-offs (20) • Bonus packs (20) • In-, on-, and near-pack premiums (20) • Games (20)	**Cell 5** (No Promotions Match Cell 5's Conditions)
Delayed	**Cell 2** • Scanner-delivered coupons (19) • Media- and mail-delivered coupons (19) • Online coupons (19) • Social (group) coupons (19) • Mail-in and online premiums (20) • Bounce-back coupons (19) • Free-with-purchase premiums (20)	**Cell 4** • In- and on-pack coupons (19) • Rebates and refunds (20) • Continuity programs (20)	**Cell 6** • Self-liquidating premiums (20) • Sweepstakes and contests (20)

© Cengage Learning 2013

*Indicates the chapter, either Chapter 19 or 20, in which this form of sales promotion is covered.

managers' major reasons for providing premiums are to increase consumer brand loyalty and to motivate new purchases.[1]

Brand managers use several forms of premium offers to motivate desired consumer behaviors: (1) free-with-purchase premiums; (2) mail-in and online offers; (3) in-, on-, and near-pack premiums; and (4) self-liquidating offers. These forms of premiums perform somewhat different objectives. Free-with-purchase, mail-in, and online offers are useful primarily for generating brand *trial* or *retrial*. In-, on-, and near-pack premiums serve *customer-holding purposes* by rewarding present consumers for continuing to purchase a liked or preferred brand. And self-liquidators perform primarily a *image-reinforcement* function, yet also can serve a *customer-holding* purpose.

Free-with-Purchase Premiums

Both marketers of durable goods and consumer packaged goods (CPG) brands provide free-with-purchase premiums (also called *free-gift-with-purchase premiums*). As shown in Table 20.1, this form of premium typically represents a delayed reward to consumers that is primarily designed to generate *trial purchases*. Examples of this type of free-with-purchase premium include an offer from Michelin to receive a $100-retail-value emergency roadside kit with the purchase of four Michelin tires. Recently, Michelin provided a $100 credit card for a purchase of four Michelin tires. Volkswagen gave away Apple iPods with purchases of New Beetle automobiles. Sun City, a nationwide developer of homes for retirees, offered a free golf cart to people who purchased a new home within 18 days from receiving the offer. Attractive premiums such as these might motivate indecisive consumers to purchase the premium-offering item rather than a competitive option.

Research has shown that the perceived value of a premium item, or gift, depends on the *value of the brand that is offering the gift*. In particular, the identical item was perceived to be of lower value when it was offered as a free gift by a lower- versus higher-priced brand.[2] This finding buttresses the point made in the previous chapter that sales promotions perform an *informational role* in addition to utilitarian and hedonic functions. This is to say that sales promotions provide signaling information consumers use to judge product quality and value. An important implication of this finding is that brands used as gift items must be cautious that their images are not damaged by the sponsoring brand. The adage "Beware of the company you keep" is as applicable in the premium-partners context as it is in social relations.

Mail-In and Online Offers

By definition, mail-in and online offers are premiums in which consumers receive a free item from the sponsoring manufacturer in the mail or online in return for submitting a required number of proofs of purchase or taking some action related to the brand. As shown in Table 20.1, this form of premium represents a *delayed* reward to consumers that is primarily designed to generate *trial purchases* (cell 2).

For example, Kellogg's brand of Smart Start cereal urged consumers to mail in for a free cholesterol and wellness kit, and its Frosted Flakes brand offered a children's book by mail with the purchase of two Kellogg's cereals (see Figure 20.1). Nestle's brand of Nesquik chocolate milk offered a free zip-up hoodie to consumers who provided six UPC bar codes from Nesquik items along with $6.99 for handling and shipping. Colgate-Palmolive offered a free SpongeBob powered toothbrush to those families that (1) purchased a regular Colgate toothbrush and (2) provided evidence of their child having visited a dentist. As noted in the *Marcom Insight*, Burger King offered a free Whopper with an online coupon if Facebook users "defriended" 10 of their friends on Facebook.

FIGURE 20.1 Illustration of a Mail-In Premium

GLOBAL FOCUS

Barq's Root Beer, Elvis, and Russian Knickknacks

Barq's root beer is a regional soft drink brand that was founded in New Orleans. Nearly a hundred years after its founding, Barq's remained a small-share brand with a limited advertising and promotion budget. In the early 1990s, Barq's decided to promote the brand in commemoration of the fifteenth anniversary of Elvis Presley's death. Barq's vice president of marketing thought up a great premium idea that would involve purchasing an old Cadillac that Elvis had owned, cutting it into thousands of small pieces, and offering each piece to a different consumer as part of a mail-in premium requiring multiple proofs of purchase of Barq's root beer. There was only one problem with this premium idea: The administrators of the Presley estate demanded a $1 million licensing fee, which exceeded tenfold Barq's budget for the promotion.

Unable to afford this, Barq's marketing vice president scrambled to find a replacement. Just about this time, the Soviet government collapsed. Seeing the news on TV, the vice president hit immediately on the idea of a replacement for the failed Elvis promotion: "The Soviet Union Going Out of Business Sale." Mind you, this had all taken place within a month or less—decision making on

the run, so to speak. With a meager $70,000 in his possession, Rick Hill, Barq's marketing vice president, boarded a plane to Russia to purchase ex–Soviet Union memorabilia. Unable to find legitimate businesspeople from whom to purchase ex-Soviet items, Hill turned to members of the Soviet Mafia. Within two weeks he spent the $70,000 acquiring 4,000 pounds of ex-Soviet stuff (Russian nesting dolls, Lenin Day pins, military medals, etc.) that was shipped back to the United States.

Barq's offered one randomly chosen Soviet knickknack with a 12-pack proof of purchase and 50 cents postage and handling charge. This last-minute, desperate promotion achieved incredible results: 5 percent of all consumers eligible for the promotion actually took advantage of it, and sales increased 30 percent versus the comparable period the previous year. This mail-in premium promotion also received the industry's top promotion award for the year. The moral of the story: A creative promotion that is of high topical interest and captures the public's imagination can be extremely successful.

Source: Adapted from Rod Taylor, "From Russia with Root Beer," *Promo*, June 2003, 143–44.

Perhaps as few as 2 to 4 percent of consumers who are exposed to free mail-in offers actually take advantage of these opportunities. However, mail-in premiums can be effective if the premium item is appealing to the target market. (See the *Global Focus* insert for a really clever promotion that used a mail-in premium.)

In-, On-, and Near-Pack Premiums

In- and on-pack premiums offer a free item inside or attached to a package or make the package itself the premium item. In general, in- and on-package premiums offer consumers *immediate value* and thereby encourage increased product consumption from consumers who like or prefer the premium-offering brand (see Table 20.1, cell 3).

For example, Colgate toothpaste sometimes attaches a free Colgate toothbrush to the package, and Pantene shampoo is occasionally packaged with a unit of free Pantene conditioner. Ford Motor Company, in conjunction with Target stores and various brands of Kellogg's cereal (Froot Loops, Apple Jacks, Frosted Flakes, and Cocoa Krispies), promoted its Fusion automobile by placing 600,000 toy Fusions into these cereal boxes. Among these 600,000 toy cars was one red model affixed with the Target logo. The person buying that particular box won a real Fusion. In a similar promotion, Ralston Purina offered tiny sports car models in about 11 million boxes of six cereal brands. Ten of these

boxes contained scale-model red Corvettes. Lucky consumers turned in the models for real Corvettes.

Near-pack premiums provide the retail trade with specially displayed premium pieces that retailers then give to consumers who purchase the promoted product. Near-pack premiums are less expensive because additional packaging is not required. Furthermore, near-pack premiums can build sales volume in stores that put up displays and participate fully.

The Special Case of "Buy X, Get 1 Free" Offers

One of the most frequent promotions CPG companies use is the "Buy X, Get 1 Free" ("BOGO") offer—where X stands for 1, 2, 3, or sometimes even 4 purchases that are needed to receive a free gift. The "gift" in this case is another unit of the same brand that is conducting the promotion or a unit of a different brand. For example, to promote their new breakfast menu, Subway offered a buy one sub sandwich and get one free before 9am in the month of April (Buy 1, Get 1 Free). Crunch Crisp candy wafers ran a Buy 2 Get 1 Free promotion. Also in the candy category, M&M's had a Buy Any 3, Get Any 1 Free offer for the consumer to buy any three of M&M's brands (e.g., M&M's, Twix, 3 Musketeers, Snickers), and receive a free M&M's candy of choice. Little Debbie, a maker of sugar-based snack items, offered a free box of any type of Little Debbie snack (e.g., Honey Buns, Oatmeal Creme Pies) when purchasing four boxes of any type of Little Debbie snack (Buy 4, Get 1 Free).

The Buy X, Get 1 Free form of premium represents an *immediate reward* to consumers, and, for manufacturers, this type of premium serves the purpose primarily of *rewarding a brand's loyal customers* or *encouraging trial* from purchasers of competitive brands who are willing to switch in order to save money—availing oneself of a Buy 1, Get 1 Free offer is tantamount to paying half price for each unit. Unlike other forms of premiums, which typically generate relatively low levels of consumer response, Buy X and Get 1 Free promotions are received heartily by consumers due to the immediacy of the reward and the attractive savings.

Self-Liquidating Offers

The name self-liquidating offers (known as SLOs by practitioners) reflects that the consumer mails in a stipulated number of proofs of purchase along with sufficient money to cover the manufacturer's purchasing, handling, and mailing costs of the premium item. In other words, consumers pay for the actual cost (not retail price) of the premium; from the manufacturer's perspective the item is *cost-free*, or, in other words, *self-liquidating*. Attractive self-liquidating premiums can serve to enhance a brand's image (see cell 6 in Table 20.1)—by associating the brand with a positively valued premium item—and also can encourage repeat purchasing by requiring multiple proofs of purchase to be eligible for the premium offer. Brand managers often use SLOs as a complement to sweepstakes offers. The combination of these two promotions enhances consumer interest in and interaction with the brand.

Gerber employed an SLO promotion when offering the Gerber Keepsake Millennium Cup. With 12 Gerber baby food proofs of purchase and $8.95, consumers received a cup engraved with their child's name and birth date. This item at retail likely would have sold for around $25. Gerber projected that many parents would purchase Gerber products exclusively until they acquired the requisite number of proofs of purchase.

It is noteworthy that very few consumers ever send for a premium. Companies expect only 0.1 percent of self-liquidators to be redeemed. A circulation of 20 million, for example, would be expected to produce only about 20,000 redemptions. Industry specialists generally concur that the most important consideration in

A Super-Successful Self-Liquidating Premium Promotion

Consumer goods giant Nabisco needed an exciting promotion that would enhance the image of its various brands among consumers and encourage retailers to provide special display space that would substantially increase sales volume. One of Nabisco's managers came up with the brilliant idea of using autographed baseball trading cards as a self-liquidating premium offer, or SLO. Trading cards are the most popular sports collectible in the United States, and thousands of people are willing to pay $50 or more to have the autograph of famous athletes signed to a trading card. In fact, sports autographs represent a half-billion-dollar business each year in the United States.

The SLO developed by Nabisco executives and its promotion agency was straightforward: Interested consumers were required to mail in two proofs of purchases of any of several Nabisco brands (Oreos, Chips Ahoy, Wheat Thins, and Ritz Crackers) along with $5 and they could get their pick of autographed cards from a lineup of famous Hall of Fame baseball players (Ernie Banks, Bob Gibson, Brooks Robinson, Willie Stargell, etc.). This was an incredible deal for consumers, considering autographed cards from these players now are worth over six times the $5 cost.

Interestingly, Nabisco paid these Hall of Fame baseball players $2 for each signed card. However, Nabisco requested 90,000 cards per player, which thus provided them with $220,000 in income—a huge signing task indeed, but one that most people would gladly undertake for earning over $200,000! To assure that the signed cards contained authentic signatures from the player depicted on the card, participants to the promotion received a certificate of authenticity, which partially explains why the cards have increased six times in value.

At a $5 charge for each card, Nabisco was able to self-liquidate the cost of the promotion and to pay for the expense of two promotions that distributed hundreds of thousands of FSI coupons to prospective purchasers of the sponsoring Nabisco brands. The promotion also generated two months of special display space in retail stores for participating Nabisco brands. All in all, this was an extremely successful sales promotion that provided value to consumers and generated increased sales and profits for Nabisco's brands.

Source: Adapted from Rod Taylor, "Signature Event," *Promo*, July 2006, 57–58.

developing a self-liquidating offer is that the premium be appealing to the target audience and represent a meaningful value. It is generally assumed that consumers look for a savings of at least 50 percent of the suggested retail price. The *IMC Focus* insert provides an illustration of a valued and highly successful SLO.

What Makes a Good Premium Offer?

It is undeniable that consumers enjoy gifts, like to receive something for free, and are responsive to offers for premium objects that are attractive and valuable. However, brand managers must be careful to select premiums that are suitable in view of the objectives that are intended to be accomplished during the promotional period. In other words, some forms of premiums serve somewhat different objectives. As always, the choice of premium object and delivery method should be based on an explicit detailing of which objective is to be accomplished. Also, managers must be careful in choosing premium items that are compatible with the brand's image and appropriate for the target market.

Price-Offs

Price-off promotions (also called *cents-off* or *price packs*) entail a reduction (typically ranging from 10 to 25 percent) in a brand's regular price. A price-off is clearly labeled as such on the package. This type of promotion is effective when the marketer's objective is: (1) to reward present brand users; (2) to get consumers to purchase larger quantities of a brand than they normally would (i.e., to load them), thereby effectively preempting the competition; (3) to establish a repeat-purchase pattern after initial trial; (4) to ensure that promotional dollars do, in fact, reach consumers (no such assurance is possible with the trade-allowance promotions covered in Chapter 18); (5) to obtain off-shelf display space when such allowances are offered to retailers; or (6) to provide the sales force with an incentive to obtain retailer support. Although price-off promotions perform multiple objectives, this text classifies price-offs as primarily representing a form of *immediate reward* for consumers to encourage *repeat purchasing* (see cell 3 in Table 20.1).

Price-offs are unable to reverse a brand's downward sales trend, produce a significant number of new users, or attract as many trial users as samples, coupons, or premium packs. Further, *retailers often dislike price-offs* because they create inventory and pricing problems, particularly when a store has a brand in inventory at both the price-off and the regular prices. Yet, despite trade problems, price-offs have strong consumer appeal.

Federal Trade Commission Price-Off Regulations

Manufacturers cannot indiscriminately promote their brands with continuous or near-continuous price-off labeling. To do so would deceive consumers into thinking the brand is on sale when in fact the announced sale price is actually the regular price.

In 1966, the Fair Packaging and Labeling Act was passed by Congress and directed the Federal Trade Commission to establish the following price-off labeling regulations:[3]

1. Price-off labels may only be used on brands already in distribution with established retail prices.
2. There is a limit of three price-off label promotions per year per brand size.
3. There must be a hiatus of at least 30 days between price-off label promotions on any given brand size.
4. No more than 50 percent of a brand's volume over a 12-month period may be generated from price-off label promotions.
5. The manufacturer must provide display materials to announce the price-off label offer.
6. The dealer is required to show the regular shelf price in addition to the new price reflecting the price-off label savings.

Bonus Packs

Bonus packs are extra quantities of a product that a company makes available to consumers at the regular price. Listerine mouthwash provided consumers with a free 250-milliliter bottle along with the purchase of a 1.7-liter bottle. Carnation offered consumers 25 percent more hot cocoa mix at the regular price. Flex-A-Min, a product designed to enhance joint flexibility, offered 33 percent more tablets for free. Electrasol dishwashing powder provided 25 percent more of the product at the regular price. Golf ball manufacturers on occasion reward consumers with an extra sleeve of three balls when they purchase a dozen.

Table 20.1 classifies this form of promotion as providing consumers with an *immediate reward* and, for manufacturers, primarily serving a *repeat purchase* objective (see cell 3). In other words, *present brand users* are the consumers most likely to avail themselves of a bonus offer; hence, receiving a bonus quantity (at no extra price) rewards these consumers for their purchase loyalty and encourages repeat purchasing.

Bonus packs are sometimes used as an *alternative to price-off deals* when the latter are either overused or resisted by the trade. The extra value offered to the consumer is readily apparent and for that reason can be effective in *loading current users* and thereby removing them from the market—a defensive tactic that is used against aggressive competitors.

Games

Promotional games represent a growing form of promotion that is being increasingly used in lieu of sweepstakes and contests. Games provide consumers with an *instant reward* and, for marketers, serve primarily to encourage *repeat purchasing* from existing brand users (see cell 3 in Table 20.1). Promotional games are capable of creating excitement, stimulating brand interest, and reinforcing brand loyalty. Many varieties of instant-win games are available online. Simply "Google" (instant-win games) and thousands of entries will appear. Playing games online requires that one provide an e-mail address and perhaps additional address information. These games are designed to increase consumer engagement with the sponsoring brand.

One of the many forms of instant-win games is the placement of winning numbers under package lids. Coca-Cola, for example, offered consumers a chance to win $1 million and a role in a movie from Universal Studios, along with thousands of other smaller prizes, if the consumer opened a can containing winning numbers. V8 vegetable juice had a look-under-the-cap contest in which winners received trips to famous resorts. Note that almost invariably, games are marketed with claims of "instant win" because consumers prefer instant gratification.

Avoiding Snafus

Brand managers and the promotion firms they recruit to execute games have to be extremely careful to ensure that a game does not go awry. There have been a number of celebrated snafus in the conduct of promotional games. For example, due to a printing error, 30,000 residents of Roswell, New Mexico, received scratch-off tickets from their local Honda dealer that pronounced each of them a winner of the dealer's $1,000 grand prize. Because the dealer was unable to pay off on the full $30,000,000 liability, the 30,000 "winners" received an apology along with an opportunity to win a $5,000 grand prize or one of twenty $1,000 prizes.[4]

A Pepsi bottler in the Philippines offered a one-million-peso grand prize (which at the time was equivalent to approximately US$36,000) to holders of bottle caps with the number *349* printed on them. To the bottler's (and PepsiCo's) great chagrin, a computer error (by the printer that produced the game numbers) created 500,000 bottle caps with the winning number *349* imprinted—making PepsiCo liable for approximately $18 billion! The botched promotion created mayhem for PepsiCo, including attacks on Pepsi trucks and bottling plants and anti-Pepsi rallies. Pepsi's sales plummeted in the Philippines, and market share fell by nine points. To resolve the problem, PepsiCo paid consumers with winning caps $19 apiece. More than 500,000 Filipinos collected about $10 million. The Filipino justice department excused PepsiCo from criminal liability and dismissed thousands of lawsuits.[5]

The Beatrice Company's Monday Night Football promotion illustrates another failed game. Contestants scratched silver-coated footballs off cards to reveal numbers, hoping to win the prize offered if the numbers on the cards matched the number of touchdowns and field goals scored in the weekly Monday night National Football League game. Game planners intended the chances of getting a match to be infinitesimal. However, to Beatrice's great surprise, a salesperson for rival Procter & Gamble (P&G) put in a claim for a great deal more money than Beatrice had planned on paying out. A computer buff, the salesperson cracked the game code and determined that 320 patterns showed up repeatedly in the cards. By scratching off just one line, he could determine which numbers were underneath the rest. Knowing the actual number of touchdowns and field goals scored on a particular Monday night, he would start scratching cards until winning numbers were located. He enlisted friends to assist in collecting and scratching the cards. Thousands of cards were collected, mostly from Beatrice salespeople. The P&G salesperson and friends identified 4,000 winning cards worth $21 million in prize money! Beatrice discontinued the game and refused to pay up.[6]

This section would be incomplete without discussing a major scandal that rocked the promotions industry in 2001. Brand managers for McDonald's restaurants and Simon Marketing, a company hired to run a summer promotion for McDonald's, created a Monopoly-type game that was to provide customers with millions of dollars in promotional prizes. Unfortunately, there was a major problem in the game's execution. An employee in charge of game security at Simon Marketing allegedly stole winning tickets and distributed them to various friends and accomplices, who obtained approximately $13 million in prize money. After learning of the theft and informing the Federal Bureau of Investigation, McDonald's immediately apologized in national advertising and introduced a different promotional game run by another promotional agency so as to make good on its promise to customers and restore its credibility. Apparently, the Simon Marketing employee who ripped off McDonald's had for several years been stealing winning game tickets from other games.[7]

A spokesperson for the Promotion Marketing Association, the trade association for the industry, characterized this debacle as a "black eye" for the promotion marketing industry. The moral is clear: Promotional games can go awry, and brand managers must go to extreme lengths to protect the integrity of the games that are designed to build, not bust, relationships with customers.

Refunds and Rebates

A refund refers to the practice in which manufacturers give *cash discounts* or reimbursements to consumers who submit proofs of purchase for CPGs (e.g., $5 refund for ten proofs of purchase for Minute Maid orange juice). The rebate (see Figure 20.2) usually refers to a cash reimbursement for purchasing a durable good (e.g., $5,000 refund on a new car). Unlike coupons, which the consumer redeems at retail checkouts, rebates are mailed to manufacturers (or their representatives) with proofs of purchase, and, unlike premiums, the consumer receives a cash reimbursement with a rebate rather than a gift item. Marketers are fond of rebates because they provide an alternative to the use of coupons and stimulate increased consumer purchasing. Rebate offers can reinforce brand loyalty, provide the sales force with something to talk about, and enable the manufacturer to flag the package with a potentially attractive deal.

There are many examples of refunds for CPG companies. For example, Campbell's offered a $5 refund to customers who provided cash register receipts indicating they had bought 10 cans of Campbell's soups and had also purchased a DVD for the movie, *Shrek the Third*. Hartz Ultra Guard (for killing fleas and ticks) offered a $3 refund on that item. For CPG brands, refunds require consumers to acquire slips at retail sites or to go online to designated websites and download appropriate forms. Some evidence indicates that consumers are more responsive to online than off-line (via traditional retail outlets) rebate and refund offers.[8]

Refunds and rebates can help broaden the accessibility of key events that are tied to one's brand. For example, in advance of the 2012 Long Beach Grand Prix Race, specially

© Justin Sullivan/Getty Images

FIGURE 20.2 Illustration of a Rebate Offer

marked packages of Tecate brands offered mail-in refunds worth $100 off two, 3-day race tickets and four 12-packs of Tecate or $10 off a single-day admission with the purchase of a 12-pack. Tecate's purpose was to make the event more affordable for their primary target market (Hispanic consumers in Southern California) and drive traffic to retail stores.[9]

Durable goods companies, especially manufacturers of electronic items, are increasing their use of rebates. Automobile companies are among the major users. For example, General Motors offered a $7,500 rebate on its premium-priced Cadillac XLR.[10] European manufacturers are increasingly using rebates when selling their cars in the United States.

Rebates offer consumers *delayed* rather than immediate value, since the consumer must wait to receive the reimbursement. In using these programs, manufacturers achieve *customer-holding objectives* by encouraging consumers to make multiple purchases (in the case of CPG items) or by rewarding previous users with cash discounts for again purchasing the manufacturer's brand. Rebate offers also can attract switchers from competitive brands who avail themselves of attractive discount offers.

Phantom Discounts

Perhaps the major reason manufacturers are using rebates more now than ever is that many consumers *never bother to redeem them.* Thus, when using rebates, manufacturers get the best of both worlds—they stimulate consumer purchases of rebated items without having to pay out the rebated amount because most consumers do not mail in rebate forms. Hence, rebates can be thought of as a form of *phantom discount.*[11] It is for this reason that some consumer advocates condemn manufacturers' use of rebates.

One may wonder why consumers purchase rebated items but then fail to take the time to submit forms to receive the rebate amount. Academic research offers an explanation. It appears that at the time of brand choice, consumers tend to exaggerate the benefit to be obtained from a rebate relative to the future effort required to redeem a rebate offer.[12] In other words, it seems that many consumers engage in a form of *self-deception* when purchasing rebated merchandise. They find rebate offers attractive and on that basis decide to purchase particular brands. Yet, later on at home, they are unwilling to commit the necessary time and effort to send in rebate forms, or simply forget to do so.

Are manufacturers exploiting consumers when offering rebates, or are consumers to be blamed for their own inaction? This should make for interesting class discussion.

Rebate Fraud

Rebate fraud occurs by manufacturers, retailers, and consumers. Manufacturers commit fraud when promoting rebate offers, but then fail to fulfill them when consumers submit rebate slips with accompanying proof of purchase. Retailers sometimes advertise attractive rebates, but then do not disclose (or disclose only in fine print) that the rebates will not arrive for several months, or that the consumer must purchase another item to be eligible for the rebate. For example, a retail advertisement may claim that a computer has a $400 rebate offer, but neglect to mention that the consumer must sign up for three years of Internet service to receive it.[13]

It is not just marketers that engage in misleading or fraudulent rebating practices. At times, some consumers undertake their own form of rebate-related fraud with bogus claims paid out to "professional" rebaters. Fraud occurs when professionals acquire their own cash registers, generate phony cash-register receipts, and send them on to manufacturers to collect refund checks without making the required product purchases. Other scam artists use computers to design phony UPC symbols, which they mail to manufacturers as evidence of purchases they actually have not made. Of course, these professionals do not send in just single refund requests; rather, they submit requests under multiple names and then have refund checks mailed to different post office boxes.

Two promotions illustrate this fraudulent practice.[14] One manufacturer ran a $3 refund offer requiring submission of a UPC to be eligible for the refund. Three out of four refund requests had the same misprinted UPC number on them. Investigators determined that *Moneytalk*, a former refunding magazine, had misprinted the product's UPC number in one of its issues. In a second case, a manufacturer's rebate forms were available in stores before its product reached store shelves. Nonetheless, this did not deter 2,200 rebate requests from flowing in immediately—all accompanied by bogus cash-register receipts and UPC numbers.

Postal authorities and marketers are taking aggressive efforts to curtail refunding fraud. Many marketers are beginning to state on their refund and rebate forms that they will not send checks to post office boxes. Others are stating that checks will be mailed only to the return address listed on the envelope. Because organized refund redeemers use computers to generate mailing and return address labels, manufacturers are further deterring fraud by stipulating on their refund and rebate forms that printed mailing labels are prohibited.

© 2012 Williams-Sonoma Inc.

FIGURE 20.3 Illustration of a Sweepstakes Offer

© Colin Underhill/Alamy

Sweepstakes and Contests

Sweepstakes and contests are widely used. Although sweepstakes (or sweeps) and contests differ in execution, both offer consumers the opportunity to win cash, merchandise, or travel prizes.

Sweepstakes

In a sweepstakes, winners are determined purely *on the basis of chance.* Accordingly, proofs of purchase *cannot* be required as a condition for entry. Two sweepstake offers are illustrative. A sweep from Pottery Barn (see Figure 20.3) encourages consumers to visit their Hawaii sweepstakes website, text "Hawaii" to a number, or scan their Quick Response (QR) code with a mobile phone to win a six-day trip for four to the island of O'ahu. (Other companies now include 2-D barcodes with promotions that can be scanned to view video demos and other information.)

Another example of a sweepstakes is from BiC razors. This ad (see Figure 20.4) provides a sweepstakes offer for entrants at the BiC Facebook site, the chance to win a 3D TV entertainment system, and other "real guy" prizes. Note that in Figure 20.4 a coupon offer (save $3.00) is provided in addition to the sweepstakes. As described later in this chapter, this form of dual promotion is known as an *overlay* promotion—one promotion "laid" on top of another.

Sweepstakes represent a very popular promotional tool. Approximately three-quarters of packaged-goods marketers use sweepstakes, and nearly one-third of

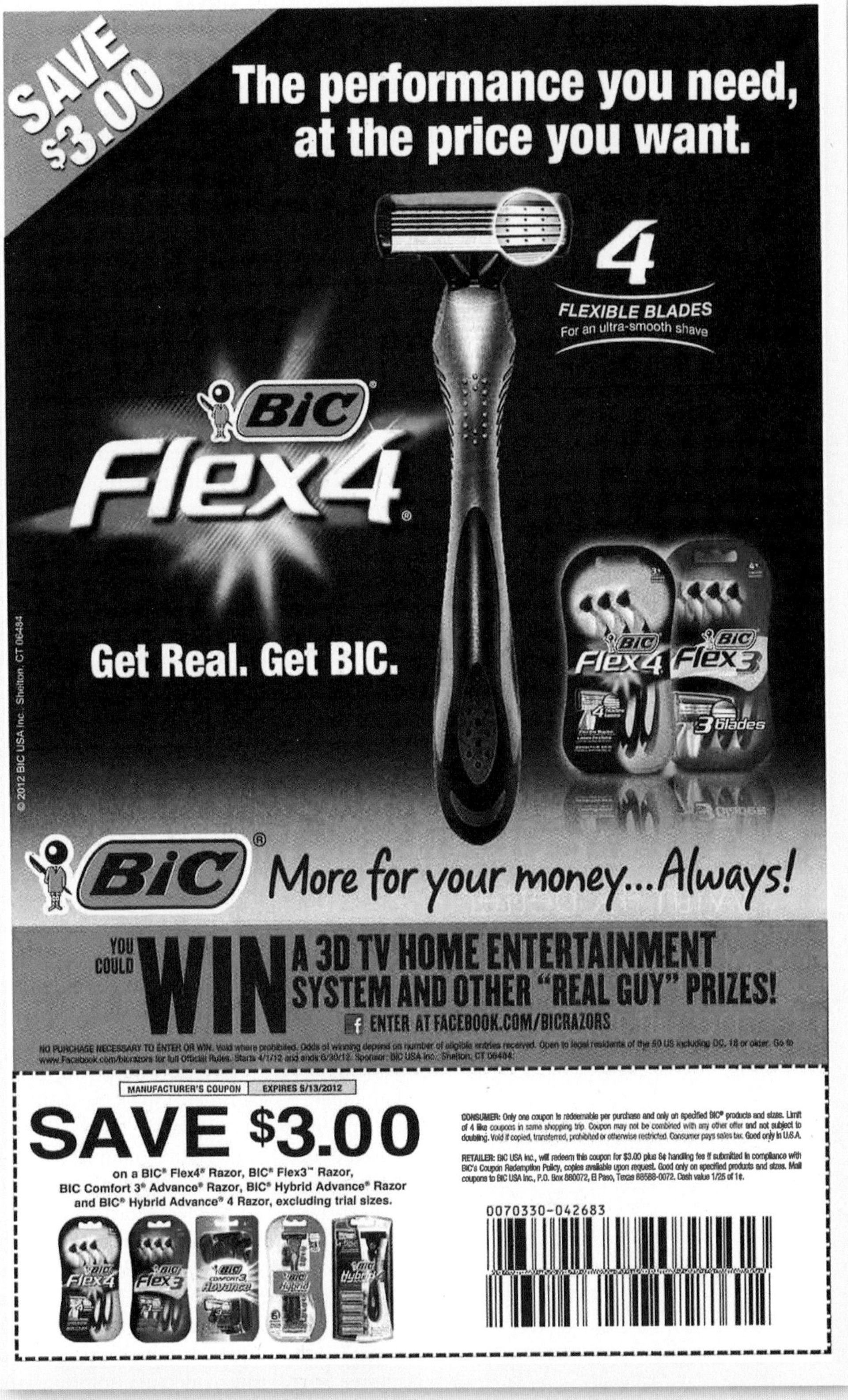

© BIC Corporation

FIGURE 20.4 Illustration of Another Sweepstakes Offer

households participate in at least one sweepstakes every year.[15] Compared with many other sales promotion techniques, sweepstakes are relatively inexpensive, simple to execute, and are able to accomplish a variety of marketing objectives. In addition to reinforcing a brand's positioning and image, well-designed sweepstakes can attract attention to advertisements, promote increased brand distribution at retail, augment sales-force enthusiasm, and reach specific groups through a prize structure that is particularly appealing to consumers in the group.

The effectiveness and appeal of a sweepstakes is generally limited if the sweepstakes is used alone. When tied in with social media, advertising, point-of-purchase displays, and other promotional tools, sweepstakes can work effectively to produce significant results. However, consumer response to sweepstakes is very low, perhaps less than 0.5 percent.[16] Nonetheless, because sweeps require less effort from consumers and generate greater participation, brand managers greatly prefer this form of promotion over contests.

Contests

In a contest, the participant must act according to the rules of the contest and may or may not be required to submit proofs of purchase. Usually, there is some "skill" or effort required on the part of participants. Illustrative of many contests is one conducted for Hershey's Syrup. Managers of this brand, in conjunction with its promotion agency, created a contest that appealed to soccer moms and their children. The contest required submission of an action photo of a 6- to 17-year-old child or teen playing soccer along with an original store receipt with the purchase price of a 24-ounce bottle of Hershey's Syrup circled. This promotion associated Hershey's Syrup with soccer, which is enjoyed by millions of families, and also encouraged brand purchasing so as to allow the consumer to participate in the contest and thus become eligible to win any of numerous prizes. A contest such as this fits with the brand's wholesome image and matches the interests of many consumers in its target market.

Contests sometimes require participants to do more than simply send in a photo. For example, in a contest for Klement's Sausage (see Figure 20.5a), if tailgaters at Milwaukee's Miller Park are spotted by the Klement's "Brat Patrol" grilling Klement's sausages or bratwurst, they could win Brewers T-shirts for six friends and their picture shown on the Miller Park Jumbotron. (Klement's is the originator of the sausage race during the sixth inning of every Milwaukee Brewers' home game.) In Johnsonville's "No Ordinary Burger Contest" held in 2012, participants were to share their unique Johnsonville burger recipes to become finalists in a live TV cook-off in order to win a $10,000 grand prize (see Figure 20.5b). Dickies, a manufacturer of work clothes, required entrants to nominate someone for the "American Worker of the Year" award and to explain in 100 words or less their reasons why the nominee deserved this recognition. A promotion for Sun-Maid raisins required entrants to create an original recipe that used at least one-half cup of raisins and could be prepared in 20 minutes or less. Pillsbury (now part of General Mills and maker of dessert baking mixes and frostings) required entrants to explain in 50 words or less, "What upcoming event would you like the Pillsbury Doughboy to help you celebrate and why?" The makers of Motrin IB ran an *Extreme Makeover: Home Edition* contest whereby participants could win an extreme makeover of their homes valued at $50,000. The contest required participants to send a photo of their homes and write an essay regarding why their homes were worthy of an extreme makeover. This contest appropriately related Motrin to the successful TV program *Extreme Makeover: Home Edition* in claiming that Motrin IB (Ibuprofen) is *Home Edition's* "partner in pain relief." One caution with contests is that some have consumers write essays praising their brand, and thus, are likely to be viewed as somewhat self-serving.[17]

(a)

(b)

FIGURE 20.5 Illustration of Promotional Contests

Consumer response to contests is typically lower than even the very low response to sweepstake offers. Nonetheless, if a standard distribution of approximately 40 million FSIs announce a contest and if, say, 0.4 percent of recipients participate in the contest, there will be a total of 160,000 participants. By virtue of participating in the contest, these individuals will have interacted with the brand more than as mere recipients of advertising messages and thus will have an opportunity to bolster their attitude toward the brand.

Online Sweeps and Contests

Online promotional events are growing in importance. Most companies now direct consumers to register online to participate in a sweepstakes or contest. Online sweeps and contests (along with online games) appeal to consumers and also further the interest of brands by creating awareness, building consumer interaction with the brand, and enabling the expansion of a brand's opt-in e-mail database. For example, recent Facebook sweepstakes for movie releases have offered grand-prize trips for two to the L.A. premier of the film (*The Hunger Games*) or a chance to win $3,000 in gift cards for one's wedding (*The Five-Year Engagement*) or other uses. You can go to the websites of some of your favorite brands and see that almost every one offers some form of online sweeps, contest, or game.

Continuity Promotions

Promotions sometimes reward consumers' repeat purchasing of a particular brand by awarding points leading to reduced prices or free merchandise. It follows from this description why continuity promotions also are referred to as *reward, loyalty,* or *point* programs. In general, continuity promotions reward consumers for purchasing a particular brand repeatedly or shopping regularly at a particular store. The program need not be based on point accumulation and instead may simply require a certain number of purchases to be eligible for prizes. For example, Budget Rent A Car ran a continuity promotion whereby renters received free Bolle ski goggles with five Budget car rentals.

Frequent-flyer programs by airlines (e.g., Air Tran A+ Rewards, Delta Sky Miles, United Mileage Plus) and frequent-guest programs by hotels (Best Western Rewards, Hyatt Gold Passport, Marriott Rewards) represent one form of loyalty program. Flyers and hotel guests accumulate points that can be redeemed eventually for free flights and lodging. These programs encourage consumers to stick with a particular airline or hotel to accumulate requisite numbers of points as quickly as possible. Renaissance Hotels, for example, provided 1,000 bonus miles per stay plus three extra miles for every U.S. dollar spent. These points were added to hotel guests' frequent-flyer point totals with designated airlines. Holiday Inn's Priority Club program rewards consumers for stays at Holiday Inn and at other hotels that InterContinental Hotels Group (IHG) owns. Priority Club members redeem these points for free stays at Holiday Inns or at other IHG hotels. IHG's website claims that in one 4-year period members redeemed over 50 billion points worth $340 million.[18]

Consumer goods companies are increasingly using a variety of loyalty programs. For example, Purina, a marketer of pet foods, has a program aimed at its Pro Club members that enables them to earn Purina Points when clipping and mailing in "weight circles" from bags of participating Purina brand dog foods. These points can be redeemed for rewards such as rebate checks (used for future purchases of Purina products), checks for veterinary services, and gift certificates for restaurants and travel.[19]

Consumers who are already loyal to a brand that offers a point program or other continuity plan are rewarded for what they would have done anyway—namely, buy a preferred brand on a regular basis. In such a case, a point program does *not* encourage repeat purchasing, although it can serve to cement an already strong relation with the customer. Conversely, point programs can encourage consumers whose loyalty is divided among several brands to purchase more frequently the brand that awards promotion points or rewards repeat purchases in some other fashion. This is perhaps where continuity programs have the greatest value.

Overlay and Tie-In Promotions

Discussion to this point has concentrated on individual sales promotions. In practice, promotions often are used in combination to accomplish objectives that could not be achieved by using a single promotional tool. Furthermore,

© Myrleen Pearson/Alamy

FIGURE 20.6 Illustration of an Overlay Program

© Lon C. Diehl/Photo Edit

these techniques, individually or in conjunction with one another, are often used to promote simultaneously two or more brands either from the same company or from different firms.

The simultaneous use of *two or more sales promotion techniques* is called an overlay, or *combination*, program. The *simultaneous promotion of multiple brands in a single promotional effort* is called a tie-in, or *group*, promotion. *Overlay* refers to the use of multiple promotional tools, whereas *tie-in* refers to the promotion of multiple brands from the same or different companies. Overlay programs and tie-ins often are used together, as the following sections illustrate.

Overlay Programs

Media clutter, as noted repeatedly in past chapters, is an ever-present problem facing marketing communicators. When used individually, consumers may never notice promotion tools (particularly coupons). A combination of tools—such as the use of a coupon with an in-pack premium offer (as shown in Figure 20.6, L'Oreal's Revitalift sample product with a $2.00 off coupon)—increases the likelihood that consumers will attend to a message and process the promotion offer. In addition, the joint use of several techniques in a well-coordinated promotional program equips the sales force with a strong sales tool and provides the trade with an attractive incentive to purchase in larger quantities (in anticipation of enhanced consumer response) and to increase display activity.

Tie-In Promotions

Growing numbers of companies use tie-ins (group promotions) to generate increased sales, to stimulate trade and consumer interest, and to gain optimal use of their promotional budgets. Tie-in promotions are cost-effective because the cost is shared among multiple brands. A tie-in involves two or more brands from the same company (an *intra*company tie-in) or from different companies (an *inter*company tie-in; see Figure 20.7).

Tie-in relationships between *complementary* brands from different companies are being used with increasing regularity. For example, the combined use of Dole (Dole Food Company, Inc.) bananas and Reese's (The Hershey Company) toppings can be shown with a coupon that might indicate purchasers of two bottles of Reese's peanut butter toppings can receive up to two pounds of Dole bananas free. Thus, knowing *how* your consumers use your brand with other brands is important. In addition to achieving strategic marcom objectives, tie-ins represent a cost-efficient promotion because multiple brands—from the same company or from different companies—share the cost of producing and distributing the FSIs that promote the brands.

FIGURE **20.7** Illustration of an Intercompany Tie-In Promotion

Implementation Problems

Tie-in promotions are capable of accomplishing useful objectives, but not without potential problems. Promotion *lead time*—the amount of time required to plan and execute a promotion—is lengthened because two or more entities have to coordinate their separate promotional schedules. Furthermore, creative conflicts and convoluted messages may result from each partner trying to receive primary attention for its product or service.

To reduce problems as much as possible and to accomplish objectives, it is important that: (1) the profiles of each partner's customers be similar with regard to pertinent demographic or other consumption-influencing characteristics; (2) the partners' images reinforce each other (e.g., Reese's and Dole both are well-known brands with images of consistent high quality); and (3) the partners be willing to cooperate rather than imposing their own interests to the detriment of the other partner's welfare.

Retailer Promotions

Discussion has thus far focused on manufacturer promotions that are directed at consumers. Retailers also design promotions for their present and prospective customers. These retailer-inspired promotions are created to increase store traffic, offer shoppers attractive price discounts or other deals, and build customer loyalty.

Retail Coupons

Couponing is a favorite promotion among many retailers in the grocery, drug, and mass-merchandise areas of business. Some grocery retailers hold special "coupon days" when they redeem manufacturer coupons at double or even triple their face value. For example, in some states, a grocery store on a "triple-coupon day" would deduct $1.50 from the consumer's bill when he or she submits a manufacturer's coupon with a face value of 50 cents. Retailers typically limit their double- or triple-discount offers to manufacturer coupons having face values of 99 cents or less.

Retailers outside the grocery industry frequently use coupons. For example, Bed Bath & Beyond, a well-known home accessories retailer, regularly offers coupons worth 20 percent off most items carried in the store. Ashley Furniture, which markets itself as the number-one home furniture brand in North America, offered coupons in one promotion ranging in value from $50 to $250. The $50-value coupon was redeemable on any purchase ranging from $499 to $999, whereas the $250-value coupon could be redeemed only on purchases of $2,500 or more.

Frequent-Shopper Programs

A number of retailers offer their customers frequent-shopper cards that entitle shoppers to discounts on select items purchased on any particular shopping occasion. For example, in a Wednesday advertising flyer, one grocery retailer offered its cardholders savings such as $2.99 on the purchase of two Mrs. Paul's fish fillets, $1.25 when buying two cans of Minute Maid juice, and $1.70 with the purchase of Freschetta pizza. Customers receive these savings on submitting their frequent-shopper cards to checkout clerks, who scan the card number and deduct savings from the shopper's bill when discounted items are scanned. These frequent-shopper cards encourage repeat purchasing from a particular retail chain. Because they are designated with labels such as "VIC" (very important customer), they also serve to elevate the shopper's sense of importance to a store. Finally, frequent-shopper card programs provide retailers with valuable databases containing information on shopper demographics and purchase habits.

In another form of loyalty program, some retailers provide customers with plastic cards that are presented to clerks for automatic scanning with every purchase made from that particular store. For example, Dick's Sporting Goods is a

retail chain that specializes in a wide variety of sporting goods products. Dick's has a "Score Card" program whereby customers submit their cards with every purchase and accumulate points enabling discounts on subsequent purchases. This is a perfect application of a loyalty, or rewards, program—one in which earning points fits perfectly with the point-scoring athletic games whose equipment and apparel is featured in this retail chain's stores.

Special Price Deals

Many retailers use a variety of creative ways of reducing prices on a temporary basis. For example, Goody's—a regional discount apparel chain—has run a price-discounting promotion in which paper shopping bags are mailed out to shoppers—paper bags of the sort that one sees in grocery stores. The bags are printed with statements such as, "20% off everything you can stuff in this bag." The deal is offered on a one-day-only basis and then repeated again at different times throughout the year. The value of a special-pricing program such as this is that it creates excitement on the part of customers, while at the same time not requiring blanket price reductions for all customers—just those who bring their bags to the store on the designated date.

Samples, Premiums, and Games

Sampling is another form of retailer-based sales promotion that is in wide use. Although many instances of store sampling represent joint programs between stores and manufacturers, retailers are sampling their own store or private label products increasingly. Club stores such as Costco are famous for providing a variety of food samples on any given purchase occasion. Such promotions serve to increase sales of the sampled items and also possess an entertainment-type value that enhances the shopping experience.

Stores also offer premiums to encourage purchases of select items. For example, Quiznos offered a free six-inch submarine sandwich when customers purchased chips and a medium fountain drink. Publix, a regional grocery chain known for its outstanding service, conducted a promotion in which consumers purchasing any of four well-known national brands (e.g., Heinz organic ketchup, Del Monte organic sweet peas) would receive a free equivalent item from Publix's Green-Wise private label (e.g., buy Heinz organic ketchup and receive a free bottle of Green-Wise organic ketchup).

Finally, games are a way for retailers to promote their store and engage their customers. For example, Roundy's Pick n' Save stores, a Midwest grocery chain, offered a Monopoly "collect and win" game promoted with their weekly coupon booklet. With the tagline, "Shop, Play & Win," this ad

combined advertising for the store, a Monopoly game which offered the chance to win over $2,800,000 in prizes, and a product coupon, all in one promotion. Of course, as discussed earlier with the national McDonald's Monopoly game, retailers should be careful with suppliers and other parties in protecting the integrity of such promotions and in delivering top prizes to consumers.

Evaluating Sales Promotion Ideas

Numerous alternatives are available to manufacturers and retailers when planning sales promotions. There also are a variety of objectives that effective promotion programs can achieve. The combination of numerous alternatives and diverse objectives leads to a staggering array of possibilities. A systematic procedure for selecting the type of sales promotion is therefore essential. The following sections outline procedures for appraising potential promotions during the idea stage and then, after they have run, for evaluating their effectiveness.

A Procedure for Evaluating Promotion Ideas

The following straightforward, three-step procedure directs a brand manager in determining which promotion ideas and approaches have the best chance of succeeding.[20]

Step 1: Identify the Objectives

The most basic yet important step toward developing a successful promotion is the clear identification of the specific objective(s) to be accomplished. Objectives should be specified as they relate both to the trade and to ultimate consumers; for example, objectives may be to generate trial, to load consumers, to preempt competition, to increase display space, and so on. Nielsen consumer panel sales data is traditionally shown as the product of the *penetration rate* (i.e., trial) and the *buy rate* (i.e., repeat purchases).[21] In turn, the buy rate can be split into the product of *purchase frequency* and *purchase size*. Thus, certain sales promotions can be matched with objectives and their measures (e.g., based on Table 20.1, sampling and online premiums with penetration or trial; bonus packs with purchase size; and in-pack premiums with purchase frequency).

Also, in this first step, the promotional planner must commit the objectives to writing and state them specifically and in measurable terms. For example, "to increase sales" is too general. In comparison, "to increase display space by 25 percent over the comparable period last year" is a specific and measurable goal.

Step 2: Achieve Agreement

Everyone involved in a brand's marcom program must agree with the objectives developed. Failure to achieve agreement on objectives results in various decision makers (such as the advertising, sales, and brand managers) pushing for different programs because they have different goals in mind. Also, in line with the following step, a promotion program can more easily be evaluated in terms of a specific objective than can a vague generalization.

Step 3: Evaluate the Idea

With specific objectives established and agreement achieved, the following five-point evaluation system can be used to rate alternative sales promotion ideas:

1. *Is the idea a good one?* Every idea should be evaluated against the promotion's objectives. For example, if increasing product trial is the objective, a sample or a coupon would be rated favorably, whereas a sweepstakes would not.
2. *Will the promotion idea appeal to the target market?* A contest, for example, might have great appeal to children, but for certain adult groups have disastrous results. In general, it is critical that the target market be treated as the benchmark against which all proposals should be judged.

3. *Is the idea unique, or is the competition doing something similar?* The prospects of receiving interest from both the trade and consumers depend on developing promotions that are not ordinary. Creativity is every bit as important to the success of promotions as it is with advertising.

4. *Is the promotion presented clearly so that the intended market will notice, comprehend, and respond positively to it?* Sales promotion planners should start with one fundamental premise: Most consumers are unwilling to spend much time and effort figuring out how a promotion works. It is critical to a promotion's success that instructions be user-friendly. Let consumers know easily and clearly what the offer is and how to respond to it.

5. *Is the proposed idea cost-effective?* This requires an evaluation of whether the proposed promotion will achieve the intended objectives at an affordable cost. Sophisticated promotion planners cost out alternative programs and know in advance the likely bottom-line payoff from each promotion option.

Postmortem Analysis

The previous section described a general procedure for evaluating proposed promotion ideas while they are in the planning stage, before actual implementation. It is essential to have a way of evaluating a promotional program after it has been implemented as well. Such an evaluation would be useful for future planning purposes, especially if the evaluation becomes part of brand management's "institutional memory" rather than discarded shortly after the evaluation is completed. As previously noted, one direct way is to examine the impact of the promotion on Nielsen consumer panel data—for example, the penetration rate (i.e., trial) and buy rate (i.e., repeat purchases consisting of purchase frequency and size). In addition, a seasoned practitioner in the promotion industry has proposed judging completed promotion programs in terms of five characteristics: expense, efficiency, execution ease, equity enhancement, and effectiveness.[22]

Expense

A promotion program's expense is the sum of the direct outlays invested in the promotion. Typical cost elements include: the expense to create the promotion; costs to advertise it; and payouts for coupons redeemed, refunds paid, game prizes awarded, samples given away, and so on.

Efficiency

Efficiency represents a promotion's *cost per unit moved*. The efficiency metric is calculated simply by dividing the total cost of the completed promotion by the number of units sold during the promotional period.

Execution Ease

This represents the total time and effort that went into the planning and execution of a promotion. Obviously, everything else held constant, promotions that require less time and effort are preferred.

Equity Enhancement

This criterion involves a subjective assessment of whether a promotion has enhanced a brand's image or possibly even detracted from it. A sweepstakes offer, for example, may serve to enhance a brand's equity by associating it with, say, a prestigious grand prize. A self-liquidating premium may accomplish the same goal. Comparatively, a game may be inappropriate for some brands by virtue of appearing tacky. As always, the evaluation depends on the brand positioning and target-market situation.

Effectiveness

A promotion's effectiveness can best be assessed by determining the total units of the promoted item that were sold during the promotional period.

Combining the Individual Factors

Having evaluated a completed promotion program along the five "E" dimensions, it is desirable that the individual evaluations be combined into a *single score*. This can be done simply enough by using a straightforward model that weights each of the five factors in importance and then summates the products of each factor's score by its weight. A model such as the following could be used:

$$\text{Program } j\text{'s Score} = \sum_{i=1}^{5}(E_{ij} \times W_i) \tag{20.1}$$

where,

Program j = A just-completed promotional program (one of many potential promotional programs that have been run for a brand and subsequently evaluated).

E_{ij} = Evaluation of the jth promotional program on the ith evaluation factor (i.e., the efficiency factor, the executional ease factor, etc.).

W_i = Weight, or relative importance, of the ith factor in determining promotion success. (Note that the weight component is subscripted just with an i, and not also a j, because the weights are constant across program evaluations. Comparatively, evaluations of the individual factors, E_{ij} require a j subscript to reflect the likelihood of varying evaluations across different promotional programs.)

Table 20.2 illustrates this straightforward model.[23] Consider a company that has run three promotional programs during a particular year. On completion, each program was evaluated with respect to the five evaluative criteria (expense, efficiency, etc.) on 10-point scales, with 1 indicating poor performance and 10 reflecting an excellent execution on each evaluative criterion. Notice also in Table 20.2 that the five criteria have been weighted as follows: Expense = 0.2, Efficiency = 0.1, Execution Ease = 0.1, Equity Enhancement = 0.3, and Effectiveness = 0.3. These weights sum to 1 and reflect the relative importance *to this particular brand manager* of the five factors. (Relative importance of these factors will obviously vary across different brands, depending on each brand's image, the company's financial standing, and so on.)

Given this particular set of weights and evaluations, it can be concluded that program 1 was the least successful of the three promotions, whereas program 3 was the most successful (see Table 20.2). Brand managers can thus archive these evaluations for reference. Eventually, norms can be established for specifying the average effectiveness level different types of promotions (samples, coupon programs, rebates, etc.) achieve.

Of course, Table 20.2 is purely illustrative. However, in actual promotion situations it is possible for brand managers to evaluate promotions formally, provided that the procedure for evaluating each criterion is clearly articulated,

TABLE 20.2 Evaluation of Three Completed Promotional Programs

Program j	Expense Weight = 0.2	Efficiency Weight = 0.1	Execution Ease Weight = 0.1	Equity Enhancement Weight = 0.3	Effectiveness Weight = 0.3	Total Score
Program 1	7	6	7	5	9	6.9
Program 2	9	8	8	7	8	7.9
Program 3	8	9	8	10	9	9.0

© Cengage Learning

systematically implemented, and consistently applied to all promotions that are appraised. The point to be appreciated is that the model on which Table 20.2 is based is suggestive of how promotional programs *can* be evaluated.

Intelligent brand managers must develop their own models to accommodate their brand's specific needs, but the point to be emphasized is that this can be accomplished with the application of thought and effort. The alternative to having a formalized evaluation system, such as the ones proposed here, is simply to run promotion events and then never to evaluate their success. Can you imagine as a student what it would be like to take courses but never to receive grades, never to be evaluated? How would you know how well you have done? How would your institution know whether grading standards have changed over the years? How would prospective employers know how well you performed in college compared with other job applicants? Like it or not, evaluation is essential. Good business practice requires it. The issue is not whether to evaluate promotions but how to do it in a valid and reliable manner.

Summary

This chapter focused on consumer-oriented promotions other than sampling and couponing. Specific topics addressed included the use of product premiums, price-off promotions, bonus packs, games, rebates and refunds, sweepstakes and contests, and continuity programs.

The discussion of premiums included the various forms of premium offers: free-with-purchase premiums; mail-in and online offers; in-, on-, and near-pack premiums, including Buy X, Get 1 Free (BOGO) offers; and self-liquidating offers (SLOs). Also described were the specific conditions necessary to execute a successful premium promotion.

Price-off promotions, which typically entail a reduction ranging from 10 to 25 percent of a brand's regular price, were described as a form of sales promotion that provides consumers with an immediate reward and serves marketers by encouraging repeat purchasing. As a result of the Fair Packaging and Labeling Act, the Federal Trade Commission was required to issue specific regulations regarding price-off promotions, and these were presented in the chapter.

Bonus packs provide consumers with extra quantities of a promoted brand for free (e.g., 25 percent more than the regular size). This form of promotion represents an immediate reward for consumers and serves to encourage repeat purchasing by rewarding consumers for their loyalty to a brand.

Games are frequently used as a means of increasing consumer enthusiasm and involvement with a brand, and in so doing perform a repeat-purchasing function by providing consumers with an instant reward. The implementation of games is fraught with the potential for snafus, so brand managers and their promotion agencies must exercise caution when using this form of promotion.

CPG companies use refunds and durable goods companies use rebates as a means of offering consumers a cash discount—but, of course, only if they go to the effort of redeeming the offer. Marketers are fond of refunds and rebates because they provide an alternative to the use of coupons and stimulate consumer purchase behavior. Rebate offers can reinforce brand loyalty, provide the sales force with something to talk about, and enable the manufacturer to flag the package with a potentially attractive deal. Because most consumers never redeem rebates, this form of promotion is referred to as a phantom discount. Consumers, in a sense, self-deceive themselves in buying a brand to take advantage of the rebate offer, but then do not undertake the necessary effort to redeem the rebate within the period allotted by the brand marketer.

Both sweepstakes and contests offer consumers the opportunity to win cash, merchandise, or travel prizes. Unlike other forms of sales promotions, sweeps and contests serve primarily image-enhancement purposes rather than generating trial usage or encouraging repeat-purchase behavior. Where sweeps require no effort on the part of the consumer other than mere entry via mail or more frequently online, contests require some "skill" or effort from the consumer (e.g., writing an essay describing why they should win). Sweeps generate higher responses from consumers than contests and thus are generally preferred by brand managers and promotion agencies.

Continuity promotions are used by many marketers to encourage brand loyalty and repeat-purchase behavior. These include the ubiquitous frequent-flyer programs offered by airlines, frequent-guest offerings from hotels, and many variants of these well-known programs that are offered to encourage consumers to continue purchasing a brand so as to accumulate points that eventually can be redeemed to receive some form of reward.

Overlay and tie-in promotions involve the use of two or more sales promotion techniques in combination with one another (an overlay, or combination, program) or the simultaneous promotion of multiple brands in a single promotional effort (a tie-in, or group, promotion). Both types of joint promotions are used as a means of spreading promotional dollars among multiple brands or multiple companies and achieving greater impact from every promotional offering.

The chapter concluded by discussing different forms of retailer-driven promotions and procedures for testing promotions, whether undertaken by manufacturers or retailers. First discussed was a three-step procedure for testing promotion ideas prior to their implementation; then the effects of promotions on consumer panel data (e.g., penetration rate [trial] and buy rate [repeat purchases]) were explained; finally a method for conducting a postmortem analysis of completed promotions was described. This latter analysis involves evaluating what can be referred to as the five "E" factors related to promotion success: expense, efficiency, execution ease, equity enhancement, and effectiveness.

Discussion Questions

1. Present a position on the following statement (voiced by a student who read a previous edition of this textbook): "I can't understand why in Table 20.1 mail-in premiums are positioned as accomplishing just a trial-impact function. It would seem that this form of promotion also accomplishes repeat-purchasing objectives."

2. Your company sells hot dogs, bologna, and other processed meats. You wish to offer a self-liquidating premium that would cost consumers approximately $25, would require five proofs of purchase, and would be appropriately themed to your product category during the summer months. Your primary market segment consists of families with school-age children crossing all socioeconomic strata. Suggest two premium items and justify your choices.

3. What is the purpose of the Federal Trade Commission's price-off regulations based on the Fair Packaging and Labeling Act?

4. Compare bonus packs and price-off deals in terms of consumer impact.

5. How can sales promotion reinforce a brand's image? Is this a major objective of sales promotion?

6. Compare sweepstakes, contests, and games in terms of how they function and their relative effectiveness.

7. Your company sells antifreeze. Sales to consumers take place in a very short period, primarily September through December. You want to tie in a promotion between your brand and the brand of another company that would bring more visibility to your brand and encourage retailers to provide more shelf space. Recommend a partner for this tie-in promotion and justify the choice.

8. Have you participated in online promotions (e.g., on Facebook), and if so, what has been your experience? Considering just a single online promotion that you participated in and considering yourself representative of the brand's target market, do you think the promotion accomplished its objective?

9. What are your thoughts regarding the future of online promotions?

10. Visit a local grocery store and identify five instances of sales promotions. Describe each promotion and comment on the objectives that promotion was intended to accomplish for the sponsoring brand or for the retailer.

11. Have you ever participated in some form of loyalty program? What has been your experience? For example, do you think the program served to increase your repeat business with the sponsoring brand?

End Notes

1. Patricia Odell, "Inventive Incentives," *Promo*, September 2006, 33–40.

2. Priya Raghubir, "Free Gift with Purchase: Promoting or Discounting the Brand?" *Journal of Consumer Psychology* 14 (1 & 2), 2004, 181–86.

3. *Code of Federal Regulations Title 16*, Volume 1, Part 502 Revised as of January 1, 2000, http://www.ftc.gov/os/statutes/fpla/part502.shtm; and *Consumer Promotion Seminar Pact Book* (New York: Association of National Advertisers, n.d.), 7.

4. Jean Halliday, "Honda Dealer Gets into Ad Accident," *Advertising Age*, July 23, 2007, 3.

5. Glenn Heitsmith, "Botched Pepsi Promotion Prompts Terrorist Attacks," *Promo*, September 1993, 10.

6. Laurie Baum, "How Beatrice Lost at Its Own Game," *BusinessWeek*, March 2, 1987, 66.

7. Bob Sperber and Karen Benezra, "A Scam to Go?" *Brandweek*, August 27, 2001, 4, 10; Kat MacArthur, "McSwindle," *Advertising Age*, August 27, 2001, 1, 22, 23; Donald Silberstein, "Managing Promotional Risk," *Promo*, October 2001, 57; and "Arch Enemies," *Promo*, December 2001, 17.

8. "Walking the Tightrope," *Promo*, March 2001, 48–51.

9. Patricia Odell, "A 12-Year Local Racing Sponsorship is Paying Off for Tecate Light," *Promo*, April 2, 2012, http://chiefmarketer.com/promotional-marketing/12-year-local-racing-sponsorship-paying-tecate-light.

10. Jonathan Welsh, "Auto Makers Pile on Buyer Incentives," *Wall Street Journal*, September 11, 2007, D1.

11. William M. Bulkeley, "Rebates' Appeal to Manufacturers: Few Consumers Redeem Them," *Wall Street Journal Online*, February 10, 1998, http://online.wsj.com.

12. Dilip Soman, "The Illusion of Delayed Incentives: Evaluating Future Effort-Money Transactions," *Journal of Marketing Research* 35 (November 1998), 427–37.

13. Ira Teinowitz and Tobi Elkin, "FTC Cracks Down on Rebate Offers," *Advertising Age*, July 3, 2000, 29.

14. Kerry J. Smith, "Postal Inspectors Target Rebate Fraud," *Promo*, April 1994, 13.

15. "Healthy, Wealthy, and Wiser," *Promo's 8th Annual SourceBook 2001*, 38–39.

16. Shari Brickin, "Stupid vs. Strategic Sweeps," *Promo*, July 2007, 61–62.

17. For discussion of the self-serving aspects of promotions and consumer psychology underlying testimonials, see Terence A. Shimp, Stacy Wood, and Laura Smarandescu, "Self-generated Advertisements: Testimonials and the Perils of Consumer Exaggeration," *Journal of Advertising Research* 47 (December 2007), 453–61.

18. Priority Club Rewards, IHG, http://www.ihgplc.com/files/pdf/factsheets/factsheet_priorityclub.pdf (accessed May 7, 2008).

19. Purina Pro Club, http://www.purinaproclub.com (accessed May 6, 2008).

20. Adapted from Don E. Schultz and William A. Robinson, *Sales Promotion Management*, Lincolnwood, IL: NTC Business Books, 1986, 436–45.

21. For an example application of Nielsen consumer panel data, see "From Clicks to Cashiers: The Effects of Online Advertising in Offline Sales," *Nielsen Catalina Solutions*, November 2011, 1–4.

22. Sara Owens, "A Different Kind of E-marketing," *Promo*, May 2001, 53–54.

23. This table is an adaptation of ibid., 53.

© Jorg Hackemann/Shuttersto

PART 5

Other IMC Tools

Part 5 includes three chapters that examine marcom tools that are somewhat less prominent than mass-media advertising and sales promotions, but nonetheless play important roles in consumer persuasion and behavior. *Chapter 21* examines the topic of public relations along with word-of-mouth influence and sponsorships. Covered in this chapter are the different activities involved in public relations, the long-term practice of reactive public relations, along with the more recent practice of proactive public relations. A special section is devoted to negative publicity, including the issue of how to handle rumors and urban legends. Also covered in Chapter 21 are the related topics of managing word-of-mouth influence, and viral and buzz marketing for brands. Chapter 21 concludes with event- and cause-oriented sponsorhships, including discussion of specific factors a company should consider when selecting an event or cause to sponsor.

Chapter 22 examines packaging, point-of-purchase (POP) communcations, and signage. First, a useful framework that describes the visual, informational, emotional, and workable features that determine packaging success is presented. Then, the valuable functions that POP performs for consumers, manufacturers, and retailers is detailed. The chapter also presents important results from the POPAI Consumer Buying Habits Study, and provides evidence regarding the impact displays can have on increasing a brand's sales volume. Finally, the strengths and limitations of billboard advertising are examined, as well as how out-of-home (OOH) audience size and characteristics are measured.

Chapter 23 is devoted to the study of personal selling and introduces students to the often challenging and rewarding job of the salesperson. The chapter describes the different types of salespeople, their duties and activities performed, advantages and disadvantages of personal selling as a career, and the basic steps involved in the personal selling process as applied to a case study. Also discussed are the determinants of salesperson performance and effectiveness, as well as characteristics of outstanding salespeople.

CHAPTER 21

Public Relations, Word-of-Mouth Influence, and Sponsorships

MARCOM INSIGHT

Rats in KFC/Taco Bell Restaurant

There are few things in life people find more appalling than rats. Imagine the disgust experienced upon viewing a televised scene of multiple rats running around a restaurant. That restaurant happened to be a KFC/Taco Bell store located in the Greenwich Village section of New York City. Following a call to its tip line from a disgruntled consumer, New York television station WNBC first reported the rats-running-wild story on its early morning news program. The initial response in a joint statement issued by KFC and Taco Bell (both restaurant chains owned by Yum Brands) was that the incident is totally unacceptable, but that it is isolated to a single restaurant that would

© Photo by Stephen Hilger/Bloomberg via Getty Images

not be allowed to reopen until it has been sanitized.

One might think: "That should do it. The company has acknowledged the problem and proposed a solution—close the store until it receives a clean bill of health." Unfortunately, in a world of YouTube, social media, and high-speed Internet connection, no problem is isolated and limited to a single store once it is broadcast worldwide through blogs linked to other blogs. A spokesperson for Nielsen BuzzMetrics, which monitors situations such as this, put it in these terms: "In the world of fast food, hygiene is the No. 1 talk driver, and rats take it to food-hygiene-on-steroids level. Rats are Defcon 5."[1]

1 Appreciate the nature and role of public relations and marketing public relations.
2 Explain the differences between proactive and reactive marketing public relations.
3 Understand the different types of commercial rumors and how to control them.
4 Discuss the importance of word-of-mouth influence.
5 Understand the role of marketing public relations in creating favorable word-of-mouth and building brand buzz and viral marketing.
6 Explain the nature of event sponsorships, including reasons for their growth, factors in selecting appropriate events, and the sponsorship agreement.
7 Understand how and why companies ambush events.
8 Appreciate the importance of measuring sponsorship performance.
9 Recognize the nature, role, and benefits of cause-related marketing.
10 Understand that accountability is a key consideration for cause-oriented as well as event-oriented sponsorships.

In fact, shortly after the story appeared on WNBC-TV more than 1,000 blogs had cited or spread the story along with the footage of rats scurrying around the restaurant.

Prior to the advent of the Internet, stories such as this would have died rather quickly in the absence of an efficient medium for their initial distribution and continuation. Nowadays, negative news about products and stores is quickly and widely disseminated—especially when it is as profoundly vivid and disgusting as a scene of rats in a restaurant. And, although company officials can claim that this is an isolated event, consumer psychology is such that people may generalize the negative scene to all KFC/Taco Bell restaurants, and all suffer some diminution in brand equity, which requires aggressive public relations efforts to restore KFC/Taco Bell's equity.

Source: Adapted from Kate MacArthur, "Taco Hell: Rodent Video Signals New Era in PR Crises," *Advertising Age*, February 26, 2007, 1, 46.

Introduction

This chapter explores the multiple roles that public relations performs in integrated marketing communications programs. Also examined are word-of-mouth influence and the role of marketing-oriented public relations in creating favorable word of mouth, and building brand buzz and viral marketing. Finally, we discuss sponsorship marketing and its two elements: event sponsorships and cause-related marketing programs.

Public relations (or PR) is an organizational activity involved with fostering goodwill between a company and its various publics. PR efforts are aimed at various corporate constituencies, including employees, suppliers, stockholders, governments, the public, labor groups, citizen action groups, and consumers. As just described, PR involves relations with *all* of an organization's relevant publics. In other words, most PR activities do *not* involve marketing per se but rather deal with general management concerns. This more encompassing aspect of public relations can be called *general PR*.

Table 21.1 lists the many general public relations activities and functions. *Advice and counsel* can be especially important as corporations and celebrities have faced PR challenges on many occasions. For example, Google has been under scrutiny for anti-trust issues; British Petroleum's contractor contributed to a major oil spill in the Gulf of Mexico; and the all-time leader in sports endorsements, Tiger Woods, was involved in a very public marital affair and divorce.[2] All of these incidents required astute advice and legal counsel. Also, companies often rely on industry lobbyists in a more proactive sense involving legislation affecting their company and/or industry. Helping to write and disseminate *publications* is part of general PR, with ethical codes of conduct and pricing guidelines (to avoid anti-trust issues) as examples. *Publicity* involves establishing positive contacts with the media. This might include press releases and press conferences in the form of product release statements, executive statement releases, and featured articles. Establishing *relationships with other publics* includes fostering goodwill with the many constituencies listed above, such as shareholders. For example, the 2012 Walmart shareholders' meeting may prove to be contentious due to allegations of bribery from a Mexican subsidiary to obtain contracts.[3] *Corporate image advertising*, covered in Chapter 10, attempts to increase a firm's name recognition, establish goodwill for the company and its products, or identify itself with some meaningful and socially acceptable activity. The PR department and/or staff will be involved in such activities. Monitoring *public opinion* is very important given the nature of general PR and is sometimes contracted through opinion research suppliers such as Harris Interactive or the Gallup organization, among others. This also may involve measuring blogs and social media for sentiments (i.e., the net of positive versus negative

TABLE 21.1	**Public Relations Activities and Functions**

- Advice and Counsel
- Publications
- Publicity
- Relationships with Other Publics
- Corporate Image Advertising
- Public Opinion Research
- Miscellaneous Activities

postings) as captured by firms such as Google Analytics, Nielsen BuzzMetrics, and Radian 6. Finally, there is a *miscellaneous* category of general PR duties, including educational efforts, speakers, scholarships, corporate donations, and other philanthropic activities.

Our primary concern in this chapter is with the more narrow aspect of public relations involving an organization's interactions with actual or prospective customers. This marketing-oriented aspect of public relations is called marketing public relations, or MPR for short.[4] MPR is performing an increasingly important marcom function for both B2C and B2B companies. Whereas advertising messages are regarded by consumers as direct attempts to influence their attitudes and behaviors, MPR messages come across not as advertisements, but as unbiased reports from journalists. An MPR message in comparison with an advertisement assumes a mantle of *credibility*. MPR messages also are considerably less expensive than advertisements because the airtime or newspaper space is provided free of charge by the newspaper, magazine, radio, television station, Internet, or social media site that transmits the message. Hence, for the dual reasons of credibility and low expense, MPR messages (and thus the PR departments and PR agencies that produce them) have achieved a more prominent position in firms' IMC efforts.

Marketing Public Relations (MPR) versus Advertising

The role that PR, or MPR, should play in a firm's marcom program has been a matter of no small debate over the years. Most marcom practitioners and brand managers have historically believed that MPR's role is specialized and limited. Some critics contend that MPR is too difficult to control and measure. However, a provocative book titled *The Fall of Advertising & the Rise of PR* has challenged prevailing beliefs and argued for an expanded role for PR.[5] The book's authors contend that public relations and its major tool, publicity, represent the most important instrument in the marketer's tool bag. The book's thesis is that new products can be introduced with little if any advertising and, instead, that a brand's marketing communicators can get the job done with creative and powerful public relations. The authors use as anecdotal evidence the success of well-known brands such as eBay, PlayStation, Starbucks, The Body Shop, Palm, and BlackBerry—all of which were introduced without large advertising budgets and focused instead on publicity and word-of-mouth buzz.

The authors of *The Fall of Advertising & the Rise of PR* have a point when stating that PR (or what we are calling *MPR*) is invaluable for introducing new products. However, two very important qualifications must be acknowledged: First, all new products cannot, contrary to the authors' omnibus claim, rely on publicity for successful introductions. Considering that most new products are *not* high in uniqueness or visibility, the news media are not interested in presenting free publicity for these mundane or ordinary products. Second, even for those truly unique new products that can benefit from MPR, when newsworthiness wears off, free publicity may not be available. At that point, the brand-equity-maintenance responsibility falls squarely on advertising's shoulders.

Proactive versus Reactive MPR

As noted, MPR is an increasingly important component in companies' marcom programs. A survey of senior marketing managers determined that MPR registers very high for purposes of increasing brand awareness, providing credibility, reaching purchase influencers, and educating consumers.[6]

MPR can be further delineated as involving both proactive and reactive initiatives. Proactive MPR is a tool for communicating a brand's merits and typically is used in conjunction with other marcom tools such as advertising and sales promotions. Dictated by a company's marketing objectives, proactive

MPR is offensively rather than defensively oriented and opportunity seeking rather than problem solving. Reactive MPR, by comparison, describes the conduct of public relations in response to outside influences. It is undertaken as a result of external pressures and challenges brought by competitive actions, shifts in consumer attitudes, or other external influences. Reactive MPR deals most often with influences having *negative consequences* for an organization. Reactive MPR attempts to repair a company's reputation, prevent market erosion, and regain lost sales.

Proactive MPR

The major role of proactive MPR is in the area of product introductions or product revisions. Proactive MPR is integrated with other IMC tools to give a product additional exposure, newsworthiness, and credibility. This last factor, *credibility*, largely accounts for the effectiveness of proactive MPR. Whereas advertising is often suspect—because we question advertisers' motives, knowing they have a personal stake in influencing us—product announcements by a newspaper editor, a television broadcaster, or blogger are notably more believable.

As previously noted, *publicity* is the major tool of proactive MPR. Like advertising, the fundamental purposes of marketing-oriented publicity are to enhance a brand's equity in a two-fold manner: (1) facilitating brand awareness by increasing recognition and recall of publicity releases and (2) augmenting brand image by forging in customers' minds strong and favorable associations with the brand. Three widely used forms of publicity are product releases, executive-statement releases, and feature articles.

Product releases announce new products, provide relevant information about product features and benefits, and inform interested listeners and readers how to obtain additional information. Product releases are often published in the product section of trade magazines (i.e., publications that cater to specific industries) and in general-interest business publications (such as *BusinessWeek, Forbes, Fortune*, and the *Wall Street Journal*), in electronic as well as hard-copy form. Product releases also are reprinted in local and national (e.g., *USA Today*) newspapers. Increasingly, product releases are made available online via social media such as YouTube, Facebook, and LinkedIn, and by means of blogs and podcasts.

Executive-statement releases are news releases quoting CEOs and other corporate executives. Unlike a product release, which is restricted to describing a new or modified product, an executive-statement release may address a wide variety of issues relevant to a corporation's publics, such as the following:

- Statements about industry developments and trends
- Forecasts of future sales
- Views on the economy
- Comments on research and development or market research findings
- Announcements of new marketing programs the company launches
- Views on foreign competition or global developments
- Comments on environmental issues or community outreach efforts

Whereas product releases are typically published in the business and product sections of newspapers and magazines along with their online versions, executive-statement releases are published in the news section. This location carries with it a significant degree of credibility. Note that any product release can be converted into an executive-statement release by changing the way it is written.

Feature articles are detailed descriptions of products or other newsworthy programs that a PR firm writes for immediate publication or airing by print or broadcast media or distribution via appropriate social media or other online sites. Materials such as these are inexpensive to prepare, yet they can provide companies with tremendous access to many potential customers.

© Courtesy of Bosch

Many newspapers often publish feature articles about new products that are of likely interest to the paper's readers. For example, the "do it yourself" section of a local newspaper published a product release for the Skil cordless screwdriver. Although this release appeared to be written by a local columnist, to the trained eye it obviously was a product release prepared by Skil's PR agency and likely was published in dozens, if not hundreds, of local newspapers. The opening paragraph and an accompanying photo of the product immediately captured the reader's attention when stating, "Don't be deceived by the size of Skil's palm-sized cordless screwdriver. The tool has a bigger punch than you'd expect." Later in the release, the do-it-yourselfer's interest was really piqued with the claim "But here's the real beauty of the tool: charge the battery, stick the screwdriver in a drawer, and it will hold the charge for two years. So it's ready to work whenever you are." It is easy to imagine that thousands of readers of this product release searched for a Skil cordless screwdriver on their next trip to their favorite store carrying products such as this.

Reactive MPR

Unanticipated marketplace developments—such as the rats-in-a-restaurant incident described in the chapter-opening *Marcom Insight*—can place an organization in a vulnerable position that demands reactive MPR. In simple terms, bad things happen and unanticipated events sometimes occur that require a public relations response. In general, the most dramatic factors underlying the need for reactive MPR are product defects and failures.

A Sampling of Celebrated Cases

Following is a sampling of negative events that have occurred over the last several decades and received widespread media attention. The ordering is chronological and ranges from the most recent events to an event occurring as far back as the early 1980s.

© Maurice Savage/Alamy

Walmart and Mexican Bribery Scandal Walmart has worked hard on its reputation in recent years. Yet, it disclosed in 2012 that its Mexican subsidiary (the retailer's largest foreign operation) had paid bribes and that an internal inquiry into the matter had been suppressed.[7]

Toyota Motor and Accelerator Pedals Toyota was forced to recall over eight million vehicles in 2010, due to problems with sticky gas pedals causing quick acceleration and damaging Toyota's reputation for quality. Toyota had to pay $48.8 million in U.S. fines and civil penalties for failing to properly disclose the safety defects.[8]

British Petroleum (BP) and the Gulf Oil Spill In 2010, BP's Macondo oil well blew out, sinking the Deepwater Horizon platform, killing 11 drill workers and spewing 5 million barrels of oil into the Gulf of Mexico. It took over 100 days for engineers to cap the well. As a result, the Gulf state's waters, inlets, and beaches were polluted, and BP fell from Interbrand's list of the top 100 global brands.[9]

Tiger Woods Arguably, Tiger Woods was one of the greatest golfers of all time, and certainly the leading endorser in all of sports for many years. Yet, in November 2009, he had a very public accident and disagreement with his wife, a disclosure of multiple affairs, all of which ended in a messy divorce. Although Nike, EA Sports, and FedEx continued their sponsorship of him, Accenture, AT&T, Gatorade, and Tag Heuer did not. Tiger went from over $100 million in annual endorsements to $60 million in 2011. (Interestingly, he still placed first on the sports endorsement list!)[10]

Mattel and Lead Paint In 2007, Mattel Inc. announced three major recalls involving products marketed under its brand names that were manufactured in China. For example, nearly 800,000 Barbie dolls were recalled due to unsafe levels of lead paint.[11]

Menu Brands and Rat Poisoning Another China-sourcing problem resulted in 2007 when over 60 million cans of pet food made by Canada's Menu Brands had to be recalled because they contained wheat imported from China that had traces of rat poison, resulting in the deaths of a number of cats and dogs and deeply disturbing pet owners.[12] A similar situation occurred in China in 2008 with milk contaminated with melamine, resulting in 13 infants dying and 860 hospitalized. Two of the perpetrators received a death sentence for their actions.

ReNu MoistureLoc Lens Cleaner In 2006, Bausch & Lomb withdrew its ReNu MoistureLoc lens-cleaner brand after allegations that the brand caused potentially blinding cornea infections. Bausch & Lomb was widely criticized after the American public learned that ReNu previously had been withdrawn from two key Asian markets. Crisis-management specialists anticipated that Bausch & Lomb's poor handling of the crisis would extend beyond the MoistureLoc brand and adversely affect other brands in the company's product portfolio.[13]

Vioxx and Heart Attacks/Strokes Vioxx, the arthritis and acute-pain medication made by the pharmaceutical giant, Merck & Co., was withdrawn from worldwide distribution in late 2004 after a scientific study revealed that patients taking Vioxx for 18 months or longer had double the risk of suffering heart attacks or strokes compared to a control group taking a placebo. With 2003 Vioxx sales of $2.5 billion, this withdrawal had significant financial implications for Merck, and the negative publicity surrounding Merck's failure to withdraw the product even sooner had damaging long-term implications for the Vioxx brand and for Merck overall.[14]

Coke, Pepsi, and Pesticide in India An Indian environmental group released a report in 2003 claiming that its laboratory tests revealed that pesticide residues in various soft-drink brands Coke and Pepsi bottled were at least 30 times higher than acceptable limits in Europe. Shortly after the report became public, sales of these two major soft-drink brands fell by over 30 percent. Officials at both companies denied that their pesticide-related standards are any different in India than elsewhere. Nonetheless, India's Supreme Court issued a ruling that both Coke and Pepsi must provide warning labels on their soft-drink containers that indicate the level of pesticide residue. In view of this publicity disaster, both companies faced the challenge of restoring the trust Indian consumers had in these high-equity brands.[15] In 2004, a similar contamination of Coke's Dasani brand occurred in the United Kingdom with residue from the chemical bromide. In 1999, an accident at Coca-Cola's bottling plant in Belgium introduced tainted carbon dioxide into some bottles of Coke.

Firestone Tires and Vehicle Rollovers Firestone tires—made by Firestone, a U.S. subsidiary of Japan's Bridgestone Corporation—was the focus of negative publicity, especially in 2000, when Ford Explorer sport-utility vehicles fitted with Firestone tires experienced numerous rollover accidents. The particular tire in question was eventually recalled, but both Firestone and the Explorer were subjected to intense public scrutiny and even scorn. More will be said about this event in a following section on crisis management.

Syringes in Pepsi: A Hoax In 1993, a New Orleans man contacted the Cable News Network (CNN) and alleged that he had found a syringe in a can of Diet Pepsi. This was only the first of several reported contaminations from different geographical areas. PepsiCo officials, knowing the reports were false, and that the Diet Pepsi bottling process was completely safe, reacted to the negative publicity by using the media. A video showing the bottling process of PepsiCo products was released shortly after the initial news broke and was seen by an estimated 187 million viewers. It demonstrated the extremely remote possibility that a foreign object, especially something as large as a syringe, could be inserted in cans in the less than one second they are open for filling and capping. That same day, PepsiCo's president and chief executive officer appeared on ABC's *Nightline* along with the commissioner of the Food and Drug Administration (FDA). PepsiCo's chief executive officer assured viewers that the Diet Pepsi can was 99.9 percent safe, and the FDA commissioner warned consumers of the penalties for making false claims.

Two days later, FDA commissioner Dr. David Kessler noted at a news conference that "it is simply not logical to conclude that a nationwide tampering has occurred" and that the FDA was "unable to confirm even one case of tampering." He also warned of fines and possible prison terms for making false complaints. These statements were later broadcast over national TV along with a video news release showing a consumer inserting a syringe into a Diet Pepsi can. She had been caught by the store's surveillance camera. With this exposure, the crisis was essentially over. Although volume case sales dropped slightly during the period immediately following the hoax, sales returned to normal in a matter of weeks.

Perrier Contaminated with Benzene Perrier was the leading brand of bottled water in the United States until 1990 when Source Perrier, the manufacturer, announced that traces of a toxic chemical, benzene, had been found in some of its products. Following multiple explanations, Perrier reluctantly recalled 72 million bottles from U.S. supermarkets and restaurants and subsequently withdrew the product from distribution elsewhere in the world. The total cost of the global recall was estimated to have exceeded $150 million. Perrier's sales in the United States declined by 40 percent, and Evian replaced it as the leading imported bottled water. Perrier's business has never fully recovered.

Tylenol and Cyanide Poisoning In 1982, seven people in the Chicago area died from cyanide poisoning after ingesting Tylenol capsules. Many analysts predicted that Tylenol would never regain its previously sizable market share. Some observers even questioned whether Johnson & Johnson ever would be able to market anything under the Tylenol name. Many pundits consider Johnson & Johnson's handling of the Tylenol tragedy as nearly brilliant. Rather than denying a problem existed, J&J acted swiftly by removing Tylenol from retail shelves. Spokespeople appeared on television and cautioned consumers not to ingest Tylenol capsules. A tamperproof package was designed, setting a standard for other companies. As a final good-faith gesture, J&J offered consumers free replacements for products they had disposed of in the aftermath of the Chicago tragedy. Tylenol regained its market share shortly after this campaign began.

In a tragic replay of the Tylenol case, two people in the state of Washington died in 1991 after ingesting cyanide-laced Sudafed capsules. Following Tylenol's lead, Burroughs Wellcome & Company, Sudafed's maker, immediately withdrew the product from store shelves, suspended advertising, established a toll-free number for consumer inquiries, and offered a $100,000 reward for information leading to the arrest of the product tamperer. Burroughs Wellcome's quick and effective response reportedly resulted in only a brief sales slump for Sudafed.

Crisis Management

As the previous examples illustrate, product crises and negative publicity can hit a company at any time and lead to strong negative reactions from consumers. It is important to note, however, that not all consumers are equally swayed by negative publicity. Unsurprisingly, consumers who hold more positive evaluations of a company are more likely to challenge negative publicity about that company and thus are less likely to experience diminished evaluations following negative publicity. In contrast, those who are less loyal are especially susceptible to the adverse effects of negative publicity.[16]

Companies often are slow to react to crises. The reason, according to one crisis-management expert, can be explained as follows:

> *When disaster strikes, the first instinct of leadership is often to worry about the company, or the stock price, or the management team, the production line, their own jobs or bonuses. The last thing they think about is, "What is that mom with two kids in the shopping cart thinking about my product right now?"*[17]

The lesson to be learned is that quick and positive responses to negative publicity are imperative. Negative publicity is something to be dealt with head-on, not denied. When done effectively, reactive MPR can virtually save a brand or a company. A corporate response immediately following negative publicity can lessen the damage that will result, damage such as a diminution in the public's confidence in a company and its brands or a major loss in sales and profits.

And in the era of online communication (e.g., social media, blogs), a company's brand image can be tarnished virtually immediately as the result of a product failure, defect, contamination problem, or any other form of negative marketing-related news.[18] Consider the Firestone/Ford Explorer debacle that

© AP Images/Al Goldis

was described previously. In the wake of news that its 15-inch tires fitted on Ford Explorer SUVs were responsible, at least in part, for hundreds of rollovers and more than 200 deaths, Bridgestone/Firestone issued a massive recall of more than 6.5 million Firestone tires.

Officials at Ford denied that that company was at fault and placed the blame squarely on the shoulders of Bridgestone/Firestone. Although Bridgestone/Firestone was incredibly slow to respond to the negative publicity being disseminated, Ford realized the power of online communication and placed an ad on about 200 websites with the potential of reaching millions of people. The ad invited viewers to click through to Ford's recall site, which included information about the specific tire models included in the recall, the tire models that were appropriate for replacement, and locations of authorized replacement dealers. The site also provided press releases from Ford and a statement from the company's CEO claiming that Ford does not take lightly its customers' safety and trust.

Whereas Bridgestone/Firestone was slow to react to the negative publicity, Ford adroitly took advantage of the speed and impact of the Internet to try to offset negative publicity directed toward it. Perhaps the Ford Explorer was not free of blame for the numerous rollover accidents, but due in large part to Ford's PR efforts, the general public placed the blame almost exclusively on Firestone. A consultancy firm reported that Firestone's score on a reputation index had plummeted by an amount never before registered in its research on company and brand reputations.[19]

One observer has compared the spread of negative product news via the Internet as equivalent to "reverse viral marketing."[20] A crisis-management authority expressed the opinion that the first thing a company needs to do when a brand is in crisis is to go online immediately and investigate what the bloggers are saying about the brand. "You want to get into the dialogue and motivate your loyal users to help you."[21]

The Special Case of Rumors and Urban Legends

You have heard them and probably helped spread them since you were a child in elementary school. They are often vicious and malicious. Sometimes they are just comical. Almost always they are false. We are talking about rumors and urban legends. As a technical aside, urban legends and rumors capture slightly different phenomena. Whereas urban legends are a form of rumor, they go beyond rumor by transmitting a story involving the use of *irony*; that is, urban legends convey subtle messages that are in contradiction of what is literally expressed in the story context.[22] As a case in point, consider the "Gucci Kangaroo" legend:

> *Have you heard about the American tourists who were driving in the outback of Australia? They had been drinking, and it seems that their car hit a kangaroo. Thinking the kangaroo to be dead, the tourists decided to take a gag photograph. They hastily propped the kangaroo up against a fence and dressed it in the driver's Gucci jacket. They proceeded to take photographs of the well-dressed marsupial. Well, it seems that the kangaroo had merely been stunned rather than dead. All of a sudden he revived and jumped away wearing the man's jacket, which also contained the driver's license, money, and airline ticket.[23]*

Technical distinction noted, hereafter we will refer simply to rumors in a sense that encompasses urban legends. It further is noteworthy that our interest involves only those rumors that involve products, brands, stores, or other objects of marketing practice.[24] A variety of Internet websites focus on rumors and urban legends, and many of these refer to products, technological developments, and even specific brands. For a review of many types of urban legends, go to Urban Legends Reference Pages (www.snopes.com) and see legends related to business and specific products such as automobiles and computers.

Commercial rumors are widely circulated but unverified propositions about a product, brand, company, store, or other commercial target.[25] Rumors are probably the most difficult problem public relations personnel face. What makes rumors so troublesome is that they spread like wildfire—especially via YouTube, Facebook, texting, and blogs—and almost always state or imply something very undesirable, and possibly repulsive, about the target of the rumor.[26] For example, the rumor spread quickly around the United States that because Mountain Dew is colored with a dye (Yellow 5), drinking the product lowers a man's sperm count. Although untrue, this urban legend influenced teenager's soft-drink consumption behavior, with some actually consuming more Mountain Dew than normal as a means of birth control and others consuming less for fear that later in life they would not be able to have children.[27]

Consider also the case of the persistent urban legend that surrounded Procter & Gamble (P&G) for years. The rumor involved P&G's famous man-in-the-moon logo, which was claimed to be a symbol of the devil. According to the rumor-mongers, when the stars in the old logo were connected, the number 666 (a symbol of the Antichrist) was formed. Also, the curls in the man-in-the-moon's beard also supposedly formed 666 when held up to a mirror. Although nonsensical, this rumor spread throughout the Midwest and South. P&G eventually decided to drop the old logo and change to a new one. The new logo retains the 13 stars, which represent the original U.S. colonies, but eliminates the curly hairs in the beard that appeared to form the number 666.

Following are some other false rumors/urban legends you may have heard at one time or another.[28] Many of these are from the past and none are true, but all have been widely circulated:

- McDonald's Corporation makes sizable donations to the Church of Satan.
- Wendy's hamburgers contain something other than beef, namely red worms. (Other versions of this rumor have substituted McDonald's or Burger King as the target.)
- Pop Rocks (a carbonated candy) explode in your stomach when mixed with soda.
- Bubble Yum chewing gum contains spider eggs.
- A woman, while shopping in a Kmart store, was bitten by a poisonous snake when trying on a coat imported from Taiwan.
- A boy and his date stopped at a Kentucky Fried Chicken (KFC) restaurant on their way to a movie. Later the girl became violently ill and the boy rushed her to the hospital. The examining physician said the girl appeared to have been poisoned. The boy went to the car and retrieved an oddly shaped half-eaten piece from the KFC bucket. The physician recognized it to be the remains of a rat. It was determined that the girl died from consuming a fatal amount of strychnine from the rat's body.
- In what is referred to as the "Gerber Myth," thousands of consumers sent letters to a post office box in Minneapolis following a rumor circulating on the Internet (as well as in church bulletins and day care centers) that Gerber, a baby food company, was giving away $500 savings bonds as part of a lawsuit settlement. Complying with the rumor's advice, parents mailed copies of their child's birth certificate and Social Security card to the Minneapolis address. For a period of time, the post office box received daily between 10,000 and 12,000 pieces of Gerber Myth mail.

The preceding examples illustrate two basic types of commercial rumors: conspiracy and contamination.[29] Conspiracy rumors involve supposed company policies or practices that are threatening or ideologically undesirable to consumers. For example, a conspiracy rumor circulated in New Orleans claiming that the founder of the Popeyes restaurant chain, Al Copeland, supported a reprehensible politician known to have Ku Klux Klan and Nazi connections. Copeland immediately called a press conference, vehemently denied any connections with the politician, and offered a $25,000 reward for information leading to the source of the rumor. This swift response squashed the rumor before it gained momentum.[30]

Contamination rumors deal with undesirable or harmful product or store features. For example, a rumor started in Reno, Nevada, that the Mexican imported beer Corona was contaminated with urine. A beer distributor in Reno who handled Heineken, a competitive brand, actually had initiated the rumor. Corona sales fell by 80 percent in some markets. The rumor was hushed when an out-of-court settlement against the Reno distributor required a public statement declaring that Corona was not contaminated. See the *IMC Focus* insert for additional examples of contamination rumors involving the artificial sweetener ingredient aspartame and plastic water bottles.

IMC FOCUS

Two Cases of Contamination Rumors: Aspartame and Plastic Water Bottles

Aspartame is the key ingredient found in artificial (non-sugar) sweeteners such as NutraSweet and Equal and is used to sweeten diet drinks such as Diet Coke and Diet Pepsi along with literally hundreds of other products. Rumors have spread, for at least a decade, that aspartame is responsible for epidemic health problems. People responsible for circulating this rumor, some of whom are scientists or claim to be, assert that aspartame is responsible for an epidemic of multiple sclerosis and systemic lupus. Lupus is claimed to be especially rampant among drinkers of Diet Coke and Diet Pepsi. Other maladies attributed to aspartame include fibromyalgia, leg numbness, vertigo, tinnitus (ear ringing), joint pain, anxiety attacks, blindness, birth defects, acute memory loss (especially among diabetics), and depression. This urban legend/rumor has been declared false by Snopes.com—an organization that monitors and researches urban legends—based largely on the fact that the legend has been debunked by the American Council on Science and Health, and the U.S. Food and Drug Administration has failed to identify any reliable pattern of symptoms that can be attributed to aspartame usage.

Another widespread urban legend/rumor involves plastic water bottles, such as those used by millions of consumers when drinking bottled mineral water. The claim, in short, is that re-using plastic bottles is dangerous because these bottles contain a potentially carcinogenic element di(2-ethylhexyl) adiphate, known by its chemical-composition initials as DEHA. Plastic bottles allegedly are safe only for one-time usage or, at most, up to a week maximum. Repeatedly washing and rinsing plastic bottles supposedly breaks down the plastic leading to the release of DEHA into the water that people drink. It also is claimed that leaving plastic water bottles in cars is particularly dangerous because the extreme heat resulting from the greenhouse effect in automobiles breaks down the plastic, releases DEHA, and causes breast cancer. Snopes.com has declared this rumor false as well based, in part, on the Food and Drug Administration's determination that DEHA does not pose a health risk. (This differs from Bisphenol A [BPA] used as a plastic food liner and banned in 26 states and Canada.)

Sources: Based on Snopes, "Aspartame," http://www.snopes.com/medical/toxins/aspartame.asp; and Snopes, "Bottle Royale," http://www.snopes.com/medical/toxins/petbottles.asp (accessed on October 19, 2012).

What Is the Best Way to Handle a Rumor?

When confronted with a rumor, some companies believe that doing nothing is the best way to handle it. This cautious approach is apparently based on the fear that an antirumor campaign will call attention to the rumor itself. An expert on rumors claims that rumors are like fires, and, like fires, time is the worst enemy. His advice is not merely to hope that a rumor will simmer down but also to combat it swiftly and decisively to put it out.[31] The suggestions for handling a false rumor are to (1) *stay alert* (e.g., noting the location, target, message, and who is making the allegation), (2) *evaluate its effects* (e.g., on sales, morale, unfair damage to image), and (3) *launch a media campaign* to combat it.[32] These elements also are suggested for social media rumors.[33]

An antirumor campaign would minimally involve the following activities: (1) deciding on the specific points in the rumor that need to be refuted; (2) emphasizing that the conspiracy or contamination rumor is untrue and unfair; (3) picking appropriate media and vehicles for delivering the antirumor message; and (4) selecting a credible spokesperson (such as a scientist, a government official as in the case of the Pepsi hoax described previously, a civic leader, or a respected theologian) to deliver the message on the company's behalf.[34]

Unfortunately, there are times in which refuting a false rumor may not always work (e.g., worm meat and McDonald's hamburgers). In this case, research has shown that positive storage (e.g., eating a great sauce made out of worms) or positive retrieval (e.g., recalling a McDonald's restaurant frequented most often) strategies may be more effective than simple refutation in the evaluation of the targeted brand.[35]

Word-of-Mouth Influence

There are times in which marketing communicators may desire to influence what people say about products and specific brands. The purpose of this section, then, is to better understand word-of-mouth influence in the marketplace and how marcom specialists can influence the dialogue in the best interests of the brands they manage. As such, word-of-mouth influence (WOM) is defined as informal communication among consumers about products and services.[36] According to PQ Media, companies spent an estimated $2.2 billion on WOM marketing in the United States in 2011, up 43 percent from 2008.[37]

Research has established that word-of-mouth influence is both complex and difficult to control.[38] Nonetheless, it is critical that brand managers attempt to control WOM in the best interests of their brands. It has been estimated that the average American consumer participates in an excess of 120 WOM conversations over the course of a typical week, with conversations focusing most often on products and services such as food and dining, media and entertainment, sports and hobbies, beverages, and shopping and retail.[39] Sometimes the influence is negative, such as was described in the previous sections on crisis management and urban legends and rumors. On other occasions WOM is beneficial to a brand, and in such an event the objective is to facilitate as much positive information as possible and to build favorable "buzz" about a brand.[40] The following sections first present some conceptual ideas about word-of-mouth influence and then discuss the practice of buzz building and viral marketing.

Strong and Weak Ties

In everyday life, people are connected in *social networks* of interpersonal relationships. Family members and friends interact on a regular basis, and people intermingle with work associates daily. This certainly has been accelerated with the use of social media (e.g., Facebook, Twitter). There also are interaction patterns that are less frequent and less strong. We thus can think of social relations in terms of *tie strength*. Consumers' interpersonal relations range along a continuum from very strong ties (such as frequent and often intimate communications between friends) to weak ties (such as rare interactions between casual acquaintances).[41] It is through these ties, both weak and strong, that information flows about new products, new restaurants, recently released movies and albums, and myriad other products and services.[42]

The important point is that marketing communications—especially via advertising media—is critical for getting the information-dissemination ball rolling. Thereafter, it is social interactions between B2C consumers or B2B customers that drive the flow of information about products, services, and brands. Although there have been exceptions, advertising usually represents the first step, followed by WOM as the second step in a two-step flow of communications that ultimately leads to people talking about and advocating particular brands.[43] Hence, marketing communicators need to orchestrate the flow of information about products using advertising and viral or "buzz" efforts (as discussed in a later section) and then the information ball will be propelled at an accelerating rate by social networks of people interacting with one another—through face-to-face interactions, via social media such as YouTube, Facebook, and Twitter, or by means of blogs. (See the *Global Focus* insert for description of how "false" blogging about products and brands is a crime in the United Kingdom.)

The Role of Opinion Leaders in WOM Dissemination

An opinion leader is a person within a social network of family, friends, and acquaintances who has particular influence on other individuals' attitudes and behavior.[44] (Viewed differently, they are people from whom others seek advice.) Opinion leaders perform several important functions: They inform other people

GLOBAL FOCUS

Create a False Blog and Go to Jail

Bloggers often say great things about new products and particular brands. Unfortunately, one cannot always be certain of the blogger's authenticity. Is the blogger a real consumer who has used a product, really likes it, and wants to tell others about it, or is this a blog created by the company that markets the product or by someone who the company has paid to say favorable things about its product?

The problem of false blogs is worldwide. In the United States, word-of-mouth regulation falls under the Federal Trade Commission's 2009 revised "Guides Concerning the Use of Endorsements and Testimonials in Advertising." For example, paid bloggers who make an endorsement must disclose material (i.e., important) connections they share with the seller of the product or service. Also, celebrity bloggers may be liable for false or unsubstantiated endorsement claims.

In the United Kingdom, legislation went into effect in 2008 that made it a criminal offense to represent oneself falsely as a consumer when blogging about brands. This regulation was designed to prevent instances such as when Sony ran an online campaign ("All I want for Christmas is a PSP") that used what appeared to be amateurish video footage with a blog falsely attributed to one of the characters in the video. In another celebrated case of false blogging, the founder of Whole Foods wrote critical comments about his competitors under an assumed name.

Writing positive messages online without making the origin of the message clear is now illegal throughout Europe. Although greater case precedent is needed, false bloggers are on alert that misrepresenting the source of a blog may lead to financial penalties and even jail time.

Sources: "FTC Publishes Final Guides Governing Endorsements, Testimonials," *FTC News Release*, October 5, 2009, 1–2; and Emma Hall, "U.K. Cracks Down on Word-of-Mouth with Tough Restrictions," *Advertising Age*, April 28, 2008, 132.

about products, they provide advice and reduce the follower's perceived risk in purchasing a product, and they offer positive feedback to support or confirm decisions that followers have already made. Thus, an opinion leader is an informer, persuader, and confirmer.

Opinion leadership influence is typically restricted to one or several consumption topics rather than applying universally across many consumption domains. That is, a person who is an opinion leader with respect to issues and products in one consumption area—such as, movies, computers, snowboarding, or cooking—is not generally influential in other unrelated areas. It would be very unlikely, for example, for one person to be respected for his or her knowledge and opinions concerning all four of the listed consumption topics.

Opinion leaders are motivated to engage in communications exchanges with others because they *derive satisfaction* from sharing their opinions and explaining what they know about products and services. Opinion leaders thus continually strive (and often feel obligated) to keep themselves informed. In general, *prestige* is at the heart of word-of-mouth influence, whether that influence is from opinion leaders or from those who follow in the information dissemination process. "We like being the bearers of news. Being able to recommend gives us a feeling of prestige. It makes us instant experts."[45] Researchers have used the term "maven" (or "market maven") to characterize people who are experts in marketplace matters.[46]

Prevent Negative WOM

Positive word-of-mouth communication is a critical element in the success of new and established brands. In fact, research indicates that consumers are much more likely to have positive than negative things to say about brands.[47] Nonetheless, unfavorable WOM can have devastating effects on a brand's image, because consumers seem to place more weight on negative than positive information in forming evaluations.[48]

Marketing communicators can do several things to minimize negative word of mouth.[49] At a minimum, companies need to show customers that they are responsive to legitimate complaints. Manufacturers can do this by providing detailed warranty and complaint-procedure information on labels or in package inserts. Retailers can demonstrate their responsiveness to customer complaints through employees with positive attitudes, store signs, and inserts in monthly billings to customers. Companies also can offer toll-free numbers and e-mail addresses to provide customers with an easy way to voice their complaints and provide suggestions. By being responsive to customer complaints, companies can avert negative—and perhaps even create positive—WOM. Moreover, researchers suggest that the use of short sentences, evidence for claims, information on important features, and avoiding hyperbole (e.g., exclamation marks) can increase the persuasiveness of WOM materials.[50]

Occasionally, certain WOM techniques that are covert or stealth in nature (e.g., identity of seller is masked) may be deceptive.[51] Interestingly, research shows that when a WOM agent's affinity is disclosed, it did not affect their credibility, nor consumer inquiries, product use, or purchases. In fact, it actually increased the pass along or relay rate of the communication.[52]

Buzz Creation and Viral Marketing

The preceding section applied traditional concepts such as opinion leadership to describe the process of word-of-mouth communication. That section may have given the impression that WOM is something that just happens and that marketing communicators are like spectators in a sporting event who passively enjoy the action but are not involved in its creation. The present section clarifies that marketing communicators are—or should be—active participants in the WOM process rather than merely idle bystanders.

Brand marketers have found it essential to influence what is said about their brands proactively rather than merely hoping that positive word of mouth is occurring. Marketing practitioners refer to this proactive effort as "creating the buzz." By definition, we can think of buzz creation as the systematic and organized effort to encourage people to talk favorably about a particular brand—either over the fence or online—and to recommend its usage to others who are part of their social network. A related term, viral marketing, refers to techniques that use social networks to increase brand awareness or other marketing objectives, through a self-replicating, viral process, similar to the spread of a virus.[53] (Terms other than *buzz creation* or *viral marketing* are used to refer to proactive efforts to spread positive WOM information; these include *guerrilla marketing*, *diffusion marketing*, and *street marketing*.)

Let us first explore the practice of buzz creation and understand why this activity is used extensively, even now to the point that major advertising agencies have created buzz-generating units.

Some Anecdotal Evidence

Before formally examining the topic of buzz creation, it will be useful first to examine some illustrations of this practice:

- Microsoft's *Halo3* game reached retail shelves several years ago with its story centering on interstellar war between twenty-sixth–century humans and alien races. However, prior to its release, Microsoft spent $40 million in marketing, including tie-ins with Mountain Dew's "Game Fuel," branded with the *Halo3* logo and main character. Copies of the *Halo3* release were leaked accidently online adding to pent-up demand. The first-day sales of *Halo3* were $170 million in the United States, setting a first-day record for the highest gross of an entertainment product within 24 hours after its launch. *Halo4*, its sequel, recently was launched successfully to the market.[54]

- In an effort to get young trendsetters to become brand evangelists, Toyota used guerilla tactics in launching its Scion model. So-called street teams were formed to distribute promotional items to large gatherings of young consumers in cities across the United States. People had the opportunity to test-drive Scion models fitted with video cameras and then e-mail copies of the drives to friends.[55]

- The marketing firm House Party (www.houseparty.com) arranges for people who really love a brand to host an event that is sponsored by the brand's company. House Party has a database of over 900,000 potential hosts and pays an average of $125 per party. Parties include the "Potty Dance Day," where hosts receive dance mats, DVDs, coupons, and coloring sheets from Kimberly Clark and get to groove to a streamed concert of the Potty Dance by children's rock band, Ralph's World. House Party has added more companies, such as Anheuser Busch InBev, McDonald's, Kraft Foods, Procter & Gamble, Ford Motor, Sony, and Reckitt Benckiser's Durex, among others.[56]

© JIM BRYANT/UPI/Newscom

- In an effort to establish Long Beach, California, as a hub for West Coast flights, marketing personnel at JetBlue undertook a buzz-building campaign. The campaign was designed to reach influential customers such as bartenders and hotel concierges in hopes they would spread the word about JetBlue Airways and its flights from the Long Beach airport. College interns were employed to visit bars, hotels, and other locales and to talk up JetBlue and

© WENN/Newscom

provide "influentials" with bumper stickers, buttons, and tote bags that served as visible reminders of JetBlue's daily flights from the Long Beach airport. To generate further interest in JetBlue and initiate buzz, interns drove Volkswagen Beetles, and painted in JetBlue's signature blue color around the streets of Long Beach.[57]

- During the opening show of the 2004 season of Oprah Winfrey's popular daytime television program, every audience member—276 in total—received a new Pontiac G6 automobile worth over $28,000. Oprah did not provide these gifts from the goodness of her heart; rather, the cars were donated by the Pontiac division of General Motors in an effort to generate gobs of free publicity about the new G6. Winfrey devoted a half hour of airtime to the Pontiac G6 and described the car as being "so cool!" Of course, Pontiac's marketing people arranged this stunt in coordination with producers of *The Oprah Winfrey Show*. As part of the arrangement, the G6 became sole sponsor of Winfrey's website for 90 days. Pontiac's marketing director claimed that the car giveaway generated $20 million in unpaid media coverage and public relations—quite a bargain considering that the actual cost to Pontiac of the donated automobiles likely was less than $5 million.[58]

Formal Perspectives on Buzz Creation

To now more fully appreciate the concept of buzz, it will be useful to introduce the concepts of networks, nodes, and links. These concepts apply not just to buzz creation but also to any type of network—including brains (nerve cells connected by axons), the Web (online sites linked with other sites), transportation systems (cities linked with other cities via roads, highways, and interstate systems), societies (people linked with other people), and so on.[59] For example, the *nodes* in an airline system are the various airports that are located in cities served by airlines; these cities, in turn, are linked by the airline routes that emanate in one city and culminate in another. Most nodes (airports) in an airline system are linked to relatively few other nodes. However, some large airports (e.g., Chicago O'Hare, Atlanta Hartsfield, and New York JFK) are *hubs* (another name for large nodes) that are linked with numerous other airports.

The notion of an airline network is applicable to social systems. Each person within his or her own social system can be considered a node. Each person (node) is potentially linked with every other person (additional nodes). Although most of us are linked with relatively few individuals, some people are linked with numerous others. Due to the large number of contacts these highly connected people have, they sometimes are referred to as *influentials*. In comparison to major hubs in airline networks, influentials represent the hubs in social networks. It obviously follows that if you, as a marketing communicator, want people to disseminate positive WOM about your brand, then getting your message to influentials is critical to your success. This is what JetBlue did when reaching out to bartenders and hotel concierges in hopes they would spread the word about JetBlue Airways and its flights from the Long Beach airport.

We now examine the special topic of viral marketing, using social networks to create brand awareness via self-replicating viral means, similar to the spread of a virus.

Viral Marketing Is Akin to Creating an Epidemic

Viral marketing can be compared to an epidemic. By analogy, consider how the common influenza (flu) virus spreads. A flu epidemic starts with a few people, who interact with other people, who in turn spread it to others until eventually, and generally quickly, thousands or even millions of people have the malady. Needless to say, flu epidemics could not occur unless people—such as school-children—were in close contact with one another. For an epidemic to occur there must be a *tipping point*, which is the moment of critical mass at which enough people are infected so that the epidemic diffuses rapidly throughout the social system.[60]

Table 21.2 shows the top 10 viral ad campaigns of all time. Blendtec's "Will it Blend?" has generated well over 173 million views (on YouTube) to the question "Will it Blend?" The campaign shows humorous views of iPhones, Justin Bieber action figures, BiC lighters, World Cup vuvuzelas, and glow sticks being pulverized in their blender. Another popular one, Evian's "Live Young" campaign, included cute babies on roller blades and has been viewed over 158 million items.

It has been conjectured that epidemics in a social context, including the spread of information about brands, can be accounted for by three straightforward rules—the law of the few, the stickiness factor, and the power of context.[61]

Law of the Few

The first rule, the law of the few, suggests that it only takes a few well-connected people to start an epidemic. These people—variously referred to as connectors, influentials, evangelists, messengers, or opinion leaders—are capable of starting "commercial epidemics" because (1) they know a lot of people,

TABLE 21.2 Top 10 Viral Video Ad Campaigns of All Time

Rank	Brand	Campaign	Agency	Views
1	Blendtec	Will it Blend?	In-house	173,200,818
2	Evian	Live Young	BETC Euro RSCG	158,185,452
3	Old Spice	Responses	Wieden+Kennedy	80,592,555
4	Volkswagen	The Force	Deutsch	58,537,201
5	DC Shoes	DC × Ken Block's Gymkhana Project	In-house with Mad Media (production)	57,868,629
6	Microsoft	Xbox Project Natal	World Famous	53,871,614
7	Pepsi	Gladiator	AMV BBDO	52,931,154
8	Old Spice	Odor Blocker	Wieden+Kennedy	52,465,193
9	Old Spice	The Man Your Man Could Smell Like	Wieden+Kennedy	51,048,338
10	Doritos	Crash The Super Bowl 2010	Goodby, Silverstein & Partners	47,267,865

Source: visiblemeasures.com, as reported in "Online Video Market 2011," *Advertising Age*, Digital Issue (Fall), September 19, 2011.

(2) they receive satisfaction from sharing information, and (3) they are innately persuasive in advocating products and brands.[62]

Paid advertising initiates the two-step process, but it alone could never accomplish the results that informal social networks achieve. Advertising might inform, but it is common people who legitimize product and brand usage. Indeed, whereas advertisements lack complete credibility—because people realize that ads are designed to influence their behavior—personal messages from friends and acquaintances are readily accepted because no vested interest typically is involved. Even strangers providing online reviews of books, albums, and other items can be highly influential on product sales.[63]

Stickiness Factor

The second rule, the stickiness factor, deals with *the nature of the message*, whereas the first rule involves the messenger. Messages that are attention catching and memorable (i.e., "sticky" messages) facilitate talk about brands. This explains why urban legends fly through the social system. Such messages are inherently interesting and thus are passed along with lightning speed.

Emotion certainly plays an important role in making online content viral. Research has found that content which evokes either high-arousal positive (e.g., awe) or negative (e.g., anger or anxiety) emotions is more viral. Content that evokes low-arousing or deactivating emotions (e.g., sadness) is less viral.[64] Thus, testing may be in order of such viral content before its release.

The point is that not all messages stick and are worth repeating, just those that are innately interesting and memorable. Millions of people talked about the giveaway of hundreds of Pontiacs on *The Oprah Winfrey Show* mentioned earlier, because that was a newsworthy and exciting event. Similarly, tens of millions of people discussed Janet Jackson's (unintentional?) breast-baring that occurred during the halftime program of the 2004 Super Bowl due to its shock value and newsworthiness.

Power of Context

The third rule of epidemics, the power of context, simply indicates that the circumstances and conditions have to be right for a persuasive message a connector conveys to have its impact and initiate an epidemic. Janet Jackson's wardrobe malfunction probably would not have spread virally among millions of viewers had it not been on the Super Bowl.

Igniting Explosive Self-Generating Demand

The foregoing account has simply described the conditions that are congenial to the spread of commercial epidemics. The present account will examine how buzz generation and viral marketing can be managed to get the message about a brand rapidly diffused throughout a social network.

© TORU YAMANAKA/AFP/Getty Images

The well-known management consulting firm, McKinsey & Company, has formulated a set of principles for igniting positive WOM momentum for new brands. McKinsey's associates refer to word-of-mouth momentum as *explosive self-generating demand*, or ESGD for short. The following principles underlie the ignition of ESGD.[65]

Design the Product to Be Unique or Visible

Products and brands that are most likely to experience ESGD have two distinguishing characteristics. First, they are *unique* in some respect—in terms of appearance (e.g., vehicles such as the Mini Cooper and the Smart Car), functionality (e.g., Apple's iPhone 5), or in any other attention-gaining manner. Second, they are highly *visible* or *confer status* on opinion leaders and connectors, who are among the first to know about new products and services. People are interested in talking only about those products and brands that have some uniqueness, excitement, or some inherent "wow" factor.[66]

Select and Seed the Vanguard

Every new product and service has a group that is out in front of the crowd in terms of the speed at which the group adopts the product. McKinsey & Company calls this group the *vanguard*. The challenge for the marketer of a new brand is identifying *which* consumer group will have the greatest influence over other consumers and then doing whatever it takes to get that group, the vanguard, to accept your brand. Athletic shoe companies often launch new brands by supplying advance pairs to local basketball heroes. In this case, vanguards might include local NBA basketball stars, area celebrities, top local AAU and high school basketball teams, and so on. The hope is that they will become "cheerleaders" for the brand.

Ration Supply

Scarcity is a powerful force underlying influencers' efforts to persuade. This is because people often want what they cannot have. Automobile companies frequently exploit this reality by producing insufficient supplies to meet immediate demand when a new model is launched, especially one that is unique in design. The supply of Apple's new iPhones in most launches has been insufficient to meet initial demand. The thinking is that people will talk more about those things they cannot immediately have.

Use Celebrity Icons

Perhaps there is no better means to generate excitement about a new product than to first get it into the hands of a celebrity. Hairstyles, clothing fashions, and product choices that celebrities adopt are often accepted by large numbers of people who emulate their behavior. In the world of golf, for example, celebrities often appear in advertisements or infomercials and tout the benefits of new golf balls, clubs, and self-help products.

Tap the Power of Lists

The media disseminate many kinds of lists that are designed to influence consumer behavior and direct action. For example, aspiring college students and their parents read magazines such as *U.S. News & World Report*'s annual lists of top colleges and universities. Newspapers regularly provide lists of the best mutual funds. Radio stations and websites regularly announce the top-drawing movies over the weekend. It has been claimed that "lists are potent tools for creating buzz because they're effective road signs for information-besieged consumers who don't know where to focus their attention."[67]

Nurture the Grass Roots

Similar to the concept of cheerleading described earlier, this tactic is based on the idea of getting adopters of a product to convert other people into users. Naturally, people who are satisfied with a product often will encourage others to use the same product. But rather than "letting it happen" (or fail to happen), the notion of nurturing the grass roots involves—as do all buzz-building tactics—some form of *proactive effort* to motivate present product adopters to recruit new members or customers. Exercise clubs sometimes provide discounts to current members when they attract additional members to the club. Brand communities can be formed (e.g., see BzzAgent, www.bzzagent.com or House Party, www.houseparty.com) so that present adopters of a product can share their enthusiasm and hopefully spread the word to others.

Summing Up

This section hopefully has provided you with an appreciation that WOM momentum can be managed in a proactive fashion rather than accepted as a *fait accompli*. Also, it should be clear that not all products and brands are appropriate for buzz-creation and viral marketing efforts. The principles identified here offer insight into when and why buzz creation and viral marketing are particularly likely and most effective. Certainly, there are cautions that buzz and "virality" may generate awareness, yet not translate into revenue and profits.[68] A number of books on the topic have been written over the years. Please refer to the following endnote for a list of several informative and well-written books on the topic.[69]

Sponsorship Marketing

This section explores the topic of sponsorship marketing and its two elements: event and cause sponsorships. Sponsorships represent a growing aspect of marketing communications and are regarded as an important marketing tool by most marketing executives. More than two-thirds of chief marketing officers indicated that event sponsorship is a vital marketing function.[70] Sponsorships involve investments in events or causes for the purpose of achieving corporate (e.g., enhancing corporate image) or marketing (e.g., improving brand equity and augmenting sales) objectives. The following definition captures the practice of sponsorship marketing:

> [S]ponsorship involves two main activities: (1) an exchange between a sponsor [such as a brand] and a sponsee [such as a sporting event] whereby the latter receives a fee and the former obtains the right to associate itself with the activity sponsored and (2) the marketing of the association by the sponsor. Both activities are necessary if the sponsorship fee is to be a meaningful investment.[71]

At least five factors account for the growth in sponsorships:[72]

1. By attaching their names to special events and causes, companies may be able to avoid the clutter inherent in advertising media. It is noteworthy that some extensively sponsored events, such as the Olympic Games (e.g., 2012 London) and the National Association for Stock Car Auto Racing (NASCAR), have become somewhat cluttered. Sponsors desiring to associate their brands with relatively uncluttered events (i.e., events with few other sponsors) must either pay huge fees to obtain exclusive sponsorship rights or select smaller, lesser known events to sponsor.

2. Sponsorships help companies respond to consumers' changing media habits. For example, with the decline in network-television viewing, sponsorships offer a potentially effective and cost-efficient way to reach customers.

3. Sponsorships help companies gain the approval of various constituencies, including stockholders, employees, and society at large. That is, these constituencies respond favorably when a brand associates itself with a desirable event or cause.

4. Relationships forged between a brand and a sponsored event can serve to enhance a brand's equity, both by increasing consumers' awareness of the brand and by enhancing its image.[73]

5. The sponsorship of special events and causes enables marketers to target their communications and promotional efforts to specific geographic regions or to specific demographic and lifestyle groups.

© John Harrelson/Getty Images for NASCAR

For example, many well-known brands sponsor riders in professional bull-riding (PBR) events—brands such as Ford Truck, the U.S. Army, Cabela's (a sporting goods retailer), Carhartt work clothing, DeWalt tools, Wrangler jeans, Dickies work and casual clothing, and Jack Daniel's (a bourbon distiller). These and many other sponsors are attracted to PBR due to the demographic composition of PBR fans, who are predominantly male (60 percent), between the ages of 21 and 49, and mostly live west of the Mississippi River (71 percent). Marketers of these rugged products find PBR sponsorship to fit well with their target markets' geographic and demographic characteristics.[74]

Now that we have provided an overview of the general features of sponsorship marketing, the following sections detail the practice of event and cause-oriented sponsorships, respectively.

Event Sponsorships

Event sponsorships include supporting athletic events (such as golf and tennis tournaments, college football bowl games, the Olympics, extreme sports such as snowboarding and professional bull riding); entertainment tours and attractions; arts and cultural institutions; and festivals, fairs, and annual events of many different forms.

Although relatively small compared to the two major components of the marcom mix—that is, advertising and sales promotions—expenditures on event sponsorship are increasing. Worldwide, brand marketers are estimated to spend close to $40 billion on event sponsorships.[75] U.S. marketers alone spent approximately $21 billion sponsoring events in 2009.[76] Well over half of that amount went toward sponsoring various sporting events such as motor sports (e.g., NASCAR), golf and tennis, professional sports leagues and teams, and the Olympics.

Thousands of companies invest in some form of event sponsorship, which is defined as a form of brand promotion that ties a brand to a meaningful athletic, entertainment, cultural, social, or other type of high-interest public activity. Event marketing is distinct from advertising, promotion, point-of-purchase merchandising, or public relations, but it generally incorporates elements from all these communications tools.

Selecting Sponsorship Events

Marketers sponsor events to develop relationships with consumers, enhance brand equity, and strengthen ties with the trade. Successful event sponsorships require a meaningful *fit* among the brand, the event, and the target market. For example, brands such as Dove and Salon Selectives sponsor Shecky's Girls Night Out (www.sheckys.com/events). This is an annual series of 35 events that take place in a number of major American cities. The target audience for these events is trend-oriented professionals who earn more than $80,000 annually. Attendees pay a modest fee of $10 to see displays of the latest fashions from up-and-coming designers and receive free samples from event sponsors. Unilever's Dove brand, for example, sponsors the event as an opportunity to introduce attendees to its new brands.[77]

Factors to Consider

What specific factors should a company consider when selecting an event? The following points identify the key issues when evaluating whether an event represents a suitable association for a brand:[78]

1. *Image matchup*—Is the event consistent with the brand image and will it benefit the image? The Coleman Company, a maker of grills and other outdoor equipment, sponsors NASCAR races, fishing tournaments, and country-music festivals. All of these events appropriately match Coleman's

© AP Images/Alden Pellett

image and also represent appropriate venues for its target customers. Unionbay, a jeans and sportswear brand, along with soft-drink brand Mountain Dew and snowboard maker Burton, sponsored the U.S. Open Snowboarding Championships. It would seem that this event matches perfectly the images of all three brands.

2. *Target audience fit*—Does the event offer a strong likelihood of reaching the desired target audience? With blue-collar customers, retailers Target and Walmart have relied on auto racing sponsorships, whereas Kohl's has aligned with U.S. Youth Soccer and Kmart with World Wresting Entertainment.[79] For the Boston Marathon, with over 26,000 runners and 500,000 spectators, major sponsors include Adidas (running shoes and apparel), John Hancock (Boston-based insurer), and the Dana-Farber Cancer Institute (based in Boston). Also, the United Parcel Service (UPS) sponsored the Triple Crown–winning racehorse Big Brown. Many of UPS's users undoubtedly had great interest in watching the last leg of the Triple Crown, the Belmont Stakes, after Big Brown previously had won the Kentucky Derby and Preakness Stakes. See the *IMC Focus* insert for further discussion.

3. *Sponsor misidentification*—Is this event one that the competition has previously sponsored, and therefore is there a risk of being perceived as "me-too-istic" and confusing the target audience as to the sponsor's identity? Sponsor misidentification is not a trivial issue and can be a problem with recent changes or corporate confusion.[80] For example, Coca-Cola paid $250 million to be the official soft drink of the National Football League (NFL) for a five-year period. After sponsoring the NFL for several years, a general

Courtesy of www.sarahfit.com

Courtesy of Craig Andrews

IMC FOCUS

Big Brown (the Thoroughbred Racehorse) and UPS

As with all aspects of life, luck plays a role in brand managers' sponsorship decisions. Consider the case of UPS and its sponsorship of the thoroughbred racehorse named Big Brown. Needless to say, the horse is a large brown stallion, and UPS, its sponsor, also is known by the nickname "big brown" due to the brown paint motif used on its fleet of trucks, airplanes, and personnel uniforms.

Why would anyone give a racehorse such a mundane name as Big Brown, the type of name a child might assign to a large dog? Well, the original owner of Big Brown also owned a Brooklyn, New York, trucking company that hauls shipments for UPS. In gratitude after his company received a contract extension from UPS, the owner picked UPS's moniker as the name for his horse. This original owner of Big Brown later sold his controlling interest in the horse to a company called IEAH Stables.

A few weeks prior to the 2008 Kentucky Derby, IEAH Stables approached United Parcel Service with the proposition that UPS sponsor Big Brown in the Kentucky Derby. UPS accepted the offer and became the exclusive sponsor of Big Brown, who went on to win the Kentucky Derby (in Louisville, Kentucky). Then, two weeks later, he won the Preakness Stakes race in Baltimore, Maryland. The third Triple Crown race, the Belmont Stakes, was three weeks later at Belmont Park outside New York City on Long Island. Big Brown was expected to become the twelfth racehorse to win America's Triple Crown.

Unfortunately (for Big Brown's owners), the horse was unable to pull off victory in the Belmont Stakes. After losing practice time due to sustaining a substantial crack in one of his hoofs that required veterinarian intervention, Big Brown ran a pathetic race and came in last in a field of just nine horses. Nonetheless, publicity was enormous, as news of Big Brown's failure to win the Triple Crown spread across all mass media outlets and the Internet. UPS's modest investment in this sponsorship undoubtedly paid for itself many times over.

Source: Adapted from Corey Dade, "UPS Extends Its Pact to Sponsor Big Brown," *Wall Street Journal*, May 17, 2008, A4.

survey (not about Coca-Cola per se) asked football fans to name brands that sponsor the NFL. Thirty-five percent of the respondents named Coke as an NFL sponsor. Unfortunately (for Coca-Cola), another 34 percent falsely identified Pepsi-Cola as a sponsor![81]

4. *Clutter*—As with most every marcom communications medium, an event sponsor typically competes for signage and attention from every other company that sponsors the event. It obviously makes little sense to sponsor an event unless live participants and television viewers are likely to notice your brand and associate it with the event that it is paying to sponsor. NASCAR, for example, attracts a large number of sponsors due to the extraordinary growth rate in fan interest. (The movie *Talladega Nights* provided a spoof of the cluttered nature of sponsorships for this sport.) However, recognizing the problem with sponsorship clutter, one observer noted that unless a brand is a prime NASCAR sponsor, it easily "can get lost on the bumper."[82]

By comparison to NASCAR's sponsorship clutter, consider a clever sponsorship undertaken by Procter & Gamble's Prilosec brand of heartburn medication. Prilosec became a sponsor of the Bunco World Championship after research revealed that millions of women are regular bunco players and that about one-third of women who play bunco suffer frequent heartburn.[83] Prilosec experienced an uncluttered sponsorship arena when it signed on to co-host the Bunco World Championship.[84]

5. *Complement other marcom elements*—Does the event complement existing sponsorships and fit with other marcom programs for the brand? Many brands sponsor multiple events. In the spirit of integrated marketing

communications, it is important that these events "speak with a single voice." (Refer back to Chapter 1 for more on speaking with a single voice.)

6. *Economic viability*—This last point raises the all-important issue of budget constraints. Companies that sponsor events must support the sponsorships with adequate advertising, point-of-purchase materials, sales promotions, and publicity in order to activate retail sales.[85] One professional in the sponsorship arena uses the rule of thumb that two to three times the cost of a sponsorship must be spent in properly supporting it and offers the following advice:

> *A sponsorship is an opportunity to spend money. But like a car without gasoline, sponsorship without sufficient funds to maximize it goes nowhere. Therein lies the biggest secret to successfully leveraging sponsorship: It's not worth spending money for rights fees unless you are prepared to properly support it.*[86]

Sponsorship Agreements

There are several other legal and business factors to consider with sponsorship agreements.[87] First, the sponsor should try to obtain some *exclusivity*, such that a competitor does not share in the same benefits of the event. A *granting of rights* should be clear as to what can and cannot be done with the sponsor's brand (e.g., to avoid disparagement). Also, the *benefits* to the sponsor (e.g., signage, co-promotion, guaranteed attendance) should be identified. In addition, the sponsor needs to *control the licensing* of their trademarks associated with the event. Finally, *options to renew*, *escape clauses* (e.g., for sponsorships with teams forced to leave town, like the 1995 Cleveland Browns), *insurance* (e.g., with event risk), accommodations for *changes in events* (e.g., marathons/half-marathons stopped due to the heat index), *payment terms*, and *publicity* all should be considered with the sponsorship agreement.

Creating Customized Events

Some firms develop their own events rather than sponsoring existing events. For example, a British "cultural entrepreneur," Damian Barr, partnered with Volvo to invent the Starlite Urban Drive-In in London with cars donated from Volvo. See the *Global Focus* for more details.

In general, there are two major reasons that brand managers choose to customize their own events rather than sponsor events another organization conducts. First, a customized event provides a brand total control over the event. This eliminates externally imposed timing demands or other constraints and also removes the problem of clutter from too many other sponsors. Also, the customized event is developed to match perfectly the brand's target audience and to maximize the opportunity to enhance the brand's image and sales. A second reason for the customization trend is that there is a good chance that a specially designed event is more effective but less costly than a preexisting event.

It would be simplistic to conclude that brand managers or higher-level marketing executives should eschew sponsoring well-known and prestigious events. Sponsoring the Olympics or another major sporting or entertainment event can greatly enhance a brand's image and boost sales volume. Indeed, successfully achieving a strong link with an event that is highly valued means that the event's stature may transfer at least in some small part to the sponsoring brand. However, achieving such an outcome requires that a strong, durable, and positive link be established between the sponsoring brand and the event. All too often individual brands are swamped by larger and better-known sponsoring brands and no solid or durable link is formed. This being

GLOBAL
FOCUS

Volvo and East London's Starlite Urban Drive-In

Perhaps when you were younger, you had a chance to go to a drive-in movie in the United States, in which you park your car and the movie is shown on a large outside screen with audio fed into a channel on your radio (or through an old portable speaker fitting into a car window). Unfortunately, the British never quite had the weather, space, or car culture needed for drive-in movies. Yet, this changed in 2010 with the idea of Damian Barr, a journalist and cultural entrepreneur, who partnered with Volvo to invent the Starlite Urban Drive-In in East London (www.starliteurbandrivein. co.uk).

With the help of Volvo, 25 brand new cars are pre-parked and a $40 ticket buys you a seat in the Volvo for the movie, a drink, and some popcorn. The nearby Brickhouse restaurant has a special Starlite menu of burgers, meatloaf, and sweet potato pie, with ice cream sundaes or brownies for dessert. In 2010, the initial

screenings at the Starlite for the movies *Grease* and *Dirty Dancing* sold out online in 30 seconds.

While a student in Texas (and based on experiences along U.S. Route 66), Mr. Barr developed his preference for drive-ins. He also wanted a "partner" (not a "sponsor") that would fit in with his vision. According to Barr, Volvo was perfect as they were very hands-off and genuinely wanted to be creative. For example, a party was held on the night before the screenings with 400 witnessing hula-hoop artists descending from a roof to the music from *Grease*. Participants were honking horns and dancing on car roofs.

According to the company, the "Volvo for Life" tagline is about enriching people's lives with building cars for a better life, so the opportunity fit well with the brand. In turn, although he has received other sponsorship offers for the Drive-In, Mr. Barr intends to remain loyal to Volvo.

Source: Emma Hall, "Volvo Parks Urban Brits at Drive-In with 'Starlite'," *Advertising Age*, July 12, 2010, 7.

the case, it is doubtful that the sponsorship represents a good return on investment.[88]

Ambushing Events

In addition to increased customization, a number of companies around the world engage in what is called *ambush marketing*, or simply *ambushing*.[89] Ambushing takes place when companies that are *not* official sponsors of an event undertake marketing efforts to convey the impression that they are.[90] For example, research following a past summer Olympics determined that 72 percent of respondents to a survey identified Visa as an official sponsor of the Olympic Games and that 54 percent named American Express as a sponsor. As a matter of fact, Visa paid $40 million to sponsor the Olympics, whereas American Express simply advertised heavily during the telecast of the Olympics.[91]

In a survey associated with the 2008 Olympics held in Beijing, nearly 1,600 consumers in 10 Chinese cities were polled to determine which brands they linked to the Olympics. Due to ambushing efforts, 5 of the top 12 brands cited were *not* Olympic sponsors, including PepsiCo, KFC, and Nike.[92] There is little doubt that ambushing efforts can be highly effective when done well.

One may question whether it is ethical to ambush a competitor's sponsorship of an event, but a counterargument can easily be made that ambushing is simply a financially prudent way of offsetting a competitor's effort to obtain an advantage over your company or brand. (The ethical aspects of ambushing would make for an interesting class discussion.)

Measuring Success

Whether participating as an official sponsor of an event, customizing your own event, or ambushing a competitor's sponsorship, the results from all these efforts must be measured to determine effectiveness. As always, *accountability* is the key. Sponsorships cannot be justified unless there is proof that brand equity and financial objectives are being achieved. Moreover, two practitioners have stated the case for sponsorship measurement:

> *Sponsorships can be an enormous waste of money and a drain on the marketing budget without a well-structured business case and a measurement plan. When it comes to sponsorship, the key question marketers need to ask is: How do you do sponsorships that build brand equity and maintain fiscal responsibility?*[93]

As always, measuring whether an event has been successful requires, first, that the brand marketer specify the objective(s) that the sponsorship is intended to accomplish. Second, to measure results, there has to be a baseline against which to compare an outcome measure. This baseline is typically a premeasure of brand awareness, brand associations, or attitudes prior to sponsoring an event. Third, it is necessary to measure the same variable (awareness, associations, etc.) after the event to determine whether there has been a positive change from the baseline level. Comparisons to control groups (e.g., for differences versus matched regions without the event) are always helpful.

The metrics used to measure sponsorship effectiveness are straightforward. The measure companies most frequently use is a simple head count of how many people attended an event.[94] The total cost of the event is then divided by the number of attendees to obtain a measure of efficiency; this measure is useful for comparison against the per-capita costs of other sponsorships. Other frequently used measures include tracking sales volume following an event, determining how many hits to the brand's Web or social media site occurred post-event, counting the number of samples or coupons that were distributed, or measuring changes in brand awareness and brand image.

Cause Sponsorships

A more minor but important aspect of overall sponsorships, cause-related marketing involves an amalgam of public relations, sales promotion, and corporate philanthropy. Cause-oriented sponsorships typically involve supporting causes deemed to be of interest to some facet of society, such as environmental protection and wildlife preservation. As of 2012, American marketers spent $1.7 billion on cause-related marketing.[95] Cause-related marketing (CRM) involves alliances that companies form with *nonprofit organizations* to promote their mutual interests. Companies wish to enhance their brands' images and sales, and nonprofit partners obtain additional funding by aligning their causes with corporate sponsors. Although CRM was initiated in the United States in the early 1980s, companies throughout the world have become active participants in supporting causes. For example, the unique Product RED licensing program that was co-founded by Irish rocker Bono and Bobby Shriver (John F. Kennedy's nephew) uses a portion of its revenue from sales of particular brands to support the Global Fund to Fight AIDS, Tuberculosis and Malaria.[96]

There are several varieties of cause-related practices, but the most common form of CRM arrangement involves a company *contributing to a designated cause every time the customer undertakes some action that supports the company and its brands.* That is, with CRM, *a company's contribution to a cause is linked to a customer's "revenue-enhancing exchanges or behaviors"* (e.g., a purchase, scanning a QR code, redeeming a coupon, texting a number, visiting a website). The company's contribution is, in other words, contingent on the customer performing a behavior (such as buying a product or redeeming a coupon) that benefits the firm. Obviously, firms aligning themselves with particular causes do so partially with philanthropic intentions, but also with interest in enhancing their brands' images and, frankly, selling more products. As always, whether cause-related alignments accomplish these goals depends very much on the specifics of the situation—in this case, the nature of the product involved and the magnitude of the contribution offered.[97] The following examples illustrate how cause-related marketing operates:

- Papa John's ran a unique code promotion during NCAA March Madness to raise funds for the V Foundation for Cancer Research and Kay Yow/WBCA Cancer Fund. Each basketball fan that entered a coach's unique code (their last name) while placing an order online for an extra-large, two-topping pizza for $12 at www.papajohns. com had $1 donated to the cancer funds.[98]
- Whirlpool Corporation's KitchenAid division has been a supporter of the Susan G. Komen Breast Cancer Foundation. In a unique program, Whirlpool donated $50 to the foundation for every purchase of a pink mixer (pink being the symbol for breast cancer awareness) that was purchased via the company's website or a toll-free telephone number. The $50 donation represented a generous 17 percent of the revenue Whirlpool obtained for this special-colored mixer priced at $289.99. In a more recent cause-oriented initiative called Cook for the Cure, KitchenAid donated a minimum of $1,000,000 to Susan G. Komen for the Cure Program in conjunction with its pink product collection (see Figure 21.1).
- General Mills' Yoplait brand yogurt also has supported the Susan G. Komen Breast Cancer Foundation. In its

FIGURE 21.1 Illustration of KitchenAid's CRM Program

© AP Images/Aaron Tyler Anderson

© G.L. Booker/Kansas City Star/MCT via Getty Images

FIGURE 21.2 Illustration of Yoplait's "Save Lids to Save Lives" CRM Program

Save Lids to Save Lives promotion, Yoplait made a 10-cent contribution to the Komen Foundation up to a total of $1.5 million for every lid that consumers mailed back to the company (see Figure 21.2).

- In support of the Share Our Strength Program that is dedicated to reducing hunger and poverty, Tyson Foods donated more than 12 million pounds of chicken and other food products. For every package purchased, Tyson donated a pound of chicken, beef, or pork to the Share Our Strength Program—up to three million pounds.
- The Campbell Soup Company has for more than 30 years sponsored the Labels for Education Program, which helps schools obtain classroom supplies by asking families to collect labels from various Campbell's brands. Since the program began, Campbell has contributed items worth over $100 million to schools and organizations in exchange for the millions of labels submitted.
- Nabisco Brands donated $1 to the Juvenile Diabetes Research Foundation for each certificate that was redeemed with a Ritz-brand proof of purchase.
- Retailer Tommy Bahama has raised significant funds for The Garden of Hope & Courage project by donating a percentage of the sale of designated items from its apparel and accessory collections.
- A number of years ago, Reynolds Metals Company, a maker of aluminum foil and other food packaging products, contributed 5 cents to local Meals on Wheels programs every time any of three Reynolds brands was purchased.
- Brand managers of Pedigree (a brand of pet food) supported the cause of sheltering and feeding abandoned dogs. Pedigree matched each purchase of a 22-pound bag of its brand of dog food by donating another 22-pound bag of food to dog shelters.

The Benefits of CRM

Cause-related marketing is corporate philanthropy based on profit-motivated giving. In addition to helping worthy causes, corporations satisfy their own tactical and strategic objectives when undertaking cause-related efforts. By supporting a deserving cause, a company can (1) enhance its corporate or brand image, (2) thwart negative publicity, (3) generate incremental sales, (4) increase brand awareness, (5) broaden its customer base, (6) reach new market segments, and (7) increase a brand's retail merchandising activity.[99]

Research reveals that consumers have favorable attitudes toward cause-related marketing efforts. One study found that the vast majority of Americans (72 percent) think it is acceptable for companies to involve a cause in their marketing. Moreover, an even larger proportion of respondents to this survey (86 percent) indicated that they would be likely to switch from one brand to another of equal quality and price if the other brand associates itself with a cause. This latter percentage takes on added significance when noting that a decade earlier the percentage of consumers indicating they would switch brands to a brand supporting a cause was only 66 percent.[100]

On the downside, about one-half of the sample in another study expressed negative attitudes toward CRM; this negativity was due in large part to consumers' cynicism about the sponsoring firm's self-serving motive.[101] Research has revealed that brands may not benefit from CRM efforts if their support is perceived as having an ulterior motive rather than authentic concern about the sponsored cause.[102] This negative effect may be diminished when multiple organizations support a cause rather than a single sponsor.[103] Also, consumers are distrustful of CRM programs that are vague in terms of exactly how much will be donated to the cause, and, in fact, the majority of CRM offers are abstract and unclear about the amount of contribution (e.g., "a portion of the proceeds will be donated").[104] It helps when there is some consistency between corporate missions and the cause donations,[105] as well as incorporating one's social mission throughout the sponsoring company (e.g., Patagonia, Whole Foods), rather than treating it just as PR.[106]

The Importance of Fit

How should a company decide which cause to support? Although there are many worthy causes, only a subset is relevant to the interests of any brand and its target audience. Selecting an appropriate cause is a matter of fitting the brand to a cause that is naturally related to the brand's attributes, benefits, or image and also relates closely to the interests of the brand's target market. When there is a natural congruence between the sponsor and the cause, the sponsoring brand is looked upon more favorably and benefits from being perceived as more socially responsible.[107] Absence of a close fit can suggest to consumers that the brand is sponsoring a cause merely for self-serving reasons. Campbell Soup Company's Labels for Education Program nicely matches the target audience of children and their parents who consume Campbell's branded products. In fact, the same can be said of all of the illustrative examples of CRM programs provided previously.

Accountability Is Critical

In the final analysis, brand marketers are obligated to show that their CRM efforts yield sufficient return on investment or achieve other important, nonfinancial objectives. Corporate philanthropy is wonderful, but cause-related marketing is not needed for this purpose—companies can contribute to worthy causes without tying the contribution to consumers' buying a particular brand.[108] However, when employing a cause-related marketing effort, a company intends to accomplish marketing goals (such as improved sales or enhanced image) rather than merely exercising its philanthropic aspirations. Hence, a CRM effort should be founded on specific objectives—just the same as any marcom campaign. Research—such as a pre- and posttest data collection, as described for event sponsorships—is absolutely essential to determine whether a CRM effort has achieved its objective and is thereby strategically and financially accountable.

Colgate-Palmolive applied a straightforward formula in measuring the effectiveness of one of its sponsorships in which the CRM program was based on consumers redeeming FSI coupons. Using scanner data, Colgate compared product sales in the three weeks following a coupon drop with the average sales for the preceding six months. The difference between these two sales figures was multiplied by the brand's net profit margin, and the event's cost on a per-unit basis was subtracted to determine the incremental profit.[109] This procedure has the virtue of being logically sound and easy to implement.

Summary

This chapter covered three major topics: marketing public relations, word-of-mouth influence (including buzz creation and viral marketing), and sponsorship marketing. An important distinction was made between general public relations (general PR), which deals with overall managerial issues and problems (such as relations with stockholders and employees), and marketing public relations (MPR).

MPR consists of proactive MPR and reactive MPR. Proactive MPR is dictated by a company's marketing objectives and seeks opportunities rather than solves problems. Reactive MPR, conversely, responds to external pressures and typically deals with changes that have negative consequences for an organization. Handling negative publicity and rumors are two areas in which reactive PR is most needed.

Opinion leadership and word-of-mouth influence are important elements in facilitating more rapid product adoption and diffusion. Opinion leaders, respected for their product knowledge and opinions, inform other people (followers) about new products and services, provide advice, reduce followers' perceived risk in purchasing, and confirm decisions that followers have already made. Positive word-of-mouth influence is often critical to new-product success. People tend to talk about new products and services because they gain a feeling of prestige from being the bearer of news. Marketing communicators can take advantage of this prestige factor by stimulating "cheerleaders," or "brand evangelists," who will talk favorably about a new product or service.

Buzz creation and viral marketing are relatively recent phenomenon as a proactive marketing practice. Firms employ the services of buzz-creation units to generate new product adoption by recruiting the efforts of connected people (influentials, opinion leaders) who will

both adopt and talk about new products. Viral marketing can be compared to a social epidemic. Online viral activity is occurring at an increasingly rapid pace with social media and blogs.

Sponsorships involve investments in events and causes to achieve various corporate objectives. Event marketing is a form of brand promotion that ties a brand to a meaningful athletic, cultural, social, or other high-interest public activity. Event marketing is growing because it provides companies with alternatives to the cluttered mass media, an ability to target consumers on a local or regional basis, and opportunities for reaching narrow lifestyle groups whose consumption behavior can be tied to the event.

The distinctive feature of cause-related marketing (CRM) is that a company's contribution to a designated cause is linked to customers engaging in revenue-producing exchanges or behaviors with the firm. Cause-related marketing serves corporate interests while helping worthy causes.

Discussion Questions

1. Assume you are the owner of a restaurant in your college or university community. A false rumor about your business has circulated claiming that your head chef has a very contagious disease. Your business is falling off. Explain precisely how you would combat this rumor.

2. What are the advantages of publicity compared with advertising?

3. Some marketing practitioners consider publicity to be too difficult to control and measure. Evaluate these criticisms.

4. Some marketing people claim that *any* news about a brand, negative or positive, is good as long as it enables the brand to get noticed and encourages people to talk about the brand. Do you agree that negative publicity is always good? Under what conditions might it *not* be good?

5. Faced with the rumor about Corona beer being contaminated with urine (see the discussion earlier in the chapter), what course of action would you have taken if the Heineken distributor in Reno had not been identified as starting the rumor? In other words, if the source of the rumor were unknown, and it continued to persist, what steps would you have taken?

6. Describe two or three commercial rumors, or urban legends, other than those mentioned in the chapter. Identify each as either a conspiracy or a contamination rumor. Describe how you think these rumors started and why people apparently consider them newsworthy enough to pass along. (You might want to locate an online urban legend site for ideas. See, for example Snopes, www.snopes.com.)

7. Suppose you are the owner of a new board shop (e.g., long boards, skateboards, kite boards,

snowboards) located in your college or university community that caters primarily to the campus population. Your fledgling store cannot yet afford media advertising, so the promotional burden rests on stimulating positive word-of-mouth communications. Present a specific strategy for how you might go about stimulating positive WOM.

8. With thoughts of the GM Volt in mind, if you were the brand manager, what would you do to generate explosive self-generating demand?

9. The researchers who conceived the concept of the market maven devised a scale to measure consumers' responses to the following six items:

(1) I like introducing new brands and products to my friends.

(2) I like helping people in providing them with Information about many kinds of products.

(3) People ask me for information about products, places to shop, or sales.

(4) If someone asked where to get the best buy on several types of products, I could tell him or her where to shop.

(5) My friends think of me as a good source of information when it comes to new products or sales.

(6) Think about a person who has information about a variety of products and likes to share this information with others. This person knows about new products, sales, stores, and so on, but does not necessarily feel he or she is an expert on one particular product. This description fits me well.

Respondents are asked to rate each item on a seven-point scale, from strongly disagree (1) to strongly agree (7); thus, total scores range from a low of 6 (strongly disagrees to all six items) to 42 (strongly agrees to all items). Administer the scale to two friends whom you regard as market mavens and to two friends who are not market mavens. See if the mavens receive predictably higher scores than the nonmavens.

10. With reference to the discussion of explosive self-generating demand, describe a current movie that *would* lend itself to buzz-creation and viral marketing efforts and another that would *not*. What is the difference between these movies that makes only one amenable to such efforts?

11. Select a brand of your choice, preferably one that you really like and purchase regularly. Assuming that this brand is not presently involved in a cause sponsorship, propose a nonprofit organization with which your chosen brand might align itself. Also, recommend a specific CRM program for this brand that would enhance the brand's sales volume and contribute to the cause.

12. Is ambushing unethical or just smart, hard-nosed marketing?

13. As mentioned in the chapter, event sponsorship expenditures in the United States far exceed investments in cause-oriented sponsorships—basically more than a tenfold differential ($21 billion versus $1.7 billion). Why, in your opinion, is the difference so large? In other words, why do you think that U.S. brand marketers much prefer to allocate their marcom budgets to sponsoring events rather than causes?

14. The National Football League (NFL) does not permit players to wear logos of sponsoring brands. For discussion sake, let us assume that the NFL suspends its prohibition of players displaying brand logos on their uniforms. Now suppose that you are the event manager for a brand of your choice and you want to sponsor a specific NFL football player to represent your brand. Which player would you sponsor and why? To justify your choice fully, you must describe your brand's target audience and indicate the image you desire to associate with your brand.

End Notes

1. DEFCON is short for Defense Readiness Condition, and DEFCON 5 designates normal peacetime military readiness.

2. Suzanne Vranica, "Public Relations Learned the Hard Way," *Wall Street Journal*, December 30, 2010, B6; and Lisa Respers France, "Tiger Woods Engulfed in PR Storm," *CNN Entertainment*, December 1, 2009, http://articles.cnn.com/2009-12-01/entertainment/tiger.woods.public.relations_1_woods-wife-elin-nordegren-tiger-woods?_s=PM:SHOWBIZ.

3. David Barstow, "Vast Mexico Bribery Case Hushed Up by Wal-Mart After Top-Level Struggle," *New York Times*, April 21, 2012, http://www.nytimes.com/2012/04/22/business/at-wal-mart-in-mexico-a-bribe-inquiry-silenced.html?pagewanted=all.

4. The dividing line between marketing PR and general PR is not perfectly clear, as described well by Philip J. Kitchen and Danny Moss, "Marketing and Public Relations: The Relationship Revisited," *Journal of Marketing Communications* 1 (June 1995), 105–18.

5. Al Ries and Laura Ries, *The Fall of Advertising & the Rise of PR* (New York: HarperBusiness, 2002).

6. Paul Holmes, "Senior Marketers Are Sharply Divided about the Role of PR in the Overall Mix," *Advertising Age*, January 24, 2005, C1.

7. Stephanie Clifford and Steven Greenhouse, "Wal-Mart's U.S. Expansion Plans Complicated by Bribery Scandal," *New York Times*, April 29, 2012, http://www.nytimes.com/2012/04/30/business/wal-mart-bribery-scandal-complicates-us-expansion-plans.html?_r=2&pa.

8. Vranica, "Public Relations Learned the Hard Way," B6.

9. Ibid.

10. "Tiger Woods Sex Scandal," NBC Sports, August 25, 2010, http://www.nbcsports.msnbc.com/id/34969596; and Jonah Freedman, "The Fortunate 50," SI.com, http://sportsillustrated.cnn.com/specials/fortunate50-2011/index.html, 2011 (accessed May 20, 2012).

11. Nicholas Casey, "Mattel Issues Third Major Recall," *Wall Street Journal*, September 5, 2007, A3.

12. Jack Neff, "Pet-Food Industry Too Slow: Crisis-PR Gurus," *Advertising Age*, March 26, 2007, 29.

13. Rich Thomaselli, "Bausch & Lomb Shortsighted in Crisis," *Advertising Age*, May 22, 2006, 3, 39.

14. "FDA Public Health Advisory: Safety of Vioxx," September 30, 2004, http://www.fda.gov/Drugs/DrugSafety/PostmarketDrugSafetyInformationforPatientsandProviders/ucm106274.htm.

15. Joanna Slater, "Coke, Pepsi Fight Charges of Product Contamination," *Wall Street Journal Online*, August 15, 2003, http://online.wsj.com.

16. Rohini Ahluwalia, Robert E. Burnkrant, and H. Rao Unnava, "Consumer Response to Negative Publicity: The Moderating Role of Commitment," *Journal of Marketing Research* 37 (May 2000), 203–14. For another related finding, see Niraj Dawar and Madan M. Pillutla, "Impact of Product-Harm Crises on Brand Equity: The Moderating Role of Consumer Expectations," *Journal of Marketing Research* 37 (May 2000), 215–26.

17. Brian Quinton quoting Gene Grabowski, "Sticky Situations," *Promo*, October 2007, 31.

18. For theoretical treatment of consumer complaining behavior on websites, see James C. Ward and Amy L. Ostrom, "Complaining to the Masses: The Role of Protest Framing in Customer-Created Complaint Web Sites," *Journal of Consumer Research* 33 (September 2006), 220–30.

19. Jean Halliday, "Firestone's Dilemma: Can This Brand Be Saved?" *Advertising Age*, September 4, 2000, 1, 54; William H. Holstein, "Guarding the Brand is Job 1," *U.S. News & World Report*, September 11, 2000; and Karen Lundegaard, "The Web @ Work? Ford Motor Company," *Wall Street Journal Online*, October 16, 2000, http://online.wsj.com.

20. Dana James quoting PR man Jack Bergen in "When Your Company Goes Code Blue," *Marketing News*, November 6, 2000, 1, 15.

21. Quinton quoting Allen Adamson in "Sticky Situations," 34.

22. For an insightful discussion of urban legends and an interesting experiment testing factors influencing the likelihood that legends will be transmitted, see D. Todd Donavan, John C. Mowen, and Goutam Chakraborty, "Urban Legends: The Word-of-Mouth Communication of Morality through Negative Story Content," *Marketing Letters* 10 (February 1999), 23–34.

23. Ibid.

24. Donavan et al.'s content analysis of 100 urban legends revealed that 45 percent included product references, 12 percent involved warnings about innovations and technology, and 10 percent identified specific brands.

25. This definition is adapted from Fredrick Koenig, *Rumor in the Marketplace: The Social Psychology of Commercial Hearsay*, Dover, MA: Auburn House, 1985, 2.

26. For a review of the academic literature related to rumors as well as inspection of three interesting studies, see Michael A. Kamins, Valerie S. Folkes, and Lars Perner, "Consumer Responses to Rumors: Good News, Bad News," *Journal of Consumer Psychology* 6, no. 2 (1997), 165–87.

27. Ellen Joan Pollock, "Why Mountain Dew Is Now Grist for Fertile Teen Gossip," *Wall Street Journal Online*, October 14, 1999, http://online.wsj.com.

28. These rumors, all of which are false, have been in circulation at one time or another since the 1970s. All are thoroughly documented and analyzed in Koenig's fascinating book, *Rumor in the Marketplace*.

29. Koenig, *Rumor in the Marketplace*, 19.

30. Amy E. Gross, "How Popeyes and Reebok Confronted Product Rumors," *Adweek's Marketing Week*, October 22, 1990, 27.

31. Koenig, *Rumor in the Marketplace*, 167.

32. Koenig, *Rumor in the Marketplace*, 171–73.

33. Abbey Klaassen, "What to Do When Your Brand is Caught in a Social-Media Firestorm," *Advertising Age*, April 20, 2009, 24.

34. These recommendations are adapted from Koening, 172–73.

35. Alice M. Tybout, Bobby J. Calder, and Brian Sternthal, "Using Information Processing Theory to Design Marketing Strategies," *Journal of Marketing Research*, 18 (February 1981), 73–79.

36. Yong Liu, "Word of Mouth for Movies: Its Dynamics and Impact on Box Office Revenues," *Journal of Marketing*, 70 (July 2006), 74–89.

37. Leslie Patton, "House Parties with a Commercial Twist," *Businessweek*, February 3, 2011, http://www.businessweek.com/magazine/content/11_07/b4215030210139.htm.

38. Dee T. Allsop, Bryce R. Bassett, and James A. Hoskins, "Word-of-Mouth Research: Principles and Applications," *Journal of Advertising Research* 47 (December 2007), 398–411.

39. Ed Keller, "Unleashing the Power of Word of Mouth: Creating Brand Advocacy to Drive Growth," *Journal of Advertising Research* 47 (December 2007), 448–52.

40. For example, WOM for movies has been demonstrated to have a significant impact on box office revenues. See Yong Liu, "Word of Mouth for Movies: Its Dynamics and Impact on Box Office Revenue," *Journal of Marketing* 70 (July 2006), 74–89.

41. For further discussion, see Everett M. Rogers, *Diffusion of Innovations*, 5th ed. (New York: Free Press, 2003), chapter 8; and Jacqueline Johnson Brown and Peter H. Reingen, "Social Ties and Word-of-Mouth Referral Behavior," *Journal of Consumer Research* 14 (December 1987), 350–62.

42. In addition to Brown and Reingen's findings, ibid., see also Jacob Goldenberg, Barak Libai, and Eitan Muller, "Talk of the Network: A Complex Systems Look at the Underlying Process of Word-of-Mouth," *Marketing Letters* 12 (August 2001), 211–24.

43. For further discussion and research evidence, see Jeffrey Graham and William Havlena, "Finding the 'Missing Link': Advertising's Impact on Word of Mouth, Web Searches, and Site Visits," *Journal of Advertising Research* 47 (December 2007), 427–35; for a different view, showing a reduction in online WOM from increased advertising, see Jie Feng and Purushottam Papatla, "Advertising: Stimulant and Suppressant of Online Word of Mouth," *Journal of Interactive Marketing*, 25 (2011), 75–84.

44. Rogers, *Diffusion of Innovations*.

45. This quote is from the famous motivational researcher Ernest Dichter, in Eileen Prescott,

"Word-of-Mouth: Playing on the Prestige Factor," *Wall Street Journal*, February 7, 1984, 1.

46. Lawrence F. Feick and Linda L. Price, "The Market Maven: A Diffuser of Marketplace Information," *Journal of Marketing* 51 (January 1987), 83–97.

47. Keller, "Unleashing the Power of Word of Mouth."

48. Paul M. Herr, Frank R. Kardes, and John Kim, "Effects of Word-of-Mouth and Product-Attribute Information on Persuasion: An Accessibility-Diagnosticity Perspective," *Journal of Consumer Research* 17 (March 1991), 454–62; Richard J. Lutz, "Changing Brand Attitudes through Modification of Cognitive Structure," *Journal of Consumer Research* 1 (March 1975), 49–59; and Peter Wright, "The Harassed Decision Maker: Time Pressures, Distractions, and the Use of Evidence," *Journal of Applied Psychology* 59 (October 1974), 555–61.

49. Marsha L. Richins, "Negative Word-of-Mouth by Dissatisfied Consumers: A Pilot Study," *Journal of Marketing* 47 (winter 1983), 76.

50. Jin Li and Lingjing Zhan, "Online Persuasion: How the Written Word Drives WOM," *Journal of Advertising Research* (March 2011), 239–57.

51. Ross D. Petty and J. Craig Andrews, "Covert Marketing Unmasked: A Legal and Regulatory Guide for Practices That Mask Marketing Messages," *Journal of Public Policy & Marketing* 27 (spring 2008), 7–18.

52. Walter J. Carl, "To Tell or Not to Tell? Assessing the Practical Effects of Disclosure for WOM Marketing Agents and Their Conversational Partners," Summary Report, Northeastern University Communication Studies, January 2006, 1–23.

53. Theresa Howard, "'Viral' Advertising Spread Through Marketing Plans," *USA Today*, June 22, 2005, http://www.usatoday.com/money/advertising/2005-06-22-viral-usat_x.htm.

54. "Halo3" Wikipedia, http://en.wikipedia.org/wiki/Halo_3 (accessed May 21, 2012).

55. Jean Halliday, "Toyota Goes Guerilla to Roll Scion," *Advertising Age*, August 11, 2003, 4; and Norihiko Shirouzu, "Scion Plays Hip-Hop Impresario to Impress Young Drivers," *Wall Street Journal Online*, October 5, 2004, http://online.wsj.com.

56. Patton, "House Parties with a Commercial Twist."

57. Chris Woodyard, "JetBlue Turns to Beetles, Beaches, Bars," *USA Today*, August 22, 2001, 3B.

58. Sholnn Freeman, "Oprah's GM Giveaway Was Stroke of Luck for Agency, Audience," *Wall Street Journal Online*, September 14, 2004, http://online.wsj.com; and Jean Halliday and Claire Atkinson, "Pontiac Gets Major Mileage Out of $8 Million 'Oprah' Deal," *Advertising Age*, September 20, 2004, 12.

59. Albert-László Barabási and Eric Bonabeau, "Scale-free Networks," *Scientific American*, May 2003, 60–69.

60. The idea of a "tipping point" is based on the popular book by journalist Malcolm Gladwell, *The Tipping Point*, Boston: Little, Brown and Company, 2000.

61. Ibid.

62. It is important to note that the notion that only a few influentials are sufficient to initiate a marketplace epidemic is not without challenge. For a sophisticated treatment of this issue, see Duncan J. Watts and Peter Sheridan Dodds, "Influentials, Networks, and Public Opinion Formation," *Journal of Consumer Research* 34 (December 2007), 441–58.

63. For example, see Judith A. Chevalier and Dina Mayzlin, "The Effect of Word of Mouth on Sales: Online Book Reviews," *Journal of Marketing Research* 43 (August 2006), 345–54.

64. Jonah Berger and Katherine L. Milkman, "What Makes Online Content Viral?" *Journal of Marketing Research* 49 (April 2012), 192–205.

65. Renée Dye, "The Buzz on Buzz," *Harvard Business Review* (November/December 2000), 139–46.

66. This expression was attributed to a marketing practitioner and cited in Justin Kirby, "Online Viral Marketing: The Strategic Synthesis in Peer-to-Peer Brand Marketing," *Brand Channel White Paper*, 2004.

67. Dye, "The Buzz on Buzz."

68. Matthew Creamer, "Virality Doesn't Translate to Payday," *Advertising Age*, March 26, 2012, 4.

69. Emanuel Rosen, *The Anatomy of Buzz: How to Create Word-of-Mouth Marketing*, New York: Doubleday, 2000; Marian Salzman, Ira Matathia, and Ann O'Reilly, Buzz: *Harness the Power of Influence and Create Demand*, New York: Wiley, 2003; Jon Berry and Ed Keiler, *The Influentials: One American in Ten Tells the Other Nine How to Vote, Where to Eat, and What to Buy*, New York: Free Press, 2003; and Greg Stielstra, *Pyro Marketing*, New York: HarperCollins, 2005. See also the following article on viral marketing: Ralf van der Lans, Gerrit van Bruggen, Jehoshua Eliashberg, Berend Wierenga, "A Viral Branching Model for Predicting Electronic Word of Mouth," *Marketing Science*, 29 (March–April 2010), 348–65.

70. Kate Maddox, "Report Finds Most CMOs View Events as 'Vital,'" *BtoB*, March 14, 2005, 6.

71. T. Bettina Cornwell and Isabelle Maignan, "An International Review of Sponsorship Research," *Journal of Advertising* 27 (spring 1998), 11.

72. The first three factors are adapted from Meryl Paula Gardner and Phillip Joel Shuman, "Sponsorship: An Important Component of the

Promotions Mix," *Journal of Advertising* 16, no. 1 (1987), 11–17.

73. T. Bettina Cornwell, Donald P. Roy, and Edward A. Steinard II, "Exploring Managers' Perceptions of the Impact of Sponsorship on Brand Equity," *Journal of Advertising* 30 (summer 2001), 41–42. See also Angeline G. Close, R. Zachary Finney, Russell Z. Lacey, and Julie Z. Sneath, "Engaging the Consumer through Event Marketing: Linking Attendees with the Sponsor, Community, and Brand," *Journal of Advertising Research* 46 (December 2006), 420–33.

74. Patricia Odell, "Running with the Bulls," *Promo*, January 2007, 6–8.

75. "Events & Sponsorship," *Marketing News' 2007 Marketing Fact Book*, July 15, 2007, 31.

76. "Global Branded Entertainment Marketing Forecast," PQ Media, Executive Summary, 4th ed., 2010, 11.

77. Amy Johannes, "Girl's Club," *Promo*, March 2008, 8–9.

78. Adapted from Mava Heffler, "Making Sure Sponsorships Meet All the Parameters," *Brandweek*, May 16, 1994, 16.

79. Rich Tomaselli, "How Discounters Use Sports as a Means to Connect with Customers," *Advertising Age*, March 19, 2012, 20.

80. Gita Venkataramani Johar, Michel Tuam Pham, and Kirk L. Wakefield, "How Event Sponsors Are Really Identified: A (Baseball) Field Analysis," *Journal of Advertising Research* 46 (June 2006), 183–98; see also Anna R. McAlister, Sarah J. Kelly, Michael S. Humphreys, and T. Bettina Cornwell, "Change in a Sponsorship Alliance and the Communication Implications of Spontaneous Recovery," *Journal of Advertising* 41 (spring 2012), 5–16.

81. James Crimmins and Martin Horn, "Sponsorship: From Management Ego Trip to Marketing Success," *Journal of Advertising Research* 36 (July/August 1996), 11–21.

82. Sam Walker, "NASCAR Gets Coup as Anheuser Is Set to Raise Sponsorship Role," *Wall Street Journal Online*, November 13, 1998, http://online.wsj.com.

83. Bunco is a simple dice game typically played in groups of four people each, who are seated at three tables. In recent years the game has spread across the United States. The simplicity of the game enables participants to eat and chat while playing. For further details, see http://www.world-bunco.com/rules.html.

84. Ellen Byron, "An Old Dice Game Catches on Again, Pushed by P&G," *Wall Street Journal*, January 30, 2007, A1.

85. For one illustration of the importance of adequately promoting event sponsorships, see Pascale G. Quester and Beverley Thompson, "Advertising

and Promotion Leverage on Arts Sponsorship Effectiveness," *Journal of Advertising Research* 41 (January/February 2001), 33–47.

86. Heffler, "Making Sure Sponsorships Meet All the Parameters."

87. Bart A. Lazar, "Weigh Sponsorship Risks, Rewards Early On," *Marketing News*, November 15, 2006, 7.

88. You may wish to examine the following two articles that address the issue of whether Olympic sponsorship is a prudent financial investment: Kathleen Anne Farrell and W. Scott Frame, "The Value of Olympic Sponsorships: Who Is Capturing the Gold?" *Journal of Market Focused Management* 2 (1997), 171–82. For a more positive perspective, see Anthony D. Miyazaki and Angela G. Morgan, "Assessing Market Value of Event Sponsoring: Corporate Olympic Sponsorships," *Journal of Advertising Research* 41 (January/February 2001), 9–15.

89. For review, see Francis Farrelly, Pascale Quester, and Stephen A. Greyser, "Defending the Co-Branding Benefits of Sponsorship B2B Partnerships: The Case of Ambush Marketing," *Journal of Advertising Research* 45 (September 2005), 339–48.

90. Dennis M. Sandler and David Shani, "Olympic Sponsorship vs. 'Ambush' Marketing: Who Gets the Gold?" *Journal of Advertising Research* 29 (August/September 1989), 9–14.

91. David Shani and Dennis Sandler, "Counter Attack: Heading Off Ambush Marketers," *Marketing News*, January 18, 1999, 10.

92. Normandy Madden, "Ambush Marketing Could Hit New High at Beijing Olympics," *Advertising Age*, July 23, 2007, 22; for the 2012 London Summer Olympics see Avril Ormsby, "Olympics-Intense Ambush Marketing Likely at London Games," *Reuters*, March 1, 2012, http://www.reuters.com/article/2012/03/01/olympics-london-ambush-idUSL5E8E1B1W20120301.

93. John Nardone and Ed See, "Measure Sponsorships to Drive Sales," *Advertising Age*, March 5, 2007, 20.

94. This is based on a survey of event marketing conducted by the magazine *Promo* and published in Patricia Odell, "Crowd Control," *Promo*, January 2005, 22–29.

95. Matt Carmichael and Dante Chinni, "Trying to Decide on a Cause-Related Marketing Category? Consumer Location is Key," *Advertising Age*, January 16, 2012, http://adage.com/article/special-report-american-consumer-project/marketers-picking-a-sponsor-location-key/232099.

96. Betsy Spethmann, "The RED Brigade," *Promo*, January 2007, 18–25.

97. Michal Strahilevitz, "The Effects of Product Type and Donation Magnitude on Willingness to Pay

More for a Charity-Linked Brand," *Journal of Consumer Psychology* 8, no. 3 (1999), 215–41.

98. "NCAA Coaches to Reveal Papa John's Promo Code," *Promo*, March 18, 2010, http://chief-marketer.com/news/ncaa-coaches-reveal-papa-johns-promo-code.

99. P. Rajan Varadarajan and Anil Menon, "Cause-Related Marketing: A Coalignment of Marketing Strategy and Corporate Philanthropy," *Journal of Marketing* 52 (July 1988), 58–74.

100. "2004 Cone Corporate Citizenship Study Results," Cause Marketing Forum, December 8, 2004, http://www.causemarketingforum.com.

101. Deborah J. Webb and Lois A. Mohr, "A Typology of Consumer Responses to Cause-Related Marketing: From Skeptics to Socially Concerned," *Journal of Public Policy & Marketing* 17 (fall 1998), 239–56.

102. Yeosun Yoon, Zeynep Gürhan-Canli, and Norbert Schwarz, "The Effect of Corporate Social Responsibility (CSR) Activities on Companies with Bad Reputations," *Journal of Consumer Psychology* 16, no. 4 (2006), 377–90; and Lisa R. Szykman, Paul N. Bloom, and Jennifer Blazing, "Does Corporate Sponsorship of a Socially-Oriented Message Make a Difference? An Investigation of the Effects of Sponsorship Identity on Responses to an Anti-Drinking and Driving Message," *Journal of Consumer Psychology* 14, nos. 1&2 (2004), 13–20.

103. Julie A. Ruth and Bernard L. Simonin, "The Power of Numbers: Investigating the Impact of Event Roster Size in Consumer Response to Sponsorship," *Journal of Advertising*, 35 (winter 2006), 7–20.

104. John W. Pracejus, G. Douglas Olsen, and Norman R. Brown, "On the Prevalence and Impact of Vague Quantifiers in the Advertising of Cause-Related Marketing (CRM)," *Journal of Advertising* 32 (winter 2003–2004), 19–28.

105. Paul Bloom, "Everyone's Waxing Philanthropic These Days, But It Pays Off – If You Do It Right," *Advertising Age*, May 26, 2008, 18.

106. Seth Stevenson, "America's Most Unlikely Corporate Guru," *Wall Street Journal*, May 2012, 86–88.

107. Debra Z. Basil and Paul M. Herr, "Attitudinal Balance and Cause-Related Marketing: An Empirical Application of Balance Theory," *Journal of Consumer Psychology* 16, no. 4 (2006), 391–403; T. Bettina Cornwell, Michael S. Humphreys, Angela M. Maguire, Clinton S. Weeks, and Cassandra L. Tellegen, "Sponsorship-Linked Marketing: The Role of Articulation in Memory," *Journal of Consumer Research* 33 (December 2006), 312–21; Carolyn J. Simmons and Karen L. Becker-Olsen, "Achieving Marketing Objectives through Social Sponsorships," *Journal of Marketing* 70 (October 2006), 154–69; Satya Menon and Barbara E. Kahn, "Corporate Sponsorships of Philanthropic Activities: When Do They Impact Perception of Sponsor Brand?" *Journal of Consumer Psychology* 13, no. 3 (2003), 316–27; and Nora J. Rifon, Sejung Marina Choi, Carrie S. Trimble, and Hairong Li, "Congruence Effects in Sponsorship: The Mediating Role of Sponsor Credibility and Consumer Attributions of Sponsor Motive," *Journal of Advertising* 33 (spring 2004), 29–42.

108. It has been argued that cause-related marketing may serve to enhance a company's goodwill, but may not improve a company's ability to compete. See Michael E. Porter and Mark R. Kramer, "The Competitive Advantage of Corporate Philanthropy," *Harvard Business Review* (December 2002), 5–16.

109. Gary Levin, "Sponsors Put Pressure on for Accountability," *Advertising Age*, June 21, 1993, S1.

CHAPTER 22

Packaging, Point-of-Purchase Communications, and Signage

If you have a smartphone, you can use it for a wide range of applications—but does that include grocery shopping? Ahold USA's Stop & Shop is a large and progressive supermarket chain in New England that has been testing the latest in in-store technology since 2004 with the introduction of the "Shopping Buddy." The Shopping Buddy was an "intelligent" cart equipped with a wireless touchscreen and a scanner that allowed shoppers to check prices, alert shoppers to sale items and coupons, check any item's location in the store (with radio frequency

identification [RFID] technology), and scan and check out purchased items. The Shopping Buddy later evolved into a handheld device provided by Stop & Shop called "Easy Shop."

Like the Shopping Buddy, another innovation, "MediaCarts," uses RFID technology to broadcast in-store ads and promotions to a shopping cart video screen as a shopper approaches an aisle. It also allows shoppers to scan purchased products, enabling a rapid checkout.

Beginning in April 2011, Modiv Mobile (now Catalina Mobile) introduced a mobile shopping app for smartphones now available in 110 Shop & Stop stores in New England. The app works with the store loyalty program in that when shoppers enter the store and open the app, they receive offers based on their shopping history. Using their smartphones, shoppers then scan barcodes of items they put into the cart and can buy the item right on their phone, thereby skipping the checkout entirely! The Catalina acquisition means that the app can be used well beyond Stop & Shop, as Catalina reaches 75 percent of U.S. households across 30,000 stores. Moreover, Coupon.com, a digital coupon giant, now is offering the coupon app Grocery iQ to shoppers for consumer-packaged goods brands. In addition, quick response (QR) codes on packages and signage can be scanned for added information for shoppers.

Critics of such mobile grocery shopping apps wonder if they will mirror "scan 'n scram" consumer behavior found with other more expensive retail products in which consumers scan barcodes to simply comparison shop among competing brands and stores, including online offerings. Yet, such comparative behavior is found to be lowest among food and medicine categories, and experts say consumers are not likely to scan dozens of boxes of Cheerios (or private label brands) between stores to see which one is cheaper.

Certainly, app checkout security and the question of reduced employment for checkout clerks (at 12 to 15 percent of grocer expenses) have been viewed as issues. Yet, on this latter point, some argue that grocers already operate on very small profit margins in a very competitive industry. Having consumers use their own smartphones for the apps does save grocers money in addition to saved labor costs at checkout. As to competition, stores also compete with online grocers, such as Peapod and Fresh Direct that estimate at least 10 percent of their customers *already* purchase their items with a mobile phone using the online apps. So, it is likely that savvy grocers will welcome the use of this state-of-the-art, in-store technology to aid shopper loyalty and efficiency in what is already an extremely competitive marketplace.

Sources: Kunur Patel, "Are Consumers Ready for Mobile Grocery Shopping?" *Advertising Age*, May 21, 2012, 8; Kathryn Koegel, "Mobile Scan 'N Scram: How Worried Should Retailers Be?" *Advertising Age*, January 18, 2012, http://adage.com/article/digitalnext/mobile-scan-n-scram-worried-retailers/232148; Dana Mattioli, "Grocers Testing Smartphones," *Wall Street Journal*, October 11, 2011, B6; "Stop & Shop to Roll Out New Intelligent Shopping Carts from IBM and Cuesol," *Yahoo! Finance*, October 13, 2004; and Jack Neff, "A Shopping-Cart-Ad Plan That Might Actually Work," *Advertising Age*, February 5, 2007.

Introduction

This chapter examines topics that represent a form of advertising but not in the same sense typically thought of when considering media such as television, radio, magazines, newspapers, and the Internet. Rather, the material covered in this chapter examines communicating with consumers at the point of purchase or close to it. In particular, we explore four general forms of marketing communications: packaging, in-store point-of-purchase (POP) messages, on-premise signage, and out-of-home advertisements (e.g., billboards). These communication modes attempt to influence consumers' store- or brand-selection decisions. On-premise store signage, out-of-home ads, and POP messages represent important forms of communications that serve in very important ways to influence consumers' awareness and images of retail outlets and the brands they carry.

We first examine "inside" forms of marcom presentation, including packaging and POP advertising. We then distinguish two general forms of "outside" marcom messages and refer to these as on-premise business signage and out-of-home advertisements, or off-premise ads. The difference between on-premise business signage and out-of-home advertising (off-premise signage) is that the former communicates information about products and services in close proximity to the store, whereas the latter provides information about goods and services that are available somewhere else.[1]

Packaging

A brand's package is, of course, the container that both protects and helps sell the product. Products available on store shelves are most always bottled, boxed, or packaged in some other manner. As the term *package* is used in the present context, beverage bottles and cereal boxes are packages; so are the jewel boxes for CDs and DVDs, the boxes in which new shoes are contained, and so on. Marcom specialists appreciate the crucial communications role performed by brand packaging, which has given rise to expressions such as, "Packaging is the least expensive form of advertising," "Every package is a five-second commercial," "The package is a silent salesperson," and "The package is the product."[2] Packaging performs key communication and sales roles at the POP inasmuch as shoppers spend an incredibly short amount of time—roughly 10 to 12 seconds—viewing brands before moving on or selecting an item and placing it in the shopping cart.[3]

There have been many recent innovations in packaging, including those that enhance the workability factor (e.g., "dip and squeeze" ketchup packs), as well

as those that are creative design innovations (e.g., decorative aluminum soda and beer bottles). For a review of the latest in packaging innovations, see the industry website WEBpackaging, www.webpackaging.com.

The growth of supermarkets, mass merchandisers (such as Walmart and Target) and other self-service retail outlets has necessitated that the package perform marketing functions beyond the traditional role of containing and protecting the product. The package also serves to (1) draw attention to a brand, (2) break through competitive clutter at the point of purchase, (3) justify price and value to the consumer, (4) signify brand features and benefits, (5) convey emotionality, and (6) ultimately motivate consumers' brand choices. Packaging is particularly important for differentiating homogenous or unexciting brands from available substitutes by working uninterruptedly to say what the brand is, how it is used, and what it can do to benefit the user.[4] In short, packages perform a major role in enhancing brand equity by creating or fortifying brand awareness and building brand images via conveying functional, symbolic, and experiential benefits (recall the brand equity model presented in Chapter 2).

Packaging Structure

A package communicates meaning about a brand via its symbolic components: color, design, shape, size, physical materials, and information labeling.[5] These components taken together represent what is referred to as the *packaging structure*. These structural elements must interact harmoniously to evoke within buyers the set of meanings intended by the brand marketer. The notion underlying good packaging is *gestalt*. That is, people react to the unified whole—the gestalt—not to the individual parts. We now describe the different package structure components from prior research, as well as use examples to illustrate each of the components.

The Use of Color in Packaging

Packaging colors have the ability to communicate various cognitive and emotional meanings to prospective buyers.[6] Research has demonstrated convincingly the important role that color plays in affecting our senses. For example, in one study researchers altered the shade of pudding by adding food colors to create dark brown, medium brown, and light brown "flavors." In actuality, the pudding was identical in all three versions, namely vanilla flavor. However, the research revealed that all three brown versions were perceived as tasting like chocolate. Moreover, the dark brown pudding was considered to have the best chocolate flavor and to be the thickest. The light brown pudding was perceived to be the creamiest, possibly because cream is white in color.[7] This study, although not conducted in a packaging context per se, certainly holds implications for the use of color in package design.

The role of color in IMC as a peripheral cue under low involvement fits in with prior research discussed in Chapter 7 on the Elaboration Likelihood Model. As an example, research shows that under low involvement, distinctive (i.e., color) ad stimuli have a significantly greater impact on ad execution thoughts, attitudes toward the brand and ad, and purchase intentions than found with the exact ad stimuli, but in a nondistinctive (i.e, black-and-white) format.[8]

In general, the strategic use of colors in packaging is effective because colors affect people psychologically and emotionally. For example, the so-called high-wavelength colors of red, orange, and yellow possess strong excitation value and induce elated mood states.[9] *Red* is often described in terms such as active, stimulating, energetic, and vital. Brands using this as their primary color include Close-Up (toothpaste), Tylenol (medicine), Coca-Cola (soft drink), Ritz (crackers), and Pringles (potato chips). *Orange* is an appetizing color that is often associated with food. Popular food brands using orange packaging include Wheaties (cereal), Uncle Ben's (rice), Sanka (coffee), Stouffer's (frozen dinners), and Kellogg's Mini-Wheats (cereal). *Yellow*, a good attention getter, is a warm color that has a cheerful effect on consumers. Cheerios (cereal), Kodak (film), Mazola (corn oil), Burt's Bees (personal care), and Pennzoil (motor oil) are just a few of the many brands that use yellow packages.

Green connotes abundance, health, calmness, and serenity. Green packaging is sometimes used for beverages (e.g., Heineken beer, 7-Up, Sprite, and Mountain Dew), often for vegetables (e.g., Green Giant), and for many other products (Irish Spring deodorant soap, Fuji film, etc.). Green also stands for environmentally friendly products and as a cue to consumers of reduced-fat, low-fat, and fat-free products (e.g., Healthy Choice products). *Blue* suggests coolness and refreshment. Blue is often associated with laundry and cleaning products (e.g., Downy fabric softener and Snuggle dryer sheets) and skin products (e.g., Nivea skin lotion, Noxzema skin cream). Finally, *white* signifies purity, cleanliness, and mildness. Gold Medal (flour), Special K (cereal), Dove (body lotion, soap), and Pantene (shampoo) are a few brands that feature white packages.

In addition to the emotional impact that color brings to a package, using polished reflective surfaces and color schemes employing white and black or silver and gold can add elegance and prestige to products. Cosmetic packages often use gold (e.g., Revlon's MoistureStay Lipcolor) or metallic silver packages (e.g., Almay Sheer makeup).

It is important to note that the meaning of color varies from culture to culture. The comments made here are based on North American culture and are not necessarily applicable elsewhere. Readers from other cultures should identify exceptions to these comments and illustrate packages that do not adhere to North American color usage. Interestingly, a website presents results from a global survey that has been conducted for more than a decade on the meanings particular colors convey. Over 30,000 people have taken the survey and identified the colors they associate with particular meanings. For example, what colors suggest the following meanings or emotions to you: dignity, happiness, dependability, high quality, and power? To see what others think and to take the survey yourself, go to www.colormatters.com/color-symbolism/global-color-survey. For additional information about color symbolism, review the website presented in the following footnote.[10]

Design and Shape Cues in Packaging

Design refers to the organization of the elements on a package. An effective package design is one that permits good eye flow, provides the consumer with a point of focus, and conveys meaning about the brand's attributes and benefits. Package designers bring various elements together to help define a brand's image. These elements include—in addition to color—shape, size, and label design.

One way of evoking different feelings is through the choice of the slope, length, and thickness of lines on a package. *Horizontal lines* suggest restfulness and quiet, evoking feelings of tranquility. There appears to be a physiological reason for this reaction—it is easier for people to move their eyes horizontally than vertically; vertical movement is less natural and produces greater strain on eye muscles than horizontal movement. *Vertical lines* induce feelings of strength, confidence, and even pride. Energizer (batteries), Aquafresh (toothpaste), and Jif (peanut butter) all feature vertical lines in their package designs. One can even think of an athletic uniform as a package of sorts, and vertical lines sometimes appear on uniforms (think, for example, of the New York Yankees' uniform with its famous pinstripes). *Slanted lines* suggest upward movement to most people in the Western world, who read from left to right and thus view slanted lines as ascending rather than descending. Armor All (automobile polish), Gatorade (power drink), and Dr. Pepper (soft drink) use slanted lines in their package designs.

Shapes, too, arouse certain emotions and have specific connotations. Generally, round, curving lines connote femininity, whereas sharp, angular lines suggest masculinity. A package's shape also affects the apparent volume of the container. In general, if two packages have the same volume but a different shape, the taller of the two will appear to hold a greater volume inasmuch as height is usually associated with volume.

For rectangular-shaped packages, research has established that different ratios among the height, width, and depth dimensions of these packages (e.g., the ratio of the box's height to its width) play a role in affecting consumers' brand choices.[11] This may seem strange, but mathematicians, architects, artists, and others have observed that the rectangular ratio of approximately 1.62 is "golden" and has appeared in the building blocks of the Great Pyramids, the Parthenon's facade, and in some master paintings.[12] Certain ratios in rectangular-shaped objects appear to promote perceptions of harmony, balance, and even beauty. In a consumer context, researchers studied actual brand packages in four grocery product categories—cereals, cookies, soaps, and detergents—and determined that the ratios of the sides of the boxes predicted the brands' market shares. This evidence suggests that the shape of a package is a strategic decision that requires careful consideration and marketplace testing. In short, a box is more than a mere container. It also is a receptacle loaded with subtle information and cues of product attractiveness and perhaps even quality.

Packaging Size

Many product categories are available in several product sizes. Soft drinks, for example, come in 8-, 12-, and 24-ounce bottles; 1-, 1.5-, and 2-liter containers; and in 6-, 12-, and 24-unit packs. Manufacturers offer different-sized containers to satisfy the unique needs of various market segments, to represent different usage situations, and to gain more shelf space in retail outlets. An interesting issue arises from the consumer's perspective with regard to the size of the container. In particular, does the amount of product consumption vary depending on the size of the container? For example, do consumers consume more content from a large package than a smaller version? Research on this matter reveals a tendency for consumers to indeed consume more content from larger packages, especially for food and drink products with contents appealing to certain sensory receptors (i.e., sugar, fat, salt).[13] One other reason for this behavior is that consumers perceive they gain lower unit prices from larger than smaller packages.[14] This finding is not universal across all products, however, because consumption for some products (such as laundry bleach or vitamins) is relatively invariant. Research also has revealed that packages with unusual shapes are perceived subconsciously as containing larger quantities compared to more conventional packages, even when these latter packages are taller—primarily because they draw more attention from consumers.[15]

Physical Materials in Packaging

Another important consideration is the materials that make up a package. Increased sales and profits often result when upgraded packaging materials are used to design more attractive and effective packages. Packaging materials can arouse consumer emotions, albeit more subconsciously. Packages constructed of metal evoke feelings of strength, durability, and, perhaps undesirably, coldness. Plastic packages connote lightness, cleanliness, and perhaps cheapness. Materials that are soft such as velvet, suede, and satin are associated with femininity. Foil can be used to convey a high-quality image and provoke feelings of prestige. Beverage products such as beers and sparkling wines often use foil with the apparent intent of appearing high end. Finally, wood sometimes is used in packages to arouse feelings of masculinity.

Evaluating the Package: The VIEW Model

A number of individual features have been discussed with regard to what a package communicates to buyers, but what exactly constitutes a good package? Although, as always, no single response is equally suitable across all packaging situations, four general features can be used to evaluate a particular package: visibility, information, emotional appeal, and workability, or VIEW.[16]

V = Visibility

Visibility signifies the ability of a package to *attract attention* at the point of purchase. The objective is to have a package stand out on the shelf, yet not be so garish that it detracts from a brand's image. Brightly colored packages are especially effective at gaining the consumer's attention. Novel packaging graphics, sizes, and shapes also enhance a package's visibility and thus serve to draw the consumer's attention. Based on principles of adaptation, though, it is important that the package be distinctive (i.e., standing out in its competitive environment).[17] For example, if all other pizza boxes are bright orange in a frozen food chest, your similarly colored pizza box may not stand out.

Many brands in product categories such as soft drinks, beer, cereal, and candy alternate packages throughout the year with special seasonal and holiday packaging as a way of attracting attention in addition to fitting in with the season. By aligning the brand with the shopping mood fitting the season or holiday, companies provide consumers with an added reason for selecting the specially packaged brand over more humdrum brands that never vary their package design. For instance, the Zipp Vitalize health drink package in the United Kingdom shows a zipper revealing fruit matching the flavor of a particular drink.

I = Information

This second element of the VIEW model deals with various forms of product information that are presented on packages (e.g., product ingredients, usage instructions, claimed benefits, nutritional information, and product warnings). The objective is to provide the right type and quantity of information without cluttering the package with excessive information that could interfere with the primary message or cheapen the look of the package.

Package labels play an influential role in affecting consumer purchase behavior. For example, research has demonstrated that presenting graphic visuals on cigarette packages for purposes of conveying the negative health consequences of smoking results in more people intending to quit smoking and willing to encourage other smokers to quit.[18] Research also has determined that low-fat labels on food products have the perverse effect of increasing food intake by up to 50 percent compared to foods not labeled as low fat.[19] This increased food consumption occurs for normal-weight consumers mostly with foods perceived as being relatively healthy, but for overweight people it increases their consumption of all foods. The reasons underlying this low-fat labeling and increased-food-intake relationship are twofold: (1) low-fat labels lead people to believe that products are lower in calories than they actually are, and (2) consumers' guilt as a result of overeating is reduced when consuming foods labeled as low fat. Some people, when eating foods labeled as low fat, infer that ingesting greater quantities is okay without considering that such foods may have lower levels of fat content, but not meaningfully fewer calories. These people consequently overeat but without experiencing the guilt of so doing.

The conveyance of clear, concrete, accurate, and standardized nutrition information from food labels (e.g., Nutrition Facts Panels, front-of-package symbols) also is important. For example, recent front-of-package nutrition research shows that although simple check symbols (e.g., "Smart Choices") are well liked, more complex traffic light symbols (used in some U.K. stores) tend to be more accurate for consumers evaluating the nutrition levels of products.[20]

In general, and in some instances, putting a short, memorable slogan on a package is a wise marketing tactic. Slogans on packages are best used when a strong association has been built between the brand and the slogan through extensive and effective advertising. The slogan on the package, a concrete reminder of the brand's advertising, can facilitate the consumer's retrieval of advertising content and thereby enhance the chances of a trial purchase. This practice of putting an advertising slogan on a package to tie in with media advertising takes advantage of a psychological principle known as *encoding specificity*. We will describe this principle in detail later in this chapter when discussing the role of POP communications.

E = Emotional Appeal

The third component of the VIEW model, emotional appeal, concerns a package's ability to evoke a desired feeling or mood. Package designers attempt to arouse feelings such as elegance, prestige, cheerfulness, and fun through the use of color, shape, packaging materials, and other devices. Packages for some brands contain virtually no emotional elements and emphasize instead informational content, whereas packages of other brands emphasize emotional content and contain very little information. Heinz ketchup's packaging well illustrates the emotional value of packaging. Heinz, like other brands in this category, had always been packaged in glass bottles. Then the company began packaging ketchup in plastic containers. Both the bottles and the plastic containers were relatively bland, however. In an appeal to children, who consume the majority of all ketchup in the United States, Heinz eventually designed an emotionally appealing, fun-oriented package with bright coloring and a multihued, striped design. Children love the different ketchup colors (red, green, and purple) and the similarly colored packages.

What determines whether information or emotion is emphasized to a greater extent in a brand's package? The major determinant is the nature of the product category and the underlying consumer behavior involved. If consumers make brand-selection decisions based on objectives such as obtaining the best buy or making a prudent choice, then packaging should provide sufficient concrete information. When, however, brand selections are made in the pursuit of amusement, fantasies, or sensory stimulation, packaging should contain the appropriate emotional content to activate purchase behavior.

W = Workability

The final component of the VIEW model, workability, refers to how a package functions rather than how it communicates. Several workability issues are prominent: (1) does the package protect the product contents, (2) does it facilitate easy storage on the part of both retailers and consumers, (3) does it simplify the consumer's task in accessing and using the product, (4) does it protect retailers against unintentional breakage from consumer handling and from pilferage, and (5) is the package environmentally friendly?

Numerous packaging innovations in recent years have enhanced workability. These include pourable-spout containers for motor oil and sugar; easy-pour and use containers (such as for Heinz ketchup); microwaveable containers for many food items; zip-lock packaging for cheese and other food items; single-serving bags and boxes; food in tubes (e.g., yogurt, applesauce, and pudding); slimmer 12-packs of beer and soft drinks that take up less room in refrigerators; and easy-to-hold, open, and pour paint containers (see Figure 22.1). Creative, environmentally-focused packages include Dial's Eco-Smart Liquid Hand Soap Refill with an easy-pour spout in a collapsible package. This innovative package allows for quick filling without spills, and uses 67 percent less plastic than other refills, resulting in reduced transportation and fuel costs.

The introduction of General Mills' Go-Gurt yogurt in a tube for children illustrates how a "workable" package can alter consumer behavior and increase sales. Because

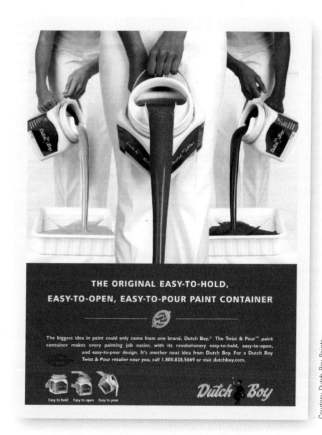

FIGURE 22.1 Illustration of Workability

eating yogurt from a standard container minimally requires the availability of a spoon, children and teens were not consuming yogurt at school. The name, Go-Gurt, also suggested that the brand was to be consumed on the go. In its first year after introduction, Go-Gurt garnered national sales in excess of $100 million and nearly doubled the proportion of yogurt users under the age of 19 to about one in six.[21]

Companies also have developed "smart packages" that include magnetic strips, bar codes, QR codes, and electronic chips (via RFID technology) that can communicate with appliances, computers, and consumers. For example, packages of microwaveable foods eventually will be programmed to "tell" microwaves how long the food item should be cooked. Procter & Gamble (P&G) has tested a smart-package program that is designed to send information about a product sale to a computer database as soon as a customer removes a P&G brand from the shelf. Small computer chips attached to the package send a signal to the store shelf, which contains printed circuit boards. The objective is, of course, to provide the company with immediate sales data that will facilitate its supply chain management.[22]

A host of packaging innovations have served to increase what might be called environmental workability. Many of the changes have involved moves from plastic to recyclable paper packages; for example, many fast-food chains eliminated the use of foam packaging, and other firms have transformed their packages from plastic to cardboard containers. Another significant environmental initiative has been the increase in spray containers as substitutes for ozone-harming aerosol cans. It is undeniable, however, that too many packages are environmentally wasteful by using excessive amounts of cardboard, plastic, and other packaging materials—all of which end up in landfills and most of which generate excessive amounts of climate-warming carbon dioxide in their manufacture. Companies need to do more work to reduce the amount of packaging materials that are used to enclose and protect their brands.

Quantifying the VIEW Components

In conclusion, most packages do not perform well on all the VIEW criteria, but packages need not always be exemplary on all four VIEW components because the relative importance of each criterion varies from one product category to another. Emotional appeal dominates for some products (e.g., perfume), information is most important for others (e.g., staple food items), while visibility and workability are generally important for all products in varying degrees. In the final analysis, the relative importance of packaging requirements depends, as always, on the particular market and the competitive situation.

Although we have provided straightforward descriptions of the four VIEW components, it would be useful to go beyond mere description and have a procedure whereby the components could be quantified on a case-by-case basis to determine whether a new package proposal stands a good chance of being successful. Figure 22.2 illustrates a procedure for accomplishing this goal and applies it to the new type of paint container that was presented in Figure 22.1. Each VIEW component could be rated first in terms of its *importance* in determining the suitability of a proposed new package and then with respect to how well the new package performs on each component, its *evaluation score*. Applying this straightforward multiplicative model to the Dutch Boy paint container generates a hypothetical set of importance and evaluation scores. Because workability is considered the most important VIEW component for this particular packaging application and because the new container for Dutch Boy paint is evaluated as performing "at the max" on this component, this new packaging design receives a highly adequate total score of 49. It should be apparent that the importance scores for each packaging component will change from packaging situation to situation, and that the evaluation scores will differ for different prototype package designs that are under consideration. A simple model of this

VIEW Component	Importance (I)*	Evaluation (E)†	I × E
Visibility	3	4	12
Information	2	5	10
Emotional Appeal	2	1	2
Workability	5	5	25
Total Score	NA	NA	49

© Cengage Learning 2013

*Importance is rated on a scale with values ranging from zero to five. A rating of zero would indicate that a specific packaging component has no importance in this particular case. Higher positive values indicate progressively increasing levels of importance.

†Evaluation is rated on a scale with values ranging from minus five to five. A rating of zero, the midpoint of the scale, would indicate that the proposed new package performs neither favorably nor unfavorably on the characteristic at hand; negative values indicate poor performance, with minus five representing the worst possible performance; positive values indicate favorable performance, with five representing the best possible performance.

FIGURE 22.2 Hypothetical Illustration of Quantifying the VIEW Model Components

sort is not intended to make what ultimately is a subjective decision but rather to structure one's thinking in arriving at such a decision.

Designing a Package

Because package design is so critical to a brand's success, a systematic approach is recommended. Figure 22.3 provides a five-step package design process. The subsequent discussion describes each step.[23]

Step 1: Specify Brand-Positioning Objectives

This initial stage requires that the brand management team specify how the brand is to be positioned in the consumer's mind and against competitive brands. What identity or image is desired for the brand? For example, when Pfizer Inc. developed Listerine PocketPaks, a dissolvable breath-strip product containing Listerine mouthwash, the objective was to design a package that was both functional and aesthetically appealing. Specifically, the package was

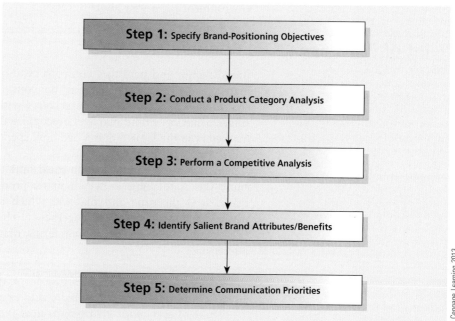

Step 1: Specify Brand-Positioning Objectives

Step 2: Conduct a Product Category Analysis

Step 3: Perform a Competitive Analysis

Step 4: Identify Salient Brand Attributes/Benefits

Step 5: Determine Communication Priorities

© Cengage Learning 2013

FIGURE 22.3 The Package Design Process

designed such that oral care could be provided outside the home, be easily transportable, and be accessible by men and women in a variety of situations.[24] The brand name, PocketPaks, describes perfectly how the package was designed literally to fit in a person's pants or jacket pocket.

Step 2: Conduct a Product Category Analysis

Having established what the brand represents (step 1), and thus what the packaging must convey, the next step is to study the product category and related categories to determine relevant trends or anticipated events that would influence the packaging decision. Consumer and competitor research is important at this stage to determine if the package is truly unique and different.

Step 3: Perform a Competitive Analysis

Armed with knowledge about competitors' use of packaging colors, shapes, graphical features, and materials, the package designer is thus prepared to create a package that conveys the desired image (step 1), yet is sufficiently unique and differentiating (step 2) to capture consumer attention.

Step 4: Identify Salient Brand Attributes or Benefits

As noted earlier, research reveals that shoppers spend an incredibly short amount of time—roughly 10 to 12 seconds—viewing brands before moving on or selecting an item. It is a good idea, therefore, that the package not be too cluttered with information and that it feature benefits that are most important to consumers. A general rule for displaying brand benefits on a package is, "The fewer, the better."[25]

Step 5: Determine Communication Priorities

Having identified the most salient brand benefits (step 4), the package designer at this phase of the process must establish verbal and visual priorities for the package. Although perhaps three benefits may have been identified in step 4 as essentially equal in importance, the designer must prioritize which of the three is to capture the greatest visual or verbal attention on the package. This is a very tough decision because it is tempting to devote equal attention to all important brand benefits. It helps if the package designer acknowledges that the package "advertisement" at the point of purchase occurs in an incredibly cluttered environment for a very short duration.

Point-of-Purchase (POP) Communications

Brand names and packages confront head-on at the point of purchase the ultimate arbiter of their effectiveness, the consumer. The point of purchase, or store environment, provides brand marketers with a final opportunity to affect consumer behavior. Brand managers recognize the value of POP advertising; indeed, marketers in the United States are now spending in excess of $21 billion on various forms of POP communications.[26]

The point of purchase is an ideal time to communicate with consumers because this is the time at which many product and brand-choice decisions are made. It is the time and place at which all elements of the sale (consumer, money, and product) come together.[27] The consumer's in-store behavior has been described in the following terms that highlight the importance of POP advertising:

> *Shoppers are explorers. They're on safari, hunting for bargains, new products and different items to add excitement to their everyday lives. Three of every four are open to new experiences as they browse the aisles of supermarkets and search for bargains at drugstores and mass merchandisers.*[28]

This translates into an opportunity to make a measurable impact just when shoppers are most receptive to new product ideas and alternative brands. Yet, as with packaging, marketers may only have a few precious seconds to engage consumers in POP communication—what some brand managers call the "first moment of truth" (FMOT).[29] Even so, savvy marketers realize that the in-store environment is the last best chance to make a difference. POP advertising often represents the culmination of a carefully integrated IMC program—at the point of purchase, consumers are reminded of previously processed mass media advertisements and now have the opportunity to benefit from a sales promotion offer.

The Spectrum of POP Materials

POP materials include various types of signs, mobiles, plaques, banners, shelf ads, mechanical mannequins, lights, mirrors, plastic reproductions of products, checkout units, full-line merchandisers, various types of product displays, wall posters, floor advertisements, in-store radio and TV advertisements, electronic billboard advertising, and other items.[30] Industry representatives classify POP materials into four categories:

- *Permanent displays:* These are displays intended for use for six months or more. (Note that the six-month dividing line is an arbitrary convention established by Point-of-Purchase Advertising International, which is known by its abbreviation, POPAI.) An illustration of a permanent display for BMW is presented in Figure 22.4.
- *Semipermanent displays:* Semipermanent POP displays have an intended life span of less than six but more than two months. Figure 22.5 presents a semipermanent display for Listerine products.
- *Temporary displays:* Temporary POP displays are designed for fewer than two months' usage. A temporary display for Kodak Inkjet products is presented in Figure 22.6.
- *In-store media:* In-store media include advertising and promotion materials such as in-store radio advertising, retail digital signage (TV-like screens at key locations), shopping cart advertising (such as discussed in the chapter-opening *Marcom Insight*), shelf advertisements (called shelf talkers), and floor graphics (advertisements placed on store floors; see illustration in Figure 22.7). A third-party company (i.e., a company other than the brand manufacturer or retailer) typically executes these in-store media. Brand marketers pay advertising rates to secure in-store radio time or shopping-cart and shelf-talker space on a nationwide basis or in specific markets. Hopefully, the in-store media is appropriately matched with the store (e.g., music not so loud as to force patrons away).

FIGURE 22.4 Illustration of a Permanent Display

FIGURE 22.5 Illustration of a Semipermanent Display

What Does POP Accomplish?

Companies are increasingly investing in POP advertising materials. As mentioned earlier, POP advertising expenditures

FIGURE 22.6 Illustration of a Temporary Display

FIGURE 22.7 Illustration of Floor Advertisements

in the United States exceed $21 billion annually. This investment is justified because in-store materials provide useful services for all participants in the marketing process: manufacturers, retailers, and consumers.

Accomplishments for Manufacturers

For manufacturers, point of purchase materials keep the company's name and the brand name before the consumer and reinforce a brand image that has been previously established through mass-media advertising or other outlets. POP signage and displays also call attention to sales promotions and stimulate impulse purchasing.

Service to Retailers

Point of purchase serves retailers by attracting the consumer's attention, increasing his or her interest in shopping, and extending the amount of time spent in the store—all of which lead to increased retail revenue and profits. Furthermore, POP materials perform a critical merchandising function by aiding retailers in maximizing available space when, for example, various products are displayed in the same unit. POP displays also enable retailers to better organize shelf and floor space and to improve inventory control and stock turnover.

Value to Consumers

Consumers are served by POP units that deliver useful information and simplify the shopping process. Permanent, semipermanent, and temporary POP units provide this value to consumers by setting particular brands apart from similar items and simplifying the selection process. Also, in-store media inform consumers of new products and brands. (See the *IMC Focus* for further discussion of in-store TV advertising.)

However, there is a downside to the growing use of in-store displays and advertising materials: consumers sometimes are overwhelmed with excessive POP stimuli. A marketing commentator has even compared the widespread usage of in-store advertising materials with online spam.[31] Like all advertising media, the in-store environment suffers from ad *clutter*, which can irritate consumers and reduce the effectiveness of brand marketers' advertising efforts. This explains why a number of retailers are implementing "clean floor" policies by reducing the number, size, and appearance of displays in an effort to enhance consumers' shopping experience.[32] In addition to benefiting all participants in the marketing process, point of purchase communication plays another important role: It serves as the capstone for an IMC program. POP by itself may have limited impact, but when used in conjunction with mass-media advertisements and promotions, POP can create a synergistic effect. Research has shown that when POP communication reinforces a brand's advertising message, the increase in sales volume can be substantial. Illustrations of this synergism appear in a later section that presents empirical evidence of POP's effectiveness.

The Growth of In-Store TV

Each of the major TV networks in the United States (ABC, CBS, NBC, Fox, and The CW) has affiliated stations throughout the country, thus representing attractive media for reaching millions of viewers for TV programs and the commercials carried therein. And now a number of retailers—Walmart, Target, Kohl's, Kroger, etc.—have their own in-store TV networks. Over 600,000 TV screens are now located in U.S. retail stores, with an expected annual growth rate of 20 percent. Unlike the major (out-of-store) TV networks, which reach consumers in the comfort of their homes or at bars and other public venues, the in-store TV networks expose consumers to ads when they are shopping and thus as close as possible to the time when they make purchase decisions.

Unsurprisingly, Walmart was one of the first retailers to recognize the potential of in-store TV as a means for exposing its customers to ads for brands carried in its stores. Currently, Walmart's "Retail Development Kit" (RDK) (including integration across the Walmart TV Network, Walmart Smart Network, Walmart.com, Shopper events, etc.) is estimated to reach as many as 200 million households weekly in 3,600 stores through its many media channels. What advertising content is carried on the Walmart TV network? You might think just ads placed by Walmart itself. In actuality, the ads are placed by national advertisers who hope to reach consumers as close as possible to the point at which they make purchasing decisions. For example, Kellogg Co. reported a significant increase in sales from advertising two new products on Walmart TV—Cheez-It Twists and Corn Flakes with bananas. TV spots on Walmart TV cost anywhere from $50,000 to $300,000 per four-week period, with the actual cost depending on the frequency with which the ads appear.

Advertisers have learned that it is best to customize ads just for in-store TV rather than running the identical ads shown on conventional television. In-store ads must be particularly attention grabbing in order to divert consumers' attention away from the primary reason they are in the store, namely to shop rather than to watch TV ads. This calls for using shorter ads than what typically appears on out-of-store TVs and also positioning TV monitors at eye level to have an optimal opportunity of diverting the shopper's attention. Integration across the many media options is key as well.

© Bob Daemmrich/Alamy

Sources: Jack Neff, "Walmart to Marketers: We Are an Experience Platform," *Advertising Age*, March 19, 2012, 18; Amy Johannes, "Timing In: In-store TV Finds Captive Audiences," *Promo*, January 2008, 11–12; Erin White, "Look Up for New Products in Aisle 5," *Wall Street Journal Online*, March 23, 2004, http://online.wsj.com; and Ann Zimmerman, "Wal-Mart Adds In-store TV Sets, Lifts Advertising," *Wall Street Journal Online*, September 22, 2004, http://online.wsj.com.

© Jim Barber/Shutterstock.com

POP's Influence on Consumer Behavior

POP materials influence consumers in four general ways: (1) by *informing* them about specific items; (2) by *reminding* them of information acquired from other advertising media; (3) by *encouraging* them to select particular brands, sometimes on impulse; and (4) aiding *merchandising* with the effective and efficient use of retail floor space.

Informing

Informing consumers is POP's most basic communications function. Signs, posters, displays, in-store advertisements, and other POP materials alert consumers to specific items and provide potentially useful information.

Motion displays are especially effective for this purpose. Motion displays, although typically more expensive than static displays, represent a potentially sound business investment if they attract significantly higher levels of shopper attention. Evidence from three studies shows that motion displays often are worth the extra expense.[33]

Researchers tested the relative effectiveness of motion and static displays for Olympia beer, a once successful but now bygone brand, by placing the two types of displays in a test sample of California liquor stores and supermarkets. Each of the sampled stores was stocked with either static or motion displays. Another sample of stores, serving as the control group, received no displays. More than 62,000 purchases of Olympia beer were recorded during the four-week test period. Static displays in liquor stores increased Olympia sales by 56 percent over stores with no displays (the control group). In supermarkets, static displays improved Olympia sales by a considerably smaller, although nonetheless substantial, amount (18 percent). More dramatic, however, was the finding that motion displays increased Olympia sales by 107 percent in liquor stores and by 49 percent in supermarkets.

A second test of the effectiveness of motion displays used S. B. Thomas' English muffins as the focal product. Two groups of 40 stores each were matched by store volume and customer demographics. One group was equipped with an S. B. Thomas' English muffin post sign that moved from side to side. The other 40 stores used regular floor displays with no motion. Sales of Thomas' muffins in the stores stocked with motion displays were more than 100 percent greater than in stores with static displays.

A third test of motion versus static displays involved Eveready batteries in tests conducted in Atlanta and San Diego. Six drugstores, six supermarkets, and six mass-merchandise stores were divided into two groups, as with the Thomas' muffin study. For mass merchandisers, the static displays increased sales during the test period by 2.7 percent over the base period, but surprisingly, sales in the drug and food outlets using the static displays were slightly less (each 1.6 percent lower) than those not using the static displays. By comparison, the motion displays uniformly increased sales by 3.7 percent, 9.1 percent, and 15.7 percent in the drugstore outlets, supermarkets, and mass merchandisers, respectively.

All three sets of results demonstrate the relative effectiveness of motion displays compared to static displays. The consumer information-processing rationale (see Chapter 6) is straightforward: (1) Motion displays attract attention. (2) Attention, once attracted, is directed toward salient product features, including recognition of the displayed brand's name. (3) Brand name information activates consumers' memories pertaining to brand attributes previously processed from media advertising. (4) Information on brand attributes, when recalled, supplies a reason for the consumer to purchase the displayed brand. It also is possible that merely seeing a display intimates that the displayed brand is on sale, whether it is or not.[34]

Thus, a moving display performs the critical in-store function of bringing a brand's name to active memory. The probability of purchasing the brand increases, perhaps substantially (as in the case of S. B. Thomas' English muffins), if the consumer is favorably disposed toward the brand. The Eveready display was less effective apparently because the selling burden was placed almost exclusively on the display. Without prior stimulation of demand through advertising, the static display was ineffective, and the motion display was not as effective as it might have been.

Reminding

A second POP function is reminding consumers of brands they have previously learned about via broadcast, print, or other advertising media. This reminder role serves to complement the job already performed by advertising before the consumer enters a store.

To appreciate the reminder role served by POP materials fully, it is important to address a key principle from cognitive psychology: the encoding specificity principle. This principle states that information recall is enhanced when the context in which people attempt to retrieve information is the same as or similar to the context in which they originally encoded the information. (Encoding is the placing of informational items into memory.) As an example, Life cereal facilitated in-store recall and retrieval of brand information when they placed "Mikey" on the package. Mikey was a hard-to-please, but cute, boy who had been featured and (hopefully) originally encoded by consumers in a long-running Life cereal commercial. By providing consumers with encoding-specific retrieval cues on the package, chances are that consumers will recall from earlier advertisements that Life is the cereal brand with the cute, but hard-to-please boy named "Mikey" who likes Life cereal.

Encouraging

Encouraging consumers to buy a specific item or brand is POP's third function. Effective POP materials influence product and brand choices at the point of purchase and encourage unplanned purchasing and even impulse buying. For example, over the years, celebrities have been featured on POP displays (e.g., John Madden for True Value Hardware, Elvira the "Mistress of Darkness" for Coors).

Merchandising

Merchandising refers to the effective and efficient use of retail space. Certainly, when matched with the retailer needs and specifications, POP displays can help with the merchandising function. Clairol's hair-coloring display for women that features color-coded labeling serves as an example.

Evidence of In-Store Decision Making

Studies of consumer shopping behavior have shown that a high proportion of all purchases are unplanned, especially in supermarkets, drugstores, and mass-merchandise outlets (such as Walmart and Target). *Unplanned purchasing* means that many product and brand choice decisions are made while the consumer is in the store rather than beforehand. POP materials play a role—perhaps the major role—in influencing unplanned purchasing. The following section discusses research on unplanned purchasing, and a subsequent section then presents impressive evidence on the role of POP displays in increasing sales volume.

The POPAI Consumer Buying Habits Study

A trade association named POPAI (Point of Purchase Advertising International) conducted this important study, which confirms that in-store media, signage, and displays heavily influence consumers' purchase decisions.[35] The study collected data from 2,400 consumers who were on a routine shopping trip in supermarket stores located in one of four major geographic regions in the United States. The number of interviews conducted per region reflected a census-balanced sample. The study was conducted in the following manner:

- Researchers screened shoppers age 18 or older to determine that they were on a "routine shopping trip."
- Researchers then interviewed qualified shoppers both before they began their shopping (10-minute entry interviews) and after they had completed their shopping trips (15- to 20-minute exit interviews). Interviews were conducted during all times of the day and every day of the week.
- During the preshopping entry interviews, researchers used an unaided questioning format to ask shoppers about their planned purchases on that particular occasion and probed for brand buying intentions. Then, during

postshopping exit interviews, researchers had access to supermarket shoppers' electronic capture of their store register tapes.

- By comparing shoppers' planned purchases obtained during entry interviews with actual purchases during exit interviews, it was possible to classify every brand purchase into one of four types of purchase behaviors: specifically planned, generally planned, substitute purchases, and unplanned purchases. Each group is defined as follows:

1. *Specifically planned*: This category represents purchases of a brand that the consumer had indicated an intention to buy. For example, the purchase of Diet Mountain Dew would be considered a specifically planned purchase if during the entry interview a consumer mentioned her or his intention to purchase that brand and in fact bought Diet Mountain Dew. According to the 2012 Consumer Buying Habits Study (see Table 22.1), 24 percent of supermarket purchases were specifically planned.

2. *Generally planned*: This classification applies to purchases for which the shopper indicated an intention to buy a particular product (say, a soft drink) but had no specific brand in mind. The purchase of Diet Mountain Dew in this case would be classified as a generally planned purchase rather than a specifically planned purchase. In 2012, generally planned purchases constituted 15 percent of those in supermarkets (see Table 22.1).

3. *Substitute purchases*: Purchases where the shopper does not buy the product or brand indicated in the entry interview constitute substitute purchases. For example, if a consumer said she or he intended to buy Diet Mountain Dew but actually purchased Vault Zero, that behavior would be classified as a substitute purchase. These represented just 6 percent of supermarket purchases in 2012.

4. *Unplanned purchases*: Under this heading are purchases for which the consumer had no prior purchase intent. If, for example, a shopper buys Diet Mountain Dew without having informed the interviewer of this intent, the behavior would be recorded as an unplanned purchase. Seventy-six percent of the purchases in supermarkets were classified as unplanned in 2012.

Notice in Table 22.1 that the summation of generally planned, substitute, and unplanned purchases constitutes the *in-store decision rate*. In other words, the three categories representing purchases that are *not* specifically planned together represent decisions influenced by in-store factors. The current in-store decision rate is 76 percent for supermarkets. This percentage indicates that in-store factors influence approximately 7.6 out of 10 purchase decisions. It is apparent that POP materials represent a very important determinant of consumers' product and brand choice behaviors!

TABLE 22.1 **Results from the POPAI Consumer Buying Habits Studies: Supermarkets 1965 to 2012**

Type of Purchase	1965	1977	1986	1995	2012
1. Specifically planned	31%	35%	34%	30%	24%
2. Generally planned	17	15	11	6	15
3. Substitute	2	3	3	4	6
4. Unplanned	50	47	52	60	55
In-store decision rate (2 + 3 + 4)	69%	65%	66%	70%	76%

Source: *The 2012 POPAI Shopper Engagement Study: Topline Report*, p. 4 (Chicago, IL: Point-of-Purchase Advertising International). Reprinted by permission.

Table 22.1 also shows how the in-store decision rate has changed over time from 1965 to 2012. The dip in the in-store rate in 1977 might be attributed to the energy crisis that led to double-digit inflation at that time. Thus, there was an increase in the number of decisions made before consumers entered the store. In the economically challenging year of 2012, the jump in the generally planned decisions may be attributed to a shift from pre-store brand decisions to in-store private label (store) products and price comparisons among brands. Still, the bulk of the purchases across these years have come from unplanned decisions made in the store.

It is important to recognize that not all purchases interviewers recorded as unplanned are truly unplanned. Rather, some purchases are recorded as unplanned simply because shoppers are *unable or unwilling* during the entry interview to inform interviewers of their exact purchase plans. This is not to imply that the POPAI research is seriously flawed, but rather that the measurement of unplanned purchases probably is somewhat overstated due to the unavoidable bias just described. Other categories may be biased also. For example, by the same logic, the percentage of specifically planned purchases is probably somewhat understated. In any event, POPAI's findings are important even if they are not precisely correct.

The summary statistics in Table 22.1 represent types of purchases aggregated over literally hundreds of product categories. It should be apparent that in-store decision rates vary greatly across product categories. To emphasize this point, Table 22.2 presents categories with the highest and lowest in-store decision rates for supermarkets in 2012.

The data presented in Table 22.2 makes it clear that in-store decision rates vary substantially. Supermarket products that are virtual staples (e.g., milk) and products that are essential and regularly purchased items (e.g., baby food/formula, laundry detergent) have the lowest in-store purchase rates because most consumers know they are going to purchase these items when they go to the

TABLE 22.2 Product Categories with the Five Highest and Five Lowest In-Store Decision Rates: Supermarket Purchases	
Category	**In-Store Decision Rate**
Highest In-Store Decision Rate [without first aid]	
Croutons	100%
Magazines	96
Gum and mints	95
Feminine hygiene	94
Air care	94
Lowest In-Store Decision Rate [without first aid]	
Milk refrigerated (including soymilk)	55
Beer	56
Baby food/formula	64
Laundry detergent	64
Isotonics sports drinks	66

Source: "Product Categories with the Five Highest and Five Lowest In-Store Decision Rates: Supermarket Purchases," *The 2012 POPAI Shopper Engagement Study* (Chicago, IL: Point-of-Purchase Advertising International). Reprinted by permission.

store. Conversely, non-necessities and items that generally do not occupy top-of-the-mind thoughts (e.g., magazines, gum) are especially susceptible to the influence of in-store stimuli. It is clear that for these types of products, brand marketers must have a distinct presence at the point of purchase if they hope to sway purchase decisions toward their brands.

Factors Influencing In-Store Decision Making Academic researchers were provided access to data from a previous POPAI's *Consumer Buying Habits Study*.[36] The researchers' objective was to determine what effect a variety of shopping-trip factors (e.g., size of shopping party, use of a shopping list, number of aisles shopped) and consumer characteristics (e.g., deal proneness, compulsiveness, age, gender, and income) have on unplanned purchasing.

The researchers determined that the rate of unplanned purchasing is elevated when consumers are on a major (versus fill-in) shopping trip, when they shop more of a store's aisles, when the household size is large, and when they are deal prone. Perhaps the major practical implication from this research is that retailers benefit from having consumers shop longer and traverse more of the store while shopping, thus increasing the odds of purchasing unintended items. One way of accomplishing this is by locating frequently purchased items (e.g., items such as bread and milk) in locations that require consumers to pass as many other items as possible.[37]

Brand Lift POPAI and a collaborating research company developed a measure—called the *brand lift index*—to gauge the average increase of in-store purchase decisions when POP materials are present versus when they are not.[38] (The term *lift* is used in reference to increasing, or lifting, sales in the presence of POP materials.) The brand lift index simply indicates how in-store POP materials affect the likelihood that customers will buy a product that they had not specifically planned to buy.

From a previous POPAI Consumer Buying Habits Study, Table 22.3 shows the products that enjoy the highest brand lift from displays. For example, the index of 47.67 for film and photofinishing products in mass-merchandise stores indicates that shoppers are nearly 48 times more likely to make in-store purchase decisions for these products when advertised with displays than if there were no displays. (Note that the index of 47.67 does *not* mean that sales of film and other photofinishing items are over 47 times greater when a display is used. Rather, this index merely reveals that consumers are nearly 48 times more likely to make in-store decisions in the presence versus absence of displays.) And supermarket shoppers are 6.47 times more likely to make in-store decisions to purchase butter or margarine when these items are displayed compared to when they are not displayed. Needless to say, displays can have incredible influence on consumer behavior.

Evidence of Display Effectiveness

Practitioners are vitally interested in knowing whether the cost of special POP displays is justified. Two important studies have examined the impact of displays and provided evidence that enlightens this issue.

The POPAI/Kmart/P&G Study

A few years ago, a notable study was conducted by a consortium of a trade association (POPAI), a mass merchandiser (Kmart), and a consumer-goods manufacturer (Procter & Gamble [P&G]).[39] The study investigated the impact that displays have on sales of P&G brands in six product categories: paper towels, shampoo, toothpaste, deodorant, coffee, and fabric softener. The test lasted for a period of four weeks, and P&G's brands were advertised in mass-media outlets and sold at their regular prices throughout the test period. Seventy-five Kmart stores in the United States were matched in terms of brand sales, store

TABLE 22.3	Supermarket and Mass Merchandise Product Categories with Highest Average Brand Lifts from Displays

Category	Brand Lift Index
Supermarket	
Butter/margarine	6.47
Cookies	6.21
Soft drinks	5.37
Beer/ale	4.67
Mixers	4.03
Sour cream/cream cheese	3.79
Cereal	3.73
Hand and body soaps	3.62
Packaged cheese	3.57
Canned fish	3.55
Salty snacks	3.50
Mass-Merchandise	
Film/photofinishing	47.67
Socks/underwear/panty hose	29.43
Cookies/crackers	18.14
Small appliances	8.87
Foils, food wraps, and bags	7.53
Adult apparel	7.45
Pet supplies	5.55
Packaged bread	5.01

Source: "Supermarket and the Mass Merchandise Product Categories with Highest Average Brand Lifts from Displays," p. 24. *The 1995 POPAI Consumer Buying Habits Study* (Washington, D.C: Point-of-Purchase Advertising International). Reprinted by permission.

volume, and shopper demographics and then assigned to three panels, or groups, of 25 stores each:

Control panel. The 25 stores in this group merchandised P&G brands in their normal shelf position *without any special displays.*

Test panel 1. These 25 stores carried the advertised brands on *display.*

Test panel 2. The 25 stores in this group carried the advertised brands on *display*; however, different displays were used than those in test panel 1, or the same displays were used as in test panel 1 but at different locations in the store.

Specific differences in displays/locations between test panels 1 and 2 are shown in Table 22.4. For example, paper towels were displayed in a mass waterfall display at two different (but undisclosed) store locations; shampoo was displayed in either a special shelf unit display or a floorstand display; and coffee was displayed either on a quarter pallet outside the coffee aisle or a full pallet at the end of the coffee aisle—called an endcap display.

Most importantly, the last column in Table 22.4 compares the percentage sales increase in each set of test stores (with displays) against the control stores where P&G brands were sold in their regular (nondisplay) shelf locations. It is

Product Category	Test Panels and Displays	Test Panel Sales versus Control Panel Sales (percentage increase)
Paper towels	Test 1: Mass waterfall (MW) display	447.1%
	Test 2: MW display in a different location	773.5
Shampoo	Test 1: Shelf unit	18.2
	Test 2: Floorstand	56.8
Toothpaste	Test 1: Floorstand in toothpaste aisle	73.1
	Test 2: Quarter pallet outside toothpaste aisle	119.2
Deodorant	Test 1: Powerwing	17.9
	Test 2: Powerwing in a different store location	38.5
Coffee	Test 1: Quarter pallet outside coffee aisle	500.0
	Test 2: Full pallet on endcap of coffee aisle	567.4
Fabric softener	Test 1: Full pallet on endcap of laundry aisle	66.2
	Test 2: Quarter pallet outside laundry aisle	73.8

TABLE 22.4 Display Information for POPAI/Kmart/P&G Study

Source: "Display Information for POPAI/Kmart/P&G Study," from "POPAI/Kmart/Procter & Gamble Study" of P-O-P Effectiveness in Mass Merchandising Stores, p. 20. *The 1995 POPAI Consumer Buying Habits Study* (Washington, D.C.: Point-of-Purchase Advertising International). Reprinted by permission.

readily apparent that positive sales increases materialized for all products and under both set of display conditions versus the nondisplay control stores. In some instances the increases were nothing short of huge. P&G's brands of shampoo and deodorant experienced modest increases during the four-week test of only about 18 percent (test panel 1), whereas paper towels and coffee experienced triple-digit increases in both display conditions—sales increases of 773.5 percent for paper towels (test panel 2) and 567.4 percent for coffee (test panel 2)!

The POPAI/Warner-Lambert Studies

Two additional studies extend the POPAI/Kmart/P&G findings obtained from mass-merchandise stores in the United States to drugstores in Canada.[40] POPAI and Warner-Lambert Canada jointly investigated the effectiveness of POP displays on sales of health items in drugstores. Eighty stores from four major drugstore chains participated (Shoppers Drug Mart, Jean Coutu, Cumberland, and Pharmaprix), and testing was conducted in three major cities: Toronto, Montreal, and Vancouver. Two brands were involved in the testing: Benylin cough syrup and Listerine mouthwash.

The Benylin Study Stores were divided into four groups for the Benylin test: Stores in group 1 offered regularly priced Benylin in its normal (nondisplay) shelf position; stores in group 2 merchandised Benylin in the normal shelf position but at a feature (i.e., discounted) price; stores in group 3 displayed Benylin at a feature price on endcap displays; and group 4 stores used in-aisle floorstand displays of Benylin at a feature price. Sales data were captured during a two-week period in each store to gauge display effectiveness.

The effectiveness of both feature pricing and displays is determined simply by comparing sales volume during the test period in store groups

2 through 4 with sales in group 1—the baseline group. These comparisons reveal the following:

- Stores in group 2 (Benylin located at its regular shelf position but feature priced) enjoyed 29 percent greater sales volume of Benylin than the stores in group 1 (Benylin at its regular price and normal shelf location). This 29 percent increment reflects simply the effect of feature pricing as both store groups sold Benylin from its regular shelf location.
- Stores in group 3 (Benylin on an endcap display and feature priced) enjoyed 98 percent greater sales of Benylin than did stores in group 1. This increment reflects the substantial impact that the endcap display and feature price combination had on the number of units sold. The large percentage increase in comparison to group 2 (i.e., 98 percent versus 29 percent) reflects the incremental impact of the endcap display location over the effect of feature pricing per se.
- Stores in group 4 (Benylin displayed in-aisle and feature priced) realized 139 percent greater sales volume than the baseline stores, which indicates that this location, at least for this product category, is more valuable than is the endcap location.

The POPAI/Warner-Lambert Listerine Study Stores were divided into four groups for this test: group 1 stores offered regularly priced Listerine in its normal shelf position; group 2 stores offered Listerine in the normal shelf position but at a feature price; group 3 stores displayed Listerine at a feature price on endcap displays at the *rear* of the store; and group 4 stores displayed Listerine at a feature price on endcap displays at the *front* of the store. Sales data were captured during a two-week period in each store to gauge display effectiveness.

Again, the effectiveness of displays can be determined by comparing sales volume of groups 2 through 4 with sales in baseline group 1:

- Stores in group 2 (Listerine located at its regular shelf position but feature priced) enjoyed 11 percent greater sales volume of Listerine than the stores in group 1 (where Listerine was regular priced and located in its regular shelf position).
- Stores in group 3 (Listerine at a rear endcap display and feature priced) experienced 141 percent greater sales of Listerine than the stores in group 1.
- Stores in group 4 (Listerine at a front endcap display and feature priced) enjoyed 162 percent greater sales volume than the baseline stores.

Both sets of results reveal that these two drugstore brands, Benylin and Listerine, benefited greatly when feature priced and merchandised from prized locations. The Listerine study results came as a bit of surprise to industry observers, however, who expected the advantage of the front endcap location to be substantially greater in comparison to the rear endcap location. The premium price that manufacturers pay for front endcap placement (versus rear endcap positioning) may not be fully justified in light of these results. Additional research with other product categories is needed before any definitive answer is possible.

Latest POPAI Research

In 2012, a subset of the 2,400 shoppers (210) were recruited to participate in electroencephalogram (EEG) and eye-tracking data collections to determine which displays make it into shoppers' line of sight and best engage shoppers' interest.[41] Although the results are not yet available, this research is invaluable in examining diagnostic, visceral, and emotional reactions to displays that are not always reflected in recall and purchase data.

The Use and Nonuse of POP Materials

Although POP materials can be very effective for manufacturers and perform several desirable functions for retailers, the fact remains that perhaps as much as 40 to 50 percent of POP materials supplied by manufacturers are never used by retailers or are used incorrectly.[42]

With the advent of RFID chips RFID attached to displays, manufacturers have acquired keen insight into retailers' use or nonuse of displays. The RFID technology enables manufacturers to track the exact location of displays and to know when display units are erected and taken down. Procter & Gamble learned in a study of display usage for its Braun's Cruzer electric razors that one-third of retailers did not comply with their agreement to erect a display for this product. P&G also found that retailers erected displays correctly only 45 percent of the time.[43] Research by Kimberly-Clark determined that its retailers used the correct POP displays only 55 percent of the time.[44] It is apparent that retailers do not always comply with manufacturers' display-usage instructions.

Reasons Why POP Materials Go Unused

Five major reasons explain why retailers choose not to use POP materials. First, at times, there is no incentive for the retailer to use certain POP materials because these materials may be inappropriately designed to their specifications and do not satisfy the retailer's needs. Second, some displays take up too much space for the amount of sales generated. Third, some materials are too unwieldy, too difficult to set up, too flimsy, or have other construction defects. A fourth reason many signs and displays go unused is because they lack eye appeal. Finally, retailers are concerned that displays and other POP materials simply serve to increase sales of a particular manufacturer's brand during the display period, but that the retailer's sales and profits for the entire product category are not improved. In other words, a retailer has little incentive to erect displays or use signage that merely serves to transfer sales from one brand to another but that does not increase the retailer's overall sales and profits for the product category.

Encouraging Retailers to Use POP Materials

Encouraging retailers to use POP materials is a matter of basic marketing. Persuading the retailer to enthusiastically use a display or other POP device means that the manufacturer must view the material from the retailer's perspective. First and foremost, POP materials must satisfy the retailer's needs and the consumers' needs rather than just those of the manufacturer. This is the essence of marketing, and it applies to encouraging the use of POP materials just as much as promoting the acceptance of the manufacturer's own brands. Hence, manufacturers must design POP materials to satisfy the following requirements:

- They are the right size and format to meet retailer specifications.
- They fit the store decor.
- They are user friendly—that is, easy for the retailer to attach, erect, or otherwise use.
- They are sent to stores when they are needed (e.g., at the right selling season).
- They are properly coordinated with other aspects of the marcom program (i.e., they should tie into a current advertising or sales promotion program).
- They are attractive, convenient, and useful for consumers.[45]

Measuring In-Store Advertising's Audience

Historically, the specific measurement of in-store (audience) exposure to POP advertising had not been available. However, a few years ago, Nielsen and the In-Store Marketing Institute had undertaken a major initiative in conjunction with a consortium of major brand marketers and retailers (e.g., Coca-Cola, Kellogg, Kroger, Miller Brewing, P&G, and Walmart), to develop a means of measuring the effectiveness of in-store advertising media.[46] This initiative, termed *PRISM* (Pioneering Research for an In-Store Metric) had devised a procedure for acquiring standard diagnostics (reach, frequency, gross impressions, etc.) for measuring the performance of in-store media. For example, gross impressions (i.e., total exposures) = traffic (i.e., frequency) × compliance (i.e., percentage of stores using the displays) × unduplicated audience (i.e., absolute number reached or net coverage). Although PRISM was discontinued in 2009 with the pullout of Walmart, it is only a matter of time before brand marketers can plan and evaluate in-store advertising using the same procedures and discipline they have used for decades in planning for and evaluating advertising placed in print and broadcast media.

On-Premise Business Signage

This section deals with a topic—on-premise signage—that is commonplace and may therefore be considered trivial. We are indeed surrounded by store signs of one variety or another. However, on-premise signs (i.e., those located on or near retail stores) are considered the most cost-effective and efficient form of communication available to retail businesses. The value of on-premise signs has been described in these optimistic terms:

> No *amount of money spent on other forms of communication media will equal the investment return of the well-designed and optimally visible on-premise sign. Surveys of new customers/clients disclose over and over that the on-premise business sign either: (1) provided the new customer with their first knowledge of the company, or (2) provided the new customer with their first impression of the company. This is true even if the customer originally learned of the business through some other communication medium, such as the Yellow Pages or "word of mouth." It is no longer [an] overstatement to assert that legible, conspicuous place-based signage, easily detectable and readable within the cone of vision of the motoring public, is essential to small business survival.*[47]

© Judith K. Shimp

Types of On-Premise Signs

Although on-premise signs include an incredible diversity of signage that is limited only by designers' creativity and governmental regulations, we can identify two general categories, free-standing and building-mounted.[48] *Freestanding signs* include monument signs, pole signs, A-frame (a.k.a. sandwich-board) signs, portable signs, inflatable signs, and other forms of signs that are *unattached* to a retail building (see Figure 22.8 for illustration). *Building-mounted signs* are *attached* to buildings and include projecting signs, wall signs, roof signs, banners, murals, and canopy or awning signs (see Figure 22.9 for illustration).

The ABCs of On-Premise Signs

On-premise signs enable consumers to identify and locate businesses and can influence their store-choice decisions and prompt impulse purchasing. These functions are conveniently referred to as the ABCs of *store signage*. That is, an effective sign should minimally perform the following functions:[49]

- Attract new customers
- Brand the retail site in consumers' minds
- Create impulse buying decisions

Of course, the specific functions performed and the importance of having eye-catching and attractive signs

FIGURE 22.8 Illustration of Free-Standing Sign

© iStockphoto.com/Luciano Mortula

FIGURE **22.9** Illustration of Building-Mounted Sign

depend on the nature of the business, whether it is a small retailer with a relatively fixed clientele—in which case, signage is relatively less critical—or a business that must constantly attract new customers. In this latter situation, signage performs a critical function because for retailers to stay in business and potentially thrive they must capture travelers, who are one-time or occasional customers.

Attracting new customers requires first and foremost that a store sign *capture the consumer's attention*. This is no small feat when considering that the retail landscape often is dense with competing signs that are attempting to achieve the same outcome: to capture attention and make a positive impression. Experts in the design of store signage use a concept, termed *conspicuity*, that refers to the ability of a sign to capture attention. By definition, conspicuity involves those signage characteristics that enable walkers or drivers and their passengers to distinguish a sign from its surrounding environment.[50] This requires that a sign be of sufficient size and the information on it be clear, concise, legible, and distinguishable from competing signage.

Seek Expert Assistance

Although the material presented on signage is basic and descriptive, it cannot be overemphasized how important it is to retail success. Signs perform an extremely important communication function, and one is well advised to seek the assistance of professionals when making such determinations as where best to locate a sign, how large it should be, what colors and graphics are best employed, and so on.

The old saying "He who represents himself has a fool for a lawyer" is likely as applicable to making an on-premise sign-selection decision as it is in all matters legal. Large retail chains include professionals on their staffs who specialize in signage, but small retailers do not have this luxury and should seek the assistance of professionals. A wealth of accumulated information is available for ready access (see endnotes 47 through 49).

Out-of-Home (Off-Premise) Advertising

The previous section dealt with on-premise advertising retailers undertake to attract attention and direct traffic to their stores. The present topic, off-premise advertising, is carried out by product and service retailers and by manufacturers of consumer-oriented brands.

Though out-of-home (OOH) advertising pales in significance compared to media such as television and is regarded as a supplementary advertising medium, OOH is nonetheless a very important form of marketing communications. PQ Media that provides custom media research for the industry, estimates that OOH advertising expenditures in the United States amounted to $6.83 billion in 2011, with $2.05 billion devoted to digital out-of-home (DOOH) advertising.[51]

Out-of-home, or outdoor, advertising is the oldest form of advertising, with origins dating back literally thousands of years. Although billboard advertising is the major aspect of out-of-home advertising, outdoor media encompasses a variety of other delivery modes: advertising on bus shelters and other street furniture; various forms of transit advertising (including ads on buses, taxis, and trucks); skywriting advertisements and advertisements on blimps; and advertising at special venues such as shopping-mall displays, at campus kiosks, and at airports. This last form of outdoor advertising is rapidly growing. For example, Terminal Five at London's Heathrow Airport—the world's busiest international airport—is inundated with 333 billboards and posters and over 200 flat-screen monitors that air short, soundless ads. This number of outdoor ad vehicles may seem excessive in just a single airport terminal, but in its first year of operation Heathrow's Terminal Five had upwards of 27 million passengers passing through it.[52] A recent academic study offers an in-depth look at the functioning and effectiveness of airport advertising.[53]

The one commonality among the various OOH media is that consumers see them outside of their homes (hence the name) in contrast to television, social media, magazines, newspapers, and radio, which typically are received in the home (or in other indoor locations). Reaching consumers with ad messages outside their homes is especially important when considering that most people spend much of their daily time at work or otherwise away from their homes. Americans report traveling an average of slightly over 300 miles in a vehicle during a typical week with an average round-trip commute totaling about 55 minutes.[54] It is obvious from these statistics that outdoor media reach millions of people in the United States as well as around the globe. In fact, global spending on outdoor advertising recently exceeded $23 billion, with $6.97 billion spent on DOOH advertising.[55] Global DOOH revenues surged 25.3 percent in 2011, primarily from the Asia-Pacific region (e.g., especially Thailand). (See the *Global Focus* insert for a discussion of billboard advertising trends in several countries outside the United States.)

Billboard advertising is the major outdoor medium and accounts for nearly two-thirds of total OOH advertising expenditures in the United States. Interestingly, the term *billboard* originates from the custom in colonial America of attaching a paper poster containing a message (known as a "bill") on a board for conveyance around town.[56] Advertising on billboards is designed with *name recognition* as the primary objective.

Forms of Billboard Ads

The major forms of billboard advertising are poster panels, painted bulletins, digital (electronic) billboards, and "specialty" billboards.

Poster Panels

These billboards are what we regularly see alongside highways and in other heavily traveled locales. Posters are silk-screened or lithographed and then pasted in sheets to the billboard. A few media conglomerates (Clear Channel Outdoor, CBS Outdoor, and Lamar Advertising) essentially control the U.S. billboard industry.

Billboard Advertising Trends in BRIC Countries

Brazil, Russia, India, and China—the so-called BRIC countries—are rapidly changing and economically advancing. Billboard advertising in these countries is changing alongside other economic transformations.

In a dramatic move in Brazil, the city of São Paulo imposed an outright ban on billboards, neon signs, and electronic panels with passage of its "Clean City" law in September 2006. Rio de Janeiro is considering implementing a similar ban. São Paulo's billboard ban has resulted in a number of outdoor advertising companies going out of business. The ban, however, does not prevent advertising on "street furniture" such as bus shelters, newsstands, and public toilets. Brand marketers denied the opportunity to use billboard advertising are increasing usage of street-furniture advertising as well as radio and newspaper advertising. Yet, in 2011, 70 percent of the city's residents found the ban to be "beneficial."

A second BRIC country, Russia, is noted for the pervasive use of billboard advertising in its major city, Moscow. Moscow's city leaders have repeatedly discussed restricting outdoor ads, although a complete São Paulo–type ban is not in the works. Yet, many billboards have been downsized and others have been removed from prominent historic buildings such as the Lenin Library. Moscow remains one of the biggest markets in Europe for outdoor ads.

Turning to China, city leaders in Beijing also have imposed restrictions on the use of billboards and other forms of outdoor advertising. It seems that these restrictions have occurred because many of the billboard ads in Beijing are directed at the city's affluent class, and city officials desire to curtail appeals to self-indulgence and luxury—in keeping with China's socialistic ideals and the desire to maintain harmony among its people.

Unlike the other BRIC countries, billboard advertising is booming in India. Billboard advertising is an outstanding medium for reaching consumers of all income levels in India. On the one hand, billboards represent one of the few media for reaching India's poor, who do not have TVs and rarely read newspapers or magazines. On the other hand, billboard ads reach the more affluent class of Indians who often ride in chauffeur-driven cars and spend hours stuck in traffic in India's clogged cities. Some restrictions have been imposed on billboard advertising in certain cities in India, but nothing of the magnitude of restrictions in other BRIC countries.

Some interesting developments in outdoor advertising are occurring in India. For example, one outdoor advertising company has developed a mobile billboard truck that parks, raises a billboard 20 feet on a pole, and then rotates the ad message to face passing traffic. The company has an inventory of 25 trucks that move to locations where they will be seen by the most prospective purchasers of the advertised brands (e.g., at train stations in the morning and in the suburbs in the evening). In rural areas of India, outdoor ad companies are utilizing a rugged vinyl that can be glued on uneven surfaces such as concrete, brick, and wood.

Sources: Amy Curtis, "Five Years After Banning Outdoor Ads, Brazil's Largest City is More Vibrant Than Ever," Center for a New American Dream, http://www.newdream.org/resources/sao-paolo-ad-ban (accessed June 14, 2012); Claudia Penteado and Andrew Hampp, "A Sign of Things to Come?" *Advertising Age*, October 1, 2007, 1, 45; Jason Leow, "Beijing Mystery: What's Happening to the Billboards?" *Wall Street Journal*, June 25, 2007, A1; and Eric Bellman and Tariq Engineer, "More Signs of India's Growth," *Wall Street Journal*, April 26, 2007, B2.

Posters can be either 8-sheet or 30-sheet, literally designating the number of sheets of paper required to fill the allotted billboard space. An 8-sheet poster is approximately 6 feet high by 12 feet wide, although the actual viewing area is slightly smaller—5 feet by 11 feet (in other words, 55 square feet of viewing space). The much larger 30-sheet poster is 12.25 feet high by 24.5 feet wide, with a viewing area of 9.6 feet by 21.6 feet (roughly 207 square feet).

Bulletins

Bulletins are either hand painted directly on billboards by artists billboard owners hire or are computer-generated vinyl images applied to the billboard space. Standard sizes for bulletins are 12 feet tall by 24 feet wide (288 square feet of viewing space) and 14 feet tall by 48 feet wide (672 square feet). Advertisers use bulletins for an extended period—from one to three years—to achieve a consistent and relatively permanent presence in heavily traveled locations. Compared to posters, bulletins are more permanent due to their rain-resistance and antifading qualities.

Digital Billboards

Digital billboards represent the biggest development in billboard advertising in many decades, perhaps ever. (In some countries, such as Thailand, DOOH now represents 50 percent of the total OOH revenue. The United States is third at 30 percent of total OOH revenue.[57]) This relatively new form of billboard is reminiscent of a huge flat-screen television that rotates ads every 4 to 10 seconds in a manner similar to a PowerPoint slideshow presentation.

Major billboard companies such as Clear Channel Outdoor are elated over the prospects for digital billboards because advertisements on these electronic billboards are frequently rotated; traditional billboards are restricted to a single advertising message throughout the course of the contract period—typically from four weeks to a full year. This has enabled billboard companies to increase their revenues substantially—perhaps as much as 6 to 10 times greater than with traditional billboards based on results from the first generation of digital billboards.[58]

It is anticipated that as many as 4,000 electronic billboards will be standing across the United States within a decade.[59] At least two factors limit the growth of digital billboards. First, they are expensive to install and cost upwards of $250,000 each.[60] Second, a number of cities and even entire states are opposed to this form of billboard due to concerns that they distract drivers, produce too much light at night, and represent visual pollution. (Whether digital billboards are unsightly and unsafe should make for interesting classroom discussion.)

In addition to offering revenue advantages for billboard companies, individual advertisers also stand to benefit from the availability of the digital billboard medium. First, digital billboards make it possible to change ads as frequently as needed. For example, an advertiser could announce a sale or special promotion one week and then the following week return to a nonpromotional sales message. A second advantage of digital billboards is the ability to rotate messages throughout the day. For example, a fast-food restaurant might promote a breakfast item during the morning drive time and then advertise other menu items during later dayparts. A third advantage of digital billboards is that they enable integration—in the best spirit of the tenets of integrated marketing communications—with other digital ads that a consumer may be exposed to during the course of a day. For example, one may see a digital billboard ad for a particular brand on the way to work, then see the same digital ad later in the day on a computer, and perhaps then again on one's mobile phone. In fact, the integration of DOOH media with mobile devices helps to extend customer engagement across media platforms.

Specialty Billboards

Resulting from the desire to attract consumer attention from the multitude of marketing messages that clutter the landscape in urban areas and along highways, specialty billboards represent different artistic and graphical techniques to present advertising messages in an especially engaging and creative way. Consider PR Newswire's interactive media wall in Times Square, used by leading consumer brands such as Pepsico and Neiman Marcus (see Figure 22.10). The massive Reuters billboard is seen by about 1.5 million people every day. Figure 22.11, for a fitness center, provides another creative use of specialty billboards in showing a billboard tilted in the direction of an overweight man who appears to be in need of the advertised service.

Buying Billboard Advertising

Outdoor advertising is purchased through companies that own billboards such as the aforementioned Clear Channel Outdoor, CBS Outdoor, and Lamar Advertising. These companies are located in all major markets throughout the

FIGURE **22.10** Illustration of an Interactive Media Wall

FIGURE **22.11** Illustration of a Specialty Billboard

nation. To simplify the national advertiser's task of buying outdoor space in multiple markets, buying organizations, or agents, facilitate the purchasing of outdoor space at locations throughout the country.

Outdoor advertising suppliers have historically sold poster-advertising space in terms of so-called *showings*. A showing is the percentage of the population that is theoretically exposed to an advertiser's billboard message. Showings are quoted in increments of 25 and are designated as #25, #50, #75, and #100. The designation #50, for example, means that 50 percent of the population in a particular market is expected to pass daily the billboards on which an advertiser's message is posted. A showing of #100 is equivalent to saying that virtually the entire population in a given market has an opportunity to see (referred to as an OTS) an advertiser's message in that particular market.

In recent years outdoor advertising companies have converted to *gross rating points (GRPs)* as the metric for quoting poster prices. As is the case with mass advertising media (TV, magazines, etc.), GRPs represent the percentage and frequency of an audience an advertising vehicle is reaching. Specifically, one outdoor GRP means reaching 1 percent of the population in a particular market a single time. Outdoor GRPs are based on the daily duplicated audience (meaning that some people may be exposed on multiple occasions each day) as a percentage of the total potential market. For example, if four billboards in a community of 200,000 people achieve a daily exposure to 80,000 people, the result is 40 gross rating points. As with traditional showings, GRPs are sold in blocks of 25, with 100 and 50 being the two levels purchased most.

Billboard Advertising's Strengths and Limitations

Billboard advertising presents marketing communicators with several unique strengths and problems.[61]

Strengths

A major strength of billboard advertising is its *broad reach* and *high frequency levels*. Billboards are effective in reaching virtually all segments of the population. The number of exposures is especially high when signs are strategically located in heavy traffic areas. Automobile advertisers are heavy users of outdoor media because they can reach huge numbers of potential purchasers with high frequency. The same can be said for telecommunications companies (such as AT&T, Verizon, and Sprint) and fast-food restaurants.

Another advantage is *geographic flexibility*. Outdoor advertising can be strategically positioned to supplement other advertising efforts (e.g., TV, radio, and newspaper ads) in select geographic areas where advertising support is most needed.

Low cost per thousand is a third advantage. The cost-per-thousand metric (abbreviated as *CPM*, where *M* is the Roman numeral for 1,000) is literally the cost, on average, of exposing 1,000 people to an advertisement. Outdoor advertising is the least expensive advertising medium on a CPM basis. However, as emphasized in Chapter 16 when discussing the relative advantages of traditional advertising media, CPM comparisons across different media can be misleading. Because the various media perform different functions, it is inappropriate to use CPM as the sole basis of evaluation.

A fourth strength of billboard advertising is that *brand identification is substantial* because billboard ads are literally bigger than life. The ability to use large representations offers marketers excellent opportunities for brand and package identification. Also, billboard companies are becoming quite ingenious in designing billboards that attract viewers' attention through the use of creative techniques and eye-catching visuals—such as those shown in Figures 22.10 and 22.11. Consider also a creative billboard ad for promoting Adidas soccer products in Japan (see Figure 22.12). Outdoor media play a more prominent role in Japan than in countries such as the United States because the average resident in a city such as Tokyo has a 70-minute commute to work, which makes billboards and other outdoor media an attractive and relatively inexpensive way of reaching them. However, the heavy spending on outdoor ads has created a major clutter problem. Sports-equipment and apparel maker Adidas came up with a novel solution: It designed faux soccer fields on billboards and suspended (via dangling ropes) two soccer players and a ball 12 stories above the ground. The two dangling soccer players played 10- to 15-minute matches at one-hour intervals during afternoons, while hundreds of pedestrians gathered below to watch. Of course, while they watched the soccer "matches," they were continuously exposed to the Adidas name and logo along with a message overlaid on the soccer "field"

FIGURE **22.12** Illustration of Billboard Advertising

proclaiming, "Own the passion and you own the game." It is difficult to imagine a more attention-gaining billboard than Adidas's use of live soccer players.[62]

A fifth advantage of billboard advertising is that it provides an excellent opportunity to reach consumers as a *last reminder before purchasing*. This explains why restaurants and products such as beer are among the heaviest billboard users. (U.S. tobacco advertisers also were heavy outdoor advertisers; in 1999, as part of a legal settlement with the state attorneys general, tobacco brands stopped advertising in outdoor media.)

Limitations

A significant problem with outdoor advertising is *demographic nonselectivity*. Outdoor advertising can be geared to general groups of consumers (such as inner-city residents) but cannot pinpoint specific market segments (say, professional African-American men between the ages of 25 and 39). Advertisers must turn to other advertising media (such as magazines and radio) to better pinpoint audience selection. However, with technology that is under development, billboard advertising is in the process of improving its ability to target customers. For example, a California company, Smart Sign Media, introduced technology that adjusts digital billboards to the radio stations playing inside passing vehicles. Using radio-station selection as an indicator of income, Smart Sign's technology calculates the average income of people who pass by and then changes the message to target the biggest cluster of people who drive by a particular billboard location.[63] Another breakthrough with outdoor boards is the use of Bluetooth technology to send video clips of new TV shows, etc. to anyone with a smartphone within a close proximity to the billboard displaying the shows and other ad information.[64]

Short exposure time is another drawback. "Now you see it, now you don't" appropriately characterizes the fashion in which outdoor advertising engages the consumer's attention. For this reason, outdoor messages that have to be read are less effective than predominantly visual ones. Bright colors, vivid images, and visual messages are essential in effective billboard advertising.

A third outdoor advertising limitation involves *environmental concerns*. Billboards, the so-called "litter on a stick," have been banned in some manner by several U.S. states (Alaska, Hawaii, Maine, and Vermont) and hundreds of local governments. Although some would argue that attractive billboards can enliven and even beautify neighborhoods and highways with attractive messages, others consider this advertising medium to be ugly and intrusive. This largely is a matter of personal taste. The articles cited in the following end note explore the issue in some depth, including a discussion of the value and potential hazards attendant to the growing use of changeable message signs—that is, digital billboards that vary the advertising message on a schedule of every 4 to 10 seconds.[65]

Measuring Billboard Audience Size and Characteristics

When placing ads in print (newspapers and magazines) and broadcast media (radio and TV), advertisers have access to so-called syndicated data sources that inform them about (1) the size of the audience to be reached when using these media, and (2) the demographic characteristics of audiences reached by media vehicles such as individual magazines (e.g., *Cosmopolitan*) or TV programs (e.g., *Saturday Night Live*). (Audience measurement techniques for the print and broadcast media were described in detail in Chapter 16.) This information is invaluable when planning for and making media buying decisions. In advance of making a media buy, an advertiser can estimate what percentage of a target audience is likely to be reached and the average frequency audience members will have an OTS (opportunity to see—or read or hear) an ad message during, say, a four-week media planning period. Print and broadcast media are, then, *measurable*, and advertisers have quite a lot of faith in the accuracy of the audience data for these media.

Comparatively, there has been no equivalent measurable audience data available for the out-of-home advertising industry. Historically, the outdoor industry has relied on traffic data the Traffic Audit Bureau collects that simply indicates how many people pass by an outdoor site such as a billboard. However, no information has been available regarding the demographic characteristics of the people who have an opportunity to see advertising messages on billboards. The lack of verified data regarding audience characteristics is widely regarded as a significant impediment that must be overcome if outdoor advertising is to become a more widely used advertising medium. Although traffic-flow data indicate the number of people who may have an opportunity to see a billboard message, it provides absolutely no information about people's demographic characteristics, which is the type of information advertisers need to make intelligent targeting decisions. This lack of information has limited the growth of the OOH industry and has prevented many advertisers from investing heavily in out-of-home media.

Nielsen Personal Outdoor Devices (Npods)

Fortunately, Nielsen Media Research, a company that specializes in the measurement of advertising audiences, is making substantial strides toward developing ways to determine the *demographic characteristics of outdoor audiences*. Nielsen's service involves selecting a representative sample of individuals, collecting from them pertinent demographic information, and equipping them with battery-operated meters called *Npods* (Nielsen Personal Outdoor Devices). Using global positioning satellite (GPS) technology, these Npod meters automatically track individuals' movements from the time they leave their homes until they return. With knowledge of the demographic characteristics of sample members and knowing literally their geographical whereabouts, it is possible to connect these two data sets and draw conclusions about the demographic characteristics of the people who have had an opportunity to see an ad carried on any particular billboard location.

Armed with verifiable knowledge about the demographic characteristics of people who pass particular billboard locations or the sites of other outdoor ads, it is likely that advertisers will increase their use of OOH advertising. Initial research by Nielsen Outdoor in Chicago determined that men age 35 to 54 have the highest exposure to outdoor advertising and that full-time-employed individuals in the upper-income categories are especially likely to be exposed to outdoor ads.[66]

A Case Study of Billboard Effectiveness

Adams Outdoor Advertising, a large Atlanta-based firm, undertook a creative campaign to demonstrate the effectiveness of billboard advertising. With the assistance of Cognetix—an advertising agency located in Charleston, South Carolina—a scheme was hatched to test the effectiveness of billboard advertising. Adams and Cognetix ran a billboard campaign for a fictitious brand of bottled water they named *Outhouse Springs*. Playing on the concept of incongruity (bottled water named Outhouse Springs?) and using potty-type humor, billboard advertisements for Outhouse Springs were located throughout the Charleston market and achieved a 75 showing at a four-week cost of approximately $25,000. Messages on the billboards included amusing, albeit incredulous, statements such as "America's First Recycled Water"; "Originally in Cans ... Now in Bottles"; "L-M-N-O-..."; and "It's #1, Not #2" (see Figure 22.13 for illustrations).[67]

To assess campaign effectiveness, brand awareness, attitudes, and purchase intentions were measured in weekly intervals. By week three, 67 percent of a large sample of consumers indicated awareness of the hypothetical Outhouse Springs brand, 77 percent had neutral or favorable attitudes toward this bottled water brand, and 85 percent indicated an intention to purchase Outhouse Springs.

Although admittedly a highly unique and viral product (recall the discussion on viral marketing and buzz-building in Chapter 21), this campaign for a fictitious brand of bottled water reveals that large numbers of people are exposed to billboard ads and can be favorably influenced. Part of the success was no doubt due to the fact that widespread buzz generated stories on TV, on radio, and in newspaper articles. Nonetheless, this test of a hypothetical brand illustrates that people are alert to billboard messages that are attention catching and memorable. For further discussion of the Outhouse Springs case along with other case studies of outdoor advertising effectiveness, go to the Outdoor Advertising Association of America's website, www.oaaa.org.

Other Forms of OOH Advertising

The emphasis to this point has focused on billboards, which are the major form of OOH advertising. However, as alluded to earlier, OOH advertising also includes various forms of transit advertising (ads on buses, taxis, and trucks), advertising on bus shelters and other "street furniture," and various miscellaneous forms of outdoor advertising.

The creativity and potential effectiveness of these forms of non-billboard OOH advertising is best illustrated with examples. Figure 22.14 is a transit

FIGURE 22.13 Illustrations from the Outhouse Springs Billboard Campaign

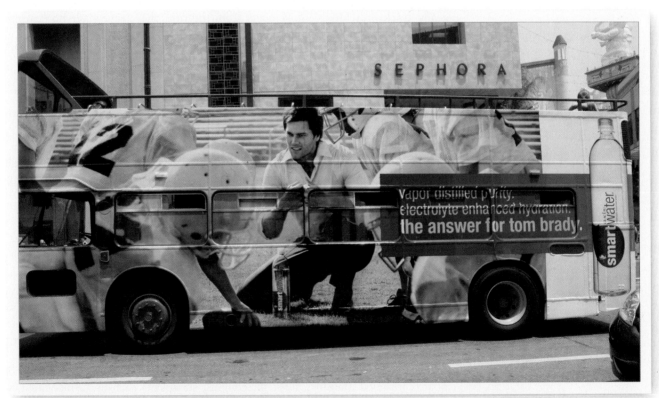

FIGURE 22.14 Illustration of a Transit Advertisement

FIGURE **22.15** Illustration of a Full-Wrap Bus Ad

FIGURE **22.16** Illustration of a Bus Bench Ad

advertisement for SmartWater, a nutrient-enhanced, vapor-distilled European brand that seems to give Tom Brady his energy. Figure 22.15 shows another transit advertisement, this one for Kodak. As a sponsor of the Olympic Games in Japan a few years ago, Eastman Kodak had marketing visibility with Japanese consumers who may never before have been exposed to their products. A fleet of 12 full-sized city buses were completely "wrapped" with Kodak or Olympic imagery promoting Kodak's involvement in the Games, and served as traveling billboards. Figure 22.16 is a bus bench ad for MADD and is another useful form of advertising directed at transit customers and passers-by.

Summary

This chapter covered four relatively minor (vis-a-vis mass-media advertising), yet important forms of marcom communications: packaging; point-of-purchase advertising; on-premise business signage; and out-of-home (off-premise) advertising. The package is perhaps the most important component of the product as a communications device. It reinforces associations established in advertising, breaks through competitive clutter at the point of purchase, and justifies price and value to the consumer. Package design relies on the use of symbolism to support a brand's image and to convey desired information to consumers. A number of package cues are used for this purpose, including color, design, shape, brand name, physical materials, and product information labeling. These cues should interact harmoniously to evoke within buyers the set of meanings intended by the marketing communicator. Package designs can be evaluated by applying the VIEW model, which contains the elements of visibility, information, emotional appeal, and workability. A concluding section described a five-step process for package design."

Major chapter coverage was devoted to POP advertising, as the point of purchase is an ideal time to communicate with consumers. A variety of POP materials—signs, displays, and various in-store media—are used to attract consumers' attention to particular brands, provide information, affect perceptions, and ultimately influence shopping behavior. POP displays—which are distinguished broadly as permanent, semipermanent, or temporary—perform a variety of useful functions for manufacturers, retailers, and consumers.

Research has documented the high incidence of consumers' in-store purchase decision making and the corresponding importance of POP materials in these purchase decisions. POPAI's *Consumer Buying Habits Study* classified all consumer purchases into four categories: specifically planned, generally planned, substitutes, and unplanned decisions. The combination of the last three categories represents in-store decisions that are influenced by POP displays and other store cues. Recently, it is estimated that in-store decisions represent as much as 76 percent of supermarket purchase decisions. Research on the effectiveness of displays—such as the joint undertaking by POPAI, Kmart, and Procter & Gamble—provides evidence that displayed brands sometimes enjoy large, triple-digit increases in sales volume during the display period.

Both off- and on-premise messages perform important functions and are capable of influencing consumers' awareness of and perceptions of stores and brands. The different forms of off- and on-premise messages are described and illustrations provided. Primary emphasis is devoted to billboard advertising. This discussion includes description of the forms of billboard advertising (e.g., digital billboards), explanation of billboard advertising's strengths and limitations, discussion of how billboard ads are purchased, and how the effectiveness of billboard advertising is measured.

Discussion Questions

1. Select a packaged-goods product category, and apply the VIEW model to three competitive brands within that category. Define all four components of the model, and explain how each applies to your selected product. Then use the following procedures to weigh each component in the model in terms of your perception of its relative packaging importance for your chosen product category:
   a. Distribute 10 points among the four components, with more points signifying more importance and the sum of the allocated points totaling exactly 10. (This weighting procedure involves what marketing researchers refer to as a constant sum scale.)
   b. Next, evaluate each brand in terms of your perception of its performance on each packaging component by assigning a score from 1 (does not perform well) to 10 (performs extremely well). Thus, you will assign a total of 12 scores: four for each VIEW component for the three different brands.
   c. Combine the scores for each brand by multiplying the brand's performance on each component by the weight of that component (from step a) and then summing the products of these four weighted scores.
   d. The summed score for each of your three chosen brands will reflect your perception of how good that brand's packaging is in terms of the VIEW model—the higher the score, the better the packaging in your opinion. Summarize the scores for the three brands for an overall assessment of each brand's packaging.

2. Choose a grocery product category and analyze the various brands in this category in terms of their packaging features designed to attract consumers' attention. Identify the packaging features that make some brands in this category more or less attention-gaining than others.

3. Considering just the workability component of the VIEW model, provide illustrations of several packages that, in your opinion, represent higher or lower levels of workability.

4. What are your personal views about the advantages and disadvantages of supermarket shopping with smartphones, or intelligent shopping carts such as the Shopping Buddy and the MediaCart (see *Marcom Insight*)?

5. What functions can POP materials accomplish that mass media advertising cannot?

6. Explain why the *POPAI Consumer Buying Habits Study* probably overestimates the percentage of unplanned purchases and underestimates the percentage of specifically planned and generally planned purchases.

7. Although not presented in the chapter, the *POPAI Consumer Buying Habits Study* revealed that the percentage of in-store decisions for coffee was 57.9 percent, whereas the comparable percentage was 87.1 percent for a group of "sauce" products (salsa, picante sauce, and dips). What might account for the 29.2 percent difference in in-store decision making between coffee and the "sauce" products? Go beyond these two product categories and offer a generalization as to what factors determine whether a particular product category would exhibit a low or high proportion of in-store decision making.

8. The *POPAI Consumer Buying Habits Study* also revealed that the highest average brand lift index from signage (rather than displays) in mass-merchandise stores was dishwashing soaps, with an index of 21.65. Provide an exact interpretation of this index value.

9. Why were motion and static displays considerably more effective at increasing Olympia beer sales in liquor stores than in supermarkets?

10. The shopping smartphone app described in the chapter-opening *Marcom Insight* is subject to criticism on grounds that it will cost checkout clerks in supermarkets their jobs. What is your perspective on this matter?

11. During past decades, cigarette advertisements were responsible for a very large percentage of all billboard advertising in the United States. The same is true for alcohol. What explanations can you offer for why these products dominated the billboard medium? What is it about consumer behavior related to these products that would make billboards an especially attractive advertising medium?

12. Changeable message signs are billboards that vary the advertising message on a schedule of every 4 to 10 seconds. What, in your opinion, is the value of this technology to the advertiser, and what are the potential hazards to society?

13. The Outhouse Springs bottled water case illustrated an effective application of billboard advertising. With reference to the material on "buzz generation" and viral marketing covered in Chapter 21, what is it about this particular campaign that may make

these results atypical and thus unrepresentative of more mundane products advertised via billboards?

14. Conduct an informal audit of on-premise business signage in your college or university community. Specifically, select five examples of on-premise signage that you regard as particularly effective. Using material from Chapter 6 on the CPM and HEM models, explain why your chosen illustrations likely stand a good chance of attracting consumer attention and influencing their behavior.

End Notes

1. R. James Claus and Susan L. Claus, *Unmasking the Myths About Signs* (Alexandria, VA: International Sign Association, 2001), 16.
2. Some of these phrases were mentioned in Michael Gershman, "Packaging: Positioning Tool of the 1980s," *Management Review* (August 1987), 33–41.
3. Peter R. Dickson and Alan G. Sawyer, "The Price Knowledge and Search of Supermarket Shoppers," *Journal of Marketing* 54 (July 1990), 42–53; and John Le Boutillier, Susanna Shore Le Boutillier, and Scott A. Neslin, "A Replication and Extension of the Dickson and Sawyer Price-Awareness Study," *Marketing Letters* 5 (January 1994), 31–42.
4. John Deighton, "A White Paper on the Packaging Industry," Dennison Technical Papers, December 1983, 5.
5. An interesting article about package meaning is available in Robert L. Underwood and Julie L. Ozanne, "Is Your Package an Effective Communicator? A Normative Framework for Increasing the Communicative Competence of Packaging," *Journal of Marketing Communications* 4 (December 1998), 207–20.
6. For an in-depth treatment of the role of color in packaging and other forms of marketing communications, see Lawrence L. Garber, Jr., and Eva M. Hyatt, "Color as a Tool for Visual Persuasion," in *Persuasive Imagery: A Consumer Response Perspective*, eds. Linda M. Scott and Rajeev Batra (Mahwah, NJ: Lawrence Erlbaum, 2003), 313–36.
7. Gail Tom, Teresa Barnett, William Lew, and Jodean Selmants, "Cueing the Consumer: The Role of Salient Cues in Consumer Perception," *Journal of Consumer Marketing* 4 (spring 1987), 23–27.
8. J. Craig Andrews, Syed Akhter, Srinivas Durvasula, and Darrel Muehling, "The Effects of Advertising Distinctiveness and Message Content Involvement on Cognitive and Affective Responses to Advertising," *Journal of Current Issues & Research in Advertising* 14 (spring 1992), 45–58.
9. This comment and parts of the following discussion are based on statements appearing in Joseph A. Bellizzi, Ayn E. Crowley, and Ronald W. Hasty, "The Effects of Color in Store Design," *Journal of Retailing* 59 (spring 1983), 21–45.
10. For information about color symbolism, go to http://www.colormatters.com/color-symbolism.
11. Priya Raghubir and Eric A. Greenleaf, "Ratios in Proportion: What Should the Shape of the Package Be?" *Journal of Marketing* 70 (April 2006), 95–107.
12. Ibid., 96.
13. Tara Parker-Pope, "The Fat Trap," *New York Times*, December 28, 2011, http://www.nytimes.com/2012/01/01/magazine/tara-parker-pope-fat-trap.html?pagewanted=all.
14. Brian Wansink, "Can Package Size Accelerate Usage Volume?" *Journal of Marketing* 60 (July 1996), 1–14; see also Brian Wansink and Craig S. Wansink, "The Largest Last Supper: Depictions of Food Portions and Plate Size Increased Over the Millennium," *International Journal of Obesity* 34, no 5 (2010), 943–44; and Brian Wansink, Collin R. Payne, and Mitsuru Shimizu, "The 100-Calorie Semi-Solution: Sub-Packaging Most Reduces Intake Among the Heaviest," *Obesity*, 19 (Spring 2011), 1098–1100.
15. Valerie Folkes and Shashi Matta, "The Effect of Package Shape on Consumers' Judgments of Product Volume: Attention as a Mental Contaminant," *Journal of Consumer Research* 31 (September 2004), 390–401.
16. Dik Warren Twedt, "How Much Value Can Be Added through Packaging," *Journal of Marketing* 32 (January 1968), 61–65.
17. See Andrews, Akhter, Durvasula, Muehling, *Journal of Current Issues & Research in Advertising*, 46.
18. Jeremy Kees, Scot Burton, J. Craig Andrews, and John Kozup, "Tests of Graphic Visuals and Cigarette Package Warning Combinations: Implications for the Framework Convention on Tobacco Control," *Journal of Public Policy & Marketing* 25 (fall 2006), 212–223; and Jeremy Kees, Scot Burton, J. Craig Andrews, and John Kozup, "Understanding How Graphic Pictorial Warnings Work on Cigarette Packaging," *Journal of Public Policy & Marketing* 29 (fall 2010), 265–76.
19. Brian Wansink and Pierre Chandon, "Can 'Low-Fat' Nutrition Labels Lead to Obesity?" *Journal of Marketing Research* 43 (November 2006), 605–17.
20. J. Craig Andrews, Scot Burton, and Jeremy Kees, "Is Simpler Always Better? Consumer Evaluations of Front-of-Package Nutrition Symbols," *Journal of Public Policy & Marketing* 30 (fall 2011), 175–90.
21. Sonia Reyes, "Groove Tube," *Brandweek's Marketers of the Year* insert, October 16, 2000, M111–M116.
22. Greg Dalton, "If These Shelves Could Talk," *The Industry Standard*, April 2, 2001, 49–51.
23. This discussion is adapted from Herbert M. Meyers and Murray J. Lubliner, *The Marketer's Guide to*

Successful Package Design (Chicago: NTC Business Books, 1998), 55–67.

24. Catherine Arnold, "Way Outside the Box," *Marketing News*, June 23, 2003, 1315.

25. Meyers and Lubliner, *The Marketer's Guide to Successful Package Design*, 63.

26. Correspondence from Richard Winter, President, Point-of-Purchase Advertising International (POPAI), Chicago, IL, May 2012.

27. John A. Quelch and Kristina Cannon-Bonventre, "Better Marketing at the Point-of-Purchase," *Harvard Business Review* (November/December 1983), 162–69.

28. "Impact in the Aisles: The Marketer's Last Best Chance," *Promo*, January 1996, 25.

29. Emily Nelson and Sarah Ellison, "Shelf Promotion: In a Shift, Marketers Beef Up Ad Spending Inside Stores," *Wall Street Journal*, September 21, 2005, A1, A8.

30. An inventory of POP advertising materials is provided in Robert Liljenwall and James Maskulka, *Marketing's Powerful Weapon: Point-of-Purchase Advertising* (Washington, D.C.: Point-of-Purchase Advertising International, 2001), 177–80.

31. Kate Fitzgerald, "In-store Media Ring Cash Register," *Advertising Age*, February 9, 2004, 43.

32. "Retail Goes Feng Shui," *Promo*, October 2007, 16, 18.

33. *The Effect of Motion Displays on the Sales of Beer; The Effect of Motion Displays on Sales of Baked Goods; The Effect of Motion Displays on Sales of Batteries* (Englewood, N.J.: Point-of-Purchase Advertising Institute, undated).

34. J. Jeffrey Inman, Leigh McAlister, and Wayne D. Hoyer, "Promotion Signal: Proxy for a Price Cut," *Journal of Consumer Research* 17 (June 1990), 74–81.

35. *The 2012 POPAI Shopper Engagement Study: Topline Report* (Chicago, IL: Point-of-Purchase Advertising International), 1–7.

36. J. Jeffrey Inman and Russell S. Winer, "Where the Rubber Meets the Road: A Model of In-store Decision Making," *Marketing Science Institute Report* No. 98–122 (October 1998).

37. Ibid., 26.

38. *Measuring the In-Store Decision Making of Supermarket and Mass Merchandise Store Shoppers* (Englewood, NJ: Point-of-Purchase Advertising Institute, 1995), 23. POPAI has since changed its name from the Point-of-Purchase Advertising Institute to Point-of-Purchase Advertising International.

39. *POPAI/Kmart/Procter & Gamble Study of P-O-P Effectiveness in Mass Merchandising Stores* (Englewood, NJ: Point-of-Purchase Advertising Institute, 1993).

40. *POPAI/Warner-Lambert Canada P-O-P Effectiveness Study* (Englewood, NJ: The Point-of-Purchase Advertising Institute, 1992).

41. *The 2012 POPAI Shopper Engagement Study: Topline Report*, 7.

42. John P. Murry, Jr. and Jan B. Heide, "Managing Promotion Program Participation within Manufacturer-Retailer Relationships," *Journal of Marketing* 62 (January 1998), 58; and *POPAI/Progressive Grocer Supermarket Retailer Attitude Study* (Englewood, NJ: Point-of-Purchase Advertising Institute, 1994), 2.

43. Amy Johannes, "RFID Ramp-Up," *Promo*, March 2008, 14.

44. Amy Johannes, "Big Brother in the Aisles," *Promo*, May 2007, 14, 16.

45. Adapted from Don E. Schultz and William A. Robinson, *Sales Promotion Management*, 278–79. For further insights on gaining retailer participation in POP programs, see Murry, Jr., and Heide (1998), "Managing Promotion Program Participation within Manufacturer-Retailer Relationships."

46. Doug Adams and Jim Spaeth, "In-store Advertising Audience Measurement Principles" (Washington, D.C.: Point-of-Purchase Advertising International, July 2003).

47. Claus and Claus, *Unmasking the Myths about Signs*, 9.

48. This distinction and the following details are from *The Signage Sourcebook: A Signage Handbook* (Washington, D.C.: U.S. Small Business Administration, 2003), 193.

49. Darrin Conroy, *What's Your Signage?* (Albany, NY: The New York State Small Business Development Center, 2004), 8.

50. Ibid., 20.

51. *Global Digital Out-of-Home Media Forecast 2012-2016*, PQ Media, http://www.pqmedia.com/globaldigitaloohforecast-2012.html (accessed May 28, 2012).

52. Aaron O. Patrick, "Mass of Messages Lands at Heathrow," *Wall Street Journal*, February 14, 2008, B3.

53. Rick T. Wilson and Brian D. Till, "Airport Advertising Effectiveness," *Journal of Advertising* 37 (spring 2008), 59–72.

54. Pierre Bouvard and Jacqueline Noel, "The Arbitron Outdoor Study," *Arbitron*, 2001, http://www.arbitron.com.

55. *Global Digital Out-of-Home Media Forecast 2012-2016*.

56. Claus and Claus, *Unmasking the Myths about Signs*, 17.

57. *Global Digital Out-of-Home Media Forecast 2012-2016*.

58. "Digital Outdoor Advertising," http://www.wikinvest.com/concept/digital_outdoor_advertising (accessed May 26, 2008).

59. The 4,000 figure is from Patrick Condon, "Digital Billboards Face Challenges from Cities," *Marketing News*, March 15, 2007, 14.

60. Joseph Popiolkowski, "Digital Billboards Get Green Light," *Stateline*, December 3, 2007,

http://www.pewstates.org/projects/stateline/headlines/ digital-billboards-get-green-light-85899386664.

61. For additional insights into why companies use billboard advertising, see Charles R. Taylor, George R. Franke, and Hae-Kyong Bang, "Use and Effectiveness of Billboards," *Journal of Advertising* 35 (winter 2006), 21–34.

62. Geoffrey A. Fowler and Sebastian Moffett, "Adidas's Billboard Ads Give Kick to Japanese Pedestrians," *Wall Street Journal Online*, August 29, 2003, http://online.wsj.com; and Normandy Madden, "Adidas Introduces Human Billboards," *Advertising Age*, September 1, 2003, 11.

63. Kimberly Palmer, "Highway Ads Take High-Tech Turn," *Wall Street Journal Online*, September 12, 2003, http://online.wsj.com.

64. Emily Steel, "CBS Touts New Shows in Video Clips; Campaign Beams Previews Via Certain Billboards to Gadgets with Bluetooth," *Wall Street Journal*, August 24, 2006, B2.

65. Myron Laible, "Changeable Message Signs: A Technology Whose Time Has Come," *Journal of Public Policy & Marketing* 16 (spring 1997), 173–76; Frank Vespe, "High-Tech Billboards: The Same Old Litter on a Stick," *Journal of Public Policy & Marketing* 16 (spring 1997), 176–79; and Charles R. Taylor, "A Technology Whose Time Has Come or the Same Old Litter on a Stick? An Analysis of Changeable Message Boards," *Journal of Public Policy & Marketing* 16 (spring 1997), 179–86.

66. "First-ever U.S. Ratings Data from Nielsen Outdoor Show that Males 35-54 Have the Highest Exposure to Outdoor Advertising," *Nielsen Media Research*, December 6, 2005, http://www.nielsenmedia.com.

67. A former graduate student, Ms. Brie Morrow, informed the first author of the Outhouse Springs billboard campaign. Brie and two of her colleagues, Jason Darby and Erin Vance, performed background work in writing a term paper for another class. We have referred to their term paper as well as additional source materials such as Jeremy D'Entremont, "Outhouse Springs and Piggly Wiggly Help Save the Light," *Lighthouse Digest*, http://www.lhdigest .com.

Some have unfairly typified salespeople as aggressive, pushy, and always relying on the "hard sell" to convince customers. This "old-school" view is certainly outdated, as some of the most important characteristics of effective salespeople today are *listening ability* and *empathy*. Moreover, recent successes for pharmaceutical sales reps have come primarily from the "soft sell" approach; that is, focusing on physician needs and wants and letting them set the agenda in meetings rather than using a "hard sell" or aggressive approach. As a result, satisfaction ratings of sales reps and sales have soared recently in the pharmaceutical industry with this softer approach.

A few years ago, a national sample of purchasing agents was surveyed to determine exactly what qualities buyers value most and least in a salesperson. Ratings from over 200 purchasing agents revealed the following:

Photographer Travis Dove

1. Discuss personal selling's role in the promotional mix and IMC.
2. Explain the advantages and disadvantages of personal selling, attitudes toward careers in this field, and some attractive features of personal selling.
3. Describe selling activities, duties, and types of selling jobs.
4. Discuss and apply the seven basic steps in personal selling.
5. Explain the determinants of salesperson performance and effectiveness.
6. Describe the characteristics of excellence in selling.

Qualities Purchasing Agents Value Most and Least in a Salesperson

Most Valued	
Reliability/credibility	98.6%
Professionalism/integrity	93.7
Product knowledge	90.7
Innovativeness in problem solving	80.5
Presentation/preparation	69.7
Least Valued	
Supplies market data	25.8%
Appropriate frequency of calls	27.3
Knowledge of competitor's products	31.2
Knowledge of buyer's business and negotiation skills (tie)	45.8

In purchasing agents' own words, here are some of the specific qualities and behaviors in salespeople that are most liked, disliked, and despised—the good, the bad, and the ugly.

The Good	The Bad	The Ugly
"Honesty"	"No follow-up"	"Wise-ass attitude"
"Loses a sale graciously"	"Walking in without an appointment"	"Calls me 'dear' or 'sweetheart'" (I am a female)
"Admits mistakes"	"Begins call by talking sports"	"Gets personal"
"Problem-solving capabilities"	"Puts down competitor's products"	"Doesn't give purchasing people credit for any brains"
"Friendly but professional"	"Poor listening skills"	"Whiners"
"Dependable"	"Too many phone calls"	"BSers"
"Adaptability"	"Lousy presentation"	"Wines and dines me"
"Knows my business"	"Fails to ask about my needs"	"Plays one company against another"
"Well prepared"	"Lacks product knowledge"	"Pushy"
"Patience"	"Wastes my time"	"Smokes in my office"

Sources: "PAS Examine the People Who Sell to Them," *Sales and Marketing Management*, November 11, 1985, 38–41; "Talk, Talk, Talk—Try A Little Listening," *Wall Street Journal*, March 22, 1990; Richard Whiteley, "How to Push Customers," *Sales and Marketing Management*, February 1994, 29–30; and Jonathan D. Rockoff, "Drug Sales Reps Try a Softer Pitch," *Wall Street Journal*, January 10, 2012, B1, B2.

Introduction

A good sales force that embodies the positive qualities identified in the opening *Marcom Insight* is crucial to corporate success. Personal selling is the last promotion-mix element covered in this textbook, but it certainly is not the least important. Indeed, popular business wisdom holds that everything starts with selling. In total, 6.5 million people are engaged in personal selling in the United States, a major contributor to the economy.[1] At times, personal selling can provide the push (as in *push strategy*) needed to get customers to carry new products, increase their amount of purchasing, and devote more effort in merchandising a company's brand. At the retail level, personal selling can determine whether a purchase is made and how often consumers shop at a particular store.

This chapter's overall objective is to present the reader with a broad array of ideas about the nature of personal selling, encouraging a greater appreciation of the opportunities and challenges for career success in this field. Toward this end, the chapter explores several dimensions of personal selling.

Personal Selling

Personal selling is a form of person-to-person communication in which a salesperson works with prospective buyers in attempting to determine their purchase needs to provide a match with his or her company's products or services. The most important feature of this definition is the idea that personal selling involves *person-to-person interaction*. This contrasts with other forms of marketing communications in which the audience typically consists of many people, sometimes millions (as in the case of mass-media advertising).

Personal Selling's Role in the Promotion Mix and IMC

As explained at various points throughout the text, all elements of the promotion mix and IMC work together to achieve overall organizational objectives. Each promotional element has its own unique characteristics, purposes, and advantages. Personal selling's primary purposes include educating customers, offering product usage and marketing assistance, and providing after-sales service and support to buyers. Personal selling, in comparison to other promotional elements, is uniquely capable of performing these functions as a result of the person-to-person interaction mode that characterizes this form of marketing communications. Consequently, various advantages accrue to personal selling compared to other promotional tools.

1. Personal selling contributes to a *relatively high level of customer attention*, since in face-to-face situations it is difficult for a potential buyer to avoid a salesperson's message.
2. It enables the salesperson to *customize the message* to the customer's specific interests and needs.
3. The two-way communication characteristic of personal selling yields *immediate feedback*, so that an alert salesperson can know whether or not his or her sales presentation is working.
4. Personal selling enables a salesperson to *communicate a larger amount of technical and complex information* than could be communicated using other promotional methods.
5. In personal selling, there is a greater ability to demonstrate a product's functioning and performance characteristics.
6. Frequent interactions with a customer permit the *opportunity for developing long-term relations* and effectively merging selling and buying organizations into a coordinated unit where both sets of interests are served.[2]

The primary disadvantage of personal selling is that it is *more costly* than other forms of promotion because sales representatives typically interact with only one customer at a time. (Typically, this might run more than $500 per sales call.[3]) Thus, when considering only the outcomes or results accomplished with the personal-selling effort (an effectiveness consideration), personal selling is generally *more effective* than other promotion elements. However, when considering the ratio of inputs to outputs (cost to results), personal selling is typically *less efficient* than other promotional and IMC tools. In practice, allocating resources to personal selling and the other promotion elements amounts to an effort at balancing effectiveness and efficiency. Integration with other IMC tools is important in providing synergistic effects.

Attitudes Toward Selling

Historically, some critics have held personal selling in low esteem. This reputation dates back at least to the time of the ancient Greek philosophers and continues to be perpetrated today by movie and television directors and playwrights. For example, Arthur Miller's classic *Death of a Salesman* and David Mamet's more recent *Glengarry Glen Ross* depict salespeople as rather pathetic characters who struggle for an existence and earn their living through ingratiation, deceit, and other unethical and immoral practices. In real life, there are indeed con men and women who rely on deception, false promises, trickery, and misrepresentation to persuade people to buy products and services they do not need or items that do not work. Although this still happens today, it represents a small percentage of the personal-selling business.

Fortunately, there is a continuing trend toward college students' holding somewhat more favorable attitudes toward selling. Table 23.1 compares results of three studies separated by a 40-year interval. It can be seen that student attitudes have improved over time, yet there still are some challenges in perceptions.[4] Overall, personal selling can be a much more attractive career option than many students previously thought. In fact, many CEOs and CMOs have made their start in personal selling.

TABLE 23.1	College Students' Changing Attitudes Toward Personal Selling		
	1958 Study	**1988 Study**	**1998 Study**
I associate a job in personal selling with:			
• Insincerity and deceit/lack of professionalism	Agree	Disagree	Disagree
• Low status/low prestige	Agree	Disagree	Agree
• Much traveling	Agree	Agree	Agree
• Low job security	Agree	Disagree	Agree
• Just a job not a career	Agree	Disagree	————
• Too little monetary reward/pay	Disagree	Disagree	Disagree
• Contributing to society	————	————	Disagree
• Opportunity for rapid advancement	————	————	Agree
• I prefer a nonsales position much more than sales	Agree	Disagree	————

Sources: Rosemary R. Lagrace and Timothy A. Longfellow, "The Impact of Classroom Style on Student Attitudes toward Sales Careers: A Comparative Approach," *Journal of Marketing Education*, 1989 (Fall), 74; and Steven Lysonski and Srinivas Durvasula, "A Cross-National Investigation of Student Attitudes Toward Personal Selling: Implications for Marketing Education," *Journal of Marketing Education*, 1998 (August), 169. Not all attitude items are measured in each survey.

Attractive Features of Personal Selling

Numerous challenging and exciting job opportunities are available in this field. The attractive features of a sales job include freedom of action, variety and challenge, opportunities for advancement, and desirable financial and nonfinancial rewards.[5]

Job Freedom. In field-sales positions (those outside of retail settings), the individual is primarily responsible for most of his or her day-to-day activities. Many sales positions involve little direct supervision. Salespeople may go days or even weeks without seeing their supervisors. Of course, with freedom comes responsibility. The unsupervised salesperson is expected to conduct his or her business professionally to achieve sales objectives.

Variety and Challenge. Managing one's own time presents a challenge that professional salespeople enjoy. Much like the person who operates his or her own business, a salesperson can invest as much time and energy into the job as desired and can generate as many rewards as possible based on hard work.

Opportunities for Advancement. More and more companies expect their middle- and upper-level managers to have had sales experience because they believe it helps an individual understand a business from the ground-level up. More corporate presidents (i.e., CEOs, CMOs) come from the sales ranks than from any other position; sales experience provides them with a knowledge of the customers, the trade, the competition, and their own company.

Attractive Compensation and Non-Financial Rewards. Personal selling is potentially both lucrative and rewarding. Nonfinancial rewards include feelings of self-worth for a job well done and the satisfaction that comes from providing a customer with a solution to a problem or with a product or service that best meets his or her needs.

Modern Selling Philosophy

Before the *modern* selling philosophy, there must have been an earlier variety. Let us label this earlier version *antiquated* and place the two in stark contrast, realizing of course that any such comparison is necessarily simplified.

Basically, *antiquated selling* is *seller-oriented*. Selling practices in this older view are undertaken with the seller's interests paramount. Manifestations of this approach include high-pressure selling tactics, little effort to understand the customer's business, and little post-sale follow through and attention to customer satisfaction.

Are these antiquated practices truly antiquated in the sense that they no longer are practiced? Certainly not. Some firms are still antiquated; although they remain in business, they no longer thrive. Their selling practices lag behind contemporary forces that have imposed a higher standard on sales performance. These forces include intense competition, narrow profit margins, sophisticated buying practices, and expectations of reliable and dependable service from vendors.

In most prospering firms, a modern selling philosophy has supplanted this seller-oriented approach. As noted previously in the pharmaceutics industry, a *partner-oriented* selling mind-set exists in most successful firms. These firms realize that their own success rests with their customers' successes. Therefore, modern partner-oriented wisdom makes customer satisfaction its highest priority. Modern selling practice is based on the following principles.[6]

1. *The sales process must be built on a foundation of trust and mutual agreement.* Selling should not be viewed as something someone does to another; rather, it should be looked upon as something two parties agree to do for their mutual benefit. In fact, it is easy to argue that modern salespeople do not sell, but rather, facilitate buying. This difference is not merely semantics— it is at the root of the transformation from the antiquated to modern selling philosophies.

2. *A customer-driven atmosphere is essential to long-term growth.* This is a corollary point to the preceding principle. Modern selling requires that the customer's welfare, interests, and needs be treated as equal to the seller's in the partnership between seller and buyer. A customer-oriented approach means avoiding high-pressure tactics and focusing on customer satisfaction. Salespeople have to be trained to know the customer and to speak in a language that the customer understands. Perhaps the preceding points are best summed up in these words: "Be product-centered, and you will make a few sales; be prospect-centered, and you will gain many customers."[7]

3. *Sales representatives should act as if they were on the customer's payroll.* The ultimate compliment a salesperson can receive is a comment from a customer to the sales supervisor along these lines: "I'm not sure whether your sales rep works for me or for you."[8] The closer salespeople are to the customer, the better they will be at providing solutions to the customer's problems.

4. *Getting the order is only the first step; after-sales service is what counts.* No problem a customer has should be too small to address. Modern selling philosophy calls for doing whatever is necessary to please the customer in order to ensure a satisfying long-term relationship. (See the *Global Focus*.)

GLOBAL FOCUS

Selling Japanese Style

Modern selling philosophy and modern selling practice are not the same thing. That is, what ought to be and what is may be worlds apart. This conflict between philosophy and practice is perhaps most acute in the United States, where organizational structures and personalities make it difficult for many Americans to behave in the fashion laid out in the six principles underlying modern selling practice. For example, the individualistic style and competitive spirit that are part of the American psyche may make it difficult for some salespeople to consider their customers' needs as important as their own.

Japanese salespeople's personalities are perhaps better suited to implementing modern selling philosophy. Respect is the foundation of Japanese selling. Being respectful (deferential to their customers and dedicated to their needs) is easy for Japanese businesspeople insofar as the feudal roots of Japan placed businessmen at the bottom of the social hierarchy. As one writer observes, "Today's Japanese sales reps, if they're good, still behave as if they're at the bottom of the social ladder, respecting and trying to satisfy their customers."

The Japanese selling style is sometimes referred to as "wet," implying that it is flexible, accommodating, caring, and human. The American style (especially "old school" or "antiquated" selling) is more likely to be "dry," or more inflexible, logical,

and cut-and-dried. A notable distinction in how the wet and dry styles are manifest is in the area of customer service. Upon being informed of a customer problem, an American sales representative might simply just pass the problem along to the technical support staff with hopes that the problem will be resolved. Japanese sales reps, on the other hand, will personally become involved in solving the problem, work with the support staff, and submit a report to the customer explaining why the product failed and what has been done to prevent that failure from happening again. They also are less likely to take credit for success or blame others for failure. Non-financial incentives to recognize, praise, or reward salespeople in Japan are found to be very important. Interestingly, commissions generally are not part of compensation packages in Japan; salespeople consider it their duty to generate extra business for their companies. Finally, Japanese buyers are very risk averse. So, it is important to be sensitive to this issue, as many Japanese buyers place a premium on doing business with honest and ethical companies providing credible goods and services.

Sources: George Leslie, "U.S. Reps Should Learn to Sell 'Japanese Style'," *Marketing News*, October 29, 1990, 6; and "Success Secrets of Selling in Japan," *Venture Japan*, 2009, http://www.venturejapan.com/japanese-corporate-sales.htm.

5. *In selling, as in medicine, prescription before diagnosis is malpractice.* This principle holds that no one solution is appropriate for all customers any more than any single diagnosis is appropriate for all patients. Customers' problems have to be analyzed by the modern salesperson and solutions customized to each problem. The days of "one solution fits all" are gone. Moreover, because most people like to make their own decisions or at least be involved in making them, a salesperson should treat the customer as a partner in the solution.

6. *Salesperson professionalism and integrity are essential.* Customers expect high standards of conduct from their salespeople and dislike unprofessional, untrustworthy, and dishonest behavior. (As evidence of this, reexamine the Bad and the Ugly in the chapter's opening *Marcom Insight*.)

Selling Activities and Types of Personal-Selling Jobs

To this point in the chapter, personal selling has been treated rather generally as if all selling jobs are identical. This section describes the different kinds of activities that salespeople perform and then identifies six types of selling jobs.

Selling Activities

What exactly does a salesperson do? The specific activities and their range of performance vary greatly from sales job to sales job. Nonetheless, the following 10 activities are common to nearly all selling jobs.[9]

Selling Function. This is the typical activity envisioned when thinking of personal selling. Selling-function activities include planning the sales presentation, making the presentation, overcoming objections, trying to close the sale, and so on.

Working with Others. Much of a salesperson's time is spent entering orders online, working with lost orders, handling shipment problems, expediting orders, and handling back orders.

Servicing the Product. These activities are performed primarily by people who sell technical products (e.g., an industrial machine). Activities include testing a newly sold product to ensure that it is working properly, training customers to use the product, and teaching safety procedures.

Information Management. These activities involve receiving feedback from customers and then relaying the information to management. Much of this is done online in the course of day-to-day selling, but some information-management work requires the salesperson to serve in the capacity of a field marketing researcher (i.e., conveying price discounts and increases, tracking customer comments and social media, collaborating with other reps, etc.). One of the best available sales information management tools is salesforce.com, which is featured in the *IMC Focus*.[10]

Servicing the Account. These activities include inventory control, stocking shelves, handling local advertising, and setting up and working with POP displays. Such activities are primarily performed by salespeople who call on retail customers such as supermarkets and drugstores.

Conferences/Meetings. Attending conferences, working at trade shows, and attending sales meetings are activities nearly all salespeople participate in to some extent.

Training/Recruiting. Salespeople who are in more advanced stages of their careers often become involved in training new salespeople, traveling with trainees, and similar duties.[11]

Entertaining. Some sales positions involve entertaining customers through activities such as dining and playing golf. Parenthetically, the antiquated view of selling would hold that you can buy customers by "wining and dining" them. Modern selling philosophy includes a role for customer entertainment, but recognizes that customers are earned (through loyal, efficient, and dependable service) rather than bought.

IMC FOCUS

Salesforce.com

Salesforce.com is a $3-billion company providing state-of-the-art cloud computing and solutions for the sales industry. It offers one-stop shopping for numerous sales software and application tools using cloud computing, storage, and connectivity tools online. Through the recent acquisition of many online business partners (e.g., Heroku, Dimdim, Radian6, Assistly), Salesforce.com has become a direct competitor with major software firms SAP and Oracle. Each of these acquisitions has resulted in much needed specialties in serving the sales industry. For example, Heroku provides application platforms supporting a multitude of programming languages. Dimdim offers salespeople online meeting collaboration, whereas Radian6's specialty is social media monitoring, metrics, sentiment analysis, and analytic dashboards (all discussed in Chapter 14). Assistly, now renamed as Desk.com, collects and organizes customer social media conversations.

Salesforce.com charges between $5 to $250 per month for a wide range of services to those working in sales, including tracking sales opportunities and e-mail, lead scoring and ranking, sales campaigns, mass e-mailing, dashboard analytics, sales forecasts, sales-to-sales collaboration, sales trends, territory management, mobile customization, 24/7 support, etc. In staying ahead of competitors, Salesforce.com is building added software ("Chatter") that works like Facebook and is intended for those in sales to share and collaborate more openly with customers, others in their firm and supply chain, and the industry as a whole. Needless to say, such information management advances have come a long way from the "old school" selling approaches of the past.

Sources: Quentin Hardy, "A Leader in the Cloud Gains Rivals," *New York Times*, December 11, 2011, http://www.nytimes.com/2011/12/12/technology/companies/salesforce-a-leader-in-cloud-computing-draws-big-rivals.html; Nick Bilton, "BITS; Social Media and Government," *New York Times*, April 30, 2012, http://query.nytimes.com/gst/fullpage.html?res=9A05E6D81E39F933A05757C0A9649D8B63; and Salesforce.com, http://www.salesforce.com, accessed June 25, 2012.

Out-of-Town Travel. Although sales jobs involve some traveling, the amount of time spent out of town is highly variable, ranging from virtually no travel to journeying thousands of miles each month. The advent of teleconferencing, online collaboration (e.g., Dimdim, Skype), real-time presentations, and webinars has lessened the need for extensive travel recently.

Working with Distributors. A final category of selling activity is selling to or establishing relations with distributors or collecting past-due accounts.

Types of Sales Jobs

The following six categories encompass the major types of sales jobs.[12]

Trade Selling

A sales representative for a food manufacturer who sells to the grocery and drug industries typifies trade selling. The primary task of trade salespeople is to build sales volume by providing customers with promotional assistance in the form of advertising and sales promotion. Trade selling requires limited prospecting and places greater emphasis on *servicing accounts*. Trade salespeople, who typically are hired out of college, may work for companies such as General Mills, Kimberly-Clark, Colgate-Palmolive, Johnson & Johnson, Campbell's Soup, Procter & Gamble, S.C. Johnson, and many other consumer packaged-goods companies.

Missionary Selling

Like trade salespeople, missionary salespeople typically are employees of manufacturers. However, the difference is that trade salespeople sell *through* their direct customers, whereas a missionary sales force sells *for* its direct customers.[13]

The pharmaceutical industry typifies missionary selling. Nearly two-thirds of all pharmaceutical sales to retailers are through wholesalers. In other words, manufacturers of pharmaceuticals typically sell their products to wholesalers who in turn sell to pharmacies and other retailers. Thus, the wholesaler is the pharmaceutical manufacturer's direct customer. Sales representatives for pharmaceutical manufacturers (called detail reps or detailers) nonetheless call on physicians and pharmacies to detail (explain) the advantages of the manufacturer's brands compared to competitive offerings. Detail reps are not selling directly to physicians (i.e., selling in the sense that a physician will place an order with the salesperson's company); rather, they are trying to get physicians to prescribe their brands and pull these brands through the channel. In so doing, they benefit both the manufacturer (via increased sales volume) and their direct customers (wholesalers).

Technical Selling

Technical salespeople ("sales engineers") are present in industries such as chemicals, machinery, electronics, computers, and sophisticated services (e.g., complicated insurance and other financial programs). They are typically trained in technical fields such as chemistry, engineering, computer science, and accounting. For example, in the chemical division of Du Pont, 95 percent of the company's salespeople start out in a technical field and then are recruited into sales.[14] Later, many sales technicians attain advanced training in business administration. Successful technical salespeople must be especially knowledgeable about their company's product lines and must be able to communicate complicated features to prospective customers.

New-Business Selling

This type of selling is prevalent with products such as office copiers, personal computers, business software, and personal insurance. Practitioners use terms such as *bird-dogging*, *cold calling*, and *canvassing* to characterize this type of selling. These terms capture the idea that new-business salespeople must call on new accounts continuously. Salespeople involved in any of the previous categories of sales jobs do some prospecting for new customers, but most of their time is spent working with and servicing existing accounts. New-business salespeople continually work to open new accounts because sales to most customers are infrequent.

Retail Selling

The distinguishing characteristic of retail selling is that the customer comes to the salesperson. Many retail sales jobs require limited training and sophistication, but others demand salespeople who have considerable product knowledge, strong interpersonal skills, and an ability to work with a diversity of customers.

Inside Sales

Inside sales, in the form of telemarketing, was discussed in some detail in Chapter 15. Suffice it to say again that telemarketing and online contacts are rapidly growing forms of selling activity. Telephone and online salespeople are especially helpful with activities such as prospecting, price quotes, and follow-up information in support of the field sales reps or for a wider range of selling activities with smaller accounts.

The Basic Steps in Personal Selling

Regardless of the specific type of sales position, all forms of personal selling can be presented by a common set of steps or phases that are performed in the process of making a sale (or in facilitating buying). There are seven basic steps involved in personal selling:[15]

1. Prospecting and qualifying
2. Preapproach
3. Approach
4. Sales presentation
5. Handling objections
6. Close
7. Follow-up

Step 1: Prospecting and Qualifying

The first step involves identifying potential buyers (prospects) who have the need, willingness, ability, and authority to buy. Specifically, the salesperson looks for names, addresses, e-mail leads, telephone numbers, social media sites (e.g., LinkedIn, Facebook, Twitter), corporate websites, and other general facts about prospective customers. Prospecting involves the identification of such customers through both *internal sources* of information (e.g., company records, membership lists, and other written documents) and *external sources* of information (e.g., referrals from existing customers, sales leads from organizations or compilers, friends, business mapping software tools, social media sites, non-competing salespeople, and so on). Prospecting is especially important for new-business sales jobs.

Once prospects have been identified, it is important to *qualify* such prospects, as they may or may not fit your current target market criteria (e.g., based on prior purchases, number of employees, shipments, geographical location, industry type, among other company statistics). Then, one can evaluate each prospect on criteria of importance to your firm. For example, databases such as the U.S. Census' North American Industrial Classification System (www.census.gov/eos/www/naics) can provide industry classification codes to target and match with the codes listed for specific prospects in business mapping software tools for a specific geographical location. Thus, not all prospects may make the best customers that fit with your firm; some qualification and targeting is first needed.

Step 2: Preapproach

The preapproach step requires the salesperson to arrange a meeting with the prospective customer and to acquire, prior to the meeting, more specific information about him or her and his or her business needs. The initial sales meeting might be arranged in a variety of ways: by sending a personal letter or e-mail to prospects, by calling to set up a meeting during designated buying times, by asking mutual friends to set up a meeting, or by having a present customer introduce the salesperson and request an interview.

Acquiring meaningful information about prospective customers and their business is an essential part of the preapproach. For example, the salesperson may learn that the prospect's business is expanding rapidly; therefore, the salesperson's product could be needed to accommodate this growing business. Salespeople use a variety of information sources for learning about prospective customers: current customers, company websites, social and other media, observing the prospect's business facilities, etc.

Step 3: Approach

The third step, approach, represents the first few moments that a salesperson spends with a prospect. This initial greeting and first impression is critical to the salesperson's chances that they will eventually make the sale. In fact, a sale is unlikely if the salesperson has failed to do his or her homework in the preapproach stage.

Salespeople can use a variety of approach techniques, often in combination with one another, to gain the prospect's attention and interest. Some of these include: (1) using a present customer's name as a reference to the prospect, (2) giving the prospect a small gift, (3) offering a benefit (e.g., cost savings, new item, research) that has appeal to the prospect's curiosity, (4) opening the sales interview with a question to gain the prospect's attention and interest (see "SPIN method" below), and (5) handing a sample product to the prospect for him or her to inspect.

Step 4: The Sales Presentation

The fourth step, the actual sales presentation, is the fundamental part of the selling activity. The salesperson presents the product or service, explains what it will do for the prospective customer, demonstrates it strengths, its value for the customer, and so forth. In this stage (as well as for the previous one), sales reps are taught the SPIN method in order to forge long-term relationships with customers with the following questions:[16]

1. *Situation questions*. These questions ask about facts or explore the prospect's present situation. For instance, "What software application are you using to create invoices for your customers?
2. *Problem questions*. These examine problems, difficulties, challenges, frustrations, and dissatisfactions that the prospect is experiencing. For example, "What parts of the system create errors?"
3. *Implication questions*. These ask about the consequences or impact of a prospect's problems, difficulties, challenges, frustrations, and dissatisfactions. As an example, "How does this problem affect your firm's return on investment (ROI)?"
4. *Need-payoff questions*. These ask about the value or usefulness of a proposed solution. For instance, "How much would you save if our company could help you reduce errors by 75 percent?"

In general, successful sales presentations result from having an *impact* on the customer.[17] This means the ability for the salesperson to get prospective customers to focus on what they are saying and eventually follow his or her lead in a buying decision. There are four fundamental tenets of *high-impact selling*. First, *prospects pay attention only to salespeople that they believe have something important to say*. As noted in Chapter 11, the credibility of the source goes a long way in ensuring a source's persuasiveness, as in the case of a salesperson's presentation. Source credibility is a function of the source's perceived expertise and trustworthiness. Thus, a salesperson's persuasiveness may be reduced if he or she is perceived by the customer to be motivated primarily by personal gain and not the customer's needs. Conversely, a sales rep that can demonstrate a high level of expertise for the product or service enhances his or her chances of being perceived as a credible source. Second, *people buy for their own reasons—not the salesperson's reasons*. The saying "What's in it for me?" certainly should be considered when evaluating a prospect's self-interests. A third tenet of high impact selling is that *people do not want to be sold; they want to buy*. That is, the true role of salespeople is to facilitate buying through understanding the buyer's needs and interests rather than pushing products on potential customers. A fourth tenet is that *buying is basically an emotional response*. Certainly, although logical criteria (e.g., price, delivery, service) and analysis are involved, even professional buying can be subject to more subjective and emotional influences.[18] For example, a corporation that purchases a new wireless phone system undoubtedly uses objective evaluative criteria such as cost, efficiency, clarity of voice transmission, range, service, etc. However, emotional considerations may come into play, such as fears that the new system may not be as reliable as the old one, that any "dead spots" in the network do not create havoc in communication, hopes that the buyer will receive praise from a superior for a smart and efficient purchase decision, etc.

Step 5: Handling Objections

In many, if not most, selling situations, prospects feel they have reasons not to buy the product or service offered by the salesperson. The salesperson must be prepared to handle objections, counterarguments, and sales resistance. At this point, the salesperson might reiterate how the product meets the customers' needs and problems, what benefits the product offers, and how the prospect can most easily make the decision (e.g., credit terms).

Different methods have been offered over the years for handling objections and reducing buying resistance. For example, the salesperson might (1) dispute the objection and offer solid reasons for this, (2) concede to parts of the objection and dispute other issues in an inoffensive manner (e.g., using a two-sided argument), or (3) address the objection later in the presentation or use humor, etc. to relieve tension brought about by conflicting issues.

Recently and briefly described earlier in the chapter, sales representatives from the pharmaceutics firm Eli Lilly & Co. have discovered that a "soft sell" to time-pressured physicians works far better than more aggressive tactics to sell pharmaceutical products.[19] For years, armies of pharmaceutical sales reps fanned out to "detail" physicians with well-rehearsed sales pitches and pressure to boost prescriptions. However, physicians have been under pressure from health plans to curb costs, and have less patience and time for hard-sell pitches. Moreover, there have been crackdowns by the FDA, etc. for aggressive and illegal marketing of drugs for non-approved uses. Pharmaceutical companies have been forced themselves to reduce expenses and find more effective selling methods. So, the new "soft sell" approach is now all about the physicians' agenda. Sales rep evaluations are no longer based on the number of prescriptions written, but now on how well physicians rate their representatives. This change has paid off for Lilly, as 85 percent of doctors are now satisfied with Lilly, up from 60 percent before the change. Sales of their pharmaceutical products have escalated as well.

Other approaches in handling objections focus on understanding not only the content of the communication, but the *form* of the communication. This notion is known as relational communications and is about the relative position of dominance, deference, or equality that buyers and sellers put themselves in as a result of dialog between the two.[20] Based on these relative positions, there may be an agreement or disagreement on the ending relationship as a result of the dialog. As depicted in Figure 23.1, a dialog in which a salesperson defers to a dominant buyer may go like this: *Buyer*: "Your prices are really quite high." *Salesperson*: "Do you really think so? I guess they are." So, there is some agreement—although the salesperson will have to work on their higher prices! In other dialogs in Figure 23.1, there may be a disagreement or conflict based on the dialog. The implication of relational communications is that certain salespeople may be more adept at recognizing the nature of the dialog with buyers, can adjust, and then better control the outcome of the dialog. Training in this area may help to recognize that the form of what is said is sometimes more important than the content.

Step 6: The Close

In the "close," the salesperson attempts to gain some type of *commitment* from the customer to purchase the product or service. In other words, the salesperson ask for the order. Salespeople use different techniques in closing the sale to make it easier for the prospect to commit to a purchase. For example, the

		SALESPERSON	
	Dominance	**Deference**	**Equality**
BUYER — **Dominance**	Salesperson: You are the most knowledgeable buyer I've met. Buyer: Actually, I know very little. Initiation/Disconfirmation —	Buyer: Your prices are really quite high. Salesperson: Do you really think so? I guess they are. Initiation/Question, Confirmation +	Buyer: Your prices are really quite high. Salesperson: Yes they are, but so are everybody's in this inflationary economy. Initiation/Extension —
Deference	Salesperson: You are the most knowledgeable buyer I've met. Buyer: Do you really think so? Initiation/Question +	Buyer: Your product really meets our needs. Salesperson: Do you really think so? Buyer: Yes, don't you? Support, Question/Support, Question —	Buyer: Your prices are really quite high. Salesperson: Yes they are, but so are everybody's. Buyer: Do you really think so? Extension/Support, Question —
Equality	Salesperson: You are the most knowledgeable buyer I've met. Buyer: Thank you. I've had 17 years of experience. Initiation/Extension —	Salesperson: You are the most knowledgeable buyer I've met. Buyer: Thank you. I've had 17 years of experience. Salesperson: Oh really! Extension/Question, Support —	Buyer: Your product really meets our needs. Salesperson: You're right. It is beautifully designed. Buyer: Yes. So is most of your line. Extension/Extension +

+ = agreement on relationship **−** = disagreement on relationship

FIGURE 23.1 Relational Communication Dialogs

Source: Gary F. Soldow and Gloria Penn Thomas, "Relational Communication: Form Versus Content in the Sales Interaction," *Journal of Marketing,* Vol. 48, Winter 1984, p. 88. Journal of Marketing by American Marketing Association; American Marketing Society; National Association of Marketing Teachers. © 1984. Reproduced with permission of American Marketing Association in the format Republish in a textbook via Copyright Clearance Center.

salesperson may (1) tell the prospect about a previous customer whose needs were similar to the prospect's and who benefitted from the salesperson's product, (2) present the prospect with two or more product versions and ask which one he or she prefers, (3) if the prospect is ready to buy, focus on purchase details such as delivery date and credit terms, (4) ask for the order in a straightforward manner, or (5) offer some incentive or cost savings (via trade-ins) to get the prospect to buy now. If the prospect is not ready to commit, leaving a demonstrator or sample may help move the prospect closer to purchase.

Step 7: The Follow-Up

Finally, in a post-sale follow-up, the salesperson attempts to reduce the consumer's post-purchase anxiety ("cognitive dissonance") that is likely especially for products requiring a high level of effort, time, or money. This may involve suggesting additional products and accessories, determining any problems the customer may be having with the product, and/or developing a stronger relationship with the customer in the hope of generating future sales.

Effective follow-up is critical for establishing long-term *relationships* with customers. Successful salespeople do not discontinue contact once they have made a sale. They make sure that the product truly fits the customer's needs, that it is being used properly, that customer complaints are remedied expeditiously, and so on. Follow-up includes sending letters of appreciation to customers, training the customer's employees in the proper use of the product, addressing the customer's complaints or product-related problems, and making adjustments if the product does not meet the customer's expectations.

In Summary

It would be erroneous to think that the preceding step-by-step presentation means that all selling efforts progress in such an orderly fashion and that each preceding step must be completed before the next one follows. Nothing could be further from the truth. The point is that the seven steps are involved to one degree or another in all selling jobs and that all must be performed at one time or another. However, rather occurring in some linear, lock-step fashion, the steps actually mingle and occur over an extended time period with iterations. For instance, a salesperson may try to close a sale early in the presentation, but find her effort rebuffed. Unable to handle the buyer's objection at that time, she courteously asks for an opportunity to do some more research (preapproach activity) and to return at a later date. Her additional study of the buyer's needs and objections leads her to develop a different presentation, to delay attempting to close the transaction, and to use a different tactic in handling the buyer's objections. Her persistence eventually pays off when the buyer is convinced that her offering is the best for his company. The following *IMC Focus* offers a direct case application of the seven basic steps in personal selling for a recently-graduated, undergraduate marketing student on his first day in his sales job.

National Business Machines Case

It was Brad Wilson's first day on the job after completing his product training with National Business Machines Inc. Two months prior to this time, Brad had graduated with a 3.0 GPA with a B.S. degree in business administration from a major university. He had taken a personal selling class as part of his marketing major.

Brad believed strongly that his most positive attribute was his outgoing and enthusiastic personality. It was the reason he had chosen sales as a career. This belief was reinforced by NBM recruiters, who remarked that it was this trait that led them to hire him over other candidates around the nation with more impressive GPAs.

Brad had been assigned to the computer laptop division of NBM, working out of an office located in a medium-sized city, and he was eager to get started. His supervisor had given him a list of customers who might be prospects for the new generation of lightweight, 11-inch computer laptops NBM had just listed for sale. Brad scanned the list and noticed Harrison Brothers was located just around the corner from the NBM building. Eager to make his first sale, he picked up his demonstration model and rushed off to Ms. Johnstone, the office manager at Harrison Brothers.

Brad (to receptionist): Good morning, I'm Brad Wilson with NBM. I would like to see Ms. Johnstone, the office manager.

Receptionist: Do you have an appointment?

Brad: Well, er, no, but we have this fantastic new line of computer laptops she'll want to hear about.

Receptionist: Ms. Johnstone, there's a Mr. Wilson here from NBM who would like to see you about some new laptops.

Mr. Wilson, Ms. Johnstone says she is busy right now. If you would like to make an appointment she'll be willing to talk to you.

Brad: Tell Ms. Johnstone I will only take 10 minutes of her time and I'm sure increasing office productivity while decreasing costs is something she'll want to hear about!

Receptionist: Ms. Johnstone says O.K. but no more than 10 minutes because she really is busy. Her office door is the last door on the left.

Brad: Hello, Ms. Johnstone, how are you doing? I'm Brad Wilson with NBM. I know you're going to be glad you agreed to see me. (Smiling with hand extended.)

Ms. Johnstone: Well, I don't know about that. Please sit down and say what you have to say. I have some things to attend to.

Brad: This is our 11-inch lightweight computer laptop which has just been introduced. It is only 2.38 pounds, is 11.8 inches wide by 7.56 inches deep, has 128 GB of flash storage, and a 1.6-GHz dual-core Intel processor.

Ms. Johnstone: That's all very nice Mr. Wilson, but we bought some of your laptops just over a year ago for $1599 each! We can't afford to buy anymore right now.

Brad: It's more a question of can you afford not to invest in this latest model, Ms. Johnstone. What we've been able to do is simplify the design so that manufacturing and servicing costs have been significantly reduced. What this means to you is that with over $574 trade-in on each of your old laptops and a total investment of only $1199 in the new laptops, your net investment is only $625. Right now you are paying $291 per year for maintenance. Maintenance on our new model is only $108 per year, a savings of $183 per year. So, in less than four years the savings on maintenance will have covered the cost of the laptops. Isn't that impressive, Ms. Johnstone?

By the way, when would you like delivery of your new laptops, next week or would the end of the month be soon enough?

Ms. Johnstone: Look, Mr. Wilson, I can see where the maintenance savings are substantial, but I'm going to have to think about it.

Brad: That's always a good idea, Ms. Johnstone, but our trade-in allowance on your current laptops is only in effect until the end of next month, and you would like to take advantage of that, wouldn't you?

Ms. Johnstone: Why, yes, I would, but I still need to consider the deal.

Brad: Let me leave this new laptop demonstrator with you so you can see its advantages over your existing laptops, and then I'll come back next week to take care of the paperwork. Is that OK, Ms. Johnstone? I promise to make an appointment with your receptionist on the way out.

Ms. Johnstone: OK, Mr. Wilson, I'll see you next week, but no promises.

Brad: Thank you for your time, Ms. Johnstone. Good-bye

NBM Case Questions

1. Based on the seven basic steps in personal selling presented earlier in the chapter, how would you evaluate Brad's sales call at Harrison Brothers?
2. Why did Brad leave the laptop demonstrator model? What was he hoping would happen when he returned?
3. What are Brad's chances of succeeding at NBM?
4. How can Brad improve his overall approach and presentation to be successful on future sales calls?

Source: This case was adapted from the original National Business Machines case in the first edition by Stephen E. Calcich, Marketing Research Consultant, Philippines. Original copyright 1984 Stephen E. Calcich. Permission granted by the author.

Salesperson Performance and Effectiveness

Regardless of the type of sales job, certain aptitudes and skills are needed to perform effectively. Indeed, people in all facets of life are ultimately judged in terms of their performance and effectiveness. Typically, these evaluations are based on quantitative assessments: number of books published by a writer, number of indictments by a prosecuting attorney, number of hits by a baseball player, number of units produced by a factory worker, number of articles published by a professor, and so on. Likewise, salespeople are typically judged in terms of the number of units sold or dollar volume. (No doubt, an argument could be made for *quality*, rather than just quantity, for each of these categories!)

Academic and business researchers have long been intrigued with explaining and predicting salesperson performance. The fundamental issue is one of identifying the specific factors that determine salesperson effectiveness—the factors that distinguish the outstanding salesperson from good, mediocre, and bad salespeople. (Stop reading for a few moments and think about your own ideas on this issue. You might jot down what you think are the most important determinants of salesperson success and later compare your thoughts with the ideas presented.)

Before a specific discussion of the determinants of salesperson performance and effectiveness, two general points require careful attention. The first is that *no single factor is able to adequately explain salesperson performance.* In a very thorough and insightful analysis of sales research conducted over a 40-year span, researchers examined over 100 separate studies and over 1,500 correlations in these studies relating salesperson performance with a wide variety of potential predictors. Their analyses revealed that, on average, no single predictor explained more than *four percent* of the variability in salesperson performance![21] The conclusion to be drawn is clear: Sales performance is based on various considerations; to expect any single factor (or even several factors) to adequately explain a complex behavior is too much.

A second general conclusion is that salesperson effectiveness is *contingent on a host of factors*; indeed, selling effectiveness depends on the total situation in which sales transactions take place. Specifically, as depicted in Figure 23.2, the effectiveness of selling behaviors (e.g., adapting to customers, establishing networks) is contingent upon (1) the salesperson's own resources (product knowledge, analytical skills, etc.), (2) the nature of the customer's buying task (e.g., whether it is a first-time or repeat decision), (3) the customer-salesperson relationship (relative power, level of conflict, etc.), and interactions among all three of these general sets of factors.[22]

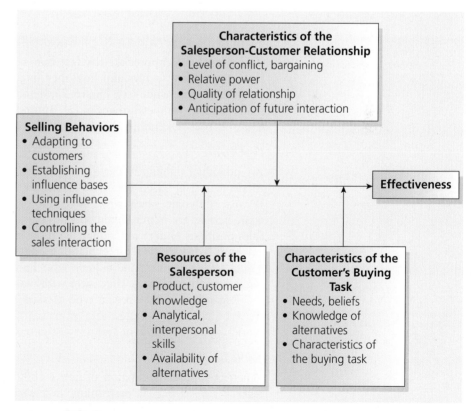

FIGURE **23.2** Contingency Model of Salesperson Effectiveness

Source: Barton A. Weitz, "Effectiveness in Sales Interactions: A Contingency Framework," *Journal of Marketing,* Vol. 45, Winter 1981, p. 90. Journal of Marketing by American Marketing Association; American Marketing Society; National Association of Marketing Teachers. © 1981. Reproduced with permission of American Marketing Association in the format Republish in a textbook via Copyright Clearance Center.

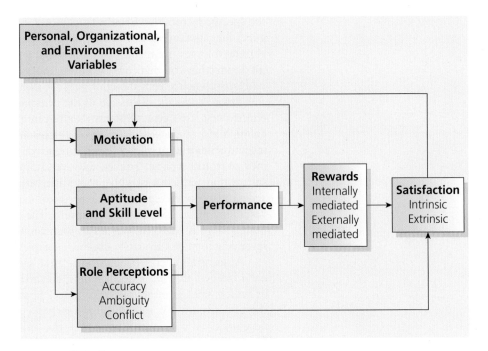

FIGURE **23.3** Determinants of Salesperson Performance

Source: Orville C. Walker, Jr., Gilbert A. Churchill, Jr., and Neil M. Ford, "Motivation and Performance in Industrial Selling: Present Knowledge and Needed Research," *Journal of Marketing Research,* 14 (May 1977), p. 158. JMR, Journal of Marketing Research by American Marketing Association. © 1977. Reproduced with permission of American Marketing Association in the format Republish in a textbook via Copyright Clearance Center.

Specific Determinants of Salesperson Performance

You now should appreciate the fact that salesperson effectiveness is contingent upon several key factors and how they interact. We will examine in greater detail six characteristics (see Figure 23.3) that have been hypothesized to determine salesperson performance: (1) aptitude, (2) skill level, (3) motivational level, (4) role perceptions, (5) personal characteristics, and (6) adaptability.[23]

Aptitude

An individual's ability to perform certain tasks depends greatly on his or her aptitude, which is based on interests, intelligence, and personality characteristics. Because different salespeople have different tasks and activities to perform, some people are better suited to one type of sales job than another. Technical sales positions require individuals with the strong analytical aptitude and technical knowledge needed for explaining complex product features to customers. Trade selling requires individuals who have good interpersonal skills and are highly adaptive, because they meet with many different types of customers.

Regardless of the specific type of sales position, all professional salespeople must be customer-oriented and empathetic. They should be able to view the world from the outside in and not just in terms of their own limited perspective.

Skill Level

Whereas aptitude is a matter of native ability, skill level refers to an individual's *learned proficiency* at performing necessary selling tasks. These skills include sales skills (such as knowing how to make a sales presentation), interpersonal skills (such as how to cope with and resolve conflict), and technical skills (such as knowledge about a product's features, performance, and benefits). These skills are partially brought to a sales job as a function of an individual's education preparation, but are also learned and fostered on the job.

Companies with effective sales programs instill in their sales force the skills needed for success. In fact, many sales organizations prefer to recruit salespeople directly out of college rather than from other sales positions so that they do not have to retrain sales candidates to overcome bad habits and conflicting skills learned elsewhere.

For example, Armstrong World Industries, a maker of carpeting, flooring, and other products, is legendary for hiring salespeople directly from college and sending them through the same basic training program that all Armstrong salespeople have undergone for over 60 years. In explaining the company's attitude toward sales training, Armstrong's director of human resources explains: "We prefer to hire people without any biases, conflicting opinions, or bad traits—and then we train them ourselves. We've had great success doing things our way, and if we're doing it that way and other companies aren't, well, then they're doing it wrong."[24] This may sound quite confident, but it merely represents the belief that it is often easier to train than it is to retrain.

Motivational Level

Motivational level refers to the *amount of time and energy* a person is willing to expend performing tasks and activities associated with a job. These tasks typically include managing sales information, calling on new accounts, creating new sales presentations, following up on sales, and so forth. An interesting thing about motivation is that it is *reciprocally related to performance*. That is, motivation is a determinant of performance and also is determined by performance—we often become even more motivated after we have enjoyed some success.

Another important characteristic of salesperson motivation is the distinction between *working hard* and *working smart*. Motivation is not simply the amount of effort but also how the effort is directed. Salespeople who work smart are typically more effective than those who just work hard.[25] Of course, a truly dynamite combination for a salesperson is to work both smart and hard.

Role Perceptions

In order to perform their jobs well, salespeople must know what is expected of them and have accurate perceptions of their role. Their jobs are defined by people both within and outside the organization, including family, sales managers, company executives, and customers. Thus, how well people perform in sales jobs depends on the accuracy of their perceptions of management's stated goals, demands, policies, procedures, organizational lines of authority and responsibilities.

Very often salespeople face *role conflicts* that inhibit their sales performance. For example, a customer may want a special price or advertising concessions that the company has policies against. Salespeople have been trained to meet customers' needs; however, they have also learned to follow company policies. What should a sales representative do in this situation? If a salesperson can negotiate differences between the two parties, he or she may be able to resolve the conflict and make the sale. In general, accurate role perceptions are a very important determinant of sales performance, effectiveness, and organizational commitment. Research has shown that role ambiguity in the early stage of employment decreases salesperson commitment to their companies and increases turnover.[26] Accurate perceptions are instilled during initial sales training and over time during periodic sales meetings and through periodic interactions with sales supervisors.

Personal Characteristics

Another determinant of salesperson effectiveness is an individual's personal characteristics—his or her age, physical size, appearance, race, and gender are some of the personal characteristics expected to affect sales performance. Research has shown that these personal factors may be even more important than the other factors in determining sales performance.[27]

It would be erroneous, however, to conclude that one's personal characteristics ensure sales success or failure. To the contrary, personal characteristics merely may make it more or less difficult to succeed in sales. Performance by any individual depends ultimately on his or her ability, skill, and motivation level, similar to the processing of message claims centrally (versus peripherally) as discussed in Chapter 7. In fact, the number of opportunities for salespeople from diverse backgrounds has increased significantly over the years.[28]

In terms of gender, the percentage of female salespeople has risen to 45 percent.[29] Yet, the question of who is better—men or women—is a fruitless one. No doubt, some women are better salespersons than some of their male colleagues and vice versa. The real determinant of sales success is not dependent on one's gender, but rather the ability to adapt oneself to situational circumstances and to call upon a repertoire of both male and female traits. This ability is called androgyny, which is "the degree to which individuals feel that they are characterized by traits associated with both men and women."[30]

Adaptability

Although not explicitly included in Figure 23.3, a final determinant of salesperson performance is one's ability to adapt to situational circumstances. This ability is due in part to personal aptitude, but also includes learned skills. Researches have built a compelling case that adaptability is an absolutely essential characteristic for success in selling.[31]

Formally, adaptive selling is the "altering of sales behaviors during a customer interaction or across customer interactions based on perceived information about the nature of the selling situation."[32] A low level of adaptability is manifest when a salesperson uses the same presentation approach and methods during a single sales encounter or across encounters. Effective salespeople adapt their presentation to fit the situation; they are able to pick up signals and *read* the situation. For example, a brief, matter-of-fact presentation may be called for when meeting with a time-pressured and impatient customer, whereas a longer, more-detailed presentation is appropriate when interacting with a customer who wants all the details before making a decision.

Thus, adaptive selling involves (1) recognizing that different selling approaches are needed in different sales situations; (2) having confidence in one's ability to use a variety of sales approaches *across* selling encounters as called for by the specifics of the situation; (3) having confidence in one's ability to alter the sales approach *during* a sales encounter; and (4) actually using different approaches in different situations.[33]

One last note, as depicted in Figure 23.3, is that a salesperson's performance is guided by the availability and type of rewards—hopefully leading to extrinsic or intrinsic satisfaction for the salesperson. No doubt, if satisfied, this can lead to greater motivation for future selling duties and tasks.

Excellence in Selling

What does it take to be a truly outstanding salesperson, to be a high performer, to excel in sales? As is always the case, there are no simple answers. Moreover, achieving excellence in one type of sales endeavor, say selling personal insurance, undoubtedly requires somewhat different aptitude and skills than achieving excellence when selling sophisticated information systems to corporate buyers. However, although there are differences from sales job to sales job, there also are similarities.

High-performing salespeople generally differ from other salespeople in terms of some general attitudes they have about the job and the manner in which they conduct their business. High-performing salespeople do the following:

- Represent the interests of their companies and their clients simultaneously to achieve *two-way advocacy*.
- Exemplify *professionalism* in the way they perform the sales job.
- Are *committed to selling* and the sales process, because they believe the sales process is in the customer's best interest.
- Actively *plan and develop strategies* that will lead to programs benefiting the customer.[34]

Specific Characteristics of High-Performers

In addition to these general practices, excellence in selling is associated with a set of specific characteristics (some of which were already mentioned briefly) that are reflected in the salesperson's personal features and job behavior. These include the first impression a salesperson makes, his or her depth of knowledge, breadth of knowledge, adaptability, sensitivity, enthusiasm, self-esteem, extended focus, sense of humor, creativity, risk taking, and sense of honesty and ethics.[35]

The First Impression

The outcome of a sales call is greatly influenced by the first impression a salesperson makes on the customer. The likelihood that a salesperson's ideas will be accepted depends largely on the initial encounter. Determinants of the first impression include personal looks, dress, body language, eye contact, handshake, punctuality, and courtesy.

Depth of Knowledge

A salesperson's depth of knowledge reflects how well he or she understands the business, products, company, competitors, and general economic climate related to the sales job. Depth of knowledge is obtained in part through an individual's self-study efforts. Knowledgeable salespeople stay alert to what is going on by listening carefully to customers, reading general business publications (*Wall Street Journal, Businessweek*, etc.), and getting the most out of company sales meetings and conferences. Another source of company knowledge is the initial training a salesperson receives.

Breadth of Knowledge

Salespeople who have a wide breadth of knowledge are conversant on a broad spectrum of subjects and, therefore, are able to interact effectively with a variety of customers. Salespeople who possess a broad scope of knowledge make customers feel relaxed and are able to share common interests (via comments or discussions concerning world events, athletics, cultural affairs, or whatever the customer's interests may be). One acquires this facet of excellence through expansive reading, taking a variety of courses while in college, continuous studying, and good listening skills. In general, breadth of knowledge is a matter of being alert, attentive, and interested in different people and events.

At a minimum, any college graduate who expects to be conversant and effective in a selling position should read a daily newspaper and a weekly magazine such as *Time*.

Adaptability

As already discussed, this fourth characteristic of excellence is the willingness and ability to adapt your interactional style to match the other person's. Because salespeople deal with a wide variety of customers, those who are more adaptable tend to be more effective. Adaptability in this sense is not to be misinterpreted as suggesting that a salesperson should alter his or her presentation to accommodate what each prospect might want to hear, regardless of the truth. Rather, the point is that people differ in terms of how open, sociable, and communicative they are, and a salesperson must adjust his or her interactional style to the customer's preferred style.

Sensitivity

The essence of this fifth characteristic of excellence is *empathy*, or the ability to place oneself in the other person's position. That is, the successful sales representative shows a genuine interest in the prospect's needs, problems, and concerns. Also, the salesperson demonstrates respect for customers and does not patronize them. Most people are quick to notice a sales representative's positive attitude toward them, and they react favorably to it.

Good listening skills are another *very important* facet of sensitivity. Listening enables the salesperson to understand the needs of the customer and to adjust the sales message accordingly. Listening is a rare skill. But why? One reason is that people are usually absorbed in their own lives, devices, and activities and listening to someone else may be boring for them. (This has become even more challenging with being constantly online through mobile devices. It is good advice to turn off one's device when interacting face-to-face with potential buyers.) Some may enjoy a conversation only when the other person is finished talking and they can start talking. The fact that so many people look upon listening as rather irksome reflects the scarcity of good listeners.

Enthusiasm

Enthusiasm, the sixth characteristic of excellence, reflects a salesperson's *deep-seated commitment to his or her company's products and to customers' needs*. Enthusiastic salespeople tend to be more motivated than less enthusiastic people, and customers are responsive to the salesperson's enthusiastic efforts.

Self-Esteem

This involves feelings of *self-worth and personal confidence*. A salesperson is more successful if he or she has a positive self-concept, likes his or her product and company, and looks forward to meeting prospects. A salesperson who does not have self-confidence may find it more challenging to be successful in selling. Furthermore, a salesperson should have a positive attitude toward the product, company, and sales message. After all, if the salesperson does not believe in the product, how can the customer?

Extended Focus

Excellent people in any endeavor have specific goals and purpose; that is, a sense of focus. Said another way, "Most people aim at nothing in life and hit it with amazing accuracy."[36] The term *extended focus* means the ability to *simultaneously focus on the specific and look at the big picture*. This eighth characteristic of excellence is based on the idea that salespeople must focus their efforts into achieving specific goals; they must not permit themselves to be distracted.

Sense of Humor

This ninth characteristic of excellence stresses the ability to laugh with others as well as to laugh at yourself. Humor helps customers relax. It also helps customers remember you. There is a difference, however, between having a sense of humor and forcing humor inappropriately.

Creativity

Salespeople who exhibit this tenth characteristic have an ability to connect seemingly unrelated ideas and to arrive at unique solutions to problems. This ability is critical in many selling positions, such as trade selling and technical selling, where the salesperson is often selling a total system rather than a single product. Often competing companies' basic products and non-product offerings (e.g., promotional programs) are very similar; therefore, what distinguishes one company from the next are the creative solutions that salespeople devise for addressing customers' needs or solving problems. Creativity does not stop with merely coming up with an idea; rather, "it is the quality of the action that puts the idea into being."[37]

Taking Risks

Closely related to creativity is the eleventh characteristic of excellence, the willingness to take risks. To be creative you must be willing to take risks, recommend solutions that might backfire or be ridiculed, and seek change rather than sameness. Excellent salespeople are always looking for new ideas, new methods, and new solutions that will benefit their customers, themselves, and their companies.

Sense of Honesty and Ethics

This twelfth characteristic is last but certainly not least. Contrary to widespread myths about personal selling, excellence in personal selling requires as high a degree of honesty and ethical behavior as in any of life's lasting relationships. The key word is *relationship*. There are some sales jobs where a single transaction between buyer and seller takes place; however, most personal-selling interactions involve building long-term relationships with customers. This is not accomplished with deceit, misrepresentation, or undependable behavior. Salespeople who are more successful are seen by customers as trustworthy and dependable. We expect these qualities in our friends, and the same expectations carry over on a professional level to the marketplace. You may recall the opening *Marcom Insight*, identifying the qualities most and least valued by purchasing agents in salespeople. The two most valued qualities are reliability/credibility and professionalism/integrity.

Summary

This chapter presents a broad array of ideas about the nature of personal selling. Personal selling's role in the promotion mix includes educating customers, encouraging product usage and marketing assistance, and providing after-sale service and support to the buyer. As a personal career, the field of sales includes the attractive features of freedom of action, variety and challenge, opportunities for advancement, and desirable financial and nonfinancial rewards.

A *partner-oriented* selling mind-set is in operation in most successful firms today. These firms realize that their success rests with their customers' successes. Hence, modern partner-oriented philosophy makes *customer satisfaction* its highest priority. Modern selling practice is based on the following principles: trust and mutual agreement must exist between buyer and seller; getting the order is only the first step—after-sales service is what counts; and professionalism and integrity are essential in a salesperson.

Personal selling is a broad field consisting of a variety of different types of sales jobs entailing different activities, including: making sales presentations, working with orders, servicing the product and the account, managing information, participating in conferences and meetings,

training, entertaining, traveling, and working with distributors. Sales jobs include trade selling, missionary selling, technical selling, new-business selling, retail selling, and telemarketing. Most sales positions involve a process explained in the seven basic steps of personal selling: (1) prospecting and qualifying, (2) the preapproach, (3) the approach, (4) the sales presentation, (5) handling objections, (6) the close, and (7) the follow-up.

A contingency model of the selling process is presented to explain that salesperson performance and effectiveness are dependent on a variety of factors, including resources of the salesperson, characteristics of the customer's buying task, and the salesperson–customer relationship. Specific determinants of salesperson performance include (1) aptitude, (2) skill level, (3) motivational level, (4) role perceptions, (5) personal characteristics, and (6) adaptability.

A final section examines excellence in selling. Twelve basic characteristics of excellence include the first impression a salesperson makes, his or her depth of knowledge, breadth of knowledge, adaptability, sensitivity, enthusiasm, self-esteem, extended focus, sense of humor, creativity, risk taking, and sense of honesty and ethics.

Discussion Questions

1. Personal selling is more effective than advertising, but may be less efficient. Explain.
2. Some people hold personal selling in low esteem. Some students rebel at the idea of taking a sales job out of college. Why do you think these attitudes persist?
3. Contrast antiquated and modern selling practices. Do you think a "soft sell" approach used by some pharmaceutical firms will work in all industries? Why or why not?
4. One form of sales presentation is called a *canned presentation*. This means that a salesperson uses the identical presentation time after time. How would

you evaluate such an approach? What are the advantages and disadvantages of this form of presentation?
5. "Sales representatives should act as if they were on the customer's payroll." Evaluate this statement by explaining in your own words what it means and by describing the advantages and disadvantages that may result when a salesperson acts in this manner.
6. In view of the different types of sales jobs described in the chapter (such as trade selling and technical selling), identify the job types you would or would not be willing to take as a first job out of college. Provide your rationale for each decision.

7. Select a friend of yours to take the role of the "buyer" with playing the role of the "salesperson." Then, go through each of the relational communication dialog boxes in Figure 23.1, playing your roles. For each dialog box, indicate whether you felt you were both in agreement with the relationship or whether there some unresolved conflict as a result of the dialog.

8. Interview a friend that has recently started a sales job and someone who has worked in sales for many years. Get each person's reaction as to how they felt Brad Wilson did on his first day of selling in the National Business Machines case.

9. No single factor is able to adequately explain salesperson effectiveness. Comment.

10. Clearly distinguish among aptitude, skill, and personal characteristics as unique determinants of salesperson performance. Considering only aptitude and personal characteristics, provide an assessment of whether you possess the aptitude and personal features for a successful career in (1) computer sales for a company like Apple or IBM, and (2) trade sales for a company such as Procter & Gamble or General Mills. Offer reasons why you think you would (or would not) succeed.

11. Distinguish between working hard and working smart. As a student, which behavior better characterizes your own performance? What behaviors would a salesperson manifest in demonstrating an ability to work smart rather than simply hard? Be specific.

12. Based on the 12 characteristics of personal excellence described in the text, which of these do you think most salespeople lack? Do you possess the potential for excellence in selling? Why or why not?

13. Interview three sales representatives and describe the differences in their philosophies and approaches to personal selling. Compare your findings with the ideas presented in the text.

14. Studies of college students' views toward personal selling were mentioned in the chapter and summarized in Table 23.1. Interview five students and ask them to rate each of the statements on a five-point scale labeled strongly agree, agree, neither agree nor disagree, disagree, and strongly disagree. Summarize the results from your small survey and draw implications based on the assumption that the five students you queried hold representative views.

15. Write a two- to three-page essay on why you would or would not be a good salesperson.

End Notes

1. Lawrence J. Gitman and Carl McDaniel, *The Future of Business: The Essentials* (Mason, OH: Cengage Southwestern, 2009), 331.

2. Gilbert A. Churchill, Jr., Neil M. Ford, and Orville C. Walker, Jr., *Sales Force Management: Planning, Implementation, and Control* (Homewood, IL: Richard D. Irwin, 1985), 67.

3. Philip Kotler and Kevin Lane Keller, *Marketing Management*, 14th ed. (Boston, MA: Prentice Hall, 2012), 426.

4. The 1958 study was conducted by the *American Salesman* magazine. The 1988 study was performed by Rosemary R. Lagace and Timothy A. Longfellow, "The Impact of Classroom Style on Student Attitudes toward Sales Careers: A Comparative Approach," *Journal of Marketing Education* (Fall 1989), 72–77. The 1998 study was part of a larger cross-national study conducted by Steven Lysonski and Srinivas Durvasula, "A Cross-National Investigation of Student Attitudes Toward Personal Selling: Implications for Marketing Education," *Journal of Marketing Education* 20 (August 1998), 161–73. Agree and disagree categories are based on whether the mean was above or below the midpoint of the belief measure. Not all measures appear in each study.

5. Churchill, Ford, and Walker, *Sales Force Management: Planning, Implementation, and Control*.

6. These points are adapted from two excellent practitioner-oriented books: Anthony Alessandra, James Cathcart, and Phillip Wexler, *Selling by Objectives* (Englewood Cliffs, NJ: Prentice-Hall, 1988); and Paul Hersey, *Selling: A Behavioral Science Approach* (Englewood Cliffs, NJ: Prentice-Hall, 1988).

7. C. Conrad Elnes, *Inside Secrets of Outstanding Salespeople* (Englewood Cliffs, NJ: Prentice-Hall, 1988), 6.

8. Hersey, *Selling: A Behavioral Science Approach*, xi.

9. William C. Moncrief III, "Selling Activity and Sales Position Taxonomies for Industrial Selling," *Journal of Marketing Research*, 23 (August 1986), 261–70.

10. The second author appreciates the suggestion of Salesforce.com by Mr. Frank O'Connor, Account Executive, Symantec Global Partner Sales, Boston, MA.

11. For a discussion of different stages of sales careers, see William L. Cron, Alan J. Dubinsky, and Ronald E. Michaels, "The Influence of Career Stages on Components of Salesperson Motivation," *Journal of Marketing*, 52 (January 1988), 78–92.

12. Ronald B. Marks, *Personal Selling: An Interactive Approach* (Boston: Allyn and Bacon, 1988), 39.

13. Ibid., 45.

14. "Du Pont Turns Scientists into Salespeople," *Sales and Marketing Management*, June 1987, 57.

15. Adapted from discussion in Alan J. Dubinsky, "A Factor Analytic Study of the Personal Selling Process," *Journal of Personal Selling & Sales Management*, 1 (Fall-Winter 1980–1981), 26–33; see also

Roseann Spiro, Gregory Rich, William Stanton, *Management of a Sales Force*, 12th ed. (New York: McGraw-Hill Irwin, 2008).

16. Neil Rackman, *SPIN Selling* (New York: McGraw-Hill, 1996); James Larcher, "Selling Salesmanship," *Business 2.0*, December 2002-January 2003, 66; Sharon Drew Morgen, *Selling Through Integrity: Re-inventing Sales through Collaboration, Respect, and Serving* (New York, Berkeley Books 1999); and Neil Rackman and John De Vincentis, *Rethinking the Sales Force* (New York, McGraw-Hill, 1996).

17. The notion of "high impact" selling and the principles that follow are based on William T. Brooks, *High Impact Selling: Power Strategies for Successful Selling* (Englewood Cliffs, NJ: Prentice-Hall, 1988).

18. Michael D. Hutt and Thomas W. Speh, *Business Marketing Management: B2B* (9th ed.), (Mason, OH: Thomson South-Western, 2007), 61–88; and Jagdish N. Sheth, "A Model of Industrial Buyer Behavior," *Journal of Marketing* 37 (October 1973), 50, 56.

19. Jonathan D. Rockoff, "Drug Sales Reps Try a Softer Pitch," *Wall Street Journal*, January 10, 2012, B1, B2.

20. Gary Soldow and Gloria Penn Thomas, "Relational Communication: Form versus Content in the Sales Interaction" *Journal of Marketing* 48 (Winter 1984), 84–93.

21. Gilbert A. Churchill, Jr., Neil M. Ford, Steven W. Hartley, and Orville C. Walker, Jr., "The Determinants of Salesperson Performance: A Meta Analysis," *Journal of Marketing Research*, 22 (May 1985), 103–118.

22. Barton A. Weitz, "Effectiveness in Sales Interactions: A Contingency Framework," *Journal of Marketing*, 45 (Winter 1981), 85–103.

23. The following discussion of the first five factors is based on Gilbert A. Churchill, Jr., Neil M. Ford, and Orville C. Walker, Jr., *Sales Force Management: Planning, Implementation, and Control* (Homewood, IL: Richard D. Irwin, 1985).

24. "Armstrong Salespeople Are to the Manor Born," *Sales and Marketing Management*, June 1987, 46.

25. Harish Sujan, "Smarter Versus Harder: An Exploratory Attributional Analysis of Salespeople's Motivation," *Journal of Marketing Research* 23 (February 1986), 41–50.

26. Mark W. Johnston, A. Parasuraman, Charles M. Futrell, and William C. Black, "A Longitudinal Assessment of the Impact of Selected Organizational Influences on Salespeople's Organizational Commitment During Early Employment," *Journal of Marketing Research*, 27 (August 1990), 333–44.

27. Churchill, Ford, Hartley, and Walker, "The Determinants of Salesperson Performance: A Meta Analysis;" see also Michael Ahearne, Thomas W. Gruen, and Cheryl Burke Jarvis, "If Looks Could Sell: Moderation and Mediation of the Attractiveness Effect on Salesperson Performance," *International Journal of Research in Marketing* 16 (1999), 269–284.

28. See, for example, Michelle Block Morse, "Rich Rewards: For Ambitious Blacks, Selling Can Mean Pride, Power, and High Pay," *Success*, 35 (March 1988), 50–61.

29. Lawrence J. Gillman and Carl McDaniel, *The Future of Business: The Essentials* (Mason, OH: Cengage South Western, 2009), 331.

30. Rosemary R. Lagrace and Jacquelyn L. Twible, "The Androgyny of Salespeople: Gooses and Ganders, or All Geese?" *Journal of Social Behavior and Personality*, 5, 6 (1990), 641–50.

31. See Siew Meng Leong, Paul S. Busch, and Deborah Roedder John, "Knowledge Bases and Salesperson Effectiveness: A Script Theoretic Analysis," *Journal of Marketing Research*, 26 (May 1989), 164–78; Rosann L. Spiro and Barton A. Weitz, "Adaptive Selling: Conceptualization, Measurement, and Nomological Validity," *Journal of Marketing Research*, 27 (February 1990), 61–69; Weitz, "Effectiveness in Sales Interactions: A Contingency Framework"; and Barton A. Weitz, Harish Sujan, and Mita Sujan, "Knowledge, Motivation, and Adaptive Behavior: A Framework for Improving Selling Effectiveness," *Journal of Marketing*, 50 (October 1986), 174–191.

32. Weitz, Sujan, and Sujan, "Knowledge, Motivation, and Adaptive Behavior: A Framework for Improving Selling Effectiveness."

33. Adapted from Spiro and Weitz, "Adaptive Selling: Conceptualization, Measurement, and Nomological Validity."

34. Thayer C. Taylor, "Anatomy of a Star Salesperson," *Sales and Marketing Management*, May 1986, 49–51.

35. These characteristics and the following discussion are based on Alessandra, Cathcart, and Wexler, *Selling by Objectives*, 59–76. A related perspective is provided by Lawrence W. Lamont and William J. Lundstrom, "Identifying Successful Industrial Salesmen by Personality and Personal Characteristics," *Journal of Marketing Research*, 14 (November 1977), 517–29.

36. Alessandra, Cathcart, and Wexler, *Selling by Objectives*, 73.

37. Ibid., 75.

Glossary

A

Ability to process Whether a person is familiar with message claims and has the necessary skills (e.g., literacy, knowledge) to help comprehend them.

Access One of the four *general privacy principles* applied to one's personal information for all advertising and marketing activities. See also **Notice, Consent,** and **Security**.

Account-specific marketing A descriptive term that characterizes promotional and advertising activity that a manufacturer *customizes* to specific retail accounts. Also called *co-marketing*.

Active synthesis The second stage of perceptual encoding, it goes beyond merely examining physical features. The context or situation in which information is received plays a major role in determining what is perceived and interpreted.

Adaptive selling Altering of sales behaviors during a customer interaction or across customer interactions based on perceived information about the nature of the selling situation.

Adnorm index Index that compares an advertisement's scores against other ads in the *same product category* as well as with the same size (e.g., full-page) and color classifications (e.g., four-color).

Advertising A paid, mediated form of communication from an identifiable source, designed to persuade the receiver to take some action, now or in the future.

Advertising plan Provides the framework for the systematic execution of advertising strategies; evaluates a brand's advertising history, proposes where the next period's advertising should head, and justifies the proposed strategy for maintaining or improving a brand's competitive situation.

Advertising strategy A plan of action of how a brand is to be advertised; involves the development of an advertising message that communicates the brand's value proposition—i.e., its primary benefit or how it can solve the consumer's problem.

Affect referral The simplest of all decision heuristics; the individual calls from memory his or her attitude, or affect, toward relevant alternatives and picks that alternative for which the affect is most positive.

Affordability method An advertising budgeting method that sets the budget by spending on advertising those funds that remain after budgeting for everything else.

Allegory A word derived from a Greek term meaning other-speak; represents a form of extended metaphor.

Ambushing An activity that takes place when companies that are *not* official sponsors of an event undertake marketing efforts to convey the impression that they are.

Androgyny The degree to which individuals feel that they are characterized by traits associated with both men and women.

Appropriateness The extent to which the message is on target for delivering the brand's positioning strategy and capturing the brand's relative strengths and weaknesses vis-à-vis competitive brands.

Attention A stage of information processing in which the consumer focuses cognitive resources on and thinks about a message to which one has been exposed.

Attitude A general and somewhat enduring positive or negative feeling toward, or evaluative judgment of, some person, object, or issue.

Attitudinal response (feelings) Television commercials and online videos (e.g., from YouTube, Tumblr) can evoke a variety of positive and negative feelings. Positive feelings might include reactions such as pride, excitement, warmth, tenderness, amazement, confidence, humor, and so on. Negative feelings might include fear, boredom, sadness, anger, disgust, and irritation.

Attractiveness An attribute that includes any number of virtuous characteristics that receivers may perceive in an endorser; consists of three related dimensions: *similarity, familiarity, and liking*.

Attributes Features or aspects of the advertised product or brand.

B

Behavioral segmentation Information about the audience's behavior—in terms of past purchase behavior or online search activity—in a particular product category or set of related categories.

Beliefs Consumer's subjective probability assessments, or expectations, regarding the likelihood that performing a certain act will lead to a certain outcome.

Bill-back ad allowance A form of trade allowance in which retailers receive allowances for featuring the manufacturer's brand in advertisements.

Bill-back display allowance A form of trade allowance in which retailers receive allowances for featuring the manufacturer's brand and providing special displays.

Bonus pack A form of sales promotion whereby extra quantities of the product that a company makes available to consumers at the regular price.

Brand Name, term, sign, symbol, design, or a combination of them intended to identify the goods or services of one seller or group of sellers and to differentiate them from those of competition.

Brand awareness An issue of whether a brand name comes to mind when consumers think about a particular product category and the ease with which the name is evoked.

Brand concept Specific meaning that brand managers create and communicate to their target market.

Brand concept management The analysis, planning, implementation, and control of a brand concept throughout the life of the brand.

Brand equity The goodwill (i.e., equity) that an established brand has built up over its existence.

Brand image The associations that are activated in memory when people think about a particular brand.

Brand image style A symbolic or experiential orientation that involves *psychological* rather than physical differentiation.

Brand loyalty A consumer's commitment to continue using or advocating a brand, as demonstrated not only by repeat purchases, but also by other positive brand behaviors (e.g., word-of-mouth advocacy, brand identification).

Brand placement A marketing strategy whereby an advertiser promotes a brand by placing it within the context (i.e., in a program scene or story) of a selected medium (e.g., a TV, film, online, or gaming program).

Brand positioning The key feature, benefit, or image that a brand stands for in the target audience's mind.

Buzz creation The systematic and organized effort to encourage people to talk favorably about a particular item—either over the fence or online—and to recommend its usage to others who are part of their social network.

C

Cause-related marketing (CRM) Involves alliances that companies form with *nonprofit organizations* to promote their mutual interests.

Central route When a receiver's motivation, ability, and opportunity to process the message arguments are high (and therefore one's elaboration likelihood is high), the receiver will focus predominately on message arguments rather than peripheral cues leading to enduring attitude change. See also **Peripheral route.**

Click fraud When a competitor or other party poses as a legitimate user and clicks on a sponsored link repeatedly in order to bias advertising effectiveness.

Co-branding Relationship that potentially serves to enhance both brands' equity and profitability.

Commercial rumor A widely circulated but unverified statement about a product, brand, company, store, or other commercial target.

Commercial specifics The elements in the execution of the advertisement such as the spokesperson or endorser, the music, the overall situation, and characters.

Communication The process whereby commonness of thought is established and meaning is shared between individuals or between organizations and individuals.

Comparative advertising The practice in which advertisers directly or indirectly compare their products against competitive offerings and claim superiority.

Compatibility The degree to which an innovation is perceived to fit into a person's way of doing things, such as consumers' needs, personal values, beliefs, and past consumption practices.

Compensatory heuristic In this situation, for a given alternative (e.g., college), the strength of one attribute (e.g., education) offsets (or compensates for) the weakness of another attribute (e.g., social life).

Competitive parity method A budgeting method that sets the advertising budget by examining what competitors are doing. Also called the *match-competitors method.*

Compiled lists Compiled (external) lists are not as desirable as (internal) house lists, however, for two important reasons. The first is because they do not contain information about the willingness of a person to purchase the specific item by mail. Second, the individuals or companies included on the list may have had to pay a fee to belong to an association representing the primary source for some lists.

Complexity An innovation's degree of perceived difficulty—the more difficult an innovation is to understand or use, the slower the rate of adoption.

Comprehend To understand and create meaning out of stimuli and symbols.

Concretizing Process of providing more concrete (versus abstract) information for consumers to process, as it is easier for them to remember and retrieve tangible rather than abstract information

Conjunctive model The consumer establishes minimum cutoffs (e.g., a "7" out of "10") on all attributes considered.

Connectedness Addresses whether an advertisement reflects *empathy*, creates a bond, and is relevant with the *target audience's* basic needs and wants as they relate to making a brand-choice decision in a product category.

Consent One of the four *general privacy principles* applied to one's personal information for all advertising and marketing activities. See also **Notice, Access,** and **Security.**

Consequences The desirable or undesirable results from consuming a particular product or brand.

Conspicuity The ability of a sign to capture attention; those signage characteristics that enable walkers or drivers and their passengers to distinguish a sign from its surrounding environment.

Conspiracy rumor A widely circulated but unverified statement that involves supposed company policies or practices that are threatening or ideologically undesirable to consumers.

Contact Any message medium capable of reaching target customers and presenting the brand in a favorable light. Interchangeable term with **touch point.**

Contamination rumor A widely circulated but unverified statement dealing with undesirable or harmful product or store features.

Contest A form of consumer-oriented sales promotion in which consumers have an opportunity to win cars, merchandise, or prizes.

Continuity A media planning consideration that involves how advertising is allocated during the course of an advertising campaign.

Continuous advertising schedule A type of schedule to allocate advertising over an advertising campaign where an equal or relatively equal number of ad dollars are invested throughout the campaign.

Copyright A set of exclusive rights, not for an actual idea or invention, but for the form in which it is expressed, and it should be in a tangible medium.

Corporate image advertising Advertising that attempts to (1) increase a firm's name recognition, (2) establish goodwill for the company and its products, or (3) identify itself with some meaningful and socially acceptable activity.

Corrective advertising Advertising that is based on the premise that a firm that misleads consumers should have to use future advertisements to rectify the deceptive impressions it has created in consumers' minds; designed to prevent a firm from continuing to deceive consumers rather than to punish the firm.

Cost-per-thousand (CPM) The cost of reaching 1,000 people who are readers, viewers, or listeners of the media vehicle.

Counterargument When the receiver challenges a message claim. See also **Support argument.**

Coupon A promotional device that rewards consumers for purchasing the coupon-offering brand by providing cents-off or dollars-off savings.

CPM-TM A refinement of CPM that measures the cost of reaching 1,000 members of the target audience, excluding those people who fall outside of the target market.

Creative brief The "blueprint," or guide, that links the advertising strategy with the execution of the ad campaign.

Customer lifetime value The net present value (NPV) of the profit that a company stands to realize on the average new customer during a given number of years.

D

Data mining To discover hidden facts and relationships contained in databases.

Database marketing (DBM) A process in which companies collect information on consumers, analyze it to predict who will buy, and then develop tailored marketing messages to those consumers.

Deal Any form of sales promotion that delivers a price reduction to consumers; retailer discounts, manufacturer cents-off offers, and the ubiquitous coupons are the most common forms of deals.

Deception A representation, omission, or practice that is likely to *mislead* the consumer *acting reasonably* and the representation, omission, or practice is a *material* one (i.e., an important characteristic likely to influence their conduct or choice).

Decoding Activities undertaken by receivers to interpret—or derive meaning from—marketing messages.

Demographics Measurable population characteristics such as age, income, and ethnicity.

Direct marketing An interactive system of marketing which uses one or more advertising media to effect a measurable response and/or transaction at any location.

Direct response TV advertising (DRTV) TV advertising that takes two basic forms: *long form* (half hour or hour-long segments explaining a product in detail, known as an infomercial) or *short form* (30-, 60-, or 120-second commercials asking viewers for an immediate response).

Disjunctive model A consumer attitude model that states for a product to be considered, it only has to meet or exceed the minimum cutoffs on just one attribute.

Diverting When a manufacturer restricts a deal to a limited geographical area rather than making it available nationally, which may result in retailers buying abnormally large quantities at the deal price and then selling off, at a small profit margin, the excess quantities through brokers in other higher-priced geographical areas.

Dual-coding theory Pictures and visuals (versus words) are better remembered because pictures are able to elicit mental images.

E

Effective rating points (ERPs) Equals the product of effective reach, or 3+ exposures, times frequency.

Effective reach The idea that an advertising schedule is effective only if it does not reach members of the target audience *too few* or *too many* times during the media scheduling period, typically a four-week period; refers to the percentage of the target audience that is exposed to the ad schedule at least three times (i.e., 3+ exposures) during the media scheduling period.

Elaboration Mental activity in response to a message such as an advertisement.

Elasticity A measure of how responsive the demand for a brand is to changes in marketing variables such as price and advertising.

Emotion-based persuasion When a consumer is highly involved in a message (such as a TV commercial), there is a tendency to relate aspects of the message to his or her personal situation.

Encoding The process of translating thought into symbolic form.

Encoding specificity principle A principle of cognitive psychology which states that information recall is enhanced when the context in which people attempt to retrieve information is the same as or similar to the context in which they originally encoded the information.

Ethics In the context of marketing communications, involves matters of right and wrong, or *moral*, conduct.

Evaluations The value, or importance, that consumers attach to consumption outcomes.

Event sponsorship A form of brand promotion that ties a brand to a meaningful athletic, entertainment, cultural, social, or other type of high-interest public activity.

Executive-statement releases News releases quoting CEOs, CMOs, and other corporate executives.

Experiential needs Needs representing desires for products that provide sensory pleasure, variety, and, in a few product circumstances, cognitive stimulation.

Expertise The knowledge, experience, or skills possessed by a source as they relate to the communications topic.

Exposure In marketing terms, signifies that consumers come in contact with the marketer's message.

External lists Mailing lists used in direct mail; from a public database, including house lists of other companies and compiled lists. See also **Internal lists**.

F

Feature analysis The initial stage of perceptual encoding whereby a receiver examines the basic features of a stimulus (such as size, shape, color, and angles) and from this makes a preliminary classification.

Feature article A detailed description of a product or other newsworthy programs that a PR firm writes for immediate publication or airing by print or broadcast media or distribution via appropriate social media or other online sites.

Feedback A way of monitoring how accurately the intended message is being received and whether it is accomplishing its intended objective(s).

Flighting schedule A type of schedule to allocate advertising over an advertising campaign where advertiser varies expenditures throughout the campaign and allocates *zero* expenditures in some months.

Followers Posts are displayed on a Twitter user's profile page and users may subscribe to other author tweets with subscribers.

Following In Twitter, an online social networking and micro-blogging service, the users can send and read text-based posts (called tweets) for up to 140 characters and these posts are displayed on a user's profile page and users may subscribe to other author tweets.

Free-with-purchase premium A form of premium that represents a delayed reward to consumers that is primarily designed to generate *trial purchases*.

Frequency The number of times, on average, during the media-planning period that members of the target audience are exposed to the media *vehicles* that carry a brand's advertiser's message. Also called *average frequency*.

Functional needs Needs involving current consumption related problems, potential problems, or conflicts.

G

Galvanometer A device (also referred to as a *psychogalvanometer*) for measuring *galvanic skin response*, or *GSR*. (*Galvanic* refers to electricity produced by a chemical reaction.)

Generation X (Gen X) To avoid overlap with the baby boom generation and Gen Y, this text defines Generation X as people born between 1965 and 1981.

Generics The major selling claim associated with the advertised brand.

Generic style An ad strategy that uses a straightforward product claim with no assertion of brand superiority.

Geodemographics Based on demographic characteristics of consumers who reside within geographic clusters such as ZIP code areas and neighborhoods.

Geo-targeting Allows mobile customers to find nearby retailers (e.g., restaurants that serve Pepsi products, including Taco Bell, Pizza Hut, Arby's, and Panda Express.)

Goals Objectives become goals when time and magnitude are included. Objectives provide the foundation for all remaining decisions.

Green marketing Responding to environmental and sustainability concerns by introducing environmentally oriented products and undertaking marcom programs to promote them.

Gross rating points (GRPs) The weight that a particular advertising schedule has delivered. GRPs are a product of reach times frequency.

H

Hierarchy-of-effects A model predicated on the idea that the marcom element move people from an initial stage of unawareness about a product/brand to a final stage of purchasing that product/brand.

House lists A form of internal lists, these are lists based on a company's own internal list of present or prospective customers.

House lists of other companies A form of external lists, these are other companies' lists that they comprise the names of people who have responded to another related company's direct-response offer.

I

Imagery The representation of sensory experiences in short-term, or working, memory—including visual, auditory, and other sensory experiences.

Infomercial A form of television advertising that serves as an innovative alternative to the conventional, short form of television commercial; full-length commercial segments that typically last 28 to 30 minutes and combine product news and entertainment.

Ingredient branding A special type of alliance between branding partners, whereby one brand (ingredient) appears on or inside another brand (the host).

In-pack premium A premium item provided inside the package of the brand that offers the free item as a promotional inducement.

Integrated information response model A model that takes its name from the idea that consumers *integrate information* from two sources—advertising and direct product usage experience—in forming attitudes and purchase intentions toward products and brands.

Intellectual property A number of different author or company creations (e.g., a new brand name and/or logo) for which a set of exclusive rights are recognized under law. This includes patents, copyrights, and trademarks.

Intense and prominent cues Cues that are louder, more colorful, bigger, brighter, and so on, thereby increasing the probability of attracting attention.

Internal lists Mailing lists used in direct mail; from a company's internal (house) database. See also **External lists.**

Internalization When an information source, such as an endorser, is perceived as credible, audience attitudes are changed through this psychological process; occurs when the receiver accepts the source's position on an issue as his or her own.

Interstitials A form of Internet advertising in which ads appear between (rather than within, as is the case with pop-ups) two content Web pages.

Involuntary attention Occurs automatically or involuntarily due to an intruding stimulus (e.g., due to the use of attention gaining techniques) rather than by the consumer's inherent interest in the topic. See also **Voluntary attention.**

Issue index Index that compares an advertisement's scores against the average scores for *all ads* in the magazine issue.

K

Keywords A feature of search engine advertising (SEA), these are specific words and short phrases that describe the nature, attributes, and benefits of a marketer's offering.

L

Laddering A marketing research technique that has been developed to identify linkages between attributes, consequences, and values; involves in-depth, one-on-one interviews that typically last 30 minutes to more than one hour.

Lexicographic model A noncompensatory heuristic where attributes are first ranked, then the alternative that is the best on the highest ranked attribute is selected.

Location-based service (LBS) Mobile service that tracks consumers location and identifies nearby places.

M

Mail-in A premium in which consumers receive a free item from the sponsoring manufacturer in the mail or online in return for submitting a required number of proofs of purchase or taking some action related to the brand. See also **Online offer.**

Marcom objectives General outcomes that the various marcom elements try to achieve individually or collectively.

Market segment A group of customers who share a similar set of needs and wants.

Market segmentation Act of dividing a market into distinct groups of customers who might require separate products and/or marketing mixes.

Marketing Human activity directed at satisfying (customer) needs and wants through exchange processes.

Marketing communications Collection of all elements in an organization's marketing mix that facilitate exchange by establishing shared meaning with its customers.

Marketing mix The collection of specific elements of a brand's 4Ps—product, place (distribution), price, and promotion—and usually aimed at a target market.

Marketing plan A written document that specifies the marketing objectives and goals, strategies, programs, budgets and controls for a company and its brands.

Marketing public relations (MPR) A narrower aspect of PR involving an organization's interactions with actual or prospective customers.

Meaning Thoughts and feelings that are evoked within a person when presented with a sign in a particular context.

Media planning The design of a strategy that shows how investments in advertising time and space will contribute to the achievement of marketing objectives.

Message A symbolic expression of what the communicator intends to accomplish.

Message-based persuasion A central-route attitude-formation process based on processing message arguments which results is an enduring change in attitudes toward a brand.

Message channel The path through which the message moves from source to receiver.

Metaphor A form of figurative language that applies a word or a phrase to a concept or an object, such as a brand, that it does not literally denote in order to suggest a comparison and to make the abstract more concrete.

Middle age Age range starting at age 35 and ending at age 54 at which point maturity is reached.

Motivation to process When a message relates to a person's present consumption-related goals and needs and is thus relevant to that individual.

N

National Do Not Call Registry Based on a Congressional mandate (and revision later in 2007), allows consumers to register (only once) to maintain their phone numbers on a do-not-call list.

Near-pack premium A premium offer that provides the retail trade with specially displayed premium pieces that retailers then give to consumers who purchase the promoted product.

Noise Extraneous and distracting stimuli that interfere with or interrupt reception of a message as it moves through a channel.

Noncompensatory heuristics In contrast to compensatory choice behavior, one attribute does not compensate for another one.

Notice One of the four *general privacy principles* applied to one's personal information for all advertising and marketing activities. See also **Consent, Access,** and **Security.**

Novel ads Unique, fresh, and unexpected; draw consumers' attention to an ad so that they engage in more effortful information processing, such as attempting to comprehend the meaning of the advertised brand.

Novel messages Messages that are unusual, distinctive, unpredictable, and somewhat unexpected; such stimuli tend to produce greater attention than those that are familiar and routine.

O

Objective-and-task method The most sensible and defendable advertising budgeting method where advertising planners specify clear objectives for the advertising, identify the tasks the advertising must perform to reach these objectives, and then set the budget accordingly. See also **Percentage-of-sales method.**

Observability The degree to which the user of a new brand or other people can observe the positive effects of new-product usage.

Off-invoice allowance A deal offered periodically to the trade that permits retailers to deduct a fixed amount from the invoice—merely by placing an order during the period which the manufacturer is "dealing" a brand.

Online marketing The promotion of product and services over the Internet.

Online offer A premium in which consumers receive a free item from the sponsoring manufacturer in the mail or online in return for submitting a required number of proofs of purchase or taking some action related to the brand. See also **Mail-in.**

Online video ads Audiovisual ads that range in length from 15 seconds to several minutes.

On-pack premium A premium item that is attached to the package of the brand that offers the free item as a promotional inducement.

Opinion leader A person within a social network of family, friends, and acquaintances who has particular influence on other individuals' attitudes and behavior.

Opportunity to process The matter of whether it is physically possible for a person to process a message.

Opt-in e-mailing The practice of marketers' asking for and receiving consumers' permission to send them messages on a particular topic.

Outcomes Aspects of product ownership that the consumer either desires to obtain or to avoid.

Overlay program The simultaneous use of two or more sales promotion techniques. Also called *combination program*.

P

Paper diaries Nielsen's alternative data collection procedure for estimating TV program ratings in some local markets. Participating households complete a 20-page diary four times a year—February, May, July, and November, which are the months known in the TV industry as "sweep" periods.

Patent Permits an author or a firm to secure a monopoly or exclusive rights to the use of an invention for a period of 20 years, which is generally not renewable.

Percentage-of-sales method A company sets a brand's advertising budget by simply establishing the budget as a fixed percentage of *past* (e.g., last year's) or *anticipated* (e.g., next year's) sales volume. See also **Objective-and-task method**.

Perceptual encoding The process of interpreting stimuli, which includes two stages: feature analysis and active synthesis.

Peripheral cues The presence of cues that are peripheral to the primary message arguments, including such elements as background music, attractive sources, scenery, and graphics.

Peripheral route When a receiver's motivation, ability, or opportunity to process the message is low (and therefore one's elaboration likelihood is low), the receiver may focus on peripheral cues leading to temporary attitude change.

Personal selling A paid, person-to-person communication in which a seller determines needs and wants of prospective buyers and attempts to persuade these buyers to purchase the company's products or services.

Phishing An illegal e-mailing practice related to spam in which criminals send e-mail messages appearing to be from legitimate corporations and direct recipients to phony Web sites that are designed to look like companies' actual Web sites, which then attempt to extract personal data from people such as their credit card and ATM numbers.

Pop-up ad A form of Internet advertising in which ads appear in a separate window that materializes on the screen, seemingly out of nowhere, while a selected Web page is loading.

Positioning The key feature, benefit, or image that a brand stands for in the target audience's collective mind.

Positioning Advertising Copy Testing (PACT) A set of nine copy testing principles developed by leading U.S. advertising agencies.

Positioning statement The key idea that encapsulates what a brand is intended to stand for in its target market's mind and then consistently delivers the same idea across all media channels.

Preemptive style A second category-dominance technique, it is employed when an advertiser makes a generic-type claim but does so with an assertion of superiority.

Preference A behavioral tendency that exhibits itself in how a person acts toward an object.

Premiums Articles of merchandise or services (e.g., travel) manufacturers offer as a form of gift to *induce action* on the part of consumers and possibly also retailers and the sales force.

Price-off promotion A form of sales promotion that entails a reduction (typically ranging from 10 to 25 percent) in a brand's regular price. Also called *cents-off* or *price packs*.

Proactive MPR A tool for communicating a brand's merits and typically is used in conjunction with other marcom tools such as advertising and sales promotions. See also **Reactive MPR**.

Product releases A publicity tool that announces new products, provides relevant information about product features and benefits, and informs interested listeners and readers how to obtain additional information.

Promotional mix The blend of advertising, public relations, personal selling, direct marketing, and online marketing/social media elements usually aimed at a specific target market.

Psychographics Information about consumers' attitudes, values, motivations, and lifestyles that relate to buying behavior in a particular product category.

Psychological reactance A theory that suggests that people react against any efforts to reduce their freedoms or choices.

Public relations (PR) An organizational activity involved with fostering goodwill between a company and its various publics (e.g., employees, suppliers, consumers, government agencies, stockholders, etc.).

Publicity Non-personal communication to a mass audience.

Pull marketing A backward tug from consumers to retailers which is the result of a manufacturer's successful advertising and consumer promotion efforts that encourage consumers to prefer, at least in the short term, the manufacturer's brand versus competitive offerings. See also **Push marketing**.

Pulsing advertising schedule A type of schedule to allocate advertising over an advertising campaign where some advertising is used *during every period* of the campaign, but the amount of advertising varies from period to period.

Pupillometer A device used to measure respondents' pupil dilation as they view a television commercial or focus on a printed advertisement, where greater dilation suggests positive reaction and smaller dilation suggests negative reaction.

Push marketing A forward thrust of effort, whereby a manufacturer directs personal selling, advertising, and trade-oriented promotions to wholesalers, distributors, and retailers. See also **Pull marketing**.

Q

Quick response (QR) code A type of matrix barcode that encodes information which can then be scanned by readers on mobile devices.

R

Rating points Represents one percent of a designated audience or entire population that has an opportunity to see an advertisement.

Reach The percentage of the target audience that is exposed, at least once, during a specified time frame to an advertiser's message.

Reactive MPR Marketing undertaken as a result of external pressures and challenges brought by competitive actions, changes in consumer attitudes, or other external influences. It typically deals with changes that have *negative consequences* for the organization. See also **Proactive MPR**.

Rebate A cash reimbursement for purchasing a durable good (e.g., $5,000 refund for purchasing a new car); usually mailed with proofs of purchase to manufacturers.

Receiver The person or group of people (target audience) with whom the source attempts to share ideas.

Refund The practice in which manufacturers give *cash discounts* or reimbursements to consumers who submit proofs of purchase for CPGs usually for a non-durable good.

Relational communications An approach to handling objections that focuses on understanding not the content of the communication, but the *form* of the communication.

Relationship An enduring link between a brand and its customers. Successful relationships between customers and brands lead to repeat purchasing and, ideally, loyalty toward a brand.

Relative advantage The degree to which consumers perceive a new brand as being better than existing alternatives with respect to specific attributes or benefits.

Reliable A test that yields *consistent* results each time an advertisement is tested.

Repeater class A function of five primary forces: personal selling, advertising and social media, price, distribution, and product satisfaction.

Resonant advertising Symbolic- or experiential-oriented, it extends from psychographic research and structures an advertising campaign to pattern the prevailing lifestyle orientation of the intended market segment.

Revenue premium The revenue differential between a branded item and a corresponding private-labeled (store brand) item.

ROMI The idea of *return on investment* (ROI), which is well known in accounting, finance, or managerial economics circles, is referred to in marketing circles as ROMI, or *return on marketing investment*.

S

Sales promotion Refers to all promotional activities (excluding advertising, public relations, personal selling, direct marketing, and online marketing/social media) that stimulate short-term behavioral responses from (1) consumers, (2) the trade (e.g., distributors, wholesalers, or retailers), and/or (3) the company's sales force.

Sales-to-advertising response function The relationship between money invested in advertising and the response, or output, of that investment in terms of revenue generated.

Sampling Any method used to deliver actual- or trial-size products to consumers.

Security One of the four *general privacy principles* applied to one's personal information for all advertising and marketing activities. See also **Notice**, **Consent**, and **Access**.

Self-liquidating offer Known as SLOs by practitioners, this form of premium requires consumer mails in a stipulated number of proofs of purchase along with sufficient money to cover the manufacturer's purchasing, handling, and mailing costs of the premium item.

Self-regulation Regulation undertaken by the advertising community itself (i.e., advertisers, industry trade associations, and ad media) rather than by governmental bodies.

Semiotics The study of signs and the analysis of meaning-producing events.

Sentiments The polarity of a text in social media.

Shaping One application by which marketers attempt to shape certain behaviors through a process of changing preceding conditions and behaviors.

Share of conversation The ratio of a brand's conversations online to the industry conversations online.

Share of market (SOM) The ratio of a brand's revenue to total category revenue.

Share of voice (SOV) The ratio of a brand's advertising expenditures to total category advertising expenditures.

Sign Something physical and perceivable that signifies something (the referent) to somebody (the interpreter) in some context.

Simile A comparative term (such as, "like," or "as") to join items from different classes of experience.

Single-source data Consists of (1) household demographic information; (2) household purchase behavior; and (3) household exposure to (or, more technically, the opportunity to see) new television commercials that are tested under real-world, *in-market* test conditions.

Slotting allowance The fees manufacturers of both consumer packaged goods and durables pay retailers for access to the slot, or location, that the retailer must make available in its distribution center (e.g., warehouse) to accommodate the manufacturer's new brand.

Social media Web-based and mobile technology used to turn communication into interactive dialogue.

Social media marketing Forms of electronic communication through which user-generated content (information, ideas, and

videos) can be shared within the user's social network.

Socialization The process through which people learn cultural values, form beliefs, and become familiar with the physical cues representing these values and beliefs.

Source A communicator in some marcom capacity—an advertiser, salesperson, blogger, etc.—who has thoughts (ideas, sales points, etc.) to share with an individual customer/prospect or an entire target audience.

Specific sales message The last or highest level of an impression viewers retain is the specific sales message.

Spin Method In personal selling, forging long-term relationships with customers with the following questions: *situation questions, problem questions, implication questions, and need-payoff questions.*

Sponsorships A growing aspect of marketing communications, which are regarded as an important marketing tool by most marketing executives.

Standardized Advertising Unit (SAU) system Enables advertisers to purchase any one of *56 standard ad sizes* to fit the advertising publishing parameters of all U.S. newspapers.

Sticky ads Ads for which the audience comprehends the advertiser's intended message; they are remembered, and they change the target audience's brand-related opinions or behaviors.

Summary dashboard A convenient summary of the social media impact of one's brand versus competitors.

Superstitials Short, animated ads that play over or on top of a Web page.

Support argument When a receiver agrees with a message argument. See also **Counterargument**.

Symbol When the object and referent have no prior intrinsic relationship but rather are arbitrarily or metaphorically related.

Symbolic needs Internal consumer needs such as the desire for self-enhancement, group membership, affiliation, altruism, and other abstract need states that involve aspects of consumption not solved by practical product benefits.

T

Target market strategies Several alternatives for actually selecting segments that have been deemed attractive or effective; includes (1) *undifferentiated marketing*, in which overall marketing mix is applied to the mass market, (2) *differentiated marketing*, in which a separate marketing mix is applied to each separate segment, or (3) *concentrated marketing*, in which one overall marketing mix is applied to one separate segment.

Target rating points (TRPs) An adaptation of gross rating points (GRPs), these adjust a vehicle's rating to reflect just those individuals who match the advertiser's target audience.

Telemarketing Sales Rule (TSR) Used to regulate against untoward telemarketing practices.

Three-exposure hypothesis The *minimum* number of exposures needed for advertising to be effective.

Tie-in The simultaneous promotion of multiple brands in a single sales-promotion effort. Also called a *joint promotion*.

Touch point See **Contact**.

Trade allowances Allowances that are used by manufacturers to reward retailers for performing activities in support of the manufacturer's brand such as featuring the brand in retail advertisements or providing special display space. Also called *trade deals*.

Trade dress The appearance and image of the product, including its packaging, labeling, shape, color, sounds, design, lettering, and style.

Trademark A distinctive sign, or indicator used by an individual, business organization, or other legal entity to *identify* the goods or services to consumers with which the trademark appears; and to *distinguish* its goods and services from competition.

Transformational advertising Brand image advertising that associates the experience of using an advertised brand with the unique set of psychological characteristics that typically would *not* be associated with the brand experience to the same degree without exposure to the advertisement.

Trialability The extent to which an innovation can be used on a limited basis prior to making a full-blown commitment.

Trier class The group of consumers who actually try a new product; the second step in which an individual becomes a new brand consumer.

Trustworthiness The perceived honesty, integrity, and believability of a source.

Tweets Messages (up to 140 words) sent by users to other users of the social network Twitter.

U

Unfair advertising Acts or practices that are likely to cause (1) substantial injury to consumers (e.g., health/safety, monetary), which is (2) not reasonably avoidable by consumers themselves, and (3) not outweighed by countervailing benefits to consumers or competition.

Unique selling proposition (USP) style An advertiser makes a superiority claim based on a unique product attribute that represents a meaningful, distinctive consumer benefit.

V

Valid A valid test assesses what it is intended to assess (e.g., being predictive of marketplace performance).

Values Enduring beliefs people hold regarding what is important in life.

Vehicles The specific broadcast programs or print choices in which advertisements are placed.

Vicarious learning (modeling) An attempt to change preferences and behavior by having an individual observe the actions of others and the consequences of those behaviors.

Viral marketing Techniques that use social networks to increase brand awareness or other marketing objectives, through a self-replicating, viral process, similar to the spread of a virus.

Voluntary attention Willful or prior attention to a message due to its perceived relevance pertinent to customers' needs (e.g., intent to purchase an advertised product). See also **Involuntary attention**.

W

Wearout The ultimate diminished effectiveness of advertising over time.

Word-of-mouth (WOM) Informal communication among consumers about products and services.

Z

Zapping When viewers switch to another channel when commercials are aired, superiority.

Zipping When ads that have been recorded along with program material using a *digital video recorder* are fast-forwarded (zipped through) when the viewer watches the prerecorded material.

Name Index

Subject Index